INTERNATIONAL

FOURTH EDITION **BUSINESS**

ENVIRONMENTS AND OPERATIONS

INTERNATIONAL
BUSINESS

FOURTH EDITION

ENVIRONMENTS AND OPERATIONS

JOHN D. DANIELS
Pennsylvania State University

LEE H. RADEBAUGH
Brigham Young University

**ADDISON-WESLEY
PUBLISHING COMPANY**

Reading, Massachusetts • Menlo Park,
California • Don Mills, Ontario
Wokingham, England • Amsterdam • Sydney
Singapore • Tokyo • Madrid
Bogotá • Santiago • San Juan

Sponsoring Editor: *Frank Burns*
Production Supervisor: *Mary Clare McEwing*
Production Coordinator: *Marcia Strykowski*
Illustrator: *George Nichols*
Text Designer: *Vanessa Piñeiro*
Cover: © *by Robert Anthony, Inc.*

Library of Congress Cataloging-in-Publication Data

Daniels, John D.
  International business.

  Includes bibliographies and index.
    1. International business enterprises.   2. Inter-
national economic relations.   3. Investments, Foreign.
I. Radebaugh, Lee H.   II. Title.
  HD2755.5.D35   1986   658.1′8   85–11127
  ISBN 0–201–10713–9

Reprinted with correction May, 1987

GHIJK-HA-898

PREFACE

CONTENT

What should be taught in a first course in international business when some of the students will thereafter have little or no direct classroom exposure to the subject and others will use the first course as background for more specialized studies in the area? This is the major question that guided us in the development of each edition of this textbook.

The growth of international business in its many forms and the resultant concern of business, government, and society as to how best to deal with this phenomenon have received so much publicity that it would be redundant to explain in great detail the need for understanding international business environments and operations. It is important, however, to explain why we selected our particular approach to the subject.

We feel strongly that introductory students should be exposed to all the essential elements of international business. But what are these essential elements? To help us answer this question, we sent out a large number of questionnaires to people who have taught introductory international business courses in a variety of types of institutions. Based on their familiarity with the third edition, we asked what topics should be added, deleted, or emphasized to a different degree. Prior to receiving these completed questionnaires, we frankly worried that we were trying to cover too much, especially since we knew that an increasing number of courses are being taught by instructors who do not have extensive specialized training in international business. What we found, though, was a near consensus that our coverage should be as broad as possible. The pervasive feeling was that the field is simply evolving too rapidly to know for sure what the future essentials will be. It is far better, our respondents reasoned, to risk covering too many things than to risk the omission of emerging issues and approaches that may well turn out to be essentials by the time that students enter the workplace and need to be informed citizens.

We have maintained the basic order of presentation from the third edition but have packed more into specific sections. Because of differences in the materials covered, the number of chapters included in each major section varies. The materials in the basic sections and the order of presentation are as follows: (1) an overview of current international business patterns, with an emphasis on what makes international different from domestic; (2) the social systems within countries as they affect the conduct of business from one country to another; (3) the major theories explaining international business transactions and the institutions influencing the activities; (4) the financial forms and institutions that measure and facilitate international transactions; (5) the interface between nation-states and the firms attempting to conduct foreign business activities; (6) the alternatives for overall corporate policy and strategy that accommodate global operations; (7) the concerns and management of international activities that fall largely within functional disciplines; and (8) the variety of alternative ways in which international business may evolve in the future.

Our perspective, exemplified throughout the presentation, is that of the manager rather than that of the social science disciplines from which international business draws its theoretical underpinnings. For example, as we talk about trade policy, we discuss not only the effects of different policies on national objectives but also the courses of action that companies and industries can take in order to influence policy and to react to whatever policy is undertaken.

PRESENTATION

Our objective was to provide a breadth and depth of coverage greater than that of many of the other introductory texts while, at the same time taking care not to overwhelm students. We considered a number of possibilities, such as the coverage of fewer details, and sought the opinion of several other instructors in our mail questionnaire. The use of a number of important pedagogical techniques as outlined in the following paragraphs provided an effective solution to this challenge.

One technique is a carry-over from the third edition—the use of short cases to introduce and end each chapter. This concept was very well received in the last edition; however, some cases were obviously better than others, some chapters lacked cases, and some cases became quickly outdated. We now have cases to introduce each chapter. Some of these are entirely new. Those that were used before have now been updated. All the introductory cases are real and identifiable situations. They are designed to accomplish two objectives: (1) to build the interest of students so that they are motivated to read what is coming in the chapter, and (2) to introduce problems and situations that will be further explained by theories and research findings presented within the chapter that follows. For instance, the first chapter starts with a case dealing with the production and marketing of the three *Star Wars* films, a topic about which almost all students should have some familiarity and interest. Elements of the case are then used as examples within the chapter to illustrate what makes international business different from its domestic counterpart, what types of international business forms were involved, and how these forms tie into a country's overall economic relations as expressed in its balance of payments.

Each chapter now also has a closing case. Like the introductory cases, some of these are new and all have been updated when situations called for alterations. These are designed to serve a different purpose than the introductory cases: to present situations for which students must analyze possible actions based on what they have learned from the chapter. In other words, the beginning cases should enhance interest and the recall of essential facts. The end cases should enhance the development of critical reasoning skills to apply the essential facts to necessary decision making.

We have also continued the use of extensive real-world examples throughout the text to illustrate diverse approaches that individuals, companies, industries, and countries have taken in specific situations. Although these examples help to enliven the presentation, they are not the types of facts that one would ordinarily expect students to remember. Yet most of us have seen examples of students' underlining the less critical facts of a chapter while skipping over those things that most instructors would consider to be more important. In order that students do not direct their memory efforts too much to the illustrative data, we are now introducing pedagogical devices to separate the more essential from the less essential. By use of a wide margin, we have now been able to outline the major points of each section. New terms are set off in boldface type and are then included in a glossary. Objectives are outlined clearly at the beginning of each chapter, and bulleted lists in the summaries recap each chapter's major points.

There is ample use of end notes to aid students and instructors in digging deeper on different subjects, yet we omit names of authors (except classics such as David Ricardo) within the chapters themselves so that students are not confused into thinking that these are names that they should remember.

There are three indexes, by subject, author, and company. A simple glance at these and at the end notes will illustrate that the content is up-to-date, worldwide, and easy to access.

Both of us come from diverse functional backgrounds and, furthermore, represent a gamut of opinions on the proper role of business and government in international affairs. In order to develop better coherence among the chapters, we each read, criticized, and contributed to each other's sections. John D. Daniels was charged with Chapters 1, 3, 4, 5, 6, 11, 12, 13, 15, 16, 17, 18, 22, and 23, and Lee H. Radebaugh was charged with Chapters 2, 7, 8, 9, 10, 14, 19, 20, and 21. The two shared responsibilities on Chapter 24.

ENHANCEMENTS (FOR THE INSTRUCTOR)

This fourth edition is supported by an expanded and improved *Instructor's Manual* prepared by the authors with the professor's needs in mind. The manual contains the following parts. The first part includes suggestions for content coverage for each chapter and provides extensive lists of audiovisual materials and supplementary articles. The second part offers a guide for classroom discussion of the end-of-chapter cases. A third important component contains ample material for evaluation of student performance. An average of 40 examination questions for test preparation are provided for each chapter; an answer key is listed as well. For convenience, a diskette containing these test questions will be available. Fourth, a supply of study questions designed to assist students in review or exam preparation is included for distribution, as you choose. Finally, we provide transparency masters from which overheads can be produced. Although the content of these visuals varies for each chapter, information pertaining to additional trade and investment figures, complementary data on cases, chapter outlines and expansion of tables or figures are just some of the items included.

To facilitate the dissemination and use of this information, the manual has been perforated for easy page removal. Also, the diskette containing examination questions affords ease and accuracy in test makeup and production. The test questions have been proofread for clarity and are classified by specific learning objectives in order to provide greater balance and fairness in the administration of exams.

Each of the above elements is offered to assist instructors in achieving a rewarding experience for their students and themselves throughout the course.

ACKNOWLEDGMENTS

The person we most wish to acknowledge is E. W. Ogram, Jr., who first conceived this introductory text and who was coauthor on the first three editions. Although other responsibilities prohibited his participation on this edition, his earlier contributions permeate large portions of the present version.

We have been fortunate from the start of the first edition to have had colleagues who would take the effort to critique draft materials, react to coverage already in print, advise on suggested changes, and send items to be corrected. Since it is the culmination of the efforts over the several editions that has brought us to where we are now, we would like to be able to acknowledge everyone's efforts. However, many more individuals than we can possibly list have helped. Those people who have been especially helpful at some point over the decade since this project first began include Jean Boddewyn, Robert Z. Bothe, Victor E. Childers, Kang Rae Cho, Refik Culpan, Robert R. Ebert, Edwin H. Flynn, Ralph Gaedeke, Robert Grosse, Phillip D. Grub, Umesh C. Gulati, Michael J. Hand, Ammik V. Hogg, William R. Hoskins, Arvind K. Jain, J. Leslie Jankovich, Robert W. Kerwin, Suresh Krishnan, Duane Kujawa, Edward M. Mazze, Richard M. Moxon, Lee C. Nehrt, Douglas W. Nigh, James A. Richardson, Fernando Robles, Ilkka A. Ronkainen, Saeed Samiee, Janice C. Shields, Robert S. Spich, Arnold Stebinger, William A. Stoever, George Sutija, Robert L. Thornton, and Craig Woodruff.

Several typists and graduate students were extremely helpful to us in the preparation of this edition, and without this anonymous support we could not have made the necessary changes. Some others were so helpful that we cannot let them remain anonymous. They are Wendy Bird, Pierre Eric Cohade, Turan Kahraman, Jan Kingston, Jeff Krug, Cindy Montgomery, Marc Niaufre, Joel Richomme, Judy Sartore, and Ruby Shepherd.

University Park, Pennsylvania   J. D. D.
Provo, Utah   L. H. R.

C O N T E N T S

PART 1

Background

Whether we are managers actively engaged in decision making within an internationally competitive environment or citizens interested in regulating international business to achieve our own objectives, it is useful to know why international business takes place, what advantages accrue to firms operating internationally, what makes this business different from purely domestic operations, and how these operations relate to a country's overall international economic position.

Chapter 1 sets the stage for a more detailed examination of the above considerations by defining essential terms and providing an overview of what will come in later chapters. The chapter begins by defining the field, explaining why the growth has been so great in recent years, and relating the field to both the functional areas of business (i.e., marketing, finance, and management) and the basic disciplines, such as geography, law, and economics. The chapter continues with an explanation of the multiple forms by which international business may take place, relating each to a nation's overall economic position by its placement within a country's balance of payments accounts. The chapter then examines recent trends in world trade and investment by product and geographic area, along with a brief explanation of the factors causing changes to take place. The chapter concludes with an overview of what will come in the following chapters.

International Business: An Overview

- To define the field of international business and emphasize the differences between business within the domestic context and business in the international context.
- To illustrate the need to rely on external disciplines (e.g., geography, history, political science, law, economics) and culture because of their impact on how international business is conducted.
- To define and discuss briefly basic terms that relate to international business.
- To introduce the different means—such as exporting, licensing, and investing—a firm can use to accomplish its international objectives.
- To relate the major events causing changes in trade and investment patterns, especially in the post–World War II period.
- To describe the changing composition of world trade in terms of countries and products.
- To examine the patterns of world investment in terms of ownership, location, products, and companies involved.
- To outline the subjects to be covered in the remainder of the text.

THE STAR WARS TRILOGY[1]

You have probably seen *Star Wars, The Empire Strikes Back,* or *Return of the Jedi.* You might not know that by the end of 1983 the three films had already grossed over U.S. $1.1 billion. This translates into an attendance of more than 300 million people, making this film sequence the most successful ever produced.

Few films enjoy success when rereleased. Those that have been successful, such as *Pinocchio,* are generally rereleased only at seven-year intervals. The 1977 film, *Star Wars,* was successfully rereleased four times by 1985. The intergalactic aspect of the trilogy is obvious. Less obvious, though, are the international dimensions, right here on planet earth, that contributed to the films' triumphs.

The deal to produce *Star Wars* was international from the start. George Lucas, the American producer, had written short summaries of two films he wished to make. He took them to every studio in Hollywood, and they all turned him down. In desperation, he decided to attend the Cannes [France] Film Festival, since it is an annual gathering place where movie moguls do business. Lucas used his last $2000 to buy an airline ticket, Eurailpass, and backpack to get to Cannes. There he made a two-picture agreement with a Hollywood studio for *American Graffiti* and *Star Wars.*

When the time came to film *Star Wars,* cost comparisons were made among technically capable interior facilities. The contract went to a studio outside London. The lower wages of British technicians more than offset the additional costs of transporting personnel from the United States to Great Britain. By the time *The Empire Strikes Back* and *Return of the Jedi* were filmed, the labor cost differentials were no longer significant, but it was convenient to stay on at the English studios, since the personnel were working so well together.

Not everything was filmed in England, however. The films' success was due largely to the fact that the extraterrestrial locales appeared authentic. At times the technicians used plates filmed elsewhere to go behind interior scenes shot in England. For instance, in *Star Wars* the Alliance leaders plot the destruction of the Death Star from the secret Rebel base on the planet Yavin. The background for Yavin was in fact the ancient Mayan ruins of Tikal in Guatemala. At other times it was necessary to film on location because of action taking place within rather than in front of scenery. For the scenes in which R2-D2 and C-3PO crash on the desert planet Tatooine, are captured by Jawas, and are sold to a local moisture farmer and his nephew (Luke Skywalker), the filming actually took place on the Sahara Desert in Tunisia. At the beginning of *The Empire Strikes Back* the Rebel force is held up in a hideout on the ice planet Hoth. In reality this was a place above the Arctic Circle in Norway.

In addition to the logistics of filming real actors in different locations, these scenes had to be combined with the miniature effects, which were made at a specially constructed monster factory in California. As shots were completed for *The Empire Strikes Back,* videocassettes had to be transported 6000 miles. This created no particular problem. Because of transportation and communications advances, global collaboration in film making has become commonplace. These advances enable us to see more realistic-looking scenes than were possible only a few years before *Star Wars.*

The actors were primarily U.S. and U.K. nationals. Carrie Fisher, Harrison Ford, and Mark Hamill who played Princess Leia Organa, Han Solo, and Luke Skywalker, respectively, were all from the United States. Alec Guinness, who played Ben (Obi-Wan) Kenobi, and Anthony Daniels, who was C-3PO, were from the United Kingdom. Lord Darth Vader could be characterized as a binational. The actor, David Prowse, is British; however, James Earl Jones, an American, did the voice because of Prowse's strong Devon farmer's accent.

The distribution of the films has been truly international. The expectation of receiving both domestic and foreign income is necessary to justify the risky investment in a high-cost film. By the end of 1983, slightly more than 38 percent of *Star Wars'* revenues and slightly more than 39 percent of those of *The Empire Strikes Back* had come from outside the United States. *Return of the Jedi* had not yet been distributed abroad long enough to have a meaningful foreign figure. Some foreign markets had not been penetrated at all, however. Most communist countries, such as the Soviet Union, Poland, and China, have simply prohibited entry. Some other countries, such as Haiti and Mali, are so poor that there are too few people who can afford to see the films. Even if attendance could be generated, the moviegoers would pay in their local currencies, which are gourdes and francs, respectively. Since the governments are also poor, especially in ownership of other currencies, they would be hard pressed to convert the gourdes and francs to a currency that the producers could use. The film distributors have made separate agreements with each country that shows one of the *Star Wars* trilogy so that revenues will come back to Lucasfilm Ltd. the producer, in U.S. dollars.

Wherever the films have been screened, there has been high public acceptance. This has been due at least partly to good reviews and shrewd marketing, but many films that have these attributes nevertheless fail to become hits in diverse countries. This difference in success has been ascribed to the fact that the films have drawn on universal themes. The noted French anthropologist Claude Levi-Strauss has observed common threads among the myths, tragedies, and fairy tales in widespread cultures. He attributes this to the fact that the mind classifies by absolute opposition, such as good versus evil. Another explanation may be that there is a bit of child in all of us, all over the world, and as George Lucas said, "*Star Wars* is a movie for children."

In spite of widespread acceptance it should not be inferred that the films and their promotion have been identical everywhere. The language dubbing of dialogue and/or the placement of subtitles is a costly but standard process necessary to appeal to a mass clientele who do not understand well the original language in films. Subtitles were necessary everywhere, in fact, for the characters speaking languages of foreign planets. These were drawn from combinations of obscure earthly dialects. In *Return of the Jedi,* for example, Jabba the Hutt's language was taken from an Inca-Indian dialect, and the Ewoks' was taken from a combination of five languages that included Mongolian, Tibetan, and Nepali.

Another standard but costly process involves the satisfaction of censors, without which a film may be either prohibited altogether or restricted to only part of the target audience. The *Star Wars* trilogy was no exception. Although intended for children, censors in a number of countries found some scenes too violent for youthful audiences. In Sweden, for example, Lucasfilm had to cut out the sequence of *Return of the Jedi* in which the monster swallows its victims and lets them die slowly and painfully during a thousand-year dinner.

Promotional techniques varied on a country-to-country basis because experienced distributors have noted what type of appeals will most likely attract film patrons. The stars were hustled to Australia for newspaper, radio, and television interviews. In Japan the advertisements were more action oriented than elsewhere. For Spain *The Empire Strikes Back* was entered into the Madrid Film Festival, which gave national recognition and acceptance.

Technically, there has been no need to alter the films. This is because 35-millimeter projection has become the worldwide standard for theatrical showings. However, no such worldwide standards exist for television, the revenues of which are important for the success of films. Television transmission is not standardized; for example, an Italian TV set cannot pick up French programs. It is very expensive to make a high-quality videotape from film, and this conversion must be done for each television transmission system where sales are to be made. Australian television rights for *Star Wars* were sold for a record sum of U.S. $2 million to cover ten runs over a ten-year period. When Canada commenced pay television services in 1983, the first film to be shown was *Star Wars.* It was repeated another 25 times during the first month.

One of the big revenue sources for the *Star Wars* trilogy has been the sale of rights to such firms as Coca-Cola, Procter & Gamble, and the Atari Division of Warner Communications to produce and sell Star Wars products. These companies have been given worldwide rights and have themselves sometimes depended heavily on foreign operations. For example,

Jedi Adventure Centers have been opened at shopping centers in twenty different countries. Rather than selling directly abroad themselves, some of the companies have made separate subcontracts with foreign firms to produce and sell particular products in the foreign countries. They have also produced abroad for the U.S. market. Take one company, the Kenner Division of General Mills. Its All Terrain Armored Transport accessories are made in Hong Kong, the *Return of the Jedi* action figures in Taiwan, and the Laser Pistol in Macao. The Chewbacca Bandolier Strap is assembled in Mexico from parts made in the United States.

THE FIELD OF INTERNATIONAL BUSINESS

International business includes all business transactions that involve two or more countries. The business relationships may be private or governmental. In the case of private firms the transactions are for profit. Government-sponsored activities in international business may or may not have a profit orientation.

In the preceding case, Lucasfilm gained operating advantages by being international. In terms of production, costs were decreased and quality was improved by the use of global locations. In terms of revenue, sales were expanded substantially through marketing abroad. Yet these advantages were not without costs. The foreign operations necessitated adjustments in the way that the production and sales took place. Thus the conduct of international business is different from the conduct of domestic business.

Time and Space Shrinkage

One of the things that sets international business apart from domestic business is that it usually encompasses greater distances. This increases operating costs and makes it more difficult to control what is taking place. But these problems are less prevalent than they used to be. The far-flung production and distribution of the three *Star Wars* films make William Shakespeare's words, "All the world's a stage, and all the men and women merely players," seem prophetic. In Shakespeare's lifetime (1564–1616), most people traveled no more than a few miles from where they were born. The time and cost of moving people or goods from one country to another was so great that sections of the world were quite isolated from each other. Many products that were commonplace in one area were either unknown or luxuries in another. Since the New World was still being explored (Australia had not even been discovered yet by Europeans), such products as tobacco and sweet potatoes were not introduced into England until after Shakespeare's birth. (One may ponder what the Italian diet must have been before Marco Polo brought pasta from Asia and the Spaniards introduced tomatoes from

South America.) European powers were still fighting to make or break trade monopolies with the Far East so that they could reap the profits from such exotic luxuries as tea. Communications between areas were very slow, although the Dutch did introduce the first airmail service during this period, via pigeon. It was not until four years after Shakespeare's death that the Mayflower sailed from Plymouth, England, to Massachusetts, a trip that took over three months. It was still another two and a half centuries before Jules Verne fantasized that one might encircle the globe in only 80 days.

- Business becoming more global
  - transport is quicker
  - communications enable control from afar

Technology and geographic expansion. So much that we take for granted today is the result of the cumulative penetration of technological and geographic frontiers over many decades. Besides the technology to make films, other technology had to be developed in order for the *Star Wars* producers to make and sell the films the way they did. The use of multiple production locations was possible only because videotapes made in the English studio could be transported to California in a day and because actors could travel quickly to locations around the world. Without the transport innovations of the twentieth century, production would have taken so long that the actors might have aged noticeably before the films were completed. Communications developments such as telephone transmission via satellites have not only speeded up interactions, they have allowed people in one country to control operations elsewhere.

- Institutional arrangements
  - by business and government
  - ease flow of goods
  - reduce risk

Institutional developments. What we take for granted today is also the result of cumulative institutional developments by business and government that let us take efficient advantage of technological innovations. While the ability to distribute films in foreign countries, for example, is due in part to transport advances, it is also due to the evolution of institutional arrangements. Take Lucasfilm's sales to Chile, for example. As soon as the films arrive in Chilean customs, a bank in Santiago would likely collect a distribution fee in pesos from the Chilean distributor and make payment to Lucasfilm in dollars at a bank in the United States. If businesses were still conducted as in the era of early caravan traders, Lucasfilm would probably have had to accept Chilean merchandise, such as copper or wine, in payment for the films. The merchandise would have been shipped back to the United States and sold before Lucasfilm could have received a useable income. While such barter transactions still do take place, they are not the most common means for making international payments. Barter transactions are usually cumbersome, time consuming, risky, and expensive. The relative ease with which most producers today can get paid for goods and services sold abroad is due to the development of a host of innovations. These include money to replace barter, clearing arrangements to convert one country's currency into another's, insurance to cover damage en route and nonpayment by the buyer, and bank credit agreements.

There are a myriad of other institutional arrangements that have facilitated the conduct of international business. One involves the transport of mail. The first international postal agreement, between France and part of what is now West Germany, was enacted during Shakespeare's life. Today you can send a letter to any place in the world by buying stamps that are denominated in your own country's currency, regardless of how many countries through which the letter passes en route. Lucasfilm could buy U.S. postage stamps for a letter sent to its Chilean distributors even though the letter might be routed on an Argentine airline that made stops en route in Colombia and Peru. Can you imagine how it would be if you had to arrange separate payment and shipment for each country though which a letter passes?

- Most large firms are highly international
  - new products become global quickly
  - firms can more easily shift production from country-to-country
  - domestic firms face international competitors

Development of global competition. The experience of Lucasfilm is typical of the film industry. Major studios from the United States distribute more than 100 films abroad each year, and foreign sales account for over 40 percent of their revenues.[2] The experience is also typical of large firms in other industries. Most are large and successful because they have multiple-country production and sales. A United Nations study indicated that the 382 largest industrial firms in the world derive an average of 40 percent of their sales from outside their home markets.[3]

Firms today can respond to many foreign opportunities more quickly than firms in the past. News about events and innovations in one place is transmitted almost simultaneously elsewhere. One of the results is a more rapid diffusion of new product information and sales in foreign countries, such as Rubik's Cube, which seemed to spread worldwide overnight from its Hungarian origin. Firms can also shift production more quickly from one country to another because of their foreign experience and because goods can be transported efficiently from most places. Coleco, for example, met unexpected demand for its Cabbage Patch Kid dolls but was able to step up output quickly through production contracts with existing associates in the People's Republic of China and Hong Kong and still have time to zip the dolls to the U.S. Christmas market by chartering three jumbo jets.[4]

Because of the ability to respond to foreign market and production opportunities, competiton has become more global. Firms that hitherto operated only domestically and defined their competitors as being domestic are now facing increased competition from foreign firms and from domestic firms that have become international. When they have not recognized and responded to the new global competition, the results have often been catastrophic. A good example is Mesta Machine's bankruptcy. Mesta Machine was one of a handful of U.S. firms that supplied equipment to the U.S. steel industry when the U.S. industry dominated world output. The firm overlooked technical advances by foreign equipment manufacturers and also the fact that foreign markets were growing more rapidly than the U.S.

market. Suddenly Mesta found competition from overseas rivals that could offer lower prices, faster delivery, and the technology demanded by the foreign and American steel industry.[5]

Drawing on Other Disciplines

- Operations in world environment
  - affected by social science disciplines
  - cover all functional business fields

Inasmuch as international business operates within the broad context of the world environment, it must draw on the contribution of a number of basic social science disciplines, including geography, history, political science, law, economics, and culture. In addition, international business covers the functional business fields such as marketing, management, and finance. These basic disciplines and functional areas play a significant role in the conduct of international business; consequently, a fundamental grasp of their importance is necessary if a manager is to function effectively in the international environment.

- Resources unevenly distributed
- Natural barriers affect trade
- Human activity affects environment

Geography is important because it determines the location, quantity, and quality of the world's resources and their availability for exploitation. The fact that these resources are unevenly distributed gives rise to the production of different products and services in different parts of the world. In our *Star Wars* example these differences led to the filming of some scenes in Tunisia and others in Norway. Geographical barriers such as high mountains, vast deserts, and inhospitable jungles affect communications and channels of distribution for companies in much of the world's economy. The distribution of human life in various areas of the world and the impact of human activity on the environment are critical in determining the nature of international business relationships.

- Accumulation of human experience
  - explains scope of business today
  - continues to evolve

History provides us with a systematic recording of the evaluation of ideas and institutions. Looking at the past gives us a clearer understanding of the functioning of international business activities in the present. It is, after all, the accumulation of human experience that determines how we can carry out business today. We have already shown how technical and institutional developments have expanded the scope of business. The creation of the three *Star Wars* films could not have occurred in the same way at an earlier period. Likewise, history continues to evolve. Certain types of transactions that are not now feasible may be possible in the future. Others may be carried out in different ways.

- World made up of nation-states
  - different country approaches to business

Political science, the study of the processes, principles, and organization of governments and political institutions, has played and will continue to play an important role in shaping international business throughout the world. It delineates the relationships between business and national political organizations and, in turn, helps to explain behavior patterns of governments and business firms in areas of potentially conflicting interests. Since we live in a world made up of nation-states, it is the political leadership in each country that decides if and under what conditions international business will occur. The prohibition by communist countries of internal distribution of the *Star Wars* films is an example of a political decision that affected international business.

- Each country has its own laws on business
- Agreements among countries set international law

Law, both domestic and international, in large measure determines what the manager of an international company can or cannot do. This includes domestic laws in both the home and host countries that regulate such matters as taxation, employment, and foreign exchange transactions. For example, when *The Empire Strikes Back* was shown in Japan, Japanese law determined how Japanese revenues would be taxed and how revenues could be exchanged from yen to U.S. dollars. U.S. law, in turn, determined how and when the earnings from Japan would be taxed in the United States. Agreements between the two countries (international law) temper how the earnings are taxed by both nations. Only by understanding the laws of each country where operations may take place and the treaties among nations can Lucasfilm determine where it is feasibly profitable to operate abroad.

- International operations impact on economy and vice versa, explaining
  - why trade takes place
  - what the products and terms are

Economics provides the analytical tools necessary for determining (1) the impact of an international company on the economy of the host and home countries and (2) the effect of a country's economic policies on the international company. Economic theory also explains why nations exchange goods and services with each other, why capital and people travel from one country to another in the conduct of business, and why one country's currency has a certain price relative to another's. For example, the decision by Lucasfilm to use British studios was economic. Economics provides a framework for understanding why, where, and when one country can produce goods or services more cheaply than another. The decision not to distribute the films in such places as Haiti was economic, based on a belief that there was insufficient economic wealth to provide a large enough market. The decision to distribute in France was also economic, based not only on France's more prosperous economy, but also on an expectation that the French francs earned from moviegoers would buy enough U.S. dollars to make the showings profitable.

- Explains behaviors acceptable in society

Culture describes the values, attitudes, and beliefs people have concerning themselves and their environment. As far as business is concerned, culture helps to explain what is and what is not acceptable behavior in society. The fact that Lucasfilm had to cut scenes from *Return of the Jedi* to get permission for children's viewing in Sweden is indicative of different cultural attitudes. Another popular film, *E.T.: The Extra-Terrestrial,* never has passed censorship for children's attendance in Sweden.

Business Operations

Each of the social science disciplines of geography, history, political science, law, economics, and culture plays a significant role in determining the type of environment that all firms in international business must deal with in at-

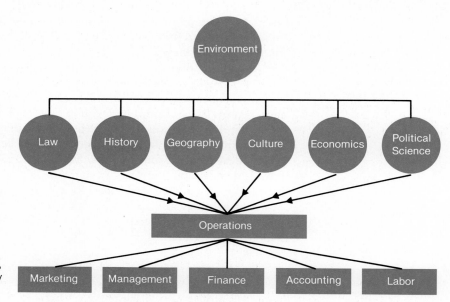

FIGURE 1.1
The Field of International Business
* The present authors wish to acknowledge that E. W. Ogram, Jr. prepared this figure originally for the third edition of this text.

- Environmental elements affect
  - how business functions can be carried out
  - the form of international operation

tempting to produce and sell their products or services in the overseas market. Figure 1.1 shows that these environmental elements affect business operations, which in turn may affect how each business function is carried out.

The specific functional adjustments then depend in part on the environment as well as on the type of operation the enterprise is undertaking. To illustrate the need for adjustments, it is useful once again to recall our *Star Wars* case. Lucasfilm had to alter its marketing by using different promotion methods for different countries. It undoubtedly had to deal with different labor and accounting regulations for its production in the United Kingdom as well. There are a number of different types of international business forms in which enterprises may choose to operate. These forms will be the subject of the next section of this chapter; however, the choice of form depends in part on the environment in which the company is operating internationally.

Types of International Business and the Balance of Payments

- Balance of payments
  - summarizes country's international economic transactions
  - most transactions involve international business

A country's **balance of payments** is a statement that summarizes all economic transactions between that country and the rest of the world during a given period of time. Although there are many common ways of presenting an account as well as the number of its subdivisions, Table 1.1 shows the major categories found in most published balance of payments statements. (Note also that in Table 1.1, credits are on the left and debits on the

TABLE 1.1 _____

BALANCE OF PAYMENTS ACCOUNTS

Credits	Debits
1. Exports of goods and services	5. Imports of goods and services
1a. Merchandise	5a. Merchandise
1b. Travel and transportation	5b. Travel and transportation
1c. Receipt of fees and royalties	5c. Payment of fees and royalties
1d. Income on assets abroad	5d. Income payment on assets owned by foreigners
2. Receipt of unilateral transfers	6. Unilateral transfers abroad
3. Inflow of foreign owned assets	7. Outflow to acquire assets abroad
3a. Ownership in government securities	7a. Ownership in government securities
3b. Direct investment	7b. Direct investment
3c. Bank liabilities to foreigners	7c. Claims on foreign banks
3d. Other investments	7d. Other investments
4. Decrease in official reserves	8. Increase in official reserves

• indication of international economic environment for business

right. This is the most common way of presenting these accounts.) The balance of payments is not synonymous with a measurement of international business activities. This is because some international business transactions are not recorded in the balance of payments and some international economic transactions are nonbusiness in nature. The balance of payments is nevertheless a convenient way of examining the types of activities that are eligible for the term "international business." All the types relate to one of the accounts, though there is not an exact correlation between the two.

The distinctions between international business and the balance of payments can be quite technical, and it is not essential for a manager to grasp all of them. To illustrate that the accounts are not synonymous, let us refer for a moment to item 2 in Table 1.1, receipt of unilateral transfers. This includes the receipt of foreign aid, gifts from people in a foreign country, and money from a country's own citizens who are working abroad. These transfers may be very important to a country's economy. For example, in recent years, Pakistan has received more foreign revenue from its citizens working in foreign countries than from any other source.[6] But this is not international business. Even though some of the balance of payments entries are not business transactions, they are all important to managers because they are indications of the economic environment in which international business takes place. The following discussion is limited to activities that qualify as international business. Other types of international economic movements will be examined later in the text, particularly in Chapters 8 and 9.

- Visible goods leaving or entering the country
  - usually a country's most important international economic transaction
  - usually a company's first international business because of least commitment and risk
  - usually a company continues even though other forms adopted

Merchandise exports and imports. Merchandise exports (item 1a in Table 1.1) are goods sent out of a country, whereas **merchandise imports** (item 5a) are goods brought in. Since these are tangible goods that visibly leave and enter countries, they are sometimes referred to as visible exports and imports. One frequently finds reference to the terms "exports" or "imports" when in reality the reference is only to the merchandise exports or imports. In the opening case the Jedi action figures are merchandise exports for Taiwan when they are sent to the United States and merchandise imports for the United States when they arrive.

Exporting and importing of goods are the major source of international revenue and expenditure for most countries. Among companies engaged in some form of international business, more are involved in importing and exporting than in any other.

Importing and/or exporting is usually the first type of foreign operation in which a firm gets involved. This is because at an early stage of international involvement these operations usually take the least commitment and least risk of a firm's resources. For example, firms may be able to export by using excess capacity, thus limiting the need to invest more capital. As will be noted in more detail in Chapter 14, firms may also be able to use the services of trade intermediaries who, for a fee, will take on the export-import functions, thus eliminating the need to have trained personnel and a department to carry out foreign sales or purchases.

The fact that exporting and importing are early means of foreign involvement should not imply that they are activities that firms abandon when they adopt other international business forms. This may sometimes occur; however, exporting and importing usually continue, either by business with other markets or to complement new types of business activities. It should also not imply that exporting and importing always precede the other forms.

- Earnings from other than goods
  - e.g., travel, transport, fees, royalties, dividends, interest
  - very important for some countries
  - involve many special international business forms
- often come after experience with merchandise trade

Services. Services (items 1b, 1c, 1d, 5b, 5c, and 5d in Table 1.1) refer to international earnings other than for goods sent to another country. Receipt of these earnings is considered a service export, whereas payment is considered a service import. Services are also referred to as **invisibles.** Many different types of services comprise international business.

Items 1b and 5b in Table 1.1 involve international travel and transportation. When prints of *Return of the Jedi* were sent from the United States to be shown in Japan, they had to travel internationally. If they were sent on Japan Air Lines, the cost of the transportation showed up as item 1b (export) on the Japanese balance of payments and as item 5b (import) on the United States' balance of payments. When the *Star Wars* actors went to Australia to publicize the film, their Australian expenses were a service export for Australia. Earnings from transportation and from foreign travel can be an important source of revenue for a country. Such countries as Greece and Norway depend heavily on revenue collected from carrying foreign cargo on their ships. The Bahamas earns more than four times as much revenue from foreign tourists as it earns from exporting merchandise.[7]

Fees (items 1c and 5c in Table 1.1) are payments for the performance of certain activities abroad. **Royalties** are the payment for use of assets abroad. Fees are charged for such services as banking, insurance, rentals (e.g., the *Star Wars* film), engineering, and management. Engineering services are often handled through a **turnkey** operation, contracts for the construction of operating facilities that are transferred to the owner when the facilities are ready to begin operations. Fees for management services are often the result of **management contracts,** an arrangement through which one firm assists another by providing management personnel to perform general or specialized management functions. Royalties may be paid for the use of such assets as trademarks, patents, copyrights, or other know-how under contracts known as **licensing agreements.** Royalties are also paid for **franchising,** a way of doing business in which one party (the franchisor) gives an independent party (the franchisee) the use of a trademark that is an essential asset for the franchisee's business. In addition, the franchisor more than nominally assists on a continuing basis in the operation of the business, such as by providing components or managerial services.

Firms often move to foreign licensing or franchising after successfully building exports to a market. This move usually involves a greater international commitment than in the early stages of exporting because the firm commonly has to send qualified technicians to the foreign country to assist the licensee or franchisee in establishing and adapting its production facilities for the new product.

Items 1d and 5d in Table 1.1 are self-explanatory. Companies may make investments abroad on which they receive interest or dividends. The particular types of investments are discussed in the next section.

- Direct investment
  - implies control
  - high commitment of capital, personnel, and technology (usually)
  - may be to gain foreign markets
  - may be to gain foreign resources
  - foreign sales often higher than from exporting
  - may be partial ownership

Investments. For **direct investment** to take place (items 3b and 7b) control must follow the investment. This can amount to a small percentage of the equity of the company being acquired, perhaps even as low as 10 percent. **Portfolio investment** (the remaining categories under items 3 and 7) can be either debt or equity, but the critical factor is that control does not follow this kind of investment. The ownership of a controlling interest in a foreign operation is the highest type of commitment to foreign operations in the given country. Not only does it imply the commitment of capital to the foreign locale, it usually means the transfer of more personnel and technology abroad than when there is no controlling interest in the foreign facility. Because of the high level of commitment, direct in-

- Portfolio investment
  - noncontrol of foreign operation
  - financial purpose, e.g., loans

vestment usually (but not always) comes after a firm has experience in exporting or importing. Direct investment operations may be set up in order to gain access to certain resources or access to a market for the firm's product. Kenner, for example, uses its Mexican direct investment to assemble the Chewbacca Bandolier Strap because this gives access to a resource, cheap labor for the product's manufacture. Kenner also has direct investments in Europe, which have been made as a means of gaining markets in the countries where the production occurs.

Since the balance of payments shows only the capital flow for a given period of time rather than the accumulated investment value, it tends to give an impression that direct investment is less important than it really is. Actually, for U.S. firms as a whole, sales from output produced abroad are many times greater than sales from U.S. production that is sent abroad as merchandise exports.[8] Today most of the world's largest firms have substantial foreign direct investments encompassing every type of business function, such as extraction of raw materials, growing of crops, manufacture of products or components, selling of output, and handling of various services.

When two or more organizations share in the ownership of a direct investment, the operation is known as a **joint venture**. In a special type of joint venture, a **mixed venture**, a government is in partnership with a private company.

Foreign portfolio investments are also important for nearly all firms operating extensively internationally. They are used primarily for financial purposes. Treasurers of companies, for example, routinely move funds from one country to another to get a higher yield on short-term investments. They also borrow funds in different countries.

- Worldwide approach to markets and production
  - also known as MNC or TNC
  - usually involved in nearly every type international business practice

Multinational enterprise. The **multinational enterprise,** referred to hereafter as MNE, has a worldwide approach to foreign markets and production and an integrated global philosophy encompassing both domestic and overseas operations. Because of the difficulty of identifying whether a firm really has a "worldwide approach," one sometimes encounters narrower operational definitions, such as requiring that a firm have production facilities in some minimum number of countries or be of a certain size in order to qualify as an MNE. The term MNE is synonymous with MNC, **multinational corporation,** which is also quite common in the literature of international business. We prefer the MNE designation because there are many internationally involved companies such as accounting partnerships that do not use a corporate form.

Another term sometimes used interchangeably with MNE, especially by the United Nations, is **transnational corporation** or TNC, a term that is also used to refer to a company owned and managed by nationals in different countries. To avoid confusion, we shall use TNC only in its latter meaning throughout the text.

Where are MNE activities included in the balance of payments? Since MNEs have global outlooks, they are usually involved in nearly every type of international business practice that we have mentioned.

INFLUENCES ON TRADE AND INVESTMENT PATTERNS

Economic Conditions

- Affect year-to-year trade volume, but trade tends to fluctuate more than economy
- Rising affluence increases portion of trade in manufactures and lessens portion in agriculture

Absolute and relative changes in world affluence since World War II have affected the total value of world trade and investment, the types of products involved, and the proportionate value of international business accounted for by individual countries. It is impossible to get definitive figures on the changes in historic world output, but indications are that international trade has remained a fairly constant percentage of gross world product (GWP) over a long period of time. This does not mean that trade and production will be related in exactly the same way every year. When economic conditions are booming, as in much of the 1970s, there is a tendency for trade to grow even more rapidly than production. Conversely, a slow growth rate, such as the period between the two world wars and the early 1980s, causes trade to increase more slowly than production. The reason for this cyclical relationship is that many foreign goods are considered marginal by consumers and government policymakers; thus imports are curtailed as the economy slackens. During the early 1980s, for example, many governments enacted measures to prevent certain imports. Producers may also attempt to export only when they have surpluses and will add capacity to serve foreign markets only if the foreign demand is sustained for a long period of time. The sustained economic growth since World War II has therefore led to the rapid expansion of trade and to direct investment in those areas where the outlook for continued growth seems promising.

Changing world affluence has affected the types of products and their relative importance in world trade. In the mid-nineteenth century, Ernst Engel, a German political economist and statistician, observed that as family incomes increase, the percentage spent on food tends to decrease, whereas the percentage spent on other items tends to remain fairly constant or increase. This is true even though the absolute amount spent on food increases because of substitution of more expensive food items. When the human body has reached the limit of its intake capacity, food purchases are replaced by nonfood items. This has had the effect of decreasing the proportion of world trade and investment accounted for by agricultural products and increasing the proportion accounted for by the manufacturing sector. In addition to consuming the traditional goods and services, the people comprising the world mass market now have access to such things as watches and foreign travel, which were once available only to the wealthy.

Technology

- Changes products traded
- Changes trading countries
- Increased trade share of industrial countries

Rapid technological changes in this century have created new products, displaced old ones, and affected the relative positions of countries in world trade and investment. The most obvious examples are new products such as jets, computers, and transistor radios, which comprise a large portion of international business. Products that existed in earlier periods have expanded in world trade because of technology in the production process, as with automobiles, or because new end uses have been found, as with soybeans and fish meal. Other products have been at least partially displaced by substitutes, such as artificial fibers for cotton, wool, and silk and synthetic rubber and synthetic nitrate for the natural products. Still other products have not grown in demand as rapidly because technology has resulted in methods of conservation. For example, because tin cans have become thinner and copper wiring used to transport telephone messages is now employed to carry more messages simultaneously, demand for these metals is not as great as it might be. Since most technical advances have emanated from the most industrialized (richer) countries, firms from these countries control a greater share of the trade and investment in the manufacturing sector, which has been the major growth area. The result has been a proportionately smaller share of international business for many of the poorer countries.

Wars and Insurrections

- Changes what is produced
- Increases international business risk
- Growing global effects on business

Military conflicts disrupt traditional international business patterns as participants divert much of their productive capacity and transportation systems to the war effort. In addition, political animosity and transport difficulties may interfere with trading channels. The composition of trade changes because of a shift from consumer goods to industrial goods that can be used in meeting military objectives. International investment is disrupted, since foreign-owned plants are frequently destroyed or expropriated. There is little capital available to move abroad, and even if there were, uncertainties and political regulations would prevent it.

An important distinction between twentieth century wars and those of earlier periods is their far-reaching impact due to increased global interrelationships. A particularly notable example was oil price increases after the Arab/Israeli war of 1973. There has been much concern in the 1980s that the Iraq/Iran war may have similar results.

Nearly every industrialized country was involved in World War II. Not until 1948, three years after the end of the war, did the volume of world trade return to the 1938 level. From a U.S. standpoint, trade with

Japan and Germany was completely halted. Trade with other parts of the world also decreased. The Axis occupation disrupted commerce, maritime ships were frequently sunk en route, most ships were converted to war use, and U.S. plants began making military equipment instead of the products they had exported in the past. Many of the foreign investments of U.S. firms in Europe and the Far East were destroyed during fighting. In turn, the U.S. government expropriated the holdings of Japanese, German, and Italian investors.

Even national disturbances may have widespread international implications. The Chilean disruptions in the early 1970s, for example, had a substantial effect on world copper production and usage. The warring within Lebanon in the 1980s has resulted in a shift in international banking from Beirut to Bahrain and Cyprus.

Political Relationships

- Increase portion of international business among member countries
- Decrease portion of business with nonmember countries
- Growth of bloc may stimulate international business

Political blocs. The major political schism in recent years has been between the communist and noncommunist countries, particularly between the industrialized nations of the world. (The subject is explored in great depth in Chapter 13.) The result is that very little trade has been conducted between the two groups. Of total world exports in 1984, about 3 percent were from communist to noncommunist countries or vice versa.[9] Direct investment is negligible between the two groups because of restrictions by communist countries on private ownership, particularly from a foreign source.

Since the 1950s, several groups of countries have banded together and removed most trade restrictions among themselves. The most notable example is the European Community (EC). Because of the greater ease of trade among members, a greater percentage of the members' total trade is being conducted within the group. Because of the growth generated within the EC, the members' portion of total world trade has grown. This growth rate along with the access to larger markets within the community has also been a major attraction to foreign investors.

- Countries' realization of interdependence with other countries
  - promote consistent and uniform rules
  - give concessions in exchange for concessions
  - promote economic growth

Multinational agreements. In recent years there have been a number of international accords and agreements affecting the conduct of world business. These have resulted from the realization that countries are increasingly interdependent and that a degree of consistency and uniformity is needed in order to assure a flow of goods and services internationally. Included among the many agreements are the International Monetary Fund (IMF), which has altered exchange regulations; the International Air Transportation Association and numerous shipping conferences, which set rates and frequencies between international ports; and the International Patent and Trade Mark Conventions, which delineate certain property rights for companies operating internationally. In addition to these multilateral activities, countries have signed numerous bilateral tax agreements that prevent international firms from being taxed by both their home and foreign countries on the same earnings. Without these provisions against double taxation, few foreign investments would be economically feasible.

The establishment in 1948 of the General Agreement on Tariffs and Trade (GATT) among twenty-three countries provided a forum for negotiating mutual reductions in trade restrictions. Since 1948, most nations in the free world have become parties to GATT. Through tariff conferences in which participants have bargained, restrictions have been reduced on most items in world trade, and countries have agreed on procedures to simplify the conduct of international trade. Political blocs and multinational agreements are discussed further in Chapter 7.

Another development in recent years has been the emergence of international agencies, such as the World Bank, the Asian Development Bank, and the Inter-American Development Bank, which give loans and assistance for government-guaranteed projects. In some cases these have been an alternative to governmental or private capital. In others the funds have been used to finance social programs, such as housing and highways, for which alternative funds would not have been readily forthcoming. In these latter cases the agency loans have undoubtedly stimulated trade and direct investment by enabling countries to buy necessary equipment from abroad and by enabling them to build the infrastructure needed for the efficient conduct of business activities. These are examined in more detail in Chapter 10.

RECENT WORLD TRADE PATTERNS

Divergent Growth Rates

- Rich, industrial countries have growing share of world trade
  - trade in manufactures growing faster
  - exception for poor countries with rapid industrialization
  - exception for oil exporters
  - largest exporters are industrial countries

Economic level of countries. One of the common ways of classifying countries is by their level of economic or industrial development. The high-income countries (Western Europe, the United States, Canada, Australia, New Zealand, and Japan) are usually referred to as either industrial or developed countries. Other noncommunist countries are referred to as developing or lesser developed countries (LDCs). Precise definitions and further subclassifications of these countries will be covered in the next chapter.

Figure 1.2 shows that the share of world exports among developed countries increased from 45.9 percent in 1948 to 64.6 percent in 1972, whereas all the pairings including LDCs decreased in world share. In absolute terms, however, LDC trade, both imports and exports, increased substantially. Several interrelated factors help to explain the loss in the world trade share by the LDCs during that period. The primary factor is that LDCs depended heavily on agricultural products and raw materials for their export earnings. Because of the economic and technical factors discussed earlier, earnings from these types of exports have not kept pace with those

Value in billions of U.S. dollars
(Percentage of world total)

1948

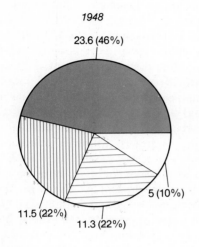

23.6 (46%)

5 (10%)

11.5 (22%)

11.3 (22%)

1972

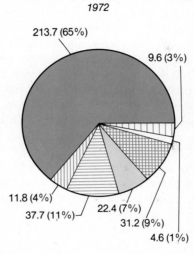

213.7 (65%)

9.6 (3%)

11.8 (4%)

37.7 (11%)

22.4 (7%)

31.2 (9%)

4.6 (1%)

1984

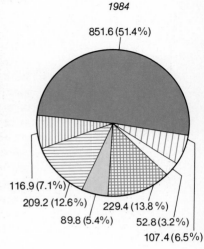

851.6 (51.4%)

116.9 (7.1%)

209.2 (12.6%)

229.4 (13.8%)

89.8 (5.4%)

52.8 (3.2%)

107.4 (6.5%)

KEY:

Exports from	Exports to
Developed	Developed
Developed	Less developed (1948)
	Oil exporters (1972, 1984)
	Others (1972, 1984)
Less developed	Developed (1948)
	Oil exporters (1972, 1984)
	Others (1972, 1984)
Less developed	Less developed (1948)
	Oil exporters (1972, 1984)
	Others (1972, 1984) and all LDC to LDC for 1984

FIGURE 1.2
Value of Free World Trade Between Developed and Less-Developed Areas, Selected Years
Source: Statistical Yearbook, 1968 (New York: United Nations, 1969), pp. 398–399; *Statistical Yearbook,* 1973 (New York: United Nations, 1974), pp. 402–409; and *Direction of Trade Statistics Yearbook,* 1985 (Washington: International Monetary Fund, 1985), pp. 5–19; and *Direction of Trade Statistics Annual* 1970–74 (Washington: International Monetary Fund, n.d.), pp. 8–35.

from manufactured goods. In manufactured production the developed countries have advantages in world markets because of their technology and their ability to reduce costs through large-scale production. In many cases the LDCs have insufficient domestic production capacity to supply their own needs, much less those of other areas.

Since 1972, however, there has been a turnaround in the LDC trade position. This has been due primarily to three factors. Foremost has been the ability of oil-exporting countries to raise the price of petroleum exports substantially. During the 1970s the price of oil exports increased more than 1200 percent.[10] A second factor has been the rapid industrialization of a number of LDCs, such as Brazil and South Korea, now referred to as newly industrialized countries (NICs). A third factor has been the easier access of LDCs' manufactured products to industrial countries' markets. At the United Nations Conference on Trade and Development (UNCTAD) in 1964 the developing countries began to pressure the industrial nations to give preference to manufactured exports from developing countries. By the end of the 1970s, every industrial country had adopted some type of policy whereby LDC manufactures could enter more easily than the same products made in another industrial country. In spite of this overall turnaround, most LDCs have been able neither to export petroleum nor to industrialize rapidly. For them the downward trend in share of world trade has continued.

Given the position of LDCs, it is not surprising that nine of the ten largest exporters are industrial countries (see Table 1.2). Six of these are members of the EC and conduct a large portion of their trade among

TABLE 1.2 _____

MAJOR EXPORTING COUNTRIES,
1984 (in billions of dollars)

Country	Exports
United States	217.9
West Germany	171.7
Japan	169.7
France	97.6
United Kingdom	93.9
Canada	90.4
Italy	73.3
Netherlands	65.8
Belgium	51.4
Saudi Arabia	46.2

Source: *Direction of Trade Statistics Yearbook,
1983* (Washington: International Monetary
Fund, 1985), pp. 2–7.

themselves, there being far fewer restrictions among EC members than between the EC and other countries.

- Since turn of century
  - generally Asian, Canadian gains
  - generally European, Latin American losses
- Shifts in recent years due to
  - petroleum trade
  - foreign policy changes
  - Asian industrialization

Twentieth century changes in United States trading partners. The major change in U.S. export markets this century has been the decline in relative importance of Europe. More than 80 percent of U.S. exports went to Europe before the turn of the century; however, the figure had dropped to about 50 percent by the 1920s and is only about 30 percent at present. The biggest gain in exports has been to Asia. Exports to Asia have grown from less than 1 percent at the turn of the century to over 30 percent now, making Asia a larger export market for U.S. products than Europe.[11]

For U.S. imports, the big losers in proportionate share in this century have been Europe and Latin America. Purchases from Europe, which constituted about half of U.S. imports at the turn of the century, have stayed between 20 and 30 percent per year since the early 1920s. Purchases from Latin America comprised about 30 percent of U.S. imports until 1960; since then the figure has fallen steadily and now accounts for about 15 percent. The major gain in imports over this long-term period has been from Canada. This growth has been fairly steady from about 5 percent early in the century to about 19 percent currently. Canada is the largest exporter to the United States, and Japan is the next largest. The proportion of imports coming from Asia has varied widely. From a turn-of-the-century figure of about 15 percent of total U.S. imports, the figure grew to one third of U.S. imports by 1940. After a substantial fall during World War II, Asia now accounts for about 35 percent of U.S. imports.

The 1970s were a particularly volatile time for the U.S. trade direction. Increases in import share and export share of specific countries from 1970 to 1981 were due primarily to three factors: shifts in petroleum trade, foreign policy changes, and greater industrialization of certain Asian countries. Because of increased revenues from oil sales, Mexico, Saudi Arabia, and Venezuela were able to import much more; together they comprised over 42 percent of the net shift in U.S. export direction. The People's Republic of China, the Soviet Union, and Egypt accounted for another 18 percent of the net shift in U.S. exports because of foreign policy changes. Increased income from industrialization in Thailand, South Korea, Taiwan, and Malaysia were responsible for their taking a larger share of total U.S. exports. The United States brought in a larger portion of its imports from Mexico and Norway because they became new oil suppliers and from Japan, Taiwan, South Korea, and Singapore because of their new industrial product capabilities. The biggest losers during the 1970s were Canada and West Germany. Together they comprised over 34 percent and 60 percent of the net decrease in U.S. export share and import share, respectively.[12] However, Canada still remains the largest importer of U.S. products.

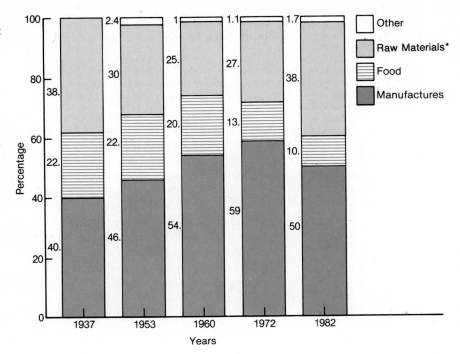

FIGURE 1.3
World Trade by Major Product Category for Selected Years in Percentage of Total World Trade
Sources: W. S. Woytinski and E. S. Woytinski, *World Commerce and Governments* (New York: Twentieth Century Fund, 1955); *United Nations Statistical Yearbook,* 1973 (New York: United Nations, 1974), p. 56; *Yearbook of International Trade Statistics,* 1982 (New York: United Nations, 1984), pp. 1114–1207.

* Includes agricultural raw materials, fuels, minerals, and chemicals.

Trade by Product Category

- Growing dependence on manufactures
- Industrial countries have largest trade share of all product categories except fuels
- Poor countries increasing trade share in some categories

Figure 1.3 shows the growing importance of manufactured goods in world trade up to 1972. Since then the raw materials category has increased substantially at the expense of manufactures because of the increased price of oil. Food exports have continued to decline as a portion of world trade. As shown in Fig. 1.4, the developed countries account for the majority of world exports in every category except fuels. The LDCs have, however, improved their world export share in chemicals, machinery, and other manufactures during recent years.

The U.S. imports and exports show a similar dependence on manufactured products. Slightly over 50 percent of exports and about 45 percent of imports are comprised of machinery, transportation equipment, and manufactured goods.

Largest Exporting Companies

- Non-U.S. firms
  - petroleum firms
  - capital-intensive industries

Tables 1.3 and 1.4 show the ten largest exporting firms from within and outside the United States. Among non-U.S. exporters, two of the largest firms are petroleum producers, yet there are no petroleum firms among

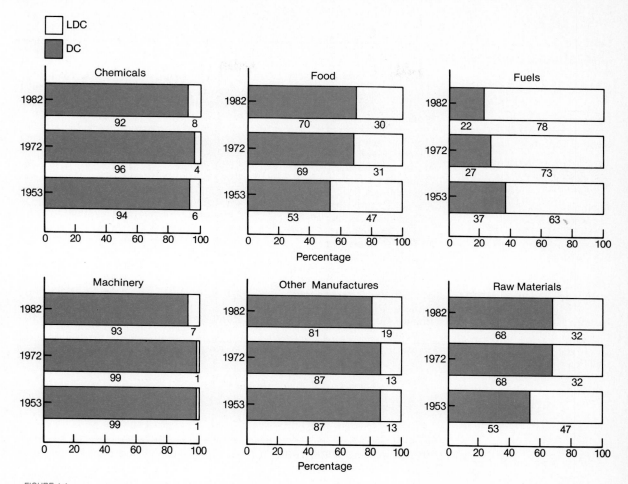

FIGURE 1.4
Percent of World Exports by Product Category Supplied by Developed and Less-Developed Countries, Selected Years

Source: Percentages derived from *Statistical Yearbook,* 1973 (New York: United Nations, 1974), p. 56, and *Yearbook of International Trade Statistics, 1984,* New York: United Nations, 1984, pp. 1130–1217.

* Includes the United States, Canada, Western Europe, Turkey, Yugoslavia, Australia, South Africa, and Japan. The LDC figures include all other countries that are not centrally planned economies.

- U.S. firms
  - technical firms
  - capital-intensive firms

the top ten U.S. exporters. This is due to the fact that the petroleum firms are based in net oil-exporting countries (United Kingdom and Venezuela), whereas the United States is a net oil importer. The remainder of the non-U.S. list consists of automobiles, chemicals, and electrical equipment—all products that require a high capital outlay and very large production runs (usually more than is possible for simply serving a domestic market) in order to minimize unit costs. Five of the largest U.S. exporters are also

TABLE 1.3 ————————————————————————————————————

LARGEST U.S. EXPORTERS (1983–1984)

Company	Products	1984 Exports (millions (of U.S. $)	1984 Exports as percent of sales	1983 Rank
General Motors	Motor vehicles and parts, locomotives	7,276,500	12.06	1
Ford Motor	Motor vehicles and parts	6,041,000	27.66	3
General Electric	Generating equipment, aircraft engines	3,935,000	6.95	4
Boeing	Aircraft	3,621,000	24.86	2
International Business Machines	Information-handling systems, equipment, and parts	3,074,000	35.12	7
Chrysler	Motor vehicles and parts	2,706,900	30.23	9
E.I. du Pont de Nemours	Chemicals, fibers, polymer products, petroleum, coal	2,650,000	15.07	6
United Technologies	Aircraft engines, helicopters	2,387,810	0.18	5
McDonnell Douglas	Aircraft, space systems, missiles	2,133,700	1.38	8
Eastman Kodak	Photographic equipment and supplies	1,949,000	10.36	10

Source: "The Fifty Leading Exporters," *FORTUNE*, Vol. 112, No. 3, August 5, 1985, p. 61. *FORTUNE* © 1985 Time, Inc. All rights reserved. Used by permission.

TABLE 1.4 ————————————————————————————————————

LARGEST NON-U.S. EXPORTERS

Company	Home Country	Major Product	Exports from Home Country (millions of U.S. $)
Petroleos de Venezuela	Venezuela	Petroleum	17,987
Volkswagenwerk	Germany	Automobiles	7758
Daimler Benz	Germany	Automobiles	6947
Peugeot	France	Automobiles	5932
Renault	France	Automobiles	5840
Siemens	Germany	Electrical equipment	5683
Hoechst	Germany	Chemicals	5607
BASF	Germany	Chemicals	5330
British Petroleum	United Kingdom	Petroleum	5325
Philips	Netherlands	Electrical equipment	5057

Source: *United Nations Centre on Transnational Corporations, Third Survey* (New York: United Nations Centre on Transnational Corporations, 1983), p. 357. Data are missing for some of the world's largest companies.

in these categories; however, the remainder derive their competitive advantage more through technical leadership, which allows them to export such products as aircraft and information-handling systems.

RECENT DIRECT INVESTMENT PATTERNS

Move to Direct Investment

Until the emergence of international firms, all private foreign investments were portfolio investments rather than direct investments. The push to direct investment began in the 1920s, but even during this period, portfolio movements were about double the direct ones. During the depression of the 1930s it became obvious that portfolio investors, especially those from the United States who were the main suppliers of foreign capital, had chosen poorly the foreign projects in which they had placed their funds. Between 1930 and 1938 the value of U.S.-owned private foreign investment fell by $3.8 billion, of which nearly 90 percent was due to the depreciation and liquidation of portfolio investments. Direct investments fared much better and actually recovered somewhat in the late 1930s.[13] Since World War II, direct investment by U.S. firms has grown substantially. Direct investment by firms from other industrial countries grew slowly for a number of years after World War II because firms from those countries were busy rebuilding their domestic markets and because they were short of funds to invest on the outside. Since about 1965, their direct investment positions have expanded rapidly.

Direct Investor Description

- Almost all ownership by firms from industrial countries
- LDC ownership starting to grow faster

Country of origin. One way of describing investors is to look at the origin of investment by country. There are no recent estimates of the value of direct investment ownership on a country-by-country basis. A recent United Nations study, did, however, estimate the number of direct investments. Table 1.5 summarizes this information and illustrates that nearly all investment has emanated from a few industrial countries. The United States and United Kingdom comprise together about 60 percent of the world total. The top dozen investing countries account for more than 95 percent.

Although direct investment from industrial countries still accounts for nearly all the world's value (about 98 percent), the fastest growing group in recent years has been from developing countries. There are now several hundred LDC direct investors that own several thousand foreign investments. Most of this movement has been from the developing countries that have experienced recent industrialization, such as Hong Kong, Singapore, Mexico, Brazil, and Argentina.[14]

TABLE 1.5 _____

FOREIGN DIRECT INVESTMENT OWNERSHIP BY COUNTRY
(Number of Affiliates, 1980)

Country	Number	Percent of World Total
United States	33,647	34.3
United Kingdom	24,928	25.4
West Germany	7,392	7.5
France	4,749	4.8
Netherlands	4,370	4.5
Switzerland	4,031	4.1
Sweden	3,369	3.4
Japan	3,029	3.1
Canada	2,991	3.1
Australia	1,885	1.9
Belgium	1,746	1.8
Italy	1,538	1.6
Other	4,289	4.5
Total	97,964	100.0

Source: Figures are compiled from United Nations Centre on Transnational Corporations, *Transnational Corporations in World Development,* Third Survey (New York: United Nations, 1983), pp. 318–326.

At the end of 1983, foreign direct investment in the United States was valued at a little over $100 billion. About 45 percent of this originated from two countries, the United Kingdom and the Netherlands. LDC direct investments comprise a substantially higher (15 percent) portion of U.S. direct investment than of total world direct investment.[15]

- Highest growth in petroleum and manufacturing
  - more stringent ownership regulations in some other sectors
  - manufacturing highest portion in industrial countries
  - petroleum highest portion in LDCs

Economic sector of investment. Between 1929 and 1973 the big shift in U.S.-owned direct investment was toward petroleum and manufacturing (see Fig. 1.5). Although the same type of historical data are not available for non-U.S. direct investment, estimates indicate that the U.S. and non-U.S. investment composition is very similar. Since the early 1970s composition has not changed appreciably. The shift toward the petroleum and manufacturing sectors has been due largely to the faster growth in world consumption of those products. Another factor has been the growing reluctance of many countries to allow foreign ownership of mineral rights, agricultural properties, and transportation and utilities systems.

The composition of U.S. direct investment abroad varies between developed countries and LDCs. The book value at the end of 1984 showed that manufacturing comprised 42 percent of the investment in developed countries but only 37 percent in LDCs. Petroleum investments were 34 percent in LDCs and only 23 percent in developed countries.[16] This divergence is partially due to circumstance, since oil investments have to be made where the oil is found. Economic conditions are also a major factor,

FIGURE 1.5
Changing Pattern of United States Direct Investment Abroad in Percentages (by Value)
Source: Survey of Current Business, various issues.

* Includes transportation, trade, utilities, and other service industries.
** Mining and smelting is included in ''other'' for 1983.

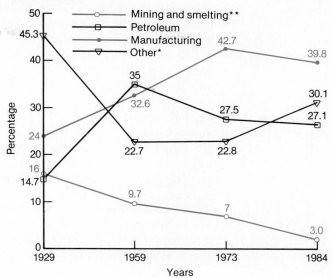

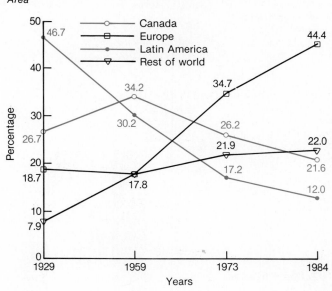

since the developed countries are the main markets for manufactured goods and are large enough to allow for efficient production. The divergence is lessening; manufacturing investments have been growing more rapidly than petroleum investments in LDCs.

At the end of 1983 the value of foreign direct investment in the United States was distributed in the following sectors: manufacturing, 35.4%; wholesale trade, 14.8%; petroleum 13.6%; and other, 36.2%.[17]

- Most are smaller firms
- Most assets are controlled by giant firms

Type of company involved. The U.S. Department of Commerce has identified over 3500 U.S. firms with almost 25,000 direct investments. Figure 1.6 shows that smaller firms make up the bulk of direct investors but that larger firms control most of the assets. This skewing is due to the fact that companies with assets of less than $50 million typically had investments in only one foreign country, whereas those with over $2.5 billion in assets had investments in over 20 foreign countries.[18] Although detailed information of this type is not available on non-U.S. direct investors, the fragmentary information that does exist indicates that the value of that investment is also heavily dominated by the very large companies.

- Most in industrial countries
  - biggest markets
  - least perceived risk
- LDC owned investment is largely regional

Location of investment. Table 1.6 shows that the major recipients of direct investment are industrial countries. Of the top fifteen recipients, only four (South Africa, Brazil, Mexico, and Hong Kong) are generally classified as

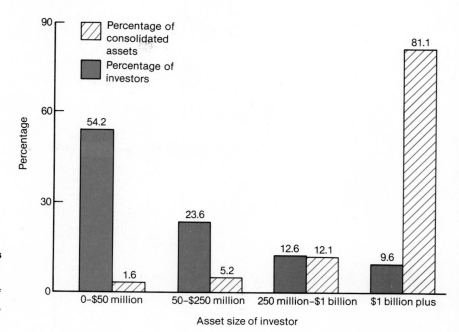

FIGURE 1.6
Profile of U.S. Direct Investors
Source: Betty L. Barker, "A Profile of U.S. Multinational Companies in 1977," *Survey of Current Business,* October 1981, p. 46.

TABLE 1.6

LOCATION OF FOREIGN DIRECT INVESTMENTS BY AREA
(number of affiliates, 1980)

Country	Number	Percent of World Total
United Kingdom	8239	8.4
Canada	6619	6.7
West Germany	6408	6.5
France	5986	6.1
Australia	5705	5.8
United States	5352	5.5
Netherlands	4084	4.2
Belgium	4014	4.1
South Africa	3873	4.0
Switzerland	2957	3.0
Brazil	2888	2.9
Italy	2535	2.6
Mexico	2355	2.4
Hong Kong	2225	2.3
Spain	2183	2.2
Remainder of Asia	10,164	10.4
Remainder of Europe	9661	9.9
Remainder of Latin America	6359	6.5
Remainder of Africa	4808	4.9
Other	1549	1.6
Total	97,964	100.0

Source: Figures are compiled from United Nations Centre on Transnational Corporations, *Transnational Corporations in World Development,* Third Survey (New York: United Nations, 1983), pp. 318–326.

LDCs. About 54 percent of foreign-owned affiliates are in Europe, and only about 31 percent are in LDCs. This pattern parallels the outward flow of direct investments owned by U.S. enterprises. At the end of 1984, U.S. ownership abroad was $233.4 billion, of which about a quarter was located in LDCs. Figure 1.5 shows that Europe has been growing as a share of U.S. direct investment, whereas Canada and Latin America have a declining portion. The portion in Latin America has been declining for a longer period; in the 1920s, nearly half was located there.

The reasons for the growing interest in developed countries are primarily two. First, more investments have been market seeking (that is, producing in a country in order to sell the output there), and the developed countries have more income to spend. Second, political turmoil in many LDCs has caused investors to shy away from those areas.

In the case of the direct investment originating from developing countries, most has thus far been to countries within the region where the parent firm is located—for example, Malaysian investments in Thailand. There is some evidence, however, that these investors are now beginning to develop footholds in more distant industrial countries.[19]

Other Forms of International Business

For most companies the two most important forms of foreign business activities are trade and direct investment. These forms also have the biggest impact on regulations governing the private flow of business among countries. That is why we have emphasized the recent patterns of these two types of activities. Other forms, such as licensing, are also important and may even be the most important for individual countries. We shall not ignore these other forms from an operational standpoint in later chapters.

SCHEME OF THE TEXT

Comparative Environmental Frameworks

Most international business takes place within the confines of countries; consequently, country-specific environments affect business somewhat differently from place to place. We have already shown how various disciplines help to understand these environments. We cannot, of course, examine every country-to-country difference, nor can we become experts in every explanatory discipline. Chapters 2 and 3 will introduce a framework of those environmental elements that appear to have the most significant impacts on differences in the way that business is normally conducted. These chapters will also illustrate types of business adjustments and suggest means whereby managers might build a better awareness of differences and decide whether to adjust to differences when they note them. Subsequent chapters will draw upon this framework as we examine alternative methods of operating abroad.

Theories and Institutions: Trade and Investment

Whereas the comparative approach above emphasizes differences within countries as they affect the conduct of business, Chapters 4–7 emphasize those factors that enhance or retard the connections among countries. We explained earlier in this chapter that trade and direct investment are the two major forms of international business. These chapters will examine why countries and businesses decide to trade as well as why and how countries influence the flow of trade. We shall also examine why companies make direct investments abroad. Some of these motives should already be intuitively apparent to you from earlier discussions in the chapter. Why, for example, did Lucasfilm decide to export movies? Why did the Soviet

Union restrict their entry? Why did Coleco produce *Return of the Jedi* Action Figures abroad for sale in the United States? Think about these questions as you examine the theories surrounding trade and direct investment. The rationale for trade versus direct investment is especially important in considering the operational choices that will be discussed in later chapters. Chapter 7 looks specifically at cross-national institutions and agreements among countries that affect the conduct of business.

World Financial Environment

The world financial environment is also a linkage among countries. However, its scope is sufficiently large to warrant a separate section. We have already mentioned that different countries have different currencies, that there may be problems in changing one currency for another, and that different currencies have different values. Chapters 8–10 explain how a company that earns revenue in one currency gets it converted to another, what determines the price of one currency in terms of another, and how to deal with the uncertainties of currency value changes and problems of convertibility. These chapters also examine the impact of different possible monetary systems on the conduct of business as well as methods of securing funds in different countries.

International Business in International Conflicts

Although we have already discussed why and how countries may influence the flow of imports and exports, trade is by no means the only international business form that countries try to influence. Of particular interest in recent years have been attempts by virtually every country of the world to regulate how international enterprises operate so that the country might gain maximum benefits with the least costs. Chapters 11 and 12 examine why countries have taken their positions, what types of actions they have adopted toward international firms, and the types of responses made by business enterprises. Chapter 13 looks specifically at business between communist and non-communist countries, since this has been so influenced by regulatory actions due to political conflicts.

Corporate Policy and Strategy

The previous sections emphasized the environments in which international business takes place. This section begins the examination of company operations. The appropriate operations depend not only on the types of environments discussed in previous sections, but also on firms' unique situations. These include such factors as the experience of the firms, their resources, the types of industries in which they operate, and their competitive situations. In Chapters 14–17 we examine the firm-specific situations in relation to their external environments in order to analyze what factors companies should consider when setting overall international strategy. By considering international operations as opposed merely to domestic operations, firms are faced with many more alternatives from which to choose. These chapters examine why they might pick one type of operational form over another and in which countries they should place their emphasis. Because of operating over larger areas, in more diverse environments, and with more types of forms, the international firms are presented with problems on how to control their far-flung operations—the subject of Chapter 17.

Functional Management, Operations, and Concerns

We have discussed the fact that in operating abroad, companies may have to adapt their functional operations to conform to practices that are acceptable where they are operating. Chapters 18–23 examine major company functions in relationship to external environments and in relationship to the policies and strategies that they pursue. Separate chapters are devoted to marketing, accounting, taxation, finance, management, and labor.

The Future

Because business decisions must be made in anticipation of what will occur in the future, the final chapter looks at methods commonly used to project future events as well as summarizing what various expert observers have predicted for the future of international business.

SUMMARY

- The cumulative penetration of technologic and geographic frontiers, coupled with institutional development, has resulted in a global competitive environment—one marked by the use of foreign countries as production bases and sales outlets and one marked by a rapid international diffusion of new products and processes.

- Because of operating in a broad global environment, a number of disciplines (geography, history, political science, law, economics, and culture) are useful to help explain the conduct of international business.

- When operating abroad, companies may have to adapt their methods of carrying out business functions. This is because the environment may dictate the appropriate operational method and because the business forms used for foreign operations may be different from those used domestically.

- The balance of payments summarizes all economic transactions between a given country and the rest of the world during a given period of time. Not all the account entries are international business activities, nor are all international business transactions accounted for in the balance of payments. The accounts are useful, however, for monitoring the environment in which international business takes place.

- Among the forms of international business are trade in goods and services, transportation, licensing, franchising, turnkey projects, management contracts, and direct and portfolio investments.

- Multinational enterprises (MNEs) take a worldwide approach to markets and production. They are sometimes referred to as multinational corporations (MNCs) or transnational corporations (TNCs).

- The major factors causing changes in world trade and investment patterns are economic conditions, technology, wars and insurrections, and political relationships.

- Most world trade and direct investment are accounted for by the developed or industrial countries. They are the major importers of all product categories and the major exporters of all except fuels. About 98 percent of direct investment originates from industrial countries, which also are the recipients of nearly 70 percent of direct investment.

- A long-term trend has been the increased portion of trade and investment accounted for by the manufacturing sector. During the 1970s, however, the value of raw material exports took a larger share of world trade because of the price increases of petroleum.

C A S E   THE 1984 OLYMPICS[20]

Every four years, athletes assemble from throughout the world to compete for medals in the summer Olympics. The purpose, according to the Olympic Charter, is "to promote development of physical and moral qualities which are the basis of sport." The Olympics are also a big business. In advance of the 1984 Los Angeles games, economic consultants estimated that the direct economic benefits (hotel space, food, games employment, and so on) accruing to Southern California would be anywhere from $970 million to $1.2 billion and that these figures understated the full economic impact because money spent is respent by those to whom it is paid. The competition affects businesses located outside the region as well, since they sell airline space, make souvenirs, and disseminate sports stories. A country hosting an Olympics competition is assured of an influx of foreign currency, thus strengthening its balance of payments position.

But the Olympics do not occur without expenses. By the time of the 1984 games in the United States, Canadian taxpayers were still paying for the more than $1 billion cost of the 1976 Montreal competition. Participation in the business of the Olympics also involves taking risks. When the United States decided to boycott the 1980 games in the Soviet Union, most Americans who had planned to attend decided to stay home instead. One travel agent in New York had already prepaid $7.2 million to the Soviets to secure space for the 18,000 American tourists that he expected to book to the Soviet Union that summer. This money was not refundable.

There were other benefits, costs, and problems in hosting the games. The Los Angeles Visitors and Convention Bureau reckoned that it could capitalize on Olympic publicity by allocating an extra $500,000 to attract potential visitors after the games because "L.A.'s the place." Some L.A. hotels reportedly were able to charge as much as $200 a day for units normally renting for $38, and airlines were able to fill their flights without offering discount fares during the games. Even areas as far away as San Francisco were able to boost their tourist promotion by advertising that their closeness was a great opportunity for an extended visit. On the negative side, people were so afraid that Los Angeles would be too crowded in 1984 that tourism fell off months in advance. Hotels feared that tourist revenues would be down for 1984 as a whole in spite of full occupancy during the Olympics.

The revenue generated from ticket sales and broadcasting rights has never been sufficient to cover even the direct costs of the games, much less the cost of constructing new facilities. Because of projected overall economic benefits and because of international publicity for the host country, governments have almost always underwritten the cost of games that they have hosted. This was not true of the 1984 Olympics in Los Angeles. When the Los Angeles Olympic Organizing Committee (LAOOC) was involved in securing the games, President Jimmy Carter declared that no federal funds would be used for support. Governor Jerry Brown pledged that "no dollar from the state of California will be used to finance them," and Los Angeles voters passed overwhelmingly a resolution that no public funds would go for the games. Although these positions were adhered to in a strict sense, there were indirect Olympic expenses that were incurred by city, state, and federal taxpayers. These included such things as payments for additional security and traffic control. The LAOOC, nevertheless, had to find private means to make the operation solvent.

One of the first things the LAOOC did was to try to minimize costs by using to the extent possible existing facilities such as stadiums (e.g., the Coliseum, the Forum) and dormitories at local universities (e.g., USC, UCLA). When new facilities were needed, private firms were asked to construct them in exchange for the advertising value. For example, McDonalds supplied a $4 million center and put its name on the facility. The LAOOC sought to fill 5000 of the 45,000 jobs with volunteers. Still, it budgeted about $500 million for direct expenses.

The LAOOC projected five primary sources of revenue: ticket sales, company sponsorship, television rights, sale of specially minted coins, and licensing of Olympic products. There were special international business problems related to each of these.

Ticket Sales. Had the LAOOC been promoting the games as a purely domestic or private event, it could have sold tickets on a first come–first served basis. The Olympic charter, however, provides that the committee "shall secure the widest possible audience for the Olympic Games" and that there is "no discrimination . . . allowed against any country." On what basis can tickets be allocated fairly among countries? The official travel agents of twelve Western European nations protested that they were discriminated against. This was not because they did not receive a fair share of tickets but rather because a large part of their ticket allocation was to sports in which their countries were not participating, for example, baseball. Interest in any given sport varies substantially on a country-to-country basis.

Company Sponsorship. Probably the most controversial means of generating revenue was from the LAOOC's designation of twenty-nine companies as official sponsors in exchange for payment of about $120 million. For example, Fuji Photo Film was designated the official film, Coca Cola the official soft drink and Anheuser-Busch the official brewery. There were even an official nursery and official purveyors of cut flowers, water, mineral water, and gasoline. The sponsorship and other commercialism led the mayor of Olympia, Greece, to threaten to withhold the Olympic torch.

The commercialism was a factor in nonparticipation by many communist countries in the games. The Soviet Union, in particular, was keen on finding some pretext to boycott the 1984 games because the United States had boycotted theirs in 1980.

Television. The major source of revenue was expected to be the sale of television rights. ABC signed the major contract for world coverage at a price of $225 million; however, ABC officials insisted on a downward arbitration of that sum if the Soviets did not attend. This downward amount could have resulted in ABC's withholding payment of as much as $60 million to the LAOOC. ABC's contract called for it to film on behalf of other countries. Because of different country-to-country preferences, it meant that ABC crews had to cover virtually all events in their entirety. These were relayed to the 1500 foreign broadcasters from more than 100 countries. These broadcasters then decided what to transmit home. For example, the Italian group broadcast the bicycle road race from start to finish, and the Pakistanis broadcast all the field hockey events.

Minted Coins. Although the U.S. federal government declared that it would not use its funds to finance the games, it nevertheless lent support by minting special $10 gold pieces and silver dollars, which were sold at many times their face value so that profits could be divided between the United States and Los Angeles Olympic Committees. U.S. law, unlike the laws of many other countries, prohibits the sale of coins through banks at more than their face value. In order to generate profits, therefore, the U.S. Treasury had to contract a private marketing specialist to handle the sales. This was a more cumbersome way of selling the coins than through banks. The chairman of the House Banking, Finance, and Urban Affairs subcommittee on consumer affairs and coinage called the work of the marketing specialist a "total and complete failure."

Licensing. The LAOOC had rights to license the words "Olympic" and "Olympiad" as well as the symbols of the interlocking rings, the star in motion, and Sam the Eagle. No one disputed that these words and symbols had commercial value; however, their use led to two unforeseen problems for the LAOOC. The first was the difficulty in controlling the usage. The LAOOC had to hire a staff of detectives to police unauthorized use. They found over 500 violators, even a Parent Teachers Association from an elementary school. The second problem concerned labor criticism that some licensed firms had contracted to make their Olympic souvenirs outside the United States and that another firm was using nonunion labor. The LAOOC listened to these allegations and agreed to form a committee to review the labor practices. Belligerent unions could, after all, do a number of things to upset the conduct or profitability of the games, such as attempting to organize the workers, prevent the use of volunteers, and picketing of facilities. The nonunion souvenir producer was persuaded to sign a union contract.

Epilogue. Just two months before the games, the Soviets announced that they would not attend. Peter Ueberroth, head of the LAOOC, later recalled that he blamed himself for not dealing directly with Soviet Party Leader Konstantin Chernenko before a close decision was made by the Soviet Politburo. After the Soviet decision, Ueberroth was fearful that many other countries would follow suit. This would increase the risk that the television viewing audience would not reach a preestablished total, thus reducing the payment by ABC to the LAOOC. Ueberroth thus set out to limit the number of boycotters. He flew to Cuba and got Fidel Castro to agree not to pressure other Latin countries to stay away, even though Cuba felt it had to follow the Soviet lead. He flew to Rumania and convinced President Nicolae Ceauşescu to attend in spite of Soviet pressure to do otherwise. In the end, more Americans watched the TV coverage than had heretofore watched any other event, so ABC paid in full. LAOOC later announced a

$215 million surplus. In terms of U.S. government participation, Ueberroth nevertheless said, "Sports is an immense force in other countries. Our Government still doesn't understand the consequence of the two Olympic boycotts in 1980 and 1984."[21]

QUESTIONS

1. How have communications and transportation technologies affected the way the business of the 1984 Olympics could be managed compared with Olympic games in earlier times?
2. How do social science disciplines explain how different countries might administer their hosting of the Olympics?
3. How do foreign environments affect the management of the Olympics?
4. What types of business and types of international business transactions are affected by the holding of the Olympics?
5. Should government at the federal, state, or local level have given more support to the 1984 Summer Olympics?

NOTES

1. We wish to acknowledge the cooperation of Robert M. Greber, Chief Executive Officer, and Susan Trembly, Publicity and Advertising Assistant, at Lucasfilm Ltd. for granting interview information. In addition to the interview data, the case relied on data from the following sources: Sid Adilman, " 'Star Wars' Heralds Dawn of Canadian Paycable Amid Ad Blitz for Blockbuster Pix," *Variety,* January 19, 1983, p. 2; Louise Sweeney, "Returns from 'Jedi': Marketing a Megahit," *Christian Science Monitor,* June 30, 1983, pp. B7–8; "$2 Mil. for 'Star Wars' on Aussie TV," *Variety,* March 10, 1982, p. 43; Timothy White, "Slaves to the Empire," *Rolling Stone,* July 24, 1980, pp. 33–37; Jean Vallely, "The Empire Strikes Back," *Rolling Stone,* June 12, 1980, pp. 31–34; Gillian MacKay, "George Lucas Launches the Jedi," *McClean's,* Vol. 96, May 30, 1983, pp. 42–44; Gerald Clarke, "Great Galloping Galaxies!," *Time,* Vol. 121, May 23, 1983, pp. 62–65; Conrad Phillip Kottak, "Social-Science Fiction," *Psychology Today,* Vol. 106, February 1978, pp. 12–18; "Fun in Space," *Newsweek,* May 30, 1977, pp. 60–61; and Aljean Harmetz, "Showing of 'Star Wars' Trilogy Set," *New York Times,* February 28, 1985, p. 20.
2. Karen Stabiner, "Selling American Films Abroad," *New York Times,* November 20, 1983, Section 6, p. 129.
3. United Nations Centre on Transnational Corporations, *Transnational Corporations in World Development,* Third Survey (New York: United Nations, 1983), p. 48.
4. Adi Ignatius, "Cabbage Patch Dolls, Believe It or Not, Begin as Bok Choy Way-Ways in China," *Wall Street Journal,* December 8, 1983, p. 34.
5. Thomas F. O'Boyle, "Rise and Fall," *Wall Street Journal,* January 4, 1984, p. 1.
6. International Monetary Fund, *Balance of Payments Statistics,* August 1983, p. 9.
7. *Ibid.,* p. 1.

8. Obie G. Whichard, "U.S. Direct Investment Abroad in 1982," *Survey of Current Business,* August 1983, p. 15 and pp. 5–16 for 1982 export and direct investment figures. The sales from the direct investment were estimated at 108 percent, which was the figure in the U.S. Department of Commerce Benchmark Study. See Ned G. Howenstine, "Gross Product of U.S. Multinational Companies, 1977," *Survey of Current Business,* February 1983, p. 25.

9. *Direction of Trade Statistics Yearbook, 1982* (Washington: International Monetary Fund, 1982), pp. 2–6.

10. *1981 Yearbook of International Trade Statistics,* Vol. 1 (New York: United Nations, 1983), p. 1224.

11. *Survey of Current Business,* December 1984, p. S16.

12. Robert T. Green, "Internationalization and Diversification of U.S. Trade: 1970 to 1981," Department of Marketing Administration Working Paper 83/84–5–1 (Austin: University of Texas, Graduate School of Business, October 1983), pp. 3–7.

13. John H. Dunning, "Capital Movements in the 20th Century," *Lloyds Bank Review,* April 1964, pp. 20–21.

14. Louis T. Wells, Jr. "Guess Who's Creating the World's Newest Multinationals," *Wall Street Journal,* December 12, 1983, p. 26.

15. *Survey of Current Business,* October 1984, p. 38.

16. *Survey of Current Business,* August 1984, p. 18.

17. *Survey of Current Business,* October 1984, p. 27.

18. Betty L. Barker, "A Profile of U.S. Multinational Companies in 1977," *Survey of Current Business,* October 1981, pp. 38–57.

19. Wenlee Ting, "The Emerging Challenge of the NIC Multinationals: Technology, Marketing and Operations," paper presented to the Academy of International Business Annual Meeting, San Francisco, December 1983, pp. 2–3.

20. Kenneth Reich, "Overall L.A. Tourism Drop Feared in Olympic Year," *Los Angeles Times,* September 14, 1983, Sec. I, p. 24; Kenneth Reich, "Olympic Ticket Policies Hit," *Los Angeles Times,* October 12, 1983, Section CC, pp. 1–3; Don Irwin, "Olympic Coin Sales Net $24 Million So Far," *Los Angeles Times,* November 3, 1983, Section II, p. 3; Kenneth Reich, "State to Study Cost of L.A. Olympics," *Los Angeles Times,* November 22, 1982, Section I, p. 21; Craig R. Whitney, "U.S. Travel Agent for Olympics Hoping to Cut Loses," *New York Times,* August 8, 1980, p. A8; "One Thing's Certain: Olympics Won't Lose Money," *Christian Science Monitor,* November 8, 1983, p. B2; Kenneth Reich, "Olympic Jobs Put at 45,000," *Los Angeles Times,* July 5, 1983, Section II, pp. 1–3; Phil Elderkin, "How Los Angeles Expects Olympics to Turn a Profit," *Christian Science Monitor,* June 3, 1981, p. 10; Kenneth Reich, "Olympic Revenue Questions Raised," *Los Angeles Times,* October 6, 1983, Section II, pp. 1–3; and Kenneth Reich, "Labor Chief Wants Olympic Souvenirs Made in America," *Los Angeles Times,* August 13, 1983, Section I, p. 13.

21. "Master of the Games," *Time,* January 7, 1985, p. 38.

PART 2

Comparative Environmental Frameworks

The firm operating internationally is affected by and has an immense impact on the environments in which it operates. International business today is conducted among organizations within virtually every conceivable value and institutional framework. Chapter 2 explores first the relationship between a country's economic and political philosophy and its business practices. Next, the adjustments and relations to these economic and political systems by international firms are discussed. Finally, the chapter examines national differences generated by varying levels of economic development. Chapter 3 analyzes the physical, demographic, and behavioral variations among nations that influence the conduct of business. The chapter concludes with recommendations and caveats for companies coming into contact with alien societies.

2

The Economic and Political Environments Facing Business

- To explain the major political and economic ideologies and how they interrelate in theoretical and practical senses.
- To evaluate the role of the foreign firm in different political and economic systems.
- To describe the major types of problems facing the developing countries.
- To discuss the importance of the North-South dialogue in determining a new international economic order.
- To show how multinational enterprises can interact with public and private enterprises in developing countries and what their major contributions can be.

GULF IN ANGOLA[1]

On November 11, 1975, Angola finally gained its long-sought independence from Portugal. Unfortunately, there was some question as to who should receive the national flag. Before and after independence a bloody civil war engulfed Angola; thousands of people on all sides lost their lives in the struggle. Three major factions had been fighting for control of Angola for a decade. The faction that gained control in late 1975 and early 1976 was the Popular Movement, which had its roots in the leftist opposition to the Portuguese regime. Supported by thousands of Cuban troops and Soviet advisors, the Popular Movement under the leadership of Agostinho Neto was able to expand its sphere of influence from the area surrounding the capitol Luanda to take control of the country.

Two other major factions at the time were UNITA (the National Union for the Total Independence of Angola) and the National Front. UNITA, led by the popular Jonas Savimbi, drew its power base from the Ovimbundu tribe, which claims approximately 40 percent of the country's population. UNITA now operates out of the south of Angola and is especially popular with the West because of Savimbi's anticommunist, moderate, nondoctrinaire form of socialism. President Gerald Ford wanted to give U.S. aid to Savimbi during the civil war, but a Vietnam-conscious Congress refused. The National Front, rooted in the north as part of the ancient Bakongo kingdom, is the third force. It is concerned with separating the northern part of the country from Angola.

Gulf Oil has operated in Angola for more than two decades. In 1975, when the civil war hit its peak, approximately 7 percent of all Gulf's oil was produced in Angola. However, the war took its toll; production in 1976 dropped to nearly half the 1975 level. In its 1975 annual report, Gulf stated, "In view of the civil strife in Angola late in December, the Company suspended its operations and temporarily withdrew its personnel from Angola at the request of the U.S. State Department." Gulf also placed royalty payments that were due Angola in a special Treasury bill fund. "Payment was withheld because of conflicting demands from parties contending for political control in Angola. The Company will disburse these funds plus interest earned on them when a government attains control and is generally recognized by the world community."

In April 1976, Gulf moved back into Angola, began operations, and paid back taxes and royalties. Pending discussions on a new long-term relationship with the new government, Gulf agreed to continue operating under the same terms that prevailed before operations were suspended in 1975. Finally, in 1978, Gulf signed a new participation agreement with the Angolan national oil company undertaking joint development and exploration projects. In 1978, Gulf drilled its first new well since the 1975–1976 civil war period.

Angola, located on the western coast of sub-Saharan Africa, is wedged in between Zaire and Namibia. Its Marxist government faces some severe problems. A poor transportation infrastructure makes two-way trade difficult for some regions of the country. Farmers are hesitant to engage in more than subsistence agriculture because of a lack of goods to buy. The agricultural sector is inefficient; Angola needs to import 90 percent of its food. France initially provided assistance in developing state grain farms.

Native managers and technicians are also in short supply. Brazilians manage hotel facilities; West Germans serve as airline pilots; and workers from Sweden, Italy, and East Germany are training auto mechanics. Not too long after independence, the Angolan government was asking the Portuguese for help in running the country.

West Africa has become one of the world's major oil-producing areas. At one time, Nigeria ranked second behind Saudi Arabia as a supplier of crude for the United States. Gulf lists Nigeria and Angola as its two largest foreign suppliers of crude. West Africa is independent of the Arab oil producers, even though Nigeria and Gabon are members of OPEC (the Organization of Petroleum Exporting Countries) and Angola aspires to be a member. This makes West Africa an attractive source of supply.

In its 1980 annual report, Gulf announced the following scenario for Angola:

> *Offshore Angola, Gulf has a 49-percent interest with Sonangol, the national oil company. Gulf's net production is expected to rise approximately 150 percent by 1985 from 37,000 barrels per day in 1980. Eleven exploration wells are planned for 1981, including three wells to appraise the recent Takula discovery. Initial production from the field this year will yield approximately 5,000 barrels per day, and the field may eventually produce more than 100 million gross barrels of crude. Also under way is a gas-reinjection project to enhance oil recovery from deep reservoirs and recover natural gas liquids. Construction is scheduled to be completed by early 1982.*

Gulf expects to invest $500 million in Angola by 1985. In addition, Texaco, Cities Service, Boeing, General Electric, General Tire and Rubber, and many other firms have major projects going in Angola.

However, the 20,000 Cuban troops in Angola present a problem. Angola's avowedly Marxist government, with its Cuban support, is very unpopular with the Reagan administration. The administration is trying to overturn the 1976 Clark Amendment so that it can provide military support for UNITA. This situation makes Gulf personnel, as well as those of several other major U.S. companies, very concerned. As was pointed out by an executive of Cities Service Company, "Time will take care of Angola. The Angolans are more and more development oriented. They aren't interested in politicizing central Africa on behalf of Cuba or the Soviet Union. Our people aren't persona non grata in Angola." A Texaco executive says, "They are pragmatic people. Although they lean toward a Marxist-style government, their Marxist friends can't give them what they need, so they turned to the West."

Gulf has argued for Angola's status quo before a House subcommittee but is afraid to do too much lobbying. Gulf points out that most African nations oppose intervention in Angola because UNITA is supported by South Africa. Any aid to UNITA could move Angola further away from the West and could precipitate an oil cutoff from Nigeria, which supplies a significant percentage of U.S. oil imports. In addition, the Angolan government encourages foreign investment and has enacted a very favorable investment code.

In demonstrating the ability of Gulf to adapt to different political situations, William E. Moffett, Vice-President of Gulf Oil Company, pointed out that Gulf had been operating in Angola with the MPLA government for seven years without any significant problems. In fact, he felt that three successive U.S. government administrations had accepted the premise that commercial relationships were acceptable, even in spite of political differences.

The early 1980s was a period of intense discussion on the role that the United States and its companies should take in Angola, especially as the guerrilla war with Savimbi continued to escalate. In response to an editorial in the *Wall Street Journal* that called for support of Savimbi in order to achieve victory in Angola and criticized the role of U.S. companies there, Mr. Moffett stated,

> *Finally, I would remind you that the presence of Western companies in Angola is not a political or foreign policy contradiction but a sign of real progress and hope. It constitutes a growing recognition by developing countries that wealth cannot be distributed until it is created. There are many ways to achieve "victory"; by helping countries such as Angola to develop their resources and meet their people's aspirations for a better life, we relieve them of the excessive dependence on outside forces that you decry, and provide them a better opportunity to make informed choices about their economic and political future.* (Wall Street Journal, *December 14, 1983, p. 31*)

- First World: nonsocialist industrial countries
- Second World: socialist countries
- Third World: developing countries

There are three major world economies in which the multinational enterprise (MNE) may operate successfully. The **First World** is made up of the nonsocialist industrial countries, the **Second World** consists of the socialist countries, and the **Third World** is comprised of the developing countries. The Third World is subdivided into various other groupings; this issue will be treated later in the chapter. In each of these three worlds there are different general economic and political frameworks, diverse levels of economic development, and a variety of economic conditions. To each of an infinite number of situations the MNE brings a frame of reference based on its own domestic experience and whatever it has learned in other foreign settings. If the firm is to be successful, it must carefully analyze the interaction of its policies with the economic environment in order to maximize efficiency.

The following important economic characteristics must be analyzed and accounted for by the MNE in the preliminary business process as well as during ongoing operations:

• Key economic characteristics that must be considered by an MNE

1. general economic framework: capitalist, socialist, etc.;
2. governmental monetary and fiscal policy;
3. economic stability: cyclical fluctuations, growth, inflation;
4. factor endowment: land, labor, and capital (quality as well as quantity);
5. market size;
6. extent of social overhead capital: power, transportation, communications, etc.;
7. international interaction: balance-of-payments positions, stability of exchange rate, trade patterns.[2]

How important is the economic environment of each country in which the firm operates? As was pointed out in one study, "No industrial enterprise or individual can exist entirely divorced from its environment, and firms both influence and are significantly influenced by the nature of the total environment."[3] The study emphasized that these environmental constraints, which include the economic characteristics listed above, limit the relative efficiency of the firm and thus the society.[4]

This chapter discusses the economic environment and its impact on the firm. Specific emphasis will be given to two major areas: (1) the general economic framework and its relationship to the political framework and (2) the level of economic development of developing countries. Many of the economic problems mentioned previously will be discussed in detail in later chapters.

POLITICAL AND ECONOMIC FRAMEWORKS

Two major segments of any society that have had an enormous impact on the way business is conducted are the political and economic systems. The **political system** is designed to integrate the society into a viable, functioning unit. The **economic system** is concerned with allocating scarce resources among competing users and involves two important matters: the control and coordination of resources and the ownership of property. In contemporary society it is very difficult, if not impossible, to separate political systems from economic systems. However, each type of system will be discussed independently, followed by a synthesis of the two.

Political Systems

- Pluralistic societies are those with a variety of ideologies

Ideology can be considered as the systematic and integrated body of constructs, theories, and aims that constitute a society. Most complex societies today are **pluralistic**—there are different ideologies held by numerous segments rather than one official ideology adhered to by all. These may be very similar, with only minor differences, or they may have widely divergent points of view. A good example would be in Angola, where the three different ethnic (and therefore political) groups formed a coalition government after independence. However, political rivalries broke down the coalition and resulted in a government supported by outside powers and harassed by an ousted member of the former coalition, who was supported by other outside interests. A similar coalition situation exists in El Salvador. The true test of any political system is its capacity to keep divergent ideologies from tearing the society apart.

Political ideologies are many and varied, and it is difficult to fit them neatly into a continuum representing degrees of citizen participation in decision making. However, Fig. 2.1 attempts to depict democratic and non-democratic forms of government. The two extremes in a theoretical sense are often considered to be democracy and totalitarianism. It is from these two theoretical extremes that various degrees of participation have emerged and evolved through time.

- Democratic systems involve wide participation of citizens in the decision-making process

Democracy. The ideology of pure **democracy** comes from the ancient Greek concept that citizens should be directly involved in the decision-making process. All citizens should be equal politically and legally and should enjoy widespread freedoms. The problem with implementing this type of system is that complexity increases with the number of citizens, creating problems in achieving full participation. As a result, most contemporary societies that espouse democracy have generated various forms of **representative democracy.**

The following features are characteristic of contemporary democratic political systems:

1. involvement of the citizens, either directly or indirectly, in making political decisions, the majority ruling;
2. in a representative democracy, majority rule through periodic elections;
3. some degree of equality among the citizens;
4. some degree of liberty, or some rights maintained by the citizens.[5]

- Totalitarianism is the absence of widespread participation in decision making, which is restricted to only a few individuals

Totalitarianism. If democracy or total participation by all citizens is at one end of the spectrum, then **totalitarianism** is at the other end. In this case a single party, individual, or group of individuals holds a monopoly of political power and does not recognize or permit opposition. In totalitarian-

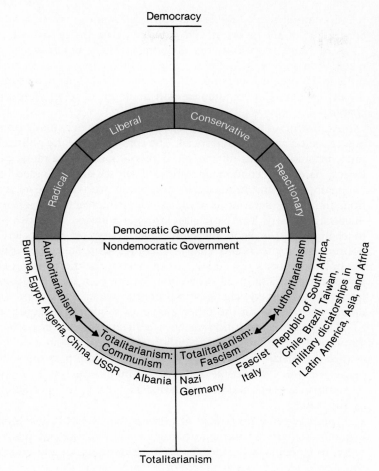

FIGURE 2.1
The Political Spectrum
Source: Endpaper
("Democracy/Totalitarianism")
from *American Democracy in
World Perspective* by William
Ebenstein, C. Herman Pritchett,
Henry A. Turner and Dean Mann,
© 1967 by Harper & Row Pub.
Co. Reprinted by permission by
the publisher.

ism (e.g., a dictatorship) the opportunity to participate in decisions is restricted to a few individuals.[6]

There are a variety of forms of totalitarianism. The form most often thought of in the Western context is communism. However, there are other forms. The sheikdoms of the Middle East thrive on a form of government that is anything but democratic. The overthrow of the Shah of Iran supposedly heralded a new era of popular consent for the Ayatollah Khomeini, but these intimations of democracy turned into a cruel joke with the subsequent repression and persecution of nonorthodox factions. South Korea's government is far from communist, but few would question its totalitarian nature. Latin American governments routinely fluctuate between nervous democracy and military dictatorships.

● Communism is a form of
totalitarianism initially
theorized by Karl Marx

Communism in a theoretical and contemporary sense is very complex. Separation of the political and economic systems is virtually impossible. As Karl Marx theorized, the economic system determines the direction taken by a society in politics, religion, philosophy, and so on. However, the actual mechanics and implications of a centrally planned economic system usually espoused in communism will be deferred to another section of the chapter.

● Bourgeoisie: the owners of
the means of production

● Proletariat: the working class
that should eventually
become the dictator class in
a communist system

According to Marx, two types of revolutions eventually occur in a capitalistic society: political and social. The completion of the political revolution precedes and touches off the social revolution, a long-range phenomenon largely based on economic inequities. Each society is divided by Marx into two major economic groups: the bourgeoisie, who own the means of production, and the proletariat or working class, which actually performs the production processes. The basic class struggle between these two groups leads to changes in the economic and social system of the society. Since the bourgeoisie try to retard change in order to protect their own position, the only way social revolution can advance is for the working class to seize power through a political revolution. As the bourgeoisie become absorbed into the new society, changes in property ownership and production techniques occur, causing the other elements of society to adjust accordingly.

The political revolution results in a dictatorship by the proletariat, which theoretically is to remain for only a short time to smooth the transition during the social revolution. A general equalization of the social and economic welfare of the people occurs, as institutions such as the family, religion, educational systems, and private business interests are replaced or dominated by the state.

● Lenin refined communism to
include a political system of
enlightened revolutionaries

Lenin added a great deal to Marxist theory in his development of the Communist party as the controlling element of the political system. The party, to be composed of professional revolutionaries and enlightened people, would serve as the vanguard of the proletariat. The top party leadership should be skilled organizers and administrators and thus would hold responsible positions in the state bureaucracy. Governmental rule was to revolve around the principle of democratic centralism, permitting absolute freedom in the discussion of issues until a decision was made. After that point the decision was to be accepted unanimously. The government would be responsible for organizing society into different groups in order to provide as much input as possible into the decision-making process. As the social revolution approached completion, the dictatorship by the proletariat would disappear, and full communism would take its place.

Contemporary political systems. Pure democracy has given way to various forms of representative government in which citizens vote for individuals to represent them and make collective decisions. Voting eligibility may depend on a certain minimum age, as in the United States, or on racial classifications, as in South Africa. The racial situation in South Africa has resulted in an interesting political system. South Africa's racial mixture is 73 percent blacks, 15 percent whites, and 12 percent Asians (primarily Indians) and coloreds. The coloreds are a racially mixed category. In 1984, elections were held in South Africa to select representatives for Asians and coloreds. The tricameral parliament has one assembly for Asians with 45 seats, one assembly for coloreds with 85 seats, and one assembly for whites with 178 seats. The whites have the majority vote in parliament and thus control all legislation. In the 1984 election, many eligible Asian and colored voters stayed away from the polls to protest the disenfranchisement of the majority black population.[7]

Multiple political parties may participate in the process, as in the United States and most other free industrial countries, or there may be a single dominant party that controls political power, as in Mexico and Singapore.

Singapore was given its freedom from British colonial rule in 1963, although it had enjoyed partial freedom since 1955. After a brief period of unification with Malaysia, Singapore became a fully independent state with a parliament and a president as constitutional head of state. The People's Action Party (PAP) has been in strong control since the establishment of the state. Prime Minister Lee Kuan Yew has been the strong ruler of Singapore for years. Although it is theoretically possible for a party other than PAP to be in power, that is highly unlikely. The 75-member Parliament elects a president for a four-year term, and the president appoints a prime minister, who leads the cabinet.[8]

It is evident from even casual observation that contemporary communism differs from theoretical communism. The political revolutions have resulted in a permanent rather than transitory dictatorship by the proletariat. Also, democratic centralism has given way to totalitarian or autocratic centralism, with no general participation in decision making—especially by those with opposing viewpoints. An important split has developed over the degree and importance of political revolution in achieving social objectives.

Economic Systems

- Market economy: resources are allocated and controlled by consumers, who "vote" through buying goods
- Command economy: resources are allocated and controlled by government decision
- Private ownership: individuals own resources

Economic systems are usually loosely defined as either capitalist, socialist, or mixed. However, it is possible to classify economic systems according to method of resource allocation and control (**market economy** or **command economy** and to type of property ownership (**private ownership** or **public ownership**). Expansion of this concept to include mixed ownership and control would result in the taxonomy indicated in Fig. 2.2.

The ownership of factors of production can be viewed as a continuum from complete private ownership at one end to complete public ownership at the other. In reality, no country belongs wholly at one end or the other.

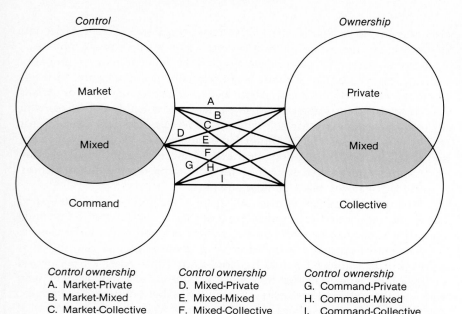

FIGURE 2.2
Interrelationships between Control of Economic Activity and Ownership of Factors of Production

Control ownership
A. Market-Private
B. Market-Mixed
C. Market-Collective

Control ownership
D. Mixed-Private
E. Mixed-Mixed
F. Mixed-Collective

Control ownership
G. Command-Private
H. Command-Mixed
I. Command-Collective

● Public ownership: the government owns resources

The United States is considered to be the prime example of private enterprise, yet the government owns some factors of production and actively produces in such sectors of the economy as education, the military, the postal service, and certain utilities. The Soviet Union, which espouses public ownership of the means of production, allows small peasant farming on a private basis. Most countries lie somewhere in the mixed category, which is very broad and includes varying degrees of public and private ownership. Likewise, the control of economic activity represents a continuum from market to command economies, the actual situation lying somewhere in between.

● Interrelationship of price, quantity, supply, and demand

Market economy. In a market economy, two societal units are very important: the household and the firm. Resources are owned and products consumed by households, while resources are used and products produced by firms. The market mechanism involves an interaction of price, quantity, supply, and demand of resources and products. Labor is supplied by the household if the firm offers an adequate wage. Products are consumed if the price is within a certain range. A firm bases its wages on the quantity of labor available to assume a job. Resources are allocated as a result of the constant interplay between households and firms, as well as the interplay between households and between firms (as when the input of one firm is the output of another). The key factors that make the market economy work are consumer sovereignty and the freedom of the enterprise to operate in the market. As long as both units are free to make decisions, the interplay of supply and demand should ensure proper resource allocation.

• Large corporations, labor unions, and the government limit freedom in a free market

The market economy has been highly successful in most industrial countries, especially in the United States. A perfect market economy does not exist in the United States owing to three major factors: large corporations, labor unions, and the government. The large corporation is able to reduce market pressures somewhat by exerting control over the purchase of resources or the sale of products. Because of the large size of the firm and the relative smallness of each individual shareholder, the gap between ownership and control of decision making is quite wide. Decisions may or may not be strictly motivated by the market.

Labor unions came about in response to the power exerted by the owners and managers of business over the labor market. Tremendous benefits in terms of salaries, fringe benefits, work conditions, and bargaining power have been won by the unions, but market forces have been seriously disrupted. Many unions control entry into the work force and restrict the freedom of workers to change occupations in response to supply and demand, thus aggravating undesirable conditions. Wages are generally considered to be one-directional—upward—under the typical union structure.

Government policies continue to shape the U.S. economy. Fiscal and monetary policies have a direct effect on employment, the production and consumption of goods and services (for example, the military), and the growth of the money supply.

• The government sets goals and decides price and quantity

Central command.   In a centrally planned economy the government harmonizes the activities of the different economic sectors. In the extreme form of central command, goals are set for every enterprise in the country and must be followed. The government determines how much is produced, by whom, and for whom. The assumption is that the government is a better judge of how resources should be allocated than is the economy in general and the consumer in particular.

Usually, the heart of a centrally planned economy is its blueprint, generally a five-year plan. Based on this overall goal, specific targets are set each year for each sector of the economy. An attempt is made to harmonize all sectors, since the output of one firm becomes the input of another. A centrally planned economy must rely on the accuracy of government targets instead of on market prices to allocate resources properly. The Soviet Union is a major example of a planned economy, yet market forces are influential to some degree in its labor market, the distribution of consumer goods, part of the production of farm products, and some privately furnished services.

• Problems of centrally planned economies

A centrally planned economy is not without problems. It has frequently been pointed out that special problems arise in production, in the procurement of materials, and in investment. In production, quotas are often given in quantitative terms; managers often find ways to meet the quotas, but at a high cost to society. For example, one firm producing cloth was given a target of length in meters but no specification for width. The manager therefore produced cloth at a very narrow width in order to meet the target. Likewise, a nail manufacturer was given a target in tonnage and ended up producing large nails rather than a proper mix of different sizes.

The procurement of materials is also a problem. If one firm fails to reach its target, other firms that depend on that firm's product as an input are severely affected. As a result, firms overorder supplies and employ special pushers to obtain them.

In the area of investment, technology and innovation entail risks that could lead to not meeting a production quota. Managers often adopt a short-run rather than a long-run perspective.

- Different mixtures of market and centrally planned economies and public and private ownership of resources

Mixed economies. By definition, no economy is purely market determined or centrally planned. The United States and the Soviet Union can be viewed as extremes of mixed economies. However, mixed economies generally have a higher degree of government intervention than is found in the United States and a greater degree of reliance on market forces than is found in the Soviet Union. Government intervention can be regarded in two ways: actual government ownership of means of production and government influence in economic decision making. The former is easy to quantify statistically, but since the latter is a matter of policy and custom, it is difficult to measure precisely.

Several industrial economies have a strong mixture of market and command economies. The French economic system, for example, has traditionally depended heavily on private enterprise, but it also relies on strong direction from the government that closely approximates limited central planning. The French planners indicate directions that general development in the economy should take but do not indicate special targets that each industry or firm should achieve. Special incentives are used to stimulate industrial growth according to the plan. These include special credit policies, depreciation allowances in certain sectors, favorable treatment of exports, and preference in government orders.

- France's mixed economy

When François Mitterand of the French Socialist Party was elected President of France in 1981 for a seven-year term of office, the economy of France took a strong turn toward central control. President Mitterand's platform included the nationalization of some of the largest companies in France, and he followed through on his promises. Most of the nationalizations took place in large industries that were important for France's strategic future. Initially, the Industry Ministry implemented strongly interventionist industrial policies. In 1983, however, President Mitterand appointed an Industry Minister (Laurent Fabius) who was much more moderate and more inclined to let the managers of the state industries make key market decisions.

However, the government has clearly set targets and goals for the future direction of the key state enterprises. A couple of examples illustrate how the government has intervened to direct investment. One of the key industries targeted for future growth is the electronics industry. In order to have a company large enough to compete with the ITTs and Siemens of the world, the French government allowed two state-owned electronics firms, Cie. Générale d'Electricité and Thomson S.A., to merge their telecommunications industries.

Another example is that of Cie. de Saint-Gobain. Like many of the large companies in industries that were not very efficient or competitive in world markets, Saint-Gobain was forced to lay off workers. In one area, however, Saint-Gobain established a development company that helped some of its laid-off managers acquire a privately owned company and then provided loans for expansion of the company, which resulted in the absorption of many of the workers let go by Saint-Gobain. The development company loaned the money at rates of interest that were substantially below market rates and then permitted some of the loan to become a direct grant if the company would hire former Saint-Gobain workers.

● Changes in Turkey

In some countries the change has been from more to less state intervention. In Turkey, for example, the government has been abandoning statist policies and adopting free enterprise and greater reliance on market forces. These policies have helped Turkey to reduce inflation from over 100 percent in 1980 to around 40 percent in 1984 and to increase GNP by about 4 percent per year during the period of 1981–1984 from a situation of almost no growth in 1980.

Another country that has been going through rapid change within a centrally planned environment is the People's Republic of China (PRC). Some of the major economic reforms enacted since 1979 are:

● Major economic reforms in China

1. greater decentralization of production and investment decisions to enterprises and farms;

2. stronger incentives with more direct links between material rewards and the work of households and individuals; and

3. greater use of market mechanisms in allocating resources. Credits are available for commercial ventures to market consumer goods and agricultural inputs in rural areas.

These changes have been very visible in the agricultural area. Farmland, draft animals, and implements are assigned to individual households for several years (usually five years). Farmers are free to farm as they wish. They have to sell an agreed amount of their crops to the government and to their village production teams. They can keep the rest for their own use if they desire. They can also sell it at the market prices determined purely by supply and demand. During 1978–1982, gross agricultural output rose at 7 percent per year, more than double the average rate in the preceding twenty years. Farmers' real income grew at an even greater rate owing to the higher prices they received from their goods. The PRC is not ready to dismantle its statist system totally, but it does allow some flexibility within the system.[10]

● Japan, Inc.

A final illustration of state intervention is that of Japan. Japan is often called "Japan, Inc."—for good reason. At the close of World War II, Japan decided to take a different approach from that of many countries. Instead of nationalizing key sectors and industries, Japan decided to let investment remain in the private sector and then focus more on setting targets and using fiscal incentives to direct investment flows. The famous Ministry of International Trade and Industry (MITI) was organized to guide industrial development through "strategic planning and authority (both formal and informal) over investment and production priorities."[11] MITI seemed to be more concerned with developing a vision than with setting up a blueprint for the economy. During the early period of MITI in the 1950s and early 1960s the key was protectionism so that industries could reach economies of scale free of outside competition. However, the 1960s was a period of selective liberalization that involved MITI-inspired industrial reorganizations resulting in industries, such as automobiles and steel, that became formidable world competitors. Structural adjustment to the oil price shocks of the 1970s was also inspired and encouraged by MITI as it helped to force companies to become more energy-efficient. Those companies on the MITI "hit list" had to become involved in a program that set out the

steps to reduce excess capacity, the timing of such reductions, and restrictions on further expansion. Where necessary, the industries were allowed to establish arrangements to maintain orderly markets under the condition of excess supply and were given government financial support to facilitate structural adjustment. [12]

Two indicators of the role of government in capitalist societies are government disbursements and revenues as a percentage of gross domestic product. Figure 2.3 compares data from several industrial countries. It is interesting to note the wide divergence among countries, with Japan showing the lowest percentages and Sweden the highest. As was noted above, however, Japan's influence in the economy extends beyond actual expenditures. It is interesting to note the large percentage for France, and it should be mentioned that the data on France are from 1980, even before the election of President Mitterand.

Political-Economic Synthesis

● General synthesis:
  ● Democratic societies: market economy and private ownership

Except for the discussion on communism, we have made no attempt to link an economic philosophy with a particular political regime, nor a particular political philosophy with any of the economic systems discussed in the

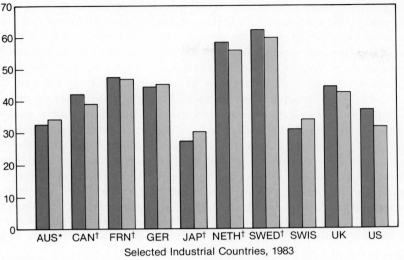

FIGURE 2.3
Government Disbursements and Revenues as a Percentage of GDP of Selected Industrial Countries, 1983
Source: OECD *Observer,* March 1985.

Over 40% considered high level of government involvement (handwritten note)

Country	Abbreviation	Disbursements	Revenues
Australia*	AUS*	32.7	34.2
Canada†	CAN†	42.2	39.0
France†	FRN†	47.5	46.9
Germany	GER	44.4	45.2
Japan†	JAP†	27.3	30.2
Netherlands†	NETH†	58.3	55.8
Sweden†	SWED†	62.2	59.7
Switzerland	SWIS	30.8	33.9
United Kingdom	UK	44.3	42.5
United States	US	36.9	31.7

*1982–1983 data
†1982 data

- Totalitarian societies: command economy and public ownership
- Exceptions to the rule

previous section. In general, one tends to think of a totalitarian political regime in connection with public ownership of factors of production and a command economy. This may not always be the case. There are many examples of totalitarian regimes and mixed (primarily capitalistic) economies. In a different type of situation, Salvador Allende attempted to institute communism in Chile after winning a democratic election. However, several problems occurred that ultimately led to his death and the failure of his experiment. First, he was elected with only 36 percent of the vote. Second, his reforms led to a rapid deterioration of the economic system and further erosion of his support. Third, it became evident that it would be more and more difficult to continue the reforms and maintain a democratic form of government. Fourth, the military decided to end the experiment before a complete Marxist social revolution could take place. Allende's failure points up the difficulties of trying to effect a social (and therefore economic) revolution without total political control.

• Democratic socialism: strong control of the economy by an elected government

It is commonly thought that a democratic form of government is best complimented by private ownership of factors of production and a market economy. However, this view does not apply to **democratic socialism.** The so-called market socialists feel that since economics and politics are so closely connected, the voters should rely on their elected government to control the economic system—that is, the part of the economy not owned by the government would be regulated by the government. The whole rationale for democratic socialism is that in order to have a democratically controlled economy and the economic security necessary for liberty, the economy must be owned or regulated by a welfare-oriented government. This is obviously what the voters had in mind when they elected François Mitterand as President of France.

Just as some Western democracies have socialist leanings, several communist countries seem to be going through a metamorphosis as well, as was pointed out in the discussion on the People's Republic of China.

It is obvious from our discussion of political and economic systems that numerous combinations are possible. It might be safe to conclude that the greater the tendency toward political totalitarianism, the greater the reliance on government intervention in ownership and control of the economy. However, most countries that experience relative freedom in political decision making have experimented with different degrees of intervention in the economic system.

Some authors have noted that the extremes are tending to converge to a more even mix of public-private interaction in ownership and control. In the case of the industrial countries the emphasis seems to be on control rather than on ownership. There are three major reasons for this increased government participation where a quasi–laissez-faire attitude previously existed:

1. the failure of the market mechanism to provide adequately for all sectors of society;

2. the problem of stagnation and inflation plaguing most industrial countries during the 1970s; and

3. increased interdependence of world economies so that world supply and demand could have a strong impact on national supply and demand.

A movement away from the centrally planned communist model can occur by decentralizing the planning and control process and by allowing certain aspects of the economy to operate on a market rather than a planned basis.

The Role of the Foreign Firm

The difficulty facing most foreign firms is one of adjustment. For example, a firm based in the United States is accustomed to the political and economic systems of that country and has devised ways to survive profitably in that particular environment. Upon entering another country for the first time the firm needs to answer certain questions such as:

• Key issues to be considered by the foreign firm

1. What is the political structure of the country?
2. Under what type of economic system does the country operate?
3. Is my industry in the public or private sector?
4. If it is in the public sector, does the government also allow private competition in that sector?
5. If it is in the private sector, is there any tendency to move it toward public ownership?
6. Does the government view foreign capital as being in competition or in partnership with public or local private enterprises?
7. In what ways does the government control the nature and extent of private enterprise?
8. How much of a contribution is the private sector expected to make in helping the government formulate overall economic objectives?

The questions appear simple, but their answers are not, owing to the dynamic nature of political and economic events.

Canada, for example, has long been the favorite of U.S. business with more foreign investment and exports going there than to any other country in the world. The downfall of Joe Clark's government and the resurrection of Pierre Trudeau in 1980 dramatically changed the picture. Tired of U.S. domination in vital industries—especially oil—Trudeau outlined a broad program of U.S. divestiture that shook the foundations of U.S.-Canadian relations. (See the case at the beginning of Chapter 11.) Just as everything was looking bleak in Canada for foreign-based MNEs, Trudeau fell from favor, and the Progressive Conservatives led by Brian Mulroney pushed the Liberal Party from power.

In all cases the foreign firm must be aware of its own experience and how that experience has helped shape its managerial philosophy and practice. In addition, the firm must determine how the new environment differs from the more familiar domestic environment and decide how managerial philosophy and practice must be changed to adapt to the new political and economic environment. It should be noted that private enterprise has been very adept at operating in any environment. Its management, marketing, production, and technical skills have been welcomed in a variety of forms in Marxist-Leninist, social democratic, and Third World socialist countries as well as in mixed economy and capitalist countries.

THE DEVELOPING COUNTRIES

At various times the poorer countries of the world have been referred to as backward, underdeveloped, less developed (LDCs), and, more recently, developing. Also, the term "Third World" is often used to distinguish those countries from the free industrial First World (industrial market economies) and socialist Second World (East European nonmarket economies). Table 2.1 provides a list of countries in five major categories as defined by the World Bank. The industrial market economies, with the exception of Australia and New Zealand, lie in the Northern Hemisphere, giving rise to the "North-South dialogue" so frequently mentioned between indus-

TABLE 2.1 _____

WORLD BANK COUNTRY CATEGORIES

I. *Industrial Market Economies* *

Australia
Austria
Belgium
Canada
Denmark
Finland
France
Federal Republic of Germany
Iceland
Ireland
Italy
Japan
Luxembourg
The Netherlands
New Zealand
Norway
Spain
Sweden
Switzerland
United Kingdom
United States

II. *East European Nonmarket Economies*

Albania
Bulgaria
Czechoslovakia
German Democratic Republic
Hungary
Poland
Romania
Soviet Union

III. *High-Income Oil Exporters*

Bahrain
Brunei
Darussalam
Kuwait†
Libya†
Oman
Qatar†
Saudi Arabia†
United Arab Emirates†

IV. *Low-Income Economies*
1982 Annual Per Capita GNP of less than $410

V. *Middle-Income Economies*
1982 Annual Per Capita GNP of more than $410

A. *Net Oil Exporters*
Algeria†
Angola
Cameroon
Congo
Ecuador†
Egypt
Gabon†
Indonesia†
Islamic Republic of Iran†
Iraq†
Malaysia
Mexico
Nigeria†
Peru
Syria
Trinidad and Tobago
Tunisia
Venezuela†

B. *Oil Importers*

1. Major Exporters of Manufactures
Argentina
Brazil
Greece
Hong Kong
Israel
Republic of Korea
Philippines
Portugal
Singapore
South Africa
Thailand
Yugoslavia

2. Other Oil Importers
The remainder of the middle income economies which are not classified as net oil importers or major exporters of manufactures.

* These twenty-one countries plus Greece, Portugal, and Turkey comprise the Organization for Economic Cooperation and Development (OECD).
† Members of the Organization of Petroleum Exporting Countries (OPEC).

Source: *World Development Report, 1984,* published for the World Bank (New York: Oxford University Press, 1984).

trial and developing countries. Spain is a relatively recent addition to the list of industrial countries. As recently as the 1979 *World Development Report* of the World Bank, Spain was considered a middle-income developing country.

The socialist Second World countries used to be in a World Bank category known as centrally planned economies. Now, however, the World Bank has put them in a category that it calls East European nonmarket economies.

A third designation of countries is the high-income oil exporters. These countries used to be in a special category of developing countries, but now they are completely separate.

The developing countries are more difficult to define. Recent publications of the World Bank and the International Monetary Fund have separated the developing countries into two groups: low-income economies and middle-income economies. The low-income economies are those with 1982 annual per capita GNP of less than $410. The middle-income developing countries are those with a per capita GNP of more than $410. The middle-income economies are divided into two categories: net oil exporters and oil importers. Many of the net oil exporters are members of the Organization of Petroleum Exporting Countries (OPEC).

A subset of the middle income oil importers is the major exporters of manufacturers. These countries are sometimes called newly industrialized countries or NICs.[13]

With only a few exceptions the low-income countries are found in Asia, Africa, and Latin America. Middle-income countries are much more widespread geographically, but a majority of Latin America's population is in middle-income countries.

Table 2.2 provides some comparative indicators for the low- and middle-income developing countries and the industrialized countries. It is interesting to note that as the groupings move from low-income to industrialized coun-

TABLE 2.2

BASIC INDICATORS (1982)

	Population (millions)	GNP Per Capita ($ 1982)	Adult Literacy Rate*	Life Expectancy at Birth	Distribution of Gross Domestic Product (percent)		
					Agriculture	Industry	Services
Low-income	2266.5	280	52%	59	37	32	31
Middle-income	1158.3	1520	65	60	15	38	47
Industrialized	722.9	11,070	99	75	3	36	61

* 1981 data from *World Development Report, 1983.*

Source: *World Development Report, 1984,* published for the World Bank (New York: Oxford University Press, 1984), pp. 218–219; 222–223.

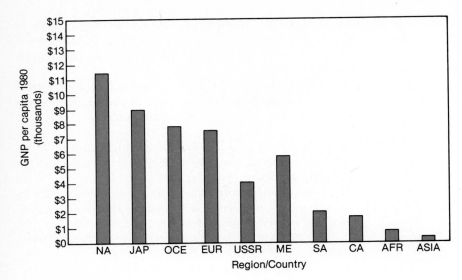

FIGURE 2.4
Per Capita GNP by Major Regions
Source: World Bank Atlas, 1983 and 1982 (Washington, D.C.: World Bank, 1983, 1982)

Country/Region	Abbreviation	GNP per capita, 1980
North America	NA	$11,460
Japan	JAP	9,020
Oceania	OCE	7,810
Europe	EUR	7,540
USSR*	USSR*	4,040
Middle East	ME	5,790
South America	SA	2,070
Central America	CA	1,740
Africa	AFR	760
Asia	ASIA	330

*1979 data

tries, the distribution of gross domestic product (GDP) shifts in emphasis from agriculture to industry to services.

The geographical distribution of wealth is even more dramatically illustrated in Fig. 2.4. With the exception of Oceania the wealth of the world is in the Northern Hemisphere.

Problems of Developing Countries

Each year, *Business Week* runs a special report on the developing countries in which it takes a look at the major problems by geographic region. Even though there are great differences among the developing countries, many shared problems and characteristics exist. Some of the most common problems mentioned are hyperinflation, external debt, weakening currencies, shortage of skilled workers, political instability, war and insurrection, mass poverty (primarily in Africa), rapid population growth, weakening commodity prices, and reliance on imported oil. Although it is not necessary to look at all of those problems right now, we will look at a few of the most important ones.

• Basic needs: health, education, water, nutrition, housing

Basic needs.   The problems of the low-income developing countries are unique. It is true that no country is without poverty, but in the low-income countries it is accute. Their per capita GNP in 1980 averaged only $250 per year, compared with the per capita GNP of developing countries in general of $650 per year.

The World Bank looks at basic needs in the following five areas: health, education, water, nutrition, and housing. In recent studies, the Bank has found that four things about basic needs must be understood in order to increase the productivity of the poor:

1. In addition to basic capital assistance—such as credit and machinery—education and health are required.

2. The landless and urban poor have no physical assets at all.

3. Even if the poor could earn an income, they rarely have adequate goods and services to spend it on.

4. It may take a long time to increase the productivity of the poor to the point at which they can meet a minimum set of their basic needs.[14]

The rapid population growth of the developing countries presents a major problem in improving the quality of life. That problem will be discussed in more detail later on. Rapid urbanization is another problem affecting the quality of life. The poor who are unable to earn a living in rural areas move to the cities in hope of finding jobs. There they find already high levels of urban unemployment and increasingly poor housing conditions. Low levels of education are often caused by and help to perpetuate underdevelopment. Any improvement in the level of literacy requires a tremendous investment in financial resources and a commitment on the part of people. In order to generate the skilled labor force necessary for development, the level of technical education needs to be increased significantly. If resources are not committed to education, sustained growth is difficult to achieve. Without sustained growth it is difficult to generate enough resources to provide adequate educational opportunities.

Population growth.   One of the major issues identified by the World Bank in 1984 was rapid population growth. Projections of growth are always dangerous to make, but it is possible to look at the past and try to measure the impact of rapid population growth on the world economy.

Starting with the year 1 A.D., it took 1500 years for the world's population to double. Between 1750 and 1900, a period of only 150 years, population doubled again. Between 1950 and 1984 the population doubled again to nearly 4.8 billion people.[15] In Chapter 24 we discuss projections of population growth into the future.

Most of the growth in the past two decades has taken place in the developing countries, where families are less likely to be able to cope with the needs of larger families. Much of the growth has taken place because of more mothers entering the fertility age and a decline in infant mortality.

The World Bank feels that rapid population growth impairs economic growth for three reasons:

● Reasons why rapid population growth impairs economic growth

First, it exacerbates the awkward choice between higher consumption now and the investment needed to bring higher consumption in the future. . . .

Second, in many countries increases in population threaten what is already a precarious balance between natural resources and people. . . .

Third, rapid increases in population make it hard to manage the adjustments that accompany and promote economic and social change. The growth of cities in developing countries, largely due to high rates of natural increase, poses serious management problems; so too does continued rapid growth that in some rural areas threatens permanent environment damage. [16]

However, some people disagree with this opinion of the World Bank. They feel that the greatest natural resource we have is people and that people tend to adjust and adapt to changing world conditions. As resources become scarce, people develop substitutes for those resources so that growth can continue. Besides, growth is difficult to achieve without a younger population to support an aging population. However, even these critics realize that the pockets of extreme population growth in the developing countries pose real problems for those countries and possibly for the world at large. The difficult problem faced by those governments is to develop government policies that will encourage slow growth in their populations. That is not an easy task.

Inflation. A major problem facing many developing countries is inflation. As will be pointed out in the Bolivian peso case at the beginning of Chapter 9, the magnitude of inflation in many developing countries is virtually incomprehensible to most people in the industrial world. Argentina suffered inflation in 1984 of between 600 and 700 percent. Brazil's inflation during that same period was over 200 percent. In that kind of environment it is difficult for firms to plan for the future and run a profitable operation. Prices change almost daily in order to maintain a sufficient cash flow to replace inventory and keep the firm operating. It is difficult to forecast inflation accurately, so firms end up underpricing or overpricing products. The result is a shortage of cash flow in the first situation and a price that is too high to maintain market share in the second situation. Inflation of the magnitude experienced by Bolivia, Argentina, and Brazil also creates problems for firms that deal in international markets. If the exchange rate changes at the same pace as inflation, then the prices that foreigners pay for exports of the inflationary country will not really change. But if the exchange rate does not change as much as inflation, companies are forced to raise their prices and soon find that they cannot compete in world markets.

Inflation also destabilizes a country politically. If the government tries to control inflation by controlling wages, the real income of the populace declines, and frustration sets in. If the government decides to do nothing, the country runs the risk of having the economy deteriorate to the point at which real incomes fall anyway. It is particularly difficult to institute fiscal rigor when the government is in a fragile position in the first place.

Oil. By far one of the biggest curses of the developing countries is oil. Some of the developing countries, such as Mexico and Venezuela, have reaped the benefits of oil revenues historically, but the ensuing inflation and more recent drop in demand and therefore revenues have created some real problems. The oil-importing developing countries were hit by rising prices of oil in the 1970s. Because they had to pay increasingly higher prices for the same volume of consumption, they were forced to forego needed imports of capital equipment for basic development.

• Problems of oil exporters

First, let's examine the problem of developing countries that export oil. Some oil-exporting developing countries, such as Saudi Arabia and Kuwait, do not really export much except oil; their export base is not diverse. In addition, their populations are fairly small, so fluctuations in export revenues are a nuisance but can be managed. Other countries such as Mexico, Venezuela, Nigeria, Indonesia, and Iran are primarily oil exporters, but they also have large population bases. Many of them set up elaborate development plans and entered into large construction projects based on projected worldwide demand for oil. As will be discussed more fully in Chapter 7, the drop in world demand for oil, followed by falling prices and revenues for the oil exporters, resulted in serious problems for many of them. Those that had borrowed in world capital markets to finance the growth that would be paid for by oil found that they did not have the resources available to pay off their debt. Those that preferred to go on a cash-and-carry basis, like Iran in recent years, found that they were not selling enough oil to finance their current development. In general, the oil exporters found that oil as a percentage of GDP increased, public expenditures as a percentage of GDP increased, and nonoil exports declined in importance. Most of the oil exporters found that their exchange rate strengthened during the 1973–1980 period, so it became more difficult for them to sell nonoil exports in world markets. As was mentioned above, those countries spent huge amounts of money in large-scale development projects, which had a tendency to experience delays and cost overruns. When oil prices began to fall after 1980, the economies of many of the oil exporters started to come unraveled.

• Problems of oil importers

The countries that import oil have found themselves in a different position. During the 1970s, when oil prices were skyrocketing and demand was firm, those countries were forced to borrow large amounts of money to import the oil necessary just to exist. These prices in turn were a major contributor to inflation in those countries. The drop in prices in the early 1980s was a real blessing to the oil importers because they could devote a larger percentage of their resources to development rather than just importing oil. Also, the oil factor was taken out of inflation. However, the countries were not necessarily out of trouble completely. The events that forced prices down—primarily recession in the industrial countries, leading to a shortfall in demand—also curtailed many of the export markets that those countries had hoped to exploit to pay their oil bills. As they, especially countries such as Brazil and Argentina, struggled to sell goods abroad to pay off their oil-induced debts, they found that the markets were insufficient to generate enough cash flow. On balance, the moderation of oil prices should be a blessing to the developing countries in general, even though the exporters will really suffer.

Debt. One of the consequences of the rapid increase in the cost of oil during the 1970s was the equally rapid increase in external debt as developing countries sought assistance in financing the import of oil and other products necessary for development. Developing country debt increased from $86.6 billion in 1971 to $393 billion in 1979 to $456 billion in 1980 to $766 billion at the end of 1982 and $810 billion at the end of 1983.[17] Of the 1983 total, it was estimated that $560 billion was owed to private lenders such as commercial banks and MNEs, and the remainder was owed to official institutions.

Figures 2.5, 2.6, and 2.7 provide some data on some of the most celebrated debtors. Note the tremendous size of the debt in countries such as Mexico and Brazil. The debt service ratio is the ratio of interest payments plus principal amortization to exports. Notice how many of the large debtors have to spend the earnings of nearly half of their exports just servicing debt. It is obviously important to have a diversified economy, as South Korea does, so that manufacturing exports can be used to help service that debt. Another interesting statistic is the debt as a percentage of GNP (or GDP for some of the countries). That percentage tends to be very high for the large debtors.

Table 2.3 provides some debt indicators for a sample of ninety developing countries, which includes those countries listed in Figs. 2.5–2.7. It is interesting to compare the overall data with those of some of the major

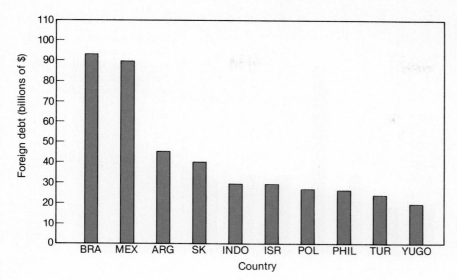

FIGURE 2.5
Foreign Debt of Major Debtor Nations, in Billions of Dollars
Source: Lawrence Rout, "World Debt in Crisis," *Wall Street Journal,* June 22, 1984, pp. 29–32.

Country	Abbreviation	Foreign debt (billions of $)
Brazil	BRA	93.1
Mexico	MEX	89.8
Argentina	ARG	45.3
S. Korea	SK	40.1
Indonesia	INDO	29.5
Israel	ISR	29.3
Poland	POL	27.0
Philippines	PHIL	26.4
Turkey	TUR	23.9
Yugoslavia	YUGO	19.5

debtors in those figures to see how severe their problems are in comparison with those of the other countries.

It is evident from the figures quoted earlier in this section and pointed out in Table 2.3 that debt to developing countries increased dramatically during the 1970s and early 1980s. The first crisis hit the international banking community when Poland was having its troubles in the 1970s. It appeared at that time that Poland would have to default, and many experts were unsure of the impact on the international financial community. However, that crisis was weathered. The real crisis hit in August 1982 when Mexico, with nearly four times the debt of Poland, simply could not fulfill its debt service obligations. It was forced to reschedule principal and interest payments. Most of the large debtors, especially Brazil and Argentina, were

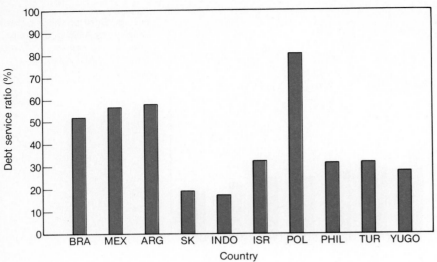

FIGURE 2.6

Debt Service Ratio of Major Debtor Nations
Source: Lawrence Rout, "World Debt in Crisis," *Wall Street Journal,* June 22, 1984, pp. 29–32.

Country	Abbreviation	Debt service ratio (%)
Brazil	BRA	51.7
Mexico	MEX	56.7
Argentina	ARG	58.1
S. Korea	SK	19.1
Indonesia	INDO	17.3
Israel	ISR	32.3
Poland	POL	80.8
Philippines	PHIL	31.6
Turkey	TUR	31.8
Yugoslavia	YUGO	28.0

in the same position and had to go through reschedulings at the same time. It is interesting to note that fourteen countries rescheduled $8 billion of debt in 1981, and ten countries rescheduled $4 billion in 1982, but it was estimated that thirty-six reschedulings involving approximately twenty-nine countries and nearly $70 billion took place in 1983.[18]

• Role of the IMF

The International Monetary Fund (IMF) has played a crucial role in helping the debtor nations. The IMF has gone into country after country and recommended rather strong economic restrictions as a precondition for receiving loans from the IMF, which are almost a necessity if the international commercial banks are to reschedule the country's loans. These restrictions have involved a combination of export expansion, import substitution, and drastic reduction in public spending. In Mexico, for example, the government deficit was running at an estimated 17.6 percent of GDP in 1982,

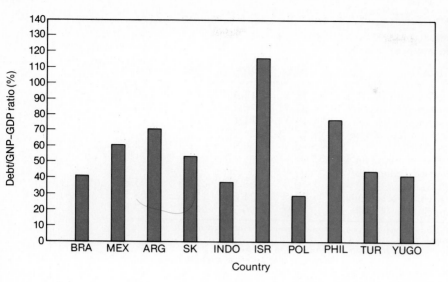

FIGURE 2.7
Debt/GNP–GDP Ratio of Major Debtor Nations
Source: Lawrence Rout, "World Debt in Crisis," *Wall Street Journal,* June 22, 1984, pp. 29–32.

Country	Abbreviation	Debt/GNP-GDP ratio (%)
Brazil	BRA	41.1
Mexico	MEX	60.5
Argentina	ARG	70.6
S. Korea	SK	53.5
Indonesia	INDO	37.3
Israel	ISR	116.1
Poland	POL	29.3
Philippines	PHIL	77.2
Turkey	TUR	44.4
Yugoslavia	YUGO	41.6

and the IMF gave the government a target of 5.5–6.5 percent, a substantial reduction in government spending.[19] In many developing countries these radical requirements have touched off heated debate and have sorely tested the political stability of the governments in power. Once the IMF sets targets, it monitors them periodically as a precondition to releasing funds. The international banks often use the results of this monitoring to determine their policies.

• **Factors contributing to the debt problem**

The 1980s is a crucial period for the developing countries' ability to survive the debt crisis. The crisis was brought on by a series of factors: imprudent decisions by lenders and borrowers, the prolonged recession in industrial countries, the strong U.S. dollar, and high interest rates.[20] The recession obviously made it more difficult for the countries to earn foreign exchange through exports in order to pay off the debt obligations.

TABLE 2.3

DEBT INDICATORS FOR DEVELOPING COUNTRIES, 1970–1983
(percent except as indicated)

Indicators	1970	1975	1980	1983*
Ratio of debt to GNP	13.3	15.4	19.2	26.7
Ratio of debt to exports	99.4	76.4	76.1	121.4
Debt service ratio†	13.5	11.1	13.6	20.7
Ratio of interest service to GNP	0.5	0.8	1.5	2.2
Total debt outstanding and disbursed (billions of dollars)	68.4	168.5	424.8	595.8
Official (billions of dollars)	33.5	71.6	157.5	208.5
Private (billion of dollars)	34.9	96.9	267.3	387.3

Note: Calculations are based on a sample of ninety developing countries.
* Estimated.
† Ratio of interest payments plus amortization to exports.
Source: *World Development Report, 1984,* published for the World Bank (New York: Oxford University Press, 1984), p. 31.

The strong U.S. dollar and high interest rates simply increased the cost of paying off the debt. Strong economic growth, moderate interest rates, a softening of the U.S. dollar, and patience on the part of the banks are key factors to monitor as the debt crisis continues.

Trade. As developing countries' economies have strengthened during the decades of the 1960s through the 1980s, there has been an attempt to shift from the export of primary products (such as food, agricultural products, and minerals) to the export of manufactures. As shown in Fig. 2.8, the manufactures and fuels groups increased in importance in relation to other product groups between 1965 and 1981. At the same time, as shown in Fig. 2.9, the low-income countries lost ground to the middle-income countries in terms of their percentage of total developing country exports. Figure 1.4 illustrated the plight of the developing countries in general when compared with the industrial countries in terms of their share of world exports by product category. Only in the case of fuels do the developing countries dominate. In all other categories, especially the noncommodities categories, the developing countries have a very small share of the world total.

The problem with relying on oil and other commodities is that the prices of those products are subject to wide swings. As will be noted in Chapter 4, this can be devastating when a country relies on one commodity for exports. As a country plans its development efforts for the future, it tries to forecast revenues from commodities exports, but that is difficult to do. Many times, the revenue estimates end up being too high because

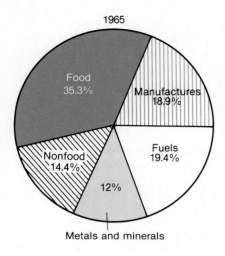

1965

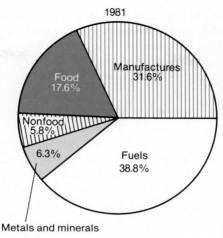

1981

FIGURE 2.8
Exports from Developing Countries by Commodity, 1965 and 1981 (Percentage of Total Exports)
Source: World Development Report, 1984, published for the World Bank (New York: Oxford University Press, 1984), p. 28.

of drops in prices of commodities. Then the country ends up with a balance of trade deficit and pressure on its currency. This situation will be discussed in more detail in Chapter 9.

Another trade problem of the developing countries is that the recession of the late 1970s and early 1980s resulted in increased protectionism by many of the industrial countries. As unemployment in basic and labor-intensive industries of the industrial countries increased, so did cries for protection from cheap imports from developing countries. This was devastating to developing countries, because, as is shown in Fig. 1.2, those countries have

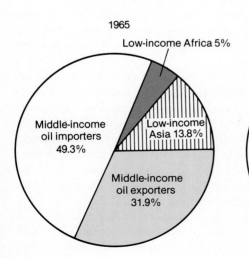

1965

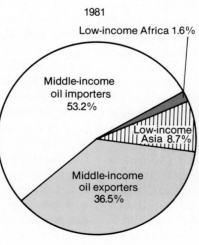

1981

FIGURE 2.9
Exports from Developing Countries by Country Group, 1965 and 1981 (Percentage of Total Exports)
Source: World Development Report, 1984, published for the World Bank (New York: Oxford University Press, 1984), p. 28.

to rely on the developed countries as the major markets for their goods. Also, the industrial countries have been trying to convince the developing countries that the long-run solution to their problems lies in diversifying exports and including more manufactured goods, yet these same industrial countries restrict imports of such goods.

The North-South Dialogue

In 1964 in Geneva the first session of the United Nations Conference on Trade and Development (UNCTAD) was held, leading to what is now called the North-South dialogue (the North reflecting the industrialized and the South the developing countries). At this time a new international economic order was identified,

> based on equity, sovereign equality, interdependence, common interest, and cooperation among all States, irrespective of their economic and social systems, which shall correct inequalities and redress existing injustices, make it possible to eliminate the widening gap between the developed and the developing countries, and ensure steadily accelerating economic and social development and peace and justice for present and future generations. [21]

None of the pronouncements emanating from the session were particularly new, but the collective resolve of the developing countries (the South) appeared to be stronger than ever before.

- **Key issues in the North-South dialogue**

Since 1974, various meetings have been held to continue the North-South dialogue. These meetings have focused on specific problems. In particular, the developing countries have expressed concern in the following areas: stabilization of export earnings and commodity prices, reduction of trade barriers in the developed countries, increased aid, debt moratorium, and additional private investment. The basic concern is how to transfer wealth from the developed to the developing countries. Even though each side has moderated its position, a fairly wide gap exists between what the developing countries want and what the developed countries want and are willing to give.

- **UNCTAD—The United Nations Conference on Trade and Development**

UNCTAD V, held in Manila in 1979, may have started a new era of cooperation and understanding in the dialogue. The four main areas of emphasis in the conference were: (1) trade and financial flow aspects of the relationships between developed and developing countries, (2) emphasis on growing interdependence between different parts of the world economy, (3) efforts to bring socialist countries into the dialogue on economic issues, and (4) emphasis on trade liberalization and concern about expanding protectionism.[22] The mood seemed to be one of greater cooperation rather than the conflict that has marred earlier sessions of UNCTAD.

The UNCTAD VI meetings held in Yugoslavia in 1983 focused on the problems of debt and protectionism. At that meeting, the Group of 77, a caucus of developing countries (which now exceeds the original number of 77 countries) organized to help the developing countries coordinate their United Nations strategy, identified the following points as the key focus for the discussions:

• Key focus of UNCTAD VI meeting held in 1983

1. automatic debt relief,
2. an increase in world liquidity through the IMF,
3. greater aid and private bank lending to developing nations, and
4. freer access for developing country exports to the markets of the rich.[23]

• Group of 77—The caucus of developing countries in UNCTAD

However, the meeting was not as fruitful as the Group of 77 had hoped. The industrial countries acknowledged that protectionism indeed hurts the developing countries, and they agreed to begin to open their markets more as the recovery took hold, but they also encouraged the richer developing countries to do the same for their poorer neighbors. This met with some resistance, since the developing countries felt that they had to set up barriers to allow their own infant industries to develop. The industrials were also against discussions of increasing liquidity because they felt that the World Bank and the IMF were better suited to deal with those issues. UNCTAD was originally organized to deal with commodity issues, whereas the World Bank and IMF were organized to deal with financial issues. In addition, the industrial countries have greater control over the latter two organizations than they do over UNCTAD. In effect, the industrial North seemed to feel that the developing South would see a lot of their problems disappear as the impact of the recovery "trickled down" (in the terminology of the United States) to the developing countries.

External Influences on Development—Multilateral Institutions

The road to development is a difficult one. The developing countries may not be able to solve their problems alone. The International Monetary Fund and the World Bank are two institutions that are instrumental in the development process. The IMF provides financial support for countries suffering severe balance of payments problems—most of the developing countries. As was noted in the section on debt, this financial assistance, although multilateral, comes with strings attached. Countries are often forced to make substantial and politically unpopular concessions for IMF support. At times, countries have felt that too much loss of sovereignty is involved in IMF financing.

The World Bank also provides financing, especially for infrastructure development in low-income developing countries. In a World Bank study, three problems were identified with respect to the economies of developing countries: overvalued currencies and trade restrictions that have discouraged local production, government pricing and tax policies that have kept the cost of imported fertilizer and equipment high and the price of agricultural products low, and overreliance on government.[24] The bank intends to take a more active role in helping countries alter their basic economic policies in return for aid. This would bring bank policy more in line with that of the IMF.

External Influences on Development—The MNE

The 1970s brought a flurry of books and articles on the impact—usually the evils—of the MNE in developing countries. MNEs were accused of every type of evil possible, including the destruction of the nation-state. However, several factors have occurred to alter this perception: (1) a shift in bargaining power toward the nation-state; (2) a dispersion in multinationals to include home countries other than the United States, thus eliminating the United States as the sole source of economic influence; (3) the development of multinationals by developing countries themselves; (4) the emergence of more multinationals, including a larger number of smaller, more flexible enterprises, and (5) greater flexibility on the part of multinationals in adapting to local situations.[25]

• Third World MNEs

One of these points is worth discussing in more detail. Third World multinationals, usually from the rapidly developing middle-income countries, have increased dramatically in recent years, as was noted in Chapter 1. These MNEs come primarily from three different types of developing countries: resource-rich countries (such as OPEC members); labor-rich, rapidly industrializing countries (such as Hong Kong, Taiwan, and South Korea); and market-rich, rapidly industrializing countries (such as Brazil, Mexico, and the Philippines).[26] These countries tend to have governments that are pro-business and committed to international business activities. MNEs from the developing countries also tend to be more readily accepted in fellow developing countries, since they are "part of the group." They are not perceived to be as much of a threat as MNEs from the industrialized countries.

The strength of these MNEs comes from their special experience with manufacturing for small home markets. They bring in skills that the host countries do not yet have and that the traditional Western MNEs have forgotten. Therefore they are more competitive in other developing countries where markets are small and labor costs are low.[27]

The impact of industrial country MNEs on developing countries is complex. Chapter 11 looks at the major issues in greater depth. Suffice it to say that MNEs have created quite a furor in recent times. They have been portrayed as vicious exploiters and as institutions bent on the destruction of the nation-state.

A humorous description of the MNE in this conflict appeared in the London *Economist:*

It fiddles its accounts. It avoids or evades its taxes. It rigs its intra-company transfer prices. It is run by foreigners, from decision centres thousands of miles away. It imports foreign labour practices. It doesn't import foreign labour practices. It overpays. It underpays. It competes unfairly with local firms. It is in cahoots with local firms. It exports jobs from rich countries. It is an instrument of rich countries' imperialism. The technologies it brings to the third world are too old-fashioned. No, they are too modern. It meddles. It bribes. Nobody can control it. It wrecks balances of payments. It overturns economic policies. It plays off governments against each other to get the biggest investment incentives. Won't it please come and invest? Let it bloody well go home. [28]

Many developing countries are finding that they need to provide a better climate for foreign investment if access to the capital and technology of the industrial country MNEs is to be a key part of their industrial strategy. For years, Mexico would not allow majority ownership for most new investment. However, the debt problems of the early 1980s caused Mexico to change its legislation in order to attract more capital. It found that incurring debt was not the best way to go. As a result, Mexico began to work in 1984 to improve the investment climate and restore the confidence of foreign investors in the hopes of attracting more capital.[29]

MNEs do have a great deal to offer developing countries in terms of capital, technology, managerial expertise, and access to world markets. As the oil companies have found out, however, MNEs need to be increasingly flexible in the way profits are to be earned. Licensing agreements, production agreements, management contracts, and joint ventures are taking the place of wholly owned direct investments. As host countries improve their basic operating environments to attract investment and the MNEs adjust their operating strategies to these environments, development will increase, and profits will be earned.

SUMMARY

- The three major "world economies" in which the multinational enterprise must operate successfully are the nonsocialist (i.e., democratic and capitalistic) industrial countries, the socialist (i.e., communist) countries, and the less-developed countries.

- Pure democracy, a political philosophy espousing the idea that all citizens should be directly involved in decision making, has evolved in most countries to various forms of representative democracy. Communism has adopted a totalitarian political framework that largely precludes citizen participation in decision making in order to ensure adherence to political, economic, and social objectives.

- Economic systems can be classified according to the ownership of factors of production and the control of economic activity. The pure extremes are considered to be the private ownership of the means of production in a market economy and the collective or public ownership of the means of production in a command economy. Realistically, contemporary economies are a mix of the two extremes.

- Generally, market economies are connected with democratic political regimes, whereas centrally planned economies are connected with totalitarian/communistic regimes. However, many theorists feel that democratic socialism incorporates the best of both worlds.

- When a firm decides to enter a new country, it must be aware of its own experience and how that experience has helped shape its managerial philosophy and practice. It must also determine how the new environment differs from the more familiar domestic situation and decide how managerial philosophy and practice must be changed to adapt to the new political and economic environment.

- The World Bank classifies countries into the following groups: industrial (developed), East European nonmarket economies, high-income oil exporters, low-income developing economies, and middle-income developing economies that are net oil importers. The last category is subdivided into countries that are major exporters of manufactured goods and those that are not. The former group is often known as newly industrialized countries, or NICs.

- Developing countries are located primarily in Latin America, Africa, and Asia. They encompass a large portion of the world's population but a small percentage of its wealth.

- Among the most serious problems facing developing countries are basic needs (health, education, water, nutrition, and housing); oil; population growth; growing debt; trade and protectionism; inflation; and political instability.

- The North-South dialogue is built around the concept of spreading wealth more uniformly among countries by allowing developing countries better access to markets of industrial countries and by expanding aid to developing countries.

- The developing countries are beginning to place greater reliance on state-owned enterprises or on more public sector participation in deciding the future of the economy. The foreign firm must be willing to cooperate with the host government and to participate in joint ventures with state-owned enterprises if it wishes to operate in those countries.

- The multinational enterprise provides (1) financial capital, (2) modern technology, (3) entrepreneurial skill, and (4) increased local employment in its direct investments in developing countries.

C A S E   BATA, LTD.[30]

As war swept across Europe in 1939, Tom Bata had an important decision to make. His father, of the ninth generation of a family of shoemakers in Czechoslovakia, had built a worldwide shoe network in 28 countries, using machinery and the mass production technology of the 1920s. But now Tom was left with the responsibility of expanding that empire during a period of great uncertainty in the world. Realizing that it was probably only a matter of time before the Nazis overran his homeland, Bata took 100 Czech families and emigrated to Canada in order to preserve his father's business in a land of freedom.

Since that time, Bata's decision has been ratified through strong growth worldwide. Bata, Ltd. is a family-owned business that operates around the globe. Its production facilities produce hundreds of millions of shoes annually, and those shoes generate over $2 billion in revenues through sales in 6000 Bata-owned retail outlets and 125 independent retailers in 115 nations. Its 85,000 employees work in over ninety factories and five engineering facilities, as well as the retail operations mentioned above. Its influence is so pervasive that it makes and sells one out of every three shoes manufactured and sold in the noncommunist world. In fact, the word for shoe in many parts of Africa is "bata."

Bata, Ltd. tends to operate as a decentralized operation that is free to adjust to the local environment, within certain parameters. Tom Bata travels extensively to check on quality control and to ensure good relations with the governments of the countries where Bata, Ltd. operates.

Although Bata, Ltd. has factories in more than ninety countries and operations of one form or another in over 100, it does not own all of those facilities. Where possible, it owns 100 percent of the operations. In some countries, however, the government requires less than majority ownership. In India, 60 percent of the stock of the local Bata operations trades on the Indian stock exchange; and in Japan, Bata, Ltd. owns only 9.9 percent of the operations. In some cases, Bata, Ltd. provides licensing and consulting and technical assistance to companies in which it has no equity interest.

Bata, Ltd.'s strategy for servicing world markets is an interesting one. Some MNEs try to lower costs by achieving economies of scale in production. That means that they produce as much as they can in the most optimal-sized factory and then service markets around the world from that single production facility. Bata, Ltd. tries to service its different national markets by producing in a given market nearly everything it sells in that market. Part of the reason for this strategy is that Bata, Ltd. can achieve economies of scale very quickly, since it has a fairly large volume in the countries where it produces.

This may seem difficult to believe, especially when Bata, Ltd. has production facilities in some African nations whose only industry it is. However, Bata, Ltd. feels that it can achieve economies of scale very easily because it is a labor-intensive operation. Bata, Ltd. also tries to get all of its raw materials locally. This is not possible in some cases, especially in some of the poorer developing countries. However, it tries to have as much value-added as possible in those countries.

Another of Bata, Ltd.'s policies is that it prefers not to export production. It prefers to use local production to service the local market. Obviously, that rule is not a fixed one, since the company produces in only ninety countries but has distribution in over 100 countries. Sometimes, Bata, Ltd. runs into trouble with local governments when it imports some raw materials but does not engage in exporting. Then it has to adjust to the local laws and requirements for operation.

One of the reasons why Bata, Ltd. avoids excessive reliance on exports is because of the risk. If an importing country were to restrict trade, Bata could possibly lose market opportunity and market share. In addition, Mr. Bata noted the benefit to the developing country of not exposing itself to possible protectionism:

> We know very well what kind of a social shock it is when a plant closes in Canada. Yet in Canada we have unemployment insurance and all kinds of welfare operations and there are many alternative jobs that people can usually go to. In most of the developing countries, on the other hand, it's a question of life and death for these people. They have uprooted themselves from an agricultural society. They've come to a town to work in an industry. They've brought their relatives with them because working in industry, their earnings are so much higher. Thus a large group of their relatives have become dependent on them and have changed their lifestyle and standard of living. For these people it is a terrible thing to lose a job. And so we are very sensitive to that particular problem.

Bata, Ltd. operates in a variety of different types of economies. It has extensive operations in both the industrial democratic countries and the developing countries. It has been soundly criticized (as have been most MNEs) for operating in South Africa and thus tacitly supporting the white minority political regime, and it has also been criticized for operating in other totalitarian regimes such as Chile. Bata counters by pointing out that the company has been operating in Chile for over forty years, during which a variety of political regimes have been in power.

Although Bata's local operations have not been nationalized very many times, the company has had some interesting experiences. In Uganda, Bata's local operations were nationalized by Milton Obote, denationalized by Idi Amin, renationalized by Amin, and finally denationalized by Amin. During that time the factory continued to operate as if nothing had happened. Mr. Bata's explanation for finally being left alone is that *shoes had to be produced and sold, materials had to be bought and wages paid. Life went on. In most cases, the governments concluded it really wasn't in their interest to run businesses, so they cancelled the nationalization arrangements.*

In spite of Bata's ability to operate in any type of political situation, Mr. Bata prefers to operate in a democratic environment. He feels that democracies and totalitarian regimes both have bureaucracies, but in a democracy there is the potential to discuss and possibly change procedures. In a totalitarian regime it is sometimes wise to not say anything.

The impact of Bata, Ltd. on a country is multifaceted. The basic strategy of the company is to provide footwear at affordable prices for the largest possible segment of the population, so a basic product is being provided. It could be argued that the product is a necessity rather than a luxury. The production facilities are very labor-intensive, so jobs are created, which tend to increase the purchasing power of the economy. Although some top levels of management may come from outside of the country, there is a tendency to train local management as quickly as possible so that they can assume responsibility. Because the company tries to get most of its raw materials locally, suppliers are usually developed. Since Bata, Ltd. likes to diversify its purchases, it usually develops more than one supplier for a given product, leading to competition and efficiencies.

Bata, Ltd. usually brings in its own capital resources when it starts up a new operation, but it is also adroit in utilizing international capital markets. On more than one occasion, Bata, Ltd. has utilized the resources of the International Finance Corporation (IFC), a division of the World Bank that provides development financing for private enterprise projects in developing countries. One of Bata's most recent attempts at IFC financing was to expand a tannery in Bangladesh. The importance of getting IFC support is that Bata, Ltd. would be much more likely to attract other debt and equity capital once it had received IFC approval. All of the five previous Bata projects supported by the IFC had been successful, and the loans had been paid back.

QUESTIONS

1. Why do you think that a developing country might be willing to allow Bata, Ltd. to operate locally?

2. Do you agree with Bata's assessment of the riskiness of exporting? How do you think the developing countries might react to that assessment?

3. What is there about Bata, Ltd.'s operations that might make it less susceptible to serious political influence than some other types of companies?

4. One country that Bata is not currently operating in is the People's Republic of China (PRC). Assume that you are assigned to write a position statement that Mr. Bata can use to help convince the leaders of the PRC that Bata, Ltd. should be allowed to set up production and distribution facilities in their country. Also, provide Mr. Bata with your impressions of the pros and cons of entering the PRC.

NOTES

1. Data for the case were taken from *Annual Reports* (Gulf, 1975–1983); *Wall Street Journal,* March 27, 1981, p. 1; *Wall Street Journal,* November 8, 1979, p. 20; *New York Times,* February 2, 1981, p. D1; *New York Times,* June 27, 1981, p. 1; *Economist,* May 22, 1976, p. 93; *Economist,* July 31, 1976, pp. 52–53; *Business Week,* August 10, 1981, pp. 52–63; "U.S. Interests, Public and Private, in Angola," *Wall Street Journal,* December 14, 1983, p. 31; "Gulf Oil's Role in Southern Africa," *Wall Street Journal,* January 26, 1984, p. 33.

2. Adapted from Richard N. Farmer and Barry M. Richman, *Comparative Management and Economic Progress* (Homewood, Ill.: Richard D. Irwin, 1965), p. 30.

3. *Ibid.,* p. 25.

4. For similar ideas, see Hans Schollhammer, "Strategies in Comparative Management Theorizing," in *Comparative Management: Teaching, Training and Research,* Jean Boddewyn, ed. (New York: Graduate School of Business Administration, New York University, 1970), p. 22; Richard W. Wright, "Organizational Ambiente: Management and Environment in Chile," *Academy of Management Journal,* March 1971; and Bernard D. Estafen, "System Transfer Characteristics: An Experimental Model for Comparative Management Research," *Management International Review,* no. 2–3 (1970).

5. Lyman T. Sargent, *Contemporary Political Ideologies* (Homewood, Ill.: The Dorsey Press, 1969), p. 87.

6. Robert A. Dahl, *Modern Political Analysis* (Englewood Cliffs, N.J.: Prentice-Hall, 1963), p. 7.

7. Steve Mufson, "South Africa's Indians and Mixed Races Increasingly Support Struggle of Blacks," *Wall Street Journal,* January 11, 1985, p. 19; S. M. Khalid, "Protests Mar Colored Vote," *USA Today,* August 23, 1984, p. 6A.

8. *The Europa Year Book 1984* (London: Europa Publications Limited, 1984), pp. 2365–2366.

9. Nicholas Bray, "Laurent Fabius Named in France as New Premier," *Wall Street Journal,* July 18, 1984, p. 31; Roger Ricklefs, "France's Big State Firms Give a Boost to Small Business," *Wall Street Journal,* August 22, 1984, p. 24.

10. *World Development Report, 1984* (Washington, D.C.: World Bank, 1984), p. 54.

11. *Ibid.,* p. 67.

12. *Ibid.,* p. 67.

13. *Ibid.,* pp. ix–x.

14. Mahbub ul Haq, "An International Perspective on Basic Needs," *Finance & Development,* September 1980, p. 12.

15. *World Development Report, 1984,* p. 2.

16. *Ibid.,* pp. 7–8.

17. "The Banker's Guide to LDC Debt," *Banker,* March 1981, pp. 90–91; *International Letter,* No. 518 (Chicago: Federal Reserve Bank of Chicago, January 27, 1984), p. 2.

18. *International Letter,* No. 518, p. 2.

19. "Will Mexico Make It?," *Business Week,* October 1, 1984, pp. 74–77.

20. *World Development Report 1984,* p. 31.

21. From "The Declaration on the Establishment of a New International Economic Order," reprinted in Paul Rogers, ed., *Future Resources and World Development* (New York: Plenum Press, 1976), p. 135.

22. Mahmud al Burney, "A Recognition of Interdependence: UNCTAD V," *Finance & Development,* September 1979, p. 18.

23. Paul Lewis, "Aid and Trade Are in the Air at North-South Talks," *New York Times,* June 12, 1983, p. 8F.

24. Art Pine, "World Bank Drafts Long-Term Aid Plan That Pressures Poor Countries to Change," *Wall Street Journal,* August 21, 1981, p. 4.

25. Paul Streeten, "Multinational Revisited," *Finance & Development,* June 1979, pp. 39–42.

26. David A. Heenan and Warren J. Keegan, "The Rise of Third World Multinationals," *Harvard Business Review,* January–February 1979, pp. 102–103.

27. Louis T. Wells, Jr., "Guess Who's Creating the World's Newest Multinationals," *Wall Street Journal,* December 12, 1983, p. 22.

28. "Controlling the Multinationals," *Economist,* January 24, 1976, p. 68.

29. "Why Only a Few Companies Are Betting on Mexico's Future," *Business Week,* October 1, 1984, p. 78.

30. The material for the case was taken from the following sources: Dean Walker, "Shoemaker to the World," *Executive,* January 1981, pp. 63–69; Gary Vineberg, "Bata Favors Free Trade but Tempers Asia Stance," *Footwear News,* Vol. 39, No. 24, June 13, 1983, pp. 2+; Ira Breskin and Gary Vinesberg, "Parent Bata Looks After Farflung Footwear Family," *Footwear News,* Vol. 39, No. 23, June 6, 1983, pp. 1+; Ira Breskin, "Globe-Trotting Bata, Ltd. A World Bank Customer," *Footwear News,* Vol. 38, No. 38, October 4, 1982, p. 23.

3

The Human and Cultural Environments Facing Business

- To demonstrate the common methods of examining human-cultural environments and some of their principal limitations.
- To illustrate differences in norms of human physical and demographic characteristics among countries and the effects these characteristics have on the efficiency of standardized business practices on a worldwide basis.
- To examine the major behavioral attributes that differentiate business practices on a country-to-country basis.
- To present guidelines on whether and how multinational firms should attempt to introduce their home country practices into foreign operations.

When Prime Minister Margaret Thatcher made an official visit to Saudi Arabia in 1981, the first ever by a British head of government, she deferred to Islamic custom on appropriate attire for women. She wore a long-sleeved, ankle-length dress throughout the day. During her talks with King Khalid, she wore a net veil over her face.

A year before Mrs. Thatcher's visit, Parris-Rogers International (PRI), a British publishing house, had to sell its floundering Bahraini operations, which had been set up to edit the first telephone and business directories for thirteen Arab states on or near the Arabian peninsula. Like many foreign firms, PRI was drawn to the Middle East in the 1970s because of the burgeoning business brought on by rising oil prices. Whereas Prime Minister Thatcher had protocol officers to advise her of expected behavior when she visited Saudi Arabia, PRI had no guidance. Lack of understanding and failure to adapt to a very different way of life contributed directly to PRI's failure.

Most of the oil-rich states have had an acute shortage of local personnel to work on their development projects. Consequently, foreign workers have comprised a large portion of their work forces, for example, 40 percent of Saudi Arabia's in 1981. When PRI could not find sufficient qualified local people, it filled four key positions through advertisements in London newspapers. In late 1978, Angela Clarke, an Englishwoman, was hired as editor and researcher, and three young Englishmen were hired as salesmen. The four left immediately for Bahrain. None of them had visited the Middle East before; all expected that they could carry out business in their accustomed way.

The salesmen were hired on a commission basis. They expected that by moving aggressively they could make the same number of calls as would be normal in Great Britain. They were used to working about eight hours a day, to commencing appointments at a scheduled time, to having the undivided attention of potential clients, and to restricting most conversation to the specifics of the business transaction.

What the salesman found instead was less time to sell because of the Moslem requirement to pray five times per day and because of a further reduction of the work day during the holy month of Ramadan. Appointments seldom began when scheduled. When the salesmen finally got in to see Arab businessmen, they were often invited to go to a cafe, where the Arabs would divert the conversation to idle chitchat. Whether in a cafe or in the office, the drinking of coffee or tea seemed to have precedence over the business matter that the Englishmen considered the meeting to be about. It seemed further to the salesmen that the Arab businessmen placed little importance on the appointments, since they frequently diverted their attention to friends who joined them at the cafe or in the office.

Angela Clarke was paid a salary instead of a commission, so PRI bore all the expense that came about because her work was thwarted in unexpected ways. PRI had based its government contract prices to prepare telephone directories on its English experience. The preparation turned out to be more time consuming and costly. In the traditional Middle Eastern social structure there were no street names or building numbers. Ms. Clarke had to do a census of Bahraini establishments, identifying each with such prepositions as "below," "above," or "in front of" some meaningful landmark, before getting to the expected directory work.

Other problems occurred because Angela Clarke was a single woman. She was in charge of the research in all thirteen states and was to have hired freelance assistants in most of them. Saudi Arabian authorities never allowed her in the country as a single female, and her visa for Oman took six weeks each time to process. In the states that she could enter, Ms. Clarke was sometimes required to stay only in a hotel that government officials had approved for a foreign woman. Therein, she was prohibited from eating in the dining room unless accompanied by the hotel manager. Her advertisements to hire assistants were met by harassment, obscene telephone calls, and visits to her hotel rooms.

The salesmen never adjusted to work in the new environment. Instead of pushing PRI to alter its commission scheme, they tried to alter the way that the Arab businessmen were dealing with them. After a few months the salesmen refused to take the time to drink coffee and tea with their potential clients. They showed their irritation at "irrelevant" conversations, delays, and interruptions from outsiders. The Arab businessmen responded negatively. PRI received so many complaints from Arab businessmen that the salesmen had to be replaced. By then, though, the harm was done to PRI's sales.

Angela Clarke fared better, at least from a personal standpoint. She overcame many of the problems of being single simply by wearing a wedding ring and registering at hotels as a married woman. When traveling, she ate meals in her room, conducted meetings in conference rooms, and had all incoming calls screened by the hotel operators. Since decency patrols could arrest immodestly dressed women, Ms. Clarke always wore long-sleeved blouses and skirts below the knees. To be on the safe side, she took to wearing plain blue or beige clothing, making certain always to have a full slip underneath. When PRI left the area, she stayed on to work for a Japanese bank. Still, because of her inability to enter Saudi Arabia, PRI sent in her place one of the salesmen, who was not trained to do the research.

The rapid growth and intrusion of foreigners into the region has created adjustment problems not only for the foreigners, but for the local societies as well. On one hand, the foreign workers are needed. On the other hand, there is fear that their presence will erode deep-seated values and traditions. In many cases the foreigners are expected to conform. In others, foreigners are allowed to pursue their own customs as long as they maintain a complete separation from the local populace. For example, most Western television programming is immoral according to the traditional Islamic standards that rule both the customs and legal systems. In some places, foreigners may acquire unscramblers to view Western television fare, but local people may not. There have also been some second thoughts about some of the culture's double standards. At one time, for example, male and female hotel guests were allowed to swim in the same pools in Saudi Arabia. This permission was rescinded, however, because Saudis frequented the hotels to eat and hold meetings; thus they could be corrupted by viewing behavior that is considered decadent by their standards. When Ms. Clarke and the salesmen first arrived in Bahrain, there were prohibitions on the sale of any pork products, even imported ones that came in cans. This prohibition was later modified, but grocers had to keep pork products in separate rooms in which only non-Muslims could work or buy.

The existence of these dual and changing standards for foreigners and citizens makes it difficult for foreigners to know how to behave. This situation has been further complicated because the Middle East is going through such substantial, but uneven, economic and social transformation. This was well described as follows:

> *Changes that in other countries have been spread out over several generations are being accomplished in a few short years. Diesel trucks and jet airplanes are replacing camel caravans, but the camel has not yet been discarded. Modern architecture and broad, tree-lined avenues are replacing mudbrick houses on twisting streets, but mudbrick buildings are still evident. Nomads (Bedouins) are beginning to drive from place to place; but it is common to see a pickup truck or a Mercedes parked beside a traditional tent.* [2]

As more contact takes place between Arabs and Westerners, there is bound to be cultural borrowing and the meshing of certain aspects of traditional behavior. This is apt to come slowly, perhaps more slowly than many think. A noted anthropologist summarized the Americans' misconception of change by the Saudis:

> *We tend to think of them as underdeveloped Americans—Americans with sheets on. We look at them as undereducated and rather poor at anything technological. All we have to do is to make believers out of them, get them the proper education, teach them English, and they will turn into Americans.*

In fact, Saudi students abroad revert to traditional behavior on returning home. Nor do foreigners, after an assignment in Saudi Arabia, follow Saudi customs when they return home. These are indications of how deeply rooted both Saudi and Western behaviors are.

INTRODUCTION

Importance of the Human Environment

A business employs, sells to, buys from, is regulated by, and is owned by people. Therefore it is important for an international company to consider differences in groups of people or societies so that it can predict and control its relationships and operations. The PRI case illustrates how human differences give rise to different business practices in varying parts of the world. When a company observes that a business practice in a foreign country differs from its home country experience or from what its management would like to see exist, it should examine the human causes underlying the divergences. This will help to determine the feasibility of introducing a new operating practice. Sears Roebuck, for instance, observed before establishing retail outlets in both Mexico and Spain that other large retailers in those countries did not give consumer credit. In Mexico the lack of credit was attributable to an unfounded distrust of clients; consequently, Sears easily introduced credit practices. In Spain, however, consumers viewed credit as a shameful inability to pay.[3] The obstacles to changing the practice in Spain were therefore formidable because the proposed change ran counter to deep-seated attitudes of the people who would be affected by the change.

Some differences, like acceptable female attire, are easily discerned. Others may be more difficult to perceive. Most of us take many things for granted. We expect that people will respond a certain way in a given situation, that they will consider certain things to be more important than others, and that their duties and privileges will be similar to those of people in similar stations or positions that we have observed in our own society. All of these expectations may be wrong in another culture. In the PRI case the British salesmen budgeted time and considered that drinking coffee and chatting about nonbusiness activities in a cafe were "doing nothing," especially if "there was work to be done." The Arab businessmen had no compulsion to finish at a given time, viewed time in a cafe as "doing something," and considered "small talk" to be a necessary prerequisite for evaluating whether they could interact satisfactorily with the other people. Because of a belief that "you shouldn't mix business and pleasure," the Englishmen were edgy when friends of the Arab businessmen intruded. The Arabs felt that "people are more important than business" and that there was nothing private about business transactions anyway.

The Nation-State

• Useful proxy of society because

There is no universally satisfactory definition of a **society;** however, the nation-state is a workable term in international business, since basic similarity among people is both a cause and effect of national boundaries. Furthermore,

- boundaries are cause and effect of national differences in norms
- laws fall primarily along national lines
- Limitations of country-by-country analysis
  - not everyone in country is alike
  - variations within some countries are great
  - commonalities link groups from different countries

the laws governing business operations apply primarily along national lines. This does not imply that everyone in a country is alike; nor does it imply that each country is unique in all respects. There are, however, certain physical, demographic, and behavioral norms that may alter methods of conducting business from one country to another.

In using the nation-state as a point of reference, one should realize that there is much greater variation within some countries than within others. Geographic and economic barriers may make it difficult for people to move from one part of a country to another, thus limiting their interactions. In addition, if government control is decentralized, the absence of a unifying legal system enhances the separation. Even if there are no substantial geographic barriers, linguistic, religious, and ethnic differences within a country usually retard a fusing of the population into a homogeneous state. India, for example, is much more diverse than Denmark for all the reasons given above.

Everyone is a member of various groups—for example, groups based on nationality, profession, age, religion, and place of residence. There are many commonalities that might in some ways link groups from different countries more closely together than groups within a country. For instance, it has been shown that people in urban areas differ in certain attitudes from people in rural areas and that managers have different work-related attitudes than production workers regardless of the country examined.[4] Therefore if one is comparing countries, one must be careful to examine relevant groups. If, for example, a firm is interested in predicting how a group of British scientists and a group of French scientists might work together, it would be more appropriate to see if there are differences in the two groups' approaches to solving problems rather than whether British and French problem-solving approaches in general are different. The common occupational bond might make scientists in the two countries more similar to each other than to nonscientists within either of the countries.

TYPES OF VARIABLES

There are too many human variables and different types of business functions for an exhaustive cause–effect discussion in one chapter. For example, one model of comparative management has classified the process of management into thirty-six distinct functions and has related these to six educational and nine cultural variables. The model thus describes 540 direct relationships.[5] One can expand the number of relationships substantially by classifying management processes differently and by using additional physical and cultural variables.[6] This chapter concentrates on a few of the physical, demographic, and behavioral variables that have been noted to influence business practices substantially. While it is possible to describe a few of the effects that these may have on the process of management, we must leave to the reader the task of anticipating the full range of possible adjustments. The latter part of the chapter highlights alternative approaches for determining and dealing with differences that exist in foreign countries as well as the changes in international firms themselves as they come in contact with new human environments.

PHYSICAL ATTRIBUTES

Variations

- Variations due primarily to genetics
  - people mix more within than outside nation-state
  - gene frequency may change over time
  - cultural environment also affects variations
- Differences influence conduct of business

Each country is comprised of people whose physical attributes vary widely; nevertheless, there are usually dominant characteristics present in a large portion of a given population. The field of **somatology,** a branch of anthropology, is concerned with the comparative study of human variation and classification, especially through measurement and observation. The variations are due largely to genetics and become less noticeable as people migrate and intermarry. Even in the absence of mixing with other groups, gene frequency—and thus physical characteristics—may change over a period of time because of natural selection as humans adapt to the changing physical environment. There is also growing evidence that the cultural environment (social norms and responses) may affect physical attributes. For example, adult male height is greater in societies in which infants are subjected to such stressful practices as periodic mother-infant separation and circumcision.[7]

It is of less importance to the international businessperson to determine whether variations are primarily hereditary or environmental than to grasp the sometimes subtle differences that may influence the conduct of business. Among the many differences that have been noted among groups are skin color; height, weight, and form of the body; color, abundance, distribution, balding, and graying of the hair; blood type; and resistance and susceptibility to certain diseases. The businessperson must also realize that some physical norms change relatively quickly. Illustrative of this change has been the growth in people's average height in most industrial countries, particularly Japan, in recent years.

Appearance

- Subtle differences, easily overlooked by outsiders, may be important to insiders
- Must consider societies' self-stereotypes

Among human variations the most noticeable are those of appearance. While most such differences are readily apparent, there are a host of subtle variations that, although important to people within a given society, may be easily overlooked by nondiscriminating outsiders. For example, Asians complain that Western films and advertisements frequently depict Orientals' national backgrounds incorrectly. They may identify a Chinese person as a Japanese or a Korean as a Thai, for example. Western selective perception simply overlooks the differences.

Size of individuals would seem to be one of the most obvious differences. However, one U.S. company attempted to sell men's slacks in Japan that were based on U.S. tailoring patterns, only to realize that the slacks fit few Japanese men because of narrower Japanese hips. Before the company discovered the error, a competitor had preempted the market. In another case a U.S. firm had good initial sales for its brassieres in West Germany but then witnessed a rapidly declining demand. At first the decline was wrongly attributed to higher labor costs, which had to be passed on to consumers, and the decision to abandon this market was almost made. Fortunately, some additional research determined that size variations between German and U.S. women resulted in an ill-fitting product. This difference was complicated by differences in buying behavior. The German women were not prone to try on merchandise in the store or to return it because of discomfort. Instead, they simply did not make repeat purchases. The result was an initial lack of the type of feedback that the firm needed.

Not only actual physical differences must be taken into consideration in such business functions as product changes, machinery height, and selection of advertising message; so must traits that a country has idealized. Groups of people often create wishful stereotypes of themselves that must be considered when creating imagery. For this reason, advertisements in the United States typically depict individuals who are somewhat younger and thinner than the bulk of the people toward whom the product is aimed. In West Germany there has been an idealization of the tall Nordic type, though most Germans are actually no taller than the average Pole or French person.[8]

DEMOGRAPHY

Demography is the statistical study of populations and their subgroups. The following discussion draws largely from Table 3.1, which includes data from seven countries that were selected because of similarity in total population. Although these countries do not represent world extremes in the types of characteristics described, the diversities are nevertheless substantial.

Population Growth Rates

- Growth rate usually higher in LDCs
- Changes in growth rate due to
  - birth rate
  - death rate
  - international migration

Low population growth rates are more typical of the countries generally regarded as more highly developed economically. This has caused great concern among development economists, who have noted that decreases in both birth rates and death rates have historically followed rather than preceded economic development. In most less-developed countries in recent

TABLE 3.1

DEMOGRAPHIC FIGURES FOR SELECTED COUNTRIES

Country	Population, 1983 (in thousands)[a]	Population Increase 1980–1985 (%)[b]	Projected Population 2000 (in thousands)[b]	Life Expectancy at Birth 1980–1985[b]	Percentage Illiteracy[a,c] (latest survey)	Percentage of 1980 Population[b]		
						Under Age 15	Age 15–64	Over Age 65
Argentina	30,094	1.6	37,197	69.7	7.4 ((1970)	30.0	61.8	8.2
Canada	25,289	1.2	29,393	74.5	3.8 (1977)	23.2	67.9	8.9
Colombia	28,110	2.1	37,999	63.6	14.8 (1981)	39.4	57.1	3.5
Rumania	22,891	0.8	25,531	70.8	11.4 (1954)	26.5	63.1	10.4
South Africa	31,586	2.5	54,456	53.5	43.0 (1960)	41.3	54.6	4.1
Yugoslavia	23,022	0.8	25,103	71.0	16.5 (1971)	24.4	66.4	9.2
Zaire	32,084	2.9	52,410	50.0	45.5 (1980)	44.8	52.3	2.9

a. *Statistical Yearbook* (London: UNESCO, 1984).
b. *The World Population Situation in 1983* (New York: United Nations, 1984).
c. Illiterate population 15 years of age and over.

● government population
programs

years, the death rate has fallen markedly because of medical advances while the birth rate has remained high. This has caused an unprecedented population explosion that has hampered efforts to raise living standards because of insufficient investment, jobs, food, and social services to compensate for the additional population. The disparity in growth rates is illustrated by the fact that Colombia, which in 1983 had about 2.8 million more inhabitants than Canada, will at present rates have an edge of 8.6 million by 2000. Not all changes are due to birth and death rates. Among the fastest increases in the 1970s were those recorded by Kuwait and Qatar. The influx of foreigners to work in the expanding economies created by oil wealth accounts for this rapid growth.

Clearly, the size of population has an important effect on markets and labor power; however, there is substantial disagreement as to what should and can be done to regulate population growth. In many LDCs, such as Sri Lanka and Bangladesh, extensive government-sponsored birth control programs have achieved mixed results. Other countries have sought to *increase* their birth rates. In the mid-1980s, for example, both Rumania and Malaysia set goals to increase their populations substantially—the former by making abortions more difficult to obtain and the latter by giving additional tax relief for working mothers with more children.[9]

Education

● Education increasingly
important to work force and
how firms operate
● LDCs generally have
● excess of unskilled
● shortage of skilled
● International transfers where
there is skill level shortage

For most industrial jobs, workers must know how to read and write. Because of increasing use of new technology, it is becoming more important that workers can read labels, manuals, and blueprints. Comparing again the seven countries of Table 3.1, one finds that, in Zaire, only 54.5 percent of those over 15 years old are literate, compared with 92.6 percent in Argentina. The literacy problem in most developing countries has resulted in large pools of unemployed people who lack the skills to perform all but the most rudimentary industrial tasks. Of the people who are classified as employed, a great number are **underemployed**—working fewer hours than they would like. At the same time there is a critical shortage of skilled labor.

Countries with low literacy rates tend to be deficient at other levels in their educational structure as well. If one looks at college education as an indicator of people qualified for managerial and technical jobs, the diversity among countries is enormous. In 1983, Canada had approximately 988,000 university students, compared to only about 32,000 in Zaire.[10] Because of such differences, international companies must transfer a larger portion of their managers to a country like Zaire than to one like Canada. Years of education are only a partial indication of skills, since the type of education may not match employment needs. Until recently, Argentina graduated more lawyers than engineers, even though there was a surplus of the former and a shortage of the latter.

Besides being a requisite for employment, education also has profound effects on advertisements, complexity of products, and explanation of financial results and measurements. Perhaps the most notable consequence is the effect that education may have on the development process itself. There is considerable disagreement as to the method and results of calculating economic returns from education. However, there is fairly widespread agreement that investment in this area results in high, though not necessarily optimal, returns.

Age Distribution

- Life expectancy lower in LDCs
  - Fewer productive workers as percent of population
- Poverty reduces efficiency

Generally, employable people are considered to be those between the ages of 15 and 65. If the age of a population consists largely of very old or very young people, a smaller than normal number will be available to do productive work. The less-developed countries usually have a larger proportion of very young people because life expectancy is lower. Canada's life expectancy at birth is 74.5 years, compared to only 50 years in Zaire. This means that Canada has many more people over age 65 than Zaire, while Zaire has many more people who are younger than 15. In total population, Zaire has 6.8 million more inhabitants than Canada. However, in the critical 15-to-65 age group the margin is 0.4 million more in Canada.

The basic causes of low life expectancy are poor health and inadequate nutrition brought about by poverty. In addition to the effect of poverty on age distribution, individuals who suffer from physical problems cannot be expected to perform over long periods as productively or as safely as healthy people. Furthermore, sickness increases absenteeism, thus creating problems of maintaining assembly and integrated work operations.

Dualism

- Urban-rural differences
- Differences by other groups, e.g., race

Dualism refers to progress that is confined to certain sectors of an economy while the rest of the sectors are left virtually untouched. Overall data for a country obscure such differences. Within less-developed countries there typically are fairly substantial groups that have the characteristics of advanced countries. (Of course, one can also find backward areas or groups within most developed countries.) For example, of the seven countries shown in Table 3.1, both Colombia and South Africa have composite figures showing low life expectancy and low levels of education. Each, though, has elements of dual development. In Colombia a few of the cities, such as Medellin, Bogota, and Cali, have fairly highly educated populations with high life expectancies. South Africa has not only the urban-rural difference of Colombia but also the great contrast between blacks and whites. Approximately

20 percent of the population, classified as white, controls most of the wealth and has the advantages that accompany wealth.

In situations such as these, firms seldom locate manufacturing and distribution centers away from the more advanced urban centers, since both the markets for the goods produced and the skilled labor force to build the products are in these areas. Locating in urban centers as a means of overcoming labor problems is becoming increasingly difficult, however, as government restrictions and incentives induce companies to locate elsewhere in the countries.

BEHAVIORAL ATTRIBUTES

- Agreement that cultural differences exist, but
  - problems of how to measure
  - disagreement on what they are
- Recent research
  - more on industrial countries than earlier
  - cultural anthropologists observe national character
  - carefully compared samples

In every society there are norms of behavior based on attitudes, values, and beliefs that constitute societal **culture.** These obviously vary from country to country. Casual visitors remark on differences as they travel; experts write about them; and people managing affairs across countries find that results cannot be fully explained by economic models.[11] There is a great deal of controversy, however, as to what these differences are. This is because of an acknowledged problem of measuring the variances.[12] It is simply very difficult to isolate culture from such factors as economic and political conditions and institutions. An opinion survey, for example, may reflect a short-term response to temporary economic conditions rather than the basic values and beliefs that will have longer-term effects on the way business can be managed. One must be very tentative and guarded in proclaiming what differences exist and how companies should react to them.

In spite of these problems, a good deal of research conducted in recent years indicates that there are aspects of culture that are significantly different across national borders and have a substantial impact on how business is normally conducted in different countries. There has also been an upsurge in studies comparing business operations in industrial countries, whereas most interest historically was in primitive areas where little international business takes place. One of the common means of research has been the reliance on trained experts, usually cultural anthropologists, to relay their observations of a national character. This method was used extensively during World War II, for example, to predict how the enemy would react to different situations. Another method is to compare carefully paired samples of attitudes or of organizational practices from two or more countries. The following discussion highlights some of the major findings of such research.

Group Affiliations

- Ascribed—by birth
- Acquired—not by birth

All countries' populations are commonly subdivided into groups, and individuals have memberships in more than one group. Affiliations determined by birth are known as **ascribed group memberships;** these include differen-

● Reflect resources and position

tiations based on sex, family, age, caste, and ethnic, racial, or national origin. Among **acquired group memberships** (not determined by birth) are religion, political affiliation, and associations. The type of membership often reflects the degree of access to economic resources, prestige, social relations, and power. The type of membership often reflects, as well, one's place in the social stratification system. Every society has stratification, such as valuing people in managerial and technical positions over production workers.

● Performance capability viewed
  ● most highly in some societies
  ● secondarily in others
● Egalitarian societies place less importance on group membership

Competence versus group affiliation. In some societies the acceptance of people for jobs and promotions is based primarily on their performance capabilities. In the United States, for example, this is the norm. This does not mean, of course, that there is no discrimination against people in the United States because of their sex, color, religion, or whatever. However, the belief that competence should prevail is valued sufficiently highly that legislative and judicial actions in recent years have aimed at instituting that value. Such a value is far from universal. In many cultures, competence is of secondary importance. Furthermore, the belief that it is right to place some criterion ahead of competence is a value held just as strongly in some countries as competence is in the United States. Whatever factor is given primary importance—such as the relative weight given to seniority, sex, or some other factor—will determine to a great extent who is eligible to fill certain positions and how their compensation will be determined.[13]

The more egalitarian or open a society, the less difference ascribed group membership will make in access to rewards. Sometimes membership rigidity actually extends to legal proscriptions. For example, in South Africa, blacks, whites, and coloureds are each eligible to fill only certain jobs. Frequently, memberships simply prevent large groups of people from getting the preparation that would make them equally qualified with others in the society. In countries with poor government education systems, elite groups send their children to private schools, while other children receive inferior educations. Even in the United States, which has free public education, it has been noted in recent years that school assignments based on neighborhood patterns perpetuate differences in both education and class.

● Country-by-country attitudes vary toward
  ● male versus female roles
  ● importance of youth vs. older age
  ● family versus nonfamily ties
● Rapid changes occurring in many places

Importance of different group memberships. Although there are almost unlimited ways of defining group memberships, three types of international contrasts (sex, age, and family) should indicate both how widespread these differences are and how important they are as business considerations.

Country-specific differences in attitudes toward males and females are especially apparent as one scans the globe. Recall the case at the beginning of this chapter and the fact that the female editor for PRI could not get permission to enter Saudi Arabia. One of the most striking features of Saudi Arabia to foreigners is the rigidity of behavior expected of people because of being male or female. Separation is maintained at a greater level even than in most other Islamic countries. Schools are separate, and so is most social life. Only about 10 percent of women work outside the home; when they do, they remain very much apart from men. To get to work, women are legally prohibited from driving cars and socially restricted from riding in a taxi without a male relative. Most jobs for women are in professions with little or no male contact, such as teaching or giving medical treatment to other women. When women do work in integrated organizations, the Saudis feel a necessity to put partitions between them and male employees.

In Saudi Arabia the sheltering of women is also reflected in education figures. The ratio of males to females in elementary school is 2.8 to 1; in universities it is 10 to 1.[14] Even between countries in which women constitute a large portion of the working population there are vast differences in the types of jobs thought of as "male" or "female." In the Sudan, 74 percent of the manufacturing employees are women; in neighboring Egypt the figure is only 5 percent. In Switzerland, 48 percent of administrative and managerial positions are filled by women, compared to only 14 percent in Canada. In terms of preparation, 25 percent of Rumania's engineering students are women, whereas in Argentina the figure is 2 percent.[15]

Age involves some curious variations. In many countries it is assumed that age and wisdom are correlated. The effect is that advancement has been based largely on seniority, with the result that upper-level managers are commonly above 70 years of age. In the United States, retirement at age 60 or 65 has been mandatory in many companies, and relative youthfulness may even be an advantage in moving ahead. (This phenomenon also helps to explain the relatively high U.S. sales of such products as toupees, hair dyes, and health club memberships.) This quest for youthfulness does not, however, carry over to U.S. politics, where one finds rather high minimum age requirements for many posts and no mandatory retirement.

In some societies, especially Mediterranean and Latin American countries, the family constitutes the most important group membership. An individual is accepted largely on the basis of the social status or respectability of his or her family rather than on individual achievement. Because family ties are so strong, there may also be a compulsion to cooperate closely within the family unit but to be distrustful of links involving others. A study of Greek business, for example, noted how family restaurants mobilize their efforts to attain success, whereas in large organizations (where people are from many different families) there is little cooperation among employees because of little trust of people outside the dominant in-group.[16]

Barriers to employment on the basis of age or sex are undergoing substantial changes in many parts of the world; thus one cannot rely on statistical and attitude studies that are even a few years old. One of these changes has involved the growing number of women and men in the United States in occupations previously dominated by the other sex. In the 1970s, for example, the number of male secretaries, telephone operators, and nurses rose substantially.[17] In terms of age, there have been movements in the United States to eliminate mandatory retirement in business, whereas in Japan and Western Europe there have been movements to lower the retirement age.[18] Even in Saudi Arabia the percent of total enrollment in universities that is female almost doubled in the 1970s.

- Local attitudes may force hiring by local norms or opinions
- Must consider to whom workers will look up

Some effects on international business hiring practices.   Even if individuals have the qualifications for a certain position and there are no legal barriers for hiring them, social obstacles may still make international firms think twice about employing them. Two examples from the work experience of one of the authors should illustrate this fact. In Panama a surface observation indicated no discrimination based on racial or ethnic background. However, a group of office personnel protested the possible hiring of a Jamaican-Panamanian. Jamaican-Panamanians have not fully assimilated into Panamanian society—they still speak English as a first language and maintain their own English-language newspapers. During the time I worked in Jamaica, the press objected to the fact that foreign firms hired too many Chinese-Jamaicans (who, by the way, have a substantially higher educational background than the nation's population as a whole and were much sought after by international employers). This was a case of social pressure to increase the utilization of black Jamaicans, who held less than their proportionate share of wealth or managerial positions. An interesting contrast in both Panama and Jamaica is the difference between the Chinese and Hindu ethnic groups. In each country, both groups hold a substantial share of the wealth. People of Chinese descent are prevalently employed in every type of organization; however, it is rare to encounter Hindus employed in other than Hindu-owned merchant activities. Their exclusion appears to be self-imposed rather than an externally imposed employment practice. When persons are hired in spite of local animosities, there is an added risk of failure due to obstacles to human acceptance.

Class structures may be so rigid within one type of group that they are difficult to overcome in other contexts. One U.S. firm set up a plant in Taiwan without realizing the strength of the class structure, built largely on the military hierarchy. The U.S. managers hired the person they thought would be the most qualified individual to head the organization. In actuality, however, he consistently deferred his decision making to a subordinate because this subordinate had outranked him during their military experience. In many African countries the tribal relationship is still very important. For instance, Firestone found that Liberians could be attracted to work on plantations only if they could get permission from their tribal chiefs. Firestone was forced to develop a system of compensating the chiefs in order to attract the workers.[19]

Importance of Work

- Most people work for more than basic necessities in industrial countries
- Different motives for work in different places

People work for a number of reasons. Most people in industrial societies could satisfy their basic needs for food, clothing, and shelter by working few hours. What motivates them to work more? The reason for working and relative importance of work among human activities may be explained largely by the interrelationship of the cultural and economic environment of the country in which one lives. The differences in motivation help to explain management styles, product demand, and levels of economic development.

- Work for salvation
  - output preferred to leisure
  - not a universal value
- Attitudes may change as economic gains change

Protestant ethic. Max Weber, a German sociologist, observed near the turn of the century that the predominantly Protestant countries were the most economically developed. This **Protestant ethic,** he reasoned, was an outgrowth of the Reformation, when work was viewed as a means of salvation. Adhering to this belief, people preferred to transform productivity gains into additional output rather than additional leisure.[20] Although few societies today hold to this strict basic concept of work for work's sake, leisure is certainly viewed more highly in some societies than in others. In the United States, for example, where incomes probably allow for more leisure than in any other country in the world, there is still much disdain for the millionaire playboy who contributes nothing to society and for the person who lives on welfare. People who are forced to give up work, such as retirees, complain strongly of their inability to do anything "useful." This may be contrasted with some other societies, such as India, where the living of a simple life with minimum material achievements is still largely looked upon as a desirable end in itself.

Industrial countries today do not look down on personal economic achievement; rather, they find it commendable. In contrast, it has been argued that many Asian economies are characterized by limited economic needs that are an outgrowth of the culture. If incomes start to rise, workers tend to reduce their efforts so that personal income remains unchanged.[21] A number of observers have argued that this may be a very short-lived phenomenon, that expectations rise slowly on the basis of past economic achievement. Most of us believe we would be happy with just "a little bit more"—until we have that "little bit more," which then turns out to be not quite enough.

- People more eager to work if
  - rewards for success are positive
  - some uncertainty of whether one will be successful

Belief in success and reward. One factor that influences the attitude toward working is the perceived likelihood of success and rewards. The concepts of success and reward are closely related. Let us first look at the concept of success. For almost any task that one might undertake, there is some probability of success and failure. For instance, the task of running a mile presumably has a greater probability of success than the running of the mile in less than four minutes. The reward for successfully completing either of the above alternatives may be high or low. Our decision to attempt to complete either the running of a mile or the running of it in less than four minutes will be based on a combination of our perceived likelihood of success and the rewards, if successful, from completing either task. In cultures where the likelihood of success from working is low *and* where the perceived rewards of success are also low, there is a tendency to view work as a necessary evil. This view may exist in harsh climates, in very poor areas, or among subcultures whose members are discriminated against. When the outcome of work is very certain, there is little enthusiasm for the work itself. This has been noted in Scandinavia, for example, where rewards tend to be both positive and not very different regardless of how hard one works. Where high uncertainty of success is combined with some probability of a very positive reward for success, one finds the greatest enthusiasm for work.[22]

- After being accustomed to work, hard to adjust to leisure
- Work ethic related to economic achievement

Work as a habit. Another factor in the trade-off between work and leisure is that the pursuit of leisure activities may itself have to be a learned process. After a long period of sustained work activity with little time for leisure, people may have problems in deciding what to do with additional free time. This undoubtedly helps to explain the continued drive for greater achievement in some societies that already have considerable material goods, such as the United States. In recent years the Soviet Union has tried to shift from a six-day to a five-day work week, with resulting problems of alcoholism and other delinquent behavior on the part of people who did not know what to do with their new-found free time. One study, attempting to determine why some parts of Latin America developed a higher economic level and desire for material achievement than others, attributed differences to the fact that some Spanish settlers worked themselves rather than using slave or near-slave labor. In such areas as Antioquia in Colombia, the Spanish settlers thus developed a work ethic and became the industrial leaders of the country.[23] Thus we cannot overlook the effects of habit when comparing the importance of work from one country to another.

- High-need achievers want personal responsibility, calculated risks, performance feedback
- Lower-need achievers prefer smooth social relationships
- International differences noted

Achievement motivation. A psychological study has concluded that there are some national differences in desire for achievement.[24] Three attributes distinguish the high-need achiever:

1. liking situations that involve personal responsibility for finding solutions to problems,
2. setting moderate achievement goals for taking calculated risks, and
3. wanting concrete feedback on performance.

Lower-need achievers are more concerned about either personal power or the gaining of affiliation (smooth social relationships). The measure considers achievement only in terms of material or career success, leaving no room for measuring a need for spiritual achievement, which may be more important in other societies.[25]

Tests of managers in five areas (the United States, northern Italy, southern Italy, Turkey, and Poland) produced significant differences in responses. For instance, U.S. and Polish managers had a substantially higher achievement need, whereas the Turks and Italians had a higher affiliation need. This helps to explain situations in which U.S. and local managers react differently. For instance, in the job of purchasing, a manager with a high affiliation need may be much more concerned with developing an amiable and continuing relationship with suppliers than in reducing costs and speeding delivery. Another study used questionnaires specifically designed to compare U.S., Japanese, and Korean managers on the importance to them of organizational goals.[26] Of the eight goals (productivity, growth, efficiency, profit maximization, stability, industry leadership, employee welfare, and social welfare), all but the last showed significant differences in response by nationality. The study thus supported the idea that managers from different countries will prioritize organizational goals differently.

Need hierarchy.   A well-known motivation theory is that there is a **hierarchy of needs,** the most fundamental being physiological, followed by safety, social, self-esteem, and self-actualization needs.[27] Basically, one tries to fulfill lower-order needs before moving on to higher ones. Furthermore, once a need is fulfilled, it is no longer a motivator. This model is helpful for differentiating the reward preferences of employees in different countries. Several studies have indicated probable differences by country in the importance attached to the different needs. There also seem to be differences in the placement of the needs within the hierarchy. One of the most extensive studies involved data from 116,000 questionnaires from employees within the same U.S. multinational firm in fifty countries. Among the findings was that the Netherlands and the Scandinavian countries gave a higher importance to social needs than to self-actualization. In such a situation, group-centered motivation methods may have a more positive impact on employees than individual job enrichment methods, which are important in the United States.[28]

Importance of Occupation

In every society, certain occupations carry a perception of greater reward than others. This perception may be due to economic, social, or prestige factors. It will determine to a great extent the numbers and qualifications

Ranking and importance of needs shown to differ among countries

"Best" people gravitate to "best" jobs

- indication that perception of "best" jobs varies somewhat by country
- self-employed versus organization
- economic rewards not the only factor
- temporary versus career job

of people who will seek employment in a given occupation as individuals compete for high-reward jobs. Although we do not have extensive data for comparative purposes, there are some indications of national differences. One study asked Japanese and U.S. high school students to rank twenty-three occupations on the basis of prestige. Although few rankings were exact duplicates, variances tended to be small. One of the interesting differences was that U.S. students placed physicians in the highest rank, probably because of the importance in the United States of financial rewards, while Japanese students put college professors on top, probably because of the importance the Japanese attach to education and their emphasis on clean occupations.[29] The reluctance of educated people to dirty their hands or associate directly with operative workers has made it difficult to get lower-level managers in Latin America. To generalize, in Latin American culture there is a class of leisure, a class that works with its mind, and a third class that works with its hands.[30] The importance of business as a profession is also predictive of the degree of difficulty that an international firm may have in hiring qualified managers. It seems that in many countries, people with the educational qualifications desired by firms prefer to work in governmental posts rather than in business.

Another international difference involves the desire to work for an organization versus being one's own boss. It is generally believed, for example, that Belgians and French people try, if possible, to go into business for themselves. Going by the number of retail establishments in these countries compared on a per capita basis with the number in most other countries, one may conclude that the belief holds true. In Mexico, as well, it has been reported that U.S. subsidiaries find it hard to keep good local managers because they want to work for themselves after gaining experience. Psychological studies also show that workers in France, Belgium, and Italy place a greater importance on personal independence from the organizations employing them than do workers in many other countries.[31] Other studies show that workers in some parts of Africa have typically joined the urban labor force for only temporary periods. After these periods the workers have returned to their old agricultural endeavors, even though these endeavors usually yielded lower economic rewards.[32]

Jobs with low prestige usually go to people whose skills are in low demand. In the United States, for example, such occupations as babysitting, delivering newspapers, and carrying groceries are largely handled by teenagers, who grow out of the jobs through additional age and training. In most less-developed countries these are not transient occupations. They are filled by adults who have very little opportunity of moving on to higher-reward positions.

Self-Reliance

- Some national differences in
  - preference for autocratic versus participatory leadership
  - trust of people outside close group
  - self-determination versus fatalism
  - what is considered to be family

Superior–subordinate relationships. Psychological studies show that there are national differences in people's preferences for autocratic versus consultative managerial styles. Austria, Israel, New Zealand, and the Scandinavian countries are among those having a strong preference for superiors to consult with subordinates before making decisions. The countries with the highest preference for autocratic leadership are Malaysia, Mexico, Panama, Guatemala, and Venezuela. It is interesting to note that there is a significant correlation between countries' preferences for autocratic leadership and the incidence of autocratic political leadership.[33] One can see that organizations may find it easier to initiate worker participation methods in some countries than in others.

Trust. Several studies indicate variances based on national cultural background in the degree to which individuals have trust in others.[34] The greater the trust, the greater the ability and eagerness of people to establish rapport with others. It has been noted that where trust is high, both managers and subordinates have more desire for participative than authoritative decision making and actually tend to function this way. Certainly the acceptance of new products, as in the United States, is enhanced by the belief that the manufacturer is not developing something simply to cheat the public. One may find similar acceptance in dealing with a new firm. Studies note that U.S. citizens have high levels of trust and get right to the point in a business discussion. Conversely, people of some other nationalities are apt to spend more time in preliminary discussion before getting down to business. This is largely due to the fact that these people seek more cues as to whether they can trust others in a business relationship. In some parts of the world, such as Greece, nearly all transactions among individuals are carried out by cash rather than check as an assurance of payment. In this type of environment it is difficult to raise funds through the sale of company shares, since people prefer to place their funds in visible assets they can control themselves.

Relationship to nature. If people believe strongly in self-determination, they may be willing to work hard to achieve goals and to blame and reward themselves and others for performance. A belief in fatalism, on the other hand, may be a barrier to the acceptance of a basic cause–effect relationship. Religious differences play a part in this. Conservative Christian, Buddhist, Hindu, and Moslem societies tend to view occurrences as "the will of God." In such an atmosphere it is difficult to persuade personnel to plan ahead. Even getting workers to cooperate in accident or damage prevention—by checking tire pressure, for example—may be hard.[35] Studies show that there are national differences even among managers in fairly developed societies.

In a comparison of five groups (United States, Greece, Spain, Central Europe, and Scandinavia) the average scores of each group indicated a belief in internal control. Yet they differed in the degree of belief in internal control. The U.S. and Greek scores indicated much more, and the Spaniards' much less, belief in internal control than the others.[36]

Family affiliations.   We have already discussed the varying degree of importance in different societies of the family unit as a group. There are also differences in what is normally conceived to constitute a family. In the United States, for example, one is accustomed to the notion of a nuclear family dwelling containing a husband, wife, and minor children; however, this is not the pattern for most people in the world. Instead, one may find in the same household a vertically extended family (several generations) and/or a horizontally extended one (aunts, uncles, and cousins). This difference has a number of effects on business. Material rewards from an individual's work may be less effective in such societies, since rewards attract and are divided among more people. Geographic mobility is reduced, since more people in a family would have to find new jobs. Purchasing decisions may be more complicated because of the interrelated roles of family members. Even where the extended family does not live together, mobility may be reduced because people prefer to remain near relatives. Security and social needs may also be met more extensively at home rather than in the work place.

Communications

- All languages are complex and reflective of environment
- Common languages among countries reduce compulsion to learn second languages
- Common language within countries is a unifying force
- Not everything can be easily translated
- Words mean different things in different places

Language.   Experts in linguistics have determined that even very primitive societies have complex languages that reflect the environment in which people live. Because of varying environments, it is often difficult to translate things directly from one language to another. For example, people living in the temperate zone of the Northern Hemisphere are accustomed to referring to summer as roughly the months of June, July, and August, whereas people in tropical zones are prone to use the term summer, whether in English or some other language, to denote their dry season, which varies substantially in time of year from one country to another. Some things simply do not translate. For instance, in Spanish there is no word to refer to everyone who works in a business organization. Instead there is one word, *empleados,* which refers to white-collar workers, and another word, *obreros,* which refers to laborers. This differentiation reflects the substantial class difference attributed to each group. Another interesting difference in phrasing between English and Spanish, which undoubtedly reflects attitudes, is that a clock *runs* in English but *walks* in Spanish.

There are many nations that have English or Spanish as the official language. When a language has such widespread acceptance, there is generally not a high compulsion for native speakers to learn other languages. Commerce and other cross-border associations can be conducted easily with other nations that have the same official language. When a second language is studied, the choice is usually based on its utility in dealing with other countries. English and French have traditionally been common choices because of the commercial links developed during colonial periods. In countries that do not share a common language with other countries—for example, Finland and Greece—there is a much greater need to study a second language or multiple languages in order to deal internationally.

Even within the same language there may be substantial differences. The terms *corn, maize,* and *graduate studies* in the United Kingdom correspond to *wheat, corn,* and *undergraduate studies,* respectively, in American English. Although the wrong choice of words is usually just a source of brief embarrassment, a poor translation may be tragic. Bad translations have been blamed for structure collapses at construction sites in the Middle East.[37] In contracts, correspondence, negotiations, advertisements, and social gatherings, one has to be very careful to ensure that what is intended is communicated.

Language itself may reflect the internal cohesion of a country as well as its relative ability to deal with other countries. In some countries, such as Japan and Portugal, almost everyone has the same native language. In about half the countries of the world, however, there are multiple language groups, which may be very difficult to unify. In some cases the official language of the country may actually be spoken by only a minority of the inhabitants. This is true in India and Zaire, where, nevertheless, most power has accrued to people who number among those few who speak the official language.[38]

- Includes such things as color, distance, time, and status cues

Silent language. Not all communication is in the form of a formal language. We all give and receive messages by a host of cues other than those of formal language—a **silent language.**[39] A particular color conjures up meanings to us based on experience within our own culture. In most Western countries, black has historically been associated with death, yet white in parts of the Far East and purple in Latin America have the same connotation. The color of products and their advertisements must relate to the consumers' frame of reference.

Distances between people during conversation is a learned process that differs by society.[40] When the distance is closer or greater than is customary, a person tends to feel very uneasy. A U.S. manager conducting business discussions in Latin America may constantly be moving backward to avoid the closer conversational distance to which the Latin American official is accustomed. At the conclusion of the session, both parties may have an unexplainable distrust of the other.

Time is another confusing area. Even in one's own society the degree of punctuality depends on the situation. For a business appointment in the United States at 2:00 P.M., one usually plans to arrive a bit early. For a dinner at someone's home, one arrives on time or a few minutes late. For a cocktail party, one may arrive a bit later. In a foreign country the accepted punctuality may differ drastically. Someone from the United States in Latin America, for example, may consider it discourteous that the Latin American with whom that person has a business appointment does not invite the visitor into the office at the appointed time. Latin Americans may find it equally discourteous if the U.S. businessperson arrives at their home at the invited time for dinner while they are still making preparations.

Cues concerning a person's relative position may be particularly difficult to grasp. A U.S. businessperson may underestimate the importance of a foreign counterpart who has no large private office with a wood desk and carpeting. The foreigner may do the same if U.S. counterparts open their own garage doors and mix their own drinks. The prestige position in the United States has been described thus

> With our habits of social informality, prestige in U.S. society is more subtle (or gross, depending on your value position). That is, one's desires for prestige are mainly satisfied not by how people behave toward you but how much they knowingly or secretly envy you. [41]

This helps to explain the greater reliance on objects as prestige cues in the United States.

Perception and processing. Anything we encounter has many more cues associated with it than we notice; this is because we perceive cues selectively. Identification may be by any of our senses (sight, smell, feel, sound, taste) and by various ways within each of these. For example, visually we can sense color, depth, and shape. There is an extensive body of work showing that there are differences in the cues used by societies to perceive things. Part of the reason is physiological—for example, genetic differences in eye pigmentation that enable some groups to differentiate colors more finely. Another reason is culture—for example, richness of vocabulary that causes people to notice differences in color.[42] Vocabulary differences reflect cultural differences. For example, there are more than 6000 different words in Arabic for camels, their body parts, and the equipment associated with camels.[43]

Although different ones are perceived by different societies, once we perceive cues, we process them. Information processing is universal in that all societies categorize, plan, and quantify. In terms of categorization, we bring objects together according to their major shared function. Something to sit upon is thus called a chair in English whether it is large or small, made of wood or plastic, upholstered or not. All societies have future and conditional tenses; thus all societies plan. All societies have numbering sys-

- Cues perceived selectively and differ among societies
- Language reflects culture and forces people to note things
- All societies categorize and plan

tems as well. But the specific ways societies go about grouping things, dealing with the future, and counting differ substantially.[44]

- No universally accepted behavior
- Hard to note subtle differences

Morals and etiquette.   The way we normally act in our native culture may be subject to different degrees of acceptance and interpretation in another society. Practices that are accepted in one locale may even be considered immoral in another. The very normal practice of depicting a male and female in close contact for an advertisement in a Western country must be changed in many Far Eastern countries to fit a moral context in which even holding hands in public is taboo. U.S. motion picture exports are illustrative of different moral conceptions. For example, the film *Kid Blue* was banned in Greece because the villain was not caught and punished. Sweden, which permits the most graphic sex pictures, prohibited showing *The Sound of Music* and *Tom Sawyer* to children because of violent scenes. In Taiwan, U.S. films that depict male actors with long hair have been banned. In Latin America, scenes showing bare breasts have been cut from U.S. films.[45] In Finland the Helsinki city council once canceled library subscriptions to Donald Duck comic books because of complaints about Donald's morals. It seems that his bare bottom and his uncertain relationship with Daisy constituted a "racy life style."[46]

   If a U.S. businessperson in the Far East fails to bring small but thoughtful gifts to the Far Eastern counterpart, that official may not only consider it a breach of etiquette, but may also feel that the U.S. businessperson places little interest or emphasis on the meeting. At the same time, if not invited into private homes, the U.S. manager may develop the same wrong opinion of the Far Eastern associate, not realizing that such invitations are not customary. Gift giving can be a real dilemma. In many places it is customary to give payments to governmental officials in order to obtain their services. While these payments are not part of coded regulations, they are well embedded in local common law practices. The going rate of payment is rather easily ascertained and is usually graduated on the basis of ability to pay. It is a fairly efficient means of taxation in countries that pay civil servants poorly and do not have means of effectively collecting income taxes. Still, these payments are frequently viewed by foreign firms and their home country constituents as bribes.

- Idealism
  - settle principles first
  - prefer mass action
- Pragmatism
  - settle small issues first
  - want specific measurable achievements

Evaluation of information.   National differences have been noted in the degree to which people try to settle principles before they try to settle small issues or vice versa (**idealism versus pragmatism**). Idealist societies tend to prefer planned economic systems; pragmatist cultures prefer free market systems. From a business standpoint, differences manifest themselves in a number of ways. The idealist sees the pragmatist as too interested in trivial details, whereas the pragmatist sees the idealist as too theoretical.

Labor, in a more pragmatist society, tends to ask for very specific things, such as a pay increase of one dollar per hour. In a more idealist society, labor tends to make vague demands, depending on mass action to demonstrate its principles.[47]

RECONCILIATION OF INTERNATIONAL DIFFERENCES

Are Cultures Converging?

- Three scenarios
  - smaller cultures absorbed by national and global ones
  - subcultures transcend national boundaries
  - organizations more similar worldwide but people in organizations holding on to cultures

There is much more contact among different areas of the world than there has ever been before. This is due, of course, to advances in transportation and communications, along with rising incomes that allow people to take advantage of these advances. There has also been a growth in global competition, so that many of the same international companies compete against each other in many different parts of the world. These factors have led to much leveling of cultures. More similar products are demanded and more similar methods are used to produce them globally. Many small cultural groups are being absorbed into more dominant national ones, and many regional languages have become extinct in recent years.

On the other hand, we see evidence of the emergence of more subcultures within countries because of the influx of people who are holding onto their traditional ways rather than assimilating into their new surroundings completely. There is also evidence that some groups accept new ideas, products, and technologies from abroad more readily than others. All of these factors might lead us in the future to define cultural segments along lines that cut across national boundaries but that do not include everyone within given countries.

There is a third possibility on how cultures are evolving as they come into greater contact with each other. On the basis of an extensive survey of recent cross-cultural studies, a management theorist concluded that organizations are becoming more similar internationally; however, people within the organizations are continuing to hold onto their national differences as strongly as ever.[48] In other words, the tangible things such as technology are becoming more universal, but the way people cooperate, attempt to solve problems, and are motivated are not becoming more universal.

Cultural Awareness

Regardless of which of the above three scenarios might emerge, there is a near consensus that at least some cultural differences will persist that will complicate the task of conducting international business. Where these differences exist, one must decide whether and to what extent one should adapt home country practices to the foreign environment. But before one can make that decision, one must be aware of what the differences are.

As was discussed near the beginning of the chapter, this is not an easy task. There is much disagreement about the differences. There is also no foolproof method of building better cultural awareness.

One should recognize that some people seem innately better equipped than others to deal with new situations. Even domestically, some people are more prone to say the right thing at the right time while others unintentionally offend. Even in our home countries, most of us are more easily aware of differences in things that we have learned consciously, such as table manners, than in things that we have learned subconsciously, such as our method of approaching problem solving. Still, there is general agreement that one can improve one's awareness and sensitivity. This chapter has presented a framework of human cultural factors that have been especially noted to cause business adjustments on a country-to-country basis. By paying special attention to these factors, one can make a start on building awareness.

One can undertake a good deal of research by reading about and discussing other countries. One can also research what people in another country think of one's own culture. One has to be very careful, though, that the opinions presented are indicative of what the situation really is. Very often they represent unwarranted stereotypes, an accurate assessment but only of a subsegment of the particular country, or a situation that has since undergone change. By getting the viewpoints of people with different perspectives, one is in a much better position to be realistic in an assessment of a different culture. One may pay special attention to the behavior of those people who are well accepted or those with whom one would like to be associated in a given society in order to emulate their behavior.

Dangers of Polycentrism

- Overwhelmed by national differences
  - risks not introducing workable changes

The term **polycentrism** characterizes an individual or organization being "overwhelmed by the differences, real and imaginary, great and small, between its many operating environments."[49] It is understandable that many managers develop this attitude. Indeed, most discussions, including the one in this chapter, have focused on uniquenesses abroad and the attendant problems that international firms have encountered. If, in reviewing domestic business practices, managers concentrated on the numerous actions that have failed because of misjudged markets, resistance to change, and misunderstood communications, they might get an overly formidable impression of their own operating environments as well. In reality we do not know for sure if companies' practices abroad are more prone to failure than their practices at home.

If a company is too polycentric in its views, it stands the risk of being so overcautious that it shies away from certain areas or from transferring intact home country practices or resources that, in fact, may work well abroad. One of the authors attended a conference in which a large U.S.-based international firm assembled its worldwide personnel managers for an exchange of views. The complaints from the overseas managers centered on certain corporate directives that "do not fit our country." The impression generated was that foreign operations were so unique that each overseas office should be independent to develop its own procedures. Additional discussions made it apparent, however, that the complaints focused on only about 5 percent of corporate directives. To delegate the proposed control would risk not introducing some of the 95 percent of practices that had worked successfully abroad. It would furthermore risk duplication of efforts, which may have been more costly than the problems of trying to administer the ill-suited corporate directives. The additional discussions also generated comments for the first time from the personnel managers in U.S. domestic offices who had received the same corporate instructions. Their conclusion was that they had as many problems with the questionable policies as had their foreign counterparts. The problem, which had originally been attributed to environmental differences, was in fact universal.

If an international firm is to have an advantage over the local firms with which it competes, it must usually perform some functions differently than the local firms. Polycentrism may lead to such extensive delegation or to such extensive imitation of domestically proven practices that innovative superiority is lost. Furthermore, control may be diminished as operations for each country move separately to foster local rather than world-wide objectives.

Dangers of Ethnocentrism

- Overlooks national differences
  - ignores important variables
  - thinks change easily introduced
  - believes home country objectives should prevail

The term **ethnocentrism** describes the firm or individual so imbued with the belief that what worked at home should work abroad that environmental differences are ignored. Since the first part of this chapter was concerned largely with pitfalls resulting from such beliefs, it would be redundant to reaffirm the need to consider physical, demographic, and behavioral variances among people. It is worth mentioning that ethnocentrism may fall into three categories. One type involves the oversight of important variables because one has become so accustomed to certain cause–effect relationships in the home country that one forgets or does not realize that differences exist abroad. The dangers of this type are obvious and may best be rectified by the use of checklists of human variables in order to assure that the major factors are at least considered. A second type of ethnocentrism involves recognizing differences but assuming that the introduction of changes is both necessary and easily achieved. The problems accompanying this type of attitude will be discussed later. A third type is manifested by the firm that, although recognizing both the environmental differences and the problems of change, operates abroad in order to achieve home country rather than foreign or worldwide objectives. This type of operation may result in adverse long-term competitive viability as (1) the company does not perform as well as competitors, and (2) it developes opposition to its practices from host governments.

Change Agent or Changed Agent?

● International firms often follow hybrid of home and foreign norms

Between the extremes of polycentrism and ethnocentrism are hybrid business practices that are not exactly like the international company's home operations and not exactly like those of the typical host country firm. These are the most common means of reconciling differences. When the host country environment is substantially different, the international firm must decide whether to get people in the host country to accept something new, in which case the firm will be acting as a change agent, or whether the firm itself will make some changes.

● Must consider own versus foreign value system

One's own value system. It is much easier for one to adapt to things that do not go against one's own value system than to things that do. Whether one eats a salad before or after the main course is usually not strongly imbedded in one's value system; therefore adjustment causes little moral dilemma. Such things as different degrees of exposing one's body may, however, present adjustment difficulties. In many of these cases, though, the foreigner or foreign firm may not be expected to adhere to the national norm.

The Society for Applied Anthropology, whose members advise agencies on means to institute change in different cultures, has adopted a code of ethics to protect foreign cultures with which it comes into contact. Among the considerations is whether or not a project of planned change will actually benefit the target population. Because of differences in value systems in terms of what is a benefit, this is no easy code to implement. One such case was the introduction of infant formula to developing countries, which resulted in very negative unforeseen results. This will be discussed more fully in Chapter 18.

● Cost of making change may exceed benefits gained

Cost-benefit of change. A firm must consider its sometimes opposite objectives of cost minimization and sales maximization along with the resources it has at its disposal. It has been noted, for example, that international firms tend to introduce the same or only slightly altered products into foreign markets instead of designing what would be best suited for and have the maximum acceptance in those markets. This may be rational, even though it is costly to convince people to buy "the next best thing" and even though sales are not maximized. The cost of designing a new product may exceed the losses from the alternative. Furthermore, the firm may lack the resources to make large-scale product changes.

● Resistance lower if number of changes is not too great

Resistance to too much change. When Sears, Roebuck decided to open its first retail store in Spain, one of its main problems was with suppliers. Sears tried to deal with these suppliers in much the same way as in the United States. Among the many changes that Sears tried to introduce at the start were payments by check, firm delivery dates, standard sizes, no manufacturer's labels, and larger orders. Suppliers balked or did things their old way, claiming forgetfulness.[50] With the benefit of hindsight, one may argue that some of these changes were not necessary for the fulfillment of Sears' objectives. Acceptance by suppliers may have been easier had fewer demands been made on them at one time, and Sears could have phased in its other policies over a period of time.

● The more the change upsets the things important in value system, the more resistance

Importance of change. A Spanish textile factory, when opening in a community in Guatemala, tried to install training methods, work hours, and a host of other production "improvements" that are commonplace in more developed areas. Not only did people refuse to work, but soldiers had to protect the factory from the community. The management retracted and gave in on those things that were most important to the potential workers. These included a four-hour period between shifts so that male workers could attend to agricultural duties and female workers could do household chores and nurse their infants. The laborers were willing to work Saturday afternoons in order to compensate for production lost during shift breaks.[51] The important lesson of this is that the more a change disrupts basic values, the more the people affected will resist the change. When changes do not interfere with deep-seated customs, then accommodation is much more likely. By giving in on the matters that were most important to the workers, the foreign firm was able to gain an effective and committed work force.

● People more willing to implement change when involved in decision

Participation. One means of avoiding undue problems if possible changes are to be introduced is to promote participation. By discussing the possibility of change, one may ascertain how strong resistance might be, stimulate the recognition of a need for improvement, and slacken fears of adverse consequences among individuals who otherwise might feel they have no say in their own destinies. One sometimes thinks of delegation or participation as a factor in successful change, primarily in highly developed countries where people have the backgrounds to make substantial contributions. Experience with economic development programs, however, indicates that participation in even the most backward communities of the world may be extremely important. Two of the most successful development programs on record are the Vicos project in Peru and the Etawah project in India.[52] Unlike some other development programs, these projects depended very heavily on participation in planning and enactment by the people of the communities.

- People more apt to support change when they see personal or reference group rewards

Reward sharing. Sometimes a proposed change may have no foreseeable benefit for the people whose support is needed to assure its success. One should guard against pseudo-improvements in products that do not fit the needs of consumers, since the company's gains may be short-lived.[53] Production workers have little incentive to shift to new work practices unless they see some benefits for themselves. A U.S. firm manufacturing electrical appliances in Mexico moved workers easily from radio to black-and-white television production. When the time came to introduce color televisions, however, defects inexplicably increased. Investigations determined that the workers were eager to turn out a high-quality black-and-white set because they or their friends might be consumers. The prices of the color set, though, were so far beyond their reach that there was no incentive to be careful in production. The firm therefore developed a bonus system for quality.[54] Rewards may be in monetary compensation or prestige.

- Convince those who can influence others

Opinion leaders. By discovering the local channels of influence, an international firm may locate opinion leaders to help speed up the acceptance of change. In Ghana, government health workers frequently ask permission and seek the help of village witch doctors before inoculating people or spraying huts to fight malaria. This way the desired result is achieved without destroying the important social structure. Opinion leaders may emerge in different places, such as among youth in a rapidly changing society. An interesting use of this concept in Mexico involved sending low-level workers rather than supervisors to the parent plant in the United States. These workers returned as heroes among their peers and were believed and emulated when they demonstrated new work habits.[55]

- Time change when there is likely to be least resistance

Timing Many good ideas never get practiced effectively because they are ill-timed. Change brings uncertainty and insecurity. A labor-saving production method creates resistance because people fear losing their jobs. There will be many fewer impediments if the labor-saving methods are introduced when there is a labor shortage rather than a surplus, regardless of what management says will happen to employment. Attitudes and needs may change slowly or rapidly, so keeping abreast of these changes helps in determining timing. Volkswagen introduced small cars in the United States when substantial numbers of consumers were ready for a small car. The Henry J. and Crosley, two other small cars, were introduced to the U.S. market a few years earlier, too soon to be successful.

- International firms
  - change some things abroad

Learning abroad. The discussion thus far has centered on the interaction between the international firm and the host society. The firm not only affects the relationship but may also be affected by it. It may not only change things abroad or alter its own activities to fit the foreign environment,

- change themselves when encountering foreign environments
- learn things abroad that they can apply at home
- Most attention on business practices of firms from countries doing best economically

it may also learn things that will be useful in its own home country or other operations.

It has been noted that the national practices most likely to be scrutinized for possible use in other countries are those from the countries that are doing best economically.[56] For example, there was a great focus on the British cultural character in the nineteenth century, when Britain was the economic leader. Then, at the turn of the century, attention was diverted to Germany and the United States. There has been a recent shift in attention toward Japan. Business theorists and practitioners have debated whether some common and successful Japanese business practices can be successfully adopted elsewhere. Whether one is importing or exporting practices, one must consider the same factors when questioning whether and how change can be introduced.

SUMMARY

- National norms for physical, demographic, and behavioral characteristics of people create the need for international firms to assess whether they must alter their business practices from one country to another.

- Although differences are often examined on a country-to-country basis, one must be aware that a given country may contain distinct societies. One must also be aware that people from some groups have much more in common with people from certain foreign countries than with people from others. They may also have more in common with similar groups in foreign countries than with people from different groups in their own countries.

- Group differences have been noted in such human physical variations as skin color, height, weight, and form of the body; color, abundance, distribution, balding, and graying of the hair; blood type; and resistance and susceptibility to certain diseases. Businesspeople not only must consider the effects that these variances may have on their practices, but must also consider the wishful stereotypes people have developed of themselves.

- Demography, the statistical description of populations and their subgroups, is a convenient way of analyzing human differences by country. Among the many descriptive measures of use are population growth rates, education, age distribution, and differences by subgroups, such as regions or ethnic backgrounds.

- Societal culture includes norms of behavior based on attitudes, values, and beliefs. There is general agreement that there are national differences but a great deal of disagreement as to exactly what these differences are.

- Group affiliation based on sex, family, age, caste, religion, political preference, associations, and ethnic, racial, or national origin often reflects a person's degree of access to economic resources, prestige, social relations, and power. Among the effects on business is the determination of who may be qualified and available for given jobs.

- Most people work far more than would be necessary for the satisfaction of basic food, clothing, and shelter needs. The relative importance of work may be explained largely by the interrelationship of the cultural and economic environment. Among the explanations for a drive to work are the Protestant ethic, the degree to which people believe that work will bring success, a work ethic based on habit, achievement motivation, and fulfillment of higher-order needs.

- Occupations carry different perceptions of economic, social, and prestige rewards in different countries. People tend to gravitate to jobs for which they perceive high rewards. The many international differences result in varied attitudes toward working for an organization, particularly business, versus working for one's self.

- Self-reliance, as opposed to reliance on outside factors, depends on one's trust of others and attitude toward nature and fate, whether one believes an autocratic or participative relationship is preferable, and on cooperative group membership, especially the family.

- We communicate through formal language, through silent language based on culturally determined cues, and through prevailing morals and etiquette. We even evaluate much information on the basis of our cultural background. The distinctions are often so subtle that much misunderstanding may develop in cross-national dealings.

- There is controversy over whether and how national cultures are converging as they come into greater contact with each other.

- In encountering a foreign environment there are dangers of excess polycentrism (becoming overwhelmed by differences) or of ethnocentrism (believing that what worked at home should work everywhere).

- In deciding whether to encourage a foreign populace to adjust to an international firm's accustomed practices or whether to develop new practices to fit a given population, the company should proceed with caution. Among the considerations are the cost and benefit to the firm of each alternative, the importance of the change to both parties, the possibility of participation in decision making, the way rewards of change may be allocated, the identity of opinion leaders, and the existence of the right timing for change.

- There has usually been more interest in diffusing business practices from those countries that are showing the most economic success. Cultural factors may determine whether or not they will work in another society.

JOHN HIGGINS*

In 1962, Leonard Prescott, vice-president and general manager of Weaver-Yamazaki Pharmaceutical of Japan, believed that his executive assistant, John Higgins, had been losing his effectiveness in representing the U.S. parent company because of his extraordinary identification with the Japanese culture.

Weaver Pharmaceutical, with extensive international operations, was one of the largest U.S. drug firms. Its competitive position depended heavily on research and development. Sales activity in Japan had begun in the early 1930s through distributorship by Yamazaki Pharmaceutical, a major producer of drugs and chemicals in Japan. World War II disrupted sales, but Weaver resumed export sales to Japan in 1948 and captured a substantial market share. To prepare itself for increasingly keen competition from Japanese producers in the foreseeable future, Weaver decided to undertake local production of some of its product lines. In 1953 the company began its preliminary negotiations with Yamazaki, which culminated in the establishment of a jointly owned and operated manufacturing subsidiary in 1954.

Through the combined effort of both parents, the subsidiary soon began to manufacture sufficiently broad lines of products to fill the general demands of the Japanese market. Importation from the United States was limited to highly specialized items. The company did a substantial amount of research and development (R&D) on its own, coordinated through a joint committee of both parents to avoid unnecessary duplication of efforts. The subsidiary had turned out many new products, some of which were marketed successfully in the United States and elsewhere. Weaver management considered the Japanese operation to be one of the most successful of its international ventures. It felt that the company's future prospects were quite promising, especially since there was steady improvement in Japan's standard of living.

The subsidiary was headed by Shozo Suzuki, who as executive vice-president of Yamazaki and president of several other subsidiaries limited his participation in Weaver-Yamazaki to determination of basic policies. Day-to-day operations were managed by Prescott, who was assisted by Higgins and several Japanese directors. Though several other Americans were assigned to the venture, they were concerned with R&D and held no overall management responsibilities.

The Weaver Company had a policy of moving American personnel from one foreign post to another with occasional tours in the international division of the home office. Each assignment generally lasted for three to five years. Since there was only a limited number of expatriates, the personnel

---

* Reprinted from *Stanford Business Cases 1963* with the permission of the publishers, Stanford University Graduate School of Business, © 1963 by the Board of Trustees of the Leland Stanford Junior University. This is a condensed version of the original by M. Y. Yoshino.

policy was flexible enough to allow an employee to stay in a country for an indefinite period of time if he or she desired. A few Americans had stayed in one foreign post for over ten years.

In 1960, Prescott replaced the former general manager, who had been in Japan since 1954. Prescott was an old hand at international work, having spent most of his twenty-five-year career with the company in its international work. He had served in India, the Philippines, and Mexico and had spent several years in the home office's international division. He was delighted with the challenge to expand the Japanese operations. After two years there, Prescott was pleased with the progress the company had made and felt a sense of accomplishment in developing a smoothly functioning organization.

He became concerned, however, with the notable changes in Higgins's attitude and thinking. Prescott felt that Higgins had absorbed and internalized the Japanese culture to such a point that he had lost the U.S. point of view. Higgins had "gone native," so to speak, and this change resulted in a substantial loss of his administrative effectiveness.

Higgins was born in a small Midwestern town; after high school in 1950, he entered his state university. Midway through college, he was drafted. Since he had shown an interest in languages by taking German and Spanish in college, he was given an opportunity to attend the Army Language School for intensive training in Japanese. After fifteen months he was assigned as an interpreter and translator in Tokyo. While in Japan, he took further courses in Japanese language, literature, and history. He made many Japanese friends, fell in love with Japan, and vowed to return there for a period to live. In 1957, Higgins returned to college. Since he wanted to use the language as a means rather than an end in itself, he finished his college work in management rather than in Japanese. He graduated with honors in 1958 and joined Weaver. After a year in the company training program he was assigned to Japan.

Higgins was pleased to return to Japan, not only because of his love for Japan, but also for the opportunity to improve the "ugly American" image abroad. Because of his language ability and interest in Japan, he was able to intermingle with broad segments of the Japanese population. He noted that Americans had a tendency to impose their value systems, ideals, and thinking patterns upon the Japanese, believing that anything American was universally right and applicable. He felt indignant about American attitudes on numerous occasions and was determined to do something about it.

Under both Prescott and his predecessor, Higgins's responsibilities included troubleshooting with major Japanese customers, attending trade meetings, negotiating with government officials, conducting marketing research projects, and helping with day-to-day administration. Both bosses sought his advice on many difficult and complex administrative problems and found him capable.

Prescott mentally listed a few examples to describe what he meant by Higgins's "complete emotional involvement" with the culture of Japan. In 1961, Higgins married a Japanese woman who had studied in the United States and graduated from a prestigious Japanese university. At that time, Higgins asked for and received permission to extend his stay in Japan for an indefinite period. This seemed to Prescott to mark a turning point in Higgins's behavior.

Higgins moved to a strictly Japanese neighborhood, relaxed in a kimono at home, used the public bath, and was invited to weddings, neighborhood parties, and even Buddhist funerals. Although Weaver had a policy of granting two months' home leave every two years with paid transportation for the employee and his or her family, Higgins declined his trips, preferring to visit remote parts of Japan with his wife.

At work, Higgins had also taken on many characteristics of a typical Japanese executive. He spent a great deal of time listening to the personal problems of his subordinates, maintained close social ties with many of the men in the organization, and had even arranged marriages for some of the young employees. Consequently, many employees sought Higgins's attention to register their complaints and demands with management. These included requests for more liberal fringe benefits in the form of recreational activities and acquisition of rest houses at resort areas. Many employees also complained to Higgins about the personnel policy that Prescott had installed. This involved a move away from promotion based on seniority to one based on superior's evaluation of subordinates. The employees asked Higgins to intercede on their behalf. He did so and insisted that their demands were justified.

Although Prescott felt it helpful to learn the feelings of middle managers from Higgins, he did not like having to deal with Higgins as an adversary rather than an ally. Prescott became hesitant to ask Higgins's opinion because he invariably raised objections to changes that were contrary to the Japanese norm. Prescott believed that there were dynamic changes taking place in traditional Japanese customs and culture. He was confident that many of the points Higgins objected to were not tied to existing cultural patterns as rigidly as Higgins seemed to think. The opinion was bolstered by the fact that many Japanese subordinates were more willing to try out new ideas than Higgins was. Prescott further thought that there was no point in a progressive American company's merely copying the local customs. He felt that the company's real contribution to Japanese society was in bringing in new ideas and innovations.

Recent incidents had raised some doubts in Prescott's mind as to the soundness of Higgins's judgment, which Prescott had never before questioned. For example, there was a case involving the dismissal of a manager who in Prescott's opinion lacked initiative, leadership, and general competency. After two years of continued prodding by his superiors, including

Prescott himself, the manager still showed little interest in self-improvement. Both Higgins and the personnel manager objected vigorously to the dismissal because the company had never done this before. They also argued that the man involved was loyal and honest and that the company was partially at fault for having kept him on for the last ten years without spotting the incompetency. A few weeks after the dismissal, Prescott learned accidentally that Higgins had interceded on behalf of the fired employee and had gotten Yamazaki Pharmaceutical to take him on. When confronted, Higgins simply said that he had done what was expected of a superior in any Japanese company.

Prescott believed these incidents to be symptomatic of a serious problem. Higgins had been an effective and efficient manager. His knowledge of the language and the people had proved invaluable. On numerous occasions, his American friends envied Prescott for having a man of Higgins's qualifications as an assistant. Prescott also knew that Higgins had received several outstanding offers to go with other companies in Japan. Prescott felt that Higgins would be far more effective if he could take a more emotionally detached attitude toward Japan. In Prescott's view, the best international executive was one who retained a belief in the fundamentals of the U.S. point of view while also understanding foreign attitudes. This understanding, of course, should be thorough or even instinctive, but it also should be objective, characterized neither by disdain nor by strong emotional attachment.

QUESTIONS

1. How would you contrast the attitudes of Higgins and Prescott toward the implementation of U.S. personnel policies in the Japanese operations?
2. What are the major reasons for these differences in attitude?
3. If you were the Weaver corporate management person responsible for the Japanese operations and the conflict between Higgins and Prescott had come to your attention, what would you do? Be sure to identify some alternatives and then make a recommendation.

NOTES

1. Most data were taken from an interview with Ms. Angela Clarke, a protagonist in the case. Additional background information came from Kenneth Friedman, "Learning the Arabs' Silent Language: Interview with Edward T. Hall," [the noted anthropologist quoted in the case] *Bridge,* Spring 1980, pp. 5–6ff.; Samira Harfoush, "Non-Traditional Training for Women in The Arab World," *Bridge,* Winter 1980, pp. 6–7ff.; "British Premier Visits Saudi Arabia," *New York Times,* April 20, 1981,

p. A2; Karen Elliott House, "Modern Arabia," *Wall Street Journal,* June 4, 1981, pp. 1ff.; David Ignatius, "A Saudi Job Offers Hordes of Foreigners a Chance to Prosper," *Wall Street Journal,* March 20, 1981, p. 1.

2. Eve Lee, "Saudis as We, Americans as They," *Bridge,* Winter 1980, pp. 6–7ff.

3. "Problems of Opening a Retail Store in Spain," *Wall Street Journal,* March 27, 1967, p. 1.

4. Marshall H. Segall, *Cross-Cultural Psychology: Human Behavior in Global Perspective* (Monterey, Calif.: Brooks/Cole Publishing Company, 1979), p. 143; Luis R. Gomez-Mejia, "Effect of Occupation on Task Related, Contextual, and Job Involvement Orientation: A Cross-Cultural Perspective," *Academy of Management Journal,* Vol. 27, No. 4, 1984, pp. 706–720.

5. Richard N. Farmer and Barry M. Richman, *Comparative Management and Economic Progress,* rev. ed. (Bloomington, Ind.: Cedarwood Publishing, 1970), pp. 20–21.

6. George P. Murdock has, for example, listed seventy-two cultural variables in "The Common Denominator of Culture," in *The Science of Man in the World Crises,* Ralph Linton, ed. (New York: Columbia University Press, 1945), pp. 123–142.

7. S. Gunders and J. W. M. Whiting, "Mother-Infant Separation and Physical Growth," *Ethnology,* Vol. 7, No. 2, April 1968, pp. 196–206; Thomas K. Landauer and J. W. M. Whiting, "Infantile Stimulation and Adult Stature of Human Males," *American Anthropologist,* Vol. 66, 1964, p. 1008.

8. James F. Downs and Herman K. Bleibtreu, *Human Variation: An Introduction to Physical Anthropology* (Beverly Hills, Calif.: Glencoe Press, 1969), p. 197.

9. "Romania Urges Big Boost in National Birth Rate," *The News* [Mexico City], March 4, 1984, p. 2; John Berthelsen, "Malaysia Promotes Idea of Big Families to Spur Economy," *Wall Street Journal,* April 10, 1984, p. 10.

10. *Statistical Yearbook: 1984* (London: UNESCO, 1984).

11. Ian Jamieson, *Capitalism and Culture: A Comparative Analysis of British and American Manufacturing Organizations* (Farnborough, England: Gower Press, 1980), Chapter 1.

12. Nancy J. Adler and Jill de Villafranca, "Epistemological Foundations of a Symposium Process: A Framework for Understanding Culturally Diverse Organizations," *International Studies of Management and Organization,* Winter 1982–83, pp. 7–22.

13. Harry C. Triandis, "Dimensions of Cultural Variation as Parameters of Organizational Theories," *International Studies of Management and Organization,* Winter 1982–83, pp. 143–144.

14. *Statistical Yearbook: 1972* (New York: United Nations, 1973), p. 804.

15. Elise Boulding et al., *Handbook of International Data on Women* (New York: John Wiley, Halstead Press, 1976), pp. 59–60, 163.

16. Triandis, *op. cit.,* p. 146.

17. Carol Hymowitz, "More Men Infiltrating Professions Historically Dominated by Women," *Wall Street Journal,* February 25, 1981, p. 31.

18. See, for example, Mike Tharp, "Youth Movement," *Wall Street Journal,* July 25, 1977, p. 1; Masayoshi Kanabayashi, "Fading Tradition," *Wall Street Journal,* December 21, 1977, p. 1.

19. Wayne Chatfield Taylor, *The Firestone Operations in Liberia* (New York: National Planning Association, 1956).

20. Max Weber, "The Protestant Ethic and the Spirit of Capitalism," and Kember Fullerton, "Calvinism and Capitalism," both in *Culture and Management,* Ross A. Webber, ed. (Homewood, Ill.: Richard D. Irwin, 1969), pp. 91–112.

21. J. H. Boeke, *Economics and Economic Policy of Dual Societies* (New York: Institute of Pacific Relations, 1953), pp. 39–41.

22. Triandis, *op. cit.,* pp. 159–160.

23. Everett E. Hagen, *The Theory of Social Change: How Economic Growth Begins* (Homewood, Ill.: Richard D. Irwin, 1962), p. 378.

24. David C. McClelland, *The Achieving Society* (Princeton, N.J.: D. Van Nostrand Company, 1961); David C. McClelland, "Business Drives and National Achievement," *Harvard Business Review,* July–August 1962, pp. 92–112.

25. M. L. Maehr and J. G. Nicholls "Culture and Achievement Motivations: A Second Look," in *Studies in Cross Cultural Psychology,* Neil Warren, ed. (London: Academic Press, 1980), Vol. 2, Chapter 6.

26. George W. England and Raymond Lee, "Organizational Goals and Expected Behavior among American, Japanese and Korean Managers—A Comparative Study," *Academy of Management Journal,* December 1971, pp. 425–438.

27. Abraham Maslow, *Motivation and Personality* (New York: Harper & Brothers, 1954).

28. Geert Hofstede, "National Cultures in Four Dimensions," *International Studies of Management and Organization,* Spring–Summer 1983, p. 68; for an earlier comparison among countries, see Mason Haire, Edwin Ghiselli, and Lyman Porter, *Managerial Thinking* (New York: John Wiley & Sons, 1966), pp. 90–103.

29. Charles E. Ramsey and Robert J. Smith, "Japanese and American Perceptions of Occupations," *American Journal of Sociology,* March 1960, pp. 475–482.

30. Robert R. Rehder, *Latin American Management Development and Performance* (Reading, Mass.: Addison-Wesley, 1968), p. 16.

31. Hofstede, *op. cit.,* pp. 54–55.

32. See, for example, Thomas R. De Gregori, *Technology and the Economic Development of the Tropical African Frontier* (Cleveland: Case Western Reserve University, 1969), pp. 217–226.

33. Hofstede, *op. cit.,* pp. 50–57.

34. See, for example, Geza Peter Lauter, "Sociological-Cultural and Legal Factors Impeding Decentralization of Authority in Developing Countries," *Academy of Management Journal,* September, 1969, Vol. 12, No. 3, pp. 367–378; Richard B. Peterson, "Chief Executives' Attitudes: A Cross-Cultural Analysis," *Industrial Relations,* May 1971, Vol. 10, No. 2, pp. 194–210. G. Katona, B. Strumpel, and E. Zahn, "The Sociocultural Environment," in *International Marketing Strategy,* H. B. Thorelli, ed. (Middlesex, England: Penguin Books, 1973).

35. Farmer and Richman, *op. cit.,* p. 195.

36. L. L. Cummings, D. L. Harnett, and D. J. Stevens, "Risk, Fate, Conciliation

and Trust: An International Study of Attitudinal Differences among Executives," *Academy of Management Journal,* September 1971, p. 294.

37. Christian Hill, "Language for Profit," *Wall Street Journal,* January 13, 1977, p. 34.

38. Vern Terpstra, *The Cultural Environment of International Business* (Cincinnati: South-Western Publishing Company, 1978), pp. 4–12.

39. This term was first used by Edward T. Hall, "The Silent Language in Overseas Business," *Harvard Business Review,* May–June 1960.

40. *Ibid.* In the United States the customary distance for a business discussion is five to eight feet; for personal business it is eighteen inches to three feet.

41. Webber, ed., *op. cit.,* p. 18.

42. For a survey of major research contributions, see Harry C. Triandis, "Reflections on Trends in Cross-Cultural Research," *Journal of Cross-Cultural Psychology,* March 1980, pp. 46–48.

43. Benjamin Lee Whorf, *Language, Thought and Reality* (New York: John Wiley & Sons, 1956), p. 13.

44. Segall, *op. cit.,* pp. 96–99.

45. Earl C. Gottschalk, Jr., "Hollywood Frets about Foreign Censorships," *Wall Street Journal,* December 28, 1973, p. 22.

46. Bill Paul, "Donald Duck Faces a Morals Charge in Western Europe," *Wall Street Journal,* February 10, 1978, p. 1.

47. E. Glenn, *Man and Mankind: Conflict and Communication between Cultures* (Norwood, N.J.: Ablex, 1981).

48. J. D. Child, "Culture, Contingency and Capitalism in the Cross-National Study of Organizations," in *Research in Organizational Behavior,* L. L. Cummings and B. M. Staw, eds. (Greenwich, Conn.: JAI Publishers, 1981), Vol. III, pp. 303–356.

49. Hans B. Thorelli, "The Multi-National Corporation as a Change Agent," *The Southern Journal of Business,* July 1966, p. 5.

50. "Problems of Opening a Retail Store in Spain," *Wall Street Journal,* March 27, 1967, p. 1.

51. Manning Nash, "The Interplay of Culture and Management in a Guatemalan Textile Plant," in *Culture and Management,* Ross A. Webber, ed., pp. 317–324.

52. Conrad M. Arensberg and Arthur H. Niehoff, *Introducing Social Change: A Manual for Americans Overseas* (Chicago: Aldine, 1964), pp. 123–125.

53. George M. Foster, *Applied Anthropology* (Boston: Little, Brown, 1969), pp. 7–8.

54. John D. Daniels, "U.S. Subsidiary Adjustments to the Mexican Labor Force," *Journal of International Business Studies,* Spring 1971, p. 19.

55. *Ibid.*

56. Ian Jamieson, "The Concept of Culture and Its Relevance for an Analysis of Business Enterprise in Different Societies," *International Study of Management and Organization,* Winter 1982, pp. 71–72.

PART 3

Theories and Institutions: Trade and Investment

Why do trade and investment take place? What are the governmental institutions that enhance or retard trade and factor mobility? What would happen if there were no institutions? These are the major questions considered in this section.

Chapter 4 considers the question of why foreign trade takes place. The theory of international trade is developed, and the advantages of specialization resulting from trade are discussed. Chapter 5 presents the arguments against a free flow of trade among countries and the mechanisms by which nations regulate both the inward and outward flow of goods across their borders.

Chapter 6 is concerned with still another essential aspect of the field of international business: the reasons behind direct foreign investment. In this context the close relationship between trade and investment is also examined. Chapter 7 deals with the major agreements, both bilateral and multilateral, by which nations have joined together to effect a unified or cooperative policy.

4

International Trade Theory

- To examine economic theories that explain what trade patterns would exist if trade could move freely among countries.
- To illustrate theories that demonstrate how global efficiency can be increased through the free movement of trade.
- To point out the assumptions underlying theories of trade.
- To introduce prescriptions for targeting trade patterns in terms of how much, with whom, and what products.
- To examine how business decisions determine what trade takes place among countries.

SRI LANKAN TRADE[1]

Sri Lanka, a term meaning "resplendent land," is an island country of four-teen million people off the southeast coast of India. Lying just above the equator, it is 270 miles long and 140 miles across at its widest points. It has a hot tropical climate with two monsoon periods; yet the central mountain region is cool enough to receive frost. Sri Lanka, which was known as Ceylon from the early sixteenth century until 1972, is in many ways typical of developing countries. It has a low per capita income (about $200 per year in 1980), a high dependence on a few primary products for earning foreign exchange, insufficient foreign exchange earnings to purchase all of the consumer and industrial imports its citizens would like, and a high unemployment rate. In many other ways, though, Sri Lanka is atypical of developing nations. By various measurements that compare the quality of life among countries, Sri Lanka ranks fairly high. Its 85 percent literacy rate is one of the highest in Asia, and its standards of nutrition, health care, and income distribution are among the best in the third world. Its life expectancy of 67 years is one of the highest in the developing world, and the population growth rate of 1.7 percent per year is one of the lowest.

Although Sri Lanka did not receive its independence until 1948, it is a country with a long recorded history of international trade. By the middle of the third century B.C., special quarters of its capital were set apart for "Ionian merchants." King Solomon sent his galleys to Sri Lanka to purchase gems, elephants, and peacocks to woo the Queen of Sheba. Sinbad and Marco Polo sailed there. Sri Lanka sent its ambassadors to Claudius Caesar in the Roman Empire and later established trade links with China. One by one the European powers came to dominate the island in order to acquire products that were not available in their own countries. The Portuguese, for example, sought such products as cinnamon, cloves, and cardamom, and the English developed the island's economy on tea, rubber, and coco-nuts, replacing rice as the major agricultural crop.

Since independence, Sri Lanka has looked to international trade policy as a means of helping to solve such problems as (1) foreign exchange short-age, (2) overdependence on one product and one market, and (3) insufficient growth of output and employment.

Foreign exchange is needed for buying imports. Advances in interna-tional communications and transportation have contributed to rising Sri Lankan expectations, which have translated into desires for foreign products or for foreign machinery to produce them. These desires have grown more rapidly than foreign exchange earnings.

Sri Lanka has also been concerned about its overdependence on a single product and market. Until 1975, more than half of Sri Lanka's export earn-ings were from tea. This made Sri Lanka vulnerable in two ways. First, the world demand for tea has not grown as rapidly as that for many other products, particularly manufactured ones; therefore tea has not offered as viable a means of increasing economic growth, employment, or foreign exchange earnings as some other products. Second, tea prices can fluctuate substantially from one year to another because of bumper crops or natural disasters in any tea-exporting country. For example, the wholesale price of tea rose over 90 percent between 1976 and 1977 but then fell 27.5 percent over the next two years. This makes it very difficult to plan or commit funds for long-term business or government projects. Because Sri Lanka is a former British colony, many Sri Lankans have also been concerned that the country cannot be politically and economically independent as long as trade is so centered on the British market. At the time of independence, for example, a third of Sri Lankan exports went to the United Kingdom. Sri Lanka is thus potentially vulnerable to British political demands and economic downturns.

Because of these varied but interrelated problems Sri Lanka has attempted since independence to earn more foreign exchange by exporting more of its traditional commodities. In addition, Sri Lanka has attempted to diversify its production. From independence in 1948 until a change of government in 1977 the emphasis was on the restriction of imports in order to encourage local production, thus saving foreign exchange. Since then the emphasis has been on the development of new industries that can export a part of their production, thus earning more foreign exchange. Whether the diversification has been for import substitution or export development, the intended outcome has been to create growth and jobs by using unemployed people and other unemployed resources. By moving to new products the country expects to be less dependent on the tea market and on sales of that product to the traditional British market.

The decision to develop exports of nontraditional products raises the questions of what those products should be and how to get firms to produce them for foreign markets. In 1977 the newly elected government in Sri Lanka was determined that any assistance should be given to those industries that would give Sri Lanka the best potential advantage of competing in world markets. In order to judge where the competitive advantages lay, the government took numerous steps to ease restrictions on imports. Authorities reasoned that the industries that could survive import competition were the most likely to become competitive in export markets.

Government authorities were not satisfied to sit back and wait for imports to determine the whole future industrial thrust. They reasoned that some entirely new industries might have to be assisted. Additionally, there was a desire to make some short-term export gains in order to develop credibility for the export development program. The export development division of the Ministry of Industries was instrumental in creating a methodology to identify appropriate products for development and promotion.

An obvious way of selecting product groups was to identify nontraditional products that were already being exported in small amount, since this ability to export was an indication of potential growth. The export development division also sought to find other products for which Sri Lanka might have a potential advantage in competing abroad. They first identified products that would have a high need for semiskilled and skilled labor. This was because labor costs in Sri Lanka were low, because the labor force was fairly educated, and because there was a good deal of unemployment and underemployment. The division narrowed that group of products to include only those for which Sri Lanka had indigenous raw materials for production and packaging. This was deemed to be an important competitive indicator because it would be costly to import materials that would have to be processed before being reexported. Finally, the division examined market conditions where Sri Lanka was most apt to be able to sell. This examination was based on an analysis of demand in two types of country markets: (1) those where Sri Lanka had special market concessions and (2) those that were geographically close to Sri Lanka. The former would have minimum trade barriers to Sri Lankan products; the latter could be served with a minimum of transport costs.

Seventeen products emerged after careful scrutiny. These were ranked according to export potential and to the expected benefits that would accrue to the country. The leading items were

- processed tea (packaged teabags and instant tea);
- ready-made garments (men's shirts, pajamas, ladies and children's dresses);
- chemical derivates of coconut oil,
- edible fats;
- bicycle tires and tubes; and
- other rubber products such as automobile tires and tubes.

Other items included canvas footwear, passionfruit juice, canned pineapple, ceramic ware, seafood (lobsters and shrimp), handicraft items, and gems.

This identification of the most likely competitive industries encouraged some businessmen to evaluate making investments in areas that they had hitherto not considered. Additionally, the government established an industrial development zone with its own power supply and international telecommunications facilities. Companies that produced in and exported their production from the zone could qualify for up to a ten-year tax holiday plus another fifteen years of tax concessions, depending on investment size and the number of employees. They could also bring in goods and components without paying import taxes on them at the time of import. The import tax was deferred until the ensuing products were sold domestically. If the items were reexported, there was no import tax at all.

The first manufacturers to take advantage of the incentives were textile and footwear producers who had special access to the U.S. and European markets. Since then the products have become more diverse, including such things as tires and semiconductors. Between 1977 and 1981, 135 new manufacturing projects representing U.S. $240 million in investment value were approved.

The change in trade policy in 1977 has not helped the shortage of foreign exchange. As imports have entered Sri Lanka more easily and as incomes have risen, consumers have demanded even more foreign products. As a result, Sri Lanka has placed restrictions on large consumer items but has allowed smaller items, such as watches, to enter freely because of a belief that they would otherwise be smuggled in anyway.

However, the move to establish new export industries is accomplishing many of its objectives. Whereas manufacturing comprised only 14.2 percent of Sri Lankan exports in 1977, the portion grew to 34.8 percent by 1981. The portion of export earnings from tea fell to 35.7 percent by 1980. There has also been a dispersion of Sri Lankan export markets, with such countries as the United States, Saudi Arabia, West Germany, and India gaining in importance. Whereas a third of exports once went to Britain, no single country now accounts for as much as 15 percent of Sri Lankan sales.

INTRODUCTION

- Universal trade questions
  - what products?
  - with whom?
  - how much?
- Some theories explain trade patterns in absence of government interference
- Some theories explain what government actions should strive for in trade

In the introductory case, Sri Lankan authorities, like authorities in all countries, wrestled with the problems of what, how much, and with whom the country should import and export. Once decisions were made, trade policies were enacted to try to achieve the desired results. These policies in turn affected business. They affected what companies might be able to sell in Sri Lanka from Sri Lankan and from foreign sources. They affected what companies might be able to produce in Sri Lanka for sale in either the domestic or the foreign market. Although Sri Lankan officials set policies to conform to the country's unique conditions and objectives, they relied on the same body of trade theory to guide them in their trading decisions as would officials anywhere else in the world.

Whereas some theories precede events (for example, Einstein's theory of relativity was a necessary antecedent to the atomic experiments that followed several decades later), international trade took place long before any theories were developed about trade. Sri Lanka, for example, had been actively exchanging goods with other parts of the world for more than 1500 years before there were any recorded essays theorizing about international trade.

Two types of trade theories have since emerged. The first type deals with the natural order of trade, that is, examining and explaining what trade patterns would exist if trade were allowed to move freely among

TABLE 4.1

EMPHASIS OF MAJOR TRADE THEORIES

Theory	Description of natural trade			Prescription of trade relationships			
	How much is traded?	What products are traded?	With whom does trade take place?	Should government control trade?	How much should be traded?	What products should be traded?	With whom should trade take place?
Mercantilism	—	—	—	Yes	X	X	X
Neomercantilism	—	—	—	Yes	X	—	—
Absolute advantage	—	X	—	No	—	X	—
Country size	X	X	—	—	—	—	—
Comparative advantage	—	X	—	No	—	X	—
Factor proportions	—	X	X	—	—	—	—
Demand similarity	—	X	X	—	—	—	—
Product life cycle (PLC)	—	X	X	—	—	—	—
Dependency	—	—	—	Yes	—	X	X

countries. These deal with questions of how much, which products, and with whom a country will trade in the absence of restrictions among nations. Not all of the theories of this type deal with all of these questions; what they do deal with are shown in Table 4.1 under the heading "Description of Natural Trade." Note that two of these theories are also prescriptive, that is, positing that free trade is the trade system that should prevail. Some other theories of the first type are merely descriptive; that is, they explain what does or will happen but do not make a value judgment about the result. The second type of theory prescribes that government should interfere with the free movement of goods and services among countries in order to alter the amount, composition, and direction of trade. These are the ones marked "Yes" under the question, "Should government control trade?" in Table 4.1.

Since no single theory explains all natural trade patterns and since all prescriptions are relevant to some of the actions taken by government policymakers, this chapter examines a variety of approaches. However, the subject of government interference in trade is such a broad one that discussion of many of the specific arguments and methods will await Chapter 6. Both the descriptive and prescriptive approaches to trade theory are of considerable importance to international business. They help one to understand where one can produce and sell a given product competitively and what kind of products one might best produce in a given locale. The theories are also helpful for understanding and predicting what kinds of government trade policies might be enacted and how they might affect competitiveness.

MERCANTILISM

- Attempt to export more than import
  - restricted imports
  - subsidized exports
  - colonies fostered policies
  - surplus paid for in gold

Why has Sri Lanka been so dependent on primary products instead of manufactured ones? Perhaps the roots of this answer lie in an economic philosophy put forward by a number of writers from approximately the period 1500–1800.[2] This economic philosophy, **mercantilism,** premised that a country's wealth was dependent on its holdings of treasure, usually in the form of gold. Trade was an integral part of this economic philosophy; consequently, mercantilism was the first theory espoused for trade.

Governments sought to export more than they imported and, if successful, would receive the value of their trade surpluses in the form of gold from the country or countries that ran deficits. This was a period when nation-states were emerging, and gold served to consolidate the power of central governments. The gold was used largely to build armies and national institutions that would solidify people's primary allegiance to the new nation rather than to such traditional units as city-states, religions, and guilds.

But how could countries export more than they imported? Trade was conducted largely by government monopolies. Restrictions were placed on most imports and subsidies on many exports. Colonies, such as Sri Lanka under British rule, served to help carry out this trade objective first by supplying many commodities that the mother country might otherwise have had to buy from a nonassociated country. Second, the colonial powers sought to run trade surpluses with their own colonies as a further means of obtaining revenue. They did this not only by monopolizing the colonial trade but also by preventing the colonies from manufacturing. This way the colonies had to export the less-valued raw materials and import the more valuable manufactured products. One of the major causes of the American Revolution, for example, was the English government's prohibition of colonial manufacturing.

Since the mercantilist philosophy went out of vogue in about 1800, few actual prohibitions were set by colonial powers on the development of industrial capabilities within their colonies; however, there were few encouragements either. Institutional and legal arrangements continued to tie the trade of colonies to their industrialized mother countries. Sri Lanka, like the many other countries that have attained independence since World War II, began its era of independence with a production structure and a trade pattern closely resembling those of colonies during the heyday of mercantilist economic thought. Efforts to alter this pattern are discussed in a later section on dependency trade theory.

Carry-over of Terminology

• "Favorable balance" not necessarily favorable

We still use some of the terminology of the mercantilist era. The term **favorable balance of trade,** for example, is still used to indicate that a country is exporting more than it is importing, whereas an unfavorable balance of trade is indicative of a trading deficit. In many ways it is unfortunate that this terminology has survived. Most of us think of the word *favorable* as meaning beneficial and the word *unfavorable* as meaning disadvantageous. It is not necessarily beneficial to run a trade surplus; nor is it necessarily disadvantageous to run a trade deficit. If a country is running a trade surplus (favorable balance of trade), it means that for the time being it is receiving goods and services from abroad of less value than it is sending out. In the mercantilist period the difference was made up by a transfer of gold. Today the difference is usually made up by granting credit to the deficit country. If that credit is not repaid in full, the so-called favorable trade balance may actually turn out to be disadvantageous for the country with the trade surplus.

Neomercantilism

• Attempt to run export surplus
  • not to bring in gold

In recent years the term **neomercantilism** has been used to describe countries that apparently try to run favorable balances of trade—not to seek an influx of gold, but rather in an attempt to achieve some social or political objective. For instance, a country may try to achieve full employment by

- to achieve some other
  political or social
  objective

sending its surplus production abroad because there is inadequate demand at home. Or a country might attempt to maintain political influence in an area by sending the area more merchandise than it receives from that area.

ABSOLUTE ADVANTAGE

So far we have ignored the question of why countries need to trade at all. Why can't Sri Lanka or any other country be content with the goods and services that are produced within its territorial confines?

- Country's wealth depends on
  available goods and services
  rather than gold
- Specialization will increase
  goods and services available
  because
  - resources shift to
    efficient industries
  - labor becomes more
    skilled
- Specialization due to natural
  or acquired advantage

Under mercantilist policy, many countries tried to become as self-sufficient as they possibly could in order to decrease their dependence on imports. They developed local production of as many things as possible. This did not mean, of course, that they were ever fully capable of self-sufficiency. Their citizens wanted many things for which they had no productive capabilities when imports were prohibited; therefore smuggling of these products tended to flourish.

In his 1776 book *The Wealth of Nations,* Adam Smith questioned many of the assumptions made by the mercantilists.[3] He questioned the mercantilists' assumption that a country's wealth depends on its holdings of treasure. He said instead that the real wealth of a country consists of the goods and services available to its citizens. Smith developed the theory of **absolute advantage,** which holds that different countries can produce different goods more efficiently than others. On the basis of this theory he questioned why the citizens of a country should have to buy domestically made goods that they could purchase more cheaply from abroad.

Smith reasoned that if trade were free to move without restrictions, each country would specialize in those products for which it had a competitive advantage. Resources would shift to the efficient industries because countries could not compete in the inefficient ones. Through specialization, countries could become even more efficient. This is because labor could become more skilled at doing the same tasks over and over, because labor would not lose time in switching from the production of one kind of product to another, and because long production runs would give incentives to the development of more effective working methods. A country could then use the excess of its specialized production to buy more imports than it could have otherwise produced. But in what products should a country specialize? Although Smith felt that the marketplace would make the determination, he thought that a country's advantage would be either natural or acquired.

Natural Advantage

- Refers to climate and natural
  resources

A country may have a **natural advantage** in the production of a product because of climatic conditions or because of access to certain natural resources. The climate may dictate, for example, what agricultural products

● Production of goods without the natural advantage means decreasing output of goods with the advantage

● No country is self-sufficient in natural resources

can be produced more efficiently. Sri Lanka's efficiency in the production of tea, rubber, and coconuts, for example, is due largely to the existence of the right climatic conditions for these products.

Sri Lanka imports wheat and dairy products. If Sri Lanka were to increase its production of wheat and dairy products, for which its climate is less suited, it would have to use land now devoted to the cultivation of tea, rubber, or coconuts, thus decreasing the output of those products. At the same time the United States could produce tea, perhaps in hothouses, but at the cost of diverting resources away from products such as wheat for which its climate is naturally suited. It is cheaper for both countries to trade tea for wheat than to seek to be self-sufficient in the production of both. The more diverse the climates of two countries, the more likely that they will have natural advantages for trading with each other.

Most countries find that they must import ores, metals, or supplies of fuel from other countries where those natural resources are in plentiful supply. No one country is large enough or sufficiently well endowed with physical resources to be independent of the rest of the world except for short periods. Sri Lanka, for example, exports natural graphite but must import its supply of natural nitrates. Another natural resource is soil, which, when coupled with topography, is an important determinant of the type of products to be produced most efficiently in different areas.

The existence of different natural advantages in different places also helps to explain where certain manufactured or processed products might be best produced, particularly if transportation costs can be reduced by processing an agricultural commodity or natural resource before exporting it. Recall that Sri Lankan authorities sought to identify industries that could use its primary commodities, such as tea. The processing to make instant tea would likely save bulk and transportation costs on tea exports. However, to make canned liquid tea could add weight, thus lessening the likelihood of being internationally competitive with this type of processed product.

Acquired Advantage

● Technology, skill development
  ● may be on differentiated product
  ● may be on process of making a product

Most of the world's trade today consists of manufactured goods rather than agricultural goods and natural resources. As was discussed above, natural advantage and transport costs are important in determining where the products can be produced most efficiently. We also find that the production location of many goods today is due to an **acquired advantage,** commonly referred to as technology. An advantage in product technology refers to an ability to produce a different or differentiated product. Denmark, for example, exports silver tableware and Italy exports leather goods, not because of the existence of Danish silver mines or Italian hides from its cattle ranches. Rather, companies from those two countries have developed distinctive products. An advantage in process technology refers to an ability to produce a homogeneous product more efficiently. Japan, for example, has been an exporter of steel in spite of having to import iron and coal, the two primary ingredients necessary for its production.

Resource Efficiency Example

The idea of absolute advantage in international or domestic trade can be explained by picturing two countries (or regions within one country) and two commodities. In this example we assume that the countries are Sri Lanka and the United States and the commodities are tea and wheat. Since we are not yet considering the concepts of money and exchange rates, we shall treat the cost of production in terms of the resources needed to produce either tea or wheat. This is a realistic treatment in that real income depends on the output of goods associated with the resources used to produce them. We may start with the assumption that Sri Lanka and the United States each have the same amount of resources (land, labor, and capital), which can be used for the production of either tea or wheat. Let us say that 100 units of resources are available in each country. This is shown in Fig. 4.1. In the case of Sri Lanka we assume that it takes four resources to produce a ton of tea and ten resources to produce a ton of wheat. In the United States it takes twenty resources per ton of tea and five resources per ton of wheat. Sri Lanka is thus more efficient (takes fewer resources to produce) in the production of tea than the United States, and the United States is more efficient than Sri Lanka in the production of wheat.

Let us start with a situation in which the two countries have no foreign trade. If Sri Lanka and the United States were each to devote half of their resources to the production of tea and half to the production of wheat, Sri Lanka would be able to produce 12.5 tons of tea and 5 tons of wheat (point A in Fig. 4.1), whereas the United States could produce 2.5 tons of tea and 10 tons of wheat (point B in Fig. 4.1). Since each country has only 100 resources, neither country can increase the production of wheat without decreasing the production of tea or vice versa. Without trade the combined production of the two countries would then be 15 tons of tea (12.5 plus 2.5) and 15 tons of wheat (5 plus 10). If each of the countries were to specialize in the commodity for which it had an absolute advantage, Sri Lanka could then produce 25 tons of tea and the United States 20 tons of wheat (points C and D in Fig. 4.1). We can see then that by specialization the production of both products can be increased (from 15 to 25 tons of tea and from 15 to 20 tons of wheat). By trading, the two countries can have more tea and more wheat than were available to them without trade.

FIGURE 4.1
Production Possibilities with Absolute Advantage

ASSUMPTIONS

Sri Lanka
1. 100 resources available
2. 10 resources to produce a ton of wheat
3. 4 resources to produce a ton of tea
4. Uses half of resources per product when there is no foreign trade

United States
1. 100 resources available
2. 5 resources to produce a ton of wheat
3. 20 resources to produce a ton of tea
4. Uses half of resources per product when there is no foreign trade

PRODUCTION	Tea	Wheat
Without Trade:		
Sri Lanka (Point A)	12.5	5
U.S. (Point B)	2.5	10
Total	15.0	15
With Trade:		
Sri Lanka (Point C)	25.0	0
U.S. (Point D)	0	20
Total	25.0	20

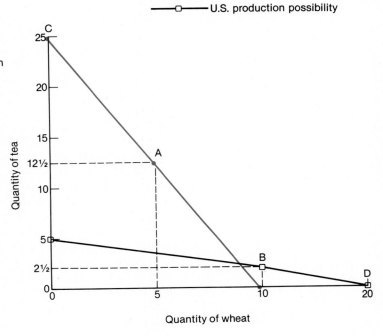

Theory of Country Size

The theory of absolute advantage did not deal with country-by-country differences in specialization; however, some recent research based on country size helps to explain how much and what type of products will be traded.

- Bigger countries tend to trade smaller portion of output or consumption
  - resources more varied
  - distances (transport cost) greater from interior to other countries
- Bigger countries tend to have advantage on products with large-scale production

Resource variety. The **theory of country size** holds that because countries with large land areas are more apt to have varied climates and natural resources, they are generally more nearly self-sufficient than smaller countries. Most of the very large countries such as Brazil, China, India, the United States, and the Soviet Union import or export less than 10 percent of the value of their national product, whereas small countries such as Iraq, the Netherlands, and Iceland have international trade of more than 40 percent of theirs.[4] Although this relationship holds generally true, there are, of course, some exceptions. South Korea, for example, is a small country for which trade is a small percentage of national income. This is because of its stringent restrictions on the importation of foreign goods.

Transport costs.   Although the theory of absolute advantage ignored transport costs, these costs do affect large and small countries differently. Transportation costs make it more likely that small countries will export. Normally, the farther the distance, the higher the transport costs. Let us assume, for example, that the normal maximum distance for transporting a given product is 100 miles because, beyond that distance, prices are increased too substantially. In a country such as the United States, very little of the production or market is located within 100 miles of the Canadian or Mexican borders. In the Netherlands, however, almost the entire population is within 100 miles of its border because the country is so small. Canada is an interesting anomaly. Although it is a very large country, foreign trade is a fairly high portion of its national income. That is because almost all of its population is near the U.S. border; thus transportation and distribution costs are minimized in getting goods to the border.

Scale economy.   In addition to the comparison of countries' size by land area, countries may also be compared on the basis of their economic size. Studies have shown that countries with large economies and big per capita incomes are more likely to develop production of goods that use technologies requiring long production runs.[5] This is because of the development of industries to serve their large domestic markets. These same industries tend to be competitive in export markets as well.

COMPARATIVE ADVANTAGE

The Logic

• Trade gains even though country may have absolute advantage on all products because

  • must give up less efficient output to produce more efficient

What happens when one country can produce all products at an absolute advantage? In 1817, David Ricardo examined this question and expanded on Adam Smith's treatise on absolute advantage. He developed the theory of **comparative advantage.** This theory holds that there may still be gains from trade if a country specializes in those products that it can produce more efficiently than other products without regard to whether or not the country has an absolute advantage vis-à-vis other countries.[6] While at first this may seem incongruous, a simple analogy should explain the logic of this theory. Imagine that the best architect in a particular town also happens to be the best carpenter. Would it make economic sense for the architect to build his or her own frame house? Definitely not. The architect can earn more money by devoting all professional energies to working as an architect, even though that means having to employ a less skillful carpenter to build the home. In the same manner a country, like the architect, will gain if it concentrates its resources on the production of the commodities that it can produce most efficiently. It will then buy, from countries less well endowed in terms of resources or skills, those commodities that it has relinquished. Like the architect who gave up carpentry, the country will concentrate its efforts on the production of those commodities for which comparative efficiency is greatest.

A Demonstration

In the following example of tea and wheat production in Sri Lanka and the United States we are assuming that the United States is more efficient in the production of both tea and wheat than Sri Lanka. The United States thus has an absolute advantage in the production of both products. In this example it takes Sri Lanka ten resources to produce either a ton of tea or a ton of wheat, whereas it takes the United States only five resources to produce a ton of tea and four resources for a ton of wheat. (See Fig. 4.2.) As in the earlier example of absolute advantage we are once again assuming that each country has a total of 100 resources available. If each country uses half of its resources in the production of each product, Sri Lanka can produce 5 tons of tea and 5 tons of wheat (point A in Fig. 4.2). The United States can produce 10 tons of tea and 12.5 tons of wheat (point B in Fig. 4.2). Without trade, neither country can increase its production of tea without sacrificing some production of wheat or vice versa.

Although the United States has an absolute advantage in the production of both tea and wheat, the United States has a comparative advantage only in the production of wheat. This is because its advantage in wheat is comparatively greater than its advantage in tea. By using the same number of resources the United States can produce 2.5 times as much wheat as Sri Lanka but only twice as much tea. Although Sri Lanka has an absolute disadvantage in the production of both products, Sri Lanka has a comparative advantage (or less of a comparative disadvantage) in the production of tea. This is because Sri Lanka is half as efficient in tea and only 40 percent as efficient in wheat production.

Without trade, the combined production would be 15 tons of tea (5 in Sri Lanka plus 10 in the United States) and 17.5 of wheat (5 in Sri Lanka plus 12.5 in the United States). By opening up trade the production of tea, wheat, or a combination of the two can be increased. If we would like to increase the production of tea without changing the amount of wheat that could have been produced before trade, the United States could now produce all 17.5 tons of wheat by using seventy resources (17.5 tons times four per ton). The remaining thirty U.S. resources could be used for the production of 6 tons of tea (thirty resources divided by five per ton). These are shown as point D in Fig. 4.2. Sri Lanka would use all of its resources in the production of 10 tons of tea (point C in Fig. 4.2). The combined wheat production has stayed at 17.5 tons, but the tea production has increased from 15 to 16 tons.

If we would like to increase the production of wheat while leaving

FIGURE 4.2
Production Possibilities with Comparative Advantage

ASSUMPTIONS

Sri Lanka
1. 100 resources available
2. 10 resources per ton of wheat
3. 10 resources per ton of tea
4. Uses half of resources per product when no foreign trade

United States
1. 100 resources available
2. 4 resources per ton of wheat
3. 5 resources per ton of tea
4. Uses half of resources per product when no foreign trade

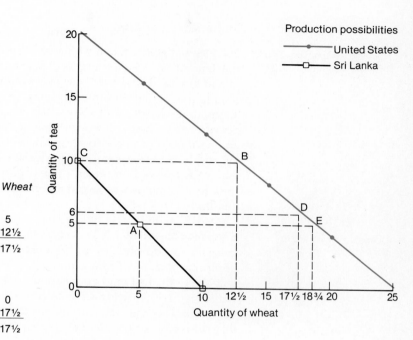

PRODUCTION	Tea	Wheat
Without trade:		
Sri Lanka (Point A)	5	5
U.S. (Point B)	10	12½
Total	15	17½
With trade (increasing tea production)		
Sri Lanka (Point C)	10	0
U.S. (Point D)	6	17½
Total	16	17½
With Trade (increasing wheat production)		
Sri Lanka (Point C)	10	0
U.S. (Point E)	5	18¾
Total	15	18¾

tea production the same as it was before trade took place between the two countries, Sri Lanka could use all its resources on the production on tea, yielding 10 tons (point C in Fig. 4.2). The United States could produce the remaining 5 tons of tea by using twenty-five units of resources. The remaining seventy-five units of U.S. resources could now produce 18.75 tons of wheat (seventy-five divided by four). These are shown as point E in Fig. 4.2. Without sacrificing the tea available before trade, wheat production has increased from 17.5 to 18.75 tons.

If the United States were to produce somewhere between points D and E in Fig. 4.2, both tea and wheat production would increase over what was possible before trade took place. Whether the production targets are for an increase of tea, wheat, or a combination of the two, both countries can gain by having Sri Lanka trade some of its tea production to the United States for some of the United States' wheat output.

Some Assumptions

● Not valid assumption, at least in short term

Full employment.   When we made our earlier analogy about the same person being both the best architect and the best carpenter, we assumed that our individual could stay busy full time by practicing architecture. If one relaxes this assumption, the advantages of specialization are less pervasive. The architect might, if unable to stay busy full time with architectural duties, do carpentry work without having to forego the added income that an architect would receive. Both the theories of absolute and comparative advantage likewise assume that resources are fully employed. Because of having many unemployed resources, some countries have sought to restrict imports in order to employ idle resources, even though they are then not employed efficiently.

● Countries may want to achieve something else

Efficiency objective.   A second assumption of the analogy is that the individual who can do both architecture and carpentry is primarily interested in profit maximization or maximum efficiency. There are a number of reasons why the individual might not choose to work full time at architectural tasks. Carpentry work might simply be very relaxing and self-fulfilling. The architect might fear that the hired carpenter will not be reliable. The architect may wish to maintain the skills of carpentry in case carpentry, rather than architecture, commands higher wages in the future. Countries also often pursue other objectives than output efficiency. They may fear too much specialization because of vulnerability to changes in technology and price fluctuations.

● Simplifies analysis

Two countries, two commodities.   For the sake of simplicity, Ricardo's and our examples assumed a very simple world of only two countries and two commodities. Although this is not realistic, it does not limit the theory. Economists have used the same reasoning, but with very complex mathematics, to demonstrate the efficiency advantages with multiproduct and multicountry situations.

● Not included in theory but can easily be accommodated

Transport costs.   Neither the theory of absolute advantage nor that of comparative advantage considered the cost of moving products from one country to another. This is not a serious limitation of the theories. Although specialization might save the number of resources necessary for producing goods, resources are also needed to move the goods internationally. If it costs more resources to transport the goods than are saved through specialization, then the advantages of trade are negated.

● Not quite as mobile or immobile as theory states

Mobility. The absolute and comparative advantage theories assume that resources can move freely from the production of one good to another domestically but are not free to move internationally. Neither of these assumptions is completely valid. The misplaced clothing worker in New England, for example, may not move easily into an aerospace job in California. This worker will have difficulty working in such a different industry and might have trouble moving to a new area. Contrary to the theories, there is some mobility of resources internationally, although not as much as there is domestically. The questions of domestic and international mobility will be discussed in the next two chapters.

FACTOR PROPORTIONS THEORY

● Factor in relative abundance is cheaper than factor in relative scarcity
  ● countries have best advantage exporting of products using abundant production factors

Although Smith and Ricardo, in their theories of absolute and comparative advantage, showed how output could be increased by having countries specialize in the products for which they have an advantage, their theories did not help to identify for which types of products a country would be most likely to have its advantage. They assumed that the free market would lead producers to move to the goods that they could make more efficiently as they were unable to compete in other areas. A century and a quarter later, two Swedish economists, Eli Heckscher and Bertil Ohlin, developed the **factor proportions theory,** which reasoned that differences in countries' endowments of labor relative to their endowments of land or capital would explain differences in factor costs. They reasoned that if labor were abundant in relation to land and capital, for example, labor costs would be low and land and capital costs high. If labor were scarce, then the price of labor would be high in relation to the price of land and capital. These factor costs would lead countries to excel in the production and export of products using their abundant and cheaper factors of productions.[7]

Land-Labor Relationship

It was on the basis of the factor proportions theory that Sri Lankan authorities reasoned that they were likely to have a competitive advantage for products using large amounts of semiskilled workers. This was a production factor that they had in abundance.

The factor proportions theory seems logical on the basis of a casual observation of worldwide production and exports. Where there are many people relative to the amount of land—for example, in Hong Kong and the Netherlands—one would expect, and one does find, that land prices are very high. One would not expect either Hong Kong or the Netherlands, regardless of their climate and soil conditions, to excel in the production of goods requiring large amounts of land, such as sheep or wheat production.

These products are left to countries like Australia and Canada, where there is abundant land relative to the number of people. Casual observation of manufacturing in relation to the labor-land proportions also seems to substantiate the theory. In Hong Kong, for example, the most successful industries are those for which technology permits the use of a minimum amount of land relative to the number of people employed; for example, clothing production can be achieved in multistoried factories where there is a small distance among workers on any level. Hong Kong does not compete in the production of automobiles, which requires much more space per worker.

Labor-Capital Relationship

- Factors not homogeneous, especially labor
  - U.S. exports have high intensity of professional labor
  - U.S. imports have high intensity of less-skilled labor
  - U.S. exports are labor intensive compared with U.S. imports

When labor is abundant in relation to capital, one would expect cheap labor rates and export competitiveness in products requiring large amounts of labor relative to capital. The opposite would be expected when labor is scarce. We find many examples of this. India, Iran, and Tunisia, for instance, excel in the production of hand-made carpets that differ in appearance as well as production method from the machine-made carpets produced in the United Kingdom and the United States using cheap capital.

Studies examining the labor-to-capital relationship have shown that export competitiveness has not always been what one would expect, however. For example, Wassily Leontief found that overall U.S. exports were less capital-intensive and more labor-intensive than U.S. imports.[8] Because of the presumption that the United States has abundant capital relative to labor, this surprising finding is known as the **Leontief paradox**. Several possible explanations have been put forward for it.

One of the most plausible explanations has been that the Heckscher-Ohlin theory assumes erroneously that production factors are homogeneous. Labor skills are, in fact, very different within and among countries, since different people have different training and education. Training and education require capital expenditures that do not show up in traditional capital measurements, which include only plant and equipment values. By modifying the Heckscher-Ohlin theory to account for different labor groups, the factor proportions theory seems to hold. If we look at labor not as a homogeneous commodity, but rather by categories of labor, we find that the United States actually has a more abundant supply of highly educated labor than of other types. In fact, this supply is abundant in relation to other production factors. U.S. exports embody a high proportion of professionals such as scientists and engineers; thus the U.S. uses its abundant production factors. U.S. imports, on the other hand, have a high intensity of less-skilled labor. The exports of such countries as India and Hong Kong display low requirements for professional and technical workers and high requirements for unskilled and semiskilled labor.[9]

Differences in skill level by country also affect where products are most likely to be produced at different times and whether they will be produced with large inputs of labor versus capital. This will be discussed in the section on the product life cycle theory of international trade.

Different Production Methods

The factor proportions analysis becomes more complicated when the same product might be produced by different methods, such as with either high inputs of labor or high inputs of capital. Canada produces wheat in a capital-intensive (lots of machinery per worker) method because of the abundance of low cost capital relative to labor. In India, on the other hand, we find the same wheat produced by using many fewer machines because there is abundant and cheap labor to work in the agriculture sector. Where there is more than one way of producing the same output, it is the relative input cost in relation to output that determines what country can produce the same product more cheaply.

THE PRODUCT LIFE CYCLE

- Production location for many products goes from one country to another in the products' life cycles

In the late 1960s a new body of theory emerged that attempts to explain world trade and investment patterns in manufactured products on the basis of stages in a product's life.[10] Only that part of the theory dealing with trade aspects is covered in this chapter. Chapter 6 will emphasize the investment aspects of the theory. Briefly, the theory of **product life cycle (PLC)** states that certain kinds of products go through a cycle consisting of four stages (introduction, growth, maturity, and decline) and that the location of production will shift internationally depending on the stage of the cycle. These four stages are a continuum rather than being fully differentiated from each other. Nevertheless, we shall describe each stage in terms of its major characteristics.

Stage 1: Introduction

- Innovation in response to observed need
  - produce and sell in same country
- Innovative country is exporter
- New product
  - made in labor-intensive way
  - little competition
  - usually in industrial country, especially U.S.

Innovation, production, and sales in the same country. New products are usually developed because of observation of a need and a market for them. Since there is generally more observation of nearby market conditions, the development is more apt to be in response to domestic than foreign needs. In other words, a U.S. firm is most apt to develop a new product because of observed needs in the U.S. market, a French firm because of perceived French needs, and so on. Once a research and development group has created a new product, that product could theoretically be manufactured anywhere in the world, even though its sales are intended primarily for the market where consumer needs were first observed. In practice, however, the early production generally occurs in a domestic location as well because the company wishes to use its excess capacity and because it is useful to locate near the intended consumers in order to get quick market feedback.

Industrial countries, especially the United States. Since the early manufacturing and sales of new products occur primarily in countries that make product innovations, it is useful to know where new products are developed. There is not a good simple indicator for comparing product innovations or technological development among countries. However, there are such indirect measurements as the income from foreign licensing, the amount of research and development expenditures, the number of new patents granted, and the identification of the most notable technological innovations. These all indicate that only about 2 percent of the world's technology emanates from the lesser developed countries and that over half originates in the United States.[11]

There are a number of reasons for the dominant position of the United States. These include the high income in the United States, which allows for risking expenditures on research that may or may not yield gainful results; an awe of science dramatized by such adjectives as "wonder," "miracle," and "magic" when referring to new products; the availability of a nucleus of scientists and engineers; and a contingent of consumers who generally believe that "new" is better than "old."

The recent supremacy of the United States does not imply that all product innovations originate in the United States. In fact there is evidence that the U.S. share of new products has been declining. For the purpose of explaining the PLC theory, however, we shall assume that the new products have originated in the United States.

Exports and labor. Although most sales are for the domestic market during the introduction stage of a product cycle, a small part of the production may be sold to customers in foreign markets who have heard about the new product and actively seek to purchase it. These foreign customers are most likely to be in other industrial countries because of similarities in income levels, which create similar market segments.

At this stage the production process is apt to be quite labor intensive in comparison to the way the product will be produced at a later stage. Because the product is not yet standardized, it is necessary to produce it by a process that permits rapid changes in product characteristics as dictated by feedback from the market. This implies high labor input as opposed to automated production, which is more capital intensive. A second factor influencing the early labor intensity is that process technology (the capital machinery necessary to produce a product on a large scale) usually comes later than the development of product technology. It is only when sales begin to develop very rapidly (stage 2) that there is an incentive to build machinery that can produce the product on a large scale. At the introductory stage, sales growth may be too uncertain to warrant the high development costs of the new process machines.

The fact that the United States excels in the development of new products that are generally made in a labor-intensive way helps us to understand the Leontief paradox, which showed that the United States generally exports labor-intensive products. Since U.S. labor rates are known to be among the highest in the world, how can the United States compete? One line of thought is that it is due to the monopoly position of original producers, which allows them to pass on costs to consumers who are unwilling to wait for possible price reductions later on. There is much evidence of this behavior based on eventual price decreases of products such as calculators and videocassette recorders. Another line of thought it that although U.S. labor is paid a high hourly wage, its education and skill level make it adept and efficient when production is not yet standardized. When production becomes highly automated, it becomes less competitive because unskilled labor may be quickly trained to perform highly repetitive tasks efficiently. It is interesting to note that the United States tends to have its best manufacturing export advantage in those industries in which production workers are most highly paid, such as aerospace. The least competitive advantage is in the industries with lower wage rates, such as clothing.[12]

Stage 2: Growth

- Innovating country increases exports
- More competition
- Increased capital intensity
- Some foreign production
  - most likely in other industrial countries
  - to serve markets where production is located

If sales begin to grow after a product is introduced, there is an incentive for competitors to find means of breaking the monopoly position. They can often do this by making slight product changes, which overcome proprietorship created through patents. At the same time, demand is liable to be growing substantially in foreign markets, particularly those of industrial countries where consumers want the new product. In fact, demand may grow sufficiently to justify the capital expenditure to produce in some foreign markets in order to overcome transfer charges and tariffs.

The higher the foreign demand, the tariff, and the transportation costs, the more likely and the faster overseas production will start. This may be done by a new producer or by the firm that had the original monopoly. Regardless of who is producing, the output at this stage is likely to stay almost entirely in the foreign country with the new manufacturing unit. Let us say, for example, that U.S. production had a monopoly that has been broken by Japanese output at this stage. The Japanese output will be sold mainly in Japan because of growth in the Japanese market, because unique product variations are being introduced for Japanese consumers, and because Japanese costs may still be high owing to production start-up problems.

Because sales are growing fast in many markets, there are greater incentives at this level for the development of process technology. However, it may not yet be well developed because of the number of product variations introduced by different competitors who are trying to take a leadership position by gaining market share. The production process may therefore still be characterized as labor intensive during this stage but becoming less so. If we assume that the United States was the original product innovator, we would expect the U.S. producers to increase their exports in this stage but face the loss of certain key export markets for which local production has commenced.

Stage 3: Maturity

- Decline in exports from innovating country
- More product standardization
- More capital intensity
- Price a more important competitive factor
- Production starts in LDCs

In stage 3, maturity, worldwide demand begins to level off, even though it may be growing in some countries and declining in others. In the mature stage of production there is often a shakeout of producers so that product models become highly standardized. Because consumers recognize the similarities among competing products, cost becomes a more important competitive weapon. Longer production runs become possible for foreign plants, and this in turn reduces per unit cost. The lower cost per unit enables sales to increase more in LDCs.

Since markets and technologies are widespread, the innovating country no longer has a production advantage. In fact, there are incentives to begin moving plants to LDCs where one can use unskilled but inexpensive labor effectively on standardized (capital-intensive) work processes.

Stage 4: Decline

- Almost all production in LDCs
- Innovating country is net importer

As a product moves to a declining stage, those factors occurring during the mature stage continue to evolve. The markets in industrial countries decline more rapidly than those in LDCs as affluent customers spend disposable income on ever newer products. By this time, market and cost factors have dictated that almost all production is situated in LDCs.

Verification and Limitations of PLC Theory

- Many products follow PLC pattern
- Types likely not to follow pattern
  - very short life cycle
  - price not an important competitive factor
  - transport costs too high for much trade
  - product differentiation

There have been a number of attempts to verify the PLC theory. Studies have found behavior to be consistent with the predictions of the PLC model for certain consumer durables, synthetic materials, and electronics.[13]

Although there are many industries for which the PLC model seems to hold, there are many other types of products for which one would not expect to find this behavior.[14] One such type would be that for which, because of very rapid innovations, the life cycle is too short to have time to achieve cost reductions by moving production from one country to another. For many electronic products today, for example, product obsolescence occurs so rapidly that there is little international diffusion of production. Another is a luxury-type product for which cost is of little concern to the consumer. A third type of product is one for which international transportation costs are so high that there is little opportunity for export sales regardless of the stage within the product life cycle. A fourth type of product is one in which a firm is able to use imaginary product differentiation, such as that created through certain advertising, in order to maintain consumer demand without competing on the basis of price.

• MNEs increasingly
  • introducing new products simultaneously at home and abroad
  • using foreign production for new products to serve home market

Regardless of the type of product, there has been an increased tendency by MNEs to introduce new products at home and abroad almost simultaneously. In so doing, they eliminate the leads and lags that are assumed to exist as a product is diffused from one country to another. Furthermore, companies are increasingly producing abroad simply to take advantage of production economies rather than in response to growing foreign markets. For example, computer monitors are produced in South Korea to feed the U.S. market, not to supply monitors to South Korea.

COUNTRY SIMILARITY THEORY

• Most trade theories emphasize differences among countries, e.g., climate, factor endowments, innovative capabilities
• Most trade today among seemingly similar countries
  • different technological emphasis
  • similar demands

Thus far in this chapter, the theories to explain why trade takes place have concentrated on differences among countries. On the basis of these theories we would expect that the greater the dissimilarity among countries, the greater potential there would be for trade. For example, big differences in climatic conditions would create different capabilities of producing agricultural products. Differences in labor or capital intensities would lead countries to be able to produce different types of products efficiently. Differences in innovative abilities would affect how a product's production will move from one country to another during its life cycle.

Yet when we observe actual trade patterns, we see that most of the world's trade occurs among countries that have similar characteristics. Most trade takes place among industrialized countries that have highly educated populations and are located in temperate areas of the world. On the basis of this observation, overall trade patterns seem to be at variance with the traditional theories that emphasize country-to-country differences.

The aforementioned theories do tend to explain most of the trade among dissimilar countries, such as trade between an industrial country and an LDC. That so much trade takes place among industrial countries is due to the growing importance of acquired (product technology) advantage as opposed to natural advantage in world trade. The **country similarity theory** holds that, having developed a new product in response to observed market conditions in the home market, a producer will then turn to markets that are perceived to be the most similar to those at home. In other words, consumers in industrial countries will have a high propensity to buy high-quality and luxury products, whereas consumers in lower income countries will buy few of these products.[15]

Although the markets within the industrial countries might have similar demand characteristics, there are differences in how these countries specialize in order to gain acquired advantages. For example, it has been noted that the British have for some time excelled in biochemistry and applied engineering, the Germans in synthetics chemistry, and the French in pharmacology. It has also been noted that there are substantial country-to-country differences in how they apportion their R&D expenditures, thus giving rise to the development of different technical and product capabilities in different industrial countries.[16]

INDEPENDENCE, INTERDEPENDENCE, AND DEPENDENCE

- No country completely dependent or independent, though some nearer one extreme or other
    - too much independence means doing without things
    - too much dependence means vulnerability to events in other countries
    - interdependence is mutual dependence
- Many LDCs trying to reduce dependence on one market or one product

This concept must be viewed along a continuum. Imagine independence at one extreme and dependence on the other, with interdependence somewhere in the middle. There are no countries located at either extreme of this continuum; however, some tend to be nearer one of the edges or the other.

Independence

Independence would be a situation in which a country would not rely at all on others. Since all countries trade, no country is completely independent economically from other countries. It is therefore hard to imagine how life would be without the accessibility of goods and services produced in a foreign country. The most recent observation of a society's economic independence was when hunters reported in 1971 on the Tasaday tribe on the island of Mindanao in the southern Philippines. Most scientists believe that this may have been the last group on earth to live in virtual isolation. Because of not having goods, services, or technologies from other societies, Tasadays had certain advantages of independence. They did not have to worry, for example, that another society might cut off their supply of essential foods or tools. At the same time, Tasadays gave up a great deal through their accidental isolation. At the time of their discovery they had no knowledge of agriculture, no traps, and no hunting weapons; they depended on gathering a few wild fruits and capturing tadpoles and frogs by hand to satisfy their food needs.[17]

The problem of government policy has been how to attain some of the advantages of independence without paying too high a price in terms of consumer deprivation. Earlier in this chapter we showed that large countries typically depend much less on foreign trade than do small countries. Even consumers in large countries could suffer through policies to promote more independence. The degree of suffering would depend on the type of product. The elimination of coffee or tea imports into the United States would probably involve less of a hardship, for example, than the cessation of foreign purchases of certain essential metals such as manganese, cobalt, and chromium. In between are products that could be produced domestically, but at a much higher price. No country today seeks complete independence. However, most try to forge their trade patterns so that they are minimally vulnerable to foreign supply and demand problems.

Interdependence

One of the ways of limiting vulnerability to problems of foreign events is through **interdependence,** the development of mutually needed trade. France and West Germany, for example, have highly interdependent economies. Each of the two countries depends about equally on the other as a trading partner. Therefore France is not too vulnerable to the possibility that West Germany would cut off supplies or markets. This is because France could counter with the cessation of essential products or markets to the West Germans.

Dependence

In recent years, many developing countries have decried their **dependency** (often written in Spanish "Dependencia"), saying that they are too dependent on the sale of one primary commodity and/or too dependent on one country as a customer and supplier. Because of the usual small size of an LDC economy, it tends to be much more dependent on a given industrial country than the industrial country is dependent on the LDC. Mexico, for example, depends on the United States for over 60 percent of its imports, whereas the United States depends on Mexico for less than 5 percent of its imports. The Mexicans view this situation as dependency rather than interdependency because Mexico can be much more adversely affected by U.S. policies than the United States can be affected by Mexican policies. This fear of dependency has led many LDCs to try to change their production and trade patterns. This was one of the concerns of Sri Lanka in the opening case.

Figure 4.3 shows that there are only three industrialized countries (Greece, Iceland, and Norway) out of twenty-three whose leading export accounts for as much as 25 percent of total export earnings. Among the developing countries, however, we find that over 80 percent are dependent

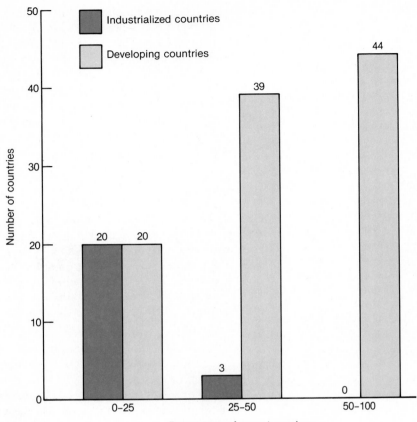

FIGURE 4.3
Dependence on Leading Commodity for Export Earnings
Source: Commodities are based on compilation of three digit Standard Industrial Classifications in *1982 Yearbook of International Trade Statistics,* Vol. I (New York: U.N. Department of International Economic and Social Affairs, 1984).

on one commodity for at least 25 percent of their export earnings. A selected list of high commodity dependencies by LDCs is given in Table 4.2.

The developing countries are also somewhat more dependent on one trading partner than are industrial countries. (See Fig. 4.4.) The trading partner on whom the developing country typically depends is almost always an industrial country. Some examples are shown in Table 4.3. Only one industrial country (Canada) conducts over half its trade with one partner, the United States.

Although theorists and policymakers wishing to lower dependency have proposed a number of different approaches, they all propose that LDCs intervene in the foreign trade markets. As was shown in the introductory case, Sri Lanka has attempted to diversify its exports by developing nontraditional products for which policymakers feel that Sri Lanka can ultimately be competitive in world markets.

TABLE 4.2 _____

SELECTED LDC DEPENDENCE ON ONE COMMODITY FOR EXPORT EARNINGS

Country	Commodity	Percent of export earnings
Burma	Rice	55.2
Colombia	Coffee	51.4
Cuba	Sugar	82.7
Ghana	Cacao	80.3
Iraq	Petroleum	98.6
Jamaica	Inorganic chemicals	77.1
Kiribati	Crude fertilizers	84.6
Macao	Clothing	61.7
Mali	Cotton	51.2
Mauritania	Iron ore	85.4
Niger	Uranium and thorium ores	79.4
Sierra Leone	Semiprecious stones	61.0
Somalia	Live animals	76.6

Source: *1982 Yearbook of International Trade Statistics,* Vol. I (New York: U.N. Department of International Economic and Social Affairs, 1984).

WHY COMPANIES TRADE

Most theories on basis of countries but trade decisions usually made by companies

Incentives to export
- use excess capacity
- reduce production costs per unit
- increase markup
- spread sales risk

Incentives to import
- find cheaper supplies
- add to product line
- reduce risk of nonsupply

Most trade theories take an approach from a country standpoint. In other words, they approach trade with a question such as, "Why should Sri Lanka trade?" Regardless of the advantages that countries may gain by trading, trade will ordinarily not reach fruition unless businesses within the country perceive that there are opportunities for exporting and importing. Since companies have a limited number of resources, they must make decisions on whether to exploit those resources domestically or internationally. Only if they see that the international opportunities might be greater than the domestic ones will they divert those resources to the foreign sector. To understand why trade takes place, it is therefore useful to understand the trade advantages accruing to individual businesses.

Export Opportunities

Use of excess capacity. Companies frequently have immediate or long-term output capabilities for which there is inadequate domestic demand. This may be in the form of known reserves of natural resources or product-specific capabilities that cannot easily be diverted to the production of other goods for which there might be an adequate domestic demand.

As was shown earlier in this chapter, small countries tend to trade more than large countries. This is partially due to their need to use excess capacity when process technology is relatively fixed to produce efficiently only on a large scale. Take automobile production, for example. Volvo

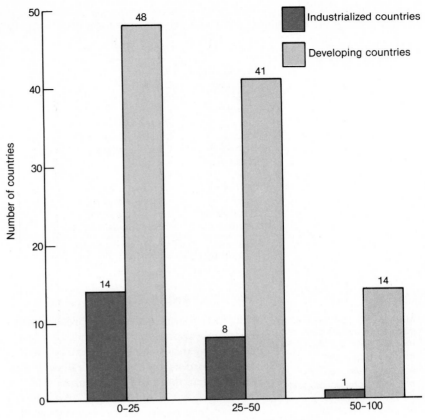

FIGURE 4.4
Dependence on Major Export Partner
Source: 1982 Yearbook of International Trade Statistics, Vol. I (New York: U.N. Department of International Economic and Social Affairs, 1984).

has a much greater need to export from the small Swedish market than does General Motors from the large U.S. market.

Cost reduction. Studies have shown that a company can generally reduce its costs by 20–30 percent each time its output is doubled, a phenomenon known as the **experience curve.**[18] For instance, if we assume a 20 percent cost reduction and an initial cost of $100 per unit, the second unit produced will cost $80, the fourth $64, the eighth $51.20, the sixteenth $40.96, the thirty-second $32.77, and so on. The reduction may come about by covering fixed costs over a larger output, by becoming more efficient because of the experience of having produced more units, and by making quantity purchases of materials and transportation. Therefore it is obvious that the market leader may garner cost advantages over competitors. One way of increasing output is by defining one's market in global rather than domestic parameters.

TABLE 4.3 _____

SELECTED LDC DEPENDENCE ON ONE TRADING PARTNER

LDC	Export market	Percent of LDC's exports
Afghanistan	U.S.S.R.	51.7
Brunei	Japan	68.2
Central African Republic	France	53.4
Mauritius	U.K.	64.9
Mexico	U.S.	53.5
Somalia	Saudi Arabia	69.9

Source: *1982 Yearbook of International Trade Statistics,* Vol. I (New York: U.N. Department of International Economic and Social Affairs, 1984).

More profitability. A producer might be able to sell the same product at a greater profit abroad than at home. This may come about because of a different foreign than domestic competitive environment. One such reason is that the product may be in a different stage of its life cycle abroad. Thus a mature stage at home may force domestic price cutting, whereas a growth stage abroad may make price reductions unnecessary there. It may also come about because of different government actions at home or abroad that affect profitability—for example, differences in the taxation of earnings or differences in regulations on prices.

Risk spreading. By spreading sales in more than one country market, a producer might be able to minimize fluctuations in demand. This may come about because of differences on a country-to-country basis in the timing of business cycles and because the life cycle of products might be in different stages in different countries. Another factor in the spreading of risks through exportation is that a producer might be able to develop more customers, thereby reducing vulnerability to the loss of any single or a few customers.

Import Opportunities

The impetus for getting involved in trade may come either from the exporter or from the importer. In either case it is necessary that there be both a seller and a buyer. Impetus may come from an importer because a firm is seeking out cheaper supplies, components, or products to be used in its home market. We discussed earlier why some countries can produce certain products more cheaply than others. Or a firm may be actively seeking new products that have been innovated abroad in order to complement its existing lines. This will give the company more to sell. It might also enable the importer to use excess capacity in its own distribution sales force.

An importer, like an exporter, might be able to spread its operating risks. In importing it is because of developing alternative suppliers, thereby making the firm less vulnerable to the dictates or problems of any single supplier. In the 1960s, for example, many large steel customers in the United States, such as the automobile industry, diversified their steel purchases to include European and Japanese suppliers. This reduced the risk of supply shortages in case of a strike among steel workers in the United States.

Trade Impediments

- Do not know of opportunities
- Do not know trade mechanics
- Fear that too risky
- Trade restrictions may prevent

Although there are often advantages for firms in commencing importation or exportation, many factors may impede firms' entry into trading relations. These in turn affect the full materialization of trade among countries. To begin with, there may be imperfect knowledge of markets in foreign countries so that a producer does not take advantage of the avenues open to it. Most of us are more aware of nearby situations than of far off ones. Or a producer might be aware of potential demand in foreign countries but nevertheless not know the mechanics of exporting and distributing in foreign markets. The process of exporting, after all, involves a whole new set of terminology and institutions. A company might also perceive that exporting or importing is too risky. A potential exporter may fear, for example, that payment will not be forthcoming, that payment will be in a currency that cannot easily be used, or that the competitive environment abroad is too unknown or disorderly. A potential importer may fear that supplies are too uncertain given the greater distance between countries and the problems of strikes and unrest abroad.

Government policies might either enhance or retard the movement of trade. Policies to remove imperfect knowledge about the foreign environment might positively increase trade. Direct restrictions on the importation or exportation of goods are detriments. It is safe to say, though, that all governments in the world have policies that both enhance and retard trade. In the Sri Lankan case at the beginning of the chapter, the Sri Lankan government sought to remove some marketing imperfections by helping to identify industries of likely international competitiveness. At the same time, however, Sri Lanka set direct import restrictions on a number of products.

SUMMARY

- Trade theory is useful to business because it helps to explain what might be produced competitively in a given locale, where one might go to produce a given product efficiently, and whether government practices will interfere with the free flow of trade among countries.
- Some trade theories deal with the question of what will happen to international trade in the absence of governmental interference; others

prescribe how government should interfere with trade flows in order to achieve certain national objectives.

- Mercantilist theory premised that a country should try to have a favorable balance of trade (export more than it imports) in order to receive an influx of gold. Neomercantilist theory also seeks a favorable balance of trade; however, the purpose is to achieve some social or political objective.

- Adam Smith developed the theory of absolute advantage, which holds that consumers will be better off if they can buy foreign-made products that are priced more cheaply than domestic ones.

- According to the absolute advantage theory, a country may produce goods more efficiently because of a natural advantage (e.g., raw materials, climate) or because of an acquired advantage (e.g., technology or skills).

- The theory of country size holds that because countries with large land areas are more apt to have varied climates and natural resources, they are generally more nearly self-sufficient than smaller countries. A second reason for their greater self-sufficiency is that their population centers are more likely to be located at a greater distance from other countries, thus raising the transport costs of foreign trade.

- The comparative advantage theory holds that total output can be increased through foreign trade even though one country may have an absolute advantage in the production of all products.

- Some of the assumptions of the absolute and comparative trade theories that have been questioned by policymakers are that full employment exists, that output efficiency is the major objective, that there are no transport costs among countries, that resources move freely within countries, and that resources are immobile internationally.

- The factor proportions theory holds that the relative factor endowments in a country of land, labor, and capital will determine the relative costs of these factors. These costs in turn will determine what goods a country can produce most efficiently.

- The analysis of the factor proportions theory is complicated when different production methods can be used to make the same product and when there are country-to-country differences in the education and skill of work forces.

- The product life cycle theory states that many manufactured products will first be produced in the countries whose research has developed the new product. This is almost always an industrialized country, with the United States accounting for the largest share in recent years. Over the life of the product, however, the production will tend to become more capital intensive and be shifted to foreign locations.

- According to the country similarity theory of trade, most trade today takes place in manufactured goods among industrial countries because there are more similar market segments among these countries.

- LDCs have increasingly been concerned that they are too vulnerable to events in other countries because of their high dependence on one export product and/or one trading partner. As they try to be more independent of the external environment, however, they face the risk that their own consumers may have to pay higher prices or do without some goods.

- Although most trade theories deal with country-to-country benefits and costs, it is usually at the firm level that trading decisions are made. Companies may perceive trading advantages because of using excess capacity, lowering production costs, and spreading risks. They may not commence foreign trading activities, however, because of not knowing about opportunities or how to take advantage of them or because they perceive foreign operations to be too risky.

C A S E　　**THE CASHEW**[19]

The cashew tree is best known today for its nuts, which account for about 20 percent of the value of world nut production—about equal to almonds or hazelnuts.

The fruit of the tree (known as the cashew apple), however, drew earlier attention. The cashew apple was harvested in the wild by the Tupi Indians of Brazil, who introduced it to early Portuguese traders. These traders in turn propagated the plant in other tropical countries, but attempts to grow the tree on plantations were not successful because of the cashew's vulnerability to insects when many cashew trees grow close together. What did happen, though, was that the tree became wild and thrived among other trees in the forests of India, East Africa, Indonesia, and Southeast Asia.

Consumption of the cashew apple precludes using the cashew nut. This is because the fruit matures before the nut, and so the fruit is spoiled by the time the nut can be usefully harvested. A second factor that inhibited the early use of the nut is that its processing is tedious and long. In about the 1920s, though, an industry developed in India to process the nuts. The nuts became more valuable than the fruit because of growing popularity among Indian consumers. India maintained a virtual monopoly on cashew processing until the mid-1970s. This monopoly was due to a combination of three factors. First, India was the largest producer of wild cashews; no other country could challenge India in volume of output. Second, early demand was in India; thus any other country would have to incur added transport charges in order to reach the Indian market. The third and probably the most important long-range factor was the process technology, at which Indian workers were particularly adept.

This cashew nut processing was performed in a very labor-intensive manner, requiring manual dexterity and low labor rates. The nut is contained beneath a layer of shell and also a layer of thin skin. To remove the shell, the nut must be placed in an open fire for a few minutes and then tapped while still hot with a wooden hammer. If the nut is broken in the tapping, its value decreases considerably. Once the shell is removed, the nut is placed in an oven for up to ten hours, after which the skin is removed by hand while the nut is still warm. The removal is without the use of fingernails or any sharp objects that can mark or break the surface. The nuts are then sorted and graded into twenty-four different categories by the size of the pieces. The highest-quality grade typically sells for about four times the price of the lowest grade, which is sold almost entirely to the confectionery industry.

Several factors through the years began to threaten India's position. One of the earliest was a shortage of Indian-grown raw nuts as demand grew in such countries as the United States and the United Kingdom. Since the nuts were grown in the wild and not suited to plantation growth, India had to look abroad for supplies. They found them in East Africa (e.g., Mozambique, Tanzania, Kenya). Since there was high unemployment and underemployment in those countries, they were at first eager to sell the raw nuts, which were gathered from the ground after the fruit had fallen from the trees. By that time, India was no longer the world's major consumer; consequently, the East African countries began to realize in the post–World War II period that they might be able to bypass India by processing the raw nuts themselves. The cashew-processing methods were well known, so there was no obstacle such as might exist in attempting to duplicate a more mechanized production method. There was another obstacle, however, that prevented early competition from East Africa. The Indian workers had worked on homemade handicrafts when they were very young. By the time they were employed in cashew processing, they could perform the delicate hand operations efficiently. Without the childhood training, it is very difficult to develop an adult adeptness. This lack of childhood training proved fatal to the African hand cashew-processing industry because workers broke too many nuts and were too slow to make the output profitable.

Although the failure gave the Indian industry a reprieve, it put them on notice that they were vulnerable to cutoffs of supply. The Indian Council for Agricultural Research, the International Society for Horticultural Sciences, and the Indian Society for Plantation Crops expanded their efforts to increase India's raw nut production. Concomitantly, three different companies developed mechanical equipment to replace hand processing. The

Sturtevant Tropical Products Institute developed a method now used by a London equipment manufacturer, Fletcher and Stewart, which cracks the shells with a steel plate. Oltremare Industria of Italy and Widmer and Ernst of Switzerland developed machines to cut the shells. Equipment was sold to East African countries and to Brazil in the 1970s. These countries decreased their raw nut exports to India in order to maintain supplies for their own processing.

Fortunately for India, two factors have kept its hand-processing industry afloat. First, the new machinery breaks many nuts, so Indian processors still have little competition in the sale of higher-grade cashew nuts. At any time, however, newer machinery might solve the breakage problem, again threatening the approximately 200 Indian processors and their 300,000 employees. Furthermore, there is increased competition for the lower-grade output, a point that will be discussed later. The second factor that has kept the Indian industry alive is that their processors have been able to obtain more raw nuts from domestic sources. From 1965 to 1974, Indian raw nut production increased by nearly 60 percent. Pesticide technology now makes cashew tree plantations feasible, thus increasing the number of trees per acre. Furthermore, Indian experimentation in hybridization, vegetative propagation, and grafting and budding techniques promises to increase the output per tree to five times what it was in the wild.

By the 1980s, Indian processors felt vulnerable to two more situations. Since India could no longer compete as well in its traditional North American and European markets for lower-grade nuts, a larger portion of those nuts was sold in the Soviet Union. By 1978, the Soviet Union was India's largest cashew nut customer in terms of tonnage. The Soviet Union bought the nuts at a price above world market levels, and its buying habits were believed to be for political purposes. By buying large quantities at a high price, the Soviet Union might have considerable political influence in India, especially in the Kerala area where the processing industry is centered. At any time these sales might decline drastically for political reasons.

The second potential problem facing the Indian industry in the 1980s has been the potential excess cashew nut supply, which can result from plantation techniques and improved technology in India and elsewhere. To find outlets for a possible nut glut, the All-India Coordinated Spices and Cashew Nut Improvement Project has been centering its efforts on finding new markets for products from the cashew tree. The cashew apple, for example, is available in far greater tonnage than the cashew nut. It has been discarded in the past because one could get either fruit or nut but not both, and the nuts have been more valuable. Work is being carried out to try to get both the fruit and the nut. The fruit is also being studied for commercial use in candy, jams, chutney, juice, carbonated beverages, syrup, wine, and vinegar. A second area of research is in the use of cashew nut shell liquid (CNSL), which was once discarded as a waste product. It is now used extensively in the production of friction dusts for formulation in brake linings and clutch facings. It has also been used in the formulation of particle board and in tanning processes. Thus far, however, the extraction of CNSL has been too costly to make it fully competitive with some other types of oils.

QUESTIONS

1. What trade theories help to explain where cashew tree products have historically been produced?
2. Might India lose its competitive advantage in future cashew nut production? Why or why not?
3. If you were an Indian processor, what alternatives might you consider to maintain future competitiveness?

NOTES

1. Data for this case were taken from *1983 Commodity Yearbook* (Jersey City, N.J.: Commodity Research Bureau, Inc. 1983), p. 340; "The Business Outlook: Sri Lanka," *Business Asia,* February 6, 1981, p. 48; "Sri Lanka Investment: inside or outside the Free Trade Zone?" *Business Asia,* April 24, 1981, pp. 134–135; P. Murugasu, "Selecting Products for Export Development," *International Trade Forum,* October–December 1979, pp. 4–7; International Monetary Fund, *Direction of Trade Statistics Yearbook 1982* (Washington, D.C.: IMF, 1982), p. 345; "United States Congress Speaks on Sri Lanka," bulletin issued by the Embassy of the Democratic Socialist Republic of Sri Lanka, Washington, April 1979; Lucien Rajakarunanayake, "Sri Lanka: Patterns of Serendipity" (Washington, D.C.: Embassy of Sri Lanka, May 1975); Colin de Silva, "Sri Lanka, the 'Resplendent Isle,' " *New York Times,* February 14, 1984, Sec. xx, p. 9.

2. The mercantilist period is not associated with any single writer. A good coverage of the philosophy of the era may be found in Eli Heckscher, *Mercantilism* (London: George Allen & Unwin, 1935).

3. The book has been reprinted by various publishers. For the specific references of this chapter the edition used was Adam Smith, *The Wealth of Nations* (New York: The Modern Library, n.d.).

4. Stephen P. Magee, *International Trade* (Reading, Mass.: Addison-Wesley Publishing Company, 1980), pp. 10–12.

5. G. C. Hufbauer, "The Impact of National Characteristics and Technology on the Commodity Composition of Trade in Manufactured Goods," in *The Technology Factor in International Trade,* Raymond Vernon, ed. (New York: Columbia University Press, 1970), pp. 145–231.

6. David Ricardo, *On the Principles of Political Economy and Taxation,* originally published in London in 1817 but since reprinted by a number of different publishers.

7. Bertil Ohlin, *Interregional and International Trade* (Cambridge, Mass.: Harvard University Press, 1933).

8. W. W. Leontief, "Domestic Production and Foreign Trade: The American Capital Position Re-examined," *Economia Internationale,* February 1954, pp. 3–32.

9. See, for example, Donald Keesing, "Labor Skills and International Trade: Evaluating Many Trade Flows with a Single Measuring Device," *Review of Economics and Statistics,* Vol. 47, 1965, pp. 287–294; H. Katrak, "Human Skills, R & D and Scale Economies in the Exports of the United Kingdom and the United States," *Oxford Economic Papers,* Vol. 25, 1973, pp. 337–360.

10. Raymond Vernon, "International Investment and International Trade in the Product Life Cycle," *Quarterly Journal of Economics,* May 1966, pp. 190–207; José de la Torre, "Product Life Cycle as a Determinant of Global Marketing Strategies," *Atlanta Economic Review,* September–October 1975, pp. 9–14.

11. See, for example, Paul Streeten, "Technology Gaps between Rich and Poor Countries," *Scottish Journal of Political Economy,* November 1972, Vol. xix, No. 3, pp. 213–230, and Theresa Tellez, "Science, Technology and the Matter of Choice," *Science and Public Affairs,* October 1973, p. 55 for LDC estimates. Estimates of the U.S. portion are from National Science Foundation studies reported in Victor K. McElheny, "U.S. Science Lead Is Found Eroding," *New York Times,* March 14, 1976, p. 1. For more recent country-by-country comparisons of R&D expenditures, see Barnaby J. Feder, "Europe's Technology Revival," *New York Times,* May 21, 1984, p. D1+.

12. Daniel J. B. Mitchell, "Recent Changes in the Labor Content of U.S. International Trade," *International Labor Relations Review,* April 1975, pp. 355–375.

13. For good summaries of the studies to test the theory as well as recent tests, see James M. Lutz and Robert T. Green, "The Product Life Cycle and the Export Position of the United States," *Journal of International Business Studies,* Winter 1983, pp. 77–93; Alicia Mullor-Sebastian, "The Product Life Cycle Theory: Empirical Evidence," *Journal of International Business Studies,* Winter 1983, pp. 95–105.

14. Ian H. Giddy, "The Demise of the Product Life Cycle in International Business Theory," *Columbia Journal of World Business,* Spring 1978, pp. 90–97.

15. Stefan B. Linder, *An Essay on Trade Transformation* (New York: Wiley Publishing, 1961).

16. Michael J. Thomas, "The Location of Research and Development in the International Corporation," *Management International Review,* No. 1, 1975, p. 39.

17. Kenneth Mac Leish, "Stone Age Cavemen of Mindanao," *National Geographic,* August 1972, pp. 219–249.

18. See, for example, Boston Consulting Group, *Perspective in Experience* (Boston: Boston Consulting Group, 1970); Robert D. Buzzell, Bradley T. Buzzell, Gale Sultaw, and Ralph G. M. Sultaw, "Market Share: A Key to Profitability," *Harvard Business Review,* Vol. 58, No. 1, 1975.

19. Data for this case were taken from "L'Anacarde ou Noix de Cajou," *Marches Tropicaux,* 13 juin 1980, pp. 1403–1405; R. J. Wilson, *The Market for Cashew Nut*

Kernels and Cashew Nutshell Liquid (London: Tropical Products Institute, 1975); J. H. P. Tyman, "Cultivation, Processing and Utilization of the Cashew," *Chemistry and Industry,* January 19, 1980, pp. 59–62; Jean-Pierre Jeannet, "Indian Cashew Processors, Ltd.," ICH Case 9-378-832 (Boston, Harvard Business School, 1977); Jean-Pierre Jeannet, "Note on the World Cashew Nut Industry," ICH Case 9-378-834 (Boston, Harvard Business School, 1977).

5

Governmental Influence on Trade

- To evaluate the rationale for governmental policies to enhance and/or restrict trade.
- To illustrate how pressure group problems and trade-offs among groups make it difficult to devise trade policies that will benefit a country's population as a whole.
- To compare the protectionist arguments used in developed versus developing countries.
- To examine the potential and actual effects of governmental intervention on the free flow of trade.
- To give an overview of the major means by which trade is restricted.
- To highlight the fact that governmental trade policies create uncertainties in the conduct of business.

AUTOMOBILE IMPORTS[1]

1985 ended a three-year agreement that had limited Japanese automobile exports to the United States to 1.68 million units per year. The year before this, 1984, was an election year. Politicians were therefore more eager than usual to please constituents who considered the automobile import question a sufficiently major issue to swing their votes one way or another. Unfortunately for the politicians there was no clear-cut consensus among potential voters on what should be done. In fact, different groups were in diametric opposition, some wanting much more stringent restrictions and others wanting no restrictions at all. The U.S. Special Trade Representative vowed to end the import restrictions. The president of the United Auto Workers (UAW) responded that it would "punish the workers for the greed of their bosses." How did this situation develop?

During the first six months of 1980, foreign automobile companies shipped 1.2 million passenger cars to the United States, an increase of 21 percent over the comparable 1979 period. The foreign share of the new car market increased from 17 percent to 25.3 percent during the period. Clearly, the U.S. automobile firms and their workers were in trouble. A beleaguered American Motors sold out to Renault, a French automaker, in an attempt to maintain operations. Chrysler was forced to sell most of its foreign subsidiaries, primarily to Peugeot, to raise working capital and then announced the largest losses ever registered by a company. Chrysler's loss record was eclipsed within a week as Ford reported its losses. General Motors' working capital was drastically reduced, and that firm had to become a heavy borrower for the first time in five years. By the end of 1980, 193,000 out of 750,000 members of the UAW were unemployed.

Pressures mounted both to restrict imports and to shore up the ailing U.S. companies. There was considerable disagreement, however, on the exact cause of the automobile import problem and on what would be the best course of action to alter the competitive situation. That managers of the U.S. automobile firms and officials of the UAW were speaking out in favor of restricting imports was itself a milestone. It was important because the automobile industry and its union had long been supporters of free-trade, having publicly opposed import restrictions on such products as steel in the past.

Although imports were rising at the same time that sales by U.S. firms were decreasing, factors other than imports were contributing to the problems of the U.S. automobile industry. U.S. consumers have historically preferred the large cars with rear-wheel drive that Detroit produced for them. Although there was a jump in small-car sales after the 1973 oil embargo, Americans largely maintained their demand for larger cars. The U.S. auto firms thus felt that they could prolong the life of present facilities rather than writing them off quickly and going through the very costly process of building new plants or converting old ones before their useful lives ran out. The rapid increase in gasoline prices during 1979 and 1980 was unexpected and led to a rapid switch in demand among those decreasing numbers of consumers who were demanding cars at all. A general recession and unprecedented high interest rates reduced car sales drastically.

The U.S. automakers were not holding their own in sales of the small cars that they had been producing for several years. Japanese producers who were the primary exporters to the U.S. were evidently just as surprised as Detroit about the sudden shift in demand; they lacked capacity to fill U.S. orders quickly. Yet many buyers were willing to wait six months for delivery of a Honda rather than purchase a U.S. manufactured model. Why Americans preferred the Japanese automobiles was debatable. One argument was that price differences created by labor cost differences were the cause. The Bureau of Labor Statistics estimated that average Japanese auto workers' wages and benefits in the first half of 1979 were only half those of U.S. auto workers. People who accepted the cost differential argument largely favored the taxing of imports in order to raise their prices. Yet on the basis of canvassing 10,000 U.S. households, the Motor and Equipment Manufacturers Association found that imports strongly outranked U.S. small cars in perceived fuel economy, engineering, and durability. People who accepted these results felt that imports should not be limited.

The arguments for protecting or aiding the U.S. auto industry were based on two premises: (1) that the costs of unemployment are higher than the increased costs to consumers of limiting imports and (2) that U.S. production can become fully competitive with imports if it is helped to get over its temporary problems. The first premise is based on such factors as personal hardships for persons displaced in the labor market; lost purchasing power, which adversely affects demand in other industries; and the high taxes needed to support unemployment insurance and food stamps. A *New York Times* poll showed that 71 percent of Americans felt that it was more important to protect jobs than to get cheaper foreign products. The second premise is based on such factors as the historical competitive capability of the U.S. producers, the possibility of scale economies of U.S. production, and the much higher productivity possible with new plants. For example, Ford estimated that conversion of its Dearborn engine plant would cost $650 million but would enable the plant to produce 250 engines per hour instead of the present 200.

Those against protection thought that the present problems were due to errors in management decisions. Thus the firms should not be rewarded by having consumers or taxpayers pay for seeing the companies through the crisis. Any assistance, even short-term, they felt, would result in at least one of the following: higher taxes because of subsidies to companies, such as the loan assistance given to Chrysler in 1980; higher prices for foreign cars (which are the preferred type), or the necessity of buying domestic cars (which are perceived as inferior). Another antiprotection group felt that government assistance in limiting imports would result in foreign retaliation, which would adversely affect other U.S. industries that were currently more competitive with foreign production. Japan, for example, might stop buying as many U.S.-made aircraft or U.S.-grown soybeans if the United States restricted Japanese auto imports.

The United Auto Workers union was clearly more interested in maintaining jobs than in protecting the U.S. auto firms. UAW representatives were instrumental in helping to convince Volkswagen and Honda to set up U.S. assembly operations. The UAW wanted much more, though; it pushed for having 75 percent of Volkswagen and Honda parts made in the United States. This push for local content ran counter to some of the policies being pursued by the U.S. auto firms that were trying to produce "global" cars in order to gain maximum economies of scale and buying specific parts that could be produced more cheaply in certain countries, such as die-cast aluminum parts in Italy. The Ford Escort, for example, which is assembled in the United States, Britain, and West Germany, contains parts from nine countries. The UAW sought public support through newspaper and radio advertisements and managed to get several states to buy U.S.-made vehicles, as the union urged (unless the purchases were "inconsistent with the public interest"). The people who opposed protection, mainly consumers, were generally unorganized; thus there was no major promotion effort to counter the UAW. The result was a negotiation with Japan in 1981 to limit its automobile exports to the U.S. to 1.68 million per year for the next three years. Japanese politicians and automakers reasoned that if they did not "voluntarily" go along with this quota, compulsory limits might be even more restrictive.

What was the outcome of the three-year experiment? The U.S. auto industry recovered and by 1984 was announcing record profits. The turnaround was partially due to recovery from the recession, which lifted auto sales. But the restrictions were also a factor. General Motors (GM), for example, was able to invest heavily in some almost fully automated plants using robots to assemble car bodies. By 1984, GM pushed for elimination of import quotas, saying that it could now compete. Critics of GM argued that the company merely wished to bring in more Japanese autos from its affiliate, Isuzu.

Another factor in the industry's recovery was an increased U.S. demand for more expensive and more profitable cars. Some people claimed that this was a natural phenomenon of the market. Others alleged that it was an outgrowth of the import restrictions, which gave U.S. consumers little choice except to buy more expensive cars. Because Japanese producers were not able to increase U.S. profits by selling more cars, they did so instead by selling more luxurious models and raising prices. During the three years of the original export restraints, the average Japanese import increased by $2600; and a Wharton Econometrics study attributed $1000 of this to import restraints. In the meantime, U.S.-made cars' prices increased by 40 percent. These price increases made both U.S. and Japanese producers more profitable. In 1984, GM gave a $1.5 million bonus and Ford a $1.4 million bonus to their chairmen because of their firms' record earnings.

Except for General Motors, U.S. producers in 1984 wanted a continuation of the quotas. The Japanese were willing to continue their restraint on sales but pushed for an increased allocation to 1.9 million units per year. In the meantime the UAW was concerned that the automobile import restrictions affected only Japan. Ford had announced that it would spend $500 million to produce 130,000 Mazda cars per year in Mexico for sale in the United States. (Ford owns 25 percent of Toyo Kogyo, which makes Mazdas.) The House of Representatives voted to require that cars sold in the United States have up to 90 percent U.S. content, but the bill did not pass the Senate.

INTRODUCTION

- All countries seek to influence trade
  - economic, social, political objectives
  - often conflicts among objectives
  - people (groups) with more at stake form strongest pressure groups

The preceding case shows why and how automobile imports were limited into the United States. This is not atypical. No country in the world permits goods and services to flow across its borders unregulated. Restrictions are commonly placed on imports and occasionally on exports. Direct or indirect subsidies are frequently given to industries to enable them to compete with foreign production either at home or abroad. In general, government influence is exerted in an attempt to satisfy economic, social, or political objectives. The objective of increasing automobile workers' employment is such an example. Often there are conflicts among objectives (e.g., increased employment versus lower consumer prices of automobiles) as well as considerable disagreement as to the potential effects of trade policies (e.g., employment increases for auto workers versus possible decreases for aircraft workers). It is not surprising, then, that any proposal for changes in trade regulations results in heated debates among individuals and interest groups who believe they will be affected. However, the interest groups that are most directly affected are apt to speak most loudly. People who depend on U.S. automobile production (workers, owners, suppliers, and local politicians) perceive losses from import competition to be very great. Workers see themselves as having to take new jobs in new industries, perhaps in new locales. There may be prolonged periods of unemployment, reduced incomes, and insecure work and social surroundings. These people are liable to become a very strong pressure group. Workers in an industry that is indirectly affected by retaliation, such as aircraft, do not perceive the same threat and are less vocal. Also, all consumers must now pay the higher prices of domestically made cars. In the aggregate these costs are great, but they are so diffused throughout society that consumers are not likely to join together to protest import limitations very strongly.

THE RATIONALE FOR GOVERNMENT INTERVENTION

Unemployment

- Unemployed form effective pressure group for import restrictions
- Import restrictions to create domestic employment
  - may lead to retaliation in other countries
  - is met by less retaliation if done by small country
  - loses jobs in importing
  - may decrease export jobs owing to price increases for components
  - may decrease export jobs owing to lower incomes abroad
- Costs of import restrictions
  - possibly include higher prices
  - possibly include higher taxes
  - should be compared with costs of unemployment
- Many countries assist workers to find new employment

Pressure groups are a reality with which governmental policymakers and businesspeople must deal. There is probably no more effective pressure group than the unemployed because no other group has quite the time and incentive to write letters to congressional representatives or walk around with pickets. As a former U.S. Special Trade Representative said, "To men wearing work shirts and drinking beer in a neighborhood bar in Gary, Indiana, their lost jobs, misery, and suffering are caused by imports."[2] Therefore it is not surprising that import restrictions are often placed on goods to create domestic jobs.

One of the problems of restricting imports to create jobs is that other countries might retaliate. The most often cited example was when the United States raised import restrictions to their highest level in history in 1930. In a matter of months, Canada, Mexico, France, Italy, and Spain countered with limitations of their own. In 1931, India, Peru, Argentina, Brazil, and China joined the parade. The United States lost rather than gained jobs as its exports diminished.[3] In recent years, new import restrictions by a major country such as the United States have almost always brought quick retaliation. When automobile imports from Japan were restricted, for example, Japanese pressure groups forced import restrictions on American orange juice.

Two things may mitigate the problems of retaliation. The first is that there may be less tendency to retaliate against a small country that places barriers on imports. Thus a small country may be able to increase employment more easily by imposing trade barriers. The second is that if redistribution because of retaliation decreases employment in a capital-intensive industry but increases it in a labor-intensive industry, employment objectives may be attained.

Even if there is no retaliation, the net number of jobs gained through producing domestically is bound to be less than the number of people who would be employed in the newly protected industry. That is because many people would otherwise be employed in handling the imports. In the case of the United States, for example, it is estimated that 194,000 jobs are directly related to the imported car industry. These include such workers as employees of importers, dealers, and distributors of foreign cars and workers in U.S. plants that make foreign car parts.[4]

Imports may also help create jobs in export industries. Take Caterpillar

Tractor, which is one of the largest exporters in the United States. It once bought its crankshafts exclusively in the United States but turned to German and Japanese suppliers in order to cut costs enough to be competitive in foreign markets.[5] A less direct way that imports stimulate exports is by increasing foreign income and foreign exchange earnings, which are then spent on new imports by the foreign country.

If import restrictions do result in a net increase in domestic employment, there will still be costs to some people in the domestic society. The potential costs to society (higher prices or higher taxes) of prohibiting free trade are most acute when the domestic product being protected is much more expensive or highly inferior in quality to the foreign product. A problem may be caused by producing goods for which the country lacks a comparative advantage or by lagging behind in technical and product development.

These costs of higher prices or higher taxes must be compared with the costs of unemployment if workers are displaced through free trade. It may be necessary to find some means by which individuals are compensated for their losses and by which they move to new employment. These are not easy tasks. To begin with, it is hard to put a price tag on anxieties created by having to be idle, change jobs, or move. Furthermore, it is difficult for people who are working to understand that they may be better off financially by having part of their taxes go to help support people whose positions were lost because of imports. In some cases it may be equally difficult to convince people to accept handouts in lieu of their old jobs.

Many countries give assistance to workers who are adversely affected by imports. In the United States, for example, workers are eligible for special federal trade adjustment benefits if four criteria are met:

1. imports of competitive products increase;
2. significant layoffs, threatened layoffs, or underemployment occurs;
3. a decline in a plant's sales or production occurs; and
4. increased imports contribute importantly to the plant's job losses.[6]

It is argued that little is done in the way of retraining and relocation. Assistance is received in the form of supplements to unemployment benefits, and workers spend the funds for living expenses in the hope that they will be recalled to old jobs.

Infant Industry Argument

• Production becomes more competitive over time
  • because of gaining economies of scale

One of the oldest arguments for protection from imports was presented as early as 1792 by Alexander Hamilton. The logic of the **infant industry argument** for protection is that initial output costs for an industry in a given country may be too high to be competitive in world markets, but

- because of efficiency of workers
- therefore protection needed in early stage but not in later stage
- Hard to choose the type of industry that can become competitive
    - if choice wrong, it may be hard to do away with restrictions
- Controversy over who should bear costs in industries' infancies
    - investors, taxpayers, consumers?

that over a period of time the costs will decrease sufficiently so that efficient production will be achieved. There are two reasons for this dynamic cost situation. First is the concept of economies of scale. Because of high fixed costs, a company may have to reach a certain level of output and sales to reduce total unit costs to the level of competition, assumed in this case to be foreign competition. The second is the learning curve concept, based on the premise that initial production may be costly because of the inexperience of workers and managers, but that as they gain experience in formal or on-the-job training, their output will grow so that unit costs of production decrease. Proponents of the infant industry argument hold that the domestic infant industry should be guaranteed a large share of the domestic market so that adulthood is ultimately reached.

While both reasons for expecting cost decreases over a period of time are well founded, there are some problems in institutionalizing the concept efficiently. The first is identification of industries having a high probability of reaching adulthood—no easy task, since a host of variables may affect future cost structures. One can certainly find examples of industries, such as automobile production in Brazil and Japan, that grew to be competitive because of government protection. In many other cases, however—for example, automobile production in Argentina and Australia—the industries are not yet out of diapers even after many years of operation. If infant industry protection is given to an industry that does not reach competitiveness, chances are that the owners, workers, and suppliers will constitute a formidable pressure group that may effectively prevent the import of a cheaper competitive product.

Even if policymakers are adept at ascertaining which industries may effectively reach adulthood, this does not necessarily mean that governmental assistance should be given. There are, of course, many examples of entrepreneurs who endure early losses in order to gain future benefits, and one may argue that assistance should be given only if entry barriers to new firms are very high. Someone in the economy must absorb the higher cost of local production during infancy. Most likely it will be the consumer who pays higher prices; however, a government may subsidize the industry so that consumer prices are not increased, in which case the taxpayer absorbs the burden. For the infant industry argument to be fully viable, future benefits should exceed early costs.

The automobile import case at the beginning of this chapter raises interesting questions about the infant industry argument. We have all heard of second childhoods, but is the automobile industry in the United States in its second infancy? Can this U.S. industry overcome some of its present disadvantages? Or has the absolute or comparative advantage shifted to other countries, thus precluding U.S. ability to compete effectively in the future? If efficiency can be reached, who should incur the short-term costs: investors, taxpayers, or consumers?

Industrialization Objectives

- Protection to promote industrial production because
  - faster demand growth than agriculture
  - brings in investment funds
  - diversifies economy
  - more price increase than primary products
- Not necessarily expect eventual competitiveness

In recent years, many countries have sought to increase their domestic industralization because they feel that

1. this will increase output more than an emphasis on agriculture,
2. inflows of foreign investment in the industrial area will promote growth,
3. diversification away from traditional agricultural products or raw materials is necessary to stabilize trade fluctuations, and
4. the prices of manufactured goods tend to rise more rapidly than the prices of primary products.

Before the 1930s, protectionist arguments of economic development (except for the infant industry argument, which was considered a minor deviation) were largely outside the central economic discussions dominated by the classical school of free trade. Since the world Depression, arguments for governmental intervention in the economy, including protection from imports, have received more widespread acceptance. A major thrust has emanated from the observations that industrial countries are better off economically than nonindustrial countries and that, since the original Industrial Revolution in England, a number of countries have developed an industrial base while largely preventing competition from foreign-based production. This, for example, was the experience of the United States, Japan, and the Soviet Union. As in the infant industry argument, the premise here is that cheaper products from abroad would prevent the establishment of domestic industry if free market conditions were allowed to prevail. The industrialization argument differs from the infant industry argument in that proponents argue that objectives will be achieved even though domestic prices do not become competitive on the world market.

- Shift from agriculture to industry
  - marginal productivity of agricultural workers very low
  - may increase demands on social and political services in cities
  - may overlook development possibilities in agricultural sector

Marginal agricultural returns.   When deciding whether to import a product or produce it locally, most observers use comparative cost as a basis of determination. It has been noted that the real test of comparative advantage should be the marginal rate of substitution within a country, that is, the amount of output gained for one product compared with the amount of output sacrificed by another as resources are shifted. Applying this concept to developing economies, it has been noted that there are frequently surpluses of population engaged in agriculture. This is particularly true in economies such as India or Egypt, which have little additional arable land available. In other words, large numbers of people may leave the agricultural sector with little or no effect on the country's agricultural output. If these surplus workers can be employed in the manufacturing sector, their output is likely to contribute a net gain to the economy because so little agricultural production is sacrificed in the process. If the money cost of the domestically produced manufactured product is higher than an imported one, it will be necessary to restrict sales of the imported product to ensure survival of the domestic output. This should result in either higher prices or higher taxes; nevertheless, real output should rise in the economy.

There are some dangers in attempting to shift people out of agriculture. One of these is that individuals' expectations may be raised and then not fulfilled, thus leading to excessive demands on social and political services. Indeed, one of the major problems facing poor countries today is the massive migration to urban areas of people who cannot be easily absorbed. There is no work for them either because the industrialization process has proceeded too slowly or because the migrants lack the rudimentary skills and work habits necessary for manufacturing employment.[7] A second problem is that agriculture may in fact be a better means of effecting additional output than industry. Not all poor countries are utilizing their lands fully. Nor is industrial development the only means of economic growth. Such countries as the United States, Canada, and Argentina grew rapidly during the nineteenth century, in large part through agricultural exports, and they continue to profit from such exports. Australia, New Zealand, and Denmark maintain high incomes along with substantial agricultural specialization. A third problem is that if protection is to be given to manufacturing enterprises, one must decide on which type so that the marginal substitution from agriculture is high and the disadvantage compared to foreign production is low. A fourth problem is that too much of a rural-to-urban shift may reduce agricultural output in developing countries, thus making it even more difficult for them to feed themselves. It is interesting to note that most of the world's agricultural production and exports come from the so-called industrial countries.

- If import restrictions keep out foreign manufacturers, foreign firms may invest to produce in restricted area
- Prices of primary products fluctuate substantially
- Dependence on one or a few manufactured products does not limit risk of market loss

Promoting investment inflows. In Chapter 6 we will show that import restrictions are a major impetus for direct investment movements, particularly those regulating the purchase of foreign-produced manufactured products. The influx of foreign firms may hasten the move from agriculture to industry as well as contribute to growth by adding to the stock of capital and technology per worker employed. It may also add to employment, an especially attractive benefit from the standpoint of most policymakers.

Diversification. According to a U.N. study of twenty-five primary products imported in world trade, annual average price fluctuations around the long-term trend were about 14 percent during the first half of this century.[8] Whether due to such uncontrollables as weather affecting supply or business cycles abroad affecting demand, fluctuations can wreak havoc on economies that are dependent on the export of primary products. This is particularly true when an economy depends very heavily on one commodity for employment of its population and for its export earnings. Recall from the preceding chapter that a large number of developing countries depend heavily on just one primary commodity. The resultant instability in earnings means that a country may be able to afford foreign luxuries one year but may be unable to afford replacement parts for essential equipment the next.

A greater dependence on manufacturing is no guarantee of stable export earnings. The gross national product of most LDCs is small; consequently, a change may simply shift dependence to one or two manufactured products from one or two agricultural ones. The basic risk of having all economic eggs in one basket has not been removed.

• Quantity of primary products will buy smaller quantity of manufactured products over a period of time because
  • quantity demanded of primary products grows more slowly
  • production cost savings in primary products more apt to be passed on to consumers
• Evidence not conclusive

Terms of trade. The **terms of trade** refer to the quantity of imports that a given quantity of a country's exports can buy. A number of spokespeople for LDCs have argued that the prices of raw materials and agricultural commodities have not risen as fast as the prices of finished products. During the 1870–1914 period, largely because of rapidly improved world transportation systems, tropical exports grew at almost exactly the same rate as industrial production in the advanced countries. However, they have not kept pace since.[9] The result is that over a period of time it will take more primary products to buy the same amount of manufactured goods. Further, the demand for primary products does not rise as rapidly, so LDCs become increasingly poorer in relation to developed countries. This supposedly warrants protection of emerging manufacturing enterprises that replace traditional products.

The declining terms of trade for LDCs have been explained in part by lagging demand for agricultural products and by changes in technology that have saved on raw material utilization. A further explanation sometimes offered is that, because of competitive conditions, savings due to technical changes that lower production costs of primary products are largely passed on to consumers, whereas cost savings in manufactured products go to higher profits and wages. Although the logic is sound, the evidence is inconclusive because of problems in quality changes of manufactured products, gaps in data, and other possible causes for LDC export problems.[10] The lack of export and import development by LDCs is primarily a function of their lag in growth, and economic growth is a complex matter, involving the interplay of many variables.

• Controversy over whether industrialization should emphasize
  • products to sell domestically that were formerly imported or
  • products that can be sold competitively in world markets

Import substitution versus export promotion. Import barriers in the industrialization process are usually instituted so that a country may produce goods locally that were formerly imported. There are substantial examples of substituting locally manufactured products that have led in turn to a declining dependence on imports as a share of GNP.[11] This process would seemingly save foreign exchange. However, it has been argued that since capital equipment must usually be imported, foreign exchange savings are

● Import substitution products may become eventual exports

minimal. Furthermore, even if import substitution efforts are successful in saving foreign exchange, they may nevertheless allocate resources inefficiently. For these reasons it is sometimes argued that countries should concentrate their industrialization efforts on industries for which export markets should logically exist. For instance, they could perform further processing of raw materials that they are now exporting.[12]

In reality, it is not so easy to distinguish between the two types of industrialization, nor is it always possible to develop exports. Industrialization for export promotion is sometimes an outgrowth of substitution, which is feasible at a later date. The fact that a country concentrates its industrialization activities on products for which it would seem to have a comparative cost advantage is no guarantee that exports can be generated. There are a variety of trade barriers, to be discussed later in this chapter, that are particularly problematic to the development of manufacturing exports from nonindustrialized countries.

Relationships with Other Countries

● Trade restrictions are more selective means
  ● may have more effect on certain industries but
  ● can choose to restrict least essential
  ● must consider retaliation

Balance of payments adjustments. In Chapter 9 we will examine in detail the fact that in order to correct balance-of-payments problems a country may change the value of its currency relative to others, adjust the rate of domestic price change, or influence individual accounts in the balance of payments. Since the trade account is a major component within the balance of payments for most countries, there are numerous attempts by governments to modify what would have been an import or export movement in a free market situation.

Trade influence differs from the other two means of adjustment primarily because of greater selectivity. This may be either an advantage or a disadvantage compared to the other adjustment mechanisms. If a country is running a deficit, for example, either a devaluation or a domestic deflation can make domestically produced goods and services less expensive than foreign ones. This has a widespread effect on both imports and exports as well as on such service accounts as tourism. Because of the breadth of industries affected, fairly small changes relative to other countries' prices may have a substantial effect on payments balances. Furthermore, this minimizes the burden of adjustment on any single industry. Direct trade influence may, however, allow a country to choose the types of products or services to be affected. For example, the importation of luxury items may be curtailed, whereas no change is made in rules or prices governing imports of needed foodstuffs. One of the problems plaguing the effectiveness of any type of attempt to solve payments imbalances is the effort by other countries to counteract the attempt. Evidence is not at all clear as to which adjustment method will provoke the most or least retaliation abroad.

- Export restrictions may keep world prices up in monopoly situation
  - may lead to substitution
  - high cost to prevent smuggling
- Export restrictions may keep domestic prices down by increasing domestic supply
  - may give producers less incentive to increase output
  - may shift foreign production and sales
- Import restrictions may
  - prevent dumping, used to put domestic producers out of business
  - get other countries to bargain away restrictions
  - get foreign producers to lower their prices

Price control objectives. A few countries hold monopoly or near-monopoly control of certain resources. To maintain control and pursuant high prices, strict export regulations are enforced. Australia, for example, has for over fifty years prohibited the export of Merino rams, considered the top-quality wool producers in the world. One problem with this type of policy is the encouragement of smuggling and the consequent high cost of preventing it. Brazil lost its world monopoly and practically its total world market position in natural rubber after a contrabandist brought rubber plants into Malaysia. South Africa and Colombia pay high prices to prevent diamonds and emeralds, respectively, from flooding world markets. A second problem is that if prices are kept too high, substitutes may be developed. High prices of Chilean natural nitrate led to the development of a synthetic. High sugar prices in 1974 led to the development of a corn derivative substitute, which firms such as Smucker's and Dr. Pepper continued to use even after sugar prices have receded.[13] The oil export controls by OPEC countries have speeded up spending for development of solar and nuclear energy in oil-importing countries.

A country may also limit exports of a product in short supply so that domestic consumers may buy the good at a lower price than if foreign purchasers were allowed to bid the price up. In recent years, Argentina has done this with wheat and the United States with hides and soybeans. The primary danger in these policies is that the lower prices at home will not entice producers to expand domestic output, whereas foreign output is expanded. This may lead to long-term market loss.

There is a fear that producers from one country will artificially price products so low in a given market that they drive other producers out of business. The result of this, it is argued, is a costly dislocation for displaced workers and industries from other countries. If entry barriers are high for new forms, the surviving producers may even be able to extract monopoly profits. The ability to price artificially low abroad may be the result of high domestic prices due to a monopoly position at home or the result of home government subsidy or sponsorship policies. The underpricing of exports (usually below cost or below the home country price) is often referred to as **dumping** or the export of unemployment. Competitors of these exporters, for example, the U.S. television and steel industries, reason that their own governments should interfere and guarantee their own market access.[14] They argue not only the problems of dislocation, but also that the price differential in no way reflects efficiency differences. Home country consumers or taxpayers seldom realize that they are in effect subsidizing foreign sales. A group of Japanese did boycott purchases of Japanese color television sets after it was disclosed that the sets were being sold in the United States at prices much below those in Japan.[15]

Another pricing concept is the use of trade restrictions as a means of forcing other countries to bargain away restrictions of their own. In 1971, for example, the United States placed a 10 percent surcharge on all dutiable imports. The surcharge was quickly negotiated away as some other countries, particularly Japan, reduced barriers to the importation of U.S. products. The danger in this mechanism is that each country may escalate restrictions rather than bargain them away.

A final price argument for governmental influence on trade is the **optimum tariff** theory, which holds that a foreign producer will lower its prices if a tax is placed on its products. If this occurs, benefits shift to the importing country. For example, assume that an exporter has costs of $500 per unit and is selling to a foreign market for $700 per unit. With the imposition of a 10 percent tax on the imported price, the exporter may choose to lower the export price to $636.36 per unit which, with a 10 percent tax of $63.64 would keep the price at $700 for the importer. The exporter may feel that a price higher than $700 would result in lost sales; thus a profit of $136.36 per unit instead of the previous $200 per unit is still better than no profit at all. An amount of $63.64 per unit has thus shifted to the importing country. While in actual practice one may find examples of products whose prices did not rise correspondingly to increased costs of taxes, the behavior is very difficult to predict in advance.

- To protect essential industries
  - hard to agree on essentiality
  - must consider costs and alternatives
- Weaken other countries
  - by making it hard or expensive for them to get goods
  - may increase rather than decrease schism
- Develop spheres of influence

Political objectives. Much governmental influence on trade cannot be explained through economic rationale. One of the major considerations is the protection of essential domestic industries during peacetime so that in case of war the country is not dependent on foreign sources of supply. This argument for protection has much appeal in rallying support for barriers to the importation of foreign-produced goods. However, in time of a real crisis or military emergency, almost any product could be considered essential. Because of the high cost of protecting an inefficient industry or domestic substitute, the international emergency argument should not be (but frequently is) accepted without a careful evaluation of costs, real needs, and alternatives. Once an industry is afforded protection, it is difficult to terminate it. On the basis of the strategic argument the United States government subsidizes its shipbuilding industry by about $500 million a year, pressured AT&T to award a fiber optics contract to a U.S. firm rather than a Japanese firm, and at this writing is considering import limits on textiles because of a need for additional domestic capacity to make military uniforms in time of war.[16]

Defense arguments are also used to prevent exports of strategic goods to potential enemies. The United States, for example, restricts the export of certain goods to communist countries. This policy may be valid—if you assume that your own country needs products from the potential enemy less than the potential enemy needs your own products. Even if this assumption is made, one should assess the possibility that the so-called enemy country may simply find sources of supply from other countries or develop a capability of its own. Closely akin to this is the restriction of exports on raw materials that could be sold competitively, because of fear that essential supplies will become depleted.

Trade controls on other than strategic goods may also be used as a foreign policy weapon to try to prevent another country from easily meeting its economic and political objectives. A good example was the cessation of trade between the United States and Cuba. Before the communists came to power in Cuba, both imports and exports with the United States accounted for more than 80 percent of Cuba's foreign trade. By cutting off imports from Cuba, the United States for many years was little affected economically, since sugar imports, which comprised most of the trade, could easily be bought from other countries that had surpluses. There was perhaps some loss of U.S. exports, although this is difficult to measure because other countries gained earnings for buying U.S. goods. Cuba, on the other hand, could no longer acquire replacement parts for its predominantly U.S.-made machinery. Furthermore, additional machinery purchases had to be diverted to other countries at a higher unit and transportation cost. While the economic consequences of trade as a foreign policy weapon might work, one can still question the political consequences. In the Cuban situation, for example, one can argue on the one hand that Cuba's weakened economy has made it more difficult for that country to export its revolutionary policies to other countries. On the other hand, one can argue that the policies perhaps widened the schism between the two countries, rather than bringing Cuba back into the alignment of Western countries. (The case at the end of Chapter 13 illustrates many of the dilemmas in U.S.–Cuban trade.)

There are many other examples of governments' influencing trade for political reasons. Aid, credits, and purchases are frequently tied into a political alliance or even to votes within international bodies. Most major powers buy at higher than world prices from certain less-developed countries in order to maintain their influence on those countries. The United States did this with sugar; France, with citrus products. In country-to-country negotiations, government officials may even trade off some of the economic advantages of their own nations' firms in order to gain political advantages.

FORMS OF TRADE CONTROL

The previous discussion centered on the end objectives sought by governmental influence on trade. Attaining any of the objectives depends in great part on groups at home who pressure for actions they believe will have the most positive or least negative influence on them. Since the actions taken on foreign trade by one country will have repercussions abroad, retaliation from foreign governments looms as another potential obstacle to the achievement of the desired objectives. The choice of alternative instruments to achieve the trade goal is therefore important, since domestic and foreign groups may respond differently to them. Basically, the types of influence may be classified into two categories: (1) those that influence quantity movements by directly influencing prices and (2) those that affect quantity movements directly and usually influence prices (but not necessarily to consumers) secondarily. Another common distinction is between tariff barriers and nontariff barriers. Tariffs influence prices, and nontariff barriers may affect either price or quantity directly.

Tariffs

- May be on goods entering, leaving, or passing through a country
- May be for protection or revenue
- May be per unit or per value
- Many LDCs claim effective tariff on their manufactured products is higher than published rate
  - raw material input to manufacturers would have entered duty free
  - manufactured LDC products usually pay higher duties than other manufactured products

The most common type of trade control is the **tariff** or **duty,** a government tax levied on goods shipped internationally. If collected by the exporting country, it is known as an export tariff; if collected by a country through which the goods have passed, it is a transit tariff. By far the most common is the import tariff.

Import duties serve primarily as a means of raising the price of imported products so that competitively produced domestic goods will gain a relative price advantage. A duty may be classified as protective in nature even though there is no domestic production in direct competition. For example, if a country wishes to reduce the foreign expenditures of its citizens because of balance-of-payments problems, authorities may choose to raise the price of some foreign products, even though there is no close domestic substitute, in order to curtail consumption temporarily.

Tariffs also serve as a means of governmental revenue. Although of little importance to the large industrial countries, the import duty is a major source of revenue elsewhere because governmental authorities may have more control over ascertaining the amount and nature of goods passing across their frontiers and collecting a tax on them than they do over determining and collecting individual and corporate income taxes. Revenue tariffs are most commonly collected on imports; however, many raw material–exporting nations use export duties extensively, such as New Caledonia's tariff on nickel. When the United States threatened to place an import tariff for protectionist reasons on compressors originating in Singapore, Singapore countered with an export tariff that afforded the protection while giving the tax revenue to Singapore rather than to the United States.[17] Transit duties were historically a major revenue source for countries but have nearly been abolished through governmental treaties.

A tariff may be assessed on the basis of a tax per unit, in which case the duty is known as a **specific duty.** It may also be assessed as a percentage of the value of the item, in which case it is known as an **ad valorem duty.** It is not uncommon for both a specific duty and an ad valorem duty to be charged on the same product. A specific duty is easier to assess because it is not necessary for customs officials to determine a value on which to calculate a percentage. During normal periods of price rises, the specific duty will, unless changed, become a smaller percentage of the value and therefore less restrictive to imported goods.

One of the major tariff controversies concerns the relationship between industrial countries and those seeking to diversify through the export of nontraditional manufactured products. Raw materials can frequently enter developed markets free of duty; however, once processed, those same materials usually have a tariff assigned to them. Since an ad valorem tariff is based on the total value of the product, nonindustrial countries have argued that the **effective tariff** on the manufactured portion is higher than would be indicated by the published tariff rate. For example, a country may charge no duty on coffee beans but assess a 10 percent ad valorem tariff on instant coffee. If $5 for a jar of instant coffee covers $2.50 in coffee beans and $2.50 in processing costs, the $0.50 duty is effectively 20 percent on the manufactured portion, since the beans could have entered free of duty. This has made it more difficult for developing countries to find markets for their products. In addition, many of the products that developing countries are best able to produce are the ones that in industrial countries are produced by employees who are ill equipped to move easily to new employment. The result is the formation of pressure groups to keep out these products. It has been estimated that the tariffs in industrial countries on items of most export interest to less-developed countries are about twice as high as those on manufactured imports as a whole.[18]

Nontariff Barriers: Direct Price Influences

- Countries give variety of assistance to help their firms be competitive
  - those to overcome market imperfections are least controversial
  - little agreement on "unfair" subsidies
  - recent increase in export credit assistance

Subsidies. Although countries sometimes resort to direct payments to producers for losses they incur by selling abroad, governments most commonly give other types of assistance to their firms to make it cheaper or more profitable for them to sell overseas. For example, most countries provide an array of services for their companies that are potential exporters. These include providing information, sponsoring trade expositions, and establishing contacts for businesses overseas. These types of service subsidies are frequently more justifiable from an economic standpoint than tariffs, since one may argue that they are designed largely to overcome market imperfections rather than create them. Furthermore, there are certainly economies to be gained by disseminating information widely. Such types of assistance are not likely to be met with complaints from other countries. On the other hand, one may contend that users should be the only ones to share the costs. At any rate, export assistance is apt to result in less opposition at home than the imposition of import restrictions.

Other types of subsidies are more controversial, and producers frequently contend that they face unfair competition from subsidized exports. But what constitutes a subsidized export? On this point there is little agreement. Does Canada subsidize exports of fish because it gives grants to fishermen to buy trawlers? Does Britain subsidize steel because the government-owned steel company has had severe losses in recent years? Has the United States prevented some automobile imports because the state of Pennsylvania made many concessions to convince Volkswagen to locate its plant there?[19] Recent questions have also been raised about various governments' support of research and development (for example, the U.S. government funds 55 percent of U.S. R&D, of which much results in exported military and commercial products)[20] and tax programs that directly or indirectly affect export profitability. Some of these tax programs will be discussed in Chapter 20.

Some other types of government assistance to exporting are sufficiently important to warrant mentioning, including foreign aid and loans. These are nearly always tied—that is, the recipient must spend the funds in the donor countries. This makes some products competitive abroad that would otherwise not be able to compete pricewise. Most industrial countries also provide repayment insurance for their exporters, thus reducing the risk of nonpayment for overseas sales. In the early 1980s, industrial countries progressively lowered their export credit rates, which were already below market rates, in an effort to stimulate their own exports. One of the schemes used has been the combining of aid with loans so that the rate on paper does not look as low to competitor nations as it really is.[21]

● An undervalued exchange rate will make a country's goods more competitive

Exchange rate manipulations. Exchange rate determination will be discussed in Chapter 9. Basically, however, if a country can manage to keep its currency value so that it buys less of foreign currency than might be the case in a free market determination, its products will have a relative cost advantage. If, for example, the United States and France each produce identical widgets at a cost of US $1 and FF 8, respectively, the costs are identical as long as the exchange rate is US $1 = FF 8. If the United States manages to undervalue the dollar so that US $1 = FF 4, the French could buy widgets from the United States at half the price of widgets produced in France at FF 8. There is much evidence that artifically maintained exchange rates have been major influences on world trade in the last few years.

Through multiple exchange rates, a country sometimes charges importers a high amount in order to get foreign exchange to purchase certain products from abroad; conversely, an exporter receives more in his or her own currency when converting foreign exchange to the local currency. In 1978, for example, in an effort to increase manufactured exports, Peru gave exporters 180 soles for each dollar exported instead of the official rate of 130. This had the effect of encouraging producers to divert output abroad as well as to charge lower export prices in order to be more competitive.

Customs valuation.   In order to determine the value of an imported product for affixing an ad valorem duty, customs officials used to have fairly wide discretion. Even though the invoice value of a shipment might be $100, customs officials might use the domestic wholesale or retail price or even an estimation of what it would cost if the product were produced domestically. This meant that they might charge a 10 percent duty on a value much higher than the $100. The discretion was permitted to prevent exporters and importers from declaring an arbitrarily low price on invoices in order to avoid paying as high a tariff. It has been argued, however, that in practice the discretionary powers were sometimes used as an arbitrary means of preventing the importation of foreign-made products by assessing the value to be too high. At the crux of the allegations was the "American selling price," which meant that U.S. customs charged a customs duty, primarily on shoes and chemicals, based on the U.S. domestic selling price of similar products.

Since 1980, most industrial countries have agreed on a sequence for assessing values. They must first use the invoice price. If there is none or if there is doubt of authenticity, they must then assess on the basis of the value of identical goods and then on the basis of similar goods coming in at about the same time. If these techniques cannot be used, then customs may compute a value based on final sales value or on reasonable cost.[22] The difficulty of arriving at a fair price is illustrated by complaints that imports of Polish golf carts were injuring U.S. domestic producers. Although tariff restrictions were first based on a higher assessment than the invoice value, there was disagreement because of the different methods of determining costs in Poland and in the United States and the fact that none of the carts was sold in Poland. The excess valuation was finally removed five years later.[23]

Another customs valuation problem is that so many different products are traded. The number is constantly increasing, and there are a myriad of variations. It is easy (by accident or on purpose) to classify a product so that it will pay a higher duty. With over 13,000 categories of products a customs agent must use discretion to determine if silicon chips should be considered as "integrated circuits for computers" or as "a form of chemical silicon."[24]

Other direct price influences.   In addition to the aforementioned means of raising the price of imported products, there are other means that countries frequently use. These include special fees, for example, for consular and customs clearance and documentation; the requirement that customs

---

- Hard for customs to determine if invoice price is honest
  - customs may arbitrarily increase duty
  - agreed-upon valuation procedures in recent years
- Hard to put products in right categories

deposits be placed in advance of shipment; and the establishment of minimum prices at which goods can be sold after they are cleared through customs.

Nontariff Barriers: Quantity Controls

- May set total amount to be traded
- May allocate amount by country

Quotas. The most common type of import or export restriction from a quantity basis is the **quota.** From the standpoint of imports, a quota most frequently sets a limit on the quantitative amount of a product allowed to be imported in a given year. The amount frequently reflects a guarantee that domestic producers will have access to a certain percentage of the domestic market in a given year. The sugar import quota of the United States was for many years set so that U.S. producers would have about half the home market. In this case the quotas were further allocated by country on the basis of political considerations rather than price. The price to consumers of imported sugar equaled the price of more expensive domestically produced sugar, since the lowering of the consumer price could not increase the predetermined market share. This restriction of supply will usually increase consumer prices, since there is little incentive to use price as a means of increasing sales. In the case of import tariffs the gains from price increases to consumers are received in the form of government revenue in the importing country. In the case of quotas, however, the gains are most likely to accrue to producers or exporters in the producing country. Windfall gains could accrue to middlemen in the importing country if they bought at a lower open market price and then sold at the higher protected domestic price.

Import quotas do not necessarily protect domestic producers. Japan, for example, maintains quotas on twenty-five agricultural products, most of which are not produced in Japan.[25] Imports are allocated as a means of bargaining for sales of Japanese exports as well as a means of avoiding excess dependence on any one country for essential food needs, which could be cut off in case of adverse climatic or political conditions.

Export quotas may be established in order to ensure that domestic consumers will have a sufficient supply at a low price, to prevent depletion of natural resources, or to attempt to raise an export price by restricting supply in foreign markets. The various commodity agreements in recent years have attempted to allocate exports by producing countries and to restrict their output so that prices will be raised to importing countries.

A specific type of quota that prohibits all trade is known as an **embargo.** As in the case of quotas, embargoes may be placed on either imports or exports, on whole categories of products regardless of destination, on specific products to specific countries, or on all products to given countries. Although embargoes are generally used for political purposes, the effects may be economic in nature.

- Government purchases give preference to domestically made goods
- Government sometimes legislates that its firms preference domestically made goods

"Buy local" legislation. As governmental purchases become a large portion of total expenditures within a country, the determination of where governmental agencies will make their purchases becomes of added importance in international competitiveness. Most national governments give preference to their own producers in the purchase of goods, sometimes in the form of content restriction (that is, a certain percentage of the product for governmental purchase must be of local origin) and sometimes through price mechanisms. For example, a governmental agency may be able to buy a foreign-made product only if the price of the foreign product is some predetermined margin below that of a domestic competitor. Sometimes the preference for local products is even more subtle. For example, the Nippon Telegraph and Telephone Public Corp. (NTT), a Japanese quasi-government telecommunications monopoly in the world's second largest telecommunications market, purchases only a very small portion of its equipment from foreign sources. Foreign firms claim that they have had superior technology and prices, but in practice they have been excluded from the market.[26] AT&T, in spite of being a private telecommunications firm, has been forced to use U.S. suppliers even though their prices have been as much as a third higher than foreign bids.[37]

There is abundant legislation worldwide that simply prescribes a minimum percentage of domestic value that must be encompassed in a given product for it to be sold legally within the country. The office of the U.S. Trade Representative says that of the fifty countries it monitors, forty have such performance requirements.[28] In the introductory case on automobile imports, the local content proposed for cars sold in the U.S. would be, if implemented, such a type of legislated protection. Among those implemented already in other countries are Mexico's requirement that 50 percent of automobile components be made there and Brazil's requirement that companies purchase domestically made computers.

- Many other types of barriers including
  - arbitrary standards, licensing arrangements, administrative delays, service restrictions

Standards. It has not been uncommon for countries to set classifications, labeling, and testing standards in a manner that allows the sale of domestic products but inhibits the sale of foreign-made products. These are sometimes ostensibly for the purpose of protecting the safety or health of the domestic populace. However, imports have often been tested under more onerous conditions (e.g., imported cars in Japan) than have domestic products.[29]

Specific permission requirements. Many countries require that potential importers or exporters secure permission from governmental authorities before they conduct trade transactions, a procedure known as a **licensing arrangement.** To gain a license, it may even be necessary to send samples abroad in advance. The use of licenses not only may restrict imports or exports directly by denial of permission, but also may result in further deterrence of trade because of the cost, time, and uncertainty involved in the process. Similar to a licensing arrangement is a foreign exchange control. For instance, in order to import a given product an importer in an exchange control country must apply to governmental authorities to secure foreign exchange to pay for the product. Once again, the failure to grant the exchange coupled with the time and expense of completing forms and awaiting replies constitute an obstacle to the conduct of foreign trade. Specific permission requirements may also be placed on exports. In an effort to prevent militarily usable technology from falling into the hands of communist countries the United States places specific export permission requirements on certain products and to certain destinations. These will be discussed further in Chapter 13.

Administrative delays. Closely akin to specific permission requirements have been intentional administrative delays on entry, which raise uncertainty and the cost of carrying inventory. In 1983, for example, France required that all imported videotape recorders arrive through a small customs entry point that was both remote and inadequately staffed. The resultant delays effectively kept Japanese recorders out of the market until there was a negotiated "voluntary export quota" whereby Japan limited its penetration of the French market.[30]

Reciprocal requirements. In recent years there has been an upsurge in requirements that exporters effectively take merchandise in lieu of money; for example, Colombia paid for buses from Spain's ENESA with coffee, and China purchased railroad engineering services from Italy's Tecnotrade with coal.[31] Since these transactions often require exporters to find markets for goods outside their lines of expertise, many firms shy away from this type of business. These barter transactions will be discussed in greater detail in Chapter 9.

Restrictions on services. Trade restrictions are usually associated with government interference with the international movement of goods. In addition to earnings from the sale of goods abroad, many countries depend substantially on revenue from the foreign sale of such services as transportation, insurance, consulting, and banking. These services are sometimes referred to as invisibles and account for about one fourth the value of all international trade. There have been recent reports of widespread discrimination by countries favoring their own firms. Among the complaints have been that Japanese airlines get cargo cleared more quickly in Tokyo than do foreign carriers, that Argentina requires automobile imports to be insured en route with Argentine firms, that West Germany requires models for advertisements in West German magazines to be hired through a West German agency, even if the advertisement is made abroad, and that Spain restricts the dubbing of foreign films so that people are forced to read subtitles.[32]

Tariffs have traditionally been placed only on the value of goods; however, South Korea recently reasoned that the cost of imported goods should also include what firms pay to advertise them once they have entered. The result was a 40 percent import tax on the advertising expenditures for Fuji and Kodak film in Korea.[33]

The Role of GATT

- Major trade liberalization organization
  - rules for negotiations
  - monitors enforcement
- Most favored nation exceptions
  - LDCs
  - trading groups
  - discrimination
- GATT rounds
  - across-the-board reductions
  - mainly tariff accords
  - nontariff barriers recently

The most important trade liberalization activity in the post–World War II period has been through GATT, the General Agreement on Tariffs and Trade. GATT has given the world a basic set of rules under which trade negotiations take place and a mechanism for monitoring the implementation of these rules. A requirement for membership in GATT is that nations adhere to the **most favored nation (MFN)** clause. MFN means that if a country, such as the United States, gives a tariff reduction to another country—for example, from 20 percent to 10 percent on wool sweaters from Australia—the United States must grant the same concession to all other countries of the world. The MFN applies to quotas and licenses as well.

There are three allowed exceptions to MFN:

1. manufactured products from developing countries may be given preferential treatment in comparison to those originating from industrial countries;

2. concessions granted to other members of a trading alliance, such as the EC, do not have to be extended to other countries; and

3. nations that arbitrarily discriminate against products from a given country may not necessarily be given MFN treatment by the country whose products are discriminated against.

It is under the second exception that the United States and Israel agreed in 1985 to remove all tariffs on each other's products without giving the same benefits to other countries. It is under the last exception that the United States does not grant MFN treatment to a number of communist countries.

GATT's most important activity has been the sponsoring of "rounds," which have led to a number of multilateral reductions in tariffs and nontariff barriers for its membership. The process of granting reductions is basically across the board. In other words, countries may agree to lower tariff rates by 50 percent over some specified period of time. Given the large number of products traded (the United States exports about 4000 different products and imports about 10,000), it would be virtually impossible to negotiate each product separately. It would be even more difficult to negotiate each product separately with each country separately. Nevertheless, each country brings to the negotiations certain products that it considers as exceptions to its own across-the-board reductions. That a series of negotiations have resulted in vast tariff reductions indicates not only that countries are committed to work jointly toward freer trade, but that tariffs are the easiest trade barrier to tackle. They are, after all, published and quantitative.

The most recently concluded conference, the Tokyo Round in 1979, resulted in an overall reduction in tariffs by about 33 percent. For example, tariffs between the United States and the EC were reduced by 35 percent each way, and U.S. imports into Japan by 40 percent. In spite of these tariff reductions the primary thrust of the negotiations involved grappling with the increasingly important and complex nontariff barriers, especially in five specific areas: industrial standards, government procurement, subsidies and countervailing duties, licensing, and customs valuation. In each of these five areas, conference members agreed on a code of conduct for GATT nations.

The Agreement on Industrial Standards provides for treating imports on the same basis as domestically produced goods. Similarly, the Agreement on Government Procurement calls for treating bids by foreign firms on a nondiscriminatory basis for most large contracts. One of the major controversies, which has continued since the signing of these agreements, is whether Japan is adhering, given that Nippon Telegraph & Telephone buys practically no imported telecommunications equipment.

The Agreement or Code of Conduct on Subsidies and Countervailing Duties recognizes domestic subsidies as appropriate policy tools whose implementation, however, should avoid any adverse impact on other countries. Export subsidies are prohibited, the only exception being agricultural products. This agreement also spells out procedures regarding the possibility of using countervailing duties against a second country if the first country believes its domestic firms are being harmed by the second country's subsidy.

The Licensing Code commits members to simplify their licensing procedures significantly and to treat both foreign and domestic firms in a nondiscriminatory manner.

The Customs Valuation Code calls for either c.i.f. or f.o.b. valuation (invoice value with or without transportation and insurance included) and specifically bans certain types of valuation methods, such as basing valuation on the selling price of a product in the importing country. The specific procedures were discussed earlier in the chapter in the section on customs valuation.

There is fairly general agreement that these agreements are difficult to enforce. There are simply too many subtle means that countries use to circumvent the intent of the Tokyo negotiations. Furthermore, there is one important area on which participants were uanble to agree in the Tokyo Round: the use of temporary safeguards against severe domestic disruptions caused by expanding imports. GATT still allows safeguard measures that can reverse the injurious effects of increases in imports that, in turn, result from trade liberalization moves. In such a situation the injured nation may cancel a previously negotiated action that liberalized trade as long as the country feels that this move is necessary to prevent further injury, particularly in the form of increased unemployment in the affected industry.

In practice very few safeguards have been imposed under the new GATT rules. However, there have been a number of "voluntary" limitations on exports, such as the example of Japanese limits on auto exports to the United States in the opening case. The voluntary restraint is a method of getting around the GATT agreement. This is the case because neither the importing country nor the exporting country complains, and GATT can do nothing without a complaint.

What can GATT do if there are complaints? First, there are investigations to determine if the allegations are valid. If they are, and if corrective steps are not taken, other GATT members may rescind MFN treatment to the violating country. This threat of export market loss, along with the mutual commitment to cooperate, has been sufficient to gain widespread compliance with GATT directives. In recent years, for example, the United States eliminated an export tax measure (DISC) after complaints from the EC that this subsidized U.S. exports and after GATT investigations upheld the allegations.

TRADE INFLUENCE AND UNCERTAINTY

● When facing import competition, firms might
  ● try to get protection
  ● make domestic output competitive
  ● move abroad
  ● All alternatives have costs and risks

Governmental actions concerning trade are usually examined in terms of their effects on such broad objectives as balance of payments, income distribution, employment, and tax receipts or on such narrow objectives as decreasing steel imports versus increasing citrus exports as a trade-balancing measure. The very fact that changes in governmental actions may substantially alter the competitiveness of facilities in given countries creates uncertainties about which businesses must make decisions.[34] These decisions affect companies that are facing import competition as well as companies whose exports are facing protectionist sentiment.

Take the case at the beginning of this chapter about automobile manufacturers in the United States during recent years. Foreign competition was taking a larger proportion of the U.S. market; consequently, a U.S. company wishing to maintain sales in the domestic market had a number of options. These included (1) pushing for import restrictions; (2) effecting internal adjustments, such as cost efficiencies, product innovations, or improved marketing; (3) moving production to a lower cost country and exporting to the United States; and (4) concentrating on market niches where there is less import competition. Clearly, there are substantial costs associated with any one of these options, as well as considerable uncertainty as to outcome.

The U.S. automobile industry was successful at lobbying for the first option. The Japanese agreed to limit their exports to the United States for the next three years; however, automobile price increases along with the inability to get all U.S. producers to join together in a protectionist coalition made continued protection nonviable. The U.S. firms also pursued the second option by instituting various cost-saving measures. Ford estimated its cost level in 1984 to be $4 billion a year less than in 1979.[35] It is not always possible to achieve cost breakthroughs; and if one does, the innovations may be short-lived as foreign competitors respond with like improvements. The effect of the movement of production abroad (option 3), such as Ford's plan to produce in Mexico, could be negated if the United States afterward prohibited importation from the foreign plant. The likelihood of import restrictions in such a situation would be inversely related to the number of producers following this option. In other words, if Ford, Chrysler, and GM all went to foreign sourcing, there would likely be no strong coalition to push for import controls on the foreign production, except from labor. Furthermore, a host of new variables are introduced when operating in a new arrangement. The Big Three auto firms have also followed the fourth option. Each has made arrangements for Japanese companies to supply small cars for them so that they can concentrate more of their production efforts on the larger cars, for which there is little foreign competition.[36] One should attempt to assess costs and probabilities of each alternative before embarking on a program.

The potential protection of the U.S. auto industry also created problems for firms that were planning to export to the U.S. market. They had choices of lobbying against the protection, trying to devise process or product technologies that would overcome the restrictive measures, or locating their production in the United States. As was the case for domestic producers, each of these options involved costs and risks. As was the case with U.S. auto firms, Japanese auto firms followed each of their alternatives to some extent. They lobbied with the Japanese government to take steps to counter U.S. actions. They developed allies, such as associations of foreign car importers, to lobby on their behalf in the United States. They continued their efforts to reduce costs in case tariffs might be imposed. They developed capabilities for adding more luxury items so that profits might not diminish if quotas were imposed. They also negotiated arrangements to produce outside Japan such as in Mexico and the United States, in case sanctions would be taken only against Japanese output.

SUMMARY

- In spite of the fact that the free movement of trade internationally would result in a more efficient utilization of resources, no country permits an unregulated flow of goods and services across its borders.

- Given the possibility of retaliation and the fact that imports as well as exports create jobs, it is difficult to determine the effect on employment of protecting an industry.

- The redistribution of income through changes in trade policy is a problem for which policymakers have not yet found a solution.

- The infant industry argument for protection holds that without governmental prevention of import competition, certain industries would not be able to pass from high-cost to low-cost production.

- Because industrial countries are generally more economically advanced than nonindustrial ones, government interference is often argued to be beneficial if it promotes industrialization. More specifically, it is reasoned that marginal output increases as people move from agriculture to manufacturing, that dependence on a few primary products is both risky and less profitable over a period of time, and that import restrictions will lead to the inflow of capital for manufacturing development.

- Direct influence on trade is used as a means of solving balance-of-payments disequilibrium. This is a more selective means than resorting to either changes in currency values or internal price adjustments.

- Trade controls are used as a means of controlling prices of goods traded internationally. This includes protection of monopoly positions, prevention of foreign monopoly prices, greater assurance that domestic consumers get low prices, and getting foreign producers to lower their profit margins.

- Much of the interference in the free flow of goods and services internationally is motivated by political rather than economic reasons. Political reasons include maintenance of domestic supplies of essential goods and prevention of potential enemies from gaining goods that would help them achieve their objectives.

- Many nonindustrial countries are seeking export markets within the industrialized world for their manufactured products but argue that the effective tariffs on their products are too high.

- The types of trade control that directly influence price and secondarily influence quantities include tariffs, subsidies, multiple exchange rates, arbitrary customs valuations, and special fees.

- The types of trade control that directly affect quantity and secondarily affect price include quotas, "buy local" regulations, licensing, foreign exchange controls, arbitrary standards, administrative delays, and requirements to take goods in exchange.

- Although the volatility of home and foreign influence on foreign trade creates additional uncertainties, firms must nevertheless proceed with operating decisions.

C A S E STEEL IMPORTS[37]

At the end of World War II the U.S. steel industry was the most powerful in the world, and there seemed no apparent chance that anyone would rise to challenge its supremacy. By 1950, U.S. raw steel production accounted for 47 percent of the world's supply. However, this share fell to 17 percent in 1976 and has fallen ever since. Not only has the U.S. world share of production fallen, the United States has become a net importer of steel. Foreign tonnage accounted for over 20 percent of U.S. consumption by 1984. Steel companies in the United States have argued that this figure understates the inroads of foreign competition because so much additional steel enters in finished products such as automobiles and pipes. Steel jobs in the United States have fallen by more than 200,000 since 1953.

On a worldwide basis, several factors are important for understanding the evolving competitive situation. One of these involves additional capacity created in countries that are fairly new to steel production. Many developing countries feel that domestic mills are essential for their industrialization objectives, and the need for steel output is viewed somewhat emotionally for security and prestige purposes. These countries have been able to increase capacity because the technology, except for certain specialty steels, has become widespread and easily attainable. Because of the high priority placed on steel, many countries have been willing to forego other development projects in order to build mills or have received financial assistance from outside for construction. Turkey, for example, received both U.S. and Soviet long-term, low-interest government loans to finance its steel output. Since the early 1970s the largest capacity increase has been among Third World countries; they have a substantial excess capacity that is growing. The world excess capacity is illustrated by estimates that the U.S., European, and Japanese steelmakers had operating rates of 50 percent or less in 1983. European steelmakers planned a 15 percent capacity cut by 1985, and U.S. makers a 34 percent cut by 1990. Given the high fixed costs of steel production, a second factor affecting steel competition is that much of the world's production is government owned. It is argued that these firms will continue operating regardless of whether they cover their short-term costs. Because of employment pressures in countries such as France, it has been politically very difficult to cut back production more rapidly in the state facilities. Export markets have been used as an instrument of maintaining more output. In 1984, for example, French workers rioted when the government attempted to cut back on steel production and 25,000 industry jobs. The state-owned companies in such countries as Britain, Spain, and Argentina have been reporting record losses but continue exporting at low prices. In addition to direct ownership, it has been argued that governmental assistance through tax incentives, reorganization schemes, provision for long-term, low-interest loans, and waiving of environmental requirements have placed U.S. steel producers at a disadvantage vis-à-vis some foreign producers.

The largest steel exporter to the United States in recent years has been Japan, which is now the third largest steel producer in the world after the Soviet Union and the United States. Steelmaking is a privately owned industry in a country without a sufficient domestic supply of either iron or coal, the two major materials needed for production.

A number of factors have contributed to the ability of the Japanese steel industry to compete effectively in the United States in recent years. One is technology. Although U.S. firms claim that their newest plants are as advanced as any in Japan, the average age of Japanese plants is much below that of U.S. plants, so, on the average, the plants are more productive. For example, it is generally recognized that the useful life of a coke oven is 25 years; however, in 1982, 41 percent of U.S. ovens exceeded that age compared with only 2 percent in Japan. In 1958 it took Japanese workers nearly 36 man-hours to produce a ton of cold-rolled sheet steel, which U.S. steelmakers could turn out in 12. Japanese productivity caught up with that of the United States in 1975; by 1983 it exceeded U.S. productivity by 25 percent. In addition, Japanese workers receive less compensation and, when on strike, typically continue working, wearing an armband. American firms have guaranteed their workers pay increases that have been exceeding increases in productivity rates in order to gain a "no strike" clause in labor contracts. By 1983, U.S. steelworkers made about $23 per hour, whereas the average worker in other U.S. manufacturing industries earned less than $13.

Another factor concerns production location. Most U.S. mills were built many years ago in the corridor of states bordering the Great Lakes. These locations minimized transportation costs for raw materials and for finished steel to be shipped to industrial users in this same corridor. These locations may no longer be optimal if a firm wants to use cheaper iron from Brazil and wants to sell to the expanding industrial and population base in the South and West. Japanese production is largely situated at deep-water ports; their industry now has an estimated cost advantage on purchases of raw materials even though they are imported. In spite of these advantages, Japan is increasingly importing steel from Taiwan and South Korea, countries with even lower labor rates and newer plants, on the average. South Korea's Pohang Iron & Steel is now considered the world's most efficient steelmaker. In addition to its efficiency advantage, the average South Korean steel worker earns only one third the salary of a Japanese steel worker.

Regardless of where the competition is from, there is a general agreement that there will have to be major new investment and restructuring of the U.S. steel industry if it is to bring its costs down to those of imported steel. The steel industry in the United States has argued the difficulty of making this investment because of poor earnings records of recent years.

This has been contested by critics who pointed to U.S. Steel's acquisition of Marathon Oil when it lacked funds for technological improvements. They have also blamed industry managers for spending funds for years at hopelessly obsolete plants rather than targeting outlays to viable facilities. These obsolete plants are now being retired, though.

Four competitive responses appear to offer some hope for the future of the steel industry in the United States. The first has been a move to so-called mini-mills, which have specialized products, the latest technology, and proximity to markets. These plants are competitive, and their combined capacity and sales are growing. The second has been a move by foreign steel firms, such as Nippon Kokan of Japan, to buy into the U.S. industry, thus infusing funds and technology while eliminating a foreign competitor. The third has been a move by U.S. producers to buy semifinished steel from abroad, thus cutting costs at an important level of production. The fourth has been a move to merge firms in the industry in order to gain administrative scale economies, to complement production, and to phase out less competitive plants while maintaining a full product line. An example of this was the Republic Steel–LTV merger plan.

In spite of these moves, the U.S. steel industry has been calling for more stringent protection. For several years the United States has used a "trigger price" mechanism that is aimed at automatic investigation of dumping whenever foreign steel comes in below a floor price. If dumping (selling below cost or below the home market price) is found, then the United States will take action against the imports. Few have been happy with the mechanism. Antiprotectionist groups argue that these procedures allow the steel companies to raise their prices without making the necessary changes to effect competitive viability and thus give added profits to Japanese producers who still compete with higher prices. The steel industry and the federal General Accounting Office have shown that the procedures break down in the bureaucratic framework and that 40 percent of steel imports come in below the floor price. In 1982 the United States worked out a "voluntary export quota" with the EC that guaranteed the EC about 5 percent of the U.S. market. This simply opened up the U.S. market for producers from Mexico and Brazil. In 1983 the United States put new restrictions on the importation of European specialty steel. However, the EC retaliated with new tariffs on a variety of U.S. chemicals, sporting equipment, and burglar and fire alarms.

QUESTIONS

1. Should the United States seek to maintain a steel industry even if it could not become cost competitive with foreign steel?

2. Should foreign producers be allowed to export steel to the United States at a price below their cost?

3. Can the United States again become cost efficient in the production of steel vis-à-vis foreign competition?

4. What types of governmental assistance might the United States give to the steel industry to help it compete more effectively with foreign steel? What are the advantages and disadvantages of each option?

5. If the steel industry in the United States does not receive assistance, what other options does it have?

6. Contrast the differences and similarities of the steel situation with those of the automobile case at the beginning of the chapter.

NOTES

1. The data for the case were taken from "Carter May Help Ailing Chrysler," *New York Times,* June 23, 1979, p. 27; "U.S. Trade Agency Facing Crucial Decision on Detroit's Plea for Auto Import Curbs," *Wall Street Journal,* November 7, 1980, p. 29; "Car Wars," *Wall Street Journal,* February 15, 1980, p. 1; "Japan Asks Its Car Firms to Limit Exports to U.S. and Start American Production," *Wall Street Journal,* February 13, 1980, p. 2; "U.S. Autos Losing a Big Segment of the Market—Forever?,"*Business Week,* March 24, 1980, pp. 78–85; "Made in U.S.A.—With Foreign Parts," *New York Times,* November 9, 1980, Sec. 3, p. 1ff.; "7 of 10 Americans Agree," *New York Times,* November 6, 1980, p. A23; "Pressure Mounts to Restrict Auto Imports by Japan," *Wall Street Journal,* November 19, 1980, p. 2; Clyde H. Farnsworth, "House, 219–199, Votes to Require U.S. Made Parts in Imported Cars," *New York Times,* November 4, 1983, p. A1; John Holusha, "New Ways at 2 G.M. Plants," *New York Times,* April 10, 1984, p. D1; Amal Nag, "The Politics of Auto-Import Quotas," *Wall Street Journal,* October 17, 1983, p. 30; Art Pine, "U.S. Bid to Limit '84 Car Imports Spurned by Japan, Which Seeks 1.9 Million Units," *Wall Street Journal,* October 26, 1983, p. 2; Donald Woutat, "GM and Ford Bonuses Raise Questions about Import Curbs, Union's Restraint," *Wall Street Journal,* April 16, 1984, p. 10; Leslie Wayne, "The Irony and Impact of Auto Quotas," *New York Times,* April 8, 1984, p. F1+; "Brock Vows to End Import Quotas on Japanese Cars," *Wall Street Journal,* May 3, 1984, p. 29.

2. John Hein, "A New Protectionism Rises," *Across the Board,* Vol. XX, No. 4, April 1983, p. 23, quoting former U.S. Special Trade Representative Robert Strauss.

3. James J. Kilpatrick, "How Not to Create Jobs," *Nation's Business,* March 1983, Vol. 77, No. 1, p. 5.

4. John Andrew, John Helyar, and Bill Johnson, "Silver Lining," *Wall Street Journal,* February 29, 1984, p. 1.

5. *Ibid.,* p. 19.

6. *United States Department of Labor News,* January 30, 1980, p. 1.

7. For an interesting account of the absorption problem, see Warren J. Bilkey, "Perceived Shortages of Unskilled Labor in Labor Surplus Economies: Costa Rica, El Salvador, Dominican Republic, and Mexico," *Journal of International Business Studies,* Fall 1972, pp. 1–16.

8. United Nations, *Instability in Export Markets in Underdeveloped Countries* (New York: United Nations, 1952), pp. 4–6.

9. Lloyd G. Reynolds, "Economic Development in Historical Perspective," *American Economic Review,* May 1980, p. 92.

10. Supportive of the premises are Raul Prebisch, *The Economic Development of Latin America and Its Principal Problems* (New York: United Nations Department of Economic Affairs, 1950); Charles P. Kindleberger, *The Terms of Trade: A European Case Study* (New York: John Wiley & Sons, 1956), and W. Arthur Lewis, *Aspects of Tropical Trade, 1883–1965* (Stockholm: Almquist and Wiksells, 1969). Nonsupportive are M. June Flanders, "Prebisch on Protectionism: An Evaluation," *Economic Journal,* June 1964; Theodore Morgan, "The Long-Run Terms of Trade between Agriculture and Manufacturing," *Economic Development and Cultural Change,* October 1959; and Gottfried Haberler, "Terms of Trade and Economic Development," in *Economic Development of Latin America,* H. Ellis, ed. (New York: St. Martin's Press, 1961).

11. R. Weisskoff and E. Wolff, "Development and Trade Dependence," *Review of Economics and Statistics,* November 1975, p. 470.

12. M. Guerard, "Fiscal Versus Trade Incentives for Industrialization," *Finance and Development,* June 1975, p. 22.

13. "Sweet Competition," *Wall Street Journal,* November 2, 1976, p. 1.

14. Clyde M. Farnsworth, "2 Latin Steel Exporters Face Duties," *New York Times,* April 20, 1984, p. D1; Eduardo Lachica, "Some South Korean and Taiwan Firms Face Possible Dumping Duties on TV Sets," *Wall Street Journal,* February 27, 1984, p. 12.

15. "A Boycott Tunes Down Japan's TV Makers," *Business Week,* No. 2166, March 6, 1971, p. 41.

16. Robert B. Reich, "Beyond Free Trade," *Foreign Affairs,* Vol. 61, No. 4, Spring 1983, p. 787.

17. "Singapore Places Duty on Company's Exports to U.S. for First Time," *Wall Street Journal,* December 12, 1983, p. 35.

18. N. Hutton, "The Salience of Linkage in International Economic Negotiations," *Journal of Common Market Studies,* Nos. 1 and 2, 1975, p. 147.

19. For these and many other examples, see "One Man's Subsidy Is Another Man's Poison," *Economist,* March 11, 1978, pp. 77–78.

20. Reich, *op. cit.,* p. 786.

21. "U.S. Fails to Get Pact Limiting Direct Aid in Trade Financing," *Wall Street Journal,* April 16, 1984, p. 32.

22. "Tokyo Round: (3) New Customs Valuation Rules," *World Business Weekly,* March 10, 1980, p. 14.

23. "Trade Unit Ruling Sets End to Penalty Duty on Poland's Golf Carts," *Wall Street Journal,* May 21, 1980, p. 10.

24. Stanley Nehmer, "The Tangled Maze of Nontariff Barriers," *New York Times,* April 15, 1973, p. 14F.

25. Clyde H. Farnsworth, "If He Says It's Broccoli, It's Broccoli," *New York Times,* May 25, 1984, p. A18.

26. Eduardo Lachica, "U.S. Bids Japan to Open Market for Phone Firms," *Wall Street Journal,* March 30, 1984, p. 33.

27. Edward Meadows, "Japan Runs into America Inc.," *Fortune,* Vol. 105, No. 6, March 22, 1982, pp. 56–61.

28. Kenneth N. Gilpin, " 'Local Content' Laws Posing New Obstacles for World's Exporters," *International Herald Tribune,* June 27, 1983, p. 17+.

29. See, for example, Jimmey S. Hillman, "Nontariff Barriers: Major Problems in Agricultural Trade," *American Journal of Agricultural Economics,* August 1978, pp. 491–501; "Wrapping up the MTN Package," *Business America,* April 23, 1979, pp. 5–6; "Japan: Barriers That Slow Ford Escort Sales," *Business Week,* December 1, 1980, p. 60.

30. "Japan to Curb VCR Exports," *New York Times,* November 21, 1983, p. D5.

31. "New Restrictions on World Trade," *Business Week,* July 19, 1982, p. 119.

32. Laura Wallace, "Rising Barriers," *Wall Street Journal,* October 5, 1981, p. 1; Nina Darnton, "Spain Restricting the Dubbing of Foreign Movies," *New York Times,* June 4, 1984, p. C11.

33. "Korean Dispute Arises over Customs Duties Levied on Ad Spending," *Wall Street Journal,* January 20, 1984, p. 54.

34. For a good discussion of alternatives when faced with import competition, see Ingo Walter and Kent A. Jones, "The Battle over Protectionism: How Industry Adjusts to Competitive Shocks," *Journal of Business Strategy,* Vol. 2, No. 2, Fall 1981, pp. 37–46.

35. "Ford Posts Record Net in Quarter," *New York Times,* April 27, 1984, p. D1.

36. "The Chrysler Deal Dooms America's Cheap Small Cars," *Business Week,* April 29, 1985, p. 27.

37. Data for this case were taken from "Why the Trigger Price Omits Specialty Steel," *Business Week,* October 20, 1980, pp. 44–45; "South Korea Goal: Join List of Top Steelmakers," *New York Times,* February 4, 1979, special section, p. 32; "Import Protection for Steel Faulted," *New York Times,* February 14, 1980, p. A7; "Basic Problems," *Wall Street Journal,* September 30, 1983, p. 1+; Steven Greenhouse, "National in Japanese Steel Deal," *New York Times,* April 25, 1984, p. D20+; Thomas F. O'Boyle and J. Ernest Beazley, "U.S. Steel Bid Stirs Debate inside Firm," *Wall Street Journal,* February 3, 1984, p. 25; Paul Lewis, "French Workers Riot over Steel Cutbacks," *New York Times,* March 30, 1984, p. D7; Steven Greenhouse, "Many E.E.C. Roles in Steel Dispute," *New York Times,* January 16, 1984, p. D8; Thomas F. O'Boyle, "Forging a Link," *Wall Street Journal,* December 20, 1983, p. 1; "The Rebirth of Steel," February 16, 1984, p. 34; Donald F. Barnett and Louis Schorsch, *Steel: Upheaval in a Basic Industry* (Cambridge, Mass.: Ballinger, 1984).

6

Why Direct Foreign Investment Takes Place

- To explain why controlled or direct investments are viewed differently by investors and governments than noncontrolled or portfolio investments.
- To demonstrate means by which foreign direct investment may be acquired.
- To evaluate the relationship and possible substitution between foreign trade and international factor mobility, especially direct investment.
- To classify the major types of direct investment motivation.
- To show why trade is often not feasible as a means for a firm to service foreign markets, thus necessitating foreign investment.
- To illustrate the circumstances that lead companies to seek foreign supplies through their direct foreign investments.
- To show how and why government actions influence the movement of direct investment.
- To introduce the advantages that direct investors have vis-à-vis domestic firms.

BRIDGESTONE TIRE COMPANY[1]

The Bridgestone Tire Company is the largest tire producer in Japan, with 50 percent of that market. During the decade of the 1970s its sales grew sixfold so that by 1981 it was the fourth largest tire company in the world. Although most of the company's sales efforts have been geared toward the Japanese market, foreign sales have been increasing for the firm. Part of these foreign sales have been indirect because Bridgestone is a major supplier to Japanese automobile firms. As part of the original equipment on Japanese automobiles that are exported, Bridgestone tires arrive in foreign markets where Bridgestone makes little or no export effort of its own. Direct exports are also important. In 1979, Bridgestone exported approximately $514 million of car and truck tires to the United States, an amount representing nearly 29 percent of its sales. Bridgestone's top management believes that it is essential to grow outside of Japan. It believes that by 1990 or 1995 there will be only four or five major tire companies in the world. The management also believes that it will be difficult for them to sustain growth in Japan because it is hard to go beyond 50 percent of the market.

In 1980 the company's president announced that the firm's number-one priority would be the establishment of a manufacturing investment in the United States. Probably the major factor influencing this priority was the firm's large amount of direct and indirect export sales to the United States. These sales gave Bridgestone a solid indication that it could compete against firms with established U.S. sales and manufacturing facilities. Many automobile dealers were already familiar with the Bridgestone product, which entered as part of the original equipment. Thus they might not be reluctant to carry Bridgestone tires as replacements. By 1980, as well, Bridgestone had become more confident about its ability to manage and control a manufacturing investment in the highly competitive U.S. market. Part of this confidence was due to Bridgestone's success with foreign manufacturing facilities in four developing countries, an indication of Bridgestone's ability to transfer such things as personnel, technology, and management systems abroad. Through these investments, Bridgestone gained 40 percent of the business in Southeast Asia, leading the company to buy out Uniroyal's 60 percent equity in an Australian plant. In addition, Bridgestone had observed the success of some other Japanese firms, such as Sony, that had introduced some Japanese managerial methods to their U.S. facilities.

But why should Bridgestone manufacture in the United States? Why not continue exporting, since sales growth by this means had been highly successful? Several factors could have a negative impact on Bridgestone's export activities to the United States. The first of these might be government-imposed restrictions. Although imports of replacement tires comprised a very small part of the U.S. market and Bridgestone had a meager 1 percent of the automobile tire market, imports could be restricted in several ways. To begin with, U.S. tiremakers had been laying off workers throughout much of 1979 and 1980 as tire sales fell 7 percent; thus protectionist sentiment could easily grow. More probable could be action taken against imports of Japanese automobiles, thus placing the sale of original equipment tires in jeopardy. It was no secret in 1980 that Honda and Toyota were seriously considering the establishment of U.S. production or assembly operations and might opt for tires made in the United States once their plants were operating. Toyota, by the way, bought 40 percent of Bridgestone's original equipment tires. Finally, because of Japan's huge trade surplus with the United States, the United States could conceivably place overall restrictions on the import of Japanese products.

Exports might also be imperiled if Japanese costs went up in relation to American costs. Because of high transportation costs for tires (they are bulky in relation to their value), it is usually difficult to ship tires over a large distance except as part of original equipment on vehicles. Bridgestone's overseas shipping expenses ranged between $3 and $12 per tire, depending on size. U.S. producers even depended on multiple U.S. plant locations in order to minimize transport costs. It was generally conceded that a one-plant firm in the United States could not maintain sales on both the east and west coasts. Bridgestone's ability to overcome the high transport costs was largely due to the falling value of the yen in recent years relative to the U.S. dollar. Since most of Bridgestone's costs were in yen, a fall in the yen value resulted in a cheaper price in terms of U.S. dollars. When the yen strengthened in 1978, Bridgestone's exports to the United States fell 12 percent. Thus the firm was understandably concerned about its ability to plan long-term exports to the United States.

A final factor affecting Bridgestone's decision to commence U.S. production was to get in on the ground floor of the growing radial truck tire market in the United States. Bridgestone had gained nearly a 10 percent share of this market in the United States through exporting. The manager of international planning and sales promotion for Bridgestone concluded that it would be far easier to gain a share of this market during the early growth stage than to wait a few years until the mature market was dominated by Goodyear and Michelin, which had already announced plans to open highly automated radial tire–making facilities in the United States.

Bridgestone was comparing the options of establishing manufactured facilities by either buying an interest in an existing firm or building its own plant(s). Because of financial problems plaguing many of the U.S. tire companies, Bridgestone found that it could probably purchase a U.S. company for a lower price than it would cost to build facilities. At early 1980 market prices, for example, Uniroyal could be purchased for about $115 million. However, facilities would have to be altered to get Bridgestone's desired mix of auto and truck tires. A single plant would cost at least $150 million to build but would be exactly to Bridgestone's specifications.

In late 1980, Firestone contacted Bridgestone about its willingness to sell its truck radial tire plant for $100 million. Bridgestone was unwilling to pay this price because of indications of plant labor problems and a belief that much of the equipment in the 1972 facility was obsolete. The final agreed-upon price in 1982 was $52 million. In addition, Bridgestone agreed to supply Firestone with private label radial truck tires for at least three years.

INTRODUCTION

An increasing portion of firms' foreign sales is being made from controlled foreign production facilities; this is termed **direct foreign investment.** This trend has led to an upsurge of studies attempting to explain why direct foreign investment takes place; not surprisingly, no one explanation or theory encompasses all the reasons.[2]

The preceding case illustrates the multiplicity of factors influencing the decision of one firm to produce in a foreign country. Before deciding to invest in the United States, Bridgestone faced a sequence of decisions. One of the first was whether or not to serve foreign markets. Bridgestone was content with the Japanese market as long as it could expand rapidly within that market. However, once the company reached a large and fairly stable share of a maturing market, the choices were either product diversification or geographic diversification if growth was to be sustained. Either type of diversification would involve new risks because of operating in new arenas. Bridgestone chose the latter because of a belief that its competitive advantage was more specific to the production of tires than to knowledge of the Japanese market. (In 1980, for example, Bridgestone spent more on R&D than Goodyear, which is the world's largest tire manufacturer. The high level and concentration of R&D expenditures has led Bridgestone to make notable breakthroughs in both product and process technologies.)[3] Bridgestone first entered foreign markets through exporting and was successful. However, management felt that it could not sustain an export market to the United States because of the high transport cost of tires, the possibility of U.S. government import restrictions or preferences by final or industrial consumers for a U.S.-made product, and an uncertain cost structure created by the changing yen–dollar relationship. Bridgestone might still have chosen to license its technologies and/or its name to producers already in the U.S. market. This would have generated revenues without the risk of having to operate in an alien environment. By this time, though, the perceived risk of operating in the United States was minimal because of Bridgestone's growing foreign experience, its observation of Japanese company successes in the United States, and its probable ability to sell output to Japanese automakers with whom the company had experience. There were also competitive reasons for not licensing. Bridgestone felt that it had to be located in growth markets if it were to survive the expected shakeout in the industry. This was especially true for radial truck tires. The transfer of technology to other tire producers might eventually undermine Bridgestone's ability to compete in other markets.

The case also illustrates that a direct investment can be acquired in alternative ways. Neither the motives nor the methods for acquiring direct investment as illustrated in the case are conclusive. This chapter will further examine these various motives and methods.

The growth of direct foreign investment has resulted in a heightened interest in two other questions:

1. What effect does the investment have on national economic, political, and social objectives?

2. What is or should be a firm's pattern of investment in terms of such variables as geographic allocation and acquisition method?

Both of these questions will be discussed from an introductory standpoint in this chapter; they will be explored more thoroughly in subsequent chapters—the former in Chapter 11 and the latter in Chapter 16.

THE MEANING OF DIRECT FOREIGN INVESTMENT

The Concept of Control

● Although direct investment implies control
  ● hard to determine what percent ownership gives control
  ● government offices usually use 10 or 25 percent to define "direct"

In Chapter 1 we said that for direct investment to take place, control must follow the investment. The amount of ownership share necessary for control is certainly not clear-cut. If stock ownership is widely dispersed, then a small percentage of the holdings may be enough to gain weight in managerial decision making. On the other hand, even a 100 percent share does not guarantee control. If a government dictates whom a firm hires, what the firm must sell at a specified price, and how earnings will be distributed, then one might rightly argue that control has passed to the government. These are all decisions that governments have frequently imposed on foreign investors operating within their confines. But it is not necessarily just governments that may wrest control from whoever holds the voting shares. If some resource needed for the firm to operate is not regulated by the owners of the firm, then whoever does control the resource may exert substantial influence. This was precisely the situation faced by Arthur G. McKee and Company with its Italian subsidiary. McKee acquired 94 percent of Compagnia Tecnica Industrie Petroli for $1.5 million in stock and cash. The really critical resource was the 850 Italian employees, who went on strike to gain control for themselves. If McKee had failed to meet their demands, the employees would have joined Technip, a French competitor, or would have begun their own company.[4] Because of the difficulty of identifying direct investments, governmental offices have had to establish arbitrary definitions, usually indicating ownership of either 10 or 25 percent of the voting stock in a foreign enterprise as minimum for an investment to be considered direct.

The Concern over Control

● Decisions of national importance may be made abroad

Government concern. Why is there concern over whether an investment is controlled from abroad? Many critics worry that the national interest will not be best served if a multinational firm makes decisions from afar on the basis of its global or its own national objectives. For example, General Motors owns 100 percent interest in Vauxhall Motors in the United Kingdom. The control of Vauxhall by General Motors in this direct investment means that GM's corporate management in the United States must be directly concerned with and make decisions about such things as staffing, export prices, and retention versus payout of profits in Vauxhall. The British populace is also concerned in this case because decisions that directly affect the British economy are being (or at least can be) made in the United States. The British government, on the other hand, owns slightly less than 1 percent of General Motors. Since this is not enough for control, the British government does not have to expend time and effort in making management decisions for General Motors. Nor is the U.S. populace concerned that vital GM decisions will be made in Britain. This should not imply that noncontrolled investments are unimportant. They may substantially affect a country's balance-of-payments situation (see Chapter 9), and they may play an important part in a firm's financial management and strategy (see Chapter 21).

● When investors control
  ● more willing to transfer technology and other competitive assets
  ● usually cheaper and faster means of transferring assets than to noncontrolled

Investor concern. Control is also very important to many investors who are reluctant to transfer certain vital resources to another domestic or foreign organization that can make all its operating decisions independently. Valuable patents, trademarks, and management know-how could then be used to undermine the competitive position of the original holders, who transferred these resources.[5] In the introductory case, for example, Bridgestone was reluctant to transfer either product technology, such as its SuperFiller radials, or process technology, such as its mold changeover methods, to other companies. Bridgestone's management is well aware of how acquired technology can be used to catch a leader. Between the end of World War II and 1979, much of Bridgestone's technology came from Goodyear, which held a noncontrolling interest in Bridgestone. This desire for control does not imply that the control of foreign operations is always preferable. There are many circumstances in which assets are transferred to noncontrolled entities; this is one of the subjects of Chapter 15.

There may also be economies of buying and selling with a controlled entity because of dealing within a common corporate culture, of using one's own managers to speed transfers, and avoiding protracted negotiations with another company.

Methods of Acquisition

- Usually involve some capital movement, but
  - may be other type of asset
  - may borrow locally
  - may exchange equity
- Ongoing business or start up

Direct investment has traditionally been considered an international capital movement that moves abroad when the anticipated return (accounting for the risk factor and the cost of transfer) is higher overseas than at home. Although most direct investments involve some type of international capital movement, an investor may transfer many other types of assets. Such organizations as Western Hotels have transferred very little capital to other countries. Instead, Western has transferred managers, hotel cost controls, and reservations capabilities in exchange for equity in foreign hotels. An example of a direct investment made completely by transferring nonfinancial resources instead of capital was the Plessey (British) acquisition of Airborne Accessories Corporation of New Jersey. Plessey had two assets that were vitally needed by Airborne Accessories: technology and established sales capabilities outside the United States. Plessey offered the owners notes in exchange for the ownership. Although the interest and principal on these notes was to be paid strictly out of the earnings of the acquired company, the owners reasoned that this interest was a higher return than they could get by continuing to own and manage Airborne themselves.[6]

Aside from committing nonfinancial resources, there are two other means of acquiring assets that do not involve international capital movements in a normal sense. First, if a business earns funds in a foreign country, these may be used to establish an investment. For example, if a firm exports merchandise but holds payment for those goods abroad, the settlement could be used to acquire an investment. In this case the company has merely exchanged goods for equity. Although this is not a method used extensively for initial investment, the use of retained earnings is a major means of expanding abroad. A firm may initially transfer assets abroad in order to establish a sales or production facility. If the earnings from the facility are used to increase the value of the foreign holdings, direct investment has increased without a new international capital movement. The second means is by trading equity between firms in different countries. For example, Naarden in the Netherlands acquired a share of Flavorex in the United States by giving the Flavorex owners stock in the Naarden Company.

In several of the preceding examples a firm in one country acquired an interest in an ongoing business operation in another country. As an alternative the investors could have established an entirely new company abroad. In either case the investors' ownership of voting shares might have been less than 100 percent; if less, the remainder could be (1) widely rather than narrowly held and (2) owned by private rather than by governmental sources. The rationale and implications of these various alternatives are too lengthy and numerous to be discussed at this point; they will be elaborated on in Chapter 15.

THE RELATIONSHIP OF TRADE AND FACTOR MOBILITY

- Both finished goods and production factors partially mobile internationally
  - cost and degree of mobility determine which will move

Whether capital or some other asset is transferred abroad initially to acquire a direct investment, the asset is a type of production factor. Eventually, the direct investment usually involves the movement of various types of production factors as investors infuse capital, technology, personnel, raw materials, or components into their operating facilities abroad. It is therefore useful to examine the relationship of trade theory to the movement of production factors.

The Trade and Factor Mobility Theory

Chapter 4 explained that trade often occurs because of differences in factor endowments among countries. A country such as Canada, with abundant arable land relative to its small but educated labor force, may cultivate wheat in a highly mechanized manner. This wheat may be exchanged for handmade Hong Kong sweaters, which require abundant semiskilled labor and little land.

Historical treatises on trade assumed that the factors of production were nearly immobile internationally and that trade could move freely. In actuality there are many natural and imposed barriers that make both finished goods and production factors partially mobile internationally. Factor movement is an alternative to trade that may or may not be a more efficient allocation of resources. If the factors of production were not free to move internationally as was assumed by early economic theorists, then trade would ordinarily be the most efficient way of compensating for differences in factor endowments. If neither trade nor the production factors could move internationally, a country would often have to forego consuming certain goods. An alternative would be to produce them in different manners. This would usually result in decreased worldwide output and higher prices. One can only speculate on the astronomical cost of coffee if it were produced in hothouses in Arctic regions. In some cases, however, the inability to utilize foreign production factors may stimulate efficient methods of substitution, such as the development of new materials as alternatives for traditional ones or of machines to do hand work. The development of synthetic rubber and rayon was undoubtedly speeded up because of wartime conditions that made silk and natural rubber, as well as silkworms and rubber plants, impractical to move.

Substitution

Pressure for most abundant factors to move to area of scarcity

Whenever the factor proportions are very different among countries, there are pressures for the most abundant factors to move to countries of greater scarcity so that they can command a better return. Thus in countries with an abundance of labor relative to land and capital, there is a tendency for laborers to be unemployed or poorly paid; if permitted, they will gravitate to countries with relatively full employment and higher wages. Likewise, capital will tend to move away from countries where it is abundant to those where it is scarce. Mexico is thus a net recipient of capital from the United States, and the United States is a net recipient of labor from Mexico.

If finished goods and production factors were both completely free to move internationally, then the comparative costs of transferring goods and factors would determine the location of production. A hypothetical example should illustrate the substitutability of trade and factor movements under different scenarios.

Assume (1) that the United States and Mexico have land that is equally productive and available at the same cost for the growing of tomatoes, (2) that the cost of transporting tomatoes from the United States to Mexico or from Mexico to the United States is $0.75 per bushel, and (3) that workers from either country pick an average of two bushels per hour during a 30-day picking season. The only differences in price between the two countries are due to labor and capital cost variations. The labor rate in the United States is assumed to be $20.00 per day or $1.25 per bushel; in Mexico it is assumed to be $4.00 per day or $0.25 per bushel. The cost of capital needed to buy seeds, fertilizers, and equipment costs the equivalent of $0.50 per bushel in Mexico and $0.30 per bushel in the United States.

If neither tomatoes nor production factors can move between the two countries, then the cost of tomatoes produced in Mexico for the Mexican market would be $0.75 per bushel ($0.25 of labor plus $0.50 of capital), whereas those produced in the United States for the U.S. market would be $1.55 per bushel ($1.25 of labor plus $0.30 of capital). If trade restrictions on tomatoes were eliminated between the two countries, the United States would import from Mexico because the Mexican cost of $0.75 per bushel plus $0.75 of transportation cost to move them to the United States would be less than the $1.55 cost of growing them in the United States.

Consider another scenario in which neither country allows the importation of tomatoes but in which both countries allow certain movements of labor and capital. An investigation shows that Mexican workers can enter the United States on temporary work permits for an incremental travel and living expense of $14.40 per day per worker or $0.90 per bushel. At the same time, U.S. capital can be enticed to invest in Mexican tomato production provided that it receives a payment equivalent to $0.40 per bushel, less than the Mexican going rate but more than it would earn in the United States. In this situation, Mexican production costs per bushel would be $0.65 ($0.25 of Mexican labor plus $0.40 of American capital). U.S. production costs would be $1.45 ($0.25 of Mexican labor plus $0.90 of travel and incremental costs plus $0.30 of American capital). Note that each country was able to reduce its production costs (Mexico from $0.75 to $0.65 and the United States from $1.55 to $1.45) by bringing in abundant production factors from abroad.

With free trade and the free movement of production factors, Mexico would produce for both markets by importing capital from the United States. According to the above assumptions, that would be a cheaper alternative than sending labor to the United States. In reality, neither production factors nor the finished goods that they produce are completely free to move internationally. Some slight changes in imposing or freeing restrictions can greatly alter how and where goods may be produced most cheaply. In the case of the United States in recent years there has been more freedom for capital to flow out than for labor to flow in. A result of this has been an increase in U.S.-controlled direct investment to produce goods that are then imported back into the United States.

Complementarity of Trade and Direct Investment

- Factor mobility via direct investment often stimulates trade movements due to
  - components
  - complementary products
  - equipment to subsidiaries

In spite of the increase in direct investments to produce goods for reimport, an interesting occurrence is that firms usually export substantially to their foreign facilities. Many of these exports would not occur if it were not for the existence of the overseas investments. In these cases, factor movements stimulate rather than substitute for trade. One reason for this phenomenon is that domestic operating units may ship materials and components to their foreign facilities for use in a finished product. For example, the Mexican government requires that all automobiles sold in Mexico be assembled there. Chrysler therefore has an investment in Mexico to which parts are shipped from the United States. The foreign subsidiaries or affiliates may also buy capital equipment or supplies from home country firms because of the confidence in performance and delivery or because of desires for maximum worldwide uniformity. A foreign facility may produce part of the product line while serving as sales agent for exports of its parent's other products. Moulinex, for instance, continues to export its small cooking utensils from France while using the sales force from its U.S. manufacturing operations to handle the imports.

DIRECT INVESTMENT MOTIVATION

- Business motivations
  - expand markets
  - acquire supplies or resources
- Government motivation may additionally be to
  - gain political advantage

The reasons that firms engage in direct investment ownership are no different from those outlined in Chapter 4 for their pursuit of international trade. These are

1. to expand markets by selling abroad,
2. to acquire foreign resources (e.g., raw materials, production efficiency, knowledge), and
3. at a government level, to attain some political advantage.

These three objectives in turn may be pursued by any one of three forms of foreign involvement. One of these, the sale of services (e.g., licensing or management contracts) is often avoided either for fear of the loss of control of key competitive assets or because of greater economies from self-ownership of production. This avoidance was discussed earlier in the chapter. The following discussion will concentrate on the remaining two forms: trade and direct investment. Emphasis will be on why the latter is chosen in view of the fact that most firms consider it riskier to operate a facility abroad than at home.

MARKET EXPANSION INVESTMENTS

Transportation

- Increases landed cost too greatly for some products
  - must produce near market

Early trade theorists usually assumed away the cost of transporting goods from one place to another. More recent location theorists have considered total landed cost (cost of production plus shipping) as being more relevant. When transportation is added to production costs, some products become impractical to ship over a great distance. In the opening case of the chapter we showed that one of the factors influencing Bridgestone's decision to invest in the United States was the high cost of transporting tires relative to the production price of tires. One can think of numerous other products that are impractical to ship great distances without a very large escalation in the price. A few of these products and their investing companies are newspapers (Thompson Newspapers, Canadian), margarine (Unilever, British-Dutch), dynamite (Nobel, Swedish), and soft drinks (Pepsico, U.S.). For these firms it is usually necessary to produce abroad if they are to sell abroad.

- Excess domestic capacity
  - usually means exporting rather than direct investment
  - may be competitive through variable cost pricing

Lack of domestic capacity. As long as a company has excess capacity at its home country plant, it might be able to compete effectively in limited export markets in spite of the high transport costs. This could be because the fixed operating expenses are covered through domestic sales; thus foreign prices can be set on the basis of variable rather than full cost. Such a pricing strategy may give way as foreign sales become more important or as output nears full plant capacity utilization. This is one of the factors that helps to explain why firms, even those with products for which transport charges are a high portion of total landed costs, typically export before producing abroad. The other major factor is that companies want to get a better indication that it will be feasible to sell a sufficient amount in the foreign country before committing resources for foreign production.

This reluctance to expand total capacity while there is still substantial excess capacity is not unlike a domestic expansion decision. Internationally as well as domestically, growth is apt to take place in increments. To understand this process, it is useful to draw a parallel of how growth may take place domestically. The simplest example is the firm that makes only one product. Most likely, this firm will begin operations near the city where its founders are already residing and will begin selling in only the local or regional area. Eventually, sales may be expanded to a larger geographic market. As capacity is reached, the firm may build a second plant in another part of the country to serve that region and save on transportation costs. Warehouses and sales offices may be located in various cities in order to assure closer contact with customers. Purchasing offices may be located close to suppliers in order to improve the probability of delivery at low prices. In fact, the company may even acquire some of its customers or suppliers in order to reduce inventories and gain economies in distribution. Certain functions may be further decentralized geographically, such as the location of financial offices near a financial center. As the product line evolves and expands, operations continue to disperse. In the pursuit of foreign business it is not surprising that firms find it necessary to acquire assets abroad.

- Large-scale process technology
  - large-scale production and export usually reduce unit landed costs, since fixed costs are covered
- Small-scale process technology
  - country-by-country production usually reduces unit landed costs, since transportation is minimized

Scale economies. Transportation costs must be examined in relation to the type of technology used to produce a good. The manufacture of some products necessitates plant and equipment that use a high fixed capital input. In such a situation, especially if the product is highly standardized or undifferentiated from competitors, the cost per unit is apt to drop significantly as output increases. Products such as ball bearings, alumina, and semiconductor wafers fall into this category. Such products are exported substantially because the cost savings from scale economies overcome the added transport expenses to get goods to foreign markets. Products that are more differentiated and labor intensive, such as pharmaceuticals and certain prepared foods, are not as sensitive to scale economies. For these types of products, transportation costs may dictate smaller plants to serve national rather than international markets.[7] David's Cookies, for example, first entered the Japanese market with ingredients mixed in the United States. However, there was little cost reduction through consolidation of Japanese and American batter preparation. Consequently, David's switched to Japanese ingredient preparation to overcome the transport cost incurred when exporting.[8]

Trade Restrictions

- If imports highly restricted
  - companies often produce locally to serve market
  - firms more prone to produce locally if market potential is high in relation to scale economies

Chapter 5 showed that for various reasons there are numerous ways in which a government can make it impractical for a firm to reach its market potential through exportation alone. The firm may find that it *must* produce in a foreign country if it is to sell there. In 1982, for example, Mexico announced that within five years, locally produced microcomputers would have to comprise 70 percent of the market. Although many producers questioned whether the same prices and quality could be maintained as when they exported, they nevertheless were reluctant to abandon a market growing at 25 percent a year.[9] Such government pronouncements are not unusual. They undoubtedly favor large companies that can afford to commit large amounts of resources abroad and make foreign competitiveness more difficult for the smaller firms, which can afford only to export as a means of serving foreign markets.

How prevalent are trade restrictions as an enticement for making direct investments? There are substantial numbers of anecdotal examples of firms' decisions to locate within protected markets, yet studies of aggregate direct investment movements have disagreed on the importance of trade barriers.[10] A possible explanation for the fact that some studies have not found import barriers to be an important enticement is that the studies have had to rely on actual tariff barriers as the measurement of restrictions. This reliance overlooks the importance of nontariff constraints, indirect entry barriers, and potential trade restrictions. In the opening case, Bridgestone reacted to these latter impediments to trade rather than to the actual existence of tariffs. It seems certain that import barriers are a major enticement to direct investment but that they must be viewed alongside other factors, such as the market size of the country imposing barriers.

Import trade restrictions, for example, have been highly influential in enticing automobile producers to locate in Mexico. Similar restrictions on automobiles by Central American countries have been ineffective because of their small markets. However, Central American import barriers on products requiring lower amounts of capital investment and therefore smaller markets (e.g., pharmaceuticals) have been highly effective at enticing direct investment.

Consumer-Imposed Restrictions

- Consumers sometimes prefer domestically made products because
  - nationalism
  - believe their own products are better

One usually thinks of government-imposed legal measures as the only trade barriers to otherwise competitive goods, but consumer desires may also dictate limitations. Consumers may have a preference for buying domestically made goods even though these are more expensive. They may also demand that merchandise be altered so substantially that foreign production becomes unfeasible. The question of preference for domestically made prod-

- fear that foreign made goods may not be delivered on time
- they are more likely geared to the latest local preferences

ucts may be due to nationalistic feelings, to a belief that foreign-made goods are inferior, or to a fear that service and spare parts will not be easily obtainable for imported wares.

Nationalism. The impact of nationalistic feelings on investment movements is not easily assessed; however, some evidence does exist. There have been active campaigns at times in many countries to persuade people to buy locally produced goods. In the United States, for instance, attempts have been made in recent years to boycott Polish hams, Japanese Christmas ornaments, and French wines. Some firms, such as Zenith, have gone so far as to advertise that since their televisions are made with domestic labor, the U.S. public should prefer them to foreign-made goods. The promotion was of questionable value, however, since Zenith finally moved production to Mexico. Fearful that adverse public opinion might lead to curbs on television imports, firms such as Mitsubishi and Toshiba announced the establishment of TV production plants in the United States.[11]

Product image. The link between product image and direct investment is a bit clearer than the one between nationalism and direct investment discussed above. The image may stem from the merchandise itself or from beliefs concerning after-sales servicing. In tests using commodities that were identical except for the label of country origin, it has been found that consumers view wares differently on the basis of product source.[12] It may be slow and costly for a company to overcome image problems created by manufacturing in a country having a lower image status for a particular product. Consequently, there may be advantages in producing in a country with an already existing high image. For example, a Canadian electronics producer found U.S. consumers reluctant to purchase its products because of a belief that Canadian electronics were inferior to U.S. electronics. When part of the output was shifted to the United States and "Made in U.S.A." was put on the label, this problem disappeared.[13]

Delivery risk. There is considerable fear that parts for foreign-made goods may be difficult to obtain from abroad. Industrial consumers often prefer to pay a higher price to a producer located nearby in order to minimize the risk of nondelivery due to distances and strikes. For instance, Hoechst Chemical of West Germany located one of its dye factories in North Carolina because that region's textile industry feared delivery problems from the cheaper German imports.

Product change. It is often essential to alter a product to suit local tastes or requirements. This may compel the use of local raw materials and market testing. It is most difficult and expensive to test market and alter a product at a great distance from the production. Coca-Cola, for example, sells abroad some drinks (made from local fruits) that are not available in the United States. It is assuredly much cheaper to make these overseas.

The necessity of product alteration has two other effects on company production. To begin with, it means an additional investment. As long as an investment is needed to serve the foreign market anyway, management might consider locating facilities abroad. Next, product alteration may mean that certain economies from large-scale production will be lost. This may cause the least-cost location to shift from one country to another. The more the product has to be altered for the foreign market, the more likely that the production will be shifted abroad. Two of the factors influencing the decision of Volkswagen to set up U.S. production facilities, for example, were the ever-increasing safety requirements set by the U.S. government and the desire for new options by U.S. consumers, which were different from those needed to sell in other parts of the world.[14]

Following Customers

● Keep customers by producing abroad when customers produce abroad

We very often find examples of companies that sell abroad indirectly— that is, they sell products, components, or services domestically that become embodied in a product or service that their domestic customer then exports. Bridgestone, for example, sold tires to Toyota and Honda, which in turn exported fully assembled cars (including the tires) to foreign markets. In these situations it is common for the indirect exporters to follow their customers when those customers make direct investments. Bridgestone's investment decision in the United States was partially based on a desire to continue selling to Honda and Toyota once those companies initiated U.S. production. Bridgestone's decision was in turn instrumental in Yasuda Fire & Marine Insurance Co.'s decision to establish a U.S. investment in order to provide workmen's compensation insurance to Bridgestone's U.S. operations.[15]

Following Competitors

● Competitors tend to make direct investments in a given country at similar times
  ● country conditions noted by all
  ● prevent competitor's advantage

Within oligopoly industries it has been observed that several investors often establish facilities in a given country within a fairly short time period.[16] Much of this concentration can be explained by internal or external changes, which would affect most oligopolists within an industry at approximately the same time. In many industries, for example, capacity expansion cycles are similar for most firms. Thus the firms would logically consider a foreign investment at approximately the same time, as their domestic capacity point is approached. Externally, they might all be faced with changes in import restrictions or market conditions that indicate a move to direct investment in order to serve consumers in a given country. In spite of the prevalence of these motivators, much of the movement by oligopolists seems better explained by defensive motives.

Much of the research done in game theory shows that people often make decisions based on the "least damaging alternative." The question for many firms is "Do I lose less by moving abroad or by staying at home?" Let us say that some foreign market may be effectively served only by an investment in the market, but the market is large enough to support only one producer. One way of facing this problem would be for competitors to set up one joint operation and divide profit among them; however, anti-trust laws might discourage or prevent this.[17] If only one firm does decide to establish facilities, it will have an advantage over its competitors by garnering a larger market, spreading its R&D costs, and making a profit that can be reinvested in other areas of the world. Once one firm decides to produce in the market, competitors are prone to follow quickly rather than let the firm gain advantages. The decision is thus based not so much on the benefits to be gained, but rather on the greater losses sustained by not entering the field. In most oligopoly industries (e.g., automobiles, tires, petroleum), one can see this pattern. It helps to explain the large number of producers relative to the size of the market in some countries.

Changes in Comparative Costs

- Least-cost production location changes due to inflation, wage rates, etc.

A company may export successfully because its home country has a cost advantage. The home country cost advantage depends on the price of the individual factors of production, the size of operations, transportation of finished goods, and the productivity of the combined production factors. None of these conditions affecting cost is static; consequently, the least-cost location may change over time. Another factor affecting Volkswagen's decision to locate in the United States was the fact that during the 1970s, German wage rates (measured in dollars) grew much faster than those in the United States, owing largely to a rise in the value of the mark relative to that of the dollar. Volkswagen estimated a 10 percent cost savings by producing in the United States for that market.[18]

The concept of shifts in comparative costs of production is closely related to that of resource-seeking investments as well. A firm may establish a direct investment to serve a foreign market but eventually import into the home country from the country to which it was once exporting. Some of these concepts will be discussed in the following section on supply-oriented investments, particularly the subsection on the product life cycle.

SUPPLY-ORIENTED INVESTMENTS

A cartoon ran a picture of Santa Claus speaking to his elves and captioned, "I'm sorry to report that after the first, I'll be moving operations to Taiwan."[19] This cartoon is consistent with the popular image of direct investments motivated by cheap foreign labor used to make imported products. While this does take place, it is only a partial picture of the direct investments that gain resources and supplies from other countries.

Vertical Integration

- Raw materials, production, and marketing often in different countries
  - control of different levels ensures smoother flow and may reduce costs
- Most vertical integration is supply oriented

Vertical integration involves gaining control of different stages as a product moves from its earliest production to its final distribution. As products and their marketing become more complicated, there is a greater need to combine resources located in more than one country. If one country has iron, a second has coal, a third has the technology and capital for making steel and steel products, and a fourth has the demand for the steel products, there is a great interdependence among the four and a strong need to establish tight relationships in order to ensure the continuance of the production and marketing flow. One way of adding assurance to this flow is by gaining a voice in the management of one of the foreign operations by investing in it. Most of the world's direct investment in petroleum may be explained through this interdependence concept. Since much of the petroleum supply is located in countries different from those with a heavy petroleum demand, the oil industry has become vertically integrated on an international basis.

Certain economies may also be gained through vertical integration. The greater assurance of supply and/or markets may allow a firm to carry smaller inventories and spend less on promotion. It may also permit considerably greater flexibility in shifting funds, taxes, and profits from one country to another through artificial intercompany transfer prices, as will be discussed more fully in Chapters 20 and 21. Let us say, for example, that a company produces raw materials in Brazil and a finished product in West Germany. The company has fairly wide discretion as to the price the Brazilian subsidiary charges the German subsidiary for the raw materials. If the German tax rate is higher than the Brazilian rate, the company may charge a higher price to the German operation so that profits are shifted to Brazil, where the tax is lower. On the other hand, if there is difficulty in taking funds out of Brazil because of exchange control problems, the company may shift profits to West Germany by charging a lower price to the German operation. This serves as a means of moving funds out of Brazil.

Advantages of vertical integration may accrue to a firm by either market-oriented or supply-oriented investments in other countries. There are examples of both. Of the two, however, there have been more in recent years among manufacturers to gain raw materials in other countries than vice versa. This is because of the growing dependence on raw materials in LDCs and the lack of resources by LDC firms to invest substantially abroad. This movement of capital and technology to LDCs is consistent with a theory that holds that factor mobility is most efficient when the more mobile factors, such as capital, move so as to be combined with the less mobile ones, such as natural resources. Without the capital movement the natural resources might otherwise not be exploited efficiently.[20]

Rationalized Production

- Different components or portions of product line in different parts of the world
  - advantage of factor cost differences
  - advantage of long production runs
  - satisfy governments that local production takes place
  - but higher risk of work stoppage
  - but record keeping more difficult

Companies increasingly produce different components or different portions of their product line in different parts of the world (**rationalized production**) to take advantage of varying costs of labor, capital, and raw materials. Such firms as Litton Industries and Fairchild Camera are among more than 200 U.S. firms that have established labor operations in northern Mexico. Semifinished goods can be exported to Mexico duty free, as long as they will be reexported from Mexico. Once the labor-intensive portion of production is accomplished in Mexico, the goods are reshipped to the United States and are subject to duties in the United States only on the amount of value added in Mexico. U.S. firms are by no means the only ones taking advantage of lower labor costs for part of their manufacturing operations. Much of the investment of Swedish companies in Poland, such as Alfa-Laval, Electrolux, SKF Ball Bearing, Atvidaperg Furniture, ASEA Engineering Combine, and Ericsson Telephone Company, is of this type.[21]

Many companies shrug off the possibility of rationalized production of parts because of the risks of work stopping in many countries due to a strike or of a change in import regulations in just one country. There is a further problem: Firms are required to keep detailed cost records to prove that duty is paid on all the costs incurred in the foreign production. Warnaco did not do this for portions of its White Stag apparel line made in Japan, Hong Kong, and Taiwan for final production in the United States. The company was fined on 150 counts.[22]

An alternative to parts rationalization is the production of a complete product in a given country but only part of the product range within that country.[23] A U.S. subsidiary in France, for example, may produce only product A, another subsidiary in Brazil only product B, and the home plant in the United States only product C. Each plant sells worldwide so that each can gain scale economies and take advantage of differences in input costs that may affect total production cost differences. Each may get concessions to import because of demonstrating that jobs and incomes are developed locally.

Access to Production Factors

- Presence in country may improve knowledge flow and access to other resources

Closely resembling the vertical integration concept is that of seeking abroad some input not easily or cheaply available in the home country. Many foreign firms have offices in New York in order to gain better access to the U.S. capital market, or at least to the knowledge of what is happening within that market that can affect other worldwide capital occurrences. The search for knowledge may take other forms as well. It may be a U.S. pharmaceutical firm in Peru conducting research that is not allowed in the United States. It may be C.F.P. (French), which bought a share in Leonard Petroleum to learn U.S. marketing in order to compete better with other U.S. oil firms outside the United States. It may be McGraw-Hill, which has an office in Europe to uncover European technical developments.

Foreign acquisitions may give firms faster and cheaper access to certain resources. Because of the technical lead of the United States in semiconductors, such firms as Siemens and Robert A. Bosch from West Germany have found it more expeditious to acquire U.S. firms with advanced capabilities than to develop them independently.[24] In a study of foreign firms with investments in the United States it was found that the ability to gain access to technology was a very important factor in the decision to invest.[25]

The Product Life Cycle Theory

- New products, main production in industrial countries
- Mature products, main production in LDCs
- Not all products go through shift in location

One explanation for changes in the location of production is called the product life cycle (PLC) theory.[26] (Recall the explanation of the theory in relation to trade in Chapter 4.) Basically, the PLC holds that new products are more apt to be made in highly developed countries, whereas developing countries should have an advantage in the fabrication of mature merchandise. This is due to several factors. First, R&D expenditures are much higher in the developed areas of the world because of larger markets and resources. Just as a company begins operating in the locale of its founders, it begins manufacturing new products near the locale of its development. The major market for advanced goods is also in the developed areas of the world, and it is useful to be near this market if alterations are needed in early production stages. New products are not too apt to have a very routinized and standardized method of manufacture. Consequently, the higher-educated labor force, which usually is available in the more advanced countries, is more adept at adjusting to new production methods as they are needed.

Once a product becomes mature, however, there is apt to be a larger market in the developing areas of the world, and there is likely to be a very standardized manufacturing method. At this point it may be advantageous to shift the output to a developing country, where lower-skilled but cheaper labor is available.

- PLC exceptions
  - product differentiation
  - rapid obsolescence

Recent tests show that this pattern holds for many but not all products.[27] There are a number of reasons why some products do not exhibit a shift in production location. If, for example, a company can successfully differentiate its product through advertising or other means, it may be able to maintain its production in a highly developed country rather than in a developing country long after product maturity is reached. In addition, some products, such as fashion items, are displaced by new products at such a fast rate that there is no time to shift production at a mature stage.[28] The PLC theory does explain much of the shift in production location to service domestic markets from multiple locations around the world.

Government Investment Incentives

● Government incentives may shift the least-cost location of production

In addition to putting restrictions on imports, countries frequently encourage direct investment inflows by offering tax concessions or a wide variety of other subsidies. Such incentives are offered by the central governments of every industrial country except the United States and Japan.[29] LDCs offer them as well. Among the direct assistance are tax holidays, accelerated depreciation, low-interest loans, loan guarantees, subsidized energy or transport, and the construction of rail spurs and roads to serve the plant facility.[30] These incentives affect the comparative cost of production among countries, enticing companies to invest in certain countries to serve national or international markets.

POLITICAL MOTIVES

● Governments take ownership in or give incentives to direct investors to
  ● gain supplies of strategic resources
  ● develop spheres of influence

In Chapter 4 we showed that trade has sometimes been undertaken historically for political motives. During the mercantilist period, for example, European powers sought colonies in order to control their foreign trade and extend the sphere of influence of the mother countries. Since colonialism is no longer an acceptable practice, it is argued that many of the old colonial aims may be achieved by having companies control vital sectors in the economies of LDCs.[31] For instance, if a U.S. firm controls the production of a vital raw material in an LDC, it can effectively prevent unfriendly countries from gaining access to the production. It may also be able to hold down prices to the home country, prevent local processing, and dictate its own terms for operating. It has been pointed out, for example, that Great Britain, France, Italy, and Japan established national oil companies with governmental participation (B.P. C.F.P., E.N.I., and J.P.D.C., respectively) in order to lessen their reliance on U.S. multinational petroleum firms, which might give preference to the United States in the allocation of supplies.[32] It has been argued that, in the process of gaining control of resources, much political control is transferred to the industrial nations.

Governmental encouragement of MNE expansion to other developed countries may be for gaining greater control over vital resources. Japan, for example, is highly dependent on foreign sources for certain foodstuffs, lumber, and raw materials. In recent years, Japanese governmental agencies have been assisting national companies to undertake foreign investments in these sectors in order to protect supplies in Japan.[33]

The control of resources is not necessarily the only political aim for encouraging direct investors. During the early 1980s, for example, the U.S. government instituted various incentives designed to increase the profitability of U.S. investment in Caribbean countries that were unfriendly to the Castro regime of Cuba. The reasoning was that the incentives would lure more investment to the area, causing the economies of the friendly nations to strengthen. This would in turn make it difficult for unfriendly leftist governments to gain control. (This situation is treated in the case at the end of Chapter 12.)

It is interesting to note that although government ownership and control of companies has been increasing, by no means have all these government enterprises become multinational. There are simply too many objectives for government ownership other than control over foreign economies. Even if the government enterprise has foreign facilities, it does not necessarily mean that the motive described above prompted the investment.[34] For example, the firm may be acting in terms of any of the rational economic motives discussed earlier in the chapter.

MULTIPLE MOTIVES

- Combination of factors, rather than one, usually explain a direct investment

Although previous discussions within this chapter have categorized investments by separate motives, in reality most decisions to invest abroad, such as the Bridgestone case at the beginning of the chapter, are based on multiple motives. One such combination of influences may be illustrated by automobile investments in Brazil.

As the automobile became a mature product, there were considerable opportunities for saving labor costs by moving operations to a country having cheap labor, such as Brazil. One problem, however, is that economies of large-scale operations are needed to reduce the total cost of the vehicles. As long as car imports were permitted by Brazil, the U.S. and European producers could serve the Brazilian market more cheaply by exporting than by manufacturing a low volume in Brazil for that market. To move *all* operations to Brazil would be too costly and would so disrupt domestic operations that some type of home government sanctions would be inevitable. However, in the next stage, Brazil required local production as a requisite for serving the Brazilian consumer. Consequently, Ford, General Motors, Chrysler, Volkswagen, Daimler Benz, Saab-Scandia, Alfa Romeo, and Fiat established facilities, and production first got underway in 1957. They built plants because the Brazilian market was deemed too important to lose and too important for competitors to have to themselves. Now output is high. Brazil is a major exporter and even sends components back to home countries.[35]

The political motives are seldom in isolation from economic motives. To encourage companies to invest abroad, governments must consider the objectives of the potential investors. U.S. policymakers, for example, reasoned that many U.S. firms might find it advantageous to tap cheap labor sources in the Caribbean. Consequently, legislation was enacted to allow the Caribbean output to enter the U.S. virtually free of restrictions. Investors, acting purely on economic motives, helped to achieve governmental objectives.

ADVANTAGES OF DIRECT INVESTORS

- Most successful domestic firms invest abroad, especially ones with unique advantages
- Direct investment makes firms more successful domestically

Are companies big because they are multinational or are they multinational because they are big? Such a "chicken-and-egg" type question has hounded direct investment theorists. On one hand, there is some evidence that the very successful domestic firms are the ones most likely to commit resources to direct investments. On the other hand, there is evidence that the ownership for foreign direct investment makes firms more successful domestically.

Monopoly Advantages before Direct Investment

One explanation for direct investment is that investors perceive a monopoly advantage over similar companies in the countries to which they go. The advantage is due to the ownership of some resource that is not available at the same price or terms to the local firm. The resource may be in the form of access to markets, patents, product differentiation, management skills, or the like. Because of the greater cost usually incurred by transferring resources abroad and the perceived greater risk of operating in a different environment, the firm will not move unless it expects a higher return than at home and a higher return than the local firm abroad.[36]

Certain monopoly advantages may accrue to large groups of firms and explain their relative ability and willingness to move abroad. One such observation has been made in reference to the cost and access to capital. When the capital component is an integral part of a new investment, the company that can borrow in a country with a low interest rate has an advantage over the company that cannot. Before World War I, Great Britain was the largest source for direct investment because of the strength of sterling and the resulting lower interest rates on borrowing sterling funds. In recent years the strength of the U.S. dollar gave an advantage to U.S. firms.[37]

Related to this is the relative power of different currencies in terms of the plant and equipment they will purchase. During the two and a half decades immediately following World War II, the U.S. dollar was very strong, and it was perhaps overvalued in later years. The result was that by converting dollars to other currencies, U.S. firms could purchase a greater output capacity in foreign countries than they could after the dollar began to slide downward in 1971. The reverse was true for firms from such countries as West Germany and Japan, which invested more heavily in the United States during the late 1970s when the yen and mark increased their purchasing power.

Currency values do not, however, provide a strong explanation of direct investment patterns. There was a two-way investment flow between the United States and West Germany and the United States and Japan when the dollar was weak as well as when the dollar was strong. Then in the first half of the 1980s, U.S. companies were not increasing investment abroad significantly, whereas foreign companies were investing heavily in the United States in spite of the strong dollar. The major reasons were high real interest rates in the United States and a relatively strong U.S. economy. The currency strength situation is therefore only a partial explanation of direct investment flows and must be viewed along with other multiple motives for direct investment.

Advantages after Direct Investment

- Firms with foreign
  investments
  - tend to be more profitable
  - tend to have more stable
    sales and earnings

In order to support large-scale expenditures, such as expenditures for R&D, that are necessary to maintain a domestic competitive viability, it is frequently necessary to sell on a global basis.[38] To do this, it is often necessary to establish direct investments abroad. The advantage accruing to multinationals rather than to purely domestic firms by spreading out some of the costs of product differentiation, research and development, and advertising is apparent in a comparison of the domestic profitability of the two types of firms. Among groups of similar size that spent comparable amounts on advertising and employed comparable numbers of scientists and engineers, the MNEs in every case earned more on their domestic investments than did the purely domestic firms.[39]

Economies in different countries are in different stages of the business cycle at different times. It has been noted that companies that operate in these different economies are more able to reduce fluctuations in year-to-year sales and earnings than firms operating only in a domestic environment.[40] This effectively reduces operating risks for them.

SUMMARY

- Direct investment is the control of a company in one country by an organization from another country. Because of the difficulty of defining control, arbitrary minimum ownership of the voting stock is used to define direct investment.

- Governments are concerned about who controls enterprises within their confines for fear that decisions will be made that are contrary to the national interest.

- Firms often prefer to control foreign production facilities because (a) the transfer of certain assets to a noncontrolled entity might otherwise undermine the competitive position and (b) there are economies of buying and selling with a controlled entity.

- Although a direct investment is usually acquired by transferring capital from one country to another, capital is not usually the only contribution made by the investor or the only means of gaining equity. The investing firm may supply technology, personnel, and markets in exchange for an interest in a company in a foreign country.

- The factors of production and finished goods are only partially mobile internationally. Moving either one is one means of compensating for differences in factor endowments among countries.

- The cost and feasibility of transferring international production factors versus finished goods will determine which alternative results in cheaper costs.

- Although a direct investment may be a substitute for trade, it may also stimulate trade through sales of components, equipment, and complementary products.

- As is the case with foreign trade, foreign direct investment may be undertaken as a means of expanding foreign markets or to gain access to supplies of resources or finished products. In addition, governments may encourage direct investments for political purposes.

- The price of some products increases too substantially if transported internationally; therefore foreign production is necessary in order to tap foreign markets.

- Companies usually try to hold out on establishing foreign production as long as they have excess domestic capacity.

- The degree to which scale economies lower production costs is one of the determinants of whether to centralize production in one or a few countries or to disperse it among many countries.

- Since most direct investments are for the purpose of selling in the country where the investments are located, governmental restrictions that prevent the effective importation of goods are probably a most compelling force causing firms to establish their direct investments.

- Consumers may feel compelled to buy domestically made products even though these products are more expensive. They may also demand that product alterations be made to fit their needs. Both of these consumer demands may dictate the need to establish foreign operations to serve foreign markets.

- Direct investment sometimes has chain effects. When one company makes an investment, some of its suppliers follow with investments of their own, followed by investments by their suppliers, and so on.

- In oligopoly industries, companies from the same industry have been noted to invest at about the same time in a foreign country. This is sometimes because they are responding to similar market conditions and sometimes because they wish to negate competitors' advantages in the markets.

- Vertical integration is needed to control the flow of goods across borders from basic production to final consumption in an increasingly interdependent and complex world distribution system. It may result in lower operating costs and may make it easier for firms to transfer funds among countries.

- Rationalized production involves the production of different components or different products in different countries to take advantage of different factor costs.

- The least-cost location of production may change over time, especially in the life cycle of a product. In general, advanced countries have a cost advantage in the production of new products, and less-developed countries have an advantage in mature products.

- The least-cost production location may change because of government incentives that effectively subsidize production.

- Governments may encourage their firms to invest abroad in order to gain advantages over other countries.

- Most investments are made because of interrelated multiple motives.

- The possibility of holding certain monopolistic advantages helps to explain why firms are willing to take what they perceive to be higher risks of operating abroad. This also helps to explain the dominance by firms from certain countries and the advantages certain currencies have in exchange.

- Foreign investment may enable firms to spread certain fixed costs vis-à-vis domestic firms. It may also enable firms to gain access to needed resources, to prevent competitors from gaining control of needed resources, and smooth sales and earnings on a year-to-year basis.

C A S E   ELECTROLUX ACQUISITIONS[41]

Electrolux is Sweden's largest manufacturer of electrical household appliances and was one of the world's pioneers in the marketing of vacuum cleaners. However, not all the products bearing the Electrolux name are controlled by the Swedish firm. Electrolux vacuum cleaners sold and manufactured in the United States, for example, have not been connected with the Swedish firm since the U.S. subsidiaries were sold in the 1960s. The Swedish firm reentered the U.S. market in 1974 by purchasing National Union Electric, which manufactures Eureka vacuum cleaners.

Electrolux pursued its early international expansion largely to gain economies of scale through additional sales. The Swedish market was simply too small to absorb fixed costs as much as the home markets for competitive firms from larger countries. When additional sales were not possible by exporting, Electrolux was still able to gain certain scale economies through the establishment of foreign production. Research and development expenditures and certain administrative costs could thus be spread out over the additional sales made possible by foreign operations. Additionally, Electrolux concentrated on standardized production to achieve further scale economies and rationalization of parts.

Until the late 1960s, Electrolux concentrated primarily on vacuum cleaners and the building of its own facilities in order to effect expansion. Throughout the 1970s, though, the firm expanded largely by acquiring existing firms whose product lines differed from those of Electrolux. The compelling force was to add appliance lines to complement those developed internally. Its recent profits ($220 million in 1983) have enabled Electrolux to go on an acquisitions binge. Electrolux acquired two Swedish firms that made home appliances and washing machines. Electrolux management felt that it could use its existing foreign sales networks to increase the sales of those firms. In 1973, Electrolux acquired another Swedish firm, Facit, which already had extensive foreign sales and facilities. Vacuum cleaner producers were acquired in the United States and in France; and to gain captive sales for vacuum cleaners, Electrolux acquired commercial cleaning service firms in Sweden and in the United States. A French kitchen equipment producer, Arthur Martin, was bought, as was a Swiss home appliance firm, Therma, and a U.S. cooking equipment manufacturer, Tappan.

Except for the Facit purchase, the above acquisitions all involved firms that produced complementary lines that would enable the new parent to gain certain scale economies. However, not all the products of acquired firms were related, and Electrolux sought to sell off unrelated businesses. In 1978, for example, a Swedish firm, Husqvarna, was bought because of its kitchen equipment lines. Electrolux was able to sell Husqvarna's motorcycle line but could not get a good price for the chain saw facility. Reconciled to being in the chain saw business, Electrolux then acquired chain saw manufacturers in Canada and Norway, thus becoming one of the world's largest chain saw producers. The above are merely the most significant Electrolux acquisitions; the firm made approximately fifty acquisitions in the 1970s.

In 1980, Electrolux announced a takeover that was very different from those of the 1970s. It offered $175 million, the biggest Electrolux acquisition, for Granges, Sweden's leading metal producer and fabricator. Granges was itself a multinational firm (1979 sales of $1.2 billion) and made about 50 percent of its sales outside of Sweden. The managing directors of the two firms indicated that the major advantage of the takeover would be the integration of Granges' aluminum, copper, plastics, and other materials into Electrolux's production of appliances. Many analysts felt that the timing of Electrolux's bid was based on indications that Beijerinvest, a large Swedish conglomerate, wished to acquire a nonferrous metals mining company. Other analysts felt that Electrolux would be better off to continue international horizontal expansion, as it had in the 1970s. The analysts pointed to large appliance makers such as AEG Telefunken of West Germany that were likely candidates for takeover because of recent poor performance.

QUESTIONS

1. How do Electrolux's reasons for direct investment differ from those of Bridgestone at the beginning of the chapter?
2. How has Electrolux's strategy changed over time? How has this affected its direct investment activities?
3. Which of Electrolux's foreign investments would be horizontal and which would be vertical? What are the advantages of each?
4. What do you see as the main advantages and possible problems of expanding internationally primarily through acquisitions as opposed to building one's own facilities?
5. Should Electrolux take over Granges?

NOTES

1. Data for the case were taken from Urban C. Lehner, "Bridgestone Looks Overseas for Growth," *Wall Street Journal,* June 17, 1981, p. 1; Edward Noga, "Bridgestone," *Automotive News,* April 20, 1981, p. E10; Edward Noga, "Bridgestone Tries U.S. Market," *Advertising Age,* April 6, 1981, p. 85; David Pauly, "Bridgestone Tire: Made in Japan," *Newsweek,* August 11, 1980, pp. 62–64; Mike Tharp, "Bridgestone, Japan's Tire Giant, Now Seeking International Role," *New York Times,* November 21, 1980, p. D4; Ralph E. Winter, "Firestone Confers with Bridgestone," *Wall Street Journal,* April 15, 1981, p. 3; "Japan: Why a Tiremaker Wants a U.S. Base," *Business Week,* January 14, 1980, p. 40; Margaret Yao, "Firestone Agrees to Sell Tire Plant to Japanese Firm," *Wall Street Journal,* February 16, 1982, p. 52; Bernard Krisher, "A Different Kind of Tiremaker Rolls into Nashville," *Fortune,* Vol. 105, No. 6, March 22, 1982, pp. 136–145.
2. Some recent surveys of the considerable number of explanations may be found in Jean J. Boddewyn, "Foreign and Domestic Divestment and Investment Decisions," *Journal of International Business Studies,* Vol. XIV, No. 3, Winter 1983, pp. 23–35;

A. L. Calvet, "A Synthesis of Foreign Direct Investment Theories and Theories of the Multinational Firm," *Journal of International Business Studies,* Spring–Summer 1981, pp. 43–60; John H. Dunning, "Toward an Eclectic Theory of International Production," *Journal of International Business Studies,* Spring–Summer 1980, pp. 9–31; Robert Grosse, "The Theory of Foreign Direct Investment," *Essays in International Business,* No. 3, December 1981, pp. 1–51; M. Z. Rahman, "Maximisation of Global Interests: Ultimate Motivation for Foreign Investments by Transnational Corporations," *Management International Review,* Vol. 23, No. 4, 1983, pp. 4–13.

3. Krisher, *op. cit.,* p. 141.

4. "The Subsidiary That Rebelled," *Time,* July 23, 1969, pp. 68–69.

5. This desire to hold a monopoly control over certain information or other proprietary assets has been noted by such writers as M. Casson, "The Theory of Foreign Direct Investment," Discussion Paper Number 50 (Reading, England: University of Reading International Investment and Business Studies, November 1980); Stephen Magee, "Information and the MNC: An Appropriability Theory of Direct Foreign Investment," in *The New International Economic Order,* Jagdish N. Bhagwati, ed. (Cambridge, Mass.: The MIT Press, 1977), pp. 317–340; Alan H. Rugman, *Inside the Multinationals: The Economics of Internal Markets* (New York: Columbia University Press, 1981).

6. "Plessey Co. Acquires Airborne Accessories for $8.9 Million Notes," *Wall Street Journal,* February 21, 1968, p. 6.

7. Yves Doz, "Managing Manufacturing Rationalization within Multinational Companies," *Columbia Journal of World Business,* Fall 1978.

8. Clyde Haberman, "Made in Japan: U.S. Cookie," *New York Times,* February 17, 1984, p. B6.

9. Lawrence Rout, "Mexico Limits U.S. Makers of Computers," *Wall Street Journal,* February 1, 1982, p. 31.

10. Studies that found import barriers to be an important enticement include Sanjaya Lall and N. S. Siddharthan, "The Monopolistic Advantages of Multinationals: Lessons from Foreign Investment in the U.S.," *The Economic Journal,* Vol. 92, No. 367, September 1982, pp. 668–683; T. Horst, "Firm and Industry Determinants of the Decision to Invest Abroad," *Review of Economics and Statistics,* August 1972, pp. 258–266; John H. Dunning, *American Investment in British Manufacturing Industry* (London: Allen and Unwin, 1958); and D. Orr, "The Determinants of Entry: A Study of the Canadian Manufacturing Industries," *Review of Economics and Statistics,* Vol. 57, 1975, pp. 58–66. Those not finding import barriers to be important include R. E. Caves, M. E. Porter, A. M. Spence, and J. T. Scott, *Competition in the Open Economy: A Model Applied to Canada* (Cambridge, Mass.: Harvard University Press, 1980); and B. Balassa, "Effects of Commercial Policy on International Trade, the Location of Production and Factor Movements," in *The International Allocation of Economic Activity,* Bertil Ohlin, ed. (New York: Holmes & Meier, 1977).

11. "Toshiba Plans to Build Color-TV Plant in U.S.," *Wall Street Journal,* April 5, 1977, p. 43; "Mitsubishi U.S. Unit to Assemble TV Sets in Irvine, California, Plant," *Wall Street Journal,* April 14, 1977, p. 7.

12. Philippe Cattin, Alain Jolibert, and Coleen Lohnes, "A Cross-Cultural Study of 'Made in' Concepts," *Journal of International Business Studies,* Vol. XIII, No. 3,

Winter 1982, pp. 131–141; Robert D. Schooler, "Bias Phenomena Attendant to the Marketing of Foreign Goods in the U.S.," *Journal of International Business Studies,* Spring 1971, pp. 71–80; A. Nagashima, "A Comparison of Japanese and U.S. Attitudes towards Foreign Products," *Journal of Marketing,* January 1970, pp. 68–74.

13. John D. Daniels, "Recent Foreign Direct Manufacturing Investment in the United States," *Journal of International Business Studies,* Summer 1970, p. 128.

14. "Why VW Must Build Autos in the U.S.," *Business Week,* February 16, 1976, p. 46.

15. Steven P. Galante, "Japanese Have Another Trade Barrier: Limiting Business to Compatriot Firms," *Wall Street Journal,* April 12, 1984, p. 36.

16. Edward B. Flowers, "Oligopolistic Reactions in European and Canadian Direct Investment in the United States," *Journal of International Business Studies,* Fall–Winter 1976, pp. 43–55; Frederick Knickerbocker, *Oligopolistic Reaction and Multinational Enterprise* (Cambridge, Mass.: Harvard University, Graduate School of Business, Division of Research, 1973). For opposing findings, see Lall and Siddharthan, *loc. cit.*

17. Carl H. Fulda and Warren F. Schwartz, *Regulation of International Trade and Investment* (Mineola, N.Y.: Foundation Press, 1970), pp. 657–670.

18. "Why VW Must Build Autos in the U.S.," *op. cit.,* p. 48.

19. "Salt and Pepper," *Wall Street Journal,* December 15, 1983, p. 31.

20. K. Kojima, *Direct Foreign Investment: A Japanese Model of Multinational Business Operations* (London: Croom Helm, 1978).

21. Herbert Lawson, "U.S. Firms Open Plants across Mexican Line to Save Labor Costs," *Wall Street Journal,* May 25, 1967, p. 1; "Comeback for Protectionism," *Time,* May 11, 1970, p. 99; Michael Gamarnikow, "Eastern Partners for Western Businessmen," in *American–East European Trade,* Phillip Grub and Karel Holbik, eds. (Washington, D.C.: The National Press, 1969), pp. 150–151.

22. "Warnaco Unit Fined $100,000 on Charge of Customs Violations," *Wall Street Journal,* February 14, 1977, p. 2.

23. Doz, *loc. cit.*

24. "Global Report," *Wall Street Journal,* January 16, 1978, p. 6.

25. Riad A. Ajami and David A. Ricks, *Motives of Non-American Firms Investing in the United States,* College of Administrative Science, Working Paper Series (Columbus: Ohio State University 1980).

26. Raymond Vernon, "International Investment and International Trade in the Product Cycle," *Quarterly Journal of Economics,* May 1966, pp. 191–207.

27. James M. Lutz and Robert T. Green, "The Product Life Cycle and the Export Position of the United States," *Journal of International Business Studies,* Vol. XIV, No. 3, Winter 1983, pp. 77–94; Alicia Mullor-Sebastian, "The Product Life Cycle Theory: Empirical Evidence," *Journal of International Business Studies,* Vol. XIV, No. 3, Winter 1983, pp. 95–106.

28. Ian Giddy, "The Demise of the Product Life Cycle Model in International Business Theory," *Columbia Journal of World Business,* Spring 1978, pp. 90–96.

29. "National Policies toward Foreign Direct Investors," *FRBNY Quarterly Review,* Winter 1979–80, p. 28.

30. Robert Weigand, "International Investments: Weighing the Incentives," *Harvard Business Review,* Vol. 61, No. 4, July–August 1983, pp. 146–152.

31. Among the many treatises on this subject is Carlos F. Diaz Alejandro, "International Markets for Exhaustible Resources, Less Developed Countries and Transnational Corporations," in *Economic Issues of Multinational Firms,* Robert G. Hawkins, ed. (New York: JAI Press, 1977).

32. M. Y. Yoshino, *Japan's Multinational Enterprises* (Cambridge, Mass.: Harvard University Press, 1976), pp. 53–57.

33. Terutomio Ozawa, "Japan's Resource Dependency and Overseas Investment," *Journal of World Trade Law,* January–February 1977, pp. 52–73.

34. For a good discussion of differences in European government-owned enterprises, see Renato Mazzolini, *Government Controlled Enterprises* (New York: John Wiley & Sons, 1979).

35. Lewis H. Diugid, "Brazil to Supply Pinto Power," *Washington Post,* October 1, 1972, p. H7; "The Brazilian Motor Vehicle Industry," *Notes on International Business Research,* No. 10 (Cambridge, Mass.: M.I.T. Press, August 1975).

36. Stephen H. Hymer, *A Study of Direct Foreign Investment* (Cambridge, Mass.: M.I.T. Press, 1976); Alan M. Rugman, "Internationalization as a General Theory of Foreign Direct Investment: A Re-Appraisal of the Literature," *Weltwirtschaftliches Archiv* Band 116, Heft 2, 1980, pp. 365–379.

37. Robert Z. Aliber, "A Theory of Direct Foreign Investment," in *The International Corporation,* Charles P. Kindleberger, ed. (Cambridge, Mass.: M.I.T. Press, 1970), pp. 28–33.

38. N. H. Prater, "Foreign Participation in the U.S. Market," *Industrial Development,* Vol. 152, No. 3, May/June 1983, pp. 20–22.

39. Thomas Horst, "American Multinationals and the U.S. Economy," *American Economic Review,* May 1976, p. 153.

40. Joseph C. Miller and Bernard Pras, "The Effects of Multinational and Export Diversification on the Profit Stability of U.S. Corporations," *Southern Economic Journal,* Vol. 46, No. 3, 1980, pp. 792–802; Alan M. Rugman, "Foreign Operations and the Stability of U.S. Corporate Earnings: Risk Reduction by International Diversification" (Vancouver: Simon Fraser University, 1974); A. Servern, "Investor Evaluation of Foreign and Domestic Risk," *Journal of Finance,* May 1974, pp. 545–550.

41. Background data on Electrolux may be found in "Why Electrolux Wants a Materials Supplier," *Business Week,* February 18, 1980, pp. 78–79; "Company Briefs," *Wall Street Journal,* October 19, 1979, p. 5; Alan L. Otten, "Electrolux, a Big Success in Appliances, Is Helped by Decentralized Operations," *Wall Street Journal,* June 4, 1980, p. 16; "Electrolux to Proceed with Granges Offer, Providing Sweden Acts," *Wall Street Journal,* June 18, 1980, p. 29; "Electrolux Suspends Its Purchases of Stock in TI Group of Britain," *Wall Street Journal,* February 21, 1984, p. 38.

7

Cross-National Cooperation and Agreements

- To help the student understand the pros and cons of regional economic integration.
- To use the European Community and other groups to illustrate how regional economic integration is actually operating.
- To describe the reasoning behind, and current trends in, commodity agreements such as those in petroleum, tin, and copper.
- To discuss other bilateral and multilateral treaties affecting international business.

DUNLOP/PIRELLI: A CROSS-BORDER MERGER[1]

Even on a personal level, one might expect problems to arise from a marriage between a rather conservative partner from Great Britain and a romanticist from Italy, but how about at the corporate level? The dawning of the European Community (EC) brought with it a rash of cross-border mergers and attempted mergers as Europe sought strength in size to counter the onslaught of U.S. multinationals. In fact, one of the great hopes of the EC was that such cross-border mergers would become commonplace as firms attempted to take advantage of economies of scale. One of the first such EC-spawned mergers was between a German firm and a Belgian firm, resulting in Agfa-Gevaert. Of course, the famous joint efforts of Royal Dutch/Shell and Unilever set the standard for large cross-border mergers. However, other European mergers seemed harder to put together. Fiat and Citroen put together a merger in the early 1970s, but it lasted only until 1975. Dunlop/Pirelli was different.

In 1971, two years before Britain was to join the EC, Dunlop and Pirelli signed their historic merger or, as some called it, "union" agreement. At the time, Dunlop was operating 135 factories in twenty-two countries, primarily **Commonwealth countries,** in tires, industrial and consumer rubber products, sports equipment, and precision engineering components. Pirelli had eighty-five factories primarily in Italy, the Mediterranean countries, and South America with sales in electric cables, tires, and rubber goods. Production facilities of the two companies overlapped in only two countries. Both companies were excited because they believed that their increased size would allow them to compete more effectively in Europe and would also open each company to new products and markets. Their combined sales would put them in second place in Europe in the tire business, behind Goodyear and ahead of Firestone.

Organizationally, each firm set up a holding company similar in style to Royal Dutch/Shell. Pirelli SpA became the holding company of the Italian operations with two other operating companies: Industrie Pirelli SpA to handle manufacturing operations in Italy and other EC countries and Société Internationale Pirelli, S.A., a Swiss holding company, for Pirelli's operations outside of the EC countries.

Initially, Dunlop acquired a 49 percent interest in Industrie Pirelli SpA and a 40 percent interest in Société Internationale Pirelli, S.A. Pirelli acquired a 49 percent interest in Dunlop's European operations and a 40 percent interest in its operations in the Commonwealth.

Each company was allowed to keep its separate identity and make decisions on day-to-day operations. However, there was to be substantial coordination at upper levels of management. All important decisions, strategies, approval of investments, and new ventures were to be examined by a top-

- Commonwealth countries—a voluntary association of 48 independent nations, including the United Kingdom and most of its former colonies

level central committee of four executives each from Dunlop and Pirelli. Below the central committee were permanent committees for tires, consumer and industrial products, finance, and personnel. The committees were responsible for strategic rather than day-to-day tactical policies. Policies and recommendations of the separate committees were to be implemented by the corporate representatives on the central committee. Other forms of cooperation were to be carried out between the two companies. English was chosen as the official language.

Right away, Dunlop and Pirelli found that they had to make some adjustments in their operating styles. Two areas of concern were research and development and long-range planning. Dunlop and Pirelli expected to gain some real economies in R&D, since they could eliminate duplication of efforts. However, they found that Pirelli tended to do R&D in separate product groups, whereas Dunlop used a large R&D center that was separate from the divisions. In the area of planning, Dunlop tended to plan in considerable detail for three years, and Pirelli used a planning horizon of five years but did not plan in as much detail.

In the first year of operations, some real schisms began to develop. The bane of most mergers is differential growth, and that plagued the merger from the first day. Industrie Pirelli lost money in the first six months of operations, owing to a severe recession in Italy, whereas Dunlop was enjoying substantial growth in a booming British economy. As Pirelli Chairman Leopoldo Pirelli put it, "No sooner were we married than the bride, namely us, caught smallpox."

However, the fortunes of the early 1970s were reversed in the late 1970s and early 1980s. By then, Dunlop found itself in the red and Pirelli on the upswing. In the end, nationalism and a lack of common strategies caused the merger's demise. In early 1981 the joint effort finally disintegrated, and the two companies went their separate ways. Together, they may have had trouble; separately, they faced some severe trials. At that time, Dunlop was short on technology and fighting off a takeover bid from a Malaysian company. Pirelli was too small to be very competitive in the European market. Although the glitter of the expanded EC spawned the merger between the two, the reality of trying to pretend that the market was more homogeneous than it was proved to be too much to handle.

INTRODUCTION

During the Depression of the 1930s the world plunged into a period of isolation, trade protection, and economic chaos. From the wreckage of World War II emerged a spirit of intergovernmental cooperation designed to promote economic growth and stability. The purpose of this chapter is to discuss some of the important forms of such cooperation. The first part of the chapter is devoted to the discussion of regional forms of economic integration, in which countries band together to improve the flow of trade and, in some cases, resources. Other forms of integration, such as commodity agreements and trade agreements, will also be discussed. Finally, any discussion of international cooperation would be incomplete without a discussion of the role of the United Nations and its impact on business worldwide.

REGIONAL ECONOMIC INTEGRATION

- Economic integration—the abolishment of economic discrimination between national economies

During the 1950s and 1960s an important cooperative movement emerged—regional economic integration. **Economic integration** can be defined

> *as a process and as a state of affairs. Regarded as a process, it encompasses measures designed to abolish discrimination between economic units belonging to different national states; viewed as a state of affairs, it can be represented by the absence of various forms of discrimination between national economies.* [2]

If one assumes that discrimination actually affects economic activity between the countries in question, integration can be seen as valuable.

- Major efforts of economic integration: EC, EFTA, LAIA, and COMECON
- Geographic proximity is an important reason for economic integration

When one considers some of the major efforts of economic integration, such as the **European Community (EC)**, the **European Free Trade Association (EFTA)**, the **Latin American Integration Association (LAIA)**, and the **Council for Mutual Economic Assistance (COMECON,** an association of communist countries), the concept of geographic proximity looms as important. The major reasons for this are:

> *(a) the distances to be traversed are shorter in the case of neighboring countries; (b) tastes are more likely to be similar, and distribution channels can be more easily established in adjacent economies; and (c) neighboring countries may have a common history, awareness of common interests, etc., and hence be more willing to coordinate policies.* [3]

Also important are the notions of ideological and historical proximity. For instance, Cuba and Mongolia are both members of COMECON because of their similar political philosophies.

There are five major forms of economic integration:

- Major forms of economic integration
  - free trade area: no internal tariffs
  - customs union: common external tariffs
  - common market: factor mobility
  - economic union: harmonization of economic policies
  - complete economic integration

1. **Free trade area (FTA).** Tariffs are abolished among the members of the FTA, but each member maintains its own external tariff against the non-FTA countries. Two examples of this form of economic integration are EFTA and the Latin American Free Trade Association (LAFTA), which was abolished in 1980 and replaced with the LAIA, a looser form of free trade association.

2. **Customs union.** In this case a common external tariff is combined with the abolishment of all internal tariffs. This was the first stage of the EC and is also descriptive of the Andean Group, the Central American Common Market (CACM), and the Caribbean Community and Common Market (CARICOM), the other major groups in Latin America.

3. **Common market.** All of the characteristics of a customs union are combined with the abolishment of restrictions on factor mobility. This is the state that the EC is currently enjoying.

4. **Economic union.** Common market characteristics are combined with some degree of harmonization of national economic policies. This is the theoretical direction in which the EC is moving.

5. **Complete economic integration.** This next evolutionary stage of the economic union "presupposes the unification of monetary, fiscal, social, and counter-cyclical policies and requires the setting up of a supranational authority whose decisions are binding for the member states."[4] Some would say that the institution of the European Parliament was a step in the direction of political unification of Europe, a condition that is almost essential for economic integration. However, this process of unification is still in its infancy.

The Economic Effects of Integration

● Tariffs disrupt trade and resource flows

In a very general sense, country A purchases goods from country B because it does not produce the goods itself or because the comparable goods from country B are less expensive and/or of higher quality. The imposition of tariffs and nontariff barriers (such as quotas) disrupts the free flow of goods and therefore resource allocation by (1) shifting production of some goods from lower-cost foreign producers to protected, higher-cost local producers and (2) shifting consumer demand from foreign goods to domestic goods in response to changes in relative prices resulting from the tariff or quantities available due to nontariff barriers.

For example, some would argue that the imposition of a quota on textile imports into the United States has resulted in the continuation of certain types of textile production in the United States, even though it would be less expensive to produce textiles in developing countries. In most developing countries where imports are limited through tariffs or nontariff barriers owing to a shortage of foreign exchange, consumption automatically shifts to local production. This is especially true with respect to luxury items such as automobiles.

The institution of a customs union reduces discrimination among participating nations even though it often increases, or at least maintains an existing level of, discrimination with nonparticipating nations. Thus the formation of the European Community resulted in a reduction of tariffs and the increased mobility of goods among EC member nations, even though outsiders, such as the United States, still had to leap a large tariff barrier to do business in the EC.

● Static effects of integration: resources flow to efficient producers

The impact of a customs union can be static or dynamic. The static effects have to do with efficiency in resource allocation. Production shifts toward more efficient industries, and consumption shifts to cheaper substitutes produced in member countries. Companies that are protected in their domestic markets tend to have real problems when the barriers are eliminated. This has happened in Argentina and Chile. The elimination in tariffs in the late 1970s and early 1980s resulted in bankruptcies as companies found that they could not compete with more efficient foreign companies. At the same time, Argentine and Chilean consumers preferred to buy cheaper foreign goods rather than the high-cost local goods.

• Dynamic effects of integration: as markets grow, firms achieve economies of scale of production

Dynamic effects account for changes in total consumption and for changes in internal and external efficiencies as a result of growth. This implies that as the market grows, firms are able to produce goods at a cheaper price, since the fixed costs of the business can be spread out over more and more units of production.

Regional economic integration often creates trade opportunities as tariff barriers fall. One example would be the recent invasion into France of inexpensive Italian wines. Although France could not use tariffs as a means of reducing barriers, it has tried to use nontariff barriers to keep out Italian wines. Regional economic integration also results in the diversion of trade from nonmember to member countries. U.S. investment in Europe in the 1960s was an effort by U.S. companies to maintain markets that had been developed by exports from the United States. Caterpillar and Ford are two companies that utilized this investment strategy, thus diverting trade from the United States to EC member countries.

• Efficiency increases due to competition

An important dynamic effect is an increase in efficiency due to increased competition. The EC has tried to encourage the merger of smaller member firms into more efficient economic units that can compete with U.S. and Japanese multinationals. In addition, the EC is trying to get firms to cooperate more in a variety of ways, such as through joint R&D and joint production efforts. One example of this is the formation of Esprit, a $1 billion joint basic research effort sponsored by European governments to encourage European computer firms to compete with IBM and other large computer companies. The EC hopes that it can foster cooperation among Great Britain's ICL, France's Bull, Italy's Olivetti, West Germany's Nixdorf, and the Netherlands' Philips.[5] On a national level, Italy's Montedison, with sales of over $2 billion, is the result of a merger between Montecatini and Edison. Rhone-Poulenc, France's largest synthetic fibers manufacturer, increased its annual sales significantly with the acquisitions of France's fourth and sixth largest chemical companies, Pechiney-Saint-Gobain and Progil. Even the smaller firms that do not compete directly with the multinationals benefit from competition with similar-sized firms in other member countries.

As was pointed out in the Dunlop/Pirelli case, however, nationalism has kept most of these cross-border mergers from approaching any level of significance. There is just too much national pride to allow significant progress to take place. It will be interesting to track the success, or lack of success, of Esprit over the next decade as the Europeans try to cooperate in a very sensitive area.

Benefits from Reducing Barriers—Some Examples

Table 7.1 lists several of the more important groups involved in one form of economic integration or another. All of the groups have achieved at least free trade area status, and some—such as the EC—are dabbling in various forms of factor mobility and harmonization of economic policies.

It is interesting to note the sizes of the different groups. The major purpose of integration is to provide a large market in which companies

TABLE 7.1

COMPARATIVE DATA ON MAJOR TRADE GROUPS, THE UNITED STATES, AND JAPAN

	1982 population[a] (in millions)	1982 GNP[b] (in billions of U.S. dollars)	Per capita GNP (in U.S. dollars)	Percent of world exports (1982)[d]
COMECON (Council of Mutual Economic Assistance)	448.9	1697	3781	8.9
LAIA (Latin American Integration Association)	320.8	670	2087	4.3
EC (European Community)	270.7	2348	8674	32.3
ASEAN (Association of South East Asian Nations)	268.7	207	771	3.7
United States	231.5	3010	13,160[c]	11.7
ECOWAS (Economic Community of West African States)	157.9	123	780	1.4
Japan	118.4	1062	10,080[c]	7.7
Andean Pact	75.0	146	1941	1.4
EFTA (European Free Trade Association)	41.5	391	9432	5.7

a. Data for the following countries were extracted from *World Bank Atlas, 1983:* Cape Verde, Guinea-Bissau, Gambia, Mongolia, and Iceland.
b. Data for the following countries were extracted from *World Bank Atlas, 1981:* Bulgaria, Czechoslovakia, East Germany, Poland, Soviet Union; *World Bank Atlas, 1983:* Iceland; *World Bank Atlas, 1980:* Cuba; *World Bank Atlas, 1979:* Mongolia and Vietnam.
c. Per capita assumptions can be found in *World Development Report,* 1984, pp 274–276.
d. Iceland, data from *Europa Year Book.*
The countries included in the above groups are as follows:
COMECON: Bulgaria, Czechoslovakia, Cuba, East Germany, Hungary, Mongolia, Poland, Romania, Soviet Union, and Vietnam.
LAIA: Argentina, Bolivia, Brazil, Chile, Colombia, Ecuador, Mexico, Paraguay, Peru, Uruguay, and Venezuela.
EC: Belgium, Denmark, France, Greece, Ireland, Italy, Luxembourg, Netherlands, United Kingdom, and West Germany. Portugal and Spain are to be included in 1986.
ASEAN: Indonesia, Malaysia, Philippines, Singapore, and Thailand.
ECOWAS: Benin, Burkina (formerly Upper Volta), Cape Verde, Gambia, Ghana, Guinea, Guinea-Bissau, Ivory Coast, Liberia, Mali, Mauritania, Niger, Nigeria, Senegal, Sierra Leone, and Togo.
Andean Pact: Bolivia, Colombia, Ecuador, Peru, and Venezuela.
EFTA: Austria, Finland, Iceland, Norway, Portugal, Sweden, and Switzerland.
SOURCE: *World Development Report, 1984* (Washington, D.C.: The World Bank, 1984).

can grow and achieve economies of scale. The United States fits right in the middle of the different groupings in terms of population, but it is the largest in terms of GNP and per capita GNP of any of the groups of countries. Thus the regional groups in reality are struggling just to achieve the same market size that the United States has as a single country. The importance of this fact is that the United States operates with a common language, common currency, and common set of laws (in spite of some differences from state to state). Thus it is easier for the United States to achieve the economies of a large market than it is for a group like the Latin American Integration Association, which contains eleven countries, or the European Community, which has ten countries.

● The EC and COMECON have a high percentage of intrazonal trade. African and Latin American groups have a low percentage

Trade liberalization. Although trade liberalization has been one of the major goals of any form of economic integration, this goal has met with varying success. The EC has been the most successful of all, over 50 percent of its exports going to its member countries. EFTA, on the other hand, exports less than 20 percent of its products to other member countries of the EFTA; interestingly enough, it exports around 50 percent of its products to EC member countries. Intraregional exports as a percentage of total exports are less than 20 percent in Latin America, and most Latin American countries trade more with the United States than they do with each other.

The various African forms of regional integration provide for free trade status, but very little intrazonal trade goes on. Their experience is very similar to that of Latin America except that their primary markets lie in Europe rather than the United States. This is because the EC has given preferential status to a number of developing countries in Africa, the Caribbean, and the Far East. They also have strong ties from former colonial status. Similar status has been accorded to EFTA and other non-EC countries in Europe. Another part of the explanation lies in the size of the market. As is noted in Table 7.1, ECOWAS has a market size of 157.9 million people and an average per capita GNP of only $780 per year, whereas ECOWAS countries can export to the EC, which has a population of 270.7 million people and a per capita GNP of $8674 per year. Since most ECOWAS countries export raw materials rather than finished goods, their intrazonal capacity is quite small. The EC countries, however, are in need of raw materials.

● Firms are able to increase the scale of operations owing to the larger market size opened up by trade liberalization

Scale of operations. One of the more interesting side benefits of trade liberalization in the regional groups is the changing scale of operations of local firms. When the EC was first organized, the U.S. multinationals had to change their method of servicing European markets. The large size of the U.S. market allowed these firms to achieve economies of scale so that they could export to the EC. After the market was established and the walls of protectionism began to grow, the firms were forced to invest in EC countries or lose their markets. They had been used to large-scale organizations and had the financial and managerial resources to handle the expansion.

One such example is Ford Motor company.[6] Ford first began operating in Europe through its British subsidiary in 1913 and its German subsidiary in 1926. During the next several decades, however, Ford's European operations were separate operating subsidiaries reporting to Ford but not coordinating their policies in any meaningful way. In its 1960 Annual Report, Ford management noted the following:

> *The historical patterns of trade and commerce among nations are undergoing significant changes. Trade groupings, such as the European Economic Community and the European Free Trade Association, are being established. Similar groupings are being considered in Latin America and by some of the African countries. Further changes in trade patterns have been brought about in a number of countries by government regulations that make it advantageous to manufacture locally.*
>
> *The company and its subsidiaries are responding to these trends, which bear promise of increasing competition for world automobile markets, by exploring opportunities to strengthen and to expand their international operations.*

It was only a few years after this that Ford changed its management structure to include the European operations under one umbrella organization in order to take advantage of the economies of scale that were beginning to develop in the EC. The two large manufacturing centers in Great Britain and West Germany were to remain the focal points of the new strategy, but no longer were they to be considered separate, independent operating companies. Ford decided that the best way to operate was literally to obliterate national boundaries (which was easier said than done because of nationalistic tendencies on the part of country management). As was noted by the German managing director,

> *The pooling of the two companies cut the engineering bill in half for each company, provided economies of scale, with double the volume in terms of purchase—commonization of purchase, common components—provided the financial resources for a good product program at a really good price that we could still make money on.*[7]

Ford began developing and selling European cars rather than engineering separate cars in each market. This strategy resulted in the Escort, Capri, and Fiesta among others. Not only did Ford design and assemble similar automobiles throughout Europe, but it also designed common components to be used in Ford cars. To show the importance of the size of the market in developing this strategy, one Ford executive commented: "Neither the British nor German company could have come up with the Capri separately, tooled it separately. Only with the whole volume of Europe in prospect did the Capri become a viable product development program."[8]

This strategy, which was tried and tested in the United States and perfected in a new international market in Europe, is now the wave of the future for the entire world. The world car, once considered a folly because of different national markets, is now a reality. The experience of the large auto manufacturers in Europe has shown that different national markets can be used to manufacture and assemble automobiles on a cross-national scale.

The EC has created other giant companies as a result of the expanded market. The one that most people hear about is Volkswagen, which is partially owned by the German government. Volkswagen has expanded primarily by growth rather than merger or acquisition. The Fiat (Italian)/Citroen (French) merger in the early 1970s alluded to in the case at the beginning of this chapter did not last five years before French and Italian nationalism killed it. The French automaker Peugeot decided to meet the market by acquiring Citroen and Chrysler's dying European operations.

However, the most interesting of the purely European companies is Renault, one of the largest car companies in Europe. Renault, which is owned by the French government but almost totally autonomous in decision making, has grown largely by good management. It was not caught up in the fashionable cross-border merger movement of the 1970s. Instead, it solidified its position in France and then began to move into other European markets. It now operates on the philosophy that the key to success is to design a good car and then produce interchangeable parts worldwide. The growth of the European market has enabled it to achieve economies of scale there that are now the springboard to expansion into the U.S. market.[9] Renault's assault on the European market was so successful that it moved to the United States, where it acquired 46 percent of the stock in American Motors.

These examples of corporate growth in the EC resulted from individual companies expanding their market share through internal growth, merger, or acquisition. The EC has also attempted to create corporate size in ways that go beyond mere encouragement. The Airbus Industrie is a collaborative effort on the part of several European airplane manufacturers to produce a product that can compete with its U.S. counterparts. However, the U.S. industry is three times the size of the entire European production. Not many such efforts have proven successful. The Esprit project mentioned above is another example of an explicit atte.apt on the part of the EC to achieve economies of scale, this time in research and development.

European Evolution to Integration

• OEEC—organization of European countries assisted by the Marshall Plan; forerunner of the OECD.

World War II left a wake of economic as well as human destruction throughout Europe. To facilitate utilization of aid from the Marshall Plan, the sixteen-nation **Organization for European Economic Cooperation (OEEC)** was established in 1948 with the encouragement of the United States. Its purposes were to improve currency stability, combine economic strength, and improve trade relations. However, the OEEC did not appear to be strong enough to provide the necessary economic growth, so further efforts at cooperation were initiated.

• EC or EEC—economic integration of European countries

One major school of thought adhered to the idea that a Common Market ought to be developed, which would result in the elimination of all restrictions to the free flow of goods, capital, and persons; allow for the harmonization of economic policies; and create a common external tariff. The result was the creation of the **European Economic Community** (EEC) through the Treaty of Rome in March 1957. It involved West Germany, Belgium, the Netherlands, Luxembourg, France, and Italy. The concept of the EEC has since been broadened to include more countries and embrace the title European Community (EC), which implies a broader form of cooperation.

• EFTA: free trade area

The second major school of thought rejected this notion of total integration and favored instead a free trade area, which would allow for the elimination of all restrictions on the free flow of industrial goods among member nations and would permit each country to retain its own external tariff structure. This approach would provide the benefits of free trade among members but would allow each country to pursue its own economic objectives with outside countries. This was especially true for Great Britain, which had developed favorable trade relationships with Commonwealth countries. From the British point of view, a common external tariff would result in too much cooperation and restriction of individual sovereignty.

Following the second line of thought, the Stockholm Convention of May 1960 resulted in the creation of the EFTA, which involved seven of the OEEC countries that were not partners in the EEC: Austria, Denmark, Norway, Portugal, Sweden, Switzerland, and the United Kingdom. The composition of the EFTA has since changed to the countries listed in Table 7.1. These countries were concerned about a unified European effort in economic integration and reaffirmed their interest in working toward a broader solution; however, there were still many problems that led to their creating the EFTA:

1. the lack of desire to harmonize social and economic policies, as would be required by the EEC;

2. the special arrangements between the United Kingdom and the Commonwealth nations; and

3. the political neutrality of Austria, Sweden, and Switzerland.

As is the case with any good idea, complexity breeds bureaucracy. The more simple forms of integration, such as a free trade area and customs union, can usually be managed by a coordinating committee that is larger than it needs to be but adequate to do the job. However, the more complex forms of integration, such as one finds in the EC, have developed a very extensive bureaucracy to look out for the goals and rules of the group of countries.

• Major institutions of the EC: the Commission, the Council of Ministers, the Parliament, and the Court of Justice

The key to the success of the EC is the balance between common and national interests monitored and refereed through four major institutions:

the Commission,

the Council of Ministers,

the Parliament,

and the Court of Justice.

The Commission is made up of individuals whose allegiance is to the EC rather than to an individual government. The Commission is the EC watchdog; it is supposed to draw up policies, implement them when approved by the Council of Ministers, and make sure that treaties and laws are adhered to by member nations.

The Council of Ministers is composed of one representative from each of the member governments. It is responsible for making the major policy decisions for the EC.

The Parliament is basically an advisory body elected directly in each member country. The representatives tend to adhere to particular philosophical persuasions rather than the wishes of the individual governments. Representatives of different countries with similar political leanings can form coalitions to increase their power base. Figure 7.1 illustrates how the composition of the Parliament changed between the first group elected in 1979 and the new group elected in 1984. The center-right coalition of Christian Democrats, Conservatives, Liberals, and Gaullists lost some members (from 240 down to 220), even though they retained a majority. In the first five years of operation the Parliament exhibited little political power, although it must approve the budget of the EC. The individual EC member governments are reluctant to surrender too much national sovereignty to the Europarliament. The Parliament serves primarily to advise on legislative proposals made by the Commission to the Council.

The Court of Justice is composed of one member from each country in the EC. It serves as a supreme appeals court for EC law. The Commission or member countries can bring other members to the Court for failing to meet treaty obligations. Likewise, member countries, firms, or institutions can bring the Commission or Council to the Court for failure to act properly under the treaty.

Obviously, not every regional economic group is so organized. In most cases there is a commission that is responsible for formulating and implementing policy and a series of committees that are responsible for making recommendations to the commission. But the EC is a more ambitious undertaking than most. In addition, it is growing. Growth brings with it various problems, which tend to keep the bureaucracy increasing. The EC has grown from the original six countries to an enlarged group of nine (with the additions of Denmark, the United Kingdom, and the Republic of Ireland

FIGURE 7.1.

Europe from Left to Right: Composition of the European Parliament, 1979 and 1984

Source: The Economist, June 23, 1984, p. 32.

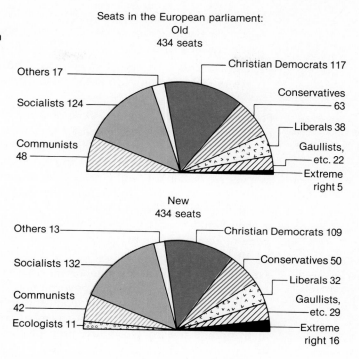

Seats in the European parliament:
Old
434 seats

Others 17

Socialists 124

Communists 48

Christian Democrats 117

Conservatives 63

Liberals 38

Gaullists, etc. 22

Extreme right 5

New
434 seats

Others 13

Socialists 132

Communists 42

Ecologists 11

Christian Democrats 109

Conservatives 50

Liberals 32

Gaullists, etc. 29

Extreme right 16

in 1973), to ten (with the addition of Greece in 1981). The next phase of expansion is designed to include Spain and Portugal in 1986.

Harmonization of Policies in Europe

Although the reduction of internal trade barriers by free trade areas and the adoption of a common external tariff by customs unions have been the major benefits of economic integration, there have been other policies as well. Once again, the EC provides some good examples to illustrate these policies.

Common agricultural policy (CAP). One of the most famous of the EC's common policies involves the agricultural policy. The farm policy features four main points:

1. Free trade of agricultural products. This policy is still slightly hampered by nontariff barriers.

2. Price supports to guarantee high prices to farmers. This is one policy that especially concerned the United Kingdom before its entry into the Common Market. The fear was that higher continental farm prices would have a damaging inflationary effect.

3. A series of variable levies or duties on farm imports. This would ensure that competitive foreign products would not be sold at less than prevailing continental prices.

4. Agricultural modernization projects. These would be undertaken to try to make farming in the EC more efficient.

• The free flow of labor has provided cheap labor but has resulted in social problems

Free flow of labor. The free flow of labor has been instrumental in the rebuilding of Europe. To compensate for a tight labor supply and to provide unskilled workers for assembly lines and some manual service industries, the EC has also opened the doors to immigrants from other countries such as Yugoslavia, Turkey, and Greece. The original idea was that the itinerant workers would move in without families and work on a short-term basis— one to three years. However, many of these unskilled workers have brought in their families and become permanent residents, causing problems in integration, citizenship, housing, education, and welfare.

• Requires better information about companies and a more stable exchange rate system

Free flow of capital. Two important aspects of the free flow of capital are information and currency convertibility. If investors are to make wise decisions, they need high-quality comparable financial information. As will be pointed out in Chapter 18, EC member countries vary considerably in their attitude toward accounting principles and practices. As a result, the EC passed the Fourth Directive, which is a positive step toward making the presentation of financial statements uniform. Additional directives have been issued in the areas of consolidation of financial statements and the qualifications and duties of auditors. The EC is also trying to get companies to present more information about their employees and about investment and disinvestment plans so that employees can have a say before, not after, the fact.

• EMS—a monetary system designed to provide more stability in currency values for EC member countries

The currency problem is no easier to solve than the uniformity of financial statements. Initially, the EC hoped to have a single Eurocurrency by 1981. However, the intervening steps have proved formidable indeed. In March 1979 the EC member countries created the **European Monetary System** (EMS) in hopes of stabilizing their own exchange rates. This union will be discussed in more detail in Chapter 9.

Competition policy. The EC has had a difficult time deciding how it feels about competition and its restraint. The reduction in tariffs is designed to promote the free flow of goods among the members of the Community. However, it is possible to use restraint of trade to eliminate competition. As a result, the EC has adopted a series of policies designed to promote competition. Three of the major series of agreements deal with horizontal transactions, vertical transactions, and dominant positions.

Horizontal agreements involve independent firms at the same level in the production and distribution chain. The agreements that create the most difficulty for firms are those involving price fixing, market sharing, discriminatory agreements, and collective boycotts.

Vertical agreements are those between firms at different levels in the production and distribution chain. The key is to avoid market sharing arrangements. A dominant position occurs when a company dominates a market and therefore dominates the pricing policies of its competitors.[10]

These concepts of competition have been difficult for the EC to administer in reality. The EC's Commissioner for Industrial Affairs has historically recommended a variety of practices to promote industrial growth that have appeared to be anticompetitive. In 1981 the EC established a steel pact that resulted in a cutback of steel production in order to stabilize prices at a higher level. At one time it also considered setting up a cartel for the fibers industry. However, that agreement was not approved.

One of the most celebrated cases involving dominant position was that of IBM. In 1977 the Commission began investigating IBM after receiving antitrust complaints from some of IBM's competitors. The case was finally resolved on August 2, 1984, when the Commission agreed to a compromise settlement with IBM and dropped its legal proceedings. The Commission had been concerned over the tremendous market advantage of IBM, which is estimated to control 55 percent of the computer market in Europe.[11] The settlement requires IBM to supply technical information to competitors within four months after announcing a new mainframe computer product so that competitors can develop compatible equipment.[12]

Latin American Cooperation

Economic integration in Latin America has taken some interesting twists over the years. As can be seen in Fig. 7.2, two of the original groups, the Latin American Free Trade Association (LAFTA) and the Caribbean Free Trade Association (CARIFTA), changed names and focus. In spite of the evolution the initial reason for integration remains. The post–World War II strategy of import substitution to resolve balance of payments problems was doomed to failure because of the small national markets in Latin America. Therefore the feeling was that some form of economic cooperation was needed to enlarge the potential market size so that national firms could achieve economies of scale and be more competitive worldwide.

• Forms of integration in Latin America

A study by the Inter-American Development Bank (IDB) identified three types of integration in Latin America: a free trade area, a common market, and a partial economic preferences model.[13] The free trade model is best illustrated by LAFTA and CARIFTA. LAFTA was formed in 1960 during the time when the European Economic Community was being organized, and CARIFTA was formed in 1965. However, neither of these efforts lasted very long.

Latin American Integration Association (LAIA)

Latin American Free Trade Association (LAFTA) from 1960 to 1980

Members	Date of Entry	
Argentina	Jan.	1981
Bolivia	Mar.	1982
Brazil	Nov.	1981
Chile	May	1981
Colombia	May	1981
Ecuador	Mar.	1982
Mexico	Feb.	1981
Paraguay	Dec.	1980
Peru	Nov.	1981
Uruguay	Mar.	1981
Venezuela	Mar.	1982

Cartagena Agreement, Andean Group

Bolivia	Nov.	1969
Chile	Sept.	1969
	(withdrew Oct. 1976)	
Colombia	Sept.	1969
Ecuador	Nov.	1969
Peru	Oct.	1969
Venezuela	Nov.	1973

Central American Common Market (CACM)

Costa Rica	Sept.	1963
El Salvador	May	1961
Guatemala	May	1961
Honduras	Apr.	1962
	(withdrew Jan. 1971)	
Nicaragua	May	1961

Caribbean Community and Common Market (CARICOM)

Caribbean Free Trade Association (CARIFTA) from 1965 to 1973

Members	Date of Entry	
Antigua and Barbuda	July	1974
Bahamas	July	1983
Barbados	Aug.	1973
Belize	July	1974
Dominica	July	1974
Grenada	July	1974
Guyana	Aug.	1973
Jamaica	Aug.	1973
Montserrat	July	1974
St. Christopher and Nevis	July	1974
St. Lucia	July	1974
St. Vincent	July	1974
Trinidad and Tobago	Aug.	1973

Legend:
- LAIA
- LAIA (Andean Group)
- CACM
- CARICOM

FIGURE 7.2
Integration Systems in Latin America
Source: "Inter-American Development Bank Predicts Renewed Push for Economic Integration in Latin America," *IMF Survey,* December 10, 1984, p. 375.

● Common market examples in Latin America

The second model came into existence in Latin America because of the failure of the free trade area model. The Andean Group was formed by several members of LAFTA that were close to each other geographically. They felt that it was necessary to have more than just free trade, so they included a common external tariff, restrictions on the inflow of foreign investment, and the integration of economic and social policies. These were similar to the objectives of the Central American Common Market (CACM) and the Caribbean Community and Common Market (CARICOM). The

Andean Group decided that it needed to develop subregional industries and to allocate these industries among the members of the group. That would enable more even development. However, the problems of the region have kept it from achieving the full benefits of integration.

The third model of partial economic preferences is best illustrated by the Latin American Integration Association (LAIA), the countries originally in LAFTA that decided not to become part of the Andean Group. LAIA gives countries an opportunity to establish a series of bilateral agreements that may be extended to other countries if desired. This allows countries with common interests to make faster progress than might be the case when disparate members have to resort to compromise that might dilute the effectiveness of the agreement.

• LAIA: provides a series of bilateral agreements

Other Regional Efforts

Economic cooperation is taking place in three other regions: Eastern Europe, Asia, and Africa.

Eastern Europe.   The Council for Mutual Economic Assistance (CMEA or COMECON) was formed in 1949 to assist in the economic development of the member nations. The current members as listed in Table 7.1 include Mongolia, Cuba, and Vietnam, which were admitted in 1962, 1972, and 1978, respectively. Albania, an original member of COMECON, ended its affiliation in 1961.

COMECON is interested in integrating economic activities and planning economic specialization within the region. Its intrazonal trade of 60 percent is the highest of any of the regional forms of integration.[14] As noted in Table 7.1, COMECON is the largest of the regional groups. However, this is deceiving because the Soviet Union has 60 percent of the population and over 70 percent of the GNP of the group. In none of the other regional economic groups is there such economic dominance by a single member of the group.

• COMECON: has a high percentage of intrazonal trade and economic domination by the Soviet Union

Asia.   The major form of integration in Asia is the Association of South East Asian Nations (**ASEAN**), which was organized in 1977. ASEAN includes Indonesia, Malaysia, the Philippines, Singapore, and Thailand. ASEAN is attempting cooperation in many areas, including industry and trade. In industry, ASEAN countries are attempting to enter into joint projects and set up medium-sized industries in different countries. These industries would be 60 percent owned by the host country and 40 percent owned by the other members of ASEAN. The two initial projects approved and under construction were urea fertilizer projects in Indonesia and Malaysia. Other initial projects ran into a series of problems and were not as successful in getting off the ground as were the two urea projects.

• ASEAN: a major form of integration in Asia that is beginning to cooperate

The other major area of cooperation is that of trade. Although ASEAN countries have not opted for a free trade area at this point, they are cooperating in reducing tariffs in a variety of areas. Their Basic Agreement on the Establishment of ASEAN Preferential Trade Arrangements was approved by the General Agreement on Tariffs and Trade and has resulted in some trade liberalization. By 1982, however, only 2 percent of intra-ASEAN trade consisted of preferentially traded items.[15]

• Africa has more different forms of integration than any other continent

Africa. Although only one form of African integration is listed in Table 7.1, there are actually several forms. These forms are not necessarily mutually exclusive. The Ivory Coast, for example, is in six different organizations in Africa that are related to political and/or economic development. The major African groups are the West African Economic Community (Burkina, Ivory Coast, Mali, Mauritania, Niger, and Senegal); the Entente Council (Benin, Burkina, Ivory Coast, Niger, and Togo); the Economic Community of West African States (ECOWAS—the countries are listed in Table 7.1), the Organisation Commune Africaine et Mauricienne (Benin, Burkina, Central African Republic, Ivory Coast, Mauritius, Niger, Rwanda, Senegal, and Togo); the Organization of African Unity, or OAU (nearly every country in Africa); and the Southern African Development Co-Ordination Conference (Angola, Botswana, Lesotho, Malawi, Mozambique, Swaziland, Tanzania, Zambia, and Zimbabwe). In addition to these specific groups there is also an African Development Bank.

As can be seen, there is a lot of overlap among the groups. Most groups try to cooperate in some form of economic integration, although it tends to be at a fairly low level. The countries in general are so poor and economic activity is so low that there is not much of a base for cooperation. Most African countries rely heavily on agriculture as a major source of export revenue, so there is not much of a reason to lower the barriers to the primary products. Most industrial effort is at a fairly low level and still needs protection before opening the doors to competition. This retards the development of a free trade area. Most of the groups are also attempting cooperation in other areas, such as transportation and other forms of infrastructure, small industrial projects, and the like.

The ECOWAS is featured in Table 7.1 because it is the largest of the groups, with the exception of the OAU, which tends to be more of a political than an economic organization. The ECOWAS has four commissions: trade, customs, immigration, monetary, and payments; industry, agriculture, and natural resources; transport, telecommunications, and energy; and social and cultural affairs. Major efforts are being made to eliminate all internal tariffs and to set up a common external tariff, which will make the ECOWAS a customs union in the same sense as the EC. However, it is doubtful that the ECOWAS will be able to achieve the other types of integration accomplished by the EC.

It was mentioned above that the Organization of African Unity is the largest form of regional cooperation in Africa. The reason that it was not highlighted in Table 7.1 is that it is really too large to be effective. It is more like a regional bloc in the United Nations than a regional economic group. Its original goals were oriented more toward the elimination of colonialism and racism in Africa than toward economic growth. A study of the principal events in the history of the OAU confirms that it tends to deal more in political than economic issues. The smaller groups mentioned above appear to be more effective in achieving economic cooperation.

Problems of Integration

Although there appear to be overwhelming arguments in favor of some form of economic integration among neighboring countries, there are some definite problems. The IDB report on Latin America referenced above noted that LAFTA fell apart for the following major reasons: it lacked a common external tariff, there were no provisions for coordinating domestic and external policies of member countries, regional industrial production was not addressed, and there was no mechanism to ensure that economic benefits would be spread out evenly among member countries.[16] These problems seemed to be particularly important in the Latin American context, but there are variety of other problems facing nearly all of the groups. Among the most important are nationalism, nontariff barriers, economic divergence, cost, and expansion.

• Major problems of integration: nationalism, nontariff barriers, economic divergence, cost, and expansion

It is important to note that the problems that keep regional groups from achieving the level of harmonization desired often create uncertainty for firms that want to invest within the group. The uncertainty makes it difficult to decide on the size of operations that a firm should build. Many firms have built large operations in Ireland to serve the entire EC, but these operations would be too large to serve just Ireland. Thus it is important for firms to have confidence in the success of a regional economic integration effort.

Nationalism. Most regional economic groups fall apart—or at least accomplish less than desired—because of nationalistic pressures. France (that is, President Charles de Gaulle) essentially kept the United Kingdom out of the EC until 1973 (after de Gaulle's death). Spain and Portugal's political as well as economic instability have also postponed their entrance into the EC. It is difficult for countries to surrender sovereign power to a supranational body. This is the reason that many of the EFTA countries have never cared to enter the EC and that many lofty EC goals have never been achieved. Chile left the Andean Group because it wanted to pursue a course that was different from the one set by the other member countries. The Central

American Common Market is literally nonexistent owing to war and insur-rection in Central America.

Nontariff barriers.   All of the regional economic groups focus on the elimi-nation of tariff barriers so that goods can flow freely from country to country. In most cases, tariffs have been reduced significantly or eliminated. However, nationalism keeps trade from flowing as freely as it should. With respect to the EC, for example,

> *Restrictions and cartels keep the price of automobiles 30 percent higher in Britain than in Belgium, while video recorders are as much as 20 percent more expensive in West Germany than in the Netherlands. Belgium won't admit margarine packed in oblongs, but insists on cubes. Ireland says foreign furniture must be labeled in Gaelic. West Germany uses a 16th-century purity law to keep out foreign beer.* [17]

Although these problems are more acute during periods of regionwide recession, they have been a part of the regional economic groups since their inception. Governments have replaced tariffs with other measures to protect industries. True integration will never exist as long as these nontariff barriers remain.

Economic divergence.   Another problem is linked to differences in the economic makeup of the members of the group. In LAIA, for example, Brazil has a population of 126.8 million people and a GNP of $248.5 billion compared with Paraguay, which has a population of 3.1 million and a GNP of $5.9 billion. ASEAN ranges from Indonesia with a population of 152.6 million and a GDP of $90.2 billion to Singapore with a population of 2.5 million and a GDP of $14.7 billion. The absolute size of the Soviet Union compared with other members of COMECON was mentioned above.

The problem with disparity in size is that it is difficult for member countries to agree on long-term development strategies. There are just too many different points of view about how to achieve economic growth. Many of the regional groups have attempted to coordinate their development strategies, with differing degrees of success. We have already mentioned the EC attempts to set up cartel arrangements for products such as steel and textiles. The Andean Group worked hard in its initial years to rationalize automobile production so that all member countries would be part of the production process. Otherwise, there might be a tendency for companies to produce automobiles in one location to achieve economies of scale. The most likely candidates for that type of production would have been those countries with large markets, leaving out the smaller countries like Bolivia and Ecuador.

Cost.   The more complicated the form of integration, the more difficult it is to maintain an equitable budget. Free trade areas and customs unions do not have too much to worry about, since they are concerned with expanding internal trade. However, other more ambitious forms of regional economic integration cannot put their programs into effect without the finances to do so. The major sources of funds for EC programs come from customs duties, levies on imports of farm products, and contributions from the collection of value-added taxes by each member government. Two problems have been plaguing the EC for a number of years: One is that Great Britain is upset over the amount it has to pay each year, and the second is that the cost of programs may soon exceed the revenues generated as outlined above. Great Britain is particularly upset because it is a heavy importer of food, and 75 percent of the EC budget goes into the Common Agricultural Policy. In essence, British consumers are subsidizing continental farmers. The other problem is that the cost of funding programs is rising faster than the revenues collected, and the member countries are not eager to increase their contributions.

Expansion. As shown in Figure 7.1, the composition of the Latin American integration systems is fairly stable. Usually, the countries desiring to affiliate with a system did so when the system was first set up. The major exception to that is the entry of Venezuela into the Andean Pact in 1973, four years after the other countries had joined.

• Spain and Portugal will be the next entrants to the EC

Earlier in the chapter we mentioned the additions to membership in COMECON and in the EC. The addition of Greece to the EC was not easy. There is a big disparity between the economy of Greece and the economies of the other members of the EC. The Greek economy may not be prepared to compete with those of the rest of Europe in manufactured goods. Spain and Portugal are to be the eleventh and twelfth members of the EC. They should make quite an impact in agriculture, textiles, and steel. Both countries have been trading with EC member nations for years under relatively tariff-free conditions, but there are some tariffs that need to be eliminated. The four countries with the lowest per capita GNP in the EC will be Portugal, Greece, Ireland, and Spain. Thus the entry of Portugal and Spain will strengthen the bloc of "have nots" in the EC.

Regional Economic Groups vis-à-vis the Rest of the World

Regional economic groups can be beneficial to outsiders as well as insiders, as was pointed out in the case of Ford mentioned earlier. However, problems can also develop. When the Andean Pact instituted its investment policies, it met with some resistance. The goal of Andean Pact policy in the areas of foreign capital, trademarks, patents, licenses, and royalties was to gradually reduce the extent of foreign ownership and control so that all businesses would eventually be majority-owned and controlled by local investors and receive greater benefits from the use of intangibles than MNEs would ordinarily grant. However, these stringent policies, considered by some to be against foreign investment, caused Chile to drop out of the Andean Pact in 1976. Since then, some of the policies have been slightly moderated.

Europe faces a difficult time in coping with import competition from Japan and the United States. Formally, the EC is represented in trade negotiations by one representative rather than by representatives from the individual nations. In practice, however, nationalism continues to hold sway. The EC has not been able to control the import policies of the individual member nations completely. In the case of automobiles, Italy, France, and Great Britain have a policy that is more restrictive than what the EC would like to implement. As a result, the three refuse to go along with a less stringent policy, and the others (notably West Germany) are not anxious to adopt quite as stringent a policy. This situation leaves the EC to flounder without any policy.

Problems with U.S. industry are potentially more difficult because of the importance of the two markets to each other. In recent years the major sources of contention have been in the areas of steel and agricultural products. In the case of steel the EC and United States negotiated quotas to relieve some of the pressure on the U.S. industry. In addition to the problems of steel and agriculture, the EC and United States have debated over general economic policy, especially with respect to trade with the Soviet Union. The United States has taken a more restrictive line than has the EC. A number of disputes arose over the building of a pipeline to carry natural gas from the Soviet Union to Western Europe and over the sale of high technology goods to the Soviet Union that could have national security implications.

A final major problem of regional economic integration is that it can slow down the movement to international economic integration. The objective of GATT is to lower trade barriers worldwide, not just on a regional basis. Regional groups such as the EC liberalize trade for the member countries at the expense of the rest of the world. Proponents of regional economic integration maintain that it is easier to reach a consensus for a smaller group of more homogeneous countries. However, the static and dynamic effects of free trade would be more beneficial if applied on a worldwide basis. The difficulty is that all of the problems discussed in the previous section on regional economic integration would be magnified on a worldwide basis.

COMMODITY AGREEMENTS

Most of the developing countries have traditionally relied on the export of one or two commodities to supply the hard currencies needed for economic development. Unfortunately, many short-run factors have caused price instability, leading to fluctuations in export earnings. The most important factors are:

1. natural forces such as floods, droughts, and weather;
2. relatively price-insensitive demand;
3. relatively price-insensitive supply (in the short run); and
4. business cycles in advanced industrial countries that can cause sudden changes in quantities demanded.

World commodity prices have fluctuated dramatically in recent years. In Chapter 5 we showed that this was a reason that countries attempt to diversify their economies. During the 1960s and 1970s the prices of seven of the ten core commodities identified by UNCTAD (coffee, cocoa, tea, sugar, cotton, rubber, jute, sisal, copper, and tin) fluctuated 10 percent around their long-term trend, and the other three fluctuated 20 percent.[18] During the late 1970s and early 1980s the major problem facing commodities was the drop in world demand due to a recession in most industrial countries. This caused the prices of commodities to fall significantly.

Some commodities, such as copper, operate in a relatively free market. Wild price fluctuations are a result of supply and demand as well as speculation. However, consumers and producers alike would often prefer a more stabilized pricing system that allows for predictions of future costs and earnings and thus facilitates planning. The types of commodity agreements that are most frequently adopted are buffer stocks, price ranges, and export/import quotas. There are five international commodity agreements with market intervention provisions such as those mentioned above: the International Sugar Agreement (1977), the International Natural Rubber Agreement (1979), the Sixth International Tin Agreement (1981), the International Cocoa Agreement (1980), and the International Coffee Agreement (1983).[19]

The **buffer stock** system provides a partially managed system monitored by a central agency. Free market forces are allowed to determine prices within a certain range, but outside of that range a central agency buys or sells the commodity to support the price. This is the type of system used in the tin market and is similar to a "dirty float" in the world currency markets, in which governments intervene to support the value of a currency.

The tin agreement is one of the longest-standing commodity agreements in existence. There are two levels at which the buffer stock manager needs to be concerned about prices: the **"net seller"** range and the **"net buyer" range.** To help maintain prices, the tin agreement has provided for export controls on producing countries. Otherwise, the buffer stock manager would not be able to manipulate the market enough. It is interesting to note that the Sixth Agreement did not include the United States, the largest tin importer, or Bolivia, a major tin producer.

● The sugar agreement

The sugar agreement is another buffer stock system. In 1980 the system was set up to buy sugar when the price hit $0.11 per pound and sell when it hit $0.22. During 1980 and 1981, however, the price skyrocketed to over $0.40 per pound, which put tremendous pressures on the buffer stock. Obviously, the stock was inadequate to handle the surge in prices. The price increase was caused by a shortfall in production coupled with an increase in demand due to normal growth and the surge in the synfuels program worldwide.[20] In August–September 1984 the price of sugar actually fell to $0.04, well below the lower intervention price range. At that price the buffer stock was inadequate to cause a sufficient price increase to reach the lower limit.

Price ranges can be handled in many different ways. In some of the metal markets, such as zinc, lead, and platinum, prices are fixed at the smelters by producers. Although most purchases are made at the smelters, a free market with prices parallel to the smelter prices but usually at a premium or discount takes care of marginal needs. Bilateral price agreements are often negotiated between two countries to guarantee maximum and minimum prices. This was the type of arrangement Great Britain entered into with other members of the Commonwealth. Multilateral agreements such as the International Wheat Agreement are often entered into by more than two countries.

● Examples of quota systems

Quota systems occur when producing and/or consuming countries divide total output and sales in order to keep up prices. Quota systems have been used for such products as coffee, tea, and sugar. They are often used in conjunction with a buffer stock system. For the quota system to work, countries must develop close ties in order to prevent sharp fluctuations in supply. The quota system is also most effective when a single country has a large share of world production or consumption. Two of the best examples from a production standpoint are wool, which is controlled by Australians, and diamonds, which are controlled by DeBeers Company in South Africa.

● International Coffee Organization

Another example of a quota system is the International Coffee Organization. In 1980 the ICO decided to set up a quota system in which world producers would limit their exports to keep coffee prices between $1.15 and $1.55 per pound, with the quotas to be loosened or tightened as prices neared the upper or lower limit. This plan involved negotiations by producing and consuming nations alike. There are two problems with the quota system, however. The first is that the quotas can be perceived as too low by some of the countries, especially those that rely on coffee as their main and maybe only major export cash crop. The other is that a surplus or shortage of coffee might make it impossible to control the quantity on the market and therefore the price. The quota-regulated price range of $1.15–1.55 is a far cry from the $3.40 per pound price that coffee carried in 1977 after the infamous Brazilian frosts.

The global quota for coffee exports was increased in 1984–1985, but the price was maintained at the same level. This was designed to allow total revenues to rise for exporting countries. However, two problems faced the members of the Coffee Agreement: sales to nonmembers of the Agreement are not covered, and countries continue to complain about their allocations. The former point is an important one because of the temptation to transship coffee from a nonmember importer to a member importer. The latter problem is one faced by all producer cartels, as will be seen in the discussion of the oil situation later in the chapter.

Many of the developing countries that export primary commodities have voiced great concern over fluctuating commodity prices. The real concern, of course, is fluctuating revenues—especially on the downward side. Prices of many commodities have fallen in recent years owing largely to sluggish demand, resulting in disastrous financial consequences for many countries. The theory behind buffer stocks in commodity agreements is that commodities would be purchased in order to support prices. However, this has not worked adequately. One of the major facets of the North-South dialogue alluded to in Chapter 2 is the creation of a common fund to support prices of all commodities. The industrial countries are not too excited over the idea, since the fund would not be earmarked for a specific commodity but would be administered by a bureaucracy. The International Monetary Fund and the EC through its Lomé Convention rely more on compensatory financing schemes to stabilize earnings of commodities exporters.

• Members of OPEC

THE ORGANIZATION OF PETROLEUM EXPORTING COUNTRIES

In 1972 the director of the U.S. State Department's Office of Fuels & Energy made the bold prediction that the average price of Middle East crude oil, which was then at $2.25 per barrel might go to $5.00 or even higher by 1980. In an understatement it was mentioned that these figures would translate into higher gasoline prices, heating bills, and industrial cost.[21] OPEC is composed of the Middle East Arab countries of Saudi Arabia, Kuwait, Qatar, the United Arab Emirates, Iraq, Libya, and Algeria and the Islamic Republic of Iran, Indonesia, Nigeria, Gabon, Venezuela, and Ecuador. The effectiveness of OPEC in controlling prices and production was first illustrated by the political and economic events of 1973 and 1974, when the price of crude oil was increased from $3.64/bbl to $11.65/bbl within one year. OPEC was able to accomplish this because:

• Reasons for OPEC control over prices

1. it produced over 50 percent of world production in 1973;

2. demand for oil was high;

3. the consuming countries were not able to supply their own oil needs; and

4. substitutes were not readily available.

World oil prices dropped a little bit in the 1975–1978 period, but they rebounded in 1979–1980, when they peaked at about $35 per barrel.

• Major reasons for OPEC's loss of power

However, OPEC's resolve began to weaken in the early 1980s. Even though oil consumption increased steadily over most of the 1970s, the oil price rise in 1979–1980 resulted in a drop in demand for oil in the industrial countries. The major reasons for the drop in decline in consumption were the world recession, the increase in crude oil prices, the substitution of other fuels for oil, the effectiveness of national energy policies aimed at conservation, and the changing structure of industry with a decline in the importance of energy-intensive industries.[22]

• Key trends in oil during 1973–1983

During the period 1973–1983, some interesting trends developed in the oil industry. The first is that the consumption of oil as a percentage of total energy consumption in the world declined from 48 percent to 40 percent. Natural gas, coal, hydroelectric power, and nuclear energy increased at the expense of oil. The second is that the percentage of world oil consumption decreased for North America and Western Europe, whereas it increased for the centrally planned economies and the rest of the world. Finally, the output of OPEC actually decreased by 50 percent over the past decade. Part of that was due to the fall in demand for oil in general, but part of it was due to the increase in oil supply by non-OPEC members, as is demonstrated in Table 7.2. The major non-OPEC increase came from the USSR (in the centrally planned economies category), Mexico, and the United Kingdom (in the rest of the world category).[23]

Because of these trends, OPEC has been losing its grip. After successive price increases over the period 1973–1980, OPEC was forced to cut prices in 1983 and 1985. These cuts in prices along with the drop in demand have been devastating to the countries of OPEC with large populations, such as Nigeria, Indonesia, Venezuela, and Iran. It was estimated that OPEC countries as a group suffered balance-of-payments deficits during the 1982–1985 period. As a result, foreign exchange reserves began to slip. The

TABLE 7.2

Total World Oil Production (Share, Percent)

	1973	1979	1983
OPEC	57%	48%	32%
USA	16	13	15
Centrally Planned Economies	17	22	27
Rest of World	10	17	26
	100%	100%	100%

SOURCE: "International Oil Markets," *Currency Profiles* (New York: The Henley Centre for Forecasting and Manufacturers Hanover Trust, December 1984), p. 7.

reserves of Saudi Arabia, which were at $150 billion in 1982–1983, had fallen to less than $100 billion by early 1985.[24] Clearly, OPEC, which had been considered the model producer cartel, was facing some serious difficulties.

TRADE AGREEMENTS

There are a variety of different kinds of trade agreements. The first part of the chapter focused on regional economic groups that were essentially multilateral trade agreements involving a limited group of countries. A more ambitious form of multilateral trade agreement is the General Agreement on Tariffs and Trade established by the United Nations after World War II. In addition to the multilateral agreements there are a number of bilateral agreements in force. Since GATT was covered in Chapter 5, we will discuss bilateral agreements in this chapter.

Bilateral Agreements

• Bilateral agreements—trade agreements between two countries

It would be impossible to identify all of the bilateral and limited multilateral trade agreements that are currently in force in the world. The United States has concluded a number of major agreements with a variety of countries. Because the EC negotiates as a bloc rather than as individual countries, agreements reached between the United States and the EC are treated as bilateral agreements. The historic steel agreement reached in 1982 is a good example of a bilateral agreement between the United States and the EC. In a similar vein the United States has concluded agreements with Canada (Automotive Products Trade), Japan (voluntary quotas on automobile imports), and the individual Caribbean countries through the Caribbean Basin Initiative. Each year the U.S. Trade Representative's Office publishes a report summarizing the major bilateral and multilateral negotiations that the United States took part in during the year and highlighting the major treaties in force at that point in time.

OTHER MULTILATERAL INSTITUTIONS

The United Nations

• United Nations—a multilateral organization that deals with social, political, and economic issues
• UNCTAD—a U.N. organization active in the dialogue between developing and industrial countries

There are numerous other bilateral and multilateral organizations, treaties, and agreements in existence. The United Nations is one of the most visible and extensive. Many of the organizations alluded to in other chapters are outgrowths of the United Nations. Some of these are the World Bank Group, the International Monetary Fund, and the General Agreement on Tariffs and Trade. The New International Economic Order referred to in Chapter 2 is also a product of the United Nations. The **United Nations**

Conference on Trade and Development (UNCTAD) has been especially active in dealing with the relationships between developing and industrial countries with respect to commodities, manufacturing, shipping, and invisibles and financing related to trade.

Another important U.N. agency is the **Economic and Social Council (ECOSOC),** which is responsible for economic, social, cultural, and humanitarian facets of U.N. policy. This group organized a Commission of Transnational Corporations to secure effective international arrangements for the operations of transnational corporations and to further global understanding of the nature and effects of their activities. The commission has looked at a variety of topics, such as transfer pricing, taxation, and international standards of accounting and reporting.

- ECOSOC—a U.N. organization that organized the Commission of Transnational Corporations

The United Nations organized a Conference on the Law of the Sea, which began working in 1973 on issues such as freedom of navigation, pollution, scientific research in coastal waters, the status of the underwater shelf that surrounds each continent, and seabed mining. The last area is one of greatest difficulty. Scientists agree that the seas are rich in mineral resources, and considerable disagreement exists over whether U.N. authority or private industry should have the mining rights. The treaty was signed in Jamaica in December 1982, but implementing it has been a struggle. One of the major problems is that even though over 100 countries signed the agreement, very few of them have ratified it. In addition, the United States, West Germany, Italy, Belgium, and Great Britain are among the countries that chose not to sign the treaty in the first place.

The Organization for Economic Cooperation and Development

- OECD—a multilateral organization that helps industrial countries formulate social and economic policies

The United Nations is the most comprehensive form of multilateral cooperation in the world today. The **Organization for Economic Cooperation and Development (OECD)** was already described briefly in Chapter 2 as well as in this chapter. However, it is worth expanding a little on discussions of those two organizations. The OECD, like the U.N., is a multilateral form of cooperation. The major difference is that the OECD is made up of primarily industrial countries. It was organized in 1961 to assist member governments in formulating policies aimed at promoting economic and social welfare and to stimulate and harmonize members' assistance to developing countries.[25] It has over 200 different committees that deal with economic issues. Three committees that deal with specific trade issues are the Trade Committee, the Executive Committee Special Session, and the Development Assistance Committee.

The Trade Committee provides a forum for considering long-range trade policies of member nations and for discussing current problems as well. This committee was useful in discussing the steel problems in the early 1970s. The Executive Committee Special Session deals with the coordination of national economic policies. This discussion has taken on increased significance over the past few years as inflation has dropped and currencies have come under pressure owing to the strong U.S. dollar. The final committee is concerned about the transfer of financial resources to the developing countries.

The OECD has issued a code of conduct relating to the operations of MNEs to ensure that the MNEs operate in such a way as to support the economic and political objectives of the individual member nations. In addition, the OECD issued a set of guidelines dealing with the disclosure of financial and operating information of MNEs. These disclosures will be mentioned in a little more detail in Chapter 19.

The U.N. and the OECD are multilateral institutions that have broader appeal than the narrower trade or economic issues described earlier in the chapter. All of these organizations, however, have a useful purpose. They provide a forum where nations can discuss political, economic, and social issues of mutual benefit and, it is hoped, come to some basis of cooperation for mutual benefit.

SUMMARY

* After a period of economic isolation and World War II, many efforts toward intergovernmental cooperation emerged.

* Regional economic integration became very important after World War II as countries began to realize the benefits of cooperation and larger market sizes. The major types of economic integration are the free trade area, customs union, common market, economic union, and complete economic integration.

* In its most limited sense, economic integration allows countries to trade goods without tariff discrimination (free trade area). In a more complex arrangement, all factors of production are allowed to move across borders, and some degree of social, political, and economic harmonization is undertaken (complete economic integration).

* The static effects of economic integration improve the efficiency of resource allocation and have an impact on both production and consumption. The dynamic effects involve internal and external economies that arise because of changes in growth of market sizes.

* The European Community is an effective common market that has abolished most of the restrictions on factor mobility and is moving toward the status of an economic union by attempting to harmonize national economic policies to a limited extent. The EC includes Belgium, Denmark, France, Greece, West Germany, Ireland, Italy, Luxembourg, the Netherlands, and the United Kingdom. The next entrants to the EC will be Spain and Portugal.

- The EC is governed by the Commission, the Council of Ministers, the Parliament, and the Court of Justice.

- Some of the major goals of the EC are (1) abolishment of intrazonal restrictions on the movement of goods, capital, services, and labor; (2) a common external tariff; (3) a common agricultural policy; (4) harmonization of tax and legal systems; (5) a uniform policy concerning antitrust; and (6) a harmonization of national currencies.

- Other forms of economic integration have occurred in other parts of the world, notably in Latin America and among the Communist countries. Various forms of free trade areas and customs unions also exist in Africa and Asia.

- Many developing countries rely on the export of commodities to supply the hard currencies needed for economic development. Instability in commodity prices has tended to result in fluctuations in export earnings. Commodity agreements, utilizing buffer stocks, price ranges, quotas, or combinations of the three, are often entered into in the hope of stabilizing prices.

- The Organization of Petroleum Exporting Countries (OPEC) was successful as a producer cartel in the 1970s and was able to force up prices of crude oil to historic highs. However, the drop in demand worldwide and the entrance of major non-OPEC producers has reduced OPEC's influence.

- A variety of multilateral and bilateral trade agreements has resulted in the increase in trade worldwide in the decades after World War II. The broadest of these agreements is the General Agreement on Tariffs and Trade.

- The United Nations has become deeply involved in international business through the World Bank Group, the International Monetary Fund, the Commission on Transnational Corporations, and the Conference on the Law of the Sea.

- The Organization for Economic Cooperation and Development is an association of the major industrial countries of the world whose major objectives are to foster economic and social development.

 **A NEW COMMON MARKET: THE UNITED STATES, CANADA, AND MEXICO**[26]

In the late 1970s, many people were looking at the possibility of establishing a common market in North America similar to the EC but involving Canada, Mexico, and the United States. The market would have all of the earmarks of a common market with the abolishment of all tariffs and quotas in intrazonal trade, a common external tariff, and mobility of factors of production. The major objective of the market would be somehow to help the United States lessen its dependence on OPEC by giving it free access to oil and natural gas in Canada and Mexico.

The new market would be a large one with much of its economic strength coming from the United States. Some of the demographics are as follows:

Demographic Data, 1982

	Population (millions)	Gross national product (billions of U.S. dollars)	Per capita GNP (U.S. dollars)
Canada	24.6	278.5	11,320
Mexico	73.1	165.9	2270
United States	231.5	3010	13,160

Intrazonal trade currently is as follows:

Exports to and from (in billions of U.S. dollars) (1982)

	United States	Canada	Mexico
United States		33.7	11.8
Canada	46.5		0.36
Mexico	29.9	0.81	

A common market involving these three countries could make them totally self-sufficient in energy. In addition, manufacturers in the three countries would have unrestricted access to each other's markets. Both agricultural and industrial sectors in Canada and Mexico would benefit from U.S.-developed technology. This infusion of technology could be very beneficial to Mexico, especially in helping the country alleviate its high unemployment.

As can be seen from the above table, the three countries already enjoy a large amount of intrazonal trade. This would be expected to increase in the future. Because of negotiations completed under the Tokyo Round of GATT in 1979, 80 percent of all Canadian exports to the United States and 65 percent of all U.S. exports to Canada are expected to be duty free by 1987. Another 15 percent of Canadian exports are to enter the United States at tariffs of 5 percent or less. However, Canada's average tariff on dutiable U.S. imports is 8.5 percent, more than double the average U.S. tariff on dutiable imports from Canada.

In recent years a variety of forms of economic cooperation have taken place between the United States and Canada. In 1965 an Automotive Products Trade agreement was implemented between the two countries. It provides for qualified duty-free trade in specified automotive products between the United States and Canada. In the early 1980s there was some discussion about the possibility of developing free trade in specific sectors, such as steel and textiles. That idea began to give way to a broader discussion of free trade, especially with the election of conservative Prime Minister Brian Mulroney in Canada and the reelection of President Reagan in the United States.

Mexico exports a significantly greater amount of goods to the United States than it does to Canada. As far as Mexico's exports to the United States are concerned, tariffs on 40 percent of the total exports (essentially from oil and coffee beans) are nonexistent, and tariffs on other goods average 6.03 percent. Mexico, on the other hand, is not a member of GATT because it is taking a very protectionist posture as a strategy to develop local industry. As a result, Mexico's complex licensing system bars many U.S.-manufactured goods. Those goods that are imported into Mexico enter at tariff rates that range from 35 to 100 percent. That situation was aggravated in the early 1980s as Mexico came under severe hard currency pressures because of its foreign debt obligations. The Mexican government was forced to choke off imports and significantly expand exports of goods and services in order to meet its international obligations. However, threatened protectionist measures on the part of the U.S. government could significantly slow down Mexico's export-driven recovery.

U.S. investment in the two countries is substantial. Mexico is slightly different from Canada, however, because it went through a period when it did not allow majority foreign ownership on new investments. The United States is the largest foreign investor in Mexico, as it is in Canada. Even though the Mexican government lifted its restrictions on foreign ownership in 1984, few foreign firms were willing to risk large investments initially in such an unstable economic environment. However, some U.S. companies were setting up assembly operations in Mexico close to the U.S. border to take advantage of low labor rates in Mexico. It was estimated that these assembly operations were supplying more foreign exchange to the Mexican economy than was tourism.

The United States is also the largest foreign investor in Canada. In 1978, U.S. companies provided 79.4 percent of all foreign direct investment in Canada. In 1979, U.S. companies controlled forty-five of the hundred largest companies in Canada. Canadian-based subsidiaries of U.S. companies accounted for 43 percent of all Canadian manufacturing and 58 percent of all oil and natural gas companies. For a few years under the leadership of Prime Minister Pierre Trudeau the Canadian government was trying to force many U.S. companies to divest ownership, especially in the oil and gas industries. However, such a negative climate for investment began to develop in Canada that the government was forced to back off from some of its demands. In addition, Prime Minister Mulroney appeared to be much more interested in encouraging foreign investment than in discouraging it.

Labor costs were considered to be lower in Mexico than in either Canada or the United States, but the productivity level was not very high. Labor costs in Canada were quite high. Northern Telecom, a Canadian communications equipment manufacturer, estimated that total labor costs at its Canadian plants were 10–50 percent higher than those at its U.S. factories. Not all wages were that high, but there was a significant difference.

Although all three countries have some degree of unemployment, the problem is most acute in Mexico. Unemployment is so high in Mexico that workers constantly cross the border into the United States, principally to settle in California and the Southwest, looking for jobs. This has given the United States a large pool of low-skilled, cheap labor, but it has also created a lot of tension between the U.S. and Mexican governments. If the free flow of goods and capital were to be extended to labor, the level of migration might increase dramatically, leading to a variety of social and economic problems.

QUESTIONS

1. List the benefits that would accrue to all three members of the new common market.
2. List the major economic problems that could arise from such a union.
3. Discuss the political and nationalistic ramifications of such a union.
4. How would this union compare with some of the others that we discussed in this chapter?
5. If you were a U.S. businessperson looking at this newly created market, what strategies might you employ to serve all three markets? What factors would you consider in making your choice?

NOTES

1. Data for the case were taken from "A Modern Merger: Joined but Separate," *International Management,* October 1971, supplement, pp. 35–37; "The Romance is over for Dunlop and Pirelli," *Business Week,* May 11, 1981, p. 46.

2. Bela Balassa, *The Theory of Economic Integration* (Homewood, Ill.: Richard D. Irwin, 1961), p. 1.

3. *Ibid.,* p. 40.

4. *Ibid.,* p. 2.

5. Joyce Heard, "IBM Finds a Club That Doesn't Want It as a Member," *Business Week,* February 11, 1985, p. 42.

6. The information in this example is from various Annual Reports of Ford Motor

Company; also from *Forbes,* July 1, 1972, pp. 22–26; *Forbes,* April 2, 1979, pp. 44–48.

7. *Forbes,* July 1, 1972, p. 23.

8. *Ibid.*

9. Robert Ball, "Renault Takes Its Hit Show on the Road," *Fortune,* May 4, 1981, pp. 275–284.

10. Price Waterhouse, *EEC Bulletin,* No. 68 (Brussels: Price Waterhouse, September 1984), p. 4.

11. Heard, *op. cit.*

12. Dennis Kneale, Beth Karlin, and Brent Bowers, "IBM Settles Antitrust Suit with Common Market," *Wall Street Journal,* August 3, 1984, p. 2.

13. "Inter-American Development Bank Predicts Renewed Push for Economic Integration in Latin America," *IMF Survey,* December 10, 1984, pp. 369, 374–376.

14. *Europa Yearbook—1984,* pp. 126–127.

15. *Ibid.,* p. 106.

16. "Inter-American Development Bank . . . ," *op. cit.,* p. 374.

17. Paul Lewis, "Common Market: An Unworkable Jigsaw Puzzle," *New York Times,* February 22, 1984, p. A3.

18. Jere R. Behrman, *Development, the International Economic Order, and Commodity Agreements* (Reading, Mass.: Addison-Wesley Publishing Company, 1978), p. 66.

19. "Markets Test Commodity Agreements' Ability to Meet Objectives of Price Stabilization," *IMF Survey,* December 10, 1984, p. 370.

20. "An Even Sweeter Sugar Outlook," *Business Week,* October 6, 1980, p. 104; F. Gerard Adams, "Price Pressures Build despite Weaker Demand," *Business Week,* October 27, 1980, p. 197.

21. "The Middle East Squeeze on Oil Giants," *Business Week,* July 29, 1972, p. 56.

22. "International Oil Market Prospects," *Currency Profiles* (New York: The Henley Centre for Economic Forecasting and Manufacturers Hanover Trust Company, December 1984), p. 6.

23. *Ibid.,* pp. 6–7.

24. Ronald Taggiasco and William Glesgell, "OPEC Still Hasn't Faced up to Reality," *Business Week,* February 11, 1985, p. 29.

25. *Europa Yearbook,* p. 184.

26. Most of the material for this case comes directly from Herbert E. Meyer, "Why a North American Common Market Won't Work—Yet," FORTUNE, September 10, 1979, pp. 118 ff., © 1979 Time, Inc. All rights reserved; "Why Only a Few Companies Are Betting on Mexico's Future," *Business Week,* October 1, 1984, pp. 78–82; Earl H. Fry and Lee H. Radebaugh, eds. *Regulation of Foreign Direct Investment in Canada and the United States* (Provo, Utah: Brigham Young University, 1983); Lee H. Radebaugh and Earl H. Fry, eds. *Canada/U.S. Trade Relations* (Provo, Utah: Brigham Young University, 1984).

PART 4

World Financial Environment

A company that operates internationally must work within the framework of diverse financial systems and yet measure and report its worldwide performance in terms of some common frame of reference. Since different nations have distinct currencies, transactions among countries must be conducted in more than one currency.

Chapter 8 defines the terms used in international currency transactions, explains how the foreign exchange markets work, examines the instruments of foreign exchange, and describes the uses of the foreign exchange market.

Chapter 9 explains how different currencies' values are determined. The emphasis is on the exchange rate arrangements that exist within the international monetary system, the theories that explain the determination of exchange rates, methods used to forecast exchange rate movements, and the effects that values and movements have on business operations.

A company operating internationally faces a more diverse group of financial institutions than is found in a domestic situation. These institutions and their scopes and limitations are described in Chapter 10.

8

Foreign Exchange

- To discuss the terms and definitions in foreign exchange.
- To describe how the foreign exchange market works for immediate and long-term transactions.
- To illustrate how countries control limited supplies of foreign exchange through licensing, multiple rates, and import deposit requirements.
- To contrast the various instruments of foreign exchange, such as commercial bills of exchange and letters of credit.
- To discuss briefly how the foreign exchange market is used in commercial and financial transactions.

THE BRAZILIAN CRUZEIRO[1]

Brazil is an interesting country that moved from revolution, despair, and hyperinflation in the 1960s to the economic miracle of the late 1960s and early 1970s. During the mid- to late 1970s, however, the economic miracle was beset with the attendant problems of spiraling oil prices, developing country debt, and a renewed outburst of inflation. By the early 1980s, Brazil's economy was in trouble again as it struggled to generate enough foreign exchange to pay off its debts and pay for imports necessary to fuel an economic recovery and, it was hoped, a repeat of the miracle.

The Brazilian cruzeiro is not freely convertible into other currencies because of restraints and restrictions imposed on it by the Central Bank of Brazil. Since 1968 the government has allowed the value of the cruzeiro to change on a relatively frequent basis in order to keep the laws of supply and demand more or less satisfied. Owing to controls, the law of supply and demand is not allowed to operate freely, however. Most foreign exchange transactions are taken care of by the Central Bank of Brazil, the Banco do Brasil, S.A., and banks and tourist agencies authorized to deal in foreign exchange.

Although the cruzeiro is devalued (the value is allowed to drop in relation to the U.S. dollar) on a relatively frequent basis, that does not mean that its value is always what it would be in a free market. In fact, outside of the official market a black market for dollars exists where the cruzeiro is traded at a substantial discount. This is a very common phenomenon in countries where the exchange rate is controlled by the government.

Because of the shortage of foreign exchange, the Central Bank is very concerned about how foreign exchange is used. In most cases, imports require a license. These licenses, or import certificates, are a necessary part of the foreign exchange allocation process. The Foreign Trade Department of the Banco do Brasil (CACEX) establishes foreign currency quotas for six-month intervals and issues import certificates based on semiannual import programs developed by importers. As a result of this requirement, importers have to do a good job of planning their foreign exchange requirements and convincing the Brazilian government that their imports are essential to the long-run viability of the nation.

During the early 1980s the Brazilian government had regulations for its citizens living temporarily abroad. These regulations permitted them to convert cruzeiros into the currency of the country where they were living, but the government allowed the equivalent only of U.S. $300 per month. Brazilian tourists were allowed to exchange cruzeiros for $500 worth of another currency without prior approval, except on trips to Central and South America, where they were permitted only $100. However, tourists were allowed to take only $100 with them in cash when they left. The rest of the money was in the form of payment orders. This practice kept tourists from cashing large amounts of cruzeiros into another currency and then cancelling the trip and keeping the foreign currency.

In spite of these controls, some firms were given special dispensation. For example, a special allowance of $20,000 a year was available for the travel and representation expenses abroad of firms whose annual exports totaled at least $200,000. In addition, firms that exported products and earned foreign exchange had an easier time getting import certificates than those that did not.

Most of the currency transactions mentioned above occur in the spot market, the market on a given day for foreign exchange. However, forward contracts are available for commercial transactions. These contracts are usually between an importer and the Banco do Brasil to provide for the conversion of cruzeiros into dollars or some other foreign currency to settle an obligation due at some point in the future. These contracts are often entered into when the Banco do Brasil issues the importer a letter of credit, a document that specifies that the Banco do Brasil will pay for the imports when it is notified that the imports have arrived or at some point in the future after arrival. The importer is often required to deposit a large percentage of the contract as a guarantee that the Banco do Brasil will have the cash necessary to convert into the foreign currency.

INTRODUCTION

As can be seen from the Brazilian example, a fundamental difference between making payment in the domestic market and making payment for goods, services, or securities purchased abroad is that in a domestic transaction only one currency is used, while two or more currencies may be used in a foreign transaction. For example, a U.S. businessperson who exports $100,000 worth of textile machinery to a Zurich textile producer will ask the Swiss buyer to remit payment in dollars unless the U.S. firm has some specific use for Swiss francs. (If the firm has a subsidiary located in Switzerland, for instance, it may wish to make the funds acquired available to this subsidiary and would accept payment in Swiss francs.)

Let us assume that the above situation is not the case and that you are a U.S. importer who has agreed to purchase a certain quantity of French perfume and to pay the French exporter 20,000 francs for it. How would you go about paying? First, you would go to the international department of your local bank to buy 20,000 French francs at the going market rate. We will assume that the dollar/franc exchange rate is FF 9.5 = $1. Your bank would then debit your demand deposit by $2105 and give you a special check payable in francs made out to the exporter. The check is then sent to the exporter, who deposits it in a Paris bank. The bank in

- Foreign exchange—currencies and other instruments of payments denominated in other currencies

turn credits the exporter's account with 20,000 francs, and the transaction is completed.

The special check and other instruments for making payment abroad are referred to collectively as **foreign exchange.** Before we discuss the instruments of foreign exchange, it is necessary to understand what is meant by the term *exchange rates.* Even though the major purpose of this chapter is to provide essential information about the nature of foreign exchange, it is important to understand that Chapters 9 and 10 are an integral part of this discussion. Chapter 9 will focus on what gives exchange rates their value and what causes those rates to change. Chapter 10 will look at the international capital markets in which foreign exchange is traded.

TERMS AND DEFINITIONS

- Exchange rate—the number of units of one currency to acquire one unit of a currency of another country

An **exchange rate** can be defined as the number of units of one currency that must be given to acquire one unit of a currency of another country. It is the price one pays in the home currency to purchase a certain quantity of funds in the currency of another country. For example, toward the end of 1984 it took only $0.0003376 to purchase one Brazilian cruzeiro. The exchange rate, then, is the link connecting different national currencies that makes international price and cost comparisons possible.

- Spot rate—the exchange rate involved for immediate delivery
- Interbank market—the foreign exchange markets between and among banks
- Forward rate—the rate quoted for future delivery

If the rate is quoted for current foreign currency transactions, it is called the **spot rate.** The spot rate is for **interbank transactions** (transactions between banks) for delivery within two business days or immediate delivery for over the counter transactions that usually involve nonbank customers. If the rate is quoted for delivery of foreign currency in the future, it is called the **forward rate.** The forward rate is a contractual rate between the foreign exchange trader and the trader's client.

The Spot Market

- The spread in the spot market is the difference between the bid (buy) and offer (sell) rates quoted by the foreign exchange trader

Since most foreign currency transactions take place with foreign exchange traders, the rates are quoted by the traders. Whether the traders quote prices in the spot or the forward market, they will always quote a **bid** (buy) and **offer** (sell) rate. The bid is what the trader is willing to buy foreign exchange for, and the offer is what the trader is willing to sell foreign exchange for. The **spread in the spot market,** the difference between the bid and offer rates, is the margin on which the trader earns a profit on overall transactions. Thus the rate quoted by a trader for the British pound might be $1.1635/45. This implies that the trader would be willing to buy pounds at $1.1635 and sell them for $1.1645. It is obvious that the trader would want to buy low and sell high.

- Direct quote—the number of units of the domestic currency for one unit of the foreign currency
- Indirect quote—the number of units of the foreign currency for one unit of the domestic currency

As was noted in the example above, the pound is quoted by the U.S. bank at the number of U.S. dollars for one unit of the foreign currency (the British pound). This is also known as the **direct quote** or **normal.** If the rate were quoted in terms of the number of units of the foreign currency for one unit of the domestic currency, it would be known as the **indirect quote** or **reciprocal.** It is reciprocal because it is the inverse of the direct quote. For example,

$$\frac{1}{\$1.1645} = 0.8587 \text{ British pounds per U.S. dollar}$$

- U.S. terms—direct quote
- European terms—indirect quote

Both the direct and indirect quotes are used. In the United States it is common to use the direct quote for domestic business. That is often referred to as **U.S. terms.** For international business, however, banks will often use **European terms,** which would be the indirect quote. The rate quoted for the Brazilian cruzeiro above was the direct rate. The indirect rate at that same time was 2962.5 cruzeiros per dollar. The reason for using the indirect quote for international business is that it is a custom internationally to use the U.S. dollar as the **base currency** for transactions; the other currency in the transaction would be the **quoted currency.**

Most large newspapers, especially those devoted to business or with business sections, quote exchange rates on a daily basis. The *Wall Street Journal,* for example, provides the direct and indirect rates for forty-four different currencies in every issue. The rates are the selling rate of Banker's Trust for interbank transactions of $1 million and more. In addition to the spot rates of each of those currencies, the forward rates are provided for the British pound, the Canadian dollar, the French franc, the Japanese yen, the Swiss franc, and the West German mark. Table 8.1 provides some quotes of several different currencies.

- Cross rate—an exchange rate computed from two other exchange rates

A final important definition for the spot market is the **cross rate.** The cross rate is an exchange rate computed from two other rates. Since most foreign currency transactions are denominated in terms of U.S. dollars, it is common to see two nondollar currencies related to each other in the cross rate. To simplify the discussion, we will use the European quotes of the Swiss franc and West German mark and will figure the cross rate with the Swiss franc as the quoted currency and the West German mark as the base currency. In Table 8.1 the spot rates for West German marks (DM) and Swiss (SwF) francs on Thursday, December 20, 1984, were:

DM 3.1200 per U.S. dollar

SwF 2.5700 per U.S. dollar

The cross rate would be:

$$\frac{\text{SwF } 2.5700}{\text{DM } 3.1200} = \text{SwF } 0.8237 \text{ per DM}$$

TABLE 8.1

FOREIGN EXCHANGE QUOTES

Country	U.S. Equivalent		Currency per U.S. Dollar	
	Thurs.	Wed.	Thurs.	Wed.
Argentina (peso)	0.006445	0.00645	115.16	155.16
Brazil (cruzeiro)	0.0003376	0.0003376	2962.5	2962.5
Canada (dollar)	0.7587	0.7573	1.3180	1.3204
30-Day Forward	0.7576	0.7561	1.3199	1.3225
90-Day Forward	0.7564	0.7545	1.3221	1.3253
180-Day Forward	0.7551	0.7529	1.3244	1.3282
France (franc)	0.1048	0.1055	9.5450	9.4825
30-Day Forward	0.1046	0.1052	9.562	9.5015
90-Day Forward	0.1043	0.1049	9.591	9.5305
180-Day Forward	0.1039	0.1045	9.628	9.5705
Great Britain (pound)	1.1645	1.1755	0.8587	0.8507
30-Day Forward	1.1634	1.1744	0.8595	0.8515
90-Day Forward	1.1613	1.1720	0.8611	0.8532
180-Day Forward	1.1600	1.1712	0.8621	0.8538
Japan (yen)	0.004037	0.004039	247.70	247.60
30-Day Forward	0.004045	0.004047	247.22	247.10
90-Day Forward	0.004062	0.004063	246.19	246.10
180-Day Forward	0.004106	0.004099	243.56	243.98
Switzerland (franc)	0.3891	0.3909	2.5700	2.5580
30-Day Forward	0.3903	0.3921	2.5620	2.5505
90-Day Forward	0.3929	0.3946	2.5455	2.5345
180-Day Forward	0.3976	0.3994	2.5145	2.5035
Venezuela (bolivar)				
Official Rate	0.1333	0.1333	7.50	7.50
Floating Rate	0.07981	0.07981	12.53	12.53
West Germany (mark)	0.3205	0.3228	3.1200	3.0980
30-Day Forward	0.3213	0.3236	3.1124	3.0905
90-Day Forward	0.3230	0.3253	3.0956	3.0738
180-Day Forward	0.3263	0.3287	3.0645	3.0425

Quotes for Thursday, December 20, 1984. The New York foreign exchange selling rates apply to trading among banks in amounts of $1 million and more, as quoted at 3 P.M. Eastern time by Bankers Trust Co. Retail transactions provide fewer units of foreign currency per dollar.

SOURCE: *The Wall Street Journal*, December 21, 1984, p. 22.

which means that one West German mark equals 0.8237 Swiss franc. It is common to see the cross rate quoted as 82.37. West German and Swiss managers keep track of the cross rate, since they trade extensively with each other. Any material shifts in the cross rate could signal a change in prices of goods. For example, assume that a product costing DM 100 sold in Switzerland for SwF 82.37 as shown in the cross rate illustration. If the cross rate were to move to SwF 85, the Swiss importer might have to increase prices to get enough Swiss francs to trade for West German marks to pay the West German exporter. If the product were especially price sensitive, the importer might lose volume.

The Forward Market

- Forward spread—the difference between the spot and forward exchange rates

As defined at the beginning of the chapter, the forward rate is the rate quoted by foreign exchange traders for the purchase or sale of foreign exchange in the future. As was noted in Table 8.1, there is a difference between the spot rate and the forward rate; it is known as the **spread in the forward market**. The reason for the difference between the spot and forward rate is discussed in the following chapter, but at this point we want to be able to determine the amount of the spread and look at two ways that we can discuss the spread—as points and as a percentage premium or discount.

In the illustration below we compute the points for 90-day contracts for the Canadian dollar and the Swiss franc quoted in U.S. terms:

	Canadian dollars	Swiss francs
Spot	$0.7587	$0.3891
90-day forward	0.7564	0.3929
Points	−23	+38

- Discount—forward rate is less than the spot rate
- Premium—forward rate exceeds the spot rate

The spread in Canadian dollars is 23 points. Because the forward rate is less than the spot rate, the Canadian dollar is at a **discount** in the 90-day forward market. The spread in Swiss francs is 38 points. Since the forward rate is greater than the spot rate, the Swiss franc is at a **premium** in the forward market.

The premium or discount can also be quoted in terms of annualized percent. The formula to determine the percentage is the following:

$$\text{Premium (discount)} = \frac{F_o - S_o}{S_o} \times \frac{12}{N} \times 100$$

where F_o is the forward rate on the day the contract is entered into, S_o is the spot rate on that day, N is the number of months forwards, and 100 is used to convert the decimal to percent amounts (e.g., $0.05 \times 100 = 5\%$).

Using Canadian dollars,

$$\text{Discount} = \frac{0.7564 - 0.7587}{0.7587} \times \frac{12}{3} \times 100 = 1.2126\%$$

which means that the Canadian dollar is selling at a discount of 1.2126 percent under the spot rate.

Using Swiss francs,

$$\text{Premium} = \frac{0.3929 - 0.3891}{0.3891} \times \frac{12}{3} \times 100 = 3.906\%$$

which means that the Swiss franc is selling at a 3.906 percent premium over the U.S. dollar.

As was noted in Table 8.1, there is no forward market for the Brazilian cruzeiro, even though the case at the beginning of the chapter mentioned that an importer could get a forward contract from the Banco do Brasil. The reason for the discrepancy is that a forward contract in cruzeiros is generally not available in the interbank market. There is an excess supply of cruzeiros, and it would be practically impossible for the interbank market to balance off its purchases of cruzeiro contracts with its sales of cruzeiro contracts. The market is too thin (not enough transactions) to warrant the forward market in the interbank market.

HOW THE FOREIGN EXCHANGE MARKET WORKS

Basic Spot and Forward Markets

> Brokers—specialists that facilitate transactions in the interbank market

The determinants of exchange rates will be discussed in the next chapter, but now we need to see how foreign exchange is traded. The dollar is the most important trading currency in the international monetary system. It is also the major reserve asset held by most countries. In 1983 a survey was conducted by the U.S. Federal Reserve Board concerning foreign exchange transactions in the U.S. market. It was found that annual volume in the United States had increased by 50% to $998.4 billion over a survey conducted in 1980.[2] The majority of those transactions, 70.4 percent, was carried out by the commercial banks, the rest being conducted by foreign exchange brokers. **Brokers** are specialists that facilitate transactions between banks rather than have the banks work directly with each other.

In terms of currencies traded, the West German mark was the most popular in the United States with 32.7 percent of the market, followed by the Japanese yen with 22 percent, the British pound with 16.6 percent, the Swiss franc with 12.2 percent, and the Canadian dollar with 7.5 percent.

> Swap—an exchange of currencies in the spot market with the agreement to reverse the transaction in the future

In that same survey it was estimated that over 63 percent of all foreign exchange trading was in the spot market, primarily in the interbank market. Only 10 percent of the spot transactions were retail (where banks deal with nonbanking institutions). For transactions not carried out in the spot market, 33 percent were in **foreign currency swaps,** and only 4 percent were in the forward and futures markets. Foreign currency swaps are a combination of a spot transaction and a forward transaction. For example, a U.S. bank could trade dollars for Swiss francs with a Swiss bank in the spot market with the agreement that it will deliver Swiss francs for dollars at a specified point in the future.

As will be pointed out in the following chapter, the foreign exchange market is a relatively efficient one that is based on the economic law of supply and demand. Sometimes governments intervene to control the flow of currency. However, the central action in the foreign exchange market revolves around the commercial banks in the major money centers of the world. From the standpoint of time zones, the following describes how the money centers of the world come on line:

> *The world's communication networks are now so good, and so many countries have fairly unrestricted markets that we can talk of a single world market. It starts in a small way in New Zealand around 9:00 A.M., just in time to catch the tail end of the previous night's New York market. Two or three hours later, Tokyo opens, followed an hour later by Hong Kong and Manila and then half an hour later by Singapore. By now, with the Far East market in full swing, the focus moves to the Near and Middle East. Bombay opens two hours after Singapore, followed after an hour and a half by Abu Dhabi, with Jeddah an hour behind, and Athens and Beirut an hour behind still. By this stage trading in the Far and Middle East is usually thin and perhaps nervous as dealers wait to see how Europe will trade. Paris and Frankfurt open an hour ahead of London, and by this time Tokyo is starting to close down, so the European market can judge how the Japanese market has been trading by the way they deal to close out positions. By lunch-time in London, New York is starting to open up, and as Europe closes down, so positions can be passed westward. During the afternoon in New York, trading tends to be quiet. The problem is that there is nowhere to pass a position to. The San Francisco market, three hours behind, is effectively a satellite of the New York market. Very small positions can be passed on to New Zealand banks, but the market there is extremely limited.*[3]

• Most foreign currency transactions are handled by traders in the commercial banks

Most of the transactions are handled in the interbank market. Even in dealings among banks, most of the transactions are handled by traders in the home offices of the major money center banks. These traders typically have responsibility for a single currency, and they end up dealing with the traders of that currency worldwide. Each money center bank, such as Chase Manhattan or Manufacturers Hanover Trust, has a trading room where the currency traders are housed. That allows them to keep in touch with each other as well as with the major traders around the world. This will be discussed further in the section on international banking in Chapter 10.

Sometimes the bankers work through brokers instead of working directly with traders of other banks. There are four major brokers in the United States and several minor ones that deal in foreign exchange transac-

FIGURE 8.1
Structure of Foreign Exchange Markets
Note: As will be described below, the International Money Market (IMM) Chicago trades foreign exchange futures and DM futures options, the London International Financial Futures Exchange (LIFFE) trades foreign exchange futures, and the Philadelphia Stock Exchange (PSE) trades foreign currency options.
SOURCE: K. Alec Chrystal, ''A Guide to Foreign Exchange Markets,'' *Bulletin* (Federal Reserve Bank of St. Louis, March 1984), p. 9.

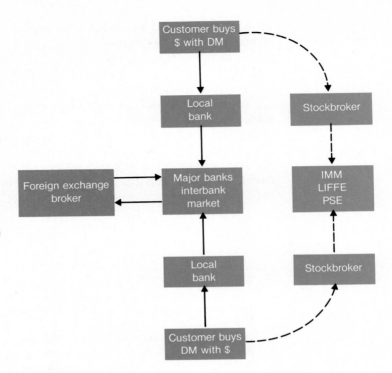

tions. These brokers typically try to link traders of different banks in foreign exchange transactions. Brokers sometimes work the corporate market as well, but that is rare in comparison with their major area of specialty.

Even though the money center banks trade most of the foreign exchange in the world, companies that are not located in these money centers can still go through regional or local banks for foreign currency transactions. However, their bank generally works through a money center bank as demonstrated in Fig. 8.1.

Specialized Markets

The commercial banks handle the majority of the spot and forward transactions. However, some specialized institutions and markets that deal in futures and options offer some variety from the banking sector. The major ones are the International Monetary Market (IMM) in Chicago, the London International Financial Futures Exchange (LIFFE), and the Philadelphia Stock Exchange (PSE). As noted in Fig. 8.1, a customer operates in these three markets through a broker, who then has access to the major money markets.

The IMM deals primarily in the futures contracts—contracts for forward delivery of currencies for specific amounts with a specific maturity date

The International Monetary Market. The **IMM** was opened in 1972 by the Chicago Mercantile Exchange. It deals primarily in futures contracts for the British pound, the Canadian dollar, the West German mark, the Swiss franc, the Japanese yen, the Mexican peso, the French franc, and the Dutch guilder. These contracts are for specific amounts and have a specific maturity date. For example, a British pound contract is for 25,000 pounds, and a Japanese yen contract is for 12.5 million yen. The "Futures Prices" section of the *Wall Street Journal* provides quotes of the contracts each day.

Although the contracts have a fixed maturity date, there is a ready market for the contracts at the IMM. Deals are made on the trading floor between brokers rather than over the telephone between traders as is the case with the forward markets for banks. The futures contracts at the IMM also tend to be relatively small in comparison with the size of the transactions that one normally encounters in the interbank market. The IMM also places limits on how much the futures prices can vary from one day to the next, whereas there are no such restrictions in the banking market. In addition, the IMM requires a margin or deposit equal to about 4 percent of the contract to be made by the purchaser of a contract.

The LIFFE deals in futures transactions similar to the IMM

The London International Financial Futures Exchange. The **LIFFE** opened in September 1982. It deals in futures contracts in British pounds, West German marks, Swiss francs, and Japanese yen in essentially the same contract sizes as are found in the IMM. The market is relatively new and not extensively developed, but it should provide an alternative to the interbank market in Europe for foreign exchange risk protection.

Option—the right to buy or sell foreign exchange within a specific period or at a specific date

The PSE initiated a foreign exchange options market in the United States for several currencies

The Philadelphia Stock Exchange. The purpose of mentioning the **PSE** is that it represents a totally new concept in foreign exchange trading, that of **options**. In the examples given above, there was a contract to buy or sell foreign exchange between a foreign exchange trader or broker and the customer. An option, however,

> is a contract specifying the right to buy or sell—in this case foreign exchange—within a specific period (American option) or at a specific date (European option). . . . The buyer of an option has the right to undertake the contract specified but may choose not to do so if it turns out to be unprofitable. The seller of the option must fulfill the contract if the buyer desires. [4]

The five currencies in which the PSE offers foreign exchange options are the West German mark, the British pound, the Swiss franc, the Japanese yen, and the Canadian dollar. Since the PSE opened the options market, others such as the IMM have entered it. Many bankers feel that the options market in foreign exchange could revolutionize foreign exchange risk protection if the transaction costs begin to come down.

CONVERTIBILITY

- Convertible currency—Residents and nonresidents of a country are able to exchange that country's currency for other currencies

The difficulty involved in exchanging one currency for others is a measure of its **convertibility**. The more difficult it is to exchange French francs for U.S. dollars, West German marks, or Japanese yen, the more inconvertible French francs become in relation to these other currencies.

There are essentially two parts to convertibility. Most countries today have nonresident (sometimes called external) convertibility. This means, for example, that all nonresidents who have deposits in French banks may at any time exchange all of their franc deposits for the currency of any other country. In other words, a U.S. exporter to France can be paid in francs and have assurance that those francs can be converted to dollars or some other currency. Not all countries permit nonresident conversion. As was noted in the opening case, Brazil is such an example. Thus export sales to Brazil that are denominated in cruzeiros create export earnings that cannot easily be spent except in Brazil. Even when an exporter or other nonresident has foreign bank balances denominated in his or her own currency, there may be problems in the absence of nonresident convertibility.

In 1982, many foreigners with dollar deposits in Mexico had those deposits converted into pesos by the Mexican government because of an acute shortage of foreign exchange. In that case, not even residents could enjoy convertibility status.

In Western Europe the trend toward convertibility was accelerated in 1958 when fourteen countries agreed to establish external convertibility for their currencies. The countries were Austria, Belgium, Denmark, Finland, France, West Germany, Italy, Ireland, Luxembourg, the Netherlands, Norway, Portugal, Sweden, and the United Kingdom. Greece adopted such a policy in 1959. This means that nonresidents of these countries as well as all exporters from these countries were free to use the proceeds of their overseas sales anywhere in the world.

Full convertibility means that both residents and nonresidents can purchase unlimited amounts of any foreign currency. Some of the countries today that have full convertibility are the United Kingdom, West Germany, and Switzerland.

- Hard currency—a currency that is usually fully convertible and strong or relatively stable in comparison with other currencies
- Black market—a free market for a currency that operates outside of the control of the government

Hard currencies are usually fully convertible. They are also relatively stable in value or tend to be rather strong in comparison with other currencies. They are desirable assets to hold.

In the absence of full convertibility a **black market** often arises. A black market is essentially a market that is parallel with the official market. The best example of the black market is an individual hanging around the central park in a developing country who is willing to convert dollars into the local currency at a substantial premium over the official rate. More will be said on that market in the next chapter.

EXCHANGE RESTRICTIONS

Governments impose various exchange restrictions in order to control their limited supplies of foreign exchange. Some of the devices they use are import licensing, multiple exchange rates, import deposit requirements, and quantity controls.[5]

Licensing

> When the government requires that all foreign exchange transactions be regulated and controlled by it through application

The exchange rate is usually fixed by governmental decree, which requires all recipients, exporters, and others who receive foreign exchange to sell it to the central bank at the official buying rate. The central bank or some other agency then rations the currency it acquires by selling it at fixed rates to those needing to make payment abroad. The test of whether an importer is permitted to buy the foreign exchange held by a central bank may be how essential the goods the importer wishes to purchase are considered by the central bank. Purchases of raw materials and basic foodstuffs would in all probability be regarded as essential; thus foreign exchange would be sold to importers of these commodities. The test of essentiality, however, is made by the government or some agency acting for the government, such as the central bank. This system allows for the purchase of foreign exchange only if the importer has obtained a license for the importation of the goods in question.

Multiple Exchange Rates

> Where a government sets different exchange rates for different transactions

Another means of conserving foreign exchange is to allow more than one rate of exchange. This is known as a multiple exchange rate system. For example, the currency of Ecuador is the sucre. As of December 31, 1983, there were two exchange markets for the sucre. In the official market the Central Bank of Ecuador maintains rates of S/54.10 buying and S/55.18 selling per U.S. dollar. This applies to most exports and imports of goods and services in the private and governmental sectors. Exchange transactions of private petroleum companies with the Central Bank take place at the official rate and, in addition, are subject to a service charge of S/0.25 per U.S. dollar on both the buying and selling sides. All remaining transactions take place at the free market rate, which fluctuates in accordance with supply and demand. The exchange rate in the free market, however, is subject to intervention of the Central Bank from time to time. On December 31, 1983, the free market buying and selling rates were S/86.88 and S/88.75, respectively, per U.S. dollar.[6]

If an importer from Ecuador wished to purchase a piece of machinery from the United States valued at $1000, the Central Bank could charge the importer S/55,180 for the funds. On the other hand, if the Ecuadorian importer happened to be importing nonessential goods, the cost to the importer would be S/88,750, an additional cost of S/33,570 over the official rate.

Import Deposit Requirement

● Where the government requires a deposit with it prior to the release of foreign exchange

Advance import deposits are another form of foreign exchange control. Nigeria, for example, has a very complicated form of licensing for imports and their eventual payment. An M form, which is an application for foreign exchange, must be filled out for all imports. Before submitting the M form, the importer must be approved as such by the government and must supply proof that it has settled all of its tax liabilities from the prior three years. Once this clearance has been given,

> Advance import deposits are required for all categories of imports other than petroleum products and rice, except for imports for which credit facilities of more than six months have been obtained. The advance deposit rates range from 10 percent of value for raw materials, 15 percent for spare parts, 50 percent for books, food (excluding rice), medicaments, building materials, and capital goods, 200 percent for motor vehicles and trucks, to 250 percent for motor cars and all other goods. For imports under letters of credit, banks must obtain the required advance deposits before opening the letter of credit. For imports requiring payment within six months of the shipment of the goods to Nigeria, the importer is required to make the advance deposits with his commercial banks not later than ten days before the arrival of the goods in Nigeria.[7]

These deposits are not interest bearing, and the payments may still be subject to delay owing to lack of foreign exchange liquidity. Import deposits of this nature are required in many developing countries.

Quantity Controls

● Where the government limits the amount of foreign exchange that can be used in a specific transaction

Governments may also limit the amount of exchange for specific purposes. This type of control is often used in conjunction with tourism. In Chile, for example, the limit for Chilean tourists going abroad is the equivalent of U.S. $200 per month for travel to Latin American and Caribbean countries and U.S. $800 a month to other countries. For travel by land to adjacent countries, 20 percent of the allowance is provided in the form of foreign exchange, and the rest is provided in money orders.[8] This procedure was adopted because some Chileans, eager to hold dollars, were buying bus tickets to adjacent countries, receiving the alloted foreign exchange, and then selling their bus tickets and cancelling the trip. This is similar to the controls in Brazil mentioned at the beginning of the case.

COMPENSATORY TRADE

- Compensatory trade—trade arrangements or commitments that link imports of foreign goods with exports of domestic goods
- Barter—the trading of goods for goods; some variations involve goods and money or other similar arrangements

Since many developing nations and countries in Eastern Europe have very small holdings of foreign currencies, a serious problem arises for them when they want to purchase much needed industrial goods from Western countries. These countries have attempted several ways to resolve this chronic problem. The idea of compensatory trade is that the importing country imposes conditions that link the imports with exports or conditions that will minimize the net outflow of foreign exchange. The oldest solution, **barter,** in which goods are traded for goods of equal value, has been used on numerous occasions in the post–World War II period.

If exchange reserves or credit are not available for a country and if there is no possibility of negotiating another type of agreement, the only alternative is barter. This is particularly true for many developing nations that do not have oil. The fourfold increase in the price of oil eliminated most of their currency reserves and, at the same time, caused their foreign borrowings to increase substantially since 1973. For them some type of barter arrangement may be the only viable alternative for economic development.

Although there are many problems in negotiating a barter agreement, Pepsico agreed to swap Pepsi syrup and bottling equipment for Russian vodka, and Occidental Petroleum arranged sales of fertilizer plants and pipelines to the Soviet Union in exchange for ammonia. In the past, Argentina has shipped wheat and frozen meat to Peru and received iron ore pellets in exchange. Indonesia bartered some of its oil for a sorely needed steel-making complex from West Germany.[9]

A slight variation of compensatory trade includes goods and money. One example is where Mitsui, one of the largest Japanese trading companies, bought tanning material in the Soviet Union and shipped it to Argentina in exchange for plastic products. Mitsui marketed these in the United States for cash.

- Offset or countertrade—a sale that involves obligations by the seller to generate foreign exchange for the buying country

A third type of compensatory trade, called **offset trade** or **countertrade,** seems to be becoming increasingly important. A good example is provided by sales of aircraft to Yugoslavia by Douglas Aircraft. The buyer and seller draw up a contract, and Douglas is paid. Then, in a separate agreement, Douglas agrees to help the Yugoslavs find new U.S. markets for their products. The dollar amount of the Yugoslav goods that Douglas must sell is a specified percentage of the aircraft purchase price. In this case the company agreed to sell goods equal to 25 percent of the invoice value of the aircraft. Developing countries view offset trade as a viable alternative to promote economic development; at the same time, it serves to provide overseas markets for their own products.

Whether firms become involved in the complexities of offset trade primarily depends on the strength of demand for their products. Apparently, Douglas thought that the only way it could market its DC9s to Yugoslavia was through this type of arrangement. Stiff competition from European companies manufacturing aircraft and other products may force more U.S. firms to negotiate such agreements in the future.

In 1978, Levi Strauss wanted to expand its European operations. At the same time, Hungary's government wanted to build a blue jeans plant but did not have sufficient hard currency to pay for it. They got together, and Levi Strauss supplied the equipment and the management know-how. The Hungarian government pays Levi Strauss with part of the output of the plant for several years and sells the balance of the output mostly in Hungary. Levi Strauss in turn supplies part of the European market from the government's plant in Hungary; the remainder helps to supply blue jeans to the African market. These forms of barter, offset, and countertrade are good ways of circumventing the shortage of foreign exchange in a particular country.

THE INSTRUMENTS OF FOREIGN EXCHANGE

The case of a U.S. exporter of cotton ginning machinery, Atlanta Ginning Company (AGCo), selling to a textile producer in Switzerland, Zurich Textile Company (ZTCo), assumes that the total invoice value of the machinery is $10,000. Since AGCo would ordinarily like to receive payment in U.S. dollars rather than Swiss francs, it would request the Swiss importer ZTCo to forward the stated dollar amount.

The primary instruments of foreign exchange by which AGCo could receive payment from ZTCo are commercial bills of exchange, bank drafts, commercial letters of credit, and cable transfers. (The term *bill of exchange* is synonymous with the term *commercial draft.*) In addition to these arrangements an exporter may wish to deal with the importer on an open account basis, especially where there is a parent subsidiary or related subsidiary basis between the exporter and importer. In especially risky situations the exporter may wish to operate on a cash-in-advance basis.

Commercial Bills of Exchange

- An instrument that instructs the importer to forward payment to the exporter
- Sight draft—payment is to be made as soon as the bill of exchange is presented to the importer
- Time draft—payment can be made at a future date

In the above example, if payment for the machinery were to be made by a **commercial bill of exchange,** the drawer (AGCo) instructs the drawee (ZTCo) to transfer the face amount on the bill of exchange at a given time. The transfer would be made to a designated payee, possibly a local Atlanta bank where the drawer has an account, or directly to AGCo. AGCo could have requested that payment be made immediately, in which case the exchange instrument is known as a **sight draft.** Or if the terms of

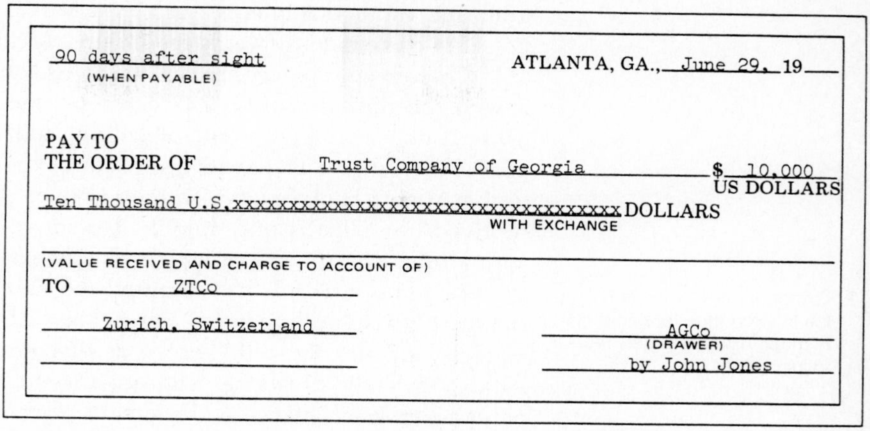

FIGURE 8.2
A 90-day Time Draft

<u>90 days after sight</u>   ATLANTA, GA., <u>June 29, 19___</u>
(WHEN PAYABLE)

PAY TO
THE ORDER OF _____ <u>Trust Company of Georgia</u> _____ $<u> 10,000 </u>
US DOLLARS

<u>Ten Thousand U.S. xxxxxxxxxxxxxxxxxxxxxxxxxxxxxxxx</u> DOLLARS
WITH EXCHANGE

(VALUE RECEIVED AND CHARGE TO ACCOUNT OF)
TO _____ <u>ZTCo</u> _____

_____ <u>Zurich, Switzerland</u> _____   _____ <u>AGCo</u> _____
(DRAWER)
<u>by John Jones</u>

agreement between AGCo and ZTCo call for payment to be in dollars at a later period (e.g., 30, 60, or 90 days after the ginning machinery was delivered to Switzerland), the instrument would be known as a commercial **time draft.** An example of a 90-day time draft as presented to ZTCo appears in Fig. 8.2.

Any export order will have three basic flows associated with it: the physical flow of the merchandise; the paper flow connected with an order but not physically accompanying the shipment (such as invoices and bills of lading); and the flow of financial documents such as the time draft. Figure 8.3 illustrates how the financial document flow operates in the case of a time draft.

AGCo sells the cotton-ginning machinery to ZTCo and ships the machinery to Switzerland (1). At the same time, AGCo forwards the 90-day time

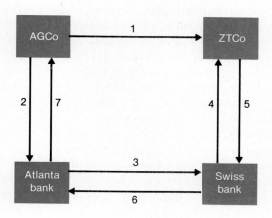

FIGURE 8.3
The Financial Document Flow

draft and other documents, such as a bill of lading, to the Atlanta bank (2). The bank then forwards these same documents to ZTCo's Swiss bank (3). When the machinery arrives, the Swiss bank notifies ZTCo and presents it with the time draft (4). ZTCo accepts the time draft, returns it to the Swiss bank, receives the bill of lading, and claims the machinery at the port of arrival (5). The Swiss bank returns the completed 90-day time draft to the Atlanta bank (6), which then notifies AGCo that the draft has been received (7). This is one simplified example of the major flows involved with a time draft; many variations of this basic example may occur.

• Discounting—the selling of a bill of exchange to a financial institution at less than face value

Once the importer has admitted the liability shown on the bill of exchange by writing "accepted" across the face of the bill, the exporter can endorse and sell the bill (known as **discounting**) in the money market. An exporter who draws the bill normally will not hold it through the entire procedure of acceptance and ultimate payment. In all probability the exporter will sell it to a local bank or to a person who is interested in investing in short-term funds. Of course, if the exporter does not hold the bill until maturity, the full face value of the bill is not obtained. The amount the exporter does receive depends on the amount the bill is discounted when first presented. This in turn is a function of the relationship between the maturity of the bill at the time it is presented for payment and the current money market conditions. There is no assurance that the bill will be accepted by an importer when it is presented. Even when it is accepted by the importer, if the creditworthiness is not known to be high, the exporter may be able to dispose of the bill only at a discount because of the credit risk involved. These disadvantages have led to an increased use of bank drafts and bankers' acceptances.

Bank Drafts

• A bill of exchange that instructs a bank rather than the importer to forward payment

The primary difference between a commercial bill of exchange and a **bank draft** is that, in the former case, the drawer (the exporter) instructs the drawee (the importer) rather than a bank to remit the amount of the invoice. In the case of a bank draft or **bank acceptance** the exporter receives payment directly from a bank designated by the importer. This would most likely involve a bank in the importer's country requesting its correspondent bank in the exporter's country to remit a specified amount to the exporter. A bank draft, then, is also a check.

An example of how a bank draft is used in international business is when a U.S. student purchases a book from Oxford University Press in London. The cost of the book is £ 10. Assuming an exchange rate of 1 pound = U.S. $1.15, a draft payable to Oxford University Press in pounds sterling could be obtained from the student's local bank and mailed by the U.S. bank directly to London. The draft will be an order on the U.S.

bank's London correspondent to pay the stipulated amount, £ 10 (U.S. $11.50), to Oxford University Press. As in all cases in which bank drafts are used, the initiative is taken by the buyer.

Letters of Credit

● Letter of credit—a precise document by which the importer's bank extends credit to the importer and agrees to pay the exporter

In the case of a commercial acceptance or bill of exchange, there is always the possibility that the importer will not be able to make payment to the exporter at the time agreed on by both parties. If in our first example the Zurich importer (ZTCo) were a new customer for the Atlanta exporter and if the exporter had not been able to secure adequate financial information on the creditworthiness of the prospective buyer, the importer could arrange for the Swiss bank to send a **letter of credit** to the exporter. The letter of credit obligates the buyer's bank in the importing country to accept a draft (a bill of exchange) presented to it, provided that the bill of exchange is accompanied by the prescribed documents.

The Atlanta exporter who receives this guarantee from the importer's bank can now rely on the credit of the bank in addition to the as yet unverified credit of the importer. The advantage of such an arrangement is that the seller can now draw a bill of exchange on the importer's bank rather than on the importer and should therefore have no difficulty in selling or discounting the draft. Figure 8.4 explains the relationships among the three parties to the letter of credit.

● A letter of credit in which a bank in the exporter's country adds its guarantee of payment

The letter of credit transactions may involve a confirming bank in addition to the parties mentioned above. A **confirmed letter of credit** means that in addition to having the guarantee of the bank in the importer's country, the exporter can have the guarantee of a bank in the exporting country. In the AGCo situation a confirmed letter of credit would involve having the Atlanta Bank add its promise to pay.

● A confirmed letter of credit that cannot be altered without permission of all parties involved

The greatest amount of protection to a shipper is provided by a **confirmed, irrevocable letter of credit,** denominated in the currency of the exporting country. An irrevocable letter of credit is one that cannot be cancelled or changed in any way without the consent of all parties to the transaction. By having the letter of credit denominated in the exporter's currency there is no risk of loss to the exporter as a result of possible exchange rate fluctuations.

Payment by Cable or Telegraphic Transfer

● A quick transfer of funds that avoids the mail transfer of money

If the Atlanta exporter desires to avoid the possible mail delay of a bank draft or letter of credit, requesting that payment be made by cable or telegraphic transfer is an alternative. If this is satisfactory to the importer in Switzerland, an arrangement is made for the local bank to cable or telegraph

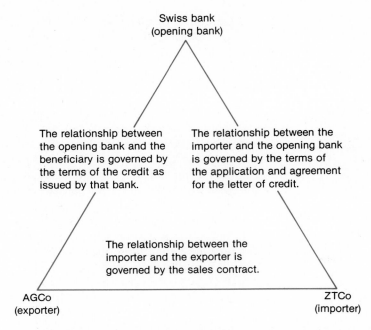

FIGURE 8.4
Three-part Letter of Credit Relationships.
SOURCE: Adapted from *Export and Import Financing Procedures,* The First National Bank of Chicago, p. 22.

Swiss bank
(opening bank)

The relationship between the opening bank and the beneficiary is governed by the terms of the credit as issued by that bank.

The relationship between the importer and the opening bank is governed by the terms of the application and agreement for the letter of credit.

The relationship between the importer and the exporter is governed by the sales contract.

AGCo
(exporter)

ZTCo
(importer)

their correspondent bank in New York or Atlanta the amount of the sale in dollars. At the same time the buyer notifies the seller or the seller's bank of the arrival of the funds.

D/A and D/P Drafts

- Release of goods is made when the obligation to pay is accepted by the importer
- Release is made when payment takes place

ZTCo cannot actually obtain possession of the machinery shipped to it unless certain documents attached to the bill, such as a bill of lading or a marine insurance certificate, are released to it. A **documentary-acceptance (D/A) draft** provides for the actual release of the goods to be made upon acceptance by the importer. The D/A draft or bill is generally used for shipments when there is little risk of nonpayment. A **documentary-on-payments (D/P) draft** indicates that the release of the goods will be made only upon payment by the importer. Exporters are more inclined to use a D/P bill if there is some question about the creditworthiness of the buyer.

Open Account

The exporter may occasionally sell on open account, in which case the necessary shipping documents would be mailed to the importer before any payment or definite obligation on the part of the buyer. It is somewhat unusual to release goods in this manner, since the exporter runs the risk of default by the buyer. An exporter would ordinarily sell under such conditions only if business with the importer had been successfully conducted for an extended period of time. Thus considerably more about the buyer's financial responsibility would be known, and there would be little question about receiving payment for the goods sold to the importer. This is generally the arrangement used when the importer and exporter are related entities.

THE USES OF THE FOREIGN EXCHANGE MARKET

- Major uses: commercial transactions, making the market, arbitrage, and risk bearing/risk reduction

- Banks collect foreign exchange, lend foreign exchange, and buy and sell foreign exchange

Up to this point, our major objective has been to define the key terms and concepts involved in foreign exchange. Now it is time to see how foreign exchange is actually used. There are four major uses of foreign exchange: commercial transactions, making the market, arbitrage, and risk bearing or risk reduction.[10]

The major facilitator of these transactions, as was mentioned earlier in the chapter, is the international department of the commercial banks. These departments perform three essential financial functions: collections, lending, and the buying and selling of foreign exchange. The collection function involves the bank in serving as a vehicle for making payments between its own customers (who are residents) and foreign nationals. In the previous example, in which the Atlanta exporter sold cotton gin machinery to a textile producer in Zurich, payment for the sale would probably be effected through the international department of a bank in either Atlanta or Zurich.

The lending function for a bank's international customers utilizes the various financing instruments available at the bank. The import letter of credit discussed above and the discounting of time drafts are illustrations of this function.

The purchase and sale of foreign exchange are undertaken by a commercial bank for many purposes. For instance, travelers going abroad or returning from a foreign country will want to purchase or sell foreign currency. Residents of one country wishing to invest abroad would also need to purchase foreign currency from a commercial bank.

Suppose that a Canadian exporter is to receive payment from a U.S. importer in U.S. dollars, and the exporter wishes to use the funds to make payment for raw materials purchased in Norway. If the Canadian firm asks the international department of its local bank to handle the transaction, the bank is simultaneously serving as a collector and acting as a dealer in foreign exchange.

Commercial Transactions

In this book we tend to focus more on commercial transactions than on any other type. These transactions involve the buying and selling of foreign exchange to facilitate the trade of goods and services. Also, these transactions are assumed to take place in the spot market. The forward market is very valuable in terms of risk bearing, which will be discussed below.

Making the Market

Making the market is another important use of foreign exchange. In essence, we are talking about transactions between brokers and traders at banks or directly between the traders at different banks. These transactions are normally undertaken to provide sufficient foreign exchange balances for the banks to conduct their normal commercial transactions as well as to bear risk in the foreign exchange market.

Arbitrage

• Buying and selling foreign exchange at a profit due to price discrepancies

Arbitrage is the process of buying and selling foreign exchange at a profit due to price discrepancies. **Triangular arbitrage** involves, for example, selling U.S. dollars for Swiss francs, Swiss francs for West German marks, and West German marks for U.S. dollars, ending up with more dollars than one started with.

For example, assume that a trader converts $100 into SwF 250 (Swiss francs) when the exchange rate is SwF 2.5 = $1.00. The trader then converts the francs into DM 400 (West German marks) at an exchange rate of DM 1.6 = SwF 1.00 and finally converts the marks into $133 at an exchange rate of DM 3 = $1.00. Thus arbitrage yields $133 from the initial sale of $100.

This is very difficult because of the sophisticated information systems that now exist in the trading rooms in banks. Sometimes triangular arbitrage can occur when dealing with foreign exchange traders in different countries.

• Investing in interest-bearing instruments in foreign exchange and earning a profit due to interest rate and exchange rate differentials

Interest arbitrage is more difficult to grasp, and it depends on concepts that we will discuss in the next chapter. Basically, however, interest arbitrage involves investing in debt instruments in different countries. For example, one could take $1000 and invest it in the United States for 90 days, or one could take the $1000, convert it into British pounds, invest the money in Great Britain for 90 days, and then convert the pounds back into dollars. The investor would pick the alternative that would provide the greater yield at the end of 90 days.

If there were no foreign exchange risks, the investor would invest in the country with the higher interest rate. For reasons that will be explained in the next chapter, however, the country with the higher interest rate will probably have a deteriorating exchange rate. Assuming in this case that Great Britain is the country with the higher interest rate, the investor could anticipate that the British pound would weaken against the dollar within 90 days. Then the investor would receive fewer dollars for the pounds than at the time the transaction was entered into. However, the investor could eliminate the foreign exchange risk by selling the sterling principal and interest in the forward market in exchange for dollars in 90 days. If the covered principal and interest yield a greater return than could be expected by investing in the United States, the investor would be able to profit from this form of arbitrage.

Risk

• Speculators—people who take positions in foreign exchange with the major objective of earning a profit

Foreign exchange transactions can be entered into in order to speculate for profit or to protect against risk. Both types of transactions are related to risk but in different ways. **Speculators** are important actors in the foreign exchange market, because they spot trends and try to take advantage of them. They can become an important source of the supply of and demand for a currency. The basic idea behind speculation is the taking of a position in a foreign currency for a profit. The difference between speculation and arbitrage is that the former involves uncertainty and the latter involves certainty. Covered interest arbitrage, for example, yields a definite risk-free profit for the investor. Speculation does not. An example of speculation would be for an investor to hold West German marks in an anticipation of the strengthening of the mark against other currencies. If the mark strengthens, the investor earns a profit. If the mark weakens, the investor incurs a loss.

On the other side of the coin would be foreign exchange transactions designed to **hedge** or protect against a potential loss due to an exchange rate change.

• Hedge—a transaction in the forward market designed to minimize a potential foreign exchange loss

The forward market as a hedge. What is the reason for transactions in the foreign exchange market for future delivery? To return to our earlier example, let us modify it to the extent of having the exporter in Atlanta sell $10,000 of cotton gin machinery to a textile producer in Liverpool, England. Let us further assume that there is an exchange rate between the pound and the dollar of £ 1 = U.S. $1.15 and that the agreement between the buyer and the seller calls for payment in pounds through the use of a commercial draft or bill of exchange payable in 90 days. The Atlanta firm will therefore draw a £ 8696 90-day bill against the British importer. At the existing exchange rate, £ 8696 sterling would be equal to U.S. $10,000. If, however, at the end of the 90 days the exchange rate is £ 1 = U.S. $1.10, the Atlanta shipper has suffered a loss of $434. This is because at the new rate, the £ 8696 sterling bill can be exchanged for only $9566. If the rate at the end of the 90-day period had changed in the opposite direction, the Atlanta exporter would have gained a windfall profit.

It should be noted that the risk of loss for the exporter is an attendant factor to receiving payment in a foreign currency. In this case it is the decline in the value of sterling relative to the U.S. dollar that has caused the exporter to suffer a loss. In the above example the British importer runs no exchange risk because the payment is denominated in sterling. If the agreement between the exporter and the importer had called for payment in U.S. dollars, the U.S. exporter would have been free of any exchange risk. The exchange risk in this case would shift to the British importer.

This type of risk can be avoided through the use of the forward market. To protect against the possibility of an exchange loss, the Atlanta exporter, at the time the initial agreement was signed, could have sold £ 8696 forward. Since the exporter has sold sterling forward for U.S. dollars, the exchange risk is shifted to the bank.

Similarly, an importer can avoid the possible increased cost of imports resulting from a rise in the exchange rate by entering the forward market, securing a contract from the commercial bank to deliver the amount of foreign exchange at a time and at a rate specified by the bank.

Ordinarily, exporters and importers do not want to run the risk of suffering the consequences of a possible adverse movement in the exchange rate. Thus in most cases they welcome the opportunity to shift this risk to someone else, namely, the international departments of their local banks. If they wish to speculate on the future of the exchange rate, they will not shift this risk.

The commercial bank that provides foreign exchange to importers will at the same time make arrangements to purchase foreign exchange from exporters. If the bank is able to match forward purchases from exporters with forward sales to importers, it avoids *taking a position* and assumes no risk.

Moreover, there is no reason to assume that the exporters' and importers' need for forward currency will exactly coincide at different points in time. If a bank agreed to deliver forward exchange to importers in amounts greater than its purchases from exporters, the bank would be taking an uncovered position. If forward sales to importers are greater than forward purchases from exporters, and these are not offset by spot purchases, the bank is speculating on the future rate of that particular currency. Normally, however, banks do not engage in speculation but confine themselves to the normal activities of dealers—namely, making their profit as importers and exporters do, on the differences between the buying and the selling prices of the commodities in which they trade. Brokers are often used to help banks match up their contract needs so that they can avoid taking a position.

• Forward contracts can be used to hedge against risk to securities, loan payments, dividends, etc.

Hedging for nontrade transactions. Entering into a forward contract to protect a specific trade transaction is one of the uses of the forward market. Investors in foreign securities, both stocks and bonds, also avail themselves of the forward market in order to hedge or protect their securities against foreign exchange fluctuations. A U.S. citizen investing in, say, Britain's ICI (Imperial Chemical Industries) may want to protect the dollar value of a sterling dividend to be received at a specified time in the future. If unsure of the spot rate in sterling at the time the dividend is received, the investor may enter into a forward contract to sell the sterling for dollars at a specified forward rate. U.S. investors holding ICI bonds might hedge their interest receipts or repayment of principal when the bonds mature.

Let us assume that this same U.S. investor chooses not to hedge the receipt of the dividend check in sterling against a decline in sterling's value. If the spot price of sterling declines in the period immediately prior to receipt of the dividend check, from U.S. $1.15 to $1.10, say, the dollar value of the £ 100,000 dividend check from ICI also declines, from $115,000 to $110,000. Of course, sterling could go up rather than down; however, the investor may prefer to take an assured rate rather than wait and see. The cost the bank would charge for purchasing the sterling probably would be less than the exchange loss brought about if there is a decline in the spot price of sterling. If the investor could enter into a forward contract at a rate of $1.1350/pound, the dividend would yield $113,500. That is less than the current spot rate but may be better than an uncertain future spot rate.

Swaps. This term signifies an exchange wherein two parties **swap** one currency for another with the understanding that, after a certain period of time, each party returns to the other the amount of currency originally received.

Swap—two parties exchange one currency for another with an agreement to reverse the transaction in the future

Swap transactions most often occur between parent and subsidiary companies. The subsidiary may wish to swap either because its demonstrated earnings record does not warrant long-term credit from the local bank or because the bank does not have sufficient funds to make the loan.

A more sophisticated version of the swap, known as the **credit swap**, is often used when the subsidiary operates in a country where there is no forward exchange market and where local credit is difficult to obtain. For example, let us assume that the parent company is located in the United States and the subsidiary is in Brazil. The U.S. parent company will make a fixed amount of dollars available to a Brazilian commercial bank for a stipulated period of time. The Brazilian commercial bank acts as an intermediary in such a transaction. On the basis of the dollars it has received, the bank makes a loan in Brazilian cruzeiros, generally at the market rate of interest, to the U.S. subsidiary. At the end of the credit period the cruzeiro loan is repaid by the subsidiary to the local commercial bank in Brazil. The Brazilian bank returns the dollars received from the U.S. parent company. Thus, the parent loan is not exposed to an exchange loss.

In this kind of arrangement the parent company gains only if the cost of the swap—that is, the opportunity cost of dollars tied up in the swap—

is less than the gain accruing to the Brazilian subsidiary. The subsidiary gains only if the cost measured in terms of the interest paid on the loan is less than the anticipated rate of return on funds invested in the subsidiary.

Since swaps are usually made by companies exchanging hard (strong) currencies for soft (weak) ones, they serve the purpose of reducing or eliminating the foreign exchange risk for the parent company and at the same time reducing the cost of local financing in the subsidiary country.

A TRANSITION

As was mentioned at the beginning of the chapter, the purpose of this chapter was to introduce some of the terms and concepts in foreign exchange. However, it is impossible to really understand foreign exchange without stepping back from the detail and looking at the international monetary system in which exchange rates function. The next chapter will examine how exchange rates obtain and maintain their values. The roles of international institutions, national institutions, and other important actors will be examined from the standpoint of the law of supply and demand and the important underlying forces that affect exchange rates. For example, why is the Brazilian cruzeiro constantly losing strength against the dollar? Do Brazil's high inflation and large foreign debt have something to do with that? Once we have mastered some of those concepts, we will take a look at how one might predict the direction, magnitude, and timing of an exchange rate change and examine what the strengthening U.S. dollar has done to international firms in recent years.

SUMMARY

- A major difference between domestic and international payments for goods and services is that more than one currency is used for international transactions.
- An exchange rate is the value of one currency in terms of another.
- A spot exchange rate is the rate quoted for current transactions, whereas the forward rate is a rate quoted by a foreign exchange trader for a contract to receive or deliver foreign currency in the future.
- The difference between the spot and forward rates at the time of a contract is the forward spread. The foreign currency is selling at a discount if the spread is negative and at a premium if the spread is positive.
- Most foreign exchange transactions take place through the traders of commercial banks, and the majority of the transactions occur in the spot market rather than the forward market. In addition, most of the

foreign exchange transactions are interbank transactions rather than between banks and nonbanking institutions.

• The International Monetary Market (IMM) is a specialized market that deals in futures contracts in the British pound, the Canadian dollar, the West German mark, the Swiss franc, the Japanese yen, the Mexican peso, the French franc, and the Dutch guilder. Other specialized markets are the London International Financial Futures Exchange (LIFFE) and the Philadelphia Stock Exchange (PSE).

• A convertible currency is one that can be freely traded for other currencies. Some countries' currencies are partially convertible in that residents are not allowed to convert to other currencies but nonresidents are.

• Some governments control access to their currencies through import licensing, multiple exchange rates, import deposit requirements, and quantity controls.

• Many developing countries and countries in Eastern Europe try to get around their small holdings of foreign currencies by using barter, the exchange of goods for goods.

• The primary instruments of foreign exchange through which payment is made in international commerce are commercial bills of exchange, bank drafts, commercial letters of credit, and cable transfers.

• The four major uses of foreign exchange are commercial transactions, making the market, arbitrage, and risk bearing or risk reduction.

C A S E   THE MEXICAN PESO[11]

On August 31, 1976, the Mexican peso was cut loose from its exchange rate of 12.5 pesos to the dollar, which was established in 1955. From 1955 to 1976 the exchange rate had been artificially maintained through a variety of mechanisms. Import controls and market intervention were used extensively to allow the peso to appear more stable than it was. These controls were a source of frustration to firms operating in Mexico. Many companies established manufacturing operations in Mexico only to find that the government would eventually phase out their ability to import needed raw materials and components.

During the 1970s the pressure began to build for a change in the value of the currency. Tourism, a major source of foreign exchange, began to taper off because of rising prices that were a direct result of general inflation in the economy.

Mexico began importing more than it was exporting, which resulted in an outflow of pesos to buy the excess imports. Exporters to Mexico did not want to hold onto pesos, preferring instead to convert them into dollars. To give so many dollars in order to buy back the pesos would have severely depleted Mexico's holdings of dollar reserves if Mexican authorities used these existing reserves to make the conversion. Mexico chose instead to maintain its level of reserves by increased short-term external borrowing of dollars, which would eventually result in principal and interest payments that could rob Mexico of what little foreign exchange it could get together.

As a result of these and other pressures, the decision was made to devalue the peso on August 31, 1976, to 20.5 pesos to the dollar. The feeling was that this devaluation would absorb some of the excess supply of pesos in the market and allow the economy to return to some level of stability. Even though devaluation was the initial solution to the problem, a number of other factors were considered as well. One consideration was to establish more elaborate foreign exchange controls so that spot transactions could be allocated according to the priorities of the government. In the final analysis, Mexico decided to go with a devaluation rather than establish an elaborate bureaucracy to administer the foreign exchange controls.

Unfortunately, the solution to the problem was short lived. From 1976 to mid-1981 the peso held its postdevaluation level pretty well, but inflation and other forces that had created the problems leading up to the 1976 devaluation began to cause more problems. The country began to develop a devaluation psychosis, imports again exceeded exports, tourism was steadily falling, foreign credit became tight and expensive, and world oil prices and demand had softened considerably. The Central Bank of Mexico steadfastly maintained that a relatively modest devaluation of 15–20 percent was all that was necessary to correct the imbalances in the economy, and officials appeared to be in no hurry to make any changes.

Meanwhile, the situation worsened. In the absence of capital controls, wealthy Mexicans were spending their money abroad on consumer durables and investments that would shelter them against another possible devaluation. With the government continuing to exude confidence up to the last hour, a devaluation of over 40 percent was announced on February 17, 1982, bringing the new rate to 38.50 pesos to the dollar. At the same time the government announced that it hoped to keep the exchange rate to a level of 38–43 pesos during the rest of the year. In an interesting move, a subsequent devaluation was announced on February 26, 1982, to 47.25 pesos, rendering obsolete the prediction of a little over a week earlier.

Unfortunately, the two devaluations did not seem to help the problem very much. In August 1982, after another devaluation, the government decided to establish two exchange rates—a preferential rate and a free market rate. Unfortunately, the official rate was only 49 pesos, and the free market rate shot up to 105 pesos.

In September 1982 the government nationalized all private banks and instituted currency controls. Among the currency controls were the following:

1. Only the Banco de Mexico can import or export foreign exchange.
2. Foreign currency is not legal tender in Mexico, and all obligations denominated in foreign currency and payable in Mexico must be paid in pesos at the rate determined by the Banco de Mexico.
3. All foreign currency is to be exchanged at the Banco de Mexico at rates indicated by the Bank.
4. The Banco de Mexico will set rules for maximum amounts to be sold to individuals for foreign travel. Foreign visitors must declare and convert to pesos all foreign currency when entering Mexico and repurchase foreign currency when they leave, all at ordinary exchange rates.

In addition to these rules, the government established a fixed priority list for determining who will get foreign exchange:

1. Public sector obligations.
2. Parastate companies in the order determined by the Finance Ministry.
3. Mexican Government dues and quotas in international organizations and expenses for Mexico's diplomatic corps.
4. Obligations of credit institutions, including insurance and finance companies.
5. Imports of high-priority basic food items, intermediate goods, and basic capital goods.
6. Imports of capital and intermediate goods to maintain the functioning of existing industrial facilities.
7. Imports of equipment, intermediate products, and capital goods for plant expansions.
8. Financial obligations of the private sector contracted before September 1.
9. Needs of entities in the border and free trade zones.
10. Payment of licensing and royalty fees and other commitments of companies with foreign ownership (presumably dividends, but not specifically mentioned).
11. Travel needs for business or health reasons.
12. Travel needs for tourism.

A preferential rate of 50 pesos was established for imports of basic foods and capital goods needed to produce food, intermediate products and capital goods needed to keep industry functioning, and capital goods for industrial expansion.

Importers found some real obstacles in getting foreign exchange, even when they were high enough on the priority list to be eligible for foreign exchange. However, one nice thing about the controls was the recognition of the contribution of exports to the generation of foreign exchange. For materials imported and incorporated in export products the preferential rate could be used even if such materials were not on the preferential list if the exported product generated more foreign exchange than the cost of the import.

QUESTIONS

1. Assume that you are the manager of the Mexican subsidiary of a U.S.-based company that has set up its operation to manufacture products that will supply the Mexican market. Currently, you are importing from the United States approximately 50 percent of the total cost of production. Each month you are required to travel to corporate headquarters in East Rutherford, New Jersey, and you are about to leave for your September 25, 1982, meeting with top management. Briefly outline what you will tell them about the implications of the foreign exchange controls on your operations, and give them some recommendations on what you think they can do to get by. One of the problems that you might want to address is the nature of the competition. With all of these exchange rate changes, you need to do a little research on how the Mexican spot rate has changed in relation to some of the countries that are your most formidable competitors. In January 1982 you had considered exporting to Brazil, Argentina, West Germany, the United Kingdom, and Canada. However, the exchange rate was not very favorable for exporting at that time. Below are some exchange rates quoted in the *Wall Street Journal* in U.S. terms that might be helpful to you.

Currencies of	Dec. 31, 1981	March 31, 1982	June 30, 1982	July 30, 1982	Sept. 15, 1982
Mexico	0.0381	0.0220	0.0212	0.0205	0.0133
Canada	0.8435	0.8140	0.7725	0.7968	0.8117
Great Britain	1.9170	1.7850	1.7340	1.7410	1.7080
West Germany	0.4460	0.4145	0.4060	0.4072	0.3975
Brazil	0.00801	0.00687	0.0059	0.005587	0.0053
Argentina	0.000103	0.000089	0.000065	0.0000488	0.000025
90-day forward rate quoted on the IMM on the above dates for the Mexican peso	0.03574	0.01955	0.01838	0.01926	0.00815

2. Given the above information, what was the premium or discount that the peso was selling for in the forward market? Would you have expected the market to be a very active one in terms of the volume of transactions completed on the IMM? Be sure to explain your answer.

NOTES

1. Most of the information about the different controls is taken from the *Annual Report on Exchange Arrangements and Exchange Restrictions, 1984* (Washington, D.C.: International Monetary Fund), pp. 105–113.

2. Federal Reserve Bank of Chicago, *International Letter,* No. 510, October 7, 1983, pp. 1–3.

3. Julian Walmsley, *The Foreign Exchange Handbook* (New York: John Wiley & Sons, 1983), pp. 7–8. Copyright © 1983 John Wiley & Sons. Used by permission.

4. K. Alec Chrystal, "A Guide to Foreign Exchange Markets," *Bulletin* (St. Louis, Mo.: Federal Reserve Bank of St. Louis, March 1984), p. 12.

5. *Annual Report, op. cit.* This publication discusses by country the types of controls and multiple exchange rates being utilized.

6. *Ibid.,* p. 168.

7. *Ibid.,* p. 361.

8. *Ibid.,* p. 131.

9. The barter examples in this section are taken from *Wall Street Journal,* May 18, 1977, p. 1.

10. Chrystal, *op. cit.,* pp. 11–16.

11. Richard Moxon, "The Mexican Peso" in Robert S. Carlson, H. Lee Remmers, Christine R. Hekman, David K. Eiteman, and Arthur I. Stonehill, eds., *International Finance Cases and Simulation* (Reading, Mass.: Addison-Wesley Publishing Co., 1980), pp. 22–32; "Acme do Mexico, S.A.," a case by Ingo Walter, Graduate School of Business, New York University, 1983; "Mexico Lists Priority Items for Imports," *Wall Street Journal,* September 20, 1982, p. 28; Lawrence Rout, "Mexican Firms May Be Able to Get Dollars . . . ," *Wall Street Journal,* September 16, 1982, p. 35; Lawrence Rout, "Mexico Names New Central Bank Head and Tightens Currency Rules Further," *Wall Street Journal,* September 3, 1982, p. 3; Lawrence Rout, "Mexicans Start Picking up the Pieces after Last Week's 30% Devaluation," *Wall Street Journal,* February 23, 1982, p. 30; Lawrence Rout, "Mexico Seeking to Hold Peso at 38 to Dollar," *Wall Street Journal,* February 22, 1982; Lawrence Rout, "Mexico Ponders the Peso's Problems," *Wall Street Journal,* January 28, 1982, p. 27; "Mexico Eases down the Peso," *Business Week,* August 31, 1981, p. 79.

9

The Determination of Exchange Rates

- To identify the major determinants of exchange rates in the spot and forward markets.
- To discuss how to forecast exchange rate movements.
- To describe the International Monetary Fund and its role in the determination of exchange rates.
- To discuss the major exchange rate arrangements under which the currencies of the world function.
- To explain the role of central banks in influencing exchange rate values.
- To explain how exchange rates influence business decisions.

THE TINY BOLIVIAN PESO[1]

Bolivia, one of the poorest countries in Latin America, is situated high in the Andes, and its elevation is exceeded only by the height of its inflation. In 1983, prices were increasing by 329 percent, but that soared to 2700 percent in 1984 and was expected to reach 40,000 percent in 1985. Inflation was so high in January 1985 that it represented an increase of 116,000 percent on an annual basis, undoubtedly the highest in the world. Prices in Germany increased 10 billionfold during the 1920s, but Bolivia's experience outdistances that of Argentina, Chile, Israel, and Brazil, the inflation leaders at one time or another in the 1970s and 1980s.

Bolivia's political and economic situation has not been a picture of stability. Its government in early 1985 was the 189th in 159 years of independence. President Siles Zuazo was elected President in 1980, but the military would not let him take office for three years. By that time the government was spending in huge deficit terms, increasing inflation through loose monetary and fiscal policy. Bolivia's largest export is the coca paste used in making cocaine; its second largest export is tin, the price of which was very depressed on world markets during the early 1980s; and its third largest export is natural gas. However, its major customer for natural gas, Argentina, was having problems of its own and was not a good market for the product.

Skyrocketing inflation has affected Bolivia in a variety of ways. One way is the constant change in prices. An egg costing 3000 pesos one week sells for 10,000 pesos the next. A candy bar sells for 35,000 pesos one minute and 50,000 the next. Youngsters standing in the back of the line to see a movie paid 20,000 pesos for a ticket; those at the front of the line beat the price increase and had to pay only 4000 pesos. The number of pesos that it would take to buy three boxes of aspirin in 1985 would have bought a luxury Toyota in 1982. A 100-peso bill was of so little value that it required three of them to gain entrance to a public toilet in 1985.

Another problem is the difficulty in having banknotes be of sufficiently large denomination to enable transactions to be completed easily. Four people having dinner in a restaurant one evening late in 1984 gave the waiter a forty-eight-inch-high stack of bills weighing over two pounds to settle the bill, which came to 200,000 pesos, or approximately $22. Until the government began issuing 50,000-peso and 100,000-peso notes in November 1984, the largest banknote was the 10,000-peso note, worth about $1.10 on the official market and 30 cents on the black market. One customer of a bank brought in 700 million pesos in 50- and 100-peso notes that took six tellers until 1 A.M. to count, and the total was worth only $77,000. The two-inch stack of money used to buy the candy bar mentioned above weighed more than the candy did.

The large number of small-denomination bills has created havoc in the banking community. The huge sacks of money brought in by business customers for deposit simply cannot be counted accurately. Banks are often forced to take the customer's word that the amount declared is accurate. Theft is not an issue, since even large sacks of money yield very little purchasing power.

It is also very difficult for wages to keep up with prices. This means that workers' purchasing power can rarely keep up in real terms. As a result, labor unrest is very high. Strikes are common as workers struggle to keep up with the staggering cost of living. This is true of white collar professionals, such as doctors, as well as in traditional blue collar areas. People suffer severe hardships as price increases often take effect before their income rises. This often leaves them temporarily without enough resources to purchase the basic necessities of life. Shortages in food products often occur, since the pricing mechanism has become ineffective in allocating scarce resources.

With inflation increasing so rapidly, credit cards are not used, and checks are not allowed. It is important to receive cash immediately so that it can be used before its value disappears. A new occupation has arisen, that of the *changador*. A *changador* is someone who carries stacks of bank notes to and from banks for companies making deposits or withdrawals. The absence of credit cards and checks coupled with the small denominations of banknotes makes such individuals indispensible.

Since Bolivia does not print money, it must import the money from other countries, primarily Germany and Great Britain. In 1984, money was the third largest import into Bolivia, after wheat and mining equipment.

INTRODUCTION

As was pointed out in the preceding chapter, an exchange rate represents the number of units of one currency needed to acquire one unit of a currency of another country. The definition seems easy enough to understand, but how is that exchange rate initially determined, and what causes it to change? This chapter takes a closer look at exchange rates and how they are determined.

The Bolivian peso is a good illustration of how domestic and international economies are intertwined. The value of the peso is so tiny that it is not even quoted in the *Wall Street Journal.* Still, it is an interesting currency. It is hard to believe, for example, that a forty-eight-inch stack of paper currency could be worth only U.S. $21.78 or that the largest bank note in circulation would be worth $1.10 on the official market but only $0.30 on the black market. This implies that inflation has gotten so far out of hand that the currency has lost significant value domestically as well as internationally. In addition, the existence of a black market, as noted in Chapter 8, implies that the government has instituted strong controls over the conversion of domestic into foreign currency. Before describing the institutions that affect currency values, we will discuss the major economic variables that affect currency values.

THE DETERMINATION OF EXCHANGE RATES

The actual exchange rate at a given point in time is partly a function of the economic situation in the country and partly a political decision. Before looking at the determinants in detail, it would be useful to look at the basic concept of supply and demand in the foreign exchange market as it affects the rates in different types of exchange systems. Then we will examine the basic determinants of exchange rates, especially two major factors: purchasing power parity and interest rates.

Major Types of Exchange Systems

• Demand for a country's currency is a function of the demand for goods, services, and financial assets of that country

Freely fluctuating. To understand the law of supply and demand as it relates to foreign exchange, let's use a two-country model involving the United States and Bolivia. Figure 9.1 illustrates the concept of equilibrium in the market and then a movement to a new equilibrium level as situations change. The demand for dollars in this example is a function of the Bolivian demand for (1) U.S. goods and services and (2) dollar-denominated financial assets. An example of the former would be the Bolivian demand for dollars to buy U.S.-made machinery. An example of the latter would be Bolivian demand for dollars to buy U.S. treasury bonds. The supply of dollars (which is tied to the demand for Bolivian pesos in this illustration) is a function of U.S. demand for (1) Bolivian goods and services and (2) peso-denominated financial assets. Initially, the supply of and demand for dollars in Fig. 9.1 is at the equilibrium exchange rate e_0 and the quantity of dollars Q_1.

Let's assume that for one reason or another (such as relatively high Bolivian inflation), there is a drop in demand for Bolivian goods and services by U.S. consumers. This would result in a reduction in the supply of dollars in the foreign exchange market, causing the supply curve to shift to S'. At the same time the rapidly increasing prices of Bolivian goods might lead to an increase in demand for U.S. goods and services by Bolivian consumers, leading to an increase in demand for dollars in the market, causing the demand curve to shift to D', leading to an increase in the quantity demanded and an increase in the exchange rate. Thus the new equilibrium exchange rate will be at e_1. From a peso standpoint we could say that the increase in demand for U.S. goods would lead to an increase in supply of pesos as more consumers tried to trade their pesos for dollars, and a reduction in demand for Bolivian goods would result in a drop in demand for pesos. This would lead to a reduction in the price of the peso, indicating a weakening or devaluation of the peso.

FIGURE 9.1
Equilibrium Exchange Rate

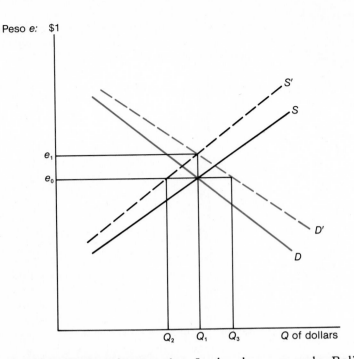

Managed fixed exchange rate. In the above example, Bolivian and U.S. authorities allowed changes in the exchange rates between their two currencies to occur in order to reach a new currency equilibrium. In fact, however, one or both of the countries might not want exchange rates to change. For example, Bolivia might not want its peso to weaken because its industrialists would be able to buy less U.S. machinery, which is needed for development. The United States might not want the dollar to strengthen because it would mean unemployment in the machinery industry. But how can they keep the values from changing when Bolivia is earning too few dollars? Somehow the dollar shortage between Q_1 and Q_3 in Fig. 9.1 must be alleviated. In a managed system the Bolivian central bank would hold foreign exchange reserves, which it had built up through the years for this type of contingency. Let us assume that some of these reserves are in dollars. The Bolivian central bank would sell enough of its dollar resources (make up the difference between Q_1 and Q_3) at the fixed exchange rate so that the exchange rate is maintained. Or the U.S. central bank might be willing to accept pesos so that Bolivians can buy U.S. goods. These pesos would then become part of the U.S. reserves.

The fixed rate can continue as long as Bolivia has reserves and/or as long as the U.S. is willing to add pesos to its holdings. Unless something occurs to change the basic imbalance in the currency supply and demand, though, the Bolivian central bank will run out of dollars and the U.S.

• Governments buy and sell their currencies in the open market as a means of influencing price

central bank will stop accepting pesos because it fears that it holds too many. At this point it would be necessary to devalue the peso, which is the same as saying that the dollar has been revalued.

The Economic Summit Meeting held in Versailles in 1982 resulted in a report on the effectiveness of foreign exchange market intervention. The report pointed out that intervention per se was not very effective, but changes in the basic economic policies of the intervening country were fairly effective in determining the long-run value of a currency. In addition, the report stated that intervention was much more valuable when carried out in conjunction with several other countries instead of being conducted unilaterally.

Once a government decides that intervention will not work, it must do something to adjust the value of its currency. If the currency is freely floating, the exchange rate will seek the correct level according to the laws of supply and demand. However, a currency that is pegged or fixed to another currency or to a group of currencies is usually changed on a formal basis with respect to its reference currency or currencies. This formal change is more accurately termed a **devaluation** or **revaluation**, depending on which direction the change takes. If the foreign currency equivalent of the home currency falls (or the home currency equivalent of the foreign currency rises), then the home currency has devalued in relation to the foreign currency. The opposite would happen in the case of a revaluation.

For example, in February 1982 the Brazilian cruzeiro was changed by 23.3 percent against the dollar in what was termed a maxi-devaluation. The Brazilian government had been using mini-devaluations, or relatively small devaluations against the dollar, at frequent intervals for a number of years. However, the mini-devaluations were inadequate to allow the cruzeiro to reach its proper value. The percentage change on February 21, 1982, can be determined as follows:

• Devaluation—foreign currency equivalent of the currency falls

	Direct quote (in the U.S.)	Indirect quote (in the U.S.)
Predevaluation	U.S. $0.003431709	Cr $291.4
Postdevaluation	U.S. $0.00263123	Cr $380.1

$$\text{Percentage change (direct)} = \frac{\text{ending rate} - \text{beginning rate}}{\text{beginning rate}} \times 100$$

$$= \frac{0.00263123 - 0.003431709}{0.003431709} \times 100 = -23.3\%$$

$$\text{Percentage change (indirect)} = \frac{\text{beginning rate} - \text{ending rate}}{\text{ending rate}} \times 100$$

$$= \frac{291.4 - 380.1}{380.1} = -23.3\%$$

Automatic fixed rate system. As in the above managed system, let us assume that the countries have agreed to maintain fixed rates by setting their domestic money supply on the basis of the amount of reserves held by the central bank and by denominating their currency value in terms of the reserve asset. Historically, the most suggested reserve asset has been gold. In the latter part of the nineteenth century, most countries approached being on such a gold standard.

Assume the Bolivian situation in which Bolivia had a shortage of dollars. Under an automatic fixed rate system it would now sell gold to get the needed dollars. However, unlike the managed system described above, there would be built-in adjustments to prevent Bolivia from running out of gold. As Bolivia sold off some of its gold, its money supply, which is tied to the amount of gold, would then fall. This would lead to higher Bolivian interest rates. It would also lead to lower Bolivian investment, followed by increased unemployment and lower prices. In the meantime, the increase in gold in the United States would be having an opposite effect. The higher interest rates in Bolivia than in the United States and the decrease in Bolivian prices relative to U.S. prices would cause an increase in Bolivian supplies of dollars as funds flowed in for investments and to purchase Bolivian goods and services. As will be pointed out later in the chapter, countries' lack of desire to subject their domestic monetary and fiscal policy to stabilizing exchange rates has led to a world of greater exchange flexibility.

Purchasing Power Parity (PPP)

● If home country inflation is lower than that of the foreign country, we would expect the home country to be stronger in value

This is the key theory that helps explain the relationships between currencies. The fundamental concept is that on the basis of a period when an equilibrium exchange rate existed (such as e_0 in Fig. 9.1), a change in the relationship between domestic and foreign prices would indicate the necessary adjustment in the exchange rate between any two currencies. The discussion accompanying Fig. 9.1 illustrates that point. Another way to illustrate the relationship between exchange rates and relative prices is found in Fig. 9.2. In Fig. 9.2 we assume that the home (domestic) currency is the U.S. dollar and the foreign currency is the Bolivian peso. According to the PPP theory, if inflation in the United States were 5 percent lower than inflation in Bolivia, one would expect the value of the peso in U.S. dollars to fall by 5 percent. That means that the peso would be worth fewer dollars than was the case before the adjustment. Another way to express this peso devaluation would be to say that the peso value of the dollar would rise by 5 percent, meaning that a dollar would yield more pesos than it would have before the adjustment.

FIGURE 9.2
Purchasing Power Parity

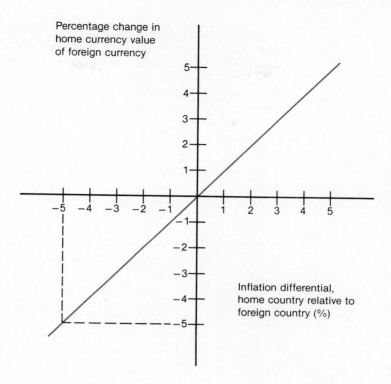

In order to relate inflation to exchange rate changes, the following formula can be used:[2]

$$\frac{e_t - e_o}{e_o} = \frac{i_{h,t} - i_{f,t}}{1 + i_{f,t}}$$

where

e equals the spot exchange quoted in terms of the number of units of the home currency for one unit of the foreign currency,

i equals the rate of inflation,

h represents the home currency,

f represents the foreign currency,

o represents the base period,

t represents the end of a period.

The anticipated future rate would equal

$$e_t = e_o \left(1 + \frac{i_{h,t} - i_{f,t}}{1 + i_{f,t}} \right)$$

For example, on August 31, 1976, the Mexican peso was devalued from 12.5 pesos per dollar ($0.08 per peso) to 20.5 pesos per dollar (approximately $0.0488 per peso), the first devaluation to take place in the peso since 1954. The consumer price index in Mexico went from 57.2 in 1955 to 176.8 in 1975; the same figures for the United States were 69.0 and 138.6. Using the formula given above,

$$i_{h,t} = \frac{138.6 - 69.0}{69.0} = 1.01$$

$$i_{f,t} = \frac{176.8 - 57.2}{57.2} = 2.09$$

$$e_t = 0.08 \left(1 + \frac{1.01 - 2.09}{1 + 2.09} \right)$$

gives $0.05204 per peso or 19.2 pesos per dollar compared with the actual amounts of $0.0488 per peso or 20.5 pesos per dollar.

The PPP theory is very useful in helping to understand the relationship between exchange rates, but it is not perfect. As was mentioned above, an assumption needs to be made about equilibrium exchange rates at some starting point. Also, currencies are rarely related accurately in a two-country world. When several currencies are involved, it is difficult to use prices to determine an equilibrium rate. Also, exchange rates are essentially a function of traded goods, whereas inflation relates to the general economy.

Interest Rates

- If the nominal interest rate in the home country is lower than that of the foreign country, we would expect the home country's inflation to be lower so that real interest rates would be equal

To relate interest rates to exchange rates, it is first necessary to relate interest rates to inflation. This is accomplished through the **Fisher Effect**. According to the Fisher Effect, the nominal interest rate is a combination of the real rate of interest and inflation. For example, it assumes that if interest rates in Country A were 5 percent higher than those in Country B, inflation in Country A would also be 5 percent higher. Thus the real interest rates (nominal rate minus inflation) would be the same. If investors knew that real interest rates in one country were higher than those in another, they would invest their money in the country with the high real interest rate until real interest rates were equal through a change in nominal interest rates or the relative rates of inflation. If inflation in the two countries was the same (zero differential) and interest rates in Country A were 5 percent higher than in Country B, investors would place their money in Country A, where they could get the higher real return.

- Implies that the currency of the country with the lower interest rate will strengthen in the future

The bridge from interest rates to exchange rates can be explained by the **International Fisher Effect (IFE)**. According to the IFE, the interest rate differential is an unbiased predictor of future changes in the spot exchange rate. An unbiased predictor is one that is neither consistently above nor below the actual future spot exchange rate. That does not mean that the interest rate differential is an accurate predictor, just that it is unbiased.

Using the United States and Bolivia as an example, the IFE states that if interest rates in the United States are 5 percent lower than those in Bolivia, the value of the peso should fall by 5 percent in the future. The fall in the value of the peso indicates a weakening or devaluation of the peso. Remember from the Fisher Effect that nominal interest rates are 5 percent lower in the United States than in Bolivia because inflation is also lower. Thus if inflation is lower in the United States than in Bolivia, the peso is expected to be 5 percent weaker as well. That flows from the discussion that accompanies Fig. 9.1, in which we learned that consumers would demand U.S. goods rather than Bolivian goods, causing an increase in demand for dollars and a contraction in supply of dollars, which would lead in turn to a strengthening of the dollar or a weakening of the peso.

Other Factors

• Currencies that are safe havens in troubled times tend to be strong currencies

There are a variety of other factors that could cause exchange rates to change. One important determinant in a world of political and economic uncertainty is that of **confidence.** During times of turmoil, people prefer to hold currencies that are considered safe haven currencies. During the early 1980s the U.S. dollar was considered a safe haven currency, and this perception was an important source of its strength. Conversely, when the Mexican peso began to slide in the early 1980s, local investors transferred large amounts of pesos out of Mexico via dollar transfers until the Mexican government clamped down. The investors had no confidence in the peso and preferred to hold dollar balances outside of Mexico.

In addition to the basic economic forces and confidence in leadership, a number of **technical factors** influence exchange rates, such as the release of national economic statistics, seasonal demands for a currency, and a slight strengthening of a currency following a prolonged weakness or vice versa.

Determinants of the Forward Rate

• Forward rates are determined primarily by interest rate differentials

As was noted in Chapter 8, forward markets do not exist for all currencies, and factors influencing the setting of rates vary from currency to currency. However, one of the most important determinants for the forward rate is the **interest rate differential,** as illustrated in the following example. Assume that the spot rate for Swiss francs as given in Table 8.1 is $0.3891, the interest rate on a 90-day U.S. treasury bill is 10 percent per annum, and the interest rate on a Swiss debt instrument of similar risk and maturity is 6.1 percent. If investors were positive that the exchange rate would not change, they would always invest in the U.S. debt instrument, since it has a higher yield. But as more dollars were invested in the United States, it would become clear that in ninety days there would be a surplus of dollars on the market as the investors liquidated their dollar investments back into Swiss francs.

This surplus of dollars would cause the spot rate to decline, and each investor would face the prospect of getting fewer Swiss francs back for each dollar invested. Of course, no one knows precisely what the future spot rates will be, and the uncertainty and risk might prevent someone from investing in the U.S. instrument.

This is where the forward rate comes in. At least in theory, the forward rate in the example would be the rate that exactly neutralizes the difference in interest rates between the United States and Switzerland. This forward rate would be computed by the foreign trader as shown below:

Interest rate in U.S. $= r_{us} = 10\%$ Spot rate $= S_o = \$0.3891$
Interest rate in Switzerland $= r_{sw} = 6.1\%$ Forward rate $= F_o = ?$
$N =$ number of months for the T bill

$$r_{us} - r_{sw} = \frac{F_o - S_o}{S_o} \times \frac{12}{N}$$

$$S_o(r_{us} - r_{sw})\left(\frac{N}{12}\right) + S_o = F_o$$

$$0.3891 \times (0.10 - 0.061)(3/12) + 0.3891 = F_o$$
$$\$0.3929 = F_o$$

At this forward rate there is no incentive for someone to invest in the United States rather than Switzerland or vice versa. For example, if someone were to invest $1000 in the United States for three months, the yield would be

$$\$1000 + \$1000[0.10 \times (3/12)] = \$1025$$

A similar investment of $1000 in Switzerland would yield $1025.08, as shown below:

1. Convert dollars to Swiss francs at the spot rate

   $$\$1000/\$0.3891 = SwF\ 2570$$

2. Invest the francs at 6.1 percent for three months

   $$2570 + 2570[(0.061 \times (3/12)] = SwF\ 2609$$

3. At the same time, enter into a forward contract to deliver SwF 2609 at $0.3929

4. At the end of three months, deliver the Swiss francs and receive dollars at the forward rate

   $$SwF\ 2609 \times \$0.3929 = \$1025.08$$

Thus the forward rate allows investors to freely trade currencies for future delivery at no exchange risk and without any differential in interest income. If a difference were to exist, traders would engage in interest arbitrage. As pointed out in Chapter 8, this means that they would sell one currency for another and invest in the latter currency if the difference in interest rates exceeded the difference in exchange rates. For example, if the interest differential were higher than the forward rate differential, arbitragers would get out of Swiss francs and invest in the United States. Eventually, the spot rate or the forward rate would change until investors were indifferent in their decision to invest in the United States or Switzerland.

Although the interest rate differential is the critical factor for a few of the most widely traded currencies, the expectation of future spot rates is also very important. Normally, a trader will automatically compute the forward rate through the interest rate differential and then adjust it for future expectations where deemed necessary. Some forward rates are quoted strictly on future expectations rather than interest rate differentials. This is especially true for currencies that are not traded very widely and for which total convertibility does not exist.

Although the theory seems very simple, its application in practice is more complex. This is because it is difficult to find debt instruments in two countries that have similar risk and maturity and that foreigners are permitted to buy, sell, and convert from. Thus the forward market exists in practice for currencies of only a few developed countries.

FORECASTING EXCHANGE RATE MOVEMENTS

- Need to be concerned with timing, size, and direction of an exchange rate movement

As was noted in the discussion above, a variety of factors have an influence on exchange rate movements. It is important for the businessperson to be able to analyze these factors in order to have a general idea of the timing, size, and direction of an exchange rate movement. However, prediction is not a precise science, and many things can cause the best of predictions to differ significantly from reality.

In the previous section we looked at the general law of supply and demand, showed how governments intervene to manage exchange rate movements, and explained how inflation and interest rates can be important determinants of exchange rates. In this section we need to look at data that can be monitored in order to get an idea of what will happen to exchange rate values.

For currencies that are freely floating, the law of supply and demand determines market value. However, very few currencies in the world are freely floating. Most currencies are managed to a certain extent. This implies that governments need to make a political decision on the value of the currency. Assuming that the governments use a rational basis for managing the value of their currencies (an assumption that may not be realistic in all cases), it is possible to monitor some of the same indicators which they do in order to try to predict values.

The following factors have been identified as important ones that should be monitored when trying to predict an exchange rate change:

1. the politics of the exchange rate change,
2. balance of payments and interest rate parity,
3. differential rates of inflation,
4. growth in the money supply (which is a good indicator of inflation),
5. business cycles,
6. a change in international monetary reserves,
7. an increase in the spread between official and free rates of exchange,
8. government policies that treat symptoms rather than causes, and
9. excessive government spending (which is a good indicator of inflation).[3]

In this discussion, reference is made to a survey of corporate practices in forecasting exchange rate changes. According to the survey, the following five factors are the ones monitored the most by corporations:

- **Key factors to monitor in forecasting exchange rate changes**

1. relative inflation rates,
2. balance of payments and trade,
3. interest rate differentials,
4. money supply growth, and
5. recent exchange rate movements.[4]

Rather than attempting to discuss all of these factors, we will focus on the following six points: balance of payments statistics, a country's reserve position, relative rates of inflation, interest rate differentials, trends in spot rates, and the forward exchange rate.

The Balance of Payments

As was noted in Chapter 1, a country's balance of payments summarizes international transactions between domestic and foreign residents. A more comprehensive definition would be as follows:

- **Definition of balance of payments**

> *The balance of payments is a statistical statement for a given period showing (a) transactions in goods, services, and income between an economy and the rest of the world, (b) changes of ownership and other changes in the economy's monetary gold, special drawing rights, and claims on and liabilities to the rest of the world, and (c) unrequited transfers and counterpart entries that are needed to balance, in the accounting sense, any entries for the foregoing transactions and changes which are not mutually offsetting.* [5]

Balance-of-payments concepts originated during the 1500s, when the primary object of trade was to accumulate as much gold and silver as possible, as we noted in the discussion on mercantilism in Chapter 4. Exports were considered very desirable, since gold and silver were received as payment. Imports were considered to be undesirable because they caused a loss of gold and silver.

● Double entry—each transaction has two entries of equal value

The concept of double entry accounting holds true in the balance of payments. This implies that each transaction has two entries of equal value that must be accounted for. Debit entries have a negative arithmetic sign, and credit entries have a positive arithmetic sign. The debit entries reflect payments by domestic to foreign residents, and credit entries reflect payments by foreign to domestic residents. Although this appears simple on the surface, the problem is that transactions are not recorded in the same way that we learn in elementary accounting. A typical firm would debit inventory and credit cash or accounts payable when purchasing inventory. In balance-of-payments statistics, export data may come from customs records, and the payment may come from a different source. In addition, errors may occur in recording transactions, and many items must be estimated, such as expenditures by tourists. Thus the balance-of-payments statistics include an account called "**Errors and omissions**," which is used to balance the total debits and credits.

● An account that is used to balance the debits and credits.

In reality, the balance of payments is a balance of transactions. The two major types of transactions that take place are exchanges and unrequited transfers.

● When a buyer and seller trade something of equal value

Exchanges. Exchanges take place when a buyer in one country and a seller in another country exchange something of equal value. For example, an equipment exporter in Canada might sell equipment to an importer in France and receive payment in return. The payment would be considered a short-term capital flow. Another example might be when a German company has invested money in Japan through a direct investment. When a dividend is declared to the German investor, the Japanese balance-of-payments statistics would record services income to the German investor matched by a short-term capital outflow to pay for that income accruing to the investor. These are examples of real transactions because they involve the trade of goods, services, and income. In addition to real transactions there are also financial transactions. An example of a financial transaction would be when a Japanese corporation makes a long-term investment in Brazil. The creation of the long-term investment would be one part of the transaction, and the other part would be the flow of capital to Brazil to finance the investment.

● When consideration is given by only one party to the transaction—such as aid to a drought-stricken country

Unrequited transfers. Unrequited transfers are transfers that take place where consideration is provided by only one party. For example, Tunisian workers in France might send part of their paychecks home to their families in Tunisia. The transaction simply involves a short-term capital flow to Tuni-

TABLE 9.1

BRAZILIAN BALANCE OF PAYMENTS STATISTICS AGGREGATED PRESENTATION, 1976–1983 (in millions of SDRs)

	Code	1976	1977	1978	1979	1980	1981	1982	1983
A. Current Account, excl. Group F	A . . C A	−5,674	−4,373	−5,616	−8,102	−9,829	−9,976	−14,793	−6,360
Merchandise: exports f.o.b.	1 A . A 4	8,635	10,214	9,944	11,792	15,474	19,795	18,287	20,508
Coffee	1 A . A W	*1,884*	*1,977*	*1,543*	*1,464*	*1,910*	*1,281*	*1,685*	*1,962*
Iron ore	1 A . A U	*861*	*776*	*821*	*996*	*1,201*	*1,483*	*1,674*	*1,415*
Other	1 A . A V	*5,890*	*7,461*	*7,581*	*9,333*	*12,363*	*17,031*	*14,927*	*17,131*
Merchandise: imports f.o.b.	1 A . B 4	−10,699	−10,298	−10,867	−13,887	−17,634	−18,742	−17,572	−14,441
Trade balance	1 A . C 4	−2,064	−84	−923	−2,095	−2,160	1,054	715	6,068
Other goods, services, and income: credit	1 S . A 4	1,146	1,358	1,604	2,132	2,418	3,096	2,987	2,288
Other goods, services, and income: debit	1 S . B 4	−4,760	−5,647	−6,354	−8,151	−10,216	−14,293	−18,489	−14,816
Investment income	1 N . B 4	*−2,499*	*−3,248*	*−3,893*	*−5,202*	*−6,466*	*−9,914*	*−13,585*	*−10,954*
Other	1 S . B Y	*−2,261*	*−2,400*	*−2,461*	*−2,950*	*−3,751*	*−4,378*	*−4,904*	*−3,862*
Total: goods, services, and income	1 T . C 4	−5,678	−4,373	−5,673	−8,115	−9,958	−10,143	−14,787	−6,461
Private unrequited transfers	1 K . C 4	6	−3	55	9	97	158	−8	99
Total, excl. official unrequited transfers	1 U . C 4	−5,672	−4,376	−5,618	−8,105	−9,861	−9,985	−14,795	−6,362
Official unrequited transfers	1 H . C 4	−3	3	2	4	32	8	2	2
B. Direct Investment and Other Long-Term Capital, excl. Groups F through H	9 Z 1 X A	5,289	5,144	8,013	4,999	5,464	9,954	7,260	1,759
Direct investment	3 . . X 4	1,188	1,441	1,498	1,718	1,186	1,965	2,311	1,285
Portfolio investment	6 Z 1 X 4	—	—	—	510	272	−1	−3	−270
Other long-term capital									
Resident official sector	4 Z 1 X 4	1,308	2,041	3,142	2,592	−8	81	1,593	2,955
Loans received by general government	4 P 1 X 2	*1,380*	*2,076*	*3,346*	*2,630*	*389*	*315*	*1,898*	*2,862*
Loans received by Central Bank	4 P 1 X 3	*−33*	*−32*	*−30*	*−24*	*−19*	*−5*	*−5*	*−6*
Other	4 Z 1 X Y	*−40*	*−3*	*−174*	*−14*	*−377*	*−229*	*−300*	*98*
Deposit money banks	5 Z 1 X 4	787	383	1,475	384	1,615	3,433	1,498	−1,419
Other sectors	8 Z 1 X 4	2,007	1,278	1,898	−205	2,398	4,476	1,861	−791
Loans received	8 P 1 X 1	*2,211*	*1,513*	*2,232*	*370*	*2,072*	*5,016*	*2,186*	*−778*
Other	8 Z 1 X Y	*−204*	*−235*	*−334*	*−575*	*327*	*−540*	*−324*	*−13*
Total, Groups A plus B	B 1 . X A	−386	771	2,397	−3,103	−4,365	−23	−7,533	−4,601

Source: International Monetary Fund, *Balance of Payments Yearbook* (Washington, D.C.: IMF, 1984).

sia. To balance that flow, a private unrequited transfer is recorded. The same kind of entry would be made when countries donate food, medical supplies, or money to Ethiopia to assist victims of the drought. No financial payment is really expected or received from Ethiopia in exchange for the goods or funds.

● Good sources of balance-of-payments statistics

Given these types of transactions, let's look at the major categories in the balance of payments. There are a variety of sources of balance-of-payments statistics. Each country usually publishes its own statistics in its currency. The *Survey of Current Business* published by the U.S. Department of Commerce is the best source of U.S. balance-of-payments statistics. A comprehensive article is published each quarter on the prior quarter's international transactions, with data and an explanation.

● SDR: a unit of account issued to governments by the International Monetary Fund

The International Monetary Fund publishes balance-of-payments statistics in two different sources: the *Balance of Payments Yearbook* and *International Financial Statistics.* The former publication provides extensive detail about every member of the IMF, and the data are presented in terms of **Special Drawing Rights (SDR).** The SDR is a unit of account issued to countries by the International Monetary Fund and accepted by the countries as something of value. Actual paper currency is not traded back and forth, but

	Code	1976	1977	1978	1979	1980	1981	1982	1983
C. Other Short-Term Capital, excl. Groups F through H	9 Z 2 X A	2,279	183	1,005	−9	1,790	884	−493	−1,076
Resident official sector	4 Z 2 X 4	395	−276	393	298	−206	−59	−85	−78
Deposit money banks	5 Z 2 X 4	939	204	713	−327	464	850	−147	−663
Other sectors	8 Z 2 X 4	945	255	−101	20	1,532	94	−260	−335
D. Net Errors and Omissions	. A . X 4	430	−529	239	950	−270	−331	−343	−573
Total, Groups A through D	D 1 . X A	2,324	424	3,641	−2,162	−2,845	531	−8,369	−6,250
E. Counterpart Items	2 . . C 4	−140	−81	−481	−21	282	515	1,288	747
Monetization/demonetization of gold	2 A . M 4	—	—	—	—	80	110	336	521
Allocation/cancellation of SDRs	2 B . M 4	—	—	—	69	69	68	—	—
Valuation changes in reserves	2 . . F 4	−140	−81	−481	−90	133	337	952	226
Total, Groups A through E	E 1 . X A	2,184	343	3,160	−2,183	−2,564	1,045	−7,081	−5,503
F. Exceptional Financing	. Y . X B	—	—	—	—	—	—	—	...
Total, Groups A through F	F 1 . X 4	2,184	343	3,160	−2,183	−2,564	1,045	−7,081	−5,503
G. Liabilities Constituting Foreign Authorities' Reserves	9 W . X 4	—	—	—	−88	185	42	3,609	4,502
Total, Groups A through G	G 1 . X 4	2,184	343	3,160	−2,271	−2,378	1,087	−3,472	−1,001
H. Total Change in Reserves	2 . . R 4	−2,184	−343	−3,160	2,271	2,378	−1,087	3,472	1,001
Monetary gold	2 A . R 4	—	−7	−3	—	−80	−110	769	−147
SDRs	2 B . R 4	−8	−2	−11	−107	−10	−87	388	—
Reserve position in the Fund	2 C . R 4	−46	2	21	−44	−86	43	−33	260
Foreign exchange assets	2 D . R 4	−2,131	−336	−3,168	2,423	2,379	−1,105	1,758	−859
Other claims	2 E . R 4	—	—	—	—	175	173	92	−279
Use of Fund credit	2 M . R 4	—	—	—	—	—	—	499	2,027
Conversion rates: cruzeiros per SDR	. . R B 4	12.32	16.51	22.62	34.81	68.61	109.81	198.19	616.86

the IMF keeps track of the sources and uses of SDRs of member countries. This concept is discussed more fully in the section of the chapter on the international monetary system. The local currency–SDR conversion rate is provided for each country in the *Yearbook*. The latter publication does not provide as much information as does the *Balance of Payments Yearbook*, but the data are provided in U.S. dollar terms and are accompanied by a variety of other types of data.

Table 9.1 provides balance-of-payments data for Brazil as presented in the *Balance of Payments Yearbook*. Our intent in providing this table is not to explain each line item, but rather to give you an idea of the information that needs to be analyzed in the balance of payments. A very detailed definition of each line item can be found in the *Balance of Payments Manual* published by the IMF.

As discussed in Chapter 1, there are several categories to the balance of payments. Table 9.1 provides eight breakdowns.

• Merchandise trade, services, and unrequited transfers

Current account. The current account balance is very important because it summarizes the real transactions that occur in a country. The current account balance includes merchandise trade; other goods, services, and income; and unrequited transfers. The merchandise trade balance is critical because of the sheer volume of transactions that takes place. The export of merchandise is a credit because it results in the receipt of payment from abroad. An import is a debit because it results in making payment to the seller abroad.

As was noted in Chapter 1, the key transactions accounted for in the services account are travel and transportation, tourism, fees and royalties, and income on investments. U.S. tourists going abroad result in a debit entry because they are transferring funds abroad to pay for the vacation. Income received from a foreign investment is treated as a credit, much like merchandise exports, because the income results in receipt of payment from foreign sources. The unrequited transfers account (sometimes referred to as unilateral transfers) was discussed above.

- Direct and portfolio investments and loans

Long-term capital. The major categories in long-term capital are direct investment, portfolio investment, and loans. These terms were all defined in Chapter 1. Note that a balance is given for the current account and long-term capital in Table 9.1. That balance is often referred to as the basic balance because it measures the long-term international economic stability of a country. It is supposedly indicative of productivity, factor endowments, buyer preferences, international competition, perception of the economy as a haven for investment, and the like.

- Supports real transactions, long-term investments, short-term investments, and speculative flows

Short-term capital. This category is the least accurately measurable category of all. It represents funds that flow as a result of real transactions, such as the payment for exports and imports, and it also represents the flow of long-term capital transactions, such as the outflow to pay for direct investments or the inflow to recognize the receipt of investment income. It also represents speculative flows that take advantage of short-term interest rates and flows that respond to such things as political uncertainty. Sometimes those flows are difficult to monitor and measure.

Other items. The net errors and omissions category was defined above as the amount of money necessary to make the debits equal the credits. The items below the line represent official financing in the balance of payments. Counterpart items relate to certain changes within the official reserves and need not be discussed in detail here. Category G in Table 9.1 refers to claims that foreign official agencies have on the assets of the country. In the case of Brazil these liabilities provided a principal source of financing for the deficit in the current and capital accounts. The final balance is that of the reserve position of the country; that balance will be discussed in more detail in the next section.

- Major balances are merchandise trade, current account, and basic

The terms *balance-of-payments deficit* and *balance-of-payments surplus* are often mentioned in the press. As was noted earlier, the balance of payments must always be in balance because of the concept of double entry accounting. Thus the idea of a surplus or deficit must be in conjunction with a specific component of the balance of payments. The balances most often cited are the trade balance, the current account balance, and the basic balance. The key in using balance-of-payments statistics to predict currency changes is to realize that the statistics reflect something fundamental about the economy. One must understand the nature of the economy to be able to use the statistics to predict exchange rates. A deficit in the balance of trade must be offset by a surplus somewhere else, so one must decide which of the two types of disequilibrium is the more unstable and thus subject to corrective action.

- Ways to restore disequilibrium in the balance of payments
- Disrupt trade and capital flows

If disequilibrium does exist under a situation of managed exchange rates, there are three major ways to restore equilibrium: (1) disrupt trade and capital flows, (2) correct internal economic imbalances, and (3) allow the exchange rate to change. It would be illogical to assume that market forces are the sole determinants of trade and capital flows. Governments can and do provide incentives and disincentives in response to their own objectives and pressure from lobbyists. Even at a given level of governmental intervention, disequilibrium can still occur, leading to even more intervention. This approach, which is a cosmetic solution to disequilibrium, requires specific identification of the determinants of the surplus or deficit and the policies to achieve equilibrium. Chapter 5 discussed many ways to restrict trade and capital flows, such as subsidies, tariffs, quotas, and restrictions on the repatriation of dividends. Earlier in the chapter it was shown how governments can intervene to support their currencies by buying and selling foreign exchange, using multiple exchange rates, and so on.

- Correct internal economic imbalances

The second major way to restore equilibrium is to correct internal economic imbalances. As will be explained in another part of the chapter, inflation is one of the major sources of a deficit in the balance of payments. Inflation can be reduced through strict monetary and fiscal policies, high interest rates, and wage and price controls. However, this approach can lead to an economic slowdown and unemployment, both of which are very unpopular politically. Exports can also be diversified through industrialization and by shifting resources to products that are more competitive in export and import markets. Import-competing industries, where economically feasible, can also be encouraged.

- Change the exchange rate

In the final analysis it may be impossible to stave off a change in the exchange rate in order to try to restore equilibrium in the balance of payments. Brazil, for example, monitors its balance of trade as a factor that it considers in changing the value of its currency. The feeling is that a devaluation will make domestic products less expensive in international markets, leading to an increase in exports. At the same time the devaluation will make imports more expensive, leading to a reduction in demand and thus a reduction in imports.

Reserve Position

• Gold, SDRs, reserve position in the IMF, foreign exchange assets, other claims, use of the Fund credit

In Table 9.1, there is a section on reserves. The major components of a country's reserves are monetary gold, SDRs, the reserve position in the IMF, foreign exchange assets, other claims, and the use of the Fund credit. The data in Table 9.1 are given in terms of changes in reserve asset positions rather than in the reserves themselves. However, this information is available in *International Financial Statistics.*

Monetary gold is an important reserve asset of each country. Originally, gold had a fixed price for monetary purposes. Since 1978, however, gold has been sold at the open market price rather than at its original official price. SDRs were defined earlier as additional liquidity created by the IMF. A country can use its SDRs in a variety of ways to get access to foreign currency that it can use in international transactions.

As was mentioned earlier in the chapter, a country is assigned a quota when it joins the IMF. Twenty-five percent of the quota is paid in dollars, SDRs, or other reserve assets, such as monetary gold. This portion of the quota is the reserve position of the country in the IMF, and a country can draw on that position for balance of payments purposes.

Foreign exchange assets refer to currencies other than the currency of the home country held by that country's central bank. These assets can be exchanged for local currency so that importers can pay for goods imported from other countries. It is important to examine the value of foreign exchange reserves in conjunction with other transactions in the balance of payments. For example, in Mexico during the mid-1970s, foreign exchange reserves were growing during a time when there was a widening of the balance-of-trade deficit and when there was very little new foreign direct investment. Foreign exchange reserves were growing because the public and private sector were borrowing foreign exchange and converting them into pesos to use for local expansion.

In Table 9.1 it appeared that Brazil was making good use of its ability to use Fund credit. That just means that it was borrowing from the IMF to help finance its severe balance-of-trade deficit and partially meet its international obligations. A similar phenomenon could be observed in Mexico and Argentina.

Relative Rates of Inflation

Purchasing power parity theory is one of the most important dimensions to consider in forecasting exchange rate changes because inflation affects not only the relative costs and therefore competitiveness of goods worldwide but also the confidence that one has in the government of a country. In looking at inflation one must study the fundamentals that underlie inflation, such as government fiscal and monetary policy, as well as the actual rates of inflation in an historical context. The example of the Bolivian peso given in the section of the chapter on purchasing power parity illustrates how inflation can be used to help predict exchange rate changes.

There are a number of good examples of how inflation affects the value of the currency. In Brazil during 1984, exports were quite strong, helping to lead to a growth in the money supply of 160 percent during that period. Most experts agreed that this was a major cause of inflation in Brazil, which was running at over 12 percent a month during the second half of 1984. It was anticipated that inflation would hit 250 percent in 1985. Since the Brazilian government has a stated policy of devaluing the cruzeiro in proportion to its inflation, the experts were predicting that the value of the cruzeiro would be between 6000 and 6500 per dollar by mid 1985, compared with approximately 2700 per dollar during the second half of 1984.[6] Similar examples could be given with respect to Argentina and Chile.

- Inflation affects trade flows and financial flows (through confidence)

We mentioned above that inflation affected trade flows and financial flows (through confidence). The impact on trade flows is not easy to predict. The general rule is that if a country's inflation is higher than that of its trading partners, its goods will be in less demand than before, and its demand for foreign goods will rise. This depends on how sensitive demand is to changes in prices. Up to a certain point in the 1970s, countries continued to import oil, even though its price was increasing dramatically. Eventually, the demand dropped off owing to the worldwide recession, conservation, and alternative energy sources. However, it took a while for this to happen. Other products are far more sensitive and can cause trade flows to change more abruptly.

Interest Rate Differentials

As was mentioned earlier, a difference in real interest rates may imply that there will be a strong demand for the currency of the country with the higher interest rate, leading to an increase in price or at least continued strength. This has been a factor in the strength of the U.S. dollar in recent years. Thus one would want to monitor trends in real interest rates and forecasts of those rates in the future. As one tries to forecast changes in interest rates, it is important to keep track of the growth in money supply, fiscal policy, and similar economic indicators. These are the same indicators to monitor when projecting inflation trends.

- Forward rate is an unbiased predictor of future spot rates

Closely connected with the monitoring of interest rates is the use of the forward rate. As was mentioned earlier, the forward rate is an unbiased predictor of the future spot rate, meaning that the forward rate is not systematically above or below the future spot rate. The forward rate also takes into account important economic fundamentals, such as interest rate differentials, so it is reasonable to assume that the forward spot rate will closely approximate the future spot rate. Earlier in the chapter, when discussing determinants of the forward rate, we showed how to use the current spot rate and interest rate differentials to determine the equilibrium forward rate. The predictive value of that exercise depends on the assumption that the forward rate is going to approximate the future spot rate fairly closely. The assumption also has to be made that funds can flow fairly freely between the capital markets of the home country and the foreign country in order to take advantage of interest rate differentials. Thus this analysis is fairly limited to the currencies of the major industrial countries of the world.

Trends in Spot Rates

Although it is always dangerous to forecast the future strictly on the basis of the past, it would also be unwise to ignore past trends. These movements can be compared with other indicators, such as rates of inflation, to help predict future movements. It is also important to monitor trends in spot rates of currencies that are critical to the currency of interest. For example, the currencies of Western Europe are affected by changes in the West German mark. In addition, they are affected by the U.S. dollar. When the dollar was especially weak during the mid-1970s, the West German mark was very strong. It was difficult for the other European countries to support their currencies to the extent that was necessary. During the early 1980s, when the dollar was quite strong, the West German mark did not exhibit as much pressure on the other Western European currencies, so there seemed to be more stability in the European Monetary System.

THE INTERNATIONAL MONETARY SYSTEM

Thus far we have focused on the major political and economic factors that determine the values of currencies. Now it is important to look at the major institutions that influence currency values: the International Monetary Fund and the central banks of the individual nations. Included in the discussion of these institutions is a discussion of the different exchange rate arrangements under which currencies such as the Bolivian peso operate.

The International Monetary Fund

The Depression, economic isolation, and trade war of the 1930s were followed by the global conflict of World War II. At the close of the war the major governments met to determine the international institutions that were needed to bring relative economic stability and growth to the free world. As a result of the many conferences, the **International Monetary Fund (IMF)** was organized.

- IMF—organized to promote exchange rate stability and facilitate the international flow of currencies

The IMF was signed into existence by 44 nations at Bretton Woods, New Hampshire, in 1944. Its aim was stability in the international monetary system. The agreement now covers over 140 countries. The basic objectives of the IMF were to promote exchange stability, maintain orderly exchange arrangements, avoid competitive currency devaluation, establish a multilateral system of payments, eliminate exchange restrictions, and create standby reserves.

- Par value—the benchmark value of a currency in terms of gold and the U.S. dollar

The Bretton Woods system operated under a principle of fixed exchange rates by which each member country established a par value for its currency based on gold and the U.S. dollar. This par value became a benchmark by which the country related its currency to the currencies of the rest of the world. Currencies were allowed to vary within 1 percent of par value (extended to 2.25 percent in December 1971), depending on supply and demand conditions. Further moves from par value and formal changes in par value (through devaluation or revaluation) were made with approval by the IMF.

Because of the strength of the U.S. dollar during the 1940s and 1950s, member currencies were denominated in terms of gold and dollars. By 1947 the United States held 70 percent of the international official gold reserves. Because of this, countries bought and sold dollars rather than gold. It was understood, although not formalized, that the United States would redeem gold for dollars, and the two became fixed with respect to each other. The dollar thus became the benchmark of the world trading currency.

Problems with liquidity   The problem with the system as envisioned by the IMF was that, in practice, rigidity replaced stability. Countries did not allow an exchange rate alteration to occur until a crisis developed. It became more and more evident that, as the world's reserve currency, the dollar was in a difficult position. As other countries' economies began to strengthen, it appeared that gold and internationally acceptable currencies (initially known as the **official reserves** of a country) could not handle the reserve requirements of a country. The freer flow of goods and capital put increasing pressure on a country's reserve assets. Also, the growing accumulation of dollars outside of the United States during the 1960s threatened to wreck the stability of the system of fixed exchange rates. The problem was that governments became increasingly uneasy about the currency (i.e., dollar) component of their reserves. Thus there was the tendency to want to replace these currencies with gold. As trade increased, the ratio of reserves to trade decreased sharply.[7]

To help increase international reserves during the period when it was

- Special Drawing Right (SDR)
  - a unit of account developed by the IMF
  - designed to increase world liquidity

- Quota—payment made by each country that joins the IMF
  - provides operating funds for the IMF
  - used as a basis for SDR allocations and a
  - country's access to the funds of the IMF
- Currencies in the SDR: dollar, West German mark, yen, French franc, pound sterling

hoped that the United States would be able to reduce its balance of payments deficit, the IMF created the Special Drawing Right (SDR), as defined earlier in this chapter. The first SDR allocation was made in 1970, and the most recent one was made in 1981. A total of SDR 21.4 billion (one SDR is worth approximately U.S. $1) was allocated during that time, based on the quota of each country.

When a country joins the IMF, it is given a **quota** that it has to contribute to the IMF reserves. The quota is determined by a formula based on the national income, gold and dollar balances, imports, and exports of a country. Twenty-five percent of the quota must be paid in dollars, SDRs, or other reserve assets and the remainder in that member's currency. That quota is used for a variety of purposes, as discussed in Chapter 2 and earlier in this chapter. It also becomes the basis on which SDR allocations are made.

The SDR was initially linked to gold, but its value through 1980 was determined as a composite value based on the trading importance of sixteen currencies. On January 1, 1981, the IMF began to use a simplified basket of five currencies for determining valuation: the U.S. dollar, West German mark, Japanese yen, French franc, and British pound sterling. The percentage weights used for each are the following: 42 for the U.S. dollar, 19 for the mark, and 13 each for the yen, pound, and franc. These specific weights were chosen because they broadly reflected the relative importance of the currencies in international trade and payments, which in turn are based on the value of the export of goods and services by the countries issuing these currencies.

The value of the SDR is calculated daily on the basis of the market basket of the above currencies, and its value is stated in terms of U.S. dollars on that day. A country can determine what the SDR value of its currency is by its dollar exchange rate on that day. For example, the value of the SDR on January 3, 1985, was U.S. $1 = SDR 1.02196. On that same day the West German mark was trading for DM 3.1605 = U.S. $1. Therefore one West German mark was worth SDR 0.32335 (1.02196/3.1605). The SDR–dollar rate is quoted daily in the Foreign Exchange section of the *Wall Street Journal.*

- SDRs can be traded for other currencies

SDRs can be used on a **designated** or **voluntary** basis. Countries exchange their SDRs for currencies of other countries and then use those currencies for market transactions. All countries are considered to be designated for this type of transaction unless the country's SDR holdings are three times greater than its allocation of SDRs. At that point the country does not have to trade its currency for SDRs unless it wants to do so. There are a variety of voluntary transactions that can take place between and among member countries.[8] Countries earn interest if their holdings of SDRs exceed their allocation, and they must pay interest if their holdings are less than their allocation.

- The SDR has become a unit of account (benchmark) for official IMF transactions

The SDR has not taken over the role of gold or the dollar as a primary reserve asset. However, it has become a **unit of account**. This simply means that the SDR has become a benchmark or reference point for a variety of transactions. The IMF uses the SDR rather than a specific national currency (such as the U.S. dollar) in most of its official reports. As will be seen later in the chapter, a number of countries quote the value of their currencies in terms of SDRs.

Evolution to floating exchange rates. As was mentioned above, the initial years of the IMF involved fixed exchange rates. Because the U.S. dollar was the cornerstone of the international monetary system, its value remained constant with respect to gold. Other countries could change the value of their currencies against gold and the dollar, but the dollar remained fixed in value.

Partly because of the inflationary pressures that began to build in the United States in the mid-1960s, the traditional U.S. trade surplus began to shrink. Continued outflow of private and governmental long-term capital, coupled with the diminishing trade surplus, caused an increasing deficit in the basic balance. As it became apparent that 1971 would see the first U.S. balance-of-trade deficit in the twentieth century, it was clear something needed to be done.

- Exchange flexibility was widened from 1 percent to 2.25 percent on either side of par value in 1971

On August 15, 1971, President Nixon announced a new economic policy that included the suspension of exchanging gold for dollars and the institution of an import surcharge. These moves were an attempt to force the other industrial countries to the bargaining table in hopes of restructuring the world monetary order. The Smithsonian Agreement of December 1971 resulted in an 8 percent devaluation of the dollar, a revaluation of some other world currencies, a widening of exchange rate flexibility (from 1 to 2.25 percent on either side of par value), and a commitment on the part of all countries to reduce trade restrictions.

This restructuring of the international monetary system did not last. World currency markets remained unsteady during 1972, and the dollar was devalued again by 10 percent in early 1973. Major currencies began to float against each other instead of relying on the Smithsonian Agreement.

- Movement to floating exchange rates

Because the Bretton Woods Agreement was based on the system of fixed exchange rates and par values, the IMF had to change its Articles of Agreement in order to permit floating exchange rates. The Jamaica Agreement of 1976 provided the amendment to the original Articles of Agreement that permitted greater flexibility in exchange rates. There was some concern that the world monetary system would collapse under the freedom of flexible exchange rates, so the Agreement reiterated the importance of pursuing exchange stability.

Exchange Rate Arrangements

The Jamaica Agreement formalized the break from fixed exchange rates. As part of this move, the IMF permitted countries to select and maintain an exchange arrangement of their choice, as long as they properly communicated their arrangement to the Fund. Each year the Fund receives information from the member countries and classifies each country into one of three broad categories:

- IMF classifications of exchange rate systems

1. currencies that are pegged to a single currency or to a composite of currencies,
2. currencies whose exchange rates have displayed limited flexibility compared with either a single currency or group of currencies, and
3. currencies whose exchange rates are more flexible.[9]

Table 9.2 identifies the countries that fit in each category. It is important to note that the countries in each category are subject to change each year. In 1983, for example, there were 38 countries pegged to the U.S. dollar, compared with only 33 in 1984; there were only 33 countries in the more flexible category, compared with 38 in 1984.

- Currencies fix their values to another currency or composite of currencies

Pegged rates.   Countries that fit in this category **peg,** or fix, the value of their currency with zero fluctuation margins (in the case of countries that peg to a single currency) or very narrow margins of 1 percent or less in the case of pegs to the SDR or other composite currency. Note that the Bolivian peso, which was discussed in the case at the beginning of the chapter, is pegged to the U.S. dollar. The "other composite" category means that the country has selected a basket of currencies that is different from the SDR. An example of this is the Swedish krona:

> In managing the exchange rate of the krona, the Sveriges Riksbank (the central bank) is guided by a trade-weighted index based on a basket of 15 currencies of Sweden's most important trading partners. In constructing the index the Swedish authorities established two criteria to be met by each country and currency included in the basket: (1) the country had to account for at least 1 percent of Sweden's total foreign trade (exports plus imports) during the previous five-year period and (2) each currency had to be quoted daily on the foreign exchange market in Stockholm. [10]

In 1984 the three most important currencies in the basket were the U.S. dollar (18.1 percent), the West German mark (16.6 percent), and the British pound sterling (13.0 percent).

- Flexibility increases to 2.25 percent around the reference point

Limited flexibility.   As noted in Table 9.2, there are two subcategories in the "limited flexibility" category. In the first of these, "limited flexibility to a single currency," the exchange rates fluctuate within a 2.25 percent margin. In all nine cases the exchange rates have shown limited flexibility against the U.S. dollar. The 2.25 percent margin is consistent with the

Smithsonian Agreement signed in 1971 that increased the flexibility in the par value system from 1 percent to 2.25 percent.

• EMS was designed to promote exchange stability in the EC

The other subcategory, "cooperative arrangements," refers to the **European Monetary System (EMS)**. The EMS was created in 1979 as a means of creating exchange stability within the members of the European Community. The major reason for this movement was to facilitate trade among the members of the Community by minimizing exchange rate fluctuations. The EMS links together the currencies of all European Community members except the United Kingdom and Greece through a parity grid. A central exchange rate is determined for the currency of each country participating in the EMS by the use of a **European Currency Unit (ECU)**. The ECU is similar to the SDR in concept, except that the basket includes the currencies of all countries in the EC except for Greece, and Greece is expected to join the EMS at the end of 1985. It is interesting to note that the British pound is used to compute the ECU, even though it does not participate in the EMS.

Once the central exchange rate is determined for the currency of each country in the EMS, a parity exchange rate is determined for each pair of countries. For example, there would be a parity rate for the French franc and West German mark, for the Italian lira and French franc, for the Dutch guilder and Italian lira, and so on. With the exception of the Italian lira, which is permitted a fluctuation of 6 percent, bilateral rates are allowed to deviate from the central parity rates by only 2.25 percent before the respective central banks must intervene to protect the integrity of the central rate. The concept of intervention was discussed earlier in the chapter.

• Frequent changes to value of currency or total freedom to float according to supply and demand

More flexibility. The final major category of currencies is that of "more flexibility." In those countries whose currencies are independently floating, government intervention occurs only to influence but not neutralize the speed of movement of the exchange rate change. In the "other managed floating" category, governments usually set rates for short intervals, such as a week at a time, and buy and sell the currency at that rate for that period. The final subcategory includes currencies that are managed according to a set of indicators. The Brazilian cruzeiro, for example, is adjusted at regularly short intervals in terms of the U.S. dollar. The degree of adjustment depends on the "movement of prices in Brazil relative to that in its main trading partners, the level of foreign exchange reserves, export performance, and the overall balance of payments positioning."[11]

Parallel markets. As can be noted in Table 9.2, only eight of the 145 countries of the IMF that reported their exchange rate arrangements have currencies that are independently floating. Many of the other countries control their currencies fairly rigidly. Some of them license their exchange,

TABLE 9.2

EXCHANGE ARRANGEMENTS BY COUNTRY AS OF MARCH 31, 1984

			Pegged			

U.S. dollar		French franc	Other currency	SDR	Other composite
Antigua and Barbuda	Lao People's Democratic Rep.	Benin	Bhutan (Indian rupee)	Burma	Algeria
Bahamas	Liberia	Cameroon	Equatorial	Burundi	Austria
Barbados	Libya	Central African Republic	Guinea	Guinea	Bangladesh
Belize	Nicaragua	Chad	(Spanish	Iran, Islamic	Botswana
Bolivia	Oman	Comoros	Peseta)	Rep. of	Cape Verde
Djibouti	Panama	Congo		Jordan	China, People's Rep.
			Gambia, The		
Dominica	Paraguay	Gabon	(£ sterling)	Kenya	Cyprus
				Rwanda	
Dominican Republic	St. Lucia	Ivory Coast	Lesotho (South	São Tomé and	Fiji
Egypt	St. Vincent and Grenadines	Mali	African	Principe	Finland
El Salvador	Sierra Leone	Niger	rand)	Seychelles	Hungary
Ethiopia	Sudan	Senegal	Swaziland		Kuwait
		Togo	(South	Vanuatu	Madagascar
			African	Viet Nam	
Grenada	Suriname	Upper Volta	rand)		Malawi
Guatemala	Syrian Arab Rep.				Malaysia
Haiti	Trinidad and Tobago				Malta
Honduras	Venezuela				Mauritania
Iraq	Yemen Arab Rep.				Mauritius
					Nepal
	Yemen, People's Democratic Rep.				Norway
					Papua New Guinea
					Romania
					Singapore
					Solomon Islands
					Sweden
					Tanzania
					Tunisia
					Zambia
					Zimbabwe

Source: International Monetary Fund, *Annual Report* (Washington, D.C.: IMF, 1984), p. 8

Flexibility limited against a single currency or group of currencies		More flexible		
Single currency	Cooperative arrangements	Adjusted according to a set of indicators	Other managed floating	Independently floating
Afghanistan	Belgium	Brazil	Argentina	Australia
Bahrain	Denmark	Chile	Costa Rica	Canada
Ghana	France	Colombia	Ecuador	Japan
Guyana	Germany, Fed.	Peru	Greece	Lebanon
Maldives	Republic of	Portugal	Guinea-	South Africa
Qatar	Ireland	Somalia	Bissau	
Saudi Arabia	Italy			United Kingdom
			Iceland	United States
Thailand	Luxembourg		India	Uruguay
United Arab	Netherlands		Indonesia	
Emirates			Israel	
			Jamaica	
			Korea	
			Mexico	
			Morocco	
			New Zealand	
			Nigeria	
			Pakistan	
			Philippines	
			Spain	
			Sri Lanka	
			Turkey	
			Uganda	
			Western	
			Samoa	
			Yugoslavia	
			Zaire	

as was noted in Chapter 8, so that full convertibility is not enjoyed by residents and nonresidents alike.

- Black markets closely approximate real supply and demand

In many of these cases a black market parallels the official market. The less flexibility there is, the more likely there is to be a black market. However, even Brazil, a country in the "more flexible" category, has a black market for its currency. The black market is more closely aligned with the forces of supply and demand than is the official controlled market. The black market exists because the government buys dollars for less than the market thinks they are worth. Thus the black market attempts to put a more realistic price on the dollar value of the local currency.

The Role of Central Banks

- Central banks often control the value of their currencies through intervention

Each country has a central bank that is responsible for the policies that affect the value of its currency on world markets. The central bank in the United States is actually the Federal Reserve System (the Fed), a system of twelve banks, each representing a region of the United States. The New York Federal Reserve Bank handles the system's intervention in the foreign exchange markets. Intervention policies are determined by the Federal Open Market Committee. However, the Fed does not act independently of the rest of government. In particular, the Secretary of the Treasury is legally responsible for stabilizing the exchange value of the dollar.[12]

- A central bank's bank

In spite of the unique nature of the central bank system in each country, there is some semblance of international cooperation through the **Bank for International Settlements (BIS)** in Basel, Switzerland. One of the functions of the BIS is to act as a central banker's bank. It gets involved in swaps and other currency transactions between central banks in the major industrial countries. In addition, it is a place where central bankers can get together to discuss monetary cooperation.

THE FUTURE OF THE INTERNATIONAL MONETARY SYSTEM

Ever since 1973, when the world abandoned the fixed exchange rate system that was instituted by the Bretton Woods agreement, there has been a tendency for some to call for a return to the past. In 1983, President François Mitterand of France harshly criticized the high volatility of exchange rates and recommended that a new Bretton Woods agreement be developed.

Major Arguments against Floating Rates

Five major arguments have been given for why the floating rate system has not worked: floating exchange rates hinder international trade, a depreciating currency generates domestic inflation, the dollar is overvalued, a decline in U.S. interest rates will cause the exchange rate to fall, and a deficit in the international merchandise trade account will cause a depreciating exchange rate.[13]

- Hinder trade

The statement made about trade is due to the assumption that unstable exchange rates make it difficult for importers and exporters to carry on a long-term relationship. However, it was found that during the 1973–1982 period, when the currencies of most industrial currencies were freely floating, trade as a percentage of GNP actually increased.[14]

- Can be inflationary

It is commonly accepted that a devaluation is inflationary. That assumes that there is a causal relationship between exchange rates and inflation and that inflation is primarily a cost-push phenomenon. However, inflation is basically a monetary phenomenon, and inflation and exchange rate changes are jointly determined by monetary policy rather than being determinants of each other.

- Keep the dollar overvalued

The complaints about the overvalued dollar have come from a variety of sectors, especially from U.S. exporters. As was mentioned earlier in the chapter, the purchasing power parity theory is the major determinant of exchange rates. However, it is possible that this principle can be violated in the short run. In the early to mid-1980s, a major determinant of the dollar appeared to be high real interest rates. This kept the value of the dollar high as investors sought to earn high yields in the United States. However, it has been argued that the high dollar was a result of a phenomenon of the U.S. capital market rather than floating exchange rates.

- Inherently unstable

The fourth criticism refers to a fall in nominal interest rates being a factor causing the U.S. dollar to fall in value. However, it was shown in the early 1980s that the U.S. dollar was more sensitive to real interest rates (the nominal interest rate minus inflation) than it was to nominal rates. When interest rates fell during a period of falling prices, the real interest rate remained virtually unchanged, and the dollar remained firm. Thus the floating exchange rates confirmed the theory that exchange rates would reflect real interest rate differentials.

The final criticism concerning merchandise trade ignores the fact that a deficit in the merchandise trade account must be made up for by a surplus in some other account. In the case of the United States, that surplus came in the capital account in the form of long-term investments in the United States as well as short-term financial flows to take advantage of the high real interest rates and relative political stability.

Call for More Stable Rates

The call for a change to a more stable exchange rate system is made under the assumption that countries will be more responsible in supporting their currencies and restructuring their economies if they are subjected to the discipline of a gold standard. Under that standard a deficit country (which traditionally suffers relatively high inflation) would be forced to use its foreign exchange reserves to purchase excess currency on foreign markets. This would decrease the country's money supply, resulting in a reduction in economic activity and inflation. Over time, the country would import less and export more, reversing its trade deficit.

The problem with this scenario is that countries did not seem to want to or be able to control exchange rates by changing monetary and fiscal policy during the early 1970s, and this led to the adoption of a floating rate system. The European Monetary System is an attempt to bring stability into the European Community, but many would argue that the stability is feasible only as long as the dollar is strong. In any event, it is doubtful that the world will return to a fixed rate system in the near future. Remember, however, that there are very few countries whose currencies are freely floating. Most are pegged to other currencies in one form or another.

BUSINESS IMPLICATIONS OF EXCHANGE RATE CHANGES

Exchange rates can affect businesses in three major ways: market decisions, production decisions, and financial decisions.

Market Decisions

- Affect business in production, marketing, and financial decisions

On the marketing side, exchange rates can affect demand for a company's products at home and abroad. It has already been mentioned that a country like Brazil will devalue its currency if it feels that its exports are becoming too expensive owing to relatively high inflation. Even though inflation would cause the cruzeiro price of the Brazilian products to rise, the devaluation means that it would take less foreign currency to buy the cruzeiros, thus allowing the Brazilian products to remain competitive in the marketplace.

On the other hand, a devaluation could result in foreign products being so expensive in Brazil that Brazilian products would soon pick up market share from imports. The key is whether or not the percentage of devaluation exceeds the relative increase in inflation.

One interesting ramification of a cruzeiro devaluation is the impact of the cheaper Brazilian goods on exporters from other countries. For example, the cheaper Brazilian goods flooding the market in Argentina might take away market share from Italian exporters, thus affecting the Italian economy.

Production Decisions

Production decisions could also be affected by an exchange rate change. A manufacturer in a country with high wages and operating expenses might be tempted to locate production in a country like Argentina, where the austral is rapidly losing value. This would be for several reasons. One reason is that a foreign currency could buy lots of australs, making the initial investment relatively cheap. Another reason is that goods manufactured in Argentina would be relatively cheap in world markets. However, a firm could accomplish the same purpose by going to any country whose currency is expected to remain weak in relation to that of the parent country currency. It would not be necessary to pick a country with high political and economic instability.

Financial Decisions

The final business area where exchange rates make a difference is in the area of finance. This subject will be discussed in more detail in Chapters 19 and 21. The areas of finance that are most affected are the sourcing of financial resources, the remittance of funds across national borders, and the financial statements. There might be a temptation to borrow money where interest rates are lowest. However, we mentioned above that interest rate differentials are often compensated for in the money markets through exchange rate changes.

In the area of financial flows, it is important for a parent company to convert local currency into the parent's own currency when exchange rates are most favorable so that it can maximize its return. It should also be noted that countries with weak currencies often have currency controls, making it difficult to manage the flow of funds optimally.

Finally, exchange rate changes can also influence the reporting of financial results. This complex topic is best left for Chapter 19. However, a simple example can illustrate the impact that exchange rates can have on income. If the Brazilian subsidiary of a U.S. company earns 100 million cruzeiros when the exchange rate is 1500 cruzeiros per dollar, the dollar equivalent of income is $66,667. If the cruzeiro devalues to 2000 cruzeiros per dollar, the dollar equivalent of income falls to $50,000. The opposite would occur if the local currency appreciates against the parent currency.

A SYNTHESIS

In this chapter we have attempted to look at the major forces leading to exchange rate values in the international monetary system. We have also attempted to explain some of the factors that could influence exchange rate changes. The fact of the matter is that even though some factors are common to each country, each country is unique. It is important to look at the system of the country as a whole to understand what is going on.

Since we started the chapter with Bolivia, it is only fitting that we end with Bolivia and see how the political and economic situation must be monitored in order to determine what might happen in the foreign exchange markets.

The following was taken from an exchange rate forecast published by Manufacturers Hanover Trust in the fourth quarter of 1984:

Reflecting on Bolivia's worsening economic, political, and social problems, last summer, in a matter of weeks, the peso plunged from around 3,500/$ to 10,000/$ on the parallel market. In response, the government, on August 16, replaced the fixed exchange rate with a two-tiered system. The "official" rate of 2,000/$ was retained for essential imports, while a rate of 5,000/$ was established for non-essential imports. Most transactions, however, continue to be based on the parallel rate.

Although the "official" peso was devalued by 60% last November and by another 75% in April (the cost of purchasing dollars in Bolivia has increased tenfold in less than a year), the devaluation pace has not kept up with the country's soaring inflation rate. As a result of economic measures taken in April, including the 75% devaluation, hikes in food, fuel, and transportation costs of 100–500%, and cuts in government subsidies, prices increased by 63% in April alone. Inflation, which is also being fueled by food shortages, uncontrolled government spending, and runaway money supply growth, was recorded at 1,041% in the year to June and is likely to reach 1,700–2,000% by year-end. Bolivia's economic problems, which also include prolonged recession and an acute shortage of foreign exchange, moreover, are exacerbated by the ability of the country's strong and militant labor unions to exert enormous pressure on a government that is too fragile to impose an effective economic program.

Because authorities have not been able to stem the plunge of the "parallel" rate (currently at 15,100/$ or almost 8 times the official rate), Bolivia's soaring inflation and acute foreign exchange shortage will force additional devaluations and possibly a merging of the official rates. An exchange rate of 20,000/$ next year is not inconceivable.[15]

The interesting thing about this forecast is that the key linkage is made between inflation and a change in the exchange rate. In addition, the key determinants of inflation—factors that one should monitor—are identified. The instability in the economy and foreign exchange markets also have resulted in multiple exchange rates and a black (parallel) market.

SUMMARY

- The demand for a country's currency is a function of the demand for that country's goods and services and financial assets denominated in that currency.

- A central bank intervenes in currency markets by creating a supply for its currency when it wants to push the value of the currency down or creating a demand for its currency when it wants to strengthen its value.

- A devaluation of a currency occurs when the foreign currency equivalent of that currency falls (or when that currency's equivalent of the foreign currency rises).

- The major factors that determine the value of a currency are purchasing power parity (relative rates of inflation), real interest rates (nominal interest rates reduced by the amount of inflation), confidence in the government's ability to manage the political and economic situation of the country, and certain technical factors that are a result of trading.

- The major determinant of the forward exchange rate is the interest rate differential between currencies.

- The major factors that one should monitor when trying to predict the direction, magnitude, and timing of an exchange rate change are the balance of payments statistics, the country's reserve position, relative rates of inflation, interest rate differentials, trends in spot rates, and the forward exchange rate. Also, it is important to look at the political situation.

- A country's balance-of-payments statement summarizes all international transactions by government, business, and private residents during a specified period of time, usually a year.

- In the system of double entry accounting, each transaction, as represented by a debit or credit, is offset by an entry that represents the financing or settling of the transaction.

- The major balances in the balance of payments that are closely monitored are the merchandise trade balance, the balance on goods and services, the current account balance, and the basic balance (the current account balance plus long-term capital flows).

- The International Monetary Fund (IMF) was organized in 1944 to promote exchange stability, maintain orderly exchange arrangements, avoid competitive currency devaluation, establish a multilateral system of payments, eliminate exchange restrictions, and create standby reserves.

- The Special Drawing Right (SDR) was instituted by the IMF to increase world liquidity.

- The value of the dollar against gold fell (i.e., the dollar was devalued) in 1971 and 1973. After the second devaluation the United States announced that the dollar would float in value on the market according to supply and demand. That finally ushered in the era of floating exchange rates.

- The currencies of countries that are members of the IMF are divided into three different categories: those that are pegged (fixed in value) to a single currency or to a composite of currencies, those that have

- displayed limited flexibility compared with either a single currency or a group of currencies, and those that are more flexible.

- Many countries that strictly control and regulate the convertibility of their currencies have a parallel or black market that maintains an exchange rate that is more indicative of supply and demand than is the official rate.

- The Bank for International Settlements (BIS) in Switzerland acts as a central banker's bank. It facilitates discussion and transactions among the central banks of the world.

- Exchange rates can affect businesses in three major ways: market decisions, production decisions, and financial decisions.

C A S E GENETITEC AND THE SUPERDOLLAR[16]

James E. Padilla, President and founder of GenetiTec, was clearly worried about the strategic direction of his company. GenetiTec was established in a western U.S. state in 1970 and had risen rapidly to a $100 million company specializing in biotechnology products. The original product line came from patents developed by Jim Padilla, but the company had since diversified into a number of product lines based on internally developed patents as well as some patents licensed from other companies in the United States.

The markets for GenetiTec's products were highly competitive in the United States and abroad. Much of the competition in recent years was coming from some very aggressive Japanese companies. Because of GenetiTec's unique patents, it held 75 percent of the world's markets in some of its product lines. However, it was beginning to lose market share in the United States and abroad.

GenetiTec produces products in the United States and abroad. About 25 percent of its total worldwide manufacturing is in Singapore and Taiwan, and Padilla is strongly considering Malaysia and Thailand as other sources of production. He could be convinced to do that if he felt that the dollar would remain firm.

Most of GenetiTec's raw materials sources for U.S. production are local. Some of its major U.S. competitors are beginning to source production abroad.

As Jim looks at his production and marketing efforts, he realizes that GenetiTec is at a very important stage in its development. Mitsubishi, a Japanese company, is interested in acquiring a controlling interest in GenetiTec to bolster its biotechnology division. Jim feels that he could expand capacity by 50 percent and be able to compete even more effectively in some product lines in which his market share is relatively small. In his other lines there is major market growth ahead if he can just expand capacity. However, he is not sure whether he should expand production in his U.S. facilities. If he decides not to expand abroad, what could this mean to the future of his company? Before making a decision, Jim decided to take a good look at the strong U.S. dollar and its history.

The dollar prior to the 1980s.   Jim was aware that the U.S. dollar was operating under a fixed exchange rate system until 1973. Before 1973 the dollar was redeemable into gold at a price fixed with the IMF. The initial price was $35 per ounce, but that value changed to $37.50 with the dollar devaluation of 1971 and to $42.20 with the devaluation in 1973. After the devaluation of 1973 the dollar was cut loose from its tie with gold and allowed to float freely according to the law of supply and demand. As can be seen in Fig. 9.3, the two devaluations resulted in a dollar exchange rate that

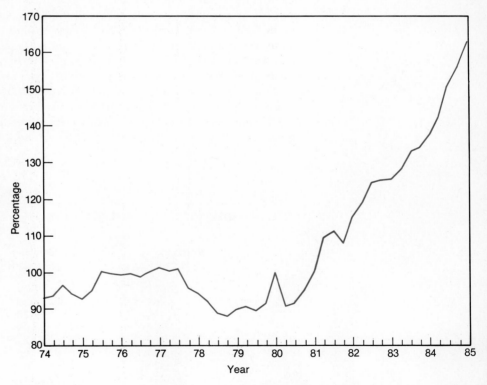

FIGURE 9.3
Indexes of Foreign Currency Price of the Dollar against 22 OECD Countries
For the indexes, 1977 = 100. The index for 1970, the year before the first dollar devaluation, would have been approximately 89.
Source: Various issues of the *Survey of Current Business.*

was considerably below that of the pre-1971 era. The effective exchange rate, which is the value of the dollar against its major trading partners weighted for the importance of trade with them, reached a low point in 1973 and again in late 1978 and early 1979.

The major reason for the dollar devaluations of the early 1970s was the merchandise trade deficit. As shown in Table 9.3, there was a trade surplus in 1970, which was a continuation of a situation that had existed ever since the Bretton Woods Agreement was signed, but the surplus turned into a deficit in 1971. As the mood began to swing against the dollar in 1971, President Nixon suspended the convertibility of the dollar into gold and forced the major industrial countries of the world to the bargaining table. The result was the realignment of currencies at the end of 1971.

The situation still looked bad at the end of 1972, so there was a lot of pressure in the foreign exchange markets in early 1973. In spite of heavy central bank intervention, the dollar continued to take a beating until it was devalued and eventually allowed to float freely.

In 1974 the dollar strengthened somewhat but began to weaken again as the impact of oil imports was felt. Oil imports increased in dollar value from $5 billion in 1973 to $17 billion in 1974, enough to change a trade surplus to a deficit. A slowdown in the U.S. economy and declining interest rates added to the deficit. A worldwide recession occurred in 1975, which greatly affected the U.S. trade balance. The trade deficit of 1974 turned to a surplus because imports to the United States fell faster than exports, agricultural exports continued at a high level, and OPEC purchases of U.S.

TABLE 9.3

THE U.S. TRADE AND SERVICES BALANCE (in millions of dollars)

	Merchandise trade balance	Services trade balance	Balance on goods and services
1970	$ 2,603	309	2,912
1971	− 2,260	1,920	− 340
1972	− 6,416	328	− 6,088
1973	911	2,609	3,520
1974	− 5,367	7,527*	2,160
1975	9,045	13,846	22,891
1976	− 9,320	18,688	9,368
1977	− 31,241	21,409	− 9,832
1978	− 33,759	24,555	− 9,204
1979	− 29,386	34,347	4,961
1980	− 27,354	34,431	7,077

Source: Geoffrey E. Wood and Douglas R. Mudd, "The Recent U.S. Trade Deficit—No Cause for Panic," Federal Reserve Bank of St. Louis *Review*, April 1976, p. 2, and *Survey of Current Business*, March 1981.

products increased. In addition, there was increasing evidence of an improving U.S. economy and an easing of inflationary pressures here. The result, as can be seen in Fig. 9.3, was a surge in the value of the dollar.

A worldwide recovery started to build in 1976, but it soon slowed down everywhere but in the United States. As a result, the U.S. balance of trade shifted between 1975 and 1976 from a surplus to a deficit. Wide differences in inflation rates and rates of economic recovery in other countries, coupled with the large U.S. trade deficit, resulted in a highly unstable foreign exchange market. In spite of widespread intervention the Italian lira, British pound, and Mexican peso deteriorated sharply. Although the dollar weakened against the Japanese yen and some Western European currencies, it strengthened against others, thereby maintaining a fairly even all-around position.

In 1977 the dollar weakened considerably as the merchandise trade deficit soared, owing largely to increased oil imports and growth in the U.S. economy relative to the rest of the world. There was a lack of confidence in the U.S. government's ability to formulate an energy program and manage the economy against impending inflation. In addition,

the continuation of other problems—the decline on Wall Street [stock prices], the higher rate of inflation in the United States than in Germany and Switzerland and the rumors that some oil-producing nations want to quit setting petroleum prices and taking payment in depreciating dollars—also has persuaded foreign investors to get out, or to stay out, of the U.S. currency.

In 1978 the dollar continued to decline in the first quarter as the same factors mentioned for 1977 continued. In February the United States registered its twenty-first consecutive monthly trade deficit and the largest in its history. Lack of confidence in the administration continued; President Carter was first accused of "benign" neglect of the dollar and finally of "malign" neglect. However, the picture began to improve slightly in the second quarter on the basis of a federal plan to sell gold, a cutback in oil imports, and a forecast for slower growth ahead in the U.S. economy.

The declining value of the dollar throughout 1978 led to a narrowing of the trade deficit toward the end of the year as U.S. exports became more competitive in the world market and U.S. imports became higher-priced in terms of U.S. dollars. Also, renewed economic strength of trading partners compared to the United States stimulated U.S. exports. Moreover, agricultural exports expanded, and Alaskan oil substituted for imports from other sources.

Despite the dramatic increase in oil prices in 1979, the U.S. trade deficit declined by over $4 billion. This was the result in part of a marked increase in the exports of U.S. manufactured goods as foreign customers continued to purchase these products because of sustained economic growth

TABLE 9.4 _____

U.S. BALANCE OF PAYMENTS STATISTICS, AGGREGATED PRESENTATION, 1976–1983 (in billions of SDRs)

	Code	1976	1977	1978	1979	1980	1981	1982	1983
A. Current Account, excl. Group F	A . . C A	3.59	−12.39	−12.52	−.72	1.49	5.17	−8.58	−39.21
Merchandise: exports f.o.b.	1 A . A 4	99.40	103.48	113.29	142.74	172.38	201.02	191.12	187.37
Merchandise: imports f.o.b.	1 A . B 4	−107.63	−130.09	−140.55	−164.04	−191.95	−224.89	−224.36	−244.74
Trade balance	1 A . C 4	−8.23	−26.61	−27.25	−21.31	−19.57	−23.87	−33.24	−57.37
Other goods, services, and income: credit	1 S . A 4	49.28	54.37	62.15	79.16	90.84	117.71	125.24	123.50
Reinvested earnings	1 E 1 A 4	*6.67*	*5.49*	*9.02*	*14.68*	*13.06*	*11.39*	*5.72*	*8.49*
Other investment income	1 N . A X	*18.70*	*22.08*	*24.63*	*34.93*	*42.66*	*61.98*	*70.25*	*63.60*
Other	1 S . A Y	*23.90*	*26.80*	*28.49*	*29.55*	*35.12*	*44.34*	*49.27*	*51.40*
Other goods, services, and income: debit	1 S . B 4	−32.85	−35.87	−42.94	−53.85	−63.95	−82.35	−92.56	−96.62
Reinvested earnings	1 E 1 B 4	*−1.44*	*−1.36*	*−2.06*	*−3.07*	*−4.72*	*−3.19*	*−1.18*	*−1.29*
Other investment income	1 N . B X	*−10.10*	*−10.81*	*−15.20*	*−22.40*	*−27.60*	*−41.29*	*−51.96*	*−48.81*
Other	1 S . B Y	*−21.31*	*−23.69*	*−25.67*	*−28.38*	*−31.63*	*−37.88*	*−41.78*	*−46.52*
Total goods, services, and income	1 T . C 4	8.19	−8.11	−8.05	4.00	7.32	11.49	−.55	−30.49
Private unrequited transfers	1 K . C 4	−.79	−.70	−.69	−.70	−.79	−.78	−1.06	−.95
Total, excl. official unrequited transfers	1 U . C 4	7.41	−8.81	−8.74	3.30	6.53	10.70	−1.61	−31.44
Official unrequited transfers	1 H . C 4	−3.82	−3.57	−3.78	−4.02	−5.04	−5.54	−6.97	−7.77
Grants (excluding military)	1 H 1 B K	*−2.72*	*−2.39*	*−2.54*	*−2.74*	*−3.63*	*−3.80*	*−4.92*	*−5.70*
Other	1 H . C Y	*−1.09*	*−1.18*	*−1.24*	*−1.28*	*−1.41*	*−1.74*	*−2.05*	*−2.06*
B. Direct Investment and Other Long-Term Capital, excl. Groups F through H	9 Z 1 X A	−13.10	−10.61	−9.37	−18.30	−6.55	−2.26	−3.54	−6.75
Direct investment	3 . . X 4	−6.57	−7.00	−6.53	−10.35	−1.83	11.74	17.92	5.97
In United States	3 Y . X 4	*3.76*	*3.19*	*6.31*	*9.18*	*12.97*	*19.81*	*13.51*	*10.58*
Abroad	3 L . X 4	*−10.33*	*−10.19*	*−12.84*	*−19.54*	*−14.80*	*−8.08*	*4.40*	*−4.61*
Portfolio investment	6 Z 1 X A	−3.99	−.44	−.29	−1.68	2.20	2.28	−.77	4.00
Other long-term capital									
Resident official sector	4 Z 1 X 4	.22	−2.45	−2.31	−2.57	−4.50	−4.31	−6.25	−4.72
Disbursements on loans extended	4 C 1 Y 4	*−5.05*	*−4.76*	*−5.28*	*−5.48*	*−6.69*	*−6.85*	*−7.81*	*−7.61*
Repayments on loans extended	4 C 1 W 4	*2.21*	*2.29*	*2.32*	*2.92*	*3.11*	*3.37*	*3.45*	*4.28*
Other	4 Z 1 X Y	*3.06*	*.03*	*.64*	*−.01*	*−.92*	*−.83*	*−1.89*	*−1.39*
Deposit money banks	5 Z 1 X 4	−1.86	−.34	−.05	−4.44	−2.42	−11.97	−14.45	−12.00
Other sectors	8 Z 1 X 4	−.90	−.38	−.19	.75	...	...	...	...
Total, Groups A plus B	B 1 . X A	−9.51	−23.00	−21.89	−19.02	−5.06	2.90	−12.12	−45.95

Source: International Monetary Fund, *Balance of Payments Yearbook*, (Washington, D.C.: 1984).

abroad, particularly in Western Europe and Japan. The improvement in the trade deficit also reflected a lagging adjustment to the depreciation of the dollar from mid-1976 through 1979.

The dollar in the 1980s. In 1980 the dollar began a substantial turnaround. The balance of trade improved somewhat over the previous year owing to the increase in agricultural and manufactured exports. Conservation efforts produced a reduction in demand for foreign oil, and oil prices began to drop precipitously in the early 1980s. In addition, higher U.S. interest rates began to be a factor as they attracted marginal capital from abroad. The trend continued in 1981 as a tight monetary policy resulted in higher interest rates and as the current account continued to improve. Table 9.4 provides more extensive balance-of-payments information on the mid- to late 1970s and early 1980s.

As Jim looked at the situation in the 1982–1984 period, he was a little perplexed. He had heard that the merchandise trade deficit was expected to hit $100 billion by the end of 1984 with no end in sight. At

	Code	1976	1977	1978	1979	1980	1981	1982	1983
C. Other Short-Term Capital, excl. Groups									
F through H	9 Z 2 X A	−8.72	−5.16	−14.77	7.18	−21.07	−22.32	−16.28	33.74
Resident official sector	4 Z 2 X 4	−.02	−1.16	.22	−.27	1.35	1.00	6.50	5.23
Deposit money banks	5 Z 2 X 4	−7.12	−3.64	−13.64	−15.96	−21.02	−18.30	−23.87	29.25
Other sectors	8 Z 2 X 4	−1.59	−.36	−1.36	−8.51	−1.41	−5.02	1.09	−.74
D. Net Errors and Omissions	. A . X 4	9.14	−1.73	10.22	19.72	19.17	18.51	30.09	8.47
Total, Groups A through D	D 1 . X A	−9.10	−29.89	−26.44	7.87	−6.96	−.91	1.69	−3.75
E. Counterpart Items	2 . . C 4	−.02	−.12	−.66	−2.22	.80	.63	−.13	−.43
Monetization/demonetization of									
gold	2 A . M 4	—	—	−.40	−2.81	−.14	−.09	−.03	−.26
Allocation/cancellation of SDRs	2 B . M 4	—	—	—	.87	.87	.86	—	—
Valuation changes in reserves	2 . . F 4	−.02	−.12	−.26	−.29	.07	−.13	−.11	−.17
Total, Groups A through F	E 1 . X A	−9.11	−30.01	−27.10	5.65	−6.16	−.27	1.56	−4.18
F. Exceptional Financing	. Y . X B	—	—	1.23	2.85	.90	—	—	—
Security issues in foreign currencies	6 Q 1 X B	—	—	1.23	2.85	.90	—	—	—
Total, Groups A through E	F 1 . X 4	−9.11	−30.01	−25.87	8.50	−5.26	−.27	1.56	−4.18
G. Liabilities Constituting Foreign Authori-									
ties' Reserves	9 W . X 4	11.31	30.21	24.62	−10.70	11.45	4.20	2.84	4.86
Total, Groups A through G	G 1 . X 4	2.20	.20	−1.25	−2.21	6.19	3.93	4.39	.68
H. Total Change in Reserves	2 . . R 4	−2.20	−.20	1.25	2.21	−6.19	−3.93	−4.39	−.68
Monetary gold	2 A . R 4	—	−.10	.35	2.76	.13	.10	.03	.25
SDRs	2 B . R 4	−.07	−.10	.97	−.87	.02	−1.47	−1.24	−.04
Reserve position in the Fund	2 C . R 4	−1.93	−.26	3.27	−.15	−1.29	−2.11	−2.32	−4.14
Foreign exchange assets	2 D . R 4	−.21	.26	−3.34	.47	−5.06	−.45	−.86	3.25
Other claims	2 E . R 4	—	—	—	—	—	—	—	—
Use of Fund credit	2 M . R 4	—	—	—	—	—	—	—	—
Conversion rates: U.S. dollars per									
SDR	. . S B Z	1.1545	1.1675	1.2520	1.2920	1.3015	1.1792	1.1040	1.0690

the same time he could see from Fig. 9.3 that the dollar was continuing to rise. In a *Wall Street Journal* story he read the following:

> *It still doesn't make very much sense, but the dollar keeps setting new records.*
> *The greenback should be showing some signs of fatigue. In fact, sages have predicted all year that the rise of the dollar against other major currencies would finally end in the face of a booming U.S. trade deficit, lower domestic interest rates and other major factors.*
> *But no. Instead of weakening, the dollar is showing almost unprecedented strength.*

In reading over some material prepared by the staff economists of his bank in New York City, Jim noticed that several factors were being mentioned as sources of strength: relatively low inflation in the United States, relatively high nominal interest rates, the perception of the United States as a safe haven from the crises in the world, a strong U.S. stock market, and demand for dollars by multinational corporations.

The strong dollar had good points and bad points both domestically and abroad. It was hurting U.S. exporters but helping U.S. importers. Foreign exporters liked the strong dollar because it gave them cheaper access to the U.S. market and helped them to compete with U.S. companies abroad. However, the strong dollar was sapping many of the industrial economies. The huge federal budget deficit in the United States was helping to keep interest rates high, a strong incentive for European investors to invest in the United States rather than Europe. These capital inflows helped offset the trade deficit outflows so that the dollar stayed strong. However, these high interest rates kept the European countries from lowering their interest rates to stimulate their weak economies. They feared that lower interest rates would force even more of their capital to the United States and thus strip their countries of capital needed for investment.

The developing countries were having a hard time because their debt burdens were denominated largely in dollars. High interest rates kept their debt servicing load high, and the strengthening dollar meant that they had to come up with more of their own currencies to purchase the dollars to pay off the debt. Both industrial and developing countries were finding that the strong dollar was making it more expensive for them to import raw materials, especially oil, since raw materials are generally priced in dollar terms. This phenomenon leads to more inflationary pressures.

Many U.S. companies were also having problems. As was pointed out in one *Business Week* article,

> *Caterpillar is for the first time selling products made by nonaffiliated foreign suppliers through its vast worldwide dealer network. GM is increasing its purchases of foreign-made cars and components. And Ingersoll-Rand has embarked on a program to shift manufacturing operations overseas. . . . Beckman Instruments Inc., a medical and laboratory-equipment subsidiary of SmithKline Beckman Corp., recently moved the production of two product lines sold overseas from the U.S. to plants in Europe. . . . Some of the parts Beckman buys from suppliers in Europe cost 33% less than what U.S. suppliers charge for the same parts. . . . It is a permanent shift.*

QUESTIONS

1. What are the major factors that have influenced the value of the dollar over the past decade?

2. What are the key factors that you would monitor if you were Jim and wanted to have a pretty good idea of the future direction of the dollar? Be sure to explain how those particular factors might influence the dollar.

3. What do you think is going to happen to the dollar, and why?

4. Assume that Jim decides to continue producing and selling as he currently is, and assume that the dollar is expected to remain firm. What do you think could happen to Jim's business?

5. Assuming a strong dollar in the near future, what strategic decisions do you think Jim should make about his business? Be sure to justify your recommendations.

NOTES

1. Eduardo Gallardo, "The 'Tiny' Bolivian Peso Can't Keep Pace with Galloping Price Increase," *Deseret News,* December 2, 1984, p. 6M; "Nicaragua, Bolivia Devalue Currencies to Avert Crises," *Arizona Republic,* February 10, 1985, p. A10; Sonia L. Nazario, "When Inflation Rate Is 116,000%, Prices Change by the Hour," *The Wall Street Journal,* February 7, 1985.

2. A more detailed discussion of the determination of the following formula can be found in Alan C. Shapiro, *Multinational Financial Management* (Boston: Allyn and Bacon, Inc., 1982), pp. 39–41.

3. David K. Eiteman and Arthur I. Stonehill, *Multinational Business Finance,* 3rd ed. (Reading, Mass.: Addison-Wesley Publishing Co., 1982), pp. 135–139.

4. Michael Jilling and William R. Folks, Jr., "A Survey of Corporate Exchange Rate Forecasting Practices," Working Paper No. 3, Center for International Business Studies, (Columbia: University of South Carolina, 1977).

5. International Monetary Fund, *Balance of Payments Statistics* (Washington, D.C.: IMF, 1984), p. xiv.

6. *Foreign Exchange Review* Vol. 8, No. 48 (New York: Manufacturers Hanover Trust, November 1984), p. 3.

7. "The Institutional Evolution of the IMF," *Finance & Development,* September 1984, p. 8.

8. Federal Reserve Bank of Chicago, *International Letter* No. 536, October 5, 1984, p. 3.

9. International Monetary Fund, *Annual Report on Exchange Arrangements & Exchange Restrictions—1984* (Washington, D.C.: IMF, 1984), p. 7.

10. *Ibid.,* p. 455.

11. International Monetary Fund, *Annual Report on Exchange Arrangements & Exchange Restrictions—1983* (Washington, D.C.: IMF, 1983), p. 111.

12. Julian Walmsley, *The Foreign Exchange Handbook* (New York: John Wiley & Sons, 1983), pp. 84–90.

13. Dallas A. Balten and Mack Ott, "Five Common Myths about Floating Exchange Rates," *Review* (St. Louis: Federal Reserve Bank of St. Louis, November 1983), pp. 7–14.

14. *Ibid.,* p. 7.

15. *Foreign Exchange Review* Vol 8, No. 43 (New York: Manufacturers Hanover Trust, October 1984), p. 3. Used by permission.

16. Data for the case were taken from Hans H. Helbling, "International Trade and Finance under the Influence of Oil—1974 and Early 1975," Federal Reserve Bank of St. Louis *Review,* May 1975, p. 13; *Wall Street Journal,* February 27, 1978, p. 1; *Wall Street Journal,* April 21, 1978, p. 1; *Federal Reserve Bulletin,* April 1981, p. 270; various issues of *Survey of Current Business;* "Strength of the Dollar Is Explained by a Mix of Economics, Psychology," *Wall Street Journal,* December 14, 1983, p. 33; "The Superdollar," *Business Week,* October 8, 1984, pp. 164–174.

10

Financial Markets for International Operations

- To show different ways in which firms can acquire outside funds for normal operations and expansion.
- To examine local debt markets, the Eurocurrency and Eurobond markets, and equity markets worldwide.
- To discuss the functions of the international banking community in facilitating the flow of funds.
- To highlight the role of development banks and similar institutions.

THE BANKS VERSUS IRAN: WHO WON?[1]

On Inauguration Day, 1981, as President Jimmy Carter turned the mantle of leadership over to Ronald Reagan, fifty-two American hostages were released from 444 days of Iranian captivity that had held the attention of the entire world. Although most of the drama concerned the individual hostages, their escape attempts, the rescue attempts, and the hostages' final release, the financial aspect of the situation had also provoked a crisis.

In early 1979, not long after the Ayatollah Ruhollah Khomeini ascended to power following the overthrow of Shah Mohammed Reza Pahlavi, David Rockefeller, chairman of Chase Manhattan Bank, expressed confidence that Iran would remain willing to pay its debts to Western banks. Rockefeller needed to be optimistic because, in 1979, Chase was the U.S. bank with the highest exposure in Iran—somewhere in the neighborhood of $200 million. In addition, Chase had lent or been agent for more than $2 billion in international loans. This was all consistent with Rockefeller's objective since becoming chairman in 1969 of dramatically increasing international operations. Chase had started too late to catch up to Citicorp's geographic spread through branches, so Rockefeller decided to make Chase a worldwide "bankers' bank"—a correspondent charging fees for handling transactions of other institutions. The developing countries in particular were picked because of their need for recycled petrodollars, the high profitability attached to these loans, and the perceived stability and low risk of lending to sovereign governments.

However, on November 14, 1979, ten days after the American hostages were taken, the banking world was turned upside down. At 5:00 A.M., U.S. Treasury Secretary G. William Miller was awakened and informed that Iranian Prime Minister Abolhassan Bani-Sadr was threatening to withdraw all of Iran's deposits from U.S. banks and place them in banking institutions of other countries. Fearful that his move would adversely affect the U.S. dollar and U.S. banks, President Carter ordered that all Iranian assets held at home or abroad by the U.S. government or private banks and corporations be immediately frozen. The total came to nearly $12 billion, consisting of $2.4 billion controlled by the U.S. government, $5.5 billion controlled by the overseas branches of U.S. banks, and $4 billion held in the United States by twelve U.S. banks.

Within hours of the announcement, Citibank seized all Iranian assets in its possession to cover its exposure. Some of these loans were syndications with other banks, and Citibank acted without consulting other syndicate members, a step that is normally taken before any syndicated loan is declared to be in default. Other syndicate members, including regional U.S. and European banks, were livid, since Citibank essentially held all of the assets.

The day after the freeze, the Iranian central bank notified Chase Manhattan that it was to draw on its accounts with several U.S. banks in London to pay interest on a loan syndicated by Chase. However, Chase stated that it could not do so owing to the freeze and that the loan was therefore in default, since the interest payment was not made. It proceeded to attach all the Iranian assets that it could. Chase polled other members of the syndicate and received their approval to declare default. Unfortunately, all U.S. banks in the syndicate (a majority) voted yes, and all non-U.S. banks voted no. This infuriated the European bankers. During the next year a pattern was set in which everything Iranian outside of Iran was taken over by banks, corporations, and individuals as protection for claims against Iran.

Most banks were very upset at the freeze because they felt that existing syndicated loan covenants adequately protected them against any potential defaults. Furthermore, Iran was up to date on its payments and appeared to have no intention of defaulting. Had Iran attempted to move any money, the banks themselves could simply have refused the transfer without prepayment of all loans. The freeze and subsequent actions by banks simply reduced flexibility and increased exposure of banks with loans outstanding but no Iranian deposits.

Tense negotiations in early 1981 led to the release of the hostages, leaving the bankers right in the middle. After a year of excessive demands, the Iranians began proposing actions that made sense. The most difficult point involved the interest that the banks would have had to pay on the Iranian funds that had been blocked for over a year. Once that was decided, the rest was easy.

The final agreement involved transferring the $12 billion to Iran in stages. The $4 billion held in the United States was gradually transferred to the Bank of England over six months and placed in a security account to satisfy over 300 legal disputes with Iran to be settled by arbitration. The remaining $7.9 billion was transferred to the Federal Reserve Bank of New York, which transferred the funds to an account with the Bank of England. The Bank of England then transferred the money to an escrow account of the Algerian Central Bank. When the balance reached $7.9 billion, the Iranians began the release of the hostages. As soon as the hostages were safe, the money was transferred to an Iranian account. The $7.9 billion was then divided as follows: $3.7 billion to U.S. and foreign banks to cover past loans, $1.4 billion to an escrow account to be used to pay off future loans, and $2.86 billion to Iran. Believe it or not, 444 days of frustration were concluded in less than ten minutes of bank transfers.

Introduction

This case illustrates a variety of interesting points such as the different strategies that banks can adopt as they pursue the international market, the role of syndication in providing loans for countries, the problems that occur when a company tries to impose the laws of its nation on companies from other nations, and the flexibility of the international financial system in moving large amounts of money. Not even addressed in the case are the problems faced by the thousands of foreign companies operating in Iran during this period that found their operations confiscated without compensation. Some of those companies may have used Iranian capital to finance growth, but many brought their funds in from the outside and found that they had to submit to arbitration to gain some form of compensation. That process is still going on.

LOCAL DEBT MARKETS

- Firms have learned to be creative in gaining access to local credit markets

As corporations expand into foreign frontiers, they need to adjust to local debt markets, both short term and long term. Since each country has different business customs, firms need to abandon strict operating procedures developed in other countries. When Caterpillar Tractor went to Brazil for the first time, it was used to operating through one bank for all of its transactions. It found out very quickly, however, that the tight credit market in Brazil required different operating procedures. So it opened accounts in several banks, which allowed it to tap several different credit sources. Caterpillar liked this so much that it exported its Brazilian policy back to Peoria.

- An IOU that used to be backed up by standby letters of credit

In the United States it is customary for U.S. companies needing cash to sell **commercial paper,** a form of IOU that used to be backed up by standby lines of bank credit. When U.S. subsidiaries of foreign corporations began to issue such paper, the market required that the paper be guaranteed by the parent company. Some giants, like Shell Oil, did not really need to rely on their parent, but most other companies did. However, Gold Fields American Corp. (GFAC), the U.S. subsidiary of the British firm of Consolidated Gold Fields, Ltd., took the first step in changing that custom. Although the parent company agreed to purchase any paper that was not paid by GFAC at its maturity date, this agreement was not considered a formal guarantee. GFAC and its parent also agreed to maintain existing lines of credit equal to the value of its commercial paper without the expense of setting up a separate line of credit specifically for the paper.[2] The U.S. market is the largest and one of the most creative markets in the world for companies to raise short-term funds, as the above example illustrates.

- Local debt markets are influenced by political and economic pressures

Even though domestic and international markets are becoming more and more like a single market—at least in the case of the industrial countries—local markets still depend a great deal on internal political and economic pressures. In Latin America, for example, high inflation has created problems for a number of firms. In some countries, efforts to control inflation have led to a curtailment in the money supply and thus the availability of funds.

- Local credit markets are affected by influences external to the local country
- Eurodollar—a U.S. dollar held outside of the United States; this term is defined and discussed in more detail in the next section

Sometimes events outside of the control of a country can affect local credit markets. This occurred in the 1960s in the United States when funds formally held as **Eurodollars** were transferred to the United States, which effectively softened a credit crunch instituted by the Federal Reserve to slow down the economy. Good corporate customers could still get their cash. Spain's preparations for entry into the European Community have revolutionized the local credit market. Before 1981 the only source of medium-term financing was the Eurodollar market, which carried with it obvious exchange risks. However, several changes in Spanish banking laws in 1981 opened up the local peseta market. The major source of influence has been the international banks, long accustomed to creative financing. Now multinationals can borrow locally without having to worry about exchange risk.[3]

- Ways that foreign companies are treated differently from domestic ones

Sometimes, foreign companies are treated differently from domestic companies when it comes to access to the credit markets. In Brazil, for example, subsidiaries of foreign-owned companies are excluded from local credit markets in order to help attract hard currency borrowings.[4]

- Factors to consider in using local credit markets

From these illustrations it is obvious that multinationals need to weigh several factors as they look at the local credit markets: (1) availability of funds, (2) cost due to interest rates, and (3) local customs and institutions. Because situations and events are dynamic, corporate treasurers must be able to react quickly.

EUROCURRENCIES

- A currency (primarily U.S. dollars) banked outside of its country of origin

The Eurocurrency market is an important source of debt available to the MNE. A **Eurocurrency** is any currency that is banked outside of its country of origin. Eurodollars, which constitute a fairly consistent 75–80 percent of the market, are dollars banked outside of the United States. Similar markets exist for Euro-German marks (about 12 percent of the market), Euro-Swiss francs (about 5 percent), and other currencies, such as pounds sterling, French francs, and Japanese yen. The Eurocurrency market is worldwide. Large transactions take place in Asia (Hong Kong and Singapore), the Caribbean (the Bahamas and the Cayman Islands), and Canada, as well as London and other European centers.

- Major sources of supply of and demand for Eurodollars

The major sources of Eurodollars are (1) foreign governments or businesspeople who want to hold dollars outside of the United States; (2) multinational corporations with cash in excess of current needs; (3) European banks with foreign currency in excess of current needs; and (4) the large reserves of oil-producing countries. The demand for Eurocurrencies comes from individuals, firms, and governments that require funds for operating capital, investment, and debt servicing.

Origin of Eurodollars

In the 1920s, European banks accepted deposits in the currencies of other countries when conditions warranted it. At that time, the pound sterling was the primary currency in the world, and financial interests borrowed and loaned sterling because of the favorable interest margins that accompanied transactions in pounds. In the 1950s, however, the U.S. dollar emerged as the leading international reserve currency, replacing the pound as a primary instrument of exchange in the money markets of the world.

The original impetus for the development of the Eurodollar market in the 1950s is believed to have come from the correspondents of Soviet banks in Europe—Moscow Narodny Bank in London and Banque Commercial pour L'Europe du Nord in Paris—rather than U.S. banks. After World War II the Soviet Union accumulated large amounts of U.S. dollars, which it needed to use in international transactions. However, it was fearful that the U.S. government would seize or freeze those assets during the Cold War period, so it transferred its dollar accounts outside of the United States.

By utilizing these and other dollar balances, the correspondent banks found a number of outlets. The dealings often involved offering these funds to other foreign banks in need of dollar financing at rates that were somewhat lower than would be charged by U.S. banks. Within a fairly short period, other holders of dollar balances took advantage of the growing demand for this relatively inexpensive dollar accommodation. Soon an active market for dollar deposits developed, notably in the Paris and London money markets.

By the middle of 1958 the market was well established, but it did not assume really significant proportions until the end of that year. At that time, interest rates paid abroad for dollar deposits rose well above the maximum interest rates that banks in the United States were permitted to pay for current deposits under Regulation Q of the Board of Governors of the Federal Reserve System. The introduction of nonresident convertibility throughout Western Europe at the end of 1958, as well as the further relaxation of exchange controls in some countries, also contributed to the growth of the Eurodollar market.

• Major sources of expansion of Eurodollar system

The expansion of the Eurodollar system in the 1960s appeared to hinge on several factors:

1. the tendency of central banks to place some of their excess dollar reserves in the Eurodollar market rather than to invest these funds in the U.S. money market;

2. the growth of the Eurobond market (to be discussed later), in which the proceeds of the bond issue were often recirculated in the Eurodollar market;

3. the growth of international trade, which caused an increase in the demand for Eurodollars to finance that trade and an increase in supply as the profitable corporations left more of their dollars in European banks;

4. the imposition of the Interest Equalization Tax in 1963 (a tax imposed on interest flowing to foreign investors);

5. restrictions on the outflow of funds from U.S. banks and corporations; and

6. the U.S. principle of deferral of taxation on income from foreign sources until dividends were repatriated to the United States (to be discussed in greater detail in Chapter 20).[5]

The growth of the market in the 1970s was fueled by the increase in world trade, the absence of restrictions on banks dealing in Eurocurrencies, and the tremendous balance-of-payments surpluses in the OPEC countries that resulted from the jump in the price of oil. The market survived a series of shocks from economic near-chaos and exchange rate instability and emerged as a strong and healthy market. However, the problems of developing country debt in the late 1970s and early 1980s again put a damper on the market.

Eurodollar Expansion

• Fractional reserve concept—very little of the deposit is held back as a precaution; most of it is loaned and reloaned to users

The key to Eurodollar expansion is the fractional reserve concept. The total size of the Eurodollar market is much greater than the actual cash deposited. Once a dollar deposit is made in a London bank, the bank may use that asset as a basis for making a dollar-denominated loan to someone else. The fraction of the original deposit not loaned out is called the fractional reserve. Since there are no reserve requirements on Eurodollar deposits, it is up to the individual bank to determine how much protection it requires in the form of reserves. The expansion occurs when the initial loan is spent, deposited in another bank, or used as a basis for another loan.

Market Size

The size of the market is difficult to determine and depends on whether one is looking at the gross or net size (the net size eliminates transfers between banks). Gross liabilities are usually just over twice as great as the net size of the market. In 1971 the total gross Eurocurrency market size was about $150 billion. As can be seen from Table 10.1, the market grew to $2.257 trillion in early 1984. It is also interesting to note from Table 10.1 that the dollar portion of the Eurocurrency market has remained in the 75–80 percent range over the past decade.

TABLE 10.1

EUROCURRENCY MARKET SIZE Based on foreign liabilities of banks in major European countries, the Bahamas, Bahrain, Cayman Islands, Panama, Canada, Japan, Hong Kong, and Singapore (in billions of dollars, rounded to the nearest $5 billion, at the end of the period).

										December
	1975	1976	1977	1978	1979	1980	1981	1982	1983	1984
Gross liabilities to:										
Nonbanks	90	109	135	174	245	327	428	474	527	500
Central banks	65	80	100	115	145	150	132	90	89	96
Other banks	330	406	505	660	843	1047	1301	1493	1537	1787
Total	485	595	740	949	1233	1524	1861	2057	2153	2383
Eurodollars as percent of total gross liabilities in all Eurocurrencies	78	80	76	74	72	75	78	79	80	82

Source: The Federal Reserve Bank of St. Louis, *International Economic Conditions,* October 1984, p. 8 and August 1985, p. 8.

● Characteristics: large, dollar-based, big corporate transactions, unregulated, short-term, time rather than demand deposits

The Eurocurrency market has several interesting characteristics. First, it is a wholesale rather than retail market, meaning that transactions involve governments, banks, and large corporations. As such, the transactions tend to be very large. Public borrowers such as governments, central banks, and public sector corporations tend to borrow the lion's share of the funds. Second, the market is virtually unregulated. A push began in the late 1970s and early 1980s to control the market, but experts could not agree on the potential dangers of the market or probable cures. Most criticisms leveled at the market have been that it is inflationary, it contributes to exchange rate instability, and it is inherently risky because it is unregulated. None of these criticisms has been borne out by empirical evidence. Some central banks, such as those in the United States and West Germany, would love to institute mandatory reserve requirements, but this sentiment is not held elsewhere.

A third characteristic is that deposits are primarily short term. About one third of the deposits by nonbanking institutions mature in eight days or less, and 90 percent have maturities of less than six months.[6] This leads to concern about risk, since most Eurocurrency loans are for longer periods of time. Fourth, the Eurocurrency market exists for savings and time deposits rather than demand deposits. That is, institutions that create Eurodollar deposits do not draw down those deposits for expenditures. Instead, they usually convert their Eurocurrency deposits into a particular national currency in order to buy goods and services. Fifth, the Eurocurrency market is primarily a Eurodollar market. As shown in Table 10.1, the percentage of the market represented by dollars began to decline somewhat in the late 1970s, but the dollar started to rebound in late 1980 and early 1981 owing to the strength of the U.S. dollar and the steady increase in OPEC reserves, which are dollar-dominated. The latter factor became less important after 1981, but the strong dollar was still the major factor.

The Eurocurrency market—excluding the Eurobond market, which will be discussed later in this chapter—has short- and medium-term characteristics. Short-term Eurocurrency borrowing has a maturity of less than one year. Anything over one year is considered a **Eurocredit.** These Eurocredits may be loans, lines of credit, or other forms of medium- and long-term credits, including **syndication** (several banks pooling resources to extend credit to a borrower).

- Eurocredit—loans that mature in one to five years
- Syndication—several banks pool resources to make a large loan in order to spread the risk

Traditionally, loans are made at a certain percentage above the London Inter-Bank Offered Rate (**LIBOR**), which is the interest rate banks charge one another on loans of Eurocurrencies. The interest rate above LIBOR depends on the creditworthiness of the customer and must be large enough to cover expenses and build reserves against possible losses. In the early 1980s, many banks began using the U.S. prime rate as an alternative to LIBOR for quoting loans. Because the U.S. prime rate was higher than LIBOR during the high-interest-rate period of 1980–1981, banks were able to increase their yields by lending at prime plus. Many borrowers, especially sovereign governments, were able to pay prime plus ⅜ percent instead of LIBOR plus 3⅓ percent and fool politicians into thinking that they were getting a better deal even though they may have been paying as much as 2 percent more for the loan.[7]

- LIBOR—the interest rates that banks charge each other
- LIBOR and the U.S. prime rate (the rate U.S. banks charge their best customers) are both used internationally as a basis for computing the cost of loans

It is important to note that LIBOR and the prime rate are simply reference rates on which loans are quoted. The prime rate is traditionally higher than LIBOR because the prime is comprised of the marginal cost of funding plus a small profit margin. LIBOR represents only the marginal cost of funding. The prime rate is also more sensitive to interest rates than is LIBOR, since LIBOR is used for very specific, large international transactions, whereas prime relates to a variety of transactions in the U.S. market. Finally, LIBOR is a market-determined price, whereas the prime tends to be managed a little more.[8]

INTERNATIONAL BONDS

Many countries have very active bond markets that are available to domestic and foreign investors. One good example is the United States. In the 1980s, given the high interest rates, relative political and economic stability, and desire of the government to finance its high budget deficits with borrowing, the U.S. market has been a ready market for foreign investors. One of the major factors that could influence foreign investors to take more U.S.-issued bonds is the repeal of the withholding tax on interest that took effect in 1984. The 30 percent withholding tax was reduced to zero, making the yield higher on U.S. bonds issued in the United States. Many experts feel that the elimination of the withholding tax could take business away from some of the bond markets in the Caribbean that have existed partly because of the lower yield in the United States.[9]

- Foreign bonds—sold outside of country of borrower but in the currency of country of issue
- Eurobonds—sold in a currency other than that of the country of issue

The international bond market can be divided into foreign bonds and Eurobonds. **Foreign bonds** are sold outside of the country of the borrower but are denominated in the currency of the country of issue. For example, a French corporation floating a bond issue in Swiss francs in Switzerland would be floating a foreign bond. A **Eurobond** is one sold in a currency other than that of the country of issue. If the French firm had floated a bond issue in West German marks in Switzerland, the issue would have been a Eurobond. Normally, however, Eurobonds are those sold in two or more markets simultaneously, usually through an international syndicate of banks.

In 1981, Dome Petroleum, Ltd. of Canada floated a $50 million bond in Swiss francs (a foreign bond) to liquidate some of its existing debt. Its rationale was that the interest rate differential between Swiss francs and Canadian dollars was so huge that the franc would have to more than double in value over the U.S. dollar and triple in value over the Canadian dollar for Dome to lose money.[10]

The Eurobond Market

- Sold in different centers simultaneously

Although the Eurobond market is centered in Europe, it has no national boundaries. Unlike most conventional bond issues, Eurobonds are sold simultaneously in several financial centers through multinational underwriting syndicates and are purchased by an international investing public that extends far beyond the confines of the countries of issue. The market has been used by a multitude of government and private borrowers from a wide range of countries.

- Different currency options sometimes available

Occasionally, Eurobond issues may provide currency options, which enable the creditor to demand repayment in one of several currencies and thereby reduce the exchange risk inherent in single-currency foreign bonds. More frequently, however, interest and principal on the bonds are payable in U.S. dollars. Over the last several years the Eurobond market has become a market for dollar-denominated obligations of foreign as well as U.S. borrowers that are purchased by non-U.S. investors.

- A way to provide access to large amounts of funds without the restrictions of local national markets

Although the need to create a more unified European capital market was recognized for many years, it became a pressing issue after mid-1963, when borrowing costs in the New York market increased substantially for European borrowers as a result of the U.S. Interest Equalization Tax. Historically, in the European capital market, individual domestic issues have been confronted with the limited capacity of the European markets to absorb large debt issues at frequent intervals. Moreover, access to these markets by foreign borrowers has long been subject to stringent restrictions. Therefore to create adequate facilities for borrowers to raise funds in Europe, a way had to be found permitting borrowers to tap several European financial centers simultaneously while avoiding restrictions on borrowing in local currencies.

- **Convertible bonds became popular**

The switch in European borrowing from New York to the London market and other European financial centers was followed toward the end of 1965 by the entry of a significant number of U.S. corporations or their foreign affiliates as large borrowers in the Eurobond market. In an effort to broaden investor appeal, U.S. and other corporate borrowers have increasingly shifted from straight debt issues to bonds that are convertible into common stock. The option of conversion rests with the holder of the convertible issue. For the nonresident investor, one of the main attractions of a convertible issue is that it usually offers a larger current return than does the dividend of the underlying stock.

- **Sources of demand for Eurobonds**
- **Primarily a dollar market**

Originally, U.S. corporations were the most important borrowers in the Eurobond market. Now, however, official borrowers such as governments and multilateral institutions are the most important borrowers, followed by foreign corporations and U.S. corporations. Although the U.S. dollar is the single most important currency of issue (75 percent of all issues in the first quarter of 1984), the West German mark, British pound, French franc, and Dutch guilder are also important.

The Eurobond market has introduced a new element of viability into the structure of the European capital market. As was noted previously, the effectiveness of Europe's national capital markets has been reduced by numerous regulations, which impede the flow of capital both within Europe and between Europe and the rest of the world. As a result of the emergence of the Eurobond market, there has been a somewhat greater degree of unity within these individual markets. Inasmuch as Eurobond issues are a significant alternative to equity investments for many European investors, the Eurobond market tends to bring long-term interest rates in Europe's national capital markets closer together than would otherwise be the case. Thus the Eurobond market is an important step toward a fully integrated European capital market.

- **Benefits: unregulated, untaxed, more flexible**

The major benefits of the Eurobond market are the fact that it is relatively unregulated, its income is essentially untaxed, and there appears to be greater flexibility in making issues than is the case in purely national markets.

- **Problems: easy to lose due to bearer form, tax evasion, lack of uniform information on issues**

However, the market also has some problems. Eurobonds are issued in bearer form, which means that if the bonds are lost or stolen, the person that ends up with the bond is essentially the owner. The use of the bearer form signifies confidentiality, which aids in tax evasion. Since there are no specific disclosure requirements for those wishing to issue bonds, it is often difficult for the potential investor to have enough information to make a good investment decision. However, this does not hamper the large companies that issue bonds. A major problem alluded to above is the elimination of the withholding tax in the United States, which could cause a large portion of the Eurobond market to shift to the United States. However, there is no guarantee of that happening.[11]

● Examples of usage by U.S. companies

A number of U.S. companies have gained access to the Eurobond market in recent years rather than use the U.S. bond market. In 1983, Texaco purchased Getty Oil and had to borrow a tremendous amount of short-term money to do that. In an effort to lighten its $10.5 billion bank debt, it issued an $800 million convertible Eurobond offering. It was so successful that it increased the offering to $1 billion and followed that up with another offering of $500 million. It was able to get a lower price and higher offering than if it had stayed in the United States. Digital Equipment, Texas Instruments, International Paper, and Illinois Power saved as much as 0.45 percentage points by issuing Eurobonds instead of U.S. bonds in 1984. ITT Financial saved about the same amount by issuing in the Eurobond market instead of in the United States.[12]

International Finance Subsidiaries

● IFS—companies set up outside of the United States to raise capital for the parent company

Before the repeal of the withholding tax on interest in 1984 a U.S. corporation that issued a bond in the United States was required to withhold 30 percent from the interest payment to the bondholder for U.S. taxes. Companies sought ways to avoid this tax, usually by setting up a finance subsidiary in a country that does not tax bond interest payments. The international finance subsidiaries (IFSs) were used extensively in the 1960s to circumvent balance-of-payments controls, since parent companies were restricted in their financing of subsidiaries. In the 1970s the major concern shifted to tax reduction to the bondholders:

● Reasons for setting up IFSs.

Typically, the terms of bonds issued by an IFS to foreign bondholders are as follows: Interest and principal are denominated in U.S. dollars. Payment of the interest and the principal are fully guaranteed by the U.S. parent, and the IFS and the U.S. parent indemnify the bondholder against U.S. withholding tax liability. Thus, the coupon amount is paid without reduction for U.S. withholding tax. The bonds normally bear a fixed rate of interest although some issues use a floating rate set at a fixed margin above the London Inter-Bank Offered Rate (LIBOR). The bonds are issued in bearer form, and the person presenting the interest coupon or presenting the bond at maturity receives payment. Some bond issues have been convertible at the option of the holder into stock of the parent corporation. The bonds are callable at any time should U.S. withholding tax be assessed by the Internal Revenue Service, and are often callable after five years should interest rates decline. The bonds are registered for trading on a European securities exchange, usually Luxembourg or London. [13]

● Popular locations for IFSs

IFSs can be set up in a number of countries; five popular ones are the Netherlands Antilles, the Netherlands, Luxembourg, the British Virgin

Islands, and Bermuda. In the Netherlands Antilles, for example, a nonresident would not be subject to Netherlands Antilles withholding taxes on payments of interest on bonds issued by the IFS. This gives the holder of the bond a higher effective yield than on a similar instrument issued in the United States. It is unclear whether the IFSs will survive the repeal of the withholding tax. However, many people feel that the Eurobond market has reached a stage of maturity at which it will remain viable whatever happens in New York. Also, the Eurobond markets offer a greater degree of anonymity than does the United States.

OFFSHORE FINANCIAL CENTERS

- Centers that provide funds other than those of their own country; markets not regulated in the same ways as domestic markets

Up to this point, allusions have been made to the major financial centers of the world. The countries with large markets, such as the major OECD countries, have large financial markets. However, this does not mean that they have large international financial markets. In addition, it does not mean that they have large offshore centers.

Offshore financial centers have one or more of the following characteristics:

1. There is a large foreign currency (Eurocurrency) market for deposits and loans (e.g., London).
2. The market is a large net supplier of funds to the world financial markets (e.g., Switzerland).
3. The market is an intermediary or pass-through for international loan funds (e.g., Bahamas, Cayman Islands).[14]

- Characteristics of offshore centers

In addition, a good offshore center must provide the following to be especially attractive to the banks:

(1) economic and political stability; (2) an efficient and experienced financial community; (3) good communications and supportive services; and (4) an official regulatory climate favorable to the financial industry, in the sense that it protects investors without unduly restricting financial institutions. [15]

Certainly the absence of official regulation and taxation are critical for the fourth point.

- Most important offshore centers

These centers can be considered as operational (functional) centers or booking (accounting) centers. London is an example of the former, and the Cayman Islands is an example of the latter. Although there are many offshore financial centers, the seven most important ones are London, the Caribbean (servicing especially Canadian and U.S. banks), Switzerland, Singapore, Hong Kong, Bahrain (for the Middle East), and New York. The New York market has been hampered until recently by restrictive regulations, but it is now moving to the front of the pack.

London is a crucial market because it offers a variety of services and has a large domestic as well as offshore market. The Caribbean centers (primarily the Bahamas, Cayman Islands, and Netherlands Antilles) are essentially offshore locations for the New York banks. Switzerland has been a primary source of funds for decades, offering stability, integrity, secrecy, and low costs. Singapore has been the center for the Asia dollar market since 1968, owing to a variety of government regulations that have facilitated the flow of funds, its strategic location geographically in terms of its time zone between Europe and the Far East, and its strong telecommunications links with the rest of the world. Hong Kong is critical because of its unique status with the United Kingdom and its geographic proximity to China and the rest of the Pacific Rim. The importance of Bahrain is obvious, given the tremendous volume of petrodollars that have been floating around the world since the explosion in oil prices in 1973 and subsequent years.

INTERNATIONAL BANKING

An important and essential aspect of the growth of international business has been the growth of international banking services. Firms would have been unable to expand as they have without the timely flow of money and other resources provided by the international banks. Not only do banks facilitate the flow of existing corporate resources, they also provide debt financing from local and international markets. A Canadian bank, for example, could loan funds to a Canadian corporation that is attempting to acquire a U.S. business, or it could provide that financing through the Eurodollar market.

Leading World Commercial Banks

U.S. MNEs dominate the list of the largest in the world, but U.S. banks do not. Only two of the top ten banks in the world are U.S.-based. Table 10.2 identifies the top ten and the countries where they are headquartered. It also shows the progress of 1984's top ten over the preceding five years.

• Rise of Japanese banks, fall of European banks

It is interesting to note the rise of the Japanese banks, the fall of the European banks, and the steadiness of the only two U.S. banks in the top ten. That phenomenon is due primarily to the strength of the U.S. dollar over the past few years, which has caused the European banks to fall and the Japanese to rise. The yen has remained fairly firm against the dollar, in fact rising against the dollar over the 1982–1983 period. Four banks that were in 1980's top ten dropped out by 1983: Credit Lyonnais (France), Société Generale (France), Deutsche Bank (West Germany), and National Westminster (England). Four banks that were not in the top ten in 1980 entered the picture by 1983: Fuji Bank, Sumitomo Bank, Mitsubishi Bank, and Sanwa Bank—all of Japan.

TABLE 10.2

TOP TEN BANKS IN THE WORLD BY ASSETS IN 1984

Bank	1979	1980	1981	1982	1983	1984
Citicorp (U.S.)	3	1	2	1	1	1
Dai-Ichi Kangyo Bank (Japan)	10	10	8	8	3	2
Fuji Bank (Japan)	14	12	13	10	4	3
BankAmerica Corp (U.S.)	2	2	1	2	2	4
Sumitomo Bank (Japan)	16	13	11	13	5	5
Mitsubishi Bank (Japan)	17	16	14	12	7	6
Sanwa Bank (Japan)	18	14	17	16	9	7
Banque Nationale de Paris (France)	4	4	3	3	6	8
Crédit Agricole (France)	1	3	4	4	10	9
Crédit Lyonnais (France)	6	5	5	5	11	10
Barclays Group (England)	9	7	6	6	8	12

Source: *The Banker*, June 1984, p. 98 and August 1985, p. 8.

Table 10.3 shows the country representation of most of the top 500 banks in the world. Even though the U.S. banks garnered 119 of the spots, they placed only three in the top twenty and eight in the top fifty, compared with eight and seventeen, respectively, for the Japanese. This is mainly because U.S. banks are not allowed to branch out nationally as non-U.S. banks can in their countries and because of the narrower range of financial activities that U.S. banks can engage in.

Structure of International Banking

MNEs find that their banks offer a variety of services worldwide through a variety of different operational modes. The major ones are representative offices, agency-affiliated banks, branches, subsidiaries, consortia, correspondents, merchant banks, Edge Act corporations, and International Banking Facilities. The latter two forms are quirks of U.S. law.

● Represents a foreign bank in a country but does not take deposits or make loans

Representative office. A **representative office** is often established in a country that does not allow direct foreign participation or while a bank is waiting approval for operations. A representative is not allowed to take deposits and make loans, but it can scout out opportunities for its parent bank. Until 1985, Sweden was the last Western European country that would not allow foreign banks to set up branches or subsidiaries. As a result, twenty-four foreign banks, including Citibank and Chase Manhattan, the two U.S. banks that figured so prominently in the Iranian case at the beginning of the chapter, had opened representative offices. These offices were expected to be converted to subsidiaries or branches with the passage of new legislation in Sweden.[16]

TABLE 10.3

COUNTRY OF REPRESENTATION OF THE
TOP 500 BANKS IN THE WORLD, 1983

Country	Number of banks
United States	119
Japan	66
West Germany	43
Italy	27
France	19
United Kingdom	19
Switzerland	13
Spain	11
Canada	10
Austria	9
Belgium	8
Korea	8
Taiwan	8
Brazil	7
India	7
Portugal	7
Yugoslavia	7
Australia	6
Kuwait	6
Luxembourg	6
Netherlands	6
Sweden	6

Source: *The Banker,* June 1984, p. 100. Used by permission.

- Like a representative but is allowed to make some loans

Agency. Agencies are more active than representative offices in foreign countries. Even though they do not accept demand deposits, they are able to accept certain specific-use deposits for short periods of time, generally in the wholesale (corporate) market. Agencies are allowed to make loans to local companies, so they must develop an asset base by raising funds in the local country or receiving funds from their parent bank.[17]

- Foreign bank holds a minority interest

Affiliated bank. An affiliated bank is a local bank in which the foreign bank holds a minority interest. It is similar to a minority joint venture, to be discussed in Chapter 15. It is a way for a bank to gain access to a market without having to come up with the capital and expertise necessary to open a branch or subsidiary.

- An office set up by a foreign bank; allowed the full range of banking activities

Branch banking. An important step in offering foreign services to multinational clients is the establishment of branches. This is true of foreign banks operating in the United States and other countries as well as of U.S. banks operating overseas.

● Factors leading to the growth of branch banking

Many reasons account for the growth of **branch banking** in the 1960s. First, the banks recognized the need to serve their domestic clients properly. They quickly realized that correspondent relationships were inadequate for serving multinational clients. Second, balance-of-payments controls instituted in the 1960s by the U.S. government encouraged the banks to develop branches overseas. One such control was the Interest Equalization Tax discussed above, a "temporary" measure instituted in 1963 and eliminated in 1974, which was an excise tax on the purchase of foreign securities by U.S. citizens. Another such control was the Direct Investment Control Program of 1968, which restricted the amount of funds that could be sent from a U.S. parent company to its foreign subsidiaries, forcing the firms to seek more extensive overseas assistance from their banks in securing medium- and long-term loans.

The growth of the Eurodollar in the 1960s was another major force leading to the establishment of foreign branches. This highly liquid and unregulated source of funds has become very important in the spread of multinationalism.

The credit crunches of 1966 and 1969–1970 in the United States led to renewed interest in foreign branches as a means of tapping the Eurodollar market for domestic use. This became a major source of concern to the U.S. government because restrictive monetary policies were being nullified by the inflow of funds formerly held as Eurodollars.

As was mentioned in the Iranian case, Citicorp is a bank that has expanded internationally through branches. Citicorp, the largest bank in the world in terms of total assets, initiated its move to international banking in 1914 by opening an office in Buenos Aires, Argentina. Now nearly half of Citicorp's 60,000 employees are located in 1490 offices in 94 foreign countries.[18] Its geographic spread has given Citicorp access to the major MNEs of the world. Citicorp's international strength has been very profitable. However, this international scope has opened Citicorp to a variety of risks. Citicorp has a large exposure in Latin America, especially Brazil, where it owned approximately 24 percent of the dollar loans and other assets of all U.S. banks in 1983.[19]

● A banking corporation set up by a foreign bank

Subsidiary. A **subsidiary** is simply a corporate form of banking. It may not be possible, for legal reasons, for a bank to operate as a branch in some countries, so it must organize a local banking corporation in which it typically holds all of the shares of stock. It is also possible to go into partnership with a local bank. As long as you have a controlling interest in the voting stock of the new bank, you can consider it a subsidiary.

● Several banks pool resources to form another bank that engages in international transactions

Consortium banking. With the growth of the Eurocurrency market and the multinational corporations, some banks began to see that branch operations would be insufficient to meet future needs. In particular, no adequate financing was being offered for medium-term loans (three to eight years).

In response to this gap in the market, four banks pooled some of their resources to establish a **consortium** called the Midland and International Banks (MAIBL). These banks were Midland, Ltd. (United Kingdom), Toronto Dominion Bank, Commercial Bank of Australia, Ltd., and Standard Bank, Ltd. (an Anglo-African Bank).

● Major reasons: need for large loans, access to multiple currencies, combination of different strengths of shareholders

Another factor giving rise to consortium banking was the need to provide large loans. For example, a consortium easily arranged a $10 million loan for a European government, a loan clearly out of reach for an individual bank. Even though syndication could have been used to raise the funds, the government was not interested in the publicity that often surrounds syndication. Multicurrency loans are more necessary for many multinational enterprises. For example, a consortium called Orion arranged financing for a client by a combined Australian dollar and West German mark public bond issue.

U.S. and continental banks have been very successful partners in consortia because of their particular skills. U.S. banks generally have size and geographic spread, but they lack the required local deposits in other currencies. Also, they often lack skills in certain types of banking that are prohibited in the United States, such as investment banking and leasing. What the continental banks lack in size and spread, they make up for in local currency deposits and non commercial-banking skills. Consortium banking has provided great opportunities for U.S. banks to develop new sidelines such as underwriting, merger brokering, and financial management.

In the late 1970s and early 1980s, some of the original consortia disbanded. Orion was bought by Royal Bank of Canada in 1981, and MAIBL was purchased by Standard Chartered Bank in 1982. Some have predicted the demise of the consortium movement and used these sellouts as proof. However, the selling banks in the consortia had reached a stage in their development at which they did not need the services of a consortium bank in London. They found that the consortium bank was actually a source of competition. However, the consortium banks have continued to operate after being sold to the new buyer in six of the seven sellouts. In spite of the celebrated sellouts, new consortium banks were formed during that same time; the total in mid-1983 was twenty-four.[20]

● Formal ties among banks; they agree to help service each other's clients

Correspondent relationships. The growth of the multinational enterprise has resulted in an expansion of the traditional services offered by domestic banks. Many banks initially developed international departments to handle the overseas needs of their domestic clients. To facilitate their financing responsibilities, international departments of commercial banks have maintained reciprocal deposits with commercial banks located in the countries where the majority of their foreign transactions take place. It is not unusual for a bank located in a regional center, such as Denver or Houston, to have some 200 **correspondent relationships** with foreign banks.

- Services performed through correspondent relationships

In addition, correspondent banks abroad perform many other services. Through frequent foreign travel by members of a bank's international department and constant communication with foreign correspondent banks, a bank's international department is well equipped to survey the overseas market potential for any company. The bank can advise a potential exporter on such matters as local competition in the foreign market, governmental regulations, credit terms, shipping, and insurance. The correspondent bank may also recommend reputable agents or distributors in their own countries. This may enable the businessperson to acquire the necessary overseas contacts to develop distribution channels for the company's product. The international department of a bank also provides travelers' letters of credit, travelers' checks, and letters of introduction for its customers.

As was pointed out in the Iranian case, Chase Manhattan, the third largest bank in the United States and the twentieth largest in the world, has expanded geographically through correspondent relationships. Thus it has tried to perform the role of the banker's bank by taking the lead in large international loans and servicing foreign banks in the United States. That strategy has allowed it to grow internationally, but its lack of international office presence when compared with Citicorp or BankAmerica will keep it number three for the foreseeable future.

- Primarily involved in placing and managing securities, activities not permissible for U.S. banks in the United States

Merchant banking. **Merchant banking** by definition involves underwriting and distributing securities, syndication of large loans, project financing, financial advisory services, and mergers and acquisitions.[21] Since many of these activities are prohibited for banks in the United States, U.S. banks initially got involved in merchant banking through consortium arrangements. Since then, many of them have also set up their own merchant banks in Europe. That is an area of tremendous growth in the future, and U.S. banks are beginning to move aggressively into it.

- Allows banks to set up offices in other money centers to perform international banking activities

Edge Act corporations. In 1919 a bill introduced by Senator Walter Edge of New Jersey was enacted as the Edge Act. It provided for the organization of a corporation that would facilitate the involvement of U.S. banks in foreign banking. Most **Edge Act companies** are of the single-bank variety and are typified by the Bank of America's Edge Act subsidiary, which in 1949 became the first major Edge Act corporation in the modern era.

Two aspects of Edge Act status differentiate the Edge Act company from the commercial bank. Commercial banks in the United States are restricted to one state and generally to a geographic area within the state. The Edge Act status allows a bank to open offices in other states in order to be close to important international contacts. Also, Edge Act status allows a bank to diversify its operations. Many lines of business that are prohibited domestically are permissible for an Edge Act company's international operations, such as leasing and managing offshore mutual funds. Aside from those different operations, Edge Act companies are involved in the typical operations of the international department of a commercial bank, such as letters of credit, bills of exchange, collections, and foreign exchange.

Originally, most Edge Act corporations were set up in New York City to be close to the pulse of international banking. Recently, however, banks have been setting up Edge Act corporations in other principal international commercial centers such as Chicago, Miami, Houston, San Francisco, Los Angeles, and New Orleans. The major banks are making this move to get access to firms in major markets where they are not allowed to set up branch operations at this point.

• Allows domestic banks to service foreign clients without many of the U.S. regulations

International Banking Facilities. In 1981, legislation was enacted in the United States that permitted the establishment of an **International Banking Facility** (IBF). An IBF is not a new banking facility (such as a building), but it is a new method of operations within a banking institution that basically results in a separate set of books. IBFs are allowed to take deposits from and make loans to nonresidents of the United States, other IBFs, and the entities that established the IBFs.

There are four major restrictions on IBFs:

• Major restrictions on IBFs

1. The initial maturity of deposits must be at least two working days to keep the account from being a checking account.

2. The minimum transaction must be for $100,000, except for the withdrawal of interest or the closing of an account, which basically keeps the IBF in the wholesale (corporate) rather than retail market.

3. IBFs are not permitted to issue negotiable instruments, such as certificates of deposit (CDs), which keeps then from competing with domestic banks in the U.S. money market.

4. Deposits and loans of IBFs cannot be related to a customer's activities in the United States, which once again keeps the IBFs from competing with U.S. banks in the domestic market.

• Major benefits of IBFs
• Primacy of New York market

The major benefits from setting up an IBF are that there are no reserve requirements, interest rate ceilings, or deposit insurance assessment, which are regulations existing in the United States that add to the cost of doing business. The early data on the first two years of operations show that most of the IBF transactions are interbank in nature. The implication is that they are becoming major actors in the Eurocurrency market. Most of the IBFs are located in New York, California, Florida, and Illinois. In terms of the volume of liabilities, however, New York leads the pack with 77 percent, followed by California with 12 percent and Illinois with 7.5 percent. Of the 477 IBFs in existence at the end of September 1983, 30.2 percent were U.S. chartered banks, 55.3 percent were agencies and branches of foreign banks, and 14.5 percent were Edge Act corporations. It appears that most of the business of IBFs has come from U.S. operations of foreign banks and from the operations of U.S. banks in the Bahamas and Cayman Islands.

The operations of IBFs have expanded faster than international banking in general in the first three years of operations, but it remains to be seen if that kind of growth can continue. However, the operations are significant in the Eurocurrency market, and they provide an opportunity for U.S. banks to engage in offshore operations without having to set up offshore facilities.[22]

Important Developments in International Banking

Although there are a variety of issues that international banks have to face and a number of key developments that have taken place in recent years, we will focus on the following: the expansion of services, communications breakthroughs, foreign exchange trading losses, foreign loans, and changes in the U.S. market.

Expansion of services. The market for financial services has virtually exploded for banks in recent years. The three major functions that are especially suited for the offshore banks are

- Major international services offered by banks

1. Money transfer and foreign exchange, which includes international money arbitrage. An ancillary activity is foreign exchange dealing and servicing.
2. International treasury. This category includes providing the source for funds, allocating funds to end users, converting funds, and providing for the reconversion of funds.
3. International loan and credit. This includes the analysis and approval of credit, monitoring loans, and establishing and revising country loan limits.[23]

- International services of BankAmerica

A good example of the variety of services offered by a large international bank is BankAmerica, the largest bank in the world. BankAmerica divides its services into three categories: international trade support, international financing services, and international money management services. International trade support includes commercial letters of credit, acceptance financing (providing bankers' acceptances), collections of international accounts, remittances and money transfers, and international trade information. International financing services includes direct financing, loan syndications (such as the ones in which Citicorp and Chase Manhattan were involved in Iran), government-sponsored trade-financing programs, lease financing, project financing, standby letters of credit, Eurobond transactions, international trust and investment services, private placements of debt and equity capital, and merger and acquisition advisory services. International money management services include international cash management services, foreign exchange trading, foreign exchange advisory services, and international treasury services (including project consulting services, educational services, and treasury management systems).[24]

What is impressive about the list of services performed by BankAmerica is their breadth. It is important for a large international bank to provide a variety of services in order to meet the needs of its corporate clients.

• Faster transfer of funds and information

Communications. One of the major services offered by multinational banks is the movement of funds across national boundaries. In spite of its importance, this service was not developed adequately until the early 1970s. In some cases, transfers of funds between European countries could take several days to several weeks, even when cable transfers were used.

• SWIFT—cooperative arrangement of banks worldwide to transfer funds instantaneously

In an effort to eliminate the time lag in carrying out international money transfers by mail or telex, a number of banks organized the **Society for Worldwide Interbank Financial Telecommunication (SWIFT)** in 1973. SWIFT has grown from an initial membership of 239 banks in fifteen countries to over 1200 banks in fifty countries. It processes around half a million transactions per day. SWIFT services primarily involve processing transactions such as customer transfers, foreign exchange confirmations, bank transfers, and documentary credits. The system offers speed and security. A special message text language allows banks to "talk" together by computer in a common language, which greatly facilitates the transfers of information.[25]

• CHIPS—a clearing mechanism for domestic and foreign currency transactions in the United States

Another important institution is the **Clearing House Interbank Payment System (CHIPS),** an international electronic check transfer system that moves money between major U.S. banks, branches of foreign banks, and Edge Act subsidiaries of out-of-state banks. The system handles a large volume of transactions per day and most of the foreign exchange trade and Eurodollar transactions. CHIPS has speeded up the settling of its transactions to the close of each business day rather than the next business day as was the custom.[26]

Foreign exchange trading losses. In recent years, U.S. banks have become much more active in foreign exchange trading. At some of the major banks, foreign exchange trading can amount to 5–10 percent of revenues. Thus it is becoming more important for the banks to predict accurately what will happen to the currencies that they are trading. In the second quarter of 1984, many of the larger banks, such as Citicorp and Bankers Trust, had a drop in foreign exchange trading revenues over the same quarter of the preceding year. J. P. Morgan actually recorded a loss in trading during that quarter. Of the big international banks, only Manufacturers Hanover and Chemical Bank recorded gains over the second quarter of

1983. The major explanation was that everyone bet on a weaker dollar, but the dollar continued to strengthen. In the third quarter of 1984 the banks had apparently learned their lesson and bet on a strong dollar. J. P. Morgan still showed a loss, and Citicorp had a small decline over the same quarter of the prior year, but the other majors recorded gains.[27] As long as the dollar remains volatile, it will be difficult for the foreign exchange trading rooms to show sustained growth.

• Nonaccrual loan—one that is at least 90 days overdue in paying principal or interest

Lending to developing countries. In Chapter 2 we discussed the problems associated with debt in developing countries. The banks have been affected by the debt problems because many of them are holding loans on which no principal and interest are being paid. New banking regulations in the United States require banks to identify the amount of nonaccrual loans they have at the end of each quarter. A **nonaccrual loan** is one for which principal or interest is 90 days past due or for which payment of interest or principal is determined to be doubtful of collection. Thus the banks anxiously await the end of their fiscal quarter to find out the status of their loans. The nonaccrual concept relates to domestic as well as foreign loans. Many banks have had more problems with the domestic loans than they have with the foreign loans.

There has been a lot of criticism of the commercial banks for lending so much money to the developing countries, as was mentioned in Chapter 2. During the 1970s the banks received large deposits from OPEC countries, which it then tried to lend. During the recession of the late 1970s and early 1980s, when interest rates also began to rise, corporate borrowing in the United States was very soft. However, the developing countries continued to demand loans and appeared to be willing to pay the high interest rates. The pressure on the banks began as the loans from the developing countries came due and the debtors found that they were not earning sufficient foreign exchange to make the payments.

One of the problems brought on by the debt crisis and recession is that many of the banks have not been able to increase their lending substantially. Also, many of the regional banks have been hesitant to get back into the international lending market because of the problems that they have had in receiving principal and interest payments. Many of them have simply written off the loans as nonperforming and then gone about their domestic business. That would be difficult for a bank like Citicorp with international loans outstanding of over $50 billion in 1983.

International bank lending averaged 23 percent a year during the period 1973–1981. In 1982, however, that increase slowed to only 10 percent. There were a variety of reasons for this slowdown, such as the recession, strong dollar, and limits on the internationalization of bank portfolios. But part of the reason was also the size of loans to risky countries. It was estimated that 40 percent of the banks' external claims were very risky—30 percent of the claims were to nonoil developing countries and 5 percent each to OPEC and COMECON.[28]

Many of the loans made to the developing countries were individual loans between banks and private or public corporations. However, many of the loans were a result of syndication, such as the ones described in the Iranian case at the beginning of the chapter. In syndication a large money center bank, such as Chase Manhattan or Citicorp, will line up the loan and then try to encourage other banks to take a percentage of the loan. The lead bank is then responsible for the details and watches over the transaction over the life of the loan. Many of the regional banks that became involved in syndications during the 1970s eventually decided to back out of the market and concentrate on the United States instead. The risk was just too great for them.

As long as the countries continue to make payments and the banks are able to keep from writing off the loans as uncollectible, the system should hold together. The case at the end of the chapter provides an interesting scenario of what could happen if a country should decide to repudiate its debt and force the banks to write off their loans.

• Reasons why the New York City market has become the best in the world

The changing U.S. market. The U.S. market has always been a competitive one because of its sheer size. However, the U.S. market has been going through some adjustments in recent years that have put it at the top of the market worldwide.

There are a variety of reasons why the United States (New York City, in reality) has become the worldwide leader in financial supremacy. Some of the reasons are due to the economic climate in the United States in the early 1980s—low inflation, high interest rates, high real growth, and a strong dollar. In addition, some banking regulations have been changed. Regulation Q, which kept a ceiling on interest rates, and reserve requirements on foreign lending were eliminated, and that has led to strong growth in banking. Furthermore, the establishment of the international banking facilities discussed above resulted in the shifting of a lot of capital from London and the Caribbean to the United States.

Foreign banks have invested large amounts of money in the United States over the past decade. Foreign banks and their branches make as many as 40 percent of the large commercial loans in New York and San Francisco and 20 percent nationwide.[29] The strong growth in the late 1970s was due to the desire of foreign banks to have instant access to U.S. banking technology, personnel, clients, and dollar deposits. Many of the investments were made without a full understanding of the nature of the acquired institution and without too much careful planning and coordinating after the purchase. As a result, many of the acquisitions turned out to be sour. However, the foreign bank presence has been strong, and foreign banks have captured a large percentage of the IBF market.

U.S. banks are also continuing their trend toward greater multinationalization. However, they are making some changes. Instead of focusing on the unstable loans of the developing countries, they are trying to focus on more specific project financing. They are also buying a larger stake in their overseas subsidiaries in an effort to gain greater control. Finally, they are turning to lines of business that do not require large capital outlays, such as barter, correspondent banking, and being the intermediaries in transactions between third parties.[30]

DEVELOPMENT BANKS

Multilateral Lending Institutions

● World Bank—organized under the U.N. charter; major subunits are the IBRD, IDA, and IFC

The World Bank. The World Bank Group, an autonomous U.N. agency, is composed of three major organizations: the International Bank for Reconstruction and Development (IBRD), the International Development Association (IDA), and the International Finance Corporation (IFC). The IBRD, also called the World Bank, was organized in 1944 along with the International Monetary Fund to aid in rebuilding the world economy. The bank's major objective was to serve as an international financing facility to function in reconstruction and development. With the Marshall Plan providing the impetus for the reconstruction of Europe, the bank was able to turn its efforts toward development.

● IBRD—lends money to governments for hard currency needs for infrastructure development

The World Bank generally lends money to a government for the purpose of developing that country's economic infrastructure, such as roads and power-generating facilities. Funds are lent only to members of the International Monetary Fund, usually when private capital is unavailable at reasonable terms. Loans are made at low rates of interest for periods of time that depend on the nature of the project and the country involved.

The bank's major concern is the development of infrastructure in less-developed countries. This foundation is essential for future industrialization. The impact of the bank's activities is less direct than that of the Eximbank, for example. However, the projects receiving World Bank assistance usually require importing heavy industrial equipment, and this provides an export market for many U.S. goods. Generally, bank loans are made to cover only hard currency import needs and must be repaid in hard currency at long-term rates.

● IDA—provides infrastructure loans for the poorest countries at very favorable terms

The International Development Association (IDA). The IDA was formed in 1960 as a part of the World Bank Group to provide financial support to less-developed countries on a more liberal basis than could be offered by the IBRD. Credit terms usually are extended to fifty years with no interest. Repayment should begin after a ten-year grace period and can be paid in the local currency, as long as it is convertible.

Although the IDA's resources are separate from the World Bank, it has no separate staff. Loans are made for the same types of projects as those carried out by the World Bank, but at easier and more favorable credit terms. The assistance rendered by IDA usually goes to the very poor countries.

As mentioned above, World Bank/IDA assistance has historically been for developing infrastructure. The present emphasis seems to be on helping the masses of poor people in the developing countries become more productive and take an active part in the development process. Greater emphasis is being put on improving urban living conditions and increasing productivity in small industries.

The International Finance Corporation (IFC). Although the World Bank was providing assistance to the less-developed countries, it recognized limitations to what it could do. Some of the major problems were that (1) all loans had to be guaranteed by the member government of the country receiving the loan; (2) the bank could only provide loans, not purchase stock; (3) the bank financed only the foreign exchange requirements for a project and was not concerned with local expenditures or working capital; and (4) the bank usually financed large projects of public importance and reached small projects in the private sector only indirectly by means of the development banks.

These problems led to the development of the IFC in 1956. Its main responsibilities are:

● Types of activities of IFC: oriented primarily toward helping corporations in productive projects

1. to provide risk capital in the form of equity and long-term loans for productive private enterprises in association with private investors and management;

2. to encourage the development of local capital markets by carrying out standby and underwriting arrangements; and

3. to stimulate the international flow of capital by providing financial and technical assistance to privately controlled finance companies.

Loans are made to private firms in the developing member countries and are usually for a period of seven to twelve years.

The key feature of the IFC is that its loans are all made to private enterprises and its investments are made in conjunction with private business. In addition to funds contributed by IFC, funds are also contributed to the same projects by local and foreign investors.

IFC investments are for the establishment of new enterprises as well as for the expansion and modernization of existing ones. They cover a wide range of projects, such as steel, textile production, mining, manufacturing, machinery production, food processing, tourism, and local development finance companies. Some projects are wholly locally owned, while others are joint ventures between investors in developing and developed countries.

In a few cases, joint ventures are formed between investors of two or more developing countries.

Regional Development Banks

- IDB provides development loans to companies in the Western Hemisphere

Although the World Bank Group can be considered a development bank, there are other smaller regional and local development banks. The Inter-American Development Bank (IDB) was organized in 1959 to give countries in the Western Hemisphere—principally the United States and Latin America—the same type of services the World Bank provides. However, the IDB projects are wider in scope and tailored for the member countries. The IDB depends on four separate sources of funds: (1) ordinary capital resources, (2) a fund for special operations, (3) the social progress trust fund, and (4) other resources. Loans are made from ordinary capital resources to private and public entities of member nations. These loans are generally made at favorable rates of interest and are repayable in the currencies lent. Procurement sources of goods and services are limited to those countries that contribute funds to the IDB.

Many development banks similar to the IDB have been instituted in other regions of the world. The African Development Bank, which was organized under the direction of the United Nations, is designed to promote the investment of public or private investment funds by making or guaranteeing loan and equity investment and by providing technical assistance to members. The European Investment Bank was created by the Treaty of Rome (European Economic Community) to provide long-term financing for projects in developing countries. The Asian Development Bank, headquartered in Manila, was organized in 1966 to provide services similar to the World Bank's. However, it is very similar to the IDB in that it provides specialized loans under unusually liberal arrangements.

In addition to regional development banks, there are also many national development banks. In the past twenty to twenty-five years, the World Bank has been involved in the creation of over fifty development banks, primarily national banks in member countries. These banks specialize in assisting profitable investment activities and small entrepreneurs and in stimulating investment in areas deemed critical by the government that are not affected by market forces. This activity is concentrated in a specific country rather than in a larger region, as is the goal of a regional development bank.

SECURITIES EXCHANGES

- Largest stock exchanges worldwide are New York, Tokyo, and London

In addition to the debt instruments represented by the Eurodollar and Eurobond markets, the equity capital market is another source of financing. The three largest international stock exchanges in the world are the New

York, Tokyo, and London stock exchanges. The New York market is by far the largest in the world. In 1984, Wall Street controlled 55 percent of the world's equity market, three times as much as Tokyo and eight times the size of the London market.[31]

• Reasons for importance of U.S. market

The U.S. market is important not only for U.S. companies looking for more equity capital, but also for foreign companies. Part of the reason for the popularity of the U.S. market is the size and speed of offerings. The large pension funds in the United States are able to take large blocks of stock at relatively low transaction costs. In the past few years, pension fund managers have looked at foreign stocks as a good form of portfolio diversification. Many companies go to the United States because it is the best place for them to raise funds. The brokerage houses are able to read the value of a company better than many European houses, so a company can get a good feeling for its true value in the capital markets.

Because so many foreign firms list their securities on the U.S. stock exchange, the Securities and Exchange Commission has set up fairly stringent registration and accounting provisions under the assumption that efficient capital markets would dictate that foreign firms should operate under the same guidelines as U.S. firms. Foreign firms may issue financial statements according to their own accounting standards, but material differences from U.S. standards should be disclosed.

• Reasons for growth of Tokyo exchange

The Tokyo Stock Exchange has enjoyed rapid growth in just the last few years. It is currently the second largest stock exchange, and it is experiencing greater and more rapid expansion than the U.S. and London exchanges. There are three major reasons for this growth:

1. the increase of foreign exchange reserves, which has had an impact on the bond and short-term lending markets especially;

2. the increasing number of foreign investors purchasing Japanese securities; and

3. the relaxation of rules allowing Japanese investment companies, insurance companies, and individual investors to acquire foreign securities. This last point is closely tied to the permission granted to foreign companies to offer stock on the Tokyo exchange.

The London Exchange is also a very important international capital market. As was mentioned earlier, it is the third largest capital market in the world and was, until recently, the world's undisputed leader. Deregulation in the United States has been a major reason for London's decline, but London is currently going through deregulation and preparing itself for a new round of competition.

In addition to the London Exchange there are a variety of European exchanges. The European exchanges have traditionally been hampered by the lack of reliable and comparable accounting data for use by the investors in decision making. However, the EC is promoting the standardization of reporting practices for security offerings, which should greatly enhance the use of European stock exchanges by foreigners.

Besides the reporting problem, subtle differences between U.S. and European exchanges hamper the free flow of capital. In the United States,

● Nature of European exchanges

TABLE 10.4

GLOBAL STOCK MARKET CHARACTERISTICS

Country	Market	Annual trading volume[a] (billions of U.S. $)	Market capitalization[b] (billions of U.S. $)	Turnover ratio (%)
Emerging Markets				
Argentina	Buenos Aires	1.1	3.9	29
Brazil	Rio de Janeiro	2.8	13.3	21
Chile	Santiago	1.5	9.4	16
Greece	Athens	0.1	3.0	3
Hong Kong	Hkg & Far East	19.0	41.9	50
Indonesia	Jakarta	0.01	0.1	14
Jordan	Amman	0.1	1.6	9
Korea	Seoul	1.9	3.8	49
Mexico	Mexico City	3.3	18.0	18
Philippines	Manila/Makati	0.6	2.0	31
Portugal	Lisbon	0.002	0.2	1
Singapore	Singapore	3.7	26.8	14
Spain	Madrid	1.5	16.3	9
Thailand	Bangkok	0.3	1.2	26
Zimbabwe	Salisbury	0.2	1.5	11
Developed Markets[c]				
Australia		5.0	60.0	8
Austria		N.A.	1.9	N.A.
Belgium		2.0	10.0	21
Canada		28.0	113.0	25
Denmark		N.A.	4.0	N.A.
France		14.0	53.0	26
West Germany		15.0	71.0	21
Italy		10.0	25.0	38
Japan		157.0	357.0	44
Netherlands		5.0	25.0	20
Norway		N.A.	2.6	N.A.
Sweden		2.0	12.2	15
Switzerland		N.A.	46.0	N.A.
U.K.		36.0	190.0	19
U.S.		475.9	1380.6	34

a. For U.S. trading volume computation, average foreign exchange rate is used.
b. Market capitalization figures are for the end of 1980.
c. Data are from IFC data bank and Ibbotson et al., "International Equity and Bond Returns," *Financial Analysts Journal*, July–August 1982.

Source: Vihang R. Errunza, "Emerging Markets: A New Opportunity for Improving Global Portfolio Performance, *Financial Analysts Journal*, September–October 1983, p. 52. U.S. data is from the NYSE *Fact Book* 1984, p. 77. Used by permission.

securities are handled by brokerage firms, while in Europe the securities are handled by banks, a practice prohibited in the United States. Also, many countries prohibit foreigners from doing business in their domestic stock markets. For example, U.S. brokerage houses are discouraged from joining the Swiss Stock Exchange and can operate in Switzerland only if they agree to do business with Swiss banks rather than directly with the individual investors.

• Emerging capital markets: old established ones, ones arising from special situations, ones recently established to accelerate economic growth

In addition to the big markets described above, there are a number of emerging markets in the developing countries. Table 10.4 identifies the major emerging markets and compares them with the primary developed country markets. There are three levels of emerging markets. The first is the old established markets, such as Greece, Spain, Mexico, and Brazil, that have been around for a long time, even though their volume has not been tremendous. The second category of emerging markets is those that have arisen because of special situations, such as Hong Kong and Singapore. The third level is markets that were specifically organized more recently to foster or accelerate economic growth, such as the market in South Korea.[32] These markets are not destined to take over the big three in the industrial world, but they are becoming more important as their economies experience industrial growth.

International capital markets can be both a source and a use of funds; that is, firms can either raise capital or invest capital. One problem of using smaller stock exchanges is that the market may be so thin that it cannot absorb the issue. Obviously, the U.S. stock market is the largest and most accessible in the world. Its lures are the economic and political stability of the United States and the size and efficiency of the market.

SUMMARY

• Local debt markets, which vary dramatically from country to country owing to local business customs and practices, are important sources of funds for MNEs.

• A Eurocurrency is any currency that is banked outside of its country of origin. The dollar comprises the bulk of the Eurocurrency market and is thus referred to as the Eurodollar.

• Eurodollars are expanded through the fractional reserve concept, whereby a bank reserves only a fraction of each Eurodollar deposited and loans the remainder of the deposit, thus "creating" more Eurodollars.

• A Eurobond is a bond issue sold in a currency other than that of the country of issue. A foreign bond is one sold outside of the country of the borrower but denominated in the currency of the country of issue.

- Offshore financial centers such as London, the Caribbean, Singapore, Hong Kong, Bahrain, and now New York City deal in international transactions that are not regulated in the same way as domestic markets.

- Because of a strong U.S. dollar and Japanese yen, the Japanese banks are growing in importance at the expense of European banks.

- The major operational modes used in international banking are representative offices, agency-affiliated banks, branches, subsidiaries, consortia, correspondents, merchant banks, Edge Act corporations, and international banking facilities.

- The Edge Act corporation is a special subsidiary of a U.S. commercial bank. An Edge Act company is allowed to invest in equity, grant loans abroad, and provide services to its clients that the parent bank cannot provide because of legal restrictions or problems of size or expertise.

- A consortium bank is an organization of several banks or other financial institutions that pool their resources to engage in international banking. The consortium bank engages in commercial and merchant banking activities and provides a good synergism of the size, currency deposits, and expertise of the member banks.

- International banks are faced with a number of challenges, such as providing adequate cash management and funds flow services, coping with increasingly risky loans, and dealing in a highly competitive environment.

- The World Bank Group includes the International Bank for Reconstruction and Development (IBRD), the International Development Association (IDA), and the International Finance Corporation (IFC). The IBRD is also known as the World Bank. These multilateral lending institutions are designed to provide financial support for less-developed countries on a private as well as public basis. The IFC is especially active in providing debt and equity financing in private sector projects.

- Most industrial countries and some developing countries have stock exchanges in which equity capital can be raised by firms. However, the three major international equity markets for the sale and purchase of securities by individuals from many countries are the New York Stock Exchange, the Tokyo Stock Exchange, and the London Stock Exchange.

C A S E   SCRIPT FOR COLLAPSE[33]

Scene 1: On December 2, 1982, a small Hong Kong lending company, Global Vista Finance Co., quietly closes its doors. For months it aggressively plunged most of its $7 million in borrowed money into the Hong Kong real estate market, which is now collapsing.

The next day, crowds of depositors begin to form outside the main office of a middle-sized Hong Kong bank, Gresham Bank Ltd. It had enjoyed a tidy business of borrowing money from bigger banks and relending it at high interest rates to little, unregulated firms like Global Vista. Suddenly, business was no longer so tidy. Gresham was discovering that other banks were refusing to lend it any more cash.

Scene 2: While there is no central bank to serve as lender of last resort in Hong Kong, an informal agreement among banks calls for the huge $30 billion Eastern Imperial Bank of Hong Kong to bail out a sister bank that gets into trouble. After lengthy negotiations that result in a hefty interest rate for a line of emergency credit to little Global Vista, Eastern Imperial comes to the rescue. As it does so, however, Eastern Imperial suddenly finds that it is having trouble. Major depositors, worried about the possibility that Eastern Imperial could have major exposure in loans to real estate developers, begin moving their money elsewhere. When Eastern Imperial looks for new sources of cash, it finds that other major banks are demanding higher-than-usual rates of interest.

Scene 3: Huge sums of money begin to move electronically around the world as banks, big investors, multinational companies, and Arab governments shift their dollars to safe havens, primarily to major banks in New York. By December 6, banks in places considered less safe in a crisis— Panama, Singapore, the Bahamas, and Canada—have become shaky.

Scene 4: The first U.S. bank to falter is the $15 billion Heartland National Bank of Chicago. It is a relatively healthy, conservatively run bank with a number of prosperous branches in Illinois. But it is owned by the now-shaky Eastern Imperial Bank of Hong Kong. This connection is extremely unsettling to Heartland National's largest depositors—three major money funds—which begin yanking millions out of the bank on December 8. The Federal Reserve Bank of Chicago moves quickly to inject new funds.

Scene 5: The following day the $3 billion Transamericana Investment Bank of London runs out of funds, having been tiered to death. It had been a major lender of Eurodollars to credit-hungry Latin American countries. After 24 hours of often-heated discussions, Transamericana can obtain no more credit from the consortium of eight private banks that owns it (one U.S., one Swiss, one West German, and four Latin American banks and Eastern Imperial of Hong Kong). The central bank of Switzerland has agreed to provide one eighth of the needed bailout funds, but its counterparts in the United States, West Germany and Great Britain say they have no legal or moral commitment. The Latin American central bankers say that they are strongly behind the bank but that they have no funds to back it up with. And so Transamericana fails.

Scene 6: On December 11, Hector Aquinas-Marx, the finance minister of Argentina's new Socialist-Labor government, assembles a group of foreign bankers and announces that Argentina is repudiating its $55 billion of foreign debt. This is a profound shock to the bankers, who for one thing thought that Argentina had only borrowed $40 billion. As Mr. Aquinas-Marx explains it, Argentina's rationale for the move is rather simple. For weeks it had been unable to obtain the new loans necessary to make interest payments on its old loans. The mishandling of the Transamericana failure, he says, is the last straw. From now on, Argentina, which has a small trade surplus, will pay for what it needs with cash. "We never needed you anyway," Mr. Aquinas-Marx tells the foreign bankers. "It was you who needed us."

Scene 7: On December 12, gloom spreads through the world banking community as banks begin to fall like bowling pins following the Argentine announcement. There is gloom in the New York headquarters of Megabank, a $54 billion institution that had pioneered the lending to Argentina. Megabank had parceled out pieces of the Argentine debt to dozens of other banks throughout the country and had lent $1 billion itself.

But there is joy in Megabank's currency-trading office in Zurich. There, Rennie Zitz, a 23-year-old trader, has made Megabank more than $1 billion by holding a "short position" in Swiss francs for several weeks. He had borrowed the currency and sold it, then reaped an enormous profit by later buying an equal number of francs back after the Swiss currency dropped sharply against the dollar.

The dollar went up because some Swiss investors were converting their Swiss bank accounts to dollars and then wiring the money to New York, where they would be protected by the Federal Deposit Insurance Corp. Swiss banking regulators did not spot Mr. Zitz's illegal transaction because he had booked it through Megabank's branch on the South Pacific island of Vanuatu, an office consisting of one clerk, one desk, and a telex machine.

Scene 8: On December 13, Youngstown (Ohio) Hope & Trust Bank joins the mounting pile of bank corpses in the United States. Neither its officers nor the federal banking authorities have been able to repair the damage caused by a run on the bank when it became known that Youngstown had participated in Megabank's lending foray into Argentina.

But Joe Lunchpail, a shop foreman at Youngstown Tube & Prong, goes to the bank anyway. He feels sure that he can rescue the $898.42 in his checking account because the bank is insured by the Federal Deposit Insurance Corp. Sure enough, the man from the FDIC is there, and Mr. Lunchpail takes his cash home to bury it in a dry place under one corner of his garage. With a sense of great relief, he flips on his Japanese TV set and opens a can of Dutch beer to sip as he watches the evening news report of the economic chaos that seems to be going on elsewhere. Then he learns that Youngstown Tube & Prong is closing. There is no longer an export market for prongs.

QUESTIONS

1. It has been stated that scenario making as it relates to a possible banking failure is serious business in Washington, D.C. Why do you feel that that is the case?

2. The improvements in communications and the speed of funds transfers have benefitted banking tremendously. Can you think of ways that the international financial system could be harmed by these improvements?

3. Discuss how international connections could help and hinder a domestic bank.

4. Discuss how you feel about the actions taken by Mr. Aquinas-Marx in Argentina. Be sure to include a discussion of whether or not such an action could actually occur as it is described.

5. Discuss different ways that an international bank failure could affect domestic business.

NOTES

1. Data for this case were taken from Edward P. Foldessy, "Chase, Rockefeller Sees Hopeful Signs Iran Will Repay Debts to Western Banks," *Wall Street Journal,* February 22, 1979, p. 12; "Look What's Happening at Chase!" *Business Week,* March 19, 1979, pp. 138–144; "The Banks Squabble over Iran's Assets," *Business Week,* December 3, 1979, pp. 110–112; "A Banking Rift over Iran's Assets," *Business Week,* December 10, 1979, p. 30; Herman Nickel, "Battling for Iran's Frozen Billions," *Fortune,* December 15, 1980, pp. 117–120; Alexander Taylor, *Time,* February 2, 1981, pp. 56–58; "How the Bankers Did It," Herman Nickel, "The Iran Deal Doesn't Look Bad," *Fortune,* February 23, 1981, pp. 57–59.

2. "The Foreign Impact on Corporate IOUs," *Business Week,* October 30, 1978, p. 170.

3. "A New Credit Market in Pesetas," *Business Week,* June 15, 1981, p. 102.

4. Rodrigo Briones, "Latin American Money Markets," in *International Finance Handbook,* Abraham M. George and Ian H. Giddy, eds. (New York: John Wiley & Sons, 1983), p. 4.9.4.

5. Boyden E. Lee, "The Eurodollar Multiplier," *Journal of Finance,* September 1973, p. 874.

6. "The Debate over Regulating the Eurocurrency Markets," Federal Reserve Board of New York *Quarterly Review,* Winter 1979–1980, p. 20.

7. "A New Peg for Eurolending," *Business Week,* March 30, 1981, p. 108.

8. Stephen J. Cosham, " 'Capped' Prime and LIBOR-Based Loans: The Comparative Costs," *The Banker,* February 1984, p. 58.

9. Linda Sandler and Matthew Winkler, "Bond Firms Try Harder to Sell American Debt to Overseas Investors," *Wall Street Journal,* August 31, 1984, p. 1.

10. *Business Week,* February 23, 1981, p. 117.

11. Matthew Winkler, "Big Eurobond Market Has Expanded Sharply but Faces Competition," *Wall Street Journal,* May 29, 1984, p. 1.

12. *Ibid.,* p. 19.

13. A. J. Alex Gelinas, "Tax Considerations for U.S. Corporations Using Finance Subsidiaries to Borrow Funds Abroad," *Journal of Corporate Taxation,* Autumn 1980, pp. 230–263.

14. Maximo Eng and Francis A. Lees, "Eurocurrency Centers," in *International Financial Handbook, op. cit.,* p. 3.6.3.

15. *Ibid.,* p. 3.6.4.

16. "A Long-Awaited Welcome for Foreign Banks," *Business Week,* June 4, 1984, p. 41.

17. Yoon S. Park and Jack Zwick, *International Banking in Theory and Practice* (Reading, Mass: Addison-Wesley Publishing Company, 1985), p. 51.

18. "Citibank's Pervasive Influence on International Lending," *Business Week,* May 16, 1983, p. 124.

19. *Ibid.,* p. 125.

20. Robert N. Bee, "London Consortium Banks in the Debt Crisis," *The Banker,* January 1984, p. 37.

21. Park and Zwick, *op. cit.,* p. 61.

22. This section is from K. Alec Chrystal, "International Banking Facilities," *Review* (St. Louis: Federal Reserve Bank, April 1984), pp. 5–11.

23. Eng and Lees, *op. cit.,* p. 3.6.4.

24. *International Services* (San Francisco: Bank of America, 1981), pp. 3–21.

25. "Banking Tomorrow—Communications," *The Banker,* October 1984, pp. 73–77.

26. "CHIPS: Goodby to Next-Day Settlements," *Business Week,* March 23, 1981, p. 98.

27. Stephen Grover, "Banks Foreign Exchange Revenues Dive after Wrong Guessing on Dollar's Strength," *Wall Street Journal,* July 20, 1984, p. 4; Stephen Grover, "Big Banks Use More Predictable Dollar to Improve Foreign-Exchange Trading," *Wall Street Journal,* October 25, 1984, p. 12.

28. Christopher Johnson, "International Bank Lending after the Slowdown," *The Banker,* January 1984, pp. 23–24.

29. Peter Truell and Linda Sandler, "Foreign Banks Hurt by U.S. Ventures," *Wall Street Journal,* June 19, 1984, p. 34.

30. Michael R. Sesit and Daniel Hertzberg, "Internationalization of U.S. Banks Falters after Decade of Expansion," *Wall Street Journal,* August 7, 1984, p. 23.

31. "Why the Big Apple Shines in the World's Markets," *Business Week,* July 23, 1984, p. 101.

32. Vitrang R. Errunza, "Emerging Markets: A New Opportunity for Improving Global Portfolio Performance," *Financial Analysts Journal,* September–October 1983, pp. 51–52.

33. John J. Fialka, "Script for Collapse," *Wall Street Journal,* November 10, 1982, p. 1. Reprinted by permission of the *Wall Street Journal,* © Dow Jones & Company, Inc. 1982. All rights reserved.

PART 5

International Business in International Conflicts

Although the international mobility of production factors and finished goods by multinational firms may allow the world's consumers to use products that would otherwise not be available and to consume others at a lower cost, all countries seek to influence factor mobility. Chapter 11 analyzes the economic and noneconomic motives and methods by which nation-states seek to influence the flow of direct investment. Chapter 12 examines the approaches by which international firms and governments may deal with each other in order to satisfy the objectives of each and to attempt to strengthen the bargaining position relative to that of the other party. Chapter 13 concludes with an illustration of the effects and uncertainties of international business between communist and noncommunist countries as political and economic objectives and policies become intertwined.

11

The Impact of the Multinational

- To examine the conflicting objectives sought by the constituencies with which international firms must come in contact.
- To indicate the major shortcomings in many of the antagonist and protagonist discussions of multinational companies' activities.
- To introduce students to the major criticisms put forward about multinational firms.
- To evaluate the major economic impacts (balance of payments and growth) of multinational firms on donor and recipient countries.
- To give an overview of the major political controversies surrounding MNE activities.

MNEs IN CANADA[1]

After decades of luring foreign capital to Canada, many Canadians became concerned. Mitchell Sharp, Canada's external affairs minister, made the following comment in early 1972:

> *Multinational corporations have brought to us a high degree of prosperity and a great fund of technology, but it is hardly surprising that a great many thoughtful and informed Canadians are concerned, nor is it surprising that the Canadian government is preoccupied with the same questions. Canadians are determined that foreign corporations will serve Canadian interests, buttress Canadian priorities, and respond to Canadian aspirations.*

At the time it was estimated that of the $58 billion of total corporate assets in Canada, $43 billion or 74 percent were foreign owned. No other advanced economy was so dominated by foreign ownership; such a degree of foreign control was unusual even among developing countries. The U.S. ownership was $35 billion or about 60 percent of the total corporate assets in Canada.

Sharp's comment mirrored a changing Canadian attitude toward foreign investment in general and especially that portion owned by U.S. firms. A survey by the University of Windsor showed that 43.7 percent of respondents considered American corporate ownership a "bad thing," up from 33.9 percent who felt that way in 1969. Twenty members of Parliament had joined the Committee for an Independent Canada, an organization that held that foreign investment was bad for the country.

The evolving public opinion of 1972 should not imply that Canada had heretofore allowed the entry of foreign firms without restrictions. There were already limitations on foreign ownership in certain industries that were considered to be particularly sensitive to national sovereignty. These included banks and other financial institutions, newspapers and magazines, broadcasting, and the uranium industry. Given these existing restrictions, what difference did it make that other firms were controlled outside of Canada? Would operations or decisions be any different than if the ownership were held by Canadians? Obviously, many Canadians thought they would be.

One such allegation concerned the level of positions and type of production taking place in Canada. The Science Council, a government advisory board, contended that even in high-technology industries, very little research and development was being performed by the Canadian subsidiaries of foreign firms. Furthermore, very little of the production of newer sophisticated products was being done in Canada. Canadian subsidiaries depended primarily on making mature products and components. These generally had a lower profit margin and employed a higher portion of lower-skilled people than the more innovative output taking place in the MNEs' home countries. Furthermore, since the corporate headquarters of the MNEs were located abroad, Canadians could seldom aspire to upper-level management positions while remaining in the Canadian subsidiary operations. (This situation in Canada has often been referred to as a truncated organization structure.) Given the high education level of the Canadian population, the result was shrinking advancement opportunities in Canada. There was a net flow abroad of technical and managerial persons with high skills—a so-called brain drain. Many of them went to work in the parent companies' operations, and Canada then had to import the costly technical advancements that its own citizens helped to develop abroad. Many Canadians thus expected that greater Canadian control would give people greater opportunity in Canada for using their skills and make the country less dependent on technology from abroad.

There was also fairly widespread agreement among critics of foreign ownership that in conflict situations the investors would do what was best for the home rather than the Canadian situation. Many believed that, if given a choice of exporting from Canada or the parent country, the MNEs would choose the latter. Critics were particularly upset that the U.S. government had prevented the Canadian subsidiaries of U.S. firms from exporting to China during the period before the United States opened trading relations with the country. These export limitations contributed to drains on Canadian foreign exchange, a drain that was substantial because of dividend remittances to parents that were exceeding the flow of foreign exchange into Canada.

Because of these contentions about foreign investment, pressure grew to place additional constraints on foreign ownership of Canadian operations. Included in discussions were proposals to require existing investors to turn over all or part of their ownership to Canadian interests, to place similar restrictions only on new entries into Canada, and to apply restrictions only on acquisitions of existing companies by foreign investors. During the period of discussions it became obvious that many Canadians did not agree with the placement of new investment limitations. Canada was experiencing an unemployment rate in excess of 6 percent, and there was fear that it would go up even further with a slowing of investment inflows. In Nova Scotia, where more than 10 percent were out of work, Premier Gerald Regan said, "We want all the foreign investment we can get." Given the mixed opinions, critics were unable to pass legislation that was as stringent as they wanted. One outspoken critic, Minister of Industry, Trade, and Commerce Jean-Luc Pepin, summed up the situation by saying, "We had to compromise. If you're going to be a politician you've got to be a realist."

The Foreign Investment Review Act (FIRA) was passed in late 1973 and provided that any foreign takeover of an existing company would have to be screened by the Foreign Investment Review Agency, which would recommend to Parliament whether or not the investment was of "significant benefit" to Canada. The procedure applied to Canadian companies with assets of at least $250,000 or annual sales exceeding $3 million. A takeover would involve acquisition of 5 percent or more of the Canadian company. By the end of 1974 the law was extended to cover new investments and expansion of foreign-controlled companies into new areas of business.

The term "significant benefit" was never specifically defined. Some of the things that were considered were the effects on employment, exports, competition, productivity, and industrial efficiency. Approval also depended on the degree of participation of Canadians in a venture, although no quota of Canadian representation in the management of a company was spelled out. Between 1974 and 1980 there was little impetus to enact new legislation or to implement the FIRA policies differently. In early 1980, in a campaign speech for the premiership, Pierre Trudeau spelled out his views on foreign investment. He mentioned that all foreign investments of large size should be reviewed periodically in such areas as export promotion and research and development. After his election in 1980 a ten-year National Energy Program was announced to reduce foreign ownership in the energy industry to 50 percent. This program led to the "benefit" of an 8 percent drop in foreign control of oil and gas but sparked a two-year outflow of direct and portfolio investment, which in turn led to downward pressure on the Canadian dollar and upward pressure on Canadian interest rates.

This simultaneous occurrence of costs and benefits has caused the foreign investment debate to continue. Some critics have claimed that the FIRA has not gone far enough; others have felt that controls should be eased on the foreign ownership of Canadian enterprises.

Those favoring more stringent regulation have pointed to the fact that by the end of 1980, foreigners still controlled 52 percent of the country's mining industry, 55 percent of its manufacturing, and 72 percent of the oil and gas business. The U.S. presence was still dominant, U.S. companies owning 32 percent of the pulp and paper industry, 36 percent of mining and smelting, and 39 percent of manufacturing as a whole. In fact, U.S. firms controlled thirty-seven of the hundred largest Canadian companies.

Some of the people favoring greater control have contended that FIRA has had a positive impact but has simply not gone far enough. They have shown that although foreign firms have increased their R&D in Canada, the 44 percent of total R&D they have undertaken is still less than their share of the economy. The percent of GNP spent on R&D in Canada is still small in comparison with the percentage in some other industrial countries (e.g., about 60% of that in Switzerland). Critics feel that Canadian control will produce increases in R&D; they point to the Canadian takeover of de Havilland from Britain's Hawker Siddeley Group in 1974 and of Canadair from General Dynamics of the United States in 1976. With Canadian ownership and management these firms have greatly increased R&D, developed new products, and increased employment, and they are competing internationally. The critics believe that Canadian takeover of other industries will lead to similar growth in Canada's technical capabilities.

Those who are against more stringent controls have questioned whether Canada will be able to fulfill its technological and capital needs if controls result in a lowering of direct investment flows into Canada. They have pointed out that Canada committed itself to reduce tariffs by 40 percent between 1983 and 1987. This could mean a lower motivation to make market-seeking direct investments in Canada anyway because of easier access to the Canadian market through exports, especially from the United States. Lower inflows might mean lower technological availability to Canadian production. These contentions have been based on two arguments. First, they have questioned whether indigenously controlled firms will undertake in Canada the kind of R&D that foreign firms have been criticized for not undertaking. As evidence they have cited the fact that Northern Telecom, Canada's telecommunications giant, itself maintains an R&D facility with 500 people in the United States. Second, they have shown that technology flows more quickly, more cheaply, and with fewer restrictions between a parent and subsidiary than by license among independent companies. In terms of restrictions, for instance, there is a high incidence of limiting output only for sale in Canada under the licensing arrangements. Among controlled operations, however, a number of investors have transferred technology so that Canada serves as the production base for worldwide sales (e.g., Westinghouse, steam turbines; Motorola, mobile radios; Honeywell, hydronic valves). In terms of capital they point to a Royal Bank of Canada estimate that by 2000, Canada will need $1.4 trillion of energy investment alone, of which $300 billion will have to come from foreign sources. The capital need argument became particularly pervasive as unemployment stayed high from the recession in the early 1980s.

Prime Minister Brian Mulroney was elected in late 1984 and soon thereafter replaced the FIRA with a new agency called Investment Canada. This agency reduces substantially the number of investment applications that are subject to scrutiny. Direct takeovers of Canadian firms with assets of less than $5 million (Canadian) and indirect takeovers of less than $50 million (Canadian) need not be examined. The old review board criterion of "significant benefit" has been replaced with a loosely defined "net benefit" to Canada.

INTRODUCTION

• Pressure groups push to restrict MNE movements
  • home and abroad

Not only in Canada, but in other countries as well, the rapid growth in recent years of international companies has obviously not occurred without controversy. There are, in fact, powerful pressure groups in both home and host countries that have pushed their governments to implement policies

• Fear size of MNE
  • economically larger than many countries
  • executives deal with heads of state

that restrict the movement of multinational firms. These critics are sure to play an even greater role in the future expansion of world business.

This chapter examines the major contentions regarding the practices of MNEs and the major evidence supporting or refuting the contentions. Chapter 12 analyzes the methods by which companies and countries react to criticisms and attempt to strengthen their positions.

The sheer size of many MNEs is cause enough for concern among the countries with which they come into contact. Of the world's fifty largest units in terms of economic output, forty-two are countries and eight are companies. This means, for example, that the sales of General Motors and Exxon exceed the GNP of such countries as Switzerland and Saudi Arabia. Of the next fifty units, thirty-one are companies, and only nineteen are countries.[2] This means that the large MNEs have considerable power in negotiating business arrangements with nation-states that may be of greater consequence than many treaties among countries. Executives of MNEs frequently deal directly with heads of state, not only in small, lesser-developed countries that approve of private ownership but also in large industrialized nations such as the Soviet Union that favor state ownership of productive facilities.

CONFLICTS AMONG CONSTITUENCIES

The Domestic Conflict

• Firm must satisfy
  • stockholders
  • employees
  • customers
  • society at large
• Aims of each in conflict, but
  • all must be satisfied for firm to survive in long run
  • power position of each varies over time
  • harder to balance abroad because managers are less familiar with foreign power groups

A firm must satisfy different groups of people—stockholders, employees, customers, and society at large—if it is to survive. In the short run, the aims of each group are in conflict. Stockholders would like additional sales and productivity increases, which result in higher profits to be passed on to them in the form of increased dividends or appreciation in equity. Employees would like additional compensation. Customers would like lower prices, and society at large may want increased corporate taxes or to have the company perform certain costly social functions. In the long run, all of the aims must be achieved adequately or none will be attained at all, since each group is powerful enough to cause the demise of the organization.

Management must be aware of the need to serve these various interests, but to serve them unevenly at any given period. The reason for the unevenness is that the relative power of each conflicting group varies over time. Thus at one moment, most gains may go to consumers; at another time, most gains may go to stockholders. The task of making necessary trade-offs is a difficult one domestically. Abroad, where corporate managers are not as familiar with customs and power groups as they are at home, the problem of choosing the best alternative is compounded. This is particularly true when dominant interests differ from country to country. In the early 1970s, for example, Ford Motor Company faced quite different priorities in various countries of the world. In Great Britain, labor was clearly in the driver's seat, while prices rose and profits suffered. In the United States, society as a whole (whether consumers or not) demanded more safety and pollution abatement equipment on automobiles, while wage and price freezes were enforced. At the same time, Ford announced that it would build very inexpensive cars in Southeast Asia for the Asian market. There, safety standards and employee compensation gave way to stockholder profits and consumer prices.

Cross-National Conflicts

● Constituencies work for own rather than global objectives

● Decisions in one country have repercussions elsewhere

The most cumbersome problem in overseas relationships, however, is not so much one of trying to serve conflicting interests within countries, but rather one of handling cross-national controversies in a manner that will achieve worldwide business objectives. The international company operates in a nationalistic world. Constituencies in any given country are interested in seeing their own, rather than global, objectives fulfilled. This complicates the task of management, since decisions in one country may have repercussions in another country as well. Among the many decisions of this type are the location of production, decision making, and research and development; the method of acquisition and operation; the markets to be served from production; the prices to charge; and the use of profits. In the opening case, for example, many Canadians were concerned about such issues. Assume that a U.S. investor has production facilities in both the United States and Canada: which facility will export to Venezuela? Clearly the decision will determine where the profits, taxes, employment, and capital flows will be located. Interests in either country, as well as in Venezuela, may claim they should have jurisdiction over the sales.

EVALUATION PROBLEMS

Isolated versus Systems Effects

● Effects of MNE's activities may be positive for one national objective and simultaneously negative for another
  ● pro or anti-MNE groups usually bias publicity on MNEs
  ● should examine systems effects

An MNE's actions may have a bearing on a wide range of economic, social, and political objectives. It is common that a positive influence on one objective, such as full employment, may be concomitant with a negative effect on another objective, such as domestic control over economic matters. In other words, trade-offs are necessary. It is difficult for nations to prioritize objectives, since it is natural to want only benefits without costs, a situation that is seldom possible. In spite of the widespread effects on various parts of the social system, much of the literature analyzing MNEs is written to attempt to isolate effects to a single given objective, sometimes because a solution is needed for a given problem, such as a balance-of-payments deficit for a country. Very often, however, it seems that proponents or opponents of an MNE choose to publicize those activities that may win over support to their way of thinking. One must therefore be very careful to analyze effects in terms of a systems perspective rather than an isolated one. One should also be aware that it is no simple task to evaluate overall effects when difficult value judgments on trade-offs must be made between, for example, a quantifiable economic objective and a political or social effect that must be argued qualitatively.

Cause–Effect Relationships

• Hard to determine if societal conditions are caused by MNE actions

It is usually obvious that, just because two things have moved in relationship to each other, there is not necessarily an interconnection between them. Yet because of the growth of MNEs, a number of occurrences in recent years have been attributed to them. Opponents have linked inequitable income and power distribution, environmental debasement, and societal deprivation to the growth of international firms. Proponents have related tax revenues, employment, and exports to the existence of MNEs. Although the data are often accurate and formidable, one cannot say with certainty what would have happened had MNEs not operated or followed certain practices. Technological developments, competitors' actions, and governmental policies are just three of the variables that encumber a cause–effect analysis.

Individual and Aggregate Effects

• Each MNE and its actions are different but
  • one-by-one examination is costly
  • uniform regulations overlook differences

One astute observer has said, "Like animals in a zoo, multinationals (and their affiliates) come in various shapes and sizes, perform distinctive functions, behave differently and make their individual impacts on the environment."[3] It is thus difficult to make statements about impacts and have these apply to all MNEs. Yet much literature, from the viewpoints of both protagonists and antagonists, has taken isolated examples and presented them as if they were typical. The examples chosen are usually the ones that make interesting reading because of their spectacular or extreme nature. There is therefore some danger that policies may be set on the basis of the exceptional rather than the usual.

There have been some attempts by countries to evaluate MNEs and their activities on an individual basis. Although this might lead to greater fairness and control through the realization that there are differences that should be treated differently, it is a cumbersome and costly process. Many of the policies and control mechanisms are therefore applied to all MNEs. Although this eliminates some of the bureaucracy, it risks throwing out some "good apples" with the "bad apples."

Relative and Absolute Gains or Losses

- Parties involved in international transaction
  - may all gain
  - may all lose
- Some may gain and some may lose
- Even when all gain, parties may disagree over share of gain
  - countries want greater share of benefits from MNE activities

In international transactions involving MNEs it is sometimes erroneously assumed that if one party gains, the other must lose. While that may happen, it is also possible that all parties will either gain or lose in economic transactions. It is inconceivable that any party would willingly participate in a cross-national transaction if it believed that the deal would harm its prioritized objectives. Controversies develop because things do not work out as anticipated, because there are changes in the precedence given to the trade-offs among objectives, and because of disagreements over the distribution of gains when it is acknowledged that both parties have benefited overall. It is in terms of the last problem that most controversies occur. In other words, many critics and governments have taken a similar position to that of Canada, first with the Foreign Investment Review Act and later with Investment Canada, trying not to discourage foreign investment but to secure the maximum benefit from it.[4]

Allegations against International Business Activities

The relationship between international firms and societies has generated so many allegations and controversies that they cannot all be examined in this chapter. A number of these deal not so much with whether international business should take place but rather with some specific practices. These latter allegations apply to specific operational areas of management and can, fortunately, be examined in later chapters of the text. They are no less important than the overall areas to be discussed in this chapter and are listed as follows so that students are aware of the wide range of criticisms:

1. In transferring technology to less-developed countries, prices are set too high and sales restricted too stringently (Chapter 15).
2. If a country attempts regulation, MNEs merely divest and move where regulations are less stringent (Chapter 16).
3. The centralization and control of key functions by MNEs in their home countries perpetuate a neocolonial dependence of less-developed countries (Chapter 17).
4. Sensitive country information is disseminated internationally by MNEs' global intelligence networks (Chapter 17).
5. MNEs introduce superfluous products that do not contribute to social needs and perpetuate class distinctions (Chapter 18).
6. MNEs avoid paying taxes (Chapter 20).
7. Through artificial transfer pricing, MNEs undermine attempts by governments to manage their economic affairs (Chapter 21).

8. The best jobs are given to citizens of the nation in which MNEs have their headquarters (Chapter 22).

9. Inappropriate technology is introduced by MNEs to less-developed countries (Chapter 23).

10. National labor interests are undermined because of the global activities of MNEs (Chapter 23).

ECONOMIC IMPACT

Balance-of-Payment Effects

• One country's surplus is another's deficit, but
  • long- and short-term goals different

Place in the economic system. Few topics elicit as much discussion in international economic relationships as the balance-of-payments effect of trade and investment transactions.[5] The discussion itself leads often to incentives, prohibitions, and other types of governmental interference as countries try to regulate the capital flows that parallel trade and investment movements.

The factor that distinguishes balance-of-payments arguments from other cross-national problems is that gains are a zero sum. In other words, one country's surplus must perforce be another country's deficit. If both countries were looking only at a limited time period and if both were interested only in the balance-of-payments effect of international transactions, then one country might justifiably be described as a winner at the expense of the other. In actuality, however, objectives are not this limited. A country may be willing to endure deficits in order to achieve other aims, such as price stability or growth. A country may also be willing to forego short-term surpluses in favor of long-term ones or vice versa.

• May be positive or negative
• Formula to determine effect is simple, but
  • figures to put in formula are questionable

Effect of individual direct investment. Two extreme hypothetical examples illustrate the need to evaluate each activity separately if one wants to determine the effect on the balance of payments. In the first case, a U.S. firm purchases a Haitian-owned company by depositing dollars in a New York bank for the former owners. No changes are made in the management or operations, so profitability remains the same. Dividends are now remitted to the U.S. owners rather than remaining in Haiti, so a net drain on foreign exchange for Haiti and an influx to the United States have ensued. In the next case a U.S. firm purchases unemployed resources (land, labor, materials, and equipment) in Haiti that it converts to the production of goods that were formerly imported. Because of rising demand, all earnings are reinvested in Haiti, so the entire import substitution is a gain in foreign exchange.

Most investments or nonequity arrangements (such as licensing or management contracts) fall somewhere between these two simplistic and extreme examples and are not so easily evaluated, particularly when policymakers attempt to apply regulations to fit aggregate investment movements. There are numerous measurement difficulties, but guidelines are gradually emerging and are being used by both recipient and donor countries. A basic equation for making an analysis is

$$m + x + c - (m^1 + x^1 + c^1)$$

when

$m =$ import displacement,
$m^1 =$ import stimulus,
$x =$ export stimulus,
$x^1 =$ export reduction,
$c =$ capital inflow for other than import and export payment, and
$c^1 =$ capital outflow for other than import and export payment.

Although the equation is simple, the problem of choosing the proper values to assign is formidable. Let us take for example the case of the net import change $(m - m^1)$, that is the result of the direct investment. To determine the value of m, one would need to know how much would be imported in the absence of the foreign production capability. Clearly, the amount the firm has produced and sold locally is only an indication, since the selling price and quality of products may be different from the imported counterpart that is now excluded. Furthermore, some of the local sales may have been at the expense of local competitors. The value of m^1 should include equipment, components, and materials that are brought in for manufacturing the product locally. It should also include estimates of import increases due to upward movements in national income caused by the capital inflow. For instance, if national income were assumed to have risen $2 million from the investment and the marginal propensity to import were calculated to be 10 percent, imports should have risen by $200,000.

The net export effect $(x - x^1)$ is particularly controversial in donor countries, since conclusions vary widely depending on the assumptions made. The argument is much like the one of whether the chicken or the egg came first, as was apparent in the mid-1960s, when outward investment controls were placed on U.S. firms, and in the more recent proposals for technology export controls. Those in favor of controls in the U.S. have argued that the development of foreign production capabilities are merely substitutes for U.S. exports. There was plenty of evidence to show that many once-exported products had been shifted abroad for production. Opponents of controls countered that the continued exportation of these products would have been impossible because of foreign government restrictions and shifts in cost advantages. They further argued that the investments stimulated exports from the United States because of the purchase by foreign subsidiaries of equipment, materials, components, and complementary products. Figures showed, in fact, that about one quarter of U.S. exports were by international companies to their controlled operations abroad. Again one must make assumptions about the amount of these exports that could have materialized had the subsidiaries not been established.

The net capital flow $(c - c^1)$ is the easiest figure to calculate because of controls at most central banks. The problem in using a given year for evaluation purposes is the time lag between the outward flow of investment funds and the inward flow of remitted earnings from the investment. Thus what appears at a given time to be a favorable or unfavorable capital flow may in fact prove to be the opposite over a longer period. The payback period is affected by differences in company philosophy, type of industry, ability to borrow locally, the host country's balance-of-payments situation, and the perception of relative risk in the recipient country. Consequently, the capital flows may vary widely from one project to another. A further complication arises because of the ability of international companies to transfer funds in disguised forms (see Chapter 19), thus misstating the real consequences of the investments.

Although the equation is useful for broadly evaluating the balance-of-payments effects of investments, it should be used with caution. In addition to some of the data problems mentioned above, an investment movement might have some indirect effects on a country's balance of payments that are not readily quantifiable. For example, an investor might bring new technological or managerial efficiencies that are then emulated by other firms. What these other firms do may therefore affect the country's external economic relations.

- Balance-of-payments effect of direct investments usually
  - positive initially for recipient country and negative for donor
  - positive later for donor country and negative for recipient

Aggregate assumptions and responses. In spite of the formidable task of evaluating investments from a balance-of-payments standpoint, there is near consensus that, while investments are initially favorable to the recipient country and unfavorable to the donor country, the situation reverses after some period of time. The reason is that nearly all investors plan to remit eventually to the parent organization more than they send abroad. If the net value of the foreign investment continues to grow through retained earnings, dividend payments for a given year may ultimately exceed the total capital transfers required for the initial investment. The time period before reversal may vary substantially, and there is much disagreement as to the aggregate time span needed.

- Donors and recipients set policies to try to improve short- or long-term effects
  - donor outflow restrictions
  - recipients set repatriation restrictions, asset valuation control, and conversion to debt as opposed to equity

In the case of U.S. firms' direct investment abroad, for example, more than 60 percent of the net value increase in recent years has typically come from the reinvestment of funds earned abroad. This means that the increase in claims on foreign assets has been coming primarily not from a flow of capital to the foreign operations. It also means that the return flow of funds to the United States from earnings greatly exceeds the outward flow to increase investment abroad. In the 1981–1982 period, for example, the U.S. direct investment position abroad (including the amount from reinvested income) increased by about $6 billion. During those same two years the U.S. investors remitted $22.2 billion back to the United States in dividends.[6]

From the standpoint of donor countries, restrictions on the outflow of capital are a means for improving short-term deficits, since there should be an immediate improvement in the capital account of the balance of payments. Such restrictions should be effective until repatriation in the absence of restrictions would begin to exceed the capital flow that is restricted. After this period, capital outflow restrictions would merely aggravate a deficit problem. Consequently, the restrictions merely buy the possible time needed to institute other means for solving payments difficulties. Both the United Kingdom and the United States have at one time limited direct investment outflows with the result that their firms may not have expanded abroad as extensively as they might have in the absence of the policies. These same firms have additionally had to learn to calculate the balance-of-payments effects of their own activities so as to argue their cases for greater international freedom of movement.

Governments have also sought to attract inflows of long-term capital as a means of developing production that will either displace imports or generate exports. This has been particularly true of less-developed countries. They have sought locally manufactured production in order to ease dependence on the traditional agricultural products and raw materials that have not comprised as important a part of world trade. The problem for recipients, then, is how to take advantage of the benefits of foreign capital while, at the same time, minimizing the long-run adverse effects on the balance of payments.

Many countries have attempted to ease their dilemmas by regulating inflows to assure that short-term positive impacts are maximized and to restrict longer-term capital exports. Countries have sometimes required that new foreign investment be made in the form of freely convertible currencies, industrial equipment, and other physical assets but not in the form of goodwill, technology, patents, trademarks, and other intangibles. These requirements are tied into regulations on maximum repatriation of earnings, which are stated as a percentage of investment. By holding down the stated amount of investment, eventual repatriation is minimized. In this respect, greater control is being exerted over the prices of equipment brought in, especially when the investor is also the equipment supplier, so that the investment value is not overstated. Governments are also becoming more interested in receiving part of the capital contribution in the form of loans and in local holdings of equity so that the future outward capital flow is reduced and has an upward limit.

• MNEs may hold sufficient liquid assets to affect currency values

Currency movements and the balance-of-payments. The United States Tariff Commission estimated in 1973 that the foreign exchange holdings of private institutions were five times those held by central banks.[7] (More recent estimates are not available; however, it is generally concluded that private liquid exchange holdings are still very formidable.) These are the funds that private holders can convert to other currencies and that central banks use to defend against unwanted currency price changes. Thus if a number of international companies perceive that a particular currency is weak and then attempt to reduce their holdings of that currency, the weakness may be aggravated to the point at which central banks are helpless to sustain existing exchange rates. If the world were truly on a system of freely fluctuating exchange rates, then large private holders of currencies, such as MNEs, would have to find other private holders (through bank intermediaries) in order to make conversion transactions. Central banks would not enter the market but would instead let private holders sustain conversion gains or losses. In reality, however, central banks have not wanted their own currencies to fluctuate either upward or downward beyond certain limits.

But do MNEs convert their vast currency holdings in anticipation of exchange rate changes? Evidence thus far suggests that they have not.[8] Nearly all their demand for other currencies has been due to needs for those currencies in order to conduct transactions rather than demanding the currencies because of expectations that exchange rates will change.

Growth and Employment Effects

- Not necessarily a zero-sum game
  - may use unemployed or underemployed resources
  - healthiest domestic firms own bulk of foreign direct investment

Unlike balance of payments, the growth and employment effects of MNEs are not necessarily a zero-sum game among countries. Early economists assumed that production factors were at full employment; consequently, a movement of any of these factors abroad would result in an increase in output abroad and a decrease at home. Even if this assumption were true, the gains in the recipient country might be greater or less than the losses in the donor country. In a nationalistic world, few nations willingly take losses in order for global economic gains to be enhanced. A belief that factor mobility will lead to decreased output for a given country will usually lead to controls by that country over mobility.

Part of this argument is premised on the industry-specific and complementary nature of capital and technology. A farm machinery manufacturer may, for example, be producing maximally for its domestic and export market. It is not easy for this firm to move into other product lines except through acquisition, and acquisition usually just transfers ownership rather than increasing output. The state of process technology may also preclude the immediate use of funds for increased capital intensity in production. By participating in the establishment of a foreign production facility the firm may be able to develop foreign sales without decreasing the employment of resources domestically. In fact the firm may hire additional personnel who are currently unemployed to replace those being transferred abroad, thus increasing income for citizens of the donor country via wages. The firm may receive dividends and royalties from its capital and technology being used abroad, thus further increasing domestic income. The foreign facility may even stimulate export sales because of a need for components and replacement parts along with the ability of the foreign operation to sell the company's related products. U.S. manufacturing MNEs have pointed to the fact that their U.S. exports and employment have increased much more rapidly than U.S. manufacturing exports and employment as a whole.[9]

- **Home country labor has claimed that jobs exported through direct investment**
  - **especially high-technology industries**

Donor country losses.   As the largest donor country for foreign licensing and investment, the United States understandably has some of the major critics of outward movements. One such critic is organized labor, whose argument is that foreign production often displaces what would have been U.S. exports. They cite many examples of highly advanced technology, at least partially developed through governmental contracts, that have been transferred abroad, and they claim that the foreign countries could acquire this technology only from U.S. sources. Among examples cited by AFL-CIO spokesmen are hardware for antimissile systems assembled by Lockheed in Hong Kong, the licensing of rocket technology for launching satellites by McDonnell Douglas to Japan, and the licensing of production of the F-5E fighter to Taiwan by Northrop.[10] According to critics, if these companies had not transferred the technology, foreign buyers would have purchased the products in the United States, thus increasing employment and output. Some critics have argued that U.S. MNEs are now moving their most advanced technologies abroad and are even, in some cases, producing abroad before they do so in the United States.[11] Although the cases cited are few and may not be typical, they may nevertheless be instances of donor country losses and simultaneous gains by recipient countries.

- **May gain through**
  - **more optimum use of production factors**
  - **utilization of idle resources**
  - **upgrade of resource quality**

Recipient country gains.   Most observers agree that an inflow of foreign resources from international firms can initiate increased local development through a more optimum combination of production factors and the utilization or upgrading of idle resources. The most common types of resource transmission are capital and technology, which investors may transfer simultaneously. The firm is motivated to move these resources because of the higher return in an area of shortage than in an area of abundance.

Recent studies have indicated that technology and knowledge transfers may be at least as important as capital in the growth process. A machine embodying new technology should contribute more to output, for example, than a machine that cost as much to build but is obsolete.

International firms may also enable idle resources to be used. The mere existence of resources is no guarantee that they will contribute to output. Oil production, for instance, requires not only the underground deposits, but also the knowledge of where to find them and the capital equipment to bring the oil to the surface. The production is useless without markets and transport facilities, which an international investor may be able to supply. Another less tangible aspect of this relationship may lead to greater resource utilization. If, through exposure to new consumer products, the local labor force develops new wants, this labor force may work longer and harder to acquire the new goods and services.

The upgrading of resources by the international firm may be brought about through the education of local personnel to utilize equipment, technology, and modern production methods. Even such seemingly minor programs as those promoting on-the-job safety may result in a reduction of lost time by workers and down time by machines. The transference of work skills increases efficiency, thereby freeing time for other activities.

- May lose if
  - merely replace local firms
  - take best resources
  - destroy local entrepreneurship

Recipient country losses. Some critics have claimed that there are examples in which MNEs have made investments that domestic firms would otherwise have undertaken. The result may be the bidding up of prices without additional output or the displacement of local entrepreneurship.

A study in the United Kingdom concluded, for example, that a major objection to foreign investors was that they acquire the best personnel at the expense of local companies.[12] Basically, part of the reasoning in the United Kingdom and elsewhere is that the foreign firm, by its ability to raise funds in various countries, can reduce its capital cost vis-à-vis local firms and apply the savings either to attracting the best personnel or to enticing customers from competitors through added promotional efforts. A further argument is that the foreign firm, because of its corporate rather than family structure and its enlightened advancement policies, can attract the best managers.[13]

The evidence to support these arguments is not conclusive. In fact, a number of observers claim that foreign firms are at a disadvantage in staffing.[14] Frequently, international firms do pay higher salaries and spend more on promotion than local firms; however, it is not certain whether this is a result of external advantages or a required added cost of entering new markets. Workers, good or bad, may demand more compensation to attract them away from their present secure positions. This may negate any external cost advantages. The contentions also assume that production would have been as high had the foreign firm not invested. This is not easily determined one way or the other. Additionally, in many instances the local competition also has access to external resources. Shell and British Petroleum, for example, should be able to raise capital in as many locales as a U.S. oil firm investing in the United Kingdom, and local firms, even in less-developed countries, may have access to low-cost government funds that foreign MNEs cannot tap.

The contention that foreign investment destroys local entrepreneurship must be argued largely intuitively. There is some evidence that entrepreneurial drives have an important effect on development and that expectation of success is necessary for the inauguration of entrepreneurial activity. One way of increasing the expectation of success is by assuming that there will be innovators that the local population is willing to emulate. In developing countries particularly the entrepreneurs are apt to begin as very small businesspeople who might even go unnoticed by observers from developed countries and who might easily be displaced by foreign enterprises. Many small cottage industries, for example, have collapsed when confronted with the consolidation efforts of large foreign enterprises because the local population has felt incapable of imitating the large firms.

Much can be said against this contention as well. To begin with, foreign enterprises buy many services, goods, and supplies locally and may thus stimulate local entrepreneurship. The Sears Roebuck experience in Latin America is a good case in point; Sears has actively developed local suppliers.[15] Furthermore, the real entrepreneur will find areas in which to compete; consequently, in any country there are success stories that can be emulated.

Finally, it is frequently contended that by borrowing locally the international firm causes a rise in interest rates and thus reduces borrowing by local firms.[16] Although the fact that subsidiaries have borrowed heavily in local markets is indisputable, the link between this debt and the ability of local firms to finance expansion is not at all clear. In order for international firms to influence interest rates, the amount borrowed would have to be large in relation to the size of the capital market. There is little evidence that this has occurred. Furthermore, there are few examples of international firms that acquire all resources locally. To determine the effect on growth, one would have to establish the net difference by subtracting the local companies' losses from the foreign companies' gains. The additional resources brought in should usually yield a gain for the economy.

Host countries have not only at times prohibited the entry of foreign companies that were believed to inhibit local firms, but they have also restricted local borrowing and have provided incentives for firms to locate in depressed areas where resources are idle rather than scarce. Of particular concern to many countries are foreign investments that involve the purchase of a local company. Canada's Foreign Investment Review Act and its Invest Canada Act, discussed in the opening case of this chapter, are typical of policies in many countries in that they treat acquisitions more carefully than foreign investments started from scratch.

General conclusions. From the prior discussions it is clear that not all MNE activities will have the same effect on growth in either the home or host country, nor are the effects easily determined. Factor mobility by MNEs has tended to generate emotional debate on both sides of the question. While there are dangers in attempting to categorize, the following generalizations from a U.S. Department of Commerce study add some insights into the variables that can determine whether a foreign investment creates a net addition or merely substitutes for other investment:

- Direct investment more likely replaces what local firms would do
  - in industrial countries
  - when technology is not advanced
  - when government stimulus is given to foreign rather than domestic firms
  - when local firms can produce very similar products

1. The part of the world in which the investment is made. Substitution is more likely in developed areas like Western Europe or Canada than in less-developed countries, since the former are more likely to have local firms capable of undertaking similar investments.

2. The degree of product sophistication. Substitution is less likely with respect to advanced technology products than to less sophisticated products because local firms may lack the technical know-how to produce the former. However, this will normally be true only for a limited period of time, since the foreign firms will eventually acquire such know-how.

3. The ability of foreign firms to undertake added investments. This involves not only technical know-how but financial capacity, the aggressiveness of the firms, their availability to needed management talents, and so on.

4. The amount of stimulus to investment provided by governments of the host countries. This may consist either of direct investment incentives or of general policies that are conducive to native investment. Where such stimulus is strong, local firms are likely to undertake investments in areas where foreign firms do not.

5. The degree of product differentiation. If rival firms can produce goods that are identical to those produced by foreign firms, domestic investment is more likely to be a close substitute for foreign investment than if the foreign firms can differentiate their products by style, quality, or brand name.[17]

POLITICAL CONFLICTS

- Concern that
  - MNE is foreign policy instrument of home government
  - MNE is independent of any government
  - MNE is pawn of host government

Because of the size of many MNEs, there is considerable concern that they will undermine through political means the sovereignty of nation-states. At the forefront of the concern is that the MNE will be used as a foreign-policy instrument of its home government.[18] Since the home country for nearly all MNEs is an industrial country, it is understandable that there has been relatively more (but not sole) concern in LDCs. Two other sovereignty questions are raised less frequently, but certainly often enough to warrant discussion. One is that the MNE may become independent of both the home country and the host country, thus making it difficult for either to do certain things that are considered to be in the best societal interest. The other is that the MNE might become so dependent on foreign operations that a host country can then use it as a foreign policy instrument against the home country or another country.

Home Country Control

- Home country laws applied abroad, e.g.,
  - subsidiaries cannot sell to certain countries
  - vague antitrust laws may prevent foreign ownership and combines
  - emerging possibilities such as safety laws

Extraterritoriality. When governments extend the application of their laws to the foreign operations of companies, the term used to describe the situation is **extraterritoriality**. Host countries generally abhor these occurrences, since their own sovereignty over local business practices is weakened. Companies likewise fear situations in which the home and foreign laws are in conflict, since settlement must inevitably be between governmental offices, with companies caught in the middle.

Trade restrictions. The U.S. government has attempted to apply its Trading with the Enemy Act to the foreign affiliates of U.S. firms to keep them from selling to certain communist countries. This puts subsidiaries in such countries as France and Canada in a real dilemma because the laws in those countries require the sales to be made.[19] More recently, a number of countries have agreed to prohibit shipments of certain goods to South Africa because of its racial policies; and through a series of presidential orders, foreign affiliates of U.S. firms have been prevented from making sales even though these orders violate the laws of some of the countries where the affiliates are operating.[20] U.S. firms' subsidiaries are also restricted from participating in the Arab boycott of Israel even though the boycott is a foreign policy instrument of the countries where the subsidiaries are located.[21]

Antitrust. In the case of antitrust the United States has at various times delayed its companies' acquiring facilities in foreign countries (e.g., Gillette's purchase of Braun in West Germany), forced firms to sell their interest in foreign operations (e.g., Alcoa's spin-off of Alcan), and restricted entry of goods produced by foreign combines in which U.S. firms participated (e.g., Swiss watches and parts).[22] The policies for which firms have been restrained have been legal in the countries where the actions took place. In 1979–1980 the Canadian cabinet, the British House of Lords, and the Australian parliament enacted laws that forbade Gulf Oil, Rio Tinto Zinc, and Westinghouse from supplying information to the U.S. Justice Department about their participation in a uranium cartel outside the United States. The Canadian government was particularly outraged because it had been one of the principal organizers of the cartel.[23]

One of the cumbersome problems for U.S. firms has been the vagueness with which the U.S. Justice Department views their associations abroad. This was partially mitigated in 1968 with a publication on foreign merger guidelines. In 1977 the Justice Department published further guidelines, which were amended in 1982.[24] These include case situations on how antitrust enforcement principles would be applied. Included in the associations that might be subject to challenge are participating in cartels to set prices or production quotas, granting exclusive distributorships abroad, and forming joint research and/or manufacturing operations in foreign countries.

Other issues. The U.S. government is by no means the only offender. When Moet-Hennessy bought California vineyards, the home country law in France prevented the use of the term "champagne" for the sparkling wine the company planned to produce.[25] Nor do laws have to be in complete conflict for extraterritoriality to exist. Laws requiring companies to remit earnings or to pay taxes at home on foreign earnings have certainly affected foreign expansion and local governments' control over the expansion.

There are a number of areas in which legal differences among countries enable or even require firms to operate differently among these countries. When home country constituents hold ethical or moral values that are very different from those abroad, there has been a growing concern as to whether home country governments should regulate their MNEs in order to institute those values abroad. As is true of most ethical and value controversies, the arguments are frequently highly emotional. A number of these issues may lead to future extraterritorial application. One of these involves pressures on MNEs to disobey apartheid laws in South Africa. They have had to move to improve conditions for blacks while simultaneously trying to avoid expulsion.[26]

Frequently, regulations in a foreign country are less stringent than those at home because the foreign country has not yet faced certain problems, is less sophisticated at anticipating the adverse effects of certain policies, or believes that the gains outweigh the adversities. For instance, a group of leading Japanese businessmen is reported to have drawn up a plan to remove polluting factories from Japan and locate them in nations of Asia, Latin America, and Africa.[27] A growing controversy in the United States is over whether products withdrawn from U.S. sales after being found too hazardous can be exported for sale abroad. On one hand, people argue that the standards are designed for the U.S. and should not be imposed on other countries, which can block the entry of hazardous products if they so choose. On the other hand, it is argued that there is no biological or ethical reason for treating people differently on safety and that "Made in America" should be a sign of quality and not a warning.[28] Pharmaceutical firms have been criticized for conducting tests on humans abroad that were not allowed in the United States and for selling items abroad that were not yet approved by the U.S. Food and Drug Administration. These situations involve not only the possible problems of extraterritoriality already discussed, but also the problems of whether home country governments or international firms should try to impose their own standards on other countries.

Key Sector Control

- Fear influence or disruption of local politics
- Exclude foreign control of sensitive sectors

Closely related to the extraterritoriality concept is the fear that if foreign ownership dominates key industries, then decisions made outside of the country may have extremely adverse effects on the local economy or may exert an influence on local politics. This suggests two questions:

1. Are the important decisions actually made outside the host countries?
2. If so, are these decisions any different from those that would be made by local companies?

There are numerous examples of decisions that can and have been made centrally, such as what, where, and how much to produce and sell and at what prices. These decisions might cause different rates of expansion in different countries and possible closing of plants with pursuant employment disruption. Furthermore, by withholding resources or accepting strikes the international firm may adversely affect other local industries as well.

It is argued that governments generally have more control over companies that are headquartered in their country than they have over a subsidiary of a foreign firm. Since home country operations usually comprise the largest single portion of activity for companies, they will generally go to further lengths to protect their home position than their foreign ones. Furthermore, since virtually all board members, upper-level corporate officers, and stockholders are nationals of the home country, the firm will tend to favor home country objectives more than foreign country objectives in conflict situations.

The political fears are based on the beliefs that international companies may serve as instruments of foreign policy for their home governments and that they may also be powerful enough to disrupt or influence local politics. The former fear is largely a carryover from colonial periods, when such firms as Levant and the British East India Company very often acted as the political arms of their home governments. One cannot find examples of recent official cooperation of this type. However, there is a fear that powerful foreign firms, by withholding resources at the request of the home government, might influence the political process. In 1975, for example, the U.S. State Department requested that Gulf Oil suspend its Angolan operations in an effort to weaken Soviet-backed factions that were taking control of the government. It was several months before Gulf received State Department permission to deal directly with the leftist government in order to resume operations.[29] Not only have newly emerging nations been concerned. The French and British have worried, for example, that if U.S. computer companies were to withhold output, they could create virtual havoc in the governmental administrations, companies, and research laboratories that depend on them.

- Government assistance to develop competitors in sensitive areas
- State-owned MNEs potentially controlled more easily by home government

Aside from establishing policies that generally restrict foreign investment entry, countries have selectively prevented foreign domination of a so-called **key industry,** one that might affect a very large segment of the economy by virtue of its size or influence on other sectors. Examples of such protection are the various nationalizations of foreign-owned mining, utility, and transportation companies. In other cases the government has required management by local personnel in order to ensure that the entities can survive, if necessary, without foreign domination. Some sensitive areas, such as radio and television transmission stations in the United States, are simply off limits for foreign investment. In a few cases, governments have supported the development of competitive local firms, such as consortia of computer manufacturers (e.g., ICL in Britain, Telefunken and Nixdorf in West Germany, and Siemens, CII, and Philips in West Germany and the Netherlands). In 1981, ICL broke off talks to sell its computer operations to a foreign firm (Sperry or Control Data) after public outcry against the sale and after approval of a U.K. government-guaranteed loan of $420 million for ICL.[30]

State-owned enterprises. MNEs in which governments own a controlling interest have been growing more rapidly in recent years than other MNEs. Furthermore, the number of state-owned enterprises is apparently growing as well. The political concern about home country control of these enterprises is different only in degree from other MNEs. Both may in time of conflict give in to the home country interests; however, the state enterprise may be more prone to do so and may do so more quickly. Home government officials may simply be able to influence these firms more easily. Renault, for example, did not hesitate to transfer production from Spain to France to avoid employment reductions in the home country.[31] A private French MNE might not have made this decision as easily.

MNE Independence

- Can play one country against another, but
  - reluctant to abandon fixed resources
  - countries can still control their own relationship

The discussion thus far has centered on the fear that international firms are unduly influenced by their home governments. Many observers also fear that these companies can manage, by playing one country against another, to avoid coming under almost any unfavorable restriction. For instance, if they do not like the wage rates, union laws, fair employment requirements, or pollution and safety codes in one country, they can move elsewhere or at least threaten to do so. They can, in addition, develop structures that will minimize the payment of taxes anywhere. However, the fact that companies are generally reluctant to abandon fixed assets in one country to move abroad indicates that these charges are probably exaggerated. Furthermore, the country from which a firm moves can easily restrict the importation of the goods produced abroad under the more favorable conditions. Specific types of conflicts concerning the movement of resources will be discussed in subsequent chapters.

Political Involvement

Historically a great influence on local politics
- **little recent evidence**

There is concern that the foreign firm will meddle in local politics to foster its own objectives rather than local ones. As recently as 1949, an association of six European firms handled 66 percent of Nigeria's imports and 70 percent of its exports. Other European firms had a virtual monopoly on shipping and banking. Because of this economic power, the foreign companies, through forced regulations, virtually forbade Nigerian competition and employment except in the more menial and less-paying activities. In spite of the headline examples, such as the discovery in 1972 of offers by ITT to support a group that planned to overthrow the Chilean government, most evidence shows that international firms have avoided local political involvement in recent years. Even in the ITT situation, one might argue that the action was no different than that taken by many locally controlled firms facing nationalization. Nevertheless, such instances kindle fears of a return to earlier periods when some foreign investors did manage to pick local leadership that was supportive of their firm's activities, regardless of the effect on the local population.

Bribery

Payments to government officials widespread
- **to secure business from competitors**
- **to assure safety**
- **by cash or products**
- **through various "laundering" methods**
- **but many government officials' downfall**

Extent. No discussion of the impact of MNEs would be complete without mentioning the disclosures in the 1970s of payments to governmental officials variously described as "scandalous," "improper," "extorted," "unauthorized," "questionable," and "illegal." Inquiries by the Securities and Exchange Commission revealed that by early 1977 a total of 288 companies had acknowledged $412 million of such payments.[32] This has led in turn to a rash of proposals and legislation that would purportedly eliminate these outlays or would make them unquestionably legal.[33]

While much of the criticism has been vented against MNEs, especially those from the United States, which have been the major confessors, it is interesting to note how widespread the practice has been. The investigations showed that officials in industrial as well as developing countries—foreign as well as U.S. nationals, communists as well as noncommunists—have all been participants in the receipt of dubious payments.[34] In the process of examining U.S. MNEs, a number of MNEs from other countries volunteered the information that they follow similar practices in order to conform to the norms of countries where they operate. The SEC study, although pointing out that few firms have been immune from questionable payments, discovered that just ten companies accounted for over half the total payments reported for the 1970–1976 period. The biggest were in millions: Boeing, $70 million; Exxon, $46 million; Northrop, $32 million; Lockheed, $25 million; and Armco Steel, $18 million.[35]

Motives. By far the biggest motive for the outlays was to secure business that might otherwise not have been forthcoming at all or to get it at the expense of competitors. These were mainly for governmental contract sales, and some of the higher fees were in the area of aerospace. Second in importance were expenditures to facilitate governmental services that firms were entitled to receive but that officials would otherwise have delayed. These included such things as product registrations, construction permits, and import clearances. Some firms acknowledged payments in order to reduce tax liabilities, and one (General Tire) paid to keep a competitor from operating in a specific country (Morocco). A group of rubber companies made payments through the Chamber of Rubber Manufacturers in Mexico to get the government to approve price increases that were controlled. Some companies reported payments because of extortion. These included Mobil's payments to stop the closing of its refinery in Naples, Italy, and expenditures by Boise Cascade, IBM, and Gillette to protect the safety of their employees. Some of the payments were contributions to political parties, a practice that is legal in certain foreign countries but not allowed in the United States.

Methods. Most payments were in cash, but in some cases they included products made by the company, such as ITT's gift of a color television set to the managing director of Belgium's state telephone system. Some payments were made directly to governmental officials by the firms; however, most involved the use of intermediaries and/or organizations in third countries. The methods were diverse. For instance, a person who was influential in a purchasing decision or a relative of that person was sometimes put on the firm's payroll as a consultant. In other cases that person was paid as a middleman at a fee that exceeded normal commissions. Another common practice was to overcharge a middleman or governmental agency and rebate the overcharge to an individual, usually in a foreign country, in order to evade taxes or exchange control. One firm (Pullman) even used its auditor to effect payment to a governmental official.

Some consequences. Bribery scandals resulted in the replacement of chiefs of state in Honduras, Japan, and Italy. Prince Bernhard of the Netherlands resigned all his public functions after charges that he had accepted a $1.1 million payoff. Officials were jailed in a number of countries, such as Venezuela, Iran, and Pakistan. Sri Lanka cancelled orders for Lockheed aircraft because of that firm's scandals elsewhere. Many observers contend that these disclosures have helped the political parties in many countries that have been opponents of large defense outlays. The treatment of corporate officers in firms that made payments in most cases confirms the adage that "it is more blessed to give than to receive"—that is, most of the donors have gone unscathed. Even when forced to resign, the officers have usually been kept on as consultants. For example, two Lockheed officers who resigned were paid $100,000 for the first five years and $50,000 for the next five years to serve as consultants.

• Present legislation is controversial because
  • some payments legal to expedite compliance with law, but others not
  • extraterritoriality
  • business may be lost

Foreign Corrupt Practices Act. In 1977 the United States passed controversial legislation making certain payments to foreign officials illegal. Part of the controversy surrounding this legislation has been over its vagueness and seeming inconsistencies. The vagueness stems from the fact that two different U.S. agencies may prosecute firms. In late 1979 the Justice Department published its interpretations of the law.[36] The Securities and Exchange Commission objected to the interpretations but offered none of its own until late 1981, when the SEC proposed to cede its enforcement to the Justice Department.[37] One of the seeming inconsistencies is that it is perfectly legal to make payments to people to expedite their compliance with the law but illegal to make payments to other government officials who are not directly responsible for carrying out the law. For example, a $10,000 payment to a customs official to clear legally permissible merchandise would be legal, but even a small payment to a government minister to influence the customs official would be illegal.[38]

Some of the objections are more fundamental. For the United States to impose its standards on its firms operating in other countries may be viewed in some cases as just another extraterritorial infringement. In fact it may be viewed as a double standard in that U.S. governmental aid is frequently given as a bribe, with the understanding that the recipient country will grant political concessions in return. Furthermore, there is little effort to blame donors or suspend these government-to-government programs when it is discovered that officials in recipient countries have siphoned off aid funds for themselves.

Although the actions of U.S. MNEs have been highly publicized, U.S. MNEs did not invent bribery. At present there are still at least two unknowns:

1. To what extent do domestic firms and MNEs of other countries engage in the activities for which U.S. MNEs have been criticized?
2. To what extent is business lost to those other firms as U.S. MNEs are heavily regulated in their activities abroad?

Host Country Captives

An allegation that is sometimes made about MNEs is that they may become so dependent on foreign operations that they begin to try to influence their home government to adopt policies that are favorable to the foreign countries even though those policies may not be in the best interests of the home government. Such an allegation is difficult to support because there is always disagreement on what policy will lead to the "best interests." However, there are certainly many examples of lobbying efforts by MNEs seeking the adoption of policies that are more palatable to the people abroad with whom they are doing business.

One such situation has involved U.S. oil companies in Angola. The Angolan officials have leaned toward a Marxist-style government, received aid from the Soviet Union, and hosted 30,000 Cuban troops and technicians. Angola has the type of regime that the U.S. government is prone to resist. Many State Department officials have openly expressed concern that Angola will be used as a base for further communist incursions into other countries. Yet such U.S. companies as Cities Service, Texaco, and Gulf have been quietly lobbying in Congress and having discussions with other U.S. MNEs that might open operations in Angola. They have been pushing for the United States to take a neutral stance toward the Angolan government. Critics say that the firms are doing this because they put their investments ahead of U.S. interests. Yet there is no consensus among U.S. governmental authorities. Donald McHenry, the U.S. ambassador to the United Nations under President Carter, agreed with the companies' assessment that a confrontation would merely push Angola closer to the communist bloc.[39]

SUMMARY

- Management must be aware of the need to compromise and satisfy the conflicting interests of stockholders, employees, customers, and society at large. Internationally, the problem is more complex because the relative strength of competing groups will vary by country. Furthermore, the satisfaction of interests in one country may cause dissatisfaction in another country.

- The effects of MNEs are difficult to evaluate because of conflicting influences on different societal objectives, intervening variables that obscure cause–effect relationships, and the differences among MNE practices. Countries are interested not only in their absolute gains or losses, but also in their performance relative to other countries.

- Since a balance-of-payments surplus in one country must result in a deficit elsewhere, trade and investment transactions have been scrutinized closely for their effects. However, countries are often willing to accept short-term deficits in favor of a long-term surplus or to achieve other economic gains.

- The basic effects on the balance of payments of a foreign investment can theoretically be determined, but there are disagreements about many assumptions that must be made concerning the relationship to trade. Projects are so different that it is difficult to generalize and set effective policies to apply to large groups of investors.

- Governments have attempted to utilize investment to improve their own balance-of-payments positions by such devices as regulation of capital flows, requirements of partial local ownership, limitation of local borrowing by foreign investors, and stipulations that a part of capital inflows be in the form of loans rather than equity.

- The growth and employment effects of MNEs do not necessarily benefit one country at the expense of another. Much of the effect is due to the relative resource employment with and/or without the MNE's activities.

- MNEs may contribute to growth and employment by enabling idle resources to be used, by using resources more efficiently, and by upgrading the quality of resources.

- Among the factors affecting growth and employment results are the part of the world where MNEs operate, the product sophistication, the ability of local firms, governmental policies, and the degree of product differentiation.

- The political concerns about MNEs center around the possibilities that they might be used as foreign policy instruments of home or host governments and that they might avoid the control of any government.

- Extraterritoriality is the application of home country laws to the operations of companies abroad. This sometimes leads to conflicts with host countries and may put the international firm in the untenable position of having to violate the law of one country or the other.

- Countries are most fearful of foreign control of key sectors in their economies, since decisions made abroad may be disruptive to the local economic and political stability. Furthermore, foreigners may then have enough power to adversely affect local sovereignty. There have been numerous moves to restrict foreign ownership in these sectors.

C A S E   FOREIGN REAL ESTATE HOLDINGS IN THE UNITED STATES[40]

In comparison with other countries the United States has been relatively free of restrictions on foreign investors. There are few industries, primarily certain types of transportation and communications, in which foreign control is prohibited. These prohibitions have been based on the sensitivity of these areas in informing the public and moving essential commodities in time of crisis. Historically, the only period in which there was a widespread concern about foreign ownership occurred in the late 1800s, when temporary prohibitions were placed on foreign ownership of agricultural land.

The United States has also been a relatively safe place to put investments. The only confiscations have been of properties held by interests from enemy countries during the two world wars. (One may argue that the Revolutionary War was a confiscation of thirteen English investments.) No wars have been fought on U.S. land for over a hundred years; thus the loss of property through political unrest has been negligible.

After World War II, direct investment flows were almost all out of the United States as U.S. companies took advantage of a strong dollar and a welcome by foreign governments to establish foreign facilities and position themselves well during the pursuant growth period. Foreign firms simply lacked the resources to make the equivalent reverse flows to the United States. In the late 1960s the U.S. Department of Commerce established offices for the purpose of luring investors to the United States, and several states began including foreign firms as part of their industrial promotion efforts. Although direct investment into the United States began to accelerate, the movement was largely unnoticed by the general public. One of the reasons was that no approval by U.S. authorities was necessary before the establishment of an investment. Furthermore, it was not even necessary to register anywhere that a foreign investment had been made. Many of the investors maintained a low profile and were not known, even by government officials, to be foreign investors.

The Arab oil embargo of 1973 and publicity attendant on the substantial influx of direct investment to the United States during the next few years led to Congress's adoption of the International Investment Survey Act of 1976. Although studies were carried out to assess the nature of direct investment in the United States and although a number of bills have been introduced to restrict foreign ownership, the United States has basically maintained an open-door policy. Subsequent legislation did become effective in 1979 that requires a foreign direct investor to report the establishment of a new U.S. business or acquisition of an interest in an existing U.S. business. This has not been enough to quiet people who are concerned about the foreign influx. Several bills were introduced in 1979 to limit foreign investment; and the House Committee on Government Operations adopted a report in 1980 entitled "The Adequacy of the Federal Response to Foreign Investment in the United States" that is highly critical of U.S. policy on foreign investment.

Some of the criticism about foreign investment in the United States is in response to the more stringent control of investment in other countries. The attitude is one of "why don't we treat them as harshly as they treat us?" Much of the concern, though, has been about specific key sectors that are deemed vital to the national interest. These have included banking, food, computers, high technology, oil, and coal. One of the areas that has been singled out has been real estate, especially agricultural land.

The Agricultural Foreign Investment Disclosure Act of 1978 now requires the reporting of agriculture land transfer to foreigners. There have been a number of reasons for the interest in real estate. To begin with, it is a sector with an historical emotional tie among Americans. The country was largely settled by landless people who were able to better themselves economically because of the availability of free or cheap land. Any threat of foreign control has traditionally been viewed negatively. Even with the so-called decline of the western frontier, Americans have placed a high priority on relatively cheap agricultural products and on housing. Numerous reports have alleged that large foreign real estate purchases tended to inflate prices. Many Americans have feared that the rising prices will put land out of reach of the average American. There has also been fear that agricultural resources will flow abroad rather than be sold to Americans. But how widespread is foreign ownership? The U.S. Department of Agriculture reported that as of late 1979, less than half of 1 percent of American farmland was owned by foreign investors. Yet the General Accounting Office (GAO) showed a trend of increased foreign ownership. The GAO estimated that 4 percent of the farmland and timberland sold between January 1977 and June 1978 was sold to foreign interests. Much of this was acquired by foreign paper companies such as Bowater of Britain and Abitibi of Canada. A good deal of publicity has also been given to foreign purchases of housing and office buildings in Miami, Houston, and Los Angeles, three areas of considerable activity by foreign purchasers. Although no federal restrictions have been enacted, twenty of the fifty states have restrictions on ownership of property by aliens. Only three states (Iowa, Missouri, and Minnesota) have singled out agricultural property for special treatment.

QUESTIONS

1. In the interests of the United States, should restrictions be placed on the foreign acquisition of real estate?
2. If restrictions were to be placed, what should be restricted (e.g., type of land, nationality of purchaser, use of land, size of holdings)?
3. Should foreign ownership be restricted in sectors other than real estate?
4. What are the likely consequences if the United States does or does not put new limitations on foreign investment?

NOTES

1. Data for the case were taken from "Limits Proposed to Canada Operations," *Wall Street Journal,* February 4, 1972, p. 8; "Foreign Ownership Bill with Tightened Rules Introduced in Canada," *Wall Street Journal,* January 26, 1973, p. 1; "Canadian Brain Drain, *Wall Street Journal,* May 22, 1973, p. 1; "Canada Passes Law to Screen Investments Made There by Foreigners Starting in '74," *Wall Street Journal,* Decem-

ber 14, 1973, p. 21; Mitchell C. Lynch, "Canada to Tighten Foreign Ownership Rein Further as Economic, Job Pictures Improve," *Wall Street Journal,* May 4, 1973, p. 24; Edward Carrigan, "Canada Must Control Own Industry If It's to Progress," *Citizen* [Ottawa], June 27, 1980, p. 6; "Getty Acquisition Rejected by Canada," *New York Times,* March 20, 1981, p. D6; John Urquhart, "Canada Drive," *Wall Street Journal,* February 18, 1981, p. 1ff.; Herbert E. Meyer, "Trudeau's War on U.S. Business," *Fortune,* April 6, 1981, pp. 74–82; John Urquhart, "End of Curb on Foreign Bank Operations in Canada Seen Urged by Commons Panel," *Wall Street Journal,* October 24, 1983, p. 34; Harold Crookell, "The Future of U.S. Direct Investment in Canada," *Business Quarterly,* Vol. 48, No. 2, Summer 1983, pp. 22–28; "Canada Takes 'Positive' Step to Attract Foreign Investment," *American Banker,* January 2, 1985, p. 2.

2. John Hein, "The Top 100 Economies," *Across the Board,* May 1980, pp. 8–11, using data for 1978.

3. John H. Dunning, "The Future of Multinational Enterprise," *Lloyds Bank Review,* July 1974, p. 16.

4. Crookell, *op. cit.,* p. 22.

5. The following discussion draws on problems reported in several studies that attempted to assess the balance-of-payments effects of direct investments. Among these are G. C. Hufbauer and F. M. Adler, *Overseas Manufacturing Investment and the Balance of Payments* (Washington, D.C.: U.S. Treasury, 1968); U.S. Department of Commerce, *The Multinational Corporation: Studies on U.S. Foreign Investment,* Vol. 1 (Washington, D.C., 1972); and Fritz Machlup, Walter S. Salant, and Lorie Tarshis, eds., *International Mobility and Movement of Capital* (New York: National Bureau of Economic Research, 1972).

6. Obie G. Whichard, "U.S. Direct Investment Abroad in 1982," *Survey of Current Business,* Vol. 63, No. 8, August 1983, pp. 14–30.

7. Charles N. Stabler, "Many Critics Charge Multinational Firms Create Money Crises," *Wall Street Journal,* April 19, 1973, p. 1.

8. Ian H. Giddy, "Measuring the World Foreign Exchange Market," paper presented for Academy of International Business, New York, 1978, that also referred to C. Dirck Keyser, Thomas H. E. Moran, and Maxwell W. Hudgins, "Exchange Market Behavior of American Firms," unpublished manuscript (U.S. Treasury Department, November 1978).

9. *The Effects of U.S. Corporate Foreign Investment, 1970–1973* (New York: Business International Corporation, 1975), p. 10.

10. U.S. Senate, Committee on Finance, Subcommittee Hearings on International Trade, *Multinational Corporations,* testimony by Andrew Biemiller, Director of Legislation, AFL-CIO, Washington, D.C., 93rd Congress, 1973, pp. 305–306.

11. Jack Baranson, "Technology Exports Can Hurt Us," *Foreign Policy,* Winter 1976–77, pp. 180–194.

12. John H. Dunning, *American Investment in the British Economy* (London: Political and Economic Planning, 1969), pp. 16–18.

13. Anant R. Nagandhi and S. Benjamin Prasad, *Comparative Management* (New York: Appleton-Century-Crofts, 1971), pp. 121–123.

14. See, for example, "NCR Makes Going Native Pay Off," *Business Week,* December 14, 1968; John Barry, "Ford's Top Britons Quit as U.S. Grip Tightens," *Sunday Times,* November 2, 1965.

15. Richardson Wood and Virginia Keyser, *Sears Roebuck de Mexico, S.A.* (New York: National Planning Association, 1953).

16. Isiah A. Litvak and Christopher J. Maule, eds., *Foreign Investment: The Experience of Host Countries* (New York: Praeger, 1970).

17. U.S. Department of Commerce, *The Multinational Corporation, op. cit.,* p. 61.

18. For a good discussion of various means of gaining political objectives through economic dependency, see Adrienne Armstrong, "The Political Consequences of Economic Dependence," *Journal of Conflict Resolution,* Vol. 25, No. 3, September 1981, pp. 401–428.

19. "Review & Outlook: Exporting Leadership," *Wall Street Journal,* April 9, 1984, p. 28 gives recent examples of disagreements.

20. "Mobil Oil Says Study of Sales to Rhodesia by South Africa Unit Is Blocked by Laws," *Wall Street Journal,* August 30, 1976, p. 22.

21. See, for example, "Anti-Boycott Charges Are Settled by Fines for Nine Companies," *Wall Street Journal,* October 13, 1983, p. 16.

22. These are but a few of the types of antitrust actions; see J. Townsend, "Extraterritorial Antitrust Revisited—Half a Century of Change," paper presented at the Academy of International Business, San Francisco, December 1983.

23. "Extraterritorial Trouble," *Wall Street Journal,* December 20, 1979, p. 7; and "Down under with the U.S. Courts," *Wall Street Journal,* May 1, 1981, p. 24.

24. "Antitrust Guide for Overseas Is Set for Firms," *Wall Street Journal,* January 27, 1977, p. 2; Eleanor M. Fox, "Updating the Antitrust Guide on International Operations—A Greener Light for Export and Investment Abroad," *Vanderbilt Journal of Transnational Law,* Vol. 15, Fall 1982, pp. 713–766.

25. "A Delicious Irony," *Wall Street Journal,* July 17, 1973, p. 44.

26. Mark Maremont, "Fire on Campus, Tremors in the Boardroom," *Business Week,* April 29, 1985, pp. 98–100.

27. Andre van Dam, "The Multinational Corporation vis-à-vis Societies in Transformation," paper presented to the 14th World Congress of Uniapac, Buenos Aires, November 2, 1972, p. 11.

28. Irvin Molotsky, "Exporting Products Recalled in the U.S.," *New York Times,* April 3, 1984, p. A17.

29. "Gulf Oil Seeks Talks to Resume Operations under Angola Regime," *Wall Street Journal,* February 24, 1976, p. 17.

30. "Reports of Sperry Offer for ICL Stoke Ire in U.K.," *Wall Street Journal,* May 5, 1981, p. 35; Barry Newman, "ICL Breaks off Talks with U.S. Firms," *Wall Street Journal,* May 12, 1981, p. 37.

31. Renato Mazzolini, "Government Policies and Government Controlled Enterprises," *Columbia Journal of World Business,* Fall 1980, pp. 47–54.

32. "Questionable Payments Total Put at $412 Million," *Wall Street Journal,* January 21, 1977, p. 2.

33. Jeff Gerth, "Easing of Bribery Law under Fire," *New York Times,* April 30, 1984, p. D1.

34. See, for example, Richard H. Heindel, "American Business Bribery Shakes the World—Can Americans Remake It?" *Intellect,* April 1977, p. 313.

35. Burt Schorr, "Trade Curb on Foreign Firms That Use Bribery Overseas Are Suggested by SEC," *Wall Street Journal,* September 10, 1976, p. 4.

36. Jerry Landauer, "Agency Will Define Corrupt Acts Abroad by U.S. Businesses," *Wall Street Journal,* September 21, 1979, p. 23.

37. Stan Crock, "SEC, to Clarify Ban on Foreign Payoffs, Would Cede Power to Justice Department," *Wall Street Journal,* June 16, 1981, p. 10.

38. John S. Estey and David W. Marston, "Pitfalls (and Loopholes) in the Foreign Bribery Law," *Fortune,* October 9, 1978, pp. 182–188.

39. Steve Mufson, "Friendly Foe," *Wall Street Journal,* March 27, 1981, p. 1ff.

40. Data for the case were taken primarily from Jim Drinkall and Janet Guyon, "Pieces of America," *Wall Street Journal,* September 26, 1979, p. 1ff.; "Alien Corporations Can't Own Property in Oklahoma, Its Attorney General Rules," *Wall Street Journal,* September 19, 1979; "Foreign Share of Farms, 0.5%," *New York Times,* January 28, 1980, p. D1; *International Report,* International Chamber of Commerce, August 29, 1980, p. 3; *International Report,* July 25, 1979, p. 3; "Overview of Restrictions on Foreign Ownership of Agricultural Land in the United States," unpublished report of the law offices of Dechert Price & Rhoads, submitted to the International Business Forum of Pennsylvania Briefing Courses, 1980.

12

International Business Diplomacy

- To demonstrate that the interests of nation-states and multinational firms may be complementary rather than antagonistic.
- To illustrate the importance and nuances of negotiations between business and government in an international context.
- To trace the changing involvements of home country governments in the settlement of MNE disputes with host governments.
- To highlight the collective means by which firms and/or governments may seek to strengthen their positions vis-à-vis the other.
- To indicate the importance of external relations in international business-government conflicts.

Saudi Arabia has one quarter of the world's known reserves, is the largest exporter, and is the second largest producer, after the Soviet Union, of petroleum. About 97 percent of the Saudi production is accounted for by one company, Aramco. Aramco's ownership, policies, and division of earnings have from the outset depended on interactions among (1) the private oil companies owning Aramco, (2) the government of the United States, and (3) the government of Saudi Arabia. As the objectives and power of these three parties have evolved, so have the operations of Aramco. In order to understand the changing relationships it is useful to review some events that preceded Aramco's first oil output in 1939.

U.S. government policy toward U.S. oil firms has historically seemed to be contradictory in many ways. This has been because the government objectives have involved trade-offs as well as changing priorities among the objectives. These have included desires to prevent domestic monopolistic practices by oil firms, ensuring sufficient and cheap oil supplies for U.S. needs, and strengthening the U.S. political position in strategic areas of the world. On one hand, U.S. action dismembered the Standard Oil Trust in order to stimulate domestic competition. On the other hand, the U.S. government has allowed and even encouraged joint actions abroad by the oil firms when it deemed that the actions would lead to the better achievement of the latter two objectives.

At least as far back as 1920 the United States has realized that in the long run it would have insufficient domestic oil supplies. In interim periods, though, oil could not easily be sold as fast as it could be produced. In this environment, U.S. oil firms were in a position to serve both U.S. and Middle East interests. In the 1920s and 1930s the U.S. government wanted its oil companies to gain concessions in the Middle East with the result that "representatives of the industry were called to Washington and told to go out and get it." Concessions would help assure a long-term U.S. supply, and an American presence would weaken the relative positions of the British and French in the area. The U.S. firms were welcomed in the Middle East as competitors to Shell Oil Company, British Petroleum (BP), and Compagnie Française des Pétroles (CFP) from Britain and France. They were also welcomed because they offered some sales in the United States that would otherwise be impossible because of the oil companies' control of distribution in a market glutted with supply.

During the 1920s and 1930s, some of the U.S. oil companies also made secret arrangements abroad that were unpopular with the U.S. public once they came to light. For example, Exxon (formerly called Esso or Standard Oil of New Jersey) agreed with BP and Shell to a system of world prices based on the U.S. price of oil. Exxon's chief executive was forced to resign in 1942 after exposure of his restrictive agreements with I. G. Farben, a major participant in Hitler's war efforts. In these situations the oil companies were not acting as instruments of American foreign policy as they were originally conceived to do. They were instead acting independently of any government. Later they were accused of becoming captive pawns of Middle East Arab policy.

The first two companies to participate in Saudi Arabian oil production were Socal (Standard Oil of California) and Texaco, which negotiated large concessions in a joint venture. At this time the U.S. government had no representatives in Saudi Arabia, and the two companies conducted some quasi-U.S. official diplomacy that continued throughout World War II. The two organized construction of a pipeline to the Mediterranean in 1945 and received U.S. government permission to use steel, which was in very scarce supply. In 1948, Exxon and Mobil joined the original two firms in what became known as Aramco. Mobil owned 10 percent; each of the others held a 30 percent interest.

These four firms along with three others (Gulf, Shell, and BP) were known as the Seven Sisters. Before the 1970s they collectively controlled such a large share of the world's oil from multiple sources that they were almost invulnerable to the actions of any single country. By 1950 the United States was well entrenched in the Cold War, and although it had military supremacy over the Soviet Union, the Truman administration wished to maintain cordial relationships with strategic countries. When King ibn-Saud demanded substantial revenue increases from Aramco, the U.S. government became directly involved in the negotiations. A plan was devised in 1951 whereby the oil companies would maintain their ownership but would pay 50 percent of Aramco's profits as taxes to Saudi Arabia. The companies could then deduct those taxes from their U.S. tax obligations so that, in effect, the increase in revenue to Saudi Arabia was entirely at the expense of the U.S. Treasury.

In 1952, Saudi Arabia was shown what might happen if demands on Aramco were pushed further. Iran expelled Shah Reza Pahlavi and nationalized British oil holdings. All major oil companies boycotted Iranian oil and brought the Mossadegh government to the brink of economic collapse. With CIA support, the Shah was brought back, and the Seven Sisters shared in 95 percent of the ownership of the new Iranian oil company.

Both Presidents Eisenhower and Kennedy proclaimed the importance to U.S. foreign policy of the oil firms' Middle East activities and intervened to prevent antitrust action against them in their joint dealings abroad. In addition to an aim of preventing Soviet entry to the Middle East, the United States was able to sidestep certain Arab-Israeli conflicts by being publicly pro-Israel and having the Aramco partners perform most of the direct interactions with Saudi Arabia. Saudi Arabia was not happy with U.S. policies toward Israel but lacked the means to influence them.

When the Seven Sisters gained 95 percent of the Iranian oil holdings, the other 5 percent went to smaller independent U.S. companies that had previously depended on the Seven Sisters for supplies. This marked the beginning of greater competition among distributors. It also meant that countries could deal directly with the independents to gain a greater portion of the spoils in concessionary agreements. Yet as late as 1960 the producing countries were still unable to prevent the major firms from unilaterally abrogating concessions by reducing the price they paid for oil. This price decrease, which reduced government revenues of petroleum-exporting countries, led to a meeting in Caracas by five governments and the formation there of the Organization of Petroleum Exporting Countries (OPEC). The purposes of OPEC were to prevent companies from unilaterally lowering prices, to gain a greater share of revenues, and to move toward domestic rather than foreign ownership of the assets. Still in the early 1960s, OPEC lacked the power to flex its muscles.

In the 1960s, three new trends weakened the Seven Sisters and strengthened Saudi Arabia's position in Aramco. The first of these was the continued emergence of other oil companies that made concessions in countries that had heretofore not been major suppliers, such as Occidental in Libya and CFP in Algeria. These smaller companies did not have the same diversification of supplies as the Seven Sisters; thus they were less able to move to other supply sources if a country tried unilaterally to change agreement terms.

The second occurrence was that, because of rapidly expanding industrial economies, oil demand was growing faster than supply. The earlier oil glut was quickly becoming an oil squeeze. Not even the Seven Sisters could afford any longer to boycott major supplier countries as they had done earlier in Iran.

The third factor was the lessened threat of military intervention to protect oil investors. The failure of the United States to support the abortive efforts of the British and French to prevent the Egyptian takeover of the Suez Canal was evidence that the major Western powers were unlikely to unify their efforts. The United States, although it had successfully invaded Lebanon in 1958, was less prone to intervene again in the Middle East. This was because the Soviet Union had become relatively much stronger than in 1958; thus the risks of setting off a major war through intervention were greater. The United States was also increasing its military involvement in an unpopular war in Vietnam, so it was less able to lend military support to its oil firms in the Middle East, should such support be requested.

In 1970, Muammar el-Qaddafi of Libya demanded increased prices from Occidental. Since Occidental was almost completely dependent on Libya for crude, the company relented. Qaddafi then confronted the major firms that no longer had sufficient alternative supplies. They gave in as well. Libya's success was noted in other countries, which used OPEC to further strengthen their negotiating positions by dealing collectively with the oil firms. The Teheran Agreement of 1971 immediately increased prices. The embargo by Arab OPEC members in 1973 demonstrated that they had sufficient power to gain further economic demands and to cause Western powers to modify their political positions, particularly in relation to Israel. OPEC now had eleven members and controlled about 93 percent of the world's oil exports.

As the largest OPEC producer, Saudi Arabia has been able to utilize its newfound strengths in several ways. In 1972 it bought a 25 percent interest in Aramco. It increased this to 60 percent in 1974 and 100 percent in 1980 as the conditions that existed in the 1960s continued to cause a power shift in the 1970s. For example, before the fall of Iran's Shah Pahlavi, 80 percent of the world's crude had been handled by a dozen big companies; this fell to 65 percent by 1980. Not only were smaller firms getting a larger stake, but national governments such as Sweden, Germany, Japan, and France were buying directly from oil-producing countries. Saudi Arabia has thus widened the number of customers for its crude from the original four Aramco partners.

But what about Exxon, Texaco, Socal, and Mobil's operations in Saudi Arabia as Aramco has come under government ownership? The companies have been able to exploit their many assets successfully in order to maintain a profitable presence vis-à-vis Saudi Arabia. They have realized that Saudi Arabia's increased oil revenues enable the Saudis to be a lucrative customer. They also know that Saudi Arabia is a vehemently anticommunist country that depends on the West, particularly the United States, for technical and defense assistance.

The Four Sisters have always maintained very cordial relationships with the Saudi government. As the major employer before government purchase into Aramco, the American partners had demonstrated an ability to attract qualified personnel from abroad, to train Saudis, and to run an efficient operation. As Aramco has expanded and moved into new activities, the oil firms have been able to continue these efforts through lucrative contract arrangements. By 1982, Aramco had a work force of over 53,000, of which only about 29,000 were Saudis. Although the number of Saudis employed by Aramco was increasing, so was the number of expatriates—up by 3000 from 1980. There was a near consensus that more foreigners would be needed in increasingly technical positions. By the early 1980s, Saudi Arabia was for the first time pumping more petroleum than it replaced with new discoveries. More advanced technology was necessary to find and extract oil.

The oil firms continue to make a major contribution to Aramco's success by contracting foreign workers, infusing technology, and training Saudi personnel. By the mid-1980s the Four Sisters could once again bargain more strongly with the Saudis because of their ability to sell oil, for which there was suddenly a supply glut brought about by new supplies (e.g., from Mexico) and by decreased demand. The escalation of war between Iran and Iraq also threatened Saudi Arabia's ability to sell.

The oil firms have also been important in helping to mold U.S. foreign policy through lobbying and advertising that "We would like to suggest that there is only one realistic possibility; if the United States were to adopt a neutral position on the Arab-Israeli dispute and a pro-American rather than a pro-Israel policy in the Middle East." Given these contributions to Saudi Arabia, the oil companies have been able to sell their Aramco interest at prices reported to be above the net book value of assets, the last 40 percent for about $2 billion. They have been able to secure a continued source of crude oil. They have been able to profit through management and technical contracts.

INTRODUCTION

- Operating terms
  - influenced by home and host governments
  - shift as priorities shift and as strengths of parties change

The Aramco case illustrates that the terms under which companies operate abroad are greatly influenced by both home and host country policies and that the terms are apt to change over time as government priorities shift and as the relative strengths of the parties evolve. The relative strengths were shown to be affected by such factors as competitive changes, the resources that parties have at their disposal, public opinion that legitimizes positions, and joint efforts with other parties.

As was discussed in the preceding chapter, the foreign operations of companies may have diverse effects on home and host countries, but there is substantial disagreement as to what these effects are and how to deal with them. However, there is agreement on the point that governments and businesses frequently attempt to follow conflicting courses. In fact a discord, if carried to the extreme, may result in a cessation of the particular business-government relationship, as either (1) firms refuse to operate in the locale or (2) governments refuse to grant original or continued operating permission. Short of the extreme are practices that, although not deemed ideal by either party, are nevertheless sufficiently satisfactory to permit a continued but changing relationship. This chapter will examine the means by which international business and governments attempt to improve their own positions vis-à-vis each other.

NEEDS AND ALTERNATIVES FOR FULFILLMENT

Nature of Assets

- Investor and country have assets useful to each other

The international firm and the host country may each control assets that are useful to the other. There is thus an inducement to agree on the establishment of operations and to ensure the operations continue functioning. As was shown in Chapter 11, the foreign firm may be able to bring in locally scarce resources in the form of capital, management talent, raw materials, and technology. These may be used to foster local growth, employment, and balance of payments. The foreign investor may also have access to or control of foreign markets through the ownership of the facilities that make import purchases. International firms may use these multiple facilities as a means to contribute positively to the export development of countries in which they do business. They may also negatively affect the exports of domestic firms by denying them sales access to their operating facilities in other countries, by aggressively competing with them, or by pressuring home country governments to erect barriers to the importation of foreign-made production. Finally, MNEs may be able to take on commercial risks that governments might otherwise have to undertake themselves with funds borrowed in international markets.

Countries likewise have assets to offer foreign investors. First, they offer access to their own markets, which may be available only by the establishment of local production—by far the major attraction, since most output is sold locally. The country also offers resources that may not be available elsewhere. These resources may consist of such things as land needed for agricultural production, raw materials, port facilities, cheap or specialized labor, and funds that can be borrowed reasonably. In fact, the acquisition of some of these resources may be necessary in order for the company to maintain a viable competitive position elsewhere in the world.

Strengths of the Parties

● Alternative sources for acquiring resources affect bargaining strength

If either a company or country has assets that the other would like strongly to acquire and if there are few if any alternatives for acquiring the assets, then negotiated concessions may be very one-sided. For example, when a few large oil companies dominated the extraction, processing, shipment, and final sale of an oversupply of petroleum, developing countries with oil deposits had little choice but to take what the oil firms offered. If a government refused, a firm could easily find another country that would accept a similar proposal. As the supply of petroleum became scarce and as petroleum-producing countries found alternative means for exploiting their resources, the terms of the concessions gradually changed and came more to favor the oil-producing countries. But shifts are not always in favor of countries. Mexico, for example, had such a growing economy during the 1970s that it could require foreign firms to accept a minority position when establishing operations. However, the early 1980s was a period of plummeting oil prices, so capital left Mexico because of fear of the economy. Mexico loosened its regulations to allow majority and even 100-percent foreign ownership.[2] As would be expected, there are vast differences in bargaining strength among countries, among industries, and among firms.

- Strongest company bargaining assets
  - technology
  - product differentiated through advertising
  - ability to export output
  - local product diversity

Company bargaining strength. Although companies have a variety of assets that they can contribute to their foreign operations, some of these have traditionally put them into better bargaining positions than others. There is much anecdotal evidence to support this. For example, IBM has been allowed 100 percent ownership in a number of countries because of the local need for its unique technology, while other firms were refused. Retailers have often had more difficulty gaining concessions than manufacturers because local governments believe (sometimes falsely) that local people can do equally well in retailing but that foreign help is needed in manufacturing. Among investment sectors there have also developed differences in local attitudes. Foreign ownership in such areas as agriculture and extractive industries is not very welcome in many countries because of historical foreign dominations of these sectors and beliefs that the land and subsoil belong to the country as a whole.

A recent study sheds some light on the relative bargaining strength of companies with different characteristics.[3] By examining the percentage of ownership that a large sample of U.S. investors was able to obtain in their Latin American subsidiaries, the study provided evidence to support the claim that the bargain struck between the foreign investor and host country is influenced by the resources brought in by the investor and the number of firms offering similar resources. Two investor assets were significant: technology and product differentiation. Companies that spent a high portion of their sales on R&D—5 percent or more—were able to gain a higher ownership percentage than other firms. The more that firms were able to differentiate their products from those of competitors, as measured by advertising expenditure as a percent of sales, the higher the percentage of ownership of the U.S. parent. The strength of technologically oriented companies is apparently due to the uniqueness of their assets and the perceived need for them by government policymakers for development. Firms that follow a strategy of product differentiation—for example, Coca Cola—have apparently been able to gain local consumer allies who believe the differentiated products to be superior. Two operating characteristics also proved significant: percentage of output exported and product diversity of the subsidiary. The higher the figures, the higher the percentage of ownership. The former, particularly when exports went to other entities controlled by the parent, gained foreign exchange that might otherwise not have been forthcoming. The strength of the latter operating characteristic is less easily explained; however, one possibility is that a variety of products may offer a greater future opportunity to save foreign exchange through import substitution. Another significant variable was the number of competing U.S. foreign investors in the industry for the country. The more competition, the less investors were able to gain in ownership share.

A variable that did not prove to be significant was the financial size of the affiliates. This was in spite of the fact that the Latin American countries have been in great need of capital. At least two factors may have influenced this. First, a large investment may be examined much more closely than a small one because of the potential impact, positive or negative, it might have on the economy. Second, the government may be more prone to borrow funds externally to invest in large enterprises. As many Third World countries have encountered debt-servicing problems in the mid-1980s, they have had to depend more on direct investment for their capital needs.[4] This may strengthen the bargaining position of firms whose primary contribution is capital.

- Biggest bargaining strengths
  - big markets
  - stability

Country bargaining strength.   Generally speaking, firms prefer to establish investments in highly developed countries, which offer large markets and a high degree of stability. On a national basis, countries such as the United States, Canada, and West Germany make few concessions to foreign investors. They are large recipients of investment without having to make special arrangements. In all three of these countries, however, there are differences in treatment between advanced and depressed areas.

Home Country Needs

- Has similar economic objectives as host country
- Has direct political relations with host country

Thus far the discussion has implied that terms of operations are highly dependent on the interplay of needs between the MNE and host country. While this is true, it overlooks the role of the home country, which seldom takes a neutral position in the relationships. Like the host government, the home country government is interested in certain economic objectives and may give incentives to or place constraints on the foreign expansion of its firms in order to gain what it sees as its due share of the rewards. The home government additionally has direct political interests with the host government that temper its position.[5]

Other External Pressures

- Decision makers in business and government must consider opinions of other affected groups

The complementary nature of the assets that international firms and countries control would seem, at first, to dictate a mutual interest in finding means to ensure that mutual benefits are developed. While there are pressures to do this, there are other pressures as well, particularly on governmental decision makers. People in office may have to accommodate those who are critical of international firms, even when doing so may not, in their belief, be in the best interest of the country. The pressure may come from local companies with which the foreign investor is currently or potentially competing, from political opponents who seize the "external" issue as a means of inciting an unsophisticated population against present political leadership, or from critics who reason that more benefits may accrue to the country through alternative means. Managers may also face pressures from stockholders, workers, consumers, government officials, suppliers, and other interest groups outside the country who are concerned with their own interests rather than the achievement of worldwide corporate objectives. These pressures may result in a business–host country relationship that is quite different from what one might expect using a purely economic rationale. Each party should be aware of the types and strengths of these external groups, since they affect the extent to which either side may be able to give in on issues under discussion.

NEGOTIATIONS IN INTERNATIONAL BUSINESS

- Terms for investment and licensing
- Often two-tiered

Increasingly, negotiations are used as a means of deciding the terms by which a company may function or terminate operations in a foreign country. At one time these negotiations were prevalent only for direct investments; more recently, however, they have been extended to the ratification of licensing agreements in some countries. This process often leads to two-tiered bargaining. An MNE must first come to an agreement with a local firm in order to purchase an interest in it or to sell technology to it. Once that accordance is set, a government agency may approve, disapprove, or propose an entirely different set of terms.

Bargaining Process

- Agreement only if overlapping acceptance zones
- Where acceptance is depends on
  - recent agreements
  - negotiating skills

Acceptance zones. Before becoming involved in overseas negotiations a manager will usually have some experience in a domestic bargaining process that is somewhat similar to those in the foreign sphere. For example, collective bargaining negotiations with labor, as well as agreements to acquire or merge facilities with another firm, usually start with an array of proposals from both sides, just as in negotiations with a foreign country. The total package of proposals undoubtedly includes provisions on which one side or the other is willing either to give up entirely or to compromise. These are used as bargaining means, permitting each side to claim that it is reluctantly giving in on some point in exchange for compromise on the part of the other. These are also face-saving devices, which allow either side to report to interested parties that it managed to extract concessions. On certain other points, it is probable that no compromise can be reached.

As in a domestic situation, the foreign negotiation will rely partly on other recent negotiations to serve as models. The domestic model may be the economy as a whole, the industry, or recent company experience. Abroad, what has recently transpired between other companies and the government or between similar types of companies or the same firm in similar countries may serve as a common reference, and negotiations are not likely to stray too far from established precedent. Finally, there are zones of acceptance and nonacceptance on the proposals presented. If the acceptance zones overlap, there is a possibility of coming to an agreement. If they do not overlap, there is no hope for positive negotiations. For example, if General Motors insisted on 100 percent ownership in Japan and the Japanese insisted on 51 percent local ownership, there would be no zone in which to negotiate. If, on the other hand, Chrysler insisted on a "controlling" interest in Mexico but would take as much as it could get, and the Mexicans required "substantial" local capital and wanted to maximize it, there is probably a wide zone of ownership that would be acceptable to both parties. Let us say that Chrysler is willing to go as low as 25 percent and the Mexican government is willing to let Chrysler go as high as 90 percent. The final decision will be based on the negotiating ability of each, their strengths, and other concessions that each makes in the process. Since each side can only speculate on how far the other is willing to go, the exact amount of ownership may fall anywhere within the overlapping acceptance range. One cannot be certain, even after an agreement is reached, that one has extracted the maximum concessions from the other party.

- Many provisions and often long period to negotiate
  - countries may give incentives
  - firms may make concessions

Provisions. The major difference in investment negotiations abroad and the domestic experience is a matter of degree. Negotiations may continue over a much longer period of time abroad and may include many provisions that are unheard of in the home country experience.

Most countries in recent years have given incentives to attract foreign investors. These incentives are usually available to local firms as well; however, local firms may often lack the resources to be in a strong bargaining position. For example, when the Hyster Corporation announced that it would build a $100 million factory in Europe, the company was wooed by representatives of various European governments. The company finally decided on Ireland, where the government agreed to pay for employee training, made a research and development grant, and set a maximum income tax rate of only 10 percent until the year 2000.[6] Other recent incentives have included tax holidays, accelerated depreciation, low-interest loans, loan guarantees, subsidized energy and transportation, and the construction of rail spurs and roads. Governments also provide indirect incentives, such as the presence of a tranquil, trained labor force.

When companies negotiate to gain concessions from a foreign government, they should be aware of some of the problems that the incentives might bring. Companies may encounter more domestic labor problems because of claims that they are exporting jobs in order to get access to cheap labor. The output from the foreign facility may be subject to claims of dumping because of the subsidies given by the host government. It may be more difficult to evaluate management performance in the subsidized operation.[7] Finally, it should be noted that there is always a risk that promises will be broken as situations change.

Negotiations are seldom a one-way street. Companies must also make concessions. In studies done for the World Bank, investors listed many different performance requirements to which they agreed. Those which they found to be the most troublesome were foreign exchange deposits to cover the cost of imports and capital repatriation, limits on payments for services, requirements to create a certain amount of jobs or exports, provisions to reduce the amount of equity held in the subsidiaries, and price controls. Requirements that were considered less bothersome included minimum local inputs into products manufactured, limits on the use of expatriate personnel and on old or reconditioned equipment, control on prices of goods imported or exported to controlled entities of the parent firms, and demands to enter joint ventures.[8]

Renegotiations

- Agreements evolve after operations begin
  - company position usually stronger before entry, but not always
- Negotiated valuation of assets when company leaving country

For early foreign investments in developing countries it was common to get concessions on fixed terms for a long period of time or to expect that the original terms would not change. This type of expectation has almost ceased to exist. Not only may the terms of operations be bargained before setting up operations, but the same terms may also be rebargained at any time after operations are underway.

Generally, a company's best bargaining position exists before it makes a foreign investment. Once the capital and technology have been imported and local nationals have been trained to direct the operations, the foreign firm is needed much less than before.[9] Furthermore, the company now has assets that are not easily moved to more favorable locales. The result is that the host government may be in a better position to extract additional concessions from the company. However, a company that is aware of and responsive to the changing needs and desires of the local economy can maintain or even improve its bargaining position by offering the infusion of additional resources that the country needs. One tactic is the promise of bringing in (or withholding) the latest technology developed abroad. Another is to use plant expansion or export markets as bargaining weapons. A host government may also be restrained from pushing too hard against established investors for fear this will make the country less attractive to other firms the government would like to entice.

A specific type of renegotiation that has been growing in importance is the valuation of company properties that have come under government ownership. The shift may be gradual, as in the case of the increased Saudi Arabian ownership of former Socal, Texaco, Exxon, and Mobil interests in Aramco, or all at once, such as Libya's nationalization of Exxon and Mobil holdings.[10] In either type of situation the amount of funds to be received by the foreign investor may depend on the negotiated valuation.

The Chilean nationalization of the ITT telephone company is indicative of some of the price issues that can arise.[11] The book value of the properties was $153 million; however, the Chilean government offered about a third of that figure because the equipment was in a run-down condition that caused customers to complain about the service. ITT countered that the book value understated the value because a high return on assets had been earned and could be expected to continue in the future. The government countered that the return on assets was due to the rates charged to customers in the monopoly industry rather than to the equipment value. Each party proposed outside appraisal of the value, but each wanted to select appraisers and valuation criteria that would be favorable to its position.

Behavioral Characteristics Affecting Outcome

Possibilities of misunderstanding due to
- different nationalities
- different professions
- different languages

Since negotiations are between investors or potential investors from one country and governmental officials of another country, there is a great possibility of misunderstanding due to cross-country cultural variance as well as possible language differences. Since the individuals involved may react on the basis of how they think their own performances are being evaluated, and since the background and expertise of governmental officials may be quite distinct from that of businesspeople, the intended direction of talks may be uncertain from the start. Finally, there is always a possibility that one side or the other would like to terminate bargaining but is hesitant to do so for fear of alienating future relationships.

Some cultural differences
- some negotiators are decision makers, some not
- some take pragmatic view, some take holistic
- use of gifts and flattery
- some things do not translate well

Cultural factors. Back in the 1930s, Will Rogers quipped, "America has never lost a war and never won a conference." Many participants and observers agree with this assessment of Americans in business negotiations abroad. Much of the problem stems from cultural differences that lead to misunderstandings and mistrust across the conference table. While we cannot delineate all the possible differences (recall Chapter 3), a few have been shown to be of sufficient importance to warrant mention. U.S. negotiators are more apt to have the power to make decisions than their counterpart negotiators from some other countries. They lose confidence when others have to keep checking at the head office. U.S. negotiators want to get to the heart of the matter quickly, whereas some others want to develop rapport and trust before getting to business details. Americans attempt to separate the issues into pragmatic parts, whereas some nationalities view the negotiations holistically.[12] On the basis of nearly 400 interviews, one study found that U.S. executives find it very difficult to know how to establish rapport with governmental officials through gifts, which are not considered bribes by the recipients, or through the flattery of asking advice and opinion.[13]

Language is a problem, particularly when translators have to be used. There may be a problem of finding words to express the exact meaning in another language, requiring occasional pauses while translators resort to dictionaries. Furthermore, facial reactions are difficult to judge because of the time lag between the original statement and receipt of the statement in a second language. Since English is so widely understood worldwide, people with a different native language may understand quite well most of the comments and discussions in English. This gives them the opportunity to eavesdrop on confidential comments and to reflect on possible responses while remarks are being translated into their language. The degree of precision in language that is desired by both groups may also be complicated by cultural factors.

The importance of many of these factors may change during renegotiations because the parties have had time to get to know each other and to know how each operates. There is much less of a risk because of the track record that has been established. If the relationship has been amicable, this quality is apt to be carried over. However, if the past relationship has been hostile, the renegotiation may involve even more suspicion and obstruction than occurred during the original process.[14]

- Business and government officials may mistrust each other
  - may not understand each other's objectives

Personal conflict of negotiators. Governmental and business negotiators may start with mistrust of each other due to historic animosity or the different status of the two professions in each other's country. The investors may come armed with business and economic data that are not well understood by the governmental officials, who may counter with sovereignty considerations that are nearly incomprehensible to the businessperson. Thus it may take considerable time before each understands and has sympathy for the other's position. Even then, there is a possibility that neither will attempt to develop a type of relationship designed to assure the achievement of long-run objectives—they see their rewards as dependent on immediate results and perhaps expect not to be closely connected with longer-run problems.[15]

- Hard to terminate without placing blame on others but
  - should find means to reinstitute future contacts

Termination of negotiations. For a variety of reasons, one or both parties may wish to terminate serious consideration of proposals. The method of cessation can be extremely important; it may affect the negotiators' positions vis-à-vis their superiors and the future transactions between the given country and firm, the company in other parts of the world, and the country with other foreign investors. Since termination is an admission of failure to achieve the objectives originally set forth, negotiators of organizations are prone to place blame publicly on others in order to save face themselves.[16] When Cerro and the Peruvian government broke off negotiations in 1974, public statements were made that would certainly hamper possibilities of any future dealings between the two. Further, the statements by Cerro officials might have made it harder for Peru to attract outside capital, and statements by government officials about Cerro might have made it more difficult for Cerro to negotiate and operate in other countries. For fear of adverse consequences from termination, negotiations sometimes drag out for excessive time periods until a proposal may eventually die unnoticed. Although difficult to do, the parties should attempt to find means whereby each can save face and to avoid publicity as much as possible when talks are terminating.

Simulation of negotiations. For several years, professors at New York University have conducted term-long role-playing negotiations based on actual case histories.[17] This technique may prove to be a valuable device for training negotiators for projects requiring approval of a foreign-government. By practicing their own roles and those of the government's negotiator and by researching the culture and history of the country to determine its attitudes toward foreign investors, business executives may be in a much better position to anticipate responses and plan their own actions.

The use of simulation presupposes that an MNE knows who will be doing the negotiations. The choice of negotiators will depend in part on the importance of the project, the functional areas being considered, and the level of government involved. It is a common practice for MNEs to use a team approach so that persons with legal, financial, and operations responsibility are involved in the decision making. One or more of these might be changed or augmented as the need arises. One factor that is not easily simulated is the possible stress effect of being abroad and away from family and co-workers for an extended period of time. The location of negotiations may thus give one side or the other an advantage in reaching the final agreement.

> • Helps to anticipate other's approach but
> > • hard to simulate stress situations

HOME COUNTRY INVOLVEMENT

The Historical Background

> • Industrial country governments used to protect investors militarily
> • Military intervention not now accepted because of
> > • several historical precedents
> > • cross-national resolutions
> > • East-West schism

In the nineteenth century the home country ensured through military force and coercion that prompt, adequate, and effective compensation would be received for investors in cases of expropriation, a concept known as the **international standard of fair dealing.**[18] The host countries had little to say about this standard. As late as the period between the two world wars, the United States on several occasions sent troops into Latin America to protect investors' property.[19] The 1917 Soviet confiscations without compensation of Russian and foreign private investment led the way to noncoercive interference by home countries in cases of expropriation. In conferences attended by developing countries at The Hague in 1930 and at Montevideo in 1933, participants concluded a treaty stating that "foreigners may not claim rights other or more extensive than nationals."[20] On the basis of this doctrine, Mexico used its own courts in 1938 to settle disputes arising from expropriation of foreign agricultural properties in 1915.[21] This same doctrine formed the precedent for later settlements and, in the absence of specific treaties, is largely adhered to today.

Except for the abortive attempt by British, French, and Israeli forces to prevent Egypt's takeover of the Suez Canal, there have been no major attempts since World War II at direct military intervention to protect property of home country citizens. (There have, however, been numerous threats or actual troop movements by large powers to developing countries during this period. One can argue that property protection was a surreptitious factor in the movements.) The concept of nonintervention has been strengthened by a series of resolutions.* Of probably greater importance than the resolutions has been the East-West political schism. Western nations have feared that excessive intervention into the affairs of developing countries would result in alliance of these countries with (or intervention by) the communist bloc. A secondary factor has been that most expropriations have been selective rather than general, involving a few rather than all foreign firms. It is thought that intervention in these cases might lead to further takeovers and jeopardize settlements for affected foreign firms.

The Use of Bilateral Agreements

- Improve climates for investments abroad
  - usually lack settlement mechanisms
  - do not protect against gradual changes

To improve the foreign investment climates for their investors, fifteen countries (Australia, Austria, Belgium, Canada, Denmark, France, West Germany, Japan, the Netherlands, Norway, Portugal, Sweden, Switzerland, the United Kingdom, and the United States) have established bilateral treaties with foreign governments.[22] Although these agreements differ in detail, they generally provide for home country insurance to investors to cover losses from expropriation, civil war, and currency devaluation or control. The recipient country, by approving an investment, agrees to settle payment on a government-to-government basis. In other words, Gillette could insure its Chinese investment against expropriation because of the bilateral agreement between the United States and the People's Republic of China. If China expropriated Gillette's facilities, the U.S. government would pay Gillette and then seek settlement with China. Other types of bilateral agreements include treaties of friendship, commerce, and navigation as well as prevention of double taxation. All these efforts help promote factor mobility for MNEs.

A major problem with these agreements to protect foreign investments is that they do not normally provide a mechanism for settlement. The host governments may simply lack the financial resources to settle in an appropriate currency, for example. Even if they have the resources, it is not clear

---

* Included among the many are U.N. General Assembly resolutions of 1952 and 1962, the U.N. Covenants on Human Rights of 1955, and the International Trade Organization Conference of 1948.

whether the amount of payment should be settled in local courts, in external courts, or through negotiations. Many recipient countries resist treaties because they imply the abrogation of sovereignty over business activities conducted within their borders and provide more protection for alien property than for that of their own citizens.[23] Another problem is that the agreements do not protect against gradual changes in operating rules, which can substantially reduce the profit of foreign operations. Revere Copper and Brass, for example, was forced by Jamaica to make payments tangibly above those provided by the original investment agreement. The result was an operating loss that the investment insurance did not cover.[24]

Home Country Aid as a Weapon

- Aid cut off when country takes property without compensation
  - does not always change host country attitude
  - not always used owing to multiple home country objectives
- Promise of aid sometimes helps investors

Home countries have effectively used the promise of aid or the threat to withhold it as a means of extracting from host governments terms that are more acceptable to their investors. The Hickenlooper Amendment of 1961, in response to Brazilian nationalizations, provides for the suspension of aid to any country that nationalizes properties of U.S. citizens or that has moved to nullify existing contracts and fails within a given period of time to take appropriate steps for settlement. The Hickenlooper Amendment has been officially used only once—after Ceylon (now Sri Lanka) nationalized certain Esso and Caltex properties in 1962. Ceylon countered by expropriating additional assets of the same companies. However, in the elections of 1965, the opposition party, which promised to settle the dispute, was elected. One day after the new government took office, a settlement was worked out.

The effectiveness of the amendment in the Sri Lanka situation as well as in the other instances is difficult to assess. In several cases, aid has been reduced after takeovers, and the consequences have varied. The possibility of aid termination was a positive factor in the settlement of claims against Argentina between 1962 and 1966. Indonesian leaders, however, seemed unconcerned about loss of aid when they took control of properties in 1965. Nor did Peru quickly change its position of no compensation to Standard Oil of New Jersey, even though U.S. aid fell drastically after the 1968 seizure of property. There is no way of ascertaining whether and to what extent property seizures or substantial changes in operating rules have been averted through threats of aid termination. The use of sanctions has also extended to international lending agencies. In response to nationalizations by Bolivia, Chile, Guyana, Iraq, and Peru, the United States has withheld its support of World Bank loans and refused to approve Export-Import Bank loans to those countries.[25]

Rather than withholding aid and loans, home governments have promised that one or both would be made available if conflict is either avoided or resolved on terms that are more acceptable to the home country foreign investors. Perhaps the best known example of this was the accord in 1965 whereby France agreed to give Algeria $400 million in economic aid over five years in exchange for continued operations by French enterprises in Algeria.[26] More recently, the U.S. governmental negotiators handling claims for W. R. Grace, Heinz, and General Mills in Peru let it be known that Peruvian applications to the Export-Import Bank would be welcomed once an agreeable settlement was reached.[27]

The use of aid and loans, either as a means of averting takeovers of properties by foreign investors or as a force in settling valuation disputes, may certainly be an effective weapon at times, especially since a country may depend heavily on funds from foreign governments and international agencies as either a supplement for or an alternative to foreign private investment. However, the problems are numerous. From the host country viewpoint, threats or promises from a foreign country may place leaders in a position of seemingly being manipulated by foreign powers, possibly forcing them to be even more adamant as public opinion becomes increasingly antiforeign. On the home country side, governments are apt to be inconsistent in their application of financial weapons, since their concerns are primarily with political alliances and concessions rather than with the properties of a few of their citizens. They may thus be willing to give aid in exchange for favorable votes on a U.N. resolution or for permission to locate foreign military bases, or simply through fear that public opinion among nonaligned countries would shift against the country trying to "buy" favorable treatment for its companies. A further problem may occur when home country taxpayers rightfully object to their payments' going abroad in order to assure the safety and continued profitability of investments of a few of their fellow citizens.

Before a home government comes to the assistance of its firms abroad, it must consider a multiplicity of objectives and possible consequences. This is well illustrated by one of the leading authorities on multinational firms:

> When Exxon's Peruvian subsidiary, the International Petroleum Company, was threatened with expropriations in Peru during the 1960s, U.S. policy makers had to ask many thorny questions before they could decide how to react. Would a U.S. response hurt American fishing interests operating off the Peruvian shores? Would it push the Peruvian government to choose French planes for its air force? Would it precipitate a clamp-down on the 600 other American firms then operating in Peru? Would it lead Peru to vote against a variety of U.S. projects in United Nations organizations and elsewhere?[28]

MULTILATERAL SETTLEMENTS

● Settlement of disputes by neutral country or group

● Use courts in third countries

When an international firm or home government is unable to reach agreement with a host country, they may agree to have a third party settle the dispute. In cases of trade disputes, the International Chamber of Commerce in Paris, the Swedish Chamber of Commerce, and specialized commodity associations in London are frequently asked to assist the parties. Since the trade transactions are generally among private groups, the disputes do not create the type of emotional environment that is often attendant upon foreign investment disputes.

Examples of active involvement by third parties in settling investment questions are extremely rare, for such involvement requires a relinquishment of sovereignty by host governments over activities within their own borders. Among the notable uses of external organizations have been the World Bank's agreement to arbitrate the compensation and to act as transfer agent for payments involving the Suez Canal nationalization. Another involved a World Bank nonbinding arbitral award that was accepted by both French bondholders and the City of Tokyo.[29] In 1969 the Center for the International Settlement of Investment Disputes was established under the auspices of the World Bank, providing a formal organization for parties wishing to submit their disputes. However, there is considerable doubt as to whether parties will use the organization extensively in the future. In 1974, Jamaica refused to use the center after seizing foreign bauxite holdings, even though the investors and the Jamaican government had agreed in earlier years to use the center in case of disputes. As yet there is no effective means of imposing international law on nations.

A notable example of a multilateral settlement involved claims between the United States and Iran. This situation differed from many other attempted settlements inasmuch as each country had large amounts of investments in the other's territory. In fact when the two governments froze each other's assets, Iran had substantially more invested in the United States than the United States did in Iran. The two countries agreed to appoint three arbitrators each to an international tribunal at The Hague, and those six selected three more. Part of the assets that the U.S. had held were set aside for the payment of arbitrated claims. By the beginning of 1985, about $300 million had been paid to settle 140 of the nearly 4000 claims of more than $5 billion against Iran.[30]

Courts in third countries may in limited cases be used by international firms as leverage. In 1972, Kennecott Copper, whose investments in Chile had been nationalized, successfully contested in French courts payment from French importers to the Chilean governments on the grounds that Kennecott still owned the operations.[31] A year later, British Petroleum initiated similar legal actions in Greece and Italy and promised litigation in other noncommunist countries to stop payments to Libya for oil from BP's nationalized properties.[32]

After expropriation of their Libyan facilities, California Standard, Texaco, and Arco placed notices in the leading newspapers and periodicals of the major oil-consuming countries. These warned that they might file lawsuits against purchasers of Libyan oil, which the oil firms claimed for themselves. They also had arbitrators appointed by the International Court of Justice at The Hague who ruled in the firms' favor and set an amount of compensation.[33] A problem with the International Court of Justice (the World Court) is that a defendant country must consent to any judgment, and there have been many examples of nonconsent. A result is that the Court handles few cases. Between 1966 and 1981 the Court handled only six new cases.[34]

CONSORTIUM APPROACHES

● Companies or countries join together to strengthen bargaining position, e.g., OPEC, oil firms, ANCOM, Arab boycott, codes of conduct, cross-organization production

● Companies have banded together, and countries have banded together

As was mentioned earlier, a company may at times be able to play one country against another, or a government may be able to do the same with international firms. When in a relatively weak position, companies or countries may be able to join together to present a united front when dealing with the previously more powerful entity.

Petroleum

The Aramco case at the beginning of the chapter offers a good example of how companies have banded together on one side and countries have joined forces on the other side. The unity has strengthened both sides and at different points has helped to give advantages to one over the other.

Ancom

● Common regulations governing foreign investment ownership

In 1969, five South American countries (Bolivia, Chile, Colombia, Ecuador, and Peru) formally initiated the Andean Common Market (ANCOM). Venezuela later joined the arrangement. What set this trading group apart from other forms of economic integration was the common policy toward foreign capital, trademarks, patents, licenses, and royalties. By unifying the policy the aim was to limit the role of MNEs and to prevent them from serving all the member countries by locating in a country with less stringent regulations. In contrast, the members of the European Community did not have a common policy in the 1960s, and there were occasions when France wished to restrict the growth of MNE penetration within its market by withholding ownership permission. Yet France was helpless, since MNEs could serve the French market through production in Belgium, where they were welcome. Basically, ANCOM sought to decrease foreign ownership to a maximum of 51 percent per enterprise, to exclude foreign investment in certain key sectors such as banking, and to restrict licensing arrangements between MNEs and their subsidiaries. The attempt to get the membership to adhere to this common stance has been less than fully successful, however. Chile has withdrawn from the group after disregarding the provisions, and Colombia and Peru in recent years have enforced the agreement less stringently than was originally intended by the member countries.

Arab Boycott

- Loose arrangement
  - may cease business with firms doing business with Israel
  - secondary boycott—may cease business with firms that do business with boycotted companies

Efforts have been made, soliciting the cooperation of all Arab states, to weaken Israel by boycotting purchases of Israeli goods and by refusing to do business with firms that sell strategic tools and certain resources to Israel.[35] This is a loose agreement among participants rather than a highly structured agreement. The looseness of the boycott is in some ways a strength in that it has allowed Arab countries to buy from some firms selling to Israel when they desperately needed the goods themselves. The prevention of trade between Israel and Arab states is not an unusual type of practice, nor does it have much impact on MNEs. What is different about this arrangement is that it often forces MNEs headquartered in other countries to make a choice of selling either to the Arab countries or to Israel, but not to both. (The People's Republic of China has at times also retaliated by disallowing certain business with a given country whose firms did sensitive business with Taiwan.)[36] By banding together, the Arab countries represent a very formidable market. Although it is impossible to measure the precise impact of the boycott activities, the big difference in market size has undoubtedly caused many MNEs to think twice about doing business with Israel. When Renault, a French state-owned vehicle maker, bought a controlling interest in American Motors, it also acquired the American Motors' contract to send Jeep assembly kits to Israel. Renault was immediately boycotted; the boycott threatened the loss of 10 percent of its truck sales.[37] Because of the voluntary nature of the boycott, however, the losses to Renault did not materialize.

Another distinguishing feature is the nature of a so-called secondary boycott. For example, Ford Motor Company is boycotted by the Arab League. In 1981, Ford was involved in negotiating a joint venture in the United States with Toyota; however, Saudi Arabia threatened retaliation against any firm that concluded a joint venture or production-licensing agreement with Ford. Since Saudi Arabia was the world's second largest importer of Japanese cars and since Toyota sold 128,000 cars there in 1980, the Saudi warning had to be considered seriously.[38] Toyota subsequently broke off the negotiations with Ford but did not indicate that the threatened boycott was a factor.

Codes of Conduct

- Clarify collective attitudes toward MNE activities
  - by a number of organizations
  - usually fairly vague
  - voluntary compliance
  - may make it easier for countries to legislate

The first widespread attempt to regulate direct investment on a multilateral basis was made in 1929 by the League of Nations. The attention at that time was on foreign exploitation of the tropical commodity industry. Proposals were quickly discarded, however, when the Great Depression preempted attention. Since World War II there have been several attempts at agreements that would deal in part with the relationship between foreign investors and governments. Among these were the International Trade Organization (ITO) of 1948, which really never became operative, attempts in 1951 by the U.N. Economic and Social Council (ECOSOC) to regulate antitrust, and the 1961 Code for Liberalization of Capital Movements established by the Organization for Economic Cooperation and Development (OECD).[39] None of these appears to have had much effect on MNE operations.

In 1975 the newly created Center on Transnational Corporations first met at the United Nations as a result of complaints issued by a large group of poor countries. (The so-called "group of 77" now comprises more than 100 less-developed countries.) The Center provides for the collection of information on MNE activities, is a forum for publicizing common complaints, and is considering the adoption of several codes of conduct for the activities of MNEs. Meanwhile, the OECD, which is comprised of industrial countries, attempted to head off complaints by writing and approving its own code in 1976. The codes requested by the Group of 77, as well as the code set by the OECD, are necessarily vague. They must be vague so that consensus may be reached among various nations as well as among groups within the nations. The codes are also voluntary; adoption does not guarantee enforcement. What the codes may do, however, is to clarify a collective attitude toward specific practices of MNEs that will make it easier to pass restrictive legislation at the national level without fear that the legislation is greatly out of step with external public opinion.[40]

Joint Production

- Used by countries to strengthen national capabilities vis-à-vis strong foreign competitor
- Used by firms
  - to spread risk
  - to deal more strongly with governments

To counter production dominance by firms from other countries, countries have fostered consolidation among their own manufacturers. They have given governmental assistance to R&D and preferred their own firms in governmental contracts. Two of the most notable efforts have been the development of a consortium in Europe to compete against Boeing in aircraft production and the development of various cooperative arrangements in Europe to counter IBM's dominance. One of the more notable efforts has been the EC's Esprit program of $1.3 billion to fund electronics research.[41]

Another approach has been for two or more firms from different countries to band together, not so much to strengthen the initial negotiating terms, but rather to improve positions in possible later negotiations. By investing a smaller amount in a given locality, each firm can invest in more countries, thus reducing the impact of loss in one. Furthermore, a host government may be more hesitant to deal simultaneously with more than one home government in conflict situations.

EXTERNAL RELATIONS APPROACHES

The Need by Countries

- Make selves known to attract investors
- Give country viewpoint when controversy with MNE

Countries that wish to attract more foreign investment have sometimes found either that they are inadequately known to investors or that investors have false impressions of business possibilities within their borders. Some potential investments are thus overlooked rather than rejected. An investment in a small country such as Mauritius may not be considered simply because the investment decision makers have never heard of the country. Other countries may be victims of publicity attendant on conditions in neighboring countries. For example, there is a tendency to stereotype the nations in Africa or in Latin America as a group. Investment flows to Costa Rica may thus suffer because of a war between El Salvador and Honduras, anti-U.S. sentiment in Nicaragua, nationalization programs in Peru, or political unrest in Guatemala.

To overcome either bad publicity or no publicity at all, many countries have established public relations programs abroad. Their activities are extremely varied. Some include participation in world fairs and exhibits so that the country becomes better known. Advertising is used to give data on the economy. For example, it is common to see full-page advertisements in the *Wall Street Journal* on such subjects as "Reasons to Invest in the Dominican Republic." In order to become better known, Morocco waged a campaign using advertisements with the slogan, "Invest in Morocco. It may never have crossed your mind." Countries have also used advertising media to overcome the problems of adverse publicity. The government of Peru, for example, took advertising space in the *New York Times* to assert its good faith and explain its position in negotiating the settlement with Cerro on expropriated properties.

Company Approaches

- Publicize good citizenship activities
  - that conduct of business satisfies societal objectives
  - that performing nonbusiness functions to help society

Many firms strongly believe that by acting as a good corporate citizen abroad they will remove local animosities and concern that might affect their short- or long-term competitive ability. Some have even gone so far as to set up their own published codes of conduct. The behavior itself may not be sufficient, however, since employees, governmental officials, consumers, and other groups may not know or understand what the company is doing. W. R. Grace's chairman, J. Peter Grace, has said, "No matter how responsi-

- Might increase number of local proponents through
  - ownership sharing
  - avoiding direct confrontation
  - local management
  - local R&D
- Too much concession may mean the MNE is no longer needed

bly a corporation behaves, it will be viewed with skepticism unless it effectively communicates its activities, its plans, and its goals to its many publics.[42]

Because of conflicting pressures on the international firm from different groups, the investor can almost always be accused of bad behavior by someone. For instance, if the company offers higher wages, it may be accused of monopolistic practices and aiding inflation by attracting workers from competitors. If it pays only the local going wage, the contention may be that workers are exploited. By understanding the relative power of competing groups served by the firm, management may at least be able to emphasize practices that benefit most of the groups that are in a position to substantially help or hurt the firm. A good rule for serving a given group is to try to maximize benefits without excessively disrupting the local situation. Within any given economy there is usually a range of prices, wages, and returns on investment. The international company may thus be able to be among the leaders (e.g., have wage rates or investment returns among the top quarter of firms) without being accused of disruptive practices, while still satisfying the groups directly involved.

Management should avoid direct confrontation whenever possible, since confrontation may merely force opponents to be adamant in their views. When a foreign company in India was accused by a governmental official of inefficiency in the construction of a turnkey fertilizer plant and the accusations were leaked to the press, the company countered by refuting charges in newspaper advertisements, a tactic that merely served to challenge authority and publicly tarnish the government employee's credentials. Conversely, in response to newspaper criticism about a U.S. pharmaceutical firm's labeling in Europe, the company decided to work with the Health Ministry, since criticisms affected not only the company but also the ministry's supervision of the matter. By jointly answering the charges, rapport was maintained between the firm and its major regulator and consumer.[43]

As in these two examples, much of the public relations efforts of companies are defensive, that is, in response to public criticism. This may not be sufficient. In fact by this time the efforts may be too little, too late. Gulf & Western, for example, reacted to adverse criticism, primarily in the United States, about its labor relations practices in the Dominican Republic by committing $100 million over a ten-year period to improve worker welfare through such things as housing construction and education programs. Several years later, however, the criticism had not subsided measurably, and Gulf & Western announced that it would cease operations in the Dominican Republic.[44]

The firm should organize means to increase the number of local proponents and dampen potential criticism. Opinion surveys of such interested parties as customers and workers can be conducted through various means so as to allay misconceptions, anticipate criticism, and thereby head off potentially more damaging accusations. In the past few years, many MNEs have begun advocacy publicity at home and abroad, which is an aggressive effort to win support for their international activities.[45] For example, Mobil has used newspaper and magazine advertisements to support its international vertical integration. Both Rohm and Haas and Caterpillar have made films to support the positive effects their activities have on home and host country societies.

While it may not always be possible to dispel criticism, the international firm can do several things to mitigate it. One method is to consider fully those things that are important to people in the host country. Or it may be something as fundamental as having the new manager continue a policy initiated by previous domestic management, such as allowing workers to leave the assembly line for a tea break. On the question of what to centralize and what to decentralize, there is much to be said for permitting the local manager to determine policies concerning local customs and social matters. On such sensitive issues as employment and worker output, changes should be made only after consultation regarding the attitudes of locally interested parties. Headquarters personnel may also serve a useful public relations function on the local scene. Since their positions are considered to be higher than those of local managers, they may be better received, and by higher governmental authorities.

The foreign company may also foster a sense of local participation designed both to reduce the image of foreignness and to develop local proponents whose personal objectives may be fulfilled by the continued operations of the foreign investor. The parent company can follow a policy that involves its subsidiary in purchasing local supplies and raw materials whenever possible. It might be feasible for the local subsidiary to subcontract part of its assembly operations. In the case of purchasing component parts or subcontracting, it may even be feasible for the parent or the subsidiary to make a loan or give technical assistance to help the local supplier initiate or expand a plant. If it is economically feasible, R&D activities may be undertaken within the host country. Another possibility for local participation would be a stock option plan for country nationals employed by the subsidiary. A company interested in improving its image in the host country may also establish a specific program for gradually replacing home country personnel with local nationals. Even local union officials may be more prone to work cooperatively with management rather than defensively if they are informed directly by management of possible company actions.

The main problem with local participation is that, if carried to an extreme, the host country becomes less dependent on the foreign firm. If supplies can be acquired locally and if local employees can manage the enterprise and develop new technology for it, the local citizenry may realistically question the continued necessity of the foreign ownership on existing terms. The company strategy might well be to hold out on some resources so that the company is still needed. For instance, a centralized R&D laboratory might be in charge of new product development, while the local R&D facility handles the adaptations for local market and production conditions.

In addition to conducting their business in a locally responsible manner and publicizing that conduct, some companies have found it useful to take on additional social functions that might build local support. For example, Dow Chemical financed a kindergarten in Chile, Citibank participated in a reforestation program in the Philippines, and McDonald's sponsored a telethon in Australia to raise funds for disabled children.[46]

It has also been noted that firms have sometimes been permitted greater latitude in their operations when they have agreed to invest in priority operations outside their normal line of business. These have been negotiated agreements, such as a mining firm's agreement to lay out two plantations in Nigeria in exchange for relative freedom in operating its mining venture.[47]

Good corporate citizenship and the publicity attendant on it may not be sufficient to guarantee the continued conduct of business activity. If public opinion is directed against foreign private ownership in general, such as in the Cuban expropriations, good citizens will lose out along with the bad ones. If one is doing business as a key firm in a key sector, criticisms may come simultaneously from so many directions that company defense gradually loses strength. Even in these exceptional situations an external affairs program may identify problem areas sufficiently in advance for the company to forestall adverse actions and to establish policies that prevent or minimize losses, such as decreasing new parent obligations, selling ownership to local governments or private investors, and shifting into less visible types of local enterprises.

There may also be occasions when an MNE finds it advantageous to be uncompromising in its dealings with a government, even when the adversary positions are reported publicly. The firm may assess its bargaining position as being sufficiently strong to afford to be adamant, or the firm may perceive that compromises will weaken its position in other countries. Even in these instances, however, the MNE should attempt to keep the government from looking as if it has given in to pressures once the company position is accepted. Gulf & Western, for example, negotiated for five years with the Thai government for a zinc mine and refinery without coming to an agreement. Then the firm closed its office in Bangkok, which was widely reported as an effort to bully the government into accepting terms. Within a week the Thai government did accept an agreement, but Gulf & Western announced that the office closing was simply a cost reduction measure during a transition period.[48]

SUMMARY

- Although host countries and international firms may hold resources that, if combined, should achieve objectives for both, conflict may cause one or both parties to withhold resources, thus preventing the full functioning of international business activities.

- Both the managers of international firms and the host country governmental officials must respond to interest groups that may see different advantages or no advantage at all to the business-government relationship. Therefore the final outcome of the relationship may not be the one expected from a purely economic viewpoint.

- Negotiations are increasingly used to determine the terms under which a company may operate in a foreign country. This negotiating process has many similarities to the domestic processes of company acquisition and collective bargaining. The major differences in the international sphere are the much larger number of provisions, the general lack of a fixed time duration for an agreement, and the need to agree on company property values in cases of nationalization.

- The terms under which an international firm may be permitted to operate in a given country will be determined to a great extent by the relative degree to which the company needs the country and vice versa. As the relative needs evolve over time, new terms of operation are apt to reflect the shift in bargaining strength.

- Generally, a company's best bargaining position is before it begins operation; once resources are committed to the foreign operation, the firm cannot easily move elsewhere. The company usually can maintain a strong bargaining position by keeping possession of additional resources the country needs but cannot easily attain from alternative sources.

- Since negotiations are conducted largely between parties whose cultures, educational backgrounds, and expectations differ, it is very difficult to understand sentiments and to present convincing arguments. Negotiation simulation offers a means for anticipating responses and for planning an approach to the actual bargaining.

- Historically, developed countries ensured through military intervention and coercion that the terms agreed upon between their investors and recipient countries would be carried out. The East-West political schism and a series of international resolutions have caused the near demise of these methods for settling disputes. The promise of giving or withholding aid has been used more recently by developed countries as a device for influencing host governments.

- A number of bilateral treaties have been established whereby host countries agree to compensate investors for losses from expropriation, civil war, and currency devaluation or control. These agreements are not clear about the mechanism or place of settlement for the losses.

- Although international organizations or groups in third countries are frequently used to arbitrate trade disputes among individuals from more than one country, this method has been used very rarely to settle investment disputes. The reason is that governments are reluctant to relinquish sovereignty over matters occurring within their borders.

- To prevent companies from playing one country against another or vice versa, groups of governments or companies have occasionally banded together to present a unified front in order to improve the terms received.

- External relations may be used by both companies and countries to develop a good image, overcome a bad one, and create useful proponents for one's position. This strategy, if successful, may result in better terms of operation for either side.

C A S E   JAMAICA LURES FOREIGN HOTELS[49]

Shortly after Ronald Reagan was inaugurated President of the United States in 1981, his first official visit by another head of state was from Prime Minister Edward P. G. Seaga of Jamaica. This "first" was no accident. One of the major foreign policy concerns of the new Reagan administration was a growing communist influence in the Caribbean area. Nicaragua and Grenada had recently swung far to the left, and guerrilla activity in El Salvador and Guatemala augured similar fates. Jamaica had recently voted out of office the regime of Michael Manley, which was pro-Cuban; thus Seaga offered the "great right hope" to the new U.S. administration. One of the major items of discussion between Reagan and Seaga was how to spur U.S. private assistance to Jamaica, especially in the ailing tourist industry. Agreement was reached whereby a private group of Americans and Jamaicans led by David Rockefeller would seek development of joint projects in Jamaica. A second agreement allowed Americans to hold tax-deductible business conventions in Jamaica, a move designed to spur tourism but one that was criticized in Puerto Rico because of expectations that any increase would be at its expense. The political objectives of future U.S. business involvement in Jamaica were highlighted by Curt Strand, president of Hilton International: "It's one of our few recent foreign policy victories. It's yanked out of the jaws of Cuba. If we can't help a little country like that, what credibility do we have as proponents of private enterprise?"

The main reason for the Seaga government's giving tourism development a high priority was that, despite an exhibited comparative advantage in attracting tourists because of climate, location, and natural beauty, the once-thriving tourist industry had fallen on hard times while Manley was in office. The situation had become so drastic, in fact, that the government had to take over fourteen hotels, primarily in the 1976–1977 period, because owners were unable to continue mortgage payments. These government hotels now comprised the largest chain in the Caribbean and half the hotel rooms in Jamaica. In the thirty-three months before Seaga took office, the hotels lost over $100 million. Therefore not only was tourism a potential source of funds for the economy, but it could also help alleviate the current drain on government budgets that was necessary to cover the loss.

Tourism also involved high visibility both inside and outside Jamaica; thus successes in tourism might build confidence among persons who could help the Jamaican economy. Mr. Seaga said, "Every segment is vital because we took over such a rotten state of affairs. But tourism has an important special spin off: people coming here, liking it and investing in the future of the country."

Not everyone has had the same opinion about the place of international tourism in development. Most of the local jobs are the low-level service type, catering to foreigners who expect luxury and who spend more per day than the worker earns in a month. One must remember that Jamaica has a history of slavery, a 90 percent black population, and a very recent (1962) throwing-off of colonial rule. The luring of primarily white foreign tourists is thus viewed by some as neocolonialism.

There are economic arguments as well. Several studies have indicated that tourism tends to reduce agricultural production in two ways. First, many agricultural workers merely shift employment to nonagricultural areas without being fully replaced. Second, foreign tourists want familiar rather than local foods. Rather than serving ackee and codfish and curried goatbelly soup, the tourist industry imports other foods, which are eventually demanded by the local population. This leakage of earnings to buy imports is further carried over in buying other hotel and restaurant supplies and stocking duty-free shops, where tourists make most of their purchases.

Hotels were not the only enterprises that had been taken over under Manley. Jamaica was expected to begin the biggest desocialization program since the Allende government was replaced in Chile. But because of the losses that the government was incurring, hotels were considered to be a good first sector in which to move to private participation. Large foreign hotel chains were in a better position to infuse efficient management systems and to attract tourists, the latter because of sales and reservations networks and because many people prefer to stay in chains that they know abroad.

Even with possible increased participation by foreign hotel organizations, the outlook for foreign tourism was mixed. From a positive standpoint, the president of the Jamaica Hotel and Tourist Association toured the United States and found renewed interest among travel agents in booking space. Political violence that killed over 700 people in 1980 and caused consternation among tourists had been quelled. The government embarked on widely publicized slogans of "Jamaica is smiling again" and "Come back to Jamaica." From a negative standpoint there was still uncertainty as to how people would perceive violence. The earlier deaths had not been in tourist areas. Nor had they affected tourists, but they did have an impact on the number of tourists. Jamaica did not permit gambling as did many other Caribbean areas that picked up Jamaica's slack. If tourists could be persuaded to come back initially, there was the chance that their negative impressions would cause another downturn. Many of the hotels had not been kept up during the Manley years, and development of infrastructure had fallen behind. There was the risk that tourists would find less-than-posh accommodations, crumbled roads, and frequent power outages.

The overall political-economic outlook was also mixed. Seaga inherited a 30 percent inflation rate and a 35 percent unemployment rate. The country was also saddled with huge foreign debts and a need for substantial foreign exchange for such necessities as oil and food. Sugar yield was going steadily down because of soil depletion and plant disease. Yet Seaga gained breathing time by negotiating a $700 million IMF loan with fewer strings attached than usual, secured a rescheduling of $450 million of commercial bank debt, and was actively negotiating aid and loans from a number of countries. These actions were not totally well received in Jamaica. A business leader said, "Every time Mr. Manley borrowed a dollar, everybody said, 'Oh my God!' Now Mr. Seaga is borrowing everywhere, and everybody says, 'What a great guy!' "

Another problem was labor. There was a substantial emigration of talented people in the late 1970s. A political scientist at the University of the West Indies said, "The loss of human resources is the most devastating problem facing Jamaica today." Citibank lost 30 percent of its staff in an eighteen-month period as personnel migrated primarily to Canada and the United States. By 1979 there was only one dentist per 24,000 people, and medical and dental personnel complained of power outages at crucial times of treating patients. By mid-1980 there were reports of large remigrations to Jamaica, but numbers were unconfirmed. There were also substantial constraints against work permits for non-Jamaicans. A U.S. Embassy report cautioned that "investors seeking skilled labor for their factories may run into problems. Skilled labor is, in general, scarce and relatively expensive. . . . Labor relations in Jamaica can be turbulent." At one hotel the English manager quit and fled to England in the midst of labor turmoil in late 1980.

The *Daily Gleaner* newspaper, which had been vehemently anti-Manley, wrote, "The honeymoon with the Seaga government is fast coming to an end. . . . So far, he has shown us that he is a good bookkeeper. After nine years, we are still looking for a prime minister." Yet by mid-1981, foreign investors were sufficiently optimistic that the government offices that approved investments had approximately 200 proposals for about $1 billion. There were further expectations of huge bauxite investments over the next few years as investors who had transferred output to Australia would return to Jamaica.

But what about foreign hotel expansion? The Jamaican government offered to lease eight of its fourteen hotels under agreements that would give guaranteed returns to the government. The government wished to use a leasing arrangement in order to get an immediate positive rather than negative return, yet hold on to properties that it believed would increase substantially in value during the next few years.

QUESTIONS

1. What types of concessions might foreign hotels request of Jamaica as a requisite for entry?
2. What might Jamaica do to improve its bargaining stance with foreign hotels?
3. If a foreign hotel group did make arrangements to take over a hotel, what practices should it follow to strengthen its position after commencing operations?
4. To what extent might or should home governments (especially that of the United States) become involved in promoting or discouraging foreign hotel entry into and subsequent operations in Jamaica?

NOTES

1. Data for the case were taken from Louis Morano, "Multinationals and Nation-States: The Case of Aramco," *Orbis,* Summer 1979, pp. 447–468; "Oil New Power Structure," *Business Week,* December 24, 1979, pp. 82–88; George C. Lodge, "Controlling Oil," ICH Case 9–378–048, 1977; "Saudi Takeover of Aramco Looms," *Wall Street Journal,* August 6, 1980, p. 21; "Saudi Arabia Buys Out U.S. Partners in Aramco," *Wall Street Journal,* September 4, 1980, p. 31; Douglas Martin, "Aramco's Tough Oil Search," *New York Times,* February 10, 1982, p. D1.

2. Richard J. Meislin, "Mexico Relaxes Rules on Foreign Ownership," *New York Times,* February 17, 1984, p. D1; and David E. Sahger, "I.B.M. Concessions to Mexico," *New York Times,* July 25, 1985, p. D5.

3. Nathan Fagre and Louis T. Wells, Jr., "Bargaining Power of Multinationals and Host Governments," *Journal of International Business Studies,* Vol. XIII, No. 2, Fall 1982, pp. 9–23.

4. Michael R. Sesit, "Foreign Investment Playing Bigger Role in Poorer Countries," *Wall Street Journal,* March 29, 1984, p. 3.

5. Many of these conflicts are discussed in "The Multinationals: An Urgent Need for New Ties to Government," *Business Week,* March 12, 1979, pp. 74–82.

6. Niles Howard, "The World Woos U.S. Business," *Dun's Business Month,* Vol. 120, No. 5, November 1982, pp. 38–45.

7. Robert Weigand, "International Investments: Weighing the Incentives," *Harvard Business Review,* Vol. 61, No. 4, July–August 1983, pp. 146–152.

8. R. Hal Mason, "Investment Incentives and Performance Requirements: A Case Study of Food Manufacturing," a paper presented to the Academy of International Business, San Francisco, December 29, 1983, which was a summary of a larger report submitted to the World Bank.

9. William A. Stoever, "Renegotiations: The Cutting Edge of Relations between MNCs and LDCs," *Columbia Journal of World Business,* Spring 1979, pp. 6–7.

10. "Exxon Agrees to Sell Oil and Gas Assets in Libya to Government for Net Book Value," *Wall Street Journal,* January 6, 1982, p. 2; Youssef M. Ibrahim, "Mobil Negotiating Pullout from Libya, Duplicating Exxon's Decision Last Year," *Wall Street Journal,* April 13, 1982, p. 2.

11. Stoever, *op. cit.*

12. These and other differences are noted in John L. Graham and Roy A. Herberger, Jr., "Negotiators Abroad—Don't Shoot from the Hip," *Harvard Business Review,* Vol. 61, No. 4, July–August 1983, pp. 160–168.

13. Ashok Kapoor and J. J. Boddewyn, *International Business-Government Relations: U.S. Corporate Experience in Asia and Western Europe* (New York: American Management Association, 1973), p. 67.

14. Stoever, *op. cit.,* pp. 12–13.

15. Kapoor and Boddewyn, *op. cit.,* pp. 67–71.

16. Ashok Kapoor, *International Business Negotiations: A Study in India* (New York: New York University Press, 1970), p. 284.

17. John Fayerweather and Ashok Kapoor, "Simulated International Business Negotiations," *Journal of International Business Studies,* Spring 1972, pp. 19–32.

18. George Schwarzenberger, "The Protection of British Property Abroad," *Current Legal Problems,* Vol. 5, 1952, pp. 295–299; Oliver J. Lissitzyn, *International Law Today and Tomorrow* (Dobbs Ferry, N.Y.: Oceana Publications, 1965), p. 77; Gillis Wetter, "Diplomatic Assistance to Private Investment," *University of Chicago Law Review,* Vol. 29, 1962, p. 275.

19. James M. Perry, "Gunboat Diplomacy Is Older Than U.S., and Its Purpose Hasn't Changed Much," *Wall Street Journal,* October 26, 1983, p. 24.

20. Ian Brownlie, *Principles of Public International Law* (Oxford, England: Oxford University Press, 1966), pp. 435–436.

21. Green H. Hackworth, *Digest of International Law* (Washington, D.C.: U.S. Government Printing Office, 1942), pp. 655–661.

22. For a country-by-country description of these agreements, see Organization for Economic Co-operation and Development, *Investing in Developing Countries* (Paris: OECD, 1972).

23. David R. Mummery, *The Protection of International Private Investment* (New York: Praeger Publishers, 1968), p. 49.

24. "OPIC Contends Levy against Revere Copper Wasn't Expropriation," *Wall Street Journal,* June 15, 1977, p. 35.

25. "Vote 'No' in the World Bank," *Wall Street Journal,* June 30, 1972, p. 7; "World Bank Used for U.S. Protest," *New York Times,* June 28, 1971, p. 47.

26. Mummery, *op. cit.,* p. 98.

27. "Carrying a Small Stick," *Time,* January 21, 1974, pp. 72–73.

28. Raymond Vernon, "The Multinationals: No Strings Attached," *Foreign Policy,* Winter 1978–1979, p. 126.

29. Mummery, *op. cit.,* p. 74.

30. William A. Stoever, "Issues Emerging in Iranian Claims Negotiations," *Wall Street Journal,* May 7, 1981, p. 26; James B. Stewart and Peter Truell, "U.S. Firms Win Some, Lose Some at Tribunal Arbitrating $5 Billion in Claims against Iran," *Wall Street Journal,* November 15, 1984, p. 38.

31. "Chile Halts Shipments to France of Copper from El Teniente Mines," *Wall Street Journal,* October 9, 1972, p. 12.

32. "British Petroleum Seen Likely to Sue Buyers of Oil from Libya Field," *Wall Street Journal,* June 13, 1974, p. 14.

33. "Arco Unit Awarded Payment from Libya's Takeover of Assets," *Wall Street Journal,* April 4, 1977, p. 4; "California Standard, Texaco Win Ruling against Libya Takeover of Oil Holdings," *Wall Street Journal,* March 3, 1977, p. 4.

34. Burton Yale Pines, "Hollow Chambers of the World Court," *Wall Street Journal,* April 12, 1984, p. 30.

35. For further discussions of the subject, see Jack G. Kaikati, "The Challenge of the Arab Boycott," *Sloan Management Review,* Winter 1977, pp. 83–100; Dan S. Chill, *The Arab Boycott of Israel* (New York: Praeger Publishers, 1976).

36. Barry Kramer, "China Warns Dutch on Selling Subs to Taiwan," *Wall Street Journal,* January 14, 1981, p. 31.

37. "The Arabs Gear up to Boycott Renault," *Business Week,* February 15, 1982, p. 54.

38. "Saudis Warn Toyota on Ford," *New York Times,* June 24, 1981, p. D5.

39. Don Wallace, Jr., *International Regulation of Multinational Corporations* (New York: Praeger Publishers, 1976), pp. 5–26.

40. For a discussion of how codes may harbinger national regulations, see Richard L. Rowan and Duncan C. Campbell, "The Attempt to Regulate Industrial Relations through International Codes of Conduct," *Columbia Journal of World Business,* Vol. 18, No. 2, Summer 1983, pp. 64–80.

41. John Tagliabue, "I.B.M. Turns up the Heat in Europe," *New York Times,* June 10, 1984, p. Fl.

42. "Corporate Citizenship: Outstanding Examples Worldwide," *Top Management Report,* 1979, p. 2.

43. Kapoor and Boddewyn, *International Business-Government Relations,* p. 32.

44. Belmont F. Haydel, "Case Study of a Social Responsibility Program: Gulf & Western Industries, Inc. in the Dominican Republic in Employee Health, Housing,

Education, Sports, and General Welfare, and Other Assistance to the Dominican Republic," paper presented to the Academy of International Business, New York, October 7, 1983; Pamela G. Hollie, "G. & W. to Sell Dominican Holdings," *New York Times,* June 13, 1984, p. D1.

45. For a discussion of the advertising part of the promotion, see S. Prakash Sethi, "Advocacy Advertising and the Multinational Corporation," *Columbia Journal of World Business,* Fall 1977, pp. 32–46.

46. "Corporate Citizenship: Outstanding Examples Worldwide," *Top Management Report,* 1979, p. 2.

47. Frans G. J. Derkinderen, "Transnational Business Latitude in Developing Countries," *Management International Review,* Vol. 22, No. 4, 1982/4, p. 58.

48. "Thailand Zinc Talks by Gulf and Western Unit Run into Snag," *Wall Street Journal,* February 25, 1977, p. 22; "Gulf and Western Thailand Unit Accepts Plan for $90 Million Zinc Mine, Refinery," *Wall Street Journal,* March 2, 1977, p. 12.

49. Data for the case were taken from Jo Thomas, "Tourism up, Violence off, Jamaica Says," *New York Times,* November 25, 1980, p. A3; John Huey, "Going Private," *Wall Street Journal,* May 29, 1981, p. 1ff.; John Huey, "Money Returns to Troubled Jamaica," *Wall Street Journal,* April 27, 1981, p. 27; Ann Crittenden, "Jamaican Economy Is Speeding Exodus," *New York Times,* September 30, 1979, p. 9; "Jamaica: A U.S. Boost in Luring Overseas Investors," *Business Week,* February 23, 1981; Frank Long, "Tourism: A Development Cornerstone That Crumbled," *Ceres,* September–October 1978, pp. 43–45.

13

East-West Business

- To contrast business between communist and noncommunist countries during periods of friendly and unfriendly political relationships.
- To survey the major problems inherent in expansion of East-West business.
- To describe the various methods by which commerce between the communist and noncommunist countries is conducted.
- To demonstrate the factors that may affect the future of U.S. business with Eastern countries.

The participation of U.S. firms in the Kama River project in the Soviet Union illustrates the vacillation of U.S. political policy regarding sales to communist countries. The project involved construction of the largest truck factory anywhere in the world. The plant site covers nine square miles. Because there was no automobile supply system as in Western industrial countries, every part has to be forged, machined, and assembled in one location. The capacity is up to 150,000 trucks and an additional 100,000 replacement engines per year. The single complex is larger than the combined capacity of all U.S. heavy truck manufacturing. In addition to the manufacturing facilities, housing was constructed for about 300,000 people.

When the Soviets announced plans for the project in 1969, they indicated that only three basic truck models of Soviet design would be produced. This was done to reduce the requirements for skilled labor and to cut costs through the use of automated manufacturing. The Soviets considered the possibility of manufacturing all the production equipment themselves but did not prefer that alternative for three reasons: (1) the effort would require designing and building specialized production equipment that they lacked and would severely tax their limited resources; (2) they lacked experience in the large-scale manufacture of heavy vehicles and feared that without assistance they might have costly problems; and (3) self-manufacture would delay truck production by several years. Therefore the Soviets sought to purchase technology and machinery abroad.

From mid-1970 through mid-1971, several U.S. firms became involved in negotiating sales for the project. However, sales to the Soviet Union required U.S. government approval, and none was forthcoming even when agreements were reached between U.S. firms and Soviet authorities. For example, Henry Ford II visited Moscow to discuss providing technical assistance; while he was there, the U.S. Secretary of Defense made public statements against Ford's participation. Ford withdrew from negotiations. Mack Truck signed a protocol agreement that would give it prime responsibility for both plant and product at the Kama River facility. This would have involved the sale of between $700 million and $1 billion of machinery and technology for U.S. firms and would have employed about 160,000 people in the United States. After three extensions to the expiration dates on the protocol agreement, Mack withdrew in September 1971 because the U.S. government had not granted permission.

In the meantime, several things were occurring that foreshadowed the eventual participation of U.S. firms. The United States had begun to open trade with China and was anxious to demonstrate to the Soviet Union that the Chinese trade would not be at the expense of Soviet trade. At the same time, the U.S. machine tool industry was both in a depressed state and facing added foreign competition. Permission to sell $88 million of machine tools to the Soviets was granted in June 1971; and by October, approval was given for over $400 million in sales. These sales were not related to the Kama River project, but they provided a precedent of equipment exports that U.S. firms could use as evidence in claiming that the Kama River project was no different.

Once Mack stepped aside, the Soviet Union had to look elsewhere for a prime contractor. Within days the Soviets announced the signing of a contract with Renault of France for an estimated $300 million. Other French firms as well as a host of European companies were also expected to provide much of the necessary machinery for the project. For example, the West German company Liebherr-Verzahntechnik negotiated a contract for $144 million worth of machine tools and other equipment for truck transmissions.

U.S. firms were now in a position to convince government authorities that the Soviet Union would get what it wanted from someone else if it could not get it from a U.S. company. The logjam was broken in late October 1971 when the Swindell-Dressler Division of Pullman received approval for a $10 million contract for foundry equipment for the Kama River facility, the first of several of its contracts. To gain that approval, Swindell-Dressler shuttled between the Commerce and Defense Departments and even had a Soviet delegation visit with the Senate Commerce Committee and with the Senate minority leader.

There were certain negotiating problems between Swindell-Dressler and the Soviets. One involved a translation error that caused Swindell-Dressler to make a proposal that was far beyond the scope of what was wanted. Another was a problem in comparing efficiencies of two different furnace systems when electricity and transportation were not treated as part of total expenses by the Soviets. The Americans were also denied permission to visit the site of the plant. The contract was much more detailed than a comparable one in the United States because the Soviets leave little to "good faith." Many other U.S. firms followed with contracts. To mention a few: Carborundum supplied shot-blasting equipment; Hallcroft, thermal equipment; and American Chain and Cable, aluminum foundry equipment. By 1974, sixty-five U.S. firms had signed contracts, and eight firms were doing over $10 million in business each.

Once the United States began giving permission for firms to sell to the Kama River project, it began assisting them by helping to finance sales. By 1974 the Export-Import Bank had financed $164.6 million in exports. Payment guarantees were also given to a number of large private bank loans to the Soviet Union, which were used to make U.S. purchases. George S. Shchukin, chairman of the Kama Purchasing Commission, said that probably not more than 20 percent of the facility could have been built without the Export-Import Bank's assistance.

In 1976 the Soviet press agency, Tass, reported that the first vehicles had been manufactured. This was confirmed when foreign businesspeople visited the plant later in the year. At that time the output was between thirty and forty vehicles per day, but output was expected to exceed 3000 per day by 1981. In 1979 a CIA intelligence officer reported that the plant was producing engines for military vehicles. This led to hearings by the House Armed Services subcommittee at which Defense and Commerce Department officials said that the production did not violate any existing trade understanding.

In early 1980, many members of the U.S. Congress were openly critical of the fact that, in its invasion of Afghanistan, the Soviet Union was using trucks that were built at the Kama River plant through assistance by U.S. companies. This led the chairman of Ingersoll Milling Machine, which built the machines to produce the engine blocks, to respond:

> To sell our machinery to the Kama River plant, we were in competition with the French and German machine builders, and the technology we offered was competitive. The Russians already had similar machines running in their country. We won the competition because of our cost effectiveness and because we had the most experience.

The United States nevertheless tightened controls on American exports of high-technology products to the Soviet Union in such areas as computers and software, manufacturing technology, and materials critical to the manufacture of high-technology defense goods. Export permission was revoked on spare computer parts for the plant.

INTRODUCTION

- Volatility of trade has occurred when
  - communist actions changed
  - different decision makers were in power in the U.S.
- Motives for restrictions
  - hurt enemy economically or militarily
  - coerce enemy to change policy
  - public displeasure about activities
- Communist countries also shift trade policies

The Kama River truck case is an example of business volatility because of changing political attitudes. Nowhere are political considerations more apparent than in the pattern of business relationships between the communist or Eastern countries and noncommunist or Western countries, especially in trade involving the United States. The volatility of trade has been so extreme that one U.S. businessman referred to U.S. policy toward communist countries as a "light switch"; it turns trade on and then off.[2] The changes have sometimes been in response to unpopular actions by communist countries, such as the invasion of Afghanistan, or to the ascendency of political decision makers who hold different philosophies about business interactions with communist countries. The change in decision makers has sometimes been the result of elections, but not always. Within the same U.S. administrations there have been many examples of in-fighting among people with opposite views that resulted in policy swings. A good example was in late 1983, when Secretary of State George Schultz sought closer economic ties while Secretary of Defense Caspar Weinberger simultaneously fought for tighter controls. Schultz won out and succeeded in reversing some policies that had been set only recently. This difference was summed up as follows: "There are theological positions on both sides. To the hawks any trade helps the Russians and zero is already too much. To the doves, trade leads politics, and more trade will improve relations."[3]

Within the ideology of a restrictive trade position, three different motives have sometimes been pursued. The first is a punitive one, focusing on controls to damage an unfriendly country economically and militarily in a type of economic warfare. The second is to try to remedy a situation through the withholding of trade, such as trying to coerce the Soviet Union into allowing the emigration of Jews to Israel. The third is to make a public declaration in order to register displeasure over certain activities, for example, the shooting down of a Korean passenger plane by the Soviet Union.[4]

We do not want to give the impression that it is only the policies of the United States or even Western countries that cause the shifts in East-West business relations. Communist countries have also altered their attitudes and practices substantially. In both the Soviet Union and the People's Republic of China, for example, changes in leadership and planning cycles have resulted in wide swings in how much each country depends on foreign business, with whom the foreign business occurs, what products are involved, and what forms of business are allowed.

EXPANSION PROBLEMS

A Brief History of Political Influence

- Trade volatility makes businesspeople reluctant to expend resources
- Trade fluctuations substantial since World War I

Most companies prefer to invest their capital and human resources in endeavors that are expected to continue for a long period of time. There is a great deal of uncertainty about the future East-West political relationship; consequently, many firms hesitate to commit their resources to developing East-West ties.[5] On one hand, businesspeople have witnessed increased peaceful political interactions, such as visits by political leaders, joint efforts to secure peace in the Middle East, and arms reduction discussions. Yet they also realize that the experience thus far in this century shows how rapidly business volume can alter because of politics and how it can continue to fluctuate over time.

The beginning of the twentieth century was characterized by peaceful trading relations between the United States and Russia. The two countries were neither allies nor enemies, so there was no official governmental effort to expand or retard the volume of trade. When the two countries became allies in World War I, U.S. exports to Russia jumped from a prewar figure of $25 million per year to $470 million in 1917, due largely to war-related credits. With the overthrow of the czarist government by the Bolsheviks, Soviet foreign trade became a state-controlled monopoly, credits nearly disappeared, and U.S. exports to the country fell to $17 million in 1918 and to $8 million in 1923. The exports recovered and grew to $84 million by 1929, only to fall to $14 million in 1930 because of the economic crash. A formal trade agreement between the countries in 1935 resulted in the Soviet Union's becoming the biggest customer for the United States during the Depression. In 1939 the German-Russian treaty and subsequent invasions of Poland and the Baltic states brought certain U.S. export embargoes, which were dropped in 1941 when the two countries again became allies. From then until the war ended in 1945 the United States exported over $9 billion in goods to the Soviet Union. In the post–World War II period the advent of the Cold War resulted in a drop in U.S. exports to the Soviet Union from $149 million in 1947 to $19 million in 1953.[6] U.S. sales to the Soviet Union have climbed since the low in 1953 but have been marked by substantial year-to-year changes because of political relationships and agreements. The most notable agreements were the special wheat sales, which caused exports to jump from $23 million in 1963 to $146 million in 1964 and from $162 million in 1971 to $550 million in 1972. Since then, exports of manufactured products from the United States have been fairly stable; however, fluctuations in U.S. agricultural sales have caused total trade to be very erratic.[7] In 1979, U.S. exports reached $3.61 billion, an increase of 60 percent over the previous year. Then the U.S. exports fell by over 60 percent in 1980 because of trade prohibitions after Afghanistan was invaded. When Mao Tse Tung headed the People's Republic of China, the United States traded little with that country; but with new Chinese leadership, trade grew rapidly. U.S. trade with both China and the Soviet Union fell sharply again in 1983 because of disputes.[8]

East-West trade fluctuations were also abrupt immediately after the establishment of communist governments in countries other than the Soviet Union. When the Eastern European countries formed a communist bloc with the Soviet Union, U.S. exports to those nations fell from $400 million in 1948 to only $2 million in 1953.[9] Exports from the United States to China and Cuba fell to nearly zero after the communist takeovers in 1949 and 1958, respectively. Exports from other Western industrialized countries have followed varied patterns, reflecting once again diverse political relationships. For example, in the critical period from 1948 to 1953, when U.S. exports to communist countries fell so sharply, the exports of Canada, the United Kingdom, and Sweden to the Eastern bloc took sharp declines as well, whereas the exports of Austria, Finland, France, and West Germany shot upward.[10]

Balance-of-Payments Deficits and Settlements

- Eastern balance-of-payments problems due to
  - lack of products to sell in the West
  - need to settle largely on bilateral basis
- Balance-of-payments adjustments
  - in Western countries by import tariffs, currency value changes, or improvement of cost-efficiency
  - in Eastern countries by ceasing to buy or selling below cost

The Eastern countries' difficulty in getting hard currency to buy imported goods is certainly one of the most serious obstacles to the rapid expansion of East-West trade. For many years the communist countries lacked products that could be marketed in the West in sufficient quantity to gain the exchange needed for imports. The result was that in spite of rigid priorities and restrictions on the importation of goods, the communist countries have generally had chronic balance-of-payments problems since World War II.

The methods for handling balance-of-payments deficits used by the Eastern countries are substantially different from those of Western countries. While Western countries use price mechanisms (for example, import tariffs, currency devaluations, or development of competitively viable export industries to alleviate trade imbalances) to solve exchange problems, the Eastern countries simply halt foreign buying by decree or sell some commodity abroad below cost. Between 1980 and 1982, for example, Rumania cut its imports from the West by 56 percent, resulting in austerity that would not be as easily accepted in countries with market economies.[11] To buy wheat in the 1963–1965 period, the Russians sold over $1.5 billion in gold abroad.[12] The world price for gold at that time was $35 per ounce, and it has been estimated that the production cost in the Soviet Union was between $75 and $85 an ounce.[13] In this same period the Soviets easily decreased their imports from several Western countries in order to divert expenditures to grain purchases. In the late 1970s the Soviets were accused of selling such products as automobiles and trucks in the West for a fraction of their costs in order to earn foreign exchange.[14]

The main reason for the difference in approach between Eastern and Western countries is the difference in their economic systems. As command economies, the communist countries do not rely much on the market to determine what to produce or what price to charge. In the Soviet Union, for example, 95 percent of prices have been changed only twice since 1955— in 1967 and in 1982. Prices therefore bear little resemblance to what prices or costs would be in a market economy. Currencies are not convertible, and their values are set arbitrarily in relation to Western ones so that trade prices may be further distorted. This makes mechanisms such as tariffs fairly meaningless. Since the countries decide centrally what will be produced and consumed domestically, they plan certain production to be in excess of domestic consumption and certain production to be less. Those excesses and shortages are their planned exports and imports, respectively. These are then varied only on an emergency basis because of supply problems.[15]

Recall from Chapter 9 that the ability to settle deficits on a multilateral rather than a bilateral basis is a major advantage for increasing the volume of world trade. The Eastern countries have generally followed a preference for balancing accounts as much as possible on a bilateral basis. This does not permit them as much discretion in using surpluses with one country to offset deficits with others. There are a few exceptions. The Eastern countries have tried in recent years to alleviate their difficulties in buying from OECD countries by building trade surpluses with LDCs.[16] Clearing arrangements have been established among several of the Eastern nations; however, these are more limited than those found in the West. The Western countries have not been invited to join in these arrangements.

Regulatory Factors

- Differ according to communist country
- Differ by product
- Strategic control problems
  - East may get product from other sources, thus U.S. loses business
  - disagreement among allies
  - hard to control smuggling

Export controls. The United States and several other Western countries maintain export controls for the purpose of ensuring national security, promoting foreign policy objectives, and preventing the reduction of imports of certain raw materials that are in short supply. While these controls may be applied to any other country, sales to the communist bloc have been most affected, especially those from the United States. Practically no goods from the United States are permitted to be shipped to Cuba, Cambodia, Vietnam, and North Korea. Nicaraguan trade embargos were instituted in 1984. Exceptions have been made at times for humanitarian products and for goods needed by friendly embassies in the countries. Poland, Rumania, and China, on the other hand, are treated quite leniently, with restrictions on only a limited number of products that could be of strategic military importance and few procedural requirements. The other Eastern bloc countries fall somewhere in between in terms of severity of U.S. export restrictions. These restrictions vary by product in addition to varying by destination. The Office of Export Control maintains a list of products for which special permission must be given before an export license is granted. The licensing requirements apply as well to controlled foreign affiliates of U.S. firms.

Many potential U.S. exporters, as in the Kama River truck case, have argued that, when permission to export certain goods is withheld, the communist countries simply buy from other countries or develop technology independently. This argument is sometimes effective in obtaining a license. Very often, though, it does not suffice. The U.S.–USSR Trade and Economic Council, which has 220 U.S. companies as members, estimates that the United States is losing $10 billion a year in exports to the Soviet Union alone.[17]

Although the United States, Japan, and allied Western European countries belong to the Coordinating Committee (Cocom), which agrees not to export high-technology goods with potential military use to the Eastern bloc, countries have increasingly gone around Cocom when it seemed in their national interests to do so. The United States, for example, protested the French delivery of a sophisticated telephone exchange to the Soviet Union. France and West Germany, in turn, complained of the 1984 U.S. trade liberalization with the People's Republic of China.[18] There has been very little dispute on military and atomic-energy products but considerable disagreement on civilian sales that could have military or strategic applications. One of the biggest controversies in recent years concerned a West German contract to build the Western European–Soviet pipeline.[19] As West European, U.S., and Japanese firms joined as subcontractors, the United States sought to have the agreement abrogated. The allies refused to do so, and the United States ultimately allowed its firms to participate. Another thorny issue has been that restricted goods—for example, sophisticated Digital computers—have been exported to countries where they can be legally sold and then reexported from those countries to communist nations where the sale is not allowed by the U.S. government. This has led to U.S. export restrictions that worry many firms because of the greater difficulty they have in selling to countries such as West Germany, Austria, and Norway.[20]

By no means are high-technology products the only ones affected. After the Soviet invasion of Afghanistan, the United States limited exports to the Soviet Union of an array of products. The most important of these involved the reduction in sales of feed grains. This was very controversial. On one hand, it was argued that the restriction was successful because it raised the price the Soviets had to pay for grain and has reportedly caused them to slaughter vast herds of beef cattle prematurely at the very time that Soviet consumers had grown to expect greater meat supplies. On the other hand, the Soviet Union has developed new sources of supply, such as Argentina, and has perhaps been pushed to greater self-sufficiency.[21]

- Not same for all communist countries
- Controversy on most-favored-nation status

Import controls. In addition to virtual embargoes on goods from Vietnam, Cambodia, North Korea, and Cuba, the United States uses the 1930 tariff rates (the highest in U.S. history) on goods coming from most Eastern countries. This failure to grant most-favored-nation status puts most Eastern-made goods at a competitive disadvantage in the U.S. market. The Soviet Union also has two tariff schedules and charges duty on U.S. goods at the higher of the two rates. There has been much opposition in the United States to negotiating tariff reductions because of the nature of Eastern buying, which may have little to do with competitive prices. For example, the president of a major U.S. shirt company could not sell shirts to the Soviets at $2.50 each, even though comparable Russian shirts were selling at $40 each.[22] Since purchases are made by governmental buying agencies, the agencies can effectively prevent the importation of any foreign-made good, regardless of price differential, by simply not purchasing it. Such mechanisms are not so easily established in the West.

Since U.S. import controls are not the same for all communist countries, there are sometimes problems of determining if goods are transshipped from one communist country to another so that they arrive in the United States from a country for which there are few import restrictions. For example, the United States has an embargo on imports from Cuba. In 1983 the United States ceased importing nickel from the Soviet Union because of claims that Cuban nickel was reaching the United States via the Soviet Union.[23]

Population, Geography, and Self-Sufficiency

- Large size means big market
- Large size also means more self-sufficiency
- COMECON countries seek to trade highest proportion with each other

The vast population of Eastern countries is a major factor in the optimism of Western businesses as to their future opportunities in communist countries. A spokesman for Monsanto Chemical summed up this attitude about China by stating, "You just can't look at a market of that size and not believe that eventually a lot of goods are going to be sold there. One aspirin tablet a day to each of those guys, and that is a lot of aspirin."[24] The communist world comprises approximately one third of the world population. China alone accounts for about one fifth of the world population, or roughly two thirds of the people in communist countries. The Soviet Union has a population that is slightly larger than that of the United States, and the other communist areas have a combined population that is slightly smaller.

Although the large size of the communist countries indicates possible opportunities, it is in some ways a deterrent to expanded East-West business. The Soviet Union and China rank as the two largest countries of the world in terms of land mass. Their natural resources are extremely diverse and, when coupled with the large populations, give them the potential of developing a wide variety of production. They, like the United States, might be expected to be much more nearly self-sufficient than a smaller country. The size is further enhanced by the existence of The Council for Mutual Economic Assistance (COMECON). COMECON is made up of ten communist countries: the Soviet Union, Poland, Czechoslovakia, Hungary, Bulgaria, Rumania, East Germany, Mongolia, Vietnam, and Cuba. As noted in Chapter 7, the group has embarked upon far-reaching economic integration by coordinating the long-term production plans of its members.[25] The size and desired mutual interdependence, when coupled with the geographic proximity of most of the member countries, makes trade within the Eastern bloc more natural than trade between Eastern and Western nations. Geographic proximity should also, in East-West transactions, favor Western European sales to Eastern European and Soviet markets, Japanese sales to China, and U.S. sales to Cuba.

One of the striking features of communist countries is their relatively small portion of world trade. Although trade with other communist countries comprised about 60 percent of their total trade, the absolute amount is smaller than might be indicated from population figures or general economic output. This is due largely to Eastern countries' policies of attaining maximum self-sufficiency because they fear that supplies from other communist countries may arrive late or be of poor quality.[26]

Marketing Problems

- Lack of reliable and comparable statistics
  - some methods of making approximations
- Buying decisions not made as in West
- Eastern countries lack expertise in Western selling

A major competitive advantage of U.S. firms in world markets is their ability to assess potential demand and then develop products and promotional campaigns to fit the assessment. Such advantages are largely diminished in selling to Eastern countries. The first stumbling block is the lack of reliable and comparable statistics on Eastern economies. Population figures alone are certainly not sufficient for determining a market potential, since people with low incomes may not be able to purchase many goods or services. Furthermore, buying behavior may differ so substantially that marketing programs that are successful elsewhere may not yield expected results. Income figures must be taken from national account statistics of individual countries. Because pricing systems are substantially different from those in the West, the comparability to Western figures is immediately suspect. Since the national account figures are calculated in local currencies, they must be converted at official exchange rates, which may bear little resemblance to either purchasing power or an exchange rate that might prevail if natural market factors were allowed to operate. In spite of these formidable obstacles, some researchers have developed means of converting Eastern figures so as to get cumbersome, but better, approximations of the value equivalents.[27]

Even reliable economic statistics for Eastern countries are of little use in demand assessment, since basic buying decisions are not determined by market forces that are familiar to Western exporters. The Eastern countries plan their economies and allow purchases only of products that are included in the plans. Although these countries make detailed long- and short-range economic plans, the details are not available to outsiders.[28] The result is that it is difficult to determine not only what will be consumed, but also how much of which products will be imported. The centralized nature of planning and importing makes it difficult to create demand among end users of products. Many Western firms that do sell to Eastern countries shy away from advertising because they feel that the real decisions are made by planning authorities and industrial ministries rather than by the ultimate consumers that the advertising would reach. When they do advertise, they usually are not able to target their messages or use flamboyant appeals. On Soviet television, for example, there are fifteen-minute advertising blocks, which broadcast such messages as "Vacuum cleaners can be bought at electrical appliance shops" while displaying on the screen a photograph of a row of vacuum cleaners.[29] The Eastern countries have also encountered problems in selling goods in the West because of unfamiliarity with the sophisticated advertising methods used by their competitors. Even though these countries have relied on Western advertising agencies, the agencies have only slowly been able to convince them of the need for such things as the targeting of budgets toward key products and key customers.[30]

The lack of profit motive within communist countries is a difficult concept for many Western businesspeople to grasp. For export sales to Western countries, one can promote sales to the import decision maker on the basis of what the product and terms will do for the decision maker's profit or profit center, since it is assumed that the importer is largely motivated by and evaluated on profits. For Eastern decision makers, one cannot be certain what motivates them in their purchase decisions. Clearly, the communist negotiators will act on the basis of how they view a transaction vis-à-vis their own positions within the bureaucratic structure. Here we have little information. How do they view their own personal risk in buying from one country instead of another or buying a tried and true product rather than an innovative one? Should the exporter emphasize price, specifications, durability, delivery time, labor- or material-saving properties, payment terms, or what? The situation is further complicated by the fact that the properties of many products are difficult to describe except in terms of cost savings in the production process. How do you describe these properties to someone who does not price inputs in the same manner, does not use depreciation accounting, and assesses no cost to transportation?

Bureaucratic Problems

- Each Eastern country buys independently of each other
  - usually work through foreign trade organizations
- Negotiations tend to be long and detailed

In spite of the seeming cohesiveness among the Eastern countries, they operate independently of each other in making their foreign purchases. The fact that a Western firm has successfully sold to one Eastern country is seldom much of an advantage in obtaining sales contracts in others. Within each country are numerous foreign trade organizations (FTOs) that operate autonomously. The Soviet Union, for example, has over fifty of these groups; they are organized along product lines and rival large Western firms in size. If one goes directly to an FTO to try to make sales, one must be certain that it is the right organization for the particular product line. Otherwise, information is likely to be greatly delayed in reaching the proper destination, if it gets there at all. One may make contact with FTOs directly or through foreign trade missions or commercial offices abroad, such as the Soviet purchasing office (Amtorg) in the United States. There is some disagreement as to whether one can effectively develop sales through Amtorg or whether one should bypass it and go directly to an FTO in the Soviet Union. The FTOs maintain technical staffs that constantly research prices and technical developments in their field. The purchases tend to be large; thus it is difficult for small firms to take part in sales.

The FTOs are known as very shrewd negotiators that attempt to secure the lowest possible prices from foreign producers. The fact that a company has sold once to an FTO is of little advantage in securing repeat sales, since the FTOs renegotiate to find the best price. It is often contended that the eagerness of Western firms and governments to penetrate Eastern markets has led to transactions with FTOs and other communist agencies that are one-sided in favor of the Eastern countries. Such a contention was made, for example, about the European pipeline arrangement—that sellers were so eager for the business that they sold equipment at "bargain basement" prices.[31] U.S. wheat sales to the Soviets in 1973 were at so low a price that the Soviets resold much of the supply in world markets at a profit. There is disagreement as to how the Soviets manage to pull off these agreements. They do appear to have made very good analyses of supply-demand conditions and to have known when political officials were vulnerable or eager to come to some type of agreement.

These examples do not mean that Western firms regard profit as less important in their Eastern transactions. It simply means that some arrangements have turned out to be very disadvantageous. If there are more of these examples in the future, Western companies will not be as interested in such business.

Much of today's Western business with Eastern countries is not exports of products but rather exports of technology through other types of agreements, which enable Eastern countries to produce the products themselves. The Eastern negotiators usually insist on a long list of clauses in the contracts, resulting in negotiations that are much more lengthy than similar ones in the West. Bargaining for less than one year is unusual, and three to four years is not uncommon when several Western firms are competing for the contract. The Soviets and the Chinese usually opt for attaining production capabilities at a set fee. Eastern European countries have been prone to seek out longer-term arrangements that include a continual transfer of new technology because of the greater dependence of these countries on international markets in which they need to be competitive.

Pressure-Group Problems

• May lobby or boycott to pressure against East-West business

In spite of official movements to encourage East-West business, ideological differences frequently lead to U.S. boycotts of merchandise produced in the East, to harassment of companies selling to communist countries, and to legislative stipulations that restrict the growth of East-West business. Leaders of these movements usually contend that expanded business relations will strengthen the Eastern countries in relation to the United States. Among the boycotts have been refusal by longshoremen to unload goods of communist origin and campaigns by citizen groups to prevent purchases of Polish hams, Czechoslovakian glass, and Yugoslavian tobacco. Both Firestone and Ford Motor Company bowed to public pressure against their proposed transactions with communist countries. Lobbyists have successfully amended the National Defense Education Act to prevent governmental purchases of teaching equipment from communist countries. They have also blocked most-favored-nation treatment for the Soviet Union until Soviet Jews are allowed to emigrate en masse to Israel.

METHODS OF EAST-WEST BUSINESS

Thus far the discussion has presented negative aspects of the future of East-West business. In spite of the obstacles, many firms have found methods to adjust to the nuances that have let them expand their business in communist countries. The result has been an overall rise in both the number and value of East-West transactions and some indications that there is potential for a substantial growth rate in the near future.

Financial Arrangements

- Financed by credit, cash, or some type of barter arrangement
- Eastern creditworthiness has been good but
    - concern that some countries are overextended
    - concern that loans to Eastern countries are subsidized

Although balance-of-payments problems in the Eastern countries have inhibited the ability of these countries to buy goods in the West, sales may be financed in several ways. When an exporter sells to a communist country, it may be for credit, for cash payment in either a convertible or a nonconvertible currency, or for a merchandise exchange. Although precise figures on the proportion of trade transactions through each of these payment mechanisms are unavailable, it is known that much business involves some type of credit arrangement. Vneshtorbank, the Soviet Foreign Trade Bank, has correspondent relations with over 1300 banks in over 100 countries and owns banks in Western Europe. Through this network, one can export by means of letters of credit or bills of exchange, which function substantially the same as the instruments used in exports to other Western countries. Since World War II, the credit reliability of the FTOs that handle import purchases, especially in the Soviet Union, has been so noteworthy that an increasing number of Western traders have been selling on unsecured credit terms ranging from 30 to 360 days.

Many sales to communist countries are so large that long-term credit arrangements through domestic governmental agencies may be necessary. All Western industrial countries have some type of export credit insurance, which enables their exporters to raise the required credit funds from government or private sources. Except for the United States, the credit insurance arrangements have been the same for the communist countries as for the rest of the world. The United States has at times allowed and at other times disallowed the Export-Import Bank to grant credit or credit guarantees to certain communist countries. As was shown in the Kama River truck case, credit may be essential in order to make sales. One of the more recent concerns is that some Eastern countries, particularly Poland, have so extended their debt that they may be economically unable to repay on schedule. Of concern, too, has been the fact that many loans are subsidized in order to secure business for one's own companies. As of 1984 the Soviet Union owed $28.8 billion, making it the third largest hard currency debtor in the world behind Brazil and Mexico; however, the Soviet Union ranked first in the world in loans subsidized by Western governments.[32]

A Western exporter may demand and receive a cash payment in a convertible currency when selling to Eastern countries. However, this is rarely the case, since the FTOs carefully compare alternative sources of Western supplies and frequently make decisions based on the financing arrangements that are available. Because of the shortage of convertible currencies, Eastern European countries will frequently, and the Soviet Union and China occasionally, try to pay for imports by means of merchandise (barter trade) or by payment in a nonconvertible Western currency. In a typical barter transaction, Terra Handels, a German textile firm, sells about $5 million worth of dresses per year to the Soviet Union in exchange for hunting rifles, pianos, cement, and marble. Payments in nonconvertible currencies necessitate added operating complexities, such as those discussed in Chapter 8. Many exporters shy away from barter types of arrangements because of these complexities; however, in so doing they may lose a competitive advantage. A number of Western banks and financial houses will now handle these transactions for a fee based on the type of merchandise or currency for which disposal is required.

Marketing Methods

- Assess demand through examination of economic plans, bilateral treaties
- Create demand through
  - trade fairs
  - straightforward advertising
  - frequent visits
  - being subcontractor

Occasionally, a Western firm has a product or technology that is so well known or so desired by Eastern FTOs that no marketing effort is needed to secure sales. There are also firms that manage to develop business by simply sending catalogs, price lists, and specifications to FTOs and Eastern trade missions. However, these situations are rare. Most firms have to develop an active approach to assessing and creating demand.

Although the assessment of communist import requirements is a formidable task, there are a number of information sources that give some indication. Even though the country plans do not include published import projections by product, the overall investment and production figures by industry do signify priorities. Consequently, one may determine, for example, that there will be an increased need to supply the steel industry or a decreased need to service farm machinery productions. One may examine Eastern foreign trade statistics in a number of different sources, such as the *IMF Statistical Yearbook* and the *OECD Foreign Trade Statistics, Series C.* These indicate recent import needs. Examination of bilateral trade treaties with various Western countries will indicate broadly the anticipated import needs for the near future. Western consular offices in the communist countries are a very good source of information both on the degree of need for a given product and on the names of other Western firms that are negotiating for a contract.

Probably the major means of creating demand for products in the Eastern countries is through exhibitions at trade fairs. The fairs sometimes are general in nature and sometimes specialize in products or goods from specific countries. For instance, 189 U.S. firms participated in an oil and gas exposition in Moscow that drew an estimated 30,000 Soviet engineers and technicians. Not only did companies such as Cabot Corporation and C.R.C. Crose International sell most of the oil-drilling equipment they had on display, but they also began negotiating future sales contracts.[33]

Unlike many Western buyers, buyers in communist countries are generally so short of funds that they are eager to compare minutely the technical capabilities of different firms and their products. A U.S. textile machinery producer has capitalized on this by having some of its top officials act as consultants, giving lectures and demonstrations to officials of research institutes and the textile industry in Eastern Europe.[34] This has led to personal contacts, which many businesspeople feel are most important for sales in communist countries. In fact, many firms believe that they must send managers to visit Eastern countries at least twice a year if they are to maintain market growth.

Advertising in communist countries lacks some of the flamboyance found in Western society. Almost every industrial branch has specialized publications in which advertising may be placed, and these advertisements should be as straightforward and give as much technical information as possible. A French chemical company was criticized because its promotion did not mention how much and what kind of residues would remain in the soil from using its herbicides.

Frequently, one Western firm receives a contract to supply most of the equipment needed for an industrial product in an Eastern country. This firm then sets out to find subcontractors to supply much of the needs. There is usually considerable publicity attendant on the signing of such a contract, with the result that potential subcontractors may easily contact the prime contractor to solicit sales. The ultimate suppliers are often companies from a number of different countries.

Cooperative Arrangements

- Forms of cooperative
  arrangements include
  - licensing
  - turnkey operations
  - management contracts
  - coproduction
    arrangements
  - joint ventures

Because they want to gain Western products and services with high-technology and management skill inputs and, at the same time, minimize the outflow of hard currencies, Eastern countries are increasingly entering into arrangements by which they license Western technology for a fee or have a Western firm build and/or run the establishment for them under turnkey or management contracts. The Secretariat of the Economic Commission for Europe estimates that there are nearly 600 industrial cooperation arrangements in Eastern Europe with Western firms.[35] There are also hundreds of such arrangements in China.[36]

Of particular interest are the **coproduction arrangements,** which involve having a Western firm provide equipment, technical input, or management for a plant owned by Eastern partners in exchange for a portion of the output or output from another Eastern plant. For instance, Siemens, a German equipment manufacturer, receives telephone relay equipment in Bulgaria in exchange for providing a telephone system.

The Eastern countries have exhibited very different preferences in terms of types of cooperative arrangements with Western firms. In recent years, for example, coproduction arrangements have accounted for the largest portion in Bulgaria, Czechoslovakia, Hungary, Poland, and the USSR. Joint ventures have been the major form in Rumania, and turnkey plants have been of most importance in the German Democratic Republic (GDR). Licensing has accounted for only about five percent of the arrangements with the GDR, Rumania, and the USSR, but about twenty percent with Czechoslovakia, Hungary, and Poland.[37]

The transfer of assets on a cooperative basis need not be paid for in the form of merchandise but may, instead, be in any one of the payment forms discussed earlier in the chapter. The types of asset transfers have been extremely varied. For instance, Kodak granted permission to Czechoslovakia to make its Super 8 movie film cartridges. Claret, the largest manufacturer of refrigerators in France, built a refrigerator plant for the Soviets. And Holiday Inn is providing training and reservations services for motels in Eastern Europe.

In 1979, China enacted legislation allowing foreign firms to set up joint ventures in China with Chinese partners. Thus far the number of ventures established has been small because of the long negotiations involved, because of concerns about the Chinese legal system, and because many firms are apparently taking a "wait and see" attitude. Unlike other cooperative arrangements in China, which have been established primarily to get resources for or output from China, these are designed primarily to serve the Chinese market. In a number of cases, however, the foreign investor has been required to sell a certain percentage of the output in export markets as a means of earning foreign exchange to cover its remittances.[38]

FUTURE OF U.S. BUSINESS IN THE EAST

Lagging U.S. Trade Share

Between 1970 and 1980 the United States ranked second among the 24 OECD countries in sales to Eastern Europe and the Soviet Union. By 1982 the United States had fallen to fourth place. In terms of the percentage of each of the countries' exports, the United States ranked nineteenth in 1982.[39] Although part of the difference is attributable to location, U.S. restrictions have been a major retarding factor. Only Japan exports more to China than the United States does. Thus far, however, the Chinese import market has been small—even less than that of little Hong Kong.

The Need for U.S. Products

- Projection of needs for high technology, plant and agricultural machinery, agricultural products, and consumer goods
- Indications of East's move to greater self-sufficiency

The composition of imports by Eastern countries from the West is indicative of the industrial emphasis of state planners. Nearly one third of imports are classified as engineering products, and the Eastern countries have been particularly eager to expend their resources on importing advanced machinery and equipment. From numerous examples it is obvious that the communist negotiators want to get the most advanced technology. This should give an advantage to U.S. firms, whether exporting or licensing, because of their R&D expenditures. China, for example, has announced that it will be searching out opportunities to increase its technology purchases over the next several years. Among other things, China plans to purchase ten nuclear plants at about $1.5 billion each; Westinghouse is expected to be a strong candidate for the sale.[40]

Of particular importance is the need for replacement machinery over the next several years. The Eastern countries have generally followed policies of expanding the stock of equipment and machinery in order to bring additional workers into the labor force, rather than increasing the output of existing workers through the introduction of replacement capital. There is a near-consensus that the communist countries have practically reached their limits of increasing output by simply adding to the work force. The recent five-year plans confirm this, as there is a new emphasis on technological innovation to save labor, materials, and fuels that involves the replacement of antiquated machinery with more productive capital.[41]

Not only do U.S. firms have the technology needed in the Eastern countries, but they also have the greatest experience in operating plants of the size needed for the amount of output required by the large Soviet and Chinese markets, or for a combined COMECON demand. Illustrative of the giant size desired for the production facilities is the Kama River truck plant discussed earlier.

Aside from machinery for industrial use, it is anticipated that the Eastern countries will have a greater need for agricultural machinery. About one third of the Soviet labor force is in agriculture, compared to only about 5 percent in the United States. Yet the Soviet farmer can feed only seven people, while the U.S. counterpart can feed forty-six. The difference in productivity is partially due to natural geographic conditions; nevertheless, the major culprit appears to be the lack of modern machinery. Not only would investment in the agricultural sector increase output there, it would also free workers for industrial jobs. The lack of agricultural productivity also points to a continued need for U.S. agricultural products, which comprise over half the U.S. sales to the Soviet Union. In 1983 the United States and the Soviet Union signed a five-year grain delivery agreement that will increase U.S. grain exports to the Soviet Union by about 50 percent.[42]

There are indications that some emphasis will shift to the production and importation of consumer goods. One of the ways the communist countries have produced growth is to force savings and investment by having few consumer goods available. In Rumania, for instance, the goal has been to plow between 30 and 35 percent of gross national product into investment. The inevitable result of these long-standing policies has been consumer resentment, followed by decisions to produce and market more of the goods that consumers want. If the trend toward consumer orientation continues, then many U.S. firms selling consumer goods that were scorned by decision makers in the past may find markets in communist countries. Already such firms as Pepsi-Cola and Coca-Cola have licensed production in some Eastern countries. Some observers believe that the United States should foster promotion of consumer products to the communist countries. It is argued that there will then be added pressures in those countries to divert funds from investment and military spending, thus making the United States relatively stronger.

Traditionally, service firms such as banks and advertising agencies have followed their production clients abroad in order to provide them with the same type of services as at home and to help them in coordinating worldwide strategies. The volume of East-West business activity has reached the level at which many service investments have taken place.

In spite of some of the above factors, which might lead one to be optimistic about future U.S. exports, the eleventh five-year plan (1981–1985) of the Soviet Union shows an overall inward rather than outward orientation by targeting a decreased proportion of foreign trade to total production and consumption. Furthermore, there have been recent indications that COMECON countries plan to conduct a larger portion of their trade with each other.[43]

Two-Way Flows

• Eastern bloc now selling technology to West

While the preceding discussion emphasizes the communist countries' needs for goods and technologies from the West, trade must inevitably be two-way to succeed. For some time, basically because of ideological differences, U.S. nationals have assumed that all communist-made products are inferior, pointing to a few items that are, in fact, of lower quality than their Western counterparts. That is like having outsiders view recent U.S. railroad operations as being typical of all U.S. industries. The reality is that perhaps as many as 25 percent of all scientists in the world are employed in the Soviet Union and that there are many technical areas in which they now lead the world. There has been an upsurge of Soviet patent registrations in the United States and of their sales of technology to U.S. firms.[44] One may conclude that communist countries could conceivably sell many products in greater abundance abroad.

Debt-Servicing Problems

Although their records for repayment have been impeccable, there is much concern that some Eastern countries may be nearing their capacities for debt servicing. Poland canceled a proposed $1 billion truck-manufacturing venture that General Motors was to build, and China canceled $1.5 billion in contracts with Japanese groups, both largely because of foreign currency shortages. Unless Eastern countries are able to increase their export earnings substantially, increased exports to them by credit may decelerate.

• Questions of payments
  • Soviet ability to sell raw materials
  • China's ability to earn from labor contracts abroad

On the subject of foreign earnings by communist countries, we have a number of question marks. One of the biggest is what will happen to commodity prices. During part of the 1970s the Soviet Union was able to mitigate its payments problems largely because of the high world prices of oil, gold, diamonds, and platinum. Since then the prices of these commodities have fallen considerably. Furthermore, a recent study financed by the National Science Foundation of the United States focuses doubt on the Soviet's ability to take advantage of its rich storehouse of minerals over the next decade. The remoteness of the bulk of these resources often make them more expensive to the Soviets even than imported ones.[45]

The Chinese have recently begun to bid on labor-intensive construction projects abroad as a means of alleviating foreign exchange shortages. The state-run companies pay workers less than the amount they receive on contracts; additionally, workers send part of their salaries to their families in China. They have worked on such projects as highway construction in Ethiopia, the construction of a power station in Hong Kong, and the building of model farms in Algeria. The labor contracts now bring China in about $1.5 billion a year.[46]

Interaction of Economic and Political Ties

- Future depends in part on
  - whether closer economic ties ease animosity
  - what other countries do

Much of the easing of economic restrictions by the U.S. government in the 1970s was based on the premise that closer economic ties will ease political animosities. There is little evidence to either support or reject this premise; consequently, events in the world power struggle over the next several years will determine to a great extent what occurs in East-West business ties.

There has also been increased pressure to allow U.S. subsidiary sales to be made to communist countries. In 1974 the United States allowed Ford Motor Company to export part of its Argentinean production to Cuba. If the United States had not allowed this, Argentina would almost certainly have taken over Ford's facilities, and there would have been animosity in other developing countries.

The United States is, of course, not the only trader with the East, or even the major one. Some of the change in U.S. policy has been due to the realization that, if U.S. firms do not sell, someone else will. What such major Western nations as Japan, West Germany, and the United Kingdom do will undoubtedly help mold U.S. policy. There are some big questions here. Japan and Europe, for example, have been hurt by raw materials shortages from less-developed countries and may thus turn more to the East for supplies and sales. West Germany has followed a policy called "ostpolitik," which was designed to increase economic relations with communist countries, particularly East Germany, in an effort to bring about eventual German reunification. A continued schism between China and the Soviet Union could have significant ramifications for East-West business as well.

OTHER TYPES OF COOPERATION

As Western companies continue to develop cooperative arrangements with state-owned Eastern enterprises, there may be increased realization of the complementary nature of their resources. By combining these resources in other countries, considerable economic advantages might be gained. For example, Soviet, West German, and Austrian firms have jointly constructed a power station in Iceland. Siemens of West Germany is already teaming up with East German partners to sell electric rail cars in Greece and control systems in developing countries.[47]

- The U.S. and USSR could
  - cooperate in third countries
  - combine basic with applied research capabilities

Several areas have been suggested as logically complementary for U.S. and Soviet interests. One of these could involve more research collaboration, since the Soviet is strong in basic technology but weak in applying that technology to new products, an area in which U.S. firms are strong. Another is the combination of vast Soviet natural resources with U.S. firms' ability

- combine natural resource holdings with management of projects
- combine transportation with marketing

to manage extraction in large projects. Still another is the Soviet strength in transporting goods over long distances, which could be complemented by U.S. abilities to market such goods.[48]

Ventures could eventually develop in which East and West each supply resources for projects in less-developed countries. It is reasoned that this might overcome some of the resentment against foreign exploitation, prevent the East and West from being played against each other, and reduce the dumping of expensive military hardware into poor countries.[49]

SUMMARY

- As political relationships have varied in this century between what is now the communist bloc and the Western countries, business relationships have fluctuated substantially. This has been especially true of trade between the United States and the Soviet Union. Trade flourished during the two world wars when the two countries were allies but fell to minimal proportions at times when animosities arose.

- Trade controls have been instituted to hurt an unfriendly country, to try to make a country change some policy, or to make a public statement of displeasure about another country's actions.

- One of the major factors inhibiting the expansion of East-West business since World War II has been the communist countries' lack of products that could be marketed in the West in sufficient quantity to gain the exchange needed for imports.

- When trade is out of balance, command and market economies use different means of restoring equilibrium. Command economies may simply terminate certain imports or sell abroad below cost.

- Many products for which U.S. producers might find sales in Eastern countries cannot be exported because of U.S. controls. Many potential exporters have argued that these policies result not in keeping things from the communists, but rather in diverting their purchases to other sources.

- The fact that the communist countries contain about one third of the world's population is indicative of a large market potential. However, the large land mass and the desire to be as independent as possible from the West mean that the Eastern bloc is more nearly self-sufficient than other areas of the world.

- It is difficult for Western firms to assess potential demand for their products in communist countries because of the lack of comparable economic indicators and the secrecy surrounding their import plans. Since most purchase decisions are made by planning authorities and industrial ministries, it is difficult to effect sales by creating a demand among the ultimate consumers of products.

- The agencies that handle import and service purchases in Eastern countries are known as shrewd negotiators that are frequently able to get the best possible terms by playing one Western firm against another and by bargaining over a very protracted period of time.

- When an exporter sells to a communist country, it may be for credit, for cash payment in either a convertible or a nonconvertible currency, or in exchange for merchandise. All Western industrial countries have some type of export credit insurance, which helps their firms to make large sales to the Eastern bloc.

- A general analysis of Eastern import requirements may be determined by examining recent trade statistics and bilateral trade treaties. Two of the major means of creating demand are through exhibitions at trade fairs and by soliciting sales to other Western firms that have become major contractors for building plants and facilities in Eastern countries.

- An increasing amount of Western business in communist countries is in the form of licensing technology or building plants or facilities to be run and owned by Eastern governments. Frequently, the Western firm is paid by receiving part of the merchandise, which is then sold in the West.

- The U.S. share of East-West business has generally been small in recent years. Certain factors indicate a possible future growth in the U.S. share. These include the communist countries' desire for products encompassing the most recent technology, plants producing on a very large scale, a need for agricultural products, and an increase in consumer goods, all areas in which U.S. production excels.

C A S E   U.S. TRADE EMBARGO ON CUBA

In the early 1980s, two disclosures brought speculation about future trading relations between the United States and Cuba. The first was that representatives of both the Carter and Reagan administrations had met since September 1977 with Fidel Castro or his intermediaries to discuss the normalization of relations between the two countries. The second was that, because of a severe shortage of foreign exchange, the Cuban government was offering foreign corporations both the ownership and the management of a new resort.

The fact that virtually no trade had taken place between the two countries since 1961 underscores some of the emotional issues on both sides that have plagued the reestablishment of commercial activities. By 1981 the United States could boast that some of its best friends (e.g., China) were communistic, but it apparently could not accept a communist country in its own neighborhood. Cuba, in turn, was buying well over $1 billion a year from Western industrial countries, including over $200 million from both Canada and Spain, but was unwilling to make direct overtures for trade with the United States.

Several factors led up to the 1961 embargo. After the Batista government was overthrown in 1959, Fidel Castro reportedly spent several months practicing his English before traveling to Washington to visit with the Secretary of State, John Foster Dulles. Dulles then refused to meet with him. Castro returned to Havana and made pronouncements about exporting his type of revolution elsewhere in Latin America. The United States countered by canceling its agreements to buy Cuban sugar, and Cuba retaliated by seizing U.S. oil refineries. The oil companies then refused to supply Cuba with crude oil, and Cuba turned to the Soviet Union for supplies. Since this occurred at the height of the Cold War, when the United States and the Soviet Union had few business relations, the United States quickly severed diplomatic relations with Cuba.

The incidents that further strained relations during the next twenty years were too numerous for us to detail. Some were so serious that they threatened peace. Others were almost ludicrous. They included the U.S. sponsorship of an invasion by exiles at the Bay of Pigs, the placement and removal of Soviet missiles in Cuba, the deployment of Cuban forces to overthrow regimes that the United States supported, and post-Watergate exposés that the CIA had tried to airlift someone to assassinate Castro and had spent thousands of dollars to develop a powder to make his beard fall out. There were also incidents that indicated a relationship that was growing closer. The countries have agreed on antihijacking measures and in 1977 established diplomatic interest sections in each other's capitals. Many travel restrictions have been removed, but in 1983 the United States imposed restrictions on taking money to Cuba.

By the early 1980s a number of prominent people in the United States had indicated publicly that they favored trade with Cuba. These people included some senators from both parties, the head of the United Auto Workers, and several heads of major firms. The primary rationale was that the embargo had not succeeded. Cuba was able to buy elsewhere. Among Latin American countries, nearly all had abandoned the 1964 Organization of American States embargo, from which only Mexico had abstained. Since Cuba had been able to buy elsewhere, trade proponents have reasoned that the United States has lost market opportunities. Before the Castro takeover, 80 percent of Cuba's imports were from the United States.

Others have been pessimistic about U.S. export possibilities if trade restrictions are eased. Since Cuba is short of foreign exchange, it may have to sell in the United States if it is to buy from the United States. About

83 percent of Cuba's recent exports have been sugar, and the possibility of selling large amounts of sugar to the United States may be unlikely. It would have to be sold either at the expense of U.S. domestic sugar producers or at the expense of other countries' production. For the former there are strong lobbies. For the latter there would be political repercussions if the United States reduced purchases from such countries as Mexico, the Dominican Republic, or the Philippines.

Proponents of trade believe that Castro might be less of a threat if trade with Cuba increases. Cuba would once again be dependent on the United States for spare parts; and Cubans, they argue, would become aware again of the benefits of capitalism to consumers. Furthermore, such countries as Nicaragua might not be so isolated from the United States if their Cuban benefactor were closer. Overtures toward Cuba might also counter some of the Soviet efforts to trade with and to openly court rightist dictatorships in Latin America.

The United States has intermittently raised a number of issues as prerequisites to commercial relations. One of these is that Cuba agree to stop sending troops, advisors, and propaganda to other countries to support leadership of its liking. Cuba's position is that as a sovereign nation it has as much right as the United States to become involved in other countries. Another U.S. objection is that the Soviet Union maintains a submarine base in Cuba. Cuba, in turn, objects to the U.S.-maintained military base at Cuba's Guantanamo Bay. Another possible hurdle is compensation for seized properties of U.S. investors. However, Cuba has settled with investors from France, Canada, Switzerland, and Liechtenstein. Furthermore, the United States trades with a number of countries that have not settled for property seized from U.S. parties.

An emotional factor is that neither country seems willing to be the first to propose trade formally. If the United States were to do so, then Cuba could propagandize that the twenty-year embargo has not worked and that Cuban policies have removed some of the shackles of dependence on the United States. If Cuba were to make proposals, the propaganda advantage would fall to the United States, which could then publicize to other developing countries that "even Cuba needs us."

QUESTIONS

1. Should the United States seek to open trade with Cuba? If so, under what terms?

2. What type of commercial relations with the United States would be in Cuba's best interest?

3. Do you feel that the Cuban situation warrants a different U.S. policy than that employed with such countries as China, the USSR, Poland, and East Germany?

NOTES

1. Data for the case were taken from many articles, with particular reference to Herbert E. Meyer, "What It's Like to Do Business with the Russians," *Fortune,* May 1972, pp. 67–69ff; and Edson I. Gaylord (Chairman of the Board and President, The Ingersoll Milling Machine Company), "Soviet Trucks and Technology Transfers," *Wall Street Journal,* March 10, 1980, p. 27.

2. This term was used by R. D. Schmidt, Vice Chairman of Control Data, in "U.S.-USSR Trade: An American Businessman's Viewpoint," *Columbia Journal of World Business,* Vol. 18, No. 4, Winter 1983, p. 36.

3. Clyde H. Farnsworth quoting Gary C. Hufbauer, senior fellow of the Institute for International Economics, in "The Doves Capture Control of Trade," *New York Times,* October 23, 1983, Section 3, p. 1.

4. Michael V. Forrestal and James H. Giffen, "U.S.-Soviet Trade: Political Realities and Future Potential," *Columbia Journal of World Business,* Vol. 18, No. 4, Winter 1983, pp. 29–31.

5. In a study of large U.S. firms not doing business with Eastern Europe or the Soviet Union, for example, one of the main reasons given for their reluctance to get involved was that there would be a high initial investment without assurance of return. See Robert D. Hisrich, Michael P. Peters, and Arnold K. Weinstein, "East-West Trade: The View from the United States," *Journal of International Business Studies,* Winter 1981, pp. 109–121.

6. See James Henry Giffen, *The Legal and Practical Aspects of Trade with the Soviet Union* (New York: Praeger, 1969), pp. 139–142; Committee for Economic Development, *A New Trade Policy toward Communist Countries* (New York: Committee for Economic Development, 1972), pp. 54–59; John E. Felber, *Manual for Soviet-American Trading* (New Jersey: International Intertrade Index, 1967), pp. 7–9.

7. "Clouds Over U.S.-Soviet Trade are Breaking Up," *Business Week,* December 17, 1984, pp. 44–45.

8. "Peking to Return to Tight Control of Foreign Trade," *Wall Street Journal,* March 16, 1984, p. 31; Theodore Shabad, "Soviet Trade Emphasis Shifted to Europe in '83," *New York Times,* April 3, 1984, p. D1.

9. Giffen, *A New Trade Policy toward Communist Countries,* p. 54.

10. *Ibid.*

11. Daniel Franklin and Edwina Moreton, "A Little Late in Learning the Facts," *The Economist,* April 20, 1985, p. 16.

12. John T. Farrell, "Soviet Payment Problems in Trade with the West," *Soviet Economic Prospects for the Seventies* (Washington, D.C.: U.S. Congress, Joint Economic Committee, June 27, 1973), p. 702.

13. "Soviets Gain from Record Gold Prices," *Wall Street Journal,* March 4, 1974, p. 6.

14. See, for example, Anne Colamosca, "It's Russian and Glitters," *New York Times,* May 23, 1976, p. 111; "Britain Jumps on Russia over Dumping of Trucks," *Wall Street Journal,* February 24, 1977, p. 24.

15. Franklyn Holzman, "Systemic Bases of the Unconventional International Trade Practices of Centrally-Planned Economies," *Columbia Journal of World Business,* Vol. 18, No. 4, Winter 1983, pp. 4–9.

16. Stephen Marris, "East-West Economic Relations: A Longer-Term Perspective," *OECD Observer,* No. 128, May 1984, pp. 11–17.

17. Raymond Bonner, "U.S.-Soviet Trade Bars Said to Cost $10 Billion," *New York Times,* May 25, 1984, p. D1; *Common Sense in U.S.-Soviet Trade* (Washington: American Committee on East-West Accord, 1983).

18. Frederick Kempe and Eduardo Lachica, "Cocom Feuds Over Trade to East Bloc," *Wall Street Journal,* July 17, 1984, p. 27.

19. D. A. Loeber and A. P. Friedland, "Soviet Imports of Industrial Installations under Compensation Agreements: West Europe's Siberian Pipeline Revisited," *Columbia Journal of World Business,* Vol. 18, No. 4, Winter 1983, pp. 51–62.

20. Jon Zonderman, "Policing High-Tech Exports," *New York Times,* November 27, 1983, pp. 100+; "U.S. Sets Trade Curb for Digital," *New York Times,* March 19, 1984, p. D1; and Eduardo Lachica, "U.S. Effort to Stiffen Export Licensing Is Costly and Confusing, Industry Says," *Wall Street Journal,* March 20, 1984, p. 10.

21. David Brand, "Soviets See Pluses in Grain Embargo," *Wall Street Journal,* February 26, 1981, p. 31; and Everett G. Martin, "Commodities," *Wall Street Journal,* May 7, 1981, p. 46.

22. Lyman E. Ostlund and Kjell M. Halvorsen, "The Russian Decision Process Governing Trade," *Journal of Marketing,* April 1972, p. 10.

23. Clyde H. Farnsworth, "U.S. Bars Soviet Nickel," *New York Times,* November 22, 1983, p. D1.

24. Jonathan Kwitny, "U.S. Concerns Export Mainland-Bound Goods as Embargo Loosens," *Wall Street Journal,* March 11, 1971, p. 1.

25. Seth Mydans, "Comecon Leaders Back Closer Economic Ties," *New York Times,* June 15, 1984, p. D1+; and H. Stephen Gardner, "Soviet Foreign Trade Decision-Making in the 1980s," *Columbia Journal of World Business,* Vol. 18, No. 4, Winter 1983, pp. 17–23.

26. Franklin and Moreton, *op. cit.,* p. 5.

27. See, for example, Elizabeth Goldstein and Jan Vanous, "Country Risk Analysis: Pitfalls of Comparing the Eastern Bloc Countries with the Rest of the World," *Columbia Journal of World Business,* Vol. 18, No. 4, Winter 1983, pp. 10–16.

28. Ostlund and Halvorsen, "The Russian Decision Process Governing Trade," pp. 3–11.

29. David K. Shipler, "Soviet Ads—Why Try Zip and Flair When a Fact Will Do?" *New York Times,* January 30, 1977, p. 27.

30. Larissa Oleson, "Soviet Advertising Techniques in the U.S.," *Columbia Journal of World Business,* Vol. 18, No. 4, Winter 1983, pp. 63–66.

31. Gordon Crovitz, "Europe Pays for Its Pipedream," *Wall Street Journal,* December 13, 1983, p. 30; "Paying the Piper," *Wall Street Journal,* September 30, 1983, p. 28.

32. "Review and Outlook," *Wall Street Journal,* May 14, 1984, p. 24.

33. "Soviet Union: A Pitch in Moscow for U.S. Oil Goods," *Business Week,* October 27, 1973, p. 46.

34. William A. Dymsza, "East-West: Types of Business Arrangements," *MSU Business Topics,* Winter 1971, p. 23.

35. Jerzy Cieslik, "Western Firms Participating in the East-West Industrial Co-operation: The Case of Poland," *Management International Review,* Vol. 23, No. 1, 1983, p. 69.

36. "China: How Trade Zones Are Luring Foreign Investors," *Business Week,* January 11, 1982, pp. 50–51.

37. OECD, *East-West Technology Transfer-Draft Synthesis* (Paris: OECD, 1984), pp. 348–350.

38. John D. Daniels, Jeffrey Krug, and Douglas Nigh, "U.S. Joint Ventures in China," *California Management Review,* Vol. XXVII, No. 4, Summer 1985, pp. 46–58.

39. Marris, *op. cit.,* p. 15.

40. Richard E. Smith, "China Plans to Spend $1 Billion This Year to Buy Technology from Western Firms," *Wall Street Journal,* January 30, 1984, p. 36; Doral P. Levin, "Westinghouse Expects Business Windfall from a U.S.-China Nuclear Plant Accord," *Wall Street Journal,* April 26, 1984, p. 32.

41. Robert Keatley, "Slower Soviet Economic Growth Is Seen Because of Labor and Weather Troubles," *Wall Street Journal,* March 3, 1977, p. 11; "Soviet Bloc Nations Alter Economic Plans with Stress on Technological Innovation," *Wall Street Journal,* April 8, 1977, p. 10.

42. Hertha W. Heiss, "The Framework for U.S.-Soviet Trade," *Columbia Journal of World Business,* Vol. 18, No. 4, Winter 1983, pp. 25–28.

43. Gardner, *op. cit.,* p. 20; Shabad, *loc. cit.*

44. Oleson, *loc. cit.,* quoting data in *U.S. News and World Report,* January 17, 1983.

45. Robert C. Jensen, ed., *Soviet Natural Resources in the World Economy.* (Chicago: University of Chicago Press, 1983).

46. Christopher S. Wren, "China's Growing Export: Its Workers," *New York Times,* June 3, 1984, p. 3.

47. John Tagliabue, "Bonn Innovating in Trade with East," *New York Times,* March 19, 1984, p. D8.

48. Forrestal and Giffen, *op. cit.,* p. 35.

49. Samuel Pisar, "East West Are Business Partners," *Wall Street Journal,* August 31, 1973, p. 4.

PART 6

Corporate Policy and Strategy

Whether a firm is heavily engaged in foreign markets or supply sources or is merely in the initial process of developing them, many interrelated alternatives must be considered. In this section we shall discuss those operational alternatives that normally transcend decision making within functional disciplines. These alternatives include where to go, what form the foreign operations should take, and how to organize the corporate structure to accommodate the international operations.

In Chapter 14 we discuss the means of moving goods from country to country, including strategies for sourcing materials and components, transportation modes, and export documentation.

Chapter 15 examines some of the major means and activities by which foreign involvement may be approached in order to ration the allocation of scarce resources.

Chapter 16 discusses methods of comparing countries when choices have to be made in terms of where to go to sell or invest.

Chapter 17 elaborates strategies that top management can follow to make the necessary changes for foreign operations while, at the same time, maintaining order and control for the organization as a whole.

14

Global Sourcing and the Movement of Goods

- To gain an overview of the various aspects of business logistics from an international perspective.

- To describe the major differences in ways that firms can source materials and components and manufacture and assemble products for international use.

- To examine the different modes of transportation by which goods can be moved from country to country.

THE AUTO INDUSTRY AND WORLDWIDE SOURCING[1]

The auto industry is one that has changed dramatically over the past two decades because of international competition. It is an industry that is significant in terms of production and employment in the industrial economies. In 1980, car manufacturing accounted for 7–10 percent of all manufacturing output and 5–8 percent of total manufacturing employment in North America, Japan, and Western Europe. At the same time, "U.S. automakers purchased almost 57 percent of the nation's synthetic rubber output and 53 percent of its malleable iron."

Historically, the U.S. market has been dominated by the major U.S. producers—General Motors, Ford, and Chrysler. Until 1960, imports held less than 1 percent of the U.S. market share. By 1970, however, that share had risen to 14.7 percent, and Japanese producers held 3.7 percent of the market. As was pointed out in the auto case in Chapter 5, the decade of the 1970s was revolutionary in the auto industry, resulting in a strong shift in demand from large cars to small, more fuel-efficient cars and an increase in imports.

As the share of imports rose, U.S. automakers scrambled to find solutions to their problems. Their strategies involved downsizing their regular line of cars, importing parts and cars produced by them abroad or by foreign producers, entering into new production arrangements, and developing whole new production technologies. They had to do something new or else give away the market entirely to foreign competition.

In addition to servicing some markets with exports, the U.S. industry had adopted a strategy of supplying the market outside of the United States with production in foreign locations. Part of that was due to tariff structures. Tariffs in Latin America made it nearly impossible to sell cars produced in the United States, except to the very wealthy. Post–World War II tariffs designed to encourage growth within the European Community forced the automakers to set up production facilities in Europe. The U.S. market, however, has been relatively open to foreign competition, and the size of the market made it an attractive place for foreign producers to sell. The Japanese strategy has been to develop economies of scale at home and use that production as an export base to supply the U.S. market.

The U.S. government has maintained a relatively free trade attitude toward auto trade since World War II. In 1965 an Automotive Agreement was negotiated with Canada, which allowed automakers to **rationalize** operations in North America. Exports of automobile components and finished products from Canada to the United States rival those from Japan, although U.S. companies also export a great deal to Canada. The integration of the industry in the two countries became evident in the early 1980s, when the United Auto Workers in Canada went on strike. Delays in Canadian

- **Rationalize**—To specialize production of components or assembly of products to achieve economies of scale; this enables a company to avoid having to produce all components or products in each country where it operates.

production eventually crippled production in some U.S. plants before the strike was finally resolved.

Because of extreme loss of U.S. market share by U.S. companies, the U.S. government entered into a voluntary quota arrangement with the Japanese in 1980, as was noted in Chapter 5. During the time of the quota, U.S. companies were expected to retool and become more competitive. As a partial measure of effort, the U.S. companies spent $50 billion on new plant and equipment during the 1979–1983 period, compared with $23 billion in the preceding four years. During the 1980–1983 period, U.S. companies cut $4 billion from inventory costs, trimmed management ranks by 15 percent, and nearly doubled the number of vehicles produced per employee per year.

As a result of the problems caused by import competition, U.S. car manufacturers are developing new strategies. Although these strategies are similar for all of the companies, each company is stressing something slightly different. One of Ford's strategies, for example, is to assemble cars in Hermosillo, Mexico, and ship them to the United States. The cars are designed by the Japanese company Toyo Kogyo Co. (Mazda) and use some Japanese parts. American Motors' major stockholder is the French government-owned company Renault (with just under 50 percent of the stock in AMC), and Renault is providing cars through import as well as jointly producing Renault autos in AMC plants in the United States. Chrysler sells Mitsubishi cars through its domestic dealers (it owns 15 percent of the stock of Mitsubishi), and it plans on having Mitsubishi build the Omni and Horizon models for sale in the United States.

The United Auto Workers (UAW) is concerned with these moves because of the potential impact on employment. In 1983, U.S. auto sales of 9,200,000 units were made up of 6,800,000 units produced domestically, 100,000 foreign-produced units (essentially produced in Japan) sold by U.S. automakers, and 2,300,000 imports. Japan supplied 1,800,000 of the imports, and Europe supplied 500,000. The UAW estimates that, in 1987, domestically produced units will drop to 6,000,000, foreign-produced autos sold by U.S. automakers will rise to 975,000 units, and imports will rise to 4,200,000. The foreign-produced autos sold by U.S. automakers will come from Japan (485,000 units), Korea (300,000 units), Mexico (130,000 units), and Europe (60,000 units). The imports will be from Japan (3,-430,000 units), Europe (620,000 units), and Korea (150,000 units). These latter figures assume the ending of voluntary import constraints on Japanese producers and no legislation protecting U.S. producers. Some feel that the Japanese will still try to hold their market share to 20 percent after the ending of the quotas so as not to start a price war or trigger increased protectionist responses by the U.S. government.

The most interesting and comprehensive moves are coming from General Motors. GM, the second largest company in the United States, with annual sales of over $75 billion, is embarked on a multifaceted program. GM's strategy involves overseas production to service overseas markets, the importation of Japanese and Korean cars sold through GM dealer networks, the importation of parts and technology, and the development of a completely new small car through the Saturn project. Its overall strategy can be summarized as follows: to

> *remain the Number One automaker in the USA and become Number One in the world by making massive investments in new technologies, product development, and automated facilities to create a broad line of sophisticated, fuel efficient cars capable of competing successfully in all major markets.*

It has also set a number of substrategies to accomplish these lofty goals. In terms of purchasing, it wants to increase sourcing from foreign suppliers and invest heavily in European components capacity. In manufacturing, it wants to

> *build new plants for new model types and components; maximize global commonality and centralize production in single divisions; locate facilities in or near target markets; increase the level of automation rapidly; overtake the Japanese in fit and finish quality; develop "flexible" tooling to allow rapid changes in product mix; source components from overseas/low cost countries (engines from Japan, Australia, Mexico, Brazil); and integrate European operations under Opel.*

GM's operations in Europe are headed up by the Adam Opel AG subsidiary in Germany. It has never been a major player in a market historically dominated by Ford, Renault, Fiat, Volkswagen, and Peugeot. However, the European market is nothing like the U.S. market, where one company (GM) controls slightly under 50 percent of the market. In 1983, Ford and Renault were neck and neck with about 12.5 percent each of the European market. GM's Opel division improved dramatically over its 1982 performance to move it into sixth place with 11.2 percent of the market, clearly within striking distance of the leaders.

- **Outsourcing**—A situation in which a domestic company uses foreign suppliers for components or finished products

It is in the U.S. market where GM's strategy is clearly international in scope. Because of the huge cost differentials in Asia, GM has adopted a so-called Asia strategy. It has entered into a variety of agreements with Japan's Suzuki Motors, Isuzu Motors Ltd., and Toyota and with Korea's Daewoo Corp. The object is to step up **outsourcing** of cheaper foreign-made components wherever possible as well as finished products. It is currently selling small cars made by Suzuki Motor Co. and Isuzu Motors Ltd. Its most ambitious Asian strategy from the standpoint of overseas production is the Daewoo operation in Korea. Korea is interesting because its wages average about $2.45 per hour, one tenth of those of the United States and one fifth of Japan's. GM will be using a lot of the technology developed by Adam Opel AG. It is contributing $100 million in capital to the project as well as advice on the design and construction of new engine, stamping, and assembly facilities. In addition, it is putting $10 million into a separate parts venture. Additional assistance is being provided in the form of production technology. The new car will be sold by the Pontiac division and will provide an important entrant in the small car market that GM cannot supply from domestic production. The parts operation could eventually have important ramifications for its entire production line.

The joint venture with Toyota is an interesting one. The venture between the world's two largest car makers was approved in 1983–1984, and the first cars are to roll off the assembly line in December 1985. The basic idea is to use a Toyota design and parts to assemble approximately 240,000 subcompacts a year in a GM assembly plant in Fremont, California. The venture uses Japanese manufacturing concepts such as a team assembly system, "the just-in-time inventory method of ordering and storing parts, non-adversary labor-management relations, management flexibility in assigning jobs, and an emphasis on building quality into a car at every stage of production." Thus parts and technology from abroad are going to be combined with capital and dealer networks in the United States to attempt to further penetrate the small car market.

The last, and most ambitious, undertaking mentioned in connection with GM is Project Saturn. The $1 billion project is being charged with developing a car and a production process that will allow GM to compete in the small car market through U.S. production. It hopes to save costs by designing new components and by radically changing the way it manufacturers cars. It will combine the Toyota concept of assembling and testing autos in production teams with the use of prefabricated modules. In some respects, Project Saturn will lean heavily on what GM learns from its Toyota venture in California.

INTRODUCTION TO LOGISTICS

Most firms have the option of where they want to source production for worldwide sales. As was shown in the auto case, for any given market the MNE can manufacture the product itself, or it can buy the product from someone else. If it decides to manufacture the product itself, it can either manufacture it in the local market or manufacture it in another country and import it into the market. The firm also has the option of buying the product from another manufacturer, which can produce the product locally or in another country and import it into the market.

Obviously, the true MNE is involved in fairly sophisticated forms of production sharing, in which it may produce and/or assemble components in one or several countries for markets all over the world. The virtual explosion of this form of business operation in the past few years has increased the complexity of the **logistics** function dramatically. It is also obvious that separating manufacturing and exporting is almost impossible. It

• Logistics—The functions involved in moving and storing raw materials, components, and finished goods from one stage of the manufacturing/sales process to another

used to be that a firm would either export finished goods or manufacture in a particular country for that market. The lines are becoming increasingly blurred, and the percentage of total exports coming from intraenterprise trade appears to be growing.

This concept of multinationality is very different from what existed even a decade ago. In a study of 156 of the world's largest multinationals, it was found that the Swiss and Benelux countries had a significantly higher proportion of their production outside of their parent countries because of the small size of the home market and lack of local resources. At that time, U.S. firms exhibited a very low ratio of exports to total parent firm production because of the large home market in the United States and the commitment to serve foreign markets through production abroad rather than through exports. The Japanese, on the other hand, tended to export more and produce less abroad.[2] Now, however, international trade is becoming a more important part of the GNP in the United States, U.S. firms are beginning to integrate their operations worldwide in a production sense, as was noted in the GM case, and Japanese firms are becoming large investors worldwide.

Definition of Logistics

Business logistics is a comprehensive system that can be defined as follows:

Business Logistics is the planning, organizing, and controlling of all move-store activities that facilitate product flow from the point of raw material acquisition to the point of final consumption, and of the attendant information flows, for the purpose of providing a sufficient level of customer service (and associated revenues) consistent with the costs incurred for overcoming the resistance of time and space in providing the service.[3]

From an international standpoint this concept can be better understood by looking at Fig. 14.1. Note that each solid line represents the physical flow of raw materials, components, and finished goods and that it also represents situations in which goods may be stored and in which they may also change in ownership. For example, raw materials may be purchased from an outside supplier rather than from a supplier owned by the firm. Then the materials may be stored in a warehouse until the manufacturing process needs them. Also, components may be manufactured in the home country and assembled there. They can be sold in the home market to wholesalers and retailers or sold to foreign markets. In the case of foreign sales, they could be sold through company distributors or through others, so that title actually passes before the goods reach the final consumers. To use the auto case again, Ford can purchase components manufactured in Japan and ship them to the United States for final assembly and sale in the U.S. market, or it can have the components shipped to Mexico for final assembly and sale in the United States and Mexico. If the components are manufactured

FIGURE 14.1
**International Logistics
Process**

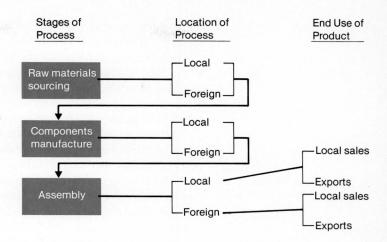

in Japan, most of the raw materials were probably imported. In the case of Mexican assembly, some of the components would come from the United States, some from Japan, and a small percentage from Mexico.

Logistics Activities

There are several logistics activities that firms must get involved in. It would be difficult to develop a comprehensive list of activities that everyone agrees on, but the major activities are transportation, storage, packaging, materials handling, order processing, forecasting, production scheduling, purchasing, and site location. We will not discuss each of these points comprehensively in this chapter, but we will touch on several of them. Most of the things that we have discussed elsewhere—such as the cultural, legal, political, and economic environments of international business—are important in determining how each of the different logistics functions are carried out. In this chapter we will concentrate on importing and exporting because of the special problems involved and the unique institutions that have developed to facilitate the international distribution of goods.

INTERNATIONAL SOURCING

Before components can be manufactured, raw materials must be procured. For Japan this can be critical, since 100 percent of its uranium, bauxite, and nickel; virtually 100 percent of its crude oil and iron ore; 92 percent of its copper; 85 percent of its coking coal; and 30 percent of its farm products are purchased from abroad. Local purchase of these items is out of the question, so trading companies (to be discussed in more detail in the section on export management companies) came into being to acquire the raw materials that are necessary to fuel the manufacturing process.

● Problems encountered in international sourcing

Anything acquired from abroad involves problems that are not present to the same extent in domestic sourcing: language, distance, currency, wars and insurrections, strikes, political problems, and tariffs, for example. Obviously, strikes can occur anywhere, but strikes related to the international transfer of goods can be maddening. Consider the refusal of longshoremen to load or unload anything related to the Soviet Union during the early years of the invasion of Afghanistan. These types of strikes are related to political events that defy the traditional negotiation process.

● Major roles of Customs: collecting fees and enforcing laws

When importing goods into any country, it is important to be totally familiar with the government customs operations. The primary duties of the U.S. Customs Service, for example, "include the assessment and collection of all duties, taxes, and fees on imported merchandise, the enforcement of customs and related laws, and the administration of certain navigation laws and treaties." As a major enforcement organization, it "combats smuggling and frauds on the revenue and enforces the regulations of numerous other Federal agencies at ports of entry and along the land and sea borders of the United States."[4]

The importer needs to know how to clear goods, what duties must be paid, and what special laws exist. For example, electronic products imported into the United States for which there are radiation performance standards are subject to the Radiation Control for Health and Safety Act of 1968. Similar laws relate to safety standards and emission standards on imported automobiles.

● Use of bonded warehouse to avoid tariffs on imports that are to be reexported

Sometimes goods are imported into a country and are immediately exported or are assembled into an intermediate or final product and exported. When imported goods are exported from a bonded customs warehouse, the entire import duty that was paid may be refunded. Likewise, when articles manufactured or produced in the United States with the use of imported merchandise are exported, 99 percent of the duties are refunded as a drawback.[5]

Foreign Trade Zones

In recent years, **foreign trade zones** have become more popular as an intermediate step in the process between import and final use.

● Foreign Trade Zones— Special zones designated by the government where tariffs can be delayed or avoided

FTZs, established by federal grants [in the United States] primarily to state and local government agencies, provide areas where domestic and imported merchandise can be stored, inspected, and manufactured free from formal customs procedures until the goods leave the zones. The intended purpose of the zones is to encourage the domestic location of firms by affording them opportunities to defer duties, pay less duties, or to avoid certain duties completely.[6]

4. function as support for the overall sales, distribution, and advertising staff of the firm.

Practically all firms can benefit at one time or another from using the services of an intermediary organization that will assume some or all of these functions. A variety of different intermediaries can be used to facilitate exports. The most important types may be grouped into four major classifications:

● Major classifications of exporters

1. agents acting for the exporter who is the principal;
2. agents purchasing for themselves as principals;
3. agents undertaking a specialized aspect of the export cycle; and
4. agents acting for other buyers as principals.[17]

Export management companies and trading companies are prominent examples of the first two types, and the freight forwarder is an example of the third type. Trading companies also illustrate the fourth type.

● Small exporters often can't justify the cost of doing all export activities themselves

Cost considerations. Before looking more specifically at the different types of intermediaries, it is important to understand the nature of the cost considerations that an exporter must face. Each of the aforementioned activities or functions involves certain fixed costs, so that at a small volume of business it is cheaper to contract the work to someone else than to handle it internally. A specialist can spread the fixed costs over services to more than one firm. If business increases enough, a firm may be able to handle the activities more cheaply itself than by buying outside services. Firms should therefore periodically reappraise the question of internal versus external handling of their varied operations.

In the international arena it is very common for companies, as they grow, to gradually absorb work that was once handled by outside specialists. Since most firms begin their international business through exporting and make initial and early sales on a small or sporadic basis, it may make little sense at this point to incur internally the fixed cost of handling exports. Direct exporting would involve training personnel in such tasks as the completion of export documents, packaging for foreign markets, and the transaction of international financing and credit arrangements. Since these tasks are highly specialized, the company may well contract them until the volume of exports increases enough to warrant the hiring or training of specialized personnel.

● Use of sales reps, agents, distributors, or retailers

Direct selling. When selling direct, the manufacturer normally ships the products overseas to a foreign firm. The firm may be a sales representative or agent that normally operates on a commission basis rather than taking actual title to the product. A foreign distributor takes title to the product and earns a profit on the final sale to the consumer. Foreign retailers are outlets for consumer goods primarily and can be serviced by company traveling salespeople or by purchases from catalogs or trade fairs. When manufacturers deal in high-technology goods or expensive machinery that is manufactured to specification, the sale is made directly to the consumer. This would be a common practice in industrial as opposed to consumer marketing.

● Export management companies—Firms that buy merchandise from manufacturers for international distribution or that sometimes act as agents for manufacturers

Indirect selling—export management companies. Indirect selling implies that the manufacturer deals through another domestic firm before entering the international marketplace. The domestic firm may act as an agent for the manufacturer and not take title, or it may choose to purchase the product from the manufacturer and sell the merchandise abroad. The latter option is common for the **export management company** (EMC). Although they originally operated on a commission basis and assumed no risks, EMCs now operate largely on a buy-and-sell basis and provide financing for export shipments. The primary function of the EMC is to obtain orders for its clients' products through the selection of appropriate markets, distribution channels, and promotion campaigns. The EMC collects, analyzes, and furnishes credit information and advice regarding foreign accounts and payment terms. Other services the EMC may handle include documentation, arrangement of transportation (including the consolidation of shipments to reduce costs), arrangement of patent and trademark protection in foreign countries, and counseling and assistance in establishing alternative forms of doing business, such as licensing or joint ventures.[18]

EMCs operate on a contractual basis, usually for two to five years, and provide exclusive representation in a well-defined overseas territory. The contract specifies such things as pricing, credit and financial policies, promotional services, and the payment basis. EMCs usually concentrate on complementary and noncompetitive products so that they can present a more complete product line to a limited number of importers.

One advantage of using an EMC is the ease of entry into a foreign market through the use of experienced export personnel and existing distribution and sales networks. A problem is that the EMC may concentrate on fast-moving or large-profit-margin items at the expense of other products. Furthermore, an EMC may lack the product specialization needed to compete effectively as it expands the number of lines handled.

Although the above description of an EMC seems to be fairly precise, it is important to note that each firm is unique. That is why the EMCs are so important in international trade. They are able to change with the conditions to provide the best possible service to firms. Some interesting facts emerged from a study of the characteristics of EMCs, although the sample was not a large one and could therefore contain some biases. EMCs tend to be fairly small with only a few people in the organization. Although nearly half of the firms said that they always take title to the goods rather than serve as agent middlemen, a fairly large number do serve as agent middlemen on occasion. Only 8 percent of the EMCs state that they only serve as agent middlemen, never taking title to the goods they sell. It has been assumed that EMCs are used primarily by small firms that have not developed any expertise in export marketing. However, the study found that a number of large firms also use EMCs. This is especially true when the firm is selling goods in a new market where it has not had any previous contact. In that way the firm is able to find an EMC that has expertise in the particular market. It is rare for EMCs to have expertise in all foreign markets; therefore it behooves firms to use several firms rather than one firm to serve its markets. After operating in foreign markets, some EMCs become importers as well.[19] This is an obvious development for a trading company.

- Sogo shosha—Japanese trading companies that import and export merchandise

Japanese trading companies.   In reality the EMCs are essentially trading companies in embryo. When one thinks of trading companies, one normally thinks of the giants such as Mitsui and Mitsubishi of Japan. The **sogo shosha,** the Japanese equivalent word for trading company, can trace their roots back to the late 1800s, when Japan embarked on an aggressive modernization process. The sogo shosha took over the primary role of acquiring raw materials for the industrialization process and then finding external markets for goods. Although there are more than 6000 trading companies in Japan, the sixteen major sogo shosha control about 55 percent of Japan's exports and 65 percent of its imports. In addition, their annual sales are slightly greater than one third of Japan's GNP, a tremendous amount of economic concentration.[20]

However, the sogo shosha are involved in much more than just trading. Their operations include financing, investment, helping to foster joint ventures between Japanese and foreign firms, technology transfer, and a variety of other activities.

- Challenges facing the trading companies

The sogo shosha face a variety of challenges in the decade of the 1980s, many of which have been brought on by changes in the domestic Japanese economy as well as the international economy. Their role in trade financing, for example, is being challenged by the banks, which are becoming more internationally oriented. Many of the marketing functions are being challenged by the manufacturers themselves. The transition appears as follows:

First, the larger and more significant the market, the sooner the manufacturer turns away from the GTC [general trading company or sogo shosha] (e.g., C. Itoh still handles auto marketing for Toyota in Saudi Arabia, a small market). Second, the more complex the technology involved, the sooner the manufacturer turns away from the GTC [because of the difficulty of the GTC dealing with the technical requirements of the product]. *Third, the more specific and involved are the marketing and service requirements, the sooner the manufacturer turns away from the GTC.* [21]

Finally, the sogo shosha are beginning to get more involved in foreign investment. Historically, the Japanese have preferred to sell abroad through exports rather than through direct investment, as has been the strategy of U.S. companies. This is obvious when comparing the strategy of a Ford with that of Toyota or Nissan. However, the nature of the international marketplace is causing the trading firms to consider more direct investments. This is because many of the trading companies have developed their own manufacturing niches and have decided to expand these operations abroad.[22] This not only illustrates a change in locational strategy, but it also shows how the trading companies have diversified their revenue base.

● Major types of U.S. export trading companies

Export trading companies. In the fall of 1982 the U.S. government enacted legislation that removed some of the antitrust obstacles to the creation of **export trading companies** in the United States. It was hoped that these ETCs would lead to greater exports of U.S. goods and services. There are four major types of ETCs: newly formed ETCs that received antitrust certification, ETCs organized by state and local governments, ETCs created by commercial banks, and ETCs organized by U.S. companies initially to handle their own exports.[23]

The first category involves business enterprises that would like to cooperate for foreign sales but would have difficulty cooperating for domestic sales owing to antitrust concerns. The government has set strict guidelines on how one would qualify for exemption from antitrust considerations. The key is that the cooperation must not lessen competition in the United States.

One example of ETCs organized by state and local governments is the Port Authority of New York and New Jersey. Their ETC, known as XPORT, is courting smaller firms with high-technology products that have an export potential.

Most of the large money center banks have applied for permission to establish ETCs. These applications must be approved by the Federal Reserve Board before the bank can start export operations. Many of the banks are concentrating on customers in their geographical market and in parts of the world where they already have a good banking network.

Some major corporations, such as Sears and Control Data, have also set up ETCs. Initially, they were designed to handle the firm's own business, but they are now expanding to include products produced by other companies as well. In the case of Control Data the ETC was initially established to handle countertrade agreements for sales of products to Eastern European countries as well as developing countries. Now the ETC of Control Data is aggressively seeking products of other companies.

Government Role in Exporting

The government plays a variety of roles in the export process, some of which support exporting and others of which appear to retard it. Several examples from the U.S. government illustrate some of these roles. These examples are not unique to the U.S. government; other countries have similar programs.

● ITA—The U.S. government agency that assists exporters

The International Trade Administration.   The International Trade Administration (ITA) of the U.S. Department of Commerce offers services to firms through four major units: the U.S. and Foreign Commercial Service (US&FCS), International Economic Policy, Trade Development, and Trade Administration.[24]

The US&FCS has overseas commercial officers that gather information for exporters. It maintains offices in 120 major foreign cities in sixty-three key countries with which the United States does business. The commercial officers can help potential exporters spot good markets and provide business, investment, and financial counseling services.

The International Economic Policy country specialists provide information on foreign market conditions, commercial policies, business practices, economic and political developments, tariffs and trade regulations, and the like. This office also provides information dealing with multilateral agreements in which the United States is a partner, such as the Tokyo Round of GATT mentioned in Chapter 8.

The Trade Development sector of the ITA provides market analysis and assistance on an industry-specific basis. Its personnel help potential exporters deal with specific obstacles and opportunities, and they also develop industry-specific strategies and programs.

The Office of Export Administration deals with controls on exports for national security and foreign policy reasons. It can be very helpful in identifying exports that may be subject to controls and then in helping the exporters qualify for export licenses.

Major services offered.   The ITA publishes a variety of documents that are helpful to the exporter. Some of these include *Business America, A Basic Guide to Exporting,* and an *Export Promotion Calendar.* These publications provide a lot of good information for the beginning as well as the experienced exporter. The ITA also provides export assistance services, market identification information, market assessment information, and market contact information.

Trade shows are sponsored and promoted by the ITA to provide opportunities for firms to exhibit their products. Many of the trade shows are sponsored by foreign governments and industry associations, but the ITA tries to help U.S. firms get involved. These shows can be an excellent marketing opportunity for firms.

The Export-Import Bank. The Export-Import Bank (Eximbank) is the oldest federal agency specializing in foreign lending. As a fully owned government corporation, it has been in existence since 1934 with the specific objective of financing U.S. foreign trade. The Eximbank provides assistance in the form of supplier credit and buyer credit programs. The supplier credit programs fall into three categories: FCIA insurance, export credit guarantees, and the discount loan program. The Foreign Credit Insurance Association (FCIA) is an association of some mutual and stock companies in the marine and casualty insurance field in partnership with and governed by the Eximbank. An exporter that secures a policy with the FCIA is insured against loss resulting from failure of the exporter's customers to pay because of commercial or political reasons. Also, the policyholder is able to arrange favorable financing of export receivables because of the security brought about by the insurance.

FCIA insurance covers short-term (to 180 days) and medium-term (181 days to five years) cases. For short-term cases there are comprehensive policies that cover 95 percent of the political losses and 90 percent of the credit losses, and political-risk-only policies that cover 90 percent of those losses. Political risks include currency inconvertibility, expropriation, cancellation of import licenses, or other actions taken by foreign governments that prevent payment by the buyer.

Under medium-term policies, at least 10 percent and sometimes 20 percent of the invoice must be paid in cash by the foreign buyer. The FCIA will then insure 90 percent of the remaining amount of the financial portion of the transaction. Political risk is also insured on a medium-term basis. The Eximbank carries 100 percent policies on political risk, while the FCIA assumes most of the credit risk.

Under the export credit guarantee program, the Eximbank will guarantee repayment of export debt obligations such as notes receivable acquired by the exporter. The bank also provides a discount loan program, in which it allows commercial banks to borrow against export paper held during times when the commercial bank may be experiencing liquidity pressures.

The buyer credit programs include the cooperative financing facility and product/project lending. Under the cooperative financing facility (CFF) the Eximbank provides loans to small- and medium-sized foreign buyers of U.S. products by way of the importer's bank. The local commercial bank must first approve the loan request of the importer. The Eximbank will then provide the buyer's bank with low-interest funds covering half of the loan. The bank may also guarantee the half not covered initially. Under product/project lending for export transactions in excess of $1 million, the bank may make a direct loan to the foreign buyer and extend financial guarantees to private lenders involved in the project.[25]

The Eximbank has not been without criticism. The guarantees are essentially an export subsidy because they allow exporters to finance operations at lower than the market rate of interest. Many problems arise when Eximbank financing supports foreign competition. For example, a U.S. airline purchasing a commercial jet from a U.S. manufacturer would have to pay more in interest to finance the purchase than would a foreign airline purchasing the same jet. Critics argue that only a handful of U.S. manufacturers benefit from Eximbank programs.

Supporters of the Eximbank say that the bank's services are invaluable to the exporters. They feel that, since the governments of most of the countries that are our major competitors in export markets have programs to assist their exporters, it is essential that our government match those efforts or try to eliminate the subsidies of those governments.

One example of an Eximbank project involves the sale of locomotives to Brazil arranged in 1984 by General Motors and General Electric. The project involves the Brazilian import of parts produced by GM and GE; final assembly will take place in Brazil. The Brazilian importer will make a 15 percent cash payment of $9.47 million and will arrange for the rest of the financing for the U.S. purchases through private financial institutions. The loans will be guaranteed by the Eximbank. It was estimated that the exports will create 832 man-years of employment for GM and 768 man-years of employment for GE.

Problems in Exporting

Many of the problems that firms face in exporting have already been mentioned. In addition, there are a number of problems that are common to international business in general and are not unique to exporting. These include language and other cultural problems. However, there are ten mistakes that are frequently made by new firms that are just getting involved in exporting:

1. Failure to obtain qualified export counseling and to develop a master international marketing plan before starting an export business.
2. Insufficient commitment by top management to overcome the initial difficulties and financial requirements of exporting.
3. Insufficient care in selecting overseas agents or distributors.
4. Chasing orders from around the world instead of establishing a basis for profitable operations and orderly growth.
5. Neglecting export business when the U.S. market booms.
6. Failure to treat international distributors on an equal basis with domestic counterparts.
7. Unwillingness to modify products to meet regulations or cultural preferences of other countries.

8. Failure to print services, sales, and warranty messages in locally understood languages.

9. Failure to consider use of an export management company or other marketing intermediary when the firm obviously does not have the personnel to handle specialized export functions.

10. Failure to consider licensing or joint venture agreements. This is especially critical in countries where there are import restrictions.[26]

Another problem faced by exporters relates to the changing nature of government policy. Although the government can provide incentives for firms, it can also withdraw those inventives at any time. In the case of the United States, for example, the Export-Import Bank has faced extinction due to government budget pressures. The Domestic International Sales Corporation, a U.S. export incentive to be discussed in Chapter 20, was eliminated because of pressure from GATT.

Building an Export Strategy

• Major elements in an export strategy: assess export potential, get expert counseling, select a market or markets, formulate a strategy, select a selling technique

As was mentioned earlier, many firms enter into exporting by accident rather than by design. When that happens, many of the problems in exporting that were listed above tend to happen. In addition, the firm never gets a chance to see how important exports could be. That is why it is important to develop a good export strategy.

The design of a strategy involves a series of steps.[27] First, it is important for a firm to assess its export potential. That involves taking a look at opportunities and resources. It would not be a smart business decision to make commitments to export if the firm did not have the production capacity to deliver the product.

Next, the firm needs to get expert counseling. For U.S. firms the best place to start is with the International Trade Administration office of the U.S. Department of Commerce in the exporter's area. That assistance is invaluable in helping the exporter get started. As the export plan increases in scale, the exporter will probably want to secure specialized assistance from banks, lawyers, freight forwarders, export management companies, and the like.

The next important step is to select a market or markets. This step often occurs by default if the exporter is responding to requests from abroad that result from trade shows, advertisements, or articles in trade publications. However, it is important to pick a market or markets in which to concentrate a push strategy. One needs to develop an expertise in a variety of factors when dealing with foreign consumers, and it is best to focus on a few key markets rather than try to develop global expertise all at once.

Once the markets have been targeted and the decision has been made to expend corporate resources in the export effort, the firm should formulate an export strategy. That strategy usually involves dealing with the following four factors: (1) export objectives, both immediate and long term; (2) specific tactics that the firm will use; (3) a schedule of activities and deadlines that will help the firm achieve its objectives; and (4) the allocation of resources to accomplish the different activities.

Finally, the firm needs to select a selling technique. The major techniques mentioned earlier in the chapter are using sales representatives or agents, distributors, foreign retailers, direct sales to end users, EMCs, or export trading companies. The key in the export plan is to approach exporting from an organized point of view rather than just to sit back and let it happen.

TRANSPORTATION

Transportation plays a very important role in the total logistics system:

> Logistics can be viewed as a series of links and nodes. The nodes are fixed points in the system where some activity occurs which temporarily halts the flow of goods in the logistics pipeline. Connecting these nodes are links which are the transportation networks that exist between the various nodes. [28]

These nodes are the raw material sources, production and demand centers, and commodity storage points that were described earlier in the chapter.

> The transportation area is filled with such complexities as many modes from which to choose, a multiplicity of carriers within each mode, varied combinations of modes and carriers to serve given links, a regulatory structure that affects the carrier operations, and a system of transportation pricing that defies all laws of logic. [29]

This section of the chapter is concerned with the problem of getting the goods from one country to another rather than moving the goods around within a particular country. The latter question is concerned with not only modes of transportation but also the selection of the proper channels within a country—such as wholesalers and retailers.

Land Freight

One normally thinks of ocean freight or air freight when dealing with export marketing, but land freight is very important for two of the United States' major trading partners—Canada and Mexico. Trade with Canada is highly developed (the United States exports more goods to Canada than to any other single country), as is Canada's transportation infrastructure. Goods frequently travel by truck and rail without much difficulty.

Mexico is a different story. Because of oil exports, Mexico was on an import binge in the late 1970s and early 1980s. However, the transportation infrastructure was inadequate to handle the increased traffic. Mexico was plagued by an overly cautious customs service, inadequate rail facilities, and outdated equipment.

Land-based transportation for export/import trade is much more common in Europe, where more than 50 percent of the trade is within the European community. The use of truck and rail transportation is much more widespread, owing to the shorter distance involved and the well-developed transportation infrastructure.

Land-based transportation is not widely used in Africa because there are very few roads and rails that connect countries. Most of the African trade is with developed countries rather than with their underdeveloped neighbors, so there is a greater reliance on ocean and air freight to service international commerce.

Ocean Freight

- Private ships—Owned by a company to transport its own goods
- Tramp ships—Independent contractors

- Liner ships—Belong to a shipping conference
- Break-bulk freight—Freight that would not fill one ship

Ocean freight can be transported in one of three major ways: private ships, tramp ships, or liner ships. **Private ships** are those owned by a company to transport its own goods. **Tramp ships** are private carriers that are not affiliated with either a shipping conference (discussed below) or a shipper (the firm contracting to have its products shipped).

Liner ships belong to steamship lines that are members of shipping conferences. These ships operate under a published tariff (shipping rate) and a published schedule so that shippers are able to plan their shipping in advance. Liner ships handle **break-bulk freight** (smaller shipments of goods that would not fill one ship) from several shippers. Bulk freight from one shipper is handled by the tramp ships.

- Shipping conferences set rates and schedules for freight traveling in one direction

Shipping conferences are one-directional agreements formulated by several liner companies. Rates and schedules are set among the companies in a very secretive fashion. The Pacific Westbound Conference is formed among liner companies doing business from U.S. Pacific coast ports to destinations west. Traffic heading *toward* U.S. Pacific coast ports is in another conference, even though most of the same liner companies could be involved. Conferences may be comprised of liners from several different countries.

- Contract shippers—Companies that sign exclusive agreements to ship goods with liner ships

Liner conferences do business with two types of shippers: contract and noncontract. The **contract shipper** signs an exclusive patronage agreement, meaning that all the break-bulk freight will be shipped with liners of the conference, and gets up to 15 percent off of the scheduled tariff. Of course, noncontract shippers cannot get the cheaper rate.

There are three major advantages to liner conferences, the first two of which may directly benefit the shipper:

- Major advantages of liner conferences

1. *Stability of liner rates.* This has the advantage of allowing a shipper to become involved in long-range planning. There is no chance that rates

could change adversely in the time between when the contracts are entered into and when the payment is made.

2. *An assured supply of shipping.* During the 1930s, rate wars actually drove many liner companies out of business, reducing the supply of ships, creating quasi-monopolies for those left, and eventually driving up prices. Although prices rose high enough to allow competitors to return, the lead time involved in getting ships back into service was too long to affect supply appreciably over the short run.

3. *Protection of the high-cost liner.* Rates are set so that the highest-cost liner can make a profit.

The disadvantages of the shipping conferences generally reflect U.S. concepts of antitrust and are as follows:

● Major disadvantages of liner conferences

1. quasi-monopoly—an individual shipper is rarely large or powerful enough to influence rates;

2. excess profits, especially to the low-cost liner company; and

3. exclusive patronage—the large independent liner companies have difficulty competing.

● Container—A large, outer package used to transport goods

Containerization. One of the most important advances in shipping in the past decade or two is that of containerization. **Containerization** amounts to using a large outer package that can be easily handled and transferred between different modes of transportation. The containers are standardized so that all transportation agencies involved in their use can develop the appropriate equipment and interface this equipment with each other. This high-technology process improves the handling time of cargo, reduces the risk of damage to and pilferage of the contents, provides potential economies of scale by changing cargo handling from a labor-intensive to a capital-intensive operation, and increases the annual capacity of ocean vessels by reducing the turnaround time in port. A container is essentially a trailer body without wheels that is easily transferred from truck or rail to ship and back again.

● Different ways to combine land and sea forms of transportation

Another way to reduce the cost of transportation and increase the speed of delivery of products involves combining different modes—such as land and sea. The **landbridge** concept could, for example, effectively bridge Europe and the Orient without having to use the Panama Canal or other such water routes. Goods could be shipped to the U.S. west coast, the container loaded on rail or trucks for overland transportation to the east coast, and the goods then transferred to ship again for the voyage to Europe. The **minibridge** concept is similar in that it involves the use of overland movement to avoid the use of water shipments via the Panama Canal. For example, a shipment from Pittsburgh to Japan would go overland under domestic transport to a port on the east coast, such as Baltimore, and then would move under international transportation overland to a west coast port for ocean shipment to Japan, instead of by water from the east coast.

A third concept, which has been used to some extent, is the **microbridge** movement. This is a direct point-to-point movement that avoids the potential backtracking involved in moving to a nearby port for shipment to another port.

Foreign freight forwarders. As was mentioned in the section of the chapter on international sourcing, dealing in ocean transportation involves a number of different institutions and documentation with which the usual exporter does not have expertise. This is true even if the manufacturer is exporting components to a foreign subsidiary that is controlled by a common parent corporation. It is common to employ the services of a **foreign freight forwarder.** Even export management companies and other types of trading companies use foreign freight forwarders for their specialized services. The foreign freight forwarder is the largest export intermediary in terms of value and weight handled; however, the services offered are more limited than those offered by an EMC. Once a foreign sale has been made, the freight forwarder will act on behalf of the exporter in recommending the best routing and means of transportation based on space availability, speed, and cost. The forwarder will secure such space and necessary storage, review the letter of credit, obtain export licenses, and prepare necessary shipping documents. Other services that may be provided include advice on packing and labeling, purchase of transport insurance, and repacking shipments damaged en route.

The freight forwarder is usually paid by the exporter on a percentage of the shipment value, with a minimum charge dependent on the number of services provided. In addition, the forwarder receives a brokerage fee from the carrier. The use of a freight forwarder is still usually less costly than providing the service internally, since most firms find it difficult both to utilize a traffic department full-time and to keep up with shipping regulations. The forwarder is able to get space because of a close relationship with carriers and can consolidate shipments in order to obtain lower rates.

Air Freight

Although air transportation is fairly expensive in comparison with land freight and ocean freight, it has the advantage of speed of delivery and can often provide access to areas of the world that are not served by any other form of transportation in a reliable way. The heart of regulation of air freight is the International Air Transport Association (IATA). IATA was created at The Hague in 1919 with one Dutch, one British, one German, and three Scandinavian airlines. The early concerns of IATA were passenger traffic, mail, navigation, and communication. It was not until 1938, when

Pan American joined IATA, that non-European airlines became involved.

In 1945, because of the rapid changes in technology and the expanding number of airlines involved in international traffic, a new IATA was formed that included airlines from all over the world. The organization is a very heterogeneous group involving many types of airlines, such as those owned by subsidized governmental departments, those owned by individuals, and the private capital airlines of the United States.

The very heart of IATA lies in the three traffic conferences: the Western Hemisphere, Europe and Africa, and the Orient and Australia. An airline can be a member of any conference and may be a member of all three conferences. The conferences are concerned with (1) an analysis of operating costs; (2) fares, rates, and charges for passengers and cargo; (3) schedules; and (4) approval of agencies, their administration, and their traffic practices.[30] At each of the annual conference meetings, the rates for the coming year are determined. Joint meetings between conferences are also held to discuss flights that take place between conference areas.

Channels within Countries

Once the goods reach the foreign market, marketing personnel need to decide the best way to get the goods to the consumer. The type of channel that is selected is a marketing question (as will be discussed in Chapter 18), but it is the responsibility of the logistics people to make sure that the goods get from the port to the proper channel—whether it be wholesaler, retailer, or customer. Although most industrial countries have adequate transportation infrastructures, the developing countries are not so fortunate, as was pointed out in discussing rail transportation in Mexico.

SUMMARY

- Business logistics involves the storage and movement of goods from the source of raw materials to the production of components, to the assembly of goods, to the distribution to consumers.

- The international firm differs from the domestic one in that goods in intermediate or final form may move from country to country rather than remain in one particular country.

- International sourcing of goods—primarily in the area of acquisition—differs from domestic sourcing in terms of such things as language, distance, currency, wars and insurrections, strikes, political problems, and tariffs.

- Foreign trade zones, long popular outside of the United States, are being used increasingly as a place to import and assemble goods for final export.

- Manufacturing strategies include servicing the world from one production facility or from many by using multiple plants that specialize in products or processes or by interchanging components for eventual assembly.

- Many firms are using offshore manufacturing centers to take advantage of cheap labor and materials. Then the finished goods are sold in the local market, shipped to the United States, or sold in third country markets.

- The Japanese have perfected the concept of just-in-time inventory management, which means that inventory shipments are planned to coincide as closely as possible with their use. That cuts down the size of inventories held and therefore the carrying costs.

- Exporters may deal directly with agents or distributors in a foreign country, or they may deal indirectly by using export management companies or other types of trading companies.

- Governments provide a variety of services for exporters. The U.S. government operates through the International Trade Administration of the U.S. Department of Commerce.

- The Export-Import Bank of the United States, like its counterparts in other countries, provides financing at low interest rates for many firms.

- Firms that are new to exporting (and also some experienced exporters) often make lots of mistakes. One way to help avoid making those mistakes is to develop a comprehensive export strategy that includes an analysis of the firm's resources as well as market opportunities.

- Goods can be transported from one country by truck or rail (to adjacent countries such as from the United States to Canada), by ocean freight, or by air freight. When ocean freight is used, it is common to use a foreign freight forwarder, which is familiar with institutions and documentation.

C A S E   THE HORNET HAS A STING[31]

In April 1980, after years of tense negotiations, McDonnell Douglas scored a stunning victory in the international weapons market by agreeing to sell 138 F-18A Hornet fighter planes to the Canadian government at somewhere near $2.5 billion, with deliveries to be made between 1982 and 1989. After the euphoria of the announcement, McDonnell Douglas management sat down and mapped a careful strategy to ensure that all facets of the complex agreement would be adhered to in the intervening decade.

In 1979 the top fifty U.S. exporters exported nearly $32 billion of goods to unaffiliated companies abroad. However, these exports were concentrated in a few industries. The top six aerospace companies, for example, were responsible for more than 25 percent of the $32 billion. The leading exporter was Boeing, and McDonnell Douglas was number four. Five of the top ten exporters dealt in aircraft or aircraft engines.

This highly competitive industry deals in big-ticket sales. Lockheed, for example, in its famous case involving payoffs of foreign government officials in Japan, sold twenty-one Tri-Stars to All Nippon Airways for $430 million. These large sales create a highly competitive atmosphere in which firms must come up with creative alternatives to the traditional goods-for-cash mode.

The rapid deterioration of the balance-of-payments position of most countries following the explosive increase in oil prices has created an additional external constraint on traditional sales. As a result, different forms of barter or countertrade agreements have arisen to meet the needs of importing countries concerned about hard currency reserves.

Historically, the use of countertrade has been a temporary solution to the lack of liquidity, and it has disappeared as the countries involved have been able to solve their liquidity problems. In the 1960s, most countertrade was short term, moderately valued, and essentially commodity-based. In the 1970s, however, countertrade became long term and involved capital goods such as machinery, plant, equipment, and technology. In 1955 it was estimated that 90 percent of the countertrade agreements involved the developing countries; by 1975, only 40 percent of such trade was with the developing countries. In the late 1960s and early 1970s the shift in emphasis in countertrade moved from the Eastern European nations to others and from commercial to industrial goods. In addition, many of the nations began to change their emphasis from import substitution to export promotion. Thus many in the U.S. government feel that the result of the increase in countertrade has been a distortion of normal trading patterns. This would especially be true when Western firms are forced to deal with state trading agencies in developing or centrally planned economies where market price is not the most relevant factor.

The four most popular forms of noncash transactions are barter agreements, clearing arrangements, switch trading, and compensation agreements. In a case in the early 1970s involving Douglas Aircraft, for example, seven DC-9 airplanes were sold to Yugoslavia for cash and a commitment by Douglas to sell nearly $9 million worth of Yugoslavian goods in the United States.

Since these early days, however, countertrade agreements have become more complex. A typical agreement might include many things such as greater participation of firms in the buyer's country in the design and production or subcontracting of components for the final product, development of assistance in export marketing for small- and medium-sized firms in the buyer's country, and promotion of tourism. This has obviously placed great organizational strains on the seller.

The race to sell the F-18A has been intense over the past few years, since the stakes have been fairly high. As McDonnell Douglas was vying for the Canadian sale, it also had its hopes up for sales to Australia, Greece, Sweden, Israel, and Spain. In preliminary talks with Australia, McDonnell Douglas had proposed selling seventy-five aircraft. The first two would be built in the United States, the remaining aircraft to be assembled in Australia. The preliminary agreement also stated that the Australian manufacturing company picked to assemble the aircraft would also be eligible to manufacture some of the parts and could thus be competitive with other parts vendors used by McDonnell Douglas in the United States. Because of the large purchase order, McDonnell Douglas would have an estimated 30 percent offset goal. The comprehensive nature of the agreement resulted in the use of the term offset rather than countertrade. Offset implies more different types of arrangements than the more narrowly defined countertrade.

The Canadian sale, of course, was huge. Because the F-18A was still in the developmental stage except for a few prototypes when the contract was signed in April 1980, the sale was expected to yield approximately $2.5 billion. By December 1980 the 138 aircraft, at a cost that had risen to $21.6 million per unit, would yield McDonnell Douglas nearly $3 billion. Over the eight-year period involved in the delivery dates, this would result in average imports for Canada of several hundred million dollars per year. Given the weakness of the Canadian dollar in recent years, this was bound to be of some concern to the Canadian government. As a result, the negotiation for the sale of the aircraft involved not only the technical capabilities of the F-18A and the attendant costs, but also the industrial benefits that McDonnell Douglas could promise the Canadian government.

As was mentioned earlier, the aircraft manufacturers in the United States also tend to be the biggest exporters. There is good reason for this that involves economies of scale as well as the fact that the dollar sale price per unit is so large. The economies of scale result from the high-technology nature of the aircraft. Aircraft have to be highly engineered and require highly skilled labor. In addition, the parts and components that are subcontracted need to be built according to precise specifications. It would be difficult to rely on production and assembly in a variety of countries, as might occur in other industries in which skills are more easily duplicable. Up to now the aircraft manufacturers have relied mainly on production and assembly in the United States and export of the finished product.

The pressures on governments due to balance-of-payments concerns has changed this picture for even the industrial countries. Canada could not afford to pay $3 billion for aircraft and receive nothing but the aircraft in return. As a result, the Canadian government began negotiating for various concessions from McDonnell Douglas.

The Canadian offset program covers a period of 15 years with a three-year grace period. The total program commitment of $2.9 billion must be covered from the following three areas: aerospace and electronics (min. 60 percent), advanced technology (min. 6 percent), and diversified activities (max. 40 percent).

The aerospace and electronics area is the most important of the three, and it involves the following types of activities: designated production, co-production, technology transfer, and joint research and development. The joint R&D activity involves production of F-18A, DC-9, and DC-10 parts as well as avionics, missile-related production, and software development training.

The diversified activities portion of the offset commitment involves three major subareas: investment/technology development, export development, and tourism development. Investment development involves helping to attract foreign investment to Canada in order to bring in foreign exchange, substitute domestic products for imports, and develop products for export. Some of the investment will involve McDonnell Douglas, but some of it will involve independent parties.

Export development is an important part of the offset commitment. The strategy involves analyzing industrial sectors in Canada, identifying product groups with export potential, identifying the specific firms that produce the products, and helping those firms to develop an export strategy and find external markets. In some cases, McDonnell Douglas is simply using Canadian goods for their purchases instead of U.S. goods or other foreign goods. In other situations the firm is trying to find external markets for Canadian goods in the United States or other countries.

Tourism is a good source of foreign exchange for most countries, and Canada is no exception. The tourism development portion of the offset commitment is designed to identify groups that hold meetings abroad and try to sell them on the concept of Canada. McDonnell Douglas does this through promotional support and technical assistance, such as counseling on accomodations, air transportation, ground services, special events, and comparisons of destinations for site selection.

When McDonnell Douglas approached the offset commitment, it had to make a strategic decision on the best way to fulfill it. The decision was made to establish an international business center that would manage the offset commitment for the sale of the F-18A. Figure 14.2 shows what the organization looks like. The center is organized within the marketing division, and it handles commercial offset programs for all McDonnell Aircraft customer countries. (McDonnell Aircraft is the defense side of McDonnell Douglas.) The center reports directly to the Vice-President of International Marketing.

FIGURE 14.2
McDonnell Aircraft International Business Center Organization Chart

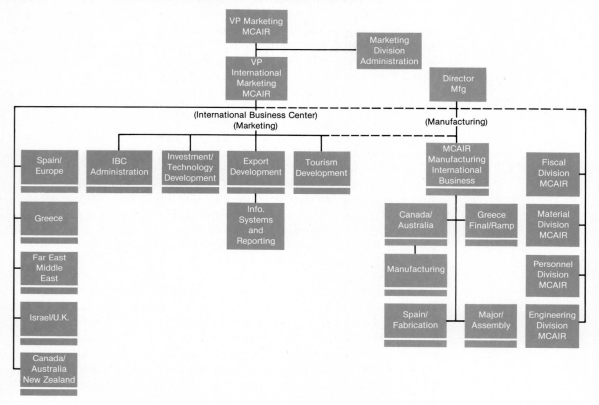

One thing that McDonnell Douglas has learned from its experience in Canada is that it is important to undertake a great deal of planning and analysis before entering into an extensive offset arrangement. In particular, McDonnell Douglas found that it had to analyze three aspects of the program: a country overview to see if the country had a sufficient industrial base to enable the offset commitment to be fulfilled; the terms and conditions of the program, especially how the program is to be monitored and credit given; and the in-house capabilities of the firm.

QUESTIONS

1. Why do you think that a country would require countertrade or offset agreements? Can you think of any other illustrations in prior chapters of countries where some form of offset might be important?

2. Assume that you are a company with annual sales of $5 million and that you have been approached by the government of Bolivia, which wants to buy $500,000 of merchandise from you. The only problem is that the government wants you to handle exports worth 50 percent of that amount in the form of Bolivian goods. Why do you think that Bolivia wants this? How would you go about deciding whether or not this is a good strategy?

3. Part of McDonnell Douglas's offset strategy involves producing parts and components in Canada. Earlier in the chapter, we discussed the concept of foreign production from the standpoint of the overall logistics strategy. Discuss whether or not McDonnell Douglas's strategy makes any sense in the context of that discussion. Are there any risks in that type of strategy?

4. Are there any ways that McDonnell Douglas could have fulfilled the export part of its offset commitment besides setting up an international business center? Is McDonnell Douglas's situation different from that of the typical exporter?

5. What do you think of the export development strategy? What could the international business center do to help an exporter once it has been identified?

NOTES

1. Data for the case were taken from the following sources: various issues of the General Motors *Annual Report;* Lawrence Ingrassia, "Europe's Auto Makers, Hurt by Low Volume, Make Dismal Showing," *Wall Street Journal,* November 5, 1984, p. 1; Douglas R. Sease, "South Korea Will Vie in U.S. Auto Market to Spur Its Economy," *Wall Street Journal,* November 16, 1984, p. 1; "Drastic New Strategies to Keep U.S. Multinationals Competitive," *Business Week,* October 8, 1984, pp. 168–172; "Showdown in Detroit," *Business Week,* September 10, 1984, pp. 102–110; Jonathan Tasini, Maralyn Edid, and John Hoerr, "The GM-Toyota Linkup Could Change the Industry," *Business Week,* December 24, 1984, p. 71; "The All-American Small Car Is Fading," *Business Week,* March 12, 1984, pp. 88–95; Mark B. Fuller, "Note on the World Auto Industry in Transition," 9-382-122 (Boston: HBS Case Services, 1982); Anne B. Fisher, "Can Detroit Live without Quotas?," *Fortune,* June 25, 1984, pp. 20–25.

2. Peter J. Buckley and Richard D. Pearce, "Overseas Production and Exporting by the World's Largest Enterprises: A Study in Sourcing Policy," *Journal of International Business Studies,* Spring/Summer 1979, pp. 11, 13.

3. John J. Coyle and Edward J. Bardi, *The Management of Business Logistics* (New York: West, 1980), p. 4.

4. Department of the Treasury, *Importing into the United States* (Washington, D.C.: Superintendent of Documents, U.S. Government Printing Office, May 1984), p. 1.

5. *Ibid.,* p. 28.

6. F. Jay Cummings and Wayne E. Ruhter, "New Life for Foreign Trade Zones," *The Collegiate Forum,* Winter 1979/80, p. 11.

7. John J. DaPonte, Jr., "Foreign-Trade Zones and Exports," *American Export Bulletin,* April 1978.

8. Philadelphia National Bank, *International Trade Procedures,* (Philadelphia, Pa., 1977), p. 30.

9. Department of the Treasury, *Importing into the United States, op. cit.,* p. 6.

10. Michael Leenders, Harold E. Fearon, and Wilbur B. England, *Purchasing and Materials Management* (Homewood, Ill.: Richard D. Irwin, 1985), pp. 350–353.

11. *Ibid.,* pp. 353–358.

12. Roger Turner, "Mexico's in-Bond Industry Continues Its Dynamic Growth," *Business America,* November 26, 1984, p. 26.

13. Robert E. Schellberg, "Kodak: A Case Study of International Distribution," *Columbia Journal of World Business,* Spring 1976.

14. G. H. Manoochehri, "Crucial Requirements for Effective Application of Just-in-Time System," unpublished paper, California State University, Fullerton, 1984.

15. *Business International,* October 3, 1980, pp. 313, 315.

16. Claude L. Simpson, Jr., and Duane Kujawa, "The Export Decision Process: An Empirical Inquiry," *Journal of International Business Studies,* Spring 1974, pp. 111–113.

17. Colin McMillan and Sydney Paulden, *Sales Manager's Guide to Selection and Control of Export Agents* (Boston: Cahners, 1969), p. 21.

18. Philip MacDonald, *Practical Exporting and Importing,* Second Edition (New York: Ronald Press, 1959), pp. 30–40.

19. John J. Brasch, "Export Management Companies," *Journal of International Business Studies,* Spring/Summer 1978, pp. 59–72.

20. "Sogo Shosha," *The Banker,* January 1984, pp. 78–84.

21. Kichiro Hayashi and Stefan H. Robock, "The Uncertain Future of the Japanese General Trading Companies," *Kajian Ekonomi Malaysia,* December 1982, p. 61.

22. Masaaki Kotabe, "Changing Roles of the Sogo Shoshas, the Manufacturing Firms, and the MITI in the Context of the Japanese 'Trade or Die' Mentality," *Columbia Journal of World Business,* Fall 1984, pp. 33–42.

23. Richard L. Barovick, "Export Trading Companies Emerge in Many Forms," *Business America,* March 19, 1984, pp. 3–7.

24. " '85 Update: ITA Export Services," *Business America,* January 21, 1985, pp. 3–13.

25. Philadelphia National Bank, *International Trade Procedures,* pp. 25–26.

26. "Ten Most Common Mistakes of New-to Export Ventures," *Business America,* April 16, 1984, p. 9.

27. Alice Gray, "Planning an Export Venture," *Business America,* April 16, 1984, pp. 3–8.

28. Coyle and Bardi, *The Management of Business Logistics,* p. 198.

29. *Ibid.,* p. 198.

30. "Antiboycott Enforcement: Commerce Steps Up Pace," *Business America,* July 13, 1981, p. 9.

31. Data from the case were taken from "Canada Orders McDonnell Jets for $2.4 Billion," *Wall Street Journal,* April 11, 1980, p. 5: "Trudeau Offers the U.S. Oil Pipeline Routes," *New York Times,* April 11, 1980, p. D1; "U.S. Agrees to Cut Price of F18 Planes Bought by Canada," *Wall Street Journal,* December 18, 1980, p. 18; Leo G.B. Welt, "Countertrade Gains Popularity as International Trade Tool," *Business America,* July 14, 1980, pp. 12–16; George Roman, "Organizing and Managing Countertrade—The CF-18A," in *Canada/U.S. Trade Relations,* Lee H. Radebaugh and Earl H. Fry, eds. (Provo, Utah: Brigham Young University, 1985), pp. 59–70; James I. Walsh, "Countertrade Megatrends: Where Are We Now? How Did We Get Here; and What Next?," presentation made at the annual meeting of the Academy of International Business, October 1984.

15

Forms of Foreign Involvement

- To explain the major motives that should guide firms in their choice of form for global business activities.
- To differentiate the major forms of operations by which firms may tap the potentials of international business.
- To describe how international agreements affect the protection of proprietary rights on assets that firms might exploit internationally.
- To describe the considerations that firms should explore when entering into contractual international arrangements with other companies.
- To emphasize that multiple forms of international operations may exist simultaneously and that firms must develop means by which to coordinate these diverse activities.

GRUPO INDUSTRIAL ALFA[1]

Mexico has long pushed for industrialization. Before 1973, import restrictions had enticed most of the world's large multinational manufacturers to establish facilities there to produce goods that Mexico might otherwise have imported. Although the direct investment inflow had the effect of increasing employment and decreasing the need for foreign exchange, the fastest growing industrial sectors in Mexico were increasingly controlled by foreign firms. The government sought to counter that foreign control in 1973 when it set restrictions on the expansion of existing investments, which were largely foreign owned.

At that time, one of the largest Mexican-owned firms was a family enterprise in Monterrey controlled by the Garza and Sada families. This firm had been little affected by foreign competition because of its major lines of business such as steel, beer, and banking. These were not easily imported into Mexico because of import restrictions on steel and the need of the others (usually) to locate near customers. These were also sectors in which there were prohibitions against foreign ownership. Although the Garza and Sada families were relatively immune from foreign competition, the outlook was for slow growth. The beer market was largely dependent on the population size, which, although growing rapidly, was not increasing demand nearly as rapidly as in some of Mexico's newer industries. In banking there was much competition. Steel sales were growing; however, more than 70 percent of output came from government-owned enterprises. This led to concern about possible governmental takeover to form a government monopoly.

The Garza-Sada families saw in the 1973 Mexicanization laws the opportunities to diversify into growth industries that foreigners would henceforth find more difficult to control. They reasoned that they might be able to buy some subsidiaries of foreign companies from firms that were unwilling to accept a minority ownership. They also reasoned that they were in a good position to share in cooperative arrangements with foreign firms that sought business activities involving Mexico. The owners felt that, to capitalize on these possibilities, they would be better off shedding the family image. Additional shares could raise capital, and good professional management could be attracted to them. In 1974 they divided the enterprise into four different companies and went public by issuing shares in each of them. Family members have subsequently maintained control through ownership equity and placement in key management positions.

One of the firms that emerged from the 1974 split is Grupo Industrial Alfa, which inherited the steel facilities and several smaller businesses. At the time of the split, Alfa's assets were estimated at $315 million (U.S.), of which 75 percent was in steel. Management of the new company was convinced of the need to diversify and sought the assistance of some of the top international consulting groups to suggest product areas into which it might move. It agreed that diversification should be based on objectives of minimizing cyclical changes in earnings, getting into growth industries, and utilizing resources for which Mexico had advantages.

During the 1974–1976 period, Alfa expanded much less than had been anticipated but did manage to acquire the television production facilities of three U.S. brands: Philco, Magnavox, and Admiral. Through these acquisitions, Alfa got 35 percent of Mexico's market for television sets as well as the continued use of the three trade names for sales in Mexico. Alfa also began moving heavily into tourism through development of areas on the Pacific.

Alfa subsequently became Mexico's largest private company. By 1980 it had assets of $1.9 billion, and its sales represented 1.2 percent of Mexico's gross domestic product. Between 1976 and 1980, Alfa's subsidiaries grew from 37 to 157, and the number of its employees tripled to over 49,000. Two events external to Alfa contributed to the growth. The first of these was the discovery of huge oil and natural gas reserves in Mexico. The second was the election of a pro–private enterprise president, Jose Lopez Portillo. He offered many incentives for industry, including nearly free energy. Suddenly, there was a rush among foreign firms to find ways of expanding their businesses in Mexico. Almost any such expansion had to involve Mexicans. In addition to being Mexico's largest private firm, Alfa had good profitability, and its management had a good reputation. It was in an excellent position to acquire the foreign resources that it wanted. In fact, the biggest problem was in how to choose among the many opportunities.

Alfa established numerous Mexican companies in which it owned a majority interest with a foreign partner holding a minority. The foreign partners came from a number of countries including Japan (Hitachi, electric motors; Yamaha, motorcycles); Canada (International Nickel, nonferrous metal exploration); the Netherlands (AKZO, artifical fibers); and West Germany (BASF, petrochemicals). For two U.S. firms the joint venture operations involved substantial departures from prior policies. Ford's 25 percent interest in a plant making aluminum cylinder heads for the U.S. and Canadian auto markets was the first minority interest Ford had ever taken in a joint venture. DuPont had taken minority interests before accepting 49 percent to Alfa's 51 percent. However, DuPont had always handled the management of the ventures. In the Mexican synthetic fibers joint venture, Alfa did the managing. Alfa's policy was to import technology but to maintain management control.

In many of the above situations the Mexican output has been produced by using the trademark that had been developed by the foreign partner. This has helped in gaining Mexican consumer acceptance. In 1979, Alfa bought 100 percent of Massey-Ferguson's tractor operation in Mexico in return for the Canadian company's receipt of a royalty fee for the use of the Massey-Ferguson trade name.

In the aluminum cylinder head joint venture previously described, it was not a captive Mexican market that attracted Ford. It was lower production costs so as to supply the American and Canadian markets. In addition to cheap energy, Mexico had offered an abundance of cheap labor and no taxes on reinvested earnings. The motors built under the Hitachi brand name have been produced in Mexico for 25 percent below the Japanese cost. Alfa has become interested in export markets. A sales arrangement was established by which the Mitsui Trading Company of Japan handles exports of Alfa's polyester chemicals abroad. Alfa opened discussions about Mexican television production with several Japanese firms in order to use known Japanese brands to penetrate the U.S. market. Because of prior contractual arrangements, Alfa could not export its "American" brands (Philco, Magnavox, and Admiral) to the United States.

Perhaps Alfa's most notable sales excursion outside of Mexico has involved steel technology. Most of the world's steel is made by the indirect process using bituminous coal to form coke, which is then mixed with limestone in blast furnaces. Alfa developed a method of producing steel by direct reduction, thus bypassing the high capital cost of blast furnaces. To transfer this patented technology to new plants in other countries would require substantial on-site personnel and construction assistance. Alfa has lacked personnel that can be spared as well as foreign construction experience. Alfa has transferred its know-how to four foreign engineering firms— West Germany's GHH-Sterkrade, Japan's Kawasaki Heavy Industries, and the United States' Pullman Swindell and Dravo. Those firms have in turn acted as agents on behalf of Alfa and have constructed steel plants in such countries as Brazil, Venezuela, Indonesia, Iran, Iraq, and Zambia. Alfa receives fees for the use of the technology in foreign mills. The engineering firms receive fees for building the plants in what are known as turnkey projects.

In order for Alfa to expand and to maintain management control during the 1976–1980 period it had to borrow and to recruit managers outside of Mexico. Alfa ended up with a debt of almost $3 billion from over 130 different banks; about 75 percent of this was payable in U.S. dollars. Alfa also had to pay highly to attract managers with the backgrounds it wanted. Then oil prices plummeted, and the Mexican peso was devalued by 40 percent. By 1981, Alfa was losing so much money that it had to receive Mexican government aid of $680 million to keep afloat. About a year later, Alfa announced that it would sell off over 100 of its companies; however, these spin-offs went more slowly than had been expected. The result was that by 1984, foreign banks had agreed to convert a part of Alfa's debt into a 30 percent stake in the company rather than have loans default. In the meantime, many of the foreign firms that had made agreements with Alfa in the 1970s found that their expected Mexican expansion (via Alfa) had been put on hold. These included, for example, BASF's and Hercules' joint ventures with Alfa. Alfa simply lacked the resources to carry out so many agreements with so many different foreign companies.

INTRODUCTION

International business may be conducted by a variety of means. The truly experienced firm with a full global orientation usually makes use of most of the forms available, differentiating them according to specific product or foreign operating characteristics.

The preceding case illustrates the use of several different methods of exploiting international opportunities. Alfa made joint ventures with foreign firms, was engaged in the acquisition and sale of technology through licensing and turnkey contracts, and gained the use of trademarks through licensing agreements. This chapter discusses the most common means by which companies commit their financial, human, and other resources to the foreign sector, methods prompted either by their own desire or by external pressures that force them to accept certain parameters. This chapter also discusses the problems of control when one company enters an agreement that makes another company responsible for handling its business objectives. For example, BASF and Hercules both lost control of their Mexican expansion plans when Alfa became unable to comply with the agreed-upon plans. The reasons for the use of two forms—trade and direct investment—will be discussed only peripherally in this chapter, since the motives were handled in Chapters 4 and 6. Export operating considerations were taken up in Chapter 14, and one form of direct investment, shared ownership, will be covered in this chapter.

SOME VARIABLES AFFECTING CHOICE

- Choice of form may necessitate trade-offs among objectives
- Factors influencing choice include legal, cost, experience, competition, risk, control, and nature of assets

In terms of resources, the modes of foreign operations differ in terms of both the amount a firm commits to foreign operations and the portion of the resources that is located at home versus abroad. Trade may, for example, result in a lower additional resource commitment than direct foreign investment if there is excess capacity that can be utilized for exporting. If it is necessary to increase capacity, then this increase may take place by investing the resources either at home or abroad. The former involves a substantial commitment to foreign operations, even though the assets are not in a foreign location. In exporting, in direct investment, and in some of the other forms of foreign operations a firm may be able to reduce its total resource commitment by making contracts with other companies to conduct activities on its behalf or by sharing ownership in international business endeavors. Before examining these other operational forms it is useful to discuss some of the major factors that firms should consider when selecting a form of operation in a given market. These considerations will be covered more intensively when we discuss the specific operational modes.

Throughout this discussion, one should be mindful that there are trade-offs. For example, a decision to own 100 percent of a foreign subsidiary will normally increase the parent's fulfillment of the objective of controlling decisions; however, it may simultaneously reduce the parent's fulfillment of the objective of minimizing exposure to political risk.[2]

Legal

- May be direct prohibitions against certain forms
- May be indirect, e.g., affecting profitability

As was indicated in the case on Grupo Industrial Alfa, a firm may be constrained in its choice of operating mode regardless of its preferences. Some of the foreign firms, such as Ford, may have preferred a wholly owned Mexican operation but were not legally permitted. In addition to the outright prohibition of certain operating forms, there are other legal means that may influence the choice. These include differences in tax rates, differences in the maximum funds that can be remitted, actual or possible enforcement of antitrust provisions, and stipulations on the circumstances in which a proprietary asset will be in the public domain and available for others to use.

Cost

- Sometimes cheaper to get another firm to handle
  - especially at small volume
  - especially if other firm has excess capacity

In order to produce or sell abroad, certain fixed costs must be incurred, so at a small volume of business it may be cheaper to contract the work to someone else than to handle it internally. A specialist can spread the fixed costs over services to more than one firm. If business increases enough, a firm may be able to handle the activities more cheaply itself than by buying outside services. Firms should therefore periodically reappraise the question of internal versus external handling of their varied operations.

Another reason that the external contracting of operations may be lower in cost is that another firm may have excess production or sales capacity that can be easily utilized. This utilization may also reduce start-up time and thus result in an earlier cash flow.

Experience

- With more experience, companies take on more direct involvement abroad

Few companies are willing in their early stages of international development to expend a large portion of their resources on foreign operations, nor may they even have sufficient resources to expand abroad rapidly. As a result, they usually—but not always—move through stages of increased levels of international involvement. In the early stages they attempt to conserve their own scarce resources and to maximize the portion of the resources that are at home rather than abroad. This leads them to operational forms that transfer the burden of foreign commitment to outsiders. As the firms and their foreign activities grow, they tend to view the foreign portion of their business differently. There is a movement then toward the internal handling of more operations and locating a larger portion of resources abroad.[3]

Competition

- More choice of form when less likelihood of competition

When a firm has a desired and unique resource, one that will not easily be copied by competitors in the near future, then that firm is in a good position to choose the operating form that it would most like to utilize. When there are competitive possibilities, then a firm may have to settle on a form that is lower on its priority list. Otherwise a competitor may preempt the market. The possibility of competition may also lead to a strategy of rapid international expansion, which may be possible (because of limited resources) only by developing external arrangements with other firms.

Minimization of competition in given markets may also be achieved through cooperative arrangements that exclude entry, share resources, or divide output. The effectiveness will depend in part on the type of mode selected as well as the permissiveness of government authorities toward the specific agreement.

Risk

- The higher the perceived risk, usually the greater the desire to set external operating forms
- External forms allow for greater spreading of assets among countries

There are many types of risk. However, the possibility of political or economic changes affecting the safety of assets and their earnings is often at the forefront of management's concern in foreign operations. One way of minimizing the loss through the seizure of assets in foreign operations is to minimize the base of assets located abroad. This may dictate external arrangements so that the asset base is shared by others. This move might also make a government less willing to move against an operation, lest it encounter opposition from more than one firm.

One possible way of spreading risk is by placing operations in a number of different countries. This means less chance that all foreign assets will simultaneously be subject to such adversities as confiscation, exchange control, or even a slowing of sales caused by a local recession. The maximum losses as well as the year-to-year changes in consolidated earnings may thus be minimized. For companies that have not yet attained widespread international operations, operational forms that minimize their own resource expenditures may permit a more rapid dispersion of operations. These forms will be less appealing to companies whose activities are already widely extended or who have ample resources to so extend.

Control

• Internal handling usually means more control and no sharing of profits

The more that a firm deals externally, the more likely that it will lose control over decisions that may affect its global optimization. These include where output will be expanded, new product directions, and quality. External arrangements also imply the sharing of revenues, a serious consideration in undertakings with high potential profits. They also risk giving information more rapidly to potential competitors. The loss of control over flexibility, over revenues, and over competition has been implied by some writers to be the most important variable guiding firms' priorities for a mode of operation.[4]

Nature of Assets

• Some assets more suited to certain forms than others

For any firm to stay in business it must have some fairly unique advantages over possible competitors. It is only when the advantage is somehow internationally mobile that there is a possibility of engaging in foreign sales. The corner grocer who exists only because of the location will have no opportunity to operate abroad successfully unless, of course, the grocer has some unique ability to choose the right locations. From a seller's standpoint a mode of operation is selected to capitalize on some asset or advantage that the seller controls. This may be achieved by either selling a product encompassing the asset or by selling the use of the asset abroad. A buyer is of course interested in improving its position by gaining access to the asset either through a product that encompasses it or through use of the asset itself.

In a general sense, the assets refer to the factors of production (e.g., raw materials, capital, or labor). Since none of these is homogeneous, one must go further to examine the quality, cost, control, and development of the resource to determine how best to capitalize on it. In order to capitalize as much as possible on the resource, it is useful to compare forms of operations that may be used. This is because some assets are simply better suited to the use of some forms than to others.

Some of the assets that are commonly involved in international transactions (process technology, product technology, know-how, and goodwill*), were demonstrated in the case at the beginning of the chapter. Process technology advantage refers to an acquired ability to produce something

---

* Goodwill is the favor that a company has acquired beyond its tangible assets.

by a nontraditional method. The direct reduction process discussed in the Alfa case is such an example. In that situation, Alfa chose to capitalize by selling the use of the process rather than exporting cheaper steel or making investments abroad to utilize the technology. The same case included several examples of the transfer of product technology and goodwill. An example of the former would be the infusion of technology to produce polyester chemicals for which Alfa had no experience. An example of the latter would be Alfa's desire to get a known Japanese trade name to help sell television sets in the United States. The four engineering firms in the case had specialized know-how in the construction of technically advanced plants in developing countries. A type of asset not mentioned in the case is the reproduction right of some marketable asset. These are primarily copyrights on such things as books, records, films, and lithographs.

LICENSING

- May be exclusive or nonexclusive
- May be used for patents, trademarks, know-how, or copyrights

There are many reasons why foreign production may be a requisite for making sales abroad. However, when firms are faced with such conditions as prohibitive home production costs, transport problems, or governmental regulations, these same firms may not desire or be able to commence foreign manufacture under their own ownership. In these circumstances a company in one country may arrange for a company in a second country to manufacture its products under a licensing agreement.

Under a licensing agreement a firm (the licensor) grants rights on intangible property to another firm (the licensee). The rights may be exclusive or nonexclusive. The U.S. Internal Revenue Service classifies intangible property into five categories:

1. Patents, inventions, formulas, processes, designs, patterns.
2. Copyrights; literary, musical, or artistic compositions.
3. Trademarks, trade names, brand names.
4. Franchises, licenses, contracts.
5. Methods, programs, procedures, systems, etc.

Usually, the licensor is obliged to furnish technical information and assistance and the licensee to exploit the rights effectively and to pay compensation to the licensor.

Economic Motives

- May be faster
- May be cheaper
- May get technology in return (cross-licensing)
- Licensor may lack resources

Frequently, a new product or process may affect only a part of a firm's total output and only for a limited period of time. The sales volume may not be large enough to warrant the establishment of overseas manufacturing and sales facilities. Furthermore, during the period of acquiring operations there is a risk that competitors will develop improvements that negate the advantages. A firm that is already operating abroad may be able to produce and sell at a lower cost and with less start-up time (thus a cash flow starts earlier) because of its ability to utilize excess capacity and its experience in coping with local problems. Risk of operating facilities and holding inventories is reduced for the licensor. The licensee may find that the cost of the arrangement is less than if the development were accomplished internally. For industries in which technological changes are frequent and affect many different products, such as chemicals and electrical goods, it is common for firms in various countries to exchange technology rather than compete with each other on every product in every market, an arrangement known as **cross-licensing.**

A possible problem with cross-licensing is that it may violate antitrust regulations if it results in the restriction of entry into a market by one of the parties. The regulations in this respect are extremely complex, and good legal assistance is a necessity for any type of agreement.[5] Another cross-licensing problem is that some of the parties may produce more innovations than others. American Home Products participated in pharmaceutical arrangements with several foreign drug makers that later terminated the arrangements because American Home's research and development produced few important drugs on its own.[6]

A second economic motive concerns the resources a firm has at its disposal. American Motors, for example, has insufficient resources to establish its own facilities everywhere that overseas production is necessary for Jeep sales. For some of the largest markets, such as India and Australia, American Motors has subsidiaries. For some smaller markets, such as Sri Lanka and Pakistan, licensing arrangements are used.

Strategic Motives

- Gives return on products not fitting the firm's strategic priority

Large diversified firms are constantly reevaluating and altering their product lines to put their efforts where their major strengths best complement their assessment of high-profit businesses. This may leave them with products or technologies that they themselves do not wish to exploit but that may be profitably transferred to other firms. Because it does not fit into General Electric's major lines of business, GE has marketed to other firms its development of a microorganism that destroys spilled oil by digesting it.[7]

Political and Legal Motives

- Keeps nonassociated firm from usurping the asset
  - gets local firm to monitor unauthorized use
  - legal factors if asset not exploited

Aside from licensing because of restrictions on trade or foreign ownership, licensing may also be a means of protecting an asset. This may come about for two reasons. First, many countries provide very little de facto protection for a foreign property right such as a trademark, patent, or copyright unless authorities are prodded consistently. To prevent the so-called "pirating" of these proprietary assets, companies have sometimes made licensing agreements with a local firm, which then monitors to make sure that no one else uses the asset locally. A second situation is in the type of country that provides protection only if the internationally registered asset is exploited locally within a specified period of time. If a firm does not exploit the registration within the country during the specified period, then whoever does so first will have the right to it. Mexico is one such country. In close proximity to each other in Mexico City are Gucci, Chemise La Coste, and Cartier shops that have no links to the European houses. The Cartier shop copies a Cartier watch dial, bracelet, presentation box, and storefront to the smallest detail. It puts cheap movements and poor-quality gold filling in the watches. This has hurt Cartier's reputation among unsuspecting buyers, who then refuse to buy in the authentic stores in New York and Paris.[8] Had Cartier licensed the use of its name in Mexico early on, it could have preempted the nonassociated use of the name there.

In the absence of licensing, a firm may find that another firm can even exclude its market entry at a later date or can compete in certain areas of the world through exploitation of the asset. Western Electric is a firm that has a liberal licensing policy in order to avoid patent litigation.

Problems and Provisions

- MNEs want return from intangible assets
- Some LDCs object to payment for intangibles that they can copy

Hardly any aspect of international business has been as controversial in recent years as licensing. Given the fact that virtually all royalties are paid to organizations in industrial countries, it is perhaps inevitable that groups within less-developed countries have criticized the amounts and methods of payments. Since MNEs view their technologies and trademarks as integral parts of their asset bases, it is perhaps just as inevitable that they are skeptical about transferring their use to other organizations. The following discussion highlights the major concerns of licensors, licensees, and host governments that might be incorporated into a formal agreement.

- Asset transference may mean loss of control, which could imply
  - asset inadequately worked
  - poor quality
  - development of competitor

Control and competition. By transferring rights to another firm the owner undoubtedly loses some control over the asset. There are a host of potential problems with this lack of control that should be settled in the original licensing agreement. Provisions should be made for the termination of the agreement if the parties do not adhere to the directives. The agreement should certainly specify methods of testing of quality, the obligations of each party concerning expenditures on sales development, and the geographic limitations on the use of the asset. Without these provisions the license may be inadequately worked, the two parties may find themselves in competition with each other, or a poor-quality product in one country may jeopardize product image and sales elsewhere. A good example of how the lack of specification led to legal suits is the case between Oleg Cassini, Inc. and the U.S. subsidiary (Jovan) of the Beecham Group from the United Kingdom. Cassini licensed Jovan to promote and extend sales throughout the world of various Cassini fragrances, cosmetics, and beauty aids. Then Jovan introduced Diane Von Furstenberg products instead and denied Cassini the right to license the Cassini name to other firms. Cassini then sued Jovan for $78 million.[9]

Depending on the nature of the asset, either the licensor or licensee stands the risk of developing a future competitor after the agreement expires. If a brand or trademark is involved, then the licensee may develop consumer preferences and then have to turn the market over to the licensor. If know-how or patents are involved, the licensee may be able to exploit the assets long after the agreement is terminated. Even before an agreement is terminated, the two parties may come into competition with each other because one has made improvements on the licensed technology that make the original patents obsolete. It has therefore become common to make provisions in the original contract for the possible use and sharing of superseding technology built on knowledge from the original transfer.

- Dilemma because
  - seller does not want to give information without payment assurance
  - buyer does not want to pay without evaluating information
- Contract terms also may be proprietary information

Secrecy. The value of many technologies would diminish if they were widely known or understood. Provisions that a licensee will not divulge this information have historically been included in agreements. Some licensors have, in addition, held on to the ownership and production of specific components so that licensees will not have the full knowledge or capability to produce an exact copy of the product on their own. Coca-Cola, for example, licenses its trademark and a portion of the production techniques to bottlers worldwide; however, the concentrate production is carried on by Coca-Cola itself. The Indian government required Coca-Cola to divulge the contents of the concentrate or lose its right to receive trademark royalties there. Rather than risk losing control over this asset, Coca-Cola chose to abandon the market.[10]

Secrecy arises as a problem for negotiating agreements to transfer process technology. Many times a firm has developed techniques that it has not yet used commercially but that it wishes to sell. A buyer is reluctant to "buy a pig in a poke," but a licensor who shows the potential licensee the process risks having the process used without payment. It has become common to set up preagreements in order to protect all parties.

An area of growing controversy is the degree of secrecy in the financial terms of licensing agreements. Within some countries, for example, governmental agencies must now approve royalty contracts once the contracts have been negotiated by the parties involved. There is much evidence that these authorities consult with their counterparts in other countries regarding similar agreements. They require approval and enter into consultation in order to improve their negotiations with MNEs, thereby reducing the countries' foreign exchange payments. Many MNEs balk at this procedure because they believe (1) that contract terms are proprietary information of competitive importance and (2) that market conditions usually dictate the need for very different terms in different countries.

- Payment varies
  - fixed fee versus usage
  - exclusive versus nonexclusive
  - market size
  - how long assets will have value
  - how taxes assessed
  - cost to transfer

Payment. There is wide variation in the amount and type of payment under licensing arrangements, and each contract tends to be negotiated very much on its own merits. The amount requested by the licensor will depend in part on whether the firm views this type of income as simply a residual for which little or no additional investment is required or whether the firm seeks to cover its R&D costs by selling to other firms. The uniqueness of the technology and the other resources that a potential licensor has at its disposal will, in addition, dictate in part the possibilities of exploiting a market in the absence of a licensing contract. The potential licensee will, of course, consider alternative possibilities. The value of a license to the licensee will depend in part on the potential sales based on present market size, degree of exclusivity within that market, the time frame before the asset becomes obsolete, and the possibility of ongoing relationships through new or cross-licensing arrangements.

One of the thorny issues as seen by LDCs is that licensees are usually prevented by contract from exporting; thus small-scale production may cause high full costs to the consumers. MNEs have countered that extending sales territories would necessitate high royalties because MNEs could not sell exclusive rights to parties in other countries. They have also argued that the development of process technologies for small-scale production would often be too costly but is done when economically feasible.[11]

Taxes may be assessed quite differently depending on the methods of arranging payments under the agreement. In the United States, earnings from the transfer of assets abroad may be treated as income or as a capital gain. Since taxes on capital gains are currently only about half those on income, the after-tax receipts are substantially different. Payment schedules may also be deferred in order to defer the payment of taxes. Fees to be paid for the use of an asset may be made in a lump sum, on a percentage of sales value, on a specific rate applied to usage, or on some combination of these methods.

There has been a trend in recent years to negotiate a "front-end" payment to cover the cost of transfer and to follow this with another set of fees based on actual or projected usage. The reason for this is the realization that few technologies may be moved abroad simply by transferring publications and reports. The negotiation process is itself expensive and must be followed by engineering, consultation, and adaptation. The early stages of production are usually characterized by low quality and slow productivity.[12] The substantial costs in the transfer process are increasingly charged to the licensee so that the licensor is motivated to assure a smooth adaptation.

Sales to controlled entities. Many licenses are given to companies connected in ownership with the licensor. U.S. firms in particular are granting licenses to their subsidiaries abroad rather than to unconnected companies. The reasons include the belief that uncontrolled licenses do not exploit patents energetically enough and that one's own management can effect higher sales because of better business know-how.[13] A license may be needed to transfer technology abroad because operations in a foreign country, even if 100 percent owned by the parent, are usually separate firms from a legal standpoint. When there is a present or potential shared ownership, a separate licensing arrangement may also be a means of compensating for contributions beyond the mere investment in capital and managerial resources.

The price at which MNEs sell to foreign operations they control is very controversial. By altering the price of product, components, patents, and so on, MNEs may effectively transfer more of their profits to low-tax countries from high-tax countries and effectively reduce current or permanent payment on a portion of their income. Since much of what is transferred among controlled entities of a multinational company is unique to that company, it is highly difficult to estimate what the competitive price would be if the company were selling the same thing to a noncontrolled entity.[14] A study concluding that firms undercharge their subsidiaries has pointed out that the royalties, management fees, rentals, and all other related charges for research and development to the foreign subsidiaries of U.S. firms are far below the portion of sales and investment that are accounted for by these foreign facilities.[15] LDCs have contended the opposite. The most influential study from this perspective demonstrated that MNEs overpriced the sale of goods and services to Colombia in spite of the fact that Colombia had low local taxes, high tariffs, and liberal deferral provisions.[16] One would have expected that, from the standpoint of tax minimization, the MNEs would have done just the opposite. A number of possible explanations have been postulated for this anomaly, such as the movement of funds to countries with a stronger currency and the understatement of Colombian profits in order to gain certain governmental concessions.[17] Regardless of the reasons or whether these results were typical, the study has been highly influential in increasing the scrutiny of MNE technology transactions. It is now more difficult for MNEs to establish licensing contracts with their controlled affiliates, and governmental approval is more likely to be required on a case-by-case basis. Governmental intervention guarantees a negotiated price, but not necessarily the price if a transaction were to occur between unrelated business parties, a so-called arm's length price.

Common because
- separate legal entities
- protects value when ownership shared
- way to avert payment or exchange limitations

Positioning the Licensing Unit[18]

- Integral part of growth strategy, then usually have separate operating unit
- Protection of asset, then usually in legal department
- Combination, then usually R&D

Although companies handle licensing in different parts of their organizations, some patterns have been observed that relate to their reasons for licensing. When licensing is an integral part of a company's growth and diversification objectives, a separate unit in the company is likely to be in charge of buying and selling. In multidivisional firms there may be more than one separate licensing unit. When the strategy is primarily the safeguarding of existing activities, licensing is apt to be a part of another unit such as a legal or patents unit. When a company combines the above two objectives, it tends to attach licensing to the research and development functions either by allying it or by setting up a parallel function reporting to the same head.

Protection of Intangible Assets

- International treaties and agreements help safeguard patents, trademarks, copyrights
  - give companies time to register
  - allow for uniform searches
  - but many countries do not adhere
  - but firms lose when others infringe on asset usage

The poet and essayist, Ralph Waldo Emerson said, "If a man can write a better book, preach a better sermon, or make a better mousetrap than his neighbor, though he builds his house in the woods, the world will make a beaten path to his door." Companies believe this, but fear that the mousetrap might be stolen if not adequately protected. Some of the most valuable assets that businesses have are their intangibles—patents, trademarks, and copyrights. Coca-Cola, for example, has a full-time legal staff to concentrate on trademark infringements. Literally millions of dollars can be used in the development of intangibles; improper protection of these assets could lead to their limited use worldwide and therefore to their limited profitability. Given the different attitudes of countries toward property rights, adequate international protection to a firm's intangibles can only come about through international cooperation. Most countries have legal procedures for registering patents, trademarks, and copyrights, but it is extremely expensive for an MNE to duplicate the application process in every country where it operates. That is why international treaties can be so important.

Patents. The first major attempt at cross-national cooperation was the Convention of Paris, initiated in 1883 and periodically revised. This convention gave rise to the International Bureau for the Protection of Industrial Property Rights (BIRPI) and involved the protection of patents, trademarks, and other property rights. The general idea behind the Paris Convention was that a nation would grant to foreigners who are members of the Convention the same status accorded its own citizens in the protection of property rights. A second major provision of the Paris Convention is that a registration in one country has a grace period of protection before filing in other member countries. The Inter-American Conference of 1910 on Inventions, Patents, Designs, and Models was initiated among the United States and Latin American countries to accomplish the same objectives as the Paris Convention.

The three most important contemporary cross-national patent agreements are the Patent Cooperation Treaty (PCT) of the World Intellectual Property Organization (WIPO), the European Patent Convention (EPC), and the EEC Patent Convention.[19] The PCT and EPC allow firms to make a uniform patent search and application, which is then passed on to all signatory countries.

Patent infringement battles are both costly and complex. The major problems on the international level are the rapid development of technology and the different patent rules and regulations in different countries. Companies are forced to change their patents from country to country to meet local needs. Patent infringement is often difficult to prove. For example, a company in Italy, where there is no patent protection on drugs, could manufacture a drug patented by a firm in the United States and sell it anywhere in the world. If the U.S. firm were to bring suit, it would have to prove patent infringement but would have difficulty getting the proof in Italy.

Owing to the high costs of patent infringement suits, many firms are attempting to settle out of court. A European company, Compagnie Générale d'Electricité, and its U.S. affiliate spent nearly $700,000 and several years fighting one suit. Although they won, the cost was high.

Trademarks. The following illustrates the importance of a trademark:

> *Failure to make reasonably certain that a trademark can be used legally can mean that thousands of dollars spent on advertising or marketing plans will go down the drain, since a trademark will not be registered if it would impair the inherent property rights in a mark already in use and registered.* [20]

In many cases, trademarks have become generic and thus in the public domain. "Yo-yo" is actually a foreign trademark that has become generic in the United States. Although "Ping-Pong" is a registered trademark in the United States, it has become generic in China and is used in place of "table tennis." Since the Japanese have no name for vulcanized rubber, they use "goodyear" to identify the product.[21]

One of the most recent developments in cross-national cooperation for trademark protection is the Trademark Registration Treaty, which was formalized at a diplomatic conference in Vienna. The United States, the United Kingdom, West Germany, and Italy were among the industrial countries that signed initially. The agreement is designed to be more universally acceptable than the Madrid Convention, which provides for the international registration of trademarks but does not include many industrial countries, such as the United States.

Traditionally, U.S. law has required the use of a trademark before an application of registration could be filed. However, pending legislation would allow application on the basis of intent rather than use. Codifiedlaw countries (those using statutory law rather than common law) have traditionally not recognized use as a precondition to registration or as a valid protection against infringement. According to the Vienna Convention, a country may not require the use of a mark as a prerequisite to obtain or maintain registration until three years after its international registration. Once the mark has been registered internationally, each country must accept it or provide grounds for refusal within fifteen months so that the firm will have sufficient time to act before its three-year period is completed.

Copyrights. Most large publishing and recording companies have extensive foreign interests and can be easily influenced by foreign competition. If there were no international copyright laws, it would be feasible for a foreign producer to copy a book or tape and then distribute it at cut-rate prices in the country where it was first produced. The Universal Copyright Convention (UCC), the major cross-national agreement, honors the copyright laws of the signatory states.

Piracy problems. Not all countries are members of the various agreements to protect intangible property rights. Of those that are, some enforce the agreements haphazardly. Many countries simply do not place a high priority on tracking down or prosecuting people who violate these property rights, preferring to put their police efforts on crimes they consider more serious.

The cost to companies has become enormous, especially to those that depend on a well known trademark to merchandise their goods. One of the enticements to trademark pirating has been the recent emphasis on designer labels. It is tempting to cash in on the massive advertising by placing well-known trademarked labels on copies of products. This has occurred on almost every type of goods. In 1983 it was estimated that $18 billion of fake merchandise entered the United States.[22] Much more goes into other countries. The Commission of the European Community estimates that pirated merchandise now accounts for about 2 percent of world trade.[23] Fake labels even go on merchandise that the copied companies do not make, such as the Jordache label on disco bags and caps, which Jordache does not market at all.

What about consumers? Sometimes they get good-quality merchandise with a prestige label for a fraction of what the legitimate product would have cost. Some firms have even contracted counterfeiters to be legitimate suppliers. Often, though, the consumer gets shoddy or even dangerous merchandise. In Britain, defective brake parts turned up in military aircraft; and in the United States a dozen people died from counterfeit tranquilizers.[24]

Various associations of manufacturers have sprung up worldwide to deal collectively with the problem. Among the things that have been proposed are greater border surveillance, criminal penalties for dealing in counterfeit goods, and the cessation of aid to countries that do not join and adhere to international agreements. One such active group has been the Association of American publishers, which estimates the value of pirated books at more than $100 million a year in Korea alone.[25] (If you are reading this book in Korea—or most other places in Asia, for that matter—you are probably reading from a pirated copy.) Companies such as Apple Computer and Union Carbide are also successfully tracking down infringers on their own and bringing cases against them. Other companies are using high technology, such as holographic images and magnetic or microchip tags, to identify the genuine products. But this has cost them millions of dollars in detective and legal fees and in payments for detecting devices.[26] Other pirating efforts occur flagrantly, and companies seem to be at a loss as to how to stop the activity. One example has been the television broadcasting of programs from satellites in countries such as Jamaica and Haiti. Not only do the original broadcasters receive no fees from this, but it also cuts in on sales to movie theaters in those countries, since films may be on television before they are distributed to the theaters.[27]

FRANCHISING

• Includes trademark and continual infusion of necessary asset

Franchising is essentially a way of doing business in which the franchisor gives an independent franchisee the use of a trademark that is an essential asset for the franchisee's business and in which the franchisor more than nominally assists on a continuing basis in the operation of the business. In many cases the franchisor also provides supplies.[28] For instance, Holiday Inn grants to franchisees the goodwill of the Holiday Inn name and the support service to get started, such as appraisal of a proposed motel site. As part of the continued relationship, Holiday Inn offers a reservations service and training programs to help ensure the success of the venture. Muzak gives franchisees permission to use its name when selling taped musical programs to business and industry. In addition, Muzak supplies the scientifically programmed tapes.[29] In a sense the franchisor and franchisee act almost like a vertically integrated firm because the parties are interdependent and each produces part of the product or service that ultimately reaches the consumer.

Some Patterns

• Many types of products and countries involved

Franchising goes back at least as far as the nineteenth century and is most associated with the United States, where one third of retail sales are handled that way. About three quarters of the sales are in three areas: car and truck dealers, gasoline service stations, and soft drink bottling. Hundreds of U.S. franchisors have thousands of foreign outlets.[30] The fastest growth areas of U.S. firms have been in the areas of food and business services, primarily in Canada, Japan, and the United Kingdom. By 1980, for example,

McDonald's had over 1000 foreign stores, and it expects to derive over half its sales from abroad by 1990.[31]

Not all franchising is by U.S. firms. Pronuptia, a French bridal wear franchisor, has 250 foreign outlets. Such firms as Wimpy's and Bake 'N' Take from the United Kingdom and Wienerwald from West Germany have been among some of the earliest and most successful food franchisors abroad. In Japan, which has been considered the most lucrative market for food franchising, U.S.-based ventures have only about half the sales.[32]

Operational Modifications

Dilemma
- the more standardization, the less acceptance in foreign country
- the more adjustment to foreign country, the less franchisor is needed

Some modifications usually necessary

A major type of modification has been in the method of recruiting foreign franchisees because (1) the franchisor and franchising are relatively less well known and (2) local financing is less readily available abroad. In order to relieve this problem, Quality Courts contracted with Universal Pictures to produce a ten-minute movie about its operations to show to potential franchisees. Another problem in foreign franchise expansion has been governmental or legal restrictions that make it difficult to gain satisfactory operating permission.

A dilemma for franchisors is that their success at home has been largely due to three factors: (1) product and service standardization, (2) high identification through promotion, and (3) effective cost controls. When entering many foreign countries, various restraints may make it difficult to conform to home country methods; yet the more adjustments that are made to the host country's nuances, the less a franchisor has to offer a potential franchisee. The success of franchisors in Japan has been due in great part to enthusiastic assimilation of Western innovations, so firms such as McDonald's have been able to copy their U.S. outlets almost intact. In Italy, however, McDonald's tested the market for two years and then decided not to enter; Wimpy's closed its outlets there after sustaining heavy losses.[33] The conclusion was that it would be too expensive to get Italians to accept the foreign food; yet if firms offered menus that were more acceptable to the Italians, there would be nothing different to offer a franchisee. Even in countries where franchises have been successful, it has usually been necessary to make some operating adjustments. For example, Kentucky Fried Chicken in Japan had to redesign its equipment and stores to save space because of the higher cost of rent. It eliminated mashed potatoes and put less sugar in its cole slaw because of Japanese tastes.

Contract Problems

Similar to those for licensing

Some of the problems that plague franchising agreements are no different from those in licensing agreements. Contracts must be spelled out in detail. But if courts must rule on disagreements, both parties are apt to lose something in the settlement. A good example was when McDonald's granted a license for up to 166 stores in France to Raymond Dayan at less than its normal fee because of doubts that the French would ever take to fast-food restaurants. M. Dayan, with the help of McDonald's, found very good Paris locations for fourteen stores, which he opened over a period of several years. He was very successful. However, McDonald's had the right to revoke the franchise agreement if its inspection found that the stores were not up to its level of cleanliness. The agreement was canceled on these grounds, leading to a court case. M. Dayan claimed that McDonald's action was simply a ruse to make him pay McDonald's usual rate. He lost out on further expansion with the McDonald's trademark. But McDonald's lost something, too. When M. Dayan took down the McDonald's signs, he immediately replaced them with signs saying O'Keefe's Hamburgers; and he had the clientele, the know-how, and the best locations in Paris.[34]

MANAGEMENT CONTRACTS

- Used primarily when
  - owned operation has been expropriated
  - firm manages a new facility
  - firm manages an operation in trouble

One of the most important assets a firm may have at its disposal is management talent. In spite of huge endowments of capital and technology, many governmental enterprises in LDCs encounter difficulties because of inadequately trained management. The transmission of management internationally has largely depended on foreign investments that deploy expatriate managers and specialists to foreign countries. Management contracts offer a means through which a firm may use part of its management personnel to assist a firm in a foreign country in general or specialized management functions for a specified period of time, for a fee.

Management contracts are established in three types of situations.[35] The first, and probably the most common, is when a foreign investment has been expropriated by a foreign government and the former owner is invited to continue supervising the operations until local management is trained. In this case the management structure may remain substantially the same, although board membership changes. A good example of this is the case on Aramco at the beginning of Chapter 12. After the Saudi Arabian government took over the ownership, the former owners continued to supply management. Some advantages of entering into contracts in this type of situation are that this may (1) facilitate getting resources out of the country in addition to those agreed upon in the expropriation discussions; (2) ingratiate the firm with local authorities so that future business operations are possible; and (3) ensure continued access to raw materials or other resources needed from the country. The second type of management contract is when a firm is asked to manage a new venture, in which case it may sell much of its own equipment to the facility. The third and least common situation occurs when an operation has run into difficulty and a foreign firm is invited in to effect a turnaround.

From the standpoint of the recipient country, the need to receive direct investment as a means of gaining management assistance is obviated. From the standpoint of the firm providing management, contracts are appropriate in order to avoid the risk of capital asset loss, when returns on investment are too low and capital outlays are too high. The contracts do have potential problems, not the least of which is the training of future competitors. Additionally, if the firm has differences of opinion on policy with the government, incurs start-up inefficiencies, or does not train local managers quickly, bad feelings may be created. Contracts are usually drawn to cover three to five years, and fixed fees or fees based on volume rather than profits are most common.

TURNKEY OPERATIONS

- Most commonly are construction firms
- May develop future competitor
- Large size of projects dictates sales to high levels
- Problems include
  - long time to complete
  - in remote areas
- New competition from LDCs

Turnkey projects involve a contract for construction of operating facilities that are transferred to the owner when the facilities are ready to commence operations, for a fee. Firms performing turnkey operations are frequently industrial equipment manufacturers that supply some of their own equipment for the project. Most commonly, they are construction firms. In addition, they may be consulting firms or manufacturers that do not find an investment on their own behalf in the country to be feasible.

The customer for a turnkey operation is very often a governmental agency that has decreed that a given product must be produced locally and under its auspices. As in the case of the management contract, a firm building a turnkey facility may be developing a future competitor. Yet many firms have chosen to perform design and construction duties, particularly in communist countries and India, where there are restrictions on foreign ownership. In recent years, most of the large projects have been in oil-exporting countries, which are moving rapidly toward infrastructure development and industrialization. Of course, not all turnkey projects are developing potential competitors. Projects to build airports and port facilities, for example, do not lend themselves to competition.

The very size of these contracts is one of the things setting this business apart from most other international business operations. Most of the contracts are for hundreds of millions of dollars, and many are for several billion. This means that a few very large firms account for most of the international market. One firm, Kellogg Rust, accounted for 11 percent of the international market and 28 percent of the U.S. portion of the market by itself in 1984.[36] This has also meant hiring executives with top-level governmental contacts abroad who can gain entry with the right decision makers to negotiate their proposals in foreign countries.

Pullman-Kellogg, for example, secured a large fertilizer plant contract in Nigeria. They sent Andrew Young, a former U.N. Ambassador who enjoys immense personal prestige in Africa, to negotiate the contract.[37] The nature of the large-scale government contracts has also placed a great importance on ceremony, such as opening a facility on a country's independence day or getting a head of state to inaugurate a facility, in order to build goodwill for future contracts. Although public relations are important, it takes much more to sell contracts of such magnitude. The U.S. Department of Commerce lists the following four factors in order of importance:

1. price,

2. export financing,

3. managerial and technological quality, and

4. experience and reputation.[38]

Payment for a turnkey operation is usually in stages, as the project develops. It is common for 10–25 percent to be made as a down payment, another 50–65 percent to be paid as the contract progresses, and the remainder to be paid once the facility is actually operating in accordance with the contract. Because of usual long time periods between conception and completion, the company performing turnkey operations is exposed to possible currency fluctuations for an extended period of time and should be covered, if possible, by escalation clauses or cost-plus contracts. Since the final payment is made only if the facility is operating satisfactorily, it is important to specify very precisely what constitutes "satisfactory." For this reason, many firms insist on performing a feasibility study as part of the turnkey contract in order not to build something that, although desired by local governmental authorities, may nevertheless be too large or inefficient. Even though the facility may be built exactly as directed, its inefficiency could create legal problems that hold up final payment.[39]

Many of the turnkey contracts are in remote areas, thus necessitating massive housing construction and importation of personnel (see Chapter 22). They may involve building an entire infrastructure under the most adverse geographic conditions. Because of the diversity and enormity of these projects, some firms, such as Bechtel, have prepared lengthy films showing their capabilities in past projects.

If a firm holds a monopoly on certain assets or resources, it will be difficult for other companies to be competitive in building facilities. As the production process becomes more known, however, the number of competitors for performing turnkey operations increases. The president of an international consulting engineering firm has listed five stages for developing countries:

1. expatriates do all the work;

2. local subcontractors develop;

3. small local contractors start up;

4. local contractors take over local work; and

5. local contractors go abroad.[40]

This evolvement has pushed U.S. firms' involvement in recent years to the high technology end of the spectrum, whereas firms from such countries as India, Korea, and Turkey can compete better for conventional projects where low labor costs are important.[41]

CONTRACT ARRANGEMENTS

- Sometimes gives similar advantages as vertical integration
- May spread risk and developmental costs

Companies that at one time would have integrated vertically by making direct investments for the extraction of raw materials in foreign countries are now finding increased desire for local ownership of the extractive process. Since the local owners frequently continue to need certain resources the foreign firms hold, contracts may be established whereby raw materials are traded for the assets held by foreign firms. For example, as the Saudi Arabian government increased its ownership share of Aramco, it still needed management and exploration assistance, which was traded for commitments of preferred status for oil sales.[42] On the basis of this precedent, several other oil-producing countries have made arrangements whereby the oil firms take all exploration and development risks in exchange for a share of the oil produced.[43]

One of the fastest growth areas for contract arrangements has been for projects that are too large for any single company to take on. This has been apparent in the development of new aircraft and weapon systems. From the inception of a project, companies from different countries frequently agree to take on the high cost and high risk of developmental work for different components needed in the final product. Afterward a lead company buys the components from the firms that did a part of the developmental work.

The major aluminum producers have developed swap contracts whereby they can save transport costs. They are all vertically integrated firms, but not in each country where they operate. Alcan might give Pechiney semiprocessed alumina in Canada in exchange for the same amount of semiprocessed alumina delivered to Alcan in France. A similar swap arrangement of oil was proposed whereby Japan would receive oil from Alaska in excess of that needed on the west coast of the United States. Japan, in turn, would divert the same amount of oil from its Middle East contracts to the Gulf Coast refineries in the United States.

ACCESSING FOREIGN TECHNOLOGY

- May help domestic and international competitiveness

In most of the aforementioned operational forms (licensing, franchising, management contracts, turnkey operations, and other contractual arrangements) an organization in one country gains access to scientific or managerial

- Ways of increasing
  - monitoring foreign developments
  - links with research organizations
  - increase visibility
  - cooperative research
  - foreign R&D

technology from an organization in another country. By gaining these assets a firm may be in a much better position to compete domestically and internationally. Because of the competitive implications, it is not surprising that many firms are establishing mechanisms whereby they may increase the likelihood of gaining advantages before their competitors.

One of the most used mechanisms has been the establishment of company units to monitor journals and technical conferences. These are not sufficient since very few patent descriptions ever appear in other than the voluminous patent office publications from each different country; therefore, firms must go to these publications as well.[44] This combined monitoring helps assure that the company is made aware of new developments, thereby enabling decision makers to decide whether to ignore the innovations, to try to counteract them through in-house developments, or to establish an operational link with the individuals or organizations that are apparently leading the field. A second mechanism is to develop formal links with academic and other research organizations at home and abroad so as to determine possible breakthroughs before they are publicized in professional journals. A third means is to increase visibility through participation in trade fairs, the distribution of brochures, and contacts with technical acquisition consultants. This visibility may encourage innovators to think of one's firm rather than another when they seek out clients. A fourth is the establishment of cooperative research projects with foreign firms, thereby gaining benefits of scale and the use of personnel from other organizations. Finally, a company may set up part of its research and development activities in foreign countries in order to utilize foreign talent that would not likely immigrate to the company's home country.[45]

THE LEVEL OF EQUITY OWNERSHIP

When a firm does establish foreign operations, it may own the entire stock or it may share the ownership. There are various types of ownership sharing, just as there are several reasons for selecting an equity amount.

The Argument for 100 Percent

- Easier to control
- No sharing of profits

Most businesspeople would prefer to have a 100 percent interest in foreign operations in order to ensure control and to prevent the dilution of profits. As long as there are no minority stockholders, corporate management has a greater freedom to enact measures that, although not in the best interest of the particular operations, are in the best interest of the company as a whole. With minority stockholders the parent firm has much less freedom of action, since these minority stockholders may become very vocal to their governments about practices that are not in the best interest of the subsidiaries. In fact, most countries have legislation to protect minority stockholders. Freuhauf-France, for example, received export orders that, although in the best interest of that subsidiary, were not considered by its U.S. majority owners to be in the best interests of Freuhauf's worldwide operations. When Freuhauf-France did not fulfill the export orders, the minority stockholders contested the action in French courts. This left the majority stockholders with the options of either filling the export order or paying damages to the minority holders.[46]

Even when the majority owners act in what they consider to be the best interest of the local company, there may be conflicts with local stockholders because of different opinions as to what businesses should be doing. Some points of possible conflict are dividend pay-out versus the retention of earnings, the degree of public disclosure of activities, and the degree of cooperation with various governmental agencies.

The argument against diluting profits is a simple one. Many firms contend that if they own all the resources that are necessary for the successful foreign operation and are willing to contribute these resources, they should not have to share ownership.

Shared Ownership Arrangements

- Internal reasons
  - spread geographically faster
  - covers R&D over larger base
- External
  - governments want local control
  - some industries more affected than others

In spite of the advantages to owning 100 percent of a foreign facility, there has been an upsurge of ownership sharing in recent years.[47] The reasons for this sharing are undoubtedly a combination of outside pressures and internal willingness to take partial ownership abroad.

From an internal standpoint there has probably been a greater need in recent years to bring outside resources into foreign operations. By sharing ownership in some existing foreign operations, many firms have been able to spread geographically at a faster rate. This has prevented competitors from gaining dominant market shares and also allowed maximum sales expansion, which helps to spread such relatively fixed costs as research and development to a larger sales base.

Externally, there has been increased pressure by many countries for ownership sharing with local shareholders, as countries feel that this policy will enhance their economic or political objectives. The types of pressures include legal requirements (the Andean countries), greater ease in getting permission to operate (Japan), and preferential tax rates for more locally controlled firms (Canada). In addition, many companies feel that by bringing local capital into the organization they take on a local character that decreases governmental and societal criticism (thus reducing the risk of nationalization or expropriation) and may bring captive sales to the participating shareholders.[48] Some industries share ownership much more than others. One study has related this to the visibility of firms in the industry. Firms with high capital outlay and few competitors, such as automobile makers, have a much higher propensity to share ownership than firms, such as pharmaceutical manufacturers, with a more atomistic market.[49] Presumably, local governments exert greater pressure for ownership sharing on those firms having the most significant impact on the economy. Or perhaps the higher capital outlay in these large investments necessitates additional outside resources.

- Hard to sustain operations when two or more partners try to control it

Equity as a control mechanism.   As was discussed in Chapter 6, the problem of deciding how much equity is necessary for control is a cumbersome one. With a few exceptions the larger the percentage of equity held, the more likely it is that the owner of this equity will control the decisions and policies of the enterprise. Many firms are willing to share ownership but will usually specify whether the sharing is with or without control. Celanese, for example, usually takes only a minority holding in its foreign operations; but because the remaining ownership is widely fragmented, Celanese can ordinarily control policies and decisions. After the 1973 Mexicanization law discussed in the Grupo Industrial Alfa case, many foreign firms sought to maintain management control in spite of minority equity positions by selling 51 percent of their shares to a broad ownership market through the Mexican stock exchange. The Mexican government, in turn, placed limits on that approach. BASF, a German chemical company, maintained management control by transferring a majority interest in its pharmaceutical company to Bancomer, a big Mexican bank. The bank was simply interested in diversifying its investment holdings and had no desire to manage.[50] When no one company has control, the operation may lack a significant direction. In discussing the problems of a company that was jointly owned by a U.S. and a Japanese firm, a Sterling Drug spokesman said, "You must decide right off the bat whether you'll control it or will put confidence in the Japanese organization."[51] This opinion is supported by studies showing that when two or more partners attempt to share in the management of an operation, there is a much higher incidence of failure than when one parent dominates.[52]

- Need not be 50–50
- Various combinations of ownership

Joint ventures.   A type of ownership sharing that is very popular among international companies is the joint venture, a company owned by more than one organization. Although it is usually formed for the achievement of a limited objective, it may continue to operate indefinitely as the objective is redefined. Joint ventures are sometimes thought of as fifty–fifty companies, but often more than two organizations participate in the ownership. Furthermore, one organization may frequently control more than 50 percent of the venture. The type of legal organization may be a partnership, corporation, or some other form of organization permitted in the country of operation. When more than two organizations participate, the resultant joint venture is sometimes referred to as a **consortium**.

One may find almost every conceivable combination of partners in joint ventures. They may include, for example, two firms from the same country joining together in a foreign market, such as Standard Oil-California and International Minerals and Chemicals in India. They may involve a foreign company joining with a local company, such as Sears Roebuck and Simpsons in Canada. Companies from two or more countries may establish a joint venture in a third country—for example, Alcan (Canadian) and Pechiney (French) in Argentina. The ventures may be formed between a private company and a local government (sometimes called mixed ventures), such as Philips (Dutch) with the Indonesian government. Even some government-controlled companies have had joint ventures abroad, such as Dutch State Mines with Pittsburgh Plate Glass in the United States. The more firms are involved in the ownership, the more complex the ownership arrangement is. For example, Australia Aluminum is owned by two U.S. companies (American Metal Climax and Anaconda), two Japanese companies (Sumitomo Chemical Company and Showa Binko), one Dutch company (Holland Aluminum), and one German company (Vereinigte Aluminum Werke).

The arguments for and against the sharing of ownership apply as well to joint ventures. Certain types of firms have a greater tolerance for joint ventures than others.[53] Firms with higher tolerance include those that are new at foreign operations and those with decentralized decision making domestically, very often the multiproduct companies. Since the latter firms are accustomed to extending control downward in their organizations, it is an easier transition to do the same thing internationally.

BUY VERSUS BUILD DECISION

A foreign direct investment may be made by acquiring an interest in an existing operation or by constructing new facilities. Each of these alternatives has advantages and disadvantages, and the preference a firm has for one or the other may affect the feasibility of investing in a given country. A firm may, for example, be willing to go only to a country in which it can acquire ongoing operations.

Reasons for Buying

- Get ongoing operation, no start-up problems
- May be easier to finance
- Does not add capacity in market

A major motive for seeking acquisitions is that a potential investor may find it difficult either to transfer some resource to a foreign operation or to acquire that resource locally for a new facility. One such resource is personnel, particularly if the local labor market is tight. Instead of paying higher compensation rates than competitors to entice employees away from their old jobs, the buy-in approach gains not only labor and management but also a whole organization structure through which these personnel may interact. Acquisitions may also be a means of gaining the goodwill and brand identification that are important for mass consumer products, especially if the cost and risk of breaking in a new brand are high. If a company must depend substantially on local financing rather than on the transfer of capital, it may be easier to gain access to local capital if an acquisition is made. For one thing, local capital suppliers may be more familiar with an ongoing operation than with the foreign enterprise. Second, an existing company may sometimes be acquired through an exchange of stock, thus circumventing home country exchange controls.

Acquisitions may in other ways reduce costs and risks as well as provide quicker results. One may be able to buy facilities, particularly of a bankrupt operation, for less than it would cost to build plants at current construction costs. If an investor fears that a market does not justify added capacity, acquisition avoids the risk of depressed prices and lower unit sales per producer that might result from new facilities. Finally, by buying a company an investor avoids the high expenses caused by inefficiencies during the start-up period and also gets an immediate cash flow rather than tying up funds for the period of construction.

Reasons for Building

- No desired firm available to acquire
- May get problems carried over
- May be harder to finance

While the aforementioned advantages may be possible through acquisitions, a potential investor will not necessarily be able to gain them. Since foreign investments are frequently made where there is little or no competition, it may be difficult to locate a company to buy. In addition, governmental restrictions may prevent the purchase of firms because of fears of such things as the lessening of competition or the dominance by foreign enterprises. Those firms that can be acquired may create substantial problems for the investor—personnel and labor relations may be both poor and difficult to change, bad will rather than goodwill may have accrued to existing brands, or facilities may be inefficient and poorly located in relationship to future potential markets. Finally, local financing may be easier rather than harder if one builds facilities, particularly if the investor plans to tap development banks for part of its financial requirements.

Some Experiences

- Buy-ins not usually as successful because
  - half-diversifications
  - get less-well-run operations

To date the most extensive study of international acquisitions included 407 acquisitions made by eighty-four firms in Europe.[54] This study concluded that, although there are some notable success stories, acquisition of an interest in foreign firms gave low payoffs in comparison with other methods of penetration. According to the firms themselves, 50 percent of the acquisitions by U.S. MNEs and 46 percent by European MNEs were "failures or not worth repeating." There was no single reason for this high perceived failure rate; however, several factors were important. One of these included "half-diversifications," which involved gaining interest in a firm that was much less similar to the MNE than would appear on the surface. In these cases, management was sometimes lulled into a false sense of security when, in fact, the acquisition meant dealing with very different types of customers or utilizing an unfamiliar technology. Another factor was that companies had a tendency to acquire not very profitable enterprises with the belief that they could turn them around with new management, an assumption that was seldom valid.

MANAGING FOREIGN ARRANGEMENTS

Chapter 17 discusses organization and control strategies for international operations. However, the forms of foreign involvement examined in this chapter have some unique characteristics that warrant discussion at this point.

Contracts with Other Firms

- When contracting another firm
  - must still monitor performance
  - must assess whether to take over operations themselves
  - work out conflicts and disputes

Even though a company may find it beneficial to rely on other firms at home or abroad to carry out a part or all of its foreign business functions, this does not relieve management of the responsibility for these functions. Management must periodically assess whether the functions should be carried out internally. Great care should be taken to ensure that the best firms are involved and that they are performing the jobs of making, selling, or servicing the product in an adequate manner.

We have already alluded to the major reason for getting other companies to perform functions overseas. If an outside firm can perform the same functions (assuming the same quality) at a cheaper rate, a company should give little consideration to taking on the duties itself. If it can do them more cheaply itself, there may still be justification for getting someone else to do the work. Every company has limited resources, which it should use to the best advantage. If the resources can be used to a better advantage in other activities, then it will pay to commit those resources to activities with a higher return and get someone else to commit resources to the pursuit of foreign business, which should yield a return to both firms. Two subjective factors also enter into the analysis. Management may simply not feel capable of doing as good a job as an outside firm. Management may also feel that the commitment of resources abroad would incur too large a risk for the firm. Since situations are fluid, decisions should be reexamined from time to time.

In choosing a firm to handle overseas business, one should consider professional qualifications, personal attributes, and motivation. Unfortunately, there is no way of precisely measuring these factors, nor is there a magic formula for weighing one qualification against another. Among professional attributes is the proven ability to handle similar business.

A myriad of possible conflicts can develop between the companies. Although any agreement should specify provisions for termination and should include means to settle disputes, these are costly and cumbersome means of achieving objectives. It is much better for both parties, if possible, to settle disagreements on a personal basis. The ability to develop a rapport with the management of another firm is thus an important consideration in choosing a representative.

Management should also estimate potential sales, determine whether quality standards are being met, and assess servicing requirements in order to check whether the other firm is doing an adequate job. Goals should be set mutually so that both parties understand what is expected, and the expectations should be spelled out in the contractual agreements.

Multiple Forms

- Same firm will usually use different forms simultaneously
  - same operation may evolve to different form over time
  - evolvement may lead to internal strains in the organization

It has been observed that most firms move through stages of increased involvement. Exporting usually precedes foreign production, and contracting for another firm to handle foreign business generally precedes handling it internally. A firm may be at different stages for different products and for different markets. A firm may also feel that differences in country characteristics necessitate diverse forms of involvement. Because of the multiproduct nature of most companies, diverse stages may accompany the varied products sold in the same country.

Dissension may develop internally as a firm's international operations evolve. For instance, a move from exporting to foreign production may reduce the size of a domestic product division. Various profit centers may all think that they have rights to the sales in a country the firm is about to penetrate. The legal, technical, and marketing personnel may have entirely different perspectives on contractual agreements. It may be feasible under these circumstances to use a team approach to evaluate decisions and performance. A firm must also develop means of evaluating performance by separating those things that are controllable and noncontrollable by personnel in different profit centers.

SUMMARY

- The forms of foreign involvement differ in terms of internal versus external handling of activities and in terms of the portion of resources committed at home versus abroad.
- Although the mode employed for foreign operations should be examined in terms of a firm's strategic objectives, the choice will often involve a trade-off among objectives.

- Among the factors that will influence the choice of operating mode are legal conditions, the firm's experience, competition factors, political and economic risk, and the nature of the assets to be exploited.

- Licensing is granting another firm the use of some rights, such as patents, trademarks, or know-how, usually for a fee. It is a means of establishing foreign production that may minimize capital outlays, prevent the free use of the assets by other firms, allow the receipt of assets from other firms in return, and allow for income in some markets where exportation or investment are not feasible.

- Among the major controversies concerning the terms of licensing agreements are the control of use of assets as they may affect future competitive relationships, the secrecy of technology and contract terms, the method and amount of payment, and how to treat transfers to a firm's controlled foreign facilities.

- International agreements have been made to protect important intangible assets—patents, trademarks, and copyrights. Since millions of dollars are often spent in the development of these assets, worldwide protection is a necessity.

- One of the big problems for firms with intangible assets in recent years has been the pirating of the assets in countries that are not signatories to international agreements or that do not actively enforce their laws on the asset protection.

- Franchising differs from licensing in that a trademark is an essential asset for the franchisee's business *and* the franchisor assists in the operation of the business on a continuing basis.

- Management contracts are a means of securing income with little capital outlay. They are usually used for expropriated properties in LDCs, for new operations, and for facilities with operating problems.

- Turnkey operations involve a contract for construction of operating facilities owned by someone else. In recent years, most of these have been very large and diverse, thus necessitating specialized skills and abilities to deal with top-level governmental authorities.

- In the absence of control of vertical operations through ownership, firms are increasingly achieving similar objectives through long-term contract and output sharing arrangements.

- Companies usually want to own 100 percent of their foreign operations, if possible, in order to secure control and to prevent the dilution of profits. However, sharing ownership is widespread because host countries want local participation and because rapid foreign expansion has necessitated that firms bring in outside resources.

- Joint ventures are a special type of ownership sharing in which equity is owned by a few organizations rather than the public at large. There are various combinations of ownership, including government and private, same or different nationalities, and two or several organizations participating.

- Contracting foreign business does not negate management's responsibility to ensure that company resources are being worked adequately. This involves constantly assessing the work of the outsiders and evaluating new alternatives.

- Firms may use different forms for their foreign operations in different countries or for different products. As diversity increases, the task of coordinating and managing the foreign operations becomes more complex.

C A S E   ## FINDING A POLYPROPYLENE LICENSE[55]

In 1974 the Northern Petrochemical Company (NPC), a subsidiary of Northern Natural Gas (now named Internorth), decided that it would like to get into polypropylene production. The decision was based on an analysis of NPC's production capabilities and on a forecast of future market demand. From a production standpoint, NPC was already making propylene, which is a precursor of and building block for polypropylene. The parent company could supply many of the raw materials for the new product. From a market standpoint, NPC estimated that, since the introduction of polypropylene in the early 1960s, the compound growth rate of sales had been somewhere between 15 and 20 percent. They also estimated that future growth would be even more rapid because of high benzene prices and possible shortages, which would depress sales of polystyrene. Polypropylene could substitute in many cases for polystyrene. The polypropylene market could be divided into two segments depending on the properties put into the product. The first, homopolymer, comprised 85 percent of the market and was used for such applications as carpet backing, packaging film, appliance moldings, and fibers. The second, copolymer, included products such as battery cases, luggage, and high-clarity bottles. The copolymer sector was of most interest to NPC because this was a newer technical area in which they could expect growth and less entrenched competition.

NPC felt that further inroads for sales were possible as continued performance and cost-effectiveness were improved. One possibility would be in automotive component fabrication. An entry into polypropylene production would necessitate a continued commitment to research and development in order to improve both product and process technology. NPC was willing to invest over $100 million in the project but lacked the technical capabilities. To use its own R&D efforts would greatly delay market entry. It would also mean the risk of legal complications because there were already numerous patent infringement cases pending because producing companies claimed that others had copied various aspects of their technology.

The total sales for Northern Natural Gas were approximately $1 billion for 1974, of which about 20 percent were accounted for by the NPC subsidiary. About 62 percent of Northern's sales was of natural gas to customers in the United States and Canada. The NPC petrochemical subsidiary was growing faster than the rest of the company and had had successes in such products as antifreeze and LDPE resins. The technology for the resins had been licensed from another firm after NPC had identified markets for use in trash can liners and leaf bags. A commercial success with technology developed externally had therefore been feasibly demonstrated.

NPC next set out to find a firm that would license the right on acceptable terms for them to use polypropylene technology. Of the nine producers in the United States, only three were believed to be in an advanced stage of copolymer development. The first of these was Hercules, which had a dominant position in the entire polypropylene market. Hercules was interested because some of its customers wanted a secondary supply source in case of problems of supply from Hercules. NPC felt that such an arrangement was not compatible with its strategy, since it would inevitably place NPC in Hercules' shadow as a secondary supplier. NPC next contacted the Rexene Division of Dart Industries. Rexene rejected outright any license because it did not want another competitor in the market. No agreement could be reached with Phillips Petroleum for two reasons. Phillips had not yet commercialized the aspect of production that NPC considered critical. Phillips was furthermore not enthusiastic about creating another competitor.

Having exhausted domestic possibilities, NPC next looked abroad. Identification of possible companies abroad was more difficult because many of those companies were believed to have a bigger lag between product development work and commercial introduction of the products. In other words, one could not depend on looking at what was currently being sold to find all the firms with a current capability. Because of market differences, some of the European and Japanese producers had been known to hold on to a development for several years before commercializing it. After some preliminary inquiries, five firms from four countries were identified as possibilities. These were Tokoyama Soda and Mitsubishi Petrochemical from Japan, Solvay from Belgium, Montedison from Italy, and BASF from West Germany. Contacts were made with all these companies and showed that none had fully commercialized advanced copolymer production. In order to proceed to some possible agreement, it was necessary for each to share with NPC its research and development data and to make special plant test runs to satisfy requests for further information. Interestingly, each was taking a very different approach to make the same product.

If NPC were to proceed to negotiations, then it would be necessary to choose the company and method that were most likely to reach the desired end results. NPC decided that BASF offered the best potential. BASF was and remains one of the giants among chemical companies. Its 1974 sales were expected to exceed $8 billion. About 55 percent of BASF's sales were outside of West Germany. In 1973 its sales in the United States were $523 million. In addition to exporting to the U.S. market, BASF had substantial U.S. investments. The most notable of these were Wyandotte Chemical, which it fully owned, and a joint venture with Dow Chemical called Dow Badische. Increases in U.S. investment had been running between $45 million and $55 million per year. This was expected to go to $90 million beginning in 1975. The chairman of BASF, Dr. Matthias Seefelder, announced that he expected no growth in the German market for 1975 because of a reluctance on the part of consumers to buy. This would make it more difficult to continue to infuse German funds into the U.S. operations, which were saddled with uncompetitive soda ash and chlorine plants. Given this cash flow problem, it was hard for BASF to make commitments for market development of new products. Dr. Seefelder also indicated that the company's main specialities (plastics, synthetic fibers, and dyestuffs) were encountering difficulties and that it would be necessary to give greater attention to other products that BASF had already developed. A strong West German mark was making German products expensive abroad, thus jeopardizing exports.

The early stages of negotiations between the two companies left the parties in opposition as to which technology would be licensed provided that an agreement on other points could be reached. BASF was willing to sell the technology that it had already developed but was not willing to make a commitment to continue copolymer research, which was not now a high priority for them because of their expectation of not being able to get substantial near-term sales in Europe. Nor was BASF willing yet to commit itself to sharing the future technology if and when it was developed. NPC wanted more than the pilot plant advancements and was in a position of having to convince BASF to alter its position if an agreement were to be reached that met NPC's original expectations.

QUESTIONS

1. What might NPC do to try to convince BASF to alter its position?
2. How do you assess the probability of the two firms coming to a mutual agreement?

3. What should NPC do if BASF is unwilling to license technology beyond the pilot plant stage?

4. What risks have the firms already incurred by going this far in their discussions?

5. From the position of BASF, what would be the pros and cons of entering an agreement along the lines that NPC has suggested?

6. In this case, NPC was seeking to buy technology. How might a search process have differed if NPC had been trying to sell a technology?

NOTES

1. Data for the case were taken from James Flanigan, "The Strategy," *Forbes,* October 29, 1979, pp. 42–52; Gerald F. Seib, "Mexican Magnates," *Wall Street Journal,* November 12, 1979, p. 1; "Yamaha Plans to Make Motorcycles in Spain, Mexico, and Nigeria," *Wall Street Journal,* January 14, 1981, p. 30; "Massey Ferguson Sets Sale of Mexican Unit," *Wall Street Journal,* September 10, 1979, p. 3; "Grupo Industrial Alfa Unit Completes Private Note Sale," *Wall Street Journal,* March 18, 1981, p. 43; "Dravo Agrees to Market Type of Plant for Grupo," *Wall Street Journal,* September 23, 1980, p. 38; Hugh O'Shaughnessy, "A Hive of Private Enterprise," *Financial Times,* May 4, 1979, p. 34; Christopher Lorenz, "A Front-Runner in Mexican Industry," *Financial Times,* June 1, 1979, p. 16; "Mexico: Exporting a Cheaper Way of Making Steel," *Business Week,* June 11, 1979, p. 53; Lawrence Rout, "Fading Miracle," *Wall Street Journal,* June 10, 1982, p. 1+; "Fresh Bailout Troubles for Mexico's Alfa," *Business Week,* March 1, 1982, p. 36; Steve Frazier, "Mexico's Grupo Alfa Wins Easier Terms from Foreign Bankers on Part of Its Debt," *Wall Street Journal,* May 1, 1984, p. 39.

2. For a discussion of the many trade-offs, see James D. Goodnow, "Individual Product: Market Transactional Mode of Entry Strategies—Some Eclectic Decision-Making Formats," paper presented at Academy of International Business meetings in New Orleans, October 24, 1980.

3. Ian H. Giddy and Stephen Young, "Do New Forms of Multinational Enterprise Require New Theories?," working paper no. 322A, Columbia University Graduate School of Business, April 1980; also, R. T. Carstairs and L. S. Welch, "Licensing and the Internationalization of Smaller Companies: Some Australian Evidence," *Management International Review,* Vol. 22, No. 3, 1982, pp. 33–44, found that firms typically export before licensing, which in turn precedes direct investment.

4. Ian H. Giddy and Alan M. Rugman, "A Model of Trade, Foreign Direct Investment and Licensing," working paper no. 274A, Columbia University Graduate School of Business, December 1979.

5. See, for example, Marcus B. Finnegan and Brian G. Brunsvold, "Antitrust Problems in Licensing," in *Current Trends in Domestic and International Licensing 1977,* Tom Arnold, ed. (New York: Practicing Law Institute, 1977), pp. 263–292.

6. "American Home Plans Drug Venture in U.S. with French Company," *Wall Street Journal,* June 3, 1981, p. 54.

7. David Ford and Chris Ryan, "Taking Technology to Market," *Harvard Business Review,* March–April 1981, p. 118.

8. Alan Riding, "Cartier's Mexican Look-Alike," *New York Times,* October 17, 1980, p. D1+.

9. "Oleg Cassini Inc. Sues Firm over Licensing," *Wall Street Journal,* March 28, 1984, p. 5.

10. "Coca Cola Ordered by India to Disclose Formula for Drink," *Wall Street Journal,* August 10, 1977, p. 11.

11. See, for example, Samuel A. Morley and Gordon W. Smith, "The Choice of Technology: Multinational Firms in Brazil," *Economic Development and Cultural Change,* January 1977, pp. 240–241.

12. Edwin Mansfield, "International Technology Transfer: Forms, Resource Requirements, and Policies," *American Economic Review,* May 1975, pp. 372–382.

13. Alfred Wolf, "Trends in International Technology License Trade," *Intereconomics,* May 1973, pp. 150–151.

14. The difficulty of choosing a fair price is discussed in Wilson B. Brown, "Islands of Conscious Power: MNCs in the Theory of the Firm," *MSU Business Topics,* Summer 1976, pp. 37–45.

15. Thomas Horst, "American Multinationals and the U.S. Economy," *American Economic Review,* May 1976, pp. 150–152.

16. Claudio V. Vaitsos, *Intercountry Income Distribution and Transnational Enterprises* (Oxford: Clarendon Press, 1974).

17. See, for example, P. Streeten, "Theory of Development Policy," in *Economic Analysis and the Multinational Enterprise,* J. H. Dunning, ed. (London: Allen and Unwin, 1974); G. F. Kopits, "Intrafirm Royalties Crossing Frontiers and Transfer Pricing Behavior," *The Economic Journal,* December 1976; and Donald R. Lessard, "Transfer Prices, Taxes, and Financial Markets: Implications of Internal Financial Transfers within the Multinational Firm," paper presented for the New York University Conference on Economic Issues of Multinational Firms, November 4, 1976.

18. This is taken from D. W. Fewkes, "Positioning the Licensing Unit," *les Nouvelles,* March 1979, pp. 28–33.

19. William T. Ryan and Doria Bonham-Yeaman, "International Patent Cooperation," *Columbia Journal of World Business,* Vol. 17, No. 4, Winter 1982, pp. 63–66.

20. "Expanded Business Volume Reflected in Trademarks Processed," *Commerce Today,* August 20, 1973, p. 16.

21. *Ibid.,* p. 19.

22. Kendall J. Wills, "Booming Underground Industry," *New York Times,* April 8, 1984, p. F6.

23. Paul Lewis, "Counterfeiting of Goods Rises," *New York Times,* October 10, 1983, p. D9.

24. *Ibid.;* and "U.S. Says Counterfeits Cost Concerns Billions of Dollars in Lost Sales," *Wall Street Journal,* February 27, 1984, p. 35.

25. "Publishers Aim New Weapon at Piracy," *Publishers Weekly.* April 27, 1984, pp. 21–22.

26. Louis Kraar, "Fighting the Fakes from Taiwan," *Fortune,* Vol. 107, No. 11, May 30, 1983, pp. 114–116; "Two Who Smuggled Counterfeit Computers Get Prison and Fines," *Wall Street Journal,* May 1, 1984, p. 62; Todd Mason, "How High Tech Foils the Counterfeiters," *Business Week,* May 20, 1985, p. 119.

27. Peter Kerr, "Foreign Piracy of TV Signals Stirs Concern," *New York Times,* October 13, 1983, p. 1A+.

28. Jerry H. Opack, "Likenesses of Licensing, Franchising," *les Nouvelles,* June 1977, pp. 102–105.

29. Philip D. Grub, "Multinational Franchising: A New Trend in Global Expansion," *Journal of International Law and Economics,* June 1972; for information on hotel franchising, see Mitchell C. Lynch, "Chain Reaction," *Wall Street Journal,* May 12, 1978, p. 48.

30. "The Growth of Universal Franchise," *International Management,* November 1979, pp. 19–21.

31. "McDonald's: The Original Recipe Helps It Defy a Down-turn," *Business Week,* May 4, 1981, p. 162.

32. "Japan: A Growing Appetite for U.S. Fast Foods," *Business Week,* April 17, 1978, pp. 48–53.

33. Linda Charlton, "Franchising, Global Venture," *New York Times,* January 27, 1974, p. 30ff.

34. "Judge Revokes License of Paris McDonald's," *International Herald Tribune* (Zurich), September 11–12, 1982, p. 14.

35. Richard Ellison, "An Alternative to Direct Investment Abroad," *International Management,* June 1976, pp. 25–27.

36. "Where Top 250 Found Business in 1984," *Engineering News Record,* July 18, 1985, pp. 41–53.

37. "Nigeria," *Business Week,* October 1, 1979, p. 60.

38. *A Competitive Assessment of the U.S. International Construction Industry* (Washington: U.S. Department of Commerce, International Trade Administration, July 1984).

39. Edgar J. Moor, "Turnkey-Plus Operations," *Business Horizons,* December 1973, pp. 39–44.

40. Louis Berger, "The Construction Scene in Southeast Asia: Who's Getting the Business?" *Worldwide P & I Planning,* January–February 1974, p. 13.

41. Joan Gray, "International Construction," *Financial Times,* April 12, 1985, pp. 13–17.

42. "Mobile Sees Further Role in Saudi Arabia for U.S. Firms after Aramco Take-Over," *Wall Street Journal,* September 25, 1974, p. 7.

43. "Exxon, Dutch-Shell Units and Malaysia Reach Initial Pact on Oil Output Sharing," *Wall Street Journal,* November 17, 1976, p. 4.

44. F. A. Sviridov, ed., *The Role of Patent Information in the Transfer of Technology* (New York: Pergamon Press, 1981), p. 137.

45. Robert Ronstadt and Robert J. Kramer, "Getting the Most out of Innovation Abroad," *Harvard Business Review,* March–April 1982, pp. 94–99; Beth Karlin and George Anders, "Importing Science," *Wall Street Journal,* October 5, 1983, p. 1+.

46. Carl H. Fulda and Warren F. Schwartz, *Regulation of International Trade and Investment* (Mineola, N.Y.: The Foundation Press, 1970), pp. 776–782.

47. A Conference Board survey quoted in "Joint Ventures," *Wall Street Journal,* October 2, 1980, p. 1.

48. Brad Heller, "U.S. Firms Must Propose Joint Ventures to Win a Slice of Huge Saudi Contracts," *Wall Street Journal,* April 13, 1984, p. 31.

49. Robert Wilson, "A Model of Foreign Minority Ownership Patterns: A Sector Analysis by Market Structure and Research and Development Intensity," DBA dissertation, School of Business Administration, Georgia State University, Atlanta, 1971.

50. George Getschow, "Foreign Investment in Mexico Swells," *Wall Street Journal,* May 1981, p. 34.

51. Mike Tharp, "Uneasy Partners," *Wall Street Journal,* November 8, 1976, p. 28.

52. J. Peter Killing, "How to Make a Global Joint Venture Work," *Harvard Business Review,* May–June 1982, pp. 120–127.

53. Lawrence G. Franko, *Joint Venture Survival in Multinational Corporations* (New York: Praeger, 1971); Richard H. Holton, "Making International Joint Ventures Work," in *The Management of Headquarters–Subsidiary Relationships in Multinational Corporations,* Lars Otterbeck, ed. (London: Cower, Aldershot, 1981), pp. 255–267.

54. John Kitching, *Acquisitions in Europe* (Geneva: Business International, 1973); John Kitching, "Winning and Losing with European Acquisitions," *Harvard Business Review,* March–April 1974, pp. 124–136.

55. Data for the case were taken from Ellen Lentz, "Chemical-Group Profits Surge in West Germany," *New York Times,* December 2, 1974, pp. 53–54; Paul Kemezis, "West German Chemical Giants Plan Additional Expansion in U.S.," *New York Times,* February 10, 1975, pp. 39–40; Northern Natural Gas Company, *Annual Report,* 1974; Lou Potempa, "Business Technology Choice," *les Nouvelles,* March 1979, pp. 24–27; Steven P. Galante, "How Foreigners Botch Their U.S. Investments," *Wall Street Journal,* June 6, 1984, p. 32.

16

Geographic Strategies

- To emphasize that firms should develop strategies for their penetration sequence by country and the portion of their resources to be committed on a country-by-country basis.

- To explain how examination of the investment climate can be used as a screening device to limit geographic alternatives to a manageable number.

- To examine the major variables that firms should consider when deciding whether and where to expand abroad.

- To examine some simplifying tools to use in the determination of global geographic strategy.

- To introduce how final investment, reinvestment, and divestment decisions are made.

By any standard, Ford is large. Its 1984 sales of 52.4 billion made it one of the five largest industrial firms in the United States and one of the ten largest in the world. It is also the world's second largest automobile company, holding about 14 percent of the worldwide market in 1984. By any standard, Ford is also highly involved internationally. The company began operations in 1903, and the sixth car it built was exported. By 1911 the company boasted that a man could drive around the world and stop every night at a garage handling Ford parts. By 1930, Ford was manufacturing or assembling automobiles in twenty foreign countries and had sales branches in another ten. In 1980, about half of the Ford's car and truck vehicles were produced and sold outside the United States. Yet as large and internationally involved as Ford is, it must allocate its limited financial and human resources so that emphasis is on those markets and production locations that are most compatible with corporate expectations and objectives.

The present locations of Ford operations are largely due to historical antecedents. Although foreign expansion was a stated objective at Ford's first annual meeting, Ford initially took a fairly passive approach as to where the emphasis would be. Ford's first foreign sales branches and assembly operations, for example, were established in Canada, England, and France because people in those countries approached Ford with proposals.

Early export sales to other countries were highly decentralized in the sense that many potential importers came to Ford to request and receive contracts to serve as distributors. Much of the European expansion was handled through the English operations and the British Commonwealth sales through the Canadian company. Where sales grew most rapidly (e.g., Argentina, Uruguay, and Brazil), Ford established assembly operations in order to save on transportation costs by limiting the bulk of shipments. Much of Ford's early expansion, through exports as well as foreign investment, was in response to external rather than internal impetuses. In other words, Ford did not scan the globe to choose the best locations. Instead, Ford took advantage of opportunities as they came along.

Ford's pattern of international activities has also been affected by criteria that management considered essential. One of these was a guiding policy that it would not manufacture or assemble anywhere without a controlling interest. The concept of control went beyond that of voting shares. In 1930, for example, a Ford group inspected potential production sites in China and reported back to Henry Ford: "This is the deal. If we buy a site in China, the site has to be in the name of a Chinaman because a foreigner can't own land in China." Henry Ford's response was simply, "No." In the 1950s and 1960s, Ford extended this concept of control to the point that nothing short of 100 percent ownership was acceptable. This further influenced Ford's geographic area of emphasis, causing Ford to expend resources to buy out a minority interest in the British company. It also meant the abandonment of production in India and Spain in 1954 (Ford recommenced Spanish production in 1976 and no longer adheres to the 100 percent policy) because the governments of those countries insisted on sharing ownership.

Political conditions have also helped to forge Ford's foreign investment pattern. For example, the French facility was bombed during World War II and was not replaced. Assembly facilities were seized by communist governments in Hungary and Rumania in 1946. It was not until 1977, however, that Ford established a separate department to evaluate the external political environment. The job of that department is to get as much information as possible from different sources in order to evaluate countries as high, medium, or low political risks. Changes in government regulations have often caused Ford to commit a high proportion of its resources to a given area during a given period. This occurred, for example, when Mexico required a higher portion of local content in vehicles, thus forcing Ford to increase its Mexican investment or lose sales there.

In spite of the extended and heavy commitment to foreign operations, Ford's production and sales are highly concentrated in a few countries. In 1984, more than 89 percent of Ford vehicles were produced in just five countries, and about 98 percent in ten countries. Sales are less concentrated; nevertheless, six countries account for about 56 percent of Ford's total. These same six countries comprised about 58 percent of the total world demand for vehicles. Because of the heavier commitments in some countries than in others, which have come about for a number of reasons, Ford's competitive position is much stronger in some markets than in others. In the United Kingdom and West Germany, where Ford has large and long-standing investments, its market share in 1984 was 27.9 percent and 12.5 percent, respectively. Elsewhere in Europe its market share was only 8.7 percent.

One of the results of Ford's international commitment is that dependence on multiple markets and facilities has had an effect of minimizing year-to-year sales and profit fluctuations. This is because demand and price levels may move differently in various countries. From 1981 to 1982, for example, Ford's U.S. vehicle production fell by 91.6 thousand. This was largely made up by a 64.9 thousand increase in EC output. In 1980, Ford lost over $2 billion in the United States, earned $775 million in Britain, and lost $200 million elsewhere in the world. This points out not only the positive effect of geographic diversification on the smoothing of earnings, but also the importance of shifting resources in order to take advantage in areas of greatest profit potential.

With huge amounts of fixed assets already in place, Ford cannot easily abandon countries and then pick them up again. What it can do, however, is to compare the attractiveness of each country with actual and potential Ford operations and move toward greater emphasis on those countries with the most promising outlooks. Ford does this separately for each of its major product groups. The reason for the separation is that different market conditions may affect various product groups. In 1979, for example, Ford tractors showed the biggest percentage unit increase in sales of the decade while car and truck sales fell.

One of the tools that Ford uses to aid decision makers in choosing where to emphasize their marketing efforts is a country comparison matrix. Ford staff members rank countries on one axis in terms of how attractive the country appears for sales of a specific type of product being considered, for example, tractors, trucks, or automobiles. On the other axis the same staff members rank the countries in terms of Ford's competitive capabilities for the specific markets. The resultant plotting helps the decision makers to narrow their major considerations primarily to the areas of the world that both look attractive and seem to offer the best fit with Ford's unique capabilities. This is by no means the end of the evaluation process. The exercise does, however, enable the decision makers to concentrate on more detailed analyses of a manageable list of alternatives. It also enables them to progress to interrelated decisions, such as where to locate production for the chosen markets.

INTRODUCTION

- Early international expansion tends to be passive
- Later expansion
  - cannot take advantage of all opportunities
- Big questions
  - where to sell?
  - where to produce?

Ford's international expansion is typical of many firms as they become more heavily involved abroad. In the early stages, companies may lack the experience and expertise to devise strategies for sequencing countries in the most advantageous way. Instead, they respond to opportunities that become apparent to them, and many of these turn out to be highly advantageous. As they gain more international experience, however, they come to realize that they seldom have enough resources to take advantage of all the opportunities. They see that the commitment of human, technical, and financial resources to one locale may result in foregoing projects in other areas. Consequently, foreign operations become an integral part of companies' decisions on how to allocate resources.

There are two interrelated questions concerning geographic areas of emphasis: Which markets should be served and where should production be located to serve these markets? Frequently, the answer to these two questions will be the same, particularly if transportation costs or governmental regulations require local production for serving the chosen market. In 1984, for example, Ford sold about 26.7 thousand vehicles in Mexico. These were produced within Mexico because, once a decision was made to serve that market, Mexican regulations dictated that the production be located there. In other cases, however, the sales and production may be in different countries. For example, Ford serves the French market in vehicles from its German production facilities.

The market and production location decisions may be highly interdependent for other reasons as well. A company may have excess production capacity already in place that will influence its relative capabilities of serving different country markets. Or a firm may find a given market very attractive but forego sales there because of an unwillingness to invest in those production locations necessary to serve the market.

A firm's international objectives should not be substantially different from those that guide actions domestically. Any foreign operations should complement domestic ones, and vice versa, so that fulfillment of overall company goals is enhanced. Because of the uniqueness of each firm's situation, the decisions of where to sell and produce are apt to be quite variable. Firms seeking foreign markets, for example, will have different considerations from firms that view foreign operations as a means of acquiring scarce or cheaper resources. Furthermore, even if the objectives and situations were similar, there would still be differences in patterns because of varying assumptions about such unknown factors as future costs and prices, reactions of competitors, technology, and a host of other internal and external constraints.

The determination of an overall geographic strategy must be dynamic. Conditions change, and results do not always conform to expectations. A plan must therefore be flexible enough to let a company (1) respond to new opportunities and (2) withdraw from activities with inadequate expected contributions. Unfortunately, there is little agreement on a comprehensive theory either for explaining past geographic patterns or for optimizing the allocation of resources among countries. Nevertheless, a number of theories frequently put forward to explain capital expenditures, trade, and strategy formulation are applicable to the international sphere.

A firm may expand its sales by marketing more of its existing product line, by adding products to its line, or by some combination of the two. Each of these alternatives has international options, and each may be more associated with certain forms of international business operating forms than with others.[2] In this chapter we will assume, for the most part, that the company has decided on its product line or product portfolio. This is a realistic assumption. Companies do frequently have to alter their product characteristics in order to satisfy foreign consumers. However, they usually start out with the question such as "Where can we sell more of our communications equipment?" rather than with the question "What new product can we make in order to maximize sales in the Greek market?" The reasons and considerations for altering products and product portfolios will be discussed in Chapter 18.

SCANNING FOR ALTERNATIVES

- May overlook opportunities
  - don't think of some locales
  - tend to think that whole region is same
  - may not examine because of conditions not *really* adverse to company
- May examine too many
  - detailed feasibility is expensive
- Certain key factors may be good indicators of likely possibilities

In the opening case, Ford used scanning techniques so that decision makers could perform a much more detailed analysis among a manageable number of geographic alternatives that looked most promising. This is a useful exercise because, without a systematic identification procedure, there is a risk that a company might consider too few or too many possibilities.

Risk of Overlooking Opportunities

As a company tries to optimize its sales or minimize its costs, it can easily overlook or disregard some viable options. Rather than being rejected, potential projects in many countries may not be carried out simply because they are never thought of. A U.S. manager thinking of foreign operations may immediately consider countries such as Canada, Japan, and West Germany; however, some very small countries may actually hold better opportunities. It is interesting to note that the tiny country of Mauritania has hired a New York public relations firm to overcome some of the market imperfections affecting it.

Even if considered, certain locales may be eliminated almost immediately for less than fully rational reasons before they are sufficiently examined for investment possibilities. A study of thirty-eight companies found that whole groups of countries were sometimes lumped together and rejected for consideration. For instance, Zambia might not be considered because "Africa is too risky."[3] Another study found that a country may be rejected because of one or two characteristics without enough examination of the company's assets, needs, or opportunities to determine whether or not these characteristics should really be given high importance. A large U.S. chemical company eliminated Brazil as a potential candidate for investment because of the rapid devaluation of the currency, even though the firm's rivals were expanding heavily there.[4]

Risk of Examining Too Many

A detailed analysis of every alternative might result in maximized sales or the pinpointing of a least-cost location; however, the cost of so many studies would erode profits. It has been noted that for a company with 1000 products that might locate in any of 100 countries, there are 100,000 different situations to be analyzed. Within each of these situations there are other alternatives as well, such as whether to export or to set up a foreign production unit. If there are conditions that would greatly enhance the probability of making or not making an investment, it is useful to examine those first, before completing a more detailed feasibility study.

The Investment Climate

In the Ford case at the beginning of the chapter, certain investments were foregone because Ford could not gain sufficient control of the operation. Decision makers' perceptions of investment climate will determine whether a detailed feasibility study will be undertaken and the terms under which a project will or will not be initiated. The term **investment climate** is elusive, meaning different things to different people at different times; however, it refers to those external conditions in host countries that could significantly affect the success or failure of a foreign business enterprise. A number of studies have queried companies as to what they see as either unacceptable terms or obstacles to foreign investment. The results have been very similar. Not all firms consider all the same variables, but certain items are mentioned by large numbers of investors as important for reaching decisions. The analysis of the investment climate serves a key role in limiting alternatives to a manageable number.

INFLUENTIAL VARIABLES

- Use of examining key indicators
  - determine order of entry
  - set allocation rate among countries
- Categories of key indicators
  - market size
  - ease and compatibility of operations for company
  - cost and resource availability
  - risk and uncertainty

The following discussion highlights the factors that are most often mentioned as influencing where sales and production emphasis will be placed. Some of the variables are more important for the sales allocation decision; some others are more important for the production location decision. Some are, of course, important for both decisions, especially when foreign investment is necessary for serving a given foreign market.

The ranking or prioritizing of countries is useful for aiding decision makers in (1) determining the order of entry into potential markets and (2) setting the allocation and rate of expansion among the different markets. The former determination assumes that a firm cannot or does not want to go everywhere at once; consequently, it chooses to allocate its resources first to the more desirable locations. The latter assumes that a firm is already selling or producing in many locales, perhaps even in all that are feasible, but wishes to decide how much of its efforts should be expended in one country versus another.

Market Size

- Expectation of sales growth probably major attraction

The importance of sales potential cannot be overlooked when comparing countries as markets or as production locations. Sales are important in ascertaining which locations will be considered and whether an investment will be made.

In a study for the U.S. Department of Commerce that involved detailed interviews with international executives of seventy-six major U.S. international companies, the National Industrial Conference Board concluded that sales growth was the major motivation for foreign investment.[5] The assumption, of course, is that sales will be made at a price above cost; consequently, where there are sales, there will be profit.

As was the situation in the Ford case, many firms begin sales to an area very passively. They may appoint an intermediate firm to promote sales for them or a licensee to produce on their behalf. If there is a demonstrated increase in sales, the company may consider investing more of its own resources. The generation of exports to a given country is an indication that sales may be made from production located in that country as well. As long as there is no threat to export sales, however, there is little to motivate a shift to production abroad. The motivating force may come about in one of several ways. Recall these from Chapter 6, "Why Direct Foreign Investment Takes Place." They include such factors as whether or not the exporter is nearing domestic capacity utilization and the likelihood of government action to restrict trade movements.

In some cases it is possible to obtain past and current sales figures on a country-to-country basis for the type product that your company would like to sell. In many cases, such figures are unavailable. Whether available or not, one has to make some projections about what will happen to sales in the future. Such data as gross national product, per capita income, growth rates, size of the middle class, and level of industrialization are often used as indicators of market size and opportunity. Methods of projecting demand from the indicators are examined in Chapter 18. There are many problems in comparing these data across countries, a subject that is discussed in the next chapter.

Ease of Operations/Compatibility

- High operating attraction to countries
  - nearby
  - with same language
  - with large population and high per capita income

Geographic, language, and market similarities. Recall in the Ford case at the beginning of the chapter that earnings and vehicle sales were smoothed because of operations in various parts of the world. Because investors generally prefer smoother performance patterns, they are even willing to pay more for assets in internationally diversified firms.[6] One might expect, therefore, that companies would seek to go first to those countries whose economies are least correlated with that of the home country. The evidence, however, is to the contrary, whether they go abroad in related or unrelated operations in terms of marketing systems, production technologies, or vertical or horizontal products.[7]

Regardless of the industry involved, it has been noted that U.S. firms usually make their first direct investment in Canada. The United Kingdom and Mexico alternate for the second and third locations. Germany, France, and Australia have most of the fourth, fifth, and sixth ranks.[8] This fairly remarkable similarity in patterns among dissimilar industries seems to be due to the fact that decision makers perceive a greater ease of operations in those countries that are near the home country. Canada and Mexico rank high because of geographic proximity. This makes it easier and cheaper to control foreign subsidiaries because of the cost and speed of traveling to the nearer-by areas. This seems to be the only explanation for two so dissimilar countries to be ranked so high. The common language helps to explain Canada, the United Kingdom, and Australia. Managers feel more comfortable in operating at early stages of international expansion in their own language and in similar legal systems evolving from British law. The language and cultural similarity may also lower operating costs and risks because of not having to work through translations. Finally, market similarity tends to exert a considerable influence on the early location of foreign operations. All the leading countries except Mexico have high per capita incomes, and all except Canada and Australia have large populations.

- Negative attraction
  - not directly measurable

Red tape. One of the things that companies frequently try to factor into their comparison of country-by-country opportunities is the degree of red tape necessary to operate in a given country. Red tape would include such things as the degree of difficulty in getting permission to bring in expatriate personnel, to obtain licenses to produce and sell certain goods, and to satisfy government agencies on such matters as taxes, labor conditions, and environmental conditions. Red tape is not directly measurable; therefore a common technique is to have people who are familiar with operating conditions in a group of countries rate them as high, medium, or low on this parameter.

- Best acceptance of proposal when
  - fit size, technology, and other factors familiar to company personnel
  - high percentage of ownership allowed
  - profits easily remitted

Fit with company capabilities and policies. After the alternatives are pared to a reasonable number, it is necessary to prepare much more detailed feasibility studies, which are quite expensive. Some management consultants have noted that firms very often get committed to locations that are far from optimal for them.[9] This is because the more time and money they invest in examining an alternative, the more likely they are to accept that project regardless of its merits. The consultants suggest that companies first examine very carefully why they are considering a commitment and to be more leery of those that are examined simply because other firms are going there or because they want to get a feel for the market. The project manager should be someone with broad experience so that a corporate point of view is maintained. The feasibility study should have from the start a series of clear-cut decision points so that sufficient information is gathered at each stage and so that, if a study is unlikely to result in an investment, it may be terminated before too much is spent on it.

One of the ways to make the surveys more manageable in scope is by ensuring that proposals fit the general framework of the organization. These proposals, if presented to management decision makers, will have a higher probability of acceptance.[10] Consideration may be limited to locales where such variables as product and plant size will be within the experience of present managers. In fact, so many guidelines and policies may be set up that very few possibilities are investigated for final feasibility. From a policy standpoint, management may find it useful to ensure that its proposal group includes personnel with backgrounds in each functional area—marketing, finance, personnel, engineering, and production. While various factors might cause ultimate decision makers to reject a proposal once a feasibility study is completed, two factors stand out as sufficiently important to sway large numbers of organizations. These are restrictions on the percentage of ownership that can be held and on maximum allowed remittance of profits.[11]

Another consideration is the perceived absorption capability of the country in relation to the company's planned or preferred type of operating characteristics. From a production standpoint the movement of capital to a foreign country usually necessitates combining that capital (or other transferred resource) with local inputs. This may place some severe restrictions on the movement by individual companies to given locales. Let us take the example of labor. The existence of a large supply of unemployed people in a capital-short country is no indication that labor of the type needed by the investor is available. The skill level may be such that the company would have to use one of several expensive alternatives (e.g., training, redesigning production or methods, or increasing supervision) in order to utilize the labor. This added expense might not only reduce the return from the capital to the point at which it would no longer be attractive, but firms might also not assent to moving so far from their production experience. Consider also a company that would need to add local capital to what it is willing to bring in. Local equity markets may be poorly developed or completely nonexistent. Furthermore, local borrowing may be prohibitively expensive.

The fit for a particular country is important regardless of whether the company is considering an initial entry or trying to decide how to allocate resources among countries where it already has operations. Take marketing capabilities, for example. Let us say that a company has already developed a product in one country that has been successfully marketed through mass advertising methods. It is normally far easier and less costly to move that product into a country where product alterations are minimal or unnecessary and where there are few restrictions on the use of advertising.

Costs and Resource Availabilities

- More important for production location decision
  - labor cost usually most important

The discussion thus far has centered on market-seeking operations. Companies are engaged internationally in the pursuit of foreign resources as well. If a resource is to be transferred, such as a raw material or technology, the analysis is somewhat simpler than that for a resource that will be used

● Should consider different ways to produce same product

in producing a product or component abroad for export into other markets. In the final analysis it will be necessary to examine the costs of labor, raw material inputs, capital, taxes, and transfer costs in relation to productivity to approximate a least-cost location. Before all of this information is collected within a final feasibility study, there are indicators that will aid decision makers in narrowing the alternatives to be considered.

It has been noted that employee compensation is for most companies the most important cost in their manufacturing facilities abroad, accounting for over 60 percent of costs other than taxes.[12] In most cases, therefore, current labor costs, trends in the costs, and unemployment rates are usually useful proxies for making comparisons. One must be aware, though, that labor is not a homogeneous commodity; the country may lack the specific skill levels required. An indication is whether the country is able to turn out competitive products embodying inputs that are similar to those required in the production being considered.

If costs other than labor are more important for the particular product in question, then it is useful to add these into the analysis. If precise data are not available, useful proxies on operating conditions may be used, such as the degree of infrastructure development and the openness to imported components.

Another problem inhibiting the manufacturing cost comparison among countries is that there has been a dramatic change in manufacturing techniques. With increases in the number of ways the same product can be made, it is necessary to compare, for example, the cost of producing by using a large labor input in Malaysia with the use of robotics in the United States.[13]

Risk and Uncertainty

● Most investors prefer certainty to uncertainty

Is a projected rate of return of 9 percent in Nigeria the same thing as a 9 percent rate in France? Should return on investment be calculated on the basis of the entire earnings of a foreign subsidiary or just on the earnings that can be remitted to the parent? Is it ever rational to invest in a country with a very uncertain political and economic future? These are but a few of the unresolved questions that firms must debate when making international capital budgeting decisions.

Given the same expected return, most decision makers prefer a more certain to a less certain outcome. An estimated rate of return on investment (ROI) is calculated by averaging the various returns deemed possible for investments. The result, as shown in Table 16.1, is that two identical projected ROIs may have quite different certainties of achievement as well as diverse probabilities around the expected return. In the table the certainty of the 10 percent projected ROI is higher for investment B than for investment A. Furthermore, the probability of earning at least 10 percent is also

TABLE 16.1 _____

COMPARISON OF ROI CERTAINTY

ROI as percentage	Investment A		Investment B	
	Probability	Weighted value*	Probability	Weighted value*
0	.15	0	0	0
5	.20	1.0	.30	1.5
10	.30	3.0	.40	4.0
15	.20	3.0	.30	4.5
20	.15	3.0	0	0
Estimated ROI		10%		10%

* Calculated by multiplying ROI as percentage by probability.

higher (70 percent versus 65 percent) for that alternative. Experience shows that most but not all investors would choose alternative B over alternative A. In fact, as uncertainty increases, the investors usually require a higher estimated ROI. For this reason, U.S. government bonds, which are considered nearly risk-free, usually yield less than U.S. corporate bonds, which in turn yield less than U.S. corporate stocks.

It is often possible to reduce risk or uncertainty, such as by insuring against the possibility of nonconvertibility of funds. However, any such actions are apt to be costly. In the first process of scanning to develop a manageable number of alternatives, it is useful to give some weight to the elements of risk and uncertainty. At a later and more detailed stage of feasibility study, one should determine whether the degree of risk is acceptable or not without the incurring of additional costs. If it is not, then one would need to calculate an ROI that includes expenditures to increase the outcome certainty of the operation.[14]

The following discussion highlights three types of risks and uncertainties: competitive, monetary, and political. Relatively more coverage will be given to the last of these three, not because it is more important, but rather because we have covered this area more sparsely in other parts of the text.

- Prefer similar operating environments
- Try to out-guess competitors

Competitive risk. National boundaries play a role in the degree of certainty of return that investors perceive for alternative investments. As long as the investors are conducting business entirely within one country, the alternative investment projects fall within very similar political and economic environments. Furthermore, the experience of having already operated within that country as well as operating abroad in general increases the probability of accurate assessments of consumer, competitor, and governmental actions.[15] This is consistent with the earlier discussion that firms generally go first to those foreign environments that are perceived to be more similar to the home country. It also helps to explain the fact that reinvestments or expanded investments within a country where the company has extensive operations are often evaluated very differently than proposed incursions into a new country. The reinvestment decision will be discussed later in the chapter.

In the previous chapter we explained that one of the reasons for using nonequity arrangements was to spread business to many markets rapidly when a firm perceives that its innovative advantage may be short-lived. Even when the firm assesses that it has a substantial competitive lead time, this lead time may be very different in different markets. One of the strategies to take advantage of temporary monopoly advantages is known as the **imitation lag,** which holds that a company should move first to those countries that are most likely to develop local production themselves and later to other countries.[16] Local technology and high freight costs generally result in a more rapid move to local production. If technology is available, local producers may start manufacturing well before foreign companies are willing to sell the technology. If freight costs are high for exports to the country, a local producer may, in spite of inefficiencies, be able to gain an advantage in cost over imported goods.

- Obstacles if
  - difficult to sell facilities
  - exchange control
  - remission restrictions

Monetary risk. One of the considerations on where to expand internationally, particularly if the expansion is via direct investment, is the access to and exchange rate on the invested capital and its earnings. The concept of liquidity preference is a common theory to help explain capital budgeting decisions in general, and this theory can be applied to the international expansion decision.

Differences in liquidity vary by type of asset and by country. One may forego maximization of expected short-term profits for a number of reasons, one of which is to maintain at least a portion of funds in highly liquid assets, which usually yield a lower return (e.g., passbook versus time certificates at a savings and loan association). Part of the liquidity need is for consumption; thus firms invest in liquid short-term securities in order to pay dividends rather than reinvesting in expected higher-yield and long-term projects and foregoing dividends. Part is for unexpected contingencies, such as to purchase stockpile materials if a strike threatens supply. To borrow for the materials might involve a cost in excess of the income lost through the investment alternatives. Finally, part is so that funds may be shifted to even more profitable opportunities, such as purchasing materials at a discount during a temporary price depression. Both individuals and businesses have different liquidity needs based on perceived present and future opportunities and risks, total assets at their disposal, and known contingencies.

Aside from types of investments, there are some real differences in liquidity by country of investment. One of these involves locating buyers for all or a portion of existing or new equity issues. A foreign investor may wish to bring in local funds for a number of reasons, such as political pressures or because it is a relatively cheaper way of financing. One may simply wish to sell a plant or portion of it so that the funds may be used for other types of expansion endeavors. The ability to find buyers depends largely on the existence of a local capital market. Here there is a big difference by country. Saint Gobain, for instance, easily found buyers for its mirror plant in Tennessee because of the nature of the U.S. capital market. Had the plant been located in Ghana, the disposal process would surely have been much more problematic. The subject of disinvestment (or divestment) will be discussed in more detail later in this chapter.

The ability to find local buyers is but one part of the liquidity difference by country. Assuming that a foreign investor does find a local purchaser, chances are that the intent is to use the funds in another country. If the funds are not convertible, then the foreign investor will be forced to spend them in the host country. Note the similarity of this with the comparison of time and passbook certificates made above. The only difference is that the time of inconvertibility may be much more indefinite than the liquidity period on the time certificate. Of more pressing concern for most investors is the ability to convert earnings from operations abroad, since earnings are generally used not only for expansion but also for dividend payments to stockholders in the home country. The discussion in Chapter 8 showed that not only does the ability to convert vary substantially among countries, but so does the cost of convertibility. It is not surprising that most investors set different minimum returns on investments for acceptance of projects in different locales, thus making potential operations in countries with strong currencies more acceptable than those in countries with weak currencies.[17]

The indicators of present or potential currency exchange problems that were discussed in Chapter 9 are the same ones that decision makers would examine when comparing potential operations among countries. They include the existence of exchange controls, whether there is a developed capital market, the inflation rate, changes in exchange rates, and the balance-of-payments situation.

- May be from wars and insurrections, takeover of property, changes in rules
- Predictions use
  - analysis of past patterns
  - experts' opinions
  - models based on instability measurements

Political risk. One of the major concerns of international firms is that the political climate will change in such a way that their operating positions deteriorate. Political actions may adversely affect company operations through governmental takeovers of property, either with or without compensation; through operational restrictions that impede the ability of the firm to take actions it would otherwise have taken; and by damage to property or personnel.[18] These types of risks were illustrated in the opening case of this chapter. Ford's operation in France was bombed, the one in Hungary taken over by the government, and the one in Mexico given very different operating requirements.

The following discussion will center on only one type of political risk—the government takeover of foreign facilities. That is because the methods to evaluate this type risk are not fundamentally different from those used to make other political risk predictions. Three approaches to predict political risk will be discussed here. These are the analysis of past patterns, the use of expert opinion, and the building of models based on instability measurements.

One cannot help but be influenced by what has been happening within a country. There are many dangers in predicting political risk on the basis of past patterns, though. Political situations in specific countries may change rapidly for the better or worse as far as foreign investors are concerned. However, the historical evolution is indicative of the broad climate for operations. Studies that have examined large numbers of takeovers in the post–World War II period give us some clues about what to expect.[19]

Almost all of the takeovers were in less-developed countries, Latin America accounting for about half. In terms of percentage of investments affected, however, Africa and the Middle East were riskier. Asia was the lowest risk area by all measurements. Even these regional categories obscure country-by-country differences. Approximately fifty countries had no takeovers, and three alone (Argentina, Chile, and Peru) accounted for about one third of the takeovers.

Governmental takeovers, except in a few countries, have been highly selective. They have usually involved land, natural resources, financial institutions, and utilities.[20] Since the early 1970s, however, manufacturing investments have been the most vulnerable. The selectivity is illustrated by the experience of investors in Peru. Cerro's mining interests and ITT's telephone company were nationalized; however, Cerro maintained several manufacturing companies there, and ITT a hotel.

Even among manufacturing industries, there are differences. One study has ranked forty types of businesses, including twenty-seven different types of manufacturers, as to their likelihood of coming under public ownership.[21] Basically, those most likely are the ones that may have a substantial and visible widespread effect on a given country because of their size, monopoly position, or necessity for national defense or because other industries depend on them. Among the manufacturing investments, near the top are ordnance (defense), tobacco (usually a monopoly public revenue generator), steel mills (usually a monopoly serving many firms), and sugar and salt (large producers selling essential products). At the other extreme are products such as household appliances, jewelry, and toys. Although the general hierarchy may be useful in determining the relative acceptability of different types of foreign ownership, one must also be aware of individual country differences in attitudes toward foreign ownership in specific types of endeavors. For instance, the fishing industry, which is placed at the midpoint on the list, was a predictable candidate for nationalization in Peru because it was highly visible—being the prime earner of foreign exchange—and because poor economic conditions in the industry, which the fishermen did not understand, were attributed to the foreign capitalists.

Both among and within industries there are variances in local need for foreign resources. This was discussed in Chapter 12. Companies that hold assets that are badly needed in a given country and for which that country has little alternative source are much less vulnerable to political actions. This points out once again the need for internal assessment in order to design types and places for foreign operations that minimize the risk of governmental control. Thus far, firms with a high technological input that produce a large amount of component parts outside the countries where investments are made have been less prone to takeovers. This was particularly noted during the Allende and Velasco expropriations in Chile and Peru.[22]

The fact that assets are taken over does not necessarily mean a full loss to investors. Most take-overs have been preceded by a formal declaration of intent by the government with a subsequent legal process to determine compensation to the foreign investor. Historical analysis of compensation and continuing relationships (e.g., purchase and management contracts) are not of much use for estimating possible losses from takeovers of facilities. Although investors receive compensation in more than 90 percent of takeovers, it is difficult to determine how adequate the compensation is.

A second approach for political risk analysis is to analyze the opinions of people who should be knowledgeable about a country situation. Two different observers, one addressing the problem of political exposure in general and the other addressing nationalization, have suggested very similar means of data gathering and analysis.[23] Basically, their approaches attempt to ascertain the evolving opinions of people who may influence future political events affecting business. The first step involves reading statements made by political leaders both in and out of office to determine their philosophies on business in general, foreign input to business, and the means of effecting economic changes and their feelings toward given foreign countries. Although published statements are fairly readily available, they may appear too late for a business to have time to react.

One should analyze the context of statements to determine whether they express true intentions or were made merely to appease particular interest groups or social strata. It is not uncommon, for example, for political leaders to make emotional appeals to the poor based on allegations that foreign business is draining wealth from the country while, at the same time, these leaders quietly negotiate entry and give incentives to new foreign firms. Examination of investment plans offers further insights to the political climate.

Visits to the country in order to "listen" are very important for determining opinions and attitudes. Embassy officials and other foreign and local businesspeople are useful for obtaining opinions as to the probability and direction of change. Journalists, academicians, middle-level local governmental authorities, and labor leaders usually reveal their own attitudes, which often reflect changing political conditions that may affect the business sector.

A more systematic method of relying on opinions is to use a panel of analysts with experience in a country and have them rate on a scale various categories of political conditions over different time frames. For example, they might rate a country on a scale from zero to seven in terms of the fractionalization of political parties that could lead to disruptive changes in government. This could be done for the present time as well as for future periods such as one, five, and ten years.[24]

A third method being used to predict political risk is to build models based on instability measurements. The greater the political instability, the greater the possibility of change in the political climate. Although political instability has been found to be one of the major concerns of businesspeople, it is difficult to reach a consensus as to what constitutes dangerous instability or how such instability can be predicted.[25] Political parties may change rapidly at times with little effect on business; on the other hand, sweeping changes for business may occur without a change in government. One measurement of political stability during a relevant time period involves seven indicators weighted from zero to six. These are (1) institutionally prescribed election, (2) fall of cabinet, (3) significant groups outlawed, (4) execution of significant political figure, (5) assassination of chief of state, (6) coup d'etat accompanied by mild amount of violence, and (7) civil war.[26] While the occurrence of these indicators may be useful for predicting what is to come, actual foreign investment activity does not correlate with the instability index.[27] Rather than political stability per se, the direction of change in government seems to be more important. About half the takeovers in the 1946–1973 period were made within three years after a leftist government took office.[28]

One theory is that frustration—the difference between the level of aspirations and the level of welfare and expectations—develops and that foreign investment is a scapegoat when a country's frustration level is high. To test this hypothesis, six proxy indicators were used for the aspiration level (urbanization, literacy, newspaper circulation and radios per capita, labor unionization, and natural resource endowment); six for welfare (infant survival rate, caloric consumption, doctors per capita, hospital beds per capita, piped water supply per capita, and per capita income); and two for expectations (change in per capita income and gross investment rates). Using 1960–1965 data on twenty-one Latin American countries, this methodology found that frustration was correlated to expropriation in the 1968–1971 period. The top three countries in terms of frustration (Chile, Boliva, and Peru) were also major expropriators.[29] This approach has considerable possibilities, since it predicts future trends rather than looking to the past and since it is predicated on a lead time that might be sufficient for managements to adjust operations to minimize losses.

SOME TOOLS FOR COMPARING COUNTRIES

Grids

- May depict acceptable or unacceptable conditions
- Rank countries by important variables

A grid may be used to compare countries on whatever factors are deemed important. Table 16.2 is an example of a grid with information placed into three major categories. Certain countries may be immediately eliminated from consideration because of characteristics that decision makers find unacceptable. These are in the first category of variables, where country I can be eliminated. Values and weights are assigned to items so that a country may be ranked according to attributes that are important to the decision maker. In the same table, for example, country II is graphically pinpointed as a high return–low risk, country III as a low return–low risk, country IV as a high return–high risk, and country V as a low return–high risk.[30]

TABLE 16.2

SIMPLIFIED GRID TO COMPARE COUNTRIES FOR MARKET PENETRATION

Variables	Weight	I	II	III	IV	V
1. Acceptable (A), Unacceptable (U) factors						
a. Allows 100 percent ownership	—	U	A	A	A	A
b. Allows licensing to majority-owned subsidiary	—	A	A	A	A	A
2. Return (higher number = preferred rating)						
a. Size of investment needed	0–5	—	4	3	3	3
b. Direct costs	0–3	—	3	1	2	2
c. Tax rate	0–2	—	2	1	2	2
d. Market size, present	0–4	—	3	2	4	1
e. Market size, 3–10 years	0–3	—	2	1	3	1
f. Market share, immediate potential, 0–2 years	0–2	—	2	1	2	1
g. Market share, 3–10 years	0–2	—	2	1	2	0
Total			18	10	18	10
3. Risk (lower number = preferred rating)						
a. Market loss, 3–10 years (if no present penetration)	0–4	—	2	1	3	2
b. Exchange problems	0–3	—	0	0	3	3
c. Political unrest potential	0–3	—	0	1	2	3
d. Business laws, present	0–4	—	1	0	4	3
e. Business laws, 3–10 years	0–2	—	0	1	2	2
Total			3	3	14	13

Both the variables and weights should vary by product and company, depending on the firm's internal situation and consequent objectives. The grid technique is of use even when comparative analysis is not made, since a minimum score may be necessary for the company to either invest additional resources or commit further funds to a more detailed feasibility study. Grids do tend to get cumbersome, however, as the number of variables increases. Furthermore, while they are useful in ranking, they often obscure interrelationships among countries.

Opportunity-Risk Matrix

- Opportunity on one axis and risk on other
  - decide indicators and weight them
  - evaluate each country by weighted indicators
  - plot to see relative placements
  - may plot size of operations differently
  - may plot expected movements

One way of showing more clearly the summary of data that could be included on a grid is to plot risk on one axis and opportunity on the other.[31] Many companies, such as Borg-Warner, use variations of this instrument.[32] Figure 16.1 is an example that is simplified to include only six countries. The grid shows that the company has current operations in four of the countries (all except countries A and E). Of the two nonexploited countries, country A has low risk but low opportunity, and country E has low risk and high opportunity. If resources are to be spent in a new area, country E appears to be a better bet than country A. In the other four countries there are large commitments in country F, medium in countries C and D, and small in country B. In the future time horizon being examined, it appears that only country F will have low risk along with high opportunity. The situation in country D is expected to improve during the studied period. Country C's situation is deteriorating, and country B's is mixed (better opportunity but more risk). Note that the averages shift during the period. The importance of the matrix is to reflect the placement of a country relative to other countries.

But how are values plotted in on such a matrix? It is up to the company to determine what factors are good indicators of risk and opportunity. These factors must then be weighted to reflect that some are more important than others. For instance, on the risk axis the company may give 40 percent of the weight to expropriation risk, 25 percent to foreign exchange controls, 20 percent to civil disturbances and terrorism, and 15 percent to exchange rate change. This makes a total allocation of 100 percent. Each country would then be rated on a scale of 1 to 10 for each of the variables, 10 indicating the best score and 1 indicating the worst. The score on each item is multiplied by the weight allocated for the variable. For instance, if country A were given a rating of 8 on the expropriation risk variable, the 8 would be multiplied by .4 for a score of 3.2. All of country A's risk variable scores are then summed to give the placement of country A on the risk axis. One would follow a similar procedure to find the plot location on the opportunity axis. Once the scores are determined for each

FIGURE 16.1
Opportunity-Risk Matrix

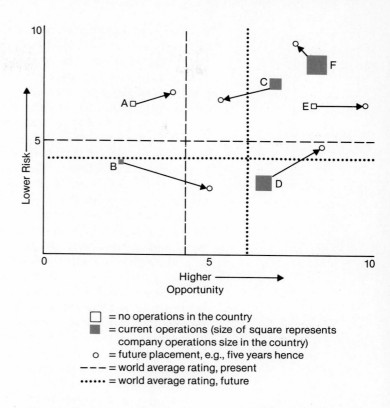

☐ = no operations in the country
■ = current operations (size of square represents
      company operations size in the country)
○ = future placement, e.g., five years hence
– – – = world average rating, present
•••••• = world average rating, future

country, one can determine the average score for risk and the average score for opportunity, thereby dividing the matrix into quadrants.

A key element of the sample matrix, one that is not always included in practice, is the projection of the future country location. The utility of such a placement is obvious if the projections are realistic. Therefore it is useful to have forecasts made by people who are not only knowledgeable about the countries but also knowledgeable about forecasting methods.

Country Attractiveness—Company Strength Matrix

- Highlights fit of company's product to country
- Plotting procedure similar as for opportunity-risk matrix

Another commonly used matrix approach has been devised to highlight a company's specific product advantage on a country-by-country basis. This was briefly explained in the case on Ford. For its tractor operations, for example, Ford uses this type of matrix. On the country attractiveness scale, countries are ranked from highest to lowest attractiveness for tractors specifically. On the other scale, Ford ranks its competitive strength in tractors by country. The method of performing the ranking is the same as for the opportunity-risk matrix. Ford's weighted scale for country attractiveness includes such variables as market size, market growth, price controls, red tape, requirements for local content and exports, inflation, trade balance, and political stability. Ford's competitive strength weighted scale includes market share, market share position, its product fit for the needs of the country, absolute profit per unit, percentage profit on cost, quality of Ford's distribution in comparison with competitors, and the fit of Ford's promotion program for the country in comparison with competitors.[33]

Figure 16.2 illustrates this type of matrix for market expansion before countries are plotted into their positions. The company should attempt to concentrate its activities in the countries that appear in the top left-hand corner of the matrix and to take as much equity as possible in investments there. It is there that the country attractiveness is the highest *and* where the firm has the best competitive capabilities to exploit the opportunities. In the top right-hand corner the country attractiveness is also high, but the company has a weak competitive strength for that market—perhaps it lacks the right product. If it is not too costly, the company might attempt to gain greater domination in those markets by rectifying its competitive weakness. Otherwise, it might consider either divestment (reducing its investment) or strengthening the position through joint venture operations with another firm whose assets are complementary. Investments should not be made in areas in the bottom right-hand corner, and divestment should be attempted. Income may be "harvested" by pulling out all possible cash that can be generated while, at the same time, not replacing depreciated facilities. Licensing still offers potential because it may generate some income without having to make investment outlays. In other areas the company must analyze situations selectively in order to decide which of the aforementioned approaches to take. These are marginal areas about which it is less easy to generalize.

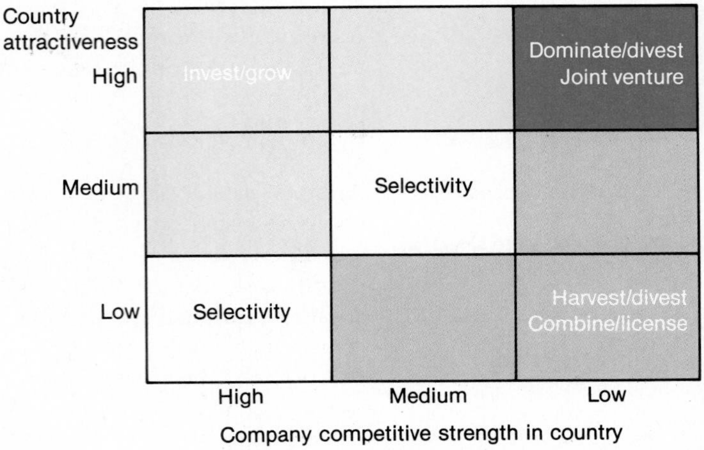

FIGURE 16.2
Country Attractiveness–Company Strength Matrix

DIVERSIFICATION VERSUS CONCENTRATION STRATEGIES

- Strategies for ultimately reaching high commitment in many countries
  - diversification—go to many fast and then build up slowly in each
  - concentration—go to one or a few and build up fast before going to another
  - may take hybrid of above two

Ultimately, a firm may gain a sizable presence and commitment in most countries of the world; however, there are different paths to reach that position. At one extreme, in a diversification strategy the company may move rapidly into most foreign markets, gradually increasing its commitments within each of them. This could be done, for example, through a liberal licensing policy for a given product so that there are sufficient resources for this initial widespread expansion. The company may eventually increase its involvement by internalizing activities that it initially had contracted to other firms. At the other extreme, in a concentration strategy the company might move only to one or a few foreign countries until it developed a very strong involvement and competitive position there. There are, of course, hybrids of these two strategies—for example, moving rapidly to most markets but increasing the commitment in only a few. The following discussion centers on those major variables that are important to consider when deciding whether to use a diversification or concentration strategy.[34] (See Table 16.3.)

Sales Response Function

- Increasing response rate favors concentration
- Decreasing favors diversification

The sales response function refers to the amount of sales created at different levels of marketing expenditures. If, for example, the first $100,000 of marketing expenditure in a given country yielded $1,000,000 of sales, the next $100,000 yielded $800,000, and the third yielded $600,000, this

TABLE 16.3

PRODUCT/MARKET FACTORS AFFECTING CHOICE BETWEEN DIVERSIFICATION AND CONCENTRATION STRATEGIES

Product/market factor	Prefer diversification if:	Prefer concentration if:
1. Sales response function*	Decreasing	Increasing
2. Growth rate of each market	Low	High
3. Sales stability in each market	Low	High
4. Competitive lead time	Short	Long
5. Spillover effects	High	Low
6. Need for product adaptation	Low	High
7. Need for communication adaptation	Low	High
8. Economies of scale in distribution	Low	High
9. Program control requirements	Low	High
10. Extent of constraints	Low	High

* The terms used in the original article for "decreasing" and "increasing" were "concave" and "S curve," respectively.

Source: Igal Ayal and Jehiel Zif, "Marketing Expansion Strategies in Multinational Marketing," *Journal of Marketing,* Vol. 43, Spring 1979, p. 89. Reprinted by permission of the American Marketing Association.

would be a decreasing response. On the other hand, if the first $100,000 in a country yielded $600,000, the second yielded $800,000, and the third yielded $1 million, it would be an increasing response. There are products that follow each pattern over similar expenditure levels. If the company had $300,000 to spend on a marketing program for which there is the same decreasing response in each country, the company would create more sales by spreading entry over three countries. This would yield $3 million ($1M + 1M + 1M), whereas a concentration on one country would yield only $2.4 million ($1M + 0.8M + 0.6M). If the same $300,000 were spent on a product with an increasing response, however, a concentration strategy would yield better results, $2.4 million ($0.6M + 0.8M + 1M) as opposed to $1.8 million ($0.6M + 0.6M + 0.6M).

Growth Rate in Each Market

- Fast growth favors concentration because
  - must use resources to maintain market share

When the growth rate in each market is high, it is usually preferable to concentrate on a few markets because it will be necessary to spend a great deal to maintain market share, and costs per unit are typically lower for the market share leader. Slower growth in each market may allow the company to have enough resources to build and maintain a market share in a number of different countries.

Growth Stability in Each Market

International diversification has been shown to have an even stronger relationship to profit stability than product diversification.[35] Recall once again the Ford case at the beginning of the chapter and the earlier discussion that earnings and sales are smoothed because of operations in various parts of the world. This is because there are leads and lags in the business cycles. Additionally, a company whose asset and earnings base are in a variety of countries will be less affected by occurrences within a single nation. A strike or expropriation will therefore affect earnings from only a small portion of total corporate assets. Currency devaluations in some countries may be offset by revaluations in other countries.

The more stable sales and profits are within a single market, the less need there is for a diversification strategy. Likewise the more interrelated markets are, the less smoothing is achieved by selling in each. One would expect, for example, that Ford would get less of a smoothing effect between France and West Germany (because their economies are so interrelated through the EC) than between either of those two countries and the United States.[36]

Competitive Lead Time

● Longer the lead time, more one can concentrate

In the preceding chapter we discussed that one of the reasons for using nonequity arrangements as a means of serving foreign markets is to beat competitors into the market. The use of these external arrangements helped the companies to spread into more markets than they could if they had had to use their own resources. If a company assesses that it has a long lead time before competitors can likely copy or supersede its advantages, then the company may be able to hold on to the control of the expansion by following a concentration strategy and still beat competitors into other markets.

Spillover Effects

Spillover effects refer to situations whereby the marketing of a program in one country results in awareness of the product in other countries. This can happen, for example, if the product is advertised through media viewed on a cross-national basis. In such situations a diversification strategy has advantages because additional customers may be reached with little additional cost.

Need for Product, Communications, and Distribution Adaptation

● Adaptation means additional costs
  ● hard to spread to many markets
  ● hard to gain economies of scale through diversification

Chapter 18 will discuss why and under what circumstances products and the marketing of them may have to be altered for foreign markets. The adaptation process is often costly and, if so, may lead to two factors that favor a concentration strategy. First, the additional costs may limit the resources the firm has for expansion in many different markets. Second, the fixed costs incurred for adaptation cannot be as easily spread over sales in other countries as a means of reducing total unit costs.

Program Control Requirements

● Diversification often implies external arrangements that may cause control to be lost

The more necessary it is that the company control what is happening in the foreign country where the product is being sold, the more likely that it should develop a concentration strategy. This is because more of the firm's resources will need to be used to maintain that control. The need for more control could come about for a number of reasons. These include fear that an external arrangement will create a competitor or that there is a need for highly technical assistance to customers.

Extent of Constraints

- Constraints limit resources for going to many places simultaneously

Constraints on what a firm can do may come about internally or externally. Take resource availability, for example. The higher the constraints, the more likely a concentration strategy is. Let us say that the key resource for introducing a new product into the foreign markets is the availability of certain specialized technical personnel. If there is a shortage of these personnel both within and outside the company, the company will be constrained in the number of countries to which it can expand rapidly. Or if there are constraints in where they can be moved, the company may find it difficult to expand into many different markets rapidly.

INVESTMENT PROPOSAL EVALUATION

- After scanning, must evaluate with precise projections
  - internal and accounting rates of return are most popular

Thus far we have examined comparative opportunities on a very broad basis. At some point it is necessary to do a much more detailed analysis of much more specific projects and proposals in order to make allocation decisions. Firms use a variety of financial criteria to evaluate foreign investments, internal rate of return and accounting rate of return being the most used measurements.[37]

Measurement Problems

- Should evaluate systems effect
- Figures sometimes don't reflect market values

The derivation of meaningful rate of return figures is no easy task when foreign operations are concerned. Profit figures from individual operations may obscure the real impact those operations have on overall company activities. For example, if a U.S. company were to establish an assembly operation in South Africa, this assembly operation could either increase or decrease exports for the United States. Assumptions would have to be made about the changed profits in the United States and elsewhere as a result of the South African project. Or let us say that by building a plant in Brazil to supply components to Volkswagen of Brazil, the investor increases the possibility of selling to Volkswagen in other countries.

The above discussion assumes that, although overall company returns are difficult to calculate, those for the operating subsidiary are fairly easily ascertained. This is not the case. A substantial portion of the sales and purchases of foreign subsidiaries may be with units of the same parent company. The prices charged on these transactions will affect the relative profitability of one unit vis-à-vis another. Furthermore, the base on which to estimate the net value of the foreign investment may not be realistically stated, particularly if part of the net value is based on exported capital equipment that is both obsolete at home and of little use elsewhere. By stating a high value the company may be permitted to repatriate a larger portion of its earnings.

Noncomparative Decision Making

- Most proposals decided on go–no go basis if meeting minimum acceptance criteria due
  - proposals not ready at same time
  - must often act quickly

Because of the limited resources firms have at their disposal, one may easily get the erroneous impression that companies maintain a storehouse of foreign investment proposals that may be ranked on the basis of some predetermined criteria. If this were so, management could simply start allocating resources to the top-ranked proposal and continue down the list until no further investments were possible. This is seldom the case, however. About three quarters of final investment proposals are evaluated separately, and a decision is made on what is commonly known as a go–no go decision.[38] This is usually made on the basis that the project meets some minimum threshold criteria. Of course, there has been a good deal of weeding out of possible projects at various scanning and decision points along the way.

One of the major factors restricting firms from comparing investment opportunities is cost. Clearly, firms cannot afford to conduct very many investigations simultaneously. Another factor inhibiting comparison of investment opportunities is that feasibility studies are apt to be in various stages of completion at a given time. Let us say that the investigation process has been finished for a possible project in Australia but that ongoing research is being conducted for New Zealand, Japan, and Indonesia. Can the company afford to wait until the results from all the surveys are completed? Probably not. The time interval between completions would probably invalidate much of the earlier results, thus necessitating an updating, added expense, and further delays.

Other time-inhibiting problems exist as well. Frequently, governmental regulations may require a decision within a given period of time. An example was the selection by the Andean Common Market countries of those automobile companies that were allowed to produce and compete for certain segments of the market. Very little lead time was given by the countries, and the automakers knew that a negative decision would preclude sales for them in the Andean area for the foreseeable future. Another external limitation may be imposed by other companies that have made partnership proposals. If no answer is forthcoming in a short period of time, a proposal may be made to a different potential partner.

Finally, few companies can afford to let resources lie idle or be employed for a low rate of return during a waiting period. Both stockholders and employees may question the waiting period. This applies not only to financial resources but also to such resources as technical competence, since the lead time over competitors is reduced by holding off a decision.

Reinvestment Decisions

- May have to make new commitments to maintain competitiveness

Most of the net value of foreign investment has come from the reinvestment of earnings abroad rather than from new international capital transfers. The decisions to replace depreciated assets or to add to the existing stock

● May be handled differently due to expertise of local managers

of capital from retained earnings in a foreign country are somewhat different from original investment decisions. Once committed to a given locale, a firm may find that there is no option to move a substantial portion of the earnings elsewhere because to do so would endanger the continued successful operation of the given foreign facility. For example, the failure to expand might result in a falling market share and a higher unit cost than competitors'.

Aside from competitive factors, a company may need several years of almost total reinvestment as well as allocation of new funds to one area in order to meet its objectives. Over a period of time the earnings may be used to expand the product line, the integration of production, and the market served from present output. A further factor for treating reinvestment decisions differently is that once there are experienced personnel within a given country, it is often assumed that they are the best judges of what is needed for their countries; therefore certain investment decisions may be delegated to them.

DIVESTMENT

● Must also decide how to get out of operations because
  ● do not fit overall strategy
  ● better alternative opportunities
● Managers less apt to propose divestments than investments

In much of the preceding discussions it was shown that firms should consider decreasing their commitments to certain areas in order to free resources when they will better fit with corporate objectives. It is now common to read that a firm is terminating its ownership in an investment in a foreign country. A short time ago, most of such headlines highlighted the conflict between MNEs and nation-states. They emphasized either governmental expropriation or moves by MNEs to gain leverage over host countries in the terms by which they operate. Studies of divestments point out that these headlined examples are decidedly in the minority.[39] The majority of incidents have involved the selling of operations that have poor performance prospects compared to alternative opportunities. Admittedly, however, some of these have been in anticipation of governmental takeovers if the firms did not move voluntarily to sell their ownership. But almost one third of divestments by U.S. firms have been neither voluntary sales nor expropriations. Instead, they have involved the liquidation of unprofitable operations.

Studies of the divestment experience have concluded that most firms might have fared better had they been more experienced and developed divestment specialists. Instead, there has been a tendency to wait too long and to be thwarted by local managers who fear the loss of their own positions if the MNE abandons an operation. In fact this question of who has something to gain or lose is a factor that sets apart decisions to invest from decisions to divest. Both types of decisions should be highly interrelated and geared to the strategic thrust of the company. The idea for investment projects typically originates with middle managers or with managers already employed in foreign subsidiary operations who are enthusiastic in collecting information to accompany a proposal as it moves upward in the organization. After all, the evaluation and employment of these people depend on growth. They have no such compulsion to propose divestments. These proposals typically originate at the top of the organization after most remedies have been tried for the salvation of the operations.[40]

Use of asset book value has been most common when selling an interest, and firms have sought to smooth their exit in a way that permitted possible reestablishment of operations at a later date. This latter desire, along with efforts to salvage as much as possible when divesting, means that it is difficult for MNEs to threaten to move to another country contrary to what is often alleged.

SUMMARY

- Because companies do not have sufficient resources to take advantage of all the opportunities that are apparent to them, two of the major considerations facing firms are which markets to serve and where to locate the production to serve those markets.

- The market and production location decisions are often highly interdependent because of requirements that markets be served from local production, because firms seek nearby outlets for excess capacity, and because firms may be unwilling to invest in those production locations necessary to serve a desired market.

- Scanning techniques are useful to aid decision makers in considering alternatives that might otherwise have been overlooked and in limiting the final detailed feasibility studies to a manageable and promising number.

- The prioritizing of countries is useful for determining the order of entry into potential markets and in setting the allocation and rate of expansion among different markets.

- Because each company has unique competitive capabilities and objectives, the makeup of factors affecting each geographic expansion pattern will be slightly different for each. There are nevertheless certain variables that have been shown to influence most firms. These include the relative size of country markets, the ease of operating in the specific foreign countries, the availability and cost of resources, and the perceived relative risk and uncertainty of operations in one country versus another.

- Some tools frequently used to compare opportunities in various countries are grids that rate country projects according to a number of separate dimensions and matrixes on which one may project one attribute on a vertical axis and another on the horizontal axis, such as risk and opportunity or country attractiveness and company capability.

- By using a similar amount of internal resources a firm may choose initially to move rapidly into many foreign markets with only a small commitment in each (a diversification strategy) or to make a strong involvement and commitment in one or a few locations (a concentration strategy).

- The major variables to consider when deciding whether to diversify or concentrate are the response of sales to incremental increases in marketing expenditures, the growth rate and sales stability in each market, the expected lead time over competitors, the degree of need for product and marketing adaptation in different countries, the need to maintain control of the expansion program, and the internal and external constraints facing the company.

- ROI figures alone do not tell the full impact a foreign investment may have on total corporate performance. One must assess such factors as effects on export and licensing income as well as what advantages competitors would gain in the absence of the investment.

- Rather than ranking investment alternatives, once a feasibility study is complete, most investors set some minimum criteria and either accept or reject a foreign project on that basis. The reason for this type of decision is that feasibility analyses are seldom finished simultaneously, and there are pressures to act quickly.

- Reinvestment decisions are normally treated separately from new investment decisions because a reinvestment may be necessary to protect the viability of existing resources and because there are people on location who presumably are in a better position to judge the worthiness of proposals.

- Not only must firms develop strategies for where new investments will be made, they must also develop the means to deemphasize certain areas and to divest if necessary.

C A S E   MITSUI IN IRAN[41]

In early 1984, Mitsui, one of Japan's largest trading companies, faced a very tough decision. Should it commit more resources in a risky project to keep it afloat? The project was a petrochemical joint venture in Iran for which planning began in 1973 and construction in 1976. A Mitsui-led group of five Japanese firms owned 50 percent of the venture, the Iranian government holding the remainder. By 1980, Mitsui had already invested $930 million directly in the project. Additionally, Mitsui had made indirect investments in the project through two of its partially owned subsidiaries that were part of the Japanese investment group. From 1980 through 1982, Mitsui was called upon on several occasions to add as much as $60 million to the project. Mitsui finally stopped work because it feared the plant would become a "bottomless pit." This led to two years of exhaustive and sharp negotiations and exchanges between Mitsui and the Iranian government. By the end of 1983 the Iranian government proposed that it would put up all additional funds, estimated to be between $1 billion and $1.5 billion, provided that the future ownership share would be adjusted to reflect the capital contribution and provided that Mitsui would send a survey team of 100 engineers and experts to the site almost immediately in order to get the project rolling again.

Work on the project had been suspended several times. The Iranian revolution first brought work to a halt in March 1979, when it was estimated that completion would be within six months. Construction resumed in the summer of 1980 but was halted again in October because of Iraqi attacks. Although the project escaped extensive damage from the attacks, the facilities were to have depended on naphtha supplies from a refinery in Abadan that was almost totally destroyed. In the meantime, Iran has put a very high priority on completion of the facility. It is the only one of the Shah's dozen or so billion-dollar projects to be continued under the regime of Khomeini. To protect the site, Iran placed antiaircraft missiles and warplanes nearby. Yet on hearing that Mitsui might send in its personnel again, the Iraqi Foreign Minister threatened renewed bombing of the construction.

The scope of the project was significant for both Japan and Mitsui. If completed, it would be the largest foreign investment anywhere in the world by Japanese interests. For Mitsui, with total assets of about $1.9 billion, the Iranian venture is already a substantial portion of its total investment. The Iranian project was even more significant in terms of Mitsui's foreign assets. Mitsui was at an early stage of developing foreign production with only new smaller projects for Chinese coal development and for natural gas in Southeast Asia and Canada. If the Iranian project is completed, Mitsui's product composition will change substantially. The present sales breakdown is as follows: iron and steel, 21 percent; metals, 11 percent; machinery, 14 percent; chemicals, 13 percent; foodstuffs, 17 percent; crude oil and gas, 12 percent; and others, 12 percent.

There was uncertainty as to the amount of loss that Mitsui would incur if it were to abandon the project. Mitsui had taken out political risk insurance that covered $474 million; but if it were to withdraw on its own volition, it might lose the right to claim most of the insurance. A court ruling could not be given before pulling out, except for war damage insurance. In spite of this uncertainty and in spite of interest payments on loans taken out for Iranian construction, there was little speculation in financial circles that Mitsui would go bankrupt. About 15 percent of Mitsui's shares were held by three powerful Japanese banks, the Mitsui Bank, Bank of Tokyo, and Fuji Bank. They were expected to support Mitsui if liquidity became a problem. Between 1982 and 1984 the Japanese government also did two things to ease Mitsui's financial problems in the project. The government bought a 5 percent equity share in the venture and also refinanced most of Mitsui's loans on the project at lower rates.

By early 1984 there were many conflicting pressures on Mitsui. Although the latest Iranian proposal lessened Mitsui's future financial requirements in Iran, the company might still be able to use its scarce technical resources more effectively elsewhere, especially if the chemical facility never reached completion. Mitsui reasoned that it would be difficult to entice technicians to work at a site that might be bombed by Iraqi aircraft and that had inadequate housing for employees. Yet Mitsui was aware of many foreign investors, even a few from the United States, that were still operating in Iran in spite of the political turmoil of recent years.

The Iranian Prime Minister told a Japanese government survey team in Teheran that the Iranian government would ensure stable supplies of crude oil to Japan if the project was completed. The question of oil supplies was a very sensitive issue because of Japan's dependence on foreign sources for over 99 percent of its needs. Japan depended more on Iran than on any other single oil source. Japan's trade with Iran was $7.5 billion in 1983. But Japan was also dependent on Iraq, trading about $1 billion in 1983. An official of Japan's Ministry of International Trade and Industry said, "The project will decide the destiny of the fiduciary relations between Japan and the Middle East and eventually, the destiny of Japan's energy security."

QUESTIONS

1. Should Mitsui try to complete its investment project in Iran?
2. What might Mitsui do to improve the safety of its assets if it does make further investments in Iran?
3. What might Mitsui have done to prevent the Iranian dilemma?

NOTES

1. Data for the case were taken from "Ford in Britain," *The Economist,* February 28, 1981, pp. 66–67; Gilbert D. Harrell and Richard O. Kiefer, *MSU Business Topics,* Winter 1981, pp. 5–15; Mira Wilkins and Frank Ernest Hill, *American Business Abroad: Ford on Six Continents* (Detroit: Wayne State University Press, 1964); Allan Nevins, *Ford: Expansion and Challenge: 1915–33,* Vol. II (New York: Charles Scribner's Sons, 1957); "Ford Annual Report 1984"; "How Safe Is It to Invest Abroad?" *International Management,* October 1979, pp. 67–70.

2. John D. Daniels, "Combining Strategic and International Business Approaches through Growth Vector Analysis," *Management International Review,* Vol. 23, No. 3, 1983, pp. 4–15.

3. Yair Aharoni, *The Foreign Investment Decision Process* (Boston: Harvard University Graduate School of Business, 1966), pp. 52–53.

4. Robert B. Stobaugh, Jr., "How to Analyze Foreign Investment Climates," *Harvard Business Review,* September–October 1969, p. 101.

5. National Industrial Conference Board, *The Multinational Corporation: Studies on U.S. Foreign Investment,* Vol. 2 (Washington, D.C.: U.S. Department of Commerce, 1973).

6. Raj Aggarwal, "Investment Performance of U.S.-Based Companies: Comments and a Perspective on International Diversification of Real Assets," *Journal of International Business Studies,* Spring-Summer 1980, pp. 98–104.

7. Karen B. Hisey and Richard E. Caves, "Diversification Strategy and Choice of Country: Diversifying Acquisitions Abroad by U.S. Multinationals, 1978–1980," *Journal of International Business Studies,* Summer 1985, pp. 51–64.

8. Irving B. Kravis and Robert E. Lipsey, "The Location of Overseas Production and Production for Export by U.S. Multinational Firms," *Journal of International Economics,* Vol. 12, May 1982, pp. 201–223.

9. Rodman L. Drake and Allan J. Prager, "Floundering with Foreign Investment Planning," *Columbia Journal of World Business,* Summer 1977, pp. 66–77.

10. Aharoni, *op. cit.,* pp. 54–56.

11. These were found in studies of reactions to the Ancom investment code by Robert E. Grosse, *Foreign Investment Codes and the Location of Direct Investment* (New York: Praeger, 1980), pp. 122–123.

12. Kravis and Lipsey, *op. cit.,* p. 212.

13. Alan Marshall, "International Facility Planning in Emerging Industries," *Industrial Development,* May–June 1983, pp. 23–25.

14. See, for example, Briance Mascarenhas, "Coping with Uncertainty in International Business," *Journal of International Business Studies,* Vol. 13, No. 2, Fall 1982, pp. 87–98; Philip J. Stein, "Should Your Firm Invest in Political Risk Insurance?," *Financial Executive,* March 1983, pp. 18–22; Pravin Banker, "You're the Best Judge of Foreign Risks," *Harvard Business Review,* Vol. 61, No. 2, March–April, 1983, pp. 157–165.

15. For an analysis of the importance of these variables in the decision-making process, see Joseph La Palombara and Stephen Blank, *Multinational Corporations in Comparative Perspective* (New York: The Conference Board, 1977), pp. x–xii.

16. Robert B. Stobaugh, Jr., "Where in the World Should We Put That Plant?," *Harvard Business Review,* January–February 1969, pp. 132–134.

17. Marie E. Wicks Kelly and George C. Philippatos, "Comparative Analysis of the Foreign Investment Evaluation Practices by U.S. Based Manufacturing Multinational Companies," *Journal of International Business Studies,* Vol. 13, No. 3, Winter 1982, p. 39.

18. Stefan H. Robock, "Political Risk—Identification and Assessment," *Columbia Journal of World Business,* July–August 1971, p. 7.

19. Robert G. Hawkins, Norman Mintz, and Michael Provissiero, "Government Takeovers of U.S. Foreign Affiliates," *Journal of International Business Studies,* Spring 1976, pp. 3–16; David G. Bradley, "Managing against Expropriation," *Harvard Business Review,* July–August 1977, pp. 75–83.

20. See, for example, U.S. Department of State, Bureau of Intelligence and Research, *Nationalization, Expropriation, and Other Takings of United States and Certain Foreign Property since 1960* (Washington, D.C., 1971); J. F. Truitt, "Expropriation of Foreign Investment: Summary of the Post–World War II Experience of American and British Investors in the Less-Developed Countries," *Journal of International Business Studies,* Fall 1970, pp. 21–34.

21. Lee C. Nehrt, "The Political Climate for Private Investment: Analysis Will Reduce Uncertainty," *Business Horizons,* June 1972, p. 56.

22. Bradley, "Managing against Expropriation," pp. 81–82.

23. Nehrt, "The Political Climate for Private Investment," pp. 52–55; Herbert Cahn, "The Political Exposure Problem: An Often Overlooked Investment Decision," *Worldwide P & I Planning,* May–June 1972, pp. 20–22.

24. F. T. Haner, "Rating Investment Risks Abroad," *Business Horizons,* April 1979, pp. 18–23. This methodology is used by a number of consulting services as well. See, for example, "As the World Twirls: BI's Ratings Show New Risks vs. Opportunities," *Business International,* April 15, 1983, pp. 113–115.

25. National Industrial Conference Board, *Obstacles and Incentives to Private Foreign Investment, 1967–1968* (New York, 1969); R. S. Basi, *Determinants of United States Private Direct Investment in Foreign Countries* (Kent, Ohio: Kent State University Press, 1963); Franklin R. Root, "Attitudes of American Executives toward Foreign Governments and Investment Opportunities," *Economic and Business Bulletin,* January 1968, pp. 14–23.

26. Ivo K. Feirabend and Rosalind L. Feirabend, "Aggressive Behavior in Politics: A Cross-National Study," *Journal of Conflict Resolution,* Fall 1966, pp. 249–271.

27. Robert F. Green, "Multinational Profitability as a Function of Political Instability," *Management International Review,* Vol. 12, No. 6, 1972, pp. 23–29.

28. Hawkins et al., "Government Takeovers of U.S. Foreign Affiliates," p. 7.

29. Harold Knudsen, "Explaining the National Propensity to Expropriate: An Ecological Approach," *Journal of International Business Studies,* Spring 1974, pp. 51–69.

30. This classification scheme is adapted from Carl Noble and Virgil Thornhill, "Institutionalization of Management Science in the Multinational Firm," *Columbia Journal of World Business,* Fall 1977, pp. 13–15.

31. The incorporation of risk and opportunity are considered essential elements in any portfolio analysis. Yoram Wind and Susan Douglas, "International Portfolio Analysis and Strategy: The Challenge of the 80s," *Journal of International Business Studies,* Vol. 12, No. 2, Fall 1981, pp. 72–73.

32. See, for example, "How Borg-Warner Uses Country-Risk Assessment as a Planning Element," *Business International,* November 9, 1979, pp. 353–356.

33. Harrell and Kiefer, *loc. cit.*

34. Igal Ayal and Jehiel Zif, "Market Expansion Strategies in Multinational Marketing," *Journal of Marketing,* Vol. 43, Spring 1979, pp. 84–94.

35. Joseph C. Miller and Bernard Pras, "The Effects of Multinational and Export Diversification on the Profit Stability of U.S. Corporations," *Southern Economic Journal,* Vol. 46, No. 3, 1980, pp. 792–805.

36. *Ibid.,* p. 804.

37. Kelly and Philippatos, *loc. cit.,* p. 32.

38. *Ibid.*

39. Jagdish C. Sachdev, "Disinvestment: A New Problem in Multinational Corporation Host Government Interface," *Management International Review,* No. 3, 1976, pp. 23–35; J. J. Boddewyn, *International Divestment* (Geneva: Business International, 1976).

40. Jean J. Boddewyn, "Foreign and Domestic Divestment and Investment Decisions: Like or Unlike?," *Journal of International Business Studies,* Vol. 14, No. 3, Winter 1983, p. 28.

41. Data for the case were taken primarily from *Japan Company Handbook* (Toyko: The Oriental Economist, 1981), p. 748; Atsuko Chiba, "Mitsui Led Group Must Pay More Money or Pull out of Iran Petrochemical Project," *The Wall Street Journal,* November 25, 1980, p. 30; "Mitsui Halts Iran Plant's Start-Up," *New York Times,* April 24, 1981, p. D1; Henry Scott Stokes, "Mitsui Said to Plan Iran Pullout," *New York Times,* November 12, 1980, p. D1; Steve Mufson, "Iran, Iraq Both Offer Oil to Japan," *The Wall Street Journal,* February 11, 1981, p. 31; James P. Sterba, "Japan Affirms Sanctions Decision," *New York Times,* April 27, 1980, p. 1; Youssef M. Ibrahim, "Japan Threatened by Iran-Iraq War," *Wall Street Journal,* November 8, 1983; Suleiman K. Kassicieh and Jamal R. Nassar, "Revolution and War in the Persian Gulf: The Effect on MNCs," *California Management Review,* Vol. 26, No. 1, Fall 1983, pp. 88–99.

17

Control

- To explain why control of foreign operations is usually more cumbersome than control of domestic ones.

- To indicate the advantages and disadvantages of decision making at the headquarters and foreign subsidiary locations.

- To highlight both the importance of and the methods commonly used for planning, reporting, and evaluating on a global basis.

- To differentiate the major sources of international information and their overall advantages and limitations.

- To describe the alternative organizational structures that may be used to encompass the international operations of firms.

- To present an overview of some specific control considerations affecting international firms, such as the handling of acquisitions, the choice of headquarters location, and the legal structure of the foreign facility.

NESTLÉ[1]

The former managing director of Nestlé, Pierre Liotard-Vogt, said, "Perhaps we are the only real multinational company existing." While this may be something of an exaggeration, one is hard pressed to find other companies with such a high dependence on foreignness. The Swiss-based company, one of the fifty largest industrials in the world, was international from the start. The modern company was formed by a 1905 merger between an American-owned and a German-owned firm. More than 96 percent of Nestlé's sales is outside of Switzerland, and about 40 percent of the top management at the Vevey headquarters is non-Swiss. The chief executive officer at various times has been a Frenchman, an Italian, a German, and a Swiss who took American citizenship. The one area in which the company stays staunchly Swiss is in ownership. Nearly two thirds of the shares are registered; if sold, they can be bought only by other Swiss. This ownership identification with neutral Switzerland, a country that never had colonies, has allowed the company to do business where some of its worldwide rivals have been restricted, such as in Chile under Allende, in Cuba, and in Vietnam.

In 1984, Nestlé's sales from over 300 factories around the world were about 31 billion Swiss francs. Approximately 37 percent of those sales were in Europe, 17 percent in North America, 15 percent in Latin America, 24 percent in Asia, 4 percent in Africa, and 3 percent elsewhere. With such a geographic spread of operations, Nestlé maintains quite clear-cut policies on where decisions will be made and what roles corporate and country managers will play.

A major responsibility of Nestlé's corporate management is to give strategic direction to the firm. To do this, the corporate management decides in which geographic areas and with which products it plans to allocate efforts. To maintain this control, Nestlé's headquarters staff handles all acquisition discussions as well as decisions as to which products will be researched at the centralized facilities in Switzerland. To support these functions, each geographic area is expected to provide a positive cash flow to the parent. Because of a heavy dependence on the introduction of new products that may take several years to become profitable, it is necessary to ensure that the more established products remain sufficiently profitable for generating needed funds. The budget that originates from the country area level is the main means used to ensure that each area carries its share within the corporation. Budgets are set up on an annual basis and must be approved in Switzerland. Adherence to budgeted goals is a main means of evaluating managerial performance. Another corporate function is to serve as a conduit for information. The successes, failures, and general experiences of product programs in one country are passed on to managers in other countries.

Information on the success of a white chocolate bar in New Zealand and on a line of Lean Cuisine frozen food in the United States was disseminated this way.

In spite of the centralized directives described above, Nestlé's area managers have a great deal of discretion in certain matters. Product research is centralized so that there is a minimum duplication of efforts. When a new product is developed, the corporate management offers it to the subsidiaries and may urge initial trials. However, they will not force the subsidiaries to launch a new product if the subsidiary managements do not find it acceptable. If the product is introduced, the local management is fairly free to make adaptations of it as long as corporate management does not find the changes poor. One of Nestlé's best selling products, Nescafé instant coffee, is slightly different from country to country in the coffee blend and the darkness of the roast.

Although budgets are set on a yearly basis, reports are much more frequent. This way, corporate management may note when something is wrong and intervene to avert a disaster. The degree of reliance on these reports and the actual content of them have evolved to reflect changing conditions as well as philosophical differences of top management at the corporate level. For instance, when a new chief executive took over in 1982, he streamlined the length of monthly reports to a few key figures that could fit on one sheet of paper and began to rely more heavily on visits to the local operations as a means of finding out about them. Several things are done to try to bring corporate and country management closer together. One is to alternate people between jobs in the field and jobs at headquarters—the "market" and the "center" in Nestlé terminology. Another is to ensure that top management can converse with area management in at least French and English and preferably in German and Spanish as well. The compensation system and management style are purposely established to limit turnover among employees. The combination of these various methods contributes to many long-term interactions designed to break down barriers between headquarters and the field.

In spite of these clear-cut policies, many company actions necessitate new decisions on where control will be vested. Nestlé's policy of expanding largely through acquisition of existing firms is one type of action that has resulted in situations not quite fitting the established lines of responsibility. The acquisition policy is premised on the belief that it is more prudent to enter an already highly competitive market by buying an existing firm and infusing resources into it. Since acquired firms are not likely to have the exact product and geographic basis to fit Nestlé's structure, these operations must be accommodated in a workable way.

For example, Nestlé acquired Libby, McNeill & Libby, a U.S. company with substantial international operations including a subsidiary in the United Kingdom. Nestlé had to iron out not only how Libby, McNeill & Libby would relate to Nestlé's existing U.S. operations, but also whether the U.K. subsidiary should continue to report to Libby or to Nestlé's European operations. Fifteen years later, in 1985, the Libby, McNeill & Libby production facilities and distribution center were closed; however, two other Nestlé divisions took on the manufacture and sale of products using the Libby name. In another case the acquisition of Stouffer Foods put Nestlé into hotel ownership for the first time. Because Stouffer had been highly profitable and because the Swiss headquarters management lacked hotel experience, many more decisions were initially made at the subsidiary level than would normally be the case. The corporate level learned from the experience and established a European joint venture hotel operation with Swissair.

Another factor that has influenced decision-making authority has been a need to share subsidiary ownership of some facilities because of host country requirements, as in Venezuela. This has reduced some of the flexibility of corporate decision making.

Its involvement in U.S. operations is a good example of Nestlé's attempt to implement a strategic growth plan. After worldwide scanning of market opportunities and business environments, Nestlé announced in 1978 that it planned for the North American operations to grow much more rapidly than operations elsewhere in the world. Specifically, North America was to increase its share of total Nestlé sales from 22 percent in 1978 to 30 percent in 1985. This was an ambitious target. Nestlé had tried unsuccessfully to break into the U.S. market with condensed milk in the late nineteenth century and succeeded in the late 1930s with instant coffee. That success was a beachhead for many other products handled through a subsidiary called Nestlé Company.

The first big acquisition was Libby, which was first operated independently of the Nestlé Company. Two other notable acquisitions in food products were Stouffer in 1973 and Beech-Nut in 1978. The most notable U.S. nonfood acquisition was Alcon, a pharmaceutical company bought in 1978 for $267 million. These acquisitions reported directly to Switzerland until 1981, when Nestlé named a head of North American operations for the first time. This move was designed to shift much decision making from Switzerland to the United States but to centralize much of the U.S. operations. The managing director of Nestlé worldwide believed this to be necessary so that he could spend time on strategic planning instead of supervising day-to-day operations.

By late 1982, however, it became apparent to top management in Vevey that the targeted goals for the U.S. operations were not going to be reached. Instead of U.S. operations comprising a growing share of worldwide operations, they were declining. Furthermore, the U.S. market share was falling for many of Nestlé's traditional products such as coffee and tea. Its only recent new product successes in the United States were coming from the Stouffer operations. Consequently, the top managers from Stouffer's were rewarded with Nestlé's top U.S. divisional jobs. At the corporate level an enormous amount was budgeted for acquisitions to put the U.S. division back on the growth track. The acquisitions were all earmarked to be compatible with the company's strategic product thrust. The 1984 announcement to acquire Carnation for $3 billion was the largest nonoil merger in history. Other acquisitions included Hills Brothers Coffee and Ward Johnston, a maker of candy bars.

INTRODUCTION

- Control questions facing all companies
  - where are decisions made?
  - how to optimize globally?
  - how country units report to headquarters?
- Foreign control usually more difficult
  - distance: more time and expense to communicate
  - diversity: country differences make it hard to compare
  - uncontrollables: more outside stockholders and government dictates
  - certainty: data problems, rapid changes

International companies take a wide variety of approaches in managing their foreign operations. Many of the problems that they face are nevertheless very similar. The Nestlé case illustrates concerns of where decisions should be made, how country operations should report to headquarters, and how to optimize on a global basis. Behind each of those concerns is a more basic one—that of control. The discussion in this chapter is broader than simply the ownership of sufficient voting shares to direct company policies. Control is the planning, implementation, evaluation, and correction of performance in order to ensure that organizational objectives are achieved. Several factors make the control process more difficult internationally. Among these factors are the following.

1. *Distance.* Both the geographic and cultural distance separating countries will increase the time, expense, and possibility of error in cross-national communications. Inquiries and control systems may not be fully understood by subsidiary managers, and the time and expense of gaining verification may make the control systems worth less than their cost.

2. *Diversity.* Throughout most of the text we have shown the need to adjust operations to find the unique situations encountered in each country in which the international firm has operations. When market size, product, labor cost, currency, and a host of other factors differentiate operations from one country to another, the task of evaluating performances or setting standards to correct or improve business functions is extremely complicated.

3. *Uncontrollables.* Performance evaluation is of little importance to control unless there is some means of attaining corrective action. The fact that many foreign operations must contend (a) with the dictates of outside stockholders, whose objectives may be somewhat different from those of the parent, and (b) with governmental regulations over which the firm has no short-term influence for change means that corrective action may be minimal.

4. *Degree of certainty.* Control implies setting goals and developing plans to meet the goals. Economic and industry data are much less complete and accurate for some countries than for others. Furthermore, political

and economic conditions are subject to rapid change in some locales. These situations impede the setting of plans, especially long-range plans, and reduce the certainty of results from the implementation of the plans.

Although the above factors make control more difficult in the international context, companies do follow procedural and structural practices in an effort to ensure that foreign operations are congruent with overall corporate goals and philosophies. This chapter discusses five aspects of the international control process: (1) location of decision making, (2) planning, (3) reporting techniques, (4) organizational structures, and (5) legal arrangements.

Location of Decision Making

- Centralization—at headquarters
- Decentralization—at country level

Any firm operating internationally must determine where decisions will be made on such diverse questions as product policy, the acquisition of funds, and placement of liquid assets. Decisions made at the foreign subsidiary level are considered to be decentralized, whereas decisions made above the foreign subsidiary level are termed centralized. There are countervailing pressures for centralization and decentralization; consequently, policies must be adapted to the firm's size, philosophy, and unique situation. Consideration must also be given to the competence of people at different levels and to the effect operations in one country can have on total corporate performance.

Complete centralization and decentralization may be thought of as the extremes. In actuality, companies neither centralize nor decentralize all decisions. Instead, they vary policies according to the type of question and the particular circumstances involved. The following discussion focuses on the rationale for locating decision control at either the corporate or the subsidiary level. Once these motivations are understood, it is easier to comprehend such elements as organization structure, planning, and evaluation, which parallel the basic centralization or decentralization philosophy.

Competence Arguments

- Early stage: generally decentralized
  - headquarters lacks foreign expertise
- Middle stage: more centralized
  - headquarters has foreign expertise and global view
- Advanced stage: both headquarters and subsidiary management have country knowledge and global view

Since a requisite for delegating authority is the belief that those selected will act responsibly, the perception of local managers' competence or lack of competence will determine to a great extent the courses of action they can pursue. While there are rational factors affecting the belief of relative capability, it has been noted that too often unrealistic attitudes lead to excessive control delegated to either the corporate or subsidiary managers. By unrealistic attitudes we mean, on one hand, a belief that only the on-the-spot person knows the situation well enough to make a decision or, on the other hand, a belief that corporate managers are the only individuals capable of handling decisions. These attitudes were referred to in Chapter

3 as polycentrism and ethnocentrism, respectively. It has been noted that firms often go through stages of centralization–decentralization. At an early period they tend to be decentralized because headquarters management does not feel confident about assessing situations abroad. Later, however, the headquarters personnel take more control as they gain capabilities and experience and strive to achieve global objectives. Finally, the operations become more decentralized again as local managers learn to understand the corporate as well as the local perspective.[2]

- More different the foreign environment from home country, the more delegation
- More confidence in foreign managers, the more delegation
  - because of size of foreign staff, experience, successes

Caliber and local conditions. In Chapter 22 we will discuss the diversities in labor markets by country and the complaints of corporate managers in charge of international operations concerning the difficulty of hiring locally or transferring capable managers to some locales. In such instances, one might expect that greater control would be exercised centrally.

The perceived difference in operating environment may also entail the establishment of different policies for different countries. Since the local management is usually in a much better position to know what will and will not work locally, they are normally given greater latitude when local conditions are perceived as quite different from the home country's operations. For example, the corporate managers of a U.S. company will probably feel more competent about dictating practices to a Canadian than to a Mexican subsidiary, since the former is presumed to parallel successful U.S. operations more closely.

There are other things that would seem to dictate differences in approaches to different local managers. Factors that would appear to favor decentralization are when the local management team is large rather than lean, when local managers have had a long time with the company, and when they have developed a successful track record. Although these factors would seem to dictate advantages in differentiating the location of decision making for operations in different countries, some evidence suggests that corporations have uniform corporate policies that apply to all their subsidiaries and that they enforce these policies on a fairly uniform basis.[3]

- More uniform the product globally, the more centralization

Product factors. The product itself may determine the relative competence of the centralized staff versus the local managers. For technically sophisticated products there is little need for local adaptations; consequently, at least for marketing policy, decisions may be made that apply to a very broad spectrum of countries. A good contrast is between Nestlé's food products, which depend on geographic differentiation, and General Electric's power generation and jet engine businesses, which are big-ticket products requiring very little adaptation to local needs. The former type of product lends itself much more to decentralization than the latter.[4] Also many products are first introduced in the largest market and later introduced to smaller markets when the country of original entry is in a later stage of the product life cycle. In such instances the centralized staff often asserts control in order to ensure that the same mistakes are not repeated in more than one country. If product technology changes rapidly, there is usually a greater need for headquarters involvement than if the product technology is stable for a long period of time.

- The larger total foreign operations are, the more likely headquarters has specialized staff with international expertise
- The larger the operations in a given country, the more likely that country has specialized staff

Time and size variables.   Usually, the longer a company operates in overseas markets, the larger its foreign sales and the greater experience it has in dealing with foreign problems. The size of total foreign operations as well as the size of operations in individual foreign countries both exert influence on the location of decision making. Studies of financial as well as marketing decisions have found that increased centralization is feasible when a corporate staff that is large enough and qualified enough has developed.[5] The company with very limited foreign operations cannot afford this centralized expertise and must therefore delegate decisions to the operating managers abroad. However, if the specific foreign country operation is very large, then that operation can afford to have its own specialized staff personnel and be treated differently than operations in some of the smaller countries. Many European firms such as Nestlé have their U.S. operations report to headquarters very differently than operations in other places because of the U.S. size. U.S. firms frequently treat their subsidiaries differently in Japan and Brazil for the same reason.[6]

- Bigger decisions at headquarters

Importance of the decision.   In any discussion of authority location, one must consider the importance of the particular decisions. The question sometimes asked is "How much can be lost through a bad decision?" The greater the potential loss, the higher the level of control, whether the problem concerns international or domestic transactions. In the case of marketing decisions, for example, local autonomy over product design is not nearly as prevalent as over advertising, pricing, and distribution.[7] Product design generally necessitates a considerably larger capital outlay than the other functions; consequently, the potential loss from a wrong decision is higher. Furthermore, advertising approaches, pricing, and distribution decisions may be more easily reversed if an error in judgment is made. Rather than delineation of the type of decision that can be made at the subsidiary level, limits may be set instead on expenditure amount, thus allowing local autonomy on small outlays while requiring corporate approval on larger transactions.

Corporate Efficiency Factors

Aside from the relative ability of managers at the corporate and subsidiary levels, the cost and benefit aspects of the decision must be considered. Furthermore, there are a number of instances in which decisions of most benefit to the subsidiary will not be best for the corporation as a whole.

- Must consider how long it takes to get help from headquarters in relation to how fast a decision must be made

Cost and expediency. Although corporate personnel may be more experienced in advising or actually making certain decisions, the time and expense involved in centralization may not justify the so-called better advice. Many decisions cannot await the lengthy period needed to transmit information from one country to another. Other decisions could not effectively be made without on-the-spot observation. To bring in corporate personnel at a high international transport expense may not be warranted.

The distance of foreign operations from headquarters is also a factor to consider. For U.S. subsidiaries in either Canada or Mexico, the time and cost of communications with the parent are low in comparison with being in a country such as the Philippines. The managers in the Philippines may be forced to make decisions on matters for which the Canadian and Mexican managers get corporate assistance.[8]

- Decision on moving goods or other resources more likely made centrally
  - affects more than one country unit

Resource transference. Both product and production factors may be moved from a company's operations in one country to its facilities in another country. The movement may be in the best interest of corporate goals, even though individual subsidiaries may not do as well if resources are transferred. Decisions involving these external relationships are usually made centrally because they require information from all operating units and the ability to mesh the various data so as to achieve overall corporate objectives. While these external relationships may involve many different types of decisions, a few examples should suffice to explain the need for centralization.

Frequently, corporate profits may be improved by moving production factors—capital, personnel, or technology—from one subsidiary to another. Without some central control point, reports would have to be disseminated from every unit to every other unit to determine the resource from one locale that could be used elsewhere. Another movement concerns exports. If exports among subsidiaries are needed to maintain a continual production flow (e.g., vertical integration or interdependent components needed in the company's end product), centralized control may be required to assure this flow. Third, exports to nonaffiliated companies involve jurisdictional questions. For example, if a firm has manufacturing facilities in the United States, Venezuela, and West Germany, which one will export to South Africa? By answering that question centrally, the firm may avoid price competition among the subsidiaries that could result in reduced corporate income. Furthermore, a number of different factors can be considered, including production costs, transportation costs, tax rates, exchange controls, and capacity utilization.

- What is best for company globally may not be best for country unit

Economies and interrelationships through standardization. Even though worldwide uniformity of products, purchases, methods, and policies may not be best for an individual operation, the overall gain may be more

● global optimization done
centrally

than sufficient to overcome the individual country losses. Standardization of machinery used in the production process, for example, may result in a more favorable purchasing price for the firm as a whole because of quantity discounts. This may also bring savings in the training of mechanics, in maintaining manuals, and in carrying inventories of spare parts. One may consider economies in almost any type of corporate activity, such as advertising programs, research and development, and purchase of group insurances. Uniformity of products also gives a firm greater flexibility in filling orders when there are supply problems, which may arise because of strikes, disasters, or sudden increases in demand. Production can simply be expanded in one country to meet shortages elsewhere.

Another argument for adhering to like policies globally is to ensure that foreign operations do not veer so drastically from the overall line or method of business that control is completely lost. If units in different countries alter products, policies, and methods even gradually but in different directions, the eventual diversity may be so great that economies are no longer possible and the interchangeability of personnel, products, and ideas becomes cumbersome.

Increasingly, the people with whom a firm must deal (government officials, employees, suppliers, consumers, and the general public) are aware of what that firm does in every country in which it operates. Concessions that have been easily granted in one country may then be demanded in other countries, where they are not as easily afforded. Let us suppose that, for public relations purposes, the management in one country decided to give preferential prices to the government and established a profit-sharing plan for employees. If the government officials and employees in a second country were to ask for similar treatment, the result might be reduced profits or poor public relations.

Even internal pricing and product decisions can affect demand in other countries. With the growing mobility of consumers, especially industrial consumers, a good or bad experience with a product in one country may eventually affect sales elsewhere. This is especially true if industrial consumers themselves want uniformity in their end products. If prices differ substantially among countries, consumers may even find they can import more cheaply than buying locally.

Global competitive strategies. A company needs to determine whether it is better off trying to emphasize country-by-country competitive positions or an integrated global one. In addition to the question of standardized versus differentiated products among countries, there are a number of other factors to consider. One is whether large scale production of components and finished goods can be exported so that costs can be reduced to buyers in various countries. The nature of the production process, transportation costs, and government import restrictions all affect the production integration advantages.

The present and potential existence of global customers and/or competitors may also dictate the making of decisions to improve global performance at the expense of a particular country's operations. Price concessions to an automobile manufacturer in Brazil, for example, may help gain business for the supplier in other countries where the buyer manufactures automobiles. A company may also attack a competitor by producing and selling where that competitor gains its major resources to compete globally. In fact, such an attack may purposely be by making little or no profit in that market. Caterpillar, for example, invested in Japan where its rival, Komatsu, had been gaining 80 percent of the cash flow needed for its global expansion.[9]

- Centralization may hurt local management
  - cannot perform as well
  - do not get training through more responsibility

Local performance considerations. Although there are clearly decisions that can be made efficiently at the corporate level, one must weigh this technical efficiency against morale problems created by taking responsibility away from the local management team. When local managers are prevented from acting in the best interest of their own operation, there is a tendency for them to think, "I could have done better, but corporate management would not let me." These managers may lose commitment to their jobs and may not gain the experience needed to move into jobs of greater responsibility. This lack of commitment may be overcome through development of a reward system that does not penalize managers for decisions that are outside of their control. In fact, a compensation system that rewards local managers partially on the basis of the corporation's total worldwide performance may enhance the development of global thinking at each country level.

- People trained at headquarters more likely to think like headquarters personnel

Selection of subsidiary managers. The degree of control imposed by corporate headquarters on the selection of top managers for foreign subsidiaries may dictate to a great extent how much formal control over the subsidiaries' operations the corporate personnel feel is necessary. For example, the use of parent country nationals in the subsidiary management—or even determining the standards of selection and training—may be perceived as a means of assuring primary loyalty to the corporate rather than subsidiary entity.[10] A study comparing U.S., British, and Japanese subsidiaries in Malaysia concluded that the Japanese firms were most apt to follow this practice. This led to control through interactions between subsidiaries and parents. This was true even though the Japanese parents were less likely to own the operations wholly or to require long-range planning from the subsidiaries.[11] Another study has concluded that frequent transfers of managers among foreign operations develops increased knowledge and commitment so that fewer procedures, less hierarchical communication, and less surveillance are needed.[12]

● LDCs argue that centralization keeps them subservient

   ● especially R&D centralization

Dependency. Many critics within the less-developed countries have contended that the centralization of decision making by MNEs is leading to an ever-increasing movement of management and technical functions to the home country, leaving the menial and low-skilled jobs in the LDCs. The critics recall colonial eras in which their own people were forbidden responsible positions and depended on the colonial powers for the control of their destinies.[13] They have been particularly disparaging about the fact that very little R&D by MNEs is done outside their home countries; and of that portion done outside, almost all is done in other industrial countries.[14]

This is a dilemma for MNEs. There are some potent arguments for centralizing most R&D in home countries, such as the availability of large numbers of people to work directly for the company, the proximity to private research organizations and universities doing related work, and the general advantages of centralized authority for less duplication of efforts.[15]

Recall that, in the Nestlé case, new product R&D was done in Switzerland to reduce duplication and to be close to the strategic planners who projected product needs further into the future than would country managers, who were more concerned with day-to-day operations. Nestlé did allow country areas the freedom to conduct adaptive R&D but controlled this carefully by requiring corporate approval of the adaptations. Thus, even when the corporation allows adaptive or new product R&D to be carried out abroad, the corporate management may exert substantial influence on it. Studies show that MNEs with substantial R&D outside the home country seldom allow the foreign affiliate complete autonomy. The corporate management may allocate budgets, approve plans, and offer suggestions. At the same time there may be substantial input from affiliates for R&D conducted centrally.[16]

PLANNING

Throughout this text we have emphasized the need to adapt the company's unique resources and objectives to the different and changing foreign situations. This is the essence of planning. Without planning, it is only by chance that a company picks the best order and method of expansion by country. Without planning, it is again by chance that a company sets policies and practices in a given locale that result in the desired performance. Since planning has been both implicitly and explicitly discussed already, this section presents merely an overview of the process.

The Planning Process

- Must mesh objectives with internal and external constraints
- Must set means to implement, monitor, and correct

Figure 17.1 indicates that planning must involve the meshing of objectives with the internal and external environment. The details in each planning section include items discussed in the environmental and operational sections of this text. Note that the first step is a self-analysis of internal resources and constraints on the total corporation along with the environmental factors that affect each company differently. Only by taking this first step can a firm set the overall rationale for its international activities. For instance, a company faced with rising domestic costs and expanded competition from imports may validly pursue one of several objectives such as cost reduction, acquisition of resources the competition needs, or diversification into new markets or products. The analysis of the internal resources will help to determine which of these objectives is feasible and most important. It will also aid in the selection of alternatives.

Since each country in which the firm is operating or contemplating operations also has certain unique elements, the local analysis will also have to be made before the final alternatives can be fully examined. For instance, local marketing factors will determine which product strategies can even be considered. Priorities must be set among alternatives so that programs may be easily added or deleted as resource availability or situations change. A company may, for example, prefer and plan to remit dividends from one of its foreign subsidiaries back to the parent; however, this may not turn out to be possible. Management should also consider what it will do with earnings if exchange controls are put into effect. Furthermore, what alternatives will then exist for the parent, which has to do without the funds? It may be necessary to borrow more at home, remit more from other subsidiaries, forego domestic expansion, or forego domestic dividends. Without the establishment of priorities, decisions may have to be made too hurriedly to fulfill company objectives even partially.

Finally, very specific objectives should be set for each operating unit, along with ways of measuring both deviations from the plan and conditions that may cause a deviation. Through timely evaluation, management may take corrective actions or at least move to contingency means for the achievement of the objectives. Evaluation methods are discussed later in the chapter.

A distinction must be made between operating plans and strategic plans. Strategic plans are longer term and involve major commitments depending on which businesses the company will be in and where. While input for a strategic plan may come from all parts of the organization, it is only at a corporate level that allocations can be made that will implement overall planned changes in geographic and product policies. It is also usual for the corporate staff to be the primary people concerned with making strategic plans, since they have information on the firm's worldwide activities, competition, and trends.

FIGURE 17.1
The International Planning Process

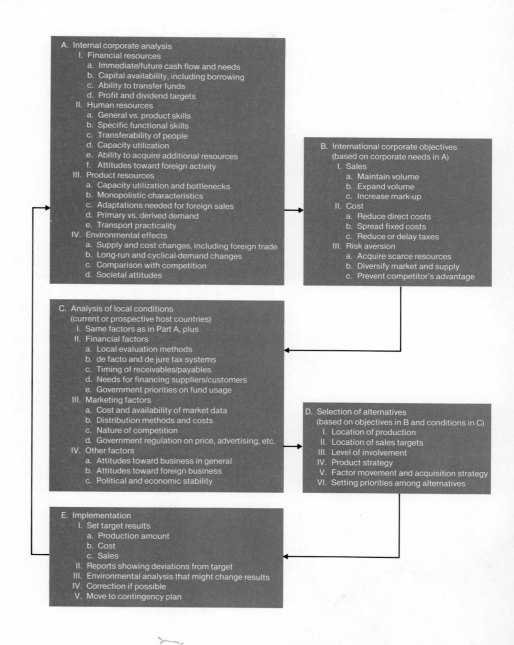

A. Internal corporate analysis
   I. Financial resources
     a. Immediate/future cash flow and needs
     b. Capital availability, including borrowing
     c. Ability to transfer funds
     d. Profit and dividend targets
   II. Human resources
     a. General vs. product skills
     b. Specific functional skills
     c. Transferability of people
     d. Capacity utilization
     e. Ability to acquire additional resources
     f. Attitudes toward foreign activity
   III. Product resources
     a. Capacity utilization and bottlenecks
     b. Monopolistic characteristics
     c. Adaptations needed for foreign sales
     d. Primary vs. derived demand
     e. Transport practicality
   IV. Environmental effects
     a. Supply and cost changes, including foreign trade
     b. Long-run and cyclical-demand changes
     c. Comparison with competition
     d. Societal attitudes

B. International corporate objectives
   (based on corporate needs in A)
   I. Sales
     a. Maintain volume
     b. Expand volume
     c. Increase mark-up
   II. Cost
     a. Reduce direct costs
     b. Spread fixed costs
     c. Reduce or delay taxes
   III. Risk aversion
     a. Acquire scarce resources
     b. Diversify market and supply
     c. Prevent competitor's advantage

C. Analysis of local conditions
   (current or prospective host countries)
   I. Same factors as in Part A, plus
   II. Financial factors
     a. Local evaluation methods
     b. de facto and de jure tax systems
     c. Timing of receivables/payables
     d. Needs for financing suppliers/customers
     e. Government priorities on fund usage
   III. Marketing factors
     a. Cost and availability of market data
     b. Distribution methods and costs
     c. Nature of competition
     d. Government regulation on price, advertising, etc.
   IV. Other factors
     a. Attitudes toward business in general
     b. Attitudes toward foreign business
     c. Political and economic stability

D. Selection of alternatives
   (based on objectives in B and conditions in C)
   I. Location of production
   II. Location of sales targets
   III. Level of involvement
   IV. Product strategy
   V. Factor movement and acquisition strategy
   VI. Setting priorities among alternatives

E. Implementation
   I. Set target results
     a. Production amount
     b. Cost
     c. Sales
   II. Reports showing deviations from target
   III. Environmental analysis that might change results
   IV. Correction if possible
   V. Move to contingency plan

Problems of Planning

- International has more complexity and uncertainty
  - environments and tasks increase
- Greater uncertainty means greater need for information but
  - problems of international information

The greater the amount of uncertainty, the more difficult it is to plan. It is generally agreed that operations in the international sphere involve more uncertainty than those in the domestic one because of the greater complexity of international operations.[17] One type of complexity is caused by the external operating environment, another by the task.[18] The more countries the company is operating in, the more environments and changes it may face. There are also different requirements for different markets in terms of task, because of different products and how they are made.

We would generally expect that greater complexity and uncertainty would lead to greater need and use for information.[19] However, there is substantial evidence that the higher the uncertainty, the lower the amount of environmental scanning to collect information.[20] This may be due to the relative inaccessibility of accurate information internationally.

BUSINESS RESEARCH

- Information needed at all levels of control

Business research is undertaken to reduce uncertainties in the decision process, to expand or narrow the alternatives under consideration, and to assess the merits of existing programs. The reduction of uncertainty would include attempts to answer such questions as: Is there a market for the product? Can qualified manpower be hired? Will the economic and political climate allow for a reasonable certainty of operations? Alternatives may be expanded by asking, "Where are possible new sources of funds or sales?" or narrowed by ascertaining, "Where among the alternatives would operating costs be lowest?" Evaluation and control are improved by assessing present and past performance: Is the distributor servicing sufficient accounts? What is our market share? Clearly, there is a myriad of details that, if ascertained, would be useful in meeting the firm's objectives.

How Much Research?

- Never have as much information as one would like
- Should compare cost versus value

A company can seldom if ever secure all of the information its managers would like. This is partially due to time constraints, since markets or raw materials may need to be secured before competitors gain control of them. Furthermore, contracts that call for bids or proposals usually have deadlines. The cost of information is another constraint. The greater area to be considered by a multinational company, of course, amplifies the number of alternatives and complexities. It is therefore useful to limit extensive information gathering to those projects that seem to have the highest potential. One method is to estimate the costs of data collection along with the probable payoff from the data in terms of revenue gains or cost savings. In this way a company may prioritize research projects on the basis of expected return from the costs of the collection.

Problems in Data

• Some countries have more than others but problems in all

The lack, obsolescence, and inaccuracy of data on many countries make much research difficult and expensive to undertake. In some countries, such as the United States, the government collects very detailed demographic and purchasing data, which is available very cheaply to any firm or individual. (But in the United States, some economists estimate that gross national product figures may be understated by as much as 15 percent; and the Census Bureau official in charge of overseeing the 1980 count was relieved of his duties because of allegations that too many millions of people were not being counted properly.)[21] Using samples based on available information, one can draw fairly accurate inferences concerning market segment sizes and locations, at least within broad categories. Also in the United States the fact that so many firms are publicly owned and are required to disclose considerable operating information is an advantage in learning competitors' strengths and weaknesses. Furthermore, one may rely on a multitude of behavioral studies dealing with U.S. consumer preferences and experience. For instance, patterns of consumption expenditures have been published to show differences among such demographic variables as age, income, education, sex, neighborhood, and race. More recently, behavior has been shown to differ by personality variables. With this available information a firm can devise questionnaires or get acknowledgments from demonstrations that reflect predictable responses. Contrast this situation with a country whose basic census, national income accounts, and foreign trade figures are suspect and where no data are collected on consumer expenditures. Business is conducted in a veil of secrecy, consumer buying behavior is speculated upon, and middlemen are reluctant to answer questions. In such a situation, expensive primary research may be required before meaningful samples and questions can be developed.

Reasons for Inaccuracies

• Lack ability to collect
• Purposely mislead
• Include only legal, reported activities

For the most part, incomplete or inaccurate published data result from the inability of many governments to collect the needed details. Poor countries may simply have such limited resources that other projects are necessarily given priority in the national budget. Why collect precise figures on the literacy rate, it is reasoned, when the same outlay of money may be used to build schools to improve that rate?

Education affects the competence of governmental officials to maintain accurate records and to analyze them. The economic factor likewise hampers the retrieval and analysis of records, since hand calculations may be used extensively instead of electronic data processing systems. (One need only witness the problem many countries have in collecting taxes to substantiate this statement.) The result may be information that is years old before it is made public. Finally, cultural factors affect responses. If there is mistrust concerning the end use of the data, the respondent may give erroneous information—particularly if questions seek financial details. Because of these differences, it has been observed that firms in the United States make much greater use of mail surveys and personal and telephone interviews than firms in Europe.[22]

Of equal concern to the researcher is the publication of information designed to persuade the businessperson to follow a certain course of action. While perhaps not purposefully publishing false statements, many governmental and private organizations may be so selective as to create false impressions. It is therefore useful to consider carefully the source of such material in the light of possible motives or biases. The government of Ethiopia, for instance, once censored outgoing reports about its drought and famine for fear that tourism might fall if foreigners knew how bad the situation was.

Not all of the inaccuracies are due to the collection and dissemination procedures of governments. A large portion of the studies by academicians that purport to describe business practices either by domestic firms in different countries or by international firms abroad are not necessarily accurate. Broad generalizations are frequently drawn on the basis of too few observations, nonrepresentative samples, and poorly designed questionnaires. There is a tendency to describe the unusual because it may make more interesting reading than the typical. Clearly, it is not enough to take the word of a scholar. One should examine the methodology as well.

The desire and ability of people to cover up data on themselves may distort published figures substantially. Part of the cover-up is attributable to unrecorded criminal activity. Economic data on Colombia, for example, do not include cocaine revenue, yet estimates are that export earnings from cocaine exceed all other Colombian exports combined.[23] In the United States, estimated illegal income from such activities as drugs, bribery, and prostitution amounted to $125 billion in 1981.[24] Part of the cover-up is attributable to tax avoidance. As much as 25 percent of the GNP in Italy and 30 percent in Israel goes unreported primarily for that reason.[25]

Some Comparability Problems

- Collection methods, definitions, base years differ
- Things outside money economy
- Currencies must be translated

One important variable to note when contrasting data from different countries is the year in which collection was made. Censuses are conducted in different years in different countries; consequently, such information as population totals cannot be easily compared. It may be necessary for the researcher to make estimates of current figures based on projected growth rates. Gross national product figures, trade statistics, and base year calculations constitute a few of the other areas that require updating.

There are also numerous definitional differences among countries; a figure as basic as "family income" might represent quite different things. Not only does the average number of children per family vary across national lines, but also whether such relatives as grandparents, uncles, and cousins are included in the definition. The number of people may make a big difference in expenditures available. Literacy is defined in some places by some minimum of formal schooling, in others by certain specified standards, and in still others as simply the ability to read and write one's name. Furthermore, percentages may be published in terms of adult population (with different ages used for adulthood) or of total population. Another definitional difference concerns depreciation, which can alter substantially the comparability of net national product figures among countries.

National income and per capita income figures are particularly difficult to compare because of differences in the dispersion of the income. A country with a large middle class will have consumption patterns that are quite distinct from those in a country where large portions of the population are excluded from the money economy. In Dahomey, for instance, at least half the population effectively earns nothing. This means that the per capita income of the remaining group is at least double what the published figure shows for the country as a whole. Those outside the money economy obviously have consumption patterns that are greater than zero, since they may grow agricultural products and produce other goods, which they consume or barter. The extent to which people in one country produce for their own consumption (e.g., having a vegetable garden, baking bread, sewing clothes, cutting hair) will distort comparisons with other countries that follow different patterns.

A further problem concerns exchange rates, which must be used to convert country data to some common currency. A 10 percent revaluation of the Japanese yen in relation to the U.S. dollar will result in a 10 percent increase in per capita income of Japanese residents when figures are reflected in dollars. Does this mean that the Japanese are suddenly 10 percent richer? Obviously not, since their yen income, which they use for about 85 percent of their purchases in the Japanese economy, is unchanged and buys no more. Even without the changes in exchange rates, it is different to make comparisons of purchasing power and living standards, since costs are so affected by climate and habit. Exchange rates constitute a very imperfect means of comparing national data.

External Sources of Information

• Specificity and cost vary by source

The number of organizations as well as publications that deal in whole or in part with information on international business is too large to explore in depth here. Instead of comparing each source, we will make some general comments about general types of information. The main sources are firms that make a living from supplying information, firms that would like to supply services connected with the conduct of international business, governmental agencies, and international organizations.

Individualized reports. In almost any country there are market research and business consulting firms that will conduct studies for a fee. Where these do not exist, some firms, such as Unilever, have gone so far as to develop them, particularly if their own research needs do not justify the maintenance of a full-time staff.[26] Naturally, the quality and cost of these studies vary widely depending on the type of information desired, the country in which the study is being conducted, and the company conducting the study. Generally, this is the most costly information source because the individualized nature of the study restricts proration among a number of firms. However, the fact that the client can specify what information is wanted often makes the expense worthwhile. To make the best use of market research groups, a company should have collected substantial data in advance so that the special studies can be designed to fit the precise needs of the client.

Specialized studies. Some research organizations prepare studies of a fairly specific nature and then sell them to any interested firm. The cost is much lower than for individualized studies. The studies are sometimes printed as directories of firms operating in a given locale, perhaps with financial or other information about the firms. The studies may also be about business in certain locales of the world, such as Brazil; about forms of business, such as licensing; or about specific products, such as baby food. They may combine any of these elements as well. For example, a title could well be "The Market for Imported Auto Parts in West Germany."

Service firms. Most firms that serve international clients, such as banks, transportation agencies, and accounting firms, publish reports that are available to potential clients. These reports are usually geared toward either the conduct of business in a given area or some specific subject of general interest, such as tax or trademark legislation. Since these are intended to reach a wide market of firms, they usually lack the specificity one would like for making a final decision. However, much of the data are useful as background information. Some of these organizations are also helpful in giving informal opinions about such things as the reputation of possible business associates and the names of people to contact. One may also discern useful information from other companies operating in a given locale.

Governmental agencies. Governments are another source of information. Statistical reports are available on many topics, although, as was mentioned earlier, the quantity and quality vary from country to country. When a government or an agency of the government has an interest in stimulating foreign business activity, the amount and type of information may be substantial. For example, the U.S. Department of Commerce not only compiles such basic data as news and regulations on individual countries, but will also help set up appointments with businesspeople in foreign countries. The Department also sponsors seminars on exporting and on other specialized topics, and at one time would even help underwrite the cost of having a graduate student do a preliminary market feasibility study for new or small exporters. Countries interested in attracting foreign investments usually have development offices at home and abroad that will supply a wealth of information.

International agencies.   There are numerous agencies supported by more than one country, such as the United Nations, the International Monetary Fund, the Organization for Economic Cooperation and Development, and the European Community. All of these organizations have large research staffs that compile basic statistics as well as reports and recommendations concerning common trends and problems. Many of the international development banks will help finance investment feasibility studies.

Trade associations.   In many product lines there are trade associations that collect, evaluate, and disseminate a wide variety of data dealing with technical and competitive factors in the industry. Much of this information is available in their trade journals; other data may or may not be made available to nonmembers.

Information service companies.   A number of companies, such as Lockheed Dialog, have in recent years established information retrieval services. These typically maintain data bases from over 100 different sources, including many of those described above. For a fee, one can access these computerized data by telephone modem and arrange for an immediate printout of studies of interest.

Internal Generation

International firms may themselves have to conduct many studies abroad. Sometimes the research may be no more than observing keenly and asking many questions. One can see what merchandise is available in stores, see who is buying in which stores, and uncover the hidden distribution points and competition. In some countries, for example, the competition for ready-made clothes may be from seamstresses in private homes rather than from retailers. The competition for vacuum cleaners may be in the form of servants who clean with mops rather than from other electrical appliance manufacturers. Traditional analysis would not reveal such matters. In many countries, even bankers have to rely more on clients' reputations than on their financial statements. Shrewd questioning may yield very interesting results.

Firms frequently set certain minimum criteria on which to base a decision. If a company regards a total market of 35 million as satisfactory, it is fruitless to spend the time and money on determining where within a range of 90 to 100 million the market actually lies.

Often it is necessary to be extremely imaginative, extremely observant, or both. A soft drink manufacturer wanted to determine the market share it held vis-à-vis its competitors in Mexico, but the competitors were not about to divulge this information. Attempts to make estimates from the points of distribution as one would do at home were just as futile because of the extremely widespread distribution of this type of product. Finally, the manufacturer hit upon two alternatives, both of which turned out to be feasible: The manufacturer of bottle caps was willing to reveal how many caps were sold to each client, and customs supplied data on the volume of imports of soft drink concentrate used by each of the competitors.

REPORTING TECHNIQUES

Need for Reports

- Must be timely in order to respond to them to
  - allocate resources
  - correct performance
- More reliance on written reports internationally

Timely reports from all operating units of an international firm are needed so that management can allocate resources properly, make corrections in plans, and reward personnel for their performances. Let us look first at resource allocation. Profits from one unit may be used within that unit or elsewhere for expansion, for dividends, to reduce the need for borrowed funds, or merely to hold for possible contingencies. One may find similar alternatives for the use of personnel, technology, and end product. The decisions on the use of any of these resources is almost continuous; consequently, reports must be frequent and show recent situations so that the resources are put to the best of use. Second, plans need to be updated in order to be realistic and to assure that there is a high probability of meeting desired objectives. Feedback of both results and conditions that might affect results are essential so that corrective action, whether in the form of new strategies to meet objectives or in the form of alteration of objectives, may be undertaken. Finally, reports are needed in order to evaluate the performance of personnel in the various operating units of the company. Not only will comparison of performance aid in determining who will receive the rewards of monetary compensation and advancement, but it also will aid in stimulating personnel to improve their own weaknesses.

The use of written reports is more important in an international than in a domestic setting because of the greater isolation of foreign subsidiaries from corporate headquarters. In Chapter 22 we show that subsidiary managers have much less personal and oral contact with line and staff personnel above them, a problem for the overseas managers. It is also a problem for the corporate managers because they miss out on much of the informal communication that can tell them about the performance of the foreign operations.

Types of Systems

- Primarily to evaluate operating units
  - secondarily to evaluate management in units
- Visits are also important control mechanism

Several studies of reporting systems utilized in international firms indicate that those used for foreign operations are similar to those used domestically.[27] There are several reasons for this. If they have been effective domestically, there is often a belief that they will be effective internationally as well—particularly if home country management believes that its know-how is superior to that abroad. Next, there are economies through carrying over the same types of reports. The need to establish new types of reporting mechanisms is eliminated, and corporate management is already familiar with the system. Finally, like reports presumably give comparability. Management may thus compare one operation against another and consolidate the reports without as much fear that they have added "apples to oranges."

The main purpose of MNEs' reporting systems is to assure adequate profitability by identifying deviations from plans that would be indications of possible problem areas. This focus may be on short-term performance or on longer-term indicators that are congruous with the strategic thrust of the organization. The emphasis is on the evaluation of the subsidiary rather than evaluation of the subsidiary manager, although the profitability of the foreign unit is one of the important ingredients in the managerial evaluation.[28]

Not all information exchange is by formalized reports. Within many MNEs, certain members of the corporate staff travel more than 50 percent of their time in order to visit with subsidiaries. Although this may do much to alleviate misunderstandings, there are some inherent dangers if visits are not done properly. If, on one hand, corporate personnel visit the tropical subsidiaries only when there are blizzards at home, the personnel abroad may perceive the trips as mere boondoggles. If, on the other hand, subsidiary managers offer too many social activities and not enough analysis of operations, the corporate staff members may consider the trip a waste of time. Also, if visitors come only when the corporate level is upset about foreign operations, the overseas managers may always be overly defensive.

Reporting Problems

Although there are some advantages in using the same reporting systems internationally and domestically, management should be aware of potential problems. These include the separation of subsidiary from management performance in the evaluation process, environmental differences, and the lack of cost and accounting comparability.

- Evaluate managers on things they can control but
  - disagreement on what is in their control

Management versus subsidiary performance. There is general agreement that subsidiaries should be evaluated separately from the management within subsidiaries. This is so that managers are not penalized for conditions and occurrences that are outside their control. Beyond this agreement, however, there is a good deal of difference among firms in what they do and do not include in the managerial performance evaluation. For instance, some firms hold managers abroad responsible for gains or losses in currency translation while others do not. Most firms deduct interest expenses before measuring the profitability of foreign operations; however, many do not.[29] These are examples of environmental factors that some, but not all, companies consider to be outside the control of the local managers.

Another area of noncontrollables is when centralized decisions are made that will optimize the performance of the total corporation. A particular subsidiary may not do as well as if it had been left to operate independently. In fact, the normal profit center records may well obscure the importance that the subsidiary plays within the total corporate entity. This may be particularly due to pricing in intercompany transactions that inflates or deflates profits of a given subsidiary.

- Hard to compare countries through standard operating ratios

Cost and accounting comparability. Different affiliate cost structures may preclude a meaningful comparison of operating results. For example, the percentage of direct labor to sales in one country may be much higher than in a subsidiary in another country if the former is more labor-intensive. There is no guarantee that the firm will produce the same product with the same set of inputs at all plants. It may have to adjust its normal production process because of available labor and capital. Different accounting practices can also create problems. Most international firms keep one set of books that are consistent with parent principles and another set of books to meet local reporting requirements.

- Want higher return in high-risk countries but may be outside control of management

Country risk. Recall from the previous chapter that, when evaluating foreign investment possibilities, most companies set a higher minimum return to invest in high-risk countries. Having done this, firms logically would expect the performance within the high-risk countries to reflect the expected higher return. Most companies agree that such an analysis would be useful; however, they also agree that they know of no reasonable means of incorporating country risk into the performance evaluation. The feeling is that the incorporation would penalize managers in risky countries and make them responsible for something outside their control.[30]

Evaluative Measurements

- Reliance on combination of measurements

Multiple measurements. Every evaluation measurement has shortcomings when applied internationally. Consequently, a system that relies on a number of different indicators may be preferable to one that relies too heavily on

- financial criteria most used
- nonfinancial used more for management than operating units

one measurement. Financial criteria tend to dominate the evaluation of foreign operations and their managers. While many different ones are used, the most important for evaluating the operations are budget compared with profit, budget compared with sales, and return on investment. The most common financial criteria for management appraisal are budget compared to profit, budget compared to sales, and return on sales. Many nonfinancial criteria are also employed. The only one commonly given much weight in subsidiary evaluation is market share increase. Several nonfinancial criteria are important for evaluating the managers, though. These include market share increase, quality control, and relationship with the host government.[31]

- Evaluate actual in relation to planned

Budget concept. One way of overcoming the problems of evaluating performance is the budget, which can help the MNE differentiate between the worth of the subsidiary and the performance of subsidiary management. The budget should include the goals for each subsidiary that will help the MNE achieve an overall objective. As long as the subsidiary manager is working toward a budgeted goal rather than a measure such as return on investment, there will be fewer problems in dealing with inflation, exchange rate changes, and transfer prices. A further discussion of budget techniques, particularly as they relate to exchange rate changes, is presented in Chapter 19.

Planning Information Acquisitions

- Should reevaluate information needs periodically to keep costs down, assure info being used

Thus far the discussion has centered on information needed to evaluate subsidiary and subsidiary management performance. Although this information is crucial, corporate management requires additional data. The information needs may be categorized as follows:

1. information generated by informal operations for centralized coordination, such as cash balances and needs;
2. information relating to external conditions, such as analyses of local political and economic conditions;
3. information for feedback from parent to local subsidiaries, such as R&D breakthroughs;
4. lateral information between related subsidiaries; and
5. external reporting needs.[32]

Since information needs are so broad, two of the problems for international firms are the cost of information relative to its value and "information glut," which refers to redundancy. One technique used by some firms is Planned Information Acquisition Analysis (PIAA), which involves reevaluating each new document or service the firm uses for information after two years.[33] By comparing the number of times sources have been retrieved and found relevant as an information input against documents in a similar category, acquisition may be limited to the items that are of most value to the firm.

Compatibility. Another problem is the compatibility of information needed by the subsidiary and by corporate management. Even when different subsidiaries are trying to solve similar problems, their information needs may be vastly different. Consequently, corporate management may be faced with dilemmas of trying to compare unlike data or of requiring different or additional data, which may be expensive. An approach that has been instituted by some firms is to allow diversity but to send copies and analysis to centralized data banks.[34] For many corporate needs, standardization is not a necessity. What is important is standardization of coding. On a centralized basis, personnel may compare the accuracy of subsidiary projects and suggest more refined models by using existing data.

Aside from the problem of data or coding uniformity, one of the major obstacles to the on-time retrieval of comparable information is that there is often such a diversity from country to country in a company's approach to data processing. They vary in terms of equipment and in software packages. Uniformity of approach is hampered by substantial cost differences in personnel, hardware, and data communications.[35]

Information centers. With the expansion of multinational telecommunications and computer linkages, managers throughout the world are now able to share information almost instantaneously.[36] On one hand, this may permit more centralization, since truly global implications of policies may be examined. On the other hand, managers in foreign locations may become more autonomous because of the greater amount of information at their disposal. Among the types of information that are readily available are engineering and design information, quality control, inventory and work-in-process levels, and data banks for scientific research and development.

Restrictions on data flows. Over sixty countries have passed or are considering legislation that directly or indirectly affects the flow of data internationally. These have been enacted for three primary reasons. The first is concern about individual privacy, particularly that the development and transmission of personnel data might give the company an undue advantage over the individual. Such restrictions, however, make it difficult for the international company to maintain centralized personnel records, which assist in making international transfers. Burroughs, for example, could not transfer its personnel records from Germany to other locations. A second concern is economic—for example, that local jobs will be lost if data processing and analysis are done abroad and that resource transmission will occur without payment to the country that created the resource. Legislation has included the require-

---

• Local needs and differences in data processing create problems of compatibility

• May permit choice of centralization or decentralization

• Many countries restricting data flows because
  • personal privacy
  • economic protection
  • strategic implications
• May become harder for companies to control globally

ment of local purchases (such as for data-processing equipment, materials, or services), that the local subsidiary maintain copies of anything transmitted, and that local authorities monitor anything transmitted. Companies worry about additional costs and that proprietary information may fall into the hands of competitors. The third reason for legislation is that corporate networks may be used to pirate military and commercial data to be sent abroad.

ORGANIZATIONAL STRUCTURE

As a firm develops international business activities, its corporate structure must adapt to the changing environment in order to accommodate foreign operations effectively. The organizational structure that emerges will depend on many factors, including the location and type of foreign facilities, the impact of international operations on total corporate performance, the nature of assets employed in pursuit of business abroad, and the time horizons for achieving international and total corporate goals.

It is necessary to establish legal and organizational structures at home and abroad to meet company objectives. Within each foreign country these arrangements may differ because of the unique nature of activities and environmental requirements. Superimposed above the country organizations may be additional structures that coordinate activities in more than one country. The form, method, and location of operational units at home and abroad will affect taxes, expenses, and control. Consequently, organizational structure has an important effect on the fulfillment of corporate objectives.

Level of Importance

- The larger the foreign operations, the higher they report in the structure
  - placement evolves as foreign operations grow

The more important the specific foreign operations are to total corporate performance, the higher the corporate level to which these units should report. The organizational structure or reporting system should therefore change over time to parallel a company's increased involvement in foreign activities.

At one end of the spectrum is the firm that merely exports temporary surpluses through a middleman who takes title and handles all the export details. Clearly, few people in the firm are concerned with the conduct of the business. Since no personnel are either overseas or engaged in export arrangement, there is no need to devise new personnel policies or training programs. Since the title to goods changes hands in the home country, there are no foreign legal or tax matters to consider. Since payment is effected in the home currency, there are no problems of transferring funds or evaluating country-by-country performance. Since no attempt is made to increase foreign sales, new marketing programs are not required. The entire operation is apt to be so insignificant to total corporate performance that top-level management is concerned very little with such transactions. The duties may be handled by anyone in the organization who knows enough and has time to discern whether or not orders can be filled. In this situation, foreign activities should be handled at a low level in the corporate hierarchy.

At the other end of the spectrum is the firm that has passed through intermediate stages and now owns and manages foreign manufacturing and sales facilities. Every functional and advisory group within the company will undoubtedly be involved in the establishment and direction of the facilities. Since sales, investments, and profits are now a more significant part of the corporate total, people very high in the corporate hierarchy are concerned with the foreign operations.

Integrated versus Separate International Activities

- International division
  - creates critical international mass
  - may have problem of getting resources from domestic divisions
- Worldwide product
  - popular among diverse product firms, especially diversity through acquisition
- Area
  - large foreign operations not dominated by a single country or region
- Functional
  - popular among extractive companies
- Matrix
  - product, function, and area given even focus
  - hard to report to two or more bosses

A controversy among observers of international organizations is whether all international activities of a given business should be grouped together (e.g., international department or division) or whether they should be grouped by the product, function, or geographic structure the company relies on domestically. Those in favor of separating the international activities argue that this allows for specialized personnel to handle such diverse matters as export documentation, foreign exchange transactions, and foreign government relations. They also argue that by putting all international operations together, the international activities constitute a large enough critical mass to wield power within the organization. When separated among product or functional units, they may be so small in comparison to domestic business that little attention is given to their development. Those in favor of integrating the domestic and foreign operations argue that a separation still may necessitate international dependence on the domestic divisions for product, personnel, technology, and other resources. Since managers in the domestic divisions are evaluated against domestic performance standards, they may withhold their best resources from the international group in order to improve their own performance.

Figure 17.2 shows simplified examples of different approaches to the placement of foreign activities within the organizational structure. Most companies broadly fit one of these categories. Part A is an example of separating international operations. Although this structure is not popular among European multinational firms, it is very common among those based in the United States.[38] One of the apparent causes for the difference is that U.S. firms are typically much more dependent on the domestic market than are European firms; therefore the international division allows U.S. firms to gain the "critical mass" discussed above.

Parts B, C, and D are types of international operations that are integrated rather than handled separately. The product organization (B) is particularly popular among companies that operate within highly diverse product groups, especially those that have become diverse primarily by acquiring other companies. Since the product groups may have little in common, even domestically, note that more than one subsidiary may exist in the same foreign country. Yet each reports to a different group. The geographic organization (C) is used primarily by firms with very large foreign operations, not dominated by a single country or area. Few U.S. firms use this structure because of the dominance of the U.S. markets. The functional organization (D) is popular among extractive companies. Companies that utilize these integrative structures may use staff departments (e.g., legal or personnel) as a means of centralizing functions common to more than one subsidiary. At Heinz, for instance, one expatriate-transfer-and-compensation policy is used by all the geographic divisions; thus, the duplication of effort is minimized.

Because of the problems inherent in either integrating or operating foreign operations, some firms are moving toward matrix organizations (E). In these a subsidiary reports to more than one group (product, function, and area). The theory is that, since each group shares responsibility over foreign operations, each group will depend on the others. The groups will become more interdependent, will exchange information, and will ultimately take strategic global perspectives as they seek to exchange resources with other groups. For example, product group managers must compete so that R&D personnel responsible to a functional group are assigned to the development of technologies that fall within their product domain. The same product group managers must compete as well to see that area managers put sufficient emphasis on their lines. Not only are product groups competing, the functional and geographic areas must also strive to draw upon resources held by others in the matrix.

Although a matrix form requires that all major perspectives be represented in strategic decision making, this form of organization is not without drawbacks. One of the problems is that groups and coalitions inevitably compete for scarce resources, and a decision must be made by an executive above the group level on how to allocate the resources when managers at the lower level fail to reach agreement. Such elements as faith in a specific executive or business group may result in more decisions being made in favor of those components.[39] As others in the organization see this occurring, they may perceive that the locus of relative power lies with a certain individual or group. This may lead managers to divert most of their energies toward the activities that are perceived as most likely to be accepted, thus perpetuating the difference in relative power. This may not represent the areas that would be the firm's best strategic choices on a global basis. Consequently, some of the advantages sought in a matrix organization may be diminished because of these interpersonal relationships. A number of alternatives may help to alleviate this problem, including the transfer of individuals

FIGURE 17.2

**Placement of International
Activities within the
Organizational Structure**

A. Separation of international

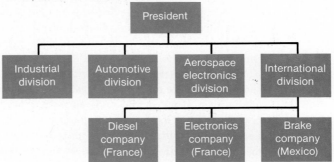

B. International within product group

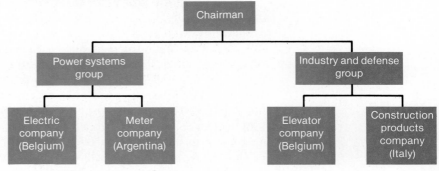

C. International within geographic group

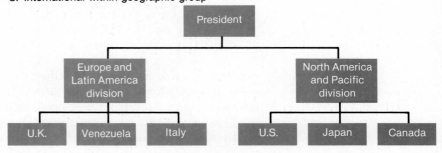

FIGURE 17.2

**Placement of International
Activities within the
Organizational Structure
(continued).**

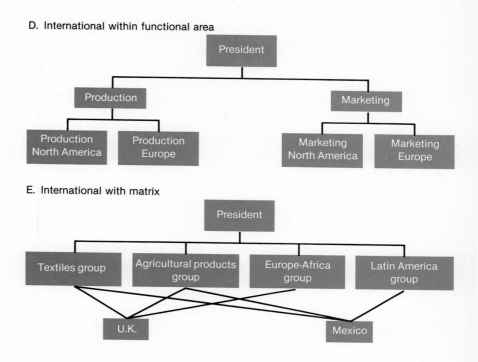

D. International within functional area

E. International with matrix

among groups and the development of additional reporting and control systems reflecting each of the three groups (product, function, and area) on a global basis. However, these alternatives are not without costs.

Coordinating Mechanisms

● Rather than changing overall structure, many companies finding mechanisms to pull product, function, and area together

Because all of the above organization structures have advantages and disadvantages, companies in recent years have been developing organization mechanisms to pull together some of the diverse functional, geographic (including international), and product perspectives without abandoning their existing structures. These have included the strengthening of corporate staffs so that people with line responsibilities are required to listen to different viewpoints whether they take advice or not, the use of more management rotation such as between line and staff and domestic and international in order to break down parochial views, the placement of international and domestic personnel in closer proximity to each other, and the establishment of liaisons among different subsidiaries within the same country so that different product groups can get synergy within an area.[40]

Locating International Headquarters

- Locating in "international" center to
  - save time in travel
  - be near international services
- Trend to locate international near domestic

Once a company develops substantial foreign operations, there may be advantages in shifting part of the headquarters staff to a new location.[41] One reason is to minimize communications and travel expense and time between the staff group and the foreign operations. Another is to be near specialized private and public institutions such as banks, factoring firms, insurance groups, public accountants, freight forwarders, customs brokers, and consular offices, which handle certain international functions. Finally, one needs to hire bilingual or multilingual personnel as well as people who are familiar with such functions as export documentation. The international transportation, institutions, and specialized personnel are greatly concentrated in a few locales. For this reason, New York is by far the most popular international headquarters location for U.S. companies that maintain corporate headquarters elsewhere. If foreign operations are substantial enough, staff may be segmented on a regional basis. Dow, Pfizer, and Exxon are among more than ninety firms that maintain Latin American regional offices in Miami.

Some companies also find it advantageous to set up regional offices abroad, such as a European headquarters somewhere in Europe. Besides the factors one would consider in locating international operations at home, such factors as amount and method of local taxation and ease of establishing operations and moving personnel in and out must be considered. Because regional headquarters usually mean an infusion of foreign exchange, an impetus to the real estate and building industries, and local employment opportunities without some of the attendant industrial problems, such as pollution, some countries actively seek these headquarters by offering various concessions.

As transportation and communications have become faster and relatively cheap, some of the advantages of locating an international group apart from headquarters have lessened. This, when coupled with moves to seek greater integration of international and domestic operations, has meant that more of the international operations are being located where the corporate headquarters is. In recent years, for example, both Bendix and Coca-Cola moved their international headquarters out of New York to Detroit and Atlanta, respectively.

SOME SPECIAL SITUATIONS

Acquisitions

- Usually not a complete fit with existing organization
- Management in acquired firm used to independence

As was noted in the Nestlé case, a policy of expansion through acquisition may create some specific control problems. In the Nestlé situation, some of the U.S. acquisitions resulted in overlapping geographic responsibilities as well as new lines of business with which corporate management had no experience. Another type of problem is that the existing management in the acquired firm is probably accustomed to a great deal of autonomy. Attempts to centralize certain decision-making procedures or to change operating methods may result in distrust, fears, and reluctance to change. This is especially true when one acquires a firm in a foreign country. A French executive put it this way:

> *To collaborate with a compatriot is easier because you know he is not different from yourself. . . . With a foreigner it is far more difficult because you often have little in common: you have to start with a harmonization of the personalities.* [42]

Resistance may come not only from the personnel, but also from governmental authorities. Authorities may use a variety of discretionary means to ensure that decision making remains vested within the country.

Moving from National to Global Strategies

It is also difficult to wrest control from other operations once their managers have become accustomed to a great deal of autonomy. This is a particular problem for companies which attempt to move from a country-to-country to a global strategy. Within Europe, for example, many U.S. firms owned very independent operations for decades in such countries as the United Kingdom, France, and West Germany. These firms have often faced formidable obstacles to the integration of these operations because the country managers perceive personal and operating disadvantages through such moves. However, Japanese firms which have invested in Europe more recently have not had to contend with these vested positions.[43]

Branch versus Subsidiary

• Tax and liability implications

When establishing a foreign operation, management may often have to decide between making that operation either a branch or a subsidiary. A foreign **branch** is legally not a separate entity from the parent; therefore branch operations are possible only if the parent owns 100 percent. A **subsidiary,** on the other hand, is legally a separate company, even though the parent may own all of the voting stock. Because of the legal separateness of the subsidiary, it is generally concluded that liability is limited to the assets of that subsidiary. Creditors or winners of legal suits may therefore not have access to other resources owned by the parent. This limited liability concept is a major factor in the choice of the subsidiary form, since otherwise, claims against a firm for its actions in one country may be settled by courts in another country. Pan American Airways' branch in Guatemala was sued for alleged infractions in Nicaragua. Since there was no legal separation of Pan Am's entities, the parent effectively lost the ability to control the assets in each country separately. There is some evidence that the subsidiary concept will not suffice in future liability disputes in which a foreign parent holds all the voting stock. Cases against Raytheon in Italy and against Swift in Argentina extended liability beyond the subsidiaries' assets.[44] At this writing, the government of India is challenging the limited liability concept even further. A case is pending against Union Carbide in a New York federal court over damages in the Bhopal accident even though the plant was operated by Union Carbide's Indian joint venture partner.[45]

Since subsidiaries are separate companies, there is also a question of how much and what decisions a parent may be allowed to dictate. Generally, this does not present a problem; however, U.S. courts ruled that Timken was in effect conspiring with another company to prevent competition when Timken dictated which markets its Canadian subsidiary could serve. Another factor related to control is public disclosure. Generally, the greater the secrecy that can be maintained, the greater the control vested by the owners. In this respect, branches are usually subject to less public disclosure because they are not covered by tight local corporate restrictions.

From the above examples it should be clear that there are conflicting control advantages with either the branch or subsidiary that should be considered when choosing the legal form of foreign operations. In addition, each form has different tax advantages and implications. Furthermore, each may have different initiation and operating costs as well as different abilities to raise capital.

Comparison of Legal Forms

• Each form has different operating restrictions

A firm establishing a subsidiary in a foreign country usually has a number of alternative legal forms from which to choose. The variety of these forms is too numerous to list in detail; however, some distinctions warrant mentioning. In addition to differences in liability, forms vary in terms of ability to transfer ownership, the number of stockholders required, the percentage of foreigners who can serve on the board of directors, the amount of required public disclosure, whether equity may be acquired by noncapital contributions, the types of businesses (products) eligible, and minimum capital required. Before making a decision an international firm should analyze all of the above-mentioned differences in terms of its corporate objectives. The nomenclature "Inc." in the United States is roughly equivalent to "S.A." in most Romance language countries, "A.G." in Germany and Switzerland, "KK" in Japan, "AB" in Sweden, and "NV" in the Netherlands. The term "PLC" is used in the United Kingdom when companies list their securities; however, "Ltd." may be used for privately held companies. There are, however, subtle differences from country to country.

Minority Control

Usually harder, but there are mechanisms

As has already been discussed, a greater share of equity usually gives a firm a better chance of controlling an operation; however, it is not always possible to gain more than 50 percent of the ownership in a foreign enterprise. Aside from the dispersion of stock not held by the foreign investor, there are several other means of gaining control with only a minority interest. One is to maintain control over some asset needed by the operation abroad, such as patents, brand name, or raw materials. This in fact is a motive for setting separate licensing, franchising, or management contract agreements with the foreign subsidiary.

Another means is to set up administrative devices. One such device is to separate equity into voting and nonvoting stock so that the minority foreign investor has a majority of the voting stock. Another is to make a side agreement with a majority holder for an operating committee in which the minority foreign investor has majority representation.

Nonequity Forms

As form of operations evolves so must structure

As was shown in Chapter 15, the use of multiple operating forms (e.g., export, license, joint venture) and the move from one to another may create needs to change areas of responsibility in the organization. It may also mean that different areas in the organization have responsibilities related to the different forms. For example, the legal department may have little day-to-day responsibility with exports but a great deal with licensing to the same foreign market. Organizational mechanisms, such as the planned sharing of information or joint committees, are useful to ensure that the activities complement each other. It is also useful to plan organization change so that obstacles are minimized when responsibilities shift from one group to another.

SUMMARY

- Control is more difficult internationally because of (a) the geographic and cultural distance separating countries, (b) the need for diversity among locales in methods of operating, (c) the larger amount of uncontrollables abroad, and (d) the higher uncertainty due to data problems and rapid change.

- Whether decisions are made at the subsidiary level or by managers above the subsidiary should depend on the relative competence of individuals at the two levels, the cost of decision making at each level, and the effects the decisions will have on total corporate performance.

- Even though worldwide uniformity of policies and other centralized decisions may not be best for an individual operation, the overall company gain may be more than sufficient to overcome the individual country losses. When top management prevents subsidiary managers from doing their best job, however, they should consider the consequences for employee morale.

- Many critics within LDCs have argued that centralization of key decision making within MNEs continues the dependency that they had in colonial periods. They are pressuring for increased control at their level.

- Good planning should include environmental analysis, strategies, and contingency strategies with inputs from both top-level and subsidiary managers.

- The amount, accuracy, and timeliness of published data vary substantially from one country to another. A researcher should be particularly aware of varied definitions, collection methods, base years for reports, and responses that may be misleading.

- Sources of published data on international business include consulting firms, governmental agencies, supranational agencies, and organizations that serve international business accounts. The cost and specificity of these publications vary widely.

- Timely reports are essential for control so that resources can be allocated properly, plans can be corrected, and personnel can be evaluated and rewarded.

- International reporting systems are similar to those used domestically because home country management is familiar with them and because uniformity makes it easier to compare different operations.

- The evaluation of subsidiaries and their managers are separate processes; however, some of the same inputs may be used for both. These include financial and nonfinancial criteria.

- Two of the growing difficulties of getting timely and comparable reports from foreign operating units are the incompatibility of data processing systems among countries and the restrictions placed on the cross-national flow of data.

- As a firm develops international business activities, the corporate structure must encompass a means for foreign operations to report. The more important the foreign operations, the higher in the hierarchy they should report.

- Whether a company separates or integrates the international activities, there is usually a need to develop some means by which (a) to prevent costly duplication and (b) to ensure that domestic managers do not withhold the best resources from the international operations.

- International or regional headquarters may be located away from corporate headquarters in order to save transport costs and gain access to specialized international talents.

- Some situations that raise special control problems include acquired operations, operations with historical autonomy, whether foreign operations are branches or subsidiaries, the legal organization form allowed in the specific country, and operations with shared ownership and nonequity arrangements.

C A S E   WESTINGHOUSE[46]

In 1969, Westinghouse's top management noted with concern that its chief rival, General Electric, gained 25 percent of its sales abroad, compared to only 8 percent by Westinghouse. Top management was determined to compete more vigorously against GE in foreign markets. At that time, Westinghouse had a separate operation, Westinghouse Electric International Company, which was located in New York, away from corporate headquarters in Pittsburgh. Between 1969 and 1971, overseas volume increased to 15 percent of sales; and the chairman, Donald C. Burnham, said, "I've set a goal that 30 percent of our business will be outside the U.S. I hope to get there and then set a bigger goal." The spurt in foreign sales was largely the result of the aggressive pursuit of overseas acquisitions. This marked a substantial change in foreign operating practice, inasmuch as Westinghouse had depended almost entirely on exports and licensing agreements for its foreign sales since World War I, when its three European subsidiaries were confiscated.

From 1969 to 1971 the International Company operated alongside four other Westinghouse divisions. These were operated as companies that were each in charge of a group of diverse products. A major complaint of the International Company was that the four other companies tended to view foreign operations as merely an appendage to which they were unwilling to give sufficient technical or even product assistance. Since the International Company had to depend on the product groups for anything that it was going to export, there were problems of gaining continued assured supplies. The product companies were quite willing to divert output abroad when they had surplus production but were reluctant when there were shortages. This was largely because the International Company rather than the product company got credit for the sales and profits. Likewise, the product groups were reluctant to lend their best personnel to the International Company to assist in exportation of highly technical orders or to lend support to production from foreign licensing and subsidiaries.

As a partial result of these complaints, Westinghouse eliminated the international division in 1971. The four product-based companies were then put in charge of worldwide control of production and sale of their goods. (Westinghouse produces more than 8000 different products.) The philosophy was that the people in those divisions would have a greater capability of selling (because of their access to product technology) than the disbanded company. Second, since they would now be evaluated on their foreign successes, they would be willing to divert resources to international development. Another factor that affected the decision to move to a worldwide product organization from that of an international division was that GE had made a similar move with apparent success a few years earlier.

At the time that responsibilities were shifted to the domestic division, many of the managers from the formerly New York–based International Company did not conceal their belief that "those unsophisticated hicks back in Steeltown couldn't be trusted to find U.S. consulates abroad, let alone customers." Although management in each of the four product companies was free to pursue foreign business or not, each chose to do so. Between 1971 and 1976, foreign sales grew to 31 percent of the Westinghouse total. During this five-year period, product diversity continued to grow. The product emphasis was further accentuated in 1976, when the company was reorganized into thirty-seven operating groups known as business units. Each unit was given a great deal of autonomy, including a free hand abroad.

From 1976 through 1978, foreign sales of Westinghouse fell to 24 percent of its total. The extension of responsibility by product units further complicated cooperation among units and created problems of duplication in foreign markets. Many horror stories surfaced. For instance, a company salesperson called on a Saudi businessman who pulled out business cards from salespeople who had visited him from twenty-four other business units. His question was, "Who speaks for Westinghouse?" In another situation, different units had established subsidiaries in the same country. One had excess cash, while another was borrowing locally at an exorbitant rate. In many cases, large projects would require the ultimate cooperation among business units to carry out different parts. At times, units could not agree in time to put together a package and lost out to foreign competitors such as Brown, Boveri from Switzerland and Hitachi from Japan. In a case in Brazil, three different sales groups were calling on the same customer for the same job.

By 1978 the vice-chairman and chief operating officer of Westinghouse was Douglas Danforth. He was highly interested in international expansion, not only because he expected greater sales and growth there, but also because he had previously worked in the Mexican and Canadian subsidiaries. In early 1979 he enlisted a Westinghouse executive to head an exhaustive study of the firm's international operations and to make a recommendation within ninety days. The study group interviewed Westinghouse personnel in the United States and abroad. It also determined how other firms were handling their international operations. The recommendation was to move to a matrix system with a head of international operations. The international operations were then to be organized along geographic lines including three regions. This was adopted. To get a consensus among the people in charge of product and geographic areas was a major departure from Westinghouse's product orientation. Danforth told the company's top 220 managers that "some of you will adjust and survive, and some of you won't."

Danforth announced that he wanted 35 percent of Westinghouse's sales to be coming from abroad by 1984. Seventeen countries were identified as having the highest potential, and these were examined in detail. To carry out the planned growth, it has been necessary to mesh country unit plans with product unit plans. In other words, if a product unit wants switchgear in Brazil increased by 40 percent and the Brazilian country manager wants to increase it by 50 percent, they must either work out an agreement or refer the decision upward in the organization to the next higher product and geographic heads. Disagreements can effectively go as high as the top-level operating committee, which consists of the chairman, vice-chairman, three presidents of product groups, the top financial officer, and the president of the international group. The 1980 annual report showed export sales of $1.2 billion and sales from foreign production of $1.1 billion. The combination comprised 27 percent of Westinghouse's total.

QUESTIONS

1. What have been the major organizational problems inhibiting the international growth of Westinghouse?

2. What organization characteristics may affect the successful implementation of the matrix management at Westinghouse?

3. How can a firm such as Westinghouse go about implementing a goal to increase the percentage of its sales accounted for by foreign operations?

NOTES

1. Data for the case were taken from "Nestlé: Centralizing to Win a Bigger Pay off from the U.S.," *Business Week,* February 2, 1981, pp. 56–58; "Nestlé—At Home Abroad: An Interview with Pierre Liotard-Vogt," *Harvard Business Review,* November 1976, pp. 80–88; Robert Ball, "Nestlé Revs up Its U.S. Campaign," *Fortune,* February 13, 1978, pp. 80–90; "For the Record," *Advertising Age,* August 2, 1976, p. 8; Robert Ball, "A Shopkeeper Shakes up Nestlé," *Fortune,* Vol. 106, No. 13, December 27, 1982, pp. 103–106; Damon Darlin, "Nestlé Hopes to Bring Its

Other U.S. Units up to Level of Its Stouffer Corp. Subsidiary," *Wall Street Journal,* March 15, 1984, p. 33; Maile Hulihan, "Nestlé Plots Aggressive Acquisition Program," *Wall Street Journal,* May 21, 1984, p. 29; James Sterngold, "Nestlé Planning to Pay $3 Billion to Acquire Carnation Company," *New York Times,* September 5, 1984, p. 1+. "Nestlé to Close Libby Units," *New York Times,* September 26, 1985, p. D5.

2. Robert L. Drake and Lee M. Caudill, "Management of the Large Multinational: Trends and Future Challenges," *Business Horizons,* May–June 1981, p. 84.

3. Donna G. Goehle, *Decision Making in Multinational Corporations* (Ann Arbor: University Research Press, 1980).

4. Drake and Caudill, *op. cit.,* p. 85.

5. Robert Stobaugh, Jr., "Financing Foreign Subsidiaries of U.S. Controlled Multinational Enterprises," *Journal of International Business Studies,* Summer 1970, pp. 48–55; R. J. Aylmer, "Who Makes Marketing Decisions in the Multinational Firm?" *Journal of Marketing,* October 1970, pp. 27–29.

6. Drake and Caudill, *op. cit.,* p. 86.

7. Aylmer, *loc. cit.*

8. For a discussion of the distance factor, see Jacques Picard, "How European Companies Control Marketing Decisions Abroad," *Columbia Journal of World Business,* Summer 1977, pp. 113–121; also Drake and Caudill, *loc. cit.* found that Canadian subsidiaries of U.S. firms did not have the same degree of autonomy as subsidiaries in other countries because of their closeness to corporate headquarters.

9. Thomas Hout, Michael E. Porter, and Eileen Rudden, "How Global Companies Win Out," *Harvard Business Review,* September–October 1982, pp. 98–108.

10. Samir M. Youssef, "Contextual Factors Influencing Control Strategy of Multinational Corporations," *Academy of Management Journal,* March 1975, pp. 136–145.

11. A. B. Sim, "Decentralized Management of Subsidiaries and Their Performance," *Management International Review,* No. 2, 1977, pp. 47–49.

12. Anders Edström and Jay R. Galbraith, "Transfer of Managers as a Coordination and Control Strategy in Multinational Organizations," *Administrative Science Quarterly,* June 1977, p. 251.

13. Among the many treatments of this subject are Osvaldo Sunkel, "Big Business and 'Dependencia': A Latin American View," *Foreign Affairs,* April 1972, pp. 517–531; Benjamin J. Cohen, *The Question of Imperialism—The Political Economy of Dominance and Dependence* (New York: Basic Books, 1973).

14. Daniel Creamer, *Overseas Research and Development by United States Multinationals, 1966–1975* (New York: The Conference Board, 1976), pp. 35, 79.

15. The arguments pro and con are summarized in Michael J. Thomas, "The Location of Research and Development in the International Corporation," *Management International Review,* No. 1, 1975, pp. 35–41.

16. William A. Fischer and Jack N. Behrman, "The Coordination of Foreign R&D Activities by Transnational Corporations," *Journal of International Business Studies,* Winter 1979, pp. 28–35.

17. B. Mascarenhas, "Coping with Uncertainty in International Business," *Journal of International Business Studies,* Fall 1982, pp. 87–98.

18. W. G. Egelhoff, "Strategy and Structure in Multinational Corporations: An Information Processing Approach," *Administrative Science Quarterly,* Vol. 27, 1982, pp. 435–458.

19. M. J. Culnan, "Environmental Scanning: The Effects of Task Complexity and Source Accessibility on Information Gathering Behavior," *Decision Sciences,* No. 14, 1983, pp. 194–206.

20. N. R. Boulton, W. M. Lindsay, S. G. Franklin, and L. W. Rue, "Strategic Planning: Determining the Impact of Environmental Characteristics and Uncertainty," *Academy of Management Journal,* Vol. 25, No. 3, 1982, pp. 500–509.

21. "The Underground Economy's Hidden Force," *Business Week,* April 5, 1982, pp. 66–67; Brooks Jackson, "Census Exceeds Projections by Millions," *Wall Street Journal,* October 29, 1980, p. 2; Robert Reinhold, "Major Census Aide Is Relieved of Post," *New York Times,* February 12, 1980, p. A-1.

22. Steven E. Permut, "The European View of Marketing Research," *Columbia Journal of World Business,* Fall 1977, p. 96.

23. Peter Nares, "Getting a Fix on Colombia's Largest Export," *Wall Street Journal,* November 25, 1983, p. 13.

24. "The Underground Economy's Hidden Force," *op. cit.,* p. 65.

25. *Ibid.,* p. 68.

26. J. S. Downham, "The Organization of Market Research in Unilever," speech at the American Marketing Association, New York City, April 5, 1972.

27. David F. Hawkins, "Controlling Foreign Operations," *Financial Executive,* February 1965; V. Mauriel, "Evaluation and Control of Overseas Operations," *Management Accounting,* May 1969; J. M. McInnes, "Financial Control Systems for Multinational Operations: An Empirical Investigation," *Journal of International Business Studies,* Fall 1971, pp. 11–28.

28. Frederick D. S. Choi and I. James Czechowicz, "Assessing Foreign Subsidiary Performance: A Multinational Comparison," *Management International Review,* Vol. 23, No 4, 1983, p. 15.

29. *Ibid.,* pp. 18–20.

30. *Ibid.,* p. 22.

31. *Ibid.,* pp. 16–17.

32. George M. Scott, *An Introduction to Financial Control and Reporting in Multinational Enterprises* (Austin, Texas: Bureau of Business Research, Graduate School of Business, The University of Texas at Austin, 1973), pp. 77–79.

33. J. Alex Murray, "Intelligence Systems of the MNCs," *Columbia Journal of World Business,* September–October 1972, pp. 63–71.

34. James Milano and Phillip D. Grub, "Problems Associated with a World Wide Information and Control System in the Multinational Environment," paper presented at the Academy of International Business Meeting, New York, December 28, 1973.

35. Martin D. J. Buss, "Managing International Information Systems," *Harvard Business Review,* Vol. 60, No. 5, September–October 1982, pp. 153–162.

36. Leland M. Wooton, "The Emergence of Multinational Information Centers," *Management International Review,* No. 4, 1977, pp. 21–23.

37. The information in this section is taken from Saeed Samiee, "Transnational Data Flow Constraints: A New Challenge for Multinational Corporations," *Journal of International Business Studies,* Vol. 15, No. 1, Spring–Summer 1984, pp. 141–150.

38. Egelhoff, *loc. cit.;* John D. Daniels, Robert A. Pitts, and Marietta J. Tretter, "Strategy and Structure of U.S. Multinationals: An Exploratory Study," *Academy of Management Journal,* Vol. 27, No. 2, June 1984, pp. 292–307.

39. C. K. Prahalad, "Strategic Choices in Diversified MNCs," *Harvard Business Review,* July–August 1976, pp. 67–78, explores in depth the problems inherent to the locus of relative power.

40. C. A. Bartlett, "MNCs: Get off the Reorganization Merry-Go-Round," *Harvard Business Review,* Vol. 61, No. 2, 1983, pp. 138–146; Robert A. Pitts and John D. Daniels, "Aftermath of the Matrix Mania," *Columbia Journal of World Business,* Vol. 19, No. 2, Summer 1984, pp. 48–54.

41. For an extensive discussion of various approaches to regional groupings, see Daniel Van Den Bulcke and Marie-Anne Van Pachterbeke, *European Headquarters of American Multinational Enterprises in Brussels and Belgium* (Brussels: Institut Catholique des Hautes Etudes Commerciales), 1984.

42. Cited in Renato Mazzolini, "European Transnational Concentration," *California Management Review,* Spring 1974, p. 46.

43. James Flanigan, " 'Multinational' As We Know It Is Obsolete," [an interview with Peter F. Drucker], *Forbes,* August 26, 1985, pp. 30–32.

44. Detlev Vagts, "A Local Economic Disaster: Can the U.S. Parent Walk away Scot-Free?," *Worldwide Projects & Installations,* November–December 1973, pp. 38–40.

45. William B. Glaberson and William J. Powell, Jr. "India's Bhopal Suit Could Change All the Rules," *Business Week,* April 22, 1985, p. 38.

46. Data for the case were taken primarily from Hugh D. Menzies, "Westinghouse Takes Aim at the World," *Fortune,* January 14, 1980, pp. 48–53; other background information may be found in "Westinghouse's Third Big Step Is Overseas," *Business Week,* October 2, 1971, pp. 64–67, and in Westinghouse's annual reports.

PART 7

Functional Management, Operations, and Concerns

In the preceding section we discussed those alternatives that normally transcend decision making within functional disciplines. In this section we will examine concerns of a more functional orientation. This does not imply that these are of less importance. In fact, they are essential considerations within the firm's global implementation of strategy. Chapter 18 emphasizes the uniqueness of each company, product, and consumer area in international marketing. Chapter 19 discusses the problems of accounting when legal systems, exchange rates, and inflationary conditions vary among countries. Chapter 20 analyzes the planning needed to interface among national tax systems. Chapter 21 examines the securement and management of funds internationally. The next two chapters deliberate "people problems"—Chapter 22 emphasizing management personnel and Chapter 23, labor.

18

Marketing

- To postulate the valid marketing philosophies that are logical for different firms in varying circumstances.
- To introduce techniques for assessing market sizes for given countries.
- To contrast practices of standardized versus differentiated programs for each country where sales are made.
- To emphasize how environmental differences complicate the management of marketing worldwide.
- To discuss the major international considerations within each of the marketing functions—product, pricing, promotion, and distribution.

MARKS & SPENCER[1]

Great Britain has often been called a nation of shopkeepers, and Marks & Spencer (M & S) is undoubtedly the shopkeeping leader. In the fiscal year ending March 1984, M & S earned $233 million on sales of $4 billion. With over 250 stores in the United Kingdom, M & S is its largest retailer. The Marble Arch store holds a place in the Guinness Book of Records as the store that takes in more revenue per square foot than any other in the world.

Soft goods (clothes and household textiles) account for 70 percent of the sales, and it is estimated that 20 percent of all the clothing manufactured in the United Kingdom is bought by Marks & Spencer. For some specific clothing items, M & S supplies over half the British market. M & S added food lines to its stores and is now the fifth largest food retailer in Britain.

How has M & S become so dominant in the British market? The operations were begun in 1884 by a Polish immigrant who believed in selling durable merchandise at a moderate price. This philosophy has seldom been altered. M & S has merchandise made to its specifications. Because of its vast buying power, it can get producers to compete by offering low prices on merchandise to be sold under M & S's St. Michael trademark. Because M & S is so well known, it has no need of many of the costly marketing expenses that other stores must undertake. There is practically no advertising. Stores are austerely decorated. There is very little personal service and no dressing rooms or public bathrooms. Customers receive no sales slips for small purchases, but merchandise is easily returned.

Another practice that has paid off for M & S in its home market has been to appeal to the nationalistic attitudes of its clientele. M & S has promoted heavily the fact that about 90 percent of the clothing it sells originates in the United Kingdom. Marks & Spencer has managed to develop an image that is as British as bed and breakfast or fish and chips. Foreign visitors to England usually do not feel that they have sopped up the local atmosphere without a visit to one of the M & S stores. One of the stores has had to put its warning signs to shoplifters in five languages.

There have been foreseeable problems to attain continued growth in the U.K. market. Not the least of the problems has been the high market share. Being already so dominant, M & S would have to add new products or appeal to new market segments to maintain its growth rate. In the late 1970s the company moved into a line of finer clothes such as silk blouses and cashmere coats. It also hoped to cash in on publicity that Margaret Thatcher used to buy her suits at M & S before becoming prime minister. This attempt was a disaster. The Harrods-type customer did not switch to M & S, and many M & S customers did trade down to even cheaper retailers.

M & S dropped its higher-priced lines; but in 1980, M & S unit sales fell for the first time.

A second problem facing M & S was its dependence on British suppliers. By 1979, 29 percent of U.K. clothing sales were of imported products, but M & S steadfastly held to its "buy British" policy. Although 60 percent of shirts sold in the U.K. were imported, 99 percent of the St. Michael brand were made in the United Kingdom. M & S's suppliers increasingly depended on imported fabrics, but it was apparent that imported finished products would be increasingly more cost competitive. An M & S executive summed up the emerging problems by saying, "Because the company is near saturation in the U.K., its growth must be overseas."

The foreign operations of Marks & Spencer have been slow to achieve success. When Britain joined the EC, management saw an opportunity to expand on the Continent because clothing from M & S suppliers could then enter other common market countries without tariffs. Paris and Brussels were selected as the first locations for stores. Before opening stores in 1975 the company sent a team of observers to Paris for 18 months so that product differences could be targeted to the French-speaking customers. The team found substantial differences. One was in sizes. They noted that "French girls always seem to wear a size less than they need with everything obviously relying on the buttons, while we [English] go for a half size too large." French women wanted skirts that were longer than the English. Frenchmen wanted single instead of double back vents in their jackets, sweaters in a variety of colors (including pastels), and jackets and slacks rather than suits. None of these men's preferences were the norm in the United Kingdom. All of these differences had implications for the merchandise mix and the establishment of supplies.

In spite of the substantial research on product, the company was not initially well received. Many fewer people entered the stores than had been anticipated. M & S believed that, since they were so well known in Britain and since so many foreign tourists visited London stores, their reputation had preceded them. Belatedly, they learned that only 3 percent of the French had even heard of Marks & Spencer or St. Michael's before the continental stores were opened. Store locations exacerbated the situation. M & S management wanted their first stores to be "flagships" and therefore sought to locate them on the most popular shopping streets. Since store space was at a premium on those streets, they had to settle for a spot in Paris where most pedestrian traffic preferred the other side of the street. In Brussels they accepted a store with a very small frontage that did not give an impression of a vast amount of merchandise on the inside. To get people to visit the stores, M & S had to depend much more heavily on advertising than in the United Kingdom. This was an added expense that made it difficult to keep prices low.

Another factor influencing costs was that M & S lacked the same kind of buying power as it enjoyed in Britain for its continental stores. Initially, the company contracted nearly 80 percent of its merchandise from continental sources that were unwilling to treat M & S any more favorably than other department stores and retail chains already in the market. Most of the remaining merchandise came from the United Kingdom, where M & S had buying clout. Since much of this was clothing made to specifications to meet the French and Belgian needs (e.g., stronger buttons, single-vent jackets, and pastel sweaters), the British producers had to make these items in short production runs. As initial large sales did not materialize, the U.K. manufacturers were reluctant to keep markups very low. Even when merchandise prices were kept low, M & S found the French to be highly suspicious of bargains.

When potential customers went into the new stores, they were unaccustomed to the starkness and lack of service. A French fashion writer summed up the customer reaction to the Paris store as "not madly joyful unless of course one is as impervious to English shopping as one is to English cooking."

To bring customers into its Paris store, M & S has had to make operating adjustments. The primary change has surprisingly been in merchandise, the area where M & S had done so much preliminary research. In trying to copy what the continentals were offering in merchandise, M & S simply could not get a more durable product to customers at a sufficiently cheaper price to attract a mass clientele. However, it fairly quickly discerned that there is a small market segment that is willing to buy the more English-type merchandise for which M & S can exert its buying power. M & S now buys only 10 percent of its merchandise from continental sources and has differentiated itself from local competitors by capitalizing on its "Englishness." It now concentrates on such items as tan and navy blue sweaters, biscuits, English beer, and even a quiche Lorraine made in the United Kingdom. In deference to French tastes, M & S has carpeted its Paris store.

It is not surprising that a large portion of the early customers turned out to be Britishers living in France. This gradually changed, though. Word leaked out that the late Princess Grace of Monaco would shop at M & S whenever she was in Paris. Parisians learned to like wandering through wide aisles with shopping carts before paying for all merchandise at one cash register. In 1983 the Paris store set the French retail store record for earnings per square foot, and about 90 percent of its business was to Parisians.

In entering the Canadian market, M & S assumed that the "Englishness" would be a greater advantage there than on the continent. M & S quickly expanded in Canada to 60 stores in order to get nationwide distribution. However, Canadians found the merchandise to be dull and the stores to be "cold and clinical." Most stores were placed in downtown locations as is the custom in the United Kingdom. The Canadians were increasingly going to suburban shopping centers, and only the M & S stores in those centers began to earn an early profit. In 1979, after eight years of Canadian operations, M & S finally made an overall small profit in Canada.

This was short-lived; losses returned the next year. In deference to Canadian tastes, M & S has added fitting rooms, wood paneling, mirrors, and wall-to-wall carpeting. There are still complaints about the merchandise, however. A former supplier opined that the British management did things "because that's the way they did it in England." This included the placement of bigger sleeves on clothing and the avoidance of livelier colors of clothing and of advertising. Management had hoped that the Canadian operations would serve as a springboard for entry into the U.S. market, but difficulties have soured that expansion dream. Management in the United Kingdom instead considered adding lines such as electrical goods and insurance services to its British stores.

INTRODUCTION

- Domestic and international marketing principles the same but
  - managers often overlook foreign environmental differences
  - managers often interpret foreign information erroneously

The Marks & Spencer case points out many of the problems a firm may face internationally. Although the company did substantial research before it began its continental operations, there were still unexpected problems that inhibited sales from growing rapidly. Marketing principles are no different in the international arena; however, environmental differences often cause managers either to overlook important variables or to misinterpret information. Marks & Spencer made mistakes in terms of such important marketing variables as the target market segment, the merchandise mix, the degree to which products would need to be altered for the markets, and the importance of the location and appearance of distribution outlets.

This chapter examines alternative approaches to the analysis of marketing size among different countries and the selection of product, pricing, promotion, and distribution strategies in international marketing. Within these areas, specific emphasis will be placed on two related problems: (1) the extent to which firms should standardize or differentiate activities among countries and (2) the controversies surrounding the economic effects of MNEs' marketing programs, particularly in less-developed countries.

MARKET SIZE ANALYSIS

- Broad scanning techniques
  - limit detailed analysis to most promising possibilities
  - good for LDCs where precise data are less available

In Chapter 16 we discussed the importance of market potential in determining a company's allocational efforts among different countries. As was emphasized in that chapter, there are other variables that must be considered in this decision. These include various cost and risk factors as well as the need to mesh future areas of expansion with the markets the company is now serving. It is not the intention of this section to discuss these other variables. Rather, we wish to explore techniques that can be used to estimate size of potential markets on a country-to-country basis. These are merely tools to help management decide which markets to emphasize.[2] In using any of the techniques, management must keep in mind the problems and limitations of data as discussed in Chapter 17.

To determine the potential demand for a given company, one must usually first estimate the sales of the category of products that the company sells and then base the company's sales on market share potential. For advanced countries, one usually finds large markets, historical consumption figures, and trained market research personnel, so costly and detailed research studies are feasible. The type of demand forecasting would therefore not be significantly different among developed countries. For LDCs, however, it is useful to develop inexpensive forecasting methods based on readily available data. Regardless of whether one is dealing with industrial or poor countries, there are different information needs depending on the precision of data required and the commitments that firms have already made in markets. For example, a firm may first scan a large number of potential markets fairly inexpensively by using published data. Only those markets that appear most promising will then be analyzed more closely, such as by test marketing in those areas. Once a firm has established sales facilities in a foreign country, it may be able to add a product to its line that has been developed elsewhere with little additional capital outlay. The techniques used in scanning might still serve a useful purpose in this situation, since they give a broad indication of product demand. The following discussions summarize some common tools and information sources that researchers may find feasible for estimating market potential.

Total Market Potential

- Input-output shows relationship of one economic sector to another
- Available for most countries but
  - may be old
  - assumes constant relationship

Existing consumption patterns. Input-output is a tool that is widely used in national economic planning to show the resources used by different industries for a given output as well as the interdependence of economic sectors. By use of tables showing all sectors on both the vertical and horizontal axes, one can see how the production (output) of one is the demand (input) of another. For instance, vehicle output becomes an input to the steel industry, households, government, foreign sector, and even to the vehicle industry itself. Most developed countries as well as many LDCs now publish input-output tables. By comparing these with economic projections for an economy as a whole or with plans for production changes in a given industry, one can project the total volume of sales changes for a given type of product as well as the purchases by each sector. The three major shortcomings of this method are that for many countries the data contained within the input-output tables and in plans or projections of economic changes are too sparse.

There is also an assumption that the relationships among sectors and resources are fixed, an assumption that may not be valid. Finally, the tables
may be many years old before they are published and readily available.

The relationship between imports and domestic production and consumption of given products is useful in determining both the existing demand for products and the country of origin of the competition. The
UNCTAD/GATT International Trade Center has published a manual de-
tailing this information and its use.[3] This information has the same shortcomings as are found in input-output tables.

• Assumes one country will
follow similar pattern to that
of another country

Data on other countries. This method assumes that product use is related
to some variable on a universal basis. For example, as incomes change in
a country, the demand for a product will change on the basis of that income
change. One method of making a projection is to collect data on the consumption of a given product in countries with different per capita gross
national products and then plot a path through which average demand
changes as incomes change (see Fig. 18.1).

Reasonably good fits for many products have been found by using
this method. However, for a few products the analysis breaks down in
some countries because other variables affect demand. For instance, the
consumption of cars in Switzerland is far lower than income would predict
because of the public transportation system, difficult terrain, and high import
duties.[4] A further problem is that this method is static. With changes in
technology and prices, a country may change its consumption pattern much
earlier or later than would be indicated by looking at a group of countries
in only one time period.

FIGURE 18.1

**Sugar Consumption and per
capita GNP for Selected
Countries: 1970**
*Source: U.N. Statistical
Yearbook, 1972.*

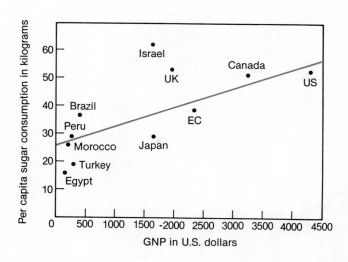

● Projects future by past trends

Time series data. This technique may be used when time series data are available and where current values move systematically with past values.[5] Figure 18.2 illustrates sugar consumption in the United States based on time series data. This contrasts with projections of sugar consumption in Fig. 18.1 based on cross-national data. The use of time series and cross-national data may also be combined. For example, one study used data from 1899 to 1957 on ten countries, plotting variations in total and proportionate breakdown of manufacturing production as per capita GNP changed in constant dollars. A conclusion was that as incomes rose, the portion of production devoted to textiles decreased and that devoted to metal products increased.[6] Such cross-sectional analyses within an economy are useful for predicting total demand and for identifying the economic sectors generating this demand.

● Demand is related to some economic or other indicator

Regression. This method is merely a means of refining data collected on numbers of countries or on a historical basis. By using data based on the historical relationship between demand for a given product and some economic indicator, or between demand and some economic indicator in a given time period, one may construct a regression equation that shows the demand (the dependent variable) based on a level of the indicator (the independent variable). This technique allows an amount of consumption that is not directly contributable to changes in the indicator to be taken

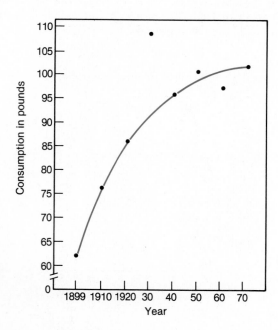

FIGURE 18.2
Per capita Sugar Consumption of the United States: 1899–1970
Source: Statistical Abstract of the United States, Supplement: 1957 and Statistical Abstract: 1972.

into consideration. It further allows for the determination of the degree of correlation between the independent and dependent variables. For instance, one study made forty-two observations of demand for radio sets based on per capita GNP. The formula was $y = a + bx$, where y is the amount of product in use per 1000 population, a is the constant of radio sets in use, and bx is radios times per capita GNP. This resulted in an equation of $y = 8.325 + 0.275x$.[7] In other words, on the basis of observed radios in use, one would expect that for an increase in per capita GNP of $100, radio sets would increase by 27.5 per 1000 population.

This equation was shown to explain 78 percent of the variation in the observations made, thus indicating a high predictability of present radios for places where income observations are made but where figures are not available on radio sets. A problem of using regression to make future projections is that tastes and technical changes may alter demand. Furthermore, there may be a saturation point in consumption that has not yet been observed. At some point, if incomes are high enough, people may merely buy radios as replacements rather than add to the amount of radios they own. If this is shown to occur, then it is possible to construct a nonlinear regression equation. Although this example used per capita GNP as the independent variable, one can construct an equation on other variables that may result in high correlations as well.

As percentage of income changes, product demand may change by a different percentage

Income elasticity.   A common predictive means is to divide the percentage of change in product demand by the percentage of change in income. If the resultant answer is greater than 1, the demand for the product is considered elastic; if the number is less than 1, demand is inelastic. Demand for products such as food is relatively less elastic than demand for products such as automobiles. In other words, upward or downward movements in income affect automobile sales more than food sales. This concept is useful in estimating the expenditures for countries at different levels of income. For instance, in the United States, only about 19 percent of personal income is spent on food, whereas Italians spend over 37 percent on food items.[8] The difference is not due to relative appetites but rather to income differences that allow people in the United States to spend more on other types of purchases. The concept is also useful for projecting changes in demand for specific products as incomes change cyclically or over a longer period. An elasticity of 1.5 would mean that a percentage change in income would result in 1.5 times that percentage change in the demand for the specific product.

Like the aforementioned methods of demand projection, income elasticity measurements must be approached with caution, especially if one is making projections in one country based on demand analysis in another. Not only are there the problems of taste but also of price differences that affect the desire of consumers to substitute cheaper for more expensive products. Italy consumes a much higher quantity of fruits and vegetables than Norway, even though Norway's income is higher, because of price differences. Genesco, when commencing clothing sales in Japan, found surprisingly that although Japan's per capita income was only about half of that in the United States, Japan's per capita consumption of suits was double that of the United States.[9] The greater formality and status ascribed to wearing suits in Japan contribute to the divergence in consumer buying behavior between the two countries.

Gap Analysis

- Difference between total market potential and companies' sales is made up of gaps
  - usage: less product sold by all competitors than potential
  - competitive: "head-to-head" competition
  - product line: company lacks some product variations
  - distribution: company misses goegraphic or intensity coverage

The above tools may be used to give an estimation of the market potential for a given product. Once this rough determination is made, a firm must calculate how well it is doing within each of the markets. A useful tool for scanning markets and comparing countries in this respect is **gap analysis**.[10] When a company's sales are lower than the estimated market potential for a given type of product, there is a company potential for increased sales, which may be due to a usage, competitive, product line, or distribution gap.

The two largest Swiss chocolate companies, Nestlé and Interfood, have found in recent years very different types of gaps in different countries.[11] This has led them to emphasize different country markets and to differentiate their types of marketing programs among nations. In some markets they have found substantial usage gaps—in other words, less chocolate is being consumed than would be expected on the basis of population and income levels. This has led them to consider trying to increase primary demand in those areas for chocolate in general. Industry specialists estimated, for example, that 80 percent of the world's poulation have never tasted a chocolate bar. Consequently, if more people can be persuaded to try chocolate bars, then the companies' sales should increase with the market increase. The U.S. market comprises another type of usage gap. Nearly everyone has tried most chocolate products, but per capita consumption fell from 20.3 pounds to 14.3 pounds between 1968 and 1978 because of increasing concern about calories. To increase chocolate consumption in general, Nestlé began promoting chocolate as an energy source for the sports-minded. In markets such as France and West Germany the companies feel that the potential market demand is being fulfilled but that there is a competitive gap; that is, Nestlé and Interfood might increase sales there but only at the expense of competitors. In some hot climates the companies have found that they have product line gaps in terms of the market for sweetened products. By working on new products, such as chocolate products that melt less easily, they may be able to garner a larger share of the present market for sweetened products. They have also found chocolate products with which they do not compete directly. Finally, there are some markets, such as Japan, where they have not yet achieved a sufficient distribution to reach their sales potentials.

PRODUCT POLICY

The Philosophies

International marketing philosophies may be categorized as

1. we sell what we make,
2. we make what we sell, and
3. we adapt what we make to the needs of foreign consumers.

This frame of reference is useful for understanding the varied approaches firms may validly take in international product policy decisions.

- Of use primarily when
  - cost and price reductions increase sales
  - spillover is high
  - desire to get rid of excess capacity
  - foreign buyers seek out product
- Will usually cut costs through standardization but
  - may lose some sales
  - may be criticized for not meeting needs

We sell what we make. Many firms begin selling abroad very passively. For some reason, often unknown to the management, requests for information on products or even actual orders simply arrive from abroad. Foreign products are learned of through numerous channels, including new developments reported in scientific and trade journals with international circulation, advertising that spills across national boundaries, and demonstration of products that consumers have bought in one country and transferred abroad. Finally, many firms send buyers abroad or actively search for new products to handle. Regardless of the reason for this initial passive involvement with overseas sales, firms do very little if any real adaptation to what consumers abroad might prefer. This approach suffices for many companies that view foreign sales as an appendage to domestic sales. This same type of company frequently exports only if it has excess inventory for the domestic market.

Whether a firm is exporting or has foreign production facilities, it may cut costs substantially by standardizing its products. This is usually done on the basis of the home country experience, since costs associated with product development, promotional programs, and distributional expertise have already been expended there. The transference abroad allows for economies as the outlays are spread over a larger volume of output.

However, this route may result in some losses in sales and thus should be employed primarily in four types of situations. The first is when cost and price reductions will increase sales substantially. For example, recall the Marks & Spencer experience in the French market. Marks & Spencer found, after its trial and error experience, that the cost savings from selling its English style clothing in France outweighed the advantages of designing new items to fit the tastes of the French mass market. Another type involves sales to countries for which the total market potential is assessed to be small regardless of whether changes are geared to unique consumer needs. In small developing countries particularly, international firms are apt to make few changes because the market size does not justify the expense. Few sales may be lost, since competitors are likely to be international firms as well, also transferring in products geared to their own domestic markets. Although this approach has thus far not resulted in significant lost sales, MNEs are being increasingly censured for it.

This is particularly true for sales within less-developed countries of labor-saving industrial equipment and luxury goods, which many critics claim are responsible for contributing to unemployment problems and to the enhancement of elitist class distinctions, respectively. Because of these criticisms, MNEs are being increasingly pressured to justify their contributions or to design and sell products that are perceived to be more in line with the needs of LDCs. The question of appropriate technology will be discussed more fully in Chapter 23. The question of luxury or superfluous products has been largely answered by MNEs through showing the positive side effects of seemingly unnecessary products. For example, soft drink manufacturers have argued that they are responsible for the establishment of glass bottle–making firms, which are essential for other industries, such as pharmaceuticals.

A third type of situation comprises sales to countries that are likely to receive marketing spillover from domestic operations. Between the United States and Canada, for example, there is a great deal of interchange and market similarity; consequently, many products and their appeals spill over easily and not only can be consistent but almost always must be. Improvements in international communications and transportation are increasingly extending the spillover effects to more distant countries so that there are more opportunities to aim the same products to groups of similar consumers in a number of different countries. The fourth situation is when a firm is able to sell essentially the same product in a foreign country by appealing to a market segment that is different from the one at home. For example, Perrier water appeals to a mass French market but to an elitist market in the United States.

- Not common strategy
- Takes geographic area as given
  - some products are standardized anyway

We make what we sell. In a firm that operates according to the dictum described in the previous section, management is usually guided by such questions as, Should we send some exports abroad? or, Where can we sell some more of product X? In other words, the product is held constant, and the location of sales is varied. The type of strategy to be described in this section is one that asks the question, What can we sell in country A? In this case the country is held constant, and the product is varied.

Sometimes a firm wants to penetrate markets in a given country because of the country's size, growth potential, proximity to home operations, currency or political stability, or a host of other reasons. The extreme of this approach would be to move to completely unrelated products. This is not a common strategy, but there are examples. Henkel of West Germany, for example, wished to diversify into the United States in order to counter an expected sluggish market at home. However, management felt that it would be difficult to compete in the United States in its major product lines, detergents and cosmetics. Henkel chose instead to buy the chemical division of General Mills.[12]

This reactive attitude to consumers does not necessarily mean that a firm has to forego the economies of standardization. One may well aim a product, such as Schweppes tonic water, Helena Rubenstein cosmetics, Boeing jets, or Brylcreem, at a global market. Instead of merely trying to transfer sales of a domestic product abroad, one designs a product to fit some global market segment. This may mean changing what is sold domestically so that it corresponds to the international standard. The possibilities of global products for industrial users may be large as well because the purchasers are apt to be technically trained decision makers. SKF, for example, introduced a line of 20,000 ball bearings to replace 50,000 on a worldwide basis.[13]

- Most common strategy
  - product changes are adaptations, by degree

We adapt what we make to the needs of foreign consumers. Most firms that are committed to continual rather than sporadic foreign sales adopt a strategy that combines the production and consumer orientations just described. Refusal to make changes for the needs of foreign markets means that too many sales may be lost. Yet expertise concerning a type of product may be very important, and companies want the foreign operations to be compatible with their product understanding. Product changes are common but tend to be in degree. A company that has been accustomed to manufacturing electric typewriters is more apt to move into the production of manual typewriters or calculators than into the production of tires or detergents. The latter products would ordinarily be too far from the management's area of expertise.

Reasons for Product Alteration

- Usually for safety or health protection
  - may be direct or indirect
  - very few international standards

Legal factors. Direct legal requirements are the most obvious reason for altering products for foreign markets, since without adhering to the regulations the company is not going to get permission to operate. The exact requirements vary widely by country but are usually for the purpose of protecting people who come into contact with a given product or service. Pharmaceuticals and foods are particularly subject to regulations concerning purity, testing, and the labeling of contents. Cars imported into the United States must conform to safety and pollution standards that are not found in many other countries.

When foreign legal requirements are less stringent than those at home, a firm may then not be legally compelled to alter its products for sales in the foreign country. However, the firm will have to weigh such questions as whether foreign sales will be lost if high domestic standards are used abroad and whether there will be domestic ill will if those standards are not used. U.S. firms have been criticized in recent years for selling abroad, especially in less-developed countries, such products as toys, automobiles, contraceptives, and pharmaceuticals that did not meet U.S. safety or quality standards. Standards and requirements are not always less stringent in LDCs. Many of the countries have content labeling and package size laws that are more strict than those found in the United States.[14]

A recurring question is to what extent it is possible to arrive at international product standards to eliminate some of the seemingly wasteful product alterations from country to country. While there has been some progress, such as agreement on the sprocket dimensions on movie film, other things (railroad gauges and electrical socket shapes, for instance) continue to vary. The reality is that there is both consumer and economic resistance. The conversion to the metric system, for example, means that U.S. consumers must learn that 236.58 milliliters is the same as 8 fluid ounces. In an economic sense a changeover is costly not only in educating people and in relabeling, but also in redesigning and tooling so that dimensions are in even numbers. At best, international standards will come very slowly.

Less apparent are the indirect legal requirements that may affect product content or demand. In some countries it may be difficult or prohibitively expensive to import certain raw materials or components, thus forcing a firm to construct an end product with local substitutes that may alter the final product substantially. Or legal requirements, such as high taxes on heavy automobiles, may shift sales to smaller models, thus altering demand indirectly for tire sales and gasoline octanes.

- Examination of cultural differences may pinpoint possible problem areas but
  - consumer buying behavior is complex

Cultural factors. Consumer buying behavior is complex. It is difficult to determine in advance if the introduction of new or different products will meet with acceptance. Some U.S. food franchisors, such as McDonald's, have been highly successful in Japan by duplicating their U.S. product and distribution almost intact—an acceptance attributed to the "enthusiastic assimilation" by the Japanese of Western ways. Yet Western cosmetic firms such as Max Factor, Revlon, and Avon have been able to garner only very small shares of the $1.5 billion-a-year Japanese cosmetics market from introducing their Western products. Among the cultural factors inhibiting their sales are the facts that perfume is hardly used in Japan, suntans are considered ugly, and bath oil is impractical in communal baths.[15] Although an examination of cultural differences will pinpoint possible problem areas, it does not ensure success.

In many countries the high fertility rate and the extended family tradition have resulted in a larger number of people per household. This has necessitated different package sizes for products oriented to families. Pillsbury's most popular package size in the United States is for two servings; yet in some markets, Pillsbury's most popular sizes are for six to eight servings.[16]

- Personal incomes and infrastructures affect product demand

Economic factors. If consumers in a foreign country lack sufficient income, they may not be able to buy in sufficient quantity the same product the international firm sells in its home market. The company may therefore have to design a cheaper model or perhaps sell a product with characteristics similar to those sold at an earlier period in the home market. National Cash Register has designed crank-operated machines that are being sold in the Philippines, Latin America, the Orient, and Spain. Where incomes are low, consumers may buy many personal use items in smaller quantities, such as one aspirin, one piece of chewing gum, or one cigarette. This usually necessitates new types of packaging.

Even if a market segment has an income that is sufficient for purchasing the same product the firm sells at home, the general level of the economy may be such that products have to be altered. The type of infrastructure (e.g., roads and utilities) may determine the necessary structural composition and tolerances of products. Factory managers will have to consider the education levels of machine operators when planning equipment purchases. This may result in product simplification because of low education levels brought about by economic conditions.

Cost of Alteration

- Some products save costs more than others through standardization
- Some product alterations are cheap

As was discussed earlier, a major argument for seeking maximum uniformity in products is the cost to be saved through standardization. This cost saving may apply to any part of the marketing program; however, product standardization is probably the area where the greatest savings are possible. If a firm is exporting, longer production runs from a centralized output may result in substantial economies of scale. Total inventories may also be lowered, since domestic and foreign sales come from the same backlog. Even if different production centers in different countries are involved, a standardized approach ordinarily reduces product development costs and should lead to easier and more comparable cost controls. Output in different countries may also be exported to substitute for domestic production when local manufacturing units cannot fill orders, as in periods of unusual demand or during strikes. The cost savings from standardization have sometimes enabled producers to cut prices and improve reliability so that markets increase in spite of differences in national and regional tastes. Examples have included personal calculators from Malaysia and housewares from Rumania.[17]

In spite of the advantages of standardization, few companies are willing to follow this approach fully because—for the legal, cultural, and economic reasons discussed—too many markets would have to be foregone.[18] Furthermore, there is a wide variance in cost-saving possibilities. For example, a production that has a need for a high fixed capital input (e.g., automobile manufacture) can gain more through long production runs than one having a high proportion of variable to fixed costs (e.g., pharmaceuticals). If a company must produce abroad in order to serve the foreign market, some of the economies of product standardization, such as from long runs or inventory centralization, will be lost anyway. In this situation there is less cost pressure to maintain uniformity.

Furthermore, some changes are cheap to effect, yet have an important influence on demand. One such area is packaging. In Panama, Aunt Jemima Pancake Mix and Ritz Crackers are sold in cans rather than in boxes because of the high humidity—a low-cost change with a high potential payoff. Before making a decision a firm should always compare the cost of alteration with the cost of lost sales if no alteration is made.

One strategy for compromising between uniformity and diversity is to standardize many components while changing the end characteristics. Coca-Cola, for example, exports concentrates to bottling plants all over the world; then carbonation, color, and sugar are added. The amounts of sugar, color, and carbonation vary slightly from country to country to conform with local preferences.[19] This type of change is practically costless, since standardization is achieved for the concentrate process and the finished product cannot feasibly be exported. Even when end products appear to be quite different, many of the gains of standardization are possible. Fiat, for instance, produces a varied line of cars for its domestic and foreign sales, yet 35 percent of the parts are interchangeable.[20]

Another strategy is to make product changes less frequently in small markets in order to spread the fixed costs associated with production over a larger amount of sales. For example, the U.S. market is large enough for firms to change models annually and still have a low cost per unit. In a small market a company may change the model only after three or four years in order to sell at a low price and yet recoup the costs associated with capital equipment and start-up.

Extent and Mix of the Product Line

- Narrowing of line allows for concentration of efforts
- Broadening may gain distribution economies

Most companies produce multiple products. It is doubtful that all of these products would generate sufficient sales in a given foreign locale to justify the expenditures to penetrate the markets. Yet of the remaining products, a company may offer only a portion in order to reduce expenditures. Instead of offering as many models and options as in the United States, General Motors in Mexico produces and sells a much more limited variety. This reduces the amount of capital investment, and sales activity can concentrate on fewer products. In other words, a firm may narrow its efforts to a few segments of a given market. A firm must also consider whether any new products need to be added to the line for sale in certain countries. Two primary considerations in reaching these decisions are the possible effects on sales and the relative cost of having one product versus a family of products. Sometimes a firm finds that it must produce and sell some unpopular items if it is to sell the more popular ones. For example, a clothing manufacturer may prefer from a profit standpoint to manufacture only the most demanded sizes. However, retailers may prefer to buy only from manufacturers that can also supply the odd sizes. The manufacturer in this situation may be forced to go to a few short production runs in order to gain the mass market on other products. This type of behavior exists abroad as well. It is especially a problem for the firm that must set up foreign production if it is to sell in the foreign market. In these circumstances a firm may be able to produce locally certain products in its line and import the other products needed to help sell the local production.

If the foreign market is small in relation to the domestic market, selling costs per unit may be high because of the fixed costs associated with selling. In Europe, for example, DuPont's textile fibers sales staff sells only about one third as much as in the United States because the typical customer in Europe operates a textile mill that is about a quarter of the size of the U.S. counterpart.[21] When faced with a situation like this, the firm can follow a strategy of broadening the product line to be handled. This may be done by grouping sales of several manufacturers or by developing new products for the local market that the same salesperson can handle. Coca-Cola, for instance, has offered a line of bar mixes in South Africa, a lemonade in Australia, a mango drink in Pakistan, a tomato juice in Belgium, and two mixed juice based drinks in Mexico.[22]

Product Life Cycle Considerations

● Differences by country in
  ● time of introduction
  ● shape of curve

Most products go through stages of growth and an eventual decline in sales. For some products, such as miniskirts, the period between the introduction and demise is relatively short. For other products, such as steam locomotives, there is a long period of fairly stable sales before demand begins to fall off. Once a product reaches the declining stage of its cycle, a firm will see its sales drop unless it has other products going through a growth stage.

The product life cycle occurs in foreign markets as well as in domestic markets. However, there may be differences among countries in either the shape or the length of the cycle. Thus a manufacturer who faces declining sales at home may be able to find a foreign market that will have growing or at least sustained sales for a product. Two companies that have used this strategy are S.S.S., a manufacturer of iron tonic, and Dixie Canning

Company, a producer of home-canning equipment. Both firms faced falling demand in the United States but found that sales in some developing countries were growing. In fact, an earlier introduction of their products in these developing countries would probably have yielded few sales. Mattel found that its Cheerful Tearful Doll had a much longer sales life span in West Germany than in the United States.[23]

Because of mass communications and transportation coupled with rising income levels, many of the differences among countries in the periods of product introduction are being lessened. The result is that companies are increasingly forced to penetrate international markets quickly with their new products or face the probability that competitors will beat them with products that are close substitutes.

Product Strategy Differences

- Within same industry
  - different firms may aim at different segments
  - firms may aim at one or multiple segments

Even within a given industry we can find numerous examples of firms that have successfully embarked on different international product strategies. The U.S., Japanese, French, and German automakers until recently pursued some contrasting strategies in this respect. The U.S. companies usually aimed at the largest market segment and generally left other producers to compete for the smaller segments. This meant that they produced medium priced but large cars for the U.S. market, leaving foreign producers to compete for the small car and luxury segments of the U.S. market. In Europe, however, since the largest market segment was for smaller cars, the same U.S. producers concentrated on smaller cars. They generally left the large car production, for which there was a small but significant demand, to others. Japanese producers have concentrated on small cars at home and abroad because these were demanded by nearly all Japanese consumers. They have continued to sell only small cars in such markets as Canada, the United States, and Mexico even though larger automobiles continue to constitute the larger (although shrinking) market segment. French firms have generally produced an array of models for the French market that range from very small economy models to large luxury ones. Abroad, they have limited introduction to one or a few models per country based on estimations of which models could compete best. Different German firms have concentrated on either the luxury or the economy market at home and have marketed similar models abroad even where the size of the luxury and economy segments of the market differ from those in West Germany.

PRICING

There is often a tendency to underestimate the importance of price in the marketing mix. Many firms simply apply a standard markup of sales anywhere in the world. This may not guarantee the proper flow of funds needed to carry on the other activities that bridge the gap between production and consumption. Pricing in the international context is more complex than in the domestic arena because of:

1. a different degree of governmental intervention,
2. a greater diversity of markets,
3. price escalation in exporting,
4. the changing relative value of currencies, and
5. differences in fixed versus variable pricing practices.

Governmental Intervention

- May set minimums or maximums
- May prohibit certain competitive price practices

Every country has laws that affect the prices of goods at the consumer level, but these laws may affect different products in different ways at different times. Restrictions may prevent firms from using the strategies they consider optimal in achieving their ends.

A governmental price control may set either maximum or minimum levels to be charged the consumer. Controls against lowering prices are usually intended to prevent firms from eliminating competitors in order to gain monopoly positions. An example of this type of control would be West Germany's Unfair Competition Law, which has been interpreted by the German courts to prohibit such items as coupons, boxtops, and giveaway articles unless these will remain a consistent policy of the company throughout the years. A firm that is accustomed to relying on such practices as a means of increasing its sales at home must develop new methods in West Germany that are consistent with the German laws. Mexico sets maximum prices on many products. If costs rise, profit margins necessarily contract. While maintaining price controls on the sale of synthetic hormones, the Mexican government increased the price of barbasco root supplies, which are needed to manufacture the steroids, by 250 percent. Such firms as Syntex from the United States, Akzona from the Netherlands, and Schering from West Germany were simply caught in the middle.[24] Price controls may also force firms to lower the quality of a product, in which case they may consider changing the brand name in order to reintroduce the higher-quality product at a later date. Price controls may even force firms to abandon formerly lucrative markets. Two Swiss firms, Schwarzenbach and Gessner, which had been selling over $3 million of chadors to Iran per year were forced to pull out of the market because of such controls.[25]

Another type of control that reduces discretionary pricing is directed specifically at imports. The General Agreement on Tariffs and Trade has a provision, the Antidumping Code, that permits countries to establish restrictions against imports that come in below the price to consumers in the exporting country. The provision makes it more difficult for firms to differentiate markets through price. For example, Volkswagen and four other European automakers were forced by the U.S. Department of the Treasury to raise the price of models exported to the United States because they were being sold below European prices.[26]

A firm might desire to export abroad at a lower price than that charged at home for several reasons. One reason might be to test sales in the foreign market. Let us say that a firm finds that it cannot export to a given country because tariffs or transportation costs make the price to foreign consumers prohibitively high. However, some preliminary calculations show that by establishing foreign production, prices may be substantially reduced to the foreign consumer. Before committing resources to produce overseas, management may wish to test the market by exporting at the price at which goods could be sold if produced in the local market. If sales do not materialize, management will know factors other than price may be preventing sale of the product. If sales do materialize, then management may go ahead and establish an investment or make a second round of exports to determine whether repeat sales develop. Other reasons for charging different prices in different countries involve competitive and demand factors. For example, a firm may feel that prices can be kept high in the domestic market by restricting supply to that market. Excess production can then be sold abroad at a lower price as long as the sales price makes some contribution to overhead.

Greater Diversity of Markets

- Consumers in some countries simply like certain products more and are willing to pay more for them
- Cash versus credit buying affects demand

Although one certainly finds numerous ways to segment the domestic market and to charge differently in each segment, the variations from country to country create even greater natural segments. These are due to such factors as economic, legal, and cultural differences within foreign countries. Few sea urchins can be sold in the United States, for example, at any price; yet they are exported to Japan, where they are considered delicacies. The Shenandoah Valley Poultry Company exports 2500 metric tons of turkey yearly from the United States to Europe largely because Europeans like the plump dark meat of turkey thighs. In the United States this meat would be sold for a lower price to cat food suppliers.[27] In some countries a firm may have many competitors and thus little discretion on its prices. In others, however, it may have a virtual monopoly due either to the stage in the product life cycle or to government-granted manufacturing rights not held by competitors. In near-monopoly situations the firm may exercise considerable pricing discretion, such as using skimming, penetration, or cost-plus strategies.

The total cost that one may pay for a product will be more than the sales price if there are additional charges because of buying on credit. How consumers view these additional charges may thus affect total demand as well as the sales price they are willing to pay. The tax treatment of interest payments as well as attitudes toward being in debt affect whether consumers will pay in cash or by credit. Japanese, for example, are much more reluctant to rely on consumer credit than Americans. About 60 percent of Japanese households owe nothing at all; and only about 10 percent of gross consumer expenditure, excluding housing, is by credit compared with 23 percent in the United States.[28] In selling to Japanese consumers it is therefore less possible than in the United States to use credit payments as a means of receiving revenue from the sale of goods.

Price Escalation in Exporting

• Price generally goes up by more than transport and duty costs

If standard markups are used within the distribution channels, lengthening the channels or adding expenses somewhere within the system will increase the price to the consumer by a greater amount than the initial increase. Let us assume that the markup is 50 percent and that a product costs $1.00 to produce. The price of the product would then be $1.50. If the cost of the production were to increase by $0.20 to $1.20, the markup of 50 percent would then make the price of the product $1.80 instead of merely $1.70. In export sales, two things happen to escalate the price of goods to the consumer. To begin with, channels of distribution are usually longer because of greater distances and because of the need to engage organizations that know export procedures and/or selling in the foreign market. Second, tariffs are an additional cost that may be passed on to consumers in an escalated form.

The implications of price escalation are several. Many seemingly exportable products turn out to be noncompetitive abroad. Furthermore, to become competitive in exporting, a firm may have to sell its product to middlemen at a lower price so that the amount of escalation will be lessened.

Currency Value and Price Changes

• Must consider replacement cost
• Frequent changes hamper selling methods
• Relative changes among countries may shift production locations

For firms that are used to operating with one currency that is relatively stable in value, pricing in highly volatile currencies can be extremely problematic. Pricing decisions should be made to ensure that sufficient funds are received to replace the inventory that has been sold and still make a profit. If this is not done, a firm may be making a "paper profit" while liquidating itself. In other words, what shows as a profit may result from failure to adjust for inflation while the merchandise is in stock. In addition to the effect of inflation on prices, a company must also consider that its income taxes may be based on the paper profits rather than on real profits. Table 18.1 illustrates a pricing plan to make a target profit (after taxes) of 30 percent on replacement cost. If a procedure similar to this one is not employed, the firm may quickly lack sufficient funds to operate.

TABLE 18.1

Effect of Tax and Inflation on Pricing

Assume: Cost at beginning of 1000
36% inflation
40% tax rate
30% profit goal on replacement cost
after taxes

If sold and collected at beginning of year		If sold and collected at end of year	
Cost	1000	Replacement cost	1360
		Markup on	
Markup	500	replacement	320
Sale prices	1500	Sales price	1680
— Cost	1000	— Original cost	1000
Taxable income	500	Taxable income	680
Tax @ 40%	200	Tax @ 40%	272
Income after taxes	300	Income after taxes	408

Explanation: The pricing structure for sales or collections at the end of the year is calculated as follows: Replacement cost is cost plus inflation until collection, or $1000 + 0.36(1000) = 1360$; income after taxes is profit goal times replacement cost, or $0.30(1360) = 408$. Since income after taxes is 60 percent of taxable income, taxable income may be calculated by $0.6x = 408$ or 680; tax is $0.4 (680) = 272$; sales price is original cost (1000) plus taxable income (680); markup on replacement is sales price (1680) less replacement cost (1360), or 320.

Westinghouse's subsidiary in Belgium nearly went bankrupt, for example, because inflation was high but payment receipts were slow.[29] The longer the collection period, the more important it is to use a graduated pricing model.

Two other pricing problems that occur because of inflationary conditions are (1) the receipt of funds in a foreign currency that, when converted, will buy less of one's own currency than had been expected and (2) the constant readjustment of prices necessary to compensate for cost changes. In the first case it is sometimes possible to specify in sales contracts an equivalency in some hard currency. For example, a sale of equipment from a U.S. manufacturer to a company in Uruguay may specify that payment be made in dollars or pesos at an equivalent price, in terms of dollars, at the time that payment is effected. Whether one can invoke an equivalency clause will depend on competitive factors and governmental regulations.

When it is necessary to change prices frequently because of inflationary conditions, it becomes more difficult to quote prices in letters or catalogues. Constant price rises may even hamper the use of what would otherwise be a preferred distribution method. Vending machine sales, for example, make price increases difficult to effect because of the need to change machines in the process and to come up with coins that correspond to the percentage increase in price desired.

Currency value changes also affect pricing decisions for any product with potential foreign competition. For example, when the U.S. dollar becomes stronger, non-U.S. made goods can be sold more cheaply in the U.S. market. In such a situation, United States producers may have to accept a lower margin in order to be competitive. When the dollar weakens, then foreign producers may have to adjust their margins downward in order to remain competitive. The need to adjust prices in such situations is dependent as well on transportation costs and on the perceived similarity between domestic and foreign made goods.

Price differences between countries must therefore not exceed by much the cost of bringing the goods in from a lower-priced country, or spillover in buying will occur. Soft drink manufacturers can easily vary their prices by a large percentage from country to country, since the cost of transportation would render large-scale movements across borders impractical. However, consumers could feasibly buy abroad and import higher-priced items. Take cameras, for example. Importers in the United States and France paid yen to buy Japanese cameras; consequently, the imported price in yen was the same in both France and the United States. But then the franc cheapened in relation to the dollar, so some U.S. dealers scurried to buy inventories located in France rather than buying from the official distributor. For example, U.S. dealers could buy the Olympus OM-10 for $224.95 through the official distributor or for $152 from inventories already in France. Such movements could undermine the longer-term viability of the distributorship system, so camera manufacturers cut camera export prices to the United States to prevent such product arbitrage from taking place.[30] Companies that produce like items in different countries have also had to adjust prices when exchange rates have moved in order not to upset drastically their sales and capacity utilization balance.

Fixed versus Variable Pricing

- Differences in
  - whether manufacturer sets prices
  - whether prices fixed or bargained in stores
  - what type establishment has bargaining

There is substantial variation from country to country in the extent to which manufacturers can or must set prices at the retail level. For instance, in Venezuela, most consumer products must have prices printed on the label, whereas in Chile it is illegal for manufacturers either to suggest retail prices or to put prices on labels.[31] There is also a substantial variation in whether consumers bargain in order to settle upon an agreed price. In a study of ten countries it was determined that bargaining takes place in about 60 percent of the stores in India and Kenya but in less than 5 percent in the People's Republic of China and South Africa. Among the ten countries there are also differences in the type of establishment in which bargaining typically takes place. For instance, bargaining is much more prevalent in purchases from street vendors in India (91 percent) than in Singapore (50 percent), whereas bargaining in high-priced specialty stores is more frequent in Singapore (73 percent) than in India (55 percent).[32]

PROMOTION

Promotion is the process of presenting messages that, it is hoped, will help to sell a product or service. The types and direction of messages and the method of presentation may be extremely diverse, depending on the company, product, or country of operation.

The Push-Pull Mix

- Push more likely when
  - self-service not predominant
  - product price is high portion of income
  - advertising is restricted

Promotion may be categorized as **push,** which involves direct selling techniques, or **pull,** which relies on mass media. An example of the former would be door-to-door selling of encyclopedias; an example of the latter would be magazine advertisements for a brand of cigarettes. Most firms use combinations of the two strategies. For each product in each country a company must determine its total promotional budget as well as the mix of the budget between push and pull.

Concerning the mix between push and pull, several factors necessitate differences among countries. These include (1) the type of distribution system, (2) the cost and availability of media to reach target markets, (3) consumer attitudes toward sources of information, and (4) price of the product relative to incomes.

Generally, the more tightly controlled the distribution system, the more likely a firm is to emphasize a push strategy. The reason is that a greater effort is required to get distributors to handle a product. Another distribution factor affecting promotion is the amount of contact between salespeople and consumers. In a self-service situation, where customers lack the opportunity of asking sales personnel their opinions on products, it becomes more important to advertise through mass media or at the point of purchase. Because of diverse national environments, the promotional problems are extremely varied. In India, for example, the large number of languages, low literacy rate, and lack of reliable media information make it very difficult and expensive to reach customers. Governmental regulations pose an even greater barrier in many countries, as is illustrated best in the communist bloc. Sales must be pushed to the governmental purchasers, since there is little or no opportunity to advertise to final consumers. A less obvious effect of government on the promotional mix is the direct or indirect tax many countries put on advertising.

France and the United States present an interesting contrast of cultural factors affecting the push-pull mix.[33] Comparative studies show that U.S.

housewives spend more time watching television and reading magazines. They also rely more on friends and advertising before purchasing a new product. French housewives spend more time shopping, examining items on shelves, and listening to the opinions of retailers. It is therefore easier to presell the U.S. housewives, whereas discounts to distributors and point-of-purchase displays are more important in France.

Finally, the price of the product relative to the income of consumers is of importance in the promotional mix. The more important the purchase is in relation to income, the more time and information the customer will usually want in order to make a decision. The information is best conveyed in a personal selling situation where two-way communication is fostered. In less-developed countries, more products will have to be pushed.

Standardization of Advertising Programs

- Advantages
  - some cost savings
  - better quality at local level
  - speeds entry to different countries.
- Frequent changes due to translation problems, legal restrictions, and what is believed

Just as there are possible economies in standardizing products worldwide, there are economies in using the same advertising programs as much as possible. These economies are not as great, however, as one finds for product standardization. The savings are more likely to occur in hidden costs of executive time spent in supervising advertising campaigns. Yet there has been a widely heralded move toward standardization in recent years.[34] One of the reasons has been to improve the quality of advertising at the local level where local agencies may lack expertise. A second reason is to speed the entry of products into different countries by not having to wait to design entirely new advertising campaigns for each one. Procter & Gamble, for example, took fifteen years to get Pampers introduced into seventy countries but feels today that technology moves too fast to wait so long.[35]

Standarized advertising usually means a program that is recognizable from market to market rather than one that is identical in each. Some problems in complete standardization relate to translation, legality, credibility or image factors, and media availability. Because of these problems, there have been very few really multinational campaigns, but rather degrees of similarity. Libby Foods succeeded entirely with pantomime, showing a clown enjoying food products. Coca-cola's "Things Go Better with Coke" was successfully transferred, but "It's the Real Thing" was not meaningful in many markets.

Obviously, if a firm is going to sell in a country with a different language, messages will have to be translated into that language. On the surface, this would seem to be an easy project; however, the number of ludicrous but costly mistakes firms have made attest to its difficulty. To begin with, countries with the "same" languages often have different words for the same object. In Latin America, for example, the word for tire changes from country to country. (This same word is spelled tyre in Great Britain.) Sometimes what is an acceptable word or direct translation in one place is obscene, misleading, or meaningless in another. Even product names may present a problem. General Motors thought that its model Nova could easily be called the same in Latin America, since it means "star" in Spanish. However, people started pronouncing it "nō vä," which is the Spanish translation for "it does not go."

What is legally allowed in one place may not be allowed elsewhere. The basic reasons for the differences are national differences in views on consumer protection, competitive protection, promotion of civil rights, standards of morality, and nationalism.[36] A few examples should illustrate the vast differences that exist. In terms of protection, policies differ on the amount of deception permitted, what can be advertised to children, whether warnings must be given of possible harmful effects, and the degree to which ingredients must be listed. The EC encourages comparisons with competitors, whereas the Philippines prohibits them. Only a few countries regulate sexism in advertising. In terms of morality, advertising of some products (e.g., contraceptives and feminine hygiene products) have been restricted in some locales. Elsewhere restrictions have been placed on ads that might prompt children to misbehave and those that show barely clad women. The nationalism issue has risen in several countries that restrict the use of foreign words, models, or themes in advertisements.

Yet in spite of these differences there is evidence that there are segments of consumers in each country that respond similarly to similar messages. (Companies typically aim different campaigns at different segments within a given country.) The size of each segment as a portion of total potential consumers may differ substantially, though, from nation to nation.[37] Because of this, companies may have to alter the portion of expenditures for different campaigns within each country.

Nationality Images

- Image of products affected by where they are made
  - may give image of more acceptable origin

A question firms should consider is whether to create a local or foreign image for their products. Certain countries tend to have images of higher quality for their products than do other countries. Studies have shown that products from developed countries are viewed more highly than those from less-developed countries.[38] Promotional messages for products from developed countries may therefore make good use of playing up the nationality of origin. Even when the goods are produced in the LDC by a foreign investor, the firm may emphasize that the technology and quality control are high because of the ability of the producing firm.

There are also image differences concerning specific products from specific countries. Because of the quality image of French wines, such U.S. wineries as Paul Masson and Gallo have used advertisements that emphasize a European's enjoyment of American wines. The French firm BSN-Gervais Dannone brews the largest selling bottled beer in Europe, and the firm's director general frankly admits that the Kroenenbourg trademark "sounds German."[39] The image that will help to sell a product in one country may have the opposite effect in another. General Foods successfully promoted Maxwell House as "the great American coffee" in some countries but belatedly discovered that Germans have little respect for U.S. coffee.[40]

Generic and Near-Generic Names

● If brand name used for class of product, firm may lose the trademark
  ● different usage by country

Companies want their product names to become household words but not so much that trademarked names can be used by competitors to describe similar products. Xerox and Kleenex are nearly synonymous in the United States with copiers and paper tissues, respectively, but have remained proprietary brands. Some other names, such as cellophane, linoleum, and cornish hens have become generic, or available for anyone to use.

Internationally, producers sometimes face substantial differences among countries that may either help or frustrate their sales. Roquefort cheese and Champagne are proprietary names in France but generic in the United States, a situation that impairs French export sales of those products. A factor impeding international sales of U.S., Canadian, Irish, and Japanese whiskies is the fact that in much of the world whisky is a synonym for Scotch whisky.[41]

LDC Criticism

● Critics argue that MNE advertising leads to superfluous and dangerous product consumption in LDCs

Related to arguments that MNEs introduce superfluous products that LDCs can ill afford is the contention that advertising for these products has led to their acceptance by people who are not equipped to understand the product implications or their needs. For example, the Zambian government banned advertising for Fanta after learning that mothers were enthusiastically weaning their children on this glamorous but not particularly nutritious drink.[42] In spite of the concern about advertising in LDCs, the evidence is that the attitudes among LDC residents are not more adverse toward advertising than those of residents of industrial countries.[43] Criticism toward practices in LDCs is therefore just as apt to come from company constituents in industrial countries.

The most famous case in this respect involved infant formula sales to developing countries. There was an increased infant mortality rate in poor countries, which was related to an increase in bottle feeding over breast feeding. Because of low incomes and poor education, mothers frequently diluted formula to the point at which there was little nutrition and gave it to their babies in unhygienic bottles and under unhygienic conditions. Critics argued that the increased bottle feeding had been the result of heavy promotion of formula by such firms as Nestlé, Bristol-Meyers, and American Home Products. The firms claimed that the rise in bottle feeding was due to factors other than their promotion, such as a rise in the number of working mothers and a general trend of fewer products and services being made in the home. The promotion, they argued, got people to give up their "home brews" in favor of the most nutritious thing available in baby bottles. In 1981 the World Health Organization overwhelmingly passed a voluntary code for restricting formula promotion in developing countries. The company most hit by criticism was Nestlé because it had the largest market share in developing countries and because it was easy to organize a boycott against Nestlé because of its products bearing the Nestlé brand name. Although formula sales in LDCs never accounted for more than 3 percent of Nestlé's worldwide business, management was most concerned about what the criticism would do to its image. In 1984 the company agreed to prohibit advertising that would discourage breast feeding, to limit free formula supplies to hospitals, and to ban personal gifts to health officials.[44] At this writing it is too early to determine whether the changes will alter formula demand in LDCs.

DISTRIBUTION

- May have to devise ways to help distributors so they give attention to your products

A company may do an excellent job at assessing market potential, designing products or services for that market, and promoting to likely consumers; however, there will be little likelihood of reaching the sales potential if the goods or services are not made conveniently available to customers. Distribution is the course—physical path or legal title—that goods take between production and consumption. In international marketing, a producer must decide on the method of distribution among countries as well as the method of distribution within the foreign country of sale. Chapters 14 and 15 discussed many distributional considerations, including where production should be located in order to serve given markets, how the title to goods gets transferred, and the forms of operations for foreign market penetration. This section will not repeat these aspects of distribution. Rather it will discuss distributional differences and conditions within foreign countries about which an international marketer should be aware.

Gaining Distribution

Both wholesalers and retailers have limited capacity in terms of storage facilities, display space, money to pay for inventories, and transportation and personnel to move and sell merchandise. Therefore they naturally try to carry only those things that have the greatest potential profits. If a firm is new to a country and wishes to introduce products that some competitors are already selling there, it may be difficult to convince distributors to handle new brands. Even established firms may sometimes find it hard to gain distribution for their new products, although they have advantages through being known and being able to use existing profitable lines as "bait" for the new merchandise.

If a firm wishes to use existing distribution channels, it may need to develop incentives for those distributors to handle the product. It is essential to analyze competitive conditions carefully in order to offer effective incentives. Kodak, for example, noted that a prevalent problem in many parts of the world was inventory control. On one hand, distributors had to scrap outdated film or paper because of overordering or because of shifts in customer demands. On the other hand, there were frequently shortages of given brands or products because of international delivery problems and the inability of distributors to project future demands with sufficient accuracy. By establishing forecasting techniques, weekly sales reports and replenishment shipments, and maintenance of regional inventories, Kodak was able to increase distribution by offering better service than had existed.[45] There are many other possibilities. These include the offering of higher margins, after-sales servicing, and promotional support. They may be offered on either a permanent or an introductory basis. The type of incentive to be offered should depend as well on the comparative costs within each market. Of course, in the final analysis, incentives will be of little help unless distributors believe that it is a viable product from a reliable company. The company must therefore sell both itself and its products to the distributors.

For companies whose products are sold only to a few final customers and for companies whose products are quite complex, it may be necessary to bypass middlemen and sell directly to the customer. This is particularly true for certain industrial products.

Distribution Segmentation

- May enter a market gradually by
    - limiting geographic coverage
    - emphasizing only certain types of middlemen

Many products and markets lend themselves to gradual development or to different distributional strategies in different areas. In many instances, geographic barriers divide countries into very distinct markets: Colombia is divided by ranges of mountains and Australia by a desert. In other countries, as in Zimbabwe and Zaire, very little wealth or few potential sales may lie outside the large metropolitan areas. In still others, advertising and distribution may be handled effectively on a regional basis. For example, when Kikkoman first began selling soy sauce in the United States, the company could not find middlemen who were willing and able to get the sauce onto the shelves of national supermarket chains. Nor did Kikkoman have the resources to bypass the middlemen. However, Kikkoman was able to target its first sales to the San Francisco area, where the product was already well known to much of the large Japanese-American population. Through a local food broker Kikkoman gained access to distribution in neighborhoods with a large Oriental population. By advertising the product to the general public on television and by showing sales results from the initial distribution, it was able to gain distribution in other neighborhoods as well. Two years later, Kikkoman moved into Los Angeles. It continued expansion gradually over the next seventeen years, using food brokers in all cases, until it had national distribution and over 50 percent of the soy sauce market.[46] It is not uncommon for a firm to use one type of middleman in one area and another elsewhere.

Foreign Selling System

> • National norms differ in
> > • number and size of stores
> > • ownership and agreements among distributors
> > • where people prefer to buy

Evidence on the comparative cost of distribution among countries is not clear. What one does find, however, is a vast array of distribution differences. Finland, for example, has few stores per capita because of the predominance of general-line retailers, whereas Italian distribution is characterized by a very fragmented retail and wholesale structure. In the Netherlands, buyers' cooperatives deal directly with manufacturers. In West Germany, cooperative ventures among retailers to perform wholesaling activities are common. Because a firm selling internationally must deal with these different situations, it must become aware of the effect the distribution system has on operating costs and on the ease of entry.

Consumer preferences toward a given form of distribution may also vary by country at a given time. For example, an estimated six million people buy by mail in West Germany; however, Portugal has offered little as a market for mail-order development. Avon, which sells door-to-door in the United States, has not found much receptiveness to this method in Japan. In some countries there is a fear that door-to-door salespeople may be thieves or tax inspectors. Finally, the type of retail establishment may be very important. Does a man prefer to buy hair dressing, for instance, in a grocery store, barber shop, drugstore, or some other type of outlet?

SUMMARY

- Although the principles of selling abroad are the same as those in the home country, the international businessperson must deal with a less familiar environment and one that may be subject to rapid change.

- Some methods for broadly assessing foreign demand for products are analysis of consumption patterns, estimates based on what has happened in other countries, of historical trends, regression, income elasticity, and gap analysis. Some problems with these tools include taste and technology changes that render past observations and observations in other countries, invalid for specific countries.

- A standardized approach to marketing implies maximum uniformity in products and programs among the countries of operation. Although this will minimize expenses, most firms make changes to fit country needs in order to increase the volume of sales.

- There are a variety of legal and other environmental conditions that may necessitate alteration of products in order to capture foreign demand. In addition to determining under what circumstances products should be altered, businesspeople also must decide how many and which products to sell abroad.

- Because of different demand characteristics, a product may be in a growth stage in one country and a mature or declining stage in another. Firms can usually exert more control over pricing during the growth stage.

- Governmental regulations may directly or indirectly affect the prices companies charge. International pricing is further complicated because of changes in the values of currencies, product preference differences, and variations in fixed versus bargaining on prices.

- For each product in each country a company must determine not only its promotional budget, but also the mix of the budget between push and pull. The relationship between push and pull promotions should depend on the distribution system, cost and availability of media, consumer attitudes, and the product relative to incomes.

- Some major problems for standardizing advertising in different countries involve translation, legal, media availability, and credibility factors.

- Distribution channels vary substantially among countries. These differences may affect not only the relative costs of operating, but also the ease of making initial sales.

C A S E   SOURCE PERRIER[47]

During the strong dollar era of the 1950s to the 1960s, when hordes of Americans flocked to France, one of their vocal complaints was the danger of drinking French tap water and the necessity to purchase bottled water. When purchasing water, they had a strong distaste for any with bubbles. The probability that, by 1980, Americans would be importing from France over $65 million per year of Perrier's naturally carbonated water seemed almost impossible. This does not imply that there was no earlier market for French water in the United States. One of the earliest customers was Benjamin Franklin, who, after returning from being ambassador in Paris, imported his drinking water. Near the turn of the century, Perrier set up

U.S. distribution; however, by 1976, sales had reached only 3.5 million bottles per year. The so-called "Perrier freaks" had to hunt in gourmet shops or a few bars to quench their thirsts. At over $1 for a 23-ounce bottle, the product had gained acceptance among only a small group of high-income people. It was a product with small sales and high retail margins.

By the early 1970s, Source Perrier was having trouble sustaining growth in France given its large share of the bottled drink market. The Chairman, Gustave Levin, whose family controlled over half of the company's stock, sought to increase sales by acquiring related companies. He bought firms producing soft drinks, milk, chocolate, and confectionery products in France. In 1972 he also purchased Poland Spring, a U.S. firm producing still (noncarbonated) spring water. None of these ventures fared well under Perrier's leadership.

Through a mutual friend, Gustave Levin met Bruce Nevins. As an executive of Levi Strauss, Nevins had been instrumental in the upsurge of jeans sales. In their conversations it was obvious that Levin coveted a niche in the U.S. market and that Nevins believed it would be possible to develop a mass market for a "non-caloric, chic alternative to soft drinks." The U.S. soft drink market at that time was about $10 billion wholesale; thus the stakes were high—so high that Perrier sold off 70 percent of its acquisitions in 1975–1976 (including Poland Spring) to finance a U.S. marketing subsidiary. The new subsidiary, Great Waters of France, was headed by Bruce Nevins.

A number of conditions made Nevins optimistic about the possible acceptance of Perrier water by U.S. consumers. The most important of these was the growing diet-consciousness. Miller Brewing had had phenomenal success a few years earlier with the introduction of Lite beer. Since cyclamates had been banned in soft drinks, producers had turned to saccharin, which many people found distasteful. There was also no popular low-calorie drink that was considered chic to order. The use of the adjective "diet" simply announced that the drinker had weight problems. If people could be persuaded that Perrier tasted good, then it could be a preferred low-calorie alternative.

Another trend was toward natural foods for health reasons. Even tap water and the 75 percent of bottled water that was processed from tap water had become suspect. In the process of purification, cancer-suspect chlorine derivatives were added to water. Furthermore, certain viruses, sodium, and heavy metals were still found in most purified water and soda water. Perrier came from natural springs and contained high levels of calcium, very little sodium, and no additives. It could be promoted as a natural drink with healthy properties, even though some of the bubbles were lost when the water was removed from the springs and put back in during the bottling process.

A third factor was a growing U.S. preference for imports. This was apparent not only in the rising ratio of imports to gross national expenditures, but also in the acceptance of "foreignness." In terms of food, so-called gourmet restaurants, cookbooks, dinner clubs, ingredients, and wines were becoming commonplace, and French items were practically synonymous with the word gourmet. Perrier might successfully capitalize on these attitudes.

The marketing program for Great Waters of France really got underway in 1977. One of the first questions was in which part of the market to position Perrier. The three trends discussed above would clearly lead to different price, promotion, and distribution strategies because of facing different competitors in each segment. In going after the diet market segment, for example, Perrier would come face-to-face with Coca-Cola and Pepsi-Cola, which between them controlled 45 percent of the soft drink market. These firms, along with the many others that competed for the remaining 55 percent of sales, fought vigorously in the market by keeping prices fairly low, advertising heavily, and clamoring for shelf space in the soft drink section of supermarkets. The difficulty of competing in this segment is evident from the experience of Schweppes, which in spite of establishing U.S. bottling facilities and engaging in heavy marketing outlays had failed to get even 1 percent of the market. Competing in this mass market segment might also cause Perrier to lose the snob appeal it held among high-income buyers.

Competing in the natural or health foods segment would pit Perrier against other bottled water producers and various tonics that contained healthful additives. This was a very small market compared with that for soft drinks. The 1976 sales of bottled water were $189 million, of which 93 percent was from purified domestic still water. This was largely sold in five-gallon containers at low prices through home or commercial delivery. Less than 20 percent of bottled water was sold in retail stores, and there was little brand identification. To expand retail sales would probably mean concentrating on gaining shelf space in the health food sections of stores. Since bottled water sales were determined to be much more geographically concentrated than soft drink sales, it would be far easier for Perrier to target its promotion and distribution for this segment. About 50 percent of sales, for example, were in California.

The gourmet market was the one to which Source Perrier had been selling for some 70 years. There were undoubtedly usage and distributional gaps in this market. The total sales of mineral water in 1976 were only $15 million. Primary demand might be increased, and Perrier might be made more readily available through increased distribution to specialty stores and new distribution to the growing gourmet sections of supermarkets.

Perrier decided to hit the mass market by competing in the soft drink market segment. One of the first problems that they had to overcome was the price of the product. They reasoned that, through massive distribution, the retail price could be cut about 30 percent from what it was when the company emphasized the gourmet segment of the market. Even at that, the price was still about 50 percent higher than the average soft drink. This price was considered "rock bottom." The cost of transporting water across the Atlantic was expensive, resulting in an East Coast retail price in 1977 of 69 cents for a 23-ounce bottle. This included a retail gross margin of 27.6 percent as compared to 22.6 percent on soft drinks. Management reasoned that the higher margin would make supermarkets more willing to handle Perrier. A low margin was maintained by Perrier not only to become more price competitive with domestic soft drinks, but also to dissuade other European firms from exporting to the United States. To get people to pay what was still a high price, it was necessary to segment the soft drink market differently than anyone had heretofore done—by aiming at an adult population and using the higher price to gain snob appeal.

Great Waters of France felt that distribution was the real key to success. A sales force of forty people, almost all of whom were formerly with soft drink firms, was hired. Through a close examination of demographics, three cities were picked for the first expansion efforts. The cities (New York, San Francisco, and Los Angeles) were those with the largest penchant for imported food items. The company made a film designed to convey to distributors and supermarket chains that Perrier water had a long-term viability. The film showed that the springs had been popular as far back as 218 B.C., when Hannibal partook of the waters, and that the present firm dates back to 1903, supplies 400 million bottles a year, and outsells the leading cola in Europe by 2 to 1. Perrier sought the most aggressive distributors for these first and subsequent market areas. These included soft-drink bottlers, alcoholic beverage distributors, and food brokers in different areas. It was essential that distributors be able to get supermarket space in the soft-drink sections, replenish stocks frequently, and set up point of purchase displays. One of the first distributors, Joyce Beverage Management, bought fifty-five trucks and hired 100 additional people to handle the Perrier account. In the introductory period, arrangements were made for secondary display stacks and in-store tastings. The company also gave cents-off coupons with purchases. Within a year, Perrier had moved from three to twenty major market areas. This was doubled in the second year.

For the big sales push, Perrier developed 11-ounce and 6.5-ounce bottles, the latter sold in multipacks. They also developed a modern logo on the bottles, later to be replaced by the original label design, which was more congruent with the old-world image that the firm wished to project. With initial distribution assured, it was necessary to get sufficient appeal so that the bottles on the shelves would be sold. In Europe the company could make therapeutic claims; however, the U.S. law very strictly forbade this. In test marketing, Perrier tried such themes as "formerly heavy drinkers such as Richard Burton and Ed McMahon are now 'hooked' on Perrier" and "contains no sodium which causes heartburn." These were abandoned in favor of messages emphasizing its qualities as a natural thirst quencher with no calories and no additives. Initial promotion was regional, relying heavily on the print media. Groups of food and beverage writers were invited for dinners and exhibitions so that they would write about Perrier. Marathons were sponsored so that the product would be associated both with "healthiness" and "thirst-quenching." As distribution became national, Perrier got Orson Welles to appear in TV spots on network channels. The advertising budget was set high—$1 million, $2 million, and $7 million for fiscal years 1977, 1978, and 1979, respectively. Throughout this period, Perrier was able to maintain snob appeal by getting tidbits in gossip columns about celebrities being seen sipping Perrier in the "right places."

Sales increased rapidly to 21 million bottles in 1977, 60 million in 1978, over 100 million in 1979, and over 200 million in 1980. The increase did not go unnoticed by either the media or competitors. By 1979 a bottling executive said, "Everyone with water seeping from a rock is buying glass, slapping a label on it, and marketing a new bottled water." In the first quarter of 1979 alone, seven new bottled waters came on the market. Some of the old bottled spring water firms suddenly sought a larger share of the growing market. They promoted blind tasting comparisons to emphasize that U.S. water was just as tasty as the imports. Nestlé's Deer Park brand made a challenge with a spring water priced 35–40 percent below Perrier. A Chicago firm, Hincley and Schmitt, introduced Premier in a bottle with a label that unashamedly copied Perrier. Its theme was, "Let your guests think it's imported." Norton Simon's Canada Dry began repositioning its club soda to be more competitive with Perrier. SAMI, a market research group, reported 104 brands of bottled waters in its territory.

By late 1980, Bruce Nevins admitted that the "U.S. market for sparkling water is in the process of maturing." He was right. Perrier's sales peaked in 1980 and began falling, largely because of competition from domestic seltzer (carbonated tap water) and domestic club soda (carbonated tap water to which mineral salts are usually added), which Perrier's U.S. president was unable to distinguish from Perrier in blind tasting. Sales of imported water in the United States fell from 28.1 million gallons in 1979 to 12.1 million in 1982. To combat U.S. domestic competition, Perrier repurchased Poland Spring in 1980. After buying Poland Spring in 1976 for $1 million, Poland Spring's new owners had carbonated the still water, modernized the facilities, and captured 6 percent of the bottled water market. The reported purchase price in 1980 was $10 million. But most of the growth in bottled waters was not for spring waters, which constituted only 11 percent of the bottled water market by 1982. Another problem was that the name Perrier was practically becoming generic as customers increasingly asked for Perrier when they simply wanted some kind of sparkling water.

In 1982, Perrier devised a new U.S. strategy, the handling of specialized imports that could be sold to market segments similar to those to which Perrier seemed to appeal. This segment was described by different Perrier officials as "aspirant people who try to improve their quality of life," as "households with incomes of $30,000 or more," and as "the same people who tend to buy better fashions, better cars and the like." Perrier took on Lindt chocolate from Switzerland in 1982 and Bonne Maman preserves from France in 1983. Both of these firms had been selling previously in the U.S. market with annual sales of $1 million and $1.5 million before the Perrier connection. By 1984 their sales were estimated to be $15 million and $5 million, respectively. While this product diversification helped Perrier in the United States, it did not solve the company's corporate problem. The capacity for bottled spring water in France was more than doubled in the 1978–1979 period in anticipation of continued growth in the U.S. market. Source Perrier began to look seriously for the first time at the British and German markets. In 1980, with little advertising, Perrier sold about 12 million bottles in Britain.

QUESTIONS

1. Might Perrier have been better off by positioning itself in a segment other than the soft drink market?
2. Should Perrier have tried a means other than exporting to penetrate the U.S. market?
3. What options are open to Perrier in the U.S.?
4. What lessons were learned in the United States that might help Source Perrier if it expands in Britain and Germany?

NOTES

1. Data for the case were taken from "M & S in Japan," *The Times* (London), August 7, 1978; "M & S Getting Their French Lessons Right," *The Times* (London), August 2, 1976, p. 16; Sandra Salmans, "Britain: How Marks & Spencer Lost Its Spark," *New York Times*, August 31, 1980, p. F3; Barbara Crossette, "British Store Shapes up for Parisians," *New York Times*, June 28, 1975, p. 14; "St. Michael Spreads the Gospel," *The Economist*, September 1977, pp. 68–69; "Super Supermarkets," *The Accountant*, June 26, 1980, pp. 981–983; Carrie Dolan, "Marks & Spencer Finds No-Frills Policy in Retailing Suits the British Just Fine," *Wall Street Journal*, April 14, 1981, p. 35; Alan Freeman, "Marks & Spencer Canada Adheres to Parent's Principles Despite Losses," *Wall Street Journal*, August 4, 1981, p. 39; Patience Wheatcroft, "Marks Looks at Sparks," *The Times* (London), October 23, 1983, p. 53; Margaret de Miraval, "British Influence Aiding French Department Stores," *Christian Science Monitor*, July 7, 1983, p. 15; "International Corporate Report," *Wall Street Journal*, May 2, 1984, p. 35; "Marks & Spencer Tries Yet Again," *Financial Times*, April 25, 1985, p. 16.

2. For a more extensive coverage of similar techniques, see Susan P. Douglas, C. Samuel Craig, and Warren J. Keegan, "Approaches to Assessing International Marketing Opportunities for Small- and Medium-sized Companies," *Columbia Journal of World Business,* Vol. 17, No. 3, Fall 1982, pp. 26–32.

3. UNCTAD/GATT, *The Compilation of Basic Information on Export Markets* (Geneva: UNCTAD/GATT, 1968). For a more detailed discussion of these procedures, see C. G. Alexandrides and George P. Moschis, *Export Marketing Management* (New York: Praeger Publishers, 1977), pp. 21–25.

4. Reed Moyer, "International Market Analysis," *Journal of Marketing Research,* November 1968, pp. 357–359.

5. Houston H. Stokes and Hugh Neuburger, "The Box-Jenkins Approach—When Is It a Cost-Effective Alternative?," *Columbia Journal of World Business,* Winter 1976, pp. 78–86.

6. Alfred Maizels, *Industrial Growth and World Trade* (Cambridge: University Press, 1963), p. 55.

7. Moyer, "International Market Analysis," pp. 357–359.

8. David Bauer, "The Dimensions of Consumer Markets Abroad," *The Conference Board Record,* June 1970, p. 45.

9. Isadore Barmash, "Genesco's Motivation," *New York Times,* November 28, 1971.

10. J. A. Weber, "Comparing Growth Opportunities in the International Marketplace," *Management International Review,* No. 1, 1979, pp. 47–54.

11. "Chocolate Makers in Switzerland Try to Melt Resistance," *Wall Street Journal,* January 5, 1981, p. 14.

12. John D. Daniels, "Combining Strategic and International Business Approaches through Growth Vector Analysis, *Management International Review,* Vol. 23, No. 3, 1983, p. 11.

13. Yves L. Doz, "Managing Manufacturing Rationalization within Multinational Companies," *Columbia Journal of World Business,* Fall 1978, pp. 82–93.

14. John S. Hill and Richard R. Still, "Adapting Products to LDC Tastes," *Harvard Business Review,* Vol. 62, No. 2, March–April 1984, pp. 92–101.

15. Andrew H. Malcolm, "On the Battlefield of Beauty," *New York Times,* May 22, 1977, p. 1.

16. Hill and Still, *op. cit.,* p. 95.

17. Theodore Levitt, "The Globalization of Markets," *Harvard Business Review,* Vol. 61, No. 3, May–June 1983, p. 94.

18. See, for example, "Colleague Says Levitt Wrong," quoting Phillip Kotler in *Advertising Age,* June 25, 1984, p. 50.

19. *Momentum* (an in-house magazine published by Coca-Cola), 1970, p. 17.

20. "The Leader from Turin," *Fortune,* September 15, 1968.

21. Roger Ricklefs, "Made for Europe," *Wall Street Journal,* April 27, 1966, p. 1.

22. *Momentum,* 1970, p. 16, and Coca Cola Annual Reports, 1982–1984.

23. Mattel, *1979 Annual Report,* p. 10.

24. "Foreign Firms Warned of Mexican Take-Over in Boycott of Barbasco," *Wall Street Journal,* March 16, 1976, p. 7.

25. "Swiss Find Iran Market for Chaders Unraveling," *Wall Street Journal,* January 26, 1981, p. 25.

26. "VW to Lift U.S. Prices an Average 2.5%, Primarily to Satisfy 'Dumping' Ruling," *Wall Street Journal,* October 14, 1976, p. 7.

27. "World Report," *Wall Street Journal,* January 20, 1977, p. 1; Patricia Wells, "Peddling Boursin to the French and Pizza to the Italians," *New York Times,* September 16, 1979, p. F3.

28. John Marcom, Jr., "Consumer Credit Expands in Japan," *Wall Street Journal,* March 3, 1981, p. 35.

29. "The Luster Dims at Westinghouse," *Business Week,* July 20, 1974, p. 58.

30. Ann Hughey, " 'Gray Market' in Camera Imports Starts to Undercut Official Dealers," *Wall Street Journal,* April 1, 1982, p. 29.

31. Hill and Still, *op. cit.,* p. 95.

32. Laurence Jacobs, Reginald Worthley, and Charles Keown, "Perceived Buyer Satisfaction and Selling Pressure versus Pricing Policy: A Comparative Study of Retailers in Ten Developing Countries," *Journal of Business Research,* Vol. 12, No. 1, March 1984, p. 67.

33. Robert T. Green and Eric Langeard, "A Cross-National Comparison of Consumer Habits and Innovator Characteristics," *Journal of Marketing,* July 1975.

34. Dennis Chase, "Global Marketing: The New Wave," *Advertising Age,* June 25, 1984, p. 49+.

35. "Multinationals Tackle Global Marketing," *Advertising Age,* June 25, 1984, p. 50.

36. "High Hurdles," *Wall Street Journal,* November 25, 1980, p. 56; Frank J. Prial, "Very, Very Bad, Pakistani Says As He Confiscates Lingerie Ad," *New York Times,* April 20, 1981, p. A11; Barry Newman, "Watchdogs Abroad," *Wall Street Journal,* April 8, 1980, p. 1+; J. J. Boddewyn, "Advertising Regulation in the 1980s: The Underlying Global Forces," *Journal of Marketing,* Vol. 46, Winter 1982, pp. 27–35; "Regulation of Advertising: Countries Starting to Eye Use of Foreign Languages," *Business International,* May 4, 1979, pp. 142–143.

37. Alfred S. Boote, "Psychographic Segmentation in Europe," *Journal of Advertising Research,* Vol. 21, December 1982/January 1983, pp. 19–25.

38. Robert D. Schooler, "Product Bias in the Central American Market," *Journal of Marketing Research,* November 1956, pp. 394–397; R. D. Schooler, "Bias Phenomena Attendant to the Marketing of Foreign Goods in the U.S.," *Journal of International Business Studies,* Spring 1971.

39. William H. Flanagan, "Big Battle Is Brewing As French Beer Aims to Topple Heineken," *Wall Street Journal,* February 22, 1980, p. 16.

40. S. Watson Dunn, "Effect of National Identity on Multinational Promotional Strategy in Europe," *Journal of Marketing,* October 1976, p. 55.

41. "Global Report," *Wall Street Journal,* April 26, 1976, p. 6.

42. Louis Turner, "There's No Love Lost between Multinational Companies and the Third World," *Business and Society Review,* Autumn 1974, p. 74.

43. James R. Wills, Jr. and John K. Ryans, Jr., "Attitudes toward Advertising: A Multinational Study," *Journal of International Business Studies,* Vol. 13, Winter 1982, p. 128.

44. "Boycott against Nestlé over Infant Formula to End Next Month," *Wall Street Journal,* January 27, 1984, p. 19.

45. Robert E. Schellberg, "Kodak: A Case Study of International Distribution," *Columbia Journal of World Business,* Spring 1976, pp. 32–38.

46. John E. Cooney, "Selling American," *Wall Street Journal,* December 16, 1977, p. 1.

47. Data for the case were taken from James F. Clarity, "Perrier, the Snob's Drink, Soon to Come in Six Packs," *New York Times,* April 27, 1977, p. C1+; Louis Botto, "Straight from the Source," *New York Times Magazine,* June 26, 1977, pp. 68–72; Roger B. May, "French Bottler Tries to Replace U.S. Pop with a Natural Fizz," *Wall Street Journal,* April 12, 1978, p. 1+; Maria Anna Ferrara, "Nestlé's Deer Park Challenges Perrier in New York Market," *Wall Street Journal,* November 27, 1978, p. 34; "Deep Chic," *Wall Street Journal,* December 7, 1979, p. 24; Carolyn Pfaff, "Perrier Fortunes Rest on Whimsical Chief," *Advertising Age,* April 14, 1980, p. 66; Peter C. DuBois, "Perrier Going Flat?" *Barron's,* May 12, 1980, p. 71; "Perrier: Putting More Sparkle into Sales," *Sales & Marketing Management,* January 1979, pp. 16–17; Bob Lederer and Martin Westerman, "How Perrier Became a Soft Drink," *Beverage World,* May 1979, pp. 37–45; "Perrier: The Astonishing Success of an Appeal to Affluent Adults," *Business Week,* January 22, 1979, pp. 64–65; "The Water Treatment," *Fortune,* January 12, 1981, p. 22; "Sales Boon for Bottled Water," *New York Times,* August 8, 1982, p. F27; Marian Burros, "Carbonated Water: More Than a Matter of Taste," *New York Times,* April 27, 1983, p. C1; Steven P. Galante, "Perrier's U.S. Marketing Know-How Put to Use for Other European Brands," *Wall Street Journal,* June 26, 1984, p. 30.

19

The Multinational Accounting Function

- To examine the major influences on the development of worldwide accounting objectives, standards, and practices.
- To investigate some of the international differences in accounting and the major efforts being made to harmonize accounting principles worldwide.
- To explain how to account for foreign currency transactions and foreign currency financial statements.
- To show how firms must disclose financial data concerning their international operations.
- To discuss some of the problems of performance evaluation in the context of foreign operations.

COLGATE-PALMOLIVE COMPANY'S INTERNATIONAL OPERATIONS[1]

In 1983, Colgate-Palmolive derived 55 percent of its sales and 48 percent of its operating profits from outside of the United States, and it had 49 percent of its identifiable assets abroad. Although Colgate-Palmolive's 1983 Annual Report does not list all of the countries where the firm has manufacturing and sales operations, it discloses the data about the firm's geographic segments shown in Table 19.1.

It is interesting to note from Table 19.1 that sales dollars actually declined from 1982 to 1983. However, the Annual Report emphasizes that the firm's unit volume actually increased during that time. This was due to "renewed economic growth" in the United States and certain overseas countries and to Colgate-Palmolive's increased market share in a variety of business categories.

In explaining why dollar sales volume fell during the year while unit sales volume increased, management pointed out that this was due to the strong U.S. dollar. Had exchange rates remained constant (everything else remaining equal), Colgate-Palmolive would actually have experienced sales growth of over 8 percent.

As noted in its *1983 Annual Report,* Colgate-Palmolive's growth in unit

TABLE 19.1 _____

COLGATE-PALMOLIVE GEOGRAPHIC SEGMENTS

Geographic area data (thousands of dollars)		1983	1982	1981
Net sales	United States	2,208,713	2,029,189	2,170,467
	Western Hemisphere	854,471	1,004,304	1,049,983
	Europe	1,156,416	1,231,568	1,378,953
	Far East and Africa	645,198	622,934	661,961
		4,864,798	4,887,995	5,261,364
Operating profit	United States	198,899	171,474	168,124
	Western Hemisphere	78,780	89,806	124,349
	Europe	46,369	71,752	81,816
	Far East and Africa	57,297	61,211	82,945
		381,345	394,243	457,234
Identifiable assets	United States	1,090,890	963,595	989,386
	Western Hemisphere	335,881	344,584	413,207
	Europe	474,766	467,485	573,364
	Far East and Africa	249,130	242,761	248,103
		2,150,667	2,018,425	2,224,060

Source: Colgate-Palmolive, 1983 Annual Report, p. 30.

sales and market share took place in a variety of countries and economic conditions:

modest recovery in most of Europe; resumed growth in many of the developing Far Eastern and African nations; and a general erosion of consumer buying power throughout Latin America.

Overseas countries where Colgate-Palmolive operates use currencies different from the U.S. dollar. For the financial statements to be prepared, they had to be translated from the local currency into the U.S. dollar. Table 19.2 provides a consolidated income statement for the firm in dollars. A consolidated statement is one that combines or consolidates the financial information from all of the firm's operations worldwide into one financial statement. In its explanation of the operating results for 1983, management points out that the $415,976,000 of general and administrative expenses contains foreign exchange gains and losses that result primarily from translating the financial statements of subsidiaries in highly inflationary economies from the local currency into U.S. dollars.

TABLE 19.2

COLGATE-PALMOLIVE COMPANY CONSOLIDATED STATEMENT OF INCOME

Thousands of dollars except per share amounts	1983	1982	1981
Net sales	$4,864,798	$4,887,995	$5,261,364
Cost of sales	2,982,200	3,044,676	3,345,448
Gross profit	1,882,598	1,843,319	1,915,916
Operating and other expenses			
Marketing	1,132,563	1,080,899	1,077,802
General and administrative	415,976	395,567	419,317
Interest expense	53,216	49,677	70,867
Interest income	(69,645)	(60,551)	(46,976)
Total operating and other expenses	1,532,110	1,465,592	1,521,010
Income before income taxes	350,488	377,727	394,906
Provision for income taxes			
United States	69,568	63,280	60,053
Foreign	83,086	117,537	126,454
Total	152,654	180,817	186,507
Net income	$ 197,834	$ 196,910	$ 208,399
Net income per common share	$ 2.42	$ 2.41	$ 2.55

Source: Colgate-Palmolive, 1983 Annual Report, p. 34.

TABLE 19.3

COLGATE-PALMOLIVE COMPANY CONSOLIDATED BALANCE SHEET

Thousands of Dollars December 31,		1983	1982
Assets	Current Assets		
	Cash	$ 13,195	$ 17,386
	Short-term investments	513,298	555,988
	Receivables (less allowance for doubtful accounts of $21,246 and $24,503)	524,228	504,586
	Inventories	676,425	630,515
	Other current assets	76,467	74,093
	Total current assets	1,803,613	1,782,568
	Property, Plant and Equipment		
	Land	32,578	33,845
	Buildings	258,971	263,253
	Machinery and equipment	1,070,739	1,012,883
		1,362,288	1,309,981
	Less: Accumulated depreciation	601,073	617,259
		761,215	692,722
	Other Assets	99,137	99,123
		$2,663,965	$2,574,413
Liabilities and Shareholders' Equity	Current Liabilities		
	Notes and loans payable to banks	$ 80,748	$ 100,978
	Current portion of long-term debt	25,263	17,409
	Accounts payable	300,242	272,642
	Accrued income taxes	88,365	98,301
	Other accruals	331,987	311,835
	Total current liabilities	826,605	801,165
	Non-Current Liabilities		
	Long-term debt	292,945	255,835
	Deferred income taxes	114,639	89,147
	Deferred staff-leaving	30,407	38,553
	Other deferred liabilities	57,701	68,389
		495,692	451,924
	Shareholders' Equity		
	Preferred stock	12,578	12,578
	Common stock	82,010	81,957
	Capital surplus	108,576	107,693
	Retained earnings	1,363,409	1,270,583
	Cumulative foreign currency translation adjustments	(224,905)	(151,487)
	Total shareholders' equity	$1,341,668	$1,321,324
		$2,663,965	$2,574,413

Source: Colgate-Palmolive, 1983 Annual Report, p. 35.

Table 19.3 contains the consolidated balance sheet for Colgate-Palmolive. Remember that each dollar balance represents not only dollars but also the dollar equivalent of foreign currency balances from around the world. Although cash is listed as $13,195,000, there is no way of knowing how much is dollars, German marks, Swiss francs, or Japanese yen. It is interesting to note that the stockholders' equity section of the balance sheet contains an account entitled "Cumulative foreign currency translation adjustments." That amount arises when the foreign currency financial statements are translated into dollars. As you will find out later in the chapter, it is the number that is used to make assets equal liabilities plus stockholders' equity. Notice that the number is negative for Colgate-Palmolive, indicating a reduction in stockholders' equity. In fact, that number is larger than the sum of the capital stock accounts.

THE ACCOUNTING FUNCTION

- The accountant is essential in providing information to decision makers.

The finance and accounting functions of Colgate-Palmolive, like those of any multinational enterprise, are very closely related. Each relies on the other in fulfilling its own responsibilities. The financial manager of any firm, domestic or international, is responsible for procuring and managing financial resources. However, these functions cannot be performed without adequate, timely information from the accountant.

The actual and potential flow of assets across national boundaries adds immense complexities to the finance and accounting functions. The MNE must learn to cope with differing rates of inflation, changes in exchange rates, currency controls, the risk of expropriation, and different customs, levels of sophistication, and local requirements.

- The international controller must be concerned about different currencies and accounting systems.

The accounting or controllership function is responsible for collecting and analyzing data for internal and external users. To manage assets, the corporate treasurer needs accounting information on the nature and extent of those assets. Performance evaluation of local managers and operations is usually performed with information provided by the controller's office. Reports must also be generated for internal consideration, local government needs, creditors, shareholders, and prospective investors. Not only must the controller be concerned about the impact of many different currencies and varied rates of inflation on the statements, but he or she also must be familiar with different accounting systems in different countries.

FACTORS INFLUENCING THE DEVELOPMENT OF ACCOUNTING WORLDWIDE

- Both form and substance of financial statements are different in foreign countries.

One of the problems that Colgate-Palmolive faces is that accounting is different around the world. This means that financial statements in France, for example, do not look the same as financial statements in the United States.

Some would argue that this is a minor matter, since we appear to be talking about form rather than substance. However, the substance is also different, as in Peru, where consolidation of related companies is not allowed; in Sweden, where significant inventory write-downs are allowed; or in France and Germany, where tax accounting and book accounting are essentially the same.

This puts the MNE in a difficult position because it needs to prepare and understand reports generated according to the local accounting standards, and it also must prepare financial statements that are consistent with generally accepted accounting principles (GAAP) in the United States in order to generate consolidated financial statements.

- **FASB: sets accounting standards in the United States.**
- **IASC: sets standards internationally.**
- **Critical users of information are creditors, stockholders, investors, and employees.**

Accounting is basically a process of identifying, recording, and interpreting economic events, and its goals and purposes should be clearly stated in the objectives of any accounting system. The **Financial Accounting Standards Board (FASB)** in the United States stated that financial reporting should provide information that is useful in investment and credit decisions; information that is useful in assessing cash flow prospects; and information about enterprise resources, claims to those resources, and changes in them.[2] The users identified by the Board are primarily investors and creditors, although other users might be considered to be important. The **International Accounting Standards Committee (IASC)**, a multinational standard-setting organization comprised of professional accounting organizations from over forty countries, includes employees as well as investors and creditors as the critical users. Also named are suppliers, customers, regulatory and taxing authorities, and many others.

- **No worldwide set of accounting standards and practices that must be adhered to.**

Although the question has been widely discussed, no consensus has been reached on whether a uniform set of accounting standards and practices exists for all classes of users worldwide or even for one class of users. To understand the different accounting principles and how they affect the MNE's operations, we must examine some of the forces leading to the development of accounting principles internationally. Figure 19.1 is an attempt to identify these major factors. The top four factors deal with the nature of the enterprise and the direct users of information. The other four represent other major factors that affect accounting objectives, standards, and practices.

Nature of the Enterprise

- **Nature and extent of information required is dependent on:**
  - **type of ownership**
  - **size of organization**

Businesses all over the world are generally organized into corporations, partnerships, or proprietorships. Ownership of enterprises can be either broadly based, as is typical of U.S. businesses; state-owned; or family-owned, as is typical of firms in most developing countries. In each country there is actually a mix of all three forms of ownership.

The nature and extent of information required by decision makers may

FIGURE 19.1
Major Domestic and Worldwide Factors Influencing the Development of Accounting Objectives, Standards, and Practices
Source: Lee H. Radebaugh, "Environmental Factors Influencing the Development of Accounting Objectives, Standards, and Practices—The Peruvian Case," *The International Journal of Accounting,* Fall 1975, p. 41.

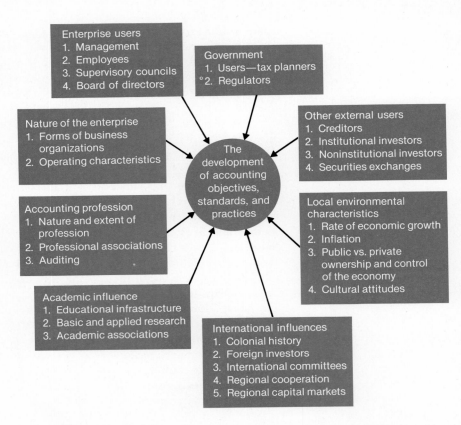

also depend on the size of the organization. In addition, different types of industries as well as different operating techniques give rise to special problems. For example, the treatment of discovery costs is a problem that is unique to the extractive industries, and the prevalence of leasing in the United States requires special standards and principles to account for this type of operating procedure.

Enterprise Users

• Managers and employees

Within every enterprise there are many users of information. The quantity and quality of information provided depends on the level of sophistication of the users as well as on the technical competence of the accountants. Managers require specialized information to assist in decision making, and this has led to a whole branch of accounting. Employees have a vested interest in the enterprise and may have an impact on the disclosure of financial data. Unions, for example, often require certain types of information before the negotiation of labor contracts.

In some countries, such as West Germany, Norway, and Finland, supervisory or works' councils are organized with special supervisory and auditing functions. In the United States as well as other countries the board of directors is a powerful policy-making group that can have strong impact on the nature and quality of reported information.

Government

• Users (such as tax authorities) and regulators

Government is one of the most pervasive forces in the development of accounting objectives, standards, and practices. Government can be divided into two groups: users and regulators. Users are tax authorities, planning commissions (such as GOSPLAN in the Soviet Union), and various agencies (such as the Bureau of Labor Statistics in the United States) that compile statistics for general use.

• Regulators are concerned with best interests of:
  • public
  • governmental users

Governmental regulators often act in response to the needs of governmental users. Regulators, such as the Securities and Exchange Commission in the United States, also act in response to the best interests of the general public.

The extent to which the government becomes involved in the setting of objectives, standards, and practices depends on the interaction of all the factors listed in Fig. 19.1. A weak and relatively unsophisticated government will probably not be too concerned about the development of accounting. If the accounting profession in a country is relatively sophisticated and appears to be meeting the needs of the users, the government may not interfere much. Where the government is an important user of information, does not feel that the accounting profession is meeting users' needs, and does not foresee much change in the near future, it will probably take a much more active role in setting or influencing the development of accounting.

Other External Users

• Creditors and investors have a strong influence on accounting principles and practices.

This category includes users other than those directly linked to the firm or government. In many countries, creditors are the most important users of corporate financial data. This is especially true in West Germany and Japan, where banks are institutional investors or provide very high leverage for expansion. In the United States, institutional investors such as insurance companies have an influential voice in the development of accounting principles and practices. This is because they are an important source of funds for corporate expansion and often control large blocs of votes in the annual shareholders' meeting. Noninstitutional investors in a broadly based capital market need good-quality information on which to base investment decisions. Investors are often represented by their stockbrokers, who are able to perform a more sophisticated analysis of financial data. In many countries, securities exchanges help to protect the investor by setting requirements for preparation and presentation of statements.

Local Environmental Characteristics

● Internal economic conditions and cultural attitudes have a big effect on accounting.

This category, probably the broadest and perhaps the most important, includes such diverse factors as cultural attitudes and the nature and state of the economy. The four factors listed in Fig. 19.1 are certainly not exhaustive. Even though the characteristics are referred to as "local," they are not independent of the world economy. The rates of economic growth and inflation depend on a country's major trading partners as well as on internal economic conditions.

Inflation may cause a country such as Brazil to begin using indexes to adjust different balance sheet and income statement accounts. Special capital accounts must then be set up to offset the adjustment. In France the government developed a uniform accounting plan as a key part of distributing Marshall Plan funds after World War II. This was part of an effort to restructure the economy in a centrally planned fashion.

International Influence

● Colonial influence, foreign investors.

Many international forces that are institutional rather than environmental have strongly influenced accounting principles worldwide. A prime example is the geographic spread of England and France in the colonial era. Each of these countries carried their business and accounting philosophies to their colonies and instituted similar systems. The United States has also tended to do this as its economic influence has spread through direct foreign investment.

Accounting Profession

● Can be influential if it is competent and well-respected.

As in countries such as the United States, Canada, the United Kingdom, and the Netherlands, the accounting profession itself can influence the development of accounting principles. Three phases of the profession are important: its nature and extent, the existence of professional associations, and the auditing function. The mere existence of a profession is not as important as its level of sophistication.

The problem with accounting in many countries is that it is not recognized as a profession, so it has trouble attracting top-flight people. By contrast, in the United Kingdom it is one of the most highly respected professions.

In the United States the American Institute of Certified Public Accountants (AICPA) was the major professional organization responsible for setting accounting standards. This responsibility has now shifted to the Financial Accounting Standards Board (FASB), which is also a private rather than a governmental group.

Academic Influence

- Quality and accessibility of education.

The academic infrastructure refers to the quality of accounting education offered as well as to the accessibility of this education. One of the typical problems in developing countries is the shortage of qualified professors in the accounting field. Since instruction in accounting is not considered a full-time profession and is generally not at a very high level, little academic research is done.

Contrast this with countries such as the United States and the Netherlands, where extensive research is conducted to develop better ways of dealing with accounting problems. The American Accounting Association (AAA) is an active educational association that provides continual input into the development of accounting principles.

HARMONIZATION OF DIFFERENCES

Many differences in worldwide accounting standards and practices impede the move to harmonization. Some of the major factors are:

1. the diversity of views regarding the purpose of financial statements,
2. differences in the extent to which the accounting profession has developed in various countries,
3. the influence of tax laws on financial reporting,
4. requirements of company laws,
5. differences among countries in basic economic facts affecting financial reporting,
6. differences among countries in practices recommended by the accounting profession,
7. the failure of professional pronouncements to accord with economic facts, and
8. the lack of an agency to enforce worldwide accounting standards.[3]

- EC is setting accounting directives that must be incorporated into the laws of each member nation.

In spite of these differences, some serious efforts have been undertaken to harmonize accounting standards on a regional as well as an international level. On a regional basis the most ambitious and potentially most effective efforts are taking place in the European Community. The EC's Commission is empowered to set directives, which are orders to the member states to bring their laws into line with the requirements within a certain transition period.

In 1978 the **Fourth Directive,** which deals with the content, object, and format of accounts, was released. That directive requires firms to select one of two different balance sheets and one of four different income statement formats. Although all EC countries were supposed to have adopted the directive by February 1982, not all did. Some countries are still wrestling with the concepts of the directive.

The effect of the Fourth Directive on a firm like Colgate-Palmolive is that the firm must adhere to the rules finally adopted in each country for reporting formats, accounting principles, and footnote disclosures. Because of numerous differences between the Fourth Directive and U.S. GAAP, subsidiaries of Colgate-Palmolive in EC countries would have to keep at least two separate sets of books.

Other directives have been issued that affect the accounting practices that European firms (and European subsidiaries of U.S. firms) would have to follow when incorporated into national law. The important thing to realize is that these directives have essentially narrowed the alternatives available rather than chosen only one best way of doing things. This is how harmonization differs from standardization.

On an international level, the United Nations has become involved in the setting of accounting standards through the Commission on Transnational Corporations of UNESCO. The commission appointed a Group of Experts on International Standards of Accounting and Reporting, a committee that has held several hearings and issued draft disclosure requirements. However, the Group of Experts has not been able to agree on a final set of standards that is acceptable to the wider membership. The disclosure concepts tend to focus on the impact of the MNE on the host society, especially in terms of employment and investment. Although the United Nations is not empowered to enforce its standards, it can attempt to persuade individual countries—especially the developing countries—to adopt its standards in local laws.

The International Accounting Standards Committee (IASC) was organized in 1973 by the professional accounting bodies of nine nation-groups: Australia, Canada, France, West Germany, Japan, Mexico, the Netherlands, the United Kingdom and Ireland, and the United States. Since that time, Italy, Nigeria, South Africa, and Taiwan (Republic of China) have been added as board members. Initially, the IASC wanted to develop standards that would have rapid and broad acceptance; thus it seemed to focus mostly on improved disclosure. More recently, it has been interested in tackling some substantive issues.

The problem with the IASC is that it has to rely on good will for acceptance of its standards. It has no legislative mandate as is the case with the directives of the EC, nor does it have emotional attachment as is the case for the developing countries with proposals adopted by the U.N. However, a number of countries have used the standards as models for their

• MNEs may have to keep several sets of books to adhere to the laws of each member nation.

• U.N. can only persuade countries to follow its standards.

• The IASC is trying to harmonize diverse standards worldwide.

• The IASC has no power or persuasion to help enforce its standards.

own legislation. Singapore, for example, has successfully adopted IASC standards.

- IASC standards closely resemble U.S. GAAP.

It should be noted that most IASC standards have been issued after the relevant U.S. standards. In addition, there are few major differences between IASC standards and U.S. GAAP. It would appear that the presence of the United States as a founding member of the IASC has allowed it considerable input and influence in the decision-making process. It would be difficult to imagine an IASC standard that was in substantial conflict with U.S. GAAP.

TRANSACTIONS IN FOREIGN CURRENCY

One of the major problems of international business is that of operating in different currencies. Chapter 21 will deal with eliminating or minimizing foreign exchange risk; this chapter helps explain the proper recording and subsequent accounting of assets, liabilities, revenues, and expenses that are measured or denominated in a foreign currency.

A company does not have to have foreign facilities to be concerned about foreign exchange. For example, any time a U.S. importer is required to pay for equipment or merchandise in a foreign currency, it must trade U.S. dollars for that currency to pay the supplier. Assume that Sundance Ski Lodge buys skis from a French supplier for FF 28,000 when the exchange rate was $0.1300/FF. Sundance would record the following on its books:

Purchases	3640	
Accounts payable		3640
FF 28,000 @ $0.1300		

- Foreign currency receivables and payables give rise to gains and losses whenever the exchange rate changes.

As long as Sundance pays immediately, there is no problem. But what happens if the exporter extends Sundance thirty days' credit? The original entry would be the same as above. During the next thirty days, anything could happen. If the rate changed to $0.1100/FF, Sundance would record a final settlement as follows:

Accounts payable	3640	
Gain on foreign exchange		560
Cash		3080

The merchandise stays at the original value of $3640. However, there is a difference between the dollar value of the account payable to the exporter ($3640) and the actual dollars that the importer must come up with in order to purchase the French francs to pay the exporter ($3080). The difference between the two accounts ($560) is the gain on foreign exchange and is recognized as income.

These gains and losses arising from foreign currency transactions must be recognized at the end of each accounting period, even if the payable (in the case of a purchase) or receivable (in the case of a sale) has not been completed. For most U.S. companies this adjustment is made every month. Using the above example, assume that the end of the month has arrived and Sundance still has not paid the French exporter. The skis continue to be valued at $3640, but the payable has to be updated to the new exchange rate of $0.1100/FF. The journal entry to record that would be

Accounts payable	560	
Gain on foreign exchange		560

The liability would now be worth $3080. If settlement were to be made at the end of the next month and the exchange rate were to remain the same, the final entry would be

Accounts payable	3080	
Cash		3080

If the U.S. firm were an exporter and anticipated receiving foreign currency, then the corresponding entries (using the above information) would be

Accounts receivable	3640	
Sales		3640
Cash	3080	
Loss on foreign exchange	560	
Accounts receivable		3640

In this case a loss results because the firm receives less cash than if it had collected its money immediately.

● Gains and losses due to exchange rate fluctuations must be recognized immediately in the income statement.

Foreign borrowing is another area in which U.S. companies incur obligations that are reported in dollars but actually denominated in a foreign currency. In the 1960s, many firms began borrowing European currencies because foreign interest rates were considerably lower than those in the United States. This made the debt cheaper, even considering the possible loss that could occur with exchange rate variations. When the dollar was devalued in 1971, many firms holding debt denominated in stronger European currencies suffered large losses. At that time, Exxon (then called Standard Oil Company of New Jersey) suffered exchange differences of $70,000,000 related to long-term obligations denominated in foreign currencies. These losses were recorded in the income statement and disclosed as foreign exchange losses to shareholders. However, many of the firms felt that the losses should be an adjustment of their interest expense (and therefore buried in the income statement), since from their viewpoint the exchange loss was merely an adjustment of the cost of the debt. This approach was not allowed by the FASB.

The procedures that U.S. firms must follow to account for foreign currency transactions are found in FASB Statement No. 52, "Foreign Currency Translation," which was adopted in December 1981. **Statement 52 requires** that firms record the initial transaction at the spot exchange rate that is in effect on that date and records receivables and payables at subsequent balance sheet dates at the spot exchange rate on that date. Any foreign exchange gains and losses that arise from carrying receivables or payables during a period when the exchange rate changes are taken directly to the income statement.[4] In its 1983 Annual Report, for example, Colgate-Palmolive disclosed that it had foreign currency transactions losses of $21,192,000 that were included in net income that year. That is a fairly substantial amount, since overseas net income before taxes was $123,700,000 during that same time.

To protect themselves from possible losses arising from changes in exchange rates between the initial recording and subsequent settlement of foreign currency receivables and payables, many firms enter into forward contracts. The use of forward contracts will be discussed in detail in Chapter 21.

TRANSLATION OF FOREIGN CURRENCY FINANCIAL STATEMENTS

- Translation—process of restating foreign currency statements into U.S. dollars.
  - recast foreign currency statements into statements consistent with GAAP.
  - translate all foreign currency into U.S. dollars.

Given that Colgate-Palmolive receives reports originally developed in a variety of different currencies, how does it eventually end up with one set of financial statements in U.S. dollars? The process of restating foreign currency financial statements into U.S. dollars is known as **translation.** The combination of all of these translated financial statements into one is known as **consolidation.**

Translation in the United States is really a two-step process. The first step involves recasting the foreign currency financial statements into statements that are consistent with U.S. GAAP. The second step involves translating all foreign currency amounts into U.S. dollars.

There used to be several ways to translate financial statements, but recent changes in financial accounting standards worldwide have resulted in the adoption of the temporal method and the current rate method as the only two options.

The Current Rate Method

- All balance sheet accounts except net worth are translated at the current rate.

The **current rate method** is the easier to apply, since it requires that all assets and liabilities be translated at the current exchange rate. Only net worth would not be translated at the current rate. This approach is easier

● Every income statement account is multiplied by the average exchange rate.

to keep track of than the temporal method, since a firm would not have to keep track of various historical exchange rates. The current rate approach results in translated financial statements that retain essentially the same ratios and relationships that exist in local currency. The income statement is translated into dollars by multiplying all income statement items by the average exchange rate during the period. This also includes depreciation expense and cost of goods sold.

The Temporal Method

● Cash, receivables, and payables at the current rate
● Historical cost assets at the historical rate.

The **temporal method** is the method that was required under FASB **Statement 8,** the standard that was in effect before Statement 52 was issued. According to the temporal method, cash, receivables, and payables (both current and noncurrent) are translated at the current exchange rate. Assets carried at historical cost (such as fixed assets and inventory carried at cost rather than market) are translated at the historical exchange rate (the exchange rate that was in effect when the transaction took place). The theoretical attractiveness of this approach is that the financial statements of the branches and subsidiaries of a U.S. company would be translated into dollars in such a way that the dollar would be the single unit of measure.

● All income statement accounts except historical cost accounts are translated at the average rate.

The income statement is translated by multiplying most of the foreign currency amounts by the average exchange rate during the period. The only major exceptions are for accounts carried at historical cost, such as inventory (in cost of goods sold) and depreciation expense. Cost of goods sold is essentially translated at the exchange rate that was in effect when the items being sold were originally purchased. Depreciation expense is translated at the exchange rate that was in effect when the underlying asset was acquired.

An Illustration

The description of the temporal and current rate methods will make more sense after we go through a numerical example. Table 19.4 provides a comparison of how one might translate a balance sheet using the current rate and temporal methods. Table 19.5 does the same thing for the income statement. Note the different exchange rates that are used for each account in the translation process.

● Temporal method: translation gain or loss is taken to income

It is important to see how the balance sheet and income statement fit together through stockholders' equity. In the case of the temporal method, the ending retained earnings balance is a plug figure that makes assets equal liabilities plus stockholders' equity. That balance is then taken to the statement of income and retained earnings to determine what the income figure should be. That is found by adding dividends to the ending retained earnings balance and subtracting the beginning retained earnings balance. Since the net income figure is essentially a plug figure and all other income statement

TABLE 19.4 _____

BALANCE SHEET, DECEMBER 31, 1985

	Local currency	Temporal method		Current rate method	
		Exchange rate	Dollars	Exchange rate	Dollars
Assets					
Cash and receivables	4,000	1.30	$ 5,200	1.30	$ 5,200
Inventory	4,500	1.32	5,940	1.30	5,850
Property, plant, and equipment (net)	14,000	1.90	26,600	1.30	18,200
	22,500		$37,740		$29,250
Liabilities and Stockholders' Equity					
Current liabilities	5,500	1.30	$ 7,150	1.30	$ 7,150
Notes payable	5,500	1.30	7,150	1.30	7,150
Capital stock	5,000	1.90	9,500	1.90	9,500
Retained earnings	6,500		13,940		13,650
Accumulated translation adjustment					(8,200)
	22,500		$37,740		$29,250

accounts are translated by using a specific exchange rate, the translation gain or loss becomes the ultimate plug figure. Under the temporal method of translation, that translation gain or loss must be taken directly to income. In the illustration in Table 19.5, that amount is a gain of $1710.

According to the current rate method, the translation gain or loss is taken to a separate component of stockholders' equity rather than to the income statement. In this case, both the income statement and retained earnings balances are computed by multiplying the foreign currency balances by the appropriate exchange rate. When the derived retained earnings figure is taken to stockholders' equity, the accounting equation of assets = liabilities + stockholders' equity will not balance. Thus the plug figure to make the balance sheet balance is the separate component of stockholders' equity. In Table 19.4 that amount is a loss of $8200.

• Current rate method: translation gain or loss taken to stockholders' equity.

Statement 52

• Statement 52 of the FASB sets the rules that must be followed by U.S. MNCs.

As was mentioned above, Statement 52 was issued by the FASB in the United States in December 1981. The British standard was issued in April 1983, and the translation standard of the International Accounting Standards

TABLE 19.5

INCOME STATEMENT, 1985

	Local currency	Temporal method Exchange rate	Dollars	Current rate method Exchange rate	Dollars
Sales	18,000	1.40	$25,200	1.40	$25,200
Expenses:					
Cost of sales	9,000	1.48	13,320	1.40	12,600
Depreciation	3,000	1.90	5,700	1.40	4,200
Other expenses	2,100	1.40	2,940	1.40	2,940
Translation loss (gain)			(1,710)		
	14,100		20,250		19,740
Income before taxes	3,900		4,950		$ 5,460
Income taxes	1,900	1.40	2,660	1.40	2,660
Net income	2,000		$ 2,290		2,800
Retained earnings (12/31/84)	5,000		12,360		11,560
	7,000		$14,650		$14,360
Dividends	500	1.42*	710	1.42*	710
Retained earnings (12/31/85)	6,500		$13,940		$13,650

Committee was issued in July 1983. The U.S. and British standards are fairly similar, but there are some significant differences between the two. The interesting thing about the international standard is that it allows enough flexibility to permit both the U.S. and British approaches.

Statement 52 introduces some new terminology that is important for an understanding of the translation process. The choice of the temporal or the current rate method of translation depends on what the functional currency is of the foreign operation. The **functional currency** is defined in Statement 52 as the "currency of the primary economic environment in which the entity operates."[5] Thus the local currency of the country where the entity is located is the functional currency if most of the operations are conducted in the currency of that country and if the entity is relatively independent of the parent company in the United States. It is also possible that the **reporting currency** of the parent company (which would be the U.S. dollar for U.S.-based MNEs) could be the functional currency. This would be the case if the foreign entity were extremely dependent on the parent company for its operations or if most of its operations were carried out in the parent company's currency.

• Functional currency— currency of the primary economic environment in which the entity operates.

- Temporal method; used when the parent's reporting currency is the functional currency.
- Current rate method: used when the local currency is the functional currency.
- In high inflation areas (cumulative 100% or more for three years), temporal method is always used.

Once the functional currency has been determined, the translation process becomes fairly mechanical. If the functional currency is the local currency, the current rate method is used to translate the financial statements into U.S. dollars. If the functional currency is the reporting currency of the parent, the temporal method is used.

The only major problem arises when the entity is operating in a highly inflationary country. This is defined as a country whose cumulative rate of inflation is approximately 100 percent or more over a three-year period. In that situation the temporal method is always used, no matter what the operating characteristics of the entity are.

Disclosure of Foreign Exchange Gains and Losses

Earlier, we mentioned that a company could experience two kinds of foreign exchange gains and losses: Those that arise from foreign currency transactions and those that arise from the translation of foreign currency financial statements into dollars. Gains and losses from foreign currency transactions are taken directly to the income statement, but a firm is not required by Statement 52 to show that on the income statement. As was noted in Table 19.2, Colgate-Palmolive does not disclose this information in the income statement. However, it does disclose the amount in management's discussion of operations.

The treatment of foreign exchange gains and losses that arise from translation depends on how the firm defines the functional currency of its operations abroad. Foreign entities that choose the local currency as the functional currency must use the current rate method of translation. Then, the translation gains and losses are taken to the separate component of stockholders' equity. The amount of $224,905,000 that appears as the December 31, 1983, balance of the cumulative foreign currency translation adjustment in Table 19.3 reflects the balance on that date rather than the amount that resulted from 1983 operations. The FASB requires that firms disclose what the opening balance of that account was each year, what amounts were added to and taken from that account during the year, and what the balance was at the end of the year. Colgate-Palmolive does that in a separate table, which can be found in the footnotes to its Annual Report.

Foreign entities that select the U.S. dollar as the functional currency must use the temporal method of translation. Then, the translation gains and losses are taken directly to income. This is the amount that Colgate-Palmolive includes in its general and administrative expenses in Table 19.2. Although the exact amount is not included on the face of the income statement, management discloses it in its discussion of operations for the year. Remember that entities in highly inflationary countries must also use the temporal method, and their translation gains and losses must be taken to income. Colgate-Palmolive management explained that most of its translation losses taken to income were from entities in highly inflationary countries.

FINANCIAL REPORTING AND CONTROL

This area is the one with the greatest overlap between the accounting and finance functions in an MNE. It is also covered in the discussion on control in Chapter 17. Generally, however, the controller is responsible for designing and implementing a good reporting and control system. In this section we will discuss some important aspects of financial reporting and information systems as well as the use of internal auditing to help achieve control.

When firms expand abroad, they have a tendency to export their domestic control systems even though these may be inadequate for the environment. Some of the reasons for this practice are that financial, budgetary, and statistical control are not initially perceived as being critical; it is cheaper to use an existing system; this practice helps standardize reporting worldwide; and it is easier for top management to use a familiar system.[6]

- Choice of currency for statements is major problem.

A number of basic problems arise in trying to develop a good reporting system, and many of them involve environmental differences. One of the most important is that of currency. Top management at the home office is used to looking at reports in dollars, while the subsidiary staff is more familiar with local currency financial statements. Which currency should be used for evaluation and control? One survey of the practices of U.S. MNEs found that 44 percent of the firms in the sample judged subsidiary performance in terms of local currency, 44 percent used U.S. dollars, and 12 percent used both dollars and local currency.[7] The problem of differential rates of inflation was mentioned; and taxation, a particularly troublesome area, will be discussed in Chapter 21.

Table 19.6 provides the results of a more recent study of the financial measures used in the performance evaluation of multinational chemical companies. Local currency was used for a number of the financial measures, but firms demonstrated a wider acceptance of dollar measures of performance evaluation. However, a number of respondents indicated that they were beginning to place greater reliance on local currency results, since these results reflect fairly accurately what is going on in the actual environment.[8]

- Need managers who can use a good information and control system.

Another environmental problem relates to personnel. Some managers in foreign countries may not have the background, capabilities, and proper attitude to fully utilize a good information and control system. This is especially common when a firm is acquired by foreign interests and the previous owner-manager is retained to run the business. This person may find it difficult to change old ways of doing business and may do everything possible to circumvent the process.

TABLE 19.6 _____

FINANCIAL MEASURES USED AS INDICATORS OF INTERNAL
PERFORMANCE EVALUATION

Financial measures	After translation in U.S. dollars (in percentage)	Before translation in local currency (in percentage)
Return on investment (assets)	80.0	52.9
Return on equity	48.6	31.4
Residual income	21.4	18.6
Profit	81.4	70.0
Cash flow potential from foreign subsidiary to U.S. operations	65.7	35.7
Budget compared to actual return on investment	45.7	38.6
Budget compared to actual profits	78.6	72.9
Budget compared to actual sales	72.9	72.9
Ratios	34.3	30.0
Others	12.9	11.4

Note: These figures represent the percentage of the total 70 firms that report using each particular measure.
Source: Helen Morsicato, *Currency Translation and Performance Evaluation in Multinationals* (Ann Arbor, Mich.: University of Michigan Research Press, 1980).

● **Transfer prices can distort financial measures.**

Intercompany transactions also complicate the process. These transactions are between related entities (such as parent and subsidiary) and involve pricing policies that may be designed to move cash from country to country rather than to help in the evaluation of performance. This issue of transfer pricing will be discussed more fully in Chapter 21.

Most MNEs standardize the format in which they are to receive reports so that comparisons of information among the various foreign operations are made easier. Generally, the reports requested will be the same as those used for domestic operations, but additional reports are often called for. These additional reports generally deal with foreign exchange positions and specific environmental information.

● **ROI budget analysis and historical comparisons are used to evaluate performances.**

The three most widely used or important techniques for performance evaluation are return on investment, budget analysis, and historical comparisons. In one study, 95 percent of the corporate officers interviewed stated that they use the same techniques for foreign and domestic operations, and they stated that return on investment (ROI) was the single most important measure. ROI, which is a ratio of net income to some investment base, provides an indicator of how efficiently the firm uses its investment in generating earnings. However, this ratio is difficult to use in foreign operations. Because of foreign currencies, different rates of inflation, different tax laws, and the use of transfer pricing, both the net income figure and the investment base may be seriously distorted. ROI may be computed in local currency, in dollars, or in both.

As a result, firms resort to supplementary measures. The budget provides a good indicator of performance relative to targets set by home office and local management. Once again, the choice of currency becomes very important in setting budgets and monitoring performance.

• Need to decide which exchange rates to use to set budgets and monitor performance.

Table 19.7 provides the major alternatives that a firm can use to set budgets and monitor performance. The areas in Table 19.7 that are the most feasible are A-1, A-3, P-2, P-3, and E-3. In cells A-1, P-2, and E-3 the same exchange rate is used to set the budget and track performance. In the case of A-1 the exchange rate that was in effect when the budget was set is used to translate actual results into dollars. Thus management sees the information in dollars, but local managers are not responsible for exchange rate changes. In area E-3 the budget in dollars is updated to reflect the current exchange rate in order to match actual performance translated at that rate. In option P-2, management is required to project exchange rates, but it is not responsible for changes in the rate during the period.

Options A-3 and P-3 require accountability for exchange rate changes, since a different rate is used to track performance than is used to set the budget. For A-3, management is accountable for the total fluctuation between the rate in effect when the budget was established and the rate in effect when actual performance was recorded. Top management needs to decide where to assign responsibility for exchange fluctuations, since A-3 will include operating as well as currency variances. The assumption is that the operating manager is responsible for currency changes.

P-3 also uses a different rate to set the budget and monitor performance. The major difference between P-3 and A-3 is that for P-3, management is required to project the exchange rate at the time the budget is set. The currency variance is the difference between the projected rate and the actual rate.[9]

TABLE 19.7

POSSIBLE COMBINATIONS OF EXCHANGE RATES IN THE CONTROL PROCESS

Rate used for determining budget	Rate used to track performance relative to budget — Actual at time of budget	Projected at time of budget	Actual at end of period
Actual at time of budget	A-1	A-2	A-3
Projected at time of budget	P-1	P-2	P-3
Actual at end of period (through updating)	E-1	E-2	E-3

Source: Donald R. Lessard and Peter Lorange, "Currency Changes and Management Control: Resolving the Centralization and Decentralization Dilemma," *Accounting Review* (July 1977). p. 630.

SUMMARY

- The MNE must learn to cope with differing rates of inflation, changes in exchange rates, currency controls, customs, levels of sophistication, and local reporting requirements in carrying out its finance and accounting functions.

- Some of the major factors that influence the development of accounting objectives, standards, and practices are the nature of the enterprise, the enterprise's users of information, governmental users and regulators, other external users (such as creditors), local environmental characteristics, international influences, academic influences, and the accounting profession.

- Many important differences in worldwide accounting standards and practices impede the move to harmonization. However, groups such as the European Community and the International Accounting Standards Committee are attempting to harmonize accounting practices and to upgrade the accounting profession.

- In translating transactions denominated in foreign currency, all accounts are initially recorded at the exchange rate that was in effect at the time of the transaction. At each subsequent balance sheet date, recorded dollar balances representing cash and amounts owed by or to the enterprise that are denominated in foreign currency are adjusted to reflect the current rate.

- The translation of financial statements involves measuring and expressing in dollars and in conformity with U.S. GAAP the assets, liabilities, revenues, and expenses that are measured or denominated in foreign currency.

- According to FASB Statement No. 52, the financial statements of foreign firms whose functional currency is the local currency must be translated into dollars by using the current rate translation method. According to that method, all balance sheet accounts except stockholders' equity are translated into dollars at the current exchange rate in effect on the balance sheet date. Stockholders' equity is translated at the historical exchange rate. All income statement accounts are translated at the average exchange rate in effect during the period.

- The financial statements of foreign firms whose functional currency is the reporting currency of the U.S. parent must translate the financial statements into dollars using the temporal method of translation. That method essentially translates monetary accounts at the current rate and nonmonetary accounts at the historical rate. All accounts in the income statement are translated at an average exchange rate, except for cost of sales and depreciation expense, which are translated at the relevant historical exchange rates.

- Foreign exchange gains and losses arising from foreign currency transactions are taken to the income statement during the period in which they occur. Gains and losses arising from translating financial statements by the current rate method are taken to a separate component of stockholders' equity. Those arising from translating according to the temporal method are taken directly to the income statement.

- Many firms use budgets to measure performance of foreign operations. Budgets can be set and performance monitored in a variety of ways. The key is to decide whether or not to isolate variances that arise from exchange rate changes.

C A S E   TIMP MANUFACTURING INC.

LaVell Ehdwords, known as Vell to his best friends, was faced with an interesting dilemma. It was June 1985, and his firm, Timp Mfg. Inc., had just acquired Inca S.A., a Peruvian company that was a potential source of supply for Timp's production process. It was Timp's first acquisition in Latin America, although it had set up several operations through acquisition and new investment in Europe and the Far East. Inca S.A. was its only acquisition in a country with a high rate of inflation (over 80% in the first two quarters of 1985) and a rapidly deteriorating currency.

Vell had just been hired by Timp management to take over as assistant controller responsible for international operations. Vell noticed that Timp had been operating up to that point with three major policies:

imports were always made in the local currency and were paid immediately rather than on time;

the current rate method of translation was used to translate the foreign currency financial statements from the local currency into U.S. dollars;

budgets were set in dollars at a forecasted exchange rate, and performance was monitored at the actual exchange rate of the period.

Local management was held responsible for any exchange rate variance.

Given those assumptions, Vell began to look at Inca S.A. from a new perspective. Timp was ready to order S/500,000,000 of merchandise from Inca S.A. with delivery to be made on July 1. (S/ is the symbol for the Peruvian sol, the currency of Peru.) The problem was that Timp was short of cash because of the acquisition and would have preferred to pay in 30 days. The exchange rate on July 1 was expected to be S/11,000/$. It would be very difficult to predict the exchange rate 30 days later, since the monetary situation in Peru was so volatile.

Another problem facing Vell was how to translate the financial statements as found in Tables 19.8 and 19.9. Vell wanted to do a quick compari-

TABLE 19.8 _____

INCA S.A. BALANCE SHEET, DECEMBER 31, 1984

	Local currency (000,000)
Assets	
Cash and receivables	1,000
Inventory	1,250
Net fixed assets	3,000
Total	5,250
Liabilities and stockholders equity	
Current liabilities	1,150
Long-term debt	1,000
Capital stock	2,200
Retained earnings	900
Total	5,250

TABLE 19.9 _____

INCA S.A. INCOME STATEMENT FOR THE YEAR ENDED DECEMBER 31, 1984

		Local currency (000,000)
Sales revenue		7,000
Less:		
Cost of sales	4,375	
Depreciation	450	
Other expenses	1,600	6,425
Net Income		575

son of translation procedures to help him decide what to do. He was told that retained earnings on January 1, 1984, was U.S. $100,000. The relevant exchange rates in Peruvian soles per dollar for 1984 were as follows:

S/5711 spot rate on December 31, 1984

S/5000 average rate in effect when the December 31 inventory was acquired

S/3000   the historical rate in effect when fixed assets were acquired, long-term debt was incurred, and capital stock was issued.

S/4000   the average exchange rate during 1984

QUESTIONS

1. What would be the difference for Timp between paying for its imports from Inca S.A. immediately and paying in 30 days? What would be the impact on Timp and Inca if Inca decides to invoice its sale to Timp in U.S. dollars rather than S/? Show appropriate journal entries to support your conclusions.

2. What would be the difference in income between translating the financial statements into U.S. dollars according to temporal method and according to the current rate method? Given the nature of the environment in Peru, which method should Timp use? What information would you want to have in order to make that decision?

3. What should Vell recommend that Timp do to evaluate the performance of Inca S.A. in the context of that environment? Be sure to discuss the strengths and weaknesses of the approach being used elsewhere by Timp and support your recommendation in the context of the environment in Peru.

NOTES

1. The data for the case are found in the Colgate-Palmolive *1983 Annual Report.*

2. Financial Accounting Standards Board, *Statement of Financial Accounting Concepts No. 1—Objectives of Financial Reporting by Business Enterprises* (Stamford, Conn: FASB, 1979), paragraphs 34–54.

3. William P. Hauworth, "Problems in the Development of Worldwide Accounting Standards," *International Journal of Accounting,* Fall 1973, p. 24.

4. Financial Accounting Standards Board, *Statement of Financial Accounting Standards No. 52: Foreign Currency Translation* (Stamford, Conn: FASB, December 1981), pp. 6–7.

5. *Ibid.,* p. 77.

6. David F. Hawkins, "Controlling Foreign Operations," *Financial Executive,* February 1965, p. 26.

7. Sidney M. Robbins and Robert B. Stobaugh, "The Bent Measuring Stick for Foreign Subsidiaries," *Harvard Business Review,* September–October 1973, p. 85.

8. *Ibid.,* p. 82.

9. Helen Morsicato, *Currency Translation and Performance Evaluation in Multinationals* (Ann Arbor, Mich.: University of Michigan Research Press, 1980).

2 0

Taxation

- To give an overview of the major historical developments of, and the philosophical attitudes toward, the taxation of foreign-source income in the United States.

- To investigate in greater depth the major aspects of the taxation of foreign-source income in the United States from export activities, branches, and foreign affiliates and subsidiaries.

- To examine some of the major non-U.S. tax practices and to show how international tax treaties can alleviate some of the impact of double taxation.

- To show what multinational enterprises need to consider in order to properly plan the tax function.

SCHERING-PLOUGH[1]

Schering-Plough, makers of the well-known pharmaceutical and consumer products Coricidin, Coppertone suntan lotion, Maybelline cosmetics, and Dr. Scholl's foot care products, has been involved in international business for decades. In 1984, the company derived 43 percent of its revenues from outside of the United States.

The Schering Corporation, as it was known, was first organized in the early 1950s. It made two organizational moves soon afterwards to bolster its international sales efforts. The first occurred in 1956, when it organized Scherico, Ltd., a wholly owned Swiss corporation. Scherico was organized to own foreign patent rights and receive foreign royalties from licensing agreements that had been entered into by Schering Corporation with other firms worldwide. This move was advantageous to Schering Corporation from a tax standpoint because royalties received in the United States were taxed at the relatively high U.S. tax rate, whereas royalties received in Switzerland were taxed at a relatively low rate. Schering Corporation transferred these rights to Scherico as a contribution to capital and at significantly below-market rates.

Schering Corporation further bolstered its worldwide sales through Essex Chemie A.G., a wholly owned subsidiary of Scherico. Essex became the distributor of Schering Corporation products in Europe, the Middle East, and the Far East. Essex purchased from Schering Corporation finished goods or substances (goods finished chemically but requiring further processing, packaging, or labeling) and then resold the items to third parties. Once again, Essex's profits in Switzerland were taxed at low Swiss tax rates. To bolster Essex's profits, Schering Corporation sold the finished goods and substances to Essex at lower-than-market prices. Essex was then able to concentrate its profits in Switzerland and pay dividends to Scherico, which functioned as a holding company for Schering Corporation.

In the mid-1960s the U.S. Internal Revenue Service (IRS) finally decided to put a stop to this large concentration of profits in Switzerland by Scherico and Essex. The IRS disliked two things about the Swiss operations. First, it felt that the royalties being received by Scherico should actually have been received by Schering Corporation and taxed in the United States. The IRS collected back taxes and interest to rectify that situation.

The other thing that the IRS disliked was the transfer price that Schering Corporation charged on sales made to Essex. It felt that the price was not an arm's length (or independent) market price and that it was too low. Thus the profits were being concentrated in Switzerland instead of the United States. Some of the profits earned by Essex were allocated back to Schering Corporation, which meant that back taxes and interest had to be paid to the U.S. government.

Schering Corporation's lawyers were able to take advantage of Swiss tax laws to minimize the payments to the U.S. IRS. For example, all dividends paid to Schering Corporation were subject to a withholding tax that had to be paid to the Swiss government. Because of a tax treaty between the U.S. and Swiss governments, that tax was reduced from 30 percent to only 5 percent. In addition, Schering Corporation was able to lower some of the back payment to the IRS by taking advantage of the Swiss reluctance to cooperate with foreign tax authorities. The Swiss government did not accept some of the U.S. government's contentions as valid and made it difficult for the U.S. government to receive what it thought it should.

INTRODUCTION

This case illustrates how MNEs can take advantage of their foreign operations to minimize tax burdens. It also shows how firms can run into problems by trying to stretch the law to the limits. The problems of taxation of foreign-source income, the use of tax haven countries (countries with low or no taxes on foreign-source income), transfer pricing, and different tax laws in different countries are among those that will be discussed in this chapter.

The area of tax planning is crucial for any business, since it can have a profound effect on profitability and cash flow. This is true in international as well as domestic business. As complex as domestic taxation seems, it is relatively simple in comparison with the intricacies of international taxation. The international tax accountant must be familiar not only with his or her country's tax policy relating to foreign operations, but also with the laws of each country in which the client operates. An understanding of the interrelationships of the tax policies involved is another essential.

Taxation has a strong impact on the choice of (1) location in the initial investment decision; (2) legal form of the new enterprise, such as branch or subsidiary; (3) method of finance, such as internal versus external sourcing and debt versus equity; and (4) method of arranging prices between related entities.[2] However, taxation is only one of many important factors. The purpose of this chapter is to examine taxation for the firm involved in international operations from a planning point of view. Emphasis will be placed on U.S. tax policy because of the nature and extent of U.S. foreign direct investment. As any country finds its firms generating more and more foreign-source income, it must make decisions on the principles of deferral, tax credits versus deductions, and so on. Therefore principles of taxation that U.S.-based MNEs face at home and abroad are, or in the future could be, applicable to firms domiciled in other countries.

TAXATION OF FOREIGN-SOURCE INCOME

When a domestic firm makes the decision to sell its products internationally, it can do so directly through the export of goods and services, through foreign branch operations (a legal extension of the parent), and through foreign corporations in which the domestic firm holds an equity interest that could vary from a small percentage to complete ownership.

Export of Goods and Services

• Sale of goods and services are included in parent company's income.

Many enterprises, such as public accounting firms, insurance firms, advertising agencies, banks, and management consulting firms, deal in services rather than goods. Many manufacturing industries also find it easier and more profitable to sell expertise, such as patents or management services, rather than goods. Generally, payment is received in the form of royalties and fees, and this payment is usually taxed by the foreign government. Since the sale of services is made by the parent, the sale must also be included in the parent's taxable income.

In spite of the large amount of foreign direct investment, U.S. firms still export a great deal of merchandise. In 1983 this export figure reached $332.2 billion. Generally, the profits from these exports are immediately taxable to the parent. However, many governments have created tax incentives to encourage exports.

The Foreign Sales Corporation.   Before the Tax Reform Act of 1984, the primary export tax incentive being used by U.S. corporations was the Domestic International Sales Corporation (DISC). The DISC legislation allowed a manufacturing firm to sell its products to a U.S. company (a DISC) that would act as a distributor worldwide. The DISC was not a taxable entity, so a percentage of its income was sheltered from taxation until a dividend was declared to the manufacturing company that owned it. However, GATT determined that the DISC violated trade subsidy principles, so the U.S. government decided to introduce substitute legislation that would provide tax incentives for exports and yet not violate international agreements. This led to the **Foreign Sales Corporation (FSC).**

• A Foreign Sales Corporation can be used by a U.S. exporter to shelter some of its income from taxation.

For a firm to qualify as an FSC, the following requirements must be satisfied:

1. It must be incorporated in and have its main offices in a foreign country or U.S. possession (except Puerto Rico).

2. It must have economic substance rather than just be a paper corporation.

3. The export services that it performs for its parent company or companies must be performed outside of the United States.

4. Up to twenty-five shareholders may own an FSC; thus export trading companies may set up FSCs if they so desire.

If the foreign corporation qualifies as an FSC, a portion of its income is exempt from U.S. corporate income tax. Also, the law provides that any dividends distributed by the FSC to its parent company are exempt from U.S. income taxation as long as that income is foreign trade income.

● The FSC must be engaged in substantial business activity.

The kinds of economic activity that qualify for the FSC legislation are the export of merchandise as well as services such as engineering services or architectural services. It is also important that substantial economic activity take place outside of the United States. The FSC cannot be a mailbox company in Switzerland that simply passes documents from the United States to the importing country. The FSC must engage in advertising and sales promotion, processing customer orders and arranging for delivery, transportation, the determination and transmittal of a final invoice or statement of account and the receipt of payment, and the assumption of credit risk.[3]

It is not necessary that all of the above economic activities be fulfilled 100 percent by the FSC, but at least one of two conditions must take place: Either 50 percent of the total direct costs of the export activity must be undertaken by the FSC, or 85 percent of the total costs of any two of the above-mentioned economic activities must take place outside of the United States.

The actual computation of taxable income and income tax liability under FSC provisions is relatively complex and beyond the scope of this chapter.[4] However, the result is to lower substantially the tax liability on income generated from export activity.

Foreign Branch

● Foreign branch income (loss) is directly included in the parent's taxable income.

A foreign branch is really an extension of the parent. It is not an enterprise incorporated in a foreign country, as is a foreign manufacturing subsidiary. Therefore any income generated by the branch is immediately taxable to the parent, whether or not cash is remitted. One important aspect of taxation of foreign branch income is that if the branch suffers a loss, the parent is allowed to deduct that loss from its taxable income, thus reducing its overall tax liability. There is no such thing as deferral in the case of a branch, since all income or loss is immediately combined with parent income or loss. Since the branch also pays corporate income tax to the government of the country in which it is operating, it may take advantage of the tax credit, which is described in more detail later in the chapter.

Foreign Corporations

The taxation of foreign corporations (as distinct from branches) is complicated in part by terminology. In an accounting sense, a corporation is the subsidiary of a parent when the parent acquires more than 50 percent of the voting stock. It is a joint venture when exactly 50 percent is owned.

The term joint venture has a variety of meanings, from the strict accounting sense to the international business concept of corporations from at least two different countries forming a separate corporation by which to do business.

- CFC—50% of *voting* stock is held by "U.S. shareholders."

CFC. From a tax standpoint it is critical to determine first of all whether the foreign subsidiary or affiliate is a **controlled foreign corporation (CFC).** A CFC is any foreign corporation in which more than 50 percent of the voting stock is held by "U.S. shareholders." A **U.S. shareholder** is a U.S. person or enterprise that holds 10 percent or more of the voting stock of the subsidiary. Table 20.1 explains how this might work.

- Active income is income from the actual conduct of business.

Foreign corporation A is a CFC because it meets both tests described above. This is the case when A is a wholly owned subsidiary of parent firm V in the United States. Foreign corporation B is also a CFC because U.S. persons V, W, and X are qualified "U.S. shareholders," and their share of the voting stock exceeds 50 percent. Foreign corporation C is not a CFC because only U.S. persons V and W are qualified "U.S. shareholders," and their combined voting shares do not exceed 50 percent.

Once a CFC has been identified, its income must be divided into two categories: active income and subpart F, or passive, income. Active income implies that it is income derived from the active conduct of trade or business. Subpart F income came about because of some very creative tax planning by multinational corporations that were rapidly expanding abroad in the post–World War II period, but the roots of the problem lie in the genesis of corporate income tax practices in the United States.

History. The nature and extent of taxation in each country depends on the government's objectives in taxing. Taxation can serve as a source of revenue to finance governmental programs and/or as a policy tool to influence the flow of goods, services, and resources. In its initial stages the U.S. government was not very large and therefore played a minor role in

TABLE 20.1 _____

DETERMINATION OF CONTROLLED FOREIGN CORPORATIONS

Shareholders and their percentage of the voting stock	Foreign corporation A	Foreign corporation B	Foreign corporation C
U.S. person V	100%	45%	30%
U.S. person W		10%	10%
U.S. person X		20%	8%
U.S. person Y			8%
Foreign person Z		25%	44%
Total	100%	100%	100%

the actual production of goods or services. Thus the revenue from excise taxes was sufficient to finance what few governmental programs existed. However, in 1909 the government instituted a corporate income tax. In 1913 this was expanded to include income from all sources, including foreign sources.

• Deferral—income of a foreign corporation is taxed in the U.S. when received as a dividend.

An important aspect of the taxation of foreign-source income was the principle of **deferral.** Deferral as it applies to foreign-source income means that income earned by a subsidiary incorporated outside of the United States is taxed only when it is remitted to the parent as a dividend, not when it is earned. Until 1918 the parent firm was permitted to deduct from taxable income those foreign taxes paid on income remitted from a foreign subsidiary. However, the tax credit became law in 1918. This allowed foreign taxes to be offset directly against U.S. taxes in determining total tax liability.[5]

During the early 1960s the U.S. government became concerned with the taxation of foreign-source income and its effect on the foreign investment policy of U.S. corporations and on the generation of revenues by the government from corporate income tax. There was a lot of concern that firms were maximizing the accumulation of profits in tax havens by artificial arrangements of intracompany pricing and other intracompany transactions.[6]

• Tax haven country—a country with low or no taxes on foreign source income.

Tax havens. One of the key areas of concern was the tax haven. A **tax haven subsidiary** is owned by the parent corporation and located in a country with special tax considerations. The following characteristics seem to typify a **tax haven country:**

a. either imposes no tax or imposes a low tax when compared with the United States;

b. has a high level of bank or commercial secrecy, which the country refused to break even under an international agreement;

c. relative high importance of banking and similar financial activites to its economy;

d. the availability of modern communication facilities;

e. lack of currency controls on foreign deposits of foreign currency; and

f. self-promotion as an offshore financial center.[7]

Tax havens can be classified into four broad categories in terms of their tax benefits:

1. countries with no taxes at all, such as the Bahamas, Bermuda, and the Cayman Islands;

2. countries with taxes at low rates, such as the British Virgin Islands and Jersey;

3. havens that tax income from domestic sources but exempt income from foreign sources, such as Hong Kong, Liberia, and Panama; and

4. countries that allow special privileges and generally are suitable as tax havens only for limited purposes.

● Purpose of tax haven: to concentrate cash to low-tax countries and avoid taxation so money could be used for expansion.

The tax haven subsidiary acted as a holding company for the parent of stock in foreign subsidiaries (often called grandchild or second-tier subsidiaries, as illustrated in Fig. 20.1), as a sales agent or distributor, as an agent for the parent in licensing agreements (an agreement whereby the parent sells patents, trademarks, or manufacturing expertise in return for royalties or fees), or as an investment company. The purpose of the tax haven subsidiary was to concentrate cash from the parent's foreign operations into the low-tax country and to use the cash for global expansion. As long as a dividend was not declared to the parent, no U.S. tax had to be paid. This accumulation of profits outside of the United States was one of President Kennedy's chief concerns.

While the debate was going on, the Treasury Department was leaning very heavily toward the elimination of deferral. However, a compromise was reached in the Revenue Act of 1962. The deferral concept was eliminated for tax haven subsidiaries involved in passive rather than active investments, and the tax credit concept was retained for subsidiaries involved in active operating investments.

As a result of this situation, Subpart F or passive income became a fact of life for MNEs after 1962.

Subpart F income. Subpart F income comes from two sources: (1) the insurance or reinsurance of U.S. risks and (2) foreign base company income. The latter is the most common type of income and is directed at the tax haven corporations. Foreign base company income comes from the following sources.

1. Base company personal holding company income—primarily passive income, such as dividends, interest, rents, royalties, and gains on sale of stocks.

2. Base company sales income—income from foreign sales subsidiaries that are separately incorporated from their manufacturing operations.

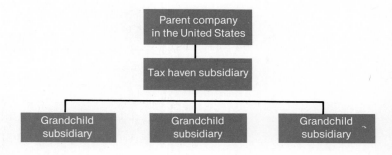

FIGURE 20.1
The Tax Haven Subsidiary Acting as a Holding Company

The sales income includes profits, fees, commissions, and the like obtained from the purchase and sale of personal property (property other than real estate) when a related person is involved. The personal property is either manufactured, produced, grown, or extracted outside and sold for use outside the CFC's country of incorporation. Any CFC performing significant operations on the property is excluded, as is any property used substantially and sold to an unrelated party.

3. Base company service income—income from the performance of technical, managerial, or similar services for a related person and performed outside the country in which the CFC is organized.

4. Base company shipping income—income derived from the use of any aircraft or vessel in foreign commerce; the performance of services directly related to the use of any such aircraft or vessel; the sale, exchange, or other disposition of any such aircraft or vessel.

- Subpart F income of a CFC is directly taxable to the parent.
- If foreign corporation is not a CFC, income is not taxable until a dividend is received.
- If CFC's income:
  - less than 10% of parent's gross, none is treated as subpart F.
  - greater than 70% of parent's gross, all becomes income to parent.

The importance of distinguishing between a CFC and non-CFC and subpart F and active income is in the application of the deferral principle, which is summarized in Fig. 20.2. As long as a foreign corporation is not a controlled foreign corporation, its income is not taxable to the parent until a dividend is received. The deferral principle applies to the active income of a CFC but not to subpart F income, which is immediately taxable to the parent. The tax credit applies to both active and subpart F income.

Exception to the rule. Most of the exceptions to subpart F income were either eliminated or modified by the Tax Reduction Act of 1975. The remaining exception is the 10–70 provision. Under this provision, if foreign base company income is less than 10 percent of gross income, none of it is treated as subpart F income. If foreign base company income exceeds 70 percent of gross income, all of the entity's income is treated as base company income.

Dave Fischbein Company and Subpart F. The Dave Fischbein Manufacturing Co. (DFMC) was organized in 1947 to produce portable bag-closing machines that were designed and built by Dave and his son, Harold. Initially, the machines were sold exclusively to Dave Fischbein Co. (DFC), which was also organized in 1947 to buy and sell new and used sewing machines. Although DFC was concerned with the domestic market, it was obvious that it had a unique advantage: in 1947 the Fischbein machine was the only one of its kind in the world.

Fischbein's initial international venture was the organization of Dave Fischbein Western Sales Corp. in 1952 to serve Latin American markets. The expansion to Europe occurred in 1956 with the organization of Compagnie Fischbein, S.A. (CFSA), a Belgian corporation that was organized to sell machines throughout the world.

FIGURE 20.2
Deferral for Different Legal Forms

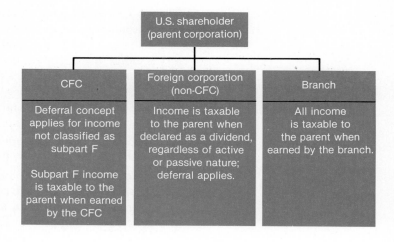

It was decided that DFSA would purchase components from DFMC and assemble them in Belgium for two major reasons: (1) if the assembled machines originated in Belgium rather than in the United States, they would get a good break in tariffs, quotas, and other related restrictions in the Common Market, and (2) lower labor and overhead costs in Belgium would increase profit margins. In addition, CFSA purchased some of the components in Belgium because they were cheaper, and less susceptible to capricious customs officials and because it was easier to comply with certain European standards.

The U.S. Internal Revenue Service, fearing that it was not getting its fair share of tax revenues, began to look more closely at CFSA. It noticed that CFSA sold 95 percent of its output outside of Belgium and that the value added to the components in Belgian assembly operation was only about 20 percent. CFSA was a controlled foreign corporation since DFC was the sole shareholder. Since CFSA did not really actively sell the products, the IRS decided that CFSA was merely earning foreign base company sales income that should be taxed to DFC as subpart F income. It contended that "the components purchased by CFSA were so perfect that they only had to be simply put together in short periods of time by not too highly skilled mechanics, whose tasks in this operation were nothing more than ministerial functions." In addition, the components were purchased (from DFMC in the United States) from outside of the country where the controlled foreign corporation was organized (Belgium) and sold outside of that country as well.

Fortunately, the tax court came to the rescue. It agreed with the IRS that CFSA was indeed a controlled foreign corporation. However, it felt that the income earned was active, not passive. This decision was based on the feeling that CFSA's operations were considered a manufacturing operation, since the work was substantial and involved the major assembly or manufacture of the product. In investigating CFSA's plant, the court found that the workers were highly skilled and that their work, which involved some custom machining of parts, was not routine.[8]

As can be seen from this example, the determination of active versus passive income is often subject to judgment. Although DFC's move to Belgium was not rooted in tax avoidance considerations, it had to show that its operations were bona fide manufacturing ones.

Tax Credit

- IRS allows a tax credit for corporate tax paid to another country.
- Credit is dollar-for-dollar reduction of tax liability.
- Credit must coincide with recognition of income.

It is considered a country's sovereign right to levy taxes on all income generated within its borders. A problem arises when a firm happens to be owned by foreigners, such as a foreign corporation, or is a branch of a foreign corporation. This problem has been an important one for U.S. firms because of the magnitude of foreign direct investment. The IRS could go one of three ways in its treatment of foreign corporate income taxes paid by the foreign subsidiary or branch of a U.S. corporation. It could (1) opt for double taxation, (2) allow the parent to claim the taxes as a deduction from adjusted gross income, or (3) allow the parent to claim the taxes as a direct credit against the U.S. tax liability. Table 20.2 is a simplified illustration of the differences among the three choices.

As can be seen from the table, double taxation is the least beneficial to the taxpayer, while the **tax credit** ensures that the taxpayer pays at least the U.S. rate. As was mentioned earlier in the chapter, tax deduction was followed until 1918, at which time the tax credit was instituted. Even though the tax credit is acceptable to the IRS, a firm may select the deduction approach.

Are all kinds of taxes paid in foreign countries eligible for the tax

TABLE 20.2 _____

TREATMENT OF FOREIGN CORPORATE INCOME TAX

	Double taxation	Deduction	Credit
Income earned by the foreign operation	$100.00	$100.00	$100.00
Foreign tax at 40% on $100	40.00	40.00	40.00
	60.00	60.00	60.00
U.S. tax at 48% on $100	48.00		
U.S. tax at 48% on $60		28.80	
U.S. tax at 48% on $100 less foreign tax at 40% on $100 (48 − 40 = $8)			8.00
Net income after tax	$ 12.00	$ 31.20	$ 52.00

credit? Unfortunately not. Indirect taxes such as sales taxes, excise taxes, and value-added taxes are not eligible for the tax credit. The major eligible tax is the corporate income tax assessed on the branch or corporation by the government of the country. As was mentioned earlier, the U.S. parent is able to defer recognition of active income until a dividend is declared to the parent. At that time it gets credit for a portion of income taxes paid. For example, if 50 percent of the income is distributed as a dividend to the parent, the parent gets to claim no more than 50 percent of the tax as a creditable tax. There are maximum limits that will be discussed shortly. Branches are not allowed the deferral privilege, so their income is immediately taxed to the parent, but all branch income taxes are eligible for inclusion in the tax credit.

Credit is also allowed for withholding taxes paid by the parent to the foreign government on dividends paid by the foreign corporation to the parent. Although most countries assess a 20–30 percent withholding tax on dividends, two countries deviate slightly. The United Kingdom collects no withholding tax, and Switzerland collects 35 percent.

- Credit is subject to upper limit of what the tax would have been in the U.S.

After the firm adds up its eligible credits, it finds that it is constrained by an upper limit imposed by the IRS. The upper limit is what the firm would have paid in taxes on that income in the United States. If the total of foreign source income is $1,000,000 and the applicable U.S. tax rate is 48 percent, then the upper limit would be $480,000. If the tax credits added up from all over the world exceeded the $480,000, the firm could carry the excess credits back two years and recompute their tax burden or carry them forward five years and try to use them. If the amount were less than the upper limit, the firm would be allowed the full amount.

Section 482—Reallocation: Transfer Pricing

- Transfer price is price on transactions between related corporate entities.
- IRS will reallocate income if it feels the transfer price was set in order to evade taxes.

Transfer pricing, also discussed in Chapter 22, is pricing the goods and services that pass between related parties, such as parent and subsidiary. One of the major factors affecting the setting of transfer prices is the minimization of taxes. For example, a parent selling goods to a subsidiary in a low-tax country would set a low transfer price on the goods so as to concentrate income in the subsidiary rather than in the parent.

However, the Internal Revenue Service has not gone along with this policy. Section 482 of the Code gives the government the power to allocate gross income, deductions, credits, or allowances between related firms where arbitrary pricing or allocation of expenses may have occurred to evade taxes. Once the reallocation has been made, the burden is on the taxpayer to prove that the reallocation was arbitrary and inconsistent and that a refund is warranted.

One important case on transfer pricing involved Eli Lilly and Company.

Eli Lilly is a large U.S. company with sales revenues in 1979 of $2.2 billion in human health, agriculture, and cosmetics products. Lilly's sales and earnings abroad in 1979 totaled 40 percent and 27 percent, respectively.

In the 1950s, Lilly instituted some interesting policies to stimulate exports. The company sold its export-destined products to Eli Lilly International Corporation (International) at a price that recovered manufacturing costs plus royalties paid by Eli Lilly to third parties and all operating expenses incurred by Eli Lilly incident to the servicing of the export business. Thus Eli Lilly essentially earned no profit on its sales to International. International sold the products to Eli Lilly Pan-American Corporation (a Western Hemisphere Trading Corporation) at cost with no provision for profits. Pan-American would then sell the goods in the Western Hemisphere outside the United States and pay a reduced tax on income because of its WHTC status. Sales by International to distributors in the Eastern Hemisphere were made at a suggested retail price less 15 percent.

The IRS, obviously, was a little upset with Eli Lilly and collected over $4 million in back taxes once profits were reallocated from Pan-American to International, which was a U.S. corporation but not a WHTC. Although Eli Lilly appealed the decision, the tax court upheld the IRS as follows:

> *Eli Lilly has adopted a pricing policy on its product destined for international markets which results in its selling organizations receiving the bulk of the overall profits from sales abroad. That policy disturbs the government only insofar as it involves Eli Lilly's products sold in the Western Hemisphere. Because one of Eli Lilly's selling subsidiaries qualifies as a Western Hemisphere Trading Corporation and therefore enjoys a reduced rate of tax on its income, the Government asserts that Eli Lilly's pricing policy results in tax avoidance and does not clearly reflect the incomes of the related organizations.* [9]

Another good illustration of the problems that a firm can run into as a result of not using an arm's length price in setting transfer prices involved the U.S. chemical manufacturer, E. I. DuPont. DuPont's Swiss subsidiary, DISA, was organized in 1959 as a marketing subsidiary that bought products from DuPont and resold them to independent distributors, which sold the products to consumers. In trying to determine what price to set on goods shipped to DISA, DuPont settled on a price that at one time was considered artificially low and another as one providing only a modest markup. An internal memorandum dealing with this pricing policy included the following statement:

> *It would seem desirable to bill the tax haven subsidiary at less than an "arm's length" price because (1) the pricing might not be challenged by the revenue agent; (2) if the pricing is challenged, we might sustain such transfer; (3) if we cannot sustain the price used, a transfer price will be negotiated which should not be more than an "arm's length" price and might well be less; thus we would be no worse off than we would have been had we billed at the higher price.* [10]

Taxation of U.S. Citizens Abroad

It is the right of every country to tax the earnings of its citizens. However, the United States goes further than most industrial countries by taxing the worldwide income of its residents.

The tax law relating to expatriates has changed several times in the past few years. The Economic Recovery Tax Act of 1981 changed the tax law to provide a series of benefits to the expatriate, such as the foreign-earned income exclusion, the foreign housing cost exclusion and/or deduction, and the foreign tax credit.

● U.S. taxes income of expatriates.

● Expatriates may exclude some income and housing allowances from taxation.

Expatriates that qualify for the provisions of the law are permitted to exclude a certain amount of their income from taxation in the United States. In 1982 they were permitted to exclude the first $75,000 of income. That amount rose by $5000 a year until 1986, when the exclusion becomes $95,000. That amount will hold after 1986.

Expatriates are also allowed to exclude from taxable income housing allowances provided by their companies in excess of a base amount determined by the IRS each year. Although a foreign tax credit is allowed for taxes paid to governments in foreign countries on income earned there, expatriates are not allowed to use as credits taxes on income excluded from U.S. taxation.

NON-U.S. TAX PRACTICES

Tax practices throughout the world differ significantly from those found in the United States. This often causes problems for the U.S. firm operating overseas. Lack of familiarity with laws and customs can create serious problems. In many countries, tax laws are rather loosely enforced, so there is great variance between the effective and statutory tax rates. In some countries, such as Spain and Italy, taxes are generally negotiated between the tax collector and the taxpayer—if they are ever reported at all.

A variance among countries in generally accepted accounting principles can lead to differences in the determination of taxable income. This could have important effects on the cash flow required to settle tax obligations. For example, France allows companies to depreciate assets very quickly and allows additional depreciation for certain assets. In Sweden, companies are allowed to write down inventories in the interest of conservatism; this tends to reduce taxable income.

● Separate entity—each unit is taxed when it earns income (U.S.).

Taxation on corporate income is accomplished by one of two approaches in most countries: the separate entity, or classical, approach and the integrated system.[11] In the former approach, which is used in the United States, each separate unit (firm or individual) is taxed when it earns income. For example, a corporation is taxed on its earnings, and shareholders are taxed on the distribution of earnings (dividends). This results in double taxation.

● Integrated system—tries to avoid double taxation of corporate income through split rates or tax credits.

Most other industrial countries use an integrated system to eliminate double taxation. In West Germany a split-rate system is used so that a lower corporate income tax rate is applied to distributed profits, since the shareholders are also taxed. The rate on retained profits is 56 percent and on distributed profits only 36 percent. The other major way to eliminate double taxation is to give a dividend credit to shareholders, as is done in the United Kingdom. Resident shareholders in West Germany are allowed a tax credit in addition to the split-rate system.

Different countries also treat differently the taxation on earnings of the foreign subsidiaries of domestic corporations. Some countries, such as France, use a territorial approach and therefore tax only domestic-source income. Other countries, such as West Germany and the United Kingdom, use a global approach; they tax branch profits and foreign subsidiary dividends. The United States is the only country to tax unremitted earnings, as in subpart F income.

Value-Added Tax (VAT)

● Each firm is taxed only on the value added to the product.

The **VAT,** often referred to as TVA, or tax on value added, has been used since 1967 by most of the countries of Western Europe (including the members of the EC as well as Sweden and Norway). One reason for the widespread use of VAT was these countries' desire to facilitate intra-European trade by agreeing to a more uniform tax system. The second reason for the adoption of VAT is its superiority to the turnover tax that had been in use throughout most of Western Europe. The turnover tax is applied to total sales at each successive stage in the production process where primary and intermediate goods are bought and sold. Thus the turnover tax is incorporated into the price many times before it reaches the ultimate consumer. The VAT, as will be shown below, is not determined in this manner and thus does not cause a pyramidal tax to be built into prices. A VAT is computed by applying a percentage rate on total sales less any purchases from other business entities. As the name implies, VAT means that each independent company is taxed only on the value added at each stage in the productive process. If one company was fully integrated vertically, the tax rate would apply to its net sales because it owned everything from raw materials to finished product.

The country rates in Europe vary significantly in spite of efforts toward a harmonization of different rates by the EC. To illustrate the use of the VAT, assume a rate of 11 percent for West Germany. Company A sells raw materials to Company B for DM 500 plus the VAT of DM 55. Although Company B pays the tax, Company A withholds it and sends it to the Treasury Department. After processing the material, Company B sells a product to Company C for DM 800 plus the VAT of DM 88. Company B sends the VAT to the government and applies for a refund of the VAT withheld by Company A so that it is only assessed on its value added in production [(800 − 500) × 11% = 33; 88 − 55 = 33]. The tax is payable to the government and is usually passed on to the consumer. However, competitive conditions may cause the firm to absorb rather than pass on the tax.

○ Many countries rebate the VAT to an exporter.

The VAT does not apply to exports, since the tax is rebated to the exporter and thus is not passed on to the consumer. This is an effective stimulus for exports. The VAT is also used as a basis for determining a border tax. A border tax in Europe is levied on imports at a rate that is approximately equal to the amount of internal excise and other indirect taxes paid by domestic producers of competing products. It is in addition to import duties. The idea behind border taxes is to put local goods and imports on the same competitive basis.

The Unitary Tax Debate

○ Unitary tax would impose a tax on a percentage of the corporation's total worldwide earnings.

The unitary tax debate has surfaced in recent years as a source of real contention between the U.S. government and other governments around the world. This is especially true of governments of countries such as the United Kingdom and the Netherlands that have a number of firms investing in the United States. The basic concept of the **unitary tax,** as developed in California, is to tax a portion of a corporation's worldwide earnings. Taxable income is determined by applying to worldwide earnings a percentage based on the average proportion of the firm's in-state sales, property, and payroll to the firm's total sales, assets, and payroll. Thus the state income tax paid by a company may have no relationship to its profitability in that state. The states like the unitary tax concept, since it minimizes the possibility of a firm's using arbitrary transfer pricing techniques among its subsidiaries to manipulate profits and therefore taxes.

○ Water's edge—the unitary tax would apply to U.S. source income only.

Although the unitary tax problem is a source of contention, there does not appear to be an easy solution. As of the fall of 1984, a number of lawsuits were pending and a variety of compromises being considered so that states would be able to collect a fair tax. One potential solution would be to use a "water's edge" philosophy so that the unitary tax concept would relate only to U.S.-source income rather than worldwide income.

Tax Incentives

○ Tax holidays are designed to attract investment.

As was noted in Chapter 6, many countries that are desirous of investment offer tax advantages to investors. Generally, these are less-developed countries that need foreign capital and technical know-how in order to develop industrially. Some countries, such as Puerto Rico, excuse investors from paying taxes for a certain period of time. Brazil has tried to develop its poverty-stricken northeast region by allowing firms operating in that area to use their earnings for expansion without paying taxes on them. These tax holiday policies are designed to influence the flow of investment funds, but their total impact is difficult to measure. Investment is usually undertaken because of market potential, market proximity, or source of raw materials. Taxation policies may affect profitability, but they are probably not a major factor in determining location. However, ignorance of tax laws, customs, and incentives could prove to be a serious and costly mistake.

Tax Treaties—The Elimination of Double Taxation

• Purpose of tax treaties is to prevent double taxation.

The primary purpose of most tax treaties is to prevent international double taxation or to provide remedies when it occurs. The United States has income tax treaties in force with approximately thirty-eight nations. The general pattern for tax withholding between two treaty countries is to grant reciprocal reductions on dividend withholding and to exempt royalties and sometimes interest payments from any withholding tax.

The United States has a withholding tax of 30 percent for owners of U.S. securities (individuals and corporations) who are from countries with which no tax treaties are in effect. Where a tax treaty is in effect, the U.S. rate on dividends is generally reduced to 15 percent, and the tax on interest and royalties either is eliminated or declines to a very low level.

A good example of a tax treaty is one between the United States and Canada. Canadian dividends, interest, and royalties are normally subject to a 25 percent withholding tax rate, but for U.S. firms they are subject to only 15 percent as a result of the tax treaty. Under a new treaty awaiting confirmation in both countries the withholding rate would drop to 10 percent.[12]

Treaty countries recognize that it is important to allow full taxing power to the country where the primary business operations occur and to allow the country of the minor activity to grant tax exemptions or tax credits. The treaties usually provide for the right of each country to reallocate items to reflect more properly the income taxed within its borders. Since each country's laws and taxing principles differ, this reallocation may result in double taxation.[13]

When disagreements arise, tax treaties usually provide for consultation and negotiation between tax officials of the countries involved. These officials, known as **competent authorities,** provide a variety of other services, such as providing information on changes and development in tax laws.[14]

PLANNING THE TAX FUNCTION

Since taxes affect both profits and cash flow, they must be considered in the investment as well as the operational decision process. When a U.S. parent decides to set up operations in a foreign country, it can do so through a branch or a foreign subsidiary. If the parent expects the foreign operations to operate at a loss for the initial years of operation, it should operate through a branch, since it can deduct branch losses against the current year's income at the parent's level. As the operations become profitable, it would be wise to switch to a foreign manufacturing subsidiary. If the nature of the subsidiary income is such that the deferral principle applies, then income of the subsidiary would not be taxed until a dividend is declared.

Tied in with the initial investment decision as well as with continuing operations is the financing decision. Both debt and equity financing have tax considerations. If parent loans are used to finance foreign operations, the repayment of principal is not taxable, but the receipt of interest income is taxable to the parent. Also, the interest expense paid by the subsidiary is generally a business expense, which reduces taxable income in the foreign country. Dividends, which are a return to equity capital, are taxable to the parent and are not a deductible business expense to the subsidiary. As was pointed out in Chapter 10, international finance subsidiaries are often set up to finance foreign operations. These subsidiaries are set up outside the United States to escape withholding tax requirements.

A multinational corporation that is trying to maximize its cash flow worldwide should try to concentrate profits in tax haven or at least low-tax countries. This can be done by carefully selecting a low-tax country for the initial investment, by setting up tax haven corporations to receive dividends, and by judicious transfer pricing. The last two are especially difficult because of U.S. tax laws. However, the government allowed some leeway with subpart F income. A firm can escape CFC status by retaining a large minority interest in the subsidiary and by spreading the remaining interest among many shareholders. This would allow the parent to maintain control but would rid the subsidiary of CFC status and the need to be concerned with subpart F income. Apparently, this occurred shortly after passage of the subpart F provision, since revenues from subpart F fell significantly below the initial projections.[15] However, it is estimated that most foreign operations are considered CFCs and are therefore subject to subpart F status.

With proper planning and timing of dividend remittances, the parent can take advantage of the minimum distribution provision. Whenever possible, the parent should also utilize the 10–70 rule. If the parent has a profitable operating subsidiary in a relatively low-tax country, it can accumulate subpart F income without worrying about U.S. taxes as long as that income does not reach 10 percent of total subsidiary income. Because of its low-tax status and its membership in the EC, Ireland can be used as a manufacturing center to supply the EC with goods and as a tax haven corporation. The subpart F income provisions have complicated tax planning, but opportunities still exist.

Even though a sales subsidiary in Switzerland might be earning all subpart F income, there may still be some tax advantage to the parent. If the parent is earning excess tax credits from foreign operations, it may be able to increase its ability to use those credits in a given year by increasing its foreign source income. Thus the Swiss subsidiary may not have any tax credits to contribute, but its income may allow the parent to capture another subsidiary's credits.

A judicious use of tax treaties could also be very helpful. For example, the treaty between the United States and the United Kingdom provides for a 15 percent withholding tax on dividends, while the treaties between the United States and the Netherlands and between the Netherlands and the United Kingdom provide for 5 percent withholding taxes. In addition, the Netherlands does not tax dividends from foreign sources. This would allow a U.S. firm to set up a holding company in the Netherlands that would receive dividends from a U.K. subsidiary and remit them to the U.S. parent at a combined withholding tax of only 10 percent rather than 15 percent.[16]

Tax law is very complicated, and a firm needs an experienced tax lawyer in order to take care of all the available situations. The following is a checklist that can assist a tax manager in proper tax planning:

1. Ask the respective controllers for tax projections that enumerate the items that are not tax-exempt. Likewise, timing differences due to accelerated depreciations, etc., should be shown.

2. Management should work out some minimum dividend distribution plan so that at year-end the group of companies can take advantage of any U.S. tax concessions.

3. Find avenues for bona fide reduction of the taxable profit (accelerated depreciation, inventory write-offs, etc.).

4. Check the local company's tax declarations.

5. Examine the local tax assessments and advise management of the non-deductibility of certain items so that corrective measures can be taken.

6. Verify that unjustified tax assessments are contested.

7. Verify that all relevant papers (tax returns, etc.) and tax receipts (photocopies) are forwarded to the parent company in order to obtain foreign tax credits.

8. See that the American management is aware of major changes in local tax legislation so that corporate policy for such matters as future investments, cash flow, dividend remittances, and minimum dividend distribution can be formed accordingly.[17]

SUMMARY

- International tax planning has a strong impact on the choice of location in the initial investment decision, the legal form of the new enterprise, the method of financing, and the method of setting transfer prices.

- The Foreign Sales Corporation (FSC) is a company incorporated in a foreign country or U.S. possession (except Puerto Rico). If it engages in substantial export services for its parent company, some of its income will be considered exempt from U.S. corporate income tax.

- Deferral means that income earned by a subsidiary incorporated outside of the home country is taxed only when it is remitted to the parent as a dividend, not when it is earned.

- Tax haven corporations are located in countries with tax rates that are substantially lower than rates in the parent company's home country. Their purpose is to concentrate cash from foreign operations and use that cash for the global expansion of the parent. The U.S. Revenue Act of 1962 was designed to limit the effectiveness of a tax haven corporation for U.S. firms.

- A controlled foreign corporation must declare its subpart F income as taxable to the parent in the year it is earned, whether or not it is remitted as a dividend. The major exception to subpart F provisions is the 10–70 rule.

- The tax credit allows a parent corporation to reduce its tax liability by the direct amount paid to foreign governments on dividends declared by its subsidiary to the parent as well as by the amount "deemed direct." This latter tax is the corporate income tax paid by the subsidiary to the foreign government.

- Transfer pricing is the pricing of goods and services between related parties, such as parent and subsidiary. Section 482 of the code attempts to ensure that prices are set on an arm's length basis so that income is properly allocated between related entities.

- U.S. tax law allows a U.S. expatriate to exclude a certain amount of foreign source income from taxation in the United States and allows the expatriate to exclude housing allowances provided by the companies in excess of a base amount.

- The unitary tax debate was initiated by states that wished to tax a portion of a firm's worldwide income rather than income earned in the states.

- Policies in other countries vary as to what is taxable income, how honest taxpayers are in filing returns, and how taxes are assessed. The United States taxes each separate unit (the classical approach), while most other industrial countries use an integrated system in which double taxation is eliminated.

- The purpose of most tax treaties is to prevent international double taxation or to provide remedies when it occurs. "Competent authorities" are officials representing negotiating countries that settle disagreements over tax policies and provide a variety of other services that aid in the implementation and interpretation of tax treaties.

C A S E   SIGNBOARD INTERNATIONAL

Cindy Montgomery was recently hired by SignBoard International's tax department to take a close look at some of S.I.'s foreign operations and to identify major tax implications. S.I. is a relatively new firm started by two engineering faculty members at the local university who developed hardware and software for electronic signs like the ones used in sports stadiums. The company grew rapidly as marketing efforts increased, and the original founders began to produce and sell products worldwide. After attending a few seminars, they set up some creative subsidiaries in different countries to minimize taxes. However, they are not sure whether they did the right thing and whether they fully understand the tax ramifications.

S.I. has production and assembly operations in Springville, Utah, and Glasgow, Scotland. The Glasgow plant was established to help serve the European market in some product lines because of low labor costs, favorable building leasing arrangements by the city government, and favorable tax incentives. Some parts and components are produced in Taiwan and shipped to Springville and Glasgow for final assembly. Foreign sales are handled primarily through a DISC set up in Delaware and an office in Switzerland.

S.I. St. Gallen, S.A. (SISG) is a sales subsidiary set up in Switzerland to expedite sales in most European markets. The products are produced in S.I.'s manufacturing facilities in Springville and Glasgow and sold to various independent distributors in Western Europe. However, the products are sold at cost to SISG and then to the distributors at market prices. About 5 percent of the products purchased by SISG are sold in Switzerland; the remainder are sold abroad. Very little value-added work is done in Switzerland, although some changes are made in packaging. Currently, sales are handled by a sales staff from the home office in Springville. The operation in Scotland is strictly for manufacturing. At this point, S.I. has not felt it necessary to establish an elaborate sales and service organization in Scotland or Switzerland. Both the Glasgow plant and SISG are wholly owned by S.I.

S.I. organized a DISC in Delaware five years ago to take care of exports of some of its products to Canada, Western Europe, and the Far East. It was using the profits from the sales to produce and store more inventory that could be exported. Currently, the sales staff that markets the products sold by the DISC are located in S.I.'s domestic operations. They travel abroad whenever they need to make sales calls. There are no sales offices or distributorships abroad for those products, with the exception of the office in St. Gallen. The DISC operation has been very useful, because S.I. has been able to shelter some of its income from the IRS and use it for expansion.

Cindy is aware that S.I.'s management team is considering establishing a manufacturing facility in Mexico near the U.S. border to assemble components manufactured in the United States and Taiwan and to export the products to the United States. Under Sections 806.3 and 807 of the U.S. Tariff Act, exports to the United States are exempt from duty in proportion to the contained value of U.S. materials. Top management hopes that low labor costs and tax incentives from the Mexican government will enable S.I. to develop a comparative advantage vis-à-vis its major competition. They are trying to decide whether to own a majority of the Mexican operation or take a minority interest. They have heard that you do not have to pay U.S. taxes on income from abroad if you own less than 50 percent of the foreign corporation.

A final situation that top management wants Cindy to look at is a financing subsidiary in the Netherlands Antilles. They are considering setting up a subsidiary there to issue bonds to potential investors in Europe. The proceeds of the bond issue would be lent to S.I. for expansion.

QUESTIONS

Assume that you are Cindy and are assigned to look at each of these situations above. Write a memo addressing each of the following questions.

1. What are the international tax principles in operation in SISG? What would you advise S.I. to do for tax purposes?

2. Of what value is the DISC now? What would you advise S.I. to do to obtain a tax break on its export sales? Why?

3. Evaluate the recommendation to establish a manufacturing operation in Mexico and address the tax concerns raised by top management.

4. Discuss the tax concepts that are raised in establishing a financing subsidiary in the Netherlands Antilles. You may have to refer to an earlier chapter for more information on that subject.

NOTES

1. Data for this case were taken from the 1980 Annual Report of Schering-Plough Corporation and from *Schering Corporation and Subsidiaries, Petitioners* v. *Commissioner of Internal Revenue,* respondent, *United States Tax Court Reports* 69 (1978), pp. 579–605; the quote at the end of the case is found on page 587.

2. Albert J. Radler, "Taxation Policy in Multinational Companies," in *The Multinational Enterprise in Transition,* A. Kapoor and Philip D. Grub, eds. (Princeton: The Darwin Press, 1972), p. 30.

3. Prentice-Hall, *A Complete Guide to the Tax Reform Act of 1984* (Englewood Cliffs, N.J.: Prentice-Hall, 1984), pp. 1791–1805.

4. For more detailed information, see Jeffrey S. Arpan and Lee H. Radebaugh, *International Accounting and Multinational Enterprises,* 2nd ed. (New York: John Wiley & Sons, 1985), Chapter 7 ("Taxation and Transfer Pricing").

5. Lawrence B. Krause and Kenneth W. Dam, *Federal Tax Treatment of Foreign Income* (Washington, D.C.: The Brookings Institution, 1964), pp. 27–35.

6. Donald W. Bacon, "Taxing Foreign Income of United States Taxpayers," *Taxes,* June 1965, pp. 362–363. This material appeared originally in the June 1965 issue of *Taxes—The Tax Magazine,* published and copyrighted by Commerce Clearing House, Inc., in Chicago, and is reproduced with their permission.

7. Commerce Clearing House, Inc., *Standard Federal Tax Reporter* (Chicago: CCH, 1983), paragraph 305.

8. *United States Tax Court Reports,* vol. 59, 1973, pp. 338–361.

9. *U.S. Tax Cases* 67–1, 1967, Commerce Clearing House, Inc., 83.535–83.544. Reproduced with permission from *U.S. Tax Cases,* Vol. 67–1, 1967, published and copyrighted by Commerce Clearing House, Inc., 4025 W. Peterson Avenue, Chicago, Illinois 60646.

10. Robert Feinschreiber, "Intercompany Pricing After DuPont," *International Tax Journal,* February 1980, pp. 222–229.

11. See M. A. Akhtar, *The Federal Reserve Board of New York Quarterly Review,* Summer 1977, pp. 27–32, for a more thorough discussion of this subject and for much of the information in this section.

12. See annual issues of Ernst & Whinney, *Foreign and U.S. Corporate Income and Withholding Tax Rates,* (New York: Ernst & Whinney International Operations) for other examples.

13. Jane O. Burns, "U.S. Federal Income Tax Implications and the Multinational Corporation," unpublished paper, The Pennsylvania State University, University Park, Pa., 1973.

14. Berhard H. Oetjen, "The Competent Authority's Role in Resolving International Tax Issues," *The Tax Executive,* October 1973, pp. 58–59.

15. Howard M. Liebman, "The Tax Treatment of Joint Venture Income under Subpart F: Some Issues and Alternatives," *The Business Lawyer,* Vol. 32, January 1977, p. 395.

16. George C. Watt, Richard M. Hammer, and Marianne Burge, *Accounting for the Multinational Corporation* (New York: Financial Executives Research Foundation, 1977), p. 410.

17. Ernst K. Briner, "International Tax Management," *Management Accounting,* February 1973, p. 50. Reprinted by permission.

21

The Multinational Finance Function

- To describe the multiple facets of the finance function and show how this function fits in the organizational structure of the multinational enterprise.

- To discuss the major internal sources of funds available to the multinational enterprise and show how these funds are managed on a global basis.

- To identify the major financial risks of inflation and exchange rate movements and examine how these risks can be measured and dealt with.

- To compare the strengths and weaknesses of using operating strategies and forward contracts to protect against exchange rate risks.

- To highlight some of the financial aspects of the investment decision.

DOLLAR VOLATILITY[1]

A major problem faced by corporate treasurers during the early to mid-1980s was the volatility of the U.S. dollar. Granted, that period was also a period of intense strength for the dollar as well. However, the volatility seemed to be the major issue, since treasurers had no idea how to plan the use of their firms' financial assets. As was pointed out in the *Wall Street Journal*,

> *In one recent three-week period, the dollar fell 2.2% against the mark and 2.8% against the British pound, only to then reverse course and climb 4.9% against the German currency and 4.5% against the British currency.*

Because of the dollar's strength and volatility, firms were using different approaches to protect liquid assets. Four companies that used four different approaches during the early part of 1984 were Westinghouse Electric Corp., Mack Trucks Inc., Borg-Warner Corp., and General Electric Co.

Westinghouse is a high-technology company that produces products worldwide in such diverse and general product categories as defense, energy, industry and construction, and broadcasting and cable. In addition, it has specialized product areas in beverage bottling, transport, refrigeration, and financing services. Over a quarter of Westinghouse's business is international, and that includes exports as well as foreign manufacturing.

Mack Trucks is a Pennsylvania-based company that manufactures and exports trucks worldwide. In addition, it has some assembly operations outside of the United States.

Borg-Warner is an international manufacturing and services company with operations on six continents. Its major product lines are transportation equipment, chemicals and plastics, protective services, air conditioning, industrial products, and financial services. Borg-Warner exports a sizable amount of product each year, and sales of its foreign manufacturing operations represent 20–25 percent of corporate sales.

Finally, General Electric is a large manufacturing company that derives only about 15 percent of its sales from foreign manufacturing operations. However, it is also one of the largest exporters in the United States with nearly 15 percent of its U.S. revenues coming from exports. It specializes in power systems, consumer products, technical systems, aircraft engines, and a general category called services and materials.

Although the four firms were very different in terms of product lines, they all had one thing in common in early 1984: a strong but volatile dollar that made the management of liquid assets from exports and foreign operations extremely complex. They also came up with different ways to meet their problems.

Westinghouse used the forward market to hedge some of its financial obligations worldwide. As was pointed out in Chapter 8, a forward contract is a contract between a company and its commercial bank to exchange U.S. dollars and foreign currency in the future at an agreed-upon contractual exchange rate. No matter what the future spot rate, the forward rate guarantees an exchange rate at which currencies can be traded. Because of substantial receivables and royalties that it was to receive in the French franc, which was weaker than the dollar during 1983–1984, the Westinghouse treasurer decided to enter into forward contracts to secure the dollar equivalent of its receipts. As a result, the treasurer saved several million dollars.

Mack Truck was faced with a serious competitive situation in Western Europe that was causing pricing problems for its European distributors. To help solve that problem, Mack Truck decided to bill its European distributors in their own currencies so that the distributors needed to worry only about their competitive situation. However, that meant that Mack was faced with the task of managing its exposure, since it would have substantial foreign currency receivables as a result of its export sales. The feeling at Mack was that it was easier to centralize the exposure and deal with it at corporate headquarters and allow the local operations to deal with general business strategy.

Borg-Warner also decided to centralize its foreign exchange exposure but for different reasons. Borg-Warner management feels that the large scale of its international operations allows it to net its exposure worldwide before going into the forward market or money markets to hedge its investments. It can balance off a sterling receivable position in one country, for example, with a sterling payable position in another.

General Electric uses the technique of "leads and lags" to manage its financial assets. For example, GE officials in early 1984 were predicting a strengthening of the Japanese yen in 1984, so it decided to take its yen dividends from Japanese operations and deposit them in yen certificates of deposit to earn interest. When the yen strengthened as anticipated, GE could convert its proceeds into dollars and remit them to the parent company at, it hoped, a greater profit than would have been the case if the dividends had been remitted and invested in the United States or elsewhere.

INTRODUCTION

It is December 8, 1979, and you awaken from a good night's sleep to face a bright, sunny day. After a brisk 5000-meter run, you take a shower and think about the trip coming up at the beginning of the next week to Rio de Janeiro, where you will spend a few days with the treasurer of your Brazilian subsidiary. You have been the Latin American regional treasurer of your firm for only one month. You are looking forward to learning more about the Brazilian operations, which constitute 20 percent of your region's sales and earnings.

As you sit down to breakfast you turn on the news, and the newscaster announces, "Last night, in a break with tradition that has extended back to the early 1970s, the Brazilian government instituted a massive devaluation of the Brazilian cruzeiro." What is your reaction? Do you have to change the new suit on which you just spilled orange juice, or are you confident that your operations have been adequately covered?

The treasury function of an MNE can be exciting and challenging, but it can also be fraught with surprises and headaches. As was pointed out by the treasurer of Volkswagen, "The function of a corporate treasurer is to integrate the various options of maintaining company liquidity. He has to integrate the entire system of cash flow, and he must be in a position to know about future liquidity needs."[2]

Organization of the Finance Function

- Parent-subsidiary relationships
  - complete decentralization at subsidiary level
  - complete centralization at parent level
  - varying degrees of centralization
- Complete decentralization
  - subsidiary is independent of parent.
- Complete centralization
  - parent dominates decision making

To optimize the flow of funds worldwide, the MNE must determine the proper parent-subsidiary relationship with respect to the finance function. There are three distinct patterns of parent-subsidiary relationships: (1) complete decentralization at the subsidiary level, (2) complete centralization at the parent level, and (3) varying degrees of centralization. These are referred to as ignoring the system potential, exploiting the system potential, and compromising with complexity.[3]

In a decentralized situation the subsidiary is fairly independent of the parent. The parent receives reports but generally issues only a few guidelines, especially when foreign sales comprise a small part of total sales and when the parent staff is relatively unfamiliar with the foreign environment. In a centralized situation the parent staff completely dominates planning and decision making, while the subsidiary merely carries out orders. The idea behind this approach is that the more sophisticated parent staff has a better feel for the intricacies of moving funds across many national boundaries in order to serve the needs of the whole system at the greatest profit.

The third approach attempts to use the best aspects of centralization and decentralization by achieving high levels of financial sophistication on both parent and subsidiary levels. Because of this expertise, the subsidiary staff is better able to act within specified guidelines. The parent staff assumes the role of coordinating system activities and monitoring results. To maintain close proximity to foreign financial information sources, many firms have organized regional financial decision-making centers.[4] The parent staff continues to issue guidelines for decision making and coordinates the entire system; however, the financial organization and management functions are turned over to the regional organizations.

As the complexities of the international environment increase, many firms are turning to the third approach described above. U.S. companies such as Chrysler, Tenneco, Universal Oil Products, Honeywell, and CBS have either created or strengthened a regional European treasury function. Usually, the treasurer reports directly to the parent treasury in order to strengthen the centralization of knowledge and decision making.[5]

Volkswagen separates its treasury function into five areas: accounting, banking (cash arrangement), taxes, insurance, and financing. The financing area is in turn broken down into domestic and international.[6] The international area has become even more critical since the addition of VW's Pennsylvania plant to its other overseas facilities in Brazil, Mexico, South Africa, France, and Canada.

Siemens, another German company and one of the world's largest electrical component companies, has production plants around the world. Each foreign subsidiary has an internal treasury department to handle day-to-day matters, but all financing and cash management are done at corporate headquarters in West Germany.[7]

The treasurer of the British firm Imperial Chemical Industries (ICI), one of the largest chemical companies in the world, is responsible for finance, accounting, and taxation. The financial group is divided into the cash management group, three regional groups, and a special duties group. Each operating division, domestic and worldwide, has a finance director who is responsible to the chief executive of the unit. However, since ICI is clearly centralized in the finance function, there is a definite liaison between corporate and divisional treasury personnel.[8] European companies such as the three described above are not as regionalized as their U.S. counterparts because they have relied more on exports than on foreign investment for international expansion.

Internal Sources of Funds

● Funds—working capital or current assets minus current liabilities.

If a firm wants to expand operations or needs additional working capital, it can look to outside sources or to sources within the firm. In the case of the MNE the complexity of internal sources is magnified because of the number of related affiliates and the diversity of environments in which they operate. "Funds" can have many different definitions, and the term usually means cash. However, the term is used in a much broader sense in business and generally refers to working capital, that is, the difference between current assets and current liabilities.

Figure 21.1 illustrates a situation involving a parent firm with two foreign subsidiaries. The parent, as well as the two subsidiaries, may be increasing funds through normal operations. The important thing is to utilize these funds on a firmwide basis. One possibility is the use of loans; the parent could loan funds directly to the French subsidiary, or it could guarantee an outside loan to the Brazilian subsidiary. Another source of funds for the subsidiary is the receipt of more equity capital from the parent. Funds

FIGURE 21.1
Internal Sources of Working Capital

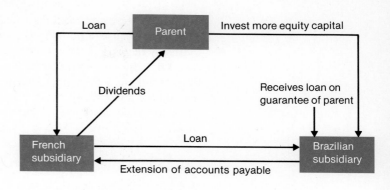

FIGURE 21.1
Internal Sources of Working Capital

can also go from subsidiary to parent. The subsidiary could declare a dividend to the parent as a return to capital or could directly loan cash to the parent.

Intersubsidiary financial links become extremely important as the MNE increases in size and complexity. In addition to loans, goods can travel between subsidiaries, thereby giving rise to receivables and payables. Although intercompany accounts can be used as sources of funds, some firms are against this practice, surprisingly. The following situation illustrates what could happen:

● Intercorporate links are a good source of funds.

> *To prevent intercompany accounts from being used as a financing tool, this particular company charges an interest rate on any account outstanding over thirty days. Since this charge is deducted from the annual bonuses of the executives responsible for the debt, it is a pretty effective deterrent.*
>
> *Nevertheless, the European treasurer of this company has tried to circumvent the rule. A few years ago the company's German subsidiary was short of funds and was reluctant to borrow from German banks at the then-going rate of 8 percent. The European treasurer tried to get the company's French affiliate, which routinely sells about $2 million worth of goods each year to the German affiliate, to forgo payment on its German receivables for nine months, covering itself by borrowing francs locally at 4 percent. The French affiliate agreed, provided the Germans paid a 5 percent interest charge. Since this charge would come out of his bonus, the German treasurer balked and instead borrowed the $2 million from a Belgian bank at 5.5 percent. The German executive saved his bonus, but the company's rigid adherence to the rulebook cost $22,500—the difference between the Belgian and French cost of borrowing $2 million for nine months.* [9]

Other firms have been much more astute at the intercompany use of funds. Olin Corporation used a complex scheme involving British, French, and Italian subsidiaries. The Italian subsidiary needed cash for expansion, but local money was costing 17 to 18 percent. At the same time, Olin's British subsidiary was stuck with a net exposed asset position and a weakening pound, which would have led to foreign exchange losses unless Olin could balance its exposure with sterling debt. Meanwhile, France was trying to encourage the use of non–French franc Eurocurrencies by allowing importers to prepay their trade payables up to one year in advance in other Eurocurrencies. Olin devised a scheme in which its French subsidiary would borrow Eurosterling at 7 percent (thereby balancing the exposure on Olin's British subsidiary) and prepay the Italian subsidiary for merchandise one year in advance. That gave the Italian subsidiary relatively cheap cash to fulfill working capital needs.[10]

Working Capital Management

The previous section emphasized the types of internal sources of funds in MNEs. The following sections look more closely at the problems of managing the components of working capital, such as cash, receivables, inventory, and payables. Working capital management is complicated on an international level because of government restrictions on the flow of funds, differing rates of inflation, and changes in exchange rates.

General principles. Some general principles of working capital management can be discussed without reference to the risks of inflation and exchange rate changes. These principles are in addition to those learned in a domestic setting. Effective cash management is one of the chief concerns of the MNE. Cash management can be decentralized, regionalized, or centralized on a firm level. Decentralization allows the local subsidiary to use excess cash in any way it sees fit. This is the most popular approach for the local manager, especially if he or she is a local partner in a joint venture with the MNE. However, decentralization has the disadvantage of not allowing use of the firm's most liquid asset on a widespread basis. Three important questions need to be raised for effective cash management:

1. What are the local and system needs for cash?
2. How can the cash be withdrawn from the subsidiary and centralized?
3. Once the cash has been centralized, what should be done with it?

● Budgets and forecasts are essential in assessing cash needs.

Before any cash is remitted to a control center, whether on a regional or parent level, local cash needs must be properly assessed. Cash budgets are essential and should reflect the needs for purchasing inventory, paying expenses, and liquidating liabilities. The timing of receivables collections and other cash receipts needs to be forecast over a relevant time frame, generally on a weekly, monthly, semiannual, and annual basis. These forecasts by each of the firm's operations will give the cash manager a feel for local and system cash needs. Since the forecasts will project the excess cash available, the manager will also know how much cash can be invested for short-term profits.

Once local needs have been adequately provided for, the cash manager must decide whether to allow the local manager to invest the excess cash or have it remitted to a central cash pool. If the latter approach is used, means of effecting the transfer must be devised. A cash dividend is the easiest way to distribute cash, but governmental restrictions may reduce the effectiveness of this tool. Exchange controls may preclude the firm's remitting as large a dividend as it would like. In some countries the size of the dividend may be tied to the investment base of the local operation. The parent needs to devise approaches, such as revaluation of fixed assets, that would increase its subsidiary's investment base. In Brazil, for example, dividend remittances in excess of an annual average of 12 percent of the foreign registered capital over a three-year period are subject to a supplementary tax, which ranges from 40 to 60 percent of the amount remitted.[11] Cash can also be remitted through management fees, royalties, and repayment of principal and interest on loans.

Transfer pricing.   Transfer pricing can also be used to move cash. A transfer price is the price on inventory sold between related entities. If the parent sells inventory to the subsidiary, a high transfer price would help concentrate cash in the central cash pool. The same effect would hold if the subsidiary were to sell inventory to the parent at a low transfer price.

In a survey on transfer pricing policies of U.S. firms, it was determined that the most important influences on transfer pricing decisions are (1) market conditions in the foreign country, (2) competition in the foreign country, (3) reasonable profit for the foreign affiliate, (4) U.S. federal income taxes, (5) economic conditions in the foreign country, (6) import restrictions, (7) customs duties, (8) price controls, (9) taxation in the foreign country, and (10) exchange controls.[12] Management of cash flows per se was not considered to be an important variable. However, when factors were grouped together according to common characteristics, influences on cash flows became the second most important factor grouping, after the internal foreign environment.

One problem with making a transfer pricing decision is that multiple objectives could conflict with each other. For example, a high transfer price from parent to subsidiary would concentrate cash in the parent and also increase income because of the higher value placed on sales. However, if the corporate tax rate to the subsidiary is considerably lower than to the parent, it might be better to concentrate profits in the subsidiary to take advantage of the tax situation. This would require an opposite transfer-pricing approach from that described above. Obviously, the overall impact of a transfer-pricing scheme needs to be analyzed before a firm policy is selected.

- Advantage of transfer pricing is that the cash is not subject to withholding taxes and restrictions.
- Arbitrary transfer prices can create difficulties in performance evaluation and with governments.

The advantage of using transfer pricing to move cash is that the cash is not subject to the withholding taxes and restrictions that dividends and royalties are. This is especially true in countries with which the United States does not have a tax treaty and where withholding taxes are relatively high.

Arbitrary transfer pricing can create problems in performance evaluation, as was pointed out in Chapter 19. Subsidiary managers find it very difficult to be motivated in a profit center context when they cannot control or influence pricing decisions. As was noted in Chapter 20, there are also definite obstacles to arbitrary transfer pricing in tax principles. The U.S. Internal Revenue Service requires firms to use some form of arm's length pricing scheme between related entities.

These uses of transfer pricing are considered abuses by some. As was mentioned in a U.N.–sponsored study:

> A parent company may drain profits from a subsidiary when the subsidiary faces tough labor negotiations (thus enabling the subsidiary to argue that it isn't in a position to meet union demands), or when a major share of the subsidiary is owned by another party (perhaps a foreign government), or when the subsidiary's profit remittances to the parent company are blocked by the foreign government's regulations.
>
> Antitrust laws may be evaded through adroit transfer pricing. As part of a market-sharing scheme, a multinational may charge a foreign affiliate such high transfer prices that the affiliate's exports of finished products aren't competitive in international sales. [13]

- Use surplus cash to retire debt, finance new investment, or acquire securities.

Once cash has been remitted to the central pool, the cash manager must decide what to do with it. Obviously, the cash manager would want to be sure that all system needs for cash are met. Then any leftover cash can be used to retire debt in the system, to finance new ventures, or simply to earn a return through the acquisition of marketable securities worldwide.

One successful example of that strategy involves the German pharmaceutical company Bayer. In the late 1970s and early 1980s, Bayer invested billions of dollars in expansion when most other pharmaceuticals were being more cautious. A large portion of the expansion was in the United States. That strategy seems to have paid off, since Bayer is using its healthy cash flow worldwide to retire much of its investment-related liabilities. It also used a lot of that liquidity to acquire inventory denominated in dollars as a hedge against rising prices and the rising dollar.[14]

By purchasing securities in countries other than that of corporate headquarters the firm might be able to diversify its risk/return on investments. As world economies diverge in their growth cycles, the return on investments in strong countries could offset relatively weak returns in stagnant countries. However, as one pension fund manager pointed out, "You're dealing with the stability of foreign governments and with expropriations, [factors] we don't feel we have the ability to cope with."[15] Thus there are risks to investing abroad that must be considered. One of the biggest, of course, is the exchange risk. An appreciation of 20 percent in the local currency value of a stock could be wiped out by a sudden fall in the value of the foreign currency relative to the currency of the investor.

In looking at the risk that one encounters in international business, it is important to consider the nature of the risk, under what circumstances the risk can occur, what the implications are to the firm, and how the risk can best be dealt with. Currency, commercial, and political risks are the major ones encountered. Currency risks encompass both inflation and exchange rate changes. Commercial risks involve the problems of extending or receiving credit and the difficulties of collection or payment of accounts in different currencies. Political risks, as was noted in Chapters 11 and 12, are extensive and cover trade relations, expropriations, and items that could be included as currency risks.

- Currency risks
  - inflation
  - exchange rate changes
- Commercial risks
  - extending and receiving credit
  - collecting and paying accounts in different currencies.
- Political risks
  - trade relations
  - expropriations

Risk Management for Inflation

Inflation occurs in varying degrees in nearly every country in which the MNE operates. Inflation has a tendency to erode the value of financial assets and make financial liabilities more attractive. The latter benefit is softened somewhat by the high interest rates that often accompany loans in countries with high inflation. In Brazil in early 1984, for example, the annualized interest rate on a 90-day cruzeiro loan was 240 percent.

- High inflation and a weak currency go hand in hand.

High-inflation countries tend to have relatively weak currencies, and it turns out that the risk management strategies for inflation and a weak foreign currency are fairly similar. These strategies will be discussed more fully in the next section. The key is to generate large amounts of cash and either get the cash out of the country or invest it in inflation-proof investments.

- Price controls can be circumvented by:
  - modifying product line
  - reintroducing products with new name
  - changing containers

Many companies faced with price controls need to find imaginative product development and pricing strategies to circumvent controls. This may involve slight product modifications and brand name changing in order to effect price rises. Quite frequently, MNEs are so brand-conscious that they refuse to take advantage of this strategy. In a study conducted in Chile it was found that Chilean firms were able to modify product line, reintroduce the product with a new brand name, and circumvent price controls more efficiently than their U.S. counterparts.[16] Where brand image is important, however, this strategy may be impossible.

One multinational firm operating in a highly inflationary Latin American country found that it could get around price controls by introducing a brand name product in a smaller container but listing the product at a significantly higher price. However, it would sell the product for quite a bit less than list price in order to attract sales. Then it could increase the price according to inflationary trends up to the upper list price limit established by the price control authorities.

One of the major problems that the firm faced was trying to correctly estimate inflation. If it predicted inflation at 200 percent and priced accordingly, it would be in serious trouble if inflation was actually 500 percent. It would have underpriced its products and sold them for less than the replacement cost of raw materials.

Risk Management for Exchange Rate Changes

If all exchange rates were fixed in relation to one another, there would be no foreign exchange risks. However, rates are not fixed, and currency values change frequently, as was discussed in Chapters 8 and 9. Instead of one-way changes on a fairly infrequent basis, currencies can fluctuate either up or down.

As was pointed out in Chapter 9, when a country's exchange rate is under pressure, the country may attempt to correct the basic economic problems, it may use cosmetic approaches (such as foreign exchange controls discussed in Chapter 8), or it may allow the value of its currency to change through formal action or through a float. All of these approaches can lead to problems in the financial flows of an MNE.

- Accounting exposure— results from translating foreign currency financial statements into parent currency.

A change in the exchange rate can result in three different exposures for a firm: accounting exposure, transaction exposure, and economic exposure. **Accounting exposure** results from translating foreign currency financial statements into the reporting currency of the parent company. Exposure occurs when the translated value of financial statement accounts changes when the exchange rate changes. This occurs for all accounts translated at the current exchange rate.

- Transaction exposure— amount of receivables and payables changes when exchange rate changes.

Transaction exposure implies that the value of amounts receivable or payable in a foreign currency changes when the exchange rate changes. This differs from accounting exposure in that transaction exposure means that the actual cash paid or received from a transaction changes because of the exchange rate change.

- Economic exposure—the overall change in value of the firm in relation to the change in exchange rate.

Economic exposure is the exposure of the value of the firm to changes in the exchange rate. For example, an exporter could be seriously damaged if its currency increases in value relative to the currency of the importers. Thus economic exposure refers to the future value or worth of the firm.

- Translation exposure:
  - as the rate changes, the value of the exposed accounts changes also.

Translation exposure. As was explained in Chapter 19, foreign currency financial statements are translated into the reporting currency of the parent company for a number of reasons, such as consolidation, performance evaluation, creditors, and taxation. The mechanics of translation were also described in Chapter 19. Exposed accounts—those translated at the balance sheet or current exchange rate—either gain or lose command over the reporting currency. For example, assume that a subsidiary operates in Mexico, where the currency is the peso. The peso, weakened by inflation, depreciates in relation to the dollar from 12.5 pesos/dollar to 20.0 pesos/dollar. The subsidiary's bank account of 100,000 pesos would be worth only $5000 after the depreciation instead of the $8000 original value.

• Translation gain or loss due to exchange rate change is not a cash flow gain or loss.

The combined effect of the exchange rate change on all exposed assets and liabilities is a gain or loss. If the foreign currency financial statements are translated according to the temporal method, the gains or losses are taken directly to the income statement. If the statements are translated according to the current rate method, the gains and losses are taken to a separate component of stockholders' equity. Whichever method is used for translation purposes, it is important to remember that this gain or loss is not a cash flow effect. The cash in the bank in Mexico is only translated, not converted into dollars.

Transactions impact.   The accounting measurement of transactions in foreign currencies was discussed in Chapter 19. The finance difficulty arises because the company has accounts receivable or payable in foreign currency. For example, assume that a U.S. exporter delivers merchandise to a British importer. If the exporter receives payment in dollars, there is no immediate impact if the dollar/sterling exchange rate changes. If payment were to be received in sterling, however, the exporter could be exposed to an exchange gain or loss.

Economic impact.   The economic impact on the firm is difficult to measure, but it is crucial to the operations of the firm in the long run. Aside from the immediate impact described above, there is a long-term impact that involves pricing strategies. The inventory sold to the British importer was probably sold to final users before the exchange rate fluctuated. Future sales would be affected, however. The following example illustrates what could happen.

	Price in Britain	Revenue to exporter
Before change	£1000	$1250
After change		
Invoice in £	£1000	$1230
Invoice in $	£1016.25	$1250

If the merchandise had been invoiced in sterling, the depreciation of sterling would have resulted in a loss of revenue to the exporter. If the merchandise had been invoiced in dollars, the price of the product in Britain would have increased to £1,016.25. In the first case the exporter would have to decide whether to increase the price to £1016.25 to maintain the same level of revenues. In the second case the importer has to decide whether to pass on the higher cost to consumers by increasing prices or absorb the cost through a lower profit margin.

Thus the economic impact includes such issues as the pricing of products, the source and cost of inputs, and the location of investments.

Several firms have noticed the economic effects of exchange rate changes in 1985. Ford Motor Company planned to close down production of tractors in Michigan and start producing the tractors in plants in England and Belgium primarily because of the strong dollar. DuPont expanded production in Britain, France, the Netherlands, West Germany, and Luxembourg rather than in the United States for the same reason.[17]

Key Issues in Risk Management

- Key elements in risk management strategy.

To adequately protect assets against risks from exchange rate fluctuations, it is important for management to (1) define and measure exposure, (2) organize and implement a reporting system that monitors exposure and exchange rate movements, (3) adopt a policy on assigning responsibility for hedging exposure, and (4) formulate a strategy for hedging exposure.

- Translation exposure can be measured by using financial statements to forecast future exposure.

Measurement. Three types of exposure were defined above. Translation exposure is easy to measure, even though it may be difficult to predict. It is usually a static concept representing the financial statements. Forecasts (via pro forma statements) can be used to predict exposure at various points in time in the future. As was mentioned above, the exposed position is net assets when the current rate method is used and net monetary assets when the temporal method is used.

- Transaction exposure can can be measured by determining actual receivables and payables.
- Economic exposure is difficult to measure and requires predicting elasticities of demand.

Transactions exposure is generally static as well. The firm can determine its actual receivable and payable flows from entries already booked in the financial records. Thus it can predict its cash flows in the foreign currency.

Economic exposure is more difficult to measure because it implies that the firm is able to predict elasticities of demand relatively accurately. This is difficult to do. In addition to price elasticities, the firm must be able to predict financial flows that are anticipated but not yet booked. This includes royalties, dividends, and sales and purchases.

- Forecasting exchange rates is complex.
- Forward rates are not an accurate predictor of future spot rates when currencies are fairly volatile.

Forecasting exchange rates. Another key aspect of measurement involves forecasting exchange rates that are applicable to the exposure identified above. Estimating future exchange rates is like using a crystal ball. Approaches range from gut feeling to sophisticated econometric models. Many firms use the forward exchange rate, which was discussed at length in Chapter 9, to approximate future spot rates. This approach is fraught with difficulties, since forward rates of some countries, such as West Germany, Canada, and the United Kingdom, are primarily determined by interest rate differentials rather than by projections of future spot rates. Also, forward markets exist only for currencies of the major industrial countries. In the short run, the period of greatest concern for most treasurers seeking protection, the predictive ability of forward rates is inconclusive. In one study covering three currencies (the British pound, the West German mark, and the Swiss franc) over three months it was found that expected rates differed from actual rates by as much as 10 percent and that movements differed in direction and magnitude. A study conducted on the same three currencies three months later concluded that the forward rate *was* a fairly accurate predictor. The difference was that markets were much more volatile in the first three-month period.[18]

Many econometric models of varying degrees of complexity are used to predict exchange rate movements. Many firms have developed their own models, while others have purchased services from their international bank or from consultants. Predicting movements properly can be just as important and certainly as difficult as measuring the level of exposure. Models basically try to use certain variables, such as levels of foreign exchange reserves, balance-of-payments trends, relative rates of inflation, and interest rates, to help predict the direction and magnitude of exchange rate movements.

As was mentioned above, firms often purchase exchange rate forecasting services from outside consultants. One such consulting firm is Multinational Computer Models, Inc. of Montclair, New Jersey, which offers a variety of services such as currency forecasts, hedging recommendations, and forward contract monitoring.

- Foreign input is important in assessing information.

Reporting system. Once the firm has decided how to define and measure exposure and estimate future exchange rates, it must design, organize, and implement a reporting system that will assist in protection against risk. Because of the nature of the problem, substantial participation from foreign operations must be combined with effective central control. Foreign input is important in order to ensure the quality of information being used in forecasting techniques. Since exchange rates move frequently, it is necessary to receive input from someone who can read the pulse of the country. In addition, the maximum effectiveness of hedging techniques will depend on the cooperation of personnel in the foreign operations.

- Exposure of several entities may offset each other.

A central control of exposure is necessary to eliminate suboptimization. Each individual organizational unit in the firm may be able to define its exposure, but the corporation itself also has an overall exposure. To set hedging policies on a separate entity basis might not take into account the fact that exposures of several entities (i.e., branches, affiliates, subsidiaries, etc.) could be offsetting.

A uniform reporting system should be devised to be used by all units reporting to the MNE. The report should identify the exposed accounts the firm wants to monitor, the exposed position by currency of each account, and the different time periods to be covered. Exposure should be separated into translation and transaction components, and the transaction exposure should be identified by cash inflows and outflows over time.

• Exposure should be considered for the long term as well as the short term.

The time periods to be covered depend upon the firm. One possibility is to look at long- as well as short-run flows. For example, staggered periods (30, 60, and 90 days; six months, nine months, and twelve months; and two, three, and four years) could be considered. The reason for the longer time frame is that operating commitments, such as plant construction and production runs, are fairly long-run decisions.[19] In identifying exposed positions by currency at each point in time, it would be good to include ranges with subjective probabilities, since frequency inevitably involves an element of error.

Once each basic reporting unit has identified its exposure, this should be sent to the next organizational level for a preliminary consolidation. That level may be a regional headquarters (such as Latin America or Europe) or a product division. The organizational structure of the firm will determine what that level is. The preliminary consolidation will allow the region or division to determine exposure by account and by currency for each time period. These reports should be routine, periodic, and standardized to ensure comparability and timeliness in formulating strategies. The final reporting should be at the corporate level. At that level, corporate exposure can be determined and strategies identified that will be in the best interests of the corporation as a whole.

Hedging policy. An important issue is to decide at what level hedging strategies will be decided on and implemented. To achieve maximum effectiveness in hedging, policies need to be established at the corporate level. With a larger overview of corporate exposure and the cost and feasibility of different strategies at different levels in the firm, the corporate treasury should be able to design and implement a cost-effective program for exposure management. As a firm increases in size and complexity, it may have to decentralize some decisions in order to increase flexibility and speed of reaction to a more rapidly changing international monetary environment. However, such decentralization should stay within a well-defined policy that has been established at the corporate level.

As was pointed out in Chapter 19, performance evaluation is complicated by foreign currencies. If hedging decisions are to be centralized and implemented at the corporate level, corporate personnel should be held accountable for foreign exchange losses and for material deviation from budgeted dollar operating results.

Hedging strategies. Once a firm has identified its level of exposure, it can hedge or protect its position from exchange rate changes. There are numerous strategies that a firm could adopt to protect itself. Each strategy has cost/benefit implications as well as operational concerns. The safest position to be in is a balanced position, in which exposed assets equal exposed liabilities. This may not be very easy. Generally, a firm will try to minimize exposure as much as possible through operational policies and then remain unhedged or enter into contractual arrangements (forward contracts) for the remainder.

To reduce exposure through operational strategies the working capital needs of the subsidiary must be determined. Although it might be wise to collect receivables as fast as possible in an inflationary country where the local currency is expected to depreciate, the firm has to consider the competitive implications of not extending credit.

In reality, working capital management under exchange risk assumes that currency values move in one direction. A weak-currency country generally, although not always, suffers from inflation. The approach to protecting assets in the face of currency depreciation also applies to protection against inflation. Inflation erodes the purchasing power of local currency, whereas depreciation erodes the foreign currency equivalent.

- **Weak currency situation**
  - **quick collection of receivables**
  - **cash should be invested**
  - **pay liabilities at latest date**

In the weak-currency situation, cash should be remitted to the parent as fast as possible or invested locally in something that appreciates in value, such as fixed assets. Accounts receivable should be collected as quickly as possible when they are denominated in the local currency and stretched out when denominated in a stronger currency. Liabilities should be treated in just the opposite manner.

A policy for inventory is difficult to determine. If inventory is considered to be exposed, it should be kept at a working level that is as low as possible. However, since its value usually increases through price rises, it can be a successful hedge against inflation and exchange rate moves. If the inventory is imported, it should be stocked before a depreciation, since it will cost more local currency after the change to purchase the same amount in foreign currency. Where price controls are in effect or where there is strong competition, the subsidiary may not be able to increase the price of inventory. In this situation, inventory can be treated in the same way as cash and receivables. These principles can be reversed when an appreciation is predicted—that is, keep cash and receivables high, and liquidate debt as rapidly as possible. However, the safest approach is to keep the net exposed position as low as possible.

- **Borrowing locally provides a trade-off between the loss from exchange rate variations and the cost of borrowing.**

The use of debt to balance exposure is an interesting phenomenon. Many firms have adopted a "borrow locally" strategy, especially in weak-currency countries. One problem is that interest rates in weak-currency countries tend to be quite high. There must be a trade-off between the cost of borrowing and the potential loss from exchange rate variations. Many firms operating in Mexico suffered huge translation losses when the peso devalued vis-à-vis the dollar in 1976 because of their net exposed asset position. This was because they were primarily dollar-financed rather than peso-financed. The dollar debt must also be paid back by peso earnings, so firms will have to generate higher revenues to purchase the more expensive dollars.

In Brazil in the late 1970s, firms had been borrowing in dollars in the Eurodollar market because of cheaper rates relative to cruzeiro rates. As the threat of devaluation became more ominous, they quickly got rid of dollar debt and began borrowing cruzeiros—even at high interest rates.

Protecting against loss from transaction exposure becomes very complex. In dealing with foreign customers it is always safest to denominate the transaction in one's own currency. The alternative would be to denominate purchases in a weaker currency and sales in a stronger currency. If forced to make purchases in a strong currency and sales in a weak currency, the firm could resort to contractual measures or try to balance its inflows and outflows through more astute sales and purchasing strategies.

Because of the decline of the dollar in 1977, many U.S. companies were being pressured by foreign suppliers to make payments in the suppliers' currencies, which were generally stronger than the dollar. Many companies were able to resist this pressure owing to their market strength. Others were able to share the risk.

- Lead strategy—collect or pay early.
- Lag strategy—collect or pay late.

Another strategy, known as "leads and lags," is often used to protect cash flows among related entities, such as a parent and its subsidiaries. The **lead strategy** involves collecting foreign currency receivables before they are due when the foreign currency is expected to weaken and paying foreign currency payables before they are due when the foreign currency is expected to strengthen. A **lag strategy** means that a firm will delay receiving foreign currency receivables if that currency is expected to strengthen and delay payables when that currency is expected to weaken.

It is much easier to use leads and lags among related entities in which a central corporate financial officer can spot the potential gains and implement a policy. The payables and receivables mentioned above could relate to intracompany purchases and sales, dividends, debt principal and interest, fees, royalties, and so on.

- Forward contract: used to lock in exchange rates for future transactions.

Sometimes, however, government controls can eliminate the use of leads and lags. When François Mitterrand became President of France in 1981, he instituted a rule that within one month of shipment, all exporters in France must exchange, for francs, foreign currency generated by those exports—even if the payment had not been made. In the case of a weak franc, most exporters would prefer to lag receipt of payment as long as feasible; that was not possible.

In addition to the operational strategies mentioned above, a firm could resort to contractual arrangements. The major approach, which was discussed at length in Chapter 9, is the forward contract. Without repeating all of the possibilities and examples in that chapter, it would be good to mention the general impact of using forward contracts to hedge against transaction exposure. In transaction exposure, an exporter might expect to receive foreign currency at some point in the future. Risk can be eliminated by entering into a contract to sell foreign currency at that same point in the future and be guaranteed the contract rate.

Money market: borrow foreign currency to hedge on exposure.

In addition to the forward market an MNE could use the money market to protect itself. Assume that a U.S. firm has a British subsidiary with a net exposed asset position and the firm expects the British pound to weaken. The parent could borrow an amount in sterling equal to the amount of exposure and invest the cash in dollars for the relevant exposure period. When the sterling weakens, the loss on exposure will be offset by the gain on the sterling loan. At the maturity of the loan the firm can cash in its dollar investment and use the proceeds to buy sterling to pay off the Eurocurrency loan. If the interest on the dollar investment exceeds the interest on the sterling loan, the firm will gain from the transaction.

Once a firm has identified its exposure and investigated the major hedging operations open to it, how does it decide what to do? One MNE believes that the most important way to hedge anticipated losses is to use aggressive pricing policies to keep profits high. Other firms are much more aggressive in their hedging strategies. The level of sophistication in analysis varies considerably, however.

FINANCIAL ASPECTS OF THE INVESTMENT DECISION

The foreign investment decision was discussed fairly extensively in Chapter 16. However, a few additional financial issues should be mentioned. As an MNE considers investing abroad, many financing options are available to it, as was explained in Chapter 10. The parent company needs to consider the mix of debt and equity that it will use. There are at least two basic reasons why the debt-equity ratio for a foreign subsidiary may differ from that of the parent. The first is that the attitude toward the debt-equity ratio in the host country may differ from that in the parent country. Firms in Japan and West Germany, for example, tend to be more highly leveraged than their U.S. counterparts. This means that they rely much more on debt than on equity capital.

Another reason is that different tax rates, dividend remission policies, and exchange controls may cause a firm to rely more on debt in some situations and on equity in others. The debt-equity ratio of the MNE will be a weighted average of the debt-equity ratios of all entities in the corporate structure.

Discounted cash flows are often used to compare and evaluate investment projects. Several aspects of capital budgeting that are unique to foreign project assessment are the following:

Unique international elements in the foreign investment decision.

1. A need exists to distinguish between project cash flows and parent cash flows.

2. Because of differing tax systems, constraints on financial flows, local norms, and differences in financial markets and institutions, financing and remittance of funds to the parent firm must be explicitly recognized.

3. Differential rates of national inflation can be important in changing competitive positions and thereby cash flows over time.

4. Foreign exchange rate changes may alter the competitive position of a foreign affiliate.

5. Foreign exchange rate changes that are not matched by differential national inflation rates may alter the value of cash flows from affiliate to parent and vice versa.

6. Segmented national capital markets may create an opportunity for financial gains or may lead to additional financial costs.

7. Political risks can drastically reduce the value of a foreign investment.

8. Terminal value is difficult to estimate because of possible divergent market values of a project to potential purchasers from the host, parent, or third countries.[20]

It is important for the parent to compare the net present value or internal rate of return of a project with that of other parent projects. At the same time, it should compare the project with others available in the host country.

Cash flows need to be viewed from two perspectives: the total flows available to the local operations and the cash available to the parent. The outflows to the parent are important to consider in light of the original investment made, especially if the investment was with parent funds. The cost of capital issue relates to the discussion above on the debt-equity ratio of the subsidiary. The parent may find that the cost of raising debt and equity funds might increase as it expands into riskier environments. That will depend on the risk return characteristics of investors and creditors and will certainly impact the attractiveness of a foreign project.

Finally, foreign political and exchange risks must be considered carefully. The best approach is to adjust forecasted cash outflows to various scenarios representing different levels of risk.

SUMMARY

* The finance or treasury function deals primarily with (1) the generation of funds for operating needs and expansion, (2) the management of working capital, and (3) the financial aspects of the foreign investment decision process.

* Three distinct patterns of parent-subsidiary relationships have surfaced with respect to the finance function: (1) complete decentralization at

the subsidiary level, (2) complete decentralization at the parent level, and (3) varying degrees of centralization.

- The major sources of internal funds for an MNE are intersubsidiary loans, loans from parent to subsidiaries, dividends, royalties, management fees, the purchase and sale of inventory, and equity from the parent to subsidiaries.

- Cash management involves determining local and system needs for cash, methods of centralizing cash, and uses for cash.

- Transfer prices (prices on goods and services sold between related entities) can be used to move cash from country to country without concern for many of the problems facing other types of flows.

- Inflation has the tendency to erode the value of financial assets and make liabilities more attractive.

- Accounts are exposed to an exchange gain or loss if their value changes when exchange rates change.

- Fluctuating exchange rates can cause the parent currency equivalent of foreign currency receivables or payables to go up or down, leading to cash flow gains or losses.

- Economic exposure occurs when the source of inputs, external markets, and operating policies are affected by exchange rate changes.

- Foreign exchange risk management involves defining and measuring exposure, setting up a good monitoring and reporting system, adopting a policy to assign responsibility for exposure management, and formulating a strategy for hedging exposure.

- A uniform reporting system and central control of exposure are important to ensure adequate protection.

- A firm can protect its position through operational strategies or financial market arrangements.

- When deciding to invest abroad, a firm needs to consider its optimal debt-equity ratio, consider local currency and investor currency rates of return, identify cash flows unique to foreign investment, calculate a multinational cost of capital, and offset foreign political and exchange risks.

CASE — WORLD TECHNOLOGIES PLC IN SOUTH AFRICA[21]

It is mid-November 1985, and Gary McKinnon, Vice President of Finance of World Technologies PLC, a Scottish high tech firm with a large manufacturing facility in South Africa, is getting very nervous. WT has been producing very profitably in South Africa for over two decades. However, it is becoming more and more difficult to get money out of South Africa, and McKinnon is considering recommending to the Board of Directors that WT sell its interest in the South African operations. Furthermore, Nittany Enterprises, a large U.S. conglomerate, bought a 25% interest in WT last year and is beginning to put more pressure on WT management in terms of its involvement in South Africa.

As companies invest abroad, they need to be concerned about the long-run potential of their operations as well as the short-run returns through dividend remissions. South Africa has long been considered a good place to invest in Africa because of its relatively large market size. In terms of population, South Africa ranks just behind Nigeria, Egypt, and Ethiopia. However, its per capita GNP is the largest in Africa. The main attraction of South Africa has been the incredibly high rate of return that companies can earn, owing largely to low labor costs and mineral wealth. The relatively large market still allows the firms to achieve economies of scale in production while taking advantage of the low labor costs.

However, the situation has deteriorated rapidly in the past several months. The system of apartheid, which has resulted in a political, social, and economic separation of blacks and whites, has been a part of South Africa for decades, and change has been slow in coming. However, the opposition has begun to galvanize around the concept of one man, one vote. The black nationalists will only settle for total voting rights, whereas the white government refuses that concept at all costs. Rioting has left hundreds dead and has heightened the uncertainty of South Africa's political future. The African National Congress (ANC), the outlawed political party that is the black majority's largest representative body, is totally against capitalism and would nationalize all industry, whether domestic or foreign owned.

The economic situation has deteriorated as well. Inflation is running at over 16 percent on an annual basis, industrial output during the first quarter of 1985 was 7 percent lower than it was a year earlier, and GNP has been stagnant since 1980. GNP is expected to drop by 2.5 percent in 1985.

Due to the crisis, the foreign exchange markets have been betting against the South African rand. Since early 1984, the rand has fallen significantly against both the U.S. dollar and the British pound. The exchange rate began to even out in mid-1985, but it began to fall in late August as the political uncertainty increased. Capital flight of over $2 billion had taken place during the first three quarters of 1985. Two-thirds of South Africa's $17 billion in debt is short-term, which places even greater pressure on the government.

Another source of pressure has been the reaction of U.S. firms. Over 300 U.S. companies have investments of around $2.5 billion in South Africa, but several have begun to divest. Apple Computer suspended all operations in August and closed down on October 1; Coca-Cola sold a majority interest in its bottling operation in 1985 and plans to transfer control over a two year period; Ford Motor Company merged its automobile operations with a South African company, reduced its stake to 40 percent, and transferred management control; International Harvester sold its truck operations in August. In all, 18 companies had divested all or significant portions of their operations during the first three quarters of 1985.

Although WT is a British firm, it is beginning to feel more and more pressure from its U.S. investors, who in turn are feeling more pressure from their shareholders. WT does not feel that it has to adopt the Sullivan Principles (a code of conduct developed by Reverend Leon Sullivan that U.S. firms are encouraged to adopt) since it is not a U.S. firm, but Nittany Enterprises is starting to put on the heat.

WT has found that the regulations influencing cash flows have changed several times over the past decades. In 1960, the South African government responded to extensive riots by freezing the proceeds of divestment sales by nonresidents so that foreign investors would not pull out of the country. Eventually, the freeze was lifted, but companies were required to use the new financial rand—which was valued at a hefty discount from the commercial rand—for repatriation of equity capital. The discount varied from time to time depending on supply and demand conditions for the financial rand. When General Tire & Rubber Co. was forced by the U.S. government to sell its South African operations because of its dealings with South Africa's security forces, it waited for the spread between the commercial and financial rands to narrow as much as possible before it sold. At that time the discount was 28 percent for one block of stock and 21 percent for another.

In 1979 the South African government decided to allow foreigners to use the financial rand market to bring in new equity capital as a means of spurring investment. International Harvester, which wanted to increase the equity capital in its South African subsidiary, brought in 5.6 million rands at a cost of only $5 million, compared with the $6.8 million it would have cost at the commercial rate. Volkswagen, which waited for the spread between rates to widen to 30–40 percent, brought in 34 million rands.

Eventually in 1983, the two-tier exchange rate was abolished and controls relaxed. In early 1985, exchange control permission was not required for the inward transfer of fixed capital to South Africa. Dividends and branch profits could be repatriated without restriction provided that such transfers were financed by available cash funds. Royalties, technical service fees, and management fees were restricted and required approval by the government. Management fees were virtually impossible to obtain permission for.

The political tensions in July and August resulted in some changes, however. South African President Pieter Botha's speech on August 15 shattered any hopes of an amicable solution to the problems. In response, the international banks announced at the end of August that they were not going to roll over South African loans. The Central Bank closed and reopened on September 2 with the announcement that it was once again instituting a two-tiered exchange rate system. Under the system, which was basically the same as the one in operation from January 1979 to early 1983, the commercial rand would be used for trade transactions, loan transactions, and dividend and interest payments. Other transactions (such as those relating to equity transactions) would be conducted at the financial rate, which trades at a discount to the commercial rand.

QUESTIONS

1. What are some of the major risks that WT faces in its operations in South Africa?
2. Discuss the major factors that you think McKinnon should consider as he decides what to recommend to the Board.
3. What affect would the two-tiered exchange-rate system have on cash-flow projections for any firm deciding to invest in South Africa?
4. What difficulties would the two-tiered system have on the different elements of the foreign exchange exposure system discussed in the chapter?

NOTES

1. Data for the case were taken from Michael R. Sesit, "Treasurers of Multinationals Plan Ways to Handle Currency Swings," *The Wall Street Journal,* January 24, 1984, p. 35; and the annual reports of the companies involved.

2. Nigel Bance, "The Man Who Manages the Finances of Europe's Largest Car Manufacturer," *Euromoney,* May 1976, p. 20.

3. Sidney M. Robbins and Robert B. Stobaugh, *Money in the Multinational Enterprise* (New York: Basic Books, 1973), pp. 37–48.

4. John T. Wooster and G. Richard Thoman, "New Financial Priorities for MNCs," *Harvard Business Review,* May–June 1974, pp. 58–68.

5. Andreas R. Prindl, "Guidelines for MNC Money Managers," *Harvard Business Review,* January–February 1976, p. 78.

6. Bance, *op. cit.,* p. 21.

7. Nigel Bance, "How Siemens Runs Its Treasury," *Euromoney,* April 1977, p. 71.

8. Nigel Bance, "Treasurer Clements: Keeping ICI's Access to Capital Markets," *Euromoney,* November 1977, p. 128.

9. "How the Multinationals Play the Money Game," *Fortune,* August 1973, p. 60.

10. "How Corporations Save by Borrowing in Sterling," *Business Week,* April 24, 1978, p. 114; see also "How a French Loophole Helps Olin Gain," *Business Week,* March 6, 1978, pp. 106–108.

11. Ernst & Whinney, *Foreign Exchange Rates and Restrictions,* (New York: Ernst & Whinney International Operations, January 1984.)

12. Jane O. Burns, "Transfer Pricing Decisions in U.S. Multinational Corporations," *Journal of International Business Studies,* Vol. 11, No. 2, Fall 1980, p. 25.

13. William M. Carley, "Investigations Beset Multinational Firms, with Stress on Pricing," *Wall Street Journal,* December 19, 1975, p. 1.

14. "Bayer: Why the High Dollar Is No Headache," *Business Week,* October 29, 1984, p. 53.

15. Daniel Hertzberg, "Pension Managers Invest More Overseas, Aware of Risks but Hopeful About Profits," *Wall Street Journal,* July 2, 1981, p. 44.

16. Richard W. Wright, "Organizational Ambiente: Management and Environment in Chile," *Academy of Management Journal,* March 1971, p. 72.

17. Gary Putka, "Strong Dollar Has Led U.S. Firms to Transfer Production Overseas," *The Wall Street Journal,* April 9, 1985, p. 1.

18. Business International Corporation, *Solving International Financial and Currency Problems* (New York: BIC, 1976), pp. 13–15.

19. Helmut Hagemann, "Anticipate Your Long-Term Foreign Exchange Risks," *Harvard Business Review,* March–April 1977, p. 82.

20. David K. Eiteman and Arthur I. Stonehill, *Multinational Business Finance* 3rd ed. (Reading, Mass.: Addison-Wesley, 1982), pp. 340–341.

21. Data for the case were taken from *Business Week,* "A Cheap Way to Invest in South Africa" November 26, 1979, pp. 104–105, *Business Week,* "South Africa's foot dragging vexes U.S. Companies" October 20, 1980, pp. 56–58, 108; *Business Week,* "How S. Africa Is Fanning Union Unrest" November 17, 1980, p. 53; Ernst & Whinney, *Foreign Exchange Rates and Restrictions* (New York: Ernst & Whinney International Operations, January 1981.) Manufacturers Hanover Trust, *Foreign Exchange Review,* Volume 9, No. 38 (New York: Manufacturers Hanover Trust, September 1985), p. 3. Ernst & Whinney, *1984 Foreign Exchange Rates and Restrictions* (New York: Ernst & Whinney International Operations, December 31, 1984), p. 14. Jonathan Kapstein, John Hoerr, and Elizabeth Weiner, "Leaving South Africa," *Business Week,* 23 September 1985, pp. 104–112. Jim Jones, Sarah Bartlett, and Elizabeth Weiner, "The Crisis Spills Into The Markets," *Business Week,* 9 September 1985, pp. 28–29.

22

Management Personnel

- To emphasize the crucial importance of qualified managers in the success of global operations.
- To enumerate the duties and conditions that necessitate different qualifications for international managers.
- To recognize the importance that nationality plays in the selection of managers in multinational firms.
- To evaluate the specific considerations and problems that occur when managers are transferred internationally.
- To examine the major alternatives in recruitment, selection, training, and compensation of international managers.

of fundamental English with a vocabulary of only 800 words and ensures that its publications use only these words.[6]

These trends should not imply that there is no advantage for an international manager in learning languages other than English. Nor does it imply that all transactions can be conducted in English. A working knowledge of the language spoken where one is operating can help in adapting to the foreign country as well as gaining acceptance by people there. However, unless fully fluent in a common language, managers should consider employing good interpreters when attempting serious discussions where the exact nuances of words and expressions are very important, even though this alternative may make it more difficult to observe nonverbal communications.

Isolation

- Less access to staff specialists
- Headquarters personnel away for extended periods of time

The manager in a foreign subsidiary may also face greater isolation in the job. Many staff functions are eliminated abroad because of the cost of duplication. At the home operation a manager can very easily walk to the next office or make a few telephone calls to get advice from specialists on problems that arise. The manager abroad may not have these specialists close at hand. Because of the cost and time to make overseas calls and cables, he or she ends up relying much more heavily on personal judgment in making decisions.

Headquarters personnel traveling abroad on assignments may face the same isolation problems as do the managers in the foreign subsidiaries. However, these managers may face more isolation in their personal lives. A perusal of advertisements for these positions indicates that at least 50 percent foreign travel is not uncommon. Although many domestic positions require commensurate traveling, the trips are apt to be of shorter duration because of the shorter time and lower expense of returning home for weekends.

NATIONALITY CHOICE FOR MANAGERS

Key Factors

International firms commonly categorize managers as **locals** (citizens of the countries where they are working) or **expatriates** (noncitizens). The expatriate group is further categorized as **home country nationals** and **third-country nationals.** These are, respectively, citizens of the country where the company is headquartered and citizens neither of the country where they are working nor of the headquarters country of the firm. The following discussion focuses on permanent or long-term assignments rather than short assignments such as business trips.

- If the foreign operating environment is very different, knowledge of environment is very important
- If worldwide uniformity is sought, knowledge of company practices is very important

Knowledge of the environment. In discussing the important role the environment plays, the vice-president of a plastics company reasoned that "it is more practical to export technical expertise and management philosophy than it is to train U.S. personnel in the subtleties of local national customs and practices, which require years of intimate contact."[7] Ideally, a firm should staff with managers who understand both the environment and the company's business specific characteristics, but this ideal combination is not always available. Whether one makes a trade-off in favor of environmental or technical knowledge will depend on several factors. The greater the difference in operating environment from the home country, the more important it is to have management that is knowledgeable about local conditions. Conversely, the greater the need for worldwide uniformity of methods and adherence to directives from the corporate headquarters, the more important it is to have local management personnel who are familiar with the usual operating methods of the firm.

- If top jobs are given only to expatriates, it may be hard to attract and keep good locals

Incentives to local personnel. Proponents of employing local nationals sometimes argue that the possibility of advancement provides an incentive to employees to perform well. Without this incentive, it is contended, they may seek employment with other firms. Opponents argue that practices that restrict the best qualified people, regardless of nationality, from positions are even more damaging to employee motivation. Anyone in the organization, they say, should have the opportunity to move up to any post, including positions in the corporate headquarters. It appears that, as yet, there is very little implementation of this one-world personnel philosophy. One study of a group of U.S. MNEs showed that although more than half of their worldwide managers were non-U.S. nationals, over 90 percent of the positions at the top four levels of the corporate hierarachy were filled by U.S. nationals. The conclusion was that part of the disparity was because foreigners were blocked from top levels.[8] At the subsidiary level as well, there is evidence that managers are often blocked from promotion because of nationality.[9]

- Locals in management may help sales and morale; however,
  - may get more involved in politics

The local image. It may sometimes be deemed useful to create as much of a local image as possible in foreign operations. This is particularly true when animosity toward foreign-controlled operations could cause loss of business, strict governmental regulations, or damage or loss of company properties. One way of helping to create a local image is to staff as much as possible with local employees who, presumably, will set company policies that are consistent with the current objectives of the area of operations.

This local image may play a role in employee morale as well. Most employees in subsidiaries have no preference as to the nationality of their supervisors. However, a substantial minority prefer to work for someone from their own country.[10] Local managers, on the other hand, are more prone than expatriates to become involved in local politics. This may have either positive or negative effects on the firm's operations, depending on whether they pick the "right" or "wrong" political party. A further problem is that if the national managers are no longer needed or wanted in their jobs, there may be legal or social restrictions that prevent termination of their employment. The use of expatriate management may thus be a risk avoidance strategy.

- More expensive to bring in expatriates

Cost. It is usually less costly to use local managers than to transfer people abroad. Firms typically pay for moving expenses (including customs duties on household effects) and settling-in expenses, such as the cost of adapting appliances to foreign electrical systems. Many companies even purchase houses from executives to ease their move overseas. It may be necessary to pay storage expenses for goods not shipped abroad, since employers may balk at moving pianos, antiques, boats, and hobby equipment. Furthermore, furniture may simply not fit in the foreign housing. U.S. companies operating in Japan, for example, often purchase local furniture for their managers who are transferred to Japan, since U.S.-style furniture simply will not fit many of the low-ceilinged, small rooms that are typical in Japan. It is also generally more expensive to maintain an expatriate than a local manager after the transfer. This problem will be discussed more fully later in the chapter.

- Permission to use expatriates may be slow or difficult to obtain

Legal impediments to transfers. Every government has laws favoring employment of its own citizens. These restrictions may simply prohibit foreign entry for specific jobs. The restrictions are usually more stringent on lower-level positions because countries seek openings for their unskilled and semi-skilled workers, who tend to have a higher unemployment rate. Recently, some governments have become more strict about the entry of foreign managers because they want more control to be vested locally.

Sometimes permission for cross-national transfers may be given—but only after such a long delay that firms are forced to fill positions, at least on a temporary basis, with local personnel.

Since government regulations and their enforcement may change drastically and quickly, considerable uncertainty is created. During 1980, for example, the United States began taking from forty to sixty days to authorize visas for Japanese supervisory officers to visit their American subsidiaries, whereas approval had previously taken from ten days to three weeks.[11]

- People transferred from headquarters more likely know headquarters policies

Control. In Chapter 17 we showed that MNEs use both transfers and visits by headquarters staff to subsidiaries for controlling the foreign operations and coordinating organizational development. These goals are accomplished because the people who are transferred are used to doing things the headquarters' way and because frequent transfers let them increase their knowledge of the global network of the company.[12] Since most of the people at headquarters are home country nationals, using them for control reduces the use of local nationals.

Long-term objectives. It has been observed that, since people transferred to subsidiaries usually expect to be there for only a few years, they are more anxious than local nationals to choose short-term projects that will materialize during their tenure in the foreign location.[13] In producing highly visible and measurable results that help satisfy personal advancement needs when the foreign assignment is terminated, they may not be best serving the longer-range corporate goals. Local nationals who stay on for a longer duration may therefore take more heed of long-term objectives because of the probability of still working there when the instituted practices reach fruition.

- Expatriates may take shorter-term perspectives

Management development. Many MNEs transfer foreigners into their home country operations and transfer home country nationals abroad to train them and to give them knowledge about the overall corporate system.[14] In firms with specialized activities only in certain countries (extraction separated from manufacturing, for example, or basic research and development separate from applied), long-term foreign assignments may be the only means of developing a manager's integrative competence. These moves also enhance managers' ability to work in a variety of social systems and are therefore valuable training for ultimate corporate responsibility, including domestic and foreign operations.

- Multicountry experience gives upward moving managers new perspectives

Home Country versus Third-Country National

Approximately 150,000 U.S. nationals working abroad file income tax returns.[15] Most estimates indicate that about two thirds of these are managers with MNEs. Since the value of direct foreign investments by non-U.S. MNEs approximates those with U.S. ownership, one can assume that the non-U.S. MNEs transfer a similar number of their own nationals abroad. Increasingly, firms are considering the option of sending a national of a third country abroad instead of a home country national.

Whereas the number of Americans employed overseas by American MNEs essentially did not change during the 1970s, the number of third-country nationals increased 150 percent to about 40,000.[16] Certain factors help to explain the actual and ideal employment of one versus the other.

Transfer decision process. A study of international transfers indicated that the decision maker, who is usually someone in the home country, generally seeks someone not only who is qualified but whose performance has been observed personally.[17] The decision maker naturally believes that this per-

- Decision makers more prone to staff foreign operations with people they know
  - now know more local managers

sonal knowledge will reduce the risk of making a wrong decision. Since foreign operations are generally more independent of corporate headquarters than domestic facilities of comparable size, there is a greater chance that a home country national rather than a foreign national will be seriously considered for a cross-national transfer. With recent improvements in travel and communications the foreign national has been exposed more to corporate personnel and thus is increasingly employed as an expatriate.

Qualifications. Most advances in technology, product, and operating procedures originate in the home country and are transferred into foreign operations at some later time. Since the use of expatriates in foreign facilities is dictated in part by a desire to infuse new methods, the personnel with recent home country experience (usually home country citizens) are apt to have the desired qualifications.

In both technical and personal adaptive qualifications, third-country nationals might be expected in some instances to perform better than home country expatriates. For example, a U.S. company used U.S. personnel to design and manage a plant in Peru until local managers could be trained. Several years later, the firm decided to commence manufacturing in Mexico. It was felt that the new plant in Mexico should more closely resemble the operations in Peru than those in the United States in terms of size, product qualities, and factor inputs. Therefore Peruvian managers were used effectively in planning, start-up, and early operating phases in Mexico. The similar language and background facilitated the adaptiveness of the Peruvians and their families in Mexico.

TRANSFER CONSIDERATIONS

Thus far the discussion has centered around nationality as a criterion for selecting managers for foreign subsidiaries. While this may be very important, individual differences must, of course, be taken into account.

Consideration of Local Prejudices

Certain individuals have in the past been excluded from consideration for transfer simply because they have characteristics that might render them ineffective in given circumstances. These characteristics had little to do with ability, but rather depended on the attitudes of people with whom the individual would have had to deal. A black manager in South Africa, a Jewish manager in Libya, a very young manager in Japan, or a female manager in Saudi Arabia, for example, would very likely encounter insurmountable problems with employees, suppliers, and customers.

There are some rational reasons for considering the acceptability factor

Margin notes:

• Third-country national may be more knowledgeable of
  • language
  • operating adjustments

• Prejudice may exist locally toward some group
  • adds problem if expatriate from discriminated group
• May be able to minimize effects of adverse attitudes
  • MNEs may overreact

in transfers because expatriates may encounter some acceptance problems regardless of who they are. Adding to these problems may compound the difficulties. For instance, it usually takes time to gain recognition of one's personal authority, and the expatriate may not be there long enough. Local employees may feel that the best jobs are given to overpaid foreigners. The expatriate may have to make unpopular decisions in order to meet global objectives. Or local management may have had experiences with expatriates who made short-term decisions and left before dealing with the longer-term implications.[18] If one adds negative stereotypes to these attitudes, it may be very difficult for the expatriate to succeed. Take stereotypes of women, for example: They should not give orders to men, they are temperamental, their place is in the home. In Western Europe there are very few women in managerial jobs. At best, women fill about 13 percent of the management positions in Portugal and Switzerland, and they fill only about 6 percent in Spain and the Netherlands.[19] Studies of managers' attitudes in MNE subsidiaries in Western Europe also indicate that about 40 percent of respondents feel that even well-qualified women will not be able to succeed in high-level management positions in their operations. This is because of such reasons as "clients will not accept them" and "employees will not take them seriously." This same study suggested means to improve the acceptability of women as expatriates. These included the selection of very well qualified older, midcareer women who could command more authority; the advance dissemination of information concerning the high qualifications; the placement of expatriate women in locations where there are already some local women in management positions; and the establishment of longer than normal assignments (e.g., seven or eight years) in order to develop role models of acceptance.[20]

But do companies overreact to these possible acceptance problems? Perhaps so. A study of 686 U.S. and Canadian companies indicated that only about 3 percent of their expatriates were women.[21] Yet there are women who have succeeded as expatriates in bastions of male management domination, such as within Japan.[22]

Technical Competence

• Usually the most important attribute

The person who is transferred to a foreign country on a regular assignment must be technically competent in the conduct of given tasks to gain the respect of fellow workers. One must make a distinction between a regular and a training assignment; in the latter, local personnel assume that the transferee is in their country temporarily to learn rather than to take responsibilities for company performance. For a regular assignment, however, local employees will resent someone coming in from a foreign country (usually at higher compensation) who, they feel, can do the job no better than themselves. The opinions of senior international executives who make transfer decisions, expatriate managers themselves, and local managers with whom expatriates will work confirm that job ability factors are the most important determinants of success or failure in overseas assignments.[23] Not only must the expatriate know the technical necessities of the tasks as performed in the home country, he or she must also be able to adapt to variations in facilities and technologies due to different levels of economic and industrial development. Some of the most common of these are scaled-down plants and equipment, varying standards of productivity, lack of efficient internal distribution, nonavailability of credit, and restrictions on type of communications media selected.

Adaptiveness

- People who don't want foreign assignments may not adapt well to them

Many individuals do not want foreign assignments and would probably not function well in them. An international move usually means a great disruption of the person's way of living, especially since the greatest shortage of managers is in the less advanced countries, those least familiar to people being transferred. It means new living and shopping habits for the executive's family, new school systems, and unfamiliar business practices. In addition, close friends and relatives—one's personal support system—are left behind. It is estimated that about one third of families transferred abroad return home prematurely. In addition, many who complete their foreign assignments may perform only marginally because of adjustment problems.[24] The importance of adaptiveness is borne out by several other studies. One of these compared corporate performance ratings of expatriates with the results of questionnaires they answered concerning cultural determinants. A positive relationship between performance ratings and such determinants as empathy, foreign travel before age twenty-one, and foreign language ability was indicated.[25] Another found that the inability of the spouse to adapt was a major factor influencing the failure of expatriate managers.[26]

However, some individuals do enjoy an expatriate experience and can easily adapt to a foreign way of life. It is certainly preferable to use these people if possible when transfers are necessary. Some firms, such as Simmons, approach this by having a specific group of international employees who are the only ones to be assigned abroad. A distinction needs to be made between a foreign assignment of fixed duration and one that is open-ended. Many more people are willing to accept a position abroad if they know that they will be returned home after a specific period of time than if the assignment may turn out to be permanent.

Repatriation Problems

- Coming home can be an adaptation

One problem concerning the expatriate manager that has received little attention until recently is that of repatriation. Most problems arise in three general areas: (1) personal finances, (2) adjustment to home country corporate structure, and (3) reacclimatization to life at home. In terms of finances, expatriates lose many of the benefits that were given to encourage the foreign assignment and may find that housing in the home country has risen substantially in price. It is estimated that a 50 percent increase in salary would be necessary to maintain the same living style in the United States that these executives enjoyed overseas. In spite of claims that foreign assignments will enhance one's career advancement, evidence to date does not always bear this out. Returning expatriates often find that many of their peers have been promoted above them in their absence, that they now have less autonomy in the job, and that they are now "little fish in a big pond." The families' social status may drop considerably on return and, along with adjustments to new schools and life-styles, may create substantial reentry problems. Some suggestions for smoothing reentry include early advice of return, maximum information on the new job, housing assistance, a reorientation program, bringing the expatriate manager frequently back to headquarters, and the use of a formal headquarters mentor who will look after the manager's interests while he or she is an expatriate.[27]

Geographic and Industry Differences

● More expatriates in LDCs
● Expatriates are larger portion of employees in services

Because of differences in availability of home country nationals, companies find a greater necessity to staff with expatriates in some locales than in others. Among U.S. multinational enterprises, for example, about 60 percent of their employees in Saudi Arabia are expatriates, but less than 1 percent of those in Western Europe. Although U.S. firms have the bulk of their investments in industrial countries, more than 70 percent of the U.S. expatriates that they employ are in the developing countries.[28]

The ratio of expatriates to total employees in foreign operations varies widely by industry. Expatriates in service industries, particularly banks, typically comprise 5–10 percent of the work force. In manufacturing, the expatriates generally make up less than 1 percent of the foreign work force.[29] There are at least two reasons for the disparity. The first is that the service industries have a much higher percentage of management positions, the most likely posts for utilizing expatriates. Second, these firms' foreign facilities are more apt to be involved in business across national boundaries than are those of manufacturers, which serve specific country markets. The need to use people with headquarters experience is therefore more important for the service industries.

Country-by-country versus global strategies. In previous chapters, particularly 17 and 18, we discussed how product and competitive factors influence the needs for corporate versus local control and for policies favoring uniformity versus differentiation among countries' operations. It has been noted that these factors and the choice of strategy also affect staffing needs and practices. Where conditions favor a country-by-country strategy, management skill needs are determined mainly by local conditions. In these circumstances, there is a general tendency to recruit more managers locally. Where there is a need to adopt a more global strategy, there is a tendency to use more expatriates. They are generally more familiar with the complexities of the business family system as a whole and tend not to see their own personal development so much in terms of what happens in the country to which they are assigned.[30]

RECRUITMENT, SELECTION, AND TRAINING

Staffing Foreign Operations

• Acquisitions and joint ventures secure staff but
  • may be inefficient
  • may be hard to control

The help of local companies.   One way of attaining personnel for foreign operations is by buying an existing firm abroad and utilizing the personnel already employed. This, in fact, has been a major reason for buying rather than building foreign facilities. Firms may also tie in closely with local companies in the expectation that these firms will contribute managers to the operation as well as hire new personnel. In countries such as Japan, where the labor market is tight and people are reluctant to move to new firms, the use of a local partner may be extremely important.

Neither of these strategies is a panacea, however. It is not always possible either to acquire facilities or to develop a partnership with a local firm. Furthermore, personnel hired through these methods may lack the product and technical knowledge that the foreign investor would like to see infused. The acquired plant itself may be old and inefficient, making a changeover difficult and expensive. If a local partner handles staffing arrangements, the employees may see their primary allegiance as to that partner rather than to the foreign investor. Finally, it is always necessary to add and replace some personnel.

• Used at home and abroad but
  • biggest need abroad is higher-level managers

College recruitment.   A few U.S. firms make a concerted effort to hire foreign graduates of U.S. universities who would like to return home to work. This method has some drawbacks. The most acute personnel shortage exists in upper-level management positions, and the individual fresh out of a university seldom has the age and experience necessary for the job. As they gain experience, however, it may be possible for them to move into higher-level management positions in the future, thus decreasing the need for expatriates. Outside the United States the number of graduate schools of business is increasing rapidly.[31] Consequently, there has been less need to look to U.S. universities as a source of personnel with formal business training.

- Identifies pool of qualified personnel
- Foreign personnel not easily encompassed because
  - subsidiaries are separate legal entitles
  - foreign operations may not be wholly owned
  - restrictions on cross-national data flows

Management inventories. Many companies are moving toward a centralized maintenance and retrieval of personnel records, which includes home and foreign-country nationals. Not only are the normal technical and demographic data maintained, but also such adaptive information as foreign language abilities, willingness to accept foreign assignments, and results of company-administered tests indicating adaptiveness. There are some problems in bringing foreign managers into these systems because, if the foreign facility is organized separately, they do not technically work for the parent. Home country management is particularly reluctant to interfere or transfer people out of an operation in which the firm owns less than 100 percent, for fear that minority stockholders will complain.[32] Furthermore, as was discussed in Chapter 17, there has been a trend toward restrictions on data flows among countries; these restrictions could inhibit future uses of centralized management inventories.

Before the 1960s there was an effort to locate and attract sons of diplomats or business expatriates for managerial ranks overseas in the belief that these people had already demonstrated adaptive ability. Recent evidence indicates that this tendency is greatly diminished because of both a growing belief that technical competence is more important than environmental adaptiveness and a growing trend toward transferring people who have already worked for the firm rather than seeking outside personnel. This trend is consistent with placing a high value on technical skills. However, a Conference Board study of U.S. expatriate managers in Canada, Nigeria, Italy, and Brazil indicates they generally rate poorly at understanding the countries in which they work.[33] This seeming necessity to trade off between technical and environmental competence may in the future be somewhat mitigated, however. A growing number of managers will be familiar with adaptive problems because of their experiences abroad as students, military personnel, Peace Corps volunteers, and the like. In fact, if mass communications and transportation result in countries becoming more similar rather than dissimilar, there may be a lessening need to adapt to different managerial styles.[34]

- Number of tests and techniques; however,
  - predictability for success in foreign assignments is not very high

Adaptability assessment. Since companies usually know more about the technical than about the adaptive capabilities of their employees, it is in the latter area that there is a great need to categorize managers for transfer purposes. People who have had success in adjusting to domestic transfers and who are not too tied to their own cultures are more likely to adapt abroad. One such technique is the Early Identification Program (E.I.P.), which, by means of sentence completion questionnaires and interviews with the manager and spouse, attempts to assess ten areas for an environmental match. Included are leisure activities, interpersonal sensitivity, culture, consideration, authoritarianism, cultural management, travel and distance acceptability, job satisfaction, motivations, and management match.

The reason for interviewing the spouse (in nearly all cases the wife) is that a foreign assignment is usually more stressful for her than for him. The foreign assignment is generally an advancement for the husband; however, the wife must start at the bottom in developing new social relations and in learning how to carry out the day-to-day management of the home. The separation from friends and family often make the wife feel a great loneliness so that she wants more time and attention from her husband on whom she may depend for her only companionship. But the husband may have less time because of having to adjust to new working conditions. This may lead to marital stress which, in turn, affects work performance. Interviewers thus look not only at likely adaptiveness, but also at whether the marriage is strong enough so that stress will not impede employment duties.[35]

Many other tests assess personality traits that are indicative of a willingness to change basic attitudes. These include the Minnesota Multiphasic Personality Inventory, the Guilford-Zimmerman Temperament Survey, and the Allport-Vernon Study of Values.[36] Some companies also conduct extensive interviews with the potential expatriate and family in order to observe possible environmental problems. Although companies that follow a rigorous procedure of selecting and training people for foreign assignments experience a somewhat lower failure rate of expatriates, the difference is not very substantial relative to the cost of testing. Consequently, few companies administer tests to determine relational abilities.[37] Instruments simply have not yet been developed that can predict adaptability with a marked degree of success.

● Used extensively for recruitment of technicians to remote areas

Personnel recruiters.   For locations where there is a need for large numbers of expatriate specialists, companies have to depend more heavily on outside recruiters to find personnel for them. One such area in recent years has been Saudi Arabia. Recruiters have used such methods as employment fairs and the direct mailing of brochures to as many as 10,000 engineers at a time to attract applications.[38]

Internationalizing the Organization

● Increase in international studies in universities

Preemployment training.   The Dow case at the beginning of the chapter showed that, until a couple of decades ago, managers had a very domestic perspective on business. This type of attitude was probably more common in U.S. companies than in firms from other countries of the world simply because the U.S. economy was so large and self-sufficient. In both the United States and other countries the amount of international business has been growing. It is probably safe to say that there is a lessened need worldwide to convince managers of the advantages in taking an international perspective on business. However, there is still a need to train managers in the differences in business operations brought about by internationalization.

One development to mitigate this need has been a move by the accrediting group for U.S. business school programs to require that all students be trained for worldwide responsibilities. A 1980 global survey of business schools showed a growing offering of international business courses.[39] Consequently, an increasing number of future employees may have had some classroom exposure to international business nuances before their employment.

There is no consensus, however, as to what students should learn to help prepare themselves for international responsibilities. For instance, the conveying of knowledge specific to foreign environments, as in area studies, may tend to remove some of the fear and aggression that are aroused through dealing with the unknown. However, the understanding of a different culture does not necessarily imply a willingness to adapt to that culture.[40]

- Include environment-specific information
- Include adaptiveness training

Postemployment training. Although more managers are gaining exposure to international business because of their firms' growth in the foreign area and although more effort is being expended in formal business school training, many employees may still escape these internationalization processes. The result may be that they place domestic performance objectives above global ones or that they feel ill-equipped to handle worldwide responsibilities as they move upward in their organizations.

One approach to training has been to include international business components as part of the overall company training programs. This means, in part, that of the managers who participate in external programs, some attend programs that have heavy international emphasis. Programs ranging in length from a day to as long as ten months have been developed at major universities and by other sponsoring agencies. Among other external executive development programs, there has been a trend toward including some international business topics.

Some companies rely primarily on their own development programs and have taken a variety of approaches. General Mills and Celanese have year-long training programs in which foreign nationals spend time in all of the companies' domestic divisions. IBM has regional training centers in which managers from several countries are brought together for specific topics. Cummins Engine provides voluntary evening language courses that any employee may take and works toward overseas business trips for more than the "privileged management elite" so that large numbers of employees develop a foreign awareness.[41] Westinghouse developed cultural awareness workshops to which enrollment was first restricted to upper-level managers.[42]

Another approach has been to emphasize adaptability rather than knowledge of another environment. The Peace Corps, for example, uses sensitivity training, which is designed to develop attitudinal flexibility. Another method is to expose a prospective candidate to subcultures within his or her own country.

Easing the Expatriate Transition

Help transferee know what to expect

The above training activities are geared toward employees, whether or not they might be deployed abroad for transfers or short-term assignments. The purposes of those activities are to break down nationalistic barriers that may prevent an organization from achieving global efficiencies. These activities may be insufficient for employees who are assigned abroad. Selecting the right people for transfers is, of course, an essential element. However, other activities may be necessary to improve the likelihood of success in foreign posts. For these reasons the vast majority of firms employing many expatriates now have formal orientation programs for potential transferees.

For the person being tapped for a foreign assignment it may be difficult to know what questions to ask. It has been noted that there are awareness levels. Satisfactory answers to the first level are sometimes sufficient for the individual to accept a transfer. These include such things as job design, compensation, and general information on housing, climate, education, and health conditions. The second awareness level comes before actual relocation takes place, including home sales, taxes, company policy on transport of goods, and job upon repatriation. The third level occurs during the relocation process and includes the mechanics of shipping goods, foreign housing arrangements, and salary distribution. Such things as the foreign social structure, communications links, kidnapping precautions, and legal advice on the law of domicile are seldom thought of before settlement abroad.[43] Because the expatriate does not usually think in advance of all those things that may affect adaptability, it is useful for companies to provide questions and answers for potential expatriates.[44]

COMPENSATION

- Must pay enough to entice people to move
- Waste if overpay
- If the number moved is high, must set policies to apply to all

People performing fairly similar jobs in different countries may receive very different amounts and forms of compensation, reflecting diversities in the productivity levels of the countries as a whole, in the costs of living, in fringe benefits, in tax rates, and in the supply and demand of certain skills. Companies must pay within a competitive range or risk either not hiring qualified persons or incurring expenses that are too high in relation to those of competitors. The determination of these amounts and forms is a problem not too unlike the determination for nonmanagerial positions and will therefore be covered in the next chapter. This section will concentrate on expatriate personnel.

For example, if a U.S. company transfers its British finance manager, who is making $50,000 per year, to Italy, where the going rate is $60,000 per year, what should the manager's salary be? Or if the Italian financial manager were to be transferred to the United Kingdom, what pay should be offered? Should the compensation be in dollars, pounds, or lire? Whose holidays should apply? Which set of fringe benefits should be used? These are but a few of the myriad questions that must be solved when moving people abroad. On one hand, the firm must try to prevent excessive costs; on the other hand, the firm must maintain high employee morale.

The amount and type of compensation difference necessary to entice a person to move to another country vary widely by person and locale. Missionaries and Peace Corps volunteers are willing to accept very little compensation in areas to which executives are reluctant to move. The problem in personnel administration is to find just the compensation package to entice the selected manager to move to the new foreign locale. For companies with very few expatriate employees a foreign compensation package may be worked out on an individual basis. This approach is used by companies with small operations abroad and by those just beginning foreign operations. As international activities expand, however, it is necessary to develop programs that will apply to the large number of international transfers. A company such as Mobil Oil, which transfers over 1000 employees internationally per year, simply cannot work out each movement on an individual basis. If this were attempted, questions of equity would be raised, since two people with quite diverse pay packages could end up in the same locale. As long as consistency is sought in transfer policy, some people inevitably will receive more than would be necessary to entice them to go abroad.

At least three factors affect the rationale for adjusting salaries upward when moving an employee to a foreign country. These are cost of living, job status, and hardship. In addition, a policy must be established concerning the currency in which the expatriate will be paid.

Cost of Living

- More expensive abroad because
  - habits change slowly
  - don't know how and where to buy

Rationale. Most people who move to another country find that their cost of living increases, primarily because they are used to living in a certain manner that is expensive to duplicate in a new environment. This does not imply that one living standard is necessarily better than another, but rather that habits are difficult and uncomfortable to change. Thus the manager who gets transferred from the United States to Mexico may find that the spouse still prefers to drive a separate car, purchase convenience foods and familiar imported brands, and own the latest appliances and entertainment equipment. The cost of these items may run double the U.S. price. If the same firm were to transfer its Mexican manager to the United States, some of the same problems would occur. The spouse might insist on fresh fruits and vegetables year round, servants to prepare them, and a chauffeur for the family's one car.

Knowledge of the local country is a second consideration. If there are children, they may have to attend private schools simply because they do not know the local language. With many transfers, children might well have to attend schools in several foreign languages if they cannot attend private schools. Food and housing may be obtained at higher than the local rate because of not knowing the language well, where to buy, or how to bargain for reductions.

• Uses various cost of living indexes
  • increase compensation when foreign cost higher
  • do not decrease when foreign cost lower
  • salary differential removed when repatriated

Differential assessment. Most firms adjust salaries temporarily upward to account for higher costs of living in the area where a person is being transferred. Once the manager returns to the home country, the differential is removed, and the salary is adjusted downward again. When moves are made to foreign areas with a lower cost of living, firms are very reluctant to attempt to reduce the size of the employee's paycheck, since this would have a negative impact on morale. For example, if a U.S.-based employee were moved to Sweden, the company would probably pay a differential to compensate for Sweden's high personal income tax rate. If the same employee were instead transferred to the Bahamas, which has a lower personal tax rate than the United States, chances are that the differential would be a windfall to the employee.

How much more does it cost to live in a foreign country? This is not an easy matter to determine, since each family has its own spending pattern or "market basket," even domestically. A company must therefore resort to some type of average measurement, which will not fit everyone's situation perfectly. One indication of price differences is the State Department's cost-of-living index for major world cities, published yearly in *Labor Developments Abroad.* Most U.S. firms use this index in one form or another or rely on U.N. indexes, consultants, or their own surveys. Some frequently used surveys are published by the *Financial Times, Business International,* and the International Monetary Fund *Staff Papers.*

In using any of these indexes, one must determine what items are included and adjust only on that basis. For example, if a family earning $4000 per month spends approximately 35 percent of this income on food, clothing, and the household services included in the index at home, then $1400 would be the base on which to calculate those differences in cost of living. If the index showed a 25 percent increase in these costs, let us say for someone being transferred from New York to Oslo, the family would receive an extra $350 to cover those items. Other items (e.g., housing and schooling) would be handled separately. If the overall cost of living is calculated to be less abroad than at home, firms are not apt to decrease salaries for those employees. On return home, however, any cost-of-living differentials are eliminated.

Differences in inflation rates and in exchange rates may quickly render surveys and indexes obsolete. It is therefore necessary to update cost-of-living adjustments frequently.

It has been suggested that cost-of-living differentials be reduced the longer the employees are in a given country. The rationale is that, as expatriates become better assimilated, they should be able to adjust more to local purchasing habits—for example, buying vegetables from a native market instead of using imported canned goods.

Job Status Payment

- Transfer is advancement and paid accordingly

If employees are transferred to a country in which the going rate for their skills is higher than that in the home country, they will probably feel that they are being treated inequitably unless compensation is brought up to the level of the new reference group. In addition, some employees may not accept a position abroad unless it is considered to be a promotion, and a promotion without a pay increase would naturally be considered inequitable by most people.

Many companies make little or no provision for reincorporating the transferred employee into the home country operation after the foreign assignment. Because overseas employees are removed from changes taking place in the home country operations, they may fall behind in advancement, even to the extent that there is no place for the transferees in the organization upon their return. To alleviate some of the anxiety of the foreign assignment, some firms pay additional money to the individuals who move abroad.

Individuals transferred abroad compare the equity of their compensation with other managers in both the country to which they are sent and the country of which they are citizens. For this reason, companies normally raise the salary for individuals while they are working in a country having a high normal salary for the task. They seldom lower the salary, though, when transferring people to a lower-salary country. Until recently, U.S. salaries were higher than anywhere else, so salary adjustments upward were never necessary for U.S. expatriates. Firms did have to adjust upward for third-country nationals and, since the dollar has fluctuated, have had to contend sometimes with upgrading U.S. expatriate salaries as well. These are adjusted downward again upon returning home. Various surveys compare executive compensation on a country by country basis.[45]

Hardship Allowances

- May encounter living problems for which extra compensation given

There are bound to be things one will have to do without when living abroad—a favorite brand of cigarettes or whiskey, certain foods, an executive's own holiday celebration, or television in the native language. Children may have to attend school away from home, perhaps even in another country. Such sacrifices can range from nuisance to hardship. And what of the problems of adjustment to new cultures? Children, feeling they are strangers at home and abroad, may suffer adverse psychological effects. A University of Colorado Medical School doctor reported a greater incidence of psychological disorders among children of expatriates.[46] The most difficult ages seem to be three to five, because of misinterpretations due to their world of fantasy, and fourteen to sixteen, because of social frustrations.[47]

Hardly anyone would deny that the living conditions in certain locations present particularly severe hardships—perhaps harsh climatic or health conditions or political insurrection or unrest that places the employee and family in danger. For instance, in recent years, antigovernment groups kidnapped expatriate employees of such companies as Ford, Kodak, and Owens-Illinois in order to collect ransoms. In fact the growing incidence of kidnapping and terrorism has caused firms not only to rethink their hardship allowances, but also to embark on training programs to advise personnel of dangers and how to deal with them. Corporations have been hit by legal suits from victims' families, which have alleged that companies have mishandled ransom negotiations. They have also been hit by shareholder suits claiming that the company has no business paying ransoms.[48]

Finally, a hardship may occur because of potential changes in total family income and status. In the home country, all members of the family may be able to work. Seldom will more than the transferred employee be given permission to work in a foreign country. If an individual is moved abroad, his or her spouse may have to give up well-paying and satisfying employment.[49] Firms realize that changes in location present various types of hardship problems and attempt to compensate their employees accordingly.

There was a time when nearly all expatriates received a premium just for being in a foreign country. However, there is a growing realization that not all foreign posts constitute a hardship and that it is easy to find people to accept jobs in the more desirable locations. The director of international personnel at Hewlett-Packard said, "We could get 50 names a day for London or Paris if we advertised it." Such thinking has prompted not only Hewlett-Packard but also such firms as IBM and Standard Oil of California to eliminate premiums for many countries.[50]

Choice of Currency

● Usually mixture of home and host currency

The potential change in currency value is another problem in expatriate compensation. For expatriate employees, salaries are usually paid partly in local currency and partly in the currency of the employee's home country. In this way the employee can save in the country considered a permanent home. Such a payment plan may also prevent the employee's having to pay taxes on the entire income, since some countries tax only on the portion of income paid in that country. Sometimes the company would likewise like to pay in local currencies to minimize additional capital outflows to the foreign investment. Some countries, such as Colombia, make it very difficult to charge hard currency expenditures to the local operation. Consequently, companies are sometimes forced to charge a part of the personnel cost to home country operations. This situation is especially applicable where exchange control exists, since virtually everything earned in local currency must be spent in the country. When exchange control exists, there is usually a difference between the official and black market rate of exchange. Employees therefore find it advantageous to draw a maximum in a convertible currency because they can buy more by exchanging it unofficially. The company must therefore establish policies that somehow fulfill both its own objectives and those of the expatriate employees.

Since expatriates seldom plan to spend their entire lives in a given foreign country, the question of the continuity of fringe benefits is a further consideration. Most large U.S. international corporations include U.S. expatriates in their home country insurance and pension plans, but few include third-country nationals in these plans. The difference between the two groups appears to be due partially to willingness to move and partially to the fact that governmental support for retirement and illness in the United States is lower than that in many other countries.

REMOTE AREAS

● Necessitate more fringe benefits and building of facilities

Many recent large-scale international projects have been in areas of the world that are so remote that MNEs would get few people to transfer to these places if the companies did not attempt to create an environment more like the one at home or make other special arrangements. Lockheed Aircraft, for example, has set up its own color television broadcasting station in Saudi Arabia for its 4000 expatriates there.[51] INCO has built schools, hospitals, churches, supermarkets, a golf course, yacht club, motel, and restaurant for its 2000 expatriates in Indonesia.[52] Instead of making such permanent investments, Reading and Bates Offshore Drilling Company has settled in Malta 350 expatriate families who commute up to 2000 miles to work by jet.[53]

Expatriate employees in these remote areas are often handled very differently from those in other locales. To attract the large number of people necessary for construction and start-up, MNEs usually offer fixed-term contract assignments at high salary and hire most people from outside the firms. Some are attracted to these assignments and are willing to undergo different living conditions because they can save amounts of money that would have been impossible at home.

SUMMARY

● Among the factors that differentiate between the tasks of international and purely domestic managers are that the former must know how to adapt home country practices to foreign locales and must deal usually with high-level government officials.

- The top-level managers of foreign subsidiaries normally perform much broader duties than domestic managers with similar cost or profit responsibilities. They must cope with communications problems between the corporate headquarters and the subsidiaries, and they must usually function with less staff assistance.

- Reasons given for preferring local to expatriate managers are that they understand regional operating conditions; they demonstrate the opportunities for local citizens and the local interests of the operations; they avoid the red tape of cross-national transfers; they are usually cheaper; and they may focus more on long-term operations and goals.

- Firms transfer people abroad to infuse home country business practices and technical competence, to control foreign operations, and to develop managers.

- When expatriates are employed, MNEs increasingly consider the option of using third-country nationals.

- When firms transfer personnel abroad, they should consider how well the people will be accepted, what to do with them when the foreign assignment is over, and how willing they are to be moved.

- Firms frequently acquire personnel abroad by buying existing companies. They may also go into business with local firms, which take on the major staffing responsibilities.

- Two of the major international training functions are to build a global awareness among managers in general and to equip managers to handle the specific nuances entailed in an expatriate assignment.

- When transferred abroad, an employee's compensation is usually changed because of differences in cost of living, job status, and hardship.

- The cost of living in a foreign country is usually higher, at least initially, than in one's own country because of purchasing habits that are difficult to break and because of not knowing how to get the best prices in a foreign country. Most companies use one of several indexes in order to adjust salaries upward.

- Expatriate employees' salaries are usually paid partly in local currency and partly in the currency of the employee's home country

- For operations in very remote areas, MNEs may have to provide many amenities in addition to the compensation package.

C A S E   THE OFFICE SYSTEMS COMPANY

In 1984, the Office Systems Company (OSC) had to replace its manager in San Salvador, El Salvador, because the present managing director (a U.S. national) announced suddenly that he would leave within a month to start his own real estate business in South Florida. OSC manufactured a wide variety of small office equipment (such as copying machines, recording machines, mail scales, and paper shredders) in eight different countries that was distributed and sold worldwide.

OSC had no manufacturing facilities in El Salvador but had been selling and servicing there since the early 1960s. OSC had first tried selling in El Salvador through independent importers but quickly became convinced that it needed to have its own staff there to make sufficient sales. It was likely that some assembly operation would be required within the next five years because of government desires to foster local employment. In spite of political turmoil, which had bordered on being a full-scale civil war over the last few years, OSC's operation in El Salvador with about 100 employees had enjoyed good and improving sales and profitability.

The option of filling the Salvadoran manager position with someone from outside the firm was alien to OSC's policy. Otherwise, the options were fairly open. OSC used a combination of home country, host country, and third-country nationals in top positions in foreign countries. It was not uncommon for managers to rotate between foreign and U.S. domestic locations. In fact, it was increasingly evident that international experience was an important factor in deciding who would be appointed to top corporate positions. The sales and service facility in El Salvador reported through a Latin American regional office located in Coral Gables, Florida. A committee at the regional office quickly narrowed its choice to five candidates whose profiles are described below.

Tom Zimmerman. He had joined the firm thirty years before and was well versed in all the technical and sales aspects required in the job. He had never worked abroad for OSC but had been on a sales team a few years earlier that visited South Africa. He was considered moderately competent in the management of the duties he had performed during the years and would retire in about four and a half years. Neither he nor his wife spoke Spanish. Their children were grown and living with their own children in the United States. He was currently in charge of a sales district about the size of the one in El Salvador. However, that district was being merged with another, so his present office would become redundant.

Brett Harrison. At age forty, Mr. Harrison had spent fifteen years with OSC. He was considered highly competent and capable of moving into upper-level management within the next few years. He had never been based abroad but had worked for the last three years in the Latin American regional office, from which he frequently traveled to Latin America. Both he and his wife spoke Spanish adequately. Their two children, ages fourteen and fifteen, were just beginning to study Spanish. His wife was a professional as well, holding a responsible marketing position with a pharmaceutical company.

Carolyn Moyer.   She had joined OSC after getting her MBA from a prestigious university twelve years before. At age 37 she had already moved between staff and line positions of growing responsibility. For two years she was second-in-command of a sales district about the size of the one in El Salvador. Her performance in that post was considered excellent. Currently she worked as a member of a planning staff team. When she joined OSC, she had indicated her eventual interest in international responsibilities because of her undergraduate major in international affairs. She had expressed a recent interest in international duties because of a belief it would help her advancement. She spoke Spanish well and was not married.

Francisco Cabrera.   He was currently one of the assistant managing directors in the larger Mexican operation. He was a Mexican citizen who had worked for OSC in Mexico for all his twelve years with the company. He held an MBA from a Mexican university and was considered to be one of the likely candidates to head the Mexican operation when the present managing director retired in seven years. He was 35, married with four children (ages two to seven). He spoke English adequately. His wife did not work outside the home and spoke no English.

Juan Moreno.   At 27 he was assistant to the present managing director in El Salvador, a position he had assumed when he joined OSC after completion of his undergraduate degree in the United States four years before. He was considered competent but lacking in experience. He had been quite successful in increasing OSC's sales, an advantage being that he was well connected with the local families who could afford to buy new office equipment for their businesses. He was not married.

QUESTIONS

1. Who should the committee choose for the assignment and why?
2. What problems might each individual encounter in the position?
3. How might OSC go about minimizing the problems that the chosen person would have in managing the El Salvador operations?

NOTES

1. Data for this case were taken from Edwin McDowell, "Making It in America: The Foreign-Born Executive," *New York Times,* June 1, 1980, Section 3, pp. 1+; Don Whitehead, *The Dow Story* (New York: McGraw-Hill, 1968); *Annual Reports*

of Dow Chemical Corporation for various years; Urban C. Lehner, "Pitfalls of Partnership," *Wall Street Journal,* January 5, 1983, p. 44; "Dow's Shifts in R & D Presage Overseas Work," *Chemical Week,* Vol. 128, No. 13, April 1, 1981, p. 17; "Lundeen Urges More Aid for Universities," *Chemical Marketing Reporter,* Vol. 224, No. 19, November 7, 1983, pp. 3+.

2. Michael G. Duerr and James Greene, *The Problems Facing International Management. Managing International Business,* No. 1 (New York: National Industrial Conference Board, 1968), pp. 1, 25.

3. United Nations Centre on Transnational Corporations, *Transnational Corporations in World Development,* Third Survey (New York: United Nations, 1983), pp. 318–326.

4. Nancy Mercinko, "Language in the Multinational Corporation," MBA thesis, The Pennsylvania State University, University Park, Pa., 1975.

5. Jean Ross-Skinner, "English Spoken Here," *Dun's Review,* March 1977, pp. 56–57; Urban C. Lehner, "When in Japan, Do as the Japanese Do, by Speaking English," *Wall Street Journal,* December 8, 1980, p. 1.

6. C. A. Verbeke, "Caterpillar Fundamental English," *Training and Development Journal,* February 1973, pp. 36–40.

7. Michael G. Duerr and James Greene, *Foreign Nationals in International Management. Managing International Business,* No. 2 (New York: National Industrial Conference Board, 1968), p. 4.

8. John D. Daniels, "The Non-American Manager, Especially as Third Country National, in U.S. Multinationals: A Separate but Equal Doctrine?," *Journal of International Business Studies,* Fall 1974, pp. 26–29.

9. Yoram Zeira and Ehud Harari, "Genuine Multinational Staffing Policy: Expectations and Realities," *Academy of Management Journal,* June 1977, pp. 327–333.

10. Dafna N. Izraeli, Moshe Banai, and Yoram Zeira, "Women Executives in MNC Subsidiaries," *California Management Review,* Vol. 23, No. 1, Fall 1980, pp. 53–63.

11. Clyde H. Farnsworth, "U.S. Tightens Japanese Visas," *New York Times,* October 7, 1980, p. D1+.

12. Anders Edström and Jay R. Galbraith, "Transfer of Managers as a Coordination and Control Strategy in Multinational Organizations," *Administrative Science Quarterly,* June 1977, pp. 248–261; A. B. Sim, "Decentralized Management of Subsidiaries and Their Performance," *Management International Review,* No. 2, 1977, p. 48.

13. Yoram Zeira and Ehud Harari, "Structural Sources of Personnel Problems in Multinational Corporations: Third-Country Nationals," *Omega,* Vol. 5, No. 2, 1977, 167–168.

14. Anders Edström and Jay R. Galbraith, "Alternative Policies for International Transfers of Managers," *Management International Review,* No. 2, 1977, pp. 13–14; Asya Pazy and Yoram Zeira, "Training Parent-Country Professionals in Host-Country Organizations," *Academy of Management Review,* Vol. 8, No. 2, 1983, pp. 262–272.

15. James S. Byrne, "Who Will Save the Boodle Boys?," *Forbes,* February 6, 1978, p. 34.

16. Calvin Reynolds, "Expatriates in a Changing World Economy," paper presented to the Academy of International Business, November 15, 1978.

17. Edwin L. Miller, "The Selection Decision for an International Assignment: A Study of the Decision Maker's Behavior," *Journal of International Business Studies,* Fall 1972, p. 63.

18. Izraeli et al., *loc. cit.*

19. Maile Hulihan, "Europe's Female Managers Still Fight Bias," *Wall Street Journal,* April 17, 1984, p. 36.

20. Izraeli et al., *loc. cit.*

21. Nancy J. Adler, "Expecting International Success: Female Managers Overseas," *Columbia Journal of World Business,* Fall 1984, pp. 79–85.

22. Jane Condon, "Asia," *Wall Street Journal,* April 2, 1984, p. 27; "Corporate Woman," *Business Week,* April 20, 1981, pp. 120–127.

23. Duerr and Greene, *The Problems Facing International Management,* p. 18; Daniels, "Non-American Managers." See also Richard D. Hays, "Behavioral Determinants of Success-Failure among U.S. Expatriate Managers," *Journal of International Business Studies,* Spring 1971, pp. 40–46.

24. Philip R. Harris and Robert L. Moran, *Managing Cultural Differences* (Houston: Gulf Publishing Company, 1979), p. 164, citing studies by the Center for Research and Education.

25. Richard J. Fleming, "Cultural Determinants for Selecting American Businessmen for Overseas Assignments," in *International Management in the Seventies: A Decisive Decade,* Richard J. Fleming, ed. (Norfolk, Va.: Old Dominion University, 1973), pp. 33–38.

26. E. K. Miller and R. E. Hill, "A Comparative Study of the Job Change Decision for Managers Selecting Domestic and Overseas Assignments," *Proceedings,* Academy of Management, 1978, pp. 287–291.

27. Among the recent articles on this subject are David M. Noer, "Integrating Foreign Service Employees to Home Organization: The Godfather Approach," *Personnel Journal,* January 1974, pp. 45–50; William F. Cagney, "Executive Reentry: The Problem of Repatriation," *Personnel Journal,* September 1975, pp. 487–488; and J. Alex Murray, "Repatriated Executives: Culture Shock in Reverse," *Management Review,* November 1973, pp. 43–45.

28. Reynolds, *loc. cit.*

29. Milton G. Holmen, "Organizing and Staffing of Foreign Operations of Multinational Corporations," paper presented to the Academy of International Business, October 25, 1980; Reynolds, "Expatriates in a Changing World Economy."

30. Anders Edström and Peter Lorange, "Matching Strategy and Human Resources in Multinational Companies," *Journal of International Business Studies,* Fall 1984, pp. 125–137.

31. For a fairly comprehensive list of these, see Zoher E. Shipchandler, ed., *International Directory: Schools of Business Administration.* (N.P.: AACSB/AIB, 1976).

32. A case of reduction of home office influence in subsidiary personnel staffing once the ownership became shared is described in Samir M. Youssef, "The Integra-

tion of Local Nationals into the Managerial Hierarchy of American Overseas Subsidiaries: An Exploratory Study," *Academy of Management Journal,* March 1973, p. 29.

33. "Corporate Aids Abroad Get Poor Marks in Study," *Wall Street Journal,* September 13, 1977, p. 18.

34. James E. Everett, Bruce W. Stening, and Peter A. Longton, "Some Evidence for an International Managerial Culture," *Journal of Management Studies,* Vol. 19, No. 2, April 1982, pp. 153–162.

35. Michael G. Harvey, "The Executive Family: An Overlooked Variable in International Assignments," *Columbia Journal of World Business,* Spring 1985, pp. 84–92.

36. E. J. Karras, Roy F. McMillan, Jr., and Thomas R. Williamson, "Interviewing for Cultural Match," *Personnel Journal,* April 1971, pp. 276–279; Rosalie L. Tung, "Selection and Training of Personnel for Overseas Assignments," *Columbia Journal of World Business,* Vol. 16, No. 1, Spring 1981, p. 72; Canadian International Development Agency (CIDA), "Going Abroad with CIDA"; Bureau of Naval Personnel, *Overseas Diplomacy: Guidelines for United States Navy: Trainer* (Washington, D.C.: U.S. Government Printing Office, 1973); M. H. Tucker, D. Raik Rossiter, and M. Uhes, *Improving the Evaluation of Peace Corps Training Activities,* Vol. 3 (Denver: Center for Research and Education, June 4, 1973).

37. Tung, *ibid.,* pp. 75–77, showed a correlation of .63 between the rigor of the selection-training process and success in foreign assignments. Only about 5 percent of firms administer tests.

38. Erik Larson, "Saudi Rigors Toughen Task of Recruiters," *Wall Street Journal,* October 15, 1980, p. 31.

39. Robert Grosse and Gerald W. Perritt, *International Business Curricula: A Global Survey* (Waco, Texas: Academy of International Business, 1980).

40. Tung, *op. cit.,* p. 71.

41. Jeffrey L. Blue and Ulrich Haynes, Jr., "Preparation for the Overseas Assignment," *Business Horizons,* June 1977, pp. 61–67.

42. Philip R. Harris and Dorothy L. Harris, "Preventing Cross-Cultural Shock," *Management and Training,* May 1976, pp. 37–41.

43. Frank L. Acuff, "Awareness Levels of Employees Considering Overseas Relocation," *Personnel Journal,* November 1974, pp. 809–812.

44. Kenneth Darrow and Bradley Palmquist, eds., *Trans-Cultural Study Guide;* (N.P.: Volunteers in Asia, 1975, Second Edition), which lists pertinent questions to ask.

45. C. Ian Sym-Smith and Mark S. White, "International Executive Compensation," *Wharton Magazine,* Winter 1980, pp. 40–42.

46. "Psychiatrist Tells of Harm in Raising U.S. Kids Abroad," *Atlanta Journal,* May 7, 1971, p. 10B.

47. Maxine Gaylord, "Relocation and the Corporate Family," *Social Work,* May 1979, pp. 186–191.

48. Sam Passow, "Manager's Journal," *Wall Street Journal,* June 18, 1984, p. 18.

49. Joann S. Lublin, "More Spouses Receive Help in Job Searches When Executives Take Positions Overseas," *Wall Street Journal,* January 26, 1984, p. 35.

50. Alfred L. Malabre, Jr., "Austerity Abroad," *Wall Street Journal,* January 8, 1973, p. 1.

51. "Global Report," *Wall Street Journal,* July 11, 1977, p. 6.

52. Barry Newman, "Mine over Matter," *Wall Street Journal,* August 25, 1977, p. 1.

53. Ray Vicker, "Malta Is a Nice Place to Live Even If Job Is 2000 Miles Away," *Wall Street Journal,* November 7, 1977, p. 1.

2|3

Labor Personnel

- To discuss how labor market differences among countries can affect optimum methods of production and how host countries prefer multinational firms to operate.
- To describe diversities in compensation policies and practices on a country-to-country basis.
- To illustrate how labor laws and practices affect management's autonomy on a national basis.
- To highlight some of the major international pressures to improve the conditions of labor worldwide.
- To examine the effect of transnational operations on collective bargaining.

INTERNATIONAL LABOR DIVISION[1]

Many developing countries have large pools of unskilled or semiskilled workers who can be easily trained for highly repetitious manual work. Since low family incomes and high unemployment rates are two of the major problems facing these countries, many of their governments have made concerted efforts to attract foreign industry to employ their people. In addition to the offer of such investment incentives as tax reductions and the building of infrastructure, some national programs have sought to project an image of peaceful and stable labor relations. Thailand sends foreign businesses brochures guaranteeing that "the relationship between employer and employee is like that of a guardian and ward. It is easy to win and maintain the loyalty of workers as long as they are treated with kindness and courtesy." Malaysia advertises "the manual dexterity of the Oriental female;" South Korea has prohibited actual walkouts during a strike, and Singapore regulates pay boosts to workers.

For many production activities that require highly repetitive tasks, mechanization has not been developed. Minimization of labor costs is the major means of gaining a competitive price advantage in these portions of production. A number of industries have found it advantageous to perform these portions of production in developing countries, where labor rates are much lower than in industrial countries and the skill levels are compatible with the job requirements. For example, it might cost $12.00 per hour to hire someone in the United States to do a task that a Korean worker might do for $1.00 per hour. At the same time tasks requiring less repetition and higher skills are maintained in countries with highly skilled labor that is cost efficient in spite of its seemingly high wage rates.

An industry that epitomizes this international labor division is electronics. Firms from Europe, Japan, and the United States have set up certain labor-intensive operations in low-wage countries. In a product such as calculators, circuits are printed on silicon wafers and tested by highly skilled workers in industrial countries. The wafers are then shipped to a low-wage country, where they are cut into tiny chips and attached to circuit boards. The circuit boards may then be returned for final assembly.

This division of tasks does not always proceed smoothly. One problem is that the least-cost production location may change, and a firm may have to move to another place to regain a competitive advantage. Two good examples of this are Malaysia and Singapore. As more than 120 foreign electronics firms set up Malaysian operations, the supply of labor became less abundant. The result was that per capita GNP rose from $370 in 1970 to $1660 in 1980, and wages have risen by over 15 percent per year since 1975. By 1979, Singapore had an estimated shortage of 15,000 workers, and the National Wage Council recommended a 23 percent across-the-board pay increase. Foreign electronics firms used a variety of gimmicks to attract workers from competitors: Luxor Industri of Sweden offered free use of a color television; GE of the United States gave bonuses to workers who stayed on the job more than two weeks; and Italy's Componenti Electronici conducted a door-to-door search for recruits. Senator U. L. Lee of Malaysia said that, "Malaysia is beginning to cost itself out of the cheap labor market," as he cited more firms turning to populous neighbors such as Indonesia and the Philippines. The chairman of Singapore's International Chamber of Commerce predicted that "within ten years, China, with its vast labor supply, will compete directly."

Of perhaps even greater potential impact for countries desiring employment for their workers is the risk of technological change, which makes a cheap labor advantage obsolete. With the introduction of advanced production technology, some companies such as Motorola and Fairchild Camera & Instrument have moved some production back to industrial countries where computer-controlled assembly is as cheap as using Asian labor.

Because countries with low labor costs are poor, a firm locating there may find itself in the middle of social and political upheavals. Take El Salvador, for example, where a number of international electronics firms operate. AVX Ceramics, which assembles components for transistors and circuits, had to reschedule shifts by shutting down during part of the night and staying open on Sunday because rebels bombed and set fire to 1200 buses. Without the rescheduling, its 1000 workers could not have gotten to the plant. Two executives of Beckman Instruments were kidnapped in El Salvador, and Beckman closed its plant after paying the ransom and getting the release of the two men. Dataram's plant was occupied by an armed group trying to unionize workers; Dataram has since built a back-up plant in Guatemala.

In operating facilities with low labor costs, firms may also encounter labor laws or practices that are difficult or unusual for them. In Malaysia, for example, companies must contend with quota systems aimed at eliminating discrimination between the Bumiputras and ethnic Chinese groups. Foreign firms operating Mexican border plants have been pressured to increase the percentage of male assembly workers, a difficult task in that jobs in the industry had come to be known as "women's work." In South Korea, since workers cannot strike, they may use slowdowns or other means to achieve their demands. At the Signetics Memory Systems plant, 3000 workers held a sit-in and hunger strike in the cafeteria to win a 23 percent pay increase.

Not the least of potential problems for companies is the growing criticism that they exploit women in developing countries. Nearly all the highly repetitious jobs in electronics and some of the other labor-intensive industries are performed by women. In many poor nations, women have had less formal education than men, have been trained since they were small in tasks requiring manual dexterity, and are willing to accept lower wages than men for the same work. Their qualifications are thus ideal for the needs of certain labor-intensive activities. Without the constraints of sex discrimination legislation, companies advertise openly that they want female production workers. It has been well publicized that, in comparison with workers in industrial countries, the pay of these women is low, they live poorly, and they work in conditions that may be dangerous to their physical well-being. One critic writing in *Ms.* summed up the situation as follows:

> *The relationship between many Third World governments and the multinational corporations is not very different between a pimp and his customers. The governments advertise their women, sell them, and keep them in line for their "johns."*

INTRODUCTION

The preceding case illustrates many of the points to be made in this chapter: that labor market differences will affect the degree of mechanization, production location, and amount of compensation; that compensation changes may lead to shifts in the location of activities; that labor relations systems vary substantially among countries; and that international criticisms of employment practices may pressure multinational firms to counter the norms and laws of certain countries. In addition to these points, the chapter will examine compensation forms, international labor mobility, and the effects of multinational ownership of production on the labor management process.

LABOR MARKET DIFFERENCES

External Reference Points

- Look to existing operations as reference for planning manpower needs in new operations abroad

Typically, a company setting up a new operation in a foreign country is duplicating, perhaps on a small or slightly altered scale, a product, process, or function that is being performed at home. A new Warnaco plant to produce bras and girdles in Belgium would be similar to other Warnaco facilities in the United States and other countries. Past experience would have shown company officials that for the size of factory being built, a certain number of cutters, machine operators, warehouse workers, drivers, salespeople, accountants, and other workers would be needed. IBM officials would have similar references for a new sales office in Tunisia, as would Shell executives for an oil refinery in Guatemala. The companies would probably have job descriptions for each category to be filled, and from past experience they would know what types of people fit best into specific positions.

Appropriate Technology

- May shift labor or capital intensities if relative costs are different
- MNEs criticized for high capital intensities in LDCs
  - sometimes costly to develop labor intensities
  - sometimes changes can be easily effected but are not
  - used machinery may be possibility
  - changes are often made

Guest Workers
USA Allows workers
from carribean to
cut sugar cane

There is some danger in attempting to duplicate organizational structures and job descriptions abroad, particularly in less-developed countries. For one thing, labor-saving devices that are economically justifiable at home, where wage rates are high, may be more costly than labor-intensive types of production in a country with high unemployment rates and low wages. Labor-intensive methods may also ingratiate the firm with governmental officials, who must cope with unrest from the portion of the population without jobs. Because of differences in labor skills and attitudes, the firm may also find it advantageous to simplify tasks and use equipment that would be considered obsolete in a more advanced economy.

The electronics firms discussed in the case at the beginning of this chapter are being criticized precisely for fitting their production methods to these differences. There seems to be no way to satisfy all the critics of the technology transfer process to less-developed countries. It is argued that MNEs have too often established production methods that are capital-intensive rather than labor-intensive, thus not contributing fully to the decrease needed in unemployment. To put this contention into perspective, it is useful to note that the unemployment and underemployment rates in LDCs average three times the rate that is found in industrial countries.[2] The result is social unrest, which makes it difficult for governmental authorities to concentrate on long-term programs leading to development. So intense is the unemployment problem in many LDCs that it is often considered the primary economic and social problem facing those countries.

The term **appropriate technology** has been coined to describe technology that is more labor-intensive than what would be cost-efficient in an industrial country.[3] It is often assumed that a more labor-intensive production method is either known or can be easily developed at little or no additional cost. There are many obvious examples of more labor-intensive methods that could be used in LDCs, such as replacing automatic bottle-washing machinery and mechanized loading equipment with human efforts.[4] In other cases, such as the extraction of petroleum, there is little latitude (except at a very high engineering cost) to substitute more labor for capital.

The evidence of whether MNEs do alter production possibilities to the extent that is cost-feasible is very mixed. On one hand, there are undoubtedly engineering biases toward duplicating facilities with which the firm has recent experience; these are the plants built to save labor in industrial countries. Management control systems may also place heavy emphasis on output per person, which is more relevant to production needs in industrial countries. Likewise, many governmental authorities within the LDCs are anxious to have showcase plants to promote the message that the countries are modernizing rapidly. On the other hand, case studies point to substantial alterations by MNEs in the LDC subsidiaries because of local costs and availabilities.[5]

As long as unemployment continues to be a major social and economic problem within LDCs, there will be controversies over the amount of labor that should be employed in the production process. A more fundamental question, one seldom raised in these controversies, is whether the benefits to be gained by modifying technologies for the unique conditions of each country are worth the costs that must be incurred. It has often been suggested that MNEs are in a much better position to make alterations than local firms would be because the cost of engineering to create more labor intensity may be amortized among production facilities located in many countries of the world.

One of the suggestions often presented for overcoming the need to engineer new techniques for LDCs is simply to revert to production methods that were used in industrial countries at an earlier period, particularly by transferring used equipment to LDCs. This suggestion presumes that older equipment and methods were labor-intensive and that know-how is still available to transfer. Neither presumption is necessarily true. However, there are sufficient examples to show that used machinery may often be utilized both efficiently and with greater labor intensity in LDCs.[6]

International Labor Mobility

• Pressure for labor to move from unemployed and low-wage areas to places of perceived opportunities

Extent. At the same time that most developing countries have faced critical unemployment problems, many industrial nations and the underpopulated oil-producing countries have been short of workers to run their factories and services. This has created a great deal of pressure for increased immigration, which in turn has been tempered by legal restrictions to minimize the economic and social problems for the countries absorbing large numbers of aliens into their societies. It is not the purpose of this section to detail the debates on the number and method of admitting aliens, although the outcomes could have profound effects on future international economic and political relationships. This section will discuss the major approaches used for admitting foreign workers and the effects on the multinational company in the process.

Reliable figures on the amount of international migration are unavailable because of the large number of people believed to be living illegally in foreign countries. However, the fragmentary evidence is rather startling. For example, in 1981 it was estimated that there were 4.3 million foreign workers and dependents in France[7] and 1.7 million foreign workers out of a population of 5.5 million in Saudi Arabia.[8] Remittances home from workers from Jordan and the Yemen Arab Republic greatly exceed the value of exports from those countries.[9] The People's Republic of China has announced its willingness to export large numbers of workers on a contract basis.[10]

Work force stability problem.   In spite of these dramatic figures, one should keep in mind that firms must rely primarily on the local labor force rather than on workers from outside the country. One of the reasons is that migrant workers in many countries, like New Zealand's workers from Fiji and Tonga, have permission to stay for only short periods of time, such as three to six months.[11] In many cases, workers leave their families behind in the hope of returning home after saving sufficient money while working in the foreign country. In the mid-1970s, for example, France had a net loss in its work force as large numbers of Spaniards returned home. Another uncertainty is the extent to which governmental authorities will restrict the number of foreign workers. This may be done by authorizing fewer work permits or by adding surveillance, such as U.S. Border Patrol roadblocks during the early 1980s, to reduce the number of illegal immigrants. Even if cutbacks are accomplished during a slack period in the economy, so that a firm may switch to the use of local rather than foreign workers, a firm may then face the costly process of training workers who may leave as soon as the economy improves.

Employment adjustments.   The ability of multinational firms to mobilize capital, technology, and management has fed the demand for migrant workers in remote parts of the globe. To construct facilities where minerals are located or in previously unoccupied areas of oil-producing countries, it has been necessary to bring in large numbers of skilled and unskilled workers from abroad. In doing this, MNEs have had to construct housing and infrastructure and to develop social services to serve the new population. Even in population areas, housing shortages might prevent the influx of temporary workers if a company did not make provisions.

Labor is, of course, neither the only factor of production nor the only one that is internationally mobile. There is only fragmentary evidence of the effect of labor mobility on the use and mobility of other production factors. One study concluded that, in many cases, the access to a seemingly endless supply of relatively cheap labor brought about by immigration in Western Europe retarded investment in capital because of the ability to substitute labor for capital, which in turn led to lower output per person than would otherwise have been the case.[12] This analysis assumes that, had there been a small labor market, firms in Western Europe would have concentrated more on making capital investments and on introducing labor-saving technologies. This is not necessarily the case. They may have chosen instead to establish more foreign investments where there was an abundance of unemployed workers. This analysis also seems at variance with more recent European experience, which has included a substantial move to robot-

---

Margin notes:

- Companies are less certain of labor supply when they depend on foreign labor imports
  - countries become restrictive
  - workers return home
  - turnover necessitates more training

- Must build infrastructure in remote areas
- Disagreement on what would have happened to production in absence of immigration
- Need to alter production setup to accommodate foreign workers

ics in spite of a large unemployed foreign population already in some of the countries.[13]

The influx and use of workers from different countries create additional problems in the work place.[14] In the United States during the early twentieth century, large numbers of foreign laborers were secured to work in city industries, for railroads, and in construction. It was common for each nationality group to work under the auspices of its own interpreters and to do particular types of tasks. Barracks and kitchens, provided by employers, were separate, so ethnic separation was perpetuated. Similar practices exist in much of Western Europe today. Some of the results are the relegation of certain nationality groups to less complex jobs owing to the language problem in training, the development of homogeneous ethnic work groups working at cross-purposes with other groups in the organization, and the emergence of go-betweens who can communicate with management and labor.

COMPENSATION

Importance of Differences

- Amount and method varies for similar skills and tasks in different countries
- MNEs may need to pay more than local firms to entice workers from existing jobs

Compensation policies and practices directly affect a firm's competitive viability, for an important competitive ingredient is a firm's ability to attract, maintain, and motivate personnel. Adequate compensation is necessary to achieve these goals. Aside from the normal staffing procedure, Chapters 5 and 6 showed that labor cost differences among countries sometimes lead to competitive advantages and motivate many firms to establish foreign production facilities. Domestically, there are vast differences in the amount and type of compensation people receive. The amount depends on the estimated contributions made to the business, supply and demand ("going wage") for particular skills in the area, cost of living, governmental legislation, and collective bargaining ability. The methods of payment (salaries, wages, commissions, bonuses, and fringe benefits) depend on customs, feelings of security, taxes, and governmental requirements. Internationally, a host of factors make the differences much greater and the planning more complex.

Such differences place the international firm in a dilemma. The firm cannot pay people less than the going wage or it will not attract sufficient personnel of the caliber desired. Yet if the firm pays the going wage in each country, there will be divergences in pay scales for people doing the same jobs in different countries. To bring everyone up to the highest level is usually too costly and might result in animosity among other firms operating in the same locale. Because employees usually compare their pay with that of other people in the country, international variances probably create little dissonance. International firms usually pay slightly better than their local counterparts in the lower-wage countries, primarily to attract people away from their present jobs, but certainly far below the salary paid for similar jobs in the highest-wage countries. Other factors leading to higher wages by international companies relate to their management philosophy and structure. For example, techniques that lead to greater efficiencies allow for higher payments to company employees. Furthermore, the international company's management philosophy, particularly in contrast to local, family-run companies, is often to attract high-level workers by offering higher relative wages.

Fringe Benefits

● Type of benefit varies substantially

● Portion of total compensation comprised of fringe benefits differs by country

The amount of compensation given in the form of fringe benefits differs radically from one country to another. Direct compensation figures therefore do not accurately reflect the amount a company must pay for a given job in a given country. The types of benefits that are either customary or have been required are also widely divergent. In Europe it has been common for employees to get added compensation according to the number of family members or because of unpleasant working conditions. Italians have gotten extra pay for each child as well as supplements for working at an open-hearth furnace or at high altitudes. In Belgium and the Netherlands, workers have been compensated for the cost of taking trains or bikes to work.[15] Finnish paper mill workers have received a "sauna premium" for missing baths when they work on Sunday.[16] Fiji Island miners have gotten a daily half-hour "sex break" to fulfill marital obligations.[17] In Japan, workers commonly receive such benefits as family allowance, housing loans and subsidies, lunches, children's education, and subsidized vacations so that fringe benefits comprise a much higher portion of total compensation than in the United States. End-of-the-year bonuses of up to three months' pay, housing, and profit sharing are other types of benefits that are common in many countries. In Britain, blue-collar workers—unless they agree otherwise—have had to be paid in currency rather than by check. This is estimated to cost industry between $58 and $74 a year per employee.[18]

● In many countries it is impossible, hard, or expensive to lay off workers

Job security benefits. Firing or laying off an employee may be either impossible or very expensive in many countries, resulting in unexpectedly higher costs for a company that is used to taking advantage of the economies of fluctuating its employment figures. In the United States, for instance, layoffs not only are permitted but have grown to be expected when demand falls seasonally or cyclically. In many countries a firm has no legal recourse except to fire workers—and then perhaps only if the firm is closing down its operations. In West Germany a fired worker may get up to eighteen months' salary. To curtail operations, a company has to come to an agreement with its unions and the government on such issues as extended benefits and the retraining and relocation of workers.[19]

There is some recent evidence that lifetime employment is breaking down, even in Japan which has been epitomized for its practices. In Japan, such practices have been customary rather than legally prescribed. Companies have been using a variety of methods to cut the size of their work forces.[20] There have also been recent increases of dismissing employees whose performance is inadequate. This in turn has led to increased voluntary mobility by workers who give precedence to outside opportunities over present loyalties.[21]

● **Workers versus company responsibility varies**
  ● **different attitudes toward safety**

Liability for injuries. Company, worker, or third-party neglect may lead to various types of injury. Physical injury may result from negligent driving by transport workers, faulty maintenance, and noninstallation of safety equipment. Monetary injury may result from careless handling of cash, embezzlement of funds, and breakage of products and equipment. A survey of liabilities in forty-six countries indicated widespread variances in the extent to which companies or workers are held responsible for injuries.[22] The determination of who is responsible should dictate how firms handle these contingencies. The amount and allocation of expenditures for insurance, training, and safety equipment thus varies substantially by country. The lack of required safety systems for employees in some countries has been well publicized of late, and MNEs have been criticized for lax practices in low-wage countries that they would be prohibited from using at home.[23] In addition to differences in safety equipment, there is evidence of some country differences in attitudes toward safety. This has been blamed for Spain's auto accident rate, which is 30 percent higher than elsewhere in Europe, and for the fact that Spain's airline, Iberia, accounted for 20 percent of in-flight errors in North Atlantic airspace that involve the risk of collision, even though the line accounts for only 1.5 percent of the traffic.[24]

● **Gives cost savings and continuity**

Internationalizing benefits. Although firms must adhere to local regulations and customs, there are potent reasons for internationalizing fringe benefit programs as much as possible. Many insurance companies have instituted worldwide programs to bring local insurance projects under a single insurance umbrella. Even without uniformity among the different areas, a program of this type allows for lower costs through insuring larger groups, centralizing insurance management, and providing a global net cost system that allows firms to obtain good worldwide insurance experience. As employees are transferred to foreign countries, greater uniformity in programs results in fewer problems with individual adjustments. The employee likewise has less risk of losing the vested benefits built up before the transfer.

How to compare. Too often, compensation expenses are compared on a per-worker basis. This may bear little relationship to the total expense of the use of these individuals. People's abilities and motivations vary widely; consequently, it is the output associated with cost that is of importance. It has often been noted that seemingly cheap labor may actually raise the total compensation expenditure because of the need for more supervision, added training expenses, and adjustments in the method of production. Not only are there differences among countries but also differences within countries. Most countries have geographic or ethnic groups with low levels of education, inadequate nutrition, or other attributes that might decrease working efficiency. Frequently, governments grant incentives for the employment of these people. These incentives may be sufficient for overcoming the added costs of locating in backward areas. However, managers must take into account not only the costs associated with inefficiencies but also the probability of continued governmental assistance.

Labor Cost Dynamics

- Relative costs change, so must consider
  - productivity change
  - labor rate change
  - conversion of labor rate to currency of competitor

Differences among countries in amount and type of compensation are not static. Salaries and wages (as well as other expenditures) may rise more rapidly in one locale than another. Therefore the relative competitiveness of operations in different countries may shift in time. Since it is the output associated with cost that is of most importance in comparing labor competitiveness, a recent example will illustrate shifting capabilities. In 1981, U.S. productivity per worker in manufacturing increased by 2.8 percent, whereas hourly compensation rates went up by 10.2 percent. The result was a unit labor cost increase of 7.2 percent ($1.102 \div 1.028$). Meanwhile, productivity in the United Kingdom increased by 5.9 percent and hourly compensation in pounds sterling by 16.2 percent, which amounted to a unit cost increase of 9.7 percent ($1.162 \div 1.059$) when measured in pounds sterling. This meant that labor costs were rising more rapidly in the United Kingdom than the United States in terms of local currencies. Because sterling fell substantially in relation to the dollar, however, the unit labor cost measured in dollars actually fell by 4.5 percent in the United Kingdom compared to the 7.2 percent increase in the U.S. This had a substantial impact on the improved international competitiveness of the United Kingdom relative to that of the United States for that year.[25]

COMPARATIVE LABOR RELATIONS

In each country where an MNE operates, it must deal with a group of workers whose approach will be affected by the sociopolitical environment of the country and by the traditions and regulations of collective bargaining.

Sociopolitical Environment

Overall attitude affects how labor and management view each other and how labor will try to improve its lot

One of the striking international differences in labor-management relations is how each group views its relationship with the other. When there is very little mobility between the two groups, there may be little direct cooperation toward reaching an overall corporate objective. This type of separation may be enhanced if a marked class difference exists between management and labor.

Certainly much of the labor strife in the United Kingdom in recent years may be traced to labor's and management's perceived involvement in a class struggle, even though labor has been gaining a greater share of total British income and wealth for some time. One of the results has been the use of governmental policy to temper relations between labor and management. This would probably not have developed had the groups been able to negotiate a more lasting agreement on the working conditions necessary to maintain production. The British situation in recent years has been further complicated by the fact that, unlike any other industrial country, a labor agreement between a company and union is not a legally enforceable contract unless the parties include a specific provision to that effect.[26] The government during the 1970s therefore played a major role in securing labor's acceptance of wage restraints.

In such countries as the United States, Brazil, and Switzerland, labor demands are largely met through an adversary process between directly affected management and labor.[27] Unions have little influence on how members actually vote in political elections. In contrast, labor groups in many countries vote largely in blocs. The result of this solidarity is that demands may be met primarily through national legislation rather than through collective bargaining with management. Such mechanisms as strikes or slowdowns to effect changes may also be national in scope. An implication of this is that a company's production or ability to distribute its product may be much more dependent on perceived labor conditions in the country as a whole. In 1984, for example, French truckers demanded lower taxes on diesel fuel and insurance and a subsidy to modernize French trucking. To make their demands known, they set up more than 250 blockades, closed off major airports, and set fire to the Paris-Lyon railway line.[28] The whole economy was affected. The use of mediation by an impartial party to try to bring opposing sides together varies as well. In Israel it is required by law. In the United States and the United Kingdom it is voluntary. Among countries that have mediation practices, attitudes toward it are diverse; for example, there is much less enthusiasm for it in India than in the United States.[29] Not all differences are settled either through changes in legislation or through collective bargaining. Another means is the labor court or government-chosen arbitrator. For example, in Australia wages in many industries are arbitrated on a semi-annual basis.[30] Settlements may be very one-sided if appointments in a country have been made by political parties that are pro- or anti-labor.

Union Structure

- National versus local
- Industry versus company
- One versus several for same company

Companies in a given country may deal with one or several different unions. A union itself may represent workers in many different industries, in many different companies within the same industry, or merely in one company. If in only one company, it may represent all plants or just one plant. There are diversities within countries; however, the most prevalent relationships vary from one country to another. For example in the United States, unions tend to be national in nature, representing certain types of workers (e.g., airline pilots, coal miners, truck drivers, or university professors) in all of a company's different plants as well as in many different organizations. A company may therefore deal with several different national unions. Each collective bargaining process is usually characterized by a single firm on one side, rather than an association of different firms, which deals with one of the unions representing a certain type of worker in all the company's plants. In Japan a union typically represents all the workers in a given company and has only very loose affiliations with unions in other companies. This is alleged to be a reason that Japanese unions tend to be less militant than those in most other industrial countries. They seldom strike, and when they do, they may stop working for only a short period of time or continue working while wearing a symbolic arm band to indicate the protest. Because of the closer company affiliation, union leaders are hesitant to do anything that might hurt the company's ability to compete in the world markets.[31] In Sweden the bargaining tends to be highly centralized in that employers from numerous companies in different industries deal together with a federation of trade unions. In West Germany employers from associations of firms in the same industries bargain jointly with union federations.[32]

Protection from Closures

- Takeover to publicize plight
  - especially on proposed closings
- Legislation to give advanced notice

The Signetics situation described in the case at the beginning of the chapter involved the occupation of a plant by workers as a means of gaining demands. This is a method increasingly used by workers in many countries.[33] These moves have usually been in response to proposed layoffs, shifts in production location, and cessation of operations. By moving into the plants, the workers have at times prevented the transfer of machinery, components, and finished goods. In fact, they have even continued to produce until they ran out of raw materials and components and sold the output on the street in order to prolong their ability to occupy the plants. The results of these efforts have been mixed. In the case of Lip, a French watch company, the occupation resulted in an eventual reorganization and the continuance of what had seemed to be an operation doomed to failure. In the case of a Philips plant in the Netherlands, however, public opinion turned against the workers, so management was able to transfer production anyway.

That workers will go so far to try to prevent a plant from closing indicates how important this issue is in some countries, particularly those in Western Europe where prenotification has been negotiated or legislated almost everywhere. The longest advanced notification is one year in West Germany. The Western European situation is in contrast to that in Canada and the United States where less than a fifth of contracts require employers to give more than a week's notice of closure.[34]

Codetermination

• Seek labor-management cooperation through sharing in leadership
  • may have unions as well

Another trend in labor relations, particularly in northern Europe, is the participation by labor in the management of firms. The most common means has been by having workers represented on the board of directors, either with or without veto power. Labor's participation has at times, as at Chrysler's U.K. facilities, been proposed by management in a belief that this would prevent constant strikes and walkouts.[35]

In spite of some voluntary moves toward codetermination, most existing examples have been mandated by legislation, such as requirements in West Germany and Sweden. These moves have been dictated not only by the philosophy of cooperative leadership but also by the opinion that labor has risks and stakes in the organization as well as shareholders. Because of a belief that the interests of blue- and white-collar workers are different, recent efforts have been made to ensure that each group is represented.[36] At this writing, it is too soon to state emphatically what effects labor's participation will have on multinational operations and management's authority and decision-making power. Already, however, there have been examples of effective blockage of investment outflows, acquisitions, and plant closures. Where layoffs have been necessary, foreign workers have been given less protection than citizens.[37] The codetermination movement seems destined to temper the ability of MNEs to optimize on a global basis.

In West Germany, for example, the system of codetermination gives workers a voice in decision making through representation on local Works' Councils and corporate supervisory boards.[38] Workers in West German firms elect representatives to serve on the Works' Council of the firm. This council makes decisions on social matters (such as the conduct of employees, hours of work, and safety) and economic and financial matters. Codetermination is in effect for social matters in that when a dispute arises between the Works' Council and the Labor Director of the firm, the dispute is settled by arbitration. In economic and financial matters the Works' Council is provided information and consulted in decisions, but the Council does not have the same strength of codetermination that it does in social matters. The members of the Works' Council are not representatives of the union, although they may be members of the union. Rather, they are representatives of and members of the work force of that particular firm.

The Works' Council and the unions have different responsibilities. For instance, collective bargaining takes place between employer associations and the unions and covers all workers within a West German state or part of that state. Since the companies in the employer associations vary in size and ability to cover different possible wage rates, the negotiated annual wage rates are minimums. These can be negotiated upward at the company level; however, the unions are barred by law from negotiating at the company or plant level. This is the task of the Works' Council.

All firms with more than 2000 employees have been required to have workers as half of the members of the supervisory board, similar to the Board of Directors in the United States. At least one of the workers' representatives must come from employees with a managerial position; and the chairman, who is elected by the shareholders' representatives, is given an extra vote in case of a tie. This pretty well ensures that the shareholders have control over decisions that are made by the board. Volkswagen's supervisory board in the early 1980s is a good illustration. It contained twenty members, ten of whom were workers' representatives. Of the nine workers' reps who were not from management, one was the national president of the Metalworkers' Union, two more were officials of that union, and the other six, who also happened to belong to the Metalworkers' Union, were members of the Works' Council. Firms with fewer than 2000 workers do not have to have a parity of worker representation on the Supervisory Board, but they must have at least one third of the board members from the workers.

Quality Circles

• Small groups meet to discuss how problems can be solved in their areas

To improve worker productivity, companies worldwide have experimented with a variety of means to commit workers to suggest means by which output can be improved. Codetermination efforts have been partially motivated by this objective, and suggestion boxes are probably the most visible symbol of the movement. Because of rapid productivity increases in Japan recently, attention naturally has focused on Japanese approaches to worker involvement. One such activity is the quality circle, with which about 8 million Japanese workers are involved. The system involves having small groups of workers meet regularly to spot and solve problems in their areas. It is a participatory effort designed to get people to say things among their peers that as individuals they would be reluctant to communicate to managers.

Team Efforts

- Small groups develop to foster productivity

In some countries, particularly Japan and its investments abroad, there has been an emphasis on work teams in order (1) to foster a group cohesiveness and (2) to get workers involved in multiple rather than a limited number of tasks. In terms of the former, it is not uncommon for a portion of the compensation to be based on the group output so that peer pressure is created to reduce absenteeism and to increase efforts. In terms of the latter, workers may rotate jobs within the group to reduce boredom and to develop replacement skills in case someone is not present. Included also have been practices whereby workers' groups control their own quality and repair their own equipment.[39]

INTERNATIONAL PRESSURES ON NATIONAL PRACTICES

- ILO monitors labor conditions worldwide
- Codes of conduct
  - on South African operations
  - by ILO and OECD on industrial relations within MNEs

In 1919 the International Labor Organization (ILO) was set up on the premise that the failure of any nation to adopt humane conditions of labor is an obstacle in the way of other nations that desire to improve the conditions in their own countries. Through ILO activities and through the general enhancement of communications globally, people are increasingly aware of differences in labor conditions among countries. Among the newsworthy reports have been legal proscriptions against collective bargaining in Malaysia and wages below minimum standards in Indonesia. Once these conditions have been noted, there have been varying efforts to pressure for changes through economic and political sanctions from abroad.

The most noteworthy example of efforts to effect internal changes in labor conditions has involved pressures on MNEs operating in South Africa. Through church groups, resolutions have been presented to stockholders proposing that firms cease, cut back, or report more fully on their South African operations. At the center in the United States has been Reverend Leon Sullivan, who set forth a list of principles on nondiscrimination and improvement of conditions for oppressed groups in the South African operations of MNEs. About half the nearly 300 U.S. firms operating in South Africa have adopted the principles. Among the developments have been Union Carbide's equalization of pay between blacks and whites doing the same tasks and GM's desegregation of cafeterias and locker rooms.[40] Meanwhile, the United Kingdom has set up a Code of Practice for its firms' operations in South Africa. Although these practices have been voluntary, there have been numerous pressures for a move toward equality in labor practices. The fact that progress has been slower than critics want has led to concern among MNEs that in the future they may be caught in the middle, between pro- and anti-apartheid pressures.

Another area influencing the labor practices of MNEs has been codes of conduct on industrial relations issued by the Organization for Economic Cooperation and Development (OECD) and the ILO. The EC and the United Nations have also been discussing their own codes. Although the OECD and ILO codes are voluntary, they may harbinger some transnational regulations of MNE activities in the future. Trade unions have been anxious to get interpretations of the guidelines and to make them legally enforceable. The present complaint mechanism is slow; however, it can give strength to national governments as they pressure MNEs. In one case, Raytheon shut down its Belgian subsidiary, which held insufficient assets to cover severance pay liabilities to its Belgian workers. Raytheon refused to bring in more assets from the outside on the grounds that the subsidiary was a separate legal entity with limited liability. The case was taken to a committee within the OECD, which suggested that the parent company has a special responsibility. Raytheon renegotiated and supplemented the assets.[41]

MULTINATIONAL OWNERSHIP AND COLLECTIVE BARGAINING

During recent years numerous articles have been written on the changing relationships between labor and management brought about by growing multinational business involvement. Much of this material has been written from a protagonist or antagonist viewpoint and should be examined with caution. In many cases, labor or MNE actions have been presented as actual or impending when in reality they are either isolated examples or merely potential means by which one of the two groups could strengthen its position vis-à-vis the other. Fortunately, some recent treatises on the subject have surveyed the literature to separate fact from fiction and actualities from potentialities.[42]

MNE Advantages

- Disagreement on home country employment effects of foreign direct investment but
  - labor push to save home country jobs

Job security. It is often argued that, when the number of jobs is not growing, the main concern of workers is employment stability rather than other work conditions. If MNEs have exported jobs from industrial countries, then it should follow that labor demands in those countries have been tempered in the process. As we showed in Chapter 11, it is difficult to conclude whether MNEs have increased or decreased home country employment by making direct investments abroad. Concomitant with investment outflows have been investment inflows and exports to the foreign facilities. Both of these tend to negate the possible net loss of jobs through foreign investment.

It is tempting to conclude that, if investment outflows had not been made, MNEs would have sustained or increased their domestic facilities by an amount comparable to that established abroad. Such domestic production may not, however, have been forthcoming, since (1) trade barriers may have prevented serving the foreign market except through foreign production facilities, and (2) competitive factors may have dictated that certain labor-intensive activities be moved away from traditional locations in industrial countries. It has been noted that, in the latter situation, the composition of work forces in industrial countries has moved more toward white-collar than toward blue-collar jobs. While some of this internal realignment in work force composition may be inevitable with or without MNE activities, the result is nevertheless a shrinking of traditional bargaining units.[43] The white-collar workers, even when organized by unions, may not be as adverse to management, since they may look forward to moving into management positions themselves. MNEs may rationalize international activities by setting up production facilities in countries with low wages and high unemployment while simultaneously concentrating such functions as accounting, R&D, and staff support in industrial countries. To the extent that they do this, they are contributing to work force composition changes that weaken the size of production bargaining units in industrial countries.

- Labor may be at disadvantage in MNE negotiations because
  - country bargaining unit only small part of MNE activities
  - MNE may continue serving customers with foreign production or resources
- MNE limitations because of capacity, legal restrictions, shared ownership, and differentiated products

Product and resource flows. If, during a strike situation in one country, an MNE is able to divert output from facilities in other countries to the consumers in the country where the strike occurs, there is less client pressure on the MNE to reach an agreement. Furthermore, since operations in a given country usually comprise a small percentage of the MNE's total worldwide sales, profits, and cash flows, a strike in that country may have minimal effects on the MNE's global performance. The MNE's geographic diversification is therefore argued to be to its advantage when bargaining with labor in a given country. It is contended that an MNE may simply hold out longer and be less affected in a strike situation.

In one well-publicized case, Hertz brought in employees to Denmark from its U.K., Italian, and French operations when its Danish employees struck.[44] While this was effective from Hertz's standpoint, the ability to move personnel across borders is extremely limited because of legal, cost, and language impediments. Other factors would seem to moderate the MNE's ability to shift other resources around. The MNE may divert output to other markets only if it has excess capacity and only if there is a homogeneous product produced in more than one market. If these two conditions are present, the MNE would still confront the cost and trade barriers that led to the establishment of multiple production facilities in the first place. If the struck operation is only partially owned by the MNE, partners or even minority shareholders may be less willing and able to sustain a lengthy work stoppage. If the idle facilities normally produce components needed for integrated production elsewhere, then a strike may have much more far-reaching effects. One may therefore conclude that the advantages of international diversification upon the collective bargaining process are present in only limited circumstances.

- MNE may threaten workers that production will be moved abroad
- Even a domestic firm faces threat of foreign competition

Production switching. There are documented examples of threats by MNEs to move production units to other countries if labor conditions and demands in one country result in changes in the least-cost location of production. A good case was when the chief executive of Hyster told employees in Scotland that the company was prepared to move two production lines from the Netherlands to Scotland and expand its Scottish operations if workers would decide within 48 hours to take a 14 percent pay cut. The following morning, workers received letters saying that the company might go somewhere else if its offer were not accepted.[45] In a speech the President of Ford Motor Company warned that, if labor did not improve the competitive position of the domestic auto industry, the company would be "forced to manufacture more and more products offshore where costs are lower and perhaps ultimately produce complete automobiles offshore."[46]

Production shifts may take place because of changes in the least-cost location whether an MNE is involved or not. This is particularly true as economies have become more open to imports. During the 1976 rubber strike, for example, Firestone advertised that U.S. worker demands would lead to more imports of foreign-made tires. Thus one may not conclude that the threat of international switches in production location is purely the result of increased MNE activities.

Although there are circumstances in which shifts would seem more plausible when MNEs are involved, one might also argue that MNEs are less likely to cause a shift in production than when national competitors are involved in various countries. The MNE must weigh the cost-saving advantages of moving its production location against the losses in terms of shutting down existing facilities, creating bad will, and becoming vulnerable through decreased diversification. A national company, such as a Korean firm producing in Korea, may not worry nearly so much about what happens to a Canadian owned plant in Canada when it exports to the Canadian market.

- Labor claims disadvantages with MNEs because
  - decision making far away
  - hard to get full data on MNEs' global operations

Structural problems. It is often contended that it is difficult for labor unions to deal with MNEs because of the complexities in the location of decision making and the difficulties involved in interpreting financial data. If the real decision makers are far removed from the bargaining location, such as at home country headquarters, it is often assumed that this will lead to arbitrarily stringent management decisions. One could conceivably argue that the opposite might take place, particularly if the demands abroad seem low in comparison with those being made at home. In reality, it is difficult to determine exactly where within an organization decisions are being made, but most research indicates that industrial relations are very much delegated to the local subsidiary levels.

The question of interpreting financial data of MNEs is complex because of disparities among managerial, tax, and public disclosure requirements in home and host countries. Labor has been particularly leery of the possibility of artificial transfer pricing to give the appearance that a given subsidiary is unable to meet labor demands. These concerns seem to place an overreliance on a company's ability to pay. Although this is an important factor, the going wage rates in the industry and the geographic area seem far more important in the final determination of a compensation package. Although MNEs may have more complex data, legal regulations are such that at least some set must satisfy local authorities. This set should be no more difficult to interpret than that involving a purely local firm. In terms of transfer pricing, it is very doubtful that MNEs set artificial levels to aid them in collective bargaining situations. To understate profits in one place would imply overstating them elsewhere, thus negating the advantage, unless changes are made to reflect different contract periods. Tax authorities would not be likely to approve sudden price changes before contract negotiation. Furthermore, any artificial prices would also have to consider income taxes, tariffs, and opinions of minority shareholders.

Labor Responses and Initiatives

- Labor might strengthen position vis-à-vis MNEs through cross-national cooperation
  - some examples, but isolated
- Most actions at national level because of competition among labor in different countries

Information sharing. The most common form of cooperation among unions in different countries is through an exchange of information. This helps them refute company claims as well as cite precedents from other countries when bargaining issues seem transferable. The exchange of information is carried out by international confederations of unions representing different types of workers and ideologies, by trade secretariats composed of unions in a single industry or in a complex of related industries, and by company councils that include representatives from an MNE's plants around the world.[47] Such information exchange has led to demands by International Nickel and Kaiser Aluminum workers in New Caledonia for the thirteen-week vacation given to their counterparts in the United States every five years. Bethlehem Steel in Liberia began collecting union dues as a result of the United Steelworkers Union's consultations with the Liberian union. In fact the same union officials who have negotiated U.S. Steel's cement industry contracts in the United States have done the negotiating for U.S. Steel's cement plant in the Bahamas.[48]

Assistance to foreign bargaining units. Labor groups in one country may support their counterparts in other countries in a number of ways. These include refusing to work overtime when that output would supply the market normally served by striking workers' production, sending financial aid to workers in other countries, and presenting demands to management through other countries. Although one can cite examples of these types of assistance, at the moment they must be classified as more potential than actual initiatives.

One can find more examples of refusals to cooperate in these matters than of successful collaboration.

Simultaneous actions.   There have been a few examples of simultaneous negotiations and strikes.[49] Among the more notable have been meetings among the unions that negotiate with General Electric worldwide, a common strategy for unions from nine countries that represent St. Gobain, and simultaneous work stoppages in England and Italy against Dunlop-Pirelli. The concept of multinational collective bargaining seems less appealing to labor leaders now than it did in the early 1970s. This is due to the relatively few successes and the national differences in union structures and demands.[50] Furthermore, there has undoubtedly been a growing nationalism of workers as their fear of foreign competition has grown.

National approaches.   Although one can uncover numerous examples of cooperation among unions of different countries, their combat against MNEs has been primarily on a national basis. There is little enthusiasm on the part of workers in one country to incur costs in order to support workers in another country. They tend to view each other instead as competitors. Even between the United States and Canada, where there has long been a common union membership, there has been a move among Canadian workers to form unions that are independent of the United States. One Canadian organizer summed up much of the attitude by saying, "An American union is not going to fight to protect Canadian jobs at the expense of American jobs." The logic was that international unions will adopt policies favoring the bulk of their membership, which is bound to be American in any joint Canadian-U.S. relationship.[51]

Through national legislation, workers have managed in places to acquire representation on boards of directors, to regulate the entry of foreign workers, to limit imports, and to limit foreign investment outflows. It is therefore probable that most foreseeable regulations will be at the national rather than the international level.

SUMMARY

- When setting up a new operation in a foreign country, firms may use existing facilities as guides for determining labor needs. They should make adjustments, however, to compensate for different labor skills, costs, and availabilities.

- It is often assumed that a more labor-intensive technology is needed to fit the needs of LDCs. There are a number of barriers to the development and infusion of such technology, although there are undoubtedly areas in which MNEs may easily make adaptations.

- For some areas of the world a substantial portion of the labor supply is imported. This creates special stability, supervision, and training problems for the companies employing them.

- Owing to the enormous variance in fringe benefits, direct compensation figures do not accurately reflect the amount a company must pay for a given job. In addition, job security benefits (no layoffs, severance pay, etc.) add substantially to compensation costs.

- Although per-worker comparisons are useful indicators of cost differences, what is relevant for international competitiveness is the output associated with total costs. The costs may shift in time, thus changing relative international competitive positions.

- The sociopolitical environment will determine to a great extent the type of relationships between labor and management.

- The number, representation, and organization of unions vary substantially among countries.

- One of labor's growing weapons has been to occupy plants in order to focus national attention on their plight and demands.

- Codetermination and quality circles are two types of participation of labor in the management of firms. The purpose is usually an attempt to bring about a cooperative rather than an adversary environment.

- In recent years there have been efforts to get firms to follow internationally accepted labor practices regardless of where they are operating or whether or not the practices are contrary to the norms and laws of the countries in which they are operating.

- It is often alleged that MNEs weaken the position of labor in the collective bargaining process because of MNEs' international diversification, their threats to export jobs, and their complex structures and reporting mechanisms.

- Cooperation between labor groups in different countries is small but has on occasion been used to combat multinational firms. Strategies include information exchanges, simultaneous negotiations or strikes, and refusals to work overtime if the intent is to compensate for a striking firm in another country.

C A S E   IMPORTATION OF FOREIGN LABOR PRACTICES[52]

As U.S. productivity increases lagged in relation to those of some of its competitors in the late 1970s, many U.S. firms considered means to reverse the trend. One such means was to observe foreign labor practices to determine whether any of them could be adopted in the United States to increase output. Some differences in practices were easily identifiable. However, it was not clear that these were the causes for the U.S. competitive deterioration—nor was it clear whether labor practices from one country would be accepted by workers in another country.

One of the things that was discernible was that, in Japan and some Western European countries, there was a more cooperative working arrangement between labor and management than existed in the United States. Among the methods illustrating this cooperation were codetermination practices, quality circles, a lifetime commitment to continue employing workers, and various profit-sharing arrangements. People who advocated the implementation of these practices argued that they lead to a joint commitment by labor and management to upgrade skills and work hard at increasing the size of the pie to be shared by employees. It was argued, for example, that as long as employees lack long-term security, they feel free to quit for better-paying positions. This mobility in turn has made companies reluctant to give employees lengthy and expensive training. It was also argued that, as long as labor and management viewed each other as adversaries, the companies got only the hands and feet of the workers and not their brains and know-how.

Not everyone agreed that labor practices were the major factor contributing to differences in productivity increases. Along with the so-called cooperative practices, many European and Japanese firms were also employing newer technology and a greater capital intensity than their U.S. counterparts. It was therefore very difficult to ascertain with certainty the real cause of productivity differences.

There were even questions as to how well some of the labor practices were working in countries with long experience in dealing with them. In West Germany, for example, the deputy chairman of Hoechst stated, "Codetermination in Germany has led to a worsening of the social climate." The chairman of Mannesmann appealed to shareholders to restructure the company to eliminate codetermination, which he felt had a negative effect on competitiveness. It was also noted that in Japan, the country that most epitomized a lifetime employment concept, there was an increase in firings, layoffs, and rewards based on merit rather than longevity.

Even among people who believed that the cooperative practices had a positive impact on productivity outside the United States there was doubt about the ability to apply these methods effectively in a U.S. context. Some observers reasoned that an historical hostility between tycoons such as Andrew Carnegie and the immigrant laborers they employed has lingered on to prevent an immediate cooperative environment regardless of what practices were introduced. Some union leaders saw that cooperative policies were at odds with the U.S. philosophy that adversary positions and confrontation techniques best serve the company and national interests. In fact, the executive assistant to the president of the AFL-CIO said, "We don't want to blur in any way the respective roles of management and labor in the plant." Another union executive took the stance that "A family approach can't work. Americans just don't think like the Japanese." Officials of Mazda, when considering the establishment of a U.S. plant in 1984, openly questioned whether U.S. production practices were different because of the nature of workers or because of the nature of their unions.

In spite of such misgivings, by the early 1980s a number of U.S. firms were beginning to employ labor practices that were deemed by them to be effective outside the United States. Experiments were made by certain non-U.S.-based MNEs (such as Sharp Electric of Japan) that were convinced that they could use certain of their home country practices in their U.S. subsidiaries. There was considerable publicity about the success of some of these experiments, such as Sanyo's television production in Arkansas. In addition, certain U.S. MNEs were willing to try out in the United States some of the practices they had adopted in their foreign subsidiaries.

One of the most publicized participating actions involved the placement in 1979 of the UAW union president, Douglas Fraser, on the board of Chrysler. Although such U.S. firms as Harman International Industries and Carborumdum had already experimented with employee participation, it was very doubtful that Chrysler would have placed the UAW man on the board if it had not been for two factors: (1) The UAW insisted on this in exchange for wage concessions as Chrysler was on the verge of bankruptcy, and (2) Chrysler had experience with codetermination through its European operations. There was far from a consensus among UAW members that this was a proper course of action. Since the UAW also represented workers in Ford and GM, the placement of the UAW president on the board of Chrysler was viewed by many as a conflict of interest. After Mr. Fraser retired and vacated his seat, the Chrysler chairman, Lee Iacocca, supported placing Owen Bieber, the new UAW president, on the board. This was after Chrysler had become profitable again.

Another participatory method gaining much attention was the use of quality circles. This was actually a U.S. innovation that caught on in Japan well before it was popular in the United States. In 1979 it was estimated that only fifteen U.S. firms employed the circles, but another fifty adopted them in 1980. Although the companies have been able to point to some cost-saving innovations, both management and labor concede that workers are not apt to suggest improvements that will lead to layoffs.

QUESTIONS

1. Which foreign participatory practices are the most and least apt to work in a U.S. context?
2. What are the potential problems of trying to adapt foreign labor practices to a domestic work situation?

NOTES

1. Data for this case were taken primarily from "El Salvador: U.S. Plants Hum along Despite the Turmoil," *Business Week,* April 13, 1981, p. 60; "Booming Malaysia Presses for Industrialization," *Business Week,* April 13, 1981, pp. 66–73; "Singapore: Cheap Labor Is on the Way out," *Business Week,* July 16, 1979, p. 48; Barbara Ehrenreich and Annette Fuentes, "Life on the Global Assembly Line," *Ms.,* January 1981, pp. 53–71; "Asia," *Business Week,* March 15, 1982, pp. 38–39; Richard J. Meislin, "Mexican Border Plants Beginning to Hire Men," *New York Times,* March 19, 1984, p. D8; Fred R. Bleakley, "Americans in Business in El Salvador: Juggling Risk, Fear and Returns," *New York Times,* March 25, 1984, pp. F6–7; Alfred L. Malabre, Jr., "Persistent Pay Gap," *Wall Street Journal,* April 18, 1984, pp. 1+.

2. Yves Sabolo, "Employment and Unemployment, 1960–90," *International Labour Review,* December 1975, p. 408.

3. For a good discussion, see Nicolas Jéquier, ed., *Appropriate Technology: Problems and Promises* (Paris: Organization for Economic Cooperation and Development, 1976).

4. Louis T. Wells, Jr., "Don't Overautomate Your Foreign Plant," *Harvard Business Review,* January–February 1974, pp. 111–118.

5. For a good survey of the various studies, see Samuel A. Morley and Gordon W. Smith, "The Choice of Technology: Multinational Firms in Brazil," *Economic Development and Cultural Change,* January 1977, pp. 240–241.

6. Dilmus D. Jones, *Used Machinery and Economic Development* (East Lansing, Mich.: Michigan State University, 1974), p. 125.

7. Felix Kessler, "Immigrants in France Anger Citizens," *Wall Street Journal,* January 22, 1981, p. 29.

8. David Ignatius, "A Saudi Job Offers Hordes of Foreigners a Chance to Prosper," *Wall Street Journal,* March 20, 1981, pp. 1+.

9. Zafer Ecevit and K. C. Zachariah, "International Labor Migration," *Finance and Development,* December 1978, p. 36.

10. "China: The Newest Export, Legions of Laborers," *Business Week,* January 28, 1980, p. 59.

11. R. J. Campbell and J. de Bres, "Temporary Labor Migration between Tonga and New Zealand," *International Labour Review,* December 1975, p. 445.

12. W. R. Böhning and D. Maillat, *The Effects of the Employment of Foreign Workers* (Paris: Organization for Economic Cooperation and Development, 1974), pp. 30–31.

13. "The Pressures Mounting over Migrant Labor," *Business Week,* May 3, 1982, p. 44.

14. For a more complete discussion of business adjustments, see John D. Daniels, "International Mobility of People," *Essays in International Business,* No. 1, March 1980, pp. 3–7.

15. "The Wages of Prosperity," *Time,* November 11, 1966, p. 102.

16. "Sauna Supplement," *Wall Street Journal,* October 5, 1976, p. 1.

17. "Cost of Loving?," *Wall Street Journal,* June 8, 1976, p. 1.

18. "Century-Old Law Setting Cash Payday Rankles British Bank," *Wall Street Journal,* December 10, 1980, p. 34.

19. "Global Report," *Wall Street Journal,* August 29, 1977, p. 6.

20. Kazutoshi Koshiro, "Lifetime Employment in Japan," *Monthly Labor Review,* August 1984, pp. 34–35.

21. "An Aging Work Force Strains Japan's Traditions," *Business Week,* April 20, 1981, p. 81.

22. Felice Morgenstern, "The Civil Liability of Workers for Injury or Damage Caused in Their Employment," *International Labour Review,* May–June 1976, pp. 317–328.

23. Barry Newman, "Danger at Work," *Wall Street Journal,* December 9, 1980, pp. 1+; Ehrenreich and Fuentes, "Life on the Global Assembly Line."

24. Ana Westley, "Spain Ponders Its Lax Safety Standards after Rash of Accidents Kills 350 People," *Wall Street Journal,* January 5, 1984, p. 26.

25. Patricia Capdevielle, Donato Alvarez, and Brian Cooper, "International Trends in Productivity and Labor Costs," *Monthly Labor Review,* Vol. 105, No. 12, December 1982, pp. 3–14.

26. Efrin Córdova, "A Comparative View of Collective Bargaining in Industrialised Countries," *International Labour Review,* July–August 1978, p. 423.

27. *Ibid.;* and Eduardo B. Gentil, "Brazil's Labor Movement," *Wall Street Journal,* November 11, 1980, p. 34.

28. "The Europarking Lot," *Wall Street Journal,* February 24, 1984, p. 32.

29. Joseph Krislov, "Supplying Mediation Services in Five Countries: Some Current Problems," *Columbia Journal of World Business,* Vol. 18, No. 2, Summer 1983, pp. 55–63.

30. Frances Bairstow, "The Trend Toward Centralized Bargaining—A Patchwork Quilt of International Diversity," *Columbia Journal of World Business,* Spring 1985, pp. 75–83.

31. Masayoshi Kanayabayasi, "Japan's Unions, Anxious to Avoid Fight, Again Likely to Accept a Modest Pay Raise," *Wall Street Journal,* February 9, 1984, p. 31.

32. Bairstow, *loc. cit.*

33. Donna Bridgeman, "Worker Take-Overs," ICCH Case 9-475-093, Harvard Business School, 1975; "Bulova Watch Plant Is Occupied to Protest Closing," *Wall Street Journal,* January 19, 1976; "ICL Workers Say They Took over Plant to Prevent Closing," *Wall Street Journal,* November 11, 1980, p. 34; Ehrenreich and Fuentes, *op. cit.*

34. Bennett Harrison, "The International Movement for Prenotification of Plant Closures," *Industrial Relations,* Fall 1984, pp. 387–409.

35. Benjamin Prasad, "The Growth of Co-Determination," *Business Horizons,* April 1977, p. 27.

36. Peter F. Drucker, "The Battle over Co-Determination," *Wall Street Journal,* August 10, 1977, p. 14; "Co-Determination Passes," *Business Europe,* March 26, 1976, pp. 99–100.

37. See, for example, "Sweden: Worker Participation Becomes the Law," *Business Week,* June 21, 1976, pp. 42–46; G. McIsaac and H. Henzler, "Co-Determination: A Hidden Noose for MNCs," *Columbia Journal of World Business,* Winter 1974, pp. 67–74; M. Warner and R. Peccei, "Worker Participation and Multinationals," *Management International Review,* No. 3, 1977, pp. 93–98.

38. Much of the information on co-determination in Germany is taken from Trevor Bain, "German Codetermination and Employment Adjustments in the Steel and Auto Industries," *Columbia Journal of World Business,* Vol. 18, No. 2, Summer 1983, pp. 40–47.

39. For two discussions of these efforts, see Duane Kujawa, "Technology Strategy and Industrial Relations: Case Studies of Japanese Multinationals in the United States," *Journal of International Business Studies,* Vol. 14, No. 3, Winter 1983, pp. 9–22; Wolf Reitsperger, "Production and Technology Issues in the International Operations," paper presented to the European International Business Association Eighth Annual Conference, Fontainebleau, France, December 20, 1982.

40. Neil Ulman, "Code on Firms in South Africa Still an Issue," *Wall Street Journal,* April 16, 1984, p. 32; Neil Ulman, "Sullivan's Code Changing South Africa," *Wall Street Journal,* June 11, 1984, p. 23.

41. Richard L. Rowan and Duncan C. Campbell, "The Attempt to Regulate Industrial Relations through International Codes of Conduct," *Columbia Journal of World Business,* Vol. 18, No. 2, Summer 1983, pp. 64–72.

42. Unless otherwise noted, information in this section is taken largely from the following treatises: Gerald B. J. Bomers and Richard B. Peterson, "Multinational Corporations and the Industrial Relations: The Case of West Germany and the Netherlands," *British Journal of Industrial Relations,* March 1977, pp. 45–62; Duane A. Kujawa, "Collective Bargaining and Labor Relations in Multinational Enterprise: A U.S. Policy Perspective," paper presented at New York University Conference on Economic Issues of Multinational Firms, November 1976; Duane Kujawa, "U.S. Manufacturing Investment in the Developing Countries: American Labour's Concerns and the Enterprise Environment in the Decade Ahead," *British Journal of Industrial Relations,* Vol. 19, No. 1, March 1981, pp. 38–48; Roy B. Helfgott, "American Unions and Multinational Enterprises: A Case of Misplaced Emphasis," *Columbia Journal of World Business,* Vol. 18, No. 2, Summer 1983, pp. 81–86.

43. For some figures on the decreased unionized share of work forces, see Rick Melcher, John Templeman, John Rossant, Steve Dryden, and Bob Arnold, "Europe's Unions Are Losing their Grip," *Business Week,* November 26, 1984, pp. 80–88.

44. Rowan and Campbell, *op. cit.,* pp. 67–68.

45. Barry Newman, "Border Dispute," *Wall Street Journal,* November 30, 1983, pp. 1+.

46. "Ford Threatens to Move More Production Abroad," *Wall Street Journal,* April 22, 1981, p. 3.

47. Martin C. Seham, "Transnational Labor Relations: The First Steps Are Being Taken," *Law and Policy in International Business,* Vol. 6, 1974, pp. 347–354.

48. "More U.S. Unions Help Foreign Workers Pressure American Companies Overseas," *Wall Street Journal,* December 7, 1970, p. 30.

49. For a fairly comprehensive list for the 1965–1971 period, see I. A. Litvak and C. J. Maule, "The Union Response to International Corporations," *Industrial Relations,* February 1972, pp. 66–67.

50. Duane A. Kujawa, "International Labor Relations: Trade Union Initiatives and Management Responses," *Personnel Administrator,* February 1977, p. 50.

51. Douglas Martin, "A Canadian Split on Unions," *New York Times,* March 12, 1984, p. D12.

52. Data for this case were taken from Earl C. Gottschalk, Jr., "Inside Counsel," *Wall Street Journal,* February 21, 1980, p. 48; William Serrin, "Nissan to Export Production Methods to Tennessee," *New York Times,* April 20, 1980, pp. A1+; John M. Geddes, "Worker-Directors: Exportable?," *New York Times,* December 17, 1979, pp. D1+; Terutomo Ozawa, "Japanese World of Work: An Interpretive Survey," *MSU Business Topics,* Spring 1980, pp. 45–55; Kenneth A. Kovach, Ben F. Sands, Jr., and William W. Brooks, "Is Codetermination a Workable Idea for U.S. Labor-Management Relations?," *MSU Business Topics,* Winter 1980, pp. 49–55; Bill Paul, "Director Conflicts," *Wall Street Journal,* December 10, 1979, pp. 1+; Eduardo Lachica, "Japanese Work Ethic and Unions Clash at Sharp of America's Memphis Factory," *Wall Street Journal,* February 26, 1981, p. 29; Douglas R. Sease and Urban C. Lehner, "Steel Blues," *Wall Street Journal,* April 2, 1981, pp. 1+; G. McIsaac and H. Henzler, "Co-Determination: A Hidden Noose for MNCs," *Columbia Journal of World Business,* Winter 1974, pp. 69–70; "Labor's Advance," *Wall Street Journal,* March 25, 1977, p. 38; "An Aging Work Force Strains Japan's Traditions," *Business Week,* April 20, 1981, pp. 72–85; Urban C. Lehner, "Mazda Ponders If U.S. Workers Can Hustle," *Wall Street Journal,* May 1, 1984, p. 38; William Serrin, "Japanese Turn Arkansas Plant into a Success," *New York Times,* November 3, 1983, p. A1; "Iacocca Supports Idea of Union Seat," *New York Times,* June 8, 1984, p. D5.

PART 8

The Future

This concluding section of the text is the shortest but by no means the least important. Companies must make decisions today on the basis of what they anticipate will occur in the future. Their ratio of accurate to erroneous predictions will determine to a great extent their ability to maintain viable operations. We begin by explaining diverse approaches toward dealing with the future. Thereafter, our framework for analysis parallels closely the organization of the text. We first examine changes in factor endowments, for these are influential on trade and investment relationships. Next we explore the evolvements of external environments facing international firms. Finally, we discuss some of the functional adjustments that are likely to take place in the future.

24

Predictions and Projections

- To make the student aware that decisions must be made today to conform with an uncertain future environment.
- To explore different future projections of the relative availability of production factors and the effects that their availability will have on business operations.
- To postulate changes in technology, transportation, and communications that may alter international relationships and methods of conducting business.
- To indicate likely changes in the share of world business accounted for by different countries and companies and pursuant relationships between firms and nation-states.
- To describe possible changes in methods by which international business will be conducted in the future.

DOW CHEMICAL EUROPE: PLANNING THE MULTINATIONAL'S FUTURE[1]

Dow Chemical is one of the largest chemical companies in the world, with sales in 1983 of $11 billion, investments in 30 countries, and sales in nearly every country in the world. It is engaged in nearly all of the major kinds of international activities mentioned in the earlier chapters: exporting, importing, direct investment abroad, licensing of technology, joint venture operations, and so on. As a result, it is affected by the different elements of the international environment and must make far more complex tactical and strategic decisions than one would have to in a purely domestic environment.

Like all MNEs, Dow must look into the future—one year, five years, ten years—and plan for the future political, social, and economic environment; the evolution of its particular industry; and how the industry must change to meet the problems and opportunities it judges it will face. However, Dow recognizes that its forecasts, while including elements common to all industries, are also unique to its own situation. Its models of the future contain a specific profile of geographic areas that the industry hopes to serve by fitting its products and services to each country's markets. The key is not to be overly pessimistic or overly optimistic. The former could lead a firm to avoid potentially profitable opportunities. The latter could lead to the unwise commitment of investment capital and management energy.

As Dow looks into the future, it needs to be concerned about markets and competition. However, Dow has found that its forecasting for change is still being done on a macro basis, rather than in detail sufficient to take the company from generalities to individual product, producer, and market analysis. More attention is given to the product mix of the future than to the nature of specific competition and customers. That is because so many changes have taken place in both competition and customers in recent years. It is difficult to predict those moves worldwide.

As it forecasts the future and attempts to set a strategy for change, Dow relies on the following four strategies and various combinations thereof: retreat, review, reduce, and restructure. The retreat strategy is often called the "greener pastures" strategy. It involves getting out of one line of business and moving into something that appears to have better profit potential. Sometimes firms move too quickly to get rid of a line of business without determining whether or not there is an adequate replacement.

The review strategy is also known as the "prune and fertilize" strategy. It is a less radical version of the retreat strategy. This strategy often involves redirecting a line of business rather than eliminating it entirely but requires a good feel for the changing market.

The reduce strategy involves sticking with a business during tough times. This is very common when a firm has invested large amounts of resources in a project and feels that the risk of taking a long-run view is better than selling assets at a huge loss. This logic flies in the face of the theory of sunk costs, but sometimes it is easier for management to postpone decisions in the face of uncertainty.

The final strategy, restructuring, involves specialization and diversification. This strategy has worked with mixed success for MNEs. It implies that the firm's real expertise is in management rather than the management of a specific technology. This has become evident in the oil industry in recent years, as well as in steel.

Historically, firms in the chemical industry have relied on a few key concepts to keep a competitive edge: making basic chemicals close to the supply of raw materials, finishing products close to end markets, conducting R&D on a centralized basis, pursuing product development on a decentralized basis, servicing markets locally, and balancing growth and investment objectives with profitability targets and social concerns. For a number of years it was assumed that the MNEs would gradually crowd everyone else out of the market because of their large financial resources. However, that has not happened for a variety of reasons: lower growth rates stemming from reduced demand; premature capital spending and resultant overcapacity; price schedules falling behind inflation rates; increased competition, especially from subsidized, state-owned or controlled enterprises; loss of export markets; difficulties with financially limited third world customers and suppliers; protectionism; overregulation; a generally poor image; deteriorating labor relations; escalating financial costs and foreign exchange risks; and reduced earnings and a devaluing balance sheet. As a result, competitors and suppliers have arisen from countries and from a scale of operations that the chemical industry and its analysts had not even considered possible a few years ago.

In spite of changing world political and economic conditions and the nature of competition and customers, Dow is planning for what it hopes to be a successful and profitable future. In its planning process it uses several guiding principles:

- In preparing for the future, Dow requires a concept, a vision of what it wants to be, to guide the development and implementation of its strategy for change. It feels that it needs to add only a few new, well-defined activities to its core operations, rather than use a shotgun approach to development.

- Dow periodically assesses how well its internal capabilities fit its basic business concept. It is important to deal from internal strength rather than rely on capabilities that it does not possess.

- It needs to make sure that it is suitably organized to take advantage of its internal resource base within the context of its business concept.

- Dow develops a worst case scenario to assess risk and determine the amount of jeopardy to which its core business might be subjected.

- It is important to communicate the concept and excitement of change and a commitment to it to all levels of the organization.

- In the crucial execution phase of change, Dow constantly fine-tunes its program, provided that it does not alter the fundamentals of its concept or its commitment to it.

Even though the future is difficult to project, a procedure must be established for developing scenarios about potential changes in corporate direction.

INTRODUCTION

- Companies must make decisions about an uncertain future
- If predictions correct, advantages over competitors
- Companies affect the future as well
- Two views on predictions
  - Trends and polls enable accurate predictions
  - Cannot predict so must use scenarios in order to be ready for best and worst occurences

Dow is not unlike other companies in that it must make decisions today about an uncertain future. If a company waits to see what happens, it is already too late, since investments in research, plant, and training may take many years to complete. The companies that guess right on what the future will bring are the ones that can make investments to produce and sell the type and price of goods and services that customers will be willing to buy. They can produce and sell them in conformity with the rules of the societies where they are operating. But it is not always possible to guess correctly. By postulating different ways that the future may evolve, companies may be better able to avoid unpleasant surprises, even though they are uncertain as to which of the multiple environments they will face.

Dow is also like other companies in that its actions will not only be affected by future events but will also affect what the future will be. This is because companies develop new products and new ways to produce old ones. As these developments are accepted by consumers and copied by competitors, their impacts may be far-reaching.

Technological change is taking place at an accelerated pace, and the changes are being diffused more rapidly on a global basis. In response to this change and diffusion, there has been an upsurge in efforts to predict and deal with the future. These include the offering of courses by universities, the emergence of journals dealing with expected things to come, and the appearance of organizations made up of prognosticators.[2]

Broadly speaking, people hold two basic philosophies on the future: that you can predict what it will be and that you cannot.[3] Those who feel that prediction is possible tend to rely on forecasts based on the extrapolation of trends or on polls among professionals to determine how they feel the future will evolve. Those who feel that the future cannot be predicted are no less concerned about what may occur. They tend to map out relevance trees or scenarios that postulate all the foreseeable ways that areas may develop so that decision makers may be aware of the best and worst things that can affect them.

Since so many people are becoming futurists, it seems not overly presumptuous for us to make some speculations on the future of international business. Our own methodology encompasses both of the above philosophies to some extent. Since international business has been explained largely from the standpoint of the supply of production factors, our discussion will begin there, followed by an exploration of transportation and communications, the means by which production and consumption come together. Finally, we will attempt to predict the changing involvements of nation-states and companies in the conduct of international business activities.

FACTORS OF PRODUCTION

Population

- Past predictions have not been very accurate
- Present predictions
  - most growth in LDCs
  - higher urban growth
  - pressure for migration to industrial countries

How many people there will be, where they will be located, and how old they will be will all have an enormous impact on the conduct of world business. Unfortunately, past projections of future populations have not been very accurate; therefore one must be wary of accepting predictions. To give an example of problems with past estimates, the U.N. forecast in 1970 that the world population in the year 2000 would be 7.5 billion. Just five years later the forecast was reduced to 5.6 billion, a drop of about one quarter.[4]

In spite of these problems, there is a near-consensus that the world's population will rise rapidly in the foreseeable future. This opinion was highlighted at the World Population Conference, which was held in Mexico City during 1984. The World Bank, for example, has estimated that the earth's population will double to about 10 billion by the year 2050.[5] This doubling is not expected to be distributed evenly. The growth is expected to come primarily in the developing countries and primarily among the poorer people within those countries. In 1984 the countries of sub-Saharan Africa accounted for 30 percent of the world's population, but that portion will reach 50 percent by the middle of the twenty-first century if present trends continue. India will displace China as the most populated country; and Bangladesh, a country the size of Wisconsin, will have 450 million people.

The population growth rate for the world as a whole is about 2 percent per year, but this is heavily weighted by the growth in developing countries, which account for three quarters of the world's population and have a growth rate of 10 percent above the world average. The population growth rate in the United States, for instance, is only about 1 percent per year. Unfortunately, the distribution and growth of the world's wealth does not correspond with that of population. For most, but not all, of the developing countries there is no indication that material improvement will be made for the growing sector of those in poverty.

Another phenomenon is the continued shifting of populations toward urban centers. The international corporation of tomorrow will be confronted with a population concentrated in huge urban conglomerates, or megalopolises. We are told that in the United States there will be linear cities stretching from San Francisco to San Diego, from Chicago to Pittsburgh, from Jacksonville to Miami, and from Boston to Washington. The Ruhr Valley of West Germany and the Tokyo-Yokohama megalopolis are two examples of linear cities that have already developed.

The trend in developing countries is even more pervasive. In 1975, only two of the ten largest cities in the world were in LDCs, but this number is expected to reach six by the year 2000. The two largest cities are expected to be Mexico City and São Paulo, which will each have over 25 million inhabitants.[6]

If the urban problems of housing, crime, utility supply, pollution, and transportation are not solved, there might be a natural tendency for people to seek locations other than large cities in which to reside. Governmental policies may also be used to stem the migration to cities. Many countries already offer incentives for businesses to locate in rural or depressed areas. Another possibility is that there will be a continued pressure for people to emigrate to industrial countries from developing ones. By the mid-1980s, all of the industrial countries except for Japan have had large groups of immigrants who were both legal and illegal residents. Furthermore, the countries seemed incapable, except at a prohibitive cost, of controlling the illegal entry and stay of poor people from the developing countries. One of the prohibitive costs, in the case of controlling Mexican aliens to the United States, could be the potential political explosion in Mexico as unemployment continues to climb.

One of the major changes that population increase will bring about is a new factor endowment relationship, to be discussed later in the chapter. In addition, market sizes and locations will shift because of the above-mentioned population trends.

Natural Resources

- Fixed supply of natural resources
- Two views
  - rapid depletion of some minerals
  - new supplies will emerge
- Recent concerns
  - less fresh water and agricultural land
  - more cost and risk to supply from remote areas

With the rising population and fixed supply of natural resources, the relative factor endowments seem destined to change substantially within the next several years. The supply of natural resources is being expended at an accelerating rate, particularly in the United States, the main consumer of ·these resources. Most of the world has never been geodetically surveyed, largely because there has not been a need or real interest on the part of countries or companies that were in a position to make explorations. In recent years, for example, we have witnessed the discovery of large reserves of raw materials in remote places or places where it is difficult to make extractions. Oil and natural gas have been found in the North Sea, oil in the north slopes of Alaska and east slopes of the Andes, and nickel in New Caledonia.

These new discoveries, especially of oil, have made many people discredit the doomsday prophesies of the early 1970s. One of the most dire forecasts was by the Club of Rome, which estimated that if the world's known reserves were only one fifth the actual reserves, continued usage at present rates would result in the depletion of aluminum by the year 2027, copper by 2020, lead by 2036, mercury by 2013, and petroleum and zinc by 2022.[7] A follow-up report in 1980, which was the most exhaustive study ever undertaken of long-term changes in the world's population, natural resources, and environment, reached pessimistic conclusions similar to those of the Club of Rome.[8]

Not everyone agrees with these pessimistic projections. In fact, a study published in 1984 in which many leading scholars participated drew an opposite conclusion. This latter study relied on much longer-term trends—for example, energy prices throughout the twentieth century rather than just the decade of the 1970s—and concluded that

> *if present trends continue, the world in 2000 will be less crowded (though more populated), less polluted, more stable ecologically, and less vulnerable to resource supply disruption than the world we live in now.* [9]

Whether one takes the optimistic or the pessimistic view, one fact seems indisputable: Many resources are finite in quantity. Already in the second half of the 1980s, we hear concerns about resources that were not voiced as loudly in the recent past. Many feel that the supply of fresh water could be inadequate in the foreseeable future. Agricultural lands are being reduced to zero productivity at the rate of about 20 million hectares per year.[10] Furthermore, the fact that new supplies of natural resources are being found where exploration and extraction are remote and/or difficult should, along with dwindling supplies, cause further price increases for these resources except for short time periods. In 1982, for example, 40 percent of the world's exploration and development of oil took place in the United States, even though the United States had only 5 percent of the free world's reserves. The cost was ten times that of finding oil elsewhere; however, the risks of other locations were deemed to be too high.[11]

Food

- Pessimism on number of future hungry people
- Multiple causes of food problem
  - despoilation of areas
  - food spoilage
  - dietary habits
  - insufficient income to purchase

There are varying estimates of the minimum recommended per capita calorie intake; however, one of the lowest is that of the Food and Agricultural Organization of the United Nations (FAO), which bases its minimum to be 80 percent of the level needed to maintain life and a light amount of activity. This corresponds to 1.2 times the basal metabolic rate. According to these figures, over 400 million people or about 10 percent of human beings were going hungry in the early 1980s.[12] Such organizations as the World Bank and the World Health Organization use a higher caloric intake minimum and estimate the number of hungry to be even higher.

The FAO has made the most extensive estimates of food consumption to the year 2000 of any organization. It has projected three different scenarios. The most pessimistic of the scenarios has food production growing at the same rate as during the decades of the 1960s and 1970s. On the basis of this projection the number of malnourished people will rise to more than 590 million by the turn of the century. Even in the FAO's optimistic scenarios, the number of people with insufficient food will not decrease significantly below present levels. Based on World Bank definitions of minimum intake, the number of the world's hungry will be about 1200 million people by the year 2000.[13]

One of the critical food supply problems has been the despoliation of previously productive areas. This includes the loss of agricultural lands because of conversion to nonagricultural use, soil erosion, salinization, and the spread of deserts. It also includes the decreased production of certain fishing areas because of excessive catches and because of pollution.

The world food problem is further complicated by pests, lack of adequate storage and transportation, and dietary habits that lead to protein shortages. The magnitude of the distribution problem is apparent in the fact that the U.N. Fund for Population Activities estimated that, in 1980, enough grain was produced to feed 1.6 billion more people than the world's population, yet 10 percent of people got too little to eat.[14] The primary reason for the disparity between production and consumption was that people lacked sufficient income to buy the food that was available. In all probability the industrial countries and their international firms will be called upon increasingly to provide the technology, capital, and jobs to alleviate food problems in LDCs.

Nonterritorial Areas

• Three areas of conflict over commercial jurisdiction
  • outer space
  • Antarctica
  • the seas

There is increasing potential for the conduct of business outside the present confines of any country's existing geographic boundaries. Outer space, for example, has advantages for the production of certain pharmaceuticals in germ-free environments. The atmosphere is also where aircraft fly and telecommunications are transmitted. There are virtually no limits to the use of space.[15] More and more of the space missions initiated by the United States include projects with commercial potential. A major problem in the use of space for commercial purposes is the increased militarization of space. A curtailment of the military aspect of space could pave the way for more international cooperation in commercial ventures.

Antarctica is another area of economic possibilities. Tourist visits by ship have reached such a magnitude that a Chilean group has proposed building a hotel there. Krill fishing in Antarctic waters is already being undertaken to such a degree that an international agreement limits quantities of the catches, and there are discussions on the jurisdiction of offshore oil exploration.[16] There have been proposals to transport icebergs to desert areas in the Middle East. Although this use of Antarctica seems far-fetched, it is known that Antarctica contains vast mineral resources. A major battle is brewing over who has control over those resources. The mining companies prefer to have that territory free and available to any enterprise, the contiguous countries prefer to extend their natural borders to include large segments of Antarctica, and other countries prefer to consider Antarctica to be the domain of all nations, so that all nations can reap the benefits of its mineral resources. That is a major problem that will not be solved easily in the coming decades, as can be foreseen from the Law of the Sea negotiations in the United Nations.

A third area, one that has received considerable attention recently, is the sea. In 1609 a Dutch jurist stated, "The sea, since it is as incapable of being seized as the air, cannot have been attached to the possessions of any particular nation."[17] In the eighteenth century the three-mile limit became recognized as the territory of the coastal state because that was the range of cannons. In 1945 the United States unilaterally extended its rights to explore and exploit mineral resources to the extent of its continental shelf. Since then, most countries bordering the sea have placed varying jurisdictional claims on territory, mineral rights, and fishing rights.[18]

As was pointed out in Chapter 7, the United Nations finally passed the Law of the Sea in 1982. However, the value of that treaty will depend on who eventually ratifies it. Several industrial countries, including the United States, have not even signed it yet, let alone made the attempt to ratify it. If the countries can agree on how the sea can be used, mining efforts should go forward at an increased pace.

Capital

- Most capital flows among developed countries
- Future flows affected by
  - political stability
  - currency strengths
  - ability of debtor nations to repay
  - growth versus recessions

Capital is a very important resource that is intensively sought by all countries. In this section, the emphasis will be on financial capital; technology or the development of physical capital is explored next. Traditionally, financial capital has been generated in and recycled among the industrial countries. Owing to high levels of per capita GNP, these countries have been able to generate the high levels of savings necessary for investment. For example, 67 percent of the increase in U.S. foreign direct investment in 1967 went to the developed countries. That percentage has increased fairly steadily over the past two decades to 71 percent in 1972 and 78.5 percent in 1976. Since 1976 the percentage of capital outflows going to developed as opposed to developing countries has remained fairly high, though not consistent. In 1980, for example, 93 percent of total private capital outflows went to the developed countries. That dropped to 62 percent in 1981 but shot up to 120 percent in 1983 as a net divestment took place in LDCs. Throughout the late 1970s and early-to-mid-1980s the percentage of U.S. foreign direct investment in the industrial countries has remained at a fairly consistent 74–75 percent of the total. The developing countries appeared to be making small inroads in the total investment pie until 1982, when the developed countries began picking up more investment capital from the United States.[19] This is not a very encouraging scenario for the developing countries, which rely on foreign investment to help offset the high principal and interest costs sustained during the heavy borrowing years of the 1970s and to help improve the unemployment situation.

It is evident that several factors are going to have a strong impact on the flow of capital in the future. Political instability in much of the world has resulted in a movement of money to safe haven countries, such as the United States. Unless greater stability ensues, it will be difficult for the developing countries and even much of Western Europe to retain large amounts of capital at home. Exchange rate instability is also causing strong demand for U.S. dollars. The U.S. trade deficit pumps more dollars abroad, but the demand for dollars to invest in the United States results in an offset to that drain. A decline in real interest rates in the United States will result in an outflow of capital, which will accentuate the U.S. trade imbalance and force the dollar down in value.

In the 1970s the key concern was how to transfer petrodollars from oil producers to oil consumers. In the 1980s the oil producers have been just as short of cash as the oil consumers. The key capital flow issue has been how to keep the debtor nations from collapsing under the weight of principal and interest payments to the international banks. As the world economy recovers and provides markets for the goods of the developing countries, the debt pressures should subside. If the world turns into another recession, another severe debt crisis will develop.

Technology

- Speed of change likely to increase

Futurists generally agree that the speed of technological change will not just continue but will accelerate, putting great pressure on international managers to interact with employees and customers to ensure that change occurs in an orderly manner. There remains a great deal of disagreement and uncertainty, however, as to the direction the changes will take. Although much has been written about such areas as artificial intelligence in computers, the creation of new materials, and the modification of hereditary characteristics, the end use of these breakthroughs as well as the types of new techniques will be determined to a great extent by the "winners" in some current and emerging arguments.

- Industrial country origin has meant labor saving emphasis but

Labor versus natural resource conservation. In recent decades the United States has spent both a larger total amount and a larger portion of its gross national product on research and development than has any other country.

- natural resource depletion may cause shift
- or competition may necessitate more labor savings

Consequently, a high percentage of new developments has originated and been institutionalized in the United States. The rest have developed in other industrialized countries whose basic characteristics are in many ways similar to those of the United States. The old axiom that "necessity is the mother of invention" helps to explain the fact that efforts have largely been directed toward methods for saving labor, which is a natural outgrowth of an economy with ample capital, land, and natural resources and the ability to relocate its highly mobile labor force to new machines, work methods, and locations. Efficiency and output have been measured in terms of people, since people were considered the scarce and expensive resource. Little effort has been made to measure efficiency in terms of other resources, such as raw materials. Until recently, for example, the automobile industry has been more concerned with output per man-hour than in measuring miles per gallon or passenger miles utilized per unit of raw material going into the automobile.

Many signs indicate that the emphasis in some industries will shift somewhat away from labor savings to natural resource savings. A good part of this projection is predicated on the changing resource endowments already discussed. As costs of raw materials rise and as a proportionately smaller amount of R&D effort is geared toward improving the output per worker in industrial countries, the real wages of these workers will probably begin to rise at a lower rate than the rate to which they have become accustomed. This may create unrest among home country employees of international companies. They will probably try various means to continue their accustomed growth in real wages, such as increasing salaries at the expense of profits or pressuring for import limitations.

Not all signs point away from a labor-saving emphasis. The last few years have seen a burgeoning global market for industrial robots.[20] One can imagine future protectionist arguments that "foreign made robots are putting our robot industry out of work" or even "foreign robots are putting our robots out of work." It is even possible to contemplate at some time in the future the designing of a completely automated assembly line that would combine robots and computers in such a manner that a plant could be in continuous operation for a period of several days without any appreciable human effort.

During the early 1980s, when the U.S. dollar began its relentless climb against nearly every major currency in the world, U.S. companies found that they could not continue to compete by doing old things. They looked for ways to cut costs by changing production methods in the United States and moving production abroad. That resulted in greater emphasis on labor-saving production or production in countries where labor was cheaper. In addition, the environmental regulatory pressures in the United States began to diminish somewhat under the Reagan administration.

Within developing countries there is also increased pressure for directing R&D efforts toward areas other than saving labor. One of the most critical problems in developing countries has been the large amount of unemployment and underemployment coupled with small domestic markets. These countries have long argued that the capital-intensive technologies developed for industrial countries are not best suited to a developing country's needs, since they augment rather than solve the unemployment problem and since high fixed costs from capital intensity lead to a high cost per unit of the finished product. Greater competition from firms in the developed countries to gain access to LDC markets may result in greater emphasis on labor-intensive methods. As labor intensity grows in both LDCs and industrial countries, new competitive relationships will have to be analyzed from the standpoint of labor cost and efficiency. In other words, there will be new comparative advantages because of new factor endowment relationships.

One problem with this analysis is that some developing countries are trying to develop export industries in addition to, or in place of, the import substitution strategy. Their desire to compete in export markets has led many of them to seek the latest technology, even if it is capital intensive, in order to be competitive. Governments can control the flow of goods into their markets and thus protect local industries, but they are at the mercy of the market when competing with industries globally. Thus we may see firms in some countries seeking high technology even though the resource endowment of their country might be more labor intensive.

- External costs, e.g., pollution, may have to be covered by producers or consumers
- National regulatory differences may change production locations
- Producers may abandon high risk production

Economic advancement versus environmental protection. We have already witnessed many conflicts between groups proposing changes they believe will have economic advantages and other groups that fear the changes will have upsetting environmental effects. One environmental argument points out that the traditional methods of ascertaining production costs are invalid in that they do not take into consideration the external costs sometimes created for others in society. For example, if fumes from automobiles create health problems, there is a cost associated with alleviating that problem. This cost, it is argued, should be charged to the production process. A second argument holds that certain irreplaceable natural habitats should not be upset simply for the sake of economic output and efficiency.

An example of the devastating impact of economic growth on the environment is the Union Carbide tragedy in Bhopal, India, on December 3, 1984. Union Carbide, the thirty-seventh largest industrial company in the United States and a chemical giant with a good safety record, was involved in an investment in India in which it held 51 percent ownership of the Bhopal plant. A poisonous cloud of methyl isocyanate gas from a pesticide plant on the outskirts of a city of over 200,000 people killed over 2000 people and injured tens of thousands. Union Carbide's operation in Bhopal was eventually shut down, and potential new investments in other countries ran into serious opposition.[21]

What does this mean for technology and international business? To the extent that environmentalists are successful, it may mean that R&D expenditures will be diverted to the achievement of environmental objectives at the expense of other performance criteria. Thus in the case of automobiles, speed, consumer cost, and gasoline utilization efficiency might give way somewhat for the achievement of cleaner air. In the production process itself, firms may have to devote greater effort and expense to ensure that they do not pollute. To the extent that pressures vary by country, production costs as well as the composition of R&D expenditures may also vary. If the United States, for example, adopts stringent rules on air pollution and West Germany does not, West German production may have an added cost advantage. Furthermore, West German producers may be able to divert their efforts to product improvements and other cost-saving techniques.

In the wake of the Bhopal tragedy it appears that governments around the world are going to be more concerned about safety and environmental regulations. In addition, many experts feel that MNEs are going to have to reconsider their whole approach to locating certain types of operations abroad where there are huge risks. As one expert said,

> *If I were a corporate manager, I would reexamine my profile of global activities, and in some cases I might pull out some products or processes where the risk is great and the profit marginal.* [22]

● "Winners" in value conflicts will determine acceptable future endeavors

Some other value convergences. In a host of other areas, value systems sharply conflict and thus make uncertain the direction of technical change as well as the institutionalization of advances that are made. One of the most deep-seated of these value differences concerns the biological manipulation of humans. In recent years we have witnessed major controversies over the transplant of human organs, the application of genetic splicing techniques, the use of birth control devices and acceptance of abortion, the testing and availability of pharmaceuticals, and the use of marijuana and hard drugs. Different pressure groups are likely to win out in different countries on changes involving value conflicts. In addition, shifts in the relative strength of groups within countries may mean that managers of international firms will face altered and evolving environments that dictate what they may do in different locations.

TRANSPORTATION AND COMMUNICATIONS

Technological advances, as well as governmental actions, may lead to changes in communications and transportation. Regardless of the cause, the effect on determining the cost and feasibility of moving products among countries may be substantial.

Technical Advances

- Technically possible to link countries more closely but
  - nationalism may prevent full linkage

Satellite communications are now a reality and, when fully operational, will cut costs significantly, especially since usage costs should be no higher for long distances than for short distances. Such a worldwide network will be able to handle not only television but also many other types of communications, such as telephone calls, telegrams, weather reports, and scientific and business data for computers.

One major problem with this data flow is the perception on the part of many countries that they are losing sovereignty. Thus a major challenge to MNEs will be to keep the barriers to data flow at a minimum. It is conceivable that firms may lose control over the flow of data if countries believe that too much sensitive data is being transferred across national lines.

Many technical advances in transportation have also been underway. Pipelines, now used even for moving solids, are increasingly competitive with shipping; landbridge concepts are evolving; new vessels are becoming larger, more automated, and more efficient. The new supertankers, for example, can pass around Cape Horn more cheaply than if they were able to go through the Panama Canal paying tolls.[23] It is estimated that, by the year 2000, about 50 percent of tankers will be too large even to use the Panama Canal.[24] Jumbo-sized airplanes are reducing the cost of air cargo, and supersonic aircraft can move passengers and cargo much faster between major cities.

Governmental Influences

- Price maintenance and subsidies retard competition
- Major waterways may come under national jurisdiction
- Panama Canal used proportionately more by Latin America

Governmental actions on highway, rail, port, and airport construction can reduce the operating costs of transportation and thus the cost of conducting business between different locales; it seems probable that governments worldwide will give a high priority to such expenditures. It also seems logical to predict that governmental subsidies and approval of price maintenance among transporters will continue. However, price maintenance at a high level may be more difficult to achieve as firms try to undercut competitors during periods of loss caused by overcapacity.

A major question for the future of international transportation concerns what will occur with the major international waterways. There is considerable disagreement among countries as to what should constitute territorial waters, even though such disagreements have had little impact on transit rights. Such important waterways as the Straits of Malacca and Gibraltar could conceivably come under national rather than international jurisdiction; thus owners could charge tolls for transit. The closing of the Suez Canal in 1967 caused substantial disruption and reallocation of earnings among nations. Continued Mideast hostilities place doubt on the future role of that artery.

It is estimated that the Panama Canal will reach a saturation point in terms of the ships it can handle by the year 2000. However, there is considerable opposition to the construction of a new canal, such as the report by the Committee of Ecological Research indicating that a sea-level canal would be a biological catastrophe.[25] Furthermore, many of the military and economic arguments that were used to justify the original canal construction are no longer valid for the United States. The major economic considerations involve the many Latin American countries (e.g., Ecuador, El Salvador, and Nicaragua) that depend heavily on the canal for their trade. Their shipments tend to be much too small to take advantage of the new larger ships that can transport goods more cheaply around South America.[26] Because of this latter consideration, it is probable that a new canal will be constructed, but not of the scale to handle the larger ships currently being built.

THE DEVELOPING COUNTRY–DEVELOPED COUNTRY INTERFACE

- Higher natural resource prices
  - help some LDCs
  - do not help most
- All scenarios show rich-poor disparities continuing

During the past two decades there has been much concern about the plight of the developing countries and their dependence on primary goods for export earnings. For many years the declining terms of trade on these products led to pessimism and resultant diversification policies. However, other equally pessimistic predictions about the future of the world may well work in favor of the developing countries and lead to a reversal in the terms of trade. The population growth and the depletion of world resources should result in a much greater demand for traditional exports, an elimination of the surplus problems, and higher prices for primary producers. As this happens, trade between the developed and developing countries as a proportion of world trade should increase. This trend will be reinforced if natural resources are depleted more rapidly in the industrial nations. But most developing countries have few natural resources and must import the most basic commodities; their plight will probably worsen.

A U.N.-commissioned study has constructed three major scenarios of the economic relationship between the rich and poor countries by the year 2000.[27] The first scenario assumes that the richer, capital-exporting regions will transfer to the poorer, capital-importing ones approximately the same fraction of their national income (in the form of credits and foreign investments) that they did in the past. Under these assumptions the gap between rich and poor countries will grow in both relative and absolute terms.

The second scenario assumes that poor countries will be freed from balance-of-payments constraints so that they will import according to their needs rather than their ability to pay. By 2000, exports of poor areas will pay for only 25 percent of their annual imports, and the other 75 percent will have to be obtained on credit. Rich countries will have to allocate 3.1 percent of their total GNP, as opposed to a current figure of less than

1 percent, to support such an effort. This will create a faster growth rate to the year 2000 for the poor than for the rich countries, but it will leave the absolute per capita income gap approximately unchanged.

The third scenario assumes a 35 percent drop in military spending, which will serve as aid to poor countries. The results will be somewhere between those of the other two scenarios.

The projections are not too hopeful. The second scenario, the most optimistic one, would still not greatly improve the plight of the developing countries on a relative basis, although all three scenarios predict an increase in absolute real income for the poor countries.

It is difficult to imagine either of the latter two scenarios as being feasible. Also, it is hard to believe that the first scenario will take place without more resources being transferred to the developing countries. Already we can see that the large international banks are providing creative financing for countries suffering severe liquidity crises. These loans and restructurings result in the transfer of financial resources to the developing countries. In addition, increased economic expansion in the industrial countries should result in more developing country exports.

FORMS OF INTERNATIONAL BUSINESS

• Same forms in future but composition may change

How will international business expand in the future? As was discussed in Chapter 15, international business has many different forms: export operations, direct investment, management contracts, licensing agreements, franchising, turnkey operations, and so on. The forms of international business will not change in the future, but their mix for a particular firm might. Although many factors could alter this mix, the following factors should be especially important:

1. host country goals and priorities,
2. home country goals and priorities,
3. the degree of intergovernmental cooperation versus conflict, and
4. the growth of trade with communist bloc countries.

All of these factors are influenced greatly by general environmental developments such as inflation, world currency stability, and world liquidity.

Factors Altering the Mix

• During rapid economic growth
  • more nonequity arrangements by MNEs abroad
  • more ownership sharing abroad by MNEs

Host country goals and priorities are constantly changing, but it is likely that economic conditions will greatly affect priorities between economic and political objectives. During periods of more rapid economic growth and low unemployment, countries are more apt to push for sovereignty concerns vis-à-vis foreign firms. During these periods they may more successfully require nonequity rather than equity operations by foreign firms. When

- LDC moves to export promotion
- Industrial countries may limit outflows
  - to save short-term capital
  - to obtain natural resources
- Questions include
  - amount of intergovernmental cooperation
  - future of East-West business

investments are allowed, countries may likely insist on shared ownership arrangements with local interests.

Foreign investment will be more welcomed, though, when host governments perceive that they need foreign capital for creating jobs and growth and as they find that they have more difficulty in borrowing abroad, such as the 1984 loosening of investment restrictions in Mexico. The current external debt situation of most developing countries indicates that foreign investment is likely to be welcomed there in the foreseeable future.

One obvious trend in recent years that should continue is the swing away from import substitution to export promotion. Import substitution is still important, but most host countries realize that the key to the future is a vital export-based economy. As markets open up for the developing countries, the feasibility of using an export-based strategy increases.

Home country goals and priorities should also contribute substantially to shaping the future. If countries begin to feel the impact of shortages in hard currency, they will tend to discourage the exportation of capital. This is a critical development for firms in countries such as the United States that have historically been active in exporting capital to finance direct investments. Important factors, such as the export of components to foreign plants, the receipt of dividends, and interest on loans from subsidiaries, may be overlooked in an effort to remedy the short-run outflow of capital. Home countries will also consider resource scarcity when determining whether a firm exports or invests abroad. They may, for example, allow capital outflows if the resultant investments bring in needed raw materials but at the same time limit outflows for market-seeking investors.

The degree of intergovernmental cooperation versus conflict is an important factor influencing growth. Countries can either open their doors to trade and investment or establish barriers to the world community. Although the world economic scene will be too shaky for the next several years to permit a free flow of goods and capital, the spirit of cooperation generated by impending global economic chaos should allow some joint undertakings to be considered. As world capital markets continue to grow in sophistication, the ownership of many large MNEs should broaden in national origin.

The growth of trade with communist bloc countries is largely a function of the previous factors. Communist bloc countries are interested in Western technology, expertise, and markets, while Western firms are interested in access to the untapped markets and abundant natural resources behind the iron and bamboo curtains. It has been pointed out that capitalist and socialist societies are evolving similarly; consequently, one might expect a growing similarity in products and methods of doing business. Among those things for which trends are in the same direction are the shift of factories to urban areas, the decrease in the number of children per family, the increase in durable goods and travel, longer commutes to work, less time spent in religious services, and later entry to and earlier departure from the labor force.[28]

It is now more likely that the brightest future of the communist countries in terms of markets for Western goods lies in the People's Republic of China (PRC). While trade between the Soviet Union and the West has been languishing in recent years, the potential of the PRC seems to be expanding. Barring a dramatic turn in political events, the PRC should continue to open up to Western business. Cooperative ventures that earn foreign exchange will continue to be the projects of greatest interest to the PRC. Even though the consumer sector is beginning to loosen up a little in the PRC, the major market will be industrial.

State Multinational Enterprises

- More state owned enterprises are multinational
  - may compete "unfairly"
  - may be slower to take advantage of foreign opportunities

Although state enterprises have been around for a long time and we know a great deal about them, those which are multinational have been around for only a short time, and we know very little about them. Historically, state multinational enterprises have acquired their present importance rather late in the evolution of the developed capitalist countries. In the case of developing countries, however, they are appearing on a significant scale earlier in the developmental process.

The reasons for establishing state multinational enterprises in recent years have varied markedly. For example, a government may have no choice but to acquire ownership of a private multinational that is threatened with bankruptcy and the possibility of mass unemployment for its workers. In such cases they may subsidize exports in order to maintain home country employment. In other situations it may result because the private sector is not willing or able to provide risk capital.

A study indicates that government ownership might have an adverse impact on the expansion of the company's base of operations into other countries. One of the distinctive features of management behavior of a government-controlled enterprise is that:

> Generally, opportunities are slow to be recognized, and formulation and implementation of plans are cumbersome. In particular, data are slow to be collected and processed: there are frequent delays in the approval of proposals, and action is plagued by many hesitations.[29]

Innovational Supremacy

- Innovative companies and countries will be world leaders
  - companies from industrial countries
  - will Japan pass the U.S.?

The companies that are most likely to dominate in the international sector are those that have some sort of innovation lead, some technical or organizational skill, or some production or marketing capability that is not widely shared by others. In discussing the future of multinational corporations, a leading scholar has stated that their prominence is likely to be concentrated *in advanced technological sectors and in the industries reliant on raw materials that are subject to oligopoly control. Multinational enterprises will be less evident with respect to the more mature and standardized products.* [30]

Because of the advantage of technical progress, it is reasonable to predict that the leading firms will continue to be located in countries where significant commitments are made to R&D expenditures. It seems safe to say that these countries will continue to be the industrial ones, although there may be some shifts among these countries. By the mid-1980s the United States was still the world's economic leader and the largest source of multinational enterprise activity. However, many observers predict that Japan will overtake the United States by the year 2000.[31] They cite recent growth trends in the United States and Japan as well as trends in support to education and research. Others have pointed out that "catch up" growth may be easier to undertake than leadership growth and that industrial employment has recently been growing more rapidly in the United States than in other industrial countries.[32] People on both sides of the U.S.-Japan debate have agreed that yielding to protectionist pressure in the United States will retard the supremacy of American industry internationally.

One of the most fascinating areas in deregulation in recent years has been in communications in the United States. The breaking up of the Bell system has increased competition for communications systems exponentially. It is doubtful that anyone could have predicted the impact of that change. The international marketplace and forms of business necessary to compete are very different from what they were a few years ago. Much of the competition is coming from abroad, but a variety of domestic firms have arisen, and Bell itself is becoming a force outside of the United States.

New Collaboration

- Large resources needed
- Concern about dominant firms
- Spreads risks

It is likely that greater collaboration among companies in foreign markets will occur in the coming years. Indeed, we are already seeing examples of joint ownership by competitors in other countries and the more common cross-licensing of technology. Three factors seem to harbinger this development. First, the large resource outlay for many new projects strains the capabilities of individual companies. In large-scale R&D projects in military equipment and in large-scale extraction projects, for example, collaborative efforts are already necessary. Second, governments are increasingly concerned about domination by a foreign market leader, such as IBM in computers or Boeing in commercial aviation. Their responses are increasingly to require these firms to contract with local suppliers and to foster consortia among their own firms to compete more vigorously. Third, multinational enterprises are likely to seek partnership arrangements as a means of putting fewer assets at risk in volatile environments. In addition, this arrangement should help the MNEs gain access to foreign technology, as is the case with the Toyota/General Motors joint venture.

Concentration or Fragmentation

Trends show concentration but
- **concern of bigness**
- **pressure for local ownership**

Some observers have predicted that, in the near future, some 300 or fewer firms will control more than half the world's production. While this might occur if past growth trends were to continue, several factors will probably prevent such heavy concentration of ownership. In industrial countries there is a move to protect consumers by limiting excessive corporate growth. In the United States, for example, such firms as IBM and Exxon are already considered too big by many individuals. Greater pressure for local ownership in enterprises is also taking place in many countries. As this continues, the large companies, instead of expanding their direct investments and sales at former rates, may increasingly sell services and technology to local firms.

Plant Location

Factors other than cost gaining in importance

It is reasonable to assume that, in the years ahead, determination of the location of plant facilities will not depend as much on measuring comparative differences in costs as it once did. Instead, as these differences are eliminated, greater attention for structuring production in the international market will be focused on the determination of market and resource accessibility, labor stability, governmental attitudes, political stability, and corporate flexibility in adapting to changes in consumer tastes. Thus it is realistic to contemplate future multinational corporate planning for production and distribution as being within a global framework of integrated markets. In this manner the firm will be able to obtain maximum efficiency in terms of production runs for finished products and component parts.

INTERFACE BETWEEN THE FIRM AND NATION-STATE

Greater interdependence limits independent government actions

Small LDCs gain support when seemingly victimized by MNEs

LDCs may
- **band together more**
- **develop own MNEs**

The relationship between the firm, the home government of the firm, and the host governments of the countries where the firm is also operating has been constantly changing. Initially, most host governments did not exercise their powers because they needed capital and expertise to develop resources. The European countries welcomed investment after World War II as part of the reconstruction process. The developing countries needed capital, expertise, and markets. Generally, home governments intervened on behalf of their firms when disputes arose and forced many foreign subsidiaries to behave according to home government wishes.

It now appears that the power balance is changing somewhat. The superpowers are going to find it increasingly tough to regulate business according to their desires. Because of the high degree of interrelatedness of the world's economies and fears of economic recession, few if any governments are permitting total laissez-faire growth in international business. Political pressures for employment and other national goals are resulting in more intervention in the economic process.

Smaller countries are very sensitive to the issues of imperialism and neocolonialism and are likely to get support from the rest of the world whenever they appear to be or actually are victimized by multinational firms. There will be continued pressure to force the foreign subsidiaries of a firm to adhere to host country goals rather than to the wishes of the parent firm or the home government.

In particular, what is going to happen to the LDCs, and what will this mean to the MNEs that operate in them? Given the rather pessimistic view of economic improvement within developing countries highlighted above, a number of implications have been suggested for MNEs.[33] For one thing, LDCs may increasingly view firms from industrial countries with suspicion. This is because these MNEs originate from the countries that many citizens from LDCs view as the cause of their economic plight through years of exploitation. The result may be the demand among LDCs for MNEs to help develop indigenous technological capabilities.

At the same time the LDCs may seek to strengthen their own positions through the development of their own MNEs, which will integrate vertically into processing and distribution to gain a larger share of the value added in the sale of their traditional products. The example of a fully integrated oil company by the government of Kuwait is a good illustration of that point.

LDCs may also band together more through cartels and other arrangements to raise the prices of their exports. The recent experience of OPEC is not a good example of the blessings of a cartel, however. If these moves fail, the environment within LDCs may be even more politically explosive than it is at present, leading MNEs to shun to a greater extent the business opportunities in poorer countries.

MICROCHANGES

Multinationalism of Business

● High potential benefits but modified by nationalism

The company that is willing to go anywhere in the world to sell or to secure production factors has been referred to variously as a multinational, supranational, transnational, and extranational corporation, as well as a cosmacorp. By whatever name, it is the type of company that is ideally suited for bridging communication gaps among nations through its network of commercial relationships. A multinational company attempts to treat the various national markets as though they were one—to the extent permitted by governments, at least.

In the years ahead, firms will confront several obstacles to full multinationalization. Probably the most significant external barrier is nationalism, which severely limits what a firm can do internationally. Nationalism may also be an internal barrier insofar as managers put their home country objectives above those of the corporation's worldwide performance. Other internal barriers include limited management horizons, a shortage of qualified management talent, and a lack of effective means for communicating across national boundaries.

The problem of nationalism, with its many ramifications, will be with us indefinitely, in both developing and industrial countries. Increased internationalism necessarily poses a threat to the control of one's own economic, political, and social destinies and generates the fear that other countries will receive a larger "piece of the pie."

Marketing

- Segmentation likely to cut through countries rather than country-to-country differences
- Rich-poor differences growing

Increasing universality. One of the trends that is most likely to have an impact on the future of international marketing is the continued growth in transportation and communications, which gives rise to the global awareness of products and life-styles. Thus a continual trend toward standardized marketing programs on a worldwide basis is probable. This does not imply that international firms will be able to narrow product lines or promotional activities. Instead, they may have to differentiate further to satisfy people's needs according to demographic, sociographic, and psychographic variables that cut across national boundaries. For example, companies may well find themselves defining a market segment as minutely as "females, age 26 to 30, working, unmarried, three to four years of college, high achievement motivation, church members, and low dogmatic personalities." As discretionary income increases, not only do exotic products become so commonplace that they lose their attractiveness, but also more products and services compete with each other (e.g., cars, travel, jewelry, and furniture competing for the same discretionary spending) so that increased segmentation is likely to be necessary.

Rich-poor disparity. Most projections are that disparities between the "haves" and "have-nots" will grow rather than diminish in the foreseeable future, both within and among countries. This is likely to mean a simultaneous growth in affluent and poor market segments. The global affluent sector will have the means of purchasing more goods and services and will not be likely to forego purchases because of antimaterial beliefs. Because of the growing education of this sector, more people will be knowledgeable about slight differences in the end utility of products. It will be less possible to segment along national lines to reach these consumers.

The rise in affluence and leisure of the "haves" will probably result in changes in the composition of expenditure. As these people take at least a part of productivity increases in the form of leisure, they will spend a proportionately larger amount of their incomes on entertainment, sports clothes and equipment, organization memberships, and travel. A further change will be a great share in service industries.

At the other extreme will be growing numbers of poor people who will have little disposable income to spend on nonnecessities. Multinational enterprises will face increasing pressures to develop standardized products to fit the needs of these people and to produce goods by labor-intensive methods so as to employ more people. This will create operational problems because of conflicting competitive pressures to differentiate products and to cut costs through capital-intensive methods.

A factor that could greatly alter this prediction is the growing belief that incomes should be equalized to a greater extent to eliminate the growing income disparity between the "haves" and the "have-nots," both within and among countries. Possibly, output may be diverted to economically less fortunate individuals rather than leisure activities. In addition, governmental influence through direct and indirect control may increase in an effort to ensure adequate demand of the type of goods and services that are available.

Product growth areas.   It is generally agreed that the generation and storage of information will continue to be one of the major growth areas during the next few decades.[34] In addition, it is probable that companies making breakthroughs in process technologies to improve productivity, such as through lasers, optics, and robotics, and those making breakthroughs in energy conservation, such as solar photovoltaics, fuel cells, and coal conversion, will be among the market growth leaders.[35]

Finance and Accounting

● Growing complexity due
  ● funds acquisition
  ● disclosure information

The international finance function can only increase in complexity. Tremendous pressures are being placed on the financial manager for large volumes of timely and accurate information relating to many different currencies.

One of the major functions of the financial manager is the acquisition of funds for operations and expansion. Capital markets are continuing to grow in size and sophistication, providing many more sources of funds from which to choose. If the dollar remains strong in relation to most major trading currencies over the next several years, the importance of the U.S. capital market centered in New York should increase. Firms should begin to shift some of their financing transactions from other countries to the offshore market established in New York City.

The different demands for disclosure of financial information will continue to be a problem for the MNE, since the firm will need to keep multiple sets of books for multiple purposes. However, the growth of a global capital market should narrow the differences in disclosure and the underlying accounting principles for the major MNEs of the world. This narrowing will take place naturally as firms compete for the same capital. U.S. standards should be guiding ones, since they were developed with the investor in mind, rather than government or the employee.

Organization

- Centralization versus decentralization tendencies due
  - global marketing and production
  - local environmental complexities

As overseas sales and profits as a percentage of total sales and profits become more important, one scenario holds that a decline in the autonomous power of subsidiary managers is likely. Their power base would erode as greater centralized control of product, marketing, and financial planning is necessitated by international interdependence of component parts required to carry through the corporate objectives of global marketing and international production.

An alternative view holds that subsidiary managements will become even more autonomous than they are now. That is because stronger leadership will be needed to cope with the complexities of the environment and nationalism as discussed above.

In all probability the centralizing tendency, within the framework of strong, capable local management, will accelerate in the years ahead. This assumes (1) that trade barriers continue to decline and (2) that it becomes economically feasible, to a greater degree than is now possible, to organize the exchange of products, components, and factors of production on a country-by-country basis. One of the advancements that may make this possible is a greater tie-in between computers and satellites for instantaneous transmission of business reports at much lower costs. Computers will be used more not only to analyze the existing flow of current activities but also to assist in organizational, financial, and personnel planning for the future. Furthermore, the close relationship between computer and satellite systems will provide marketing research specialists with an invaluable tool for studying changing market variables. The overall effect will be to increase the potential of international trade and investment.

Personnel

- Need to use human beings effectively

In 1980 a group of about 650 participants from business, government, and education attended a conference in Paris, where they discussed managerial needs for the twenty-first century.[36] They concluded that the overriding

Limits due
- immigration barriers
- changes in life styles
- fear of terrorism

managerial challenge will be to use human beings effectively. The truly multinational firm selects the best individuals, regardless of nationality, for positions throughout the worldwide organization. The institutionalization of this concept is consistent with the effective use of human beings. However, there seem to be a number of barriers to prevent the full implementation of the concept.

One of the major barriers is likely to be government regulations that prevent the free movement of people to where they can be used most efficiently. Developing countries are particularly apt to push for the use of their own citizens in managerial positions within subsidiaries even though MNEs may find it more efficient to bring in expatriates. Likewise, industrial countries are apt to prevent the full influx of labor from LDCs, thus forcing MNEs to move to the LDCs in order to secure the labor supply. Government regulations are not likely to be the only barriers to the movement of people internationally. Changes in life-styles—for example, both spouses working—may make it more difficult to transfer people anywhere, particularly to a foreign country. Publicity about international terrorism may further hamper willingness to move abroad.

At the regional level, however, there has been an upsurge in recent years of utilizing managers of various nationalities to oversee operations in a group of countries, a trend that is expected to continue. At corporate headquarters the use of nonnationals, especially in very top-level positions, has occurred only in exceptional circumstances. While there should be an upward trend in internationalizing these offices, nonnationals will probably remain an insignificant proportion of total managers at corporate headquarters during the next several decades.

Within multinational firms there will undoubtedly be a growing need to find managers who understand the nuances of country differences in conducting business operations. This will involve an understanding of different cultures, of functional adjustments, and especially of the home and host country attitudes that can affect the MNE's freedom of action.

SUMMARY

- Even though some human resources are continuing to expand, this is happening more rapidly in developing countries, thereby putting pressure on countries to find ways to use this work force in the economic mainstream. The result will be an emphasis on labor-intensive technologies.

- Natural resources are being exploited and depleted, while financial capital is stagnating through inflation and general economic uncertainty and instability. More efficient utilization of both resources is required to ensure future growth.

- Efficiency in transportation and communication can reduce the cost of goods flowing between markets as well as open up options for the utilization of previously unknown or expensive resources.

- Owing to problems of population growth, poor transportation, and inadequate storage of food in developing countries, the industrial countries and their international firms will be called upon more and more often to provide capital and technology to help find solutions.

- It will be critical for the nations of the world to agree on how to use nonterritorial areas so that the areas can be exploited.

- The trend for the mix in international business activities will be affected in part by home and host country goals and priorities, intergovernmental conflict versus cooperation, and East-West developments.

- Among the major obstacles to full multinationalization will be nationalism, limited management horizons, a shortage of qualified managerial talent, and a lack of effective means of communicating across national boundaries.

- Global consumers are more likely to increase their awareness of global products. However, despite the awareness, growing income disparities will probably increase both the high-income and low-income segments to which products can be targeted.

- An emerging pattern for state-owned multinational companies has evolved because the governments have no choice but to acquire ownership of a private multinational that is threatened with bankruptcy. In other cases, state-owned MNEs may come about because the private sector is not willing or able to provide risk capital.

- The companies that are most likely to dominate the international sector are those that have some sort of innovational lead, some technical or organizational skill, or some production or marketing capability that is not widely shared by others.

- The interface between the firm and the nation-state is a dynamic and frictional one. The major factors influencing future events appear to be (1) the growing interdependence of world economies, (2) a departure from laissez-faire economic growth, (3) the high visibility of world superpowers coupled with political realities, and (4) the growing nationalism and power of developing countries.

- As world economic instability continues to affect the cross-national flow of capital and undermine world liquidity, the multinational financial manager will be under a great deal of pressure to provide accurate, timely information and to manage funds profitably in an atmosphere where the probability of error is quite large.

- The development of the "multinational person" is an important element in the increased centralization and coordination of the multinational enterprise. Central headquarters will have to become much more expert in the environmental nuances of each country where subsidiaries are operating.

C A S E   XEROX[37]

The name Xerox is practically synonomous with copiers. This is understandable. Xerox dominated the early development of copiers in the 1960s and held 70 percent of the U.S. copier market by 1970. By that time, Xerox was also well established abroad, with subsidiaries in over 40 foreign countries. About half of these subsidiaries were owned by Xerox's joint venture with Rank from the United Kingdom. But the Xerox position began to slide. By 1984, Xerox held only 48 percent of the U.S. copier market. Such firms as Cannon, Ricoh, and Savin were competing against Xerox globally for a share of the lower-priced copier market. IBM and Kodak were doing the same for the high-priced end of the market. Xerox had moved to diversify its product lines, primarily to other types of office equipment, but it remained essentially depedent on copying equipment.

When a company's market share falls so quickly and drastically for its mainstay product line, there are usually multiple factors at play. Analysts agree that this was the case with Xerox. However, these same analysts agree that Xerox overlooked likely future events in terms of competitors and market dictates. This inattention occurred in several areas. First, Xerox concentrated its research efforts on technology that might yield major breakthroughs. This emphasis was undoubtedly influenced by the company's early experience of capitalizing on its xerography techniques. But the continuation of such a research strategy brings risks and possible problems. One obvious risk is that high costs are incurred without the development of new products. The same amount of research effort is less likely to yield a major breakthrough than an evolutionary change. In reference to Xerox, one analyst said, "They were putting blind faith in another home run by research while the Japanese were just killing them with bunts and singles."

A second problem is that when a major technical advancement does occur, it may not correspond with the readiness of the market to accept the advancement. Such was the case with Xerox's development of a long-distance office communications system in 1978. It was simply too advanced and too early for the needs of the customers for whom Xerox had planned its developments.

Finally, Xerox did not forecast the speed with which price competition would become an important consideration. As the market share leader, the company was further along the production learning curve than competitors and was therefore complacent that other copier manufacturers could not match Xerox's cost and price structure. This led to a slowness in moving to cheaper labor cost production locations in developing countries where competitors set up operations before Xerox.

Even when Xerox management did note market directions in the 1970s, the company seemed slow in responding to them. The organization structure was such that ideas were discussed by managers from various divisions within a matrix structure. But managers were seldom confident that they had the authority to make decisions about the ideas. Projects became backlogged as they were pushed upward in the organization. Once decisions were made, it was even more difficult to abandon them and change directions. One of the first things that Xerox did in the 1980s in an attempt to keep in step with future changing environments was to replace its matrix structure so that decisions could be made more quickly. Xerox also pushed decision authority down further in the organization.

But a streamlined structure was not deemed to be sufficient. Xerox additionally sought means to align its technical emphasis with those evolving conditions at home and abroad that were likely to affect its success. One means was to have the Palo Alto Research Center hire philosophers and anthropologists to work alongside engineers. Thus long-term research effort is aimed at activities that society is liable to accept. In the meantime, product divisions have been directed to work more on evolutionary changes in existing products. These are short-term modifications for which customer moods are more easily predicted. To proceed on technical ventures, whether long or short term, a number of questions must now be answered first. These include:

1. Are researchers available within or outside the company?
2. What is the likelihood that research efforts will yield advances?
3. How long will it take before there are useful results?
4. How many failures and successes have others had?
5. Can technology be obtained externally?
6. What costs will be incurred if other research projects must be displaced to accommodate this one?

Information on the probable future environment is disseminated by the Department of the Vice-President of Strategy to managers who have functional responsibilities. One office within that department, for example, is in charge of economic forecasting. This office compiles macroeconomic projections for six years into the future on eighteen countries that comprise 95 percent of the Xerox world market. These projections rely on external economic surveys that are modified to reflect internally generated assumptions about political and economic events. These assumptions are summarized within each report.

The group projects domestic and international sales for fifty products within ten industries, including expectations of technical changes as well as the economic and political assumptions outlined above. They also simulate the effects of different market shares for Xerox for each of these products. This simulation forms part of the input for future cost projections because, for most products and components, costs fall as output increases. Other cost computations are based on price level projections for over 100 different input factors across six country markets.

QUESTIONS

1. What are the major reasons why Xerox lost market share so quickly?
2. What was the problem with the matrix form of organization? What did Xerox management do to correct that problem?
3. Using the guiding principles from the Dow case at the beginning of the chapter, what are some things that you would do in addition to what was already done by Xerox management in planning for the future?

NOTES

1. Data for this case were taken from the 1983 *Annual Report* of Dow and from Frank P. Popoff, "Planning the Multinational's Future," *Business Horizons,* March–April 1984, pp. 64–68.

2. See, for instance, John E. Cooney, "Crystal Balling, 101; Colleges Now Offer Courses on the Future," *Wall Street Journal,* April 18, 1972, p. 1; *The Future: A Guide to Information Sources,* Second Edition (Washington: World Future Society, 1979); and John McHale and Magda Cordell McHale, comps., *The Futures Directory* (Boulder, Colo.: Westview Press, 1977). Three recent journals are *Long Range Planning, Journal of Forecasting,* and *Futurist.*

3. Reed Moyer, "The Futility of Forecasting," *Long Range Planning,* Vol. 17, No. 1, February 1984, pp. 65–72.

4. Julian L. Simon, *The Ultimate Resource* (Princeton, N.J.: Princeton University Press, 1981), p. 7.

5. Clyde H. Farnsworth, "A Doubling of the World's People to 10 Billion Seen by the Year 2050," *New York Times,* July 11, 1984, p. 1A.

6. "The Most Populous Cities in Year 2000," *Wall Street Journal,* February 16, 1982, p. 29.

7. Donella H. Meadows, Dennis L. Meadows, Jørgen Randers, and William W. Behrens III, *The Limits to Growth* (New York: Universe Books, 1972), pp. 56–58.

8. Gerald O. Barney, study director, *The Global 2000 Report to the President of the U.S.: Entering the 21st Century* (New York: Pergamon Press, 1982).

9. Julian L. Simon and Herman Kahn, eds., *The Resourceful Earth* (New York: B. Blackwell, 1984).

10. James Gustave Speth, "Questions for a Critical Decade," *Columbia Journal of World Business,* Vol. 19, No. 1, Spring 1984, pp. 5–9.

11. Frederick Gluck, "Global Competition in the 1980s," *Journal of Business Strategy,* Vol. 3, No. 4, Spring 1983, pp. 22–27.

12. "Food 1983," *U.N. Chronicle,* Vol. 20, No. 1, January 1983, pp. 65–80.

13. *Ibid.*

14. Alan Cowell, "UN Predicts World Population Will Level at 10.5 Billion in 2110," *New York Times,* June 15, 1981, p. A6.

15. "Communications," *Business Week,* December 17, 1979, p. 36.

16. Richard Bernstein, "U.N. Urges a Study of Antarctica," *New York Times,* December 1, 1983, p. A4.

17. John Temple Swing, "Who Will Own the Oceans?," *Foreign Affairs,* April 1976, p. 528, quoting Hugo Grotius.

18. *Ibid.,* p. 532.

19. U.S. Department of Commerce, *Survey of Current Business,* August 1977, p. 33; September 1973, p. 23; and November 1984, p. 24.

20. For a good overview of emerging technologies, see "Technologies for the '80's," *Business Week,* July 6, 1981, p. 48–56.

21. Judith H. Dobrzynski, William B. Glaberson, Resa W. King, William Powell, Jr., and Leslie Helm, "Union Carbide Fights for Its Life," *Business Week,* December 24, 1984, p. 53.

22. John Pearson and Leslie Helm, "For Multinationals, It Will Never Be the Same," *Business Week,* December 24, 1984, p. 57.

23. U.S. Congress, House Committee on Merchant Marine and Fisheries, "Panama Canal Traffic, Capacity, and Tolls," 89th Congress, Washington, D.C., Report 466, p. 6.

24. Atlantic-Pacific Interoceanic Canal Study Commission, "Interoceanic Canal Studies—1970," Washington, D.C., 1970, pp. iv–7.

25. Meredith L. Jones and Raymond B. Manning, "A Two Ocean Bouillabaise Can Result If and When Sea-Level Canal Is Dug," *Smithsonian,* December 1971, p. 19.

26. "Interoceanic Canal Studies—1970," p. 15.

27. Wassily W. Leontief, "The World Economy of the Year 2000," *Scientific American,* September 1980, pp. 207–223.

28. Clark Kerr, *The Future of Industrial Societies* (Cambridge, Mass.: Harvard University Press, 1983).

29. Renato Mazzolini, *Government Controlled Enterprises* (New York: John Wiley & Son, 1979), p. 378.

30. Raymond Vernon, "Future of the Multinational Corporation," in *The International Corporation,* Charles Kindleberger, ed. (Cambridge, Mass.: M.I.T. Press, 1970), p. 389.

31. See, for example, Robert U. Ayres, *The Next Industrial Revolution* (Cambridge, Mass.: Ballinger Publishing Company, 1984).

32. Leonard Silk, "Economic Scene," *New York Times,* August 10, 1984, p. 30, quoting a New York Stock Exchange study, "U.S. International Competitiveness" and a Brookings Institution study by Robert Z. Lawrence, "Can America Compete?"

33. Peter Wright, David Townsend, Jerry Kinard, and Joe Iverstine, "The Developing World to 1990: Trends and Implications for Multinational Business," *Long Range Planning,* Vol. 15, No. 4, August 1982, pp. 116–125.

34. See, for example, John Naisbitt, *Megatrends: Ten New Directions Transforming Our Lives* (New York: Warner Books, 1982).

35. For a discussion of these technologies, see George F. Mechlin, "Seven Technologies for the 1980's," *U.S.A. Today,* Vol. 111, No. 2452, January 1982, pp. 62–65.

36. William A. Dymsza, "The Education and Development of Managers for Future Decades," *Journal of International Business Studies,* Vol. 13, No. 3, Winter 1982, pp. 9–18, discusses the conference held at the UNESCO headquarters, June 15–18, 1980.

37. Data for this case were taken from Bro Uttal, "Xerox Xooms toward the Office of the Future," *Fortune,* Vol. 103, No. 10, May 18, 1981, pp. 44–52; Richard S. Rosenbloom and Alan M. Kantrow, "The Nurturing of Corporate Research," *Harvard Business Review,* Vol. 60, No. 1, January–February 1982, pp. 115–123; "How Xerox Speeds up the Birth of New Products," *Business Week,* No. 2888, March 19, 1984, pp. 58–59; Lynn Adkins, "What Happened to Xerox," *Dun's Business Month,* Vol. 121, No. 5, May 1983, pp. 56–60; and Richard N. Dino, Donald E. Riley, and Pan G. Yatrakis, "The Role of Forecasting in Corporate Strategy: The Xerox Experience," *Journal of Forecasting,* Vol. 1, No. 4, October–December 1982, pp. 335–348.

Glossary

Absolute advantage: A theory first presented by Adam Smith, which holds that because different countries can produce different goods more efficiently than others, they should specialize and export those things which they can produce more efficiently in exchange for those things which they cannot.

Accounting exposure: Exposure that results from translating foreign currency financial statements into the parent currency.

Acquired advantage: Commonly referred to as technology.

Acquired group membership: Refers to affiliations not determined by birth, such as religion, political affiliation, and associations.

Ad valorem duty: A duty (tariff) that is assessed as a percentage of the value of the item.

Affiliated bank: A local bank in which the foreign bank holds a minority interest.

Agency bank: An office that a bank has in a foreign country that is able to accept certain specific-use deposits for short periods of time.

Appropriate technology: The term used to describe technology that is more labor-intensive than what would be cost efficient in an industrial country.

Arbitrage: To exchange foreign currency in more than one market and end up with more money at the end of the exchange than was had at the start of the exchange.

Ascribed group memberships: The affiliations determined by birth. These include differentiations based on sex, family, age, caste, and ethnic, racial, or national origin.

Balance of payments: Summarizes all economic transactions between a country and the rest of the world during a given period of time.

Bank draft: A financial document in which the drawer instructs a bank to remit money to a drawee.

Bank of International Settlements: A bank in Switzerland which facilitates transactions among central banks.

Barter: The exchange of goods for goods instead of for money.

Base currency: The currency whose value is one whenever a quote is made between two currencies. For example, if the cruzeiro were trading at 2962.5 cruzeiros per dollar, the dollar would be the base currency, and the cruzeiro would be the quoted currency.

Bid rate: The rate at which the foreign exchange trader is willing to buy foreign exchange.

Bill of lading: A shipping document which gives instructions to the company transporting the goods.

Black market: The market for foreign exchange which lies outside of the official market.

Branch (foreign): A branch is a foreign operation which is not a separate entity from the parent.

Branch bank: An office that a bank has in a foreign country that is a legal extension of the parent bank and which engages in banking activities in the host country.

Break-bulk freight: Freight that is shipped in small enough quantities that the shipper is not able to lease an entire mode of transportation (such as a ship) for that freight.

Buffer stock: A supply of a commodity that a commodity manager is allowed to sell in the open market in order to control the price of that commodity.

Clearing House Interbank Payment System (CHIPS): An international electronic check transfer system that moves money between major U.S. banks, branches of foreign banks, and other institutions.

Command economy: An economy where resources are allocated and controlled by government decision.

Commercial bill of exchange: An instrument of payment in international business which instructs the importer to forward payment to the exporter.

Commercial paper: A form of IOU backed up by standby letters of credit.

Common market: A form of regional economic integration where countries abolish internal tariffs, use a common external tariff, and abolish restrictions on factor mobility. The term "Common Market" is also used to represent the European Economic Community (see definition below).

Commonwealth Nations: A voluntary association of 48 independent nations, including the United Kingdom and most of its former colonies.

Communism: A form of totalitarianism initially theorized by Karl Marx.

Comparative advantage: The theory that there may still be gains from trade if a country specializes in those products that it can produce more efficiently than other products, whether or not the country has an absolute advantage or disadvantage vis-a-vis other countries.

Complete economic integration: A theoretical form of regional integration which presupposes the unification of monetary, fiscal, social, and counter-cyclical policies and requires the setting up of a supranational authority whose decisions are binding for the member states.

Confirmed letter of credit: A letter of credit [see definition below] in which a bank in the exporter's country adds its guarantee of payment.

Consolidation: An accounting process whereby the financial statements of related entities (such as a parent and its subsidiaries) are added together to yield a unified set of financial statements. In the process, transactions among the related enterprises are eliminated so that the statements reflect transactions with outside parties.

Consortium bank: Several banks may pool resources to form another bank [the consortium bank] that engages in international transactions. The parent banks retain their separate operating identities, and the consortium bank becomes a new entity controlled by the parent banks.

Containerization: The use of a large outer package [the container] that can be easily handled and transferred between different modes of transportation.

Contract shipper: A company that signs an exclusive agreement to ship goods with liner ships [see definition of liner ships below].

Controlled foreign corporation: A foreign corporation in which more than 50 percent of the voting stock is owned by "U.S. Shareholders" [taxable entities that own at least 10 percent of the voting stock of the foreign corporation].

Convertibility: When a currency can be exchanged into another currency without restrictions.

Correspondent relationship: A relationship between two banks from different countries where those banks agree to perform banking functions for each other. This allows each bank to have a presence in the other bank's country without having to open an office.

Council for Mutual Economic Assistance (COMECON): A regional form of economic integration that is an association of communist countries. The members are essentially those considered to be within the Soviet bloc of influence.

Countertrade: A sale that involves obligations by the seller to generate foreign exchange for the buying country.

Country similarity theory: A new product is developed in response to observed market conditions in the home market, then a producer will turn to markets that are perceived to be the most similar to those at home.

Credit swap: A swap [see definition below] involving a parent company, a subsidiary in a foreign country, a bank in that foreign country, and a branch of that bank in the parent company's country. The parent loans money to the local branch of the foreign bank, and the foreign bank loans money to the foreign subsidiary. This provides local currency for the subsidiary and the local branch of the foreign bank.

Cross rate: An exchange rate between two currencies that is computed from the exchange rate of each of those two currencies in relation to the U.S. dollar.

Culture: The norms of a society's behavior based on attitudes, values, and beliefs.

Current rate method: Translating foreign currency financial statements into the reporting currency. All assets and liabilities are translated by using the current exchange rate, also known as the exchange rate in effect on the balance sheet date. Income statement accounts are translated by the average exchange rate for the period.

Customs union: A form of regional economic integration which eliminates tariffs among member nations and establishes common external tariffs.

Deferral: Foreign source income is not taxed until that income is declared as a dividend to the parent company.

Democracy: A political system which involves wide participation of citizens in the decision-making process.

Democratic socialism: A political-economic philosophy where elected officials are responsible for the ownership, allocation, and control of economic resources.

Demography: The statistical study of populations and their subgroups.

Dependency: When one country is too dependent on the sale of one primary commodity and/or too dependent on one country as a customer and supplier.

Devaluation: The value of a currency is formally reduced in relation to another currency. The foreign currency equivalent of the devalued currency falls.

Direct foreign investment: The controlled foreign production facilities.

Direct investment: See direct foreign investment.

Direct quote: The number of units of the domestic currency is given for one unit of the foreign currency.

Discount: A foreign currency sells at a discount in the forward market when the forward rate is less than the spot rate, assuming that the domestic currency is quoted on a direct basis.

Discounting: The selling of a bill of exchange to a financial institution at less than face value.

Documentary acceptance (D/A) Draft: A bill of exchange where goods can be released to the importer

when the bill is accepted by the importer, i.e., when the importer accepts the responsibility to make payment.

Documentary on payments (D/P) Draft: A bill of exchange which provides for the release of the goods when they are paid for.

Dualism: Progress that is confined to certain sectors of an economy while the rest of the sectors are left virtually untouched.

Dumping: The underpricing of exports (usually below cost or below the home country price).

Duty: A governmental tax (tariff) levied on goods shipped internationally.

Economic and Social Council (ECOSOC): A U.N. organization that organized the Commission of Transnational Corporations.

Economic exposure: Results in an overall change in value of the firm in relation to the change in exchange rate.

Economic integration: The abolishment of economic discrimination between national economies.

Economic union: A form of regional economic integration which combines the characteristics of a common market [see definition above] with some degree of harmonization of national economic policies.

Edge Act Corporation: A banking corporation that allows banks to set up offices in money centers in the U.S. other than those where the bank is legally allowed to operate with the purpose in mind of performing international banking activities.

Effective tariff: An argument used by developing countries which says that the real (effective) tariff on the manufactured portion of their exports is higher than indicated by the published rates because the ad valorem tariff is based on the total value of the product which includes raw materials which would have had duty free entry.

Embargo: A specific type of quota that prohibits all trade.

Errors and omissions: An account that is used in balance of payments accounting to make the debits equal the credits. The necessity for this account comes about due to the methods used in the U.S. to gather statistics.

Ethnocentrism: Characteristic of the firm or individual imbued with the belief that what worked at home should work abroad.

Eurobond: A bond that is sold in a currency other than that of the country of issue.

Eurocredit: A eurodollar loan that has a medium term maturity of 3–5 years.

Eurocurrency: A currency that is banked outside of its country of origin.

Eurodollar: A dollar that is banked outside of the U.S.

European Community (EC): A form of regional economic integration comprised of 12 countries in Europe. It most closely resembles the economic union form of regional integration. The EC is also known as the European Economic Community (EEC).

European Currency Unit: A basket of currencies comprised of the currencies of most of the members of the EC.

European Economic Community (EEC): See definition of European Community.

European Free Trade Association (EFTA): A form of regional economic integration involving European countries that are not members of the EC. These countries have established a free trade area [see definition below].

European monetary system: A cooperative foreign exchange arrangement involving most of the members of the EC that was designed to promote exchange stability within the EC.

European terms: When foreign exchange traders quote currencies on an indirect basis [see definition below].

Exchange rate: The price of one currency in terms of another currency.

Expatriates: Noncitizens of the countries where they are working.

Experience curve: The measurement of percentage production cost reductions as output increased.

Export management company: A firm that buys merchandise from manufacturers for international distribution or that sometimes acts as an agent for manufacturers.

Export trading company: A trading company sanctioned by law to become involved in international commerce. The law that established the ETC in the United States was designed to eliminate some of the antitrust barriers to cooperation.

Extraterritoriality: When governments extend the application of their laws to foreign operations of companies.

Factor proportions theory: Differences in countries' proportionate holdings of factors (land, labor, and capital) will explain differences in the costs of the factors so that the best export advantages are in production which uses the most abundant factors.

Favorable balance of trade: A country is exporting more than it is importing.

Fees: Payments for the performance of certain activities abroad.

Financial Accounting Standards Board (FASB): The private-sector organization in the United States that sets financial accounting standards.

First world countries: Nonsocialist industrial countries.

Fisher effect: The relationship between inflation and interest rates in two countries such that if the nominal interest rate in the home country is lower than that of the foreign country, one would expect the home country's inflation to be lower so that real interest rates would be equal.

Foreign bond: A bond sold outside of the country of the borrower but in the currency of the country of issue.

Foreign currency swap: Where one currency is traded for another currency with the agreement that the transaction would be reversed at some point in the future.

Foreign exchange: Currency from another country.

Foreign freight forwarder: A firm that facilitates the movement of goods from one country to another.

Foreign sales corporation: A special corporation established by U.S. tax law that can be used by a U.S. exporter to shelter some of its income from taxation.

Foreign trade zone: Special physical sites in the United States where the U.S. government allows firms to delay or avoid paying tariffs on imports.

Forward rate: A contractually-established exchange rate between a foreign exchange trader and his/her customer for delivery of foreign exchange at a specific date in the future.

Franchising: A way of doing business in which one party (the franchisor) gives an independent party (the franchisee) (1) the use of a trade-mark that is an essential asset for the franchisee's business and (2) continual assistance in the operation of the business.

Free trade area: A form of regional economic integration where internal tariffs are abolished but where countries set their own external tariffs.

Functional currency: Translating foreign currency financial statements; refers to the currency of the primary economic environment in which the entity operates.

Gap analysis: A tool used to estimate why a market potential for a given produce is less than a company's sales in a country. The reasons may be due to a usage, competitive, product line, or distribution gap.

Hard currency: A currency that is freely traded without many restrictions and for which there is usually strong external demand. Hard currencies are often called freely convertible currencies.

Hedge: A form of protection against an adverse movement of an exchange rate.

Hierarchy of needs: A well-known motivation theory states that there is a hierarchy of needs, the most fundamental being physiological, followed by safety, social, self-esteem, and self-actualization.

Home country nationals: The citizens of the country where the company is headquartered.

Idealism versus pragmatism: In the former, people try to settle principles before they try to settle small issues; whereas, in the latter, people approach problem solving from the opposite direction.

Imitation Lag: One of the strategies to take advantage of temporary monopoly advantages by moving first to those countries most likely to develop competitors.

Import broker: A specialist in import laws, documentation, and procedures.

Indirect quote: A foreign exchange quote that is given in terms of the number of units of the foreign currency for one unit of the domestic currency. This is also known as European terms.

Infant industry argument: Initial output costs for an industry in a given country may be too high to be competitive in world markets, but that over a period of time, the costs will decrease sufficiently so that efficient production will be achieved.

Input-output: Input-output is a tool that is widely used in national economic planning to show the resources used by different industries for a given output as well as the interdependence of economic sectors.

Interbank transactions: Foreign exchange transactions that take place between banks as opposed to those between banks and nonbank clients.

Interdependency: The development of mutually needed economic relations among countries.

Interest arbitrage: Investing in interest-bearing instruments in foreign exchange and earning a profit due to interest rate and exchange rate differentials.

International Accounting Standards Committee (IASC): The international private-sector organization established to set financial accounting standards that can be used worldwide.

International banking facility: A banking facility established by U.S. law that allows domestic banks to service foreign clients without many of the U.S. regulations.

International business: Includes all business transactions involving two or more countries. The business relationships may be private or governmental.

International Fisher effect: The relationship between interest rates and exchange rates that implies that the currency of the country with the lower interest rate will strengthen in the future.

International standard of fair dealing: A concept that prompt, adequate, and effective compensation would be received for investors in cases of expropriation.

Investment climate: Those external conditions in host countries that could significantly affect the success or failure of a foreign enterprise.

Invisibles: See services

Irrevocable letter of credit: A letter of credit that cannot be changed without consent of all parties involved in the letter.

Joint venture: Two or more organizations share in the ownership of a direct investment.

Just-in-time inventory management: An inventory control system perfected by Japanese manufacturing companies that controls the inflow and outflow of parts, components, and finished goods so that very little inventory is kept on hand.

Key industry: An industry that might affect a very large segment of the economy by virtue of its site or influence on other sectors.

Lag strategy: A foreign exchange management strategy that results in delaying payments or delaying receipts in a foreign currency. This strategy usually occurs because the local currency is expected to strengthen against the foreign currency.

Landbridge: A transportation concept that would permit lower transportation rates to be charged on goods shipped overland that are received by ocean transport and that will be transferred to ocean freight on the other end.

Latin American Integration Association (LAIA): A free trade area form of regional economic integration that involves most of the Latin American nations.

Lead strategy: The opposite of the lag strategy defined above. This strategy implies that firms would pay off foreign currency debts early and collect foreign currency receipts early. This is typically because the local currency is expected to weaken.

Leontief paradox: A surprising finding by Wassily Leontief that overall U.S. exports were less capital intensive and more labor intensive than U.S. imports.

Letter of credit: A precise document by which the importer's bank extends credit to the importer and agrees to pay the exporter.

Licensing agreements: Agreements whereby one firm gives rights to another for the use, usually for a fee, of such assets as trademarks, patents, copyrights, or other know-how.

Licensing arrangement (on trade): A procedure that requires potential importers or exporters to secure permission from governmental authorities before they conduct trade transactions.

Liner ships: Ships owned by steamship companies that belong to a shipping conference.

Locals: Citizens of the country where they are working.

London interbank offered rate (LIBOR): The interest rate for large interbank transactions in the international banking market.

Management contracts: An arrangement through which one firm assists another by providing management personnel to perform general or specialized management functions for a fee.

Maquiladora industry: Also known as in-bond industry. An industry concept developed by the Mexican government in which U.S.-source components are shipped to Mexico duty-free for assembly and are reexported to the United States.

Market economy: An economic philosophy where resources are allocated and controlled by consumers, who "vote" through buying goods.

Mercantilism: An economic philosophy, premised that a country's wealth is dependent on its holdings of treasure, usually in the form of gold. In order to increase wealth, countries attempt to export more than they import.

Merchandise exports: Goods sent out of a country.

Merchandise imports: Goods brought in a country.

Merchant bank: A bank primarily involved in placing and managing securities, activities not permitted for U.S. banks in the United States.

Microbridge: A landbridge concept [as defined above] which could allow goods to be transferred at low shipping rates from an inland point directly to the port of exit for ocean transportation.

Minibridge: Similar to microbridge. However, goods would have to be transferred overland to the nearest ocean port on one coast before they could be shipped overland at the cheap rates to the port of exit for ocean transportation.

Mixed venture: A special type of joint venture, where a government is in a partnership with a private company.

Most favored nation: If a country, such as the U.S. gives a tariff reduction to another country, the U.S. must grant (with a few exceptions) the same concession to all other countries of the world.

Multinational corporation: See Multinational Enterprise.

Multinational enterprise (MNE): An integrated global philosophy encompassing both domestic and overseas operations. It is also sometimes used synonymously with Multinational Corporation and Transnational Corporation.

Natural advantage: A country may have a natural advantage in the production of a product because of climatic conditions or because of access to certain natural resources.

Neomercantilism: Countries that apparently try to run favorable balances of trade, not to seek an influx of gold, but rather in an attempt to achieve some social or political objective.

Net buyer range: The price range in which the commodity buffer stock manager must buy more of the commodity than is sold in order to keep prices from falling too low.

Net seller range: The price range in which the buffer stock manager must sell more of the commodity than is bought in order to keep the price from rising too high.

Newly industrialized countries (NICS): A group of developing countries that are importers of oil but are also major exporters of manufactured goods.

Nonaccrual loan: A loan by a bank on which principal and/or interest have not been paid for 90 days.

Normal quote: Also known as a direct quote in foreign exchange [see definition of Direct Quote above].

Offer rate: The rate at which a foreign exchange trader is willing to sell foreign exchange for domestic currency.

Official reserves: Monetary gold, Special Drawing Rights, and internationally acceptable currencies held by a country.

Offset trade: Also known as countertrade [defined above].

Offshore financial centers: Countries that provide funds other than those of their own country. Their financial markets are usually not regulated in the same ways as domestic markets.

Optimum tariff: When a foreign exporter lowers its prices when an import tax is placed on its products.

Option (in foreign exchange): The right to buy or sell foreign exchange within a specific period or at a specific date.

Organization for Economic Cooperation and Development (OECD): A multilateral organization of 24 industrial countries that helps industrial countries formulate social and economic policies. All but three of the OECD countries (Greece, Portugal, and Turkey) are industrial market economies, also known as First World countries, as defined by the World Bank.

Organization for European Economic Cooperation (OEEC): A sixteen nation organization established in 1948 to facilitate the utilization of aid from the Marshall Plan. It evolved into the EEC and EFTA forms of regional economic integration.

Outsourcing: A situation in which a domestic company uses foreign suppliers for components or finished products.

Pluralistic societies: Societies where different ideologies are held by numerous segments of society rather than one ideology adhered to by all.

Polycentrism: Characterizes an individual or organization being overwhelmed by the differences, real and imaginary, great and small, between its many operating environments.

Portfolio investment: This can be either debt or equity, but the critical factor is that control does not follow the investment.

Premium (in foreign exchange): The difference between the spot and forward exchange rate in the forward market. A foreign currency is selling at a premium when the forward rate exceeds the spot rate, and when the domestic currency is quoted on the direct basis.

Private ownership: Individuals rather than the government own economic resources.

Private ships: Ocean ships owned by a company to transport its own goods.

Product life cycle: Certain kinds of products go through a cycle consisting of four stages (introduction, growth, maturity, and decline), and the location of production will shift internationally depending on the stage of the cycle.

Protestant ethic: When work is viewed as a means of salvation and when people prefer to transform productivity gains into additional output rather than additional leisure, then there is more economic growth.

Public ownership: The government rather than individuals own economic resources.

Pull: A promotion method which relies on mass media.

Push: A promotion method which involves direct selling techniques.

Quota: Sets a limit on the quantitative amount of a product allowed to be imported into or exported out of a country.

Quota (in the IMF): The payment made by each country that joins the IMF. The quota is determined by a formula based on the national income, gold and dollar balances, imports, and exports of a country. Twenty-five percent is paid in dollars, SDRs, or other reserve assets, and the remainder is paid in that member's currency.

Quoted currency: An exchange rate is usually quoted by relating one currency to the other. The currency whose numerical value is one is the base currency, and the other currency is the quoted currency. For example, if the exchange rate between the pound and dollar were to be quoted at $1.40 per pound, the pound would be the base currency, and the dollar would be the quoted currency.

Rationalized production: Companies increasingly produce different components or different portions of their product line in different parts of the world to take advantage of varying costs of labor, capital, and raw materials.

Reciprocal quote: The quote in foreign exchange that is also referred to as the indirect quote. This quote is the reciprocal of the direct quote. It is determined by dividing the direct quote into the number one.

Reporting currency: The parent company issues its financial statements to its primary shareholders.

Representative democracy: Individual citizens elect representatives to make decisions.

Representative office: An office that a bank establishes in a foreign country to represent the interests of the bank and its clients. That office is not allowed to take deposits or make loans.

Revaluation: A formal change in an exchange rate where the foreign currency value of the reference currency rises. A revaluation results in a strengthening of the reference currency.

Royalties: Payment for use of assets abroad.

Second world countries: Socialist countries (often referred to as centrally-planned economies or communist countries).

Services: International earnings other than for goods sent to another country. Also referred to as invisibles.

Shipping conferences: One-directional agreements formulated by several liner companies to set rates and schedules for ocean freight.

Sight draft: A bill of exchange that requires payment to be made as soon as it is presented to the party that is obligated to pay.

Silent language: Messages by a host of cues other than those of formal language.

Society: A broad grouping of people having common traditions, institutions, and collective activities and interests. The nation-state is often used as a workable term to denote society in international business.

Society of Worldwide Interbank Financial Telecommunication (SWIFT): A cooperative arrangement of banks worldwide to transfer funds instantaneously.

Sogo Sosha: Japanese trading companies that import and export merchandise.

Somatology: A branch of anthropology, concerned with the comparative study of human variation and classification, especially through measurement and observation.

Special Drawing Right (SDR): A unit of account issued to governments by the International Monetary Fund.

Specific duty: A duty (tariff) is assessed on the basis of a tax per unit.

Speculator: A person who takes positions in foreign exchange with the major objective of earning a profit.

Spot rate: The exchange rate quoted for immediate delivery (usually within two business days).

Spread (in the forward market): The difference between the spot and forward rate.

Spread (in the spot market): The difference between the bid (buy) and offer (sell) rates quoted by the foreign exchange trader.

Subsidiary bank: A bank which is incorporated in a country by a parent bank that is located in another country.

Swap: See Foreign Currency Swap.

Syndication: Where several banks pool resources to extend credit to a borrower.

Tariff: A governmental tax (usually on imports) levied on goods shipped internationally. It is the most common type of trade control. (see also duty)

Tax haven country: A country with low income taxes or no taxes on foreign source income.

Tax haven subsidiary: A subsidiary of a company that is established in a tax haven country for the purpose of minimizing income tax.

Temporal method: A method of translating foreign currency financial statements into the reporting currency of the parent company. It basically requires that monetary assets and liabilities be translated at the current balance sheet exchange rate, and other assets, liabilities, and owner's equity accounts be translated at historical exchange rates. Translation gains and losses are taken directly to the income statement.

Terms of trade: The quantity of imports that can be bought by a given quantity of a country's exports.

Theory of country size: Larger countries are generally more nearly self-sufficient than smaller countries.

Third-country nationals: Citizens neither of the country where they are working nor of the country where the firm is headquartered.

Third world countries: Developing countries, or those not considered socialist countries or nonsocialist industrial countries.

Totalitarianism: A political system characterized by the absence of widespread participation in decision making, which is restricted to only a few individuals.

Tramp ships: Private ocean carriers that are not affiliated with either a shipping conference or a firm that is contracting to have its products shipped.

Transaction exposure: As the exchange rate changes, the value of the exposed accounts also changes.

Transfer price: A price that is charged on goods sold between entities that are related to each other through stock ownership, such as a parent and its subsidiaries or subsidiaries owned by the same parent.

Translation: The restatement of financial statements from one currency to another.

Transnational corporation: A company owned and managed by nationals in different countries. It is also synonymous with a multinational enterprise. This text uses the former definition.

Triangular arbitrage: The process of buying and selling foreign exchange at a profit due to price discrepancies where three different currencies are involved.

Turnkey: A contract for the construction of an operating facility that is transferred to the owner when the facility is ready to begin operations.

Underemployed: People who are working fewer hours than they would like.

United Nations Conference on Trade and Development (UNCTAD): A U.N. organization that is active in the dialogue between developing and industrial countries.

U.S. terms: The quotation of exchange rates using the direct method [see definition above].

Unrequited transfers: This is used in balance of payments terminology to refer to transfers where consideration is given by only one party to the transaction, such as aid to a drought-stricken country.

Value added tax: Each firm is taxed only on the value added to the product by that firm.

Vertical integration: Involves gaining control of different stages as a product moves from its earliest production to its final distribution.

Company Index

Name Index

Subject Index